Harvard Business School Core Collection

1995 Harvard Business School Core Collection

An Author, Title, and Subject Guide

Baker Library Reference Series
Harvard Business School

Copyright © 1995
by the President and Fellows of Harvard College

Text design by
Wilson Graphics & Design
(Kenneth J. Wilson)

Harvard Business School
Baker Library
Distributed by the Harvard Business School Press
Boston, Massachusetts 02163-1098

CONTENTS

FOREWORD   vii

LISTINGS BY SUBJECT   1

APPENDIX   309
PUBLISHERS' NAMES AND ADDRESSES   311

INDEXES   319
AUTHOR INDEX   321

TITLE INDEX   361

FOREWORD

BAKER LIBRARY'S CORE COLLECTION was established in 1969 to provide a compact, easily browsed selection of choice books reflecting the research and teaching interests of the Harvard Business School. The Collection continues to meet its original purpose by assuring students, faculty, and alumni ready access to a manageable selection of current and classic books on topical issues.

Since the inception of the Core Collection, the students and alumni of the School have used it to discover the serendipitous, become informed about a business topic, or seek enlightenment about a field of research. For the past 25 years, researchers, bibliographers, and book selectors outside the School have used the catalog of the Core Collection to identify selected titles of value to their endeavors.

This edition of the catalog contains approximately 4,200 titles, including those of selected textbooks, business classics, handbooks, recent Harvard Business School faculty publications, biographies, company histories, and current business books. As always, books have been added throughout the year and those no longer in demand have been removed. Each new title is indicated by a plus sign beside the item number in the right-hand margin.

Prior editions of the Core Collection catalog arranged titles first by geographic area, then by subject within each area. With the increased globalization of business, however, geographic distinctions within the literature of business have become less significant and books less apt to focus on narrow geographic areas. Reflecting this change, the 1995 edition of the catalog now arranges the Collection's titles first by subject. Each entry contains full bibliographic information and, for the benefit of book selectors, price at the time of purchase if available. An appendix supplies publishers' addresses. Two indexes provide access to the Collection by author and title.

When Baker Library was built in 1925, there was no body of business literature as we now know it. The creation of the Core Collection in the late 1960s reflected the growth and maturing of business literature. Today, in an era of burgeoning business publications, the Core Collection and its catalog continue to serve by identifying a selected subset of books on a cross-section of important business-related topics.

Baker Library is indebted to Florence Bartoshesky Lathrop for her professional and careful attention to the titles included in the Core Collection since 1992. Thanks are also due to Pat Johnson, David Baldwin, and Kathy Moody for their invaluable production assistance for this catalog. Baker Library welcomes your comments and suggestions about the Core Collection catalog.

Ann J. Wolpert

LISTINGS BY SUBJECT

ACCOUNTANTS

Managing your accounting and consulting practice. by Mary Ann Altman and Robert I. Weil. New York: M. Bender, 1978. ca. 600 p. in various pagings: ill. (A Business reports publication) *Notes:* Includes a bibliography and index. Loose-leaf for updating. [LC 78073556]   HF5627. A45   1

ACCOUNTING

Accountant's desk handbook. Albert P. Ameiss and Nicholas A. Kargas. 3rd ed. Englewood Cliffs, N.J.: Prentice Hall, c1988. xxv, 724 p. : ill. *Notes:* Includes bibliographical references and index. [LC 87029213; ISN 0130018775]   HF5635. A474 1988   2

Accountant's encyclopedia, revised. Prentice-Hall editorial staff; Jerome K. Pescow, general editor. Englewood Cliffs, N.J.: Prentice-Hall, 1981. 2 v.: ill. *Notes:* Edition for 1962 published under title: Accountant's encyclopedia. Includes index. [LC 80011391; ISN 0130013056; $49.95]   HF5635. P87 1980   3

Accountants' handbook. edited by D.R. Carmichael, Steven B. Lilien, Martin Mellman. 7th ed. New York: Wiley, c1991. 1 v. (various pagings): ill. *Notes:* Includes bibliographical references and index. [LC 90037693; ISN 0471619795; $115.00]   HF5621. A22 1991   4

Accounting. Charles T. Horngren, Walter T. Harrison, Jr. 2nd ed. Englewood Cliffs, N.J.: Prentice Hall, 1992. 1 v. (various pagings): ill. *Notes:* Includes bibliographical references and indexes. [LC 91035032; ISN 0130056049; $43.00]   HF5635. H8125 1992   5

Accounting handbook for nonaccountants. Clarence B. Nickerson. 3rd ed. New York: Van Nostrand Reinhold, c1986. xiii, 695 p. *Notes:* Includes index. [LC 85011068; ISN 0442267541]   HF5635. N63 1986   6

Accounting information systems. Barry E. Cushing, Marshall B. Romney. 6th ed. Reading, Mass.: Addison-Wesley, c1994. 1 v. (various pagings): ill. *Notes:* Includes bibliographical references and index. [LC 93006598; ISN 020158025X]   HF5679. A34 1994   +7

Accounting information systems: concepts and practice for effective decision making. Stephen A. Moscove, Mark G. Simkin, Nancy A. Bagranoff. 4th ed. New York: Wiley, c1990. xix, 774 p. : ill. *Notes:* Includes bibliographical references. [LC 89070583; ISN 0471504491; $51.95]   HF5679. M62 1990   8

Accounting principles. Philip E. Fess, Carl S. Warren. 16th ed. Cincinnati, OH: South-Western Pub. Co., c1990. xxi, 1128, [112] p. : ill. *Notes:* Includes bibliographical references and index. [LC 88063689; ISN 0538806001; $47.25]   HF5635. F386 1990   9

Accounting principles. Robert N. Anthony, James S. Reece. 5th ed. Homewood, Ill.: R. D. Irwin, c1983. xvi, 646 p. : ill. (Willard J. Graham series in accounting) *Notes:* Published in 1975 under title: Management accounting principles. Includes bibliographies and index. [LC 82083418; ISN 0256027854]   HF5635. A68 1983   10

Accounting principles. Robert N. Anthony, James S. Reece. 4th ed. Homewood, Ill.: R. D. Irwin, 1979. xvi, 612 p. : ill. (Willard J. Graham series in accounting) *Notes:* Published in 1975 under title: Management accounting principles. Includes bibliographies and index. [LC 78072054; ISN 0256021473]   HF5635. A68 1979   11

Accounting, text and cases. Robert N. Anthony, James S. Reece. 6th ed. Homewood, Ill.: R. D. Irwin, 1979. xxv, 928 p. : ill. (The Willard J. Graham series in accounting) *Notes:* Fifth ed. published 1975 under title: Management accounting. Includes bibliographies and index. [LC 78071959; ISN 0256021481]   HF5635. A69 1979   12

Accounting, text and cases. Robert N. Anthony, James S. Reece. 8th ed. Homewood, Ill.: Irwin, 1989. xxvi, 1030 p. : ill. *Notes:* Includes bibliographical references and index. [LC 88008995; ISN 0256035709; ISN 0256066744; $53.50]   HF5635. A69 1989   13

Accounting: the basis for business decisions. Robert F. Meigs, Walter B. Meigs. 8th ed. New York: McGraw-Hill, c1990. xxxv, 1081 p. : ill. *Notes:* Authors' names in reverse order in earlier editions. [LC 89037383; ISN 0070416893; $43.95]   HF5635. M4887 1990   14

Accounting, the basis for business decisions. Walter B. Meigs, Robert F. Meigs. 7th ed. New York: McGraw-Hill, c1987. xxiii, 1059, 14 p. : col. ill. *Notes:* Includes index. [LC 86021104; ISN 0070416400; $37.95]   HF5635. M49 1987   15

Accounting theory. Eldon S. Hendriksen, Michael F. van Breda. 5th ed. Homewood, IL: Irwin, c1992. xvi, 905 p. : ill. *Notes:* Includes bibliographical references and index. [LC 91027330; ISN 0256081468; ISN 025611269X; $50.95]   HF5625. H45 1992   16

Advanced accounting. Andrew A. Haried, Leroy F. Imdieke, Ralph E. Smith. 5th ed. New York: John Wiley & Sons, c1991. xxviii, 1005 p. *Notes:* Includes bibliographical references and index. [LC 90042915; ISBN 0471518239; $54.95]   HF5635. H256 1991   17

Advanced accounting. Floyd A. Beams. 5th ed. Englewood Cliffs, N.J.: Prentice Hall, 1992. xiv, 960 p. : ill. *Notes:* Includes bibliographical references and index. [LC 91035225; ISBN 0130104892]   HF5635. B41517 1992   18

Advanced accounting. Floyd A. Beams. 4th ed. Englewood Cliffs, N.J.: Prentice Hall, c1988. xii, 968 p. : ill. *Notes:* Includes bibliographies and index. [LC 87026226; ISBN 0130101826]   HF5635. B35 1988   19

Essentials of accounting. Robert N. Anthony. 5th ed. Reading, Mass.: Addison-Wesley, c1993. 211 p. : ill. *Notes:* Page sequence runs from front to back, then back to front with book inverted. Index included in separate booklet attached inside back cover. [LC 92025517; ISBN 0201513854]   HF5635. A6879 1993   20

Financial accounting. Kermit D. Larson. 4th ed. Homewood, IL: Irwin, 1989. xxix, 766 p. : ill. (some col.) *Notes:* Rev. ed. of: Financial accounting / Kermit D. Larson, William W. Pyle. 3rd ed. 1986. Includes bibliographical references and index. [LC 88023151; ISBN 0256067813; $44.95]   HF5635. P974 1989   21

Financial accounting. Walter T. Harrison, Jr., Charles T. Horngren. Englewood Cliffs, N.J.: Prentice Hall, c1992. xxiii, 894, [23] p. : ill. (some col.) *Notes:* Includes indexes. [LC 91035800; ISBN 0133185699]   HF5635. H333 1992   22

Financial accounting and reporting desk handbook. David L. Gittes. Englewood Cliffs, N.J.: Prentice-Hall, c1980. 253 p. : ill. *Notes:* Includes bibliographies and index. [LC 79028544; ISBN 0133148564]   HF5635. G494   23

Financial accounting: principles and issues. Michael H. Granof, Philip W. Bell. 4th ed. Englewood Cliffs, N.J.: Prentice Hall, c1991. xv, 750 p. : ill. (some col.) *Notes:* Includes bibliographical references and index. [LC 90037830; ISBN 013321852X; $52.75]   HF5635. G772 1991   24

Financial accounting theory: issues and controversies. edited by Stephen A. Zeff, Thomas F. Keller. 3rd ed. New York: McGraw-Hill, c1985. xi, 660 p. : ill. *Notes:* Rev. ed. of: Financial accounting theory I. 2nd ed. c1973. Includes bibliographies. [LC 84019398; ISBN 0070727910; $20.95]   HF5635. F535 1985   25

Financial statement analysis: a strategic perspective. Clyde P. Stickney. San Diego: Harcourt Brace Jovanovich, c1990. xiii, 594 p. : ill. [LC 89017199; ISBN 0155274708; $50.00]   HF5635. S857 1990   26

Finney and Miller's Principles of accounting, intermediate. by Glenn L. Johnson and James A. Gentry, Jr. 7th ed. Englewood Cliffs, N.J.: Prentice-Hall, c1974. xv, 988 p. : ill. *Notes:* Includes bibliographical references and index. [LC 73021; ISBN 0133175863]   HF5635. F538 1974   +27

Finney and Miller's Principles of accounting-introductory. 8th ed. / Glenn L. Johnson, James A. Gentry, Jr. Englewood Cliffs, N.J.: Prentice-Hall, c1980. xiv, 754 p. : ill. *Notes:* Includes bibliographical references and index. [LC 79020369; ISBN 0133173704; $15.95]   HF5635. F537 1980   28

Fundamental accounting principles. Kermit D. Larson. 12th ed. Homewood, IL: Irwin, c1990. xxxi, 1278, 13 p. : ill. *Notes:* Previous edition by William W. Pyle and Kermit D. Larson. Includes bibliographical references. [LC 89015560; ISBN 0256073422; $47.95]   HF5635. P975 1990   29

Fundamentals of financial accounting. Daniel G. Short. 7th ed. Homewood, IL: Irwin, c1993. xxii, 810 p. : ill. *Notes:* Includes index. [LC 92019025; ISBN 0256103178]   HF5635. S56 1993   +30

Handbook of accounting and auditing. editors, Robert S. Kay, D. Gerald Searfoss, with Bruce N. Willis, Alfred M. Yates. 2nd ed. Boston: Warren, Gorham & Lamont, c1989. 1 v. (various pagings): ill. *Notes:* Kept up-to-date by cumulative supplements. Includes bibliography and index. [LC 88062092; ISBN 0791300447]   HF5635. H22 1989   31

Handbook of accounting practice. Jay Ruben. Englewood Cliffs, N.J.: Prentice Hall, c1992. xvii, 676 p. : ill. *Notes:* Includes index. [LC 92016992; ISBN 0133761126; $79.95]   HF5635. R894 1992   +32

HBJ Miller comprehensive European accounting guide. David Alexander, Simon Archer. U.S. ed. San Diego: HBJ Professional Publishing, 1991. xiv, 1097 p. *Notes:* "HBJ Miller Accounting Publications, Harcourt Brace Jovanovich"—from T.p. Includes index.; ISBN 0156023547; $65.00]   HF5616.E85 A54 1991   33

Intermediate accounting. A.N. Mosich. Rev. 6th ed. New York: McGraw-Hill, c1989. xxiv, 1364 p. : ill. *Notes:* Includes index. [LC 88027140; ISBN 0070418551; $49.95]   HF5635. M8754 1989   34

Intermediate accounting. Donald E. Kieso, Jerry J. Weygandt. 7th ed. New York: Wiley, c1992. xxvi, 1459 p. : ill. *Notes:* Includes bibliographical references and index. [LC 92003732; ISBN 0471540099; $64.95]   HF5635. K5 1992   35

Intermediate accounting. Glenn A. Welsch, Charles T. Zlatkovich. 8th ed. Homewood, IL: Irwin, 1989. xxxii, 1406 p. : ill. *Notes:* Includes index. [LC 88039984; ISBN 0256066604; $59.95]   HF5635. W46 1989   36

Intermediate accounting: comprehensive volume. Jay M. Smith, K. Fred Skousen; consulting editors, Earl K. Stice, James D. Stice. 11th ed. Cincinnati, Ohio: College Division, South-Western Pub. Co., c1992. xviii, 1147 p. : ill. *Notes:* Includes index. [LC 91037662; ISN 0538813377; $61.95]
    HF5635. S5946 1992   37

Introduction to financial accounting. Kirkland A. Wilcox, Joseph G. San Miguel. New York: Harper & Row, c1980. xxvi, 758 p. *Notes:* Includes index. [LC 79022411; ISN 0060457074]   HF5635. W69   38

Making accounting policy: the quest for credibility in financial reporting. David Solomons. New York: Oxford University Press, 1986. xviii, 261 p. : ill. (Wharton executive library) *Notes:* Includes bibliographical references and index. [LC 85018933; ISN 0195037014]   HF5635. S6896 1986   39

Modern advanced accounting. E. John Larsen, A.N. Mosich. 4th ed. New York: McGraw-Hill, c1988. xx, 1002 p. *Notes:* Rev. ed. of: Modern advanced accounting / A.N. Mosich, E. John Larsen. 3rd ed. 1983. Includes bibliographical references and index. [LC 87022621; ISN 0070365083; $45.95]
    HF5635. M8756 1988   40

Rational accounting concepts: the writings of Willard J. Graham. edited with an introduction by Harold Q. Langenderfer, Grover L. Porter. New York: Garland, 1988. xvi, 508 p. : ill. *Notes:* Includes bibliographical references. [LC 88024439; ISN 082406125X; $72.00]   HF5635. G767 1988   41

Should business and nonbusiness accounting be different? Robert N. Anthony. Boston, Mass.: Harvard Business School Press, c1989. x, 118 p. *Notes:* Bibliography: p. 115-118. [LC 88030494; ISN 0875842127; $14.95]   HF5616.U5 A599 1989   42

A survey of financial and managerial accounting. James Don Edwards, Roger H. Hermanson, R.F. Salmonson. 5th ed. Homewood, Ill.: Irwin, 1989. xii, 836 p. : ill. *Notes:* Rev. ed. of: A survey of basic accounting / R.F. Salmonson, James Don Edwards, Roger H. Hermanson. 4th ed. 1985. Includes index. [LC 88019835; ISN 025606976X; $41.95]   HF5635. S17 1989   43

Tell it like it was: a conceptual framework for financial accounting. Robert N. Anthony. Homewood, Ill.: R.D. Irwin, 1983. xxiii, 313 p. (The Anthony-Graham series in accounting) *Notes:* Includes indexes. Bibliography: p. 280-302. [LC 83081733; ISN 0256030901]   HF5681.B2 A57   44

The Wall Street journal on accounting. Lee Berton, Jonathan B. Schiff. Homewood, Ill.: Dow Jones-Irwin, c1990. viii, 471 p. : ill. [LC 89036247; ISN 155623225X; $39.95]   HF5616.U5 B47 1990   45

ACCOUNTING FIRMS

The accounting wars. Mark Stevens. New York: Macmillan, c1985. x, 261 p. : ill. *Notes:* Includes bibliographical references and index. [LC 84027357; ISN 0026144700; $16.95]   HF5616.U5 S74 1985   46

The big six: the selling out of America's top accounting firms. Mark Stevens; research by Carol Bloom Stevens. New York: Simon & Schuster, c1991. 271 p. : ill. *Notes:* Includes index. [LC 91008914; ISN 0671695495; $19.95]   HF5616.U5 S754 1991   47

ACCULTURATION

Robert T. Moran's cultural guide to doing business in Europe. Michael Johnson and Robert T. Moran. 2nd ed. Oxford; Boston: Butterworth-Heinemann, 1992. xiv, 138 p. *Notes:* Includes bibiographical references.; ISN 0750608315; $19.55]   HC240. M715 1992   48

ACTIVITY-BASED COSTING

Activity-based costing for marketing and manufacturing. Ronald J. Lewis. Westport, Conn.: Quorum Books, 1993. 239 p. : ill. *Notes:* Includes bibliographical references (p. [235]-236) and index. [LC 92031710; ISN 0899308015]   HF5686.C8 L45 1993   +49

ADMINISTRATIVE AGENCIES

Reinventing government: how the entrepreneurial spirit is transforming the public sector. David Osborne and Ted Gaebler. New York: Plume, c1992 (1993 printing). xxii, 405 p. *Notes:* Originally published: Reading, Mass.: Addison-Wesley, c1992. [LC 92030557; ISN 0452269423]   JK469 1993   50

ADVERTISING

Advertising. William M. Weilbacher. 2nd ed. New York: Macmillan, c1984. xvii, 605 p., [16] p. of plates: ill. (some col.), maps *Notes:* Includes bibliographical references and index. [LC 83005380; ISBN 0024252506]   HF5821. W38 1984   51

The advertising advantage. Boston, Mass.: Harvard Business School Press, c1991. vi, 73 p. : ill. *Notes:* Articles reprinted from Harvard Business Review. Includes bibliographical references. *Contents:* Getting the most out of advertising and promotion / Magid M. Abraham and Leonard M. Lodish—Ad spending, maintaining market share / John Philip Jones—Ad spending, growing market share / James C. Schroer—Marketing in an age of diversity / Regis McKenna—Critical issues for issue ads / David Kelley—When to advertise your company / Thomas F. Garbett—Us vs. them, the minefield of comparative ads / Bruce Buchanan and Doron Goldman—Can you pass the comparative ad challenge? / Bruce Buchanan—Research on advertising techniques that work, and don't work / David Ogilvy and Joel Raphaelson—Your own brand of advertising for nonconsumer products / Herbert L. Kahn.; ISBN 0875842801]   HF5823. A22 1991   +52

The advertising and promotion challenge: vaguely right or precisely wrong? Leonard M. Lodish. New York: Oxford University Press, 1986. xiii, 188 p. : ill. (The Wharton executive library) *Notes:* Includes index. Includes bibliographies. [LC 85018864; ISBN 0195037022]   HF5821. L58 1986   53

Advertising in contemporary society: perspectives toward understanding. Kim B. Rotzoll, James E. Haefner; consulting author, Charles H. Sandage. 2nd ed. Cincinnati, OH: South-Western Pub. Co., c1990. xiii, 190 p. : ill. *Notes:* Includes bibliographical references. [LC 89011394; ISBN 0538805943; $25.75]   HF5821. R67 1990   54

Advertising: its role in modern marketing. S. Watson Dunn. . . et al. 7th ed. Chicago: Dryden Press, c1990. xxxi, 605 p. : ill. (some col.) *Notes:* Sixth ed. by S. Watson Dunn and Arnold M. Barban. Includes bibliographies and index. [LC 89007767; ISBN 0030307481; $45.00]   HF5823. D78 1990   55

The advertising kit: a complete guide for small businesses. Jeanette Smith. New York: Toronto: New York: Lexington Books; Maxwell Macmillan Canada; Maxwell Macmillan Internatinal, c1994. viii, 292 p. *Notes:* Includes index. *Contents:* Business advertising: a portrait—Start with the inside information—Targeting your customers—Sneak peak—Check the competition—The plan—Choosing media—Writing advertising messages—Newspapers—Radio—TV: is it the impossible dream?—Is it true what they say about cable TV?—Direct mail advertising—Yellow pages—Billboards and transit—Magazines—Publicity—From the pros nest. [LC 93040134; ISBN 0029295157; $19.95]   HF5823. S619 1994   +56

Advertising management. David A. Aaker, Rajeev Batra, John G. Myers. 4th ed. Englewood Cliffs, N.J.: Prentice Hall, c1992. xiii, 593 p. : ill. *Notes:* Includes bibliographical references and index. [LC 91024126; ISBN 0130141011; $69.00]   HF5823. A13 1992   57

Advertising theory & practice. C.H. Sandage, Vernon Fryburger, Kim Rotzoll. 12th ed. New York: Longman, c1989. xiii, 483 p., [8] p. of plates: ill. (some col.) *Notes:* Includes bibliographical references and index. [LC 88024041; ISBN 080130184X; $33.55]   HF5823. S25 1989   58

Advertising's hidden effects: manufacturers' advertising and retail pricing. Mark S. Albion. Boston, Mass.: Auburn House Pub. Co., c1983. xxi, 311 p. *Notes:* Includes index. Bibliography: p. 292-298. [LC 82006776; ISBN 0865691118; $21.95]   HF5821. A398 1983   59

"Are they selling her lips?": advertising and identity. Carol Moog. 1st ed. New York: Morrow, c1990. 236 p. : ill. [LC 89012965; ISBN 0688087043; $18.95]   HF5822. M66 1990   60

Cases in advertising and communications management. Stephen A. Greyser; with the collaboration of Robert J. Kopp. 3rd ed. Englewood Cliffs, N.J.: Prentice-Hall, c1992. xvii, 680 p. : ill. *Notes:* Includes bibliographical references. [LC 90049388; ISBN 0131161385; $45.00]   HF5827. G75 1992   61

Cases in advertising and promotion management. John A. Quelch, Paul W. Farris. 4th ed. Burr Ridge, Ill.: Irwin, c1994. xiii, 746 p. : ill. *Notes:* Includes bibliographical references and index. [LC 93005170; ISBN 0256122725]   HF5823. Q44 1994   +62

Channels of desire: mass images and the shaping of American consciousness. Stuart Ewen and Elizabeth Ewen. 2nd ed. Minneapolis: University of Minnesota Press, c1992. xxii, 247 p. *Notes:* Includes bibliographical references (p. 221-235) and index. [LC 91046917; ISBN 0816618909]   HF5813.U6 E95 1992   63

Contemporary advertising. Courtland L. Bovée, William F. Arens. 4th ed. Homewood, IL: Irwin, c1992. xxxi, 718, [58] p. : ill. (some col.) *Notes:* Includes bibliographical references and indexes. [LC 91028798; ISBN 025609196X; $53.50]   HF5821. B62 1992   64

The Dartnell advertising manager's handbook. by Richard H. Stansfield. 3rd ed. Chicago: Dartnell, 1982. 1088 p. : ill. *Notes:* Title on spine: Advertising manager's handbook. Running title: The Dartnell advertising handbook. [LC 68021; ISBN 0850131286]   HF5823. S78 1982   65

Kleppner's advertising procedure. J. Russell Thomas, W. Ronald Lane. 11th ed. Englewood Cliffs, N.J.: Prentice Hall, 1990. xviii, 718 p. : ill. *Notes:* Rev. ed. of: Kleppner's advertising procedure / Thomas Russell, Glenn Verrill, W. Ronald Lane. 10th ed. c1988. Includes bibliographical references. [LC 89025588; ISN 0135163374; $44.40] HF5823. K45 1990   66

Satisfaction guaranteed: the making of the mass market. Susan Strasser. 1st ed. New York: Pantheon Books, 1989. xi, 339 p. : ill. *Notes:* Bibliography: p. [294]-326. [LC 89042675; ISN 039455292X; $24.95] HF5813.U6 S79 1989   67

Whatever happened to Madison Avenue?: advertising in the '90s. by Martin Mayer. 1st ed. Boston: Little, Brown, c1991. xix, 269 p. *Notes:* Includes bibliographical references and index. [LC 90024150; ISN 0316551546; $22.95] HF5813.U6 M32 1991   68

What's in a name?: advertising and the concept of brands. John Philip Jones; forward by Don Johnston. Lexington, Mass.: Lexington Books, c1986. xxii, 292 p. : ill. *Notes:* Includes bibliographical references and index. [LC 85045039; ISN 0669111422] HF5823. J718 1986   69

ADVERTISING AGENCIES

Emperors of adland: inside the advertising revolution. Nancy Millman. New York, NY: Warner Books, c1988. viii, 225 p., [8] p. of plates: ill. *Notes:* Includes bibliographical references and index. [LC 87037190; ISN 0446514039] HF6182.U5 M56 1988   70

ADVERTISING, DIRECT-MAIL

The Dartnell direct mail and mail order handbook. by Richard S. Hodgson. 3d ed. Chicago Dartnell Corp., 1980. 1538 p. : ill. *Notes:* Includes index. Bibliography: p. 1312-1323. [LC 73090752; ISN 0850131162] HF5861. H6 1980   71

ADVERTISING LAWS

Corporate and commercial free speech: first amendment protection of expression in business. Edwin P. Rome and William H. Roberts. Westport, Conn.: Quorum Books, 1985. x, 269 p. *Notes:* Includes indexes. Bibliography: p. [239]-250. [LC 84026496; ISN 0899300413] KF1614. R65 1985   72

ADVERTISING MEDIA PLANNING

Advertising media planning. Jack Z. Sissors, Lincoln Bumba. 3rd ed. Lincolnwood, IL: NTC Business Books, c1989. xii, 461 p. : ill. *Notes:* Includes bibliographies and index. [LC 88062122; ISN 0844231584] HF5826.5. S57 1989   73

AERONAUTICS, COMMERCIAL

Collision course: the truth about airline safety. Ralph Nader, Wesley J. Smith. 1st ed. Blue Ridge Summit, PA: Tab Books, c1994. xxii, 378 p. *Notes:* Includes bibliographical references (p. [365]-366) and index. *Contents:* The system—The FAA follies—Air traffic control—The equipment—Airports—Man, nature, & safety—Safety first. [LC 93008266; ISN 0830642714; $21.95] TL553.5. N25 1994   +74

Deregulating the airlines. Elizabeth E. Bailey, David R. Graham, Daniel P. Kaplan. Cambridge, Mass.: MIT Press, c1985. ix, 243 p. : ill. *Notes:* Includes index. Bibliography: p. [235]-240. [LC 84021816; ISN 0262022133] HE9803.A4 B32 1985   75

Deregulation and the new airline entrepreneurs. John R. Meyer and Clinton V. Oster, Jr., with Marni Clippinger... et al. Cambridge, Mass.: MIT Press, c1984. xvi, 240 p. : ill. *Notes:* Includes bibliographical references and index. [LC 84007935; ISN 0262131986] HE9803.A35 D47 1984   76

AFRO-AMERICAN BANKERS

Black managers: the case of the banking industry. Edward D. Irons and Gilbert W. Moore; foreword by Phyllis Wallace. New York: Praeger, 1985. xviii, 184 p. : ill. *Notes:* Bibliography: p. 179-184. [LC 84018304; ISN 0030719380; $27.95 (est.)]   HG1615.7.M5 I76 1985   77

AFRO-AMERICAN EXECUTIVES

The Black manager: making it in the corporate world. Floyd Dickens, Jr., Jacqueline B. Dickens. Rev. ed. New York, NY: American Management Association, c1991. xvii, 446 p. : ill. *Notes:* Includes bibliographical references (p. 433-437) and index. [LC 91053055; ISN 0814477704; $22.95]
HD38.25.U6 D53 1991   78

The black manager: making it in the corporate world. Floyd Dickens, Jr., Jacqueline B. Dickens. New York: AMACOM, c1982. xiii, 333 p. : ill. *Notes:* Includes index. Bibliography: p. 323-326. [LC 81069377; ISN 0814456782]   HF5500.3.U54 D6   79

AFRO-AMERICAN WOMEN EXECUTIVES

My soul is my own: oral narratives of African American women in the professions. Gwendolyn Etter-Lewis. New York: Routledge, 1993. xvii, 213 p. *Notes:* Includes bibliographical references (p. 207-210) and index. [LC 92039044; ISN 0415905605; $14.95]   HD6054.4.U6 E88 1993   +80

Stressors, beliefs, and coping behaviors of Black women entrepreneurs. Lois Harry. New York: Garland Pub., 1994. x, 141 p. : ill. *Notes:* Includes bibliographical references (p. 121-138) and index. [LC 93049086; ISN 0815316550]   HD6057. H37 1994   +81

AFRO-AMERICANS

Success runs in our race: the complete guide to effective networking in the African-American community. George C. Fraser. 1st ed. New York: Morrow, c1994. 348 p. : ports. *Notes:* Includes bibliographical references (p. 327-328) and index. [LC 93051512; ISN 0688129153; $25.00]
E185.86. F725 1994   +82

AGED AS CONSUMERS

Transgenerational design: products for an aging population. James J. Pirkl. New York: Van Nostrand Reinhold, c1994. xvii, 260 p. : ill. (some col.) *Notes:* Includes bibliographical references and index. [LC 93009870; ISN 0442010656]   HC110.C6 P57 1994   +83

AGNELLI, GIOVANNI

Agnelli and the network of Italian power. Alan Friedman. London: Harrap, 1988. 304 p., [8] p. of plates: ill., ports. *Notes:* Includes bibliographical references and index.; ISN 0245546553; $20.59]
HD9710.I82 A652 1988   84

AGRICULTURAL INDUSTRIES

Agribusiness management. W. David Downey, Steven P. Erickson. 2nd ed. New York: McGraw-Hill, c1987. xi, 477 p. : ill. *Notes:* Includes bibliographical references and index. [LC 86020036; ISN 0070176671; $33.95]   HD9000.5. D63 1987   85

Principles of agribusiness management. James G. Beierlein, Kenneth C. Schneeberger, Donald D. Osburn. Englewood Cliffs, N.J.: Prentice-Hall, c1986. xx, 441 p. : ill. *Notes:* "A Reston book." Includes bibliographies and index. [LC 85028325; ISN 0835955990; $25.95]   HD9000.5. B416 1986   86

AGRICULTURAL PRICES

What price food?: agricultural price policies in developing countries. Paul Streeten. New York: St. Martin's Press, 1987. viii, 127 p. : ill. *Notes:* Includes bibliographical references and index. [LC 87009577; ISN 0312007396; $35.00]   HD1417. S73 1987   87

AGRICULTURE

Financial management in agriculture. Peter J. Barry, John A. Hopkin, C.B. Baker. 4th ed. Danville, Ill.: Interstate Printers & Publishers, c1988. xii, 500 p. : ill. *Notes:* Includes bibliographies and indexes. [LC 88080270; ISN 0813427908; $34.60]   HD1437. B37 1988   88

AIDS (DISEASE)

AIDS in the workplace: legal questions and practical answers. William F. Banta. Updated and expanded ed. New York: Toronto: New York: Lexington Books; Maxwell Macmillan Canada; Maxwell Macmillan International, c1993. xxi, 422 p. *Notes:* Includes bibliographical references and index. [LC 92033947; ISN 0669280569; $29.95]   KF3570. B36 1993   89

We are all living with AIDS: how you can set policies and guidelines for the workplace. Earl C. Pike. Minneapolis: Deaconess Press, c1993. xix, 395 p. : ill. *Notes:* Includes bibliographical references (p. 360-365). [LC 93026894; ISN 0925190683; $14.95 ($16.95 Can.)]   RA644.A25 P52 1993   +90

AIR

The toxic cloud. Michael H. Brown. 1st ed. New York: Harper & Row, c1987. 307 p. *Notes:* Includes index. [LC 87045027; ISN 0060158018; $18.95]   TD883.2. B66 1987   91

AIR QUALITY MANAGEMENT

What price clean air?: a market approach to energy and environmental policy. New York: Committee for Economic Development, 1993. x, 96 p. : ill. *Notes:* "A statement by the Research and Policy Committee of the Committee for Economic Development." Includes bibliographical references. [LC 93013301; ISN 087186097X; $15.00]   HC110.A4 W45 1993   +92

AIRLINES

An introduction to airline economics. William E. O'Connor. 4th ed. New York: Praeger, 1989. xiii, 216 p. *Notes:* Bibliography: p. 203-207. [LC 88034249; ISN 0275931293; $39.85]   HE9803.A4 O26 1989   93

AMERICAN EXPRESS COMPANY

American Express: the unofficial history of the people who built the great financial empire. Peter Z. Grossman. 1st ed. New York: Crown Publishers, c1987. x, 389 p., [16] p. of plates: ill. *Notes:* Includes index. Bibliography: p. 370-380. [LC 86019925; ISN 0517562383]   HE5903.A55 G76 1987   94

House of cards: inside the troubled empire of American Express. Jon Friedman and John Meehan. New York: Putnam, 1992. 272 p., [8] p. of plates: ill. *Notes:* Includes index. [LC 91042477; ISN 0399136541; $24.95]   HE5903.A55 M44 1992   95

AMERICAN LITERATURE

Making Americans: an essay on individualism and money. Quentin Anderson. 1st ed. New York: Harcourt Brace Jovanovich, c1992. 264 p. *Notes:* Includes bibliographical references (p. [239]-254) and index. [LC 92008693; ISN 0151559414; $21.95]   PS169.N35 A5 1992   96

AMERICAN MOTORS CORPORATION

Beijing Jeep: the short, unhappy romance of American business in China. Jim Mann. New York: Simon and Schuster, c1989. 333 p. *Notes:* Includes bibliographical references (p. 313-319). [LC 89021862; ISN 0671620274; $19.95]   HD9710.U54 A6574 1989   97

AMERICAN TELEPHONE AND TELEGRAPH COMPANY

The adaptive corporation. Alvin Toffler. New York: McGraw-Hill, c1985. vi, 217 p. *Notes:* Includes a report entitled Social dynamics and the Bell System prepared with the assistance of Marilyn Shapiro, originally submitted to Bell System. Includes index. Bibliography: p. 181-188. [LC 84007181; $15.95]   HE8846.A55 T64 1985   98

The anatomy of a business strategy: Bell, Western Electric, and the origins of the American telephone industry. George David Smith. Baltimore: Johns Hopkins University Press, c1985. xxii, 237 p. : ill. (The Johns Hopkins/AT&T series in telephone history) *Notes:* Includes index. Bibliography: p. 183-230. [LC 84023419; ISN 0801827108]   HE8846.A55 S65 1985   99

Chronicles of corporate change: management lessons from AT&T and its offspring. Leonard A. Schlesinger... et al. Lexington, Mass.: Lexington Books, c1987. xiv, 254 p. : ill. *Notes:* Includes index. Bibliography: p. [233]-238. [LC 86045555; ISN 0669136859]   HE8846.A55 C47 1987   100

The deal of the century: the breakup of AT&T. by Steve Coll. 1st ed. New York: Atheneum, 1986. xiv, 400 p., [1] leaf of plates: ill. *Notes:* Includes index. Bibliography: p. 381-385. [LC 86047676; ISN 0689117574; $18.95]   HE8846.A55 C58 1986   101

The fall of the Bell system: a study in prices and politics. Peter Temin with Louis Galambos. Cambridge; New York: Cambridge University Press, 1987. xviii, 378 p. : ill. *Notes:* Includes bibliographical references and index. [LC 87010293; ISN 052134557X]   HE8846.A55 T44 1987   102

Incredibly American: releasing the heart of quality. Marilyn R. Zuckerman and Lewis J. Hatala. Milwaukee, Wis.: ASQC Quality Press, c1992. xvii, 283 p. : ill. *Notes:* Includes bibliographical references (p. [273]-276) and index. [LC 92017210; ISN 0873891929; $19.95]   HE8846.A55 Z83 1992   103

Managerial lives in transition: advancing age and changing times. Ann Howard, Douglas W. Bray. New York: Guilford Press, c1988. xvi, 462 p. : ill. (Adult development and aging) *Notes:* Includes index. Bibliography: p. 449-454. [LC 86018441; ISN 0898621267]   HE8846.A55 H68 1988   104

The rape of Ma Bell: the criminal wrecking of the best telephone system in the world. by Constantine Raymond Kraus and Alfred W. Duerig. Secaucus, N.J.: Lyle Stuart, c1988. 270 p. *Notes:* Includes index. Bibliography: p. [259]-261. [LC 88020036; ISN 081840468X; $19.95]   HE8846.A55 K73 1988   105

Telecommunications in turmoil: technology and public policy. Gerald R. Faulhaber. Cambridge, Mass.: Ballinger Pub. Co., c1987. xviii, 186 p. *Notes:* Includes bibliographies and index. [LC 87001377; ISN 0887301576]   HE8846.A55 F38 1987   106

Wrong number: the breakup of AT&T. Alan Stone. New York: Basic Books, c1989. xi, 381 p. *Notes:* Includes index. Bibliography: p. [339]-370. [LC 88047895; ISN 0465092772; $19.95]   HE8846.A55 S73 1989   107

ANDREAS, DWAYNE

Supermarketer to the world: the story of Dwayne Andreas, CEO of Archer Daniels Midland. E.J. Kahn, Jr. New York: Warner Books, 1991. viii, 320 p. : ill. *Notes:* Includes index. [LC 90050535; ISN 0446514950; $24.95]   HD9235.S6 A545 1991   108

ANGLO AMERICAN CORPORATION OF SOUTH AFRICA, LTD

South Africa Inc.: the Oppenheimer empire. David Pallister, Sarah Stewart, and Ian Lepper. Rev. and updated ed. New Haven: Yale University Press, 1988. 382 p. : ill. *Notes:* Includes index. Bibliography: p. 360-370. [LC 88050650; ISN 0300042515; $27.50]   HD9506.S74 A536 1988   109

ANTITRUST LAW

The antitrust laws: a primer. John H. Shenefield and Irwin M. Stelzer. Washington, D.C.: AEI Press, 1993. xi, 118 p. *Notes:* Includes bibliographical references. [LC 93017994; ISN 0844738085]
KF1650. S53 1993   110

APPLE COMPUTER, INC

Accidental millionaire: the rise and fall of Steven Jobs at Apple Computer. Lee Butcher. 1st ed. New York: Paragon House, c1988. xii, 224 p., [4] p. of plates: ports. *Notes:* Includes index. [LC 87009414; ISN 0913729795]
HD9696.C64 A664 1988   111

Defying gravity: the making of Newton. Doug Menuez, photography; Markos Kounalakis, text; Paul Saffo, introduction. Hillsboro, Or.: Beyond Words Pub., c1993. 176 p. : ill. (some col.) *Notes:* Pagination begins with p. 176 and ends with p. 1. [LC 93028081; ISN 0941831949; $29.95]
HD9696.C64 A866 1993   +112

The Macintosh way. Guy Kawasaki. Glenview, Il. : Scott, Foresman, c1990. xi, 209 p. : ill. *Notes:* Includes index. Includes bibliographical references. [LC 89010249; ISN 0673461750; $19.95]
HD9696.C64 A6645 1990   113

West of Eden: the end of innocence at Apple Computer. Frank Rose. New York, N.Y., U.S.A.: Viking, 1989. 356 p. *Notes:* Includes index. [LC 88040302; ISN 0670812781; $19.95]
HD9696.C64 A867 1989   114

APPLICATIONS FOR POSITIONS

Executive jobs unlimited. by Carl R. Boll. Updated ed. New York: Macmillan, 1979. xix, 197 p. [LC 79022953; ISN 002512790X]
HF5383. B55 1979   115

ARBITRAGE

Merger mania: arbitrage, Wall Street's best kept money-making secret. Ivan F. Boesky; edited by Jeffrey Madrick. 1st ed. New York: Holt, Rinehart and Winston, c1985. xiv, 242 p. *Notes:* Includes index. [LC 84025193; ISN 0030026024]
HG4521. B565 1985   116

ARCHITECTURE

Architecture and the corporation: the creative intersection. Thomas Walton. New York: Macmillan, c1988. xv, 218 p. : ill. (Studies of the modern corporation) *Notes:* Includes index. Bibliography: p. 197-208. [LC 88013062; ISN 0029339316]
NA1996. W35 1988   117

ART

The business of art. edited by Lee Caplin. 2nd ed. Englewood Cliffs, N.J.: Prentice-Hall, c1989. xx, 347 p. : ill. *Notes:* "Published in cooperation with the National Endowment for the Arts'. Includes bibliographical references. [LC 89015978; ISN 0130916463; $14.95]
N8600. B875 1989   118

ARTHUR D. LITTLE, INC

The problem solvers: a history of Arthur D. Little, Inc. E.J. Kahn, Jr. 1st ed. Boston, MA: Little, Brown and Company, c1986. 234 p. [16] p. of plates: ill., ports. *Notes:* Includes index. [LC 85082421; ISN 0316482129]
HD69.C6 K35   119

ARTIFICIAL INTELLIGENCE

AI: the tumultuous history of the search for artificial intelligence. Daniel Crevier. New York: BasicBooks, c1993. xiv, 386 p. : ill. *Notes:* Includes bibliographical references and index. [LC 91055461; ISBN 0465029973; USA $27.50 (Canada $37.95)] Q335. C66 1993 120

Artificial intelligence applications for manufacturing. written by Richard K. Miller. Madison, GA: SEAI Technical Publications, c1985. 202 p. : ill. *Notes:* Includes bibliographical references.; ISN 0896710629] Q335. M54 121

The muse in the machine: computerizing the poetry of human thought. David Gelernter. New York: Toronto: New York: Free Press; Maxwell Macmillan Canada; Maxwell Macmillan International, c1994. ix, 211 p. : ill. *Notes:* Includes bibliographical references (p. 195-203) and index. [LC 93049721; ISBN 0029116023; $22.95] Q335. G366 1994 +122

ASIA, SOUTHEASTERN—COMMERCIAL POLICY

The economic development of the Pacific Basin: growth dynamics, trade relations, and emerging cooperation. Willy Kraus, Wilfried Lütkenhorst. New York: London: St. Martin's Press; C. Hurst, 1986. x, 180 p., [1] leaf of plates: map *Notes:* Includes index. Bibliography: p. 162-177. [LC 86026292; ISBN 0312004524; $32.50] HF1591. K73 1986 123

ASIA, SOUTHEASTERN—FOREIGN RELATIONS—UNITED STATES

Japan, the United States, and a changing Southeast Asia. Charles E. Morrison. Lanham, MD: New York: University Press of America; Asia Society, c1985. xi, 69 p. : ill. *Notes:* Bibliography: p. 67. [LC 85003164; ISBN 0819145947; ISBN 0819145955; $13.50 / $4.75] HF1456.5.A7 M67 124

ASIA—COMMERCE

Global business: Asia-Pacific dimensions. edited by Erdener Kaynak and Kam-Hon Lee. London; New York: Routledge, 1989. xxxii, 443 p. : ill. *Notes:* Includes bibliographies and index. [LC 88023996; ISBN 0415012708; £45.00] HF3752. G58 1989 125

ASPIRIN

The aspirin wars: money, medicine, and 100 years of rampant competition. by Charles C. Mann and Mark L. Plummer. Boston, MA: Harvard Business School Press, c1991. viii, 420 p., [16] p. of plates: ill. *Notes:* Includes bibliographical references (p. [387]-404) and index.; ISBN 0875844014] HD9675.A72 M36 1991 126

ASSESSMENT CENTERS (PERSONNEL MANAGEMENT PROCEDURE)

Competence at work: models for superior performance. Lyle M. Spencer, Signe M. Spencer. New York: Wiley, c1993. xii, 372 p. : ill. *Notes:* Includes bibliographical references (p. 349-358) and index. [LC 92031255; ISBN 047154809X] HF5549.5.A78 S67 1993 127

Managing managers: strategies and techniques for human resource management. Ed Snape, Tom Redman, and Greg J. Bamber. Oxford, UK; Cambridge, Mass., USA: Blackwell Business, 1994. ix, 210 p. *Notes:* Includes bibliographical references (p. [189]-203) and index. [LC 93001480; ISBN 0631186751; $39.95] HF5549.5.A78 S64 1994 +128

ASSET-BACKED FINANCING

Active asset allocation: state-of-the-art portfolio policies, strategies & tactics. Robert D. Arnott and Frank J. Fabozzi editors. [Revised edition]. Chicago: Probus Publishing Co., c1992. *Notes:* Rev. ed. of: Asset location. c1988. Includes bibliographical references and index.; ISBN 1557382379; $65.00] HG4028.A84 A76 1992 129

AUDITING

Audit sampling: an introduction to statistical sampling in auditing. Dan M. Guy, D.R. Carmichael. 2nd ed. New York: Wiley, c1986. xiv, 257 p. : ill. *Notes:* Includes bibliographical references (p. 221-222) and index. [LC 85026570; ISN 0471815403; $60.00] HF5667. G87 1986 −130

Auditing. Jack C. Robertson. 6th ed. Homewood, IL: BPI/Irwin, c1990. xvii, 765 p. : ill *Notes:* Includes bibliographical references and index. [LC 89031753; ISN 025607724X; $47.95] HF5667. R72 1990 131

Auditing, an integrated approach. Alvin A. Arens, James K. Loebbecke. 4th ed. Englewood Cliffs, N.J.: Prentice Hall, c1988. xvi, 832 p. : ill. (Prentice Hall series in accounting) *Notes:* Includes index. [LC 87026359; ISN 013051814X] HF5667. A69 1988 132

Auditing concepts and methods: a guide to current auditing theory and practice. D.R. Carmichael, John J. Willingham. 5th ed. New York: McGraw-Hill, c1989. xii, 591 p. : ill. *Notes:* Includes index. [LC 89030526; ISN 0070099995; $40.95] HF5667. C2766 1989 133

Auditing, integrated concepts and procedures. Donald H. Taylor, G. William Glezen. 4th ed. New York: Wiley, c1988. xxviii, 845 p. : ill. *Notes:* Includes bibliographical references and index. [LC 88006402; ISN 0471856517; $52.50] HF5667. T295 1988 134

Montgomery's Auditing. 11th ed. / [rev. by] Vincent M. O'Reilly... [et al.]. New York: John Wiley & Sons, Inc., 1990. xxxiv, 1150 p. : ill. [LC 84027103; ISN 0471505226; $115.00] HF 5667. M7 1990 135

Principles of auditing. O. Ray Whittington... et al. 10th ed. Homewood, IL: Irwin, c1992. xxi, 824 p. : ill. *Notes:* Includes bibliographical references and index. [LC 91003925; ISN 0256084084; $57.95] HF5667. M43 1992 136

AUDITING, INTERNAL

Handbook of internal accounting controls. Wanda A. Wallace. 2nd ed. Englewood Cliffs, N.J.: Prentice-Hall, c1991. lxi, 1068 p. : ill. *Notes:* Includes bibliographical references and index. [LC 91025621; ISN 0133880591; $89.95] HF5668.25. W35 1991 137

Internal auditing manual. James D. Willson, Steven J. Root. Boston: Warren, Gorham & Lamont, c1983. 1 v. (loose leaf): ill. (Simonoff accounting series) *Notes:* Includes bibliographies and index. [LC 83060087; ISN 0882628984] HF5668.25. W54 138

Sawyer's internal auditing. Lawrence B. Sawyer, assisted by Glenn E. Sumners. 3rd ed., re-titled, rev. and enl. Altamonte Springs, Fla.: Institute of Internal Auditors, 1988. xviii, 1291 p. : ill. *Notes:* Rev. ed. of: The practice of modern internal auditing. 2nd ed., rev. and enl. 1981. Includes bibliographies and index. [LC 88080092; ISN 0894131788] HF5668.25. S28 1988 139

AUTOMATIC CONTROL EQUIPMENT INDUSTRY

Computer integrated manufacturing systems: selected readings. edited by John W. Nazemetz, William E. Hammer, Jr., and Randall P. Sadowski. Norcross, Ga.: Industrial Engineering and Management Press, Institute of Industrial Engineers, c1985. xii, 303 p. : ill. *Notes:* Includes bibliographical references and index.; ISN 0898060664] TJ213. C65 140

AUTOMATION

Dreams betrayed: working in the technological age. by Carlton Rochell with Christina Spellman. Lexington, Mass.: Lexington Books, c1987. 138 p. *Notes:* Includes index. Bibliography: p. 121-132. [LC 85045019; ISN 0669111058] HD6331.2.U5 R63 1987 141

In the age of the smart machine: the future of work and power. Shoshana Zuboff. New York: Basic Books, c1988. xix, 468 p. : ill. *Notes:* Includes index. Bibliography: p. [430]-457. [LC 87047777; ISN 0465032125; $24.95] HD45.2. Z83 1988 142

AUTOMOBILE INDUSTRY AND TRADE

Changing alliances. Davis Dyer, Malcolm S. Salter, and Alan M. Webber; the Harvard Business School Project on the Auto Industry and the American Economy. Boston, Mass.: Harvard Business School Press, c1987. xvi, 333 p. *Notes:* Includes index. Bibliography: p. 311-324. [LC 86033619; ISN 0875841759] HD9710.U52 D94 1987 143

Collision: GM, Toyota, Volkswagen and the race to own the 21st century. Maryann Keller. 1st ed. New York: Currency Doubleday, c1993. xii, 287 p. *Notes:* Includes bibliographical references (p. [271]-275) and index. [LC 93011071; ISN 038546777X; $25.00 ($31.95 Can.)]
HD9710.A2 K45 1993 +144

Comeback: the fall and rise of the American automobile industry. Paul Ingrassia and Joseph B. White. New York: Simon & Schuster, c1994. 496 p., [16] p. of plates: ill. *Notes:* Includes bibliographical references and index. [LC 94022354; ISN 0671792148] HD9710.U52 I54 1994 +145

Engines of growth: the state and transnational auto companies in Brazil. Helen Shapiro. Cambridge England; New York: Cambridge University Press, 1994. xi, 267 p. : ill. *Notes:* Revision of the author's thesis (doctoral)—Yale University. Includes bibliographical references and index. [LC 92039226; ISN 052141640X; $54.95] HD9710.B82 S48 1994 +146

Entrepreneurship in a "mature industry". edited by John Creighton Campbell. Ann Arbor: Center for Japanese Studies, University of Michigan, c1986. xi, 131 p., [2] p. of plates: ill. *Notes:* Proceedings of the 5th U.S.-Japan Automotive Industry Conference, held at the University of Michigan in Mar. 1985. Includes bibliographies. *Contents:* Simulating and managing corporate entrepreneurship: the auto industry connection / Rosabeth Moss Kanter. [LC 85029128; ISN 093951222X; $9.00] HD9710.A2 E58 1986 147

Government, technology, and the future of the automobile. edited by Douglas H. Ginsburg, William J. Abernathy; in association with the Division of Research, Harvard Graduate School of Business Administration. New York: McGraw-Hill, c1980. xi, 483 p. : ill. *Notes:* Consists of rev. papers and excerpts from discussions presented at the Harvard Business School Symposium on Government, Technology, and the Automotive Future held Oct. 19-20, 1978. Includes index. Bibliography: p. 455-460. [LC 79014448; ISN 0070232911; $29.95] HD9710.U52 H34 1978 148

The Japanese automobile industry: technology and management at Nissan and Toyota. Michael A. Cusumano. Cambridge, Mass.: Published by the Council on East Asian Studies, Harvard University and distributed by the Harvard University Press, 1985. xxi, 487 p. : ill. *Notes:* Includes index. Bibliography: p. 434-452. [LC 85014033; ISN 0674472551] TL105. C77 1985 149

Product development performance: strategy, organization, and management in the world auto industry. Kim B. Clark, Takahiro Fujimoto. Boston, Mass.: Harvard Business School Press, c1991. xi, 409 p. : ill. *Notes:* Includes bibliographical references (p. 357-368) and index. [LC 90047967; ISN 0875842453; $29.95] HD9710.A2 C57 1991 150

The productivity dilemma: roadblock to innovation in the automobile industry. William J. Abernathy. Baltimore: Johns Hopkins University Press, c1978. xii, 257 p. : ill. *Notes:* Includes bibliographical references and index. [LC 78001034; ISN 0801820812] HD9710.U52 A56 151

The reckoning. David Halberstam. New York: Morrow, c1986. 752 p. *Notes:* Includes index. "A Thomas Congdon book." Bibliography: p. [735]-740. [LC 86016427; ISN 0688048382]
HD9710.U52 H28 1986 152

Worker protection, Japanese style: occupational safety and health in the auto industry. Richard E. Wokutch. Ithaca, N.Y.: ILR Press, c1992. xiv, 263 p. : ill. *Notes:* Includes bibliographical references (p. [245]-253) and index. [LC 91048201; ISN 0875461875; $18.95] HD7269.A82 J38 1992 153

AUTOMOBILE SUPPLIES INDUSTRY

Beyond partnership: strategies for innovation and lean supply. Richard Lamming. New York: Prentice Hall, 1993. xvii, 299 p. : ill. *Notes:* Includes bibliographical references and index. [LC 92038797; ISN 0131437852; $35.00] HD9710.3.A2 L35 1993 154

AUTOMOBILES

Regulating the automobile. Robert W. Crandall... et al. Washington, D.C.: Brookings Institution, 1986. xii, 202 p. : ill. (Studies in the regulation of economic activity) *Notes:* Includes bibliographical references and index. [LC 85048171; ISN 0815715943; ISN 0815715935; $28.95; $10.95]
KF2209. C73 1986 155

AVON PRODUCTS, INC

Staying at the top: the life of a CEO. Sonny Kleinfield. New York, N.Y.: New American Library, c1986. 298 p. *Notes:* Includes index. "NAL Books." [LC 86008657; ISN 0453005217]
    HD9970.5.C674 A95 1986   156

BALANCE OF TRADE

Beyond blue economic horizons: U.S. trade performance and international competitiveness in the 1990s. Allen J. Lenz; foreword by Peter G. Peterson. New York: Praeger, 1991. xxi, 262 p. : ill. *Notes:* Includes bibliographical references (p. [251]-255) and index. [LC 90007625; ISN 0275936244; $45.00]
    HF3031. L38 1991   157

Beyond the twin deficits: a trade strategy for the 1990s. Robert A. Blecker. Armonk, N.Y.: M.E. Sharpe, c1992. 177 p. : ill. *Notes:* Includes bibliographical references (p. 157-167) and index. [LC 92009033; ISN 1563240904; $42.50]
    HF3031. B54 1992   158

Understanding the Japanese industrial challenge: from automobiles to software. by Francis M. Jeffries. Poolesville Md. (17200 Hughes Rd., Poolesville, Md. 20837): Jeffries & Associates, Inc., c1987. 404 p. : ill. *Notes:* Includes index. Bibliography: p. 385-389. [LC 85090]   HF3127. J44 1987   159

BANK EMPLOYEES

The training investment: banking on people for superior results. Margaret Rahn Keene. Homewood, Ill.: Business One Irwin, c1991. xiv, 334 p. : ill. *Notes:* Includes bibliographical references and index. [LC 90035839; ISN 1556233183; $50.00]
    HG1615.7.T7 K44 1991   160

BANK FAILURES

Bailout: an insider's account of bank failures and rescues. Irvine H. Sprague. New York: Basic Books, c1986. xii, 299 p. *Notes:* Includes index. Bibliography: p. [271]-280. [LC 85073883; ISN 0465005772; $17.95]
    HG2491. S67 1986   161

BANK MANAGEMENT

High performance in the 90s: leading the strategic and cultural revolution in banking. Cass Bettinger. Homewood, Ill.: Business One Irwin, 1991. xvii, 311 p. : ill. *Notes:* Includes bibliographical references and index. [LC 90041580; ISN 1556234252; $47.50]
    HG1615. B47 1991   162

The new business of banking. George M. Bollenbacher. Chicago, Ill.: Bankers Pub. Co.; Probus Pub. Co., c1992. xii, 237 p. : ill. *Notes:* Includes bibliographical references and index.; ISN 1557383316; $37.50]
    HG1615. B64 1992   163

BANK MARKETING

Bank marketing: a guide to strategic planning. R. Eric Reidenbach, Robert E. Pitts. Englewood Cliffs, N.J.: Prentice-Hall, c1986. ix, 245 p. : ill. *Notes:* "A Reston book." Includes bibliographical references and index. [LC 85025621; ISN 0835904083]
    HG1616.M3 R45 1986   164

Bank marketing handbook: how to compete in the financial services industry. Robert J. McMahon. Boston: Bankers Pub. Co., c1986. xviii, 339 p. : ill. *Notes:* Includes index. Bibliography: p. 321-323. [LC 86020555; ISN 087267102X; $55.00]
    HG1616.M3 M385 1986   165

BANK OF AMERICA

Roller coaster: the Bank of America and the future of American banking. Moira Johnston. New York: Ticknor & Fields, 1990. 417 p., [16] p. of plates: ill. *Notes:* Includes bibliographical references (p. 401-403) and index. [LC 90034521; ISN 0899199550; $22.95]
    HG2613.S54 B275 1990   166

BANK OF CREDIT AND COMMERCE INTERNATIONAL

False profits: the inside story of BCCI, the world's most corrupt financial empire. Peter Truell and Larry Gurwin. Boston: Houghton Mifflin, 1992. xix, 522 p. [8] p. of plates: ill., ports *Notes:* Includes bibliographical references and index. [LC 92037248; ISN 0395623391] HG1978. T78 1992   167

A full service bank: how BCCI stole billions around the world. James Ring Adams and Douglas Frantz. New York: Pocket Books, 1992. xi, 381 p. : ill. *Notes:* Includes bibliographical references (p. 335-363) and index. [LC 91044520; ISN 067172911X; $22.00] HG1978. A34 1992   168

The outlaw bank: a wild ride into the secret heart of BCCI. Jonathan Beaty and S.C. Gwynne. 1st ed. New York: Random House, c1993. xxix, 399 p. *Notes:* Includes bibliographical references (p. [363]-372) and index. [LC 92050153; ISN 0679413847; $25.00] HG1978. B4 1993   169

BANK OF ENGLAND

Portrait of an old lady: turmoil at the Bank of England. Stephen Fay. Harmondsworth; New York: Viking, 1987. 208 p. *Notes:* Includes index. Bibliography: p. 199. [LC 87027360; ISN 0670819344; £10.95] HG2994. F39 1987   170

BANKAMERICA

Breaking the bank: the decline of BankAmerica. by Gary Hector. 1st ed. Boston: Little, Brown, c1988. viii, 363 p., [16] p. of plates: ill., ports. *Notes:* Includes index. Bibliography: p. 353-355. [LC 88008878; ISN 0316353922; $18.95] HG2613.S54 B334 1988   171

BANKERS

Gentlemen of fortune: the world's merchant and investment bankers. Paul Ferris. London: Weidenfeld and Nicolson, 1984. 260 p. *Notes:* Includes bibliographical references and index. [LC 85146003; ISN 0297783807; £10.95] HG1552.A1 F47 1984   172

BANKING LAW

The Financial services resolution: policy directions for the future. edited by Catherine England and Thomas F. Huertas. Norwell, Mass.: Kluwer Academic Publishers, c1988. 361 p. : ill. (Innovations in financial markets and institutions series) *Notes:* Proceedings of a conference held Feb. 26-27, 1987, sponsored by the Cato Institute. Includes bibliographies and index. [LC 87024143; ISN 0898382513; $50.00 (est.)] KDZ260. A6 1988   173

Wall Street and regulation. edited by Samuel L. Hayes, III. Boston, Mass.: Harvard Business School Press, c1987. vii, 260 p. : ill. *Notes:* Includes bibliographies and index. [LC 87008654; ISN 087584183X] KF974. W35 1987   174

Why bank regulation failed: designing a bank regulatory strategy for the 1990s. Helen A. Garten. New York: Quorum Books, 1991. xxii, 179 p. *Notes:* Includes bibliographical references (p. [175]-176) and index. [LC 91000030; ISN 0899305806; $45.00] KF974. G37 1991   175

BANKRUPTCY

As we forgive our debtors: bankruptcy and consumer credit in America. Teresa A. Sullivan, Elizabeth Warren, Jay Lawrence Westbrook. New York: Oxford University Press, 1989. xii, 370 p. *Notes:* Includes bibliographies and index. [LC 88034503; ISN 0195055780; $29.95] HG3766. S79 1989   176

BANKS AND BANKING

American banking in crisis: views from leading financial services CEOs. Richard B. Miller. Homewood, IL: Dow Jones-Irwin, c1990. xiv, 178 p. : ill. [LC 89038531; ISN 1556232217; $34.95] HG2491. M54 1990   177

The bankers' handbook. edited by William H. Baughn, Thomas I. Storrs, Charls E. Walker. 3rd ed. Homewood, Ill.: Dow Jones-Irwin, c1988. xxxix, 1347 p. : ill. *Notes:* Includes bibliographical references and index. [LC 87073024; ISN 1556230435] HG2491. B36 1988 178

Banking deregulation and the new competition in financial services. Kerry Cooper, Donald R. Fraser. Student ed. Cambridge, Mass.: Ballinger Pub. Co., c1986. xix, 318 p. : ill. *Notes:* Includes index. Bibliography: p. 293-303. [LC 85029655; ISN 0887300901] HG2491. C67 1986 179

Banking in the Far East, 1990: structures and sources of finance. edited by Anne Hendrie. London: Financial Times Business Information, c1990. xv, 318 p. *Notes:* "A Financial Times management report."; ISN 1853341274; $259.00] HG3320.5.A6 B36 1990 180

Banking markets and financial institutions. Edited by Thomas G. Gies, and Vincent P. Apilado. Homewood, Ill. R. D. Irwin, 1971. x, 406 p. (The Irwin series in finance) *Notes:* Includes bibliographical references. [LC 76149901] HG2481. G5 +181

Bankrupt: restoring the health and profitability of our banking system. Lowell L. Bryan. New York, NY: HarperBusiness, c1991. x, 315 p. *Notes:* Includes bibliographical references (p. 299) and indexes. [LC 91009045; ISN 0887305113; $22.95 USA ($29.95 Can.)] HG2491. B77 1991 182

Banks, finance and investments in Germany. Jeremy Edwards and Klaus Fischer. Cambridge England New York, NY, USA: Cambridge University Press, c1994. xiv, 252 p. : ill. *Notes:* "Centre for Economic Policy Research." Includes bibliographical references (p. 241-246) and index. [LC 93025115; ISN 0521453488] HG3048. E38 1994 +183

Behind closed doors: wheeling and dealing in the banking world. Hope Lampert. 1st ed. New York: Atheneum, 1986. 386 p. *Notes:* Includes index. Bibliography: p. 377-386. [LC 86047683; ISN 0689117477; $18.95] HG2481. L34 1986 184

Breaking up the bank: rethinking an industry under siege. Lowell L. Bryan. Homewood, Ill.: Dow Jones-Irwin, c1988. xvii, 209 p. : ill. *Notes:* Includes index. Bibliography: p. 197-198. [LC 88014908; ISN 155623144X; $42.50] HG2491. B78 1988 185

Changes in western European banking. by Edward P.M. Gardener and Philip Molyneux. London; Boston: Unwin Hyman, 1990. xix, 300 p.; *Notes:* Includes bibliographical references and index. [LC 90034538; ISN 0044452209; $85.00] HG2974. G37 1990 186

Commercial banking in the economy. Paul S. Nadler. 4th ed. New York: Random House, c1986. xii, 199 p. : ill. *Notes:* Includes index. Bibliography: p. 191-192. [LC 85019630; ISN 0394354001; $10.00] HG2491. N3 1986 187

Commercial banking. 4th ed. / Edward W. Reed, Edward K. Gill. Englewood Cliffs, N.J.: Prentice Hall, c1989. xvi, 472 p. : ill. *Notes:* Rev. ed. of: Commercial banking / Edward W. Reed... et al. 3rd ed. c1984. Includes bibliographies and index. [LC 88015735; ISN 0131543601; $42.36] HG2491. C64 1989 188

Competitive strategies in European banking. Jordi Canals. Oxford: New York: Clarendon Press; Published in the United States by Oxford University Press, 1993. xvii, 284 p. : ill. *Notes:* Includes bibliographical references and index. [LC 92028440; ISN 0198773498] HG2974. C3613 1993 189

Deregulating financial services: public policy in flux. editors, George G. Kaufman, Roger C. Kormendi. Cambridge, Mass.: Ballinger Pub. Co., c1986. xiii, 223 p. *Notes:* "A Mid America Institute for Public Policy Research book." Includes bibliographies and index. [LC 86003355; ISN 0887301118] HG2491. D47 190

The future of American banking. James R. Barth, R. Dan Brumbaugh, Jr., Robert E. Litan. Armonk, N.Y.: M.E. Sharpe, c1992. xxiii, 207 p. : ill. *Notes:* Includes bibliographical references (p. 173-177) and index. [LC 91042825; ISN 1563240343; $49.95] HG2491. B39 1992 191

The future of American banking: managing for change. David Rogers. New York: McGraw-Hill, 1992, c1993. xx, 346 p. *Notes:* Includes bibliographical references (p. 336-340) and index. [LC 92017338; ISN 0070535388; $24.95] HG2491. R62 1992 192

The future of banking. James L. Pierce; foreword by Richard C. Leone. New Haven: Yale University Press, 1991. ix, 163 p. *Notes:* "A Twentieth Century Fund report." Includes bibliographical references (p. 153-157) and index. [LC 91000158; ISN 0300050585; $25.00] HG2491. P54 1991 193

The impact of computers on banking. by James A. O'Brien. Boston Bankers Pub. Co., 1968. xvii, 202 p. illus. *Notes:* Bibliography: p. 185-191. [LC 67028514] HG1709. O2 +194

Money & banking. David H. Friedman. 2nd ed. Washington, D.C.: Education Policy & Development, American Bankers Association, 1989. xvi, 611 p. : ill. *Notes:* Includes index. [LC 88038453; ISN 0899823580; $45.00] HG1601. F75 1989 195

Money and banking. David R. Kamerschen. 9th ed. Cincinnati: South-Western Pub. Co., c1988. xiii, 663 p. : ill. (some col.) *Notes:* Includes bibliographical references and index. [LC 87060482; ISN 0538082712; $37.05] HG1601. K26 1988 196

Money, banking, and the United States economy. Harry D. Hutchinson. 6th ed. Englewood Cliffs, NJ: Prentice Hall, 1988. xv, 558 p. : ill. *Notes:* Includes bibliographical references and index. [LC 87019299; ISN 0136001564]   HG2491. H8 1988   197

Perspectives on safe & sound banking: past, present, and future. by George J. Benston... et al. 1st MIT Press ed. Cambridge, Mass.: MIT Press, 1986. xxi, 358 p. *Notes:* Includes index. "A study commissioned by the American Bankers Association." Bibliography: p. 327-345. [LC 85023882; ISN 026202246X]   HG2481. P47 1986   198

Pricing financial services. G. Michael Moebs, with Eva Moebs. Homewood, Ill.: Dow Jones-Irwin, 1986. xviii, 246 p. : ill. *Notes:* Includes index. Bibliography: p. 231-232. Bibliography: p. 231-232. [LC 85073688; ISN 0870945947]   HG1616.S4 M69   199

Principles of banking. Eric N. Compton. 4th ed. Washington, D.C.: Education Policy & Development, American Bankers Association, c1991. xii, 461 p. : ill. *Notes:* Includes bibliographical references and index. [LC 91008412; ISN 0899823688; $42.55]   HG2461. C64 1991   200

BANKS AND BANKING, CENTRAL

Monetary sovereignty: the politics of central banking in western Europe. John B. Goodman. Ithaca, N.Y.: Cornell University Press, 1992. xii, 239 p. (Cornell paperbacks) *Notes:* Includes bibliographical references and index. [LC 91057897; ISN 0801480132]   HG2980.5.A7 G66 1992   201

BANKS AND BANKING, INTERNATIONAL

The environment of international banking. Charles W. Hultman. Englewood Cliffs, NJ: Prentice Hall, c1990. xv, 288 p. *Notes:* Includes index. Includes bibliographical references. [LC 89008681; ISN 0132828561; $22.00]   HG3881. H837 1990   202

The global bankers. Roy C. Smith. 1st ed. New York: Truman Talley Books, c1989. viii, 405 p. *Notes:* Subtitle on jacket: A top investment banker explores the new world of international dealmaking and finance. Includes index. Bibliography: p. 381-385. [LC 89004724; ISN 0525247971; $22.50]   HG3881. S553 1989   203

Global electronic wholesale banking. by Ajay S. Mookerjee and James I. Cash. London; Boston: Graham & Trotman, 1990. xv, 156 p. : ill. *Notes:* Includes bibliographical references. [LC 90035164; ISN 1853334154; $70.00]   HG3881. M622 1990   204

In whose interest?: international banking and American foreign policy. Benjamin J. Cohen. New Haven: Yale University Press, c1986. xi, 347 p. *Notes:* "A Council on Foreign Relations book." Includes index. Bibliography: p. 317-339. [LC 86009210; ISN 0300036140]   HG3881. C586 1986   205

International money and banking: the creation of a new order. A.W. Mullineux. New York: New York University Press, 1987. xii, 207 p. *Notes:* Includes index. Bibliography: p. 193-200. [LC 87012393; ISN 0814754368; $45.00]   HG3881. M815 1987   206

BARNARD, CHESTER IRVING

Chester I. Barnard and the guardians of the managerial state. William G. Scott. Lawrence, Kan.: University Press of Kansas, c1992. xvii, 233 p. : ports. *Notes:* Includes bibliographical references (p. 217-224) and index. [LC 92009978; ISN 0700605509; $27.50]   HD31.B363 S37 1992   207

BASEBALL

Lords of the realm: the real history of baseball. by John Helyar. 1st ed. New York: Villard Books, 1994. xiii, 576 p. *Notes:* Includes index. [LC 93041944; ISN 0679411976; $23.50]
    GV863.A1 H45 1994   +208

BECHTEL GROUP

Friends in high places: the Bechtel story: the most secret corporation and how it engineered the world. Laton McCartney. New York: Simon and Schuster, c1988. 273 p. : ill. *Notes:* Includes bibliographical references and index. [LC 87034562; ISN 0671474154]   TA217.B4 M38 1988   209

BECK, JEFFREY P

Rainmaker: the saga of Jeff Beck, Wall Street's mad dog. Anthony Bianco. 1st ed. New York: Random House, c1991. 486 p., [8] p. of plates: ill. Notes: Includes index. [LC 88042821; ISN 0394570235; $25.00]   HG4928.5. B53 1991   210

BEEF INDUSTRY

Technological change in Japan's beef industry. James R. Simpson...et al. Boulder, Colo.: Westview Press, 1985. xiii, 264 p.: ill. (Westview special studies in agricultural science and policy) [LC 84015260; ISN 086531876X; $18.50]   HD9433.J32 T43 1984   211

BENCHMARKING (MANAGEMENT)

Benchmarking for competitive advantage. Robert J. Boxwell, Jr. New York: McGraw-Hill, c1994. xiv, 224 p.: ill. Notes: Includes index. [LC 94003940; ISN 0070068992; $34.95]   HD62.15. B69 1994   +212

BIG BUSINESS

The big boys: power and position in American business. Ralph Nader and William Taylor. 1st ed. New York: Pantheon Books, 1986. xix, 571 p. Notes: Includes index. Bibliography: p. 523-553. [LC 85025979; ISN 0394533380; $24.95]   HD2785. N33 1986   213

The essential Alfred Chandler: essays toward a historical theory of big business. edited and with an introduction by Thomas K. McCraw. Boston, Mass.: Harvard Business School Press, c1988. vi, 538 p., [14] p. of plates: ill., maps Notes: "A list of Chandler's publications": p. 505-517. Includes index. [LC 87029754; ISN 0875841767]   HD2785. C4732 1988   214

The revolutionary corporations: engines of plenty, engines of growth, engines of change. John Desmond Glover. Homewood, Ill.: Dow Jones-Irwin, c1980. xvii, 492 p. Notes: Includes bibliographical references. [LC 80066021; ISN 0870942174]   HD2785. G556   215

Scale and scope: the dynamics of industrial capitalism. Alfred D. Chandler, Jr. with the assistance of Takashi Hikino. Cambridge, Mass.: Belknap Press, 1990. xv, 860 p.: ill. Notes: Includes bibliographical references. [LC 89036288; ISN 0674789946; $35.00]   HD2785. C474 1990   216

The third industrial age: strategy for business survival. Charles H. Tavel; translated from the French by Donald C. Caldwell. 2d ed. Oxford; New York: Pergamon Press, 1980. xix, 335 p.: ill. Notes: Translation of L'ère de la personnalité. Includes bibliographical references and indexes. [LC 79040199; ISN 0080225063; £10.00 ($25.00 U.S.)]   HD2351. T3813 1980   217

BIOTECHNOLOGY

The biotechnological challenge. edited by S. Jacobsson, A. Jamison, H. Rothman. Cambridge Cambridgeshire; New York: Cambridge University Press, c1986. 181 p.: ill. Notes: Includes bibliographical references and index. [LC 85021303; ISN 0521307759]   TP248.2. B38 1986   218

Biotechnology: an industry comes of age. by Steve Olson; for the Academy Industry Program...et al. Washington, D.C.: National Academy Press, 1986. viii, 120 p., 8 p. of plates: ill. (some col.) Notes: Based on a conference held in Washington, D.C., Feb. 27-28, 1985, and sponsored by the Academy Industry Program of the National Academy of Sciences, National Academy of Engineering, and Institute of Medicine. Includes bibliographies and index. [LC 85028442; ISN 0309036313]   TP248.14. B56 1986   219

Biotechnology, the science and the business. edited by Vivian Moses and Ronald E. Cape. Chur, Switzerland; New York: Harwood Academic Publishers, c1991. xiii, 596 p.: ill. Notes: Includes bibliographical references and index. [LC 90026538; ISN 3718651114]   TP248.2. B576 1991   220

Biotechnology: the university-industrial complex. Martin Kenney. New Haven: Yale University Press, c1986. xv, 306 p.: ill. Notes: Includes bibliographical references and index. [LC 86001694; ISN 0300033923]   TP248.2. K46 1986   221

Technology and transition: a survey of biotechnology in Russia, Ukraine, and the Baltic States. Anthony Rimmington with Rod Greenshields. Westport, Conn.: Quorum Books, 1992. ix, 227 p. *Notes:* Includes bibliographical references and index. [LC 92020948; ISN 089930804X]
TP248.195.R8 R56 1992   222

BIOTECHNOLOGY INDUSTRIES

Biotechnology and economic development: [papers from the Economic Commission for Europe Symposium on the Importance of Biotechnology for Future Economic Development, June 1985, Szeged, Hungary? edited by United Nations Economic Commission for Europe. 1st ed. Oxford; New York: Pergamon Press, 1986. 209 p. : ill. *Notes:* Published as volume 38 number 1 of the journal Economic bulletin for Europe. . . [LC 86017040; ISN 0080342558; $26.00 (U.S.)]
HD9999.B442 S96 1985   223

Economic aspects of biotechnology. Andrew J. Hacking. Cambridge Cambridgeshire; New York: Cambridge University Press, c1986. x, 306 p. : ill *Notes:* Includes index. Bibliography: p. 289-296. [LC 85012729; ISN 0521258936]
HD9999.B442 H33   224

BLOOMINGDALE'S (FIRM)

Like no other store—: the Bloomingdale's legend and the revolution in American marketing. Marvin Traub and Tom Teicholz. 1st ed. New York: Times Books, c1993. xvi, 428 p., 16 p. of plates: ill. *Notes:* Includes index. [LC 93028035; ISN 0812919637; $25.00 ($32.50 Can.)]
HF5465.U6 B588 1993   +225

BOARD OF GOVERNORS OF THE FEDERAL RESERVE SYSTEM (U.S.)

Fed watching and interest rate projections: a practical guide. David M. Jones. 2nd ed. New York: New York Institute of Finance, 1989. xxi, 225 p. : ill. *Notes:* Includes index. Includes bibliographical references. [LC 88031236; ISN 013313735X; $39.95]
HG2563. J66 1989   226

Leadership at the Fed. Donald F. Kettl. New Haven: Yale University Press, c1986. xiii, 218 p., [6] p. of plates: ill. *Notes:* Includes bibliographical references and index. [LC 86001551; ISN 0300036582]
HG2563. K45 1986   227

Monetary policy and investment opportunities. Laura S. Nowak. Westport, Conn.: Quorum Books, 1993. xii, 214 p. : ill. *Notes:* Includes bibliographical references and index. *Contents:* Pt.I. The central bank's effect on the financial system and the economy. 1. The power and structure of the central bank—2. Federal Reserve open market operations and the government securities market—3. The effect of Federal Reserve open market operations on short-term and long-term interest rates—4. The structure of interest rates—Pt.II. Monetary policy and fixed income, equity, and other investments. 5. The effect of monetary policy on the stock and bond markets—6. Short-term fixed income securities—7. Intermediate- and long-term fixed income securities—8. The effect of monetary policy on particular industries and companies—9. Derivative and hybrid instruments—10. Hedges against monetary policy. [LC 92018366; ISN 089930611X]
HG2565. N68 1993   +228

Secrets of the temple: how the Federal Reserve runs the country. William Greider. New York: Simon and Schuster, c1987. 798 p. *Notes:* Includes index. Bibliography: p. [733]-768. [LC 87016712; ISN 067147989X; $24.95]
HG2563. G72 1987   229

BODY SHOP (FIRM)

Body and soul: profits with principles, the amazing success story of Anita Roddick & the Body Shop. Anita Roddick. 1st American ed. New York: Crown, 1991. 256 p. : ill. (some col.) [LC 91012772; ISN 0517585421; $22.00]
HD9970.5.C674 B637 1991   230

BONDS

Advances in bond analysis & portfolio strategies. edited by Frank J. Fabozzi and T. Dessa Garlicki. Chicago: Probus, 1987. xvi, 682 p. : ill. *Notes:* Spine title: Bond analysis & portfolio strategies. Includes bibliographical footnotes and index.; ISN 0917253620; $40.50 (est.)]   HG4651. A28 1987   231

Corporate senior securities: analysis and evaluation of bonds, convertibles, and preferreds. Richard S. Wilson. Chicago, Ill.: Probus Pub. Co., c1987. xiv, 459 p. : ill. *Notes:* Includes bibliographies and index. [LC 87006980; ISN 0917253795; $42.50]   HG4963. W56 1987   232

Emerging European bond markets. London: IFR Pub., 1991. vi, 212 p. : ill. *Notes:* "Spain, Italy, Scandinavia"—Cover. Includes bibliographical references and index. Erratum slip inserted. [LC 91032972; ISN 1873446152; $185.00]   HG5635. E43 1991   +233

The European bond markets: an overview and analysis for money managers and traders. Stuart K. McLean, editor. 5th ed. Chicago, Ill.: Probus Pub. Co., c1993. xxi, 1616 p. : ill., charts *Notes:* At head of title: "A standing Commission of the European Federation of Financial Analyst Societies, The European Bond Commission in association with International Securities Market Association." Includes bibliographical references and index.; ISN 1557382867; $75.00]   HG5422. E94 1993   234

The handbook of fixed income securities. Frank J. Fabozzi, editor; T. Dessa Fabozzi, associate editor. 4th ed. Burr Ridge, Ill.: Irwin Professional Publishing, 1995. xxxiii, 1402 p. : ill. *Notes:* Includes bibliographical references and index. [LC 93048217; ISN 0786300019]   HG4651. H265 1995   −235

How to invest in bonds. Hugh C. Sherwood. Rev. and updated. New York: Walker, 1983. 161 p. *Notes:* Includes index. [LC 82024716; ISN 0802707327; $13.95]   HG4651. S47 1983   236

Investing: the collected works of Martin L. Leibowitz. Frank J. Fabozzi, editor; foreword by William F. Sharpe. Chicago, Ill.: Probus Pub. Co., c1992. xxxiv, 1168 p. : ill. *Notes:* Spine title: Investing: Leibowitz. Includes bibliographical references and index.; ISN 1557381984; $75.00]   HG4529.5. L44 1992   237

The Japanese bond markets: an overview and analysis. Frank J. Fabozzi, editor. Chicago, Ill.: Probus Publishing, 1990. viii, 537 p. *Notes:* Includes bibliographical references and index.; ISN 1557381127; $47.50]   HG5772. J37 1990   238

The new corporate bond market: a complete and insightful analysis of the latest trends, issues, and advances. Richard S. Wilson, Frank J. Fabozzi Chicago, Ill.: Probus Pub. Co., c1990. x, 453 p. : ill. *Notes:* Includes bibliographical references. [LC 90008078; ISN 1557381283; $55.00]   HG4963. W564 1990   239

Standard & Poor's ratings guide: corporate bonds, commercial paper, municipal bonds, international securities. New York: McGraw-Hill, c1979. xxiii, 417 p. : ill. *Notes:* Includes index. [LC 79015373; ISN 0070518831; $19.95]   HG4651. S7 1979   240

BRAND NAME PRODUCTS

Branding in action: cases and strategies for profitable brand management. Graham Hankinson and Philippa Cowking. London; New York: McGraw-Hill, c1993. xiv, 226 p. : ill. *Notes:* "Based on in-depth discussion with managers of leading UK and international branded products and services..."—Back cover. Includes bibliographical references and index. [LC 93026441; ISN 0077078128; £24.95]   HF5415.13. H348 1993   +241

World class brands. Chris Macrae. Wokingham, England; Reading, Mass.: Addison-Wesley, c1991. xii, 196 p. : ill. *Notes:* "54407"—Spine. Includes bibliographical references (p. 187-188) and indexes. [LC 91009557; ISN 0201544075; $34.00 (U.S.: est.)]   HD69.B7 M33 1991   242

BREAK-EVEN ANALYSIS

Break-even analyses: basic model, variants, extensions. Marcell Schweitzer, Ernst Trossmann, Gerald H. Lawson. Chichester England; New York: Wiley, c1992. xvi, 306 p. : ill. *Notes:* Translation of: Break-even analysen: Grundmodels, varianten, erweiterungen. Includes bibliographical references (p. [291]-297) and indexes. [LC 91000609; ISN 0471930652; $84.95 (U.S.)]   HD47.25. S3913 1992   243

BROADCAST ADVERTISING

The new ad media reality: electronic over print. Barton C. White. Westport, Conn.: Quorum Books, 1993. xxiv, 236 p. : ill. *Notes:* Includes bibliographical references (p. [227]-230) and index. [LC 93018242; ISN 0899307957; $55.00]   HF6146.B74 W48 1993   +244

BROKERS

The money culture. by Michael Lewis. 1st ed. New York: W.W. Norton, 1991. xv, 282 p. [LC 91013331; ISN 0393030377; $19.95]   HG4621. L48 1991   245

Sex and money: behind the scenes with the big-time brokers. John D. Spooner. Boston: Houghton Mifflin, 1985. 258 p. [LC 84022570; ISN 0395354080]   HG4621. S745 1985   246

BUDGET DEFICITS

Red ink II: a guide to understanding the continuing deficit dilemma. Alfred J. Watkins; introduction by William A. Galston. Lanhan: Washington, D.C.: Hamilton Press; Roosevelt Center for American Policy Studies, c1988. xii, 107 p. [LC 87036000; ISN 0819168386; ISN 0819168394]
HJ2052. W38 1988   247

BUDGET IN BUSINESS

Budgeting: profit planning and control. 5th ed. / Glenn A. Welsch, Ronald W. Hilton, Paul N. Gordon. Englewood Cliffs, NJ: Prentice Hall, c1988. xx, 661 p. : ill. (Prentice-Hall series in accounting) *Notes:* Includes bibliographies and index. [LC 88004030; ISN 0130857548; $32.00]
HG4028.B8 W45 1988   248

BUFFETT, WARREN

The midas touch: the strategies that have made Warren Buffet America's pre-eminent investor. by John Train. 1st ed. New York: Harper & Row, c1987. xi, 207 p. *Notes:* Includes index. Bibliography: p. [193]-195. [LC 86045157; ISN 0060156430; $17.95]   HG172.B84 T72 1987   249

Warren Buffett: the good guy of Wall Street. by Andrew Kilpatrick. New York: Donald I. Fine, c1992. 304 p. : ill. *Notes:* Includes index. [LC 92053078; ISN 155611334X]   HG4928.5.B84 K54 1992   250

The Warren Buffett way: investment strategies of the world's greatest investor. Robert G. Hagstrom. New York: J. Wiley, c1994. xii, 274 p. : ill. *Notes:* Includes bibliographical references and index. [LC 94020586; ISN 0471044601]   HG172.B84 H34 1994   +251

BUITONI, BRUNO

Pasta e cioccolato: una storia imprenditoriale. Bruno Buitoni; intervista di Giampaolo Gallo; postfazione di Giulio Sapelli. Perugia: Protagon, c1992. 509 p. : ill., geneal. table *Notes:* Includes index. [LC 93143695; ISN 8878910619; L38000]   HD9330.M322 B34 1992   252

BURANDT, GARY

Moscow meets Madison Avenue: the adventures of the first American adman in the U.S.S.R. Gary Burandt with Nancy Giges. 1st ed. New York: HarperBusiness, c1992. xiv, 222 p. : ill. [LC 92052609; ISN 0887305709; $22.50]   HF5810.B87 A3 1992   253

BUREAUCRACY

The vulnerable fortress: bureaucratic organization and management in the information age. James R. Taylor and Elizabeth J. Van Every; with contributions from Hélène Akzam, Margot Hovey, Gavin Taylor. Toronto: University of Toronto Press, c1993. xxiii, 283 p. : ill. *Notes:* Includes bibliographical references (p. [263]-277) and index [LC 93184304; ISN 0802077730]
HD38.4. T39 1993 +254

BURGMASTER CORPORATION

When the machine stopped: a cautionary tale from industrial America. Max Holland. Boston, Mass.: Harvard Business School Press, c1989. xiii, 335 p. *Notes:* Includes index. Bibliography: p. 317-325. [LC 88031566; ISN 0875842089]
HD9703.U54 B875 1989 255

BUSINESS

Business and society: economic, moral, and political foundations: text and readings. compiled by Thomas G. Marx. Englewood Cliffs, NJ: Prentice-Hall, c1985. xii, 370 p. *Notes:* Cover title: Business & society. Includes index. Includes bibliographies. [LC 84017961; ISN 0131075667]
HD60. B872 1985 256

Business in the age of information. John Diebold. New York, N.Y.: American Management Association, c1985. xi, 145 p. *Notes:* Includes index. [LC 84045782; ISN 0814457924]
HF5548.2. D5113 1985 257

Business information systems: an introduction. David Kroenke, Richard Hatch. 5th ed. New York: Mitchell McGraw-Hill, c1993. xxvii, 516 p. : ill. (some col.) *Notes:* Previous editions published under title: Business computer systems. Includes index. [LC 93023376; ISN 0070358710]
HF5548.2. K74 1993 258

Business systems for microcomputers: concept, design, and implementation. William D. Haueisen, James L. Camp. Englewood Cliffs, N.J.: Prentice-Hall, c1982. xvi, 416 p. : ill. (Prentice-Hall series in data processing management) *Notes:* Includes index. [LC 81021025; ISN 0131078054]
HF5548.2. H396 1982 259

Business telematics: corporate networks for the information age. Byron Belitsos, Jay Misra. Homewood, Ill.: Dow Jones-Irwin, c1986. xviii, 460 p. : ill., ports. *Notes:* Includes bibliographies and index. [LC 86070719; ISN 087094777X]
HD30.335. B44 260

The business value of computers. Paul A. Strassmann. New Canaan, Conn.: Information Economics Press, c1990. xix, 522 p. : ill. *Notes:* Includes bibliographical references and index. [LC 88080753; ISN 0962041327; $56.35]
HF5548.2. S825 1990 261

The corporate conscience: money, power, and responsible business. David Freudberg. New York, NY: American Management Association, c1986. vi, 248 p. [LC 85048223; ISN 0814458106]
HD60.5.U5 F67 1986 262

Corporate information systems management: the issues facing senior executives. James I. Cash, Jr., F. Warren McFarlan, James L. McKenney. 3rd ed. Homewood, Ill.: Business One Irwin, c1992. xv, 301 p. *Notes:* Includes bibliographical references and index. [LC 92004192; ISN 1556236158; $42.75]
T58.6. C3672 1992 263

Corporate revolution: new strategies for executive leadership. Roger Hayes and Reginald Watts. New York: Nichols Pub. Co., 1986. 246 p. *Notes:* Includes index. [LC 86012499; ISN 089397255X; $28.50]
HD60. H394 1986 264

Creating expert systems for business and industry. Paul Harmon, Brian Sawyer. New York: Wiley, c1990. xvii, 329 p. : ill. *Notes:* Includes index. Bibliography: p. 315-318. [LC 89014834; ISN 0471614955; $34.95]
HF5548.2. H366 1990 265

Dial 9 to get out!: commentaries on business life as heard on public radio's Marketplace. David Graulich. 1st ed. San Francisco: Berrett-Koehler Publishers, c1994. xv, 111 p. [LC 94003958; ISN 1881052503; $9.95]
HF5007. G72 1994 −266

Did you know?: fascinating facts & fallacies about business. D. Keith Denton, Charles Boyd. Englewood Cliffs, N.J.: Prentice Hall, 1994. viii, 255 p. : ill. *Notes:* Includes bibliographical references (p. 227-255). [LC 93047947; ISN 013032194X]
HF5341. D46 1994 −267

An exaltation of business and finance. James Lipton; designed by Kedakai Lipton. 1st ed. New York: Villard, 1993. 64 p. : ill. [LC 93018267; ISN 0679418695; $10.00]
HF5391. L57 1993 268

Expert systems: tools and applications. Paul Harmon, Rex Maus, William Morrissey. New York: Wiley, c1988. xii, 289 p. : ill. *Notes:* Includes index. Bibliography: p. 272-274. [LC 87017608; ISN 0471839507; ISN 0471839515]　　　　　　　　　　　　　　　　QA76.9.E96 H38 1988　　269

Fortune cookies: management wit and wisdom from Fortune magazine. edited by Alan Deutschman; conceived by Leslie Gaines-Ross. 1st ed. New York, N.Y.: Vintage Books, 1993. viii, 86 p. *Notes:* Collection of material previously published 1987-1993. [LC 92050705; ISN 0679745920; $8.00]　　　　　　　　　　　　　　　　　　　　　　　　　　　　　　　HD38. F67 1993　　270

Guides to corporate responsibility series. Boston c1958-1972. 163 p. illus. (part col.) *Notes:* Cover title. Reprints from the Harvard Business Review, 1958-1972.]　　　HD60. H38 1958　　+271

The heart of business: ethics, power, and philosophy. by Peter Koestenbaum. San Francisco: New York, NY: Saybrook Pub. Co.; Distributed by Norton, c1987. xiii, 368 p. : ill. [LC 87013665; ISN 0933071159; $19.95]　　　　　　　　　　　　　　　　　　　　HF5351. K586 1987　　272

How to build business-wide databases. John E. Gessford. New York: Wiley, c1991. vii, 424 p. : ill. *Notes:* Includes bibliographical references and index. [LC 91026726; ISN 0471532274]　　　　　　　　　　　　　　　　　　　　　　　　　　　　　　HF5548.2. G478 1991　　273

Information systems for management: a book of readings. edited by Hugh J. Watson, Archie B. Carroll, Robert I. Mann. 4th ed. Homewood, IL: Irwin, 1991. xi, 436 p. : ill. *Notes:* Includes bibliographical references. [LC 90028255; ISN 0256093903]　　HF5548.2. I42433 1991　　274

Introduction to computers. Elias M. Awad. [2nd ed.] Englewood Cliffs, N.J.: Prentice-Hall, c1983. ix, 491 p. : ill. *Notes:* Rev. ed. of: Introduction to computers in business. c1977. Includes bibliographical references and index. [LC 82016652; ISN 0134794443]　　HF5548.2. A92 1983　　275

Introduction to information systems in business management. James A. O'Brien. 6th ed. Homewood, IL: Irwin, c1991. 1 v. (various pagings): ill. (some col.) *Notes:* Rev. ed. of: Information systems in business management. Includes bibliographical references and index. [LC 90038637; ISN 0256088551; $44.95]　　　　　　　　　　　　　　　　　　HF5548.2. O23 1991　　276

The invisible powers: the language of business. John J. Clancy. Lexington, Mass.: Lexington Books, c1989. xi, 331 p. *Notes:* Includes index. Bibliography: p. [319]-325. [LC 88023109; ISN 0669195421]　　　　　　　　　　　　　　　　　　　　　　　　　HF1002.5. C57 1989　　277

Issues in business and society: capitalism and public purpose. Grover Starling, Otis W. Baskin. Boston, Mass.: Kent Pub. Co., c1985. viii, 499 p. : ill. *Notes:* Includes bibliographical references. [LC 84021851; ISN 053403098X; $13.50 (est.)]　　　　　　　　　　　HD60. S69 1985　　278

Knowledge processing and applied artificial intelligence. Soumitra Dutta. Oxford: Butterworth-Heinemann, 1993. xvii, 352 p. : ill. *Notes:* Title on cover and spine: Knowledge processing & applied artificial intelligence. Includes bibliographical references and index. [LC 93053133; ISN 0750616121]　　　　　　　　　　　　　　　　　　　　　　　　　HF5548.2. D87 1993　　+279

Managing information: the challenge and the opportunity. John Diebold. New York, NY: AMACOM, American Management Associations, c1985. 131 p. *Notes:* Includes index. [LC 84045223; ISN 0814457932]　　　　　　　　　　　　　　　　　　　　　　　　　HF5548.2. D512 1985　　280

Managing the corporate social environment: a grounded theory. Robert H. Miles. Englewood Cliffs, N.J.: Prentice-Hall, c1987. xvi, 319 p. : ill. *Notes:* Includes indexes. Bibliography: p. 305-309. [LC 86012245; ISN 0135508800; ISN 013550872X]　　　　　　HD60.5.U5 M55 1987　　281

Raising the bottom line: business leadership in a changing society. Carlton E. Spitzer. New York: Longman, c1982. xiv, 226 p. (Longman series in public communication) *Notes:* Includes index. [LC 81014308; ISN 0582282411]　　　　　　　　　　　　　　　　　HD60.5.U5 S64　　282

Research methods for business: a skill-building approach. Uma Sekaran. 2nd ed. New York: Wiley, c1992. xvi, 428 p. : ill. *Notes:* Includes bibliographical references (p. 393-397) and index. [LC 91038872; $59.29]　　　　　　　　　　　　　　　　　　　　　　　HD30.4. S435 1992　　283

Shaping the future: business design through information technology. Peter G.W. Keen. Boston, Mass.: Harvard Business School Press, c1991. xi, 264 p. : ill. *Notes:* Includes bibliographical references and index. [LC 90049732; $24.95]　　　　　　　　　　　　　　　HF5548.2. K395 1991　　284

BUSINESS AND POLITICS

Corporate strategy, public policy, and the Fortune 500: how America's major corporations influence government. Mike H. Ryan, Carl L. Swanson and Rogene A. Buchholz. Oxford, Oxfordshire; New York, NY, USA: Blackwell, 1987. vi, 249 p. : ill. *Notes:* Includes bibliographical references and index. [LC 86026437; ISN 0631153454; $49.95]　　　　　　JK467. R9 1987　　285

Fluctuating fortunes: the political power of business in America. David Vogel. New York: Basic Books, 1989. xi, 337 p. *Notes:* Includes index. Bibliography: p. [301]-322. [LC 88047904; ISN 046502470X; $20.95]　　　　　　　　　　　　　　　　　　　　　JK467. V64 1989　　286

Money talks: corporate PACs and political influence. Dan Clawson, Alan Neustadtl, Denise Scott. New York, NY: BasicBooks, c1992. xvi, 272 p. : ill. *Notes:* Includes bibliographical references (p. 251-261) and index. [LC 91059019; ISN 046502680X; $25.00 (Canada $33.50)]　　JF467. C53 1992　　287

The structure of power in America: the corporate elite as a ruling class. edited by Michael Schwartz. New York: Holmes & Meier, 1987. xiii, 256 p. : ill. *Notes:* Includes index. Bibliography: p. 218-244. [LC 87014849; ISN 0841907641; ISN 084190765X]　　JK467. S77 1987　　288

BUSINESS COMMUNICATION

Business communication: a process approach. Caroline L. Bloomfield, Irene R. Fairley. San Diego: Harcourt Brace Jovanovich, c1991. xx, 549 p. : ill. *Notes:* Includes bibliographical references and index. [LC 90083123; ISN 0155056689]　　HF5718. B55 1991　　289

Communicate with confidence!: how to say it right the first time and every time. Dianna Booher. New York: McGraw-Hill, c1994. xv, 413 p. *Notes:* Includes bibliographical references (p. 401-412). [LC 94013665; ISN 007006606X; ISN 0070064555; $12.95; $39.95]　　HF5718. B654 1994　　+290

Communicating in business: an action-oriented approach. F. Stanford Wayne, David P. Dauwalder. Homewood, IL: Burr Ridge, Ill.: Austen Press: Irwin, c1994. xviii, 669, 46 p. : col. ill. *Notes:* Includes bibliographical references (p. 15-22, 2nd sequence) and index. Focuses on the decision-making/business action purposes of comunication and how to shape communication and action using modern business tools. [LC 93037481; ISN 0256133638; ISN 0256158959]　　HF5718. W39 1994　　+291

Communication for management and business. Norman B. Sigband, Arthur H. Bell. 5th ed. Glenview, Ill.: Scott, Foresman, c1989. 633, [150] p. : ill. (some col.) *Notes:* Includes bibliographical references and index. [LC 88029679; ISN 0673383229; $34.00 (est.)]　　HF5718. S53 1989　　292

Excellence in business communication. John V. Thill, Courtland L. Bovée. 2nd ed. New York: McGraw-Hill, c1993. xix, 542, [14] p. : col. ill., ports. *Notes:* Includes bibliographical references and indexes. [LC 92033421; ISN 0070068674]　　HF5718.2.U6 T45 1993　　293

Guide to managerial communication. Mary Munter. 3rd ed. Englewood Cliffs, N.J.: Prentice Hall, c1992. xv, 174 p. : ill. *Notes:* Includes bibliographical references (p. 163-166) and index. [LC 91019471; ISN 0133659909; $13.95]　　HF5718. M86 1992　　294

Profiting in America's multicultural marketplace: how to do business across cultural lines. by Sondra Thiederman. New York: Toronto: New York: Lexington Books; Maxwell Macmillan Canada; Maxwell Macmillan International, c1991. xxiv, 262 p. *Notes:* Includes bibliographical references (p. [253]) and index. [LC 91010833; ISN 0669219290; $24.95]　　HF5718. T457 1991　　295

BUSINESS COMMUNICATION AND PRESENTATION

Presenting for women in business. Carole McKenzie. London: Mercury, 1991. x, 213 p. : ill. *Notes:* Includes bibliographical references (p. 203-204) and index. [LC 91088383; ISN 1852511400; £14.95]　　HF5718.22. M324 1991　　296

BUSINESS CONSULTANTS

The business plan guide for independent consultants. Herman Holtz. New York: Wiley, c1994. xi, 228 p. : ill. *Notes:* Includes bibliographical references and index. [LC 94006924; ISN 047159735X]　　HD69.C6 H6185 1994　　+297

The complete guide to consulting success. Howard Shenson, Ted Nicholas. Chicago, Ill.: Enterprise-Dearborn, c1993. x, 205 p. : ill. *Notes:* Includes bibliographical references (p. 189-200) and index. [LC 92036901; ISN 0793104920]　　HD69.C6 S516 1993　　298

The consultant's proposal, fee, and contract problem-solver. Ron Tepper. New York: Wiley, c1993. vii, 245 p. : ill. *Notes:* Includes index. [LC 92034607; ISN 0471582131]　　HD69.C6 T473 1993　　+299

The consulting process in action. Gordon Lippitt, Ronald Lippitt. 2nd ed. San Diego, Calif.: University Associates, c1986. ix, 213 p. : ill. *Notes:* Bibliography: p. 211-213. [LC 86019693; ISN 088390201X]　　HD69.C6 L54 1986　　300

Handbook of management consulting services. Sam W. Barcus III, editor, Joseph W. Wilkinson, editor. New York: McGraw-Hill, c1986. xiv, 439 p. *Notes:* Includes index. Bibliography: p. 421-426. [LC 85023144; ISN 0070036586]　　HD69.C6 H36 1986　　301

How to make it big as a consultant. William A. Cohen. 2nd ed. New York, NY: AMACOM, c1991. xiii, 319 p. : ill. *Notes:* Includes bibliographical references and index. [LC 90055203; ISN 0814459412; $24.95] HD69.C6 C595 1991 302

How to succeed as an independent consultant. Herman Holtz. 3rd ed. New York: Wiley, c1993. xv, 397 p. : ill. [LC 92036040; ISN 047157581X] HD69.C6 H63 1993 303

Management advisory services manual. Glenn H. Van Doren, Stephen D. Nadler. Boston: Warren, Gorham & Lamont, c1987- 1 v. (loose-leaf): ill. *Notes:* Includes index. Kept up to date with supplements. [LC 87050240; ISN 0887125050] HD69.C6 V36 1987 304

Management consulting, 1990: the state of the profession: a symposium-in-print on the occasion of our 20th anniversary. Kennedy Publications, Consultants News. Fitzwilliam, NH: Kennedy Publications, c1990. 127 p. : ill. *Notes:* Published on the occasion of the 20th anniversary of Consultants News. Includes bibliographical references.; ISN 0916654656] HD69.C6 M365 1990 305

Management consulting: a game without chips. Thomas G. Cody. Fitzwilliam, N.H.: Consultants News, c1986. xii, 180 p.; ISN 0916654362] HD69.C6 C59 306

The management consulting idea book. editor, James H. Kennedy [1st ed.] Fitzwilliam, N.H.: Consultants News, 1988. v.: ill. *Notes:* Spine title: MC idea book. Contains articles published in "Consultants News" between 1970-1979. Library has: v.1; ISN 0916654583] HD69.C6 M363 1988 307

BUSINESS CYCLES

The American business cycle: continuity and change. edited by Robert J. Gordon. Chicago: University of Chicago Press, 1986. xiv, 868 p. : ill. *Notes:* Includes bibliographies and index. [LC 85029026; ISN 0226304523] HB3743. N37 1984 308

Business cycles and forecasting. Lloyd M. Valentine, Dennis F. Ellis. 8th ed. Cincinnati: South-Western Pub. Co., c1991. vii, 586 p. : ill. *Notes:* Includes bibliographical references and index. [LC 90033876; ISN 0538805757; $48.99] HB3730. V29 1991 309

Business cycles: theory and evidence. Andy Mullineux, David G. Dickinson and WenSheng Peng. Oxford, UK; Cambridge, USA: Blackwell, 1993. xiii, 162 p. : ill. *Notes:* Includes bibliographical references (p. [131]-155) and index. [LC 92026627; ISN 0631185666; ISN 0631185674] HB3711. M82 1993 +310

Financial dynamics and business cycles: new perspectives. edited by Willi Semmler. Armonk, N.Y.: M.E. Sharpe, c1989. xxi, 251 p. : ill. *Notes:* Includes bibliographical references. [LC 88030857; ISN 0873325311; $47.50] HB3722. F56 1989 311

The handbook of economic cycles: Jake Bernstein's comprehensive guide to repetitive price patterns in stocks, futures, and financials. Homewood, IL: Business One Irwin, c1991. xvii, 282 p. : ill. *Notes:* Includes bibliographical references (p. 273-277) and index. [LC 91008285; ISN 1556232942; $65.00] HB3711. B46 1991 312

Meltdown: the great '90s depression and how to come through it a winner. William Houston. London: Smith Gryphon Publishers, 1993. xi, 211 p. *Notes:* Includes bibliographical references (p. 203-204) and index.; ISN 185685034X; £15.99] HB3722. H68 1993 313

Models of business cycles. Robert E. Lucas, Jr. Oxford Oxfordshire; New York, NY, USA: B. Blackwell, 1987. 115 p. (Yrjö Jahnsson lectures) *Notes:* Includes bibliographical references and index. [LC 86017622; ISN 0631147896; £16.50 ($34.95 U.S.)] HB3711. L82 1987 314

BUSINESS EDUCATION

The monster under the bed: how business is mastering the opportunity of knowledge for profit. Stan Davis and Jim Botkin. New York: Simon & Schuster, c1994. 189 p. : ill. *Notes:* Includes bibliographical references and index. [LC 94012549; ISN 0671871072] HF1106. D38 1994 +315

BUSINESS ENTERPRISES

The art of reckoning: analysis of performance criteria. Samuel Eilon. London; Orlando: Academic Press, 1984. xv, 507 p. : ill. (Decision science series) *Notes:* Includes bibliographical references and index. [LC 84253143; ISN 0122340809] HG4026. E44 1984 316

Basic financial management. John D. Martin... et al. 5th ed. Englewood Cliffs, NJ: Prentice Hall, c1991. xxiii, 952 p. : col. ill. *Notes:* Includes bibliographical references and index. [LC 90007178; ISN 0130608076] HG4026. B318 1991 317

Challenges & opportunities for business in post-apartheid South Africa. edited by Meg Voorhes. Washington, DC: Investor Responsibility Research Center, c1994. v, 118 p. : ill. *Notes:* Edited transcripts from a conference held by the Investor Responsibility Research Center on October 12, 1993 in Washington, D.C.; ISN 1879775182] HF3901.A46 C52 1994 +318

The coming of managerial capitalism: a casebook on the history of American economic institutions. Alfred D. Chandler, Jr., Richard S. Tedlow. Homewood, Ill.: R.D. Irwin, 1985. xiv, 877 p. : ill. (The Irwin series in management and the behavioral sciences) *Notes:* Includes bibliographical references and index. [LC 84082470; ISN 0256032853] HD2785. C47 1985 319

Corporate valuation: a business and professional guide. Gordon V. Smith. New York: Wiley, c1988. xiv, 224 p. : ill. (Wiley/Ronald-National Association of Accountants professional book series) *Notes:* Includes index. Bibliography: p. 215-217. [LC 87023114; ISN 0471858269] HG4028.V3 S58 1988 320

Doing business on the Internet: how the electronic highway is transforming American companies. Mary J. Cronin. New York: Van Nostrand Reinhold, c1994. xi, 308 p. *Notes:* Includes bibliographical references and index. [LC 93037806; ISN 0442017707; $26.95] HD30.335. C76 1994 +321

Financial forecasting and planning: a guide for accounting, marketing, and planning managers. Sharon Hatten Garrison, Wallace N. Davidson, Jr., and Michael A. Garrison. New York: Quorum, c1988. 160 p. : ill. *Notes:* Includes index. [LC 87036097; ISN 0899302653] HG4026. G37 1988 322

Financial planning and control. edited by M.A. Pocock and A.H. Taylor. 2nd ed. Aldershot, Hants, England; Brookfield, Vt., U.S.A.: Gower, 1988. xxiv, 459 p. : ill. *Notes:* Rev. ed. of: Handbook of financial planning and control. c1981. Spine title: Financial planning & control. Includes bibliographies and index. [LC 88010888; ISN 0566027135; $90.00 (U.S.)] HG4026.5. F575 1988 323

Guide to financial analysis. Oswald D. Bowlin, John D. Martin, David F. Scott, Jr. 2nd ed. New York: McGraw-Hill, c1990. xiii, 417 p. : ill. *Notes:* Includes bibliographical references. [LC 89028400; ISN 0070068054; $22.93] HG4011. B655 1990 324

Handbook for raising capital: financing alternatives for emerging and growing businesses. edited by Lawrence Chimerine, Robert F. Cushman, Howard D. Ross. Homewood, Ill.: Dow Jones-Irwin, c1987. xxiv, 666 p. : ill., ports. *Notes:* Includes bibliographical references. [LC 86071216; ISN 0870947052] HG4061. H36 325

Handbook of business valuation. by Thomas L. West and Jeffrey D. Jones. New York: Wiley, c1992. xxvi, 438 p. : ill. *Notes:* Includes bibliographical references and index. [LC 91024759; ISN 0471537551; $75.00] HG4028.V3 B77 1992 326

Intermediate financial management. Eugene F. Brigham, Louis C. Gapenski. 3rd ed. Chicago: Dryden Press, c1990. xxiii, 923, [36] p. : ill. *Notes:* Includes bibliographies and index. [LC 89001495; ISN 0030305527; $55.71] HG4026. B6694 1990 327

Modern business financing: a guide to innovative strategies and techniques. Robert Douglas Colman. Englewood Cliffs, N.J.: Prentice-Hall, c1986. xxii, 281 p. : ill. *Notes:* Includes index. [LC 85020490; ISN 0135890608] HG4027.3. C64 1986 328

Risks: reading corporate signals. Haig J. Boyadjian and James F. Warren. Chichester; New York: Wiley, c1987. xii, 392 p. : ill. *Notes:* Includes index. [LC 86015661; ISN 0471912077; $23.00 (U.S.)] HG4026. B66 1987 329

BUSINESS ETHICS

American business values. Gerald F. Cavanagh. 3rd ed. Englewood Cliffs, N.J.: Prentice Hall, c1990. xvi, 286 p. : ill. *Notes:* Includes bibliographical references. [LC 89037484; ISN 0130255297; $19.44] HF5387. C379 1990 330

Business environment and business ethics: the social, moral, and the political dimensions of management. edited by Karen Paul. Cambridge, Mass.: Ballinger, c1987. xi, 151 p. (Ballinger series in business in a global environment) *Notes:* Includes index. Bibliography: p. 131-140. [LC 87003573; ISN 0887302041] HF5387. B867 1987 331

Business ethics & common sense. edited by Robert W. McGee. Westport, Conn.: Quorum Books, 1992. viii, 302 p. *Notes:* Includes bibliographical references and index. [LC 92009568; ISN 0899307280] HF5387. B871 1992 332

Business ethics. Norman E. Bowie, Ronald F. Duska. 2nd ed. Englewood Cliffs, N.J.: Prentice Hall, 1990. viii, 120 p. : *Notes:* Includes bibliographical references. [LC 89038973; ISN 0130959103; $19.60] HF5387. B68 1990 333

Business ethics. Richard T. De George. 3rd ed. New York: London: Macmillan; Collier Macmillan, c1990. x, 486 p. *Notes:* Includes index. Bibliography: p. 465-476. [LC 89030478; ISN 0023280115; $26.00] HF5387. D38 1990 334

Business ethics. Thomas M. Garrett, Richard J. Klonoski. 2nd ed. Englewood Cliffs, N.J.: Prentice-Hall, c1986. xii, 171 p. *Notes:* Includes index. Bibliography: p. 161-166. [LC 84024927; ISN 0130958379]
HF5387. G37 1986   335

Business ethics: a managerial, stakeholder approach. Joseph W. Weiss. Belmont, Calif.: Wadsworth Pub. Co., c1994. xv, 287 p. *Notes:* Includes bibliographical references and index. [LC 93027746; ISN 053492512X; $19.95]
HF5387. W45 1994   +336

Business ethics: a philosophical reader. edited by Thomas I. White. New York: Toronto: Macmillan Pub.; Maxwell Macmillan Canada, c1993. xvii, 867 p. *Notes:* Includes bibliographical references. [LC 92019146; ISN 0024272213]
HF5387. B8713 1993   337

Business ethics: concepts and cases. Manuel G. Velasquez. 3rd ed. Englewood Cliffs, N.J.: Prentice Hall, c1992. x, 448 p. : ill. *Notes:* Includes index. [LC 91040468; ISN 013096025X]
HF5387. V44 1992   338

Business ethics: Japan and the global economy. edited by Thomas W. Dunfee and Yukimasa Nagayasu. Dordrecht: Boston: Kluwer Academic Publishers, c1993. xi, 275 p. *Notes:* "In cooperation with the Institute of Moralogy, Kashiwa City, Japan." "Edited versions of papers given at two conferences in Japan"—Verso t.p. Includes bibliographical references. [LC 93027884; ISN 0792324277; $85.00]
HF5387. B8724 1993   +339

Business ethics: reflections from a Platonic point of view. Sherwin Klein. New York: P. Lang, c1993. xv, 160 p. *Notes:* Includes bibliographical references and index. [LC 92022662; ISN 0820419486]
HF5387. K575 1993   +340

Business ethics: the state of the art. edited by R. Edward Freeman. New York: Oxford University Press, 1991. x, 225 p. *Notes:* Includes bibliographical references and index. *Contents:* Business ethics as a discipline: the search for legitimacy / Norman E. Bowie—Will success spoil business ethics? / Richard T. DeGeorge—Commentary on business ethics as a discipline: the search for legitimacy / William C. Frederick—Autonomy and the legitimacy of the liberal arts / Jennifer Moore—Ethics as character development: reflections on the objective of ethics education / Lynn Sharp Paine—Ethical imperatives and corporate leadership / Kenneth E. Goodpaster—Respect for persons, management theory, and business ethics / Daniel R. Gilbert, Jr.—Institutionalizing ethical motivation: reflections on Goodpaster's agenda / Robbin Derry—Rights in the global market / Thomas J. Donaldson—Donaldson on rights and corporate obligations / Edwin M. Hartman—The role of business in three levels of literacy / Ezra F. Bowen—Business ethics, literacy, and the education of the emotions / Robert C. Solomon—Business ethics as moral imagination / Joanne B. Ciulla. [LC 90007372; ISN 0195081986]
HF5387. B876 1991   341

The business of ethics and business. Harvard Business Review. Boston, Mass.: The Review, 1986. iv, 175 p. : ill. *Notes:* Reprints from the Harvard Business Review, 1957-1986. Includes bibliographical references.]
HF5387. H3 1986   342

Can ethics be taught?: perspectives, challenges, and approaches at Harvard Business School. Thomas R. Piper, Mary C. Gentile, Sharon Daloz Parks. Boston, Mass.: Harvard Business School, c1993. xvii, 178 p. *Notes:* Includes bibliographical references and index. [LC 92027077; ISN 0875844006; $12.00]
HF5387. P56 1993   343

Case studies in business ethics. edited by Thomas Donaldson and A.R. Gini. 2nd ed. Englewood Cliffs, NJ: Prentice Hall, c1990. xiv, 284 p. *Notes:* Includes bibliographical references. [LC 89036667; ISN 013116211X; $20.34]
HF5387. C36 1990   344

Contemporary issues in business ethics. Joseph R. DesJardins, John J. McCall. Belmont, Calif.: Wadsworth Pub. Co., c1985. x, 510 p. *Notes:* Includes bibliographies and index. [LC 84010446; ISN 0534036937]
HF5387. D39 1985   345

Critical issues in business conduct: legal, ethical, and social challenges for the 1990s. Walter W. Manley II and William A. Shrode; foreword by Robert H. Stovall; foreword by Leroy Collins. New York: Quorum Books, 1990. xxii, 309 p. *Notes:* Includes bibliographical references. [LC 90030009; ISN 0899305709]
HF5387. M335 1990   346

The destructive achiever: power and ethics in the American corporation. Charles M. Kelly. Reading, Mass.: Addison-Wesley Pub. Co., c1988. xii, 222 p. : ill. *Notes:* Includes bibliographies and index. [LC 87031910; ISN 0201090392; $19.95]
HF5387. K46 1988   347

Essays on ethics in business and the professions. Jack N. Behrman. Englewood Cliffs, N.J.: Prentice Hall, c1988. x, 358 p. *Notes:* Bibliography: p. 356-358. [LC 87013697; ISN 0132836238]
HF5387. B44 1988   348

Ethical decision making in everyday work situations. Mary E. Guy. New York: Quorum Books, 1990. xx, 185 p. : ill. *Notes:* Includes bibliographical references (p. [169]-176) and index. [LC 89024348; ISN 0899304184; $39.95]
HF5387. G89 1990   349

Ethical dilemmas in the modern corporation. Gerald F. Cavanagh, Arthur F. McGovern. Englewood Cliffs, NJ: Prentice Hall, 1988. x, 198 p. : ill. *Notes:* Includes bibliographies and index. [LC 87025726; ISN 0132900580] HF5387. C38 1988 350

Ethical issues in business: a philosophical approach. edited by Thomas Donaldson, Patricia H. Werhane. 4th ed. Englewood Cliffs, N.J.: Prentice Hall, c1993. x, 502 p. : ill. *Notes:* Includes bibliographical references and index. [LC 92020811; ISN 0132827166] HF5387. E8 1993 351

Ethical theory and business. . edited by Tom L. Beauchamp, Norman E. Bowie. 3rd ed. Englewood Cliffs, N.J.: Prentice Hall, 1988. xi, 596 p. *Notes:* Includes bibliographies. [LC 87025457; ISN 0132905035] HF5387. E82 1988 352

Ethics and excellence: cooperation and integrity in business. Robert C. Solomon. New York: Oxford University Press, 1992. xiv, 288 p. *Notes:* Includes bibliographical references (p. 267-275) and index. [LC 91032363; ISN 0195064305] HF5387. S614 1992 353

Ethics and leadership: putting theory into practice. William D. Hitt. Columbus: Battelle Press, c1990. ix, 236 p. : ill. *Notes:* Includes bibliographical references (p. 225-232) and indexes. [LC 89037967; ISN 0935470522; $24.95] HF5387. H58 1990 354

Ethics and the investment industry. edited by Oliver F. Williams, Frank K. Reilly, & John W. Houck. Savage, MD: Rowman & Littlefield Publishers, 1989. 259 p. *Notes:* Includes bibliographies and index. [LC 89034176; ISN 0847676137; $16.95] HF5387. E835 1989 355

Ethics in practice: managing the moral corporation. edited, with an introduction by Kenneth R. Andrews, Donald K. David. Boston, Mass.: Harvard Business School Press, c1989. vi, 294 p. : ill. *Notes:* Includes bibliographies and index. [LC 88032878; ISN 0875842070] HF5387. E857 1989 356

The ethics of management. LaRue Tone Hosmer. 2nd ed. Homewood, IL: Irwin, 1990. xi, 204 p. : ill. *Notes:* Includes bibliographical references and index. [LC 90045093; ISN 0256084890] HF5387. H67 1991 357

Executive integrity: the search for high human values in organizational life. Suresh Srivastva and associates 1st ed. San Francisco: Jossey-Bass, 1988. xxii, 354 p. : ill. (The Jossey-Bass management series) *Notes:* Includes index. Bibliography: p. 321-337. [LC 87046332; ISN 1555420850] HF5387. E94 1988 358

Executive's handbook of model business conduct codes. Walter W. Manley II. Englewood Cliffs, NJ: Prentice Hall, c1991. xxxi, 266 p. *Notes:* Includes bibliography (p. 249-253) and index. [LC 91011244; ISN 013296757X] HF5387. M336 1991 359

Good intentions aside: a manager's guide to resolving ethical problems. Laura L. Nash. Boston, Mass.: Harvard Business School Press, c1993. xvii, 259 p. *Notes:* Originally published: Boston: Harvard Business School Press, 1990. With new introd. Includes bibliographical references and index. [LC 93014788; ISN 0875844294; $14.95] HF5387. N35 1993 360

The hard problems of management: gaining the ethics edge. Mark Pastin. 1st ed. San Francisco, Calif.: Jossey-Bass, c1986. xxvi, 239 p. (The Jossey-Bass management series) *Notes:* Includes index. Bibliography: p. 229-234. [LC 85045911; ISN 087589688X] HF5387. P37 1986 361

It's good business. Robert C. Solomon, Kristine R. Hanson. 1st ed. New York: Atheneum, 1985. xiv, 282 p. *Notes:* Includes index. [LC 84045631; ISN 0689116462; $17.95] HF5387. S625 1985 362

Just rewards: the case for ethical reform in business. David Olive. Toronto: Key Porter Books, c1987. 298 p. *Notes:* Includes index. Bibliography: p [280]-291. [LC 87094121; ISN 1550130536; $24.95] HF5387. O45 1987 363

Key issues in business ethics. John Donaldson. London; San Diego: Academic Press, c1989. xxiv, 227 p. *Notes:* Bibliography: p. 211-219.; ISN 0122205405] HF5387. D66 1989 364

The Legitimate corporation: essential readings in business ethics and corporate governance. edited by Brenda Sutton. Cambridge, Mass.: Blackwell Business, 1993. xiii, 242 p. : ill. *Notes:* Includes bibliographical references (p. 236-239) and index. [LC 92047388; ISN 0631187480; $29.95] HF5387. L44 1993 +365

Making the right decision: ethics for managers. William D. Hall. New York: Wiley, c1993. xiii, 248 p. : ill. *Notes:* Includes bibliographical references (p. 247-248). [LC 93014651; ISN 0471586331] HF5387. H35 1993 +366

Managing corporate ethics: learning from America's ethical companies how to supercharge business performance. Francis J. Aguilar. New York: Oxford University Press, 1994. viii, 177 p. : ill. *Notes:* Includes bibliographical references and index. [LC 93005803; ISN 0195085345; $21.00] HF5387. A4 1994 +367

The moral manager. Clarence C. Walton. Cambridge, Mass.: Ballinger Pub. Co., c1988. vii, 278 p. : ill. *Notes:* Includes index. Bibliography: p. 225-266. [LC 88011966; ISN 0887303099] HF5387. W324 1988 368

Moral mazes: the world of corporate managers. Robert Jackall. New York: Oxford University Press, 1988. ix, 249 p. *Notes:* Includes index. Bibliography: p. 235-238. [LC 87031845; ISN 0195038258]
HF5387. J29 1988   369

Poor Richard's Legacy: American business values from Benjamin Franklin to Donald Trump. Peter Baida. 1st ed. New York: W. Morrow, 1990. 360 p. *Notes:* Includes bibliographical references. [LC 89013792; ISN 0688077293; $22.95]
HF5387. B33 1990   370

The power of ethical management. Kenneth Blanchard, Norman Vincent Peale. 1st ed. New York: W. Morrow, 1988. 139 p. [LC 87024210; ISN 0688070620]
HF5387. B56 1988   371

The responsible manager: practical strategies for ethical decision making. Michael Rion. 1st ed. San Francisco: Harper & Row, c1990. x, 134 p. *Notes:* Includes bibliographical references (p. [130]-134). [LC 89045187; ISN 0060668644; $15.95]
HF5387. R56 1990   372

Systems of survival: a dialogue on the moral foundations of commerce and politics. Jane Jacobs. 1st ed. New York: Random House, c1992. xiii, 236 p. *Notes:* Includes bibliographical references. [LC 92050157; ISN 039455079X; $22.00 ($27.50 Can.)]
HF5387. J32 1992   373

Tough choices: managers talk ethics. compiled by Barbara Ley Toffler. New York: Wiley, c1986. xiv, 372 p. *Notes:* Includes index. Bibliography: p. 348-349. [LC 86013195; ISN 0471830224; $19.95]
HF5387. T67   374

Working ethics: strategies for decision making and organizational responsibility. Marvin T. Brown. 1st ed. San Francisco: Jossey-Bass Publishers, 1990. xvii, 219 p. : ill. *Notes:* Bibliography: p. 205-209. [LC 90037973; ISN 1555422802; 25.95]
HF5387. B76 1990   375

BUSINESS ETIQUETTE

Business in Mexico: managerial behavior, protocol, and etiquette. Candace Bancroft McKinniss, Arthur Natella, Jr. New York: Haworth Press, c1994. x, 156 p. *Notes:* Includes bibliographical references (p. 143-147) and index. [LC 93023222; ISN 1560244062; ISN 1560244070; $45.94]
HF5389. M38 1994   +376

Doing business with Japanese men: a woman's handbook. Christalyn Brannen & Tracey Wilen. Berkeley, CA: Stone Bridge Press, c1993. 174 p. *Notes:* Includes index. [LC 92036102; ISN 1880656043; $9.95]
HF5389. B73 1993   377

A guide to successful business relations with the Chinese: opening the Great Wall's gate. Huang Quanyu, Richard S. Andrulis, Chen Tong. Binghamton, N.Y.: International Business Press, c1994. xii, 254 p. *Notes:* Includes bibliographical references and index. [LC 93019379; ISN 1560248688; ISN 1560248696]
HF5389. H83 1994   +378

Korean etiquette & ethics in business. Boye De Mente. Lincolnwood, Ill.: NTC Business Books, c1988. xi, 156 p. *Notes:* Bibliography: p. 113-114. [LC 87062403; ISN 0844285226; $14.95]
HF5389. D46 1988   379

On track with the Japanese: a case-by-case approach to building successful relationships. Patricia Gercik. 1st ed. New York: Kodansha International, 1992. xiii, 241 p. [LC 92011939; ISN 4770016026; $19.95]
HF5387. G47 1992   380

The Wall Street Journal book of chief executive style. editors of the Wall Street journal; contributors, David Diamond... et al. 1st edition. New York: W. Morrow, 1989. 285 p. : ill. [LC 89034468; ISN 0688079229; $24.95]
HF5389. W35 1989   381

BUSINESS FAILURES

The Icarus paradox: how exceptional companies bring about their own downfall. Danny Miller. New York, NY: Harper Business, c1990. xiii, 306 p. : ill. *Notes:* "New lessons in the dynamics of corporate success, decline, and renewal"—T.p. Includes bibliographical references. [LC 90005039; ISN 0887304532; $19.95]
HD2785. M54 1990   382

BUSINESS FORECASTING

Business forecasting. John E. Hanke, Arthur G. Reitsch. 4th ed. Boston: Allyn and Bacon, c1992. xii, 532 p. : ill. *Notes:* Includes bibliographical references and index. [LC 91032555; ISN 0205137326; ISN 0205137075]
HD30.27. H37 1992   383

Business forecasting. John E. Hanke, Arthur G. Reitsch. 3rd ed. Boston: Allyn and Bacon, c1989. xiii, 530 p. : ill. *Notes:* Includes bibliographies and index. [LC 88020956; ISN 0205118100; $44.00]
 HD30.27. H37 1989 384

Business forecasting methods. Jeffrey Jarrett. 2nd ed. Oxford, UK; Cambridge, Mass.: B. Blackwell, 1991. viii, 463 p. : ill. *Notes:* Includes bibliographical references and index. [LC 90032587; ISN 0631173293; $30.00 (U.S.)]
 HD30.27. J38 1991 385

Business without economists: an irreverent guide. William J. Hudson. New York, N.Y.: AMACOM, c1987. 178 p. : ill. *Notes:* Includes index. Bibliography: p. 167-169. [LC 86047812; ISN 0814458963; $14.95]
 HB3730. H83 1987 386

Economic forecasting for business: concepts and applications. John J. McAuley. Englewood Cliffs, N.J.: Prentice-Hall, c1986. xiv, 418 p. : ill. *Notes:* Includes bibliographical references and indexes. [LC 85006548; ISN 0132315564]
 HD30.27. M36 1986 387

Forecasting, planning, and strategy for the 21st century. Spyros G. Makridakis. New York: London: Free Press; Collier Macmillan, c1990. x, 293 p. : ill. *Notes:* Includes bibliographical references (p. 271-277) and index. [LC 90030733; ISN 0029157813; $29.95]
 HD30.27. M343 1990 388

The handbook of forecasting: a manager's guide. edited by Spyros Makridakis and Steven C. Wheelwright. 2nd ed. New York: Wiley, c1987. xviii. 638 p. : ill. *Notes:* "A Wiley-Interscience publication." Includes bibliographies and index. Non-circulating. [LC 86028137; ISN 0471839035]
 HD30.27. H36 1987 389

Introductory business forecasting. Paul Newbold, Theodore Bos. Cincinnati, OH: South-Western Pub. Co., c1990. xi, 497 p. : ill. *Notes:* Includes bibliographical references. [LC 88092877; ISN 0538802472; $43.95]
 HD30.27. N49 1990 390

Nonextrapolative methods in business forecasting: scenarios, vision, and issues management. edited by Jay S. Mendell; F. John Pessolano, associate editor. Westport, Ct.: Quorum, 1985. viii, 222 p. : ill. *Notes:* Includes index. Bibliography: p. [213]-214. [LC 84018093; ISN 0899300669]
 HD30.27. N66 391

The Popcorn report: Faith Popcorn on the future of your company, your world, your life. 1st ed. New York: Doubleday, c1991. xiv, 226 p. *Notes:* "A Currency book"—T.p. verso. Includes index. [LC 90028832; ISN 0385400004; $22.50]
 HD30.27. P66 1991 392

The practical forecasters' almanac: 137 reliable indicators for investors, hedgers, and speculators. edited by Edward Renshaw. Homewood, IL: Business One Irwin, c1992. xxi, 272 p. *Notes:* Includes bibliographical references and index. [LC 92006758; ISN 1556234708; $49.95]
 HD30.27. P73 1992 393

The world in 2020: power, culture, and prosperity. Hamish McRae. Boston, Mass.: Harvard Business School Press, c1994. xiii, 302 p. *Notes:* Includes bibliographical references and index. [LC 94024545; ISN 0875846041]
 HD30.27. M385 1994 +394

BUSINESS INTELLIGENCE

Competitor intelligence manual and guide: gathering, analyzing, and using business intelligence. Kirk W.M. Tyson. Englewood Cliffs, N.J.: Prentice Hall, c1990. xxi, 376 p. : ill. *Notes:* Cover title: Competitor intelligence manual & guide. [LC 89070970; ISN 0131552929; $79.95]
 HD38.7. T96 1990 395

Corporate intelligence and espionage: a blueprint for executive decision making. Richard Eells and Peter Nehemkis. New York: London: Macmillan; Collier Macmillan, c1984. xiii, 267 p. (Studies of the modern corporation) *Notes:* Includes index. Bibliography: p. 244-251. [LC 83043214; ISN 002909240X]
 HD38.7. E34 1984 396

Friendly spies: how America's allies are using economic espionage to steal our secrets. Peter Schweizer. New York: Atlantic Monthly Press, c1993. x, 342 p. *Notes:* Includes bibliographical references and index. [LC 92034924; ISN 0871134977]
 HD38.7. S39 1993 397

Monitoring the competition: find out what's really going on over there. Leonard M. Fuld. New York, N.Y.: Wiley, c1988. xiii, 204 p. *Notes:* Includes index. Bibliography: p. 168. [LC 87021607; ISN 0471852619]
 HD38.7. F86 1988 398

Outsmarting the competition: practical approaches to finding and outsmarting the competition. John J. McGonagle, Jr. and Carolyn M. Vella; adapted by John Pearson. London; New York: McGraw-Hill, c1993. xv, 320 p. : ill. *Notes:* Originally published: Naperville, Ill.: Sourcebooks, c1990. Includes bibliographical references (p. [301]-314) and index. [LC 92046122; ISN 0077077555; £25.00]
 HD38.7. M39 1993 +399

Real-world intelligence: organized information for executives. Herbert E. Meyer. 1st ed. New York: Weidenfeld & Nicolson, c1987. 102 p. [LC 87020787; ISN 1555841473]
 HD38.7. M47 1987 400

The steal: counterfeiting and industrial espionage. Brian Freemantle. London: Joseph, 1986. xi, 224 p. *Notes:* Includes index. Bibliography: p. 235-236. [LC 86017196; ISN 0718125843; £10.95: CIP confirmed]   HD38.7. F73   401

BUSINESS LAW

Executive's guide to business law. William A. Hancock. New York: McGraw-Hill, c1979. ca. 1000 p. *Notes:* Includes indexes. [LC 79001350; ISN 007025978X; $25.59]   KF889.3. H36   402

BUSINESS LOGISTICS

Business logistics management. Ronald H. Ballou. 3rd ed. Englewood Cliffs, N.J.: Prentice Hall, 1992. xiv, 688 p. : ill. *Notes:* Includes bibliographical references (p. 669-673) and indexes. [LC 91018762; ISN 0131055453; $64.40]   HD38.5. B35 1992   403

Corporate profitability & logistics: innovative guidelines for executives. by Ernst & Whinney National Distribution/Logistics Group. Montvale, NJ: National Association of Accountants, c1987. viii, 192 p. : ill. (Bold step series) *Notes:* Includes bibliographical references.; ISN 0866410929]   HD38.5. C67 1987   404

The logistics handbook. editors-in-chief, James F. Robeson, William C. Copacino; associate editor, R. Edwin Howe. New York: Toronto: New York: The Free Press; Maxwell Macmillan Canada; Maxwell Macmillan International, c1994. xiv, 953 p. : ill., maps *Notes:* Includes bibliographical references and index. [LC 93048859; ISN 0029265959]   HD38.5. L615 1994   +405

Logistics strategy: cases and concepts. Roy D. Shapiro, James L. Heskett. St. Paul, Minn.: West Pub. Co., c1985. x, 602 p. : ill. *Notes:* Includes index. Bibliography: p. 589-597. [LC 84015308; ISN 0314852972; $26.95]   HD38.5. S53 1985   406

Strategic logistics management. Douglas M. Lambert, James R. Stock. 3rd ed. Homewood, IL: Irwin, 1992, c1993. xxvi, 862 p. : ill. *Notes:* Stock's name appears first on the earlier edition. Includes bibliographical references and indexes. [LC 91032656; ISN 0256088381]   HF5415.7. S86 1992   407

BUSINESS MATHEMATICS

Accountant's handbook of formulas and tables. Lawrence Lipkin, Irwin K. Feinstein, Lucile Derrick. 3rd ed. Englewood Cliffs, N.J.: Prentice Hall, c1988. xii, 627 p. : ill. *Notes:* Includes bibliographies and index. [LC 88019837; ISN 0130029572; $59.95]   HF5699. L56 1988   408

The Economist guide to business numeracy. Richard Stutely; The Economist Books. New York: Wiley, c1993. 237 p. : ill. *Notes:* Originally published under the title: The Economist numbers guide. Includes index. [LC 93013998; ISN 0471305545]   HF5695. S83 1993   +409

Financial mathematics handbook. Robert Muksian. Englewood Cliffs, N.J.: Prentice-Hall, c1984. xx, 486 p. : ill. *Notes:* Includes index. [LC 83013963; ISN 0133164063]   HF5691. M84 1984   410

Mathematics for business and economics. Robert H. Nicholson. New York: McGraw-Hill, c1986. xx, 524 p. : ill. *Notes:* Includes index. [LC 85015190; ISN 007046491X; $26.95 (est.)]   HF5691. N45 1986   411

Mathematics for management and finance. Stephen P. Shao, Stephen P. Shao, Jr. 5th ed. Cincinnati: South-Western Pub. Co., c1986. x, 813 p. : ill. *Notes:* Includes index. [LC 84051155; ISN 0538133406]   HF5691. S432 1986   412

Mathematics, with applications in management and economics. Earl K. Bowen, Gorden D. Prichett, John C. Saber. 6th ed. Homewood, Ill.: Irwin, 1987. xxii, 993 p. : ill. *Notes:* Includes index. [LC 86081793; ISN 0256031401]   HF5691. B69 1987   413

Schaum's outline of theory and problems of mathematical methods for business and economics. Edward T. Dowling. New York: McGraw-Hill, c1993. ix, 384 p. : ill. (Schaum's outline series) *Notes:* Includes index. [LC 92011962; ISN 0070176973]   HF5691. L64 1993   414

BUSINESS NAMES

The name is the game: how to name a company or product. by Henri Charmasson. Homewood, Ill.: Dow Jones-Irwin, c1988. xiv, 171 p. : ill. *Notes:* Includes index. Bibliography: p. 157. [LC 87071545; ISN 1556230699]   HD69.B7 C47 1988   415

BUSINESS PRESENTATIONS

Say it with charts: the executive's guide to successful presentations in the 1990s. Gene Zelazny. 2nd ed. Homewood, Ill.: Business One Irwin, c1991. viii, 161 p. : ill. (some col.) *Notes:* Includes index. [LC 90019543; ISN 1556234473; $34.95]   HF5718.22. Z45 1991   416

BUSINESS RELOCATION

Corporate site selection for new facilities: a study conducted among the largest U.S. companies, 1989. New York: Time Inc. Magazine Company, c1989. 35 , [14] p. *Notes:* Survey conducted by Fortune Magazine.]   HT175. C67 1989   417

BUSINESS REPORT WRITING

Report writing for business. Raymond V. Lesikar, John D. Pettit, Jr. 8th ed. Homewood, IL: Irwin, c1991. xx, 460 p. : ill. *Notes:* Includes index. [LC 90004884; ISN 0256069484; $33.95]   HF5719. L45 1991   418

Writing for decision makers: memos and reports with a competitive edge. Marya W. Holcombe, Judith K. Stein. 2nd ed. New York: Van Nostrand Reinhold Co., c1987. xi, 219 p. : ill. *Notes:* Includes index. [LC 86024700; ISN 0442232683; $21.95]   HF5719. H64 1987   419

BUSINESS TEACHERS

Teaching and the case method: text, cases, and readings. C. Roland Christensen with Abby J. Hansen. Boston, Mass.: Harvard Business School, c1987. xiii, 290 p. : ill. *Notes:* Rev. ed. of: Teaching by the case method. 1981. Bibliography: p. 287-290. [LC 86022732; ISN 0875841783; ISN 0875841791]   HF1131. C48 1987   420

Teaching and the case method: text, cases, and readings. Louis B. Barnes, C. Roland Christensen, and Abby J. Hansen. 3rd ed. Boston, Mass.: Harvard Business School Press, 1994. xiii, 333 p. *Notes:* Rev. ed. of: Teaching and the case method / C. Roland Christensen. c1987. Includes bibliographical references. [LC 94000766; ISN 0875844030; $35.00]   HF1131. C48 1994   +421

BUSINESS WRITING

Business writing at its best. Minerva Neiditz. Burr Ridge, Ill.: Irwin, c1994. xiii, 267 p. : ill. *Notes:* Includes bibliographical references. [LC 93023668; ISN 0786301376]   HF5718.3. N45 1994   +422

Business writing with style: strategies for success. John Tarrant. New York: Wiley, c1991. 184 p. *Notes:* Includes index. [LC 90024548; ISN 0471532126; $9.95]   HF5718.3. T37 1991   423

The elements of business writing. Gary Blake and Robert W. Bly. New York: Toronto: New York: Macmillan Pub. Co.; Maxwell Macmillan Canada; Maxwell Macmillan International, c1991. xvii, 140 p. *Notes:* Includes index. [LC 91007838; ISN 002511445X; $17.95]   HF5718.3. B53 1991   424

BUSINESSMEN

The Alexander complex: the dreams that drive the great businessmen. Michael Meyer. 1st ed. New York, N.Y.: Times Books, 1989. xiv, 258 p. *Notes:* Includes index. [LC 89004401; ISN 081291662X; $19.95]   HC102.5.A2 M482 1989   425

The decision makers: the men and the million-dollar moves behind today's great corporate success stories. Robert Heller. 1st ed. New York: E P. Dutton, c1989. xii, 385 p. *Notes:* "Truman Talley books." Includes index. Bibliography: p. 365-367. [LC 89001133; ISN 052524798X; $22.50]   HC29. H45 1989   426

The dynamos: who are they anyway? Brett Kingstone. New York: Wiley, c1987. xx, 256 p. : ill., ports. *Notes:* Includes index. Bibliography: p. 251-252. [LC 87001754; ISN 0471858277]   HC102.5.A2 K56 1987   427

The entrepreneur. by James D. Nisbet. Charlotte, N.C.: Capital Technology, 1976. 221 p. : ill., ports.]   HF5500.2. N57   428

Entrepreneurial megabucks: The 100 greatest entrepreneurs of the last 25 years and how they did it: A. David Silver. New York: Wiley, 1985. ix, 467 p. : ill. (Small business management series) *Notes:* Includes index. [LC 85012089; ISN 0471821845; $19.95 (est.)]   HC102.5.A2 S54 1985   429

Entrepreneurs, the men and women behind famous brand names and how they made it. Joseph J. Fucini and Suzy Fucini. Boston: G.K. Hall, c1985. xviii, 297 p. : ill., ports. *Notes:* Includes index. Bibliography: p. 261-288. [LC 84015846; ISN 0816187088; ISN 0816187401]   HC29. F83 1985   430

Experience, Inc.: men and women who founded famous companies after the age of 40. Joseph J. Fucini, Suzy Fucini. New York: London: Free Press; Collier Macmillan, c1987. xi, 244 p. : ill. *Notes:* Includes index. Bibliography: p. 228-236. [LC 87011984; ISN 002910971X]   HC29. F834 1987   431

The innovators: the essential guide to business thinkers, achievers and entrepreneurs. William Davis. New York: AMACOM, c1987. vii, 408 p., [8] p. of plates: ill., ports. *Notes:* Includes index.; ISN 0814459331; $19.95]   HC29. D385 1987   432

Merchants of vision: people bringing new purpose and values to business. James E. Liebig. 1st ed. San Francisco: Berrett-Koehler, c1994. x, 242 p. : ill. *Notes:* "Published in cooperation with the World Business Academy." Includes bibliographical references (p. 229) and index. [LC 93043269; ISN 1881052427; $24.95]   HD60. L54 1994   +433

Profiles of genius: thirteen creative men who changed the world. Gene N. Landrum. Buffalo, N.Y.: Prometheus Books, 1993. 263 p. : ill. *Notes:* Includes bibliographical references (p. 253-260) and index. *Contents:* Steven Jobs—Fred Smith—Tom Monaghan—Nolan Bushnell—William Gates III—Marcel Bich—Solomon Price—Howard Head—William Lear—Soichiro Honda—Akio Morita—Arthur Jones—Ted Turner. [LC 93018637; ISN 0879758325; $22.95]   HC29. L36 1993   +434

The risk takers - five years on. Jeffrey Robinson. Rev. ed. London: Mandarin, 1990. viii, 470 p. *Notes:* Includes index. [LC 90040274; ISN 0749304553; £4.99]   HC252.5.A2 R633 1990   435

Starting at the top: America's new achievers: twenty-three success stories told by men and women whose dreams of being boss came true. compiled by John Mack Carter and Joan Feeney. 1st ed. New York: Morrow, c1985. 252 p. *Notes:* Includes index. [LC 85004826; ISN 0688045200]   HC102.5.A2 S64 1985   436

Tycoons: where they came from and how they made it. William Kay. London: Piatkus, 1985. 208 p. : ill. [LC 85034738; ISN 0861883470; £9.95 (Sept.)]   HC256.6. K39   437

The whiz kids: the founding fathers of American business—and the legacy they left us. John A. Byrne. 1st ed. New York: Currency, 1993. viii, 581 p. : ill. *Notes:* Includes bibliographical references and index. [LC 93005816; ISN 0385248040]   HC102.5.A2 B95 1993   438

CABLE TELEVISION

Toward competition in cable television. Leland L. Johnson. Cambridge, Mass.: Washington, D.C.: MIT Press; American Enterprise Institute for Public Policy Research, c1994. xii, 214 p. : ill. *Notes:* Includes bibliographical references (p. [195]-204) and indexes. [LC 94015795; ISN 0262100541]   HE8700.72.U6 J64 1994   +439

CAMPAIGN FUNDS

Corporate PACs and federal campaign financing laws: use or abuse of power? Ann B. Matasar. Westport, Conn.: Quorum Books, c1986. x, 161 p. *Notes:* Includes index. Bibliography: p. [147]-158. [LC 85012280; ISN 0899300863]   JK1991. M28 1986   440

CAPITAL

Accounting for fixed assets. Raymond H. Peterson. New York: Wiley, c1994. xix, 199 p. : ill. *Notes:* Includes bibliographical references (p. 189-192) and index. [LC 93009023; ISN 0471537039]   HF5681.C25 P48 1994   +441

CAPITAL ASSETS PRICING MODEL

Modern portfolio theory, the capital asset pricing model, and arbitrage pricing theory: a user's guide. Diana R. Harrington. 2nd ed. Englewood Cliffs, N.J.: Prentice-Hall, c1987. x, 229 p. : ill. Notes: Previous ed. published as: Modern portfolio theory and the capital asset pricing model. 1983. Includes bibliographies and index. [LC 86022693; ISN 0135972612]   HG4637. H37 1987   442

CAPITAL BUDGET

The capital budgeting handbook. edited by Mike Kaufman. Homewood, Ill.: Dow Jones-Irwin, c1986. xxi, 776 p. : ill. Notes: Includes bibliographies and index. [LC 85070803; ISN 087094522X]
HG4028.B8 C26   443

Capital budgeting: planning and control of capital expenditures. John J. Clark, Thomas J. Hindelang, Robert E. Pritchard. 3rd ed. Englewood Cliffs, N.J.: Prentice Hall, c1989. xvi, 620 p. : ill. Notes: Includes bibliographies and index. [LC 88038561; ISN 013114877X; $31.50]
HG4028.C4 C585 1989   444

Capital investment series. Boston c1954-1969. 2 v. illus. (part col.) Notes: Cover title. First printing of pt. 1 had title: Capital investment decisions. Reprints from the Harvard Business Review, 1954-1969.]   HG4028.C4 H34 1954   −445

CAPITAL INVESTMENTS

The capital budgeting decision: economic analysis of investment projects. Harold Bierman, Jr., Seymour Smidt. 7th ed. New York: London: Macmillan; Collier Macmillan, c1988. xvi, 557 p. : ill. Notes: Includes bibliographies and index. [LC 87015257; ISN 0023099410]   HG4028.C4 B54 1988   446

Capital choices: changing the way America invests in industry. Michael E. Porter. Washington, D.C.: Council on Competitiveness, c1992. 135 p. : ill. Notes: Cover title. "A research report presented to the Council on Competitiveness and co-sponsored by the Harvard Business School." Includes bibliographical references.]   HC110.C3 P67 1992   447

Handbook of capital expenditure management. Bernard D. Marino. Englewood Cliffs, N.J.: Prentice-Hall, c1986. xiv, 258 p. Notes: Includes index. [LC 86016992; ISN 0133725413]
HG4028.C4 M215 1986   448

The handbook of capital investing: analyses and strategies for investment in capital assets. Anthony F. Herbst. New York: Harper Business, c1990. xii, 396 p. : ill. Notes: Includes bibliographical references and index. [LC 90004569; ISN 0887304494; $65.00]   HG4028.C4 H453 1990   449

Investment demand and U.S. economic growth. by Bert G. Hickman. Washington Brookings Institution, 1965. xv, 264 p. illus. Notes: Bibliographical footnotes. [LC 65016626]   HC110.C3 H5   +450

Project evaluation: a unified approach for the analysis of capital investments. J. Morley English. New York: London: Macmillan; Collier Macmillan, c1984. xiv, 401 p. : ill. Notes: Includes index. Bibliography: p. 389-394. [LC 84011204; ISN 0029492408; $29.95]   HG4028.C4 E53 1984   451

ROI: practical theory and innovative applications. Robert A. Peters. Rev. ed. New York: AMACOM, c1979. xi, 173 p. Notes: Includes index. [LC 78011327; ISN 0814454968; $19.95]
HG4028.C4 P38 1979   452

CAPITAL MARKET

Capital markets and institutions. Herbert E. Dougall, Jack E. Gaumnitz. 5th ed. Englewood Cliffs, N.J.: Prentice-Hall, c1986. x, 294 p. : ill. (Prentice-Hall foundations of finance series) Notes: Includes index. Bibliography: p. 280-283. [LC 85019295; ISN 0131137131]   HG181. D59 1986   453

Capital markets: institutions and instruments. Frank J. Fabozzi, Franco Modigliani. Englewood Cliffs, N.J.: Prentice Hall, 1992. xxvi, 726 p. : ill. Notes: Includes bibliographical references and index. [LC 91018056; ISN 0136014364; $69.00]   HG4523. F33 1992   454

A guide to the financial markets. Charles R. Geisst. 2nd ed. New York: St. Martin's Press, 1989. xv, 164 p. : ill. Notes: Includes bibliographies and index. [LC 89030825; ISN 0312031637; $14.95]
HG4523. G44 1989   455

International capital markets. Morris Goldstein... et al. Washington, D.C.: International Monetary Fund, c1993. vii, 80 p. : ill. *Notes:* "April 1993." Includes bibliographical references (p. 79). *Contents:* Pt. 1. Exchange rate management and international capital flows.; ISN 1557752907; $20.00]

HG4523. I566 1993   456

Restructuring Japan's financial markets. edited by Ingo Walter and Takato Hiraki. Homewood, Ill.: Business One Irwin, c1993. xxiv, 456 p. : ill. *Notes:* "New York University Salomon Center, Leonard N. Stern School of Business." Papers presented at a conference held in Tokyo in May 1992. Includes bibliographical references and index. [LC 93011393; ISN 1556236360]

HG5772. R47 1993   +457

Technology and the regulation of financial markets: securities, futures, and banking. edited by Anthony Saunders, Lawrence J. White. Lexington, Mass.: Lexington Books, c1986. 193 p. : ill. (Lexington Books/Salomon Brothers Center series on financial institutions and markets) *Notes:* Papers from a conference sponsored by the Salomon Brothers Center for the Study of Financial Institutions and held on May 13, 1985. Includes bibliographies. [LC 85045040; ISN 0669111430]

HG4910. T38 1986   458

CAPITAL MOVEMENTS

International capital movements: based on the Marshall lectures given at the University of Cambridge, 1985. Charles P. Kindleberger. Cambridge Cambridgeshire; New York: Cambridge University Press, 1987. vi, 99 p. *Notes:* Includes index. Bibliography: p. [88]-95. [LC 86032733; ISN 0521341329]

HG3891. K55 1987   459

CAPITALISM

Behind the veil of economics: essays in the worldly philosophy. Robert L. Heilbroner. 1st ed. New York: W.W. Norton, 1988. 207 p. *Notes:* Includes bibliographical references and index. [LC 87020392; ISN 039302542X]

HB501. H396 1988   460

Capitalism against capitalism. Michel Albert; translated by Paul Haviland; foreword by Lord Donoughue. London: Whurr, 1993. x, 260 p. : ill. [LC 93002741; ISN 1870332547; £22.57]

HB501. A6213 1993   461

Capitalism versus pragmatic market socialism: a general equilibrium evaluation. James A. Yunker. Boston: Kluwer Academic Pub., c1993. 152 p. *Notes:* Includes bibliographical references (p. [141]-146) and index. [LC 93023360; ISN 0792393996]

HB501. Y864 1993   +462

The capitalist revolution: fifty propositions about prosperity, equality, and liberty. Peter L. Berger. New York: Basic Books, c1986. v, 262 p. *Notes:* Includes index. Bibliography: p. 225-252. [LC 85073882; ISN 0465008674; $17.95]

HB501. B4518 1986   463

Corporations and the common good. edited by Robert B. Dickie and Leroy S. Rouner. Notre Dame, Ind.: University of Notre Dame Press, c1986. xii, 147 p. *Notes:* "Published with the School of Management, Boston University." Includes bibliographical references. [LC 85040597; ISN 0268007543; $16.95]

HB501. C7614 1986   464

Macroeconomics and monopoly capitalism. Ben Fine, Andy Murfin. New York: St. Martin's Press, 1984. 170 p. *Notes:* Includes index. Bibliography: p. [159]-167. [LC 84016034; ISN 0312503369; $22.50]

HB501. F49 1984   465

The market economy: from micro to mesoeconomics. Stuart Holland. New York: St. Martin's Press, 1987. xiv, 363 p. : ill. *Notes:* Includes index. Bibliography: p. [345]-353. [LC 87020908; ISN 0312013248; $30.00 (est.)]

HB501. H56 1987   466

Markets or governments: choosing between imperfect alternatives. Charles Wolf, Jr. 2nd ed. Cambridge, Mass.: MIT Press, c1993. xiii, 238 p. *Notes:* Includes bibliographical references and index. [LC 93018730; ISN 0262231727]

HB501. W89 1993   +467

The nature and logic of capitalism. Robert L. Heilbroner. 1st ed. New York: Norton, c1985. 225 p. *Notes:* Includes index. Bibliography: p. 209-214. [LC 85005656; ISN 0393022277; $15.95]

HB501. H398 1985   468

The spirit of Japanese capitalism and selected essays. Yamamoto Shichihei; translated by Lynne E. Riggs and Takechi Manabu; introduction by Frank Gibney. Lanham, Md.: Madison Books: Distributed by National Book Network, 1992. x, 263 p. *Contents:* A protestant ethic in a non-Christian context—Consanguineous and territorial context—Contract versus consensus—Roots of the modern ethos—Zen and the economic animal—Theology and Japanese pragmatism—The capitalist logic of the samurai—Economic efficiency and the capitalist ethic—The tradition of Japanese capitalism—Shibusawa Eiichi and his times—Whence the economic animal—The rise of non-kin groups—Forerunners of Japan's modern thinking. [LC 91043856; ISN 081918294X; $24.95] HC462.9. Y2545 1992   469

21st century capitalism. Robert Heilbroner. 1st ed. New York: Norton, c1993. 175 p. *Notes:* Includes bibliographical references and index. [LC 93007662; ISN 0393035166]   HB501. H395 1993   +470

CAPITALISTS AND FINANCIERS

Capitalist fools: tales of American business, from Carnegie to Forbes to the Milken gang. Nicholas von Hoffman. 1st ed. New York: Doubleday, c1992. xix, 313 p. *Notes:* Includes bibliographical references (p. 279-302) and index. [LC 92011597; ISN 0385416741; U.S. $22.50 (Canada $28.00)]   HG172.A2 V66 1992   471

The fortune builders. Edwin Darby. 1st ed. Garden City, N.Y.: Doubleday, 1986. x, 276 p. *Notes:* Includes index. [LC 86006284; ISN 0385123698; $17.95]   HG184.C4 D37 1986   472

The money lords; the great finance capitalists, 1925-1950. New York Weybright and Talley, 1972. x, 374 p. *Notes:* Includes bibliographical references. [LC 72084210]   HG172.A2 J67   +473

The new money masters. John Train. 1st ed. New York, N.Y.: Harper & Row, c1989. vi, 385 p. : ill. *Notes:* "An Edward Burlingame book." [LC 89045071; ISN 0060159669; $22.50]   HG172.A2 T73 1989   474

CAREER CHANGES

The battle-weary executive: a blueprint for new beginnings. Lawrence W. Tuller. Homewood, Ill.: Dow Jones-Irwin, c1990. xiv, 310 p. *Notes:* Includes bibliographical references (p. 276-279) and index. [LC 89071411; ISN 1556232462]   HF5384. T85 1990   475

Becoming a manager: mastery of a new identity. Linda A. Hill. Boston, Mass.: Harvard Business School Press, c1992. xi, 331 p. *Notes:* Includes bibliographical references and index. [LC 91040612; ISN 0875843026; $22.95]   HF5384. H55 1992   476

Career crash: America's new crisis—and who survives. Barry Glassner. New York: Simon & Schuster, c1994. 223 p. : ill. *Notes:* Includes bibliographical references (p. 201-218) and index. [LC 93032705; ISN 0671690264; $21.00 ($27.00 Can.)]   HF5384. G55 1994   +477

In transition: from the Harvard Business School Club of New York Personal Seminar in Career Management. Mary Lindley Burton, Richard A. Wedemeyer. New York, N.Y.: HarperBusiness, c1991. xv, 248 p. *Notes:* Includes bibliographical references (p. 241-242) and index. [LC 91005065; ISN 0887305172; $20.00]   HF5382.5.U5 B876 1991   478

CAREER DEVELOPMENT

Career development in organizations. Douglas T. Hall and associates. 1st ed. San Francisco: Jossey-Bass, 1986. xxv, 366 p. : ill. (The Jossey-Bass management series) (The Jossey-Bass social and behavioral science series) *Notes:* Includes indexes. Includes bibliographies. [LC 86002932; ISN 0875896312]   HF5549.5.C35 H35 1986   479

Designing career development systems. Zandy B. Leibowitz, Caela Farren, Beverly L. Kaye. 1st ed. San Francisco, Calif.: Jossey-Bass, 1986. xviii, 323 p. : ill. (The Jossey-Bass management series) (The Jossey-Bass social and behavioural science series) *Notes:* Includes index. Bibliography: p. 305-312. [LC 86045623; ISN 1555420249]   HF5549.5.C35 L45 1986   480

Organizational career development: benchmarks for building a world-class workforce. Thomas G. Gutteridge, Zandy B. Leibowitz, Jane E. Shore; foreword by Stephen K. Merman. 1st ed. San Francisco: Jossey-Bass, c1993. xxxi, 266 p. : ill. *Notes:* Includes bibliographical references (p. 245-258) and index. [LC 93000029; ISN 1555425267]   HF5549.5.C35 G88 1993   +481

Self-assessment and career development. James G. Clawson... et al. 3rd ed. Englewood Cliffs, NJ: Prentice Hall, c1992. xi, 444 p. : ill. *Notes:* Includes bibliographical references. [LC 90014191; ISN 0138031800] HF5381. S473 1992   482

CARGILL, INC

Cargill: trading the world's grain. Wayne G. Broehl, Jr. Hanover N.H.: Dartmouth College: University Press of New England, c1992. xx, 1007 p. : ill. *Notes:* Includes bibliographical references and index. [LC 91031608; ISN 0874515726; $35.00] HD9039.C37 B76 1992   483

CARTELS

The cooperative edge: the internal politics of international cartels. Debora L. Spar. Ithaca: Cornell University Press, 1994. xii, 273 p. *Notes:* Includes bibliographical references and index. *Contents:* Of cooperation, competition, and cartels—The power to persuade and the success of the international diamond cartel—Yellowcake: the rise and decline of the international uranium cartel—Howling like wolves: cooperation in the international gold market—Stockpiles, speculators, and the international silver market—The internal sources of cooperation. [LC 93034801; ISN 0801426588] HD2757.5. S68 1994   +484

CASH FLOW

Financial accounting: an events and cash flow approach. George H. Sorter, Monroe J. Ingberman, Hillel M. Maximon. New York: McGraw-Hill, c1990. xiii, 480 p. *Notes:* Includes index. [LC 89012566; ISN 0070597391; $42.95] HF5681.C28 S67 1990   485

CASH MANAGEMENT

Cash, cash, cash: the three principles of business survival and success. Leslie N. Masonson. New York: Harper Business, c1990. xxiii, 296 p. : ill. [LC 90004460; ISN 0887304109; $27.50] HG4028.C45 M2275 1990   486

Global cash management. Louis J. Celi, Barry Rutizer. New York, NY: HarperBusiness, c1991. xii, 401 p. : ill. [LC 90027091; ISN 0887304680; $65.00 ($87.95 Can.)] HG4028.C45 C47 1991   487

Liquidity analysis and management. by George W. Gallinger, P. Basil Healey. Reading, Mass.: Addison-Wesley Pub. Co., c1987. xxiv, 605 p. : ill. *Notes:* Includes index. Bibliography: p. 570-588. [LC 86003322; ISN 0201105187; $30.00] HG4028.C45 G34 1987   488

Managing corporate liquidity: an introduction to working capital management. James H. Vander Weide, Steven F. Maier. New York: Wiley, c1985. vi, 307 p. : ill. *Notes:* Includes bibliographies and index. [LC 84013232; ISN 0471877700] HG4028.C45 V36 1985   489

CASINOS

Temples of chance: how America Inc. bought out Murder Inc. to win control of the casino business. David Johnston. New York: Doubleday, 1992. viii, 312 p. : ill. *Notes:* Includes index. [LC 92008727; ISN 0385419201; $22.50 ($28.00 Can.)] HV6711. J64 1992   490

CATHOLIC CHURCH

The Catholic bishops and the economy: a debate. Douglas Rasmussen and James Sterba. Bowling Green, Ohio: New Brunswick, USA: Social Philosophy & Policy Center; Transaction Books, 1987. xiv, 118 p. *Notes:* Series statement from jacket. Bibliography: p. [103]-118. [LC 86027269; ISN 0912051159; ISN 0912051167] BX1795.E27 C37 1987   491

CBS INC

This—is CBS: a chronicle of 60 years. Robert Slater. Englewood Cliffs, N.J.: Prentice-Hall, c1988. xiv, 354 p., [16] p. of plates: ill. *Notes:* Includes index. Bibliography: p. 327-330. [LC 88002520; ISN 0139192344] PN1992.92.C38 S57 1988   492

CENTRAL PLANNING

The turning point: revitalizing the Soviet economy. by Nikolai Shmelev and Vladimir Popov; with a preface by Richard E. Erickson; translated by Michele A. Berdy. 1st ed. New York: Doubleday, 1989. xvii, 330 p. : ill. *Notes:* Translated from the Russian. Includes bibliographical references. [LC 89001082; ISN 0385246544; $19.95] HC336. S444 1989   493

CHARITIES, MEDICAL

Unhealthy charities: hazardous to your health and wealth. James T. Bennett and Thomas J. DiLorenzo. New York: BasicBooks, c1994. xii, 269 p. *Notes:* Includes bibliographical references (p. 235-255) and index. [LC 94006191; ISN 0465029108; $25.00 ($33.50 Can.)] HV687.5.U5 B45 1994   +494

CHARITIES

Modern American philanthropy: a personal account. John J. Schwartz. New York: Wiley, c1994. xxi, 218 p. *Notes:* Includes index. [LC 93005464; ISN 0471592838] HV91. S296 1994   +495

CHASE MANHATTAN BANK, N.A

The Chase: the Chase Manhattan Bank, N.A., 1945-1985. John Donald Wilson. Boston, Mass.: Harvard Business School Press, c1986. x, 432 p., [24] p. of plates: ill., ports. *Notes:* Includes bibliographical references and index. [LC 86011962; ISN 0875841341] HG2613.N54 C538 1986   496

CHIAT-DAY, INC

Inventing desire: inside Chiat/Day: the hottest shop, the coolest players, the big business of advertising. Karen Stabiner. New York: Simon & Schuster, c1993. 351 p. : ill. (some col.) *Notes:* Includes index. [LC 93016263; ISN 0671723464; $25.00] HF6181.C49 S73 1993   497

CHICAGO (ILL.)—ECONOMIC CONDITIONS

Rusted dreams: hard times in a steel community. David Bensman and Roberta Lynch. New York: McGraw-Hill, c1987. iv, 250 p. *Notes:* Includes index. Bibliography: p. 236-244. [LC 86021047; ISN 0070047812] HC108.C4 B45 1987   498

CHICAGO MERCANTILE EXCHANGE

The Merc: the emergence of a global financial powerhouse. Bob Tamarkin. 1st ed. New York, NY: HarperBusiness, c1993. xiii, 465 p., [32] p. of plates: ill. *Notes:* Includes bibliographical references (p. 435-451) and index. [LC 91031500; ISN 0887305164] HG6049. T35 1993   499

CHICAGO SCHOOL OF ECONOMICS

Not so free to choose: the political economy of Milton Friedman and Ronald Reagan. Elton Rayack. New York: Praeger, 1987. x, 215 p. : ill. *Notes:* Includes index. Bibliography: p. 203-208. [LC 86021276; ISN 0275923630; $35.85 (est.)]   HB98.3. R39 1987   500

CHICAGO TRIBUNE

Read all about it!: the corporate takeover of America's newspapers. James D. Squires. 1st ed. New York: Times Books, c1993. xi, 244 p. *Notes:* Includes index. [LC 92050498; ISN 0812921011; $20.00 ($25.00 Can.)]   PN4899.C4 S68 1993   501

CHIEF EXECUTIVE OFFICERS

CEO: who gets to the top in America. by David L. Kurtz, Louis E. Boone, C. Patrick Fleenor. East Lansing, Mich.: Michigan State University Press, 1989. xxiii, 204 p. *Notes:* Includes bibliographical references (p. 195-204). [LC 88042902; ISN 087013261X; $20.00]   HD38.25.U6 K87 1989   502

Corporate mobility and paths to the top: studies for human resource and management development specialists. J. Benjamin Forbes and James E. Piercy. New York: Quorum Books, 1991. xvi, 208 p. *Notes:* Includes bibliographical references (p. [195]-201) and index. [LC 90042967; ISN 0899305245; $42.95]   HD38.25.U6 F67 1991   503

Determinants of executive compensation: corporate ownership, performance, size, and diversification. Ellen L. Pavlik and Ahmed Belkaoui. New York: Quorum Books, 1991. xii, 163 p. : ill. *Notes:* Includes bibliographical references and index. [LC 90026407]   HD4965.2. P38 1991   504

Facts against fictions of executive behavior: a critical analysis of what managers do. Joe Kelly. Westport, CT: Quorum Books, 1993. xiv, 225 p. : ill. *Notes:* Includes bibliographical references (p. [211]-217) and indexes. [LC 92041607; ISN 089930737X]   HD38.25.U6 K45 1993   +505

General managers in action. Francis Joseph Aguilar. New York: Oxford University Press, 1988. viii, 498 p. : ill. *Notes:* Includes bibliographical references and index. [LC 87012503; ISN 019504083X]   HD38.2. A39 1988   506

General managers in action: policies and strategies. Francis Joseph Aguilar. 2nd ed. New York: Oxford University Press, 1992. 1 v. (various pagings) *Notes:* Includes bibliographical references and index. [LC 91025992; ISN 0195073673; $49.95]   HD38.2. A39 1992   507

The hero's farewell: what happens when CEOs retire. Jeffrey Sonnenfeld. New York; Oxford: Oxford University Press, 1988. viii, 324 p. : ill. *Notes:* Includes indexes. Bibliography: p. 295-312. [LC 88001542; ISN 0195050916]   HD38.25.U6 S66 1988   508

Leaders on leadership: interviews with top executives. with a preface by Warren Bennis. Boston, MA: Harvard Business School Pub., c1992. xiv, 275 p. *Notes:* Includes index. [LC 91040754; ISN 0875843077; $29.95]   HD38.25.U6 L4 1992   509

Passing the baton: managing the process of CEO succession. Richard F. Vancil; foreword by Alonzo L. McDonald. Boston, Mass.: Harvard Business School Press, c1987. xxii, 318 p. : ill. *Notes:* Includes index. [LC 87011962; ISN 0875841821]   HD38.25.U6 V36 1987   510

Top dog. J. David Pincus, J. Nicholas DeBonis. New York: McGraw-Hill, c1994. xvi, 362 p. *Notes:* Includes bibliographical references (p. 349-356) and index. [LC 94000217; ISN 0070501297; $24.95]   HD38.2. P53 1994   +511

Value at the top: solutions to the executive compensation crisis. Ira T. Kay. 1st ed. New York, NY: HarperBusiness, c1992. x, 246 p. : ill. *Notes:* Includes bibliographical references (p. 234-237) and index. [LC 91058497; ISN 0887305016; $25.00 ($33.50 Canada)]   HD4965.5.U6 K39 1992   512

CHINA—ECONOMIC CONDITIONS—1976-

China wakes: the struggle for the soul of a rising power. Nicholas D. Kristof and Sheryl WuDunn. New York: Times Books, c1994. 501 p. : ill., maps *Notes:* Includes bibliographical references (p. [461]-484) and index. [LC 94010609; ISN 0812922522; $25.00 (Can. $33.50)]   HC427.92. K75 1994   +513

The rise of China: how economic reform is creating a new superpower. William H. Overholt. 1st ed. New York: Norton, c1993. 431 p. : ill., maps *Notes:* Includes bibliographical references and index. [LC 93004634; ISN 0393035336]   HC427.92. O93 1993   +514

CHINA—ECONOMIC POLICY—1976-

The new China: comparative economic development in Mainland China, Taiwan, and Hong Kong. Alvin Rabushka. San Francisco: Boulder, Colo.: Pacific Research Institute for Public Policy; Westview Press, 1987. xii, 254 p. *Notes:* Includes index. Bibliography: p. 233-242. [LC 87010574; ISN 0936488158; ISN 0813305195]   HC427.92. R33 1987   515

CHRYSLER CORPORATION

Going for broke: Lee Iacocca's battle to save Chrysler. Michael Moritz and Barrett Seaman. Garden City, N.Y.: Anchor Press/Doubleday, 1984. viii, 350 p., [16] p. of plates: ill., ports. *Notes:* Includes index. Bibliography: p. [331]-332. [LC 83020826; ISN 0385193696; $10.95]   HD9710.U54 C47 1984   516

Masters of deception: a corporate giant confronted by its stockholders. by Edward A. Gallaway. Bryn Mawr, Pa.: Dorrance, c1985. xi, 216 p. : ill. [LC 86100842; ISN 0805929983; $15.95]   HD9710.U54 C466 1985   517

New deals: the Chrysler revival and the American system. Robert B. Reich, John D. Donahue. 1st ed. New York: Times Books, c1985. 359 p. *Notes:* Includes bibliographical references and index. [LC 84040640; ISN 0812911806; $15.50]   HD9710.U54 C475 1985   518

CITIBANK (NEW YORK, N.Y.)

Off the books. Robert A. Hutchison. 1st ed. New York: W. Morrow, c1986. 416 p. *Notes:* Includes bibliographical references and index. [LC 85021376; ISN 0688048811]   HG2613.N54 F674 1986   519

CITIES AND TOWNS

The new heartland: America's flight beyond the suburbs and how it is changing our future. John Herbers. 1st ed. New York, N.Y.: Times Books, c1986. xii, 228 p. *Notes:* Includes index. Bibliography: p. 215-218. [LC 86000236; ISN 0812912284; $16.95]   HT384.U5 H47 1986   520

CLIENT/SERVER COMPUTING

Beyond LANs: client/server computing. Dimitris N. Chorafas. New York: McGraw-Hill, 1993, c1994. xxvii, 419 p. : ill. *Notes:* Includes index. [LC 93032977; ISN 0070110573; $50.00]   QA76.9.C55 C48 1994   +521

CLOSE CORPORATIONS

Managing and operating a closely held corporation. Michael Diamond. New York: J. Wiley, c1991. xi, 243 p. *Notes:* Includes index. [LC 90024802; ISN 0471521078; $69.95]   HD62.25. D53 1991   522

Painter on close corporations: corporate, securities, and tax aspects. William H. Painter. 3rd ed. Boston: Little, Brown and Co., c1991. 2 v. (loose-leaf) *Notes:* Rev. ed. of: Corporate and tax aspects of closely held corporations. 2nd ed. 1981. Includes bibliographical references and indexes. [LC 91061351; ISN 0316688746; $240.00]   KF1466. P3 1991   523

Smart growth: critical choices for business continuity and prosperity. Ernesto J. Poza. 1st ed. San Francisco: Jossey-Bass, c1989. xx, 211 p. : ill. *Notes:* Includes index. Bibliography: p. 199-206. [LC 89008191; ISN 1555421709; $19.95]   HD62.25. P69 1989   524

The valuation of privately-held businesses: state-of-the art techniques for buyers, sellers, and their advisors. by Irving L. Blackman. Chicago, Ill.: Probus Pub. Co., c1986. 1 v. (various pagings) *Notes:* Includes index. [LC 86020498; ISN 0917253272; $40.00]   HG4028.V3 B48 1986   525

COCA-COLA COMPANY

For God, country and Coca-Cola: the unauthorized history of the great American soft drink and the company that makes it. Mark Pendergrast. New York: Toronto: New York: Scribner's; Macmillan Canada; Maxwell Macmillan International, c1993. xvii, 556 p. : ill. *Notes:* Includes bibliographical references and index. [LC 92030317; ISN 0684193477]   HD9349.S634 C674 1993   526

The real Coke, the real story. Thomas Oliver. 1st ed. New York: Random House, 1986. 195 p. *Notes:* Includes bibliographical references. [LC 86010151; ISN 0394552733; $17.95]   HD9349.C6 O44   527

The real ones: four generations of the first family of Coca-Cola. Elizabeth Candler Graham and Ralph Roberts. Fort Lee, N.J.: Emeryville, CA: Barricade Books; Distributed by Publishers Group West, c1992. viii, 344 p., [16] p. of plates: ill., ports. [LC 92018778; ISN 0942637623; $21.95]   HD9349.S634 C6336 1992   528

COHEN, BEN

Ben & Jerry's, the inside scoop: how two real guys built a business with social conscience and a sense of humor. Fred "Chico" Lager. 1st ed. New York: Crown Publishers, c1994. xiv, 242 p., [16] p. of plates: ill., maps *Notes:* Includes index. [LC 93039176; ISN 0517597160; $22.50 ($29.50 Can.)]   HD9281.U53 V558 1994   +529

COLLECTIVE BARGAINING

A behavioral theory of labor negotiations: an analysis of a social interaction system. Richard E. Walton, Robert B. McKersie. 2nd ed. Ithaca, N.Y.: ILR Press, 1991. xxvi, 437 p. : ill. *Notes:* Reprint, with new introduction. Originally published: New York: McGraw-Hill, 1965. Includes bibliographical references (p. 421-430) and indexes. [LC 91003561; ISN 0875461794; $23.95]   HD6971.5. W35 1991   530

Collective bargaining. Neil W. Chamberlain, James W. Kuhn. 3rd ed. New York: McGraw-Hill, c1986. xvi, 493 p. : ill. *Notes:* Includes bibliographical references and index. [LC 85007814; ISN 0070104417; $31.95 (est.)]   HD6971.5. C43 1986   531

Front stage, backstage: the dramatic structure of labor negotiations. Raymond A. Friedman. Cambridge, Mass.: MIT Press, c1994. xi, 257 p. : ill. *Notes:* Includes bibliographical references (p. [239]-247) and index. [LC 93044591; ISN 0262061678]   HD6971.5. F75 1994   +532

The practice of collective bargaining. James P. Begin, Edwin F. Beal. 8th ed. Homewood, IL: Irwin, 1989. xii, 638 p. *Notes:* Beal's name appears first on earlier editions. Includes bibliographies and index. [LC 88013421; ISN 0256071160; $37.95]   HD6508. B375 1989   533

COLLEGE PRESIDENTS

Leadership and ambiguity: the American college president. Michael D. Cohen, James G. March. 2nd ed. Boston, Mass.: Harvard Business School Press, c1986. xxi, 298 p. : ill. *Notes:* Includes index. Bibliography: p. 231-234. [LC 85027268; ISN 0875841740; ISN 0875841317]   LB2341. C56 1986   534

COLLEGE TEACHING

Education for judgment: the artistry of discussion leadership. edited by C. Roland Christensen, David A. Garvin, Ann Sweet. Boston, Mass.: Harvard Business School Press, c1991. xxvi, 312 p. *Notes:* Includes bibliographical references and index. [LC 90026961; ISN 0875842550; $29.95]   LB2331. E376 1991   535

COMMERCE

The rise of the trading state: commerce and conquest in the modern world. Richard Rosecrance. New York: Basic Books, c1986. xiii, 268 p. : ill. *Notes:* Includes index. Bibliography: p. 240-249. [LC 85047558; ISN 0465070353; $19.95]   HF1007. R549 1986   536

COMMERCIAL BUILDINGS

Corporate real estate handbook. Robert A. Silverman, editor-in-chief. New York: McGraw-Hill, c1987. xii, 202 p. : ill. *Notes:* "Strategies for improving bottom-line performance"—Jacket. Includes bibliographical references and index. [LC 86015337; ISN 0070459002; $24.95]
  HD1393.25. C67 1987 537

COMMERCIAL CORRESPONDENCE

Basic business communication. Raymond V. Lesikar. 5th ed. Homewood, IL: Irwin, c1991. xxi, 666 p. : ill (some col.) *Notes:* Includes bibliographical references and index. [LC 90033272; ISN 0256083274; $44.95] HF5721. L37 1991 538

Communications in business. Walter Wells. 5th ed Boston: PWS-Kent Pub. Co., c1988. xvi, 632 p. : ill. *Notes:* Includes index. [LC 87022721; ISN 0534871674; $40.80] HF5721. W36 1988 539

Effective business communications. Herta A. Murphy, Herbert W. Hildebrandt. 5th ed. New York: McGraw-Hill, c1988. xx, 730 p. : col. ill. *Notes:* Includes bibliographical references and index. [LC 87017330; ISN 0070440948] HF5721. M85 1988 540

Writing and speaking in business. Gretchen N. Vik, Clyde W. Wilkinson, Dorothy C. Wilkinson. 10th ed. Homewood, IL: Irwin, c1990. xv, 636 p. : ill. *Notes:* Rev. ed. of: Communicating through writing and speaking in business / C.W. Wilkinson. 9th ed. 1986. Includes bibliographical references and index. [LC 89002177; ISN 0256068127; $45.95] HF5726. W667 1990 541

Writing for results in business, government, the sciences, and the professions. David W. Ewing. 2d ed. New York: Wiley, c1979. xvi, 448 p. : ill. *Notes:* Edition of 1974 published under title: Writing for results in business, government, and the professions. Includes bibliographical references and index. [LC 79011756; ISN 0471050369] HF5721. E9 1979 542

COMMERCIAL LAW

Business law and the regulatory environment: concepts and cases. Michael B. Metzger. . . et al. 7th ed. Homewood, IL: Irwin, 1989. xx, 1563 p. ill. *Notes:* Includes bibliographical references and indexes. [LC 88015312; ISN 0256068526; $41.00] KF888. B8 1989 543

Fundamentals of business law. Robert N. Corley, Peter J. Shedd. 5th ed. Englewood Cliffs, N.J.: Prentice Hall, c1990. xxii, 1018 p. [LC 89023122; ISN 0133343359; $44.40] KF889. C64 1990 544

Principles of business law. Robert N. Corley, Peter J. Shedd. 14th ed. Englewood Cliffs, N.J.: Prentice Hall, c1989. ix, 1203 p. *Notes:* Includes index. [LC 88025436; ISN 0137052790; ISN 013710443X; $39.95] KF888. C63 1989 545

COMMERCIAL STATISTICS

Basic statistics for business and economics. Leonard J. Kazmier, Norval F. Pohl. 2nd ed. New York: McGraw-Hill, c1984. xvi, 592 p. : ill. *Notes:* Includes bibliographical references and index. [LC 83014958; ISN 007033448X; $25.00 (est.)] HF1017. K38 1984 546

Elementary business statistics: the modern approach. John E. Freund, Frank J. Williams, Benjamin M. Perles. 5th ed. Englewood Cliffs, N.J.: Prentice Hall, c1988. xiii, 738 p. : ill. *Notes:* Includes index. [LC 87020586; ISN 0132531968] HF1017. F73 1988 547

Fundamentals of business statistics. John E. Hanke, Arthur G. Reitsch. Columbus: C.E. Merrill Pub. Co., c1986. xii, 371 p. : ill. *Notes:* Includes index. Bibliography: p. 315-316. [LC 85062478; ISN 0675203333] HF1017. H29 1986 548

Practical business statistics. Andrew F. Siegel. 2nd ed. Burr Ridge, Ill.: Irwin, c1994. xxviii, 820 p. : ill *Notes:* Rev. ed. of: Practical business statistics with STATPAD. c1990. Includes index. [LC 93020292; ISN 0256109745] HF1017. S525 1994 +549

Statistical analysis for business decisions. Gary E. Meek, Stephen J. Turner. Boston: Houghton Mifflin, c1983. xiv, 783 p. : ill. *Notes:* Includes index. [LC 82080074; ISN 039532274X]
  HF1017. M43 1983 550

COMMODITY EXCHANGES

Charting commodity market price behavior. L. Dee Belveal. 2nd ed. Homewood, Ill.: Dow Jones-Irwin, c1985. xxi, 174 p. : ill. *Notes:* Includes index. [LC 85070189; ISN 087094651X]
HG6046. B368 1985   551

Commodities trading: the essential primer. Russell R. Wasendorf, with Pat Stahl. Homewood, Ill.: Dow Jones-Irwin, c1985. viii, 197 p. : ill., forms *Notes:* Includes index. [LC 84072289; ISN 0870942921]
HG6046. W37   552

Commodity futures: markets, methods of analysis, and management of risk. Anthony F. Herbst. New York: Wiley, c1986. xii, 289 p. : ill. *Notes:* Includes bibliographies and index. [LC 85031503; ISN 0471097691; $39.95 (est.)]
HG6046. H47 1986   553

Commodity trading manual. Prepared by the Education and Marketing Services Department of the Chicage Board of Trade; executive editor Patrick J. Catania... et al. Chicago: Chicago Board of Trade, c1989. 382 p. : ill., charts *Notes:* Includes bibliographical references.; $20.72]
HG6049. C65 1989   554

Contrary opinion: how to use it for profit in trading commodity futures. R. Earl Hadady. 1st ed. Pasadena, Calif.: Hadady Publications, c1983. 1 v. (various pagings): ill. *Notes:* Includes bibliographical references. [LC 83090283; ISN 0961139005; $37.50]
HG6046. H193 1983   555

The economics of futures markets. Jerome L. Stein. Oxford Oxfordshire; New York: B. Blackwell, 1986. vi, 247 p. : ill. *Notes:* Includes index. Bibliography: p. [240]-244. [LC 86012924; ISN 0631151397; $45.00]
HG6046. S674   556

The European options and futures markets: the overview and analysis for money managers and traders. the European Bond Commission. New York; London: McGraw-Hill, 1990. xxv, 1086 p. : ill. *Notes:* "A Probus guide to world markets." Includes index. [LC 90022858; ISN 007707369X; £47.50]
HG6042. E87 1990   557

The futures game: who wins? Who loses? Why? Richard J. Teweles, Frank J. Jones. 2nd ed. New York: McGraw-Hill, c1987. xxii, 649 p. : ill. *Notes:* Rev. ed. of: The commodity futures game. 1974. Includes index. Bibliography: p. 609-639. [LC 86010509; ISN 0070637288; $39.95]
HG6046. T46 1987   558

Futures trading: concepts and strategies. Robert E. Fink, Robert B. Feduniak. New York, N.Y.: New York Institute of Finance, c1988. xiv, 685 p. : ill. *Notes:* Includes index. Bibliography: p. 669-670. [LC 87024030; ISN 0133457451; $35.00]
HG6046. F56 1988   559

Inside the commodity option markets. John Labuszewski, Jeanne Cairns Sinquefield. New York: Wiley, c1985. xxii, 374 p. : ill. *Notes:* "Wiley-Interscience"—Spine. Includes index. Bibliography: p. 361. [LC 84025808; ISN 0471896071; $29.95]
HG6046. L225 1985   560

The McGraw-Hill handbook of commodities and futures. edited by Martin J. Pring. New York: McGraw-Hill, c1985. 1 v. (various pagings): ill. *Notes:* Includes bibliographies and index. [LC 84029617; ISN 0070509158]
HG6046. M374 1985   561

The new commodity trading systems and methods. Perry J. Kaufman. New York: Wiley, c1987. xvi, 521 p. : ill. *Notes:* Includes index. Bibliography: p. 499-505. [LC 87006073; ISN 0471878790]
HG6036. K34 1987   562

Technical analysis of the futures markets: a comprehensive guide to trading methods and applications. John J. Murphy. New York, NY: New York Institute of Finance, 1986. xx, 556 p. : ill. *Notes:* Includes index. Bibliography: p. 548-549. [LC 85025958; ISN 013898008X; $35.00]
HG6046. M87 1986   563

The theory and practice of futures markets. Raymond M. Leuthold, Joan C. Junkus, and Jean E. Cordier. Lexington, Mass.: Lexington Books, c1989. xviii, 410 p. *Notes:* Includes bibliographies and index. [LC 87045248; ISN 0669162604; $39.95]
HG6024.A3 L48 1989   564

COMMODITY FUTURES

The Dow Jones-Irwin guide to trading systems. by Bruce Babcock, Jr. Homewood, Ill.: Dow Jones-Irwin, c1989. xix, 316 p. : ill. *Notes:* Includes index. [LC 88031441; ISN 1556231261; $55.00]
HG6024.A3 B33 1989   565

Investment strategy and the money connection: tracking the monetary and business cycles—and making them work for you. Edward J. Cousin. New York: Wiley, c1990. xiii, 301 p. : ill. *Notes:* Includes bibliographical references. [LC 90030056; ISN 0471515485; $42.50]   HG6046. C673 1990   566

COMMUNICATION

The coming information age: an overview of technology, economics, and politics. Wilson P. Dizard, Jr. 3rd ed. New York: Longman, 1989. xi, 250 p. Notes: Includes bibliographical references. [LC 88020939; ISBN 0801303052; $20.88] P92.U5 D5 1989 567

The control revolution: technological and economic origins of the information society. James R. Beniger. Cambridge, Mass.: Harvard University Press, 1986. x, 493 p. : ill. *Notes:* Includes index. Bibliography: p. [439]-476. [LC 85031743; ISBN 0674169859] HM258. B459 1986 568

Information anxiety. Richard Saul Wurman. 1st ed. New York: Doubleday, 1989. 356 p. : ill. (some col.) *Notes:* Bibliography: p. 339-348. [LC 88025787; ISBN 0385243944; $19.95] P90. W8 1989 569

Shared minds: the new technologies of collaboration. Michael Schrage. New York: Random House, c1990. xxv, 227 p. : ill. *Notes:* Includes bibliographical references (p. 215-222) and index. [LC 89043430; ISBN 0394565878; $19.95] P90. S363 1990 570

COMMUNICATION AND TRAFFIC

The future of transportation and communication: visions and perspectives from Europe, Japan and the U.S.A. Roland Thord, (ed.); with contributions by A.E. Andersson... et al. Berlin; New York: Springer-Verlag, c1993. viii, 265 p. : ill. *Notes:* Includes bibliographical references. [LC 92046064; ISBN 3540563776; ISBN 0387563776] HE151. F38 1993 +571

COMMUNICATION IN MANAGEMENT

Communicating for managerial effectiveness. Phillip G. Clampitt. Newbury Park, Calif.: SAGE Publications, c1991. xi, 323 p. : ill. *Notes:* Includes bibliographical references and indexes. [LC 90015581; ISBN 0803937598] HD30.3. C52 1991 572

Corporate communication. Paul A. Argenti. Burr Ridge, Ill.: Irwin, c1994. xix, 200 p. : ill. *Notes:* Includes bibliographical references (p. 193-196) and index. [LC 93001310; ISBN 0256057052] HD30.3. A73 1994 +573

Corporate legends and lore: the power of storytelling as a management tool. Peg C. Neuhauser. New York: McGraw-Hill, c1993. xvi, 234 p. *Notes:* Includes bibliographical references and index. [LC 93014759; ISBN 0070463263; $22.95] HD30.3. N48 1993 574

Corporate networking: building channels for information and influence. Robert K. Mueller. New York: Free Press, c1986. x, 160 p. : ill. *Notes:* Bibliography: p. 141-151. Includes index. [LC 86018347; ISBN 0029221501] HD30.3. M84 1986 575

Getting the word out: how managers can create value with communications. Frank M. Corrado. Homewood, Ill.: Business One Irwin, c1993. xi, 212 p. : ill. *Notes:* Includes bibliographical references and index. [LC 92023730; ISBN 1556237855] HD59. C638 1993 576

The handbook of executive communication. edited by John Louis DiGaetani. Homewood, Ill.: Dow Jones-Irwin, c1986. xxvii, 894 p. : ill. *Notes:* Includes bibliographies and index. Non-circulating. [LC 85071301; ISBN 0870945262; $45.00] HD30.3. H355 1986 577

Handbook of organizational communication: an interdisciplinary perspective. editors, Fredric M. Jablin... et al. Newbury Park, Calif.: Sage Publications, c1987. 781 p. : ill. *Notes:* Includes bibliographies and indexes. [LC 87023417; ISBN 0803923872; $60.00] HD30.3. H3575 1987 578

Information strategies: new pathways to management productivity. Gerald M. Goldhaber... et al. Rev. ed. Norwood, N.J.: Ablex Pub. Corp., c1984. xii, 366 p. (Communication and information science) *Notes:* Bibliography: p. 355-366. [LC 84236816; ISBN 0893911518] HD30.3. I533 1984 579

Managerial communication: a finger on the pulse. Paul R. Timm. 2nd ed. Englewood Cliffs, N.J.: Prentice-Hall, c1986. xiii, 397 p. : ill. *Notes:* Includes bibliographies and index. [LC 85006514; ISBN 0135500052; $22.95] HF5718. T55 1986 580

Managing by storying around. David M. Armstrong. 1st ed. New York: Doubleday, 1992. xvii, 249 p. *Notes:* "A Currency book"—T.p. verso. [LC 91026223; ISBN 0385421540; $20.00] HD30.3. A76 1992 581

Networking smart: how to build relationships for personal and organizational success. Wayne E. Baker. New York: McGraw-Hill, 1993, c1994. xxii, 374 p. : ill. *Notes:* Includes index. [LC 93022704; ISBN 0070050929; $22.95] HD30.3. B364 1993 +582

Organizational communication: the essence of effective management. Phillip V. Lewis. 3rd ed. New York: Wiley, c1987. xix, 345 p. : ill. *Notes:* Includes bibliographies and indexes. [LC 86005571; ISBN 0471841315; $27.95] HD30.3. L49 1987 583

Planning, implementing, and evaluating targeted communication programs: a manual for business communicators. Gary W. Selnow and William D. Crano. New York: Quorum Books, 1987. vi, 291 p. : ill. *Notes:* Includes bibliographies and index. [LC 86030418; ISN 0899302084]
                     HD30.3. S46 1987 584

Write to the top: writing for corporate success. Deborah Dumaine. 1st ed. New York: Random House, c1983. xii, 141 p. : ill. *Notes:* Bibliography: p. 141. [LC 82040145; ISN 0394712269; $9.95]
                     HF5718. D84 1983 585

COMMUNICATION IN MARKETING

Integrated marketing communications. Don E. Schultz, Stanley I. Tannenbaum, Robert F. Lauterborn. Lincolnwood, Ill.: NTC Business Books, 1992, c1993. xvii, 218 p. : ill. *Notes:* Includes index. [LC 91044518; ISN 0844233633] HF5415.123. S38 1992 586

Public relations in the marketing mix: introducing vulnerability relations. Jordan Goldman. Chicago, IL: Crain Books, c1984. xviii, 165 p. *Notes:* Includes index. [LC 83071076; ISN 0872510840]
                   HF5415.123. G65 1984 587

COMMUNICATION IN ORGANIZATIONS

The digital workplace: designing groupware platforms. Charles E. Grantham with Larry D. Nichols. New York: Van Nostrand Reinhold, c1993. x, 248 p. : ill. *Notes:* Includes bibliographical references and index. [LC 92046201; ISN 0442011237; $39.95] HD30.3. G73 1993 +588

Handbook of organizational communication. edited by Gerald M. Goldhaber, George A. Barnett. Norwood, N.J.: Ablex Pub. Corp., c1988. 502 p. : ill. *Notes:* Includes bibliographies and indexes. [LC 87019380; ISN 0893914460; $65.00] HD30.3. H357 1988 589

Inside organizational communication. International Association of Business Communicators; edited by Carol Reuss and Donn Silvis. 2nd ed. New York: Longman, 1984 c1985. xi, 368 p. : ill. (Longman series in public communication) *Notes:* Includes index. Bibliography: p. 343-348. [LC 84007896; ISN 0582285380; ISN 0582285402] HD30.36.U5 I56 1985 590

Interpersonal communication in the modern organization. Ernest G. Bormann... et al. 2nd ed. Englewood Cliffs, N.J.: Prentice-Hall, c1982. xii, 287 p. : ill. *Notes:* Includes bibliographies and index. [LC 81013927; ISN 0134750616; $18.95] HF5549.5.C6 I57 1982 591

The new organization: growing the culture of organizational networking. Colin Hastings. London; New York: McGraw-Hill, c1993. xvii, 178 p. : ill. *Notes:* Includes bibliographical references and index. [LC 93000890; ISN 0077077849; £21.95] HD30.3. H375 1993 +592

On organizational learning. Chris Argyris. Cambridge, Mass.: Blackwell Business, 1993. xi, 450 p. : ill. *Notes:* Includes bibliographical references and index. [LC 92021822; ISN 1557862621]
                     HD30.3. A74 1993 593

COMMUNICATION IN PERSONNEL MANAGEMENT

Bridging cultural barriers for corporate success: how to manage the multicultural work force. Sondra Thiederman. Lexington, Mass.: Lexington Books, c1991. xxiii, 256 p. : ill. *Notes:* Includes index. Includes bibliographical references (p. [245]-251). [LC 90040664; ISN 0669219304; $34.95]
                    HF5549.5.C6 T49 1991 594

Handbook of human resources communications. Myron Emanuel, Arthur M. York. Greenvale, N.Y.: Panel Publishers, c1988. xvi, 363 p. : ill. [LC 88039103; ISN 0916592820; $89.00]
                    HF5549.5.C6 E49 1988 595

COMMUNICATION, INTERNATIONAL

Hidden differences: doing business with the Japanese. Edward T. Hall and Mildred Reed Hall. 1st ed. in the U.S.A. Garden City, N.Y.: Anchor Press/Doubleday, 1987. xx, 172 p. *Notes:* Includes index. Bibliography: p. [161]-166. [LC 86020610; ISN 0385238835; $15.95] P96.I52 J335 1987 596

COMPARATIVE ACCOUNTING

Comparative international accounting. edited by Chris Nobes and Robert Parker. 3rd ed. New York: Prentice Hall, 1991. xix, 520 p. : ill. *Notes:* Includes bibliographical references and index. [LC 90027398; ISN 0131562908] HF5625. C74 1991   597

COMPARATIVE MANAGEMENT

Global management principles. Ronnie Lessem. New York: Prentice Hall, 1989. xxiv, 727 p. : ill. *Notes:* Includes bibliographical references. [LC 89023194; ISN 0133573443; $40.00] HD30.55. L47 1989   598

International management and production: survival techniques for corporate America. by Gerhard Johannes Plenert. 1st ed. Blue Ridge Summit, PA: TAB Books, 1990. xiv, 184 p. *Notes:* Includes index. Includes bibliographical references. [LC 89033690; ISN 0830673911; $24.60] HD30.55. P54 1990   599

Models of management: work, authority, and organization in a comparative perspective. Mauro F. Guillén. Chicago: University of Chicago Press, c1994. xiii, 424 p. *Notes:* Includes bibliographical references (p. 335-405) and index. [LC 94003887; ISN 0226310353; ISN 0226310361] HD30.55. G85 1994   +600

Riding the waves of culture: understanding diversity in global business. Fons Trompenaars. Burr Ridge, Ill.: Irwin Professional Pub., c1994. xii, 215 p. : ill. *Notes:* Includes bibliographical references and index. [LC 93048785; ISN 0786302909] HD30.55. T76 1994   +601

COMPENSATION MANAGEMENT

Compensation. George T. Milkovich, Jerry M. Newman. 3rd ed. Homewood, IL: BPI/IRWIN, c1990. xxii, 627 p. : ill. *Notes:* Includes bibliographical references. [LC 89037682; ISN 0256076715; $43.95] HF5549.5.C67 M54 1990   602

Compensation. Robert E. Sibson. 5th ed. New York, NY: American Management Association, c1990. xiv, 400 p. : ill. *Notes:* Includes bibliographical references and index. [LC 90055210; ISN 0814459773; $65.00] HF5549.5.C67 S588 1990   603

The compensation handbook: a state-of-the-art guide to compensation strategy and design. Milton L. Rock, Lance A. Berger, editors in chief. 3rd ed. New York: McGraw-Hill, c1991. xi, 628 p. : ill. *Notes:* Rev. ed. of: Handbook of wage and salary administration. Includes bibliographical references and index. [LC 90040324; ISN 0070533520; $59.95] HF5549.5.C67 H36 1991   604

Compensation management: rewarding performance. Richard I. Henderson. 5th ed. Englewood Cliffs, N.J.: Prentice Hall, c1989. xiv, 578 p. : ill. *Notes:* Includes bibliographical references and index. [LC 88004160; ISN 0131549235; $28.50] HF5549.5.C67 H46 1989   605

Compensation theory and practice. Marc J. Wallace, Jr., Charles H. Fay. 2nd ed. Boston, Mass.: PWS-Kent Pub. Co., c1988. xii, 423 p. : ill. *Notes:* Includes bibliographies and indexes. [LC 88012609; ISN 0534871984; $23.75] HF5549.5.C67 W35 1988   606

Handbook of compensation management. Matthew J. DeLuca. Englewood Cliffs, N.J.: Prentice Hall, c1993. xxv, 373 p. : ill. *Notes:* Includes bibliographical references (p. 359-363) and index. [LC 93013378; ISN 0131596586; $79.95] HF5549.5.C67 D45 1993   +607

New perspectives on compensation. editors, David B. Balkin, Luis R. Gomez-Mejia. Englewood Cliffs, NJ: Prentice-Hall, 1987. xviii, 263 p. : ill. *Notes:* Includes bibliographies. [LC 86025534; ISN 0136152120] HF5549.5.C67 N49 1987   608

Performance pay as a competitive weapon: a compensation policy model for the 1990s. K. Richard Berlet, Douglas M. Cravens. New York: Wiley, c1991. x, 228 p. : ill. *Notes:* "Published simultaneously in Canada"—T.p. verso. Includes bibliographical references (p. 221) and index. [LC 90043501; ISN 0471524263; $55.00] HF5549.5.C67 B48 1991   609

Strategic pay: aligning organizational strategies and pay systems. Edward E. Lawler III. 1st ed. San Francisco: Jossey-Bass Publishers, 1990. xvii, 308 p. : *Notes:* Includes bibliographical references and index. [LC 90037168; ISN 1555422624; $26.95] HF5549.5.C67 L383 1990   610

COMPETITION

Commitment: the dynamic of strategy. Pankaj Ghemawat. New York: Toronto: New York: Free Press; Maxwell Macmillan Canada; Maxwell Macmillan International, c1991. xiii, 178 p. : ill. *Notes:* Includes bibliographical references (p. 157-173) and index. [LC 91006527; ISN 0029115752; $29.95]
HD41. G48 1991   +611

Competing for the future. Gary Hamel, C.K. Prahalad. Boston, Mass.: Harvard Business School Press, c1994. xv, 327 p. : ill. *Notes:* Includes bibliographical references (p. 303-306) and index. [LC 94018035; ISN 0875844162; $24.95]
HD41. H24 1994   +612

Competitive advantage: creating and sustaining superior performance. Michael E. Porter. New York: London: Free Press; Collier Macmillan, c1985. xviii, 557 p. : ill. *Notes:* Includes index. Bibliography: p. 537-540. [LC 83049518; ISN 0029250900]
HD41. P668 1985   613

Competitive strategy: techniques for analyzing industries and competitors. Michael E. Porter. New York: London: Free Press; Collier Macmillan, c1980. xix, 396 p. : ill. *Notes:* Includes index. Bibliography: p. 383-387. [LC 80065200; ISN 0029253608]
HD41. P67   614

The corporate warriors. Douglas K. Ramsey. Boston: Houghton Mifflin, 1987. xxi, 261 p. *Notes:* Bibliography: p. 261. [LC 86020954; ISN 0395354870; $17.95]
HD41. R27 1987   615

Innovation and entrepreneurship in organizations: strategies for competitiveness, deregulation, and privatization. edited by Richard M. Burton and Børge Obel. Amsterdam; New York: New York, NY, U.S.A.: Elsevier; Distributors for the U.S. and Canada, Elsevier Science Pub. Co., 1986. vii, 207 p. : ill. *Notes:* Chiefly papers presented at a seminar held at the European Institute for Advanced Studies in Management, Brussels, in May 1985. "Has been published in a special issue of Technovation, vol 5 (1986), issues 1-3." Includes bibliographies and index. [LC 86024207; ISN 0444427163; fl 160.00 (Netherlands: est.)]
HD41. I56 1986   616

Leading edge logistics: a competitive positioning for the 1990's: comprehensive research on logistics organization strategy and behavior in North America. by Donald J. Bowersox... et al. .. of Michigan State University Materials and Logistics Management Program, Department of Marketing and Transportation Administration, for the Council of Logistics Management. Oak Brook, Ill.?: Council of Logistics Management?, c1989. 1 v. (various pagings): ill. *Notes:* "Prepared by Michigan State University for Council of Logistics Management"—cover. Bibliography: p. 307-309.]
HD38.5. B69 1989   617

Making organizations competitive: enhancing networks and relationships across traditional boundaries. edited by Ralph H. Kilmann, Ines Kilmann and associates. 1st ed. San Francisco: Jossey-Bass Publishers, 1991. xxx, 477 p. : ill. *Notes:* Includes bibliographical references and indexes. [LC 90040516; ISN 1555422853; $35.95]
HD41. M3 1991   618

Modern competitive analysis. Sharon M. Oster. 2nd ed. New York: Oxford University Press, 1994. xii, 411 p. : ill. *Notes:* Includes bibliographical references (p. 355-389) and index. [LC 93009826; ISN 019507579X]
HD41. O85 1994   +619

Offensive strategy: forging a new competitiveness in the fires of head-to-head competition. Lee Tom Perry. New York: Harper Business, c1990. xi, 224 p. *Notes:* Includes bibliographical references. [LC 90004381; ISN 0887304354; $32.95]
HD41. P45 1990   620

Rivalry: in business, science, among nations. Reuven Brenner. Cambridge; New York: Cambridge University Press, c1987. xi, 244 p. *Notes:* Includes index. Bibliography: p. 211-234. [LC 86024415; ISN 0521331870]
HD41. B743 1987   621

Structural holes: the social structure of competition. Ronald S. Burt. Cambridge, Mass.: Harvard University Press, 1992. 313 p. : ill. *Notes:* Includes bibliographical references and index. [LC 91043396; ISN 067484372X]
HD41. B88 1992   622

COMPETITION, INTERNATIONAL

Competition in global industries. edited by Michael E. Porter. Boston, Mass.: Harvard Business School Press, c1986. x, 581 p. : ill. (Research colloquium (Harvard University. Graduate School of Business Administration)) *Notes:* Includes bibliographies and index. [LC 86018377; ISN 0875841406]
HF1414. C66 1986   623

Enhancing American competitiveness: a progress report to the President and Congress. Competitiveness Policy Council. Washington, DC: The Council, 1993. 1 v. (various pagings): ill. *Notes:* Running title: A progress report of the Competitiveness Policy Council. "October 1993." *Contents:* Enhancing American competitiveness: a progress report to the President and Congress / Competitiveness Policy Council—Implementing technology policy for a competitive America: status report of the Critical Technologies Subcouncil to the Competitiveness Policy Council—Restoring public confidence in infrastructure investment: interim report of the Public Infrastructure Subcouncil to the Competitiveness Policy Council—Forging a strong trade policy: interim report of the Trade Policy Subcouncil to the Competitiveness Policy Council—Investing in our workforce: interim report of the Training Subcouncil to the Competitiveness Policy Council.]
                           HF1414. U55 1993 +624

The global marketplace. edited by Jerome M. Rosow. New York: Facts on File, c1988. 225 p. *Notes:* Includes index. [LC 88016279; ISN 081601633X; $21.95] HF1414. G56 1988 625

Ideology and national competitiveness: an analysis of nine countries. edited by George C. Lodge and Ezra F. Vogel. Boston, Mass.: Harvard Business School Press, c1987. x, 350 p. *Notes:* Includes index. Bibliography: p. 327-342. [LC 86019569; ISN 0875841473] HF1414. I34 1987 626

Reassessing American competitiveness. Peter Morici Washington, D.C.: National Planning Association, c1988. iv, 164 p. : ill. *Notes:* Appendix tables included. Bibliography p. 153-160. [LC 88060937; ISN 0890680957] HF1455. M67 1988 627

The silent war: inside the global business battles shaping America's future. Ira C. Magaziner and Mark Patinkin. 1st ed. New York: Random House, c1989. xii, 415 p. : ill. *Notes:* Includes bibliographical references and index. [LC 88042822; ISN 0394569792; $19.95] HF1414. M34 1989 628

COMPUTER ASSOCIATES INTERNATIONAL

Twenty-first-century management: the revolutionary strategies that have made Computer Associates a multibillion-dollar software giant. by Hesh Kestin. New York, NY: Atlantic Monthly Press, c1992. xviii, 189 p. *Notes:* Includes bibliographical references. [LC 92004089; ISN 0871135248] HD9696.C64 C63 1992 629

COMPUTER CRIMES

Approaching zero: the extraordinary underworld of hackers, phreakers, virus writers, and keyboard criminals. by Paul Mungo and Bryan Clough. 1st American ed. New York: Random House, c1992. xix, 247 p. *Notes:* Includes bibliographical references. [LC 91053159; ISN 0679409386; $22.00] HV6773. M86 1992 630

The hacker crackdown: law and disorder on the electronic frontier. Bruce Sterling. New York: Bantam Books, 1992. xiv, 328 p. *Notes:* Published simultaneously in the United States and Canada. Includes index. [LC 92017496; ISN 055308058X; $23.00 ($28.00 Can.)] HV6773.2. S74 1992 631

COMPUTER ENGINEERING

The soul of a new machine. Tracy Kidder. 1st ed. Boston: Little, Brown, c1981. 293 p. *Notes:* "An Atlantic Monthly Press book." "A portion of this book, in different form, first appeared in The Atlantic." [LC 81006044; ISN 0316491705] TK7885.4. K53 632

COMPUTER ENGINEERS

Portraits in silicon. Robert Slater. Cambridge, Mass.: MIT Press, c1987. xiv, 374 p. : ill., ports. *Notes:* Includes index. Bibliography: p. [359]-361. [LC 87002868; ISN 0262192624] TK7885.2. S57 1987 633

COMPUTER INDUSTRY

Accidental empires: how the boys of Silicon Valley make their millions, battle foreign competition, and still can't get a date. Robert X. Cringely. Reading, Mass.: Addison-Wesley, c1992. xi, 324 p. *Notes:* "A William Patrick Book." Includes index. [LC 91027089; ISN 0201570327; $19.18]
    HD9696.C63 U51586 1992   634

Computer strategies, 1990-9: technologies, costs, markets. Georges Anderla and Anthony Dunning. Chichester West Sussex; New York: Wiley, c1987. xxi, 299 p. : ill. *Notes:* Includes index. [LC 87008173; ISN 0471915858; $38.00]   HD9696.C62 A53 1987   635

Creating the computer: government, industry, and high technology. Kenneth S. Flamm. Washington, D.C.: Brookings Institution, c1988. xi, 282 p. : ill. *Notes:* Includes bibliographical references and index. [LC 87032644; ISN 0815728506; ISN 0815728492; $28.95; $10.95]   HD9696.C62 F55 1988   636

Information technology: the trillion-dollar opportunity. Harvey L. Poppel, Bernard Goldstein; with foreword by John Sculley. New York: McGraw-Hill, c1987. xx, 207 p. : ill. *Notes:* Includes bibliographical references and index. [LC 86027782; ISN 007050511X; $19.95]   HD9696.C62 P623 1987   637

Innovation and market structure: lessons from the computer and semiconductor industries. Nancy S. Dorfman. Cambridge, Mass.: Ballinger Pub. Co., c1987. xiv, 263 p. : ill. *Notes:* Includes bibliographies and index. [LC 86021619; ISN 0887301851]   HD9696.C62 D67 1987   638

Keeping the U.S. computer industry competitive: defining the agenda: a colloquium report. by the Computer Science and Technology Board, Commission on Physical Sciences, Mathematics, and Resources, National Research Council. Washington, D.C.: National Academy Press, 1990. vii, 77 p. : ill. *Notes:* Includes bibliographical references. [LC 89063507; ISN 0309041767; $16.00]
    HD9696.C63 U5212 1990   639

Newgames: strategic competition in the PC revolution. John Steffens. 1st ed. Oxford England; New York: Pergamon Press, 1994. xxix, 489 p. : ill. *Notes:* Includes bibliographical references (p. 475-478) and index. [LC 93043104; ISN 0080407919; $39.50]   HD9696.C62 S73 1994   +640

Strategic management in information technology. David B. Yoffie. Englewood Cliffs, N.J.: Prentice Hall, c1994. xi, 380 p. : ill. *Notes:* Includes discussion of Intel Corporation, Microsoft Corporation, Apple Computer, Inc., Mips Computer Systems, McCaw Cellular Communications, Motorola, Inc., Sun Microsystems, Sony Corporation: Workstation Division, IBM, Acer Inc., and Sharp Corporation. Includes bibliographical references and index. [LC 93005827; ISN 0130985597]
    HD9696.C62 Y63 1994   +641

Targeting the computer: government support and international competition. Kenneth Flamm. Washington, D.C.: Brookings Institution, c1987. xiii, 266 p. : ill. *Notes:* Includes bibliographical references and index. [LC 87011706; ISN 0815728522; ISN 0815728514; $31.95; $11.95]
    HD9696.C63 U516466 1987   642

Technomics: the economics of technology and the computer industry. William H. Inmon. Homewood, Ill.: Dow Jones-Irwin, c1986. xx, 361 p. : ill. *Notes:* Includes index. [LC 85071960; ISN 0870946889]   HD9696.C62 I55   643

COMPUTER NETWORKS

Broadband: business services, technologies, and strategic impact. David Wright. Boston: Artech House, c1993. xviii, 476 p. : ill. *Notes:* Includes bibliographical references and index. [LC 93028367; ISN 0890065896; $85.00]   TK5105.5. W75 1993   +644

The virtual community: homesteading on the electronic frontier. Howard Rheingold. Reading, Mass.: Addison-Wesley, 1993. viii, 325 p. *Notes:* "A William Patrick book." Published simultaneously in Canada. Includes bibliographical references (p. [301]-306) and index. [LC 93020910; ISN 0201608707; $22.95 ($29.95 Canada)]   TK5105.5. R48 1993   +645

COMPUTER SOFTWARE INDUSTRY

International trade in computer software. Stephen E. Siwek and Harold W. Furchtgott-Roth. Westport, Conn.: Quorum Books, 1993. xiv, 176 p. : ill. *Notes:* Includes bibliographical references (p. [167]-171) and index. [LC 92044687; ISN 0899307116]   HD9696.C63 U58357 1993   +646

Japan's software factories: a challenge to U.S. management. Michael A. Cusumano. New York: Oxford University Press, 1991. ix, 513 p. : ill. *Notes:* Includes bibliographical references. [LC 90007287; ISN 0195062167; $35.00]   HD9696.C63 J3134 1991   647

Software industry accounting. Joseph M. Morris; contributing authors, Richard P. Graff... et al. New York: Wiley, c1993. xviii, 299 p. : ill. *Notes:* Includes index. [LC 92021904; ISN 0471559318]
HF5686.C54 M67 1993 +648

COMPUTERS

Computer briefing: using the trends for better managerial decisions. Lynn M. Salerno. New York: Wiley, c1986. ix, 224 p. *Notes:* Includes index. Bibliography: p. 189-195. [LC 85017966; ISN 0471896098; $19.95] QA76. S275 1986 649

Computers and the information society. Richard S. Rosenberg. New York: Wiley, c1986. xv, 397 p. : ill. *Notes:* Includes bibliographies and index. [LC 85024680; ISN 0471826391] QA76.5. R58 1986 650

Computers on the job: managing the human side. C. Patrick Fleenor & Robert E. Callahan. 1st ed. New York, NY: Random House, c1986. xi, 178 p. : ill. *Notes:* Includes index. Bibliography: p. 169-175. [LC 85028338; ISN 0394553209] QA76.9.P75 F55 1986 651

The mystical machine: issues and ideas in computing. John E. Savage, Susan Magidson, Alex M. Stein. Reading, Mass.: Addison-Wesley, c1986. xvi, 407 p. : ill. *Notes:* Ill. on lining papers. Includes bibliographies and index. [LC 85006096; ISN 0201064626; $21.95] QA76. S334 1986 652

The universal machine: confessions of a technological optimist. Pamela McCorduck. New York: McGraw-Hill, c1985. xi, 305 p. *Notes:* Includes index. Bibliography: p. 287-295. [LC 85006654; ISN 0070448825] QA76. M367 1985 653

Using computers: the human factors of information systems. Raymond S. Nickerson. Cambridge, Mass.: MIT Press, c1986. xiv, 434 p. : ill. *Notes:* "A Bradford book." Includes indexes. Bibliography: p. [361]-417. [LC 85024163; ISN 0262140403] QA76. N497 1986 654

COMPUTERS AND CIVILIZATION

Computerization and controversy: value conflicts and social choices. edited by Charles Dunlop, Rob Kling. Boston: Academic Press, c1991. xvi, 758 p. : ill. *Notes:* Includes bibliographical references and index. [LC 90019415; ISN 0122243560; ISN 0122243552] QA76.9.C66 C656 1991 655

The cult of information: the folklore of computers and the true art of thinking. Theodore Roszak. New York: Pantheon, 1986. xii, 238 p. *Notes:* Includes biliographical references and index. [LC 85043453; ISN 0394546229] QA76.9.C66 R66 1986 656

The electronic word: democracy, technology, and the arts. Richard A. Lanham. Chicago: University of Chicago Press, 1993. xv, 285 p. : ill. *Notes:* Includes bibliographical references and index. [LC 93013884; ISN 0226468836; $22.50] QA76.9.C66 L363 1993 +657

The high cost of high tech: the dark side of the chip. by Lenny Siegel and John Markoff. 1st ed. New York: Harper & Row, c1985. 247 p. *Notes:* "A Cornelia and Michael Bessie book." Includes index. [LC 84048622; ISN 006039045X; $16.50] QA76.9.C66 S537 1985 658

High-tech society: the story of the information technology revolution. Tom Forester. 1st MIT Press ed. Cambridge, Mass.: MIT Press, 1987. viii, 311 p.; ill., maps *Notes:* Includes index. Bibliography: p. 290-296. [LC 86027499; ISN 0262061074] QA76.9.C66 F66 1987 659

The information technology revolution. edited and introduced by Tom Forester. 1st MIT Press ed. Cambridge, Mass.: MIT Press, 1985. xvii, 674 p. : ill. *Notes:* Includes bibliographies and index. [LC 84023422; ISN 0262060957; ISN 0262560333; $14.95] QA76.9.C66 I53 1985 660

Technology 2001: the future of computing and communications. edited by Derek Leebaert. Cambridge, Mass.: MIT Press, c1991. xvi, 392 p. : ill. *Notes:* Includes bibliographical references and index. [LC 90040022; ISN 0262121506; $29.95] QA76.9.C66 T34 1991 661

The third apple: personal computers & the cultural revolution. Jean-Louis Gassée; translated from the French by Isabel A. Leonard. 1st ed. San Diego: Harcourt Brace Jovanovich, c1987. viii, 212 p. *Notes:* Translation of: La troisième pomme. [LC 86019557; ISN 0151898502]
QA76.9.C66 G3713 1987 662

CONFLICT MANAGEMENT

Conflict management: the courage to confront. Richard J. Mayer. Columbus, Ohio: Battelle Press, 1990. xi, 143 p. : ill. *Notes:* Includes bibliographical references. [LC 89038236; ISN 0935470514; $24.50] HD42. M39 1990 663

Learning to manage conflict: getting people to work together productively. Dean Tjosvold. New York: Toronto: New York: Lexington Books; Maxwell Macmillan Canada; Maxwell Macmillan International, c1993. xiv, 176 p. : ill. *Notes:* Includes bibliographical references (p. [165]-171) and index. [LC 92038942; ISN 0029324912; $24.95] HD42. T583 1993 664

Managing conflict in organizations. M. Afzalur Rahim. 2nd ed. Westport, Conn.: Praeger, 1992. xvi, 228 p. : ill. *Notes:* Includes bibliographical references (p. [197-215) and indexes. [LC 92007479; ISN 0275936805] HD42. R34 1992 665

Managing conflict: interpersonal dialogue and third-party roles. Richard E. Walton. 2nd ed. Reading, Mass.: Addison-Wesley Pub. Co., c1987. xi, 160 p. : ill. (The Addison-Wesley series on organization development) *Notes:* Includes bibliographies. [LC 86020679; ISN 0201088592; $12.95 (est.)] HD42. W35 1987 666

The politics of management. Douglas Yates, Jr. 1st ed. San Francisco: Jossey-Bass, 1985. xii, 269 p. (The Jossey-Bass management series) (The Jossey-Bass social and behavioral science series) *Notes:* Includes index. Bibliography: p. 251-257. [LC 85045067; ISN 0875896715] HD42. Y38 1985 667

Solving costly organizational conflicts. Robert R. Blake, Jane Srygley Mouton. 1st ed. San Francisco: Jossey-Bass Publishers, 1984. xx, 327 p. (The Jossey-Bass management series) (The Jossey-Bass social and behavioral science series) *Notes:* Subtitle on half-t.p. and verso of t.p. : Achieving intergroup trust, cooperation, and teamwork. Includes indexes. Bibliography: p. 313-316. [LC 84047980; ISN 087589612X] HD42. B58 1984 668

Taking charge/managing conflict. Joseph B. Stulberg. Lexington, Mass.: Lexington Books, c1987. xii, 175 p. *Notes:* Includes index. Bibliography: p. [169] [LC 86045597; ISN 0669140147] HD42. S78 1987 669

CONGLOMERATE CORPORATIONS

The chaebol: Korea's new industrial might. Richard M. Steers, Yoo Keun Shin, Gerardo R. Ungson. New York: Harper & Row, Ballinger Division, c1989. xv, 164 p. : ill. *Notes:* Title supplies pronunciation on t.p.: The Chaebol (Jaé boI). Includes bibliographical references. [LC 89045774; ISN 0887303722; $24.95] HD2756.2.K8 S74 1989 670

The conglomerate commotion. by the editors of Fortune. New York Viking Press, 1970. ix, 180 p. illus. *Notes:* "A majority of the chapters were originally published in 1968 or 1969. . . in Fortune." [LC 79104152; ISN 0670237167] HD2756.U5 C64 +671

Corporate-level strategy: creating value in the multibusiness company. Michael Goold, Andrew Campbell, Marcus Alexander. New York: J. Wiley, c1994. xiv, 450 p. : ill. *Notes:* Includes bibliographical references and indexes. [LC 94006805; ISN 0471047163; $34.95] HD2756. G658 1994 +672

The invisible link: Japan's sogo shosha and the organization of trade. M.Y. Yoshino and Thomas B. Lifson. Cambridge, Mass.: MIT Press, c1986. x, 291 p. : ill. *Notes:* Includes index. Bibliography: p. [279]-285. [LC 85030033; ISN 0262240254] HD2756.2.J3 Y675 1986 673

Japan Inc.: global strategies of Japanese trading corporations. Max Eli. London; New York: McGraw-Hill, c1990. viii, 134 p. : ill. *Notes:* Translation of: Japans Wirtschaft im Griff der Konglomerate. Includes bibliographical references. [LC 90036826; ISN 0077073371; £27.50] HD2756.2.J3 E44 1990 674

Keiretsu: inside the hidden Japanese conglomerates. Kenichi Miyashita, David W. Russell. New York: McGraw-Hill, c1994. x, 225 p. : ill. *Notes:* Includes bibliographical references and index. [LC 93021388; ISN 0070425833] HD2756.2.J3 M59 1994 +675

Managing the unmanageable: strategies for success within the conglomerate. Milton Leontiades. Reading, Mass.: Addison-Wesley, 1985, c1986. vii, 193 p. : ill. *Notes:* Includes bibliographies and index. [LC 85011262; ISN 0201155958; $16.95] HD2756. L46 1986 676

The rise and fall of the conglomerate kings. Robert Sobel. New York: Stein and Day, 1984. 240 p. *Notes:* Includes index. Bibliography: p. [219]-221. [LC 83040358; ISN 0812829611; $19.95] HD2756. S62 1984 677

Strategies and styles: the role of the centre in managing diversified corporations. Michael Goold and Andrew Campbell. Oxford, UK; New York, NY, USA: B. Blackwell, 1988, cl987. x, 374 p. : ill. *Notes:* Includes bibliographical references and index. [LC 87012151; ISN 0631158294; $39.95] HD2756. G66 1987 678

CONSOLIDATION AND MERGER OF CORPORATIONS

Acquiring and merging businesses. by J. H. Hennessy, Jr. Englewood Cliffs, N.J. Prentice-Hall, 1966. xii, 274 p. [LC 66022082] HD2741. H45 +679

Acquisitions and mergers. New York Ronald Press Co., 1963. 353 p. *Notes:* Includes bibliography. [LC 63015017] HD2741. M17 +680

The acquisitions manual. edited by Sumner N. Levine. New York, N.Y.: New York Institute of Finance, c1989. xx, 599 p. *Notes:* Includes index. [LC 89032615; ISN 0134059298; $49.95] HD2746.5. A263 1989 681

After the merger: managing the shockwaves. Price Pritchett. Homewood, Ill.: Dow Jones-Irwin, c1985. xii, 140 p. : ill. *Notes:* Includes bibliographical references and index. [LC 84073046; ISN 0870946277; $19.95] HD2746.5. P74 1985 682

The art of M&A: a merger acquisition buyout guide. by Stanley Foster Reed and Lane and Edson, P.C. Homewood, Ill.: Dow Jones-Irwin, c1989. xv, 960 p. : ill. *Notes:* Includes index. [LC 88025741; ISN 155623113X; $67.50] HD2746.5. R44 1989 683

The Arthur Young management guide to mergers and acquisitions. Richard S. Bibler, editor. New York, N.Y.: John Wiley & Sons, c1989. xvii, 330 p. *Notes:* Includes index.; ISN 0471631043] HD2746.5. A788 1989 684

Autopsy of a merger. by William M. Owen. 1st ed. Deerfield, Ill.: W.M. Owen, c1986. xii, 341 p. *Notes:* Bibliography: p. 325-341. [LC 83091307; ISN 0961324708; $19.95] HD2746.5. O96 1986 685

Beyond the deal: optimizing merger and acquisition value. Peter J. Clark. New York: HarperBusiness, c1991. xii, 315 p. : ill. *Notes:* Includes bibliographical references. [LC 90024367; ISN 0887304400; $39.95] HD2746.5. C55 1991 686

Board games: the changing shape of corporate power. Arthur Fleischer, Jr., Geoffrey C. Hazard, Jr., Miriam Z. Klipper. 1st ed. Boston: Little, Brown & Co., c1988. 236 p. *Notes:* Includes index. Bibliography: p. [219]-228. [LC 88009471; ISN 0316285323; $19.95 ($27.95 Can.)] HD2746.5. F64 1988 687

Business merger and acquisition strategies: a handbook for entrepreneurs and managers. John J. Clark. Englewood Cliffs, N.J.: Prentice-Hall, c1985. xi, 223 p. : ill. *Notes:* "A Spectrum book." Includes bibliographies and index. [LC 84015963; ISN 0131063456] HG4028.M4 C35 1985 688

Corporate anti-takeover defenses: the poison pill device. by Paul W. Richter; with an introduction by Harold S. Bloomenthal. New York, N.Y.: Clark Boardman Co., c1987. 1 v. (various pagings): ill. [LC 87182020; ISN 0876325401] KF1477. R53 1987 689

Corporate takeovers: causes and consequences. edited by Alan J. Auerbach. Chicago: University of Chicago Press, 1988. ix, 343 p. (National Bureau of Economic Research project report) *Notes:* Papers originally presented at a National Bureau of Economic Research conference in Feb. 1987 in Key Largo. "A National Bureau of Economic Research report." Includes bibliographies and indexes. [LC 87037497; ISN 0226032116] HD2746.5. C675 1988 690

Dangerous pursuits: mergers and acquisitions in the age of Wall Street. Walter Adams and James W. Brock. 1st ed. New York: Pantheon Books, c1989. xiv, 208 p. : ill. *Notes:* Includes index. Bibliography: p. 183-201. [LC 89042653; ISN 0394579674; $18.95] HD2785. A686 1989 691

The deal decade: what takeovers and leveraged buyouts mean for corporate governance. Margaret M. Blair, editor. Washington, D.C.: Brookings Institution, c1993. xiii, 390 p. : ill. *Notes:* Includes bibliographical references and index. [LC 92039450; ISN 0815709455; $19.95] HG4028.M4 D42 1993 692

Debt, taxes, and corporate restructuring. John B. Shoven, Joel Waldfogel, editors. Washington, D.C.: Brookings Institution, 1990. xii, 210 p. : ill. *Notes:* Includes bibliographical references. [LC 90002168; ISN 0815778848; $28.95] HD4028.M4 D43 1990 693

The Ernst & Young management guide to mergers and acquisitions. Stephen L. Key, editor. New York: J. Wiley & Sons, c1989. xvii, 330 p. *Notes:* Previous ed.: The Arthur Young guide to mergers and acquisitions. New York: J. Wiley & Sons, 1989. Includes index.; ISN 0471528285; $29.95] HD2746.5. E76 1989 694

The handbook of international mergers and acquisitions. David J. BenDaniel, Arthur H. Rosenbloom. Englewood Cliffs, N.J.: Prentice Hall, c1990. xxiv, 375 p. : ill. [LC 89048291; ISN 0134724992; $55.00] K1362. B46 1990 695

Handbook of strategic growth through mergers and acquisitions. William K. Smith; Touche Ross & Co. Englewood Cliffs, N.J.: Prentice-Hall, c1985. 128 p. : ill. *Notes:* Includes index. [LC 84022273; ISN 0133818152; $49.95] HD2746.5. S65 1985 696

Hostile takeovers: issues in public and corporate policy. edited by David L. McKee. New York: Praeger, 1989. xiii, 179 p. : ill. *Notes:* Papers originally presented at a conference sponsored by the Kent State University Graduate School of Management and the Dept. of Economics, and held Sept. 28, 1988. Includes index. Includes bibliographical references. [LC 89030900; ISN 0275931811] HD2746.5. H69 1989   697

Hothouse management: acquisitions, takeovers, and LBOs. Boston, MA: Harvard Business Review, c1991. vii, 116 p. : ill. *Notes:* Articles reprinted from Harvard Business Review. Includes bibliographical references.; ISN 0875842968; $19.95] HD2746.5. H73 1991   698

How to acquire the perfect business for your company. Joseph Krallinger. New York: J. Wiley, c1991. xii, 224 p. : ill. *Notes:* Includes index. [LC 90034548; ISN 0471526797; $65.00] HG4028.M4 K73 1991   699

The human side of mergers and acquisitions: managing collisions between people, cultures, and organizations. Anthony F. Buono, James L. Bowditch. 1st ed. San Francisco: Jossey-Bass Publishers, 1989. xxii, 317 p. *Notes:* Includes indexes. Bibliography: p. 273-300. [LC 88007853; ISN 1555421350] HD2746.5. B79 1989   700

Integrating acquired companies: management accounting and reporting issues. edited by Clark H. Johnson; contributors, Tarun K. Bhatia... et al. New York: Wiley, c1985. xii, 181 p. (Professional management accounting series) *Notes:* "A Ronald Press publication." Includes index. [LC 84023698; ISN 0471809608; $39.95 (est.)] HF5686.C7 I54 1985   701

International mergers and acquisitions. edited by Terence E. Cooke in association with Arthur Young International. Oxford, UK; New York, NY, USA: Blackwell, 1988. 516 p. : ill. *Notes:* Bibliography: p. [498]-507. [LC 87029364; ISN 0631147489; $49.95 (U.S.)] HD2746.5. C66 1988   702

Irreconcilable differences: Ross Perot versus General Motors. by Doron P. Levin. 1st ed. Boston: Little, Brown, c1989. 357 p., [8] p. of plates: ill. *Notes:* Includes index. Bibliography: p. [347]. [LC 89030354; ISN 0316522112; $18.95 ($23.95 Can.)] HD2785. L46 1989   703

Japanese takeovers: the global contest for corporate control. W. Carl Kester. Boston, Mass.: Harvard Business School Press, c1991. xxii, 298 p. *Notes:* Includes bibliographical references and index. [LC 90040430; ISN 0875842356; $29.95] HD2907. K45 1991   704

Leveraged buyouts. edited by Stephen C. Diamond. Homewood, Ill.: Dow Jones-Irwin, c1985. xv, 180 p. : ill. *Notes:* Includes index. [LC 84073255; ISN 0870945793] HD2746.5. L48   705

Making acquisitions work: lessons from companies' successes and mistakes. prepared and published by Business International. Geneva, Switzerland; New York, N.Y.: Business International, c1988. 118 p. : ill. (Research report / Business International) *Notes:* Includes bibliographical references.] HD2746.5. M24 1988   706

Management guides to mergers & acquisitions. edited by John L. Harvey and Albert Newgarden. New York Wiley-Interscience, 1969. xii, 319 p. *Notes:* Bibliographical footnotes. [LC 79082978; ISN 0471357987] HD2741. H37   +707

Marrying for money: the path from the first hostile takeover to megamergers, insider trading, and the Boesky scandal. Jeff Madrick. London: Bloomsbury, 1987. x, 310 p. *Notes:* Includes index. [LC 87035551; ISN 0747500584; $23.02] HD2785. M34 1987   708

Mega-mergers: corporate America's billion-dollar takeovers. Kenneth M. Davidson. Cambridge, MA: Ballinger Pub. Co., c1985. xv, 412 p. *Notes:* Includes index. Bibliography: p. 399-402. [LC 85004025; ISN 0887300588] HD2746.5. D38 1985   709

Megalomania, managers & mergers. John Roberts. London: Pitman, 1987. ix, 146 p. : ill., ports. *Notes:* Includes index. [LC 87031526; ISN 0273028383; £9.95] HD2746.5. R62 1987   710

Merchants of debt: KKR and the mortgaging of American business. George Anders. New York, NY: BasicBooks, c1992. xx, 328 p. [8] p. of plates: ill. *Notes:* Includes bibliographical references and index. [LC 91058601; ISN 0465045227; $23.00] HG4028.M4 A56 1992   711

Mergers & acquisitions. Ernst & Young. 2nd ed. New York, NY: J. Wiley, c1994. xix, 336 p. *Notes:* Includes index. [LC 93007648; ISN 0471578185; $79.95] HD2746.55.U5 M47 1994   +712

The mergers & acquisitions handbook. editors, Milton L. Rock, Robert H. Rock, Martin Sikora. 2nd ed. New York: McGraw-Hill, c1994. xxiii, 551 p. : ill. *Notes:* Rev. ed. of: The Mergers and acquisitions handbook. c1987. Includes index. [LC 93028601; ISN 0070533539; $79.50] HD2746.5. M465 1994   +713

Mergers & acquisitions: will you overpay? Joseph H. Marren. Homewood, Ill.: Dow Jones-Irwin, c1985. xii, 220 p. : ill. *Notes:* Includes bibliographies and index.] HD2746.5. M27 1985   714

Mergers and acquisitions. edited by Alan J. Auerbach. Chicago: University of Chicago Press, 1988. xi, 108 p. : ill. (A National Bureau of Economic Research project report) *Notes:* Includes bibliographies and index. [LC 87019035; ISN 0226032094] HD2746.5. M455 1988   715

Mergers and acquisitions. Terence E. Cooke. Oxford Oxfordshire; New York, NY: B. Blackwell, USA, 1986. xv, 284 p. : ill. *Notes:* Includes index. Bibliography: p. [269]-273. [LC 85026732; ISN 0631147470; $60.00] HD2746.5. C665 1986   716

Mergers: motives, effects, policies. Peter O. Steiner. Ann Arbor: University of Michigan Press, c1975. xiii, 359 p. : graphs *Notes:* Includes index. Bibliography: p. 337-349. [LC 74078991; ISN 0472087991; $12.50] HD2741. S764 1975   +717

Mergers, restructuring, and corporate control. J. Fred Weston, Kwang S. Chung, Susan E. Hoag. Englewood Cliffs, NJ: Prentice Hall, c1990. xxvii, 762 p. *Notes:* Includes bibliographical references. [LC 89049014; ISN 0135771722; $47.00] HG4028.M4 W47 1990   718

The money wars: the rise and fall of the great buyout boom of the 1980s. Roy C. Smith. New York: Dutton, c1990. ix, 370 p. *Notes:* "Truman Talley books." Includes bibliographical references. [LC 90032257; ISN 052524929X; $19.95] HG4028.M4 S64 1990   719

Playing by different rules. Ellen Wojahn. New York, NY: American Management Association, c1988. xiv, 306 p. *Notes:* Includes bibliographical references and index. [LC 88011684; ISN 0814458610] HD2746.5. W65 1988   720

The Predators' Ball: the junk-bond raiders and the man who staked them. Connie Bruck. New York: American Lawyer: Simon and Schuster, c1988. 385 p. *Notes:* Includes index. [LC 88011572; ISN 067161780X] HD2746.5. B78 1988   721

Public policy toward corporate takeovers. edited by Murray L. Weidenbaum and Kenneth Chilton. New Brunswick, U.S.A.: Transaction Books, c1988. xvi, 176 p. *Notes:* Papers resulting from a research project conducted in the winter and spring of 1986 by the Center for the Study of American Business at Washington University in St. Louis, Mo. Includes bibliographies and index. [LC 87010750; ISN 0887381669; $29.95] HD2795. P825 1988   722

Restructuring American corporations: causes, effects, and implications. Abbass F. Alkhafaji. New York: Quorum Books, c1990. xii, 194 p. : ill. *Notes:* Includes bibliographical references. [LC 90032699; ISN 0899305733; $42.95] HD2746.5. A38 1990   723

The smart way to buy a business: an entrepreneur's guide to questions that must be asked. by John C. Kohl, Sr. and Atlee M Kohl. Irving, Tex.: Woodland, c1986. vii, 69 p.; ISN 0939857006; $19.95] HD2746.5. K64 1986   724

Successful corporate acquisitions: a complete guide for acquiring companies for growth and profit. Jerold Freier. Englewood Cliffs, NJ: Prentice Hall, c1990. vii, 401 p. *Notes:* Includes index. [LC 90041679; ISN 0138605033; $69.95] HD2746.5. F736 1990   725

The takeover game. John Brooks. 1st ed. New York: Dutton, c1987. x, 390 p. *Notes:* "Truman Talley books." "A Twentieth Century Fund book." Includes index. Bibliography: p. 359-372. [LC 87005967; ISN 0525245863; $19.95] HD2746.5. B76 1987   726

Takeover madness: corporate America fights back. Allen Michel, Israel Shaked. New York: Wiley, c1986. xii, 397 p. *Notes:* Includes index. [LC 85032315; ISN 0471010790; $22.95] HD2746.5. M53 1986   727

Tender offer: the sneak attack in corporate takeovers. Dorman L. Commons; foreword by Earl Cheit. Berkeley: University of California Press, c1985. xix, 159 p. *Notes:* Includes index. [LC 85001182; ISN 0520055837] HD2746.5. C64 1985   728

Three plus one equals billions: the Bendix-Martin Marietta war. by Allan Sloan. New York: Arbor House, 1983. 270 p. : ports. [LC 83070468; ISN 0877955042; $15.95] HD2746.5. S56   729

The titans of takeover. Robert Slater. Englewood Cliffs, N.J.: Prentice-Hall, c1987. ix, 230 p. : ports. *Notes:* Includes index. Bibliography: p. 219-222. [LC 86025364; ISN 0139220550] HD2785. S44 1987   730

CONSTRUCTION INDUSTRY

The McGraw-Hill construction business handbook: a practical guide to accounting, credit, finance, insurance, and law for the construction industry. edited by Robert F. Cushman and John P. Bigda. 2nd ed. New York: McGraw-Hill, c1985. 1079 p. : ports. *Notes:* Includes bibliographical references and index. [LC 83026792; ISN 0070149541] HD9715.A2 M27 1985   731

CONSULTANTS

Advice, a high profit business: a guide for consultants and other entrepreneurs. Herman Holtz. Englewood Cliffs, N.J.: Prentice-Hall, c1986. xii, 242 p. : ill. *Notes:* Includes index. [LC 85024405; ISN 013011958X] HD69.C6 H618 1986   732

Choosing and using a consultant: a manager's guide to consulting services. Herman Holtz. New York: Wiley, c1989. xiii, 208 p. *Notes:* Includes lists of names and addresses of consulting, technical, and related associations. Includes bibliographical references and index. [LC 88031693; ISN 0471602876; $22.95] HD69.C6 H619 1989   733

The consultant's calling: bringing who you are to what you do. Geoffrey M. Bellman. 1st ed. San Francisco: Jossey-Bass, 1990. xxv, 238 p. : ill. [LC 90053092; ISN 1555422535; $24.95] HD69.C6 B43 1990   734

The consultant's manual: a complete guide to building a successful consulting practice. Thomas L. Greenbaum. New York: Wiley, c1990. xii, 228 p. : ill. [LC 89036303; ISN 0471501190; $49.95] HD69.C6 G72 1990   735

Consulting: the complete guide to a profitable career. Robert E. Kelley. Rev. ed. New York: C. Scribner's Sons, c1986. xvii, 283 p. : ill. *Notes:* Includes bibliographies and index. [LC 86003912; ISN 0684186179; $19.95] HD69.C6 K45 1986   736

How to select and manage consultants: a guide to getting what you pay for. Howard L. Shenson. Lexington, Mass.: San Diego: Lexington Books; University Associates, c1990. xvi, 244 p. *Notes:* Includes bibliographical references. [LC 89035306; ISN 066921129X; $39.95] HD69.C6 S54 1990   737

Million dollar consulting: the professional's guide to growing a practice. Alan Weiss. New York: McGraw-Hill, c1992. xiii, 274 p. : ill. *Notes:* Includes bibliographical references and index. [LC 92006613; ISN 0070691029; $24.95] HD69.C6 W46 1992   738

Shenson on consulting: success strategies from the consultant's consultant. Howard L. Shenson. New York: Wiley in association with University Associates, c1990. xv, 200 p. : ill. *Notes:* Includes bibliographical references and index. [LC 90030240; ISN 0471506613; $24.95] HD69.C6 S56 1990   739

CONSUMER BEHAVIOR

Consumer behavior. James F. Engel, Roger D. Blackwell, Paul W. Miniard. 6th ed. Chicago: Dryden Press, c1990. 1 v. (various pagings): ill. (some col.) *Notes:* Includes index. Includes bibliographical references. [LC 89007696; ISN 0030229790; $45.00] HF5415.3. E53 1990   740

Consumer behavior. Leon G. Schiffman, Leslie Lazar Kanuk. 4th ed. Englewood Cliffs, NJ: Prentice Hall, c1991. xxiii, 680 p. : ill. (some col.) *Notes:* Includes bibliographical references and indexes. [LC 90042934; ISN 0131705318; $56.07] HF5415.32. S35 1991   741

Consumer behavior: concepts and applications. David L. Loudon, Albert J. Della Bitta. 4th ed. New York: McGraw-Hill, c1993. xxiii, 788 p. : ill. (some col.) *Notes:* Includes bibliographical references (p. 733-782) and index. [LC 92027875; ISN 0070387672] HF5415.32. L677 1993   +742

Consumer behavior: implications for marketing strategy. Del I. Hawkins, Roger J. Best, Kenneth A. Coney. 5th ed. Homewood, IL: Irwin, 1992. xv, 674 p. : ill. *Notes:* Includes bibliographical references and indexes. [LC 91003223; ISN 0256094098; $54.95] HF5415.33.U6 H38 1992   743

Consumer behavior in marketing strategy. John A. Howard. Englewood Cliffs, NJ: Prentice Hall, c1989. xix, 375 p. : ill. *Notes:* Includes bibliographical references and indexes. [LC 88015542; ISN 0131696661; $28.00] HF5415.32. H68 1989   744

Morality and the market: consumer pressure for corporate accountability. N. Craig Smith. London; New York: Routledge, 1989. x, 351 p. *Notes:* Includes index. [LC 89010239; ISN 0415004373; $45.00] HF5415.32. S56 1989   745

Perspectives in consumer behavior. edited by Harold H. Kassarjian, Thomas S. Robertson. 4th ed. Englewood Cliffs, N.J.: Prentice Hall, 1991. viii, 616 p. : ill. *Notes:* Previously published: Glenview, Ill.: Scott, Foresman, c1989. Includes bibliographical references and indexes. [LC 90040458; ISN 0136604404; $42.00] HF5415.32. P47 1991   746

CONSUMER EDUCATION

Read the label: reducing risk by providing information. Susan G. Hadden. Boulder: Westview Press, c1986. xviii, 275 p. : ill. *Notes:* "Published in cooperation with the American Association for the Advancement of Science." Includes bibliographies and index. [LC 85022633; ISN 0813302447; $28.00] TX335. H33 1986   747

CONSUMER SATISFACTION

Customer retention through quality leadership: the Baxter approach. Deborah G. Fliehman, David D. Auld. Milwaukee, Wis.: ASQC Quality Press, c1993. xii, 233 p. : ill. *Notes:* Includes bibliographical references (p. 221-224) and index. [LC 92029575; ISN 0873891678] HF5415.5. F58 1993 +748

Marketing for keeps: building your business by retaining your customers. Carla B. Furlong. New York: Wiley, c1993. xii, 244 p. : ill. *Notes:* Includes bibliographical references (p. 227-239) and index. [LC 92040872; ISN 047154017X; $24.95] HF5415.5. F87 1993 749

Turning lost customers into gold: —and the art of achieving zero defections. Joan Koob Cannie. New York: AMACOM, c1994. ix, 131 p. : ill. *Notes:* Includes bibliographical references and index. [LC 93023362; ISN 0814451101; $19.95] HF5415.5. C363 1994 +750

CONSUMERS

Cases in consumer behavior. F. Stewart Debruicker, John A. Quelch, Scott Ward. 2nd ed. Englewood Cliffs, N.J.: Prentice-Hall, c1986. xii, 345 p. : ill. *Notes:* Includes bibliographical references. [LC 86004943; ISN 013118332X; $19.95] HF5415.3. D42 1986 751

Consumer behavior: marketing strategy perspectives J. Paul Peter, Jerry C. Olson. Homewood, Ill.: Irwin, 1987. xvii, 698 p., [16] p. of plates: ill. (some col.) (The Irwin series in marketing) *Notes:* Includes bibliographies and indexes. [LC 86081801; ISN 0256031770] HF5415.3. P468 1987 752

The role of affect in consumer behavior: emerging theories and applications. edited by Robert A. Peterson, Wayne D. Hoyer, William R. Wilson. Lexington, Mass.: Lexington Books, c1986. ix, 196 p. : ill. *Notes:* Papers from a symposium held Sept. 21-22, 1984, at the University of Texas at Austin and sponsored by the College of Business Administration and the IC^2 Institute of the University of Texas at Austin. Includes index. Bibliography: p. [161]-184. [LC 85046042; ISN 0669128740] HF5415.3. R65 1986 753

Why they buy: American consumers inside and out. Robert B. Settle, Pamela L. Alreck. New York: Wiley, c1986. xiv, 351 p. *Notes:* Includes index. [LC 86013303; ISN 0471844578; $22.95] HC110.C6 S48 1986 754

CONSUMPTION (ECONOMICS)

The green consumer. John Elkington, Julia Hailes, and Joel Makower. Updated ed. New York, N.Y., U.S.A.: Penguin Books, 1990. xii, 342 p. : ill *Notes:* "A Tilden Press book." Includes bibliographical references. [LC 89048639; ISN 0140127089; $37.95] HC110.C6 E44 1990 755

Pursuing happiness: American consumers in the twentieth century. Stanley Lebergott. Princeton, N.J.: Princeton University Press, c1993. xiii, 188 p. : ill. *Notes:* Includes bibliographical references (p. [171]-185) and index. [LC 92040491; ISN 0691043221; $24.95] HC110.C6 L393 1993 756

CONTINENTAL ILLINOIS NATIONAL BANK AND TRUST COMPANY OF CHICAGO

The Continental affair: the rise and fall of the Continental Illinois Bank. James P. McCollom. 1st ed. New York: Dodd, Mead, c1987. xv, 393 p. *Notes:* Includes index. [LC 87021471; ISN 0396088090; $21.95 ($31.95 Can.)] HG2613.C44 C686 1987 757

CONTROLLERSHIP

Control in business organizations. Kenneth A. Merchant. Boston: Pitman, c1985. xii, 161 p. : ill. (Pitman series in the role of accounting in organizations and society) *Notes:* Includes index. Bibliography: p. 139-151. [LC 84011374; ISN 0273019147] HG4026. M47 1985 758

Controller involvement in management. Vijay Sathe; with the research assistance of Srinivasan Unapathy. Englewood Cliffs, N.J.: Prentice-Hall, c1982. xviii, 189 p. : ill. *Notes:* Includes index. Bibliography: p. 177-182. [LC 81008515; ISN 0131716603] HG4026. S268 759

Controllership: the work of the managerial accountant. James D. Willson and James P. Colford. 4th ed. New York: Wiley, c1990. x, 1218 p. : ill. *Notes:* 2nd ed. by J.B. Heckert and J.D. Willson published in 1963. Rev. ed. of: Controllership, the work of the management accountant. 3rd ed. c1981. Includes bibliographical references and index. [LC 90012215; ISN 0471632783; $105.00]
HG4026. H43 1990   760

Corporate controller's manual. editor: Paul J. Wendell. 2nd ed. Boston: Warren, Gorham & Lamont, c1989. 1 v. (various pagings) [LC 88062093; ISN 0791300846; $113.40]
HF5550. C755 1989 [non-][circ.]   761

CONVERTIBLE SECURITIES

The handbook of convertibles. Simon R. McGuire. New York: New York Institute of Finance, c1991. x, 163 p. : ill. *Notes:* Includes index. [LC 90043523; ISN 0133760626; $34.95]   HG4651. M38 1991   762

COPYRIGHT

Softwars: the legal battles for control of the global software industry. Anthony Lawrence Clapes. Westport, Conn.: Quorum Books, 1993. x, 325 p. *Notes:* Includes bibliographical references and index. [LC 92024223; ISN 0899305970]
K1443.C6 C56 1993   763

CORPORATE CULTURE

Business and the culture of the enterprise society. John Deeks. Westport, Conn.: Quorum Books, 1993. x, 256 p. *Notes:* Includes bibliographical references (p. [233]-243) and index. [LC 92034951; ISN 0899307914]
HD58.7. D427 1993   +764

The constraints of corporate tradition: doing the correct thing, not just what the past dictates. Alan M. Kantrow. 1st ed. New York: Harper & Row, c1987. xvii, 216 p. *Notes:* Includes index. Bibliography: p. 203-207. [LC 86046075; ISN 0060157534; $19.95]   HD58.7. K375 1987   765

Corporate culture and organizational effectiveness. Daniel R. Denison. New York: Wiley, c1990. xvii, 267 p. : ill. *Notes:* Includes bibliographical references. [LC 89027938; ISN 047180021X; $39.95]
HD58.7. D46 1990   766

Corporate culture and performance. John P. Kotter, James L. Heskett. New York: Toronto: New York: Free Press; Maxwell Macmillan Canada; Maxwell Macmillan International, c1992. viii, 214 p. : ill. *Notes:* Includes bibliographical references and index. [LC 91042893; ISN 0029184673; $24.95 (est.)]   HD58.7. K68 1992   767

Corporate philosophies and mission statements: a survey and guide for corporate communicators and management. Thomas A. Falsey. New York: Quorum Books, 1989. ix, 160 p. : ill. *Notes:* Includes index. [LC 88018257; ISN 0899303137; $39.95]   HD58.7. F35 1989   768

The cultures of work organizations. Harrison M. Trice, Janice M. Beyer. Englewood Cliffs, N.J.: Prentice Hall, 1992, c1993. xvii, 510 p. *Notes:* Includes bibliographical references (p. 429-491) and index. [LC 92009291; ISN 0131914383; $25.50]   HD58.7. T74 1992   769

Gaining control of the corporate culture. edited by Ralph H. Kilmann, Mary J. Saxton, Roy Serpa, and associates. 1st ed. San Francisco: Jossey-Bass, 1985. xxxi, 451 p. : ill. (A Joint publication in the Jossey-Bass management series and the Jossey-Bass social and behavioral science series) *Notes:* "From October 24 to 27, the Program in Corporate Culture, Graduate School of Business, University of Pittsburgh sponsored a conference"—P. x. Includes bibliographies and indexes. [LC 85045059; ISN 0875896669]   HD58.7. G34 1985   770

Making capitalism: the social and cultural construction of a South Korean Conglomerate. Roger L. Janelli with Dawnhee Yim. Stanford, Calif.: Stanford University Press, 1993. x, 276 p. : *Notes:* Includes bibliographical references (p. [245]-262) and index. [LC 92018093; ISN 0804716099; $35.00 (est.)]   HD58.7. J36 1993   771

Management in transition. Philip R. Harris. 1st ed. San Francisco: Jossey-Bass, 1985. xxvii, 404 p. : ill. (The Jossey-Bass management series) (The Jossey-Bass social and behavioral science series) *Notes:* "Transforming managerial practices and organizational strategies for a new work culture"—P. [vii]. Includes index. Bibliography: p. 369-384. [LC 85045055; ISN 087589660X]
HD58.7. H3695 1985   772

Mission and business philosophy. Andrew Campbell and Kiran Tawadey. Oxford; Boston: Butterworth-Heinemann, 1992. ix, 353 p. : ill. *Notes:* "Selections... from the writings of top management thinkers including Maslow, Herzberg, Peters and Waterman, Ouchi and Drucker."— Cover p. [4]. Cover title: Mission & business philosophy. Earlier ed. published in 1990. Includes bibliographical references (p. [340]-350) and index. [LC 93153667; ISN 075060509X]
                           HD58.7. C346 1992 +773

Organizational climate and culture. Benjamin Schneider, editor. 1st ed. San Francisco: Jossey-Bass, 1990. xxv, 449 p. : ill. *Notes:* Includes bibliographical references and index. [LC 90041779; ISN 155542287X; $25.95] HD58.7. O7635 1990 774

Organizational culture and leadership. Edgar H. Schein. 2nd ed. San Francisco: Jossey-Bass, c1992. xix, 418 p. *Notes:* Includes bibliographical references (p. 393-406) and index. [LC 92023849; ISN 1555424872] HD58.7. S33 1992 775

Organizational structure and information technology. by Jon Harrington. New York: Prentice Hall, 1991. xiv, 250 p. : ill. *Notes:* Includes bibliographical references and index. [LC 90035517; ISN 0134651626; $40.00] HD58.7. H3693 1991 776

The rice-paper ceiling: breaking through Japanese corporate culture. Rochelle Kopp. Berkeley, Calif.: Stone Bridge Press, c1994. 270 p. *Notes:* Includes bibliographical references and index. [LC 94027608; ISN 1880656140; $25.00] HD58.7. K656 1994 +777

Strategies for cultural change. Paul Bate. Oxford England; Boston: Butterworth-Heinemann, 1994. viii, 308 p. : ill. *Notes:* Includes bibliographical references and indexes. [LC 93034325; ISN 0750605197; £25.00] HD58.7. B375 1994 +778

Why your corporate culture change isn't working—and what to do about it. Michael Ward. Aldershot, Hampshire, England; Brookfield, Vt., USA: Gower, c1994. xiii, 149 p. : ill. [LC 93048280; ISN 0566074346; $44.95] HD58.7. W33 1994 +779

CORPORATE DIVESTITURE

The divestiture option: a guide for financial and corporate planning executives. Richard J. Schmidt. New York: Quorum Books, 1990. vi, 188 p. : ill. *Notes:* Includes bibliographical references (p. [175]-183) and index. [LC 89010879; ISN 0899303978; $39.95] HD2746.6. S36 1990 780

Strategic divestment. New York AMACOM, 1974. vi, 147 p. [LC 73085193; ISN 0814453473]
                              HD2741. V54 +781

CORPORATE GOVERNANCE

Contemporary issues in corporate governance. edited by D.D. Prentice and P.R.J. Holland. Oxford: London: New York: Clarendon Press; Allen & Overy; Oxford University Press, 1993. xx, 226 p. *Notes:* "The origins of this book lie in the Second Oxford Law Colloquium held in St. John's College, Oxford, on 10-11 September 1992, organized by the Faculty of Law of the University of Oxford and Allen & Overy"—Pref. Includes bibliographical references and index. [LC 93000443; ISN 0198258593; $52.00] KD2089.A75 C66 1993 +782

Corporate control and accountability: changing structures and the dynamics of regulation. edited by Joseph McCahery, Sol Picciotto, and Colin Scott. Oxford: New York: Clarendon Press; Oxford University Press, 1993. xv, 450 p. *Notes:* Includes bibliographical references (p. [407]-444) and index. [LC 93019420; ISN 0198258275; $45.00] HD2741. C77 1993 +783

The director's & officer's guide to advisory boards. Robert K. Mueller. New York: Quorum Books, c1990. xii, 277 p. *Notes:* Includes index. Includes bibliographical references. [LC 89032858; ISN 0899304672; $49.95] HD2745. M834 1990 784

Inside the boardroom: governance by directors and trustees. William G. Bowen. New York: Wiley, c1994. xx, 184 p. *Notes:* Includes bibliographical references and index. [LC 93042717; ISN 0471025011] HD2745. B627 1994 +785

Keeping good company: a study of corporate governance in five countries. Jonathan P. Charkham. Oxford: New York: Clarendon Press; Oxford University Press, 1994. xvii, 389 p. : ill. *Notes:* Includes bibliographical references (p. [374]-379) and index. [LC 93030539; ISN 019828828X; £19.95] HD2741. C457 1994 +786

CORPORATE IMAGE

Communicating when your company is under siege: surviving public crisis. by Marion K. Pinsdorf. Lexington, Mass.: Lexington Books, c1987. xv, 171 p. *Notes:* Includes index. Bibliography: p. [157]-161. [LC 85045473; ISN 0669117900]   HD59.2. P55 1987   787

Corporate identity: making business strategy visible through design. Wally Olins. Boston, Mass.: Harvard Business School Press, 1990, c1989. 224 p. : ill. *Notes:* First published in Great Britain by Thames and Hudson. Bibliography: p. 216-217. [LC 90004526; ISN 087584250X]   HD59.2. O39 1990   788

The Economist Intelligence Unit guide to building a global image. Andrea Mackiewicz. New York: McGraw-Hill, c1993. xvi, 184 p. : ill. *Notes:* Includes bibliographical references and index. [LC 93006485; ISN 0070093504; $39.95]   HD59.2. M33 1993   789

How to build a corporation's identity and project its image. Thomas Garbett. Lexington, Mass.: Lexington Books, c1988. xx, 271 p. : ill. *Notes:* Includes index. [LC 86045370; ISN 0669133124]   HD59.2. G37 1988   790

Rumor in the marketplace: the social psychology of commercial hearsay. Fredrick W. Koenig. Dover, Mass.: Auburn House Pub. Co., 1985. xii, 180 p. : ill. *Notes:* Includes bibliographical references and index. [LC 84012379; ISN 0865691177; $22.95]   HD59.2. K63 1985   791

CORPORATE PLANNING

Anatomy of a business plan. by Linda Pinson & Jerry Jinnett. 3rd print., rev. Fullerton, CA: Out of Your Mind . . . and into the Marketplace, c1989. 134 p. : forms *Notes:* On t.p. the registered trademark symbol "TM" is superscript following 'Marketplace' in the publisher's name. Includes index. [LC 87091257; ISN 0944205178; $24.00]   HD30.28. P45 1989   792

Building your business plan: a step-by-step approach. Harold J. McLaughlin. New York: Wiley, c1985. xi, 297 p. : ill. (Small business management series, 0737-7290) *Notes:* "A Ronald Press publication." Includes index. Bibliography: p. 289-290. [LC 84011938; ISN 0471883581; $24.95 (est.)]   HD30.28. M27 1985   793

Business policy and strategic management. Lawrence R. Jauch, William F. Glueck. 5th ed. New York: McGraw-Hill, c1988. xix, 940 p. : ill. (McGraw-Hill series in management) *Notes:* Glueck's name appears first on the earlier edition. Includes bibliographies and index. [LC 87016859; ISN 070322347X; $38.95]   HD30.28. J375 1988   794

The concept of corporate strategy. Kenneth R. Andrews. 3rd ed. Homewood, Ill.: Irwin, 1987. xviii, 132 p. *Notes:* Includes bibliographical references and index. [LC 86081803; ISN 0256036292]   HD30.28. A54 1987   795

Corporate imagination plus: five steps to translating innovative strategies into action. James F. Bandrowski. New York: London: Free Press; Collier Macmillan, c1990. xiv, 313 p. : ill. *Notes:* Includes bibliographical references (p. 291-302). [LC 89023261; ISN 0029015014; $22.95]   HD30.28. B349 1990   796

Corporate strategy and the search for ethics. R. Edward Freeman and Daniel R. Gilbert, Jr. Englewood Cliffs, NJ: Prentice Hall, 1988. xv, 222 p. *Notes:* Includes index. Bibliography: p. 204-213. [LC 87029144; ISN 0131754726]   HD30.28. F729 1988   797

The corporate strategy matrix. Thomas H. Naylor. New York: Basic Books, c1986. xii, 290 p. : ill. *Notes:* Includes index. Bibliography: p. 276-280. [LC 84045316; ISN 0465014259; $24.95]   HD30.28. N394   798

Defining the business: the starting point of strategic planning. Derek F. Abell. Englewood Cliffs, N.J.: Prentice-Hall, 1979. ix, 257 p. : ill. *Notes:* Includes bibliographical references and index. [LC 79014013; ISN 0131978144]   HD30.28. A24   799

The definitive guide to long range planning. Thomas Hatcher, Rosemary Hatcher. 2nd ed. Dubuque, Iowa: Kendall/Hunt Pub. Co., c1988. viii, 92 p. : ill.; ISN 0840350627; $30.00]   HD30.28. H3825 1988   800

The entrepreneurial manager: decisions, goals, and business ideas. A.L. Minkes. Harmondsworth, Middlesex, England; New York, N.Y., U.S.A.: Penguin Books, 1987. 221 p. : ill. *Notes:* Includes index. Bibliography: p. [201]-216. [LC 87170540; ISN 0140091165; £3.95 ($6.95 U.S.)]   HD30.28. M55 1987   801

The entrepreneur's guide to building a better business plan: a step-by-step approach. Harold J. McLaughlin. New York: Wiley, c1992. xiv, 289 p. *Notes:* Includes bibliographical references (p. 279-280) and index. [LC 91034353; ISN 0471552135]   HD30.28. M3853 1992   802

Fast-growth strategies: how to maximize profits from start-up through maturity. Mack Hanan. New York: McGraw-Hill Book Co., c1987. ix, 164 p. : ill. *Notes:* Includes index. [LC 86021673; ISN 0070259720; $17.95 (est.)] HD30.28. H363 1987   803

Handbook of business strategy. editor, Harold E. Glass. 2nd ed. Boston: Warren, Gorham & Lamont, c1991. 1 v. (various pagings): ill. *Notes:* Includes bibliographies and index. [LC 90071266; ISN 0791306984; $98.00] HD30.28. H366 1991   804

Henderson on corporate strategy. Bruce D. Henderson. Cambridge, Mass.: Abt Books, c1979. xi, 189 p. [LC 78072889; ISN 0890115265] HD30.28. H4   805

Implementing strategy. Lawrence G. Hrebiniak, William F. Joyce. New York: London: Macmillan; Collier Macmillan, c1984. xv, 252 p. *Notes:* Includes bibliographical references and index. [LC 83000852; ISN 0023575409; ISN 0023572906] HD30.28. H73 1984   806

Introducing corporate planning: guide to strategic management. David E. Hussey. 4th ed. Oxford; New York: Pergamon Press, 1991. xviii, 245 p. : ill. *Notes:* Includes bibliographical references (p. 237-239) and index. [LC 91010515; ISN 008041343X; $29.75] HD30.28. H88 1991   807

The logic of business strategy. Bruce Henderson. Cambridge, Mass.: Ballinger Pub. Co., c1984. viii, 114 p. : ill. *Notes:* Includes index. "An Abt Books/Ballinger publication." [LC 84011119; ISN 0884109836] HD30.28. H47 1984   808

Long-range planning of Japanese corporations. Toyohiro Kono. Berlin; New York: Walter de Gruyter, 1992. xiii, 390 p. : ill. *Notes:* Includes bibliographical references and index. [LC 92018407; ISN 3110129140] HD30.28. K66 1992   809

A problem-finding approach to effective corporate planning. Robert J. Thierauf. New York: Quorum Books, c1987. xiv, 220 p. : ill. *Notes:* Includes index. Bibliography: p. [213]-214. [LC 87005971; ISN 0899302629] HD30.28. T45 1987   810

Rejuvenating the mature business: the competitive challenge. Charles Baden-Fuller, John M. Stopford. [Rev. ed.]. Boston, Mass.: Harvard Business School Press, c1994. xv, 281 p. : ill. *Notes:* Originally published: London: Routledge, 1992. Includes bibliographical references (p. 263-271) and index. [LC 93036706; ISN 0875844766; $27.95] HD30.28. B323 1994   +811

Strategic management: an integrative perspective. Arnoldo C. Hax, Nicolas S. Majluf. Englewood Cliffs, N.J.: Prentice Hall, c1984. xvii, 468 p. : ill. *Notes:* Includes bibliographies and index. [LC 84006939; ISN 0138512701] HD30.28. H388 1984   812

Strategic management and organizational decision making. Alan Walter Steiss. Lexington, Mass.: Lexington Books, c1985. viii, 240 p. *Notes:* Includes bibliographical references and indexes. [LC 85040319; ISN 0669109657] HD30.28. S724 1985   813

The strategic management handbook. Kenneth J. Albert, editor in chief. New York: McGraw-Hill, c1983. 546 p. in various pagings: ill. *Notes:* Includes index. [LC 82017110; ISN 0070009546; $49.95] HD30.28. S725 1983   814

Strategic market planning: the pursuit of competitive advantage. George S. Day. St. Paul: West Pub. Co., c1984. xvi, 237 p. : ill. *Notes:* Includes index. Bibliography: p. 215-223. [LC 84002282; ISN 0314778845; $9.95] HD30.28. D39 1984   815

The technology connection: strategy and change in the Information Age. Marc S. Gerstein. Reading, Mass.: Addison-Wesley, c1987. xiv, 194 p. : ill. (The Addison-Wesley OD series) *Notes:* Includes bibliographical references. [LC 86022343; ISN 0201121883; $12.95 (est.)] HD30.28. G47 1987   816

Thinking strategically: planning for your company's future. William L. Shanklin, John K. Ryans, Jr. 1st ed. New York: Random House, c1985. xvii, 332 p. : ill. *Notes:* Bibliography: p. 317-321. [LC 84017964; ISN 039439500X; $39.95] HD30.28. S4 1985   817

Time horizons and technology investments. Committee on Time Horizons and Technology Investments, National Academy of Engineering. Washington, D.C.: National Academy Press, 1992. viii, 108 p. : ill. *Notes:* Includes bibliographical references (p. 74-77). [LC 92080242; ISN 0309046475] HD30.28. N388 1992   818

The total business plan: how to write, rewrite, and revise. Patrick D. O'Hara. New York: Wiley, c1990. xiii, 288 p. *Notes:* Includes index. [LC 89077520; ISN 0471524506; $49.95] HD30.28. O35 1990   819

Total business planning: a step-by-step guide with forms. E. James Burton, W. Blan McBride. Rev. ed. New York: Wiley, c1991. x, 245 p. : ill. [LC 91191832; ISN 0471528269; $19.95] HD30.28. B84 1991   820

Winning on the marketing front: the corporate manager's game plan. William A. Cohen. New York: Wiley, c1986. x, 381 p. : ill. (Wiley series on business strategy) *Notes:* Includes index. "Sources of secondary research": p. 283-321. [LC 85012220; ISN 0471819352; $19.95] HD30.28. C58   821

CORPORATE PROFITS

The handbook of corporate earnings analysis: company performance and stock market valuation. edited by Brian R. Bruce, Charles B. Epstein. Chicago, Ill.: Probus Pub. Co., c1994. ix, 369 p. : ill. *Notes:* Spine title: Corporate earnings analysis. Includes bibliographical references and index. [LC 94171048; ISN 1557385408; $51.60] HG4028.P7 H36 1994 +822

The vital corporation: how American businesses—large and small—double profits in two years or less. Garry Jacobs and Robert Macfarlane. Englewood Cliffs, N.J.: Prentice-Hall, c1990. xii, 264 p. : ill. *Notes:* Includes bibliographical references (p. 253-254). [LC 89028975; ISN 0139464506; $19.95] HG4028.P7 J33 1990 823

CORPORATE TURNAROUNDS

How to turn round a manufacturing company. Brian Halford Walley. New York: E. Horwood, 1992. xiv, 258 p. : ill. *Notes:* Includes bibliographical references and index. *Contents:* The manufacturing framework—The product market—Technology—Resource utilization and cost control—Work organization and training—Systems and information technology—Motivation and reward systems—Formulating a manufacturing strategy for the nineties—Appendix 1: Ferodo—Appendix 2: List of definitions and explanation of terms and acronyms used—Appendix 3: Training. [LC 93132488; ISN 0133959228; £35.00] HD58.8. W35 1992 +824

The turnaround experience: real-world lessons in revitalizing corporations. Frederick M. Zimmerman. New York: McGraw-Hill, c1991. xii, 335 p. : ill. *Notes:* Includes bibliographical references (p. 305-327) and index. [LC 91003509; ISN 0070728992; $24.95] HD58.8. Z55 1991 825

The turnaround prescription: repositioning troubled companies. Mark R. Goldston. New York: Toronto: New York: Free Press; Maxwell Macmillan Canada; Maxwell Macmillan International, c1992. xix, 198 p. : ill. *Notes:* Includes index. [LC 92010752; ISN 002912395X; $22.95] HD58.8. G63 1992 826

The unnatural act of management: when the great leader's work is done, the people say "We did it ourselves". Everett T. Suters. 1st ed. New York: HarperCollins Publishers, 1992. xv, 288 p. *Notes:* Includes index. [LC 91040225; ISN 0887305512; $20.00] HD58.8. S88 1992 827

Workouts and turnarounds: the handbook of restructuring and investing in distressed companies. edited by Dominic DiNapoli, Sanford C. Sigoloff, Robert F. Cushman. Homewood, Ill.: Business One Irwin, c1991. xxxi, 778 p. : ill. *Notes:* Includes bibliographical references and index. [LC 90043802; ISN 1556233353; $75.00] HD58.8. W68 1991 828

CORPORATION LAW

Basic legal forms for business. by Morris A. Nunes. New York: Wiley, c1990. xiv, 242 p. : ill. [LC 89022578; ISN 0471520217; $59.95] KF1411. N86 1990 829

Corporate law. Robert Charles Clark. Boston: Little, Brown, c1986. xxviii, 837 p. : ill. *Notes:* Includes bibliographical references and indexes. [LC 85081681; ISN 0316144940] KF1414. C5 1986 830

Corporate power and responsibility: issues in the theory of company law. J.E. Parkinson. Oxford: New York: Clarendon Press; Oxford University Press, 1993. [xxviii], 464 p. *Notes:* Includes bibliographical references and index. [LC 93022583; ISN 0198252889] KD2079. P37 1993 +831

Corporations and society: power and responsibility. edited by Warren J. Samuels and Arthur S. Miller. New York: Greenwood Press, 1987. xv, 328 p. *Notes:* Includes index. Bibliography: p. [313]-318. [LC 86019451; ISN 0313250723] KF1414. C675 1987 832

Interactive corporate compliance: an alternative to regulatory compulsion. Jay A. Sigler and Joseph E. Murphy. New York: Quorum Books, c1988. xii, 211 p. *Notes:* Includes index. Bibliography: p. [199]-204. [LC 87032596; ISN 0899302432] KF1414. S45 1988 833

Setting up a company in the European Community: a country by country guide. compiled by Brebner and Co., International Division. Phoenix, AZ: Oryx Press, 1989. 251 p. : ill. *Notes:* Includes index. [LC 89008691; ISN 0897746015; $49.50] KJE2448. S47 1989 834

Start-up companies: planning, financing, and operating the successful business. planned and edited by Richard D. Harroch. New York, N.Y.: Law Journal Seminars-Press, 1985. 2 v. (loose-leaf) *Notes:* "00592." Includes bibliographical references and index. Kept up to date by cumulative releases. [LC 85010088; $100.00] KF1414. S73 1985 835

CORPORATION REPORTS

The effectiveness of the annual report as a communication vehicle: a digest of the relevant literature. by David F. Hawkins, Barbara A. Hawkins. Morristown, N.J. (10 Madison Ave., P.O. Box 1938, Morristown, N.J. 07960): Financial Executives Research Foundation, c1986. xiii, 162 p. *Notes:* Bibliography: p. 103-162.]   HG4028.B2 H38   836

CORPORATIONS

Accounting and its legal implications: a guide for managers, business owners, and entrepreneurs. David W. Tate. Burr Ridge, IL: Irwin Professional Pub., c1994. xii, 210 p. *Notes:* Includes bibliographical references (p. 195-200) and index. [LC 93039278; ISBN 1556237618]
                                                                                 HF5686.C7 T37 1994   +837

Accounting for corporate reputation. Ahmed Riahi-Belkaoui and Ellen L. Pavlik. Westport, Conn.: Quorum Books, 1992. xii, 253 p. : ill. *Notes:* Includes bibliographical references and index. [LC 92008401; ISBN 0899307175]   HF5686.C7 R5 1992   838

Advances in business financial management: a collection of readings. edited by Philip L. Cooley. Chicago: Dryden Press, 1990. xvi, 634 p. : ill. *Notes:* Includes bibliographies. [LC 88033602; ISBN 0030099439; $22.00]   HG4026. A34 1990   839

Analysis for financial management. Robert C. Higgins. 3rd ed. Homewood, IL: Business One Irwin, c1992. xi, 387 p. : ill. *Notes:* Includes bibliographical references and index. [LC 91016089; ISBN 1556235496; $39.95]   HG4026. H496 1992   840

Art for work: the new renaissance in corporate collecting. Marjory Jacobson. Boston, Mass.: Harvard Business School Press, c1993. 224 p. : ill. (some col.) *Notes:* Simultaneously published: The art of business. London: Thames & Hudson, 1993. Includes bibliographical references (p. 217-220) and index. [LC 93018707; ISBN 0875843638; $60.00]   N5206. J23 1993   +841

Automating global financial management. by Business International; sponsored by Financial Executives Research Foundation. New York: Wiley, c1988. xiv, 364 p. *Notes:* Includes index. [LC 88017339; ISBN 0471612847; $49.95]   HG4012.5. A93 1988   842

Beyond the bottom line: 15 key strategies for today's financial manager. Boston, MA: Harvard Business Review, Reprint Service, c1985. 122 p. : ill. *Notes:* Includes bibliographical references.]
                                                                               HG4026. B49 1985   843

Business enterprise in American history. Mansel G. Blackford, K. Austin Kerr. Boston: Houghton Mifflin, c1986. xi, 456 p. : ill. *Notes:* Includes bibliographies and index. [LC 85060780; ISBN 0395351553]   HD2785. B52 1986   844

Business policy: text and cases. C. Roland Christensen... et al. 5th ed. Homewood, Ill.: R.D. Irwin, 1982. xvii, 838 p., [1] folded leaf of plates: ill. *Notes:* Rev. ed. of: Business policy / C. Roland Christensen, Kenneth R. Andrews, Joseph L. Bower. 4th ed. 1978. Includes bibliographical references and index. [LC 81086114; ISBN 0256026262]   HD2785. B78 1982   845

Business policy: texts and cases. C. Roland Christensen... et al. 6th ed. Homewood, Ill.: Irwin, 1987. xx, 940 p. : ill., ports. *Notes:* Includes bibliographical references and index. [LC 86082216; ISBN 0256033587]   HD2785. B78 1987   846

Case problems in finance. edited by William E. Fruhan, Jr.... et al. 10th ed. Homewood, IL: Irwin, c1992. xi, 692 p. : ill. *Notes:* Includes index. [LC 91031237; ISBN 0256083460; $53.95]
                                                                               HG4026. C279 1992   847

The CFO's handbook. edited by Richard F. Vancil assisted by Marianne D'Amico and Benjamin R. Makela. Homewood, Ill.: Dow Jones-Irwin, c1986. xxxiii, 642 p. : ill. *Notes:* Includes bibliographical references and index. [LC 85071161; ISBN 0870945912]   HG4027.3. C46 1986   848

Changing roles of financial management: getting close to the business. Patrick J. Keating, Stephen F. Jablonsky. Morristown, N.J.: Financial Executives Research Foundation, c1990. 224 p. : ill. *Notes:* Bibliography: p. [215]-224. [LC 90081172; ISBN 0910586780]   HG4026. K43 1990   849

Corporate restructuring: managing the change process from within. Gordon Donaldson. Boston, Mass.: Harvard Business School Press, c1994. xii, 227 p. : ill. *Notes:* Includes bibliographical references and index. [LC 93030462; ISBN 0875843395; $29.95]   HG4061. D578 1994   +850

Corporate capital structures in the United States. edited by Benjamin M. Friedman. Chicago: University of Chicago Press, 1985. xi, 390 p. : ill. (A National Bureau of Economic Research project report) *Notes:* Papers presented at a conference held at Palm Beach, Fla., Jan. 6-7, 1983, sponsored by the National Bureau of Economic Research. Includes bibliographies and indexes. *Contents:* Contingent claims valuation of corporate liabilities / E. Philip Jones, Scott P. Mason, and Eric Rosenfeld. [LC 84016138; ISBN 0226264114; $55.00]   HG4061. C66 1985   851

Corporate crime and violence: big business power and the abuse of the public trust. Russell Mokhiber. San Francisco: Sierra Club Books, c1988. 450 p. *Notes:* Includes bibliographies and index. [LC 87004730; ISN 0871567237]   HV6769. M65 1988   852

The corporate director's financial handbook. John P. Fertakis. New York: Quorum Books, 1988. xiv, 186 p. : ill. *Notes:* Includes bibliographies and index. [LC 88011318; ISN 0899302890]   HG4026. F475 1988   853

Corporate finance. Stephen A. Ross, Randolph W. Westerfield, Jeffrey F. Jaffe. 3rd ed. Homewood, IL: Irwin, 1992, c1993. 1 v. (various pagings): ill. *Notes:* Includes bibliographical references and indexes. [LC 92025582; ISN 025609487X]   HG4026. R675 1992   854

Corporate finance and the securities laws. Charles J. Johnson, Jr. Englewood Cliffs, N.J.: Prentice Hall Law & Business, 1990. xxvii, 819 p. *Notes:* Includes bibliographical references. [LC 90007841; ISN 0131738577]   KF1428. J58 1990   855

Corporate financial analysis: a comprehensive guide to real-world approaches for financial managers. John D. Finnerty. New York: McGraw-Hill, c1986. xiii, 566 p. : ill. *Notes:* Includes bibliographies and index. [LC 85013255; ISN 0070210403]   HG4026. F524 1986   856

Corporate financial reporting and analysis: text and cases. David F. Hawkins. 3rd. ed. Homewood, Ill.: Irwin, 1986. xx, 1051 p. : ill. (The Robert N. Anthony/Willard J. Graham series in accounting) *Notes:* Previous eds. published under the title: Corporate financial reporting: text and cases. Includes indexes. [LC 85082418; ISN 0256025878]   HF5686.C7 H35 1986   857

Corporate growth in Japan. Shimizu Ryūei. Tōkyō (1-16-15, Hirakawa-cho, Chiyoda-ku, Tokyo, Japan): Japan Research Institute, 1986. 54 *Notes:* Includes bibliographical references and index.]   HD2907. S539   858

Corporate makeover: reshaping the American economy. Harvey Segal. New York, NY: Viking, 1989. xii, 269 p. *Notes:* Bibliography: p. 207-251. [LC 88040419; ISN 0670820997; $19.95]   HD2785. S4127 1989   859

The corporate survivors. G. Harry Stine. New York, NY: American Management Association, 1986. 230 p. : ill. *Notes:* Includes index. Bibliography: p. 215. [LC 86047597; ISN 0814458319]   HD2785. S73 1986   860

The corporation as anomaly. David E. Schrader. Cambridge; New York: Cambridge University Press, 1993. xi, 202 p. *Notes:* Includes bibliographical references (p. 186-195) and index. [LC 92013629; ISN 0521412412]   HD2741. S43 1993   861

The debt/equity choice. Ronald W. Masulis. Cambridge, Mass.: Ballinger Pub. Co., c1988. xi, 141 p. *Notes:* Includes indexes. Bibliography: p. 93-127. [LC 88022214; ISN 0887303609; ISN 0887303684; $34.95]   HG4011. M38 1988   862

Decision support systems in finance and accounting. H.G. Heymann and Robert Bloom. New York: Quorum Books, 1988. xiv, 195 p. : ill. *Notes:* Includes index. Bibliography: p. [179]-189. [LC 87032609; ISN 0899302696]   HG4012.5. H49 1988   863

The desktop encyclopedia of corporate finance & accounting. Charles J. Woelfel. Chicago, Ill.: Probus Pub. Co., c1987. viii, 518 p. : ill. *Notes:* Spine title: Corporate finance & accounting. Includes bibliographies. [LC 87002302; ISN 0917253655; $27.50]   HG4027.3. W64 1987   864

Directors of industry: the British corporate network, 1904-76. John Scott and Catherine Griff. Cambridge: New York, NY, USA: Polity Press; B. Blackwell, 1984. 226 p. : ill. *Notes:* Includes index. Bibliography: p. [188]-212. [LC 84018186; ISN 0745600190; $34.95]   HD2845. S36 1984   865

Doing best by doing good: how to use public purpose partnerships to boost corporate profits and benefit your community. Richard Steckel and Robin Simons. New York: Dutton, 1992. viii, 278 p. : ill. [LC 92052877; ISN 0525934901]   HG4028.C6 S716 1992   866

The Dow Jones-Irwin guide to financial modeling. James R. Morris. Homewood, Ill.: Dow Jones-Irwin, 1987. xi, 394 p. : ill. *Notes:* Includes bibliographical references and index. [LC 86071214; ISN 0870947486]   HG4012. M67   867

The entrepreneur's guide to capital: the techniques for capitalizing and refinancing new and growing businesses. Jennifer Lindsey. Chicago, Ill.: Probus Pub., c1986. vii, 310 p. : ill. *Notes:* Includes index. [LC 86004930; ISN 0917253345; $18.95]   HG4061. L52 1986   868

The Ernst & Young guide to financing for growth. Daniel R. Garner, Robert R. Owen, Robert P. Conway. New York: Wiley, c1994. xii, 361 p. : ill. *Notes:* Includes index. [LC 93034164; ISN 0471599042; ISN 0471599034; $34.95]   HG4061. G368 1994   +869

The Ernst & Young guide to raising capital. Daniel R. Garner, Robert R. Owen, Robert P. Conway. New York: Wiley, c1991. xii, 355 p. *Notes:* Includes bibliographical references and index. [LC 90043834; ISN 0471530050; $14.95]   HG4061. G37 1991   870

Essentials of managerial finance. J. Fred Weston, Eugene F. Brigham. 9th ed. Chicago: Dryden Press, c1990. xxiv, 931 p. : ill. *Notes:* Tables (4 p.) inserted. Includes bibliographical references and index. [LC 89016780; ISN 0030307333; $55.71]   HG4026. W448 1990   871

Essentials of managerial finance. J. Fred Weston, Eugene F. Brigham. 8th ed. Chicago: Dryden Press, c1987. xxii, 840 p. : col. ill. Notes: One folded sheet (4 p.) laid in. Includes bibliographical references and index. [LC 86019614; ISN 0030099676]   HG4026. W448 1987   872

Evaluating corporate investment and financing opportunities: a handbook and guide to selected methods for managers and finance professionals. Sherman L. Lewis. New York: Quorum Books, c1986. xiv, 295 p. Notes: Includes index. [LC 86000623; ISN 0899301444]   HG4026. L49 1986   873

Financial management and policy. James C. van Horne. 8th ed. Englewood Cliffs, N.J.: Prentice-Hall, 1989. xxii, 852 p. : ill. Notes: Includes bibliographies and index. [LC 88019662; ISN 0133169103; $44.10]   HG4011. V34 1989   874

Financial management classics. edited by Carroll D. Aby, Jr. and Donald E. Vaughn. Santa Monica, Calif.: Goodyear Pub. Co., c1979. xv, 397 p. : ill. Contents: Donaldson, G. Financial management in an affluent society.—Anthony, R. N. Some fallacies in figuring return on investment. [LC 79010710; ISN 0876202881]   HG4011. F444   875

Financial management for decision making. Harold Bierman, Jr., Seymour Smidt. New York: London: Macmillan; Collier Macmillan, c1986. xix, 842 p. : col. ill. Notes: Includes bibliographies and index. [LC 85007160; ISN 0023100303]   HG4026. B534 1986   876

Financial management handbook. edited by Philip A. Vale. 3rd ed. Aldershot, Hants, England Brookfield, Vt., U.S.A.: Gower, c1988. xxii, 395 p. : ill. Notes: Includes index. Bibliography: p. 383-386. [LC 87000040; ISN 0566026236; $75.00 (U.S.)]   HG4027.3. F53 1988   877

Financial management: theory and practice. Eugene F. Brigham, Louis C. Gapenski. 6th ed. Chicago: Dryden Press, c1991. 1 v. (various pagings): ill. Notes: Includes bibliographical references. [LC 90002882; ISN 0030326729; $52.00]   HG4026. B669 1991   878

The financial manager. Jerome B. Cohen, Sidney M. Robbins, Allan Young. Columbus, Ohio: Pub. Horizons, c1986. xv, 748 p. Notes: Includes bibliographies and index. [LC 86009298; ISN 0942280318; $36.95]   HG4026. C534 1986   879

Financial strategy: studies in the creation, transfer, and destruction of shareholder value. William E. Fruhan, Jr. Homewood, Ill.: R. D. Irwin, 1979. ix, 301 p. : graphs Notes: Includes index. Bibliography: p. 287-296. [LC 78070005; ISN 0256022283]   HG4026. F78   880

Financial theory and corporate policy. Thomas E. Copeland, J. Fred Weston. 3rd ed. Reading, Mass.: Addison-Wesley, c1988. xiv, 946 p. : ill. Notes: Includes bibliographies and indexes. [LC 87012595; ISN 0201106485; $39.95]   HG4011. C833 1988   881

Foundations of financial management. Stanley B. Block, Geoffrey A. Hirt. 6th ed. Homewood, IL: Irwin, 1992. xxxvi, 700 p. : col. ill. Notes: Appendixes A-D (4 p.) inserted. Includes bibliographical references and index. [LC 91016931; ISN 025608355X; $52.95]   HG4026. B589 1992   882

Fundamentals of finanacial management. James C. Van Horne, John M. Wachowicz, Jr. 8th ed. Englewood Cliffs, N.J.: Prentice Hall, 1992. xiv, 816 p. : ill. Notes: Tables (4 p.) inserted. [LC 90026486; ISN 0133518345; $69.00]   HG4011. V36 1992   883

Fundamentals of financial management. Eugene F. Brigham. 6th ed. Fort Worth: Dryden Press, c1992. xxiii, 904, [77] p. : ill. (some col.) Notes: Tables (4 p.) inserted. Includes bibliographical references and index. [LC 91018634; ISN 0030550270; $55.29]   HG4026. B6693 1992   884

Fundamentals of financial management. James C. Van Horne. 5th ed. Englewood Cliffs, N.J.: Prentice-Hall, c1983. xvii, 615 p. : ill. Notes: Includes bibliographies and index. [LC 82010123; ISN 0133394654; $24.95]   HG4011. V36 1983   885

Handbook of corporate finance. edited by Edward I. Altman, associate editor, Mary Jane McKinney. New York: Wiley, c1986. 1 v. (various pagings): ill. (Wiley professional banking and finance series) Notes: Rev. ed. of: Financial handbook. 5th ed. c1981. Includes bibliographical references and index. [LC 86015978; ISN 0471819573]   HG4026. H288 1986   886

The handbook of financial engineering: new financial product innovations, applications, and analyses. editors, Clifford W. Smith, Jr. and Charles W. Smithson. New York: Harper & Row, c1990. xii, 675 p. : ill. Notes: Includes bibliographical references. [LC 90033922; ISN 0887304486; $59.95]   HG4026. H289 1990   887

The handbook of financial modeling: the financial executive's reference guide to accounting, finance, and investment models. John Guerard, H.T. Vaught. Chicago, Ill.: Probus Pub. Co., 1989. x, 366 p. : ill. Notes: Includes bibliographies and index. [LC 87032868; ISN 0917253450; $55.00]   HG4012. G84 1989   888

The improvement of corporate financial performance: a manager's guide to evaluating selected opportunities. Sherman L. Lewis. New York: Quorum Books, c1989. xvi, 379 p. Notes: Includes index. [LC 88035684; ISN 089930432X; $49.95]   HG4026. L493 1989   889

Inc. yourself: how to profit by setting up your own corporation. Judith H. McQuown. 7th ed. New York: HarperCollins, c1992. xvi, 268 p. : ill. Notes: Includes index. [LC 91058366; ISN 0060183276; $25.00 ($33.50 Can.)]   HD2741. M38 1992   890

Inside America's fastest growing companies. M. John Storey. New York: Wiley, c1989. xiii, 268 p. *Notes:* Includes index. Bibliography: p. 254-255. [LC 88015520; ISN 0471602493]

HD2746. S76 1989   891

Introduction to financial management. B.J. Campsey, Eugene F. Brigham. 3rd ed. Chicago: Dryden Press, 1991. 1 v. (various pagings): ill. *Notes:* Includes bibliographical references and index. [LC 90043973; ISN 0030510082; $53.57]

HG4026. C23 1991   892

Introduction to financial management. Lawrence D. Schall, Charles W. Haley. 4th ed. New York: McGraw-Hill, c1986. xviii, 790 p. : ill. (McGraw-Hill series in finance) *Notes:* Includes index. Bibliography: p. 737-743. [LC 85016646; ISN 007055109X; $35.95 (est.)]

HG4011. S33 1986   893

Introduction to financial management. Lawrence D. Schall, Charles W. Haley. 5th ed. New York: McGraw-Hill, c1988. xvii, 856 p. : ill. (some col.) *Notes:* Includes index. Bibliography: p. 797-803. [LC 87021450; ISN 007055112X]

HG4011. S33 1988   894

Issues and readings in managerial finance. edited by Ramon E. Johnson. 3rd ed. Chicago: Dryden Press, c1987. xi, 448 p. : ill. (Dryden Press series in finance) *Notes:* Rev. ed. of: Issues in managerial finance / edited by Eugene F. Brigham, Ramon E. Johnson. 2nd ed. 1980. Includes bibliographies. [LC 86013578; ISN 0030094879]

HG4026. I77 1987   895

Kaisha, the Japanese corporation. James C. Abegglen, George Stalk, Jr. New York: Basic Books, c1985. x, 309 p. : ill. *Notes:* Includes index. Bibliography: p. 289-290. [LC 85047552; ISN 0465037119; $22.50]

HD2907. A23 1985   896

Managerial finance. J. Fred Weston, Thomas E. Copeland. 9th ed. Fort Worth: Dryden Press, c1992. xxi, 1182 p. : ill. *Notes:* Includes bibliographical references and indexes. [LC 91017511; $56.57]

HG4026. W45 1992   897

Managing big business: essays from the Business History Review. edited by Richard S. Tedlow and Richard R. John, Jr. Boston, Mass.: Harvard Business School Press, c1986. xxvii, 425 p. *Notes:* Includes bibliographies and index. [LC 86007683; ISN 0875841422; ISN 0875841457]

HD2785. M353 1986   898

Managing corporate wealth: the operation of a comprehensive financial goals system. Gordon Donaldson, with the editorial assistance of Nan Dundes Stone. New York: Praeger, 1984. vii, 198 p. : ill. *Notes:* Includes index. Bibliography: p. 191-192. [LC 84004779; ISN 0030634148; ISN 0030634164; $16.95 (est.); $7.95 (est.)]

HG4061. D58 1984   899

Modern corporate finance. Alan C. Shapiro. New York: London: Macmillan; Collier Macmillan, c1990. xxvi, 1045, [46] p. : ill. *Notes:* Includes bibliographical references and index. [LC 89002503; ISN 0024095303; $54.00]

HG4026. S44 1990   900

The modern corporation and private property. Adolf A. Berle and Gardiner C. Means; with a new introduction by Murray L. Weidenbaum and Mark Jensen. New Brunswick N.J. U.S.A.: Transaction Publishers, c1991. iv, 380 p. *Notes:* "Originally published in 1968." Includes bibliographical references and index. [LC 90048752; ISN 0887388876; $24.95]

HD2795. B53 1991   901

The modern theory of corporate finance. edited by Clifford W. Smith, Jr.; with the assistance of North-Holland Publishing Company. 2nd ed. New York: McGraw-Hill, c1989. xi, 695 p. *Notes:* Bibliographiy: p. 693-695. [LC 89008167; ISN 0070591091; $19.95]

HG4026.5. M62 1989   902

The 'nice' company. Tom Lloyd. London: Bloomsbury, c1990. xx, 235 p. *Notes:* Includes bibliographical references (p. 227-228); ISN 074750346X]

HD2731. L56 1990   903

The Price Waterhouse guide to financial management: tools for improving performance. Ralph G. Loretta. New York: John Wiley, c1990. xv, 197 p. [LC 90106403; ISN 0471620440; $45.00]

HG4011. L674 1990   904

Principles of corporate finance. Richard A. Brealey, Stewart C. Myers. 4th ed. New York: McGraw-Hill, c1991. xxvii, 924, 15, 11 19, 21 p. : ill. (some col.) *Notes:* Includes bibliographical references and index. [LC 90028919; ISN 0070074054; $55.50]

HG4026. B667 1991   905

Principles of corporate finance. Ward S. Curran. San Diego, CA.: Harcourt Brace Jovanovich, c1988. xix, 742 p. : ill. *Notes:* Includes bibliographical references and index. [LC 87081160; ISN 015571550x]

HG4011. C94 1988   906

Principles of managerial finance. Lawrence J. Gitman. 6th ed. New York: Harper Collins Publishers, c1991. xxxvi, 886, A1-I13 p. : ill.; 1 computer disk (5 1/4 in.). *Notes:* System requirements for computer disk: IBM PC or true compatible; at least 256Kb RAM; MS-DOS 2.1; at least 1 disk drive or hard disk; monochrome, Hercules, CGA, EGA, or VGA card and monitor. Includes bibliographical references and index. [LC 90044747; ISN 0060424168; $58.57]

HG4011. G5 1991   907

Recent advances in corporate finance. edited by Edward I. Altman, Marti G. Subrahmanyam. Homewood, Ill.: R.D. Irwin, 1985. xiv, 438 p. : ill. *Notes:* Includes bibliographies and indexes. [LC 84082468; ISN 0870945602]

HG4011. R43   908

Recent developments in corporate finance. edited by Jeremy Edwards...et al. Cambridge Cambridgeshire; New York: Cambridge University Press, 1986. xiv, 240 p. : ill. *Notes:* Includes bibliographical references. [LC 86008241; ISN 0521329647] HG4026.5. R43 1986 909

Redefining excellence: the financial performance of America's "best-run" companies. Arabinda Ghosh. New York: Praeger, 1989. xvi, 157 p. *Notes:* Includes bibliographical references. [LC 89003859; ISN 0275933393; $39.95] HG4061. G46 1989 910

The revolution in corporate finance. edited by Joel M. Stern and Donald H. Chew, Jr. 2nd ed. Cambridge, MA: Blackwell Finance, c1992. xv, 634 p. : ill. *Notes:* Essays previously published in the Midland corporate finance journal and the Chase financial quarterly. Includes bibliographical references and index. [LC 92024567; ISN 0631185542] HG4026.5. R48 1992 911

The search for value: measuring the company's cost of capital. Michael C. Ehrhardt. Boston, Mass.: Harvard Business School, c1994. xii, 232 p. *Notes:* Includes bibliographical references and index. [LC 93021411; ISN 0875843808] HG4028.V3 E37 1994 +912

Six roundtable discussions of corporate finance with Joel Stern. edited by Donald H. Chew, Jr. New York: Quorum Books, 1986. xvi, 329 p. : ill. *Notes:* Includes index. [LC 86012382; ISN 0899301622] HG4026.5. S59 1986 913

The suicidal corporation. Paul H. Weaver. New York: Simon and Schuster, c1988. 270 p. *Notes:* Includes index. A Cato Institute book. Bibliography: p. 255-258. [LC 87023468; ISN 0671523783] HD2785. W38 1988 914

Sustainable corporate growth: a model and management planning tool. John J. Clark, Thomas C. Chiang, and Gerard T. Olson. New York: Quorum Books, 1989. xiv, 307 p. : ill. *Notes:* Includes bibliographies and index. [LC 88006755; ISN 0899302386; $49.95] HD2746. C56 1989 915

Techniques of financial analysis. Erich A. Helfert. 7th ed. Homewood, IL: Irwin, c1991. xv, 506 p. : ill. *Notes:* "Free instructor's copy"—Cover p. [4]. Includes bibliographical references and index. [LC 90041101; ISN 0256079269; $24.95] HG4026. H44 1991 916

The U.S. business corporation: an institution in transition. edited by John R. Meyer and James M. Gustafson. Cambridge, Mass.: Ballinger Pub. Co., c1988. xv, 249 p. : ill. *Notes:* "Published for the American Academy of Arts and Sciences." Includes index. [LC 88022062; ISN 0887303544] HD2785. U6 1988 917

Valuation: measuring and managing the value of companies. Tom Copeland, Tim Koller, Jack Murrin. 2nd ed. New York: Wiley, c1994. xviii, 558 p. : ill. (Wiley frontiers in finance) *Notes:* Includes bibliographical references and index. [LC 94008304; ISN 0471009938] HG4028.V3 C67 1994 +918

Valuation reference manual: putting a price tag on a business when you're buying, when you're selling, when you're valuing. Thomas J. Martin. Hicksville, NY (383 S. Broadway, Hicksville 11801): Business Owner, c1991. xx, 194 leaves] HG4028.V3 M33 1991 919

Valuing a business: the analysis and appraisal of closely-held companies. Shannon P. Pratt. 2nd ed. Homewood, Ill.: Dow Jones-Irwin, 1989. xxx, 737 p. *Notes:* Includes index. Bibliography: p. 705-724. [LC 88028308; ISN 155623127X; $60.00] HG4028.V3 P72 1989 920

What every manager should know about financial analysis. Alan S. Donnahoe. New York: Simon and Schuster, c1989. 223 p. : ill. *Notes:* Includes index. [LC 89006313; ISN 0671610988; $19.95] HG4026. D645 1989 921

CORPORATIONS, AMERICAN

Second to none: American companies in Japan. Robert C. Christopher. 1st ed. New York: Crown Publishers, c1986. xi, 258 p. *Notes:* Includes index. Bibliography: p. 240. [LC 86006378; ISN 0517562863] HD2907. C45 1986 922

CORPORATIONS, JAPANESE

Does ownership matter?: Japanese multinationals in Europe. edited by Mark Mason and Dennis Encarnation. Oxford: New York: Clarendon Press; Oxford University Press, 1994. xxvi, 456 p. : ill. *Notes:* Revised papers initially presented at a conference hosted by the Euro-Asia Centre of the European Institute of Business Administration (INSEAD), plus subsequent presentations at the Academy of International Business in Brussels and at the Council on Foreign Relations in New York. Includes bibliographical references and index. [LC 93037553; ISN 0198288271; £30.00] HD2844. D63 1994 +923

The internationalization of Japanese business: European and Japanese perspectives. Malcolm Trevor, editor. Boulder: Frankfurt a. M.: Westview Press; Campus Verlag, 1987. 209 p. : ill. *Notes:* Sponsored by Nomura International Ltd., London. Includes bibliographies [LC 87008186; ISN 0813305314; $30.00] HD2844.5. S43 1985   924

Invasion of the salarymen: the Japanese business presence in America. Jeremiah J. Sullivan. Westport, Conn.: Praeger, 1992. xi, 359 p. *Notes:* Includes bibliographical references (p. [339]-345) and index. [LC 91043435; ISN 0275944042; $29.95] HD38. S785 1992   925

The Japan syndrome—is there one?: cases to the point. by Richard D. Robinson, assisted by Michael A. Connolly and Carol A. Robinson. Atlanta, Ga.: Business Publishing Division, CBA, Georgia State University, c1985. vi, 225 p. *Notes:* Includes bibliographies. [LC 84021056; ISN 0884061825; $20.00] HD38. R573 1985   926

Japanese and European management: their international adaptability. edited by Kazuo Shibagaki, Malcolm Trevor, and Tetsuo Abo. Tokyo: University of Tokyo Press, c1989. xii, 272 p. : ill. *Notes:* "... based on the papers submitted to the fourth International Conference of the Euro-Japanese Management Studies Association held in Tokyo in 1987"—Intro. Includes bibliographical references and index. [LC 89187840; ISN 086008440X; $59.50] HD62.4. J35 1989   927

Zaibatsu America: how Japanese firms are colonizing vital U.S. industries. Robert L. Kearns; foreword by Clyde V. Prestowitz. New York: Toronto: New York: Free Press; Maxwell Macmillan Canada; Maxwell Macmillan International, 1992. xv, 256 p. *Notes:* Includes bibliographical references (p. 241-245) and index. [LC 91035868; ISN 0029172454; $22.95] HD2785. K37 1992   928

COST ACCOUNTING

Accountants' cost handbook: a guide for management accounting. 3rd ed. / edited by James Bulloch, Donald E. Keller, Louis Vlasho. New York: Wiley, c1983. 790 p. in various pagings: ill. *Notes:* "A Ronald Press publication." Includes bibliographical references and index. [LC 82024781; ISN 047105352X; $49.95 (est.)] HF5686.C8 A384 1983   929

Cost accounting: a managerial emphasis. Charles T. Horngren, George Foster, Srikant M. Datar. 8th ed. Englewood Cliffs, N.J.: Prentice Hall, c1994. xxii, 969 p. : ill. (some col.) *Notes:* Includes bibliographical references and indexes. [LC 93031195; ISN 0131810669] HF5686.C8 H59 1994   +930

Cost accounting desk reference book: common weaknesses in cost systems and how to correct them. Thomas S. Dudick with Lawrence C. Best and George Kraus. New York: Van Nostrand Reinhold Co., 1986. xiii, 262 p. : ill. *Notes:* Includes index. [LC 86007836; ISN 0442217900] HF5686.C8 D88 1986   931

Cost accounting for the '90s: the challenge of technological change: conference proceedings. Montvale, N.J.: National Association of Accountants, 1986. v, 164 p. : ill. *Notes:* Cover title. Proceedings of conference held at Parker House Hotel, Boston, April 28-29, 1986.; ISN 0866411453] HF5686.C8 C67 1986   932

Cost accounting: planning and control. Milton F. Usry, Lawrence H. Hammer, Adolph Matz. 9th ed. Cincinnati: South-Western Pub. Co., c1988. xii, 899 p. : ill. (some col.) *Notes:* Matz's name appears first on the previous edition. "A88." Includes bibliographical references and index. [LC 87063017; ISN 053801881X; $44.53] HF5686.C8 U87 1988   933

Cost accounting: planning and control. Milton F. Usry, Lawrence H. Hammer; consulting editor, William K. Carter. 10th ed. Cincinnati: College Division, South-Western Pub. Co., c1991. xix, 903 p. : ill. *Notes:* Includes bibliographical references and index. [LC 90044820; ISN 0538809256; $53.95] HF5686.C8 U97 1991   934

Cost accounting: processing, evaluating, and using cost data. Wayne J. Morse, Harold P. Roth. 3rd ed. Reading, Mass.: Addison-Wesley Pub. Co., c1986. xxix, 993 p. : ill. (some col.) *Notes:* Glossary: p. 969-980. Includes bibliographies and index. [LC 85006153; ISN 0201139952; $37.00 (est.)] HF5686.C8 M674 1986   935

FMC corporation's use of current cost accounting. by Julie H. Hertenstein. Montvale, N.J.: National Association of Accountants, c1988. ix, 82 p. : ill. *Notes:* "A study carried out on behalf of the National Association of Accountants." Includes bibliographical references. [LC 88118305; ISN 0866411631; $30.12] HF5686.C8 H463 1988   936

Handbook of cost accounting theory and techniques. Ahmed Belkaoui. New York: Quorum Books, 1991. xvi, 381 p. *Notes:* Includes bibliographical references and index. [LC 90045142; ISN 0899305830] HF5686.C8 B355 1991   937

Implementing activity-based cost management: moving from analysis to action: implementation experiences at eight companies. by Robin Cooper... et al. Montvale, NJ: Institute of Management Accountants, c1992. xviii, 336 p. : ill. *Notes:* "A joint study by the Institute of Management Accountants, KPMG Peat Marwick, Robert S. Kaplan and Robin Cooper, Maisel Consulting Group"—Cover. Includes bibliographical references (p. 327-332). [LC 93120682; ISN 0866412069] HF5686.C8 I442 1992 +938

The managerial and cost accountant's handbook. edited by Homer A. Black, James Don Edwards. Homewood, Ill.: Dow Jones-Irwin, c1979. xxv, 1297 p. : ill. *Notes:* Includes bibliographies and index. [LC 78061201; ISN 0870941739] HF5686.C8 M263 939

Principles of cost accounting: using a cost management approach. Letricia Gayle Rayburn. 4th ed. Homewood, IL: Irwin, 1989. xxiv, 1464 p. : ill. (some col.) *Notes:* Includes bibliographies and indexes. [LC 88021834; ISN 0256068275; $42.95] HF5686.C8 R364 1989 940

Strategic cost analysis: the evolution from managerial to strategic accounting. John K. Shank, Vijay Govindarajan. Homewood, IL: Irwin, 1989. xvi, 161 p. : ill. *Notes:* Includes bibliographical references. [LC 88036882; ISN 0256070423; $17.95] HF5686.C8 S458 1989 941

Total quality accounting. Michael D. Woods. New York: Wiley, c1994. xii, 225 p. : ill. *Notes:* Includes index. [LC 94000334; ISN 0471311855] HF5686.C8 W74 1994 +942

COST AND STANDARD OF LIVING

American living standards: threats and challenges. Robert E. Litan, Robert Z. Lawrence, Charles L. Schultze, editors. Washington, D.C.: Brookings Institution, c1988. xvi, 250 p. : ill. *Notes:* Includes bibliographical references and index. [LC 88026238; ISN 0815752741; ISN 0815752733; $29.95; $10.95] HD6983. A69 1988 943

COST CONTROL

Cost containment: the ultimate strategic advantage. Peter R. Richardson. New York: London: Free Press; Collier Macmillan, c1988. xi, 238 p. : ill. *Notes:* Includes index. Bibliography: p. [227]-231. [LC 88002809; ISN 0029264324] HD47.3. R53 1988 944

Cost control handbook. R.M.S. Wilson. 2nd ed. Aldershot, Hants, England: Gower, 1983. xvii, 610 p. : ill. *Notes:* "A Gower Handbook." Includes index.; ISN 0566022508] HD47.5. W484 1983 945

The cost reduction and profit improvement handbook. Harry E. Figgie, Jr. Boston, Mass.: CBI Pub. Co., c1983. xiv, 231 p. *Notes:* Includes index. [LC 83002658; ISN 0843608943; $23.95] HD47.3. F55 1983 946

Strategic cost reduction: how international companies achieve cost leadership. Geneva, Switzerland: Business International S.A., c1987. 150 p. : ill. (Business International research report) *Notes:* Includes bibliographical references.] HD47.3. S77 1987 947

COST EFFECTIVENESS

Cost-benefit analysis. edited by Richard Layard and Stephen Glaister. 2nd ed. Cambridge England; New York, NY, USA: Cambridge University Press, 1994. x, 497 p. : ill. *Notes:* Includes bibliographical references and index. "... Covers all the main problems that arise in a typical cost-benefit exercise. Part I covers the main theoretical issues, including shadow pricing, discount rates, and problems of risk, uncertainty, and income distribution. Part II considers the problem of how to ascribe a monetary value to things like safety and physical risk, time, and environmental damages. The third part covers six separate case studies. Actual examples drawn, amongst others, from transport pricing, the allocation of health care, and water vending in developing countries are described."—Back cover. [LC 93037740; ISN 0521461286; ISN 0521466741] HD47.4. C668 1994 +948

How to prepare a feasibility study: a step-by-step guide including 3 model studies. Robert E. Stevens, Philip K. Sherwood. Englewood Cliffs, N.J.: Prentice-Hall, c1982. viii, 232 p. *Notes:* "A Spectrum book." Includes bibliographical references and index. [LC 82007480; ISN 0134292413; ISN 0134292588] HD47.4. S76 1982 949

COSTS, INDUSTRIAL

Cost management for today's advanced manufacturing: the CAM-I conceptual design. edited by Callie Berliner and James A. Brimson. Boston, Mass.: Harvard Business School Press, c1988. xvi, 253 p. : ill. *Notes:* Includes bibliographies and index. [LC 88010959; ISN 087584197X]
  TS167. C67 1988 950

COUNTERTRADE

Countertrade, barter, and offsets: new strategies for profit in international trade. Pompiliu Verzariu. New York: McGraw-Hill, c1985. xii, 208 p. : ill. *Notes:* Includes bibliographical references and index. [LC 84014385; ISN 0070673314] HF1412. V47 1985 951

The countertrade handbook. Dick Francis. New York: Quorum Books, 1987. ix, 270 p. : ill. *Notes:* Includes index. Bibliography: p. 262-263. [LC 87011867; ISN 089930320X] HF1414.3. F72 1987 952

Countertrade: practices, strategies, and tactics. Costas G. Alexandrides, Barbara L. Bowers. New York: J. Wiley, c1987. xx, 235 p. (Wiley professional banking and finance series, 0733-8945) *Notes:* Includes index. Bibliography: p. 227-229. [LC 87012966; ISN 0471847119] HF1414.3. A44 1987 953

International countertrade. edited by Christopher M. Korth. New York: Quorum Books, 1987. xii, 191 p. : ill. *Notes:* Results of a conference held at the College of Business, University of South Carolina, Spring, 1985; co-sponsored by the U.S. Dept. of Education. Includes index. Bibliography: p. [179]-180. [LC 86025319; ISN 0899302130] HF1410.5. I5716 1987 954

COUPLE-OWNED BUSINESS ENTERPRISES

In love and in business: how entrepreneurial couples are changing the rules of business and marriage. Sharon Nelton. New York: Wiley, c1986. x, 278 p. *Notes:* Includes index. Bibliography: p. 270-271. [LC 86015997; ISN 0471839493] HD62.27. N45 1986 955

COURTS

Judicial jeopardy: when business collides with the courts. Richard Neely. Reading, Mass.: Addison-Wesley, c1986. xviii, 189 p. *Notes:* Includes bibliographical references and index. [LC 86007945; ISN 0201057360; $19.95] KF8700. N44 1986 956

CREATIVE ABILITY

The creative attitude: learning to ask and answer the right questions. Roger Schank with Peter G. Childers. New York: London: Macmillan; Collier Macmillan, c1988. xii, 372 p. : ill. *Notes:* Includes index. [LC 87029717; ISN 0026071703] BF408. S35 1988 957

CREATIVE ABILITY IN BUSINESS

The care and feeding of ideas. Bill Backer. 1st ed. New York: Times Books, c1993. xii, 284 p. : ill. [LC 92038389; ISN 0812919696; $23.00 ($30.00 Can.)] HD38. B185 1993 +958

Conceptual toolmaking: expert systems of the mind. Jerry Rhodes; with a foreword by Ronnie Lessem. Oxford, UK; Cambridge, MA, USA: Blackwell, 1994. vii, 206 p. : ill. [LC 93048378; ISN 0631193219; $74.76] HD53. R46 1994 +959

The creative corporation. Karl Albrecht with Steven Albrecht. Homewood, Ill.: Dow Jones-Irwin, c1987. x, 218 p. *Notes:* Includes index. Bibliography: p. 209-210. [LC 86051668; ISN 0870949292; $21.95] HD53. A42 1987 960

The creative edge: fostering innovation where you work. William C. Miller. Reading, Mass.: Addison-Wesley, c1987. xix, 252 p. : ill. *Notes:* Includes index. Bibliography: p. 240-246. [LC 86014097; ISN 020115045X; $19.95] HD53. M55 1987 961

The creative mystique: how to manage it, nurture it, and make it pay. John M. Keil. New York: Wiley, c1985. ix, 231 p. *Notes:* Includes index. [LC 84027059; ISN 0471879614; $16.95]
  HD53. K45 1985 962

Creativity at work. Dorothy S.M. Yep. Burr Ridge Ill.: Irwin Professional Pub., Mirror Press, c1994. xviii, 86 p. : ill. [LC 93038859; ISBN 0786302232] HD53. Y47 1994 −963

Creativity in business. Michael Ray, Rochelle Myers. 1st ed. Garden City, N.Y.: Doubleday, 1986. xviii, 222 p. : ill. *Notes:* Includes bibliographical references and index. [LC 86006392; ISBN 0385233760; $16.95] HD53. R39 1986 964

The creativity infusion: how managers can start and sustain creativity and innovation. R. Donald Gamache and Robert Lawrence Kuhn. New York: Harper & Row, 1989. xii, 210 p. [LC 89027595; ISBN 0887303439; $24.95] HD53. G36 1989 965

Creativity: the art and science of business management. edited by A. Dale Timpe. New York, N.Y.: Facts on File Publications, c1987. xvi, 383 p. : ill. *Notes:* Includes index. Bibliography: p. 372-376. [LC 86029320; ISBN 0816014639; $24.95] HD53. C745 1987 966

Frontiers in creative and innovative management. edited by Robert Lawrenc Kuhn. Cambridge, Mass.: Ballinger, 1985. xxv, 391 p. : ill. *Notes:* "Volume 4 of Series on econometrics and management sciences." "Papers presented at the Second International Conference on Creative and Innovative Management, held in Miami on 7-9 November 1984. . . sponsored by the RGK Foundation and the IC² Institute of the University of Texas at Austin"—t.p. Verso. Includes bibliographical references and index. [LC 8501525; ISBN 088730057X] HD53. F76 1986 967

Generating creativity and innovation in large bureaucracies. edited by Robert Lawrence Kuhn. Westport, Conn.: Quorum Books, 1993. xv, 413 p. : ill. *Notes:* Includes bibliographical references and index. [LC 92015684; ISBN 0899307744] HD53. G46 1993 968

Managing creativity. John J. Kao. Englewood Cliffs, N.J.: Prentice Hall, c1991. xii, 210 p. : ill. *Notes:* Includes bibliographical references and index. [LC 90034673; ISBN 013556705X; $20.00] HD53. K36 1991 969

New directions in creative and innovative management: bridging theory and practice. edited by Yuji Ijiri, Robert Lawrence Kuhn. Cambridge, Mass.: Ballinger, 1988. xiv, 355 p. : ill. *Notes:* Papers presented at the Third International Conference on Creative and Innovative Management, held in Pittsburgh, Pa. June 2-3, 1987, sponsored by the IC² Institute of the University of Texas at Austin. Includes bibliographies and indexes. [LC 88021998; ISBN 088730365X] HD53. N49 1988 970

Pure instinct: business' untapped resource. Kathy Kolbe. New York: Times Books, Random House, c1993. xiv, 347 p. : ill. [LC 93008571; ISBN 0812920694; $25.00] HD53. K65 1993 +971

Winning the innovation game. Denis E. Waitley, Robert B. Tucker. Old Tappan, N.J.: F.H. Revell, c1986. 256 p. *Notes:* Includes index. Bibliography: p. 244-251. [LC 86017879; ISBN 0800714946; $15.95] HD53. W35 1986 972

CREDIT

The cashless society. by Robert A. Hendrickson. New York Dodd, Mead, 1972. 254 p. *Notes:* Bibliography: p. 247-254. [LC 72003928; ISBN 0396065384] HG355. H44 +973

Consumer and commercial credit management. Robert H. Cole. 9th ed. Homewood, Il: Irwin, c1992. xxiii, 536 p. : ill. *Notes:* Includes bibliographical references and index. [LC 91009218; ISBN 0256091870; $48.95] HG3751. C64 1992 974

Money of the mind: borrowing and lending in America from the Civil War to Michael Milken. James Grant. 1st ed. New York: Farrar Straus Giroux, c1992. viii, 513 p. : ill., ports. *Notes:* Includes bibliographical references (p. [475]-490) and index. [LC 92070747; ISBN 0374169799; $27.50] HG3754.5.U6 G72 1992 975

CRISIS MANAGEMENT

Crisis management: planning for the inevitable. Steven Fink. New York, NY: American Management Association, c1986. 245 p. : ill. *Notes:* Includes index. Bibliography: p. 226-234 [LC 85048220; ISBN 0814458599] HD49. F56 1986 976

Transforming the crisis-prone organization: preventing individual, organizational, and environmental tragedies. Thierry C. Pauchant, Ian I. Mitroff. 1st ed. San Francisco: Jossey-Bass Publishers, c1992. xviii, 255 p. : ill. *Notes:* Includes bibliographical references (p. 229-244) and index. [LC 91037910; ISBN 1555424074; $28.95] HD49. P38 1992 977

We're so big and powerful nothing bad can happen to us: an investigation of America's crisis prone corporations. by Ian I. Mitroff and Thierry (Terry) C. Pauchant. Secaucus, NJ: Carol Pub. Group, c1990. xvi, 208 p. *Notes:* "A Birch Lane Press book." Includes bibliographical references and index. [LC 90002378; ISBN 1559720514; $19.95] HD49. M57 1990 978

When it hits the fan: managing the nine crises of business. Gerald C. Meyers with John Holusha. Boston: Houghton Mifflin, 1986. xvi, 271 p. : ill. *Notes:* Includes index. [LC 86010433; ISN 0395411718; $17.95]   HD49. M48 1986   979

CRITICAL PATH ANALYSIS

The new critical path method: the state-of-the-art in project modeling and time reserve management. Dennis H. Busch. Chicago, Ill.: Probus Pub. Co., c1991. iv, 459 p. : ill. *Notes:* Includes index. [LC 90021309; ISN 1557381178; $55.00]   TS158. B87 1991   980

CUSTOMER RELATIONS

Aftermarketing: how to keep customers for life through relationship marketing. Terry G. Vavra. Homewood, Ill.: Business One Irwin, c1992. xv, 292 p. : ill. *Notes:* Includes bibliographical references (p. 276-279) and index. *Contents:* A change of orientation: retention instead of conquest—Appendix 1. A survey of the top 100 advertisers to assess attitudes about retention versus conquest marketing—What you need to know: collecting the right information—Appendix 2. Suppliers of external databases and mass-compiled databases—The value of a customer information file—Blueprinting customer contact opportunities—Encouraging an informal dialogue with customers—Appendix 5. Analysis of customer communications—Establishing a formal dialogue: follow-up after sale—Appendix 6. Who's satisfying their customers—Maintaining customer contact: communication programs—Appendix 7. Sponsorships of special events by U.S. and international marketers—What to do when you fail: lost customer programs—Building an internal organization to support aftermarketing—Quality, servicing, and aftermarketing—the components of relationship marketing—Appendix 10. How to determine if your business or organization is conquest or retention oriented. [LC 92001295; ISN 1556236050]
   HF5415.5. V38 1992   +981

Customer bonding. Richard Cross and Janet Smith. Lincolnwood, Ill.: NTC Business Books, c1995. xix, 254 p. : ill. *Notes:* Includes bibliographical references and index. [LC 94011504; ISN 0844233188; $25.95]   HF5415.5. C8 1995   +982

The customer-driven company: moving from talk to action. Richard C. Whiteley. Reading, Mass.: Addison-Wesley, c1991. 308 p. : ill. *Notes:* Includes bibliographical references and index. [LC 90023765; ISN 0201570904; $21.95 ($24.95 Can.)]   HF5415.5. W56 1991   983

CUSTOMER SERVICE

Creating a customer-centered culture: leadership in quality, innovation, and speed. Robin L. Lawton. Milwaukee, Wis.: ASQC Quality Press, c1993. xix, 177 p. : ill. *Notes:* Includes bibliographical references (p. [165]-168) and index. [LC 93015572; ISN 0873891511]   HF5415.5. L39 1993   +984

Creating value for customers: designing and implementing a total corporate strategy. by William A. Band. New York: Wiley, c1991. xi, 340 p. *Notes:* Includes bibliographical references and index. [LC 90048557; ISN 0471525936; $29.95]   HF5415.5. B36 1991   985

Customers as partners: building relationships that last. Chip R. Bell. 1st ed. San Francisco: Berrett-Koehler, c1994. xv, 235 p. *Notes:* Includes bibliographical references (p. 219-225) and index. [LC 94016999; ISN 1881052540; $24.95]   HF5415.5. B434 1994   +986

Keeping customers. edited, with an introduction by John J. Sviokla and Benson P. Shapiro. Boston, MA: Harvard Business School Press, c1993. xx, 384 p. : ill. *Notes:* "A Harvard Business Review book." Articles originally published in the Harvard Business Review, 1968-1992. Companion volume to: Seeking customers. Includes bibliographical references and index. [LC 92039229; ISN 0875843336; $29.95]   HF5415.5. K45 1993   987

Managing service as a strategic profit center. Donald F. Blumberg. New York: McGraw-Hill, c1991. vii, 232 p. : ill. *Notes:* Includes bibliographical references (p. 226) and index. [LC 90005797; ISN 0070061890; $22.50]   HF5415.5. B57 1991   988

Managing to keep the customer: how to achieve and maintain superior customer service throughout the organization. Rev. ed. / Robert L. Desatnick, Denis H. Detzel. San Francisco: Jossey-Bass Publishers, c1993. xxi, 289 p. : ill. *Notes:* Includes bibliographical references (p. 277-281) and index. [LC 93006842; ISN 1555424155]   HF5415.5. D47 1993   +989

The only thing that matters: bringing the power of the customer into the center of your business. Karl Albrecht. 1st ed. New York: HarperBusiness, c1992. xii, 240 p. : ill. *Notes:* Includes bibliographical references (p. 231-232) and index. [LC 91038324; ISN 0887305415; $23.00 ($31.00 Can.)]
    HF5415.5. A425 1992   990

Practical handbook of distribution/customer service. Warren Blanding. 1st ed. Washington: Traffic Service Corporation, c1985. xx, 564 p. : ill. *Notes:* Includes index. Bibliography: p. 554-556. [LC 85050345; ISN 0874080339]   HF5415.5. B52   991

Product plus: how product + service = competitive advantage. Christopher Lovelock. New York: McGraw-Hill, c1994. xiv, 382 p. : ill. *Notes:* Includes bibliographical references (p. 360-373) and index. [LC 93028217; ISN 0070387982; $24.95]   HF5415.5. L68 1994   +992

Quality management in service organizations: an interpretation of the service quality phenomenon and a synthesis of international research. Evert Gummesson. Stockholm?: ISQA, c1993. xii, 274 p. : ill. *Notes:* Includes bibliographical references (p. 241-255) and index.]   HF5415.5. G85 1993   993

The real heroes of business—and not a CEO among them. Bill Fromm and Len Schlesinger. 1st ed. New York: Currency/Doubleday, 1994. xxiv, 337 p. : ill. *Notes:* "World-class frontline service workers: How do you find them? Train them? Manage them? Retain them?" "A Currency book." Includes index. [LC 93039817; ISN 0385425554]   HF5415.5. F76 1994   +994

The service advantage: how to identify and fulfill customer needs. Karl Albrecht, Lawrence J. Bradford. Homewood, Ill.: Dow Jones-Irwin, c1990. ix, 240 p. : ill. *Notes:* Includes bibliographical references. [LC 89016953; ISN 1556232470; $24.95]   HF5415.5. A43 1990   995

Service breakthroughs: changing the rules of the game. James L. Heskett, W. Earl Sasser, Jr., Christopher W.L. Hart. New York: London: Free Press; Collier Macmillan, 1990. xii, 306 p. : ill. *Notes:* Includes bibliographical references. [LC 90034202; ISN 0029146755; $27.95]   HF5415. H43 1990   996

The service era: leadership in a global environment. Franco D'Egidio. Cambridge, Mass.: Productivity Press, c1990. xv, 155 p. : ill. *Notes:* Translation of: Il global service management. Includes bibliographical references (p. 151-153). [LC 90041842; ISN 0915299682; $34.95]
    HF5415.5. D4413 1990   997

Service quality: new directions in theory and practice. editors, Roland T. Rust, Richard L. Oliver. Thousand Oaks, Calif.: Sage Publications, c1994. ix, 289 p. : ill. *Notes:* Includes bibliographical references and indexes. *Contents:* Service quality: insights and managerial implications from the frontier / Roland T. Rust, Richard L. Oliver—The nature of customer value: an axiology of services in the consumption experience / Morris B. Holbrook—Encounter satisfaction versus overall satisfaction versus quality: the customer's voice / Mary Jo Bitner, Amy R. Hubbert—Price and advertising as market signals for service quality / Jan-Benedict E.M. Steenkamp, Donna L. Hoffman—How consumers predict service quality: what do they expect? / Valerie S. Folkes—Managing services when the service is a performance / John Deighton—Beyond smiling: social support and service quality / Mara B. Adelman, Aaron Ahuvia, Cathy Goodwin—Linking customer satisfaction to service operations and outcomes / Ruth N. Bolton, James H. Drew—On the measurement of perceived service quality: a conjoint analysis approach / Wayne S. DeSarbo. . . [et al.]—Explanations for the growth of services / Steven M. Shugan—A customer satisfaction research prospectus / Eugene W. Anderson, Claes Fornell. [LC 93031228; ISN 0803949200; $21.95]   HF5415.5. S468 1994   +998

The service/quality solution: using service management to gain competitive advantage. David A. Collier. Milwaukee: Burr Ridge, Ill.: ASQC Quality Press; Irwin, c1994. xiv, 310 p. : ill. *Notes:* Includes bibliographical references and index. [LC 93041421; ISN 1556237537]
    HF5415.5. C62 1994   +999

When America does it right: case studies in service quality. Jay W. Spechler. Norcross, Ga.: Industrial Engineering and Management Press, c1988. xii, 599 p. : ill. *Notes:* Includes bibliographies and index. [LC 88013300; ISN 0898061008; $49.95 ($34.95 to members)]   HF5415.5. S625 1988   1000

DATABASE MANAGEMENT

An introduction to database systems. C.J. Date. 4th ed. Reading, Mass.: Addison-Wesley Pub. Co., c1986- v.: ill. (Addison-Wesley systems programming series) *Notes:* Includes bibliographies and index. [LC 85001422; ISN 0201142015; $31.95]   QA76.9.D3 D37 1986   1001

An introduction to database systems. C.J. Date. 5th ed., repr. with corrections. Reading, Mass.: Addison-Wesley, 1991- v.: ill. *Notes:* Includes bibliographical references and index. [LC 90000001; ISN 0201513811]   QA76.9.D3 D37 1991   1002

DATAFLEX CORPORATION

How to make a buck and still be a decent human being: a week with Rick Rose at Dataflex. Richard C. Rose and Echo Montgomery Garrett. 1st ed. New York: HarperBusiness, c1992. xxiv, 246 p. : ill. *Notes:* Includes index. [LC 92052611; ISN 0887305849; $20.00 ($26.76 Can.)]
    HD9696.C64 D377 1992   1003

DEBTS, EXTERNAL

Banks, borrowers, and the establishment: a revisionist account of the international debt crisis. Karin Lissakers. New York, N.Y.: BasicBooks, c1991. xii, 308 p. *Notes:* Includes bibliographical references and index. [LC 91070406; ISN 0465006051; $23.00 USA ($31.00 CAN)]
    HJ8046. L57 1991   1004

Coping is not enough!: the international debt crisis and the roles of the World Bank and International Monetary Fund. Morris Miller. Homewood, Ill.: Dow Jones-Irwin, c1986. xiii, 268 p. : ill. *Notes:* Includes bibliographical references and index. [LC 86071358; ISN 0870949330]
    HJ8899. M55 1986   1005

Debt and danger: the world financial crisis. by Harold Lever and Christopher Huhne. 1st American ed. Boston: Atlantic Monthly Press, c1986. xii, 160 p. : ill. *Notes:* Includes bibliographical references and index. [LC 86070573; ISN 087113067X]
    HG3891.5. L48   1006

Till debt do us part: who wins, who loses, and who pays for the international debt crisis. Alfred J. Watkins. Lanham, MD: Roosevelt Center for American Policy Studies: University Press of America, c1986. xvi, 87 p. *Notes:* Includes bibliographical references. [LC 85040999; ISN 0819151769; ISN 0819151750]
    HG3891.5. W27   1007

DEBTS, PUBLIC

The debt and the deficit: false alarms/real possibilities. Robert Heilbroner and Peter Bernstein. 1st ed. New York: Norton, c1989. 144 p. *Notes:* Includes index. Bibliography: p. 139-140. [LC 89003260; ISN 039302752X; ISN 0393306119; $12.95]
    HJ8119. H43 1989   1008

DECENTRALIZATION IN MANAGEMENT

Demass: transforming the dinosaur corporation. M.M. Stuckey; publisher's message by Norman Bodek. Cambridge, Mass.: Productivity Press, c1993. xxiii, 259 p. : ill. *Notes:* Includes bibliographical references (p. 239-249) and index. [LC 92028998; ISN 1563270420; $24.95]
    HD50. S783 1993   1009

Making the most of entrepreneurial management: decentralizing America's corporations. Robert E. Levinson. 1st AMACOM paperback ed. New York: AMACOM, 1986, c1983. viii, 196 p. *Notes:* Rev. ed. of: The decentralized company. c1983. Includes bibliographical references and index. [LC 85030615; ISN 0814476562]
    HD50. L483 1986   1010

Memoirs of a recovering autocrat: revealing insights for managing the autocrat in all of us. Richard W. Hallstein. San Francisco: Berrett-Koehler, c1992. xii, 156 p. : port *Notes:* Includes index. [LC 93008187; ISN 1881052354; $17.95]
    HD50. H35 1992   +1011

DECISION SUPPORT SYSTEMS

Decision support and executive information systems. edited by Paul Gray. Englewood Cliffs, N.J.: Prentice Hall, c1994. x, 469 p. : ill. *Notes:* A selection of papers from International Conferences on Decision Support Systems, DSS-81—DSS-92. Includes bibliographical references and index. [LC 93001929; ISN 0132357895; $35.00]
    HD30.213. D43 1994   +1012

Executive information systems and decision support. edited by Clive Holtham. 1st ed. London; New York: Chapman & Hall, 1992. viii, 246 p. : ill. *Notes:* Includes bibliographhical references. [LC 92026880; ISN 0442315708]
    HD30.23. E94 1992   +1013

DECISION-MAKING

Charting the corporate mind: graphic solutions to business conflicts. Charles Hampden-Turner. New York: London: Free Press; Collier Macmillan, c1990. xiii, 240 p. : ill. *Notes:* Includes bibliographical references. [LC 89025437; ISN 0029137063; $24.95]   HD30.23. H34 1990   1014

Choices: an introduction to decision theory. Michael D. Resnik. Minneapolis: University of Minnesota Press, c1987. xiii, 221 p. : ill. *Notes:* Includes index. Bibliography: p. 215-216. [LC 86011307; ISN 0816614393; ISN 0816614407; $25.00; $10.95]   T57.95. R45 1987   1015

Crucial decisions: leadership in policymaking and crisis management. Irving L. Janis. New York: London: Free Press; Collier MacMillan, 1989. xi, 388 p. : ill. *Notes:* Includes indexes. Bibliography: p. 353-371. [LC 88021292; ISN 0029161614; $27.95]   HD30.23. J37 1989   1016

Decision analysis and behavioral research. Detlov von Winterfeldt, Ward Edwards. Cambridge Cambridgeshire; New York: Cambridge University Press, 1986. xv, 604 p. : ill. *Notes:* Includes indexes. Bibliography: p. 575-594. [LC 85031393; ISN 052125308X; ISN 0521273048]   BF441. V66 1986   1017

Decision sciences: an integrative perspective. Paul R. Kleindorfer, Howard C. Kunreuther, Paul J.H. Schoemaker. Cambridge, England; New York, N.Y.: Cambridge University Press, 1993. ix, 470 p. : ill. *Notes:* Includes bibliographical references (p. [429]-459) and index. [LC 92045149; ISN 0521338123]   HD30.23. K46 1993   +1018

Decisions and organizations. James G. March. New York, N.Y.: Blackwell, 1988. vi, 458 p. : ill. *Notes:* Collection of previously published essays. Includes bibliographies and index. [LC 87029362; ISN 063115812X; $49.95]   HD30.23. M366 1988   1019

Evaluating complex business reports: a guide for executives. Eli P. Cox, III. Homewood, Ill.: Dow Jones-Irwin, c1984. viii, 86 p. : ill. *Notes:* Includes index. Bibliography: p. 81-84. [LC 83073363; ISN 0870944312]   HD30.23. C69 1984   1020

Hearing the voice of the market: competitive advantage through creative use of market information. Vincent P. Barabba and Gerald Zaltman. Boston, Mass.: Harvard Business School Press, c1991. xiv, 294 p. : ill. *Notes:* Includes bibliographical references and index. [LC 90044491; ISN 0875842410; $29.95]   HD30.23. B358 1991   +1021

Judgement and choice: the psychology of decision. Robin M. Hogarth. 2nd ed. Chichester West Sussex; New York: Wiley, c1987. xii, 311 p. : ill. *Notes:* "A Wiley-Interscience publication." Includes index. Bibliography: p. 286-305. [LC 86032481; ISN 0471914797; $14.00]   BF448. H64 1987   1022

Judgment calls: high-stakes decisions in a risky world. John C. Mowen. New York: Simon & Schuster, c1993. 303 p. *Notes:* Includes index. [LC 93011011; ISN 0671728385]   HD30.28. M69 1993   +1023

A logic for strategy. Daniel R. Gilbert, Jr... et al. Cambridge, Mass.: Ballinger, 1988. xv, 172 p. : ill. *Notes:* Includes bibliographies and index. [LC 88011972; ISN 088730205X; ISN 088730222X]   HD30.23. L64 1988   1024

Making tough decisions: tactics for improving managerial decision making. by Paul C. Nutt. 1st ed. San Francisco: Jossey-Bass Publishers, 1989. xxiii, 611 p. : ill. *Notes:* Includes index. Bibliography: p. 585-602. [LC 88046079; ISN 1555421385]   HD30.23. N88 1989   1025

The managerial decision-making process. E. Frank Harrison. 3rd ed. Boston: Houghton Mifflin Co., c1987. xiii, 542 p. : ill. *Notes:* Includes index. Bibliography: p. 500-527. [LC 86081982; ISN 039542481X; $46.36]   HD30.23. H368 1987   1026

Managerial decisions under uncertainty: an introduction to the analysis of decision making. Bruce F. Baird. New York: Wiley, c1989. xiii, 530 p. : ill. *Notes:* "A Wiley-Interscience publication." Includes index. Includes bibliographical references. [LC 88033842; ISN 0471858919; $40.45]   HD30.23. B32 1989   1027

Managing with power: politics and influence in organizations. Jeffrey Pfeffer. Boston, Mass.: Harvard Business School Press, c1992. viii, 391 p. *Notes:* Includes bibliographical references (p. 367-377) and index. [LC 91026237; ISN 087584314X]   HD30.23. P47 1992   1028

Managing with style: a guide to understanding, assessing, and improving decision making. Alan J. Rowe, Richard O. Mason. 1st ed. San Francisco: Jossey-Bass, 1987. xviii, 225 p. (Jossey-Bass management series) *Notes:* Includes index. Bibliography: p. 207-218. [LC 87045570; ISN 1555420745]   HD30.28. R676 1987   1029

Modern decision making: a guide to modeling with decision support systems. Samuel E. Bodily. New York: McGraw-Hill, c1985. xi, 300 p. : ill. *Notes:* Includes index. Bibliography: p. 285-286. [LC 84012623; ISN 0070063605; $26.95]   HD30.23. B645 1985   1030

The new science of management decision. Herbert A. Simon. Rev. ed. Englewood Cliffs, N.J.: Prentice-Hall, c1977. xi, 175 p. *Notes:* Edition of 1965 published under title: The shape of automation for men and management. Includes bibliographical references and index. [LC 76040414; ISN 0136161448] HD30.23. S49 1977 +1031

The organization game: an interactive business game where you make or break the company. by Craig R. Hickman. Englewood Cliffs, N.J.: Prentice Hall, c1994. xvi, 354 p. : ill. [LC 94005924; ISN 0130390666] HD30.23. H533 1994 +1032

Organizational strategy and change. edited by Johannes M. Pennings, and associates. 1st ed. San Francisco: Jossey-Bass, 1985. xxi, 563 p. (The Jossey-Bass management series) (The Jossey-Bass social and behavioral science series) *Notes:* Includes indexes. Bibliography: p. 495-538. [LC 84047994; ISN 087589626X] HD30.23. O75 1985 1033

A primer on decision making: how decisions happen. James G. March, with the assistance of Chip Heath. New York: Toronto: New York: Free Press; Maxwell Macmillan Canada; Maxwell Macmillan International, c1994. ix, 289 p. : ill. *Notes:* Includes bibliographical references (p. 275-281) and index. [LC 94004414; ISN 0029200350; $29.95] HD30.23. M368 1994 +1034

The professional decision-thinker: America's new management and education priority. Ben Heirs with Peter Farrell. New York: Dodd Mead, c1987. xiv, 294 *Notes:* Originally published: Great Britain: Sidgwick & Jackson, 1986. Bibliography: p. [293]-294. [LC 87015575; ISN 0396092039; $24.95] HD30.23. H432 1987 1035

Quantitative decision making for business. Gilbert Gordon, Israel Pressman, Sanford Cohen. 3rd ed. Englewood Cliffs, NJ: Prentice Hall, c1990. xii, 670 p. : ill. *Notes:* Includes bibliographical references and index. [LC 89036565; ISN 0137467931; $54.29] HD30.23. G67 1990 1036

Quantitative methods for business decisions: with cases. Lawrence L. Lapin. 4th ed. San Diego: Harcourt Brace Jovanovich, c1988. xvi, 847 p. *Notes:* Includes index. Bibliography: p. 803-808. [LC 87081158; ISN 0155743279; $38.40] HD30.23. L36 1988 1037

Research-based decisions. Charles H. Fay, Marc J. Wallace, Jr. 1st ed. New York: Random House, 1987. xi, 399 p. : ill. *Notes:* Includes bibliographies and index. [LC 86011925; ISN 0394328698; $28.00] HD30.23. F39 1987 1038

Strategy and choice. edited by Richard J. Zeckhauser. Cambridge, Mass.: MIT Press, c1991. viii, 402 p. : ill. *Notes:* Includes bibliographical references and index. *Contents:* Coping with common errors in rational decision making / Howard Raiffa. [LC 91015837; ISN 0262240335; $35.00] HD30.23. S75 1991 1039

Top decisions: strategic decision-making in organizations. David J. Hickson...et al. 1st ed. San Francisco: Jossey-Bass Publishers, 1986. xxiii, 290 p. : ill. (The Jossey-Bass management series) *Notes:* Based on studies carried out at the Bradford Management Centre in Britain, 1970-1984. Includes indexes. Bibliography: p. [273]-281. [LC 85010071; ISN 0875896537] HD30.23. T67 1986 1040

Value-focused thinking. Ralph L. Keeney. Cambridge, Mass.: Harvard University Press, 1992. xvi, 416 p. *Notes:* Includes bibliographical references and index. [LC 91031496; ISN 0674931971; $35.00] HD30.23. K354 1992 1041

Whatever it takes: decision makers at work. Morgan W. McCall, Robert E. Kaplan. Englewood Cliffs, N.J.: Prentice-Hall, c1985. xx, 132 p. : ill. *Notes:* Includes indexes. Bibliography: p. 119-123. [LC 84011773; ISN 0139520864; $21.00] HD30.23. M39 1985 1042

DEFENSE INDUSTRIES

The price of peace: the future of defense industry and high technology in a post-cold war world. William H. Gregory. New York: Toronto: New York: Lexington Books; Maxwell Macmillan Canada; Maxwell Macmillan International, c1993. x, 225 p. *Notes:* Includes bibliographical references (p. [211]-215) and index. [LC 92029050; ISN 0669279501; $24.95] HD9743.U6 G7 1993 1043

DEMING, W. EDWARDS

The Deming guide to quality and competitive position. Howard S. Gitlow, Shelly J. Gitlow. Englewood Cliffs, N.J.: Prentice-Hall, c1987. vii, 247 p. *Notes:* Bibliography: p. 244-247. [LC 86018762; ISN 0131984411] HD38.D439 G58 1987 1044

Deming management at work. Mary Walton. New York: G.P. Putnam's, c1990. 249 p. : ill. *Notes:* Includes index. [LC 90038289; ISN 039913557X; $21.95] HD38.D439 W34 1990 1045

The Deming management method. by Mary Walton; foreword by W. Edwards Deming. 1st ed. New York: Dodd, Mead, c1986. xviii, 262 p. : ill. *Notes:* Includes index. Bibliography: p. 251-256. [LC 86006187; ISN 0396086837]   HD38.D439 W35 1986   1046

DEMOCRACY

A world fit for people: thinkers from many countries address the political, economic, and social problems of our time. edited by Üner Kirdar and Leonard Silk. New York: New York University Press, c1994. xxii, 481 p. *Notes:* United Nations Development Programme Publications, UN sales no. E.93.III.B.2. Includes bibliographical references. [LC 93008945; ISN 0814746489; $50.00]   JC423. W64 1994   +1047

DEPARTMENT STORES

Land of desire: merchants, power, and the rise of a new American culture. William Leach. 1st ed. New York: Pantheon Books, c1993. xvii, 510 p. ill. *Notes:* Includes bibliographical references (p. [391]-486) and index. [LC 92050785; ISN 0394543505; $30.00]   HF5465.U63 L4 1993   +1048

DEPRECIATION

Handbook of depreciation methods, formulas, and tables. James M. Johnson. Englewood Cliffs, N.J.: Prentice-Hall, c1981. 714 p. *Notes:* Includes index. [LC 80022258; ISN 0133773906]   HF5681.D5 J59 1981   1049

DEREGULATION

The deregulated society. Larry N. Gerston, Cynthia Fraleigh, Robert Schwab. Pacific Grove, Calif.: Brooks/Cole Pub. Co., c1988. xvii, 244 p. : ill. *Notes:* Includes bibliographies and index. [LC 87005116; ISN 0534082084; $10.00]   HD3616.U47 G47 1988   1050

DESIGN

Design for society. Nigel Whiteley. London: Seattle, Wash.: Reaktion Books; Distributed in USA and Canada by the University of Washington Press, 1993. ix, 182 p. : ill. *Notes:* Includes bibliographical references (p. [177]-180) and index. [LC 94016675; ISN 0948462477]   TS171. W44 1993   +1051

DESIGN, INDUSTRIAL

The design dimension: product strategy and the challenge of global marketing. Christopher Lorenz. New York, N.Y.: Blackwell, 1986. xi, 167 p. : ill. *Notes:* Includes index. Bibliography: p. [156]-159. [LC 85015830; ISN 0631137475; $17.95]   TS171. L67 1986   1052

Design management: a handbook of issues and methods. edited by Mark Oakley; advisory editors Brigitte Borja de Mozota, Colin Clipson. Cambridge, MA: Blackwell Reference, 1990. x, 446 p. : ill. *Notes:* Includes bibliographical references. [LC 89037145; ISN 0631154043; $64.95]   TS171.4. D483 1990   1053

Green gold: Japan, Germany, the United States, and the race for environmental technology. Curtis Moore and Alan Miller. Boston: Beacon Press, c1994. viii, 279 p. *Notes:* Includes bibliographical references (p. 223-264) and index. [LC 93049354; ISN 0807085308; $25.00]   TS171.4. M66 1994   +1054

Industrial design: reflection of a century. edited by Jocelyn de Noblet. Paris: Flammarion/APCI, c1993. 431 p. : ill. (some col.) *Notes:* "Publication sponsored by: A.F.A.A., Association Française d'Action Artistique, Ministère des Affaires Etrangères, Ministère de la Culture et de la Francophonie, Délégation aux Arts Plastiques (FIACRE)." "Published in conjunction with the exhibition Design, miroir du siècle at the Grand Palais, Paris, 19 May to 25 July 1993"—T.p. verso. Published in French under the title: Design, miroir du siècle. Contents translated from French, Italian, German. Includes bibliographical references (p. 426) and index.; ISN 2080135392]
  TS171.4. I573 1993 +1055

Product assurance principles: integrating design assurance and quality assurance. Eugene R. Carrubba, Ronald D. Gordon. New York: McGraw-Hill, c1988. viii, 278 p. : ill. *Notes:* Sponsored by the American Society for Quality Control. Bibliography: p. 269-272. Includes index. [LC 87016876; ISN 0070101485]
  TS171.4. C38 1988 1056

DEUTSCHE BUNDESBANK

The most powerful bank: inside Germany's Bundesbank. David Marsh. 1st U.S. ed. New York: Times Books, 1993, c1992. xx, 331 p. *Notes:* Includes bibliographical references and index. [LC 92056830; ISN 0812921585; $25.00]
  HG3054. M37 1993 +1057

DEVELOPING COUNTRIES—ECONOMIC CONDITIONS

Economic growth in the Third World, 1850-1980. Lloyd G. Reynolds. New Haven: Yale University Press, c1985. xii, 469 p. (A Publication of the Economic Growth Center, Yale University) *Notes:* Includes index. Bibliography: p. 441-456. [LC 84019542; ISN 0300032552]   HC59.7. R475 1985 1058

DEVELOPING COUNTRIES—ECONOMIC POLICY

Economics of development. Malcolm Gillis. . . et al. 2nd ed. New York: Norton, c1987. xv, 623 p. : ill. *Notes:* Includes index. Bibliography: p. [587]-610. [LC 87005701; ISN 0393955486; $29.95]
  HC59.7. E314 1987 1059

DIAMOND MINES AND MINING

The last empire: De Beers, diamonds, and the world. Stefan Kanfer. 1st ed. New York: Farrar Straus Giroux, 1993. ix, 409 p. : ill., maps *Notes:* Includes bibliographical references and index. [LC 92035976; ISN 0374152071; $25.00]   HD9677.S64 D42 1993 +1060

DIGITAL COMMUNICATIONS

Computers and communications: a vision of C&C. Kōji Kobayashi. Cambridge, Mass.: MIT Press, c1986. xvi, 190 p. : ill. *Notes:* Translation of: C&C modern communications. Bibliography: p. [187]-190. [LC 85024144; ISN 026211111X]   TK5103.7. K6313 1986 1061

DIGITAL TELEVISION

Life after television. by George Gilder. New York: W.W. Norton, 1992. 126 p. *Notes:* Originally published: Knoxville, Tenn.: Whittle Direct Books, 1990. [LC 91046205; ISN 0393033856; $14.95]
  TK6678. G55 1992 1062

DIRECT MARKETING

The business-to-business direct marketing handbook. Roy G. Ljungren. New York: American Management Association, c1989. vi, 456 p. : ill. *Notes:* Includes index. [LC 88047707; ISN 0814458343; $65.00]
  HF5415.126. L57 1989 1063

Direct marketing: strategy, planning, execution. Edward L. Nash. 2nd ed. New York: McGraw-Hill, c1986. xxiii, 445 p. : ill. *Notes:* Includes index. [LC 85015188; ISN 0070460248]
HF5415.126. N37 1986   1064

Power direct marketing: how to make it work for you. "Rocket" Ray Jutkins. Lincolnwood, Ill., USA: NTC Business Books, c1994. xxi, 314 p. : ill. *Notes:* Includes bibliographical references (p. 305-306) and index. [LC 92034248; ISN 0844232548; $39.95]
HF5415.126. J874 1994   +1065

Successful direct marketing methods. Bob Stone. 5th ed. Lincolnwood, Ill.: NTC Business Books, c1994. xvii, 654 p. : ill. *Notes:* Includes index. [LC 93006716; ISN 0844235105; $39.95]
HF5415.126. S757 1994   +1066

DIRECT SELLING

The direct marketing handbook. Edward L. Nash, editor in chief. 2nd ed. New York: McGraw-Hill, c1992. xxxiii, 827 p. : ill. *Notes:* Includes bibliographical references index. [LC 91025694; ISN 0070460272; $69.95]
HF5438.25. D555 1992   1067

DIRECTORS OF CORPORATIONS

Behind the boardroom door. Robert Kirk Mueller; illustrated by Robert Manley. 1st ed. New York: Crown Publishers, c1984. 242 p. : ill. *Notes:* Includes bibliographical references and index. [LC 83025173; ISN 0517552558]
HD2745. M79 1984   1068

Boards of directors and the privately owned firm: a guide for owners, officers, and directors. Roger H. Ford. New York: Quorum Books, 1992. xiv, 210 p. *Notes:* Includes bibliographical references (p. [201]-205) and indexes. [LC 91024854; ISN 0899305679]
HD2745. F49 1992   1069

Boards of directors: their changing roles, structure, and information needs. Charles N. Waldo. Westport, Conn.: Quorum Books, c1985. xii, 213 p. : ill. *Notes:* Includes bibliographical references and index. [LC 84026455; ISN 0899300618]
HD2745. W25 1985   1070

Boards that make a difference: a new design for leadership in nonprofit and public organizations. John Carver. 1st ed. San Francisco: Jossey-Bass Publishers, 1990. xxii, 242 p. *Notes:* Bibliography: p. 229-234. [LC 89077419; ISN 1555422314; $22.95]
HD2745. C37 1990   1071

Creating effective boards for private enterprises: meeting the challenges of continuity and competition. John L. Ward. 1st ed. San Francisco: Jossey-Bass Publishers, 1991. xvii, 261 p. *Notes:* Includes bibliographical references (p. 255-256) and index. [LC 91008358; ISN 1555423523; $25.95]
HD2745. W35 1991   1072

The essential guide to effective corporate board committees. Louis Braiotta, Jr., A.A. Sommer, Jr. Englewood Cliffs, NJ: Prentice-Hall, 1987. xiii, 175 p. *Notes:* Includes bibliographies and indexes. [LC 87002265; ISN 0132861399]
HD2745. B63 1987   1073

Information for corporate directors: the role of the board in the management process. by John D. Aram, Scott S. Cowen. New York, N.Y.: National Association of Accountants, c1983. vii, 119 p. : ill. *Notes:* "A study carried out on behalf of the National Association of Accountants..." Includes bibliographical references. [LC 83209394; ISN 0866410953]
HD2745. A72 1983   1074

The new elite: Britain's top chief executives. Walter Goldsmith and Berry Ritchie; line drawings by Matthew Ritchie. London: Weidenfeld and Nicolson, 1987. ix, 179 p. : ports.; ISN 0297789902]
HD38.25.G73 G64 1987   1075

On the board. Geoffrey Mills. 2nd ed. London; Boston: G. Allen & Unwin, c1985. viii, 290 p. : ill. *Notes:* Includes index. Bibliography: p. [280]-283. [LC 85018666; ISN 0046582509]
HD2745. M54 1985   1076

On the edge of the organisation: the role of the outside director. Anne Spencer. Chichester; New York: Wiley, c1983. xii, 137 p. *Notes:* Includes index. Bibliography: p. 131-134. [LC 82011135; ISN 0471900184; $35.00]
HD2745. S67 1983   1077

Pawns or potentates: the reality of America's corporate boards. Jay W. Lorsch with Elizabeth MacIver. Boston, Mass.: Harvard Business School Press, c1989. 200 p. *Notes:* Includes bibliographical references. [LC 89020036; ISN 087584216X]
HD2745. L56 1989   1078

DISCLOSURE IN ACCOUNTING

A guide to financial statement disclosures. Paul Munter and Thomas A. Ratcliffe. New York: Quorum Books, 1986. ix, 273 p. : ill. *Notes:* Includes index. Bibliography: p. 267-270. [LC 85009603; ISN 0899300324]   HF5658. M86 1986   1079

DISCRIMINATION IN EMPLOYMENT

Equal opportunity in business. Cambridge, Mass.: Harvard Business Review, 1975. 168 p. : ill. (Reprint series—Harvard Business Review; no. 21132) (A Harvard Business Review reprint series) *Notes:* Includes bibliographical references.]   HD4903.5.U58 H34   +1080

Gender & racial inequality at work: the sources and consequences of job segregation. Donald Tomaskovic-Devey. Ithaca, N.Y.: ILR Press, c1993. xi, 212 p. : ill. *Notes:* Includes bibliographical references (p. [196]-205) and index. [LC 93016551; ISN 0875463053]   HD4903.5.U58 T66 1993   +1081

DISSERTATIONS, ACADEMIC

A manual for writers of term papers, theses, and dissertations. Kate L. Turabian. 5th ed. / revised and expanded by Bonnie Birtwistle Honigsblum. Chicago: University of Chicago Press, 1987. ix, 300 p. (Chicago guides to writing, editing, and publishing) *Notes:* Includes index. Bibliography: p. 281-282. [LC 86019128; ISN 0226816249; ISN 0226816257]   PE1408. T87 1987   1082

DIVERSIFICATION IN INDUSTRY

Diversification through acquisition: strategies for creating economic value. Malcolm S. Salter, Wolf A. Weinhold. New York: London: Pree Press; Macmillan, c1979., xvi, 330 p. : ill. *Notes:* Includes index. Bibliography: p. 309-320. [LC 79007370; ISN 0029280206]   HD38. S31374 1979   1083

Downscoping: how to tame the diversified firm. by Robert E. Hoskisson and Michael A. Hitt. New York: Oxford University Press, 1994. vii, 212 p. : ill. *Notes:* Includes bibliographical references and indexes. [LC 93021408; ISN 0195078438; $24.95]   HD2756. H67 1994   +1084

DOW JONES NEWS/RETRIEVAL (INFORMATION RETRIEVAL SYSTEM)

How to get the most out of Dow Jones News/Retrieval. Charles Bowen and David Peyton. Toronto; New York: Bantam Books, c1986. xix, 345 p. *Notes:* "Bantam computer books." Includes index.; ISN 0553343270; $19.95]   HF5343. B68 1986   1085

DOW JONES-IRWIN

Dow Jones industrial average: history and role in an investment strategy. Richard J. Stillman. Homewood, Ill.: Dow Jones-Irwin, 1986. xvi, 217 p. : ill., ports., charts, facsims. *Notes:* Includes index. Bibliography: p. 191-198. [LC 85073873; ISN 0870945866; $19.95]   HG4910. S76   1086

DREXEL BURNHAM LAMBERT INCORPORATED

April fools: an insider's account of the rise and collapse of Drexel Burnham. by Dan G. Stone. New York: D.I. Fine, c1990. xv, 249 p., [8] p. of plates: ill. *Notes:* Includes index. [LC 90055339; ISN 1556112289; $19.95]   HG4928.5. S76 1990   1087

DRIED MILK INDUSTRY

The politics of baby foods: successful challenges to an international marketing strategy. Andrew Chetley. New York: St. Martin's Press, 1986. xv, 189 p. *Notes:* Includes index. Bibliography: p. [166]-184. [LC 85030363; ISN 0312626339; $25.00]   HD9282.A2 C45 1986   1088

DRUCKER, PETER FERDINAND

Adventures of a bystander. Peter F. Drucker. 1st ed. New York: Harper & Row, c1979. viii, 344 p. Notes: Includes index. [LC 78002120; ISN 0060111011; $12.95] H59.D75 A33 1979   1089

DWELLINGS

Smart house: the coming revolution in housing. Ralph Lee Smith. Columbia, Md.: GP Pub., 1988. 127 p.: ill. [LC 87021262; ISN 0876839189; ISN 0876839197; $18.95; $11.95] TH4812. S63 1988   1090

EAST ASIA—ECONOMIC CONDITIONS

Capital markets in Korea and the Far East. Sung-soo Koh and Zannis Res. London: IFR, 1989? 157 p. Notes: Includes index. Bibliography: p. 131-151. [LC 89004246; ISN 0946559554; $135.00] HC460.5. K65 1989   1091

Sea change: Pacific Asia as the new world industrial center. James C. Abegglen. New York: Toronto: New York: Free Press; Maxwell Macmillan Canada; Maxwell Macmillan International, c1994. xiv, 290 p.: ill., maps Notes: Includes bibliographical references (p. 267-277) and index. [LC 93036426; ISN 0029001552; $24.95] HC460.5. A516 1994   +1092

EAST ASIA—ECONOMIC POLICY

The East Asian miracle: economic growth and public policy. Oxford; New York, N.Y.: Oxford University Press, 1993. xvii, 389 p.: ill. Notes: Includes bibliographical references. [LC 93063842; ISN 0195209931; $19.95] HC460.5. E275 1993   +1093

EAST ASIA—HISTORY

The Pacific century: America and Asia in a changing world. Frank Gibney. New York: Toronto: New York: C. Scribner's Sons; Maxwell Macmillan Canada; Maxwell Macmillan International, c1992. xi, 596 p., [16] p. of plates: ill. (some col.), maps Notes: "A Robert Stewart book." Includes bibliographical references and index. [LC 92013862; ISN 0684193493] DS511. G54 1992   1094

EAST ASIA—INDUSTRIES

The Pacific challenge in international business. edited by W. Chan Kim and Philip K.Y. Young; with a foreword by Vern Terpstra. Ann Arbor, Mich.: UMI Research Press, 1987. viii, 342 p. Notes: Includes bibliographies and index. [LC 87005008; ISN 0835716201] HC460.5. P32 1987   1095

EASTERN AIR LINES, INC

Eastern's armageddon: labor conflict and the destruction of Eastern Airlines. Martha Dunagin Saunders. Westport, Conn.: Greenwood Press, 1992. xi, 164 p. Notes: Includes bibliographical references (p. [153]-159) and index. [LC 92009581; ISN 0313284547] HE9803.E2 S28 1992   1096

EASTMAN KODAK COMPANY

Team Zebra: how 1500 partners revitalized Eastman Kodak's black & white film-making flow. by Stephen J. Frangos, with Steven J. Bennett. Essex Junction, Vt.: Omneo, c1993. xxv, 226 p., [16] p. of plates: ill. Notes: Includes index. Names on front and back lining papers. [LC 93060668; ISN 0939246384; $27.00] HD9708.5.F54 F72 1993   +1097

ECONOMETRICS

The econometric analysis of time series. A.C. Harvey. 1st MIT Press ed., 2nd ed. Cambridge, Mass.: MIT Press, 1990. xiii, 387 p. : ill. Notes: Includes bibliographical references (p. 371-379) and indexes. [LC 89012371; ISN 026208189X; $47.50] HB139. H37 1990   1098

Econometrics. by Ronald J. Wonnacott and Thomas H. Wonnacott. New York J. Wiley, 1970. ix, 445 p. illus. Notes: Includes bibliographical references. [LC 77093485; ISN 047195960X]   HB74.M3 W64   +1099

A guide to econometrics. Peter Kennedy. 2nd ed. Cambridge, Mass.: MIT Press, 1985. x, 238 p. : ill. Notes: Bibliography: p. 216-231. [LC 85016677; ISN 0262111101; ISN 0262610434] HB139. K46 1985   1100

Introduction to statistics and econometrics. Takeshi Amemiya. Cambridge, Mass.: Harvard University Press, 1994. xiii, 368 p. : ill. Notes: Includes bibliographical references and index. [LC 93003777; ISN 0674462254]   HB139. A513 1994   +1101

The practice of econometrics: classic and contemporary. Ernst R. Berndt. Reading, Mass.: Addison-Wesley Pub. Co., 1991. xviii, 702 p. : ill.; 1 computer disk. Notes: Includes bibliographical references and index. [LC 90046332; ISN 0201176289; $47.50]   HB139. B47 1991   1102

ECONOMIC DEVELOPMENT

Agenda 21: the Earth Summit strategy to save our planet. introduction by Paul Simon; edited by Daniel Sitarz. Boulder, Colo.: EarthPress, c1993. x, 321 p. Notes: "The main text of this abridged version... is based on the final official United Nations document Agenda 21 and the United Nations Guide to Agenda 21"—T.p. verso. Includes index. [LC 92074303; ISN 093575511X; $24.95] HD75.6. A37 1993   1103

Beyond the limits: confronting global collapse, envisioning a sustainable future. by Donella H. Meadows, Dennis L. Meadows, Jørgen Randers. Mills, Vt.: Chelsea Green Pub., 1992. xix, 300 p. Notes: Includes index. [LC 91046920; ISN 0930031555; $24.95]   HD75.6. M43 1992   1104

By way of advice: growth strategies for the market driven world: a view from the garden. Marcel Côté. Oakville, Ont.; New York: Lanham, MD: Mosaic Press; National Book Network, distributor, 1991. vi, 331 p. : ill. Notes: At head of title: Corporations, entrepreneurs, policy makers. Includes bibliographical references and index. [LC 91095083; ISN 0889624933; $16.95] HD82. C67 1991   1105

Changing course: a global business perspective on development and the environment: executive summary. Stephan Schmidheiny with the Business Council for Sustainable Development. Cambridge, Mass.: MIT Press, 1992. 46 p.]   HD75.6. S35 1992, Summary   1106

The Economic growth controversy. Edited by Andrew Weintraub, Eli Schwartz, and J. Richard Aronson. White Plains, N.Y. International Arts and Sciences Press, 1973. xv, 229 p. Notes: "Proceedings of a symposium held at Lehigh University in Bethlehem, Pennsylvania, on October 17-19, 1972, under the auspices of the Center for Social Research and the Department of Economics." Includes bibliographical references. [LC 73075076; ISN 0873320387]   HD82. E285   +1107

The economics of development. Everett E. Hagen. 4th ed. Homewood, Ill.: Irwin, 1986. xx, 472 p. : ill. (Irwin publications in economics) Notes: Includes bibliographies and indexes. [LC 85080014; ISN 0256032173]   HD82. H15 1986   1108

The economics of hope: essays on technical change, economic growth, and the environment. Christopher Freeman. London; New York: New York: Pinter Publishers; Distributed exclusively in the USA and Canada by St. Martin's Press, 1992. 249 p. : ill. Notes: Includes bibliographical references and index. [LC 92015155; ISN 1855670836]   HD74.5. F74 1992   1109

For the common good: redirecting the economy toward community, the environment, and a sustainable future. Herman E. Daly and John B. Cobb, Jr.; with contributions by Clifford W. Cobb. 2nd ed., updated and expanded. Boston: Beacon Press, c1994. viii, 534 p. Notes: Includes bibliographical references (p. 508-520) and index. [LC 93024460; ISN 0807047058; $17.00]   HD75.6. D35 1994   +1110

Leading issues in economic development. edited by Gerald M. Meier. 5th ed. New York: Oxford University Press, 1989. xvi, 560 p. : ill. Notes: Includes bibliographical references and index. [LC 88012560; ISN 0195055721; $22.95]   HD82. L3273 1989   1111

Management for a small planet: strategic decision making and the environment. W. Edward Stead, Jean Garner Stead. Newberry Park, Calif.: Sage Publications, c1992. xii, 212 p. : ill. Notes: Includes bibliographical references (p. 192-201) and indexes. [LC 92002644; ISN 0803946341]   HD75.6. S74 1992   1112

Valuing the earth: economics, ecology, ethics. edited by Herman E. Daly and Kenneth N. Townsend. Cambridge, Mass.: MIT Press, c1993. x, 387 p. *Notes:* Includes bibliographical references and index. [LC 92022098; ISN 0262540681] HD75.6. V36 1993 +1113

ECONOMIC FORECASTING

America in the global '90s: the shape of the future—how you can profit from it. by Austin H. Kiplinger & Knight A. Kiplinger with the staff of the Kiplinger Washington letter. Washington, D.C.: Kiplinger Books, c1989. 239 p. *Notes:* Includes index. [LC 89008187; ISN 0938721070; $12.95] HC106.8. K54 1989 1114

Bankruptcy 1995: the coming collapse of America and how to stop it. Harry E. Figgie, Jr., with Gerald J. Swanson; foreword by Warren B. Rudman. 1st ed. Boston: Little, Brown, c1992. xv, 206 p. : ill. *Notes:* Includes bibliographical references and index. [LC 92018143; ISN 0316282057] HC106.8. F54 1992 1115

The coming global boom: how to benefit now from tomorrow's dynamic world economy. by Charles R. Morris. New York, NY: Bantam Books, 1990 xx, 267 p. *Notes:* Includes bibliographical references. [LC 90000034; ISN 0553058983; $19.95] HC106.8. M69 1990 1116

Economic trend analysis for executives and investors. Howard G. Schaefer. Westport, Conn.: Quorum Books, 1993. xiii, 221 p. : ill. *Notes:* Includes bibliographical references (p. 205-209) and index. [LC 92044686; ISN 0899308228] HB3730. S32 1993 +1117

Econoquake!: how to survive & prosper in the coming global depression. Barry Howard Minkin. Englewood, N.J.: Prentice Hall, c1993. xviii, 265 p. : ill. *Notes:* Includes bibliographical references and index. [LC 92033486; ISN 0132248662; $18.95] HC106.8. M573 1993 1118

The first global revolution: a report by the Council of the Club of Rome. by Alexander King & Bertrand Schneider. New York: Pantheon Books, 1991. xxvii, 259 p. *Notes:* Includes bibliographical references. [LC 91020410; ISN 0679738258; $15.00] HC59. K479 1991 1119

Forecasting in business amd economics. C.W.J. Granger. 2nd ed. Boston: Academic Press, c1989. xii, 279 p. *Notes:* Includes bibliographical references and index. [LC 88030262; ISN 0122951816; $34.95] HB3730. G68 1989 1120

Forecasting methods for management. Spyros Makridakis, Steven C. Wheelwright. 5th ed. New York: Wiley, c1989. x, 470 p. : ill. *Notes:* Includes bibliographies and index. [LC 88026178; ISN 0471600636] HD30.27. W46 1989 1121

Future tense: the business realities of the next ten years. Ian Morrison and Greg Schmid. 1st ed. New York: Morrow, c1994. 304 p. : ill. *Notes:* Includes bibliographical references and index. [LC 93046875; ISN 0688123511; $25.00] HC106.82. M67 1994 +1122

Judgmental forecasting. edited by George Wright and Peter Ayton. Chichester; New York: Wiley, c1987. ix, 293 p. : ill. *Notes:* Includes bibliographical references and index. [LC 87001310; ISN 0471913278; £17.95] HB3730. J84 1987 1123

Land of opportunity: the entrepreneurial spirit in America. by Donald Lambro. 1st ed. Boston: Little, Brown, c1986. xv, 176 p. *Notes:* Includes index. [LC 86010566; ISN 0316512893; $17.95] HC106.8. L34 1986 1124

Long-term prospects for the world economy. Paris, France: Washington, D.C. OECD; OECD Publications and Information Centre, distributor, 1992. 193 p. : ill. *Notes:* Papers presented at a conference on Long-term Prospects for the World Economy in June 1991. Includes bibliographical references (p. 188-189). *Contents:* Long-term prospects for the world economy: overall outlook, main issues and summary of discussions / by Michel Andrieu, Wolfgang Michalski and Barrie Stevens—Scanning the future: a long-term scenario study of the world economy 1990-2015 / by André de Jong and Gerrit Zalm—Long-term prospects for the US economy / by Maurice Ernst and Jimmy W. Wheeler—North American economic integration in the 1990s / by Wendy Dobson—European economic integration in a long-term perspective / by Emilio Fontela—The evolution of Europe 1990-2010 / by Jacques Lesourne—Long-term economic issues in Japan and the Asia-Pacific region / by Masaru Yoshitomi and Naohiro Yashiro—The Asia-Pacific region in the 1990s / by Steven Wong.; ISN 9264136754; $34.00] HB3730. L67 1992 1125

Megatraumas: America at the Year 2000. Richard D. Lamm. Boston: Houghton Mifflin, 1985. xii, 290 p. *Notes:* Includes index. Bibliography: p. [249]-275. [LC 85010692; ISN 0395379121; $16.95] HC106.8. L35 1985 1126

100 predictions for the baby boom: the next 50 years. Cheryl Russell. New York: Plenum Press, c1987. 249 p. *Notes:* Includes index. Bibliography: p. 209-238. [LC 87002443; ISN 0306425270] HC106.8. R87 1987 1127

Recollecting the future: a view of business, technology, and innovation in the next 30 years. by Hugh B. Stewart. Homewood, Ill.: Dow Jones-Irwin, c1989. xvi, 356 p. : ill. *Notes:* Includes index. Bibliography: p. 347-352. [LC 88016232; ISN 1556231431; $24.95] HB3730. S75 1989 1128

Regular economic cycles. Ravi Batra. New York: St. Martin's Press, 1989, c1985. xvi, 192 p. : ill. *Notes:* First published in the U.S. as: Regular cycles of money, inflation, regulation, and depressions. c1985. An expanded version of the earlier book: The great depression of 1990. c1985. Includes index. Includes bibliographical references. [LC 89032348; ISN 0312032609; $19.95] HC106.8. B393 1989 1129

The third century: America's resurgence in the Asian era. Joel Kotkin and Yoriko Kishimoto. 1st ed. New York: Crown, c1988. xv, 286 p. *Notes:* Includes index. Bibliography: p. 235-276. [LC 88000281; ISN 0517569841; $19.95] HC106.8. K68 1988 1130

ECONOMIC HISTORY

Change and challenge in the world economy. Bela Balassa. New York: St. Martin's Press, 1985. xxviii, 484 p. *Notes:* Includes bibliographies and indexes. [LC 85001854; ISN 0312128541; $29.95] HC59. B18 1985 1131

A concise economic history of the world: from Paleolithic times to the present. Rondo Cameron. 2nd ed. New York: Oxford University Press, 1993. xxi, 454 p. : ill., maps *Notes:* Includes bibliographical references and index. [LC 92014539; ISN 0195074467] HC21. C33 1993 1132

Economics and world history: myths and paradoxes. Paul Bairoch. New York: Harvester Wheatsheaf, 1993. xvi, 184 p. *Notes:* Includes bibliographical references and index. [LC 93033060; ISN 074500654X; $45.00] HC51. B33 1993 1133

Global economy in the age of science-based knowledge. Mirko Bunc. New York: UNITAR, c1992. xv, 296 p. *Notes:* U.N. sales no. E.92.III.K.RR.37. Includes bibliographical references.; ISN 9211571847] HC54. B86 1992 +1134

Head to head: the coming economic battle among Japan, Europe, and America. Lester C. Thurow. New York: Morrow, 1992. 336 p. *Notes:* Includes bibliographical references and index. [LC 91033300; ISN 0688111505; $24.50] HC59. T5157 1992 1135

International industry and business: structural change, industrial policy and industry strategies. Robert H. Ballance. London; Boston: Allen & Unwin, 1987. xxi, 357 p. *Notes:* Includes indexes. Bibliography: p. 330-347. [LC 86028793; ISN 0043390374; ISN 0043390382] HC59. B3537 1987 1136

A journey through economic time: a firsthand view. John Kenneth Galbraith. Boston: Houghton Mifflin, 1994. xiii, 255 p. *Notes:* Includes bibliographical references and index. [LC 94004816; ISN 0395637511] HC54. G23 1994 +1137

The limits to growth; a report for the Club of Rome's project on the predicament of mankind. by Donella H. Meadows and others New York Universe Books, 1972. 205 p. illus. *Notes:* "A Potomac Associates book." Bibliography: p. 198-200. [LC 73187907; ISN 0876631650] HC59. L54 +1138

The making of economic society. Robert L. Heilbroner. 7th ed., Rev. for the mid-1980s. Englewood Cliffs, N.J.: Prentice-Hall, c1985. xvii, 268 p. : ill. *Notes:* Includes bibliographical references and index. [LC 84015912; ISN 0135462010] HC51. H44 1985 1139

The money mandarins: the making of a new supranational economic order. Howard M. Wachtel. 1st ed. New York: Pantheon Books, 1986. xvi, 254 p. *Notes:* Includes index. Bibliography: p. [227]-245. [LC 85028455; ISN 0394542991; $16.95] HC59. W23 1986 1140

The new global economy in the information age: reflections on our changing world. Martin Carnoy et al. University Park, Pa.: Pennsylvania State University Press, c1993. 170 p. : ill. *Notes:* Includes bibliographical references and index. *Contents:* The informational economy and the new international division of labor / Manuel Castells—Multinationals in a changing world economy: whither the nation-state? / Martin Carnoy—Geo-economics: lessons from America's mistakes / Stephen S. Cohen—North-South relations in the present context: a new dependency? / Fernando Henrique Cardoso—Epilogue: the resurgence of national identity and national interests. [LC 92033652; ISN 0271009098] HC59. N415 1993 +1141

The political economy of global restructuring. edited by Ingrid H. Rima. Aldershot, Hants, England; Brookfield, Vt.: E. Elgar Pub., c1993. 2 v.: ill. *Notes:* Includes bibliographical references and index. Library has: v. 1. *Contents:* v. 1. Economic organization and production—v. 2. Trade and finance. [LC 93012027; ISN 1852786388; ISN 1852788089; ISN 1852788178; $79.95 (approx.); $79.95 (approx.)] HC59.15. P65 1993 +1142

Post-capitalist society. Peter F. Drucker. 1st ed. New York: HarperBusiness, c1993. 232 p. *Notes:* Includes bibliographical references and index. [LC 92054323; ISN 0887306209; $25.00] HC59.15. D78 1993 1143

Rebuilding capitalism: alternative roads after socialism and dirigisme. edited by Andrés Solimano, Osvaldo Sunkel, Mario I. Blejer. Ann Arbor, Mich.: University of Michigan Press, c1994. viii, 409 p. : ill. *Notes:* Includes bibliographical references and index. [LC 93033321; ISN 0472105205]
  HC59.15. R42 1994 +1144

ECONOMIC INDICATORS

The atlas of economic indicators: a visual guide to market forces and the Federal Reserve. W. Stansbury Carnes and Stephen D. Slifer. New York, NY: HarperBusiness, c1991. vii, 232 p. : ill. [LC 91011050; ISN 0887305008; $24.95 ($32.95 Can.)] HC59. C28 1991 1145

Guide to economic indicators. by Norman Frumkin. Armonk, N.Y.: M.E. Sharpe, c1990. xxix, 242 p. *Notes:* Includes bibliographical references. [LC 89035917; ISN 0873325214; $15.95]
  HC103. F9 1990 1146

Handbook of key economic indicators. R. Mark Rogers. Burr Ridge, Ill.: Irwin Professional Pub., c1994. xiii, 274 p. : ill. *Notes:* Includes bibliographical references and index. [LC 94009328; ISN 0786301937] HC103. R64 1994 +1147

Leading indicators for the 1990s. Geoffrey H. Moore. Homewood, Ill.: Dow Jones-Irwin, c1990. 150 p. : ill. *Notes:* Includes index. Includes bibliographical references. [LC 89034886; ISN 1556232586; $25.00] HC106.8. M66 1990 1148

ECONOMICS

The armchair economist: economics and everyday life. Steven E. Landsburg. New York: Toronto: New York: Free Press; Maxwell Macmillan Canada; Maxwell Macmillan International, c1993. ix, 241 p. *Notes:* Includes bibliographical references (p. 233-235) and index. [LC 93004008; ISN 0029177758; $22.95] HM35. L35 1993 +1149

The business researcher's handbook. by Leila K. Kight. Washington, D.C.: Washington Researchers, 1980. vii, 153 p. [LC 80054127; ISN 0934940037] HB74.5. K53 1150

Capital for profit: the triumph of Ricardian political economy over Marx and the neoclassical. Paul Fabra. Savage, Md.: Rowman & Littlefield Publishers, c1991. xxviii, 345 p. : ill. *Notes:* Translation of: L'anti-capitalisme. Includes bibliographical references (p. 339-340) and index. [LC 90023004; ISN 0847676579] HB75. F313 1991 1151

Choosing the right pond: human behavior and the quest for status. Robert H. Frank. New York; Oxford Oxfordshire: Oxford University Press, 1985. x, 306 p. : ill. *Notes:* Includes index. Bibliography: p. 281-293. [LC 84019099; ISN 0195035208; $22.95] HB71. F6955 1985 1152

Data in doubt: an introduction to Bayesian statistical inference for economists. John D. Hey. Oxford: M. Robertson, 1983. xii, 320 p. : ill. *Notes:* Includes index. Bibliography: p. 316. [LC 83179419; ISN 0855205598; £19.50] HB137. H48 1983 1153

Economic heresies; some old-fashioned questions in economic theory. New York Basic Books, 1971. xix, 150 p. *Notes:* Includes bibliographical references. [LC 71147012; ISN 046501786X]
  HB171. R626 +1154

The economic problem. Robert L. Heilbroner, James K. Galbraith. 9th ed. Englewood Cliffs, NJ: Prentice-Hall, c1990. xviii, 716 p. : ill. *Notes:* Includes index. Includes bibliographical references. [LC 89015929; ISN 0132251949; $43.20] HB171.5. H39 1990 1155

Economics. Paul A. Samuelson, William D. Nordhaus. 14th ed. New York: McGraw-Hill, c1992. xlii, 784 p. : ill. (some col.) *Notes:* Includes index. [LC 91037800; ISN 007054879X; $59.70]
  HB171.5. S25 1992 1156

Economics. Paul Wonnacott, Ronald Wonnacott. 4th ed. New York: Wiley, c1990. xxix, 804 p. : col. ill. *Notes:* Includes bibliographical references. [LC 89035541; ISN 0471616273; $47.95]
  HB171.5. W76 1990 1157

Economics. Richard G. Lipsey, Peter O. Steiner, Douglas D. Purvis. 8th ed. New York: Harper & Row, c1987. xxvii, 942 p. : ill. *Notes:* Includes index. [LC 86029422; ISN 0060439173]
  HB171.5. L733 1987 1158

Economics. Stanley Fischer, Rudiger Dornbusch, Richard Schmalensee. 2nd ed. New York: McGraw-Hill, c1988. xlii, 813 p. : ill. (some col.) *Notes:* Includes bibliographical references and index. [LC 87021333; ISN 0070177813; $39.95] HB171.5. F458 1988 1159

Economics: a general introduction. Lloyd G. Reynolds. 5th ed. Homewood, Ill.: Irwin, 1988. xx, 892 p. : ill. *Notes:* Includes bibliographical references and index. [LC 87083129; ISN 0256062285]
  HB171.5. R38 1988 1160

Economics: analysis, decision making, and policy. George Leland Bach; with Robert Flanagan... et al. 11th ed. Englewood Cliffs, N.J.: Prentice-Hall, c1987. xv, 752 p. : ill. *Notes:* 10th ed. entitled: Economics: an introduction to analysis and policy. Includes bibliographies and indexes. [LC 86025576; ISN 0132272407]   HB171.5. B13 1987   1161

Economics explained: everything you need to know about how the economy works and where it's going. Robert Heilbroner and Lester Thurow. Rev. and updated. New York: Simon & Schuster, c1994. 285 p. : ill. *Notes:* "A Touchstone book." Includes bibliographical references and index. [LC 93021329; ISN 0671884220; $12.00 ($15.50 Can.)]   HB171. H479 1994   +1162

Economics for a civilized society. by Greg Davidson and Paul Davidson. 1st ed. New York: Norton, c1988. x, 213 p. *Notes:* Includes index. Bibliography: p. 201-204. [LC 88012559; ISN 0393026531]   HB171. D28 1988   1163

Economics from the heart: a Samuelson sampler. Paul Samuelson; edited and with introductory remarks and notes, by Maryann O. Keating. San Diego: Harcourt Brace Jovanovich, c1983. xiv, 284 p. [LC 82023318; ISN 0156275511]   HB171. S259 1983   1164

Economics in perspective: a critical history. John Kenneth Galbraith. Boston: Houghton Mifflin, 1987. 324 p. *Notes:* Includes bibliographical references and index. [LC 87003644; ISN 0395355729; $19.95]   HB75. G274 1987   1165

Economics in plain English. Leonard Silk. Updated and expanded, Rev. Touchstone ed. New York: Simon & Schuster, 1986. 237 p. : ill. *Notes:* A Touchstone book. Includes index. Bibliography: p. 219-223. [LC 85022226; ISN 0671606131; $7.95]   HB171. S5625 1986   1166

Economics: principles, problems, and policies. Campbell R. McConnell, Stanley L. Brue. 11th ed. New York: McGraw-Hill, c1990. xlii, 866, 34, 33 p. : ill. *Notes:* Includes bibliographical references. [LC 89012570; ISN 0070449678; $39.95]   HB171.5. M47 1990   1167

The end of economic man: principles of any future economics. George P. Brockway. Rev. New York: Norton, c1993. 320 p. *Notes:* Originally published: New York: Cornelia & Michael Bessie Books, c1991. Includes bibliographical references and index. [LC 92010782; ISN 0393034615; $29.95 ($37.99 Can.)]   HB171. B6499 1993   +1168

Essays on economics and economists. R.H. Coase. Chicago: University of Chicago Press, c1994. viii, 222 p. *Notes:* Includes 15 previously published papers and an original preface. Includes bibliographical references and index. [LC 93026174; ISN 0226111024; $27.95]   HB34. C54 1994   +1169

Essays on entrepreneurs, innovations, business cycles, and the evolution of capitalism. Joseph A. Schumpeter; edited by Richard V. Clemence; with a new introduction by Richard Swedberg. New Brunswick N.J., U.S.A.: Transaction Publishers, 1988. xxxix, 341 p. : *Notes:* Reprint. Originally published: Essays. Cambridge, Mass.: Addison-Wesley, 1951. "Bibliography of the writings of Joseph A. Schumpeter": p. 330-341. [LC 88027415; ISN 0887387640]   HB171. S385 1988   1170

Ethics and economic progress. by James M. Buchanan. Norman: University of Oklahoma, c1994. ix, 156 p. : ill. *Notes:* Includes bibliographical references (p. 147-150) and index. [LC 93031846; ISN 0806125969; $19.95]   HB72. B833 1994   +1171

The fairness of markets: a search for justice in a free society. Richard B. McKenzie. Lexington, Mass.: Lexington Books, c1987. xiv, 235 p. : ill. *Notes:* Includes bibliographies and index. [LC 86045958; ISN 0669148016]   HB72. M35 1987   1172

The Fortune encyclopedia of economics. edited by David R. Henderson. New York: Warner Books, c1993. xx, 876 p. : ill. *Notes:* Includes bibliographical references and index. *Contents:* Basic concepts—Economic systems and schools of economic thought—Macroeconomics—Economic policy—Taxes—Money and banking—Economic regulation—Environmental regulation—Discrimination and labor issues—International economics—Corporations and financial markets—The marketplace—The economics of special markets—Economies outside the United States—Biographies. [LC 92050535; ISN 0446516376; $49.95 ($59.95 in Canada)]   HB61. F67 1993   +1173

Frontiers of economics. edited by Kenneth J. Arrow and Seppo Honkapohja. Oxford, UK; New York, NY, USA: B. Blackwell, 1985. viii, 458 p. *Notes:* Papers presented at a symposium honoring Hilma Gabriella Jahnsson, organized by the Yrjö Jahnsson Foundation. Includes bibliographies and indexes. [LC 84021610; ISN 0631134085; ISN 0631145990; $34.95 (U.S.)]   HB21. F76 1985   1174

The growth of economic thought. Henry William Spiegel. 3rd ed. Durham: Duke University Press, 1991. xxviii, 868 p. : ill. *Notes:* Includes bibliographical references (p. [678]-845) and index. [LC 89028556; ISN 0822309734; $29.95]   HB75. S64 1991   1175

Hard heads, soft hearts: tough-minded economics for a just society. Alan S. Blinder. Reading, Mass.: Addison-Wesley Pub. Co., c1987. xi, 236 p. : ill. *Notes:* Includes index. Bibliography: p. 216-227. [LC 87014078; ISN 0201115042; $17.95]   HB171. B535 1987   1176

A history of economic theory and method. Robert B. Ekelund, Jr., Robert F. Hébert. 3rd ed. New York: McGraw-Hill, c1990. xv, 688 p. : ill. *Notes:* Includes bibliographical references. [LC 89012626; ISN 0070194165; $39.95]   HB75. E47 1990   1177

The instant economist. John Charles Pool, Ross M. LaRoe. Reading, Mass.: Addison-Wesley Pub. Co., c1985. 120 p. *Notes:* Bibliography: p. 120. [LC 84024568; ISN 0201168847; $12.95] HB171. P69 1985   1178

International finance. Keith Pilbeam. Basingstroke, Hampshire: Macmillan, 1992. xxvi, 446 p. : ill. *Notes:* Includes bibliographical references and indexes. [LC 92357460; ISN 0333545281; £14.99] HG3881. P54 1992   1179

A lexicon of economics. Kenyon A. Knopf. San Diego: Academic Press, c1991. xii, 314 p. : ill. [LC 91019658; ISN 0124169554; $29.95] HB61. K57 1991   1180

Lost prophets: an insider's history of the modern economists. Alfred L. Malabre, Jr. Boston, Mass.: Harvard Business School Press, 1993, c1994. ix, 256 p., [8] p. of plates: ill. *Notes:* Includes bibliographical references and index. [LC 93004616; ISN 0875844413; $27.95] HB119.A2 M34 1993   1181

The methodology of economics, or, How economists explain. Mark Blaug. 2nd ed. Cambridge; New York, NY: Cambridge University Press, 1992. xxviii, 286 p. *Notes:* Includes bibliographical references (p. 255-273) and indexes. [LC 92004375; ISN 0521430615; $54.00] HB131. B56 1992   1182

Microeconomics. Richard G. Lipsey, Peter O. Steiner, Douglas D. Purvis. 8th ed. New York: Harper & Row, c1988. xii, 493 p. : ill. *Notes:* Selections from the authors' Economics. Includes index. [LC 87026975; ISN 0060440996] HB171. L7333 1988   1183

The moral dimension: toward a new economics. Amitai Etzioni. New York: London: Free Press; Collier Macmillan, c1988. xvi, 314 p. *Notes:* Includes index. Bibliography: p. 259-300. [LC 88000368; ISN 0029099005; $24.95] HB72. E8 1988   1184

The portable MBA in economics. Philip K.Y. Young, John J. McAuley. New York: Wiley, c1994. x, 286 p. : ill. *Notes:* Includes bibliographical references (p. 273-276) and index. [LC 93041321; ISN 0471595268; $27.95] HB71. Y68 1994   +1185

Profits, priests, and princes: Adam Smith's emancipation of economics from politics and religion. Peter Minowitz. Stanford, Calif.: Stanford University Press, 1993. xv, 345 p. *Notes:* Includes bibliographical references (p. [331]-340) and index. [LC 93018798; ISN 0804721661; $32.50] HB72. M53 1993   +1186

Statistical analysis for business and economics. Donald L. Harnett, James L. Murphy. 3rd ed. Reading, Mass.: Addison-Wesley, c1985. xvii, 907, 99, 5 p. : ill. *Notes:* Includes bibliography and index. [LC 84018502; ISN 0201106833; $27.95] HB137. H376 1985   1187

Statistical analysis for business and economics. Ya-lun Chou. New York: Elsevier, c1989. xxiii, 1157 p. : ill. *Notes:* Includes index. [LC 88010958; ISN 0444013016] HB137. C485 1989   1188

Statistics for economics, business administration, and the social sciences. Erling B. Andersen, Niels-Erik Jensen, Nils Kousgaard. Berlin; New York: Springer-Verlag, c1987. xi, 439 p. : ill. *Notes:* Includes indexes. [LC 87009423; ISN 0387177205] HB137. A525 1987   1189

Thinking economically: how economic principles can contribute to clear thinking. Maurice Levi. New York: Basic Books, c1985. xviii, 281 p. *Notes:* Includes index. [LC 83046090; ISN 0465085539; $16.95] HB71. L53 1985   1190

Understanding the new economy. Alfred L. Malabre, Jr. Homewood, Ill.: Dow Jones-Irwin, c1989. ix, 174 p. *Notes:* Includes index. [LC 88015529; ISN 1556231172; $19.95] HB171. M323 1989   1191

ECONOMICS LITERATURE

If you're so smart: the narrative of economic expertise. Donald N. McCloskey. Chicago: University of Chicago Press, 1990. ix, 180 p. *Notes:* Includes bibliographical references (p. 165-176) and index. [LC 90033041; ISN 0226556700; $17.95] HB199. M385 1990   1192

ECONOMISTS

Economic principals: masters and mavericks of modern economics. David Warsh. New York: Free Press, c1993. xviii, 525 p. *Notes:* Most of the articles were previously published in the Boston globe. [LC 92032152; ISN 0029339960] HB76. W37 1993   1193

The worldly philosophers: the lives, times, and ideas of the great economic thinkers. Robert L. Heilbroner. 6th ed. New York: Simon & Schuster, c1986. 365 p. (A Touchstone book) *Notes:* "A guide to further reading: p. 327-33. Includes index. Bibliography: p. 335-348. [LC 86022003; ISN 0671634828; ISN 067163318X; $17.95; $9.95] HB76. H4 1986   1194

ECOTOURISM

Ecotourism: a sustainable option? edited by Erlet Cater, Gwen Lowman. Chichester; New York: Wiley, 1994. x, 218 p. : ill., maps Notes: "Published in association with the Royal Geographical Society." Includes bibliographical references and index. *Contents:* Introduction / E. Cater—Societal change and the growth in alternative tourism / R. Prosser—Environmentally responsible marketing of tourism / P. Wight—Tourism: environmental relevance / R. Sisman—Ecotourism in the Third World: problems and prospects for sustainability / E. Cater—Ecotourism: on the trail of destruction or sustainability?: a minister's view / Baroness Chalker—Tourism and a European strategy for the alpine environment / Prince Sadruddin Aga Khan—Ecotourism in Eastern Europe / D. Hall and V. Kinnaird—Ecotourism in Australia, New Zealand and the South Pacific: appropriate tourism or a new form of ecological imperialism? / C.M. Hall—Ecotourism in the Caribbean Basin / D. Weaver—The Annapurna Conservation Area project: a pioneering example of sustainable tourism? / C.P. Gurung and M. De Coursey—Ecotourism in Antarctica / B. Stonehouse. [LC 94015985; ISN 0471948969; £37.50]
G155.A1 E285 1994   +1195

EDUCATION, HIGHER

Higher learning. Derek Bok. Cambridge, Mass.: Harvard University Press, 1986. 206 p. *Notes:* Includes bibliographical references and index. [LC 86009876; ISN 0674391756]   LA227.3. B63 1986   1196

EDUCATION

Human capital: a theoretical and empirical analysis, with special reference to education. Gary S. Becker. 2nd ed. Chicago: University of Chicago Press, 1983, c1975. xviii, 268 p. : ill. *Notes:* Reprint. Originally published: New York: National Bureau of Economic Research, 1975. Includes bibliographical references and index. [LC 80014; ISN 0226041093; $14.95]   LC66. B44 1983   1197

Human capital: a theoretical and empirical analysis, with special reference to education. Gary S. Becker. 3rd ed. Chicago: University of Chicago Press, c1993. xxii, 390 p. : ill. *Notes:* Includes bibliographical references and indexes. [LC 93024690; ISN 0226041204]   LC66. B43 1993   +1198

The Japanese school: lessons for industrial America. Benjamin C. Duke. New York: Praeger, 1986. xx, 242 p. : ill. *Notes:* Includes index. Bibliography: p. 233-235. [LC 86005002; ISN 0275920534; ISN 0275920038]
LA1312. D85 1986   1199

E.F. HUTTON & COMPANY

Burning down the house: how greed, deceit, and bitter revenge destroyed E.F. Hutton. James Sterngold. New York: Summit Books, c1990. 305 p., [8] p. of plates: ill. *Notes:* Includes bibliographical references and index. [LC 90043747; ISN 0671709011; $19.45]   HG4928.5. S72 1990   1200

The fall of the house of Hutton. Donna Sammons Carpenter and John Feloni. 1st ed. New York: Holt, c1989. vii, 322 p. *Notes:* Includes index. [LC 89001768; ISN 0805009469; $19.95]
HG4928.5. C37 1989   1201

Sudden death: the rise and fall of E.F. Hutton. Mark Stevens. New York: New American Library, 1989. 298 p. *Notes:* "NAL books." [LC 89009454; ISN 0453006736; $19.95]   HG4928.5. S74 1989   1202

EFFICIENT MARKET THEORY

Efficient capital markets and accounting: a critical analysis. Thomas R. Dyckman, Dale Morse. 2nd ed. Englewood Cliffs, N.J.: Prentice-Hall, c1986. xiv, 128 p. : ill. (Contemporary topics in accounting series) *Notes:* Includes index. Bibliography: p. 92-105. [LC 84026630; ISN 0132469928]
HG4915. D95 1986   1203

ELECTRIC UTILITIES

Electric power: deregulation and the public interest. edited by John C. Moorhouse; foreword by Harold Demsetz. San Francisco, CA: Pacific Research Institute for Public Policy, 1986. xviii, 516 p. : ill. (Pacific studies in public policy) *Notes:* Includes index. Bibliography: p. 477-483. [LC 85063556; ISN 0936488115; ISN 0936488026; $34.95; $14.95] HD9685.U5 E42 1204

The power makers: the inside story of America's biggest business—and its struggle to control tomorrow's electricity. by Richard Munson. Emmaus, Pa.: Rodale Press, c1985. xi, 260 p. : ill. *Notes:* Includes index. Bibliography: p. 226-254. [LC 85008243; ISN 0878575502; $16.95] HD9685.U5 M86 1985 1205

ELECTRONIC DATA INTERCHANGE

EDI guide: a step by step approach. Edward Cannon New York: Van Nostrand Reinhold, c1993. x, 181 p. : ill. *Notes:* Includes bibliographical references and index. [LC 93012398; ISN 0442004753] HF5548.33. C36 1993 +1206

Open systems: a business strategy for the 1990s. Pamela A. Gray. London; New York: McGraw-Hill, c1991. xii, 263 p. : ill. *Notes:* Includes index. [LC 90013273; ISN 0077072448; $40.95] HF5548.33. G73 1991 1207

ELECTRONIC DATA PROCESSING

The computer impact. Edited by Irene Taviss. Englewood Cliffs, N.J. Prentice-Hall, 1970. xi, 297 p. (Series in automatic computation) *Notes:* Includes bibliographical references. [LC 74128776; ISN 0131659693] QA76. T36 +1208

Computer models in management. Barbara Bund Jackson. Homewood, Ill.: R. D. Irwin, 1979. xiv, 442 p. : ill. *Notes:* Includes bibliographical references and index. [LC 78061189; ISN 0256022259] HF5548.2. J227 1209

Distributed computing: implementation and management strategies. Raman Khanna, editor. Englewood Cliffs, N.J.: PTR Prentice Hall, c1994. x, 518 p. : ill. *Notes:* Includes bibliographical references and index. [LC 93006077; ISN 0132201380] QA76.9.D5 D515 1994 +1210

Information systems management: analytical tools and techniques. Phillip Ein-Dor, Carl R. Jones. New York: Elsevier, c1985. xvi, 230 p. : ill. *Notes:* Includes bibliographies and index. [LC 85013013; ISN 0444009574] QA76.9.M3 E4 1985 1211

ELECTRONIC DATA PROCESSING DEPARTMENTS

EDP, controls and auditing. W. Thomas Porter, William E. Perry. 5th ed. Boston, Mass.: Kent Pub. Co., c1987. xviii, 617 p. : ill. *Notes:* Includes index. Bibliography: p. 587-589. [LC 86027564; ISN 0534070922; $33.00] HF5548.35. P67 1987 1212

ELECTRONIC DIGITAL COMPUTERS

Data systems and management: an introduction to systems analysis and design. Alton R. Kindred. 3rd ed. Englewood Cliffs, NJ: Prentice-Hall, c1985. xi, 436 p. : ill. *Notes:* Includes index. [LC 84024785; ISN 0131961896] QA76.5. K488 1985 1213

Intelligent machinery: theory and practice. edited by Ian Benson. Cambridge Cambridgeshire; New York: Cambridge University Press, 1986. xi, 168 p. : ill. *Notes:* Papers presented at a conference organized by SRI International and held in Cambridge, September 1984. Includes bibliographical references and index. [LC 85012838; ISN 0521308364] QA76.5. I4886 1986 1214

Programmers at work. Redmond, Wash.: New York: Microsoft Press; Distributed in the U.S. by Harper and Row, c1986. 1 v.: ill. *Contents:* 1st ser. Interviews / by Susan Lammers. [LC 86005175; ISN 0914845713; $14.95] QA76.6. P751345 1986 1215

ELECTRONIC FUNDS TRANSFERS

Electronic funds transfers and payments: the public policy issues. edited by Elinor Harris Solomon. Boston: Norwell, MA, USA: Kluwer-Nijhoff Pub.; Distributors for the U.S. and Canada, Kluwer Academic Publishers, c1987. xi, 244 p. : ill. *Notes:* Includes bibliographies and index. [LC 86010416; ISN 0898381797]   HG1710. E45 1987   1216

ELECTRONIC INDUSTRIES

Japanese electronics technology: enterprise and innovation. by Gene Gregory. 2nd ed. Chichester; New York: Wiley, 1986. xiv, 458 p. : ill. *Notes:* Includes bibliographical references and index. [LC 86009189; ISN 0471910384; $19.00]   HD9696.A3 J29 1986   1217

Venture capital in high-tech companies: the electronics industry in perspective. George Young. Westport, Conn.: Quorum Books, 1985. vii, 213 p. : ill. *Notes:* Includes bibliographies and index. [LC 85012057; ISN 0899301460]   HD9696.A2 Y68 1985   1218

ELECTRONIC MAIL SYSTEMS

Connections: new ways of working in the networked organization. Lee Sproull, Sara Kiesler. Cambridge, Mass.: MIT Press, 1991. xiii, 212 p. : ill. *Notes:* Includes bibliographical references (p.189-204) and index. [LC 90047611; ISN 026219306X; $19.95]   HE6239.E54 S68 1991   1219

ELECTRONIC PUBLISHING

Chicago guide to preparing electronic manuscripts: for authors and publishers. 2nd ed. Chicago: University of Chicago Press, 1987. xi, 143 p. : ill. (Chicago guides to writing, editing, and publishing) *Notes:* Includes index. Bibliography: p. 131. [LC 86019343; ISN 0226103927; ISN 0226103935]   Z286.E43 U54 1987   1220

ELITE (SOCIAL SCIENCES)

Controlling interest: who owns Canada? Diane Francis. Toronto, Ont.: Macmillan of Canada, c1986. 352 p. *Notes:* Includes index.; ISN 0771597444]   HD2809. F73   1221

EMOTIONS

Passions within reason: the strategic role of the emotions. Robert H. Frank. 1st ed. New York: Norton, c1988. xiii, 304 p. : ill. *Notes:* Includes index. Bibliography: p. 279-293. [LC 88001224; ISN 0393026043; $19.95]   BF531. F73 1988   1222

EMPLOYEE FRINGE BENEFITS

Employee benefits handbook. editor, Jeffrey D. Mamorsky. 3rd ed. Boston: Warren, Gorham & Lamont, c1992. 1 v. (various pagings): forms *Notes:* Kept up to date by cumulative supplements. Includes bibliographical references and index. [LC 91066207; ISN 0791310698]   KF3509. E56 1992   1223

Fundamentals of employee benefit programs. 4th ed. Washington, DC: Employee Benefit Research Institute, 1990. xxiii, 355 p. : ill. *Notes:* Includes bibliographical references. [LC 90031748; ISN 0866430695; $29.95]   HD4928.N62 U634 1990   1224

The handbook of employee benefits: design, funding, and administration. edited by Jerry S. Rosenbloom. 2nd ed. Homewood, Ill.: Dow Jones-Irwin, c1988. xxviii, 1170 p. *Notes:* Includes bibliographies and index. [LC 88000487; ISN 1556230680; ISN 155623175X; $60.00]
     HD4928.N62 U6353 1988   1225

EMPLOYEE MOTIVATION

Getting the best out of yourself and others. by Buck Rodgers with Irv Levey. 1st ed. New York: Harper & Row, c1987. xi, 227 p. [LC 86046125; ISN 0060156708; $18.95]   HF5549.5.M63 R63 1987   1226

Making people productive. Michael Nash. 1st ed. San Francisco: Jossey-Bass, 1985. xv, 266 p. (A joint publication in the Jossey-Bass management series and the Jossey-Bass social and behavioral science series) *Notes:* Includes index. Bibliography: p. 219-251. [LC 85045292; ISN 0875896707]
HF5549.5.M63 N37 1985   1227

The new bottom line: people and loyalty in business. William B. Walton, Sr., with Mel Lorentzen. 1st ed. San Francisco: Harper & Row, c1986. 242 p. [LC 85045369; ISN 0062509101]
HF5549.5.M63 W35 1986   1228

Patterns of high performance: discovering the ways people work best. Jerry L. Fletcher. 1st ed. San Francisco: Berret-Koehler, 1993. xvii, 252 p. *Notes:* Includes bibliographical references (p. 245) and index. *Contents:* A practical definition of high performance—Rebecca Allen's high performance patterns—Nick Rostov's high performance pattern—Answers to typical questions about discovering patterns—Revitalizing a task you are stuck with and sick of—Finding a winning strategy in a corporate power struggle—Getting a critical project back on track—Deciding which job to go after and getting it—Finding time for the family while holding a demanding executive position—Making the best of the only job available in a downsizing—Finding an unconventional niche that fits—Cutting a staff to its best performers—Holding to strong values while executing a tough corporate decision—Giving something your best shot even if it doesn't work—Answers to typical questions about applying patterns—Finding a new way of working with a colleague in a difficult situation—Suggesting new ways to divide tasks—Using patterns to change the focus within a group—Answers to typical questions about applying patterns to pairs. [LC 93017921; ISN 1881052338; $27.95]   HF5549.5.M63 F58 1993   +1229

People, performance, and pay: a full report on the American Productivity Center/ American Compensation Association National survey of non-traditional reward and human resource practices. Carla O'Dell in collaboration with Jerry McAdams. Houston: American Productivity Center, 1987. [x], 98 p. : ill. [LC 86727263]   HD5549.5.M63 O33 1987   1230

EMPLOYEE OWNERSHIP

Employee ownership: a reader. National Center for Employee Ownership. Updated. Arlington, Va.: The Center, 1985. 75 p. in various pagings *Notes.* Cover title. Includes bibliographical references.]   HD5660.U6 E46   1231

Employee ownership in America: the equity solution. Corey M. Rosen, Katherine J. Klein and Karen M. Young. Lexington, Mass.: Lexington Books, c1986. x, 270 p. ([Issues in organization and management series]) *Notes:* Includes index. Bibliography: p. [247]-250. [LC 85040000; ISN 0669103071]   HD5660.U5 R67 1986   1232

Employee ownership: revolution or ripoff? Joseph Raphael Blasi. Cambridge, Mass.: Ballinger Pub. Co., 1988. xiv, 334 p. : ill. *Notes:* Includes index. Bibliography: p. [287]-314. [LC 87035402; ISN 0887300650]   HD5660.U5 B569 1988   1233

A preface to economic democracy. Robert A. Dahl. Berkeley: University of California Press, c1985. 184 p. *Notes:* Includes index. Bibliography: p. [165]-173. [LC 84008483; ISN 0520053451]
HD5660.U5 D34 1985   1234

EMPLOYEE RIGHTS

Can they do that?: a guide to your rights on the job. Michael A. Zigarelli. New York: Toronto: New York: Lexington Books; Maxwell Macmillan Canada; Maxwell Macmillan International, c1994. ix, 191 p. *Notes:* Includes bibliographical references and index. [LC 94013199; ISN 002935823X]
KF3319.6. Z54 1994   +1235

Justice in the workplace: approaching fairness in human resource management. edited by Russell Cropanzano. Hillsdale, N.J.: L. Erlbaum Associates, 1993. viii, 298 p. : ill. *Notes:* Includes bibliographical references and index. [LC 91044766; ISN 0805810552]   HF5549.5.E428 J87 1993   1236

EMPLOYEES

Corporate quality universities: lessons in building a world-class work force. Jeanne C. Meister. Alexandria, Va.: Burr Ridge, Ill.: American Society for Training and Development; Irwin, 1993, c1994. xix, 255 p. : ill. *Notes:* Includes bibliographical references and index. [LC 93001268; ISN 1556237901]   HF5549.5.T7 M423 1994   +1237

Designing training and development systems. William R. Tracey. 3rd ed. New York: American Management Association, c1992. x, 532 p. : ill. *Notes:* Includes bibliographical references and index. [LC 91041477; ISN 0814450806]   HF5549.5.T7 T648 1992   1238

Developing human resources. Leonard Nadler, Zeace Nadler; foreword by Chip R. Bell. 3rd ed. San Francisco: Jossey-Bass Publishers, 1989. xxvi, 298 p. : ill. *Notes:* Includes index. Bibliography: p. 259-290. [LC 88046096; ISN 1555421555; $24.95]   HF5549.5.T7 N29 1989   1239

Employers large and small. Charles Brown, James Hamilton, and James Medoff. Cambridge, Mass.: Harvard University Press, 1990. 109 p. : ill. *Notes:* Includes bibliographical references. [LC 89020080; ISN 0674251628]   HD5724. B725 1990   1240

Employment and technical change in Europe: work organization, skills, and training. edited by Ken Ducatel. Aldershot, Hants, England; Brookfield, Vt., USA: E. Elgar, c1994. xii, 262 p. : ill. *Notes:* Includes bibliographical references (p. 229-248) and index. [LC 94015927; ISN 1852787759]   HD6331.2.E85 E47 1994   +1241

No one need apply: getting and keeping the best workers. Lee Bowes. Boston, Mass.: Harvard Business School Press, c1987. xiv, 268 p. *Notes:* Includes bibliographies and index. [LC 86029512; ISN 087584149X]   HF5549.5.R44 B69 1987   1242

Staffing problem solver for human resource professionals and managers. Marc Dorio. New York: Wiley, c1994. xii, 288 p. : ill. *Notes:* Includes index. [LC 93029367; ISN 0471006300; $49.95]   HF5549.5.R44 D67 1994   +1243

Successful personnel recruiting & selection. Erwin S. Stanton. New York: AMACOM, c1977. x, 214 p. *Notes:* Includes index. Bibliography: p. 205-207. [LC 77021384; ISN 081445450X; $14.95]   HF5549.5.R44 S74   +1244

Training and development in organizations. Irwin L. Goldstein, and associates. 1st ed. San Francisco: Jossey-Bass Publishers, c1989. xxviii, 525 p. *Notes:* Includes bibliographical references. [LC 89045587; ISN 1555421865; $34.95]   HF5549.5.T7 G542 1989   1245

Training for impact: how to link training to business needs and measure the results. Dana Gaines Robinson, James C. Robinson. 1st ed. San Francisco: Jossey-Bass Publishers, 1989. xxi, 308 p. : ill. *Notes:* Includes bibliographical references and index. [LC 88046088; ISN 1555421539; $26.95]   HF5549.5.T7 R527 1989   1246

Workplace basics: the essential skills employers want. Anthony P. Carnevale, Leila J. Gainer, Ann S. Meltzer. 1st ed. San Francisco: Jossey-Bass Publishers, 1990. xxviii, 477 p. : ill. *Notes:* Includes bibliographical references (p. 425-464) and indexes. [LC 89048804; ISN 1555422020; $34.95]   HF5549.5.T7 C2985 1990   1247

EMPLOYER-SUPPORTED DAY CARE

Companies that care: the most family-friendly companies in America, what they offer, and how they got that way. Hal Morgan and Kerry Tucker. New York: Simon & Schuster, c1991. 351 p. *Notes:* "A Fireside book." Includes indexes. *Contents:* AT&T—Alley's General Store—BE&K, inc.—Dunning, Forman, Kirrane & Terry—Fel-Pro Incorporated—Grieco Bros., Inc.—International Business Machines Corporation (IBM)—Johnson & Johnson—S.C. Johnson & Son, Inc.—Joy Cone Co.—The Little Tikes Company—Lost Arrow Corp./Patagonia, Inc.—NCNB Corporation—SAS Institute Inc.—The Stride Rite Corporation—United States Hosiery Corporation—America's other work-and-family leaders—Family-friendly options. [LC 91006655; ISN 0671735985; $12.95]   HF5549.5.D39 M67 1991   1248

The politics and reality of family care in corporate America. John P. Fernandez. Lexington, Mass.: Lexington Books, c1990. xxv, 276 p. : ill. *Notes:* Includes bibliographical references. [LC 89029170; ISN 0669215627; $18.95]   HF5549.5.D39 F47 1990   1249

The work and family revolution: how companies can keep employees happy and business profitable. Barbara Schwarz Vanderkolk and Ardis Armstrong Young. New York: Facts on File, c1991. xii, 212 p. : ill. *Notes:* Includes bibliographical references (p. 197-206) and index. [LC 91010785; ISN 0816023646; $22.95 ($28.95 Can.)]   HF5549.5.D39 V36 1991   1250

EMPLOYMENT INTERVIEWING

The evaluation interview. Richard A. Fear; Robert J. Chiron. 4th ed. New York: McGraw-Hill, c1990. x, 246 p. : ill. [LC 89048122; ISN 0070202206; $29.95]   HF5549.5.I6 F4 1990   1251

Hiring the best: a manager's guide to effective interviewing. Martin John Yate. Boston: B. Adams, c1988. 222 p.; ISN 1558509569; ISN 1558509577]   HF5549.5.I6 Y369 1988   1252

The smart interviewer. Bradford D. Smart. New York: Wiley, c1989. xii, 205 p. : ill. *Notes:* Includes bibliographical references. [LC 89037359; ISN 0471513318; ISN 0471513326; $24.95]
    HF5549.5.I6 S63 1989   1253

ENERGY POLICY

Energy aftermath. Thomas H. Lee, Ben C. Ball, Jr., Richard D. Tabors. Boston, Mass.: Harvard Business School Press, c1990. xiii, 274 p. : ill. *Notes:* Includes bibliographical references. [LC 89039842; ISN 0875842194]   HD9502.U52 L44 1990   1254

The energy crisis ten years after. edited by David Hawdon. London: New York: Croom Helm; St. Martin's Press, 1984. 137 p. : ill. *Notes:* Papers presented at a conference held at the University of Surrey in April, 1983. Includes bibliographical references. [LC 83040189; ISN 0312251238; $25.00 (est.)]   HD9502.A2 E54374 1984   1255

Energy future: report of the energy project at the Harvard Business School. Robert Stobaugh & Daniel Yergin, editors; with I. C. Bupp . . . et al. [Rev. ed.] New York: Ballantine, c1980. xv, 493 p. : ill. *Notes:* Another copy. Includes bibliographical references and index. [LC 78021329; ISN 0394501632; $12.95]   HD9502.U52 E4914 1980   1256

Energy future: report of the energy project at the Harvard Business School. Robert Stobaugh & Daniel Yergin, editors; with I. C. Bupp . . . et al. [Rev. ed.]. New York: Ballantine, c1980. xv, 493 p. : ill. *Notes:* Includes bibliographical references and index. [LC 78021329; ISN 0345293495; $2.95]   HD9502.U52 E4914 1980   1257

Energy future: report of the Energy Project at the Harvard Business School. Robert Stobaugh, Daniel Yergin, editors; I.C. Bupp . . . et al. New rev. 3rd ed. New York: Vintage Books, 1983. xii, 459 p. : ill. *Notes:* Includes bibliographical references and index.]   HD9502.U52 E4914 1983   1258

Energy, politics, and public policy. Walter A. Rosenbaum. 2nd ed. Washington, D.C.: CQ Press, c1987. viii, 221 p. : maps *Notes:* Includes index. Bibliography: p. 211. [LC 87005301; ISN 0871874121; $13.95]   HD9502.U52 R64 1987   1259

ENGINEERING

Machine-age ideology: social engineering and American liberalism, 1911-1939. by John M. Jordan. Chapel Hill: University of North Carolina Press, c1994. xiii, 332 p. : ill. *Notes:* Includes bibliographical references and index. [LC 93002108; ISN 0807821233; $39.95]   TA23. J67 1994   +1260

ENGINEERING ECONOMY

Engineering economy: analysis of capital expenditures. Gerald W. Smith. 4th ed. Ames, Iowa: Iowa State University Press, 1987. x, 584 p. : ill. *Notes:* Includes index. Bibliography: p. 576-578. [LC 87002751; ISN 0813805538]   TA177.4. S57 1987   1261

Principles of engineering economy. Eugene L. Grant, W. Grant Ireson, Richard S. Leavenworth. 8th ed. New York: Wiley, c1990. xiv, 591 p. : ill. *Notes:* Includes index. Includes bibliographical references. [LC 89033571; ISN 0047163526; $47.95]   TA177.4. G7 1990   1262

ENGLISH LANGUAGE

How to use the power of the printed word: thirteen articles packed with facts and practical information, designed to help you read better, write better, communicate better. Malcolm Forbes... et al.; preface by Clifton Fadiman; edited by Billings S. Fuess, Jr. 1st ed. Garden City, N.Y.: Anchor Press, c1985. xvi, 110 p. : ill. Notes: "Articles have appeared... in magazine and newspaper advertisements sponsored by International Paper Company"—T.p. verso. Includes index. Bibliography: p. 108-110. [LC 82045195; ISN 0385182155; ISN 0385182163; $14.95; $7.95]
LB1576. H674 1985   1263

ENTREPRENEURSHIP

Bear hunting with the Politburo: a gritty first-hand account of Russia's young entrepreneurs—and why Soviet-style capitalism won't work. A. Craig Copetas. New York: Simon & Schuster, 1991. 270 p. [LC 91031692; ISN 0671703137]   HB615. C65 1991   1264

Corporate venturing: creating new businesses within the firm. Zenas Block and Ian C. MacMillan. Boston, Mass.: Harvard Business School Press, c1993. x, 371 p. Notes: Includes bibliographical references and index. [LC 92028830; ISN 0875843212]   HB615. B625 1993   1265

Enterprise and competitiveness: a systems view of international business. Mark Casson. Oxford: Clarendon, 1990. [xv], 229 p. : ill. Notes: Bibliography: p. [209]-215. [LC 90026362; ISN 0198283261; $52.00]   HB615. C36 1990   1266

The enterprising man. by Orvis F. Collins and David G. Moore with Darab B. Unwalla. Project director: David G. Moore. East Lansing Bureau of Business and Economic Research, Graduate School of Business Administration, Michigan State University, 1964. xvii, 254 p. Notes: "Prepared by Michigan State University under the Small Business Administration Management Research Grant Program." "Notes and References": p. 247-250. [LC 64063821]   HB601. C5686   +1267

The entrepreneur: mainstream views & radical critiques. Robert F. Hébert, Albert N. Link. 2nd ed. New York: Praeger, 1988. xviii, 178 p. Notes: Includes index. Bibliography: p. 161-171. [LC 87038188; ISN 0275928101]   HB615. H34 1988   1268

Entrepreneurial behavior. Barbara J. Bird. Glenview, Ill.: Scott, Foresman, c1989. 418 p. : ill. Notes: Includes bibliographical references (p. 383-408). [LC 88038218; ISN 0673397912; $15.95]   HB615. B57 1989   1269

Entrepreneuring in established companies: managing toward the year 2000. Steven C. Brandt. Homewood, IL: Dow Jones-Irwin, c1986. x, 252 p. Notes: Includes bibliographical references and index. [LC 85071433; ISN 0870946641]   HB615. B7 1986   1270

Entrepreneurship. edited by Mark Casson. Aldershot: Elgar, 1990. 6121 p. : Notes: Includes bibliographical references and index. [LC 90018554; ISN 1852782099; $118.95]   HB615. E623 1990   1271

Entrepreneurship, creativity & organization: text, cases & readings. John Kao. Englewood Cliffs, NJ: Prentice Hall, c1989. xv, 543 p. : ill. Notes: Includes bibliographies and index. [LC 88032101; ISN 0132830116; $39.00]   HB615. K36 1989   1272

Entrepreneurship research: global perspectives: proceedings of the Second Annual Global Conference on Entrepreneurship Research, London, UK, 9-11 March, 1992. edited by Sue Birley, Ian C. MacMillan. Amsterdam; New York: North-Holland, 1993. xvii, 515 p. : ill. Notes: Includes bibliographical references. [LC 93015465; ISN 044489988X; $111.50]   HB615. G58 1992   +1273

Entrepreneurship: what it is and how to teach it: a collection of working papers based on a colloquium held at Harvard Business School, July 5-8, 1983. edited by John J. Kao and Howard H. Stevenson. Boston, Mass.: Harvard Business School, c1985. 328 p. Notes: Includes bibliographical references.]   HB615. E634   1274

The naked entrepreneur. David Robinson. London: Kogan Page, 1990. 122 p. : ill. Notes: Includes index. Bibliography: p. 116-118. [LC 90007214; ISN 0749400846; £14.95]   HB615. R63 1990   1275

Rare breed: the entrepreneur, an American culture. William MacPhee. Chicago: Probus Pub. Co., c1987. 227 p. Notes: Bibliography: p. 227.; ISN 0917253752]   HC102.5.A2 M226 1987   1276

Recapturing the spirit of enterprise. George Gilder. [Rev. ed.] San Francisco, Calif.: Lanham, Md.: ICS Press; Distributed to the trade by National Book Network, c1992. x, 338 p. Notes: "Updated for the 1990s"—Cover. "A publication of the Center for Self-Governance." Rev. ed. of: The spirit of enterprise. c1984. Includes bibliographical references (p. [317]-325) and index. [LC 92023850; ISN 1558152016; $12.95]   HB615. G54 1992   1277

The state of the art of entrepreneurship. edited by Donald L. Sexton, John D. Kasarda. Boston: PWS-Kent Pub. Co., c1992. xxvii, 607 p. : ill. Notes: Includes bibliographical references and index. [LC 91039075; ISN 0534928684]   HB615. S725 1992   +1278

The wealth creators: an entrepreneurial history of the United States. Gerald Gunderson. 1st ed. New York: Dutton, c1989. viii, 278 p. *Notes:* "Truman Talley books." Includes bibliographies and index. [LC 88030963; ISN 0525247297; $18.95] HB615. G86 1989   1279

ENVIRONMENTAL ECONOMICS

Competitive & green: sustainable performance in the environmental age. Dennis C. Kinlaw. Amsterdam; San Diego: Pfeiffer & Co., c1993. xvii, 341 p. : ill. *Notes:* Includes bibliographical references and indexes. [LC 92051018; ISN 0893842273; $21.95] HD75.6. K55 1993   +1280

ENVIRONMENTAL POLICY

Business, ethics, and the environment: the public policy debate. edited by W. Michael Hoffman, Robert Frederick, and Edward S. Petry, Jr. New York: Quorum Books, 1990. xxiii, 253 p. *Notes:* "From the Eighth National Conference on Business Ethics sponsored by the Center for Business Ethics at Bentley College." Includes bibliographical references. [LC 90008390; ISN 0899305504; $45.00] HC110.E5 N335 1990   1281

Costing the earth: the challenge for governments, the opportunities for business. Frances Cairncross. Boston, Mass.: Harvard Business School Press, 1992. vii, 341 p. *Notes:* Includes bibliographical references (p. 319-326) and index. [LC 91033750; ISN 0875843158] HC79.E5 C36 1992   1282

Energy and the ecological economics of sustainability. John Peet. Washington, D.C.: Island Press, c1992. xviii, 309 p. : ill. *Notes:* Includes bibliographical references (p. [277]-298) and index. [LC 91041207; ISN 1559631619; $40.00] HC79.E5 P42 1992   1283

Environmental economics: an introduction. Barry C. Field. New York: McGraw-Hill, c1994. xiv, 482 p. : ill. *Notes:* Includes bibliographical references and indexes. [LC 93014507; ISN 0070207976; $28.95] HC79.E5 F47 1994   +1284

The global partnership for environment and development: a guide to Agenda 21. Post Rio ed. New York: United Nations, 1993. xiv, 239 p. : ill. *Notes:* U.N. sales no.: E.93.I.9; ISN 9211004977] HC79.E5 G545 1993   +1285

Principles of environmental management: the greening of business. Rogene A. Buchholz. Englewood Cliffs, N.J.: Prentice Hall, 1992, c1993. xiv, 433 p. : ill. *Notes:* Includes bibliographical references and index. [LC 92000247; ISN 0137205414] HC79.E5 B82 1992   1286

Proceedings of a conference on linking local and global commons held at Harvard University, April 23-25, 1992. Robert Keohane, Michael McGinnis, Elinor Ostrom. Cambridge, Mass.: Bloomington, IN: Harvard University, Center for International Affairs; Indiana University, Workshop in Political Theory and Policy Analysis, 1993. iii, 170 p. : ill., map *Notes:* "January 10, 1993." Includes bibliographical references.] HC79.E5 K46 1992   1287

EQUAL PAY FOR EQUAL WORK

A comparable worth primer. Steven L. Willborn. Lexington, Mass.: Lexington Books, 1986. x, 128 p. : ill. *Notes:* Includes index. Bibliography: p. [111]-119. [LC 85040329; ISN 0669110183] KF3467. W55 1986   1288

Comparable worth: the myth and the movement. Elaine Johansen. Boulder: Westview Press, 1984. xi, 173 p. : ill. (A Westview special study) *Notes:* Includes index. Bibliography: p. 143-167. [LC 84051747; ISN 0813300835] HD6061.2.U6 J64 1984   1289

ERRORS, POPULAR

Ponzi schemes, invaders from Mars & other extraordinary popular delusions, and the madness of crowds. by Joseph Bulgatz. 1st ed. New York: Harmony Books, c1992. viii, 437 p. : ill. *Notes:* Includes bibliographical references (p. 419-426) and index. *Contents:* Ponzi and company—The Florida land boom—The tulipmania revisited—Invaders from Mars and Bat-men on the moon—The destruction of the Xhosas—Soccer—Lotteries—Dowsing—Perpetual motion—Musical madness—Jonestown and other cults—War: the ultimate delusion. [LC 91039585; ISN 0517588307; $12.00 ($15.00 Can.)] AZ999. B85 1992   1290

ESM GOVERNMENT SECURITIES, INC

Bankers, builders, knaves, and thieves: the $300 million scam at ESM. Donald L. Maggin. Chicago: Contemporary Books, c1989. x, 308 p., 8 p. of plates: ill. *Notes:* Includes bibliographical references. [LC 89037336; ISN 0809245477; $21.95] HG2153.O3 M34 1989   1291

ETHICS

Applied ethics: a reader. edited by Earl R. Winkler and Jerrold R. Coombs. Oxford England; Cambridge Mass.: Blackwell, 1993. xii, 427 p. *Notes:* Includes bibliographical references and index. [LC 92036936; ISN 0631188339] BJ1031. A67 1993 +1292

The moral sense. James Q. Wilson. New York: Toronto: New York: Free Press; Maxwell Macmillan Canada; Maxwell Macmillan International, c1993. xviii, 313 p. *Notes:* Includes bibliographical references (p. 267-300) and index. [LC 93018520; ISN 0029354056; $22.95] BJ1012. W5375 1993   1293

EURO-BOND MARKET

ECU: European currency unit. edited by Richard M. Levich. London: Euromoney Publications, 1987. 172 p. : ill. *Notes:* Bibliography: p. 167-168.; ISN 1870031504] HG3896. E33   1294

Eurobonds. Michael Bowe. Homewood, Il.: Dow Jones-Irwin, c1988. 240 p. : ill. *Notes:* Includes index. Bibliography: p. [235]-238. [LC 88072076; ISN 1556231792; $25.00] HG3896. B68 1988   1295

The new Euromarkets: a theoretical and practical study of international financing in the eurobond, eurocurrency, and related financial markets. Brian Scott Quinn. New York: Wiley, 1975. xxii, 274 p. : ill. *Notes:* "A Halsted Press book." Includes index. Bibliography: p. [269]-271. [LC 75004755; ISN 0470702664] HG3881. Q56 1975 +1296

EURO-DOLLAR MARKET

Eurodollars and international banking. edited by Paolo Savona and George Sutija. London?: Macmillan, in association with International Banking Center, Florida International University, 1985. xiii, 226 p. : ill. *Notes:* A conference on Eurodollars was held in Miami organized by the International Banking Centre at Florida International University. Includes bibliographical references and indexes.; ISN 0333365534] HG3897. E918   1297

EUROPE 1992

1992. London: Euromoney Publications, c1990. 166, [31] p. : col. ill., 1 map *Notes:* "A Euromoney book."; ISN 1870031296; £75.00] HC241.2. N558 1990   1298

1992: understanding the new European market. James W. Dudley. Rev. ed. Chicago, IL: Dearborn Financial Pub., 1990. 430 p. : ill. *Notes:* "International bestseller." Includes bibliographical references (p. [421]-422) and index.; ISN 0793102650; $21.95] HF1532.92. D835 1990   1299

Europe 1992 and the new world power game. by Michael Silva and Bertil Sjögren. New York: Wiley, c1990. xviii, 301 p. *Notes:* Includes bibliographical references. [LC 90033731; ISN 0471515507; $22.95] HC241.2. S517 1990   1300

Inside the new Europe. by Axel Krause. 1st ed. New York, NY: HarperCollins Publishers, c1991. xxiv, 356 p. : map *Notes:* "Cornelia & Michael Bessie books." Includes bibliographical references (p. 341-344) and index. [LC 90056379; ISN 0060391014; $25.00 ($32.95 Can.)] HC241.2. K698 1991   1301

EUROPE, EASTERN—ECONOMIC CONDITIONS—1989—CONGRESSES

The transition in Eastern Europe. edited by Olivier Jean Blanchard, Kenneth A. Froot, and Jeffrey D. Sachs. Chicago: University of Chicago Press, c1994- v.; *Notes:* Includes bibliographical references and indexes. Library has: v. 1 *Contents:* v. 1. Country studies [LC 93036585; ISN 0226056600; $39.95] HC244. T6989 1994 +1302

EUROPE, EASTERN—ECONOMIC POLICY—1989—CONGRESSES

Trials of transition: economic reform in the former Communist bloc. edited by Michael Keren and Gur Ofer. Boulder, Colo.: Westview Press, 1992. xx, 308 p. *Notes:* Includes bibliographical references and indexes. [LC 92026065; ISN 0813315654; $16.95]   HC244. T73 1992   1303

EUROPE, EASTERN—ECONOMIC POLICY—1989-

Making markets: economic transformation in Eastern Europe and the post-Soviet states. edited by Shafiqul Islam and Michael Mandelbaum. New York: Council on Foreign Relations Press, c1993. ix, 238 p. : ill. *Notes:* Includes bibliographical references and index. [LC 92040676; ISN 087609129X; $14.95]   HC244. M256 1993   1304

EUROPE, EASTERN—FOREIGN ECONOMIC RELATIONS—CONGRESSES

External economic relations of the central and east European countries: colloquium, 8-10 April 1992, Brussels = Relations économiques extérieures des pays d'Europe centrale et orientale: colloque, 8-10 avril 1992, Bruxelles. Reiner Weichhardt, editor. 1st ed. Brussels: NATO, 1992. 222 p. : ill. *Notes:* English and French. "The 1992 NATO Economics Colloquium"—Pref. Includes bibliographical references.; ISN 9284500699]   HF1532.7. N37 1992   1305

EUROPEAN COOPERATION

The European adventure: tasks for the enlarged Community. London C. Knight, 1972. ix, 194 p. [LC 73155482; ISN 0853141843]   D1053. S64   +1306

EUROPEAN ECONOMIC COMMUNITY

EC/EFTA, the future European economic area. study written by the Club de Bruxelles under the direction of Patrick Baragiola. Bruxelles: The Club, 1991. f, 171 leaves]   HC241.25.E84 E88 1991   1307
The European Community and the challenge of the future. edited by Juliet Lodge. 2nd ed. New York: St. Martin's Press, c1993. xxvi, 403 p. : maps *Notes:* Includes bibliographical references and index. [LC 93017954; ISN 0312099789]   HC241.2. E83412 1993   +1308
The European marketplace. edited by James Hogan. Basingstoke: Macmillan, 1991. xii, 554 p. [LC 89054768; ISN 0333518586; £45.00]   HC241.2. E828 1991   1309
European markets after 1992. by Timothy M. Devinney, William C. Hightower. Lexington, Mass.: Lexington Books, 1991. xiii, 322 p. : ill. *Notes:* Includes bibliographical references (p. [297]-314) and index. [LC 90021844; ISN 0669214663; $24.95]   HC241.2. D44 1991   1310
Winning in the new Europe: taking advantage of the single market. Liam Fahey. Englewood Cliffs, N.J.: Prentice Hall, c1992. xv, 352 p. : ill. *Notes:* Includes bibliographical references and index. [LC 92016119; ISN 0133576337]   HC241.2. F263 1992   1311

EUROPEAN ECONOMIC COMMUNITY COUNTRIES—COMMERCE—UNITED STATES

Marketing strategies for the new Europe: a North American perspective for 1992. by John K. Ryans, Jr. and Pradeep A. Rau; contributors, James R. Krum, Cynthia C. Ryans. Chicago, IL: American Marketing Association, c1990. xvi, 202 p. : ill *Notes:* Includes bibliographical references (p. 193-202). [LC 89018279; ISN 0877572038; $29.95]   HF3092.8. R93 1990   1312

EUROPEAN ECONOMIC COMMUNITY COUNTRIES—COMMERCIAL POLICY

The world's largest market: a business guide to Europe, 1992. Robert Williams, Mark Teagan, José Beneyto. New York, N.Y.: American Management Association, 1990. xx, 280 p. : ill. *Notes:* Includes bibliographical references and index. LC 90055216; ISN 0814459897; $29.95]
HF1532.5. W55 1990   1313

EUROPEAN ECONOMIC COMMUNITY COUNTRIES—ECONOMIC CONDITIONS

The 1992 challenge from Europe: development of the European Community's internal market. Michael Calingaert. Washington, D.C.: National Planning Association, 1988. xv, 148 p. *Notes:* Includes index. Bibliography: p. 138.; ISN 0890680965; $15.00]   HC241.2. C35 1988   1314

The new Europe: into the 1990s. G. N. Minshull. 4th ed. London: Hodder & Stoughton, 1990. 348 p. : ill. *Notes:* Previous ed.: 1985. Includes index. Bibliography: p. 343-345. [LC 89045918; ISN 0340505125; £7.95]   HC241.2. M55 1990   1315

EUROPEAN ECONOMIC COMMUNITY COUNTRIES—ECONOMIC POLICY

Single market to social Europe: the European Community in the 1990s. Mark Wise and Richard Gibb. Harlow, Essex, England: New York, NY: Longman Scientific & Technical; Wiley, 1993. xvi, 337 p. : ill., maps *Notes:* Includes bibliographical references (p. [314]-327) and index. [LC 92030437; ISN 0470220287]   HC241.2. W495 1993   1316

EUROPEAN ECONOMIC COMMUNITY COUNTRIES—FOREIGN ECONOMIC RELATIONS—JAPAN

The next battleground: Japan, America, and the new European market. Tim Jackson. Boston: Houghton Mifflin, 1993. xvii, 332 p. *Notes:* Includes bibliographical references and index. [LC 92041918; ISN 0395615941; $22.95]   HF1532.5.Z4 J34 1993   1317

EUROPE—ECONOMIC CONDITIONS

How the West grew rich: the economic transformation of the industrial world. Nathan Rosenberg & L.E. Birdzell, Jr. New York: Basic Books, c1986. xii, 353 p. *Notes:* Includes bibliographies and index. [LC 85047551; ISN 0465031080; $19.95]   HC240. R67 1986   1318

EUROPE—ECONOMIC CONDITIONS—1945-

Europe in the year 2000. London: Euromonitor, 1990. xviii, 357 p. [LC 90010108; ISN 0863382428; £135.00]   HC240. E826 1990   1319

EUROPE—ECONOMIC CONDITIONS—20TH CENTURY

The European economy, 1914-1990. Derek H. Aldcroft. 3rd ed. London; New York: Routledge, 1993. vii, 300 p. : ill. *Notes:* Rev. ed. of: The European economy, 1914-1980. 2nd ed. c1980. Includes bibliographical references (p. 279-290) and index. [LC 92038193; ISN 0415091608]   HC240. A6657 1993   +1320

EUROPE—ECONOMIC INTEGRATION

Managing in the single market. Richard Brown. Oxford; Boston: Butterworth-Heinemann in association with the Institute of Management, 1993. xii, 184 p. : ill. *Notes:* Cover and spine title: Managing in the single European market. Includes bibliographical references (p. [176]-[180]) and index. [LC 94166168; ISN 0750615753; £15.95]   HC241. B765 1993   +1321

1992, one European market?: a critical analysis of the Commission's internal market strategy. the European Policy Unit at the European University Institute, Florence; eds., Roland Bieber. . . et al. 1. Aufl. Baden-Baden: Nomos, 1988. 463 p. *Notes:* Papers originally presented at a colloquium held by the European University Institute at Florence in June 1986 on the subject of completing the internal market. Includes bibliographical references. [LC 89114923; ISN 3789015229]   HC241.2. N554 1988   1322

EUROPE—HISTORY, LOCAL

Europe: road to unity. Flora Lewis. 1st Touchstone rev. ed. New York: Simon & Schuster, 1992. 590 p. : 2 maps *Notes:* Rev. ed. of: Europe: a tapestry of nations. 1987. "Revised and updated"—Cover. "A Touchstone book." Includes bibliographical references (p. 557-566) and index. [LC 92234710; ISN 0671778285] D20. L593 1992   1323

EXECUTIVE ABILITY

The anatomy of a great executive. John Wareham. New York, NY: HarperCollins, c1991. viii, 261 p. : ill. [LC 91007999; ISN 0887305059; $21.95] HD38.2. W369 1991   1324

Charismatic leadership: the elusive factor in organizational effectiveness. contributions by Jay A. Conger, Rabindra N. Kanungo, and associates; foreword by Warren Bennis. 1st ed. San Francisco: Jossey-Bass Publishers, 1988. xxii, 352 p. (The Jossey-Bass management series) *Notes:* Includes bibliographies and indexes. [LC 88042734; ISN 1555421024] HD38.2. C43 1988   1325

The Economist Intelligence Unit global manager. Michael Moynihan. New York: McGraw-Hill, c1993. xiv, 216 p. *Notes:* Includes index. [LC 93001942; ISN 0070093512; $29.95] HD38.2. M69 1993   1326

The lessons of experience: how successful executives develop on the job. Morgan W. McCall, Jr., Michael M. Lombardo, Ann M. Morrison. Lexington, Mass.: Lexington Books, c1988. xiii, 210 p. : ill. (The Issues in organization and management series) *Notes:* Includes index. Bibliography: p. [201]-204. [LC 87046405; ISN 0669180955] HD38.2. M36 1988   1327

The making of the achiever: how to win distinction in your company. by Allan Cox. 1st ed. New York: Dodd, Mead, c1985. xxiii, 258 p. *Notes:* Includes index. Bibliography: p. 252-253. [LC 84013729; ISN 0396084710] HF5500.2. C679 1985   1328

Power and influence. John P. Kotter. New York: Free Press, c1985. ix, 218 p. : ill. *Notes:* "Based on the highly acclaimed Harvard Business School course."—Jacket. Includes index. Bibliography: p. 207-212. [LC 85001574; ISN 0029183308] HD38.2. K68 1985   1329

Practical intelligence: working smarter in business and everyday life. Roger Peters. 1st ed. New York, N.Y.: Harper & Row, c1987. x, 341 p. *Notes:* Includes index. Bibliography: p. 306-336. [LC 86046096; ISN 0060156813; $17.95] HD38.2. P47 1987   1330

Predicting executive success: what it takes to make it into senior management. Melvin Sorcher. New York: Wiley, c1985. ix, 280 p. *Notes:* Includes index. [LC 85003293; ISN 0471815659; $19.95] HD38.2. S67 1985   1331

The success profile: a leading headhunter tells you how to get to the top. by Lester Korn. New York: Simon and Schuster, c1988. 287 p. : ill. *Notes:* Includes index. [LC 87023249; ISN 0671552635] HD38.2. K67 1988   1332

EXECUTIVE POWER

Taming the prince: the ambivalence of modern executive power. Harvey C. Mansfield, Jr. New York: London: Free Press; Collier Macmillan, c1989. xxiv, 358 p. *Notes:* Bibliography: p. 299-345. [LC 89000669; ISN 0029199808; $22.95] JF251. M29 1989   1333

EXECUTIVES

Ambitious men: their drives, dreams, and delusions. Srully Blotnick. New York: Viking, 1987. 388 p. *Notes:* Includes bibliographical references and index. [LC 86040274; ISN 0670810614] HD38.25.U6 B55   1334

Balancing act: how managers can integrate successful careers and fulfilling personal lives. Joan Kofodimos. 1st ed. San Francisco: Jossey-Bass, c1993. xix, 167 p. *Notes:* Includes bibliographical references (p. 155-162) and index. [LC 93004589; ISN 1555425089] HD38.2. K63 1993   +1335

Becoming a courageous manager: overcoming career problems of new managers. Ross Arkell Webber. Englewood Cliffs, NJ: Prentice Hall, c1991. xv, 304 p. : ill. *Notes:* Includes bibliographical references (p. 280-304). [LC 90042463; ISN 0130863726; $24.95] HD69.T54 W43 1991   1336

Beyond ambition: how driven managers can lead better and live better. Robert E. Kaplan with Wilfred H. Drath and Joan R. Kofodimos. 1st ed. San Francisco: Jossey-Bass, 1991. xxii, 269 p. *Notes:* Includes bibliographical references (p. 247-259) and index. [LC 91012695; ISN 1555423159; $27.95] HD38.2. K37 1991   1337

Beyond the trust gap: forging a new partnership between managers and their employers. Thomas R. Horton, Peter C. Reid. Homewood, Ill.: Business One Irwin, c1991. xiii, 249 p. *Notes:* Includes bibliographical references. [LC 90042474; ISN 1556232691] HD38.25.U6 H66 1991   1338

The change of a lifetime: employment patterns among Japan's managerial elite. John C. Beck, Martha N. Beck. Honolulu: University of Hawaii Press, c1994. vii, 286 p. : ill. *Notes:* Includes bibliographical references (p. 273-281) and index. [LC 93041946; ISN 0824815297; $18.95] HD38.25.J3 B43 1994   +1339

Climbing the corporate Matterhorn. James A. Newman, Roy Alexander. New York: Wiley, c1985. xvi, 311 p. *Notes:* Includes index. [LC 84015357; ISN 0471807648; $16.95] HD38.2. N49 1985   1340

Confessions of a corporate headhunter. by Allan J. Cox. New York Trident Press, 1973. 189 p. *Notes:* Includes bibliographical references. [LC 72096812; ISN 0671271040] HF5549.5.R44 C64   +1341

The corporate couple: living the corporate game. by Peggy J. Berry. New York: Watts, 1985. 296 p. *Notes:* Includes index. Bibliography: p. [293]-296. [LC 85013576; ISN 0531095924] HD38.2. B47 1985   1342

The cost of talent: how executives and professionals are paid and how it affects America. Derek Bok. New York: Toronto: New York: Free Press; Maxwell Macmillan Canada; Maxwell Macmillan International, c1993. vii, 342 p. *Notes:* Includes bibliographical references (p. 299-333) and index. [LC 93027892; ISN 0029037557; $24.95] HD4965.5.U6 B65 1993   +1343

Critical path hiring: how to employ top-flight managers. Philip R. Matheny. Lexington, Mass.: Lexington Books, c1986. xx, 194 p. : ill. *Notes:* Includes index. [LC 85045472; ISN 0669117897] HD38.2. M37 1986   1344

Designing and managing your career. edited by Harry Levinson. Boston, Mass.: Harvard Business School Press, c1988. vii, 391 p. *Notes:* Includes bibliographies and index. [LC 88030099; ISN 0875841805] HD38.2. D475 1989   1345

Developing managers. Manuel London. 1st ed. San Francisco: Jossey-Bass, 1985. xvii, 259 p. (The Jossey-Bass management series) (The Jossey-Bass social and behavioral science series) *Notes:* Includes index. Bibliography: p. 241-247. [LC 84043030; ISN 0875896464] HD30.4. L66 1985   1346

The effective executive. Peter F. Drucker. 1st Harper Colophon ed. New York: Harper & Row, 1985, c1967. viii, 178 p. *Notes:* Includes index. [LC 84048156; ISN 006091209X; $9.95] HD38.25.U6 D78 1985   1347

Executive compensation: a strategic guide for the 1990s. edited by Fred K. Foulkes. Boston, Mass.: Harvard Business School Press, c1991. xxiv, 550 p. : ill. *Notes:* Includes bibliographical references and index. [LC 90044176; ISN 0875842100; $75.00] HD4965.5.U6 E87 1991   1348

Executive compensation in large industrial corporations. by Wilbur G. Lewellen. New York National Bureau of Economic Research; distributed by Columbia University Press, 1968. xxv, 371 p. illus. *Notes:* Bibliography: p. 363-366. [LC 67029643] HD4965.5.U6 L4   +1349

Executive compensation: who, how much, and when? A Harvard Business Review reprint series. Boston Harvard Business Review Reprint Service, 1973? 100 p. illus.] HD4965.2. H37   +1350

Executive development series; reprints from Harvard Business Review. Boston c1955-71. 3 v. in 1. illus. *Notes:* Includes bibliographical references.] HF5549.5.T7 H365   +1351

Executive musical chairs. William R. Wilkinson. San Mateo, Calif.: Warrington & Co., c1983. xvi, 190 p. *Notes:* Includes bibliographical references and index.; ISN 0911735003] HF5549.5.R44 W46 1983   1352

Executive power. Suresh Srivastva and associates. 1st ed. San Francisco: Jossey-Bass Publishers, 1986. xxii, 360 p. *Notes:* Includes index. "A joint publication in the Jossey-Bass management series and the Jossey-Bass social and behavioral science series." Bibliography: p. 331-351. *Contents:* Why power and influence issues are at the very core of executive work / John P. Kotter. [LC 85045914; ISN 087589691X] HD38.2. S75 1986   1353

The executive search collaboration: a guide for human resources professionals and their search firms. edited by Janet Jones-Parker and Robert H. Perry. New York: Quorum Books, c1990. vi, 252 p. *Notes:* Includes bibliographical references. [LC 90030006; ISN 0899302831] HD38.25.U6 E935 1990   1354

Executive talent: developing and keeping the best people. Eli Ginzberg, editor. New York: J. Wiley, c1988. vii, 184 p. *Notes:* Includes bibliographical references and index. [LC 87024946; ISN 0471634220] HD38.2. E94 1988   1355

The functions of the executive. Cambridge Harvard University Press, 1968. xxxvi, 334 p. *Notes:* "Thirtieth anniversary edition, with an introduction by Kenneth R. Andrews." "Representative works of writers mentioned [in the introduction]": p. [xxii]-xxiii. [LC 68028690]   HD31. B36 1968   1356

The headhunters. John A. Byrne. New York: Macmillan, c1986. 280 p. *Notes:* Includes index. [LC 86000129; ISN 0025179500]   HD38.25.U6 B97 1986   1357

In search of excess: the overcompensation of American executives. by Graef S. Crystal. 1st ed. New York: W.W. Norton, 1992. 272 p. *Notes:* Includes bibliographical references and index. [LC 91025569; ISN 039303089X; $19.95]   HD4965.5.U6 C77 1991   1358

The intuitive manager. Roy Rowan. 1st ed. Boston: Little, Brown, c1986. xii, 188 p. [LC 85028517; ISN 0316759740]   HD38.2. R68 1986   1359

The leader-manager. John N. Williamson, editor. New York: Wiley, c1986. xi, 511 p. : ill. *Notes:* Bibliography: p. 507-508. [LC 86001316; ISN 0471836931; $19.95 (est.)]   HD38.2. L42 1986   1360

Management laureates: a collection of autobiographical essays. by H. Igor Ansoff... et al.; editor, Arthur G. Bedeian. Greenwich, Conn.: Jai Press, c1992- v. *Notes:* Includes bibliographical references. [LC 92034213; ISN 1559384697]   HC102.5.A2 M32 1992   1361

Managerial job change: men and women in transition. Nigel Nicholson and Michael A. West. Cambridge Cambridgeshire; New York: Cambridge University Press, 1988. xi, 274 p. : ill. *Notes:* Includes indexes. Bibliography: p. 254-264. [LC 87011752; ISN 0521334594]   HD38.2. N53 1988   1362

Managing career systems: channeling the flow of executive careers. Jeffrey A. Sonnenfeld. Homewood, Ill.: R.D. Irwin, 1984. xxi, 942 p. (The Irwin series in management and the behavioral sciences) *Notes:* Includes bibliographical references and indexes. [LC 83083331; ISN 0256031436]   HF5500.2. S66   1363

Masculinity and the British organization man since 1945. Michael Roper. Oxford; New York: Oxford University Press, 1994. xi, 259 p. : ill. *Notes:* Includes bibliographical references (p. 245-253) and index. [LC 93015075; ISN 0198256930; £25.00]   HD38.25.G7 R66 1994   +1364

MBAs on the fast track: the career mobility of young managers. Phyllis A. Wallace. New York, NY: Ballinger Pub. Co., c1989. xviii, 220 p. : ill. *Notes:* Includes index. Bibliography: p. 195-212. [LC 88034180; ISN 0887301207; $34.95]   HD38.25.U6 W35 1989   1365

The new competitors: a report on American managers from D. Quinn Mills of the Harvard Business School. D. Quinn Mills. New York: Wiley, c1985. xiii, 391 p. *Notes:* Includes bibliographical references and index. [LC 85000616; ISN 0471810266; $10.95 (est.)]   HD38.25.U6 M55 1985   1366

Outperformers: super achievers, breakthrough strategies, high-profit results. Mack Hanan, Tim Haigh. New York, NY: AMACOM, c1989. vii, 161 p. : ill. *Notes:* Includes index. [LC 89045451; ISN 0814459528; $18.95]   HD38.2. H35 1989   1367

Power and the corporate mind. Abraham Zaleznik, Manfred F.R. Kets de Vries. 2nd ed. Chicago: Bonus Books, 1985. xv, 288 p. : ill. *Notes:* Includes index. Bibliography: p. [269]-279. [LC 85071835; ISN 0933893051; $17.95]   HF5500. Z34 1985   1368

Quiet desperation: the truth about successful men. Jan Halper. New York, NY: Warner Books, c1988. x, 279 p. *Notes:* Bibliography: p. 279. [LC 87031585; ISN 0446513598]   HD38.25.U6 H34 1988   1369

Rewarding results: motivating profit center managers. Kenneth A. Merchant. Boston, Mass.: Harvard Business School Press, c1989. xvi, 272 p. *Notes:* Includes index. Bibliography: p. [253] - 260. [LC 89032888; ISN 0875842151]   HD4965.2. M47 1989   1370

Stalking the headhunter: the smart job-hunter's guide to executive recruiters. John Tarrant. Toronto; New York: Bantam Books, c1986. xii, 270 p. *Notes:* Includes index. "A Stonesong Press book." [LC 86047579; ISN 0553051814]   HD38.25.U6 T37 1986   1371

Tradeoffs: executive, family, and organizational life. Barrie S. Greiff, Preston K. Munter. New York: New American Library, c1980. xxi, 201 p. : ill. [LC 79028530; ISN 0453003745]   HF5500.2. G75   1372

What works for me: 16 CEOs talk about their careers and commitments. Thomas R. Horton. 1st ed. New York: Random House, 1986. 436 p. : ports. *Notes:* Includes index. Bibliography: p. 423-429. [LC 86006677; ISN 0394550722; $19.95]   HD38.25.U6 H67 1986   1373

EXPERT SYSTEMS (COMPUTER SCIENCE)

Expert system technology: development and application. Robert Keller. Englewood Cliffs, NJ: Yourdon Press, c1987. xxii, 246 p. : ill. (Yourdon Press computing series) *Notes:* Includes index. Bibliography: p. 237. [LC 86024742; ISN 0132955776]   QA76.76.E95 K43 1987   1374

Expert systems: techniques, tools, and applications. edited by Philip Klahr and Donald A. Waterman. Reading, Mass.: Addison-Wesley Pub. Co., 1986. v, 441 p. : ill. *Notes:* Includes bibliographical references and index. [LC 85028595; ISN 0201141868; $35.00 (est.)]   QA76.76.E95 E96   1375

A guide to expert systems. Donald A. Waterman. Reading, Mass.: Addison-Wesley, c1986. xviii, 419 p. : ill. (The Teknowledge series in knowledge engineering) *Notes:* Includes bibliographies and index. [LC 85006022; ISN 0201083132; $24.95]   QA76.9.E96 W369 1986   1376

Introduction to expert systems. Peter Jackson. Wokingham, England; Reading, Mass.: Addison-Wesley Pub. Co., c1986. ix, 246 p. : ill. (International computer science series) *Notes:* Includes index. Bibliography: p. 237-243. [LC 86001050; ISN 0201142236; £14.95]   QA76.9.E96 J33   1377

EXPORT CREDIT

Export finance. David Bowen, Dominic Mills and Martin Knight. London: Euromoney Publications, 1986. xiv, 232 p. : ill.; ISN 1870031458]   HG3753. B78 1986   1378

The McGraw-Hill handbook of global trade and investment financing. Lawrence W. Tuller. New York: McGraw-Hill, c1992. xxiv, 535 p. *Notes:* Includes index. [LC 92006034; ISN 0070654352; $64.95]   HG3753. T85 1992   1379

EXPORT MARKETING

The essence of international marketing. Stanley J. Paliwoda. New York: Prentice Hall, 1994. x, 164 p. : ill. *Notes:* Includes bibliographical references and index. [LC 93036374; ISN 0132848031]
     HF1416. P348 1994   +1380

The global business: four key marketing strategies. Erdener Kaynak, editor. New York: International Business Press, c1993. xxv, 432 p. : ill. *Notes:* Includes bibliographical references and index. [LC 91034596; ISN 1560242485]   HF1416. G55 1993   +1381

Global marketing management. Warren J. Keegan. 4th ed. Englewood Cliffs, N.J.: Prentice-Hall, 1988. xvi, 783 p. : ill. (The Prentice-Hall series in marketing) *Notes:* Rev. ed. of: Multinational marketing management. 3rd ed. c1984. Includes bibliographies and indexes. [LC 88015137; ISN 0133572609]   HF1009.5. K39 1988   1382

Going global: new opportunities for growing companies to compete in world markets. Lawrence W. Tuller. Homewood, Ill.: Business One Irwin, c1991. xvii, 398 p. *Notes:* Includes bibliographical references (p. 389) and index. [LC 90046849; ISN 1556234120; $69.95]   HF1416.5. T85 1991   1383

International dimensions of marketing. Vern Terpstra. 2nd ed. Boston, Mass.: PWS-Kent Pub. Co., c1988. xiv, 185 p. *Notes:* Includes bibliographies and index. [LC 88000802; ISN 0534872018]
     HF1416. T47 1988   1384

International marketing. Philip R. Cateora. 7th ed. Homewood, IL: Irwin, 1990. xxiii, 870 p. : ill. *Notes:* Includes bibliographical references. [LC 89037430; ISN 0256079536]   HF1009.5. C35 1990   1385

International marketing. Vern Terpstra, Ravi Sarathy. 5th ed. Chicago: Dryden Press, c1991. xxii, 714 p. : ill.; 1 map. *Notes:* Includes bibliographies and indexes. [LC 90003403; ISN 0030327679; $77.86]   HF1416. T48 1991   1386

International marketing: a cultural approach. Jean-Claude Usunier. New York: Prentice Hall, c1993. xiii, 494 p. : ill. *Notes:* Includes bibliographical references and index. [LC 92033999; ISN 0131945807; $40.00]   HF1416. U85 1993   1387

International marketing and export management. Gerald Albaum. . . et al. Wokingham, England; Reading, Mass.: Addison-Wesley, c1989. xiii, 407 p. : ill. (International business series) *Notes:* Includes bibliographies and index. [LC 89031462; ISN 0201175711; $45.75]   HF1416. I617 1989   1388

International marketing management. Subhash C. Jain. 3rd ed. Boston: PWS-Kent Pub. Co., c1990. xviii, 758 p. : ill. *Notes:* Includes bibliographical references. [LC 89039150; ISN 0534921310]
     HF1009.5. J336 1990   1389

International marketing: managerial perspectives. edited by Subhash C. Jain and Lewis R. Tucker, Jr. 2nd ed. Boston, Mass.: Kent Pub. Co., c1986. xii, 466 p. : ill. *Notes:* Bibliography: p. 459-466. [LC 85019820; ISN 0534062709; $17.50]   HF1009.5. I546   1390

Marketing: an international perspective. Philip R. Cateora, Susan M. Keaveney. Homewood, Ill.: Irwin, 1987. xi, 172 p. : ill. *Notes:* Includes bibliographies and index. [LC 86083392; ISN 0256056269]   HF1009.5. C355 1987   1391

Marketing in the international environment. Edward W. Cundiff, Marye Tharp Hilger. 2nd ed. Englewood Cliffs, NJ: Prentice-Hall, c1988. xvi, 608 p. : ill. *Notes:* Includes bibliographical references and index. [LC 87032708; ISN 0135573491; $28.00]   HF1009.5. C86 1988   1392

Multinational marketing management: cases and readings. compiled by Robert D. Buzzell, John A. Quelch. Reading, Mass.: Addison-Wesley, c1988. x, 500 p. : ill. *Notes:* Bibliography: p. 499-500. [LC 87012599; ISN 0201079968; $26.95]   1393

Strategic international marketing. Philip R. Cateora. Homewood, Ill.: Dow Jones-Irwin, 1985. xi, 428 p. : ill. *Notes:* Includes bibliographical references and index. [LC 85071302; ISN 0870946412; $37.50]
HF1009.5. C36   1394

Strategies for international industrial marketing: the management of customer relationships in European industrial markets. edited by Peter W. Turnbull and Jean-Paul Valla. London; Dover, N.H.: Croom Helm, c1986. 310 p. : ill. *Notes:* Includes index. Bibliography: p. 301-305. [LC 85029047; ISN 0709924941; $50.00 (U.S.)]
HF1009.7.E85 S77 1986   1395

EXPORT SALES CONTRACTS

Marketing by agreement: a cross-cultural approach to business negotiations. J.B. McCall and M.B. Warrington. 2nd ed. Chichester; New York: Wiley, c1989. xi, 326 p. : ill. *Notes:* Includes indexes. Bibliography: p. 311-316. [LC 88033642; ISN 0471921513; ISN 0471921521; $25.00]
K1030.4. M38 1989   1396

EXPORTS

Export-import financing. Harry M. Venedikian, Gerald A. Warfield. 3rd ed. New York: Wiley, c1992. x, 469 p. : ill. *Notes:* Includes index. [LC 91004771; ISN 047153675X; $60.00]
HG3754.U5 V46 1992   1397

FACTORY MANAGEMENT

Manufacturing organization and management. Harold T. Amrine... et al. 6th ed. Englewood Cliffs, N.J.: Prentice Hall, c1993. xvi, 623 p. : ill. *Notes:* Rev. ed. of: Manufacturing organization and management / Harold T. Amrine, John A. Ritchey, Colin L. Moodie. c1987. Includes bibliographical references and index. [LC 92012867; ISN 0135548586]
TS155. M333365 1993   1398

FAMILY

The Japanese overseas: can they go home again? Merry White. New York: London: Free Press; Collier Macmillan, c1988. x, 179 p. : ill. *Notes:* Includes index. Bibliography: p. 161-174. [LC 87033836; ISN 0029350913]
HQ682. W48 1988   1399

A treatise on the family. Gary S. Becker. Enl. ed. Cambridge, Mass.: Harvard University Press, 1991. xii, 424 p. : ill. *Notes:* Includes bibliographical references (p. 383-409) and index. [LC 90004975; ISN 0674906993]
HQ518. B35 1991   +1400

FAMILY CORPORATIONS

Family pride: profiles of five of America's best-run family businesses. Thomas Goldwasser. 1st ed. New York: Dodd, Mead, c1986. 226 p. *Notes:* Includes index. [LC 86004546; ISN 0396085873]
HD62.25. G64 1986   1401

Keeping the family business healthy: how to plan for continuing growth, profitability, and family leadership. John L. Ward; foreword by Leon A. Danco. 1st ed. San Francisco, Calif.: Jossey-Bass, c1986. xxix, 266 p. : ill. (Jossey-Bass management series) *Notes:* Includes index. Bibliography: p. 255-259. [LC 86045624; ISN 1555420265]
HD62.25. W37   1402

Zaibatsu: the rise and fall of family enterprise groups in Japan. Hidemasa Morikawa; foreword by Alfred D. Chandler, Jr. Tokyo: University of Tokyo Press, c1992. xxiv, 283 p. *Notes:* Includes bibliographical references (p. [249]-273) and index.; ISN 4130470558; $52.50]   HD2907. M67 1992   1403

FARM MANAGEMENT

Farm business management: the decision-making process. Emery N. Castle, Manning H. Becker, A. Gene Nelson. 3rd ed. New York: Macmillan, c1987. xiii, 413 p. : ill. *Notes:* Includes bibliographical references and index. [LC 86000126; ISN 0023202009; $41.00]
S561. C34 1987   1404

FEDERAL RESERVE BANKS

Inside the Fed: making monetary policy. William C. Melton. Homewood, Ill.: Dow Jones-Irwin, c1985. x, 226 p. : ill. *Notes:* Includes bibliographical references and index. [LC 84071297; ISN 0870945440]　　　HG2563. M38 1985　　1405

FEDERAL SAVINGS AND LOAN INSURANCE CORPORATION

Crisis resolution in the thrift industry: a Mid America Institute report. by Roger C. Kormendi... et al. Boston: Kluwer Academic Publishers, c1989. xvi, 109 p. : ill. *Notes:* Includes bibliographical references (p. [93]-101). [LC 89028734; ISN 0792390598; $42.00]　　　HG2152. C76 1989　　1406

FEMINISM

The feminization of America: how women's values are changing our public and private lives. Elinor Lenz & Barbara Myerhoff. 1st ed. Los Angeles: New York: J. P. Tarcher; Distributed by St. Martin's Press, c1985. 276 p. *Notes:* Includes index. Bibliography: p. 257-262. [LC 85009752; ISN 0874773695; $14.95]　　　HQ1420. L46 1985　　1407

FEYNMAN, RICHARD PHILLIPS

Genius: the life and science of Richard Feynman. James Gleick. New York: Pantheon Books, c1992. x, 532 p. : ill. *Notes:* Includes bibliographical references (p. 499-516) and index. [LC 92006577; ISN 0679408363; $27.50 ($34.50 Can.)]　　　QC16.F49 G54 1992　　1408

FIELDS, DEBBI

One smart cookie: how a housewife's chocolate-chip recipe turned into a multimillion dollar business: the story of Mrs. Field's cookies. by Debbi Fields and Alan Furst. New York: Simon and Schuster, c1987. 173 p. : ill. [LC 87015172; ISN 0671618385]　　　HD9058.C65 F544 1987　　1409

FINANCE

Accounting, budgeting, and finance: a reference for managers. Charles J. Woelfel. New York, NY: AMACOM, c1990. xv, 620 p. : ill. *Notes:* Includes bibliographical references. [LC 89077450; ISN 0814459889; $59.95]　　　HG151. W62 1990　　1410

Capital ideas: the improbable origins of modern Wall Street. Peter L. Bernstein. New York: Toronto: New York: Free Press; Maxwell Macmillan Canada; Maxwell Macmillan International, c1992. xi, 340 p. [8] p. of plates: ill. *Notes:* Includes bibliographical references (p. 319-329) and indexes. [LC 91023269; ISN 0029030110; $24.95]　　　HG173. B47 1992　　1411

The city revolution: causes and consequences. Maximilian Hall. New York: St. Martin's Press, 1987. xiii, 147 p. : ill. *Notes:* Includes index. Bibliography: p. 141-142. [LC 87009684; ISN 0312009860; $25.00 (est.)]　　　HG186.G7 H35 1987　　1412

Continuous-time finance. Robert C. Merton; foreword by Paul A. Samuelson. Cambridge, Mass.: B. Blackwell, 1990. xix, 700 p. : ill. *Notes:* Includes bibliographical references (p. [649]-678) and index. [LC 89018169; ISN 0631158472; $58.75]　　　HG173. M54 1990　　1413

The economics of money, banking, and financial markets. Frederic S. Mishkin. 3rd ed. New York, NY: HarperCollins, c1992. 1 v. (various pagings): ill. (some col.) *Notes:* Includes bibliographical references and index. [LC 91024472; ISN 0673521419; $57.14]　　　HG173. M632 1992　　1414

The economics of money, banking, and financial markets. Frederic S. Mishkin. 2nd ed. Glenview, Ill.: Scott, Foresman, c1989. 1 v. (various pagings): ill. *Notes:* Includes bibliographies and index. [LC 88018549; ISN 0673398315; $45.63]　　　HG173. M632 1989　　1415

The emerging power of Japanese money. Aron Viner. Homewood, Ill.: Dow Jones-Irwin, c1988. x, 254 p. *Notes:* Includes index. Bibliography: p. 239-243. [LC 87073190; ISN 1556230710; $21.95]　　　HG187.J3 V56 1988　　1416

Finance: environment and decisions. Peyton Foster Roden, George A. Christy. 4th ed. New York: Harper & Row, c1986. xi, 612 p. : ill. *Notes:* Rev. ed. of: Finance / George A. Christy. 3rd ed. 1981. Includes indexes. Bibliography: p. 42. [LC 85007610; ISN 0060413107]   HG173. R58 1986   1417

Finance for the nonfinancial manager. Herbert T. Spiro. 3rd ed. New York: Wiley, c1988. xviii, 282 p. : ill. *Notes:* Includes index. [LC 88005780; ISN 0471610593; ISN 0471610585]   HG173. S67 1988   1418

Finance theory. Robert A. Jarrow. Englewood Cliffs, N.J.: Prentice-Hall, c1988. xiv, 298 p. : ill. *Notes:* Includes bibliographies and index. [LC 87002359; ISN 0133148653]   HG173. J34 1988   1419

Financial assets, markets, and institutions. Gary Smith. Lexington, Mass.: D.C. Heath, c1993. xxxi, 802, 70 p. : ill. (some col.) *Notes:* Includes bibliographical references and index. [LC 92081881; ISN 0669297836]   HG173. S59 1993   +1420

The Financial development of Japan, Korea, and Taiwan: growth, repression, and liberalization. edited by Hugh T. Patrick and Yung Chul Park. New York: Oxford University Press, 1994. xii, 384 p. : ill. *Notes:* Includes bibliographical references and index. [LC 93031448; ISN 0195087666]   HG187.J3 F557 1994   +1421

A financial history of western Europe. Charles P. Kindleberger. 2nd ed. New York: Oxford University Press, 1993. xix, 524 p. : ill., maps *Notes:* Includes bibliographical references (p. [470]-501) and index. [LC 92024425; ISN 0195077385]   HG186.A2 K56 1993   1422

Financial institutions, markets, and money. David S. Kidwell, Richard L. Peterson, David W. Blackwell. 5th ed. Fort Worth: Dryden Press, c1993. xxiv, 840 p. : ill. *Notes:* Includes bibliographical references and index. Intended as a primary text in a school of business administration, the goal of this book is to give students a broad introduction to the operation, mechanics, and structure of the financial system in the United States, emphasizing its institutions, markets, and instruments and giving special attention to the Federal Reserve System and monetary policy. [LC 92070697; ISN 003075478X]   HG181. K48 1993   +1423

Financial markets and the economy. Charles N. Henning, William Pigott, Robert Haney Scott. 5th ed. Englewood Cliffs, N.J.: Prentice Hall, c1988. xvi, 638 p. : ill. *Notes:* Includes bibliographies and index. [LC 87024413; ISN 0133168948]   HG181. H37 1988   1424

Financial markets: the accumulation and allocation of wealth. Roland I. Robinson, Dwayne Wrightsman. 2d ed. New York: McGraw-Hill, c1980. xiv, 507 p. : ill. (McGraw-Hill series in finance) *Notes:* Includes index. Includes bibliographical index. [LC 79021955; ISN 0070532745; $17.95]   HG181. R59 1980   1425

The financial samurai: the emerging power of Japanese money. Aron Viner. London: Kogan Page, 1988. 233 p. *Notes:* Includes index. Bibliography: p. 221-225. [LC 88038906; ISN 1850916144; £12.95 (July)]   HG187.J3 V563 1988   1426

The financial system. J. O. Light, William L. White. Homewood, Ill.: Irwin, 1979. xiii, 639 p. : graphs *Notes:* Includes bibliographies and index. [LC 78062626; ISN 0256021201]   HG181. L48   1427

Financing East Asia's success: comparative financial development in eight Asian countries. Michael T. Skully and George J. Viksnins. New York: St. Martin's; in association with the American Enterprise Institute for Public Policy Research, 1987. xiii, 242 p. *Notes:* Includes index. Bibliography: p. 224-235. [LC 86031527; ISN 0312005369; $25.00 (est.)]   HG187.E37 S68 1987   1428

Frontiers of finance: the Batterymarch Fellowship papers. edited by Deborah H. Miller and Stewart C. Myers. Cambridge, MA: Blackwell, 1990. xix, 747 p. : ill. *Notes:* Includes bibliographical references. *Contents:* An empirical analysis of the interfirm equity investment process / Richard S. Ruback. [LC 89018620; ISN 1557860858]   HG173. F76 1990   1429

Handbook of financial markets and institutions. edited by Edward I. Altman; associate editor Mary Jane McKinney. 6th ed. New York: Wiley, c1987. 1197 p. in various pagings: ill. (Wiley professional banking and finance series) *Notes:* Rev. ed. of: Financial handbook, 5th ed. c1981. Includes bibliographies and index. *Contents:* 14. Investment banking / Warren Law. [LC 86011125; ISN 0471819549]   HG173. H33 1987   1430

Handbook of modern finance. editor, Dennis E. Logue. 3rd ed. Boston: Warren Gorham Lamont, c1994. 1 v. (various pagings): ill. *Notes:* Kept up to date by supplements with cumulative index. Includes bibliographical references and index. [LC 93060975; ISN 0791317625]   HG173. H34 1994   +1431

Inside Japanese financial markets. Aron Viner. Homewood, Ill.: Dow Jones-Irwin, c1988. xvi, 364 p. : ill. *Notes:* Includes index. Bibliography: p. 346-347. [LC 87071357; ISN 1556230206]   HG187.J3 V57 1988   1432

Interest rates, the markets, and the new financial world. Henry Kaufman. 1st ed. New York, N.Y.: Times Books, c1986. xiii, 258 p. : ill. *Notes:* Includes index. Bibliography: p. 240-244. [LC 86005865; ISN 0812913337]   HG173. K364 1986   1433

Keys to understanding the financial news. Nicholas G. Apostolou, D. Larry Crumbley. 2nd ed. Hauppauge, N.Y.: Barron's, c1994. 140 p. : ill. *Notes:* Includes bibliographical references and index. [LC 93023233; ISN 0812016947; $4.95 ($6.50 Can.)] HB3743. A66 1994 +1434

Leo Melamed on the markets: twenty years of financial history as seen by the man who revolutionized the markets. Leo Melamed. New York: Wiley, c1993. xxii, 278 p. *Notes:* Includes bibliographical references and index. [LC 92022150; ISN 0471575240] HG181. M45 1993 +1435

Money and banking: contemporary practices, policies, and issues. Tyrone Black, Donnie Daniel. 3rd ed. Plano, Tex.: Business Publications, 1988. xviii, 552 p. : ill. *Notes:* Includes bibliographies and indexes. [LC 87072016; ISN 0256061750] HG173. B57 1988 1436

Money and capital markets: the financial system in an increasingly global economy. Peter S. Rose. 5th ed. Burr Ridge, Ill.: Irwin, c1994. xxvii, 771, A6, B9, D17, I13 p. : ill. *Notes:* Includes bibliographical references and index. [LC 93030804; ISN 0256121990] HG181. R66 1994 +1437

Money, banking and the Canadian financial system. H.H. Binhammer. 5th ed. Scarborough, Ont.: Nelson Canada, 1988. xxvi, 689 p. : ill. *Notes:* Includes bibliographies and index. [LC 88093561; ISN 0176034110; $39.95] HG185.C2 B5 1988 1438

Money, finance, and macroeconomic performance in Japan. Yoshio Suzuki; translated by Robert Alan Feldman. New Haven: Yale University Press, c1986. xvii, 218 p. : ill. *Notes:* Translation of: Nihon kin'yū keizairon. Includes indexes. Bibliography: p. 203-211. [LC 85026375; ISN 0300033877] HG187.J3 S96 1986 1439

Pacific growth and financial interdependence. edited by Augustine H.H. Tan and Basant Kapur. Sydney; Boston: Allen and Unwin in association with the Pacific Trade and Development Conference Secretariat, Australian National Uuniversity, 1986. 405 p. *Notes:* "Papers written for the Fourteenth Pacific Trade and Development (PAFTAD) Conference, held in Singapore during June 18-21 1984." Includes index. Bibliography: p. 388-394. [LC 85073060; ISN 0868619043] HG190.A2 P32 1986 1440

Susan Lee's ABZs of money & finance. by Susan Lee. New York: Poseidon Press, c1988. 219 p. [LC 88009800; ISN 0671557122] HG151. L38 1988 1441

Tokyo 2000: the world's third international financial centre? by Economists Advisory Group Limited in association with Gerrard & National, PLC. London: Economist Publications Ltd., c1986. 93 p. : ill.] HG187.J3 T64 1442

Trading on the edge: neural, genetic, and fuzzy systems for chaotic financial markets. Guido J. Deboeck, editor. New York: Wiley, c1994. xxxvii, 377 p. : ill. *Notes:* Includes bibliographical references (p. 363-371) and index. [LC 94002364; ISN 0471311006] HG4012.5. T7 1994 +1443

The U.S. financial system: money, markets, and institutions. George G. Kaufman. 5th ed. Englewood Cliffs, N.J.: Prentice Hall, c1992. xviii, 654 p. : ill. (some col.) *Notes:* Includes bibliographical references and index. [LC 91030965; ISN 0139283188; $57.14] HG181. K34 1992 1444

The way it was: an oral history of finance, 1967-1987. compiled by the editors of Institutional investor. 1st ed. New York: Morrow, c1988. 815 p. [LC 88009679; ISN 0688080057] HG171. W33 1988 1445

FINANCE, PERSONAL

Everyone's money book. Jordan E. Goodman, Sonny Bloch. Chicago, Ill.: Dearborn Financial Pub., c1994. xxii, 824 p. : ill. *Notes:* Includes bibliographical references and index. *Contents:* Giving yourself a financial checkup—Maximizing returns on cash instruments—Picking winning stocks—Selecting mutual funds—All about bonds—Speculating with futures and options—Investing in gold and collectibles—Inside real estate—Finding the best limited partnerships—You and your credit—managing it wisely—Getting the most for your money when buying a car—All about insurance—How to finance a college education—The basics of tax planning—Retirement—how to get there from here—Estate planning—keeping your assets in the family—Making the most of your employee benefits—Finding financial advisers who are right for you—Smart money strategies for every age and situation. [LC 93028917; ISN 0793107210; $24.95] HG179. G675 1994 +1446

Guide to personal finance: a lifetime program of money management. Richard J. Stillman. 5th ed. Englewood Cliffs, N.J.: Prentice Hall, c1988. xxii, 504 p. : ill. *Notes:* Includes index. Bibliography: p. 486-492. [LC 87019298; ISN 0133702146; $27.50] HG179. S84 1988 1447

How to avoid a mid-life financial crisis. Richard Eisenberg. Updated ed. New York, N.Y., U.S.A.: Penguin Books, 1988. xxiii, 293 p. : forms *Notes:* Includes index. [LC 87029175; ISN 0140110119; $8.95 ($11.95 Can.)] HG179. E39 1988 1448

Making the most of your money: smart ways to create wealth and plan your finances in the '90s. Jane Bryant Quinn. New York: Simon & Schuster, c1991. 934 p. : ill. *Notes:* Includes index. [LC 90025050; ISN 0671659529; $27.50]   HG179. Q57 1991   1449

Personal financial planning. G. Victor Hallman, Jerry S. Rosenbloom. 4th ed. New York: McGraw-Hill, c1987. xix, 475 p. : ill. *Notes:* Includes index. [LC 87002584; ISN 0070256500; $29.95]   HG179. H24 1987   1450

Personal financial planning. Harold A. Wolf. 8th ed. Boston: Allyn & Bacon, c1989. xviii, 696 p. : ill. *Notes:* Rev. ed. of: Personal finance. 7th ed. c1984. Includes bibliographies and index. [LC 88026716; ISN 0205117279; $36.00]   HG179. W573 1989   1451

Sylvia Porter's your finances in the 1990s. Sylvia Porter. New York: Prentice Hall, c1990. vi, 346 p. : ill. *Notes:* Includes index. [LC 90042572; ISN 0138797765; $22.95]   HG179. P572 1990   1452

FINANCE, PUBLIC

Accounting for governmental and nonprofit entities. Leon E. Hay, Earl R. Wilson. 9th ed. Homewood, IL.: Irwin, c1992. xxi, 867 p. : ill. *Notes:* Includes bibliographical references and index. [LC 91009143; ISN 0256083134; $55.95]   HJ9733. H38 1992   1453

Effective financial management in public and non-profit agencies: a practical and integrative approach. Jerome B. McKinney. New York: Quorum Books, c1986. xiv, 378 p. : ill. *Notes:* Includes index. Bibliography: p. [367]-370. [LC 86000624; ISN 0899301541]   HJ197. M35 1986   1454

Foundations of public economics. David A. Starrett. Cambridge Cambridgeshire; New York: Cambridge University Press, 1988. xvi, 315 p. : ill. *Notes:* Includes indexes. Bibliography: p. 294-306. [LC 87027892; ISN 0521342562; ISN 0521348013]   HJ141. S66 1988   1455

FINANCIAL CORPORATION OF AMERICA

Overdrawn: the collapse of Financial Corporation of America. Michael A. Robinson. New York, N.Y., U.S.A.: Dutton, c1990. x, 303 p. *Notes:* Includes bibliographical references. [LC 90036825; ISN 0525249036; $19.95]   HG2626.S76 R63 1990   1456

FINANCIAL ENGINEERING

Financial engineering: a complete guide to financial innovation. John F. Marshall, Vipul K. Bansal. New York: New York Institute of Finance, c1992. xxiv, 728 p. : ill. *Notes:* Includes bibliographical references and index. [LC 91038920; ISN 0133125882; $65.00]   HG176.7. M37 1992   1457

Financial innovation and risk sharing. Franklin Allen and Douglas Gale. Cambridge, Mass.: MIT Press, c1994. x, 379 p. : ill. *Notes:* Includes bibliographical references and index. [LC 93051058; ISN 0262011417]   HG176.7. A44 1994   +1458

FINANCIAL FUTURES

Advanced strategies in financial risk management. Robert J. Schwart, Clifford W. Smith, Jr., editors. New York: New York Institute of Finance, c1993. xxiv, 663 p. : ill. *Notes:* "Companion to The handbook of currency and interest rate risk management"—Dustjacket. Includes bibliographical references and index. [LC 92047036; ISN 0130688835; $65.00]   HG6024.3. A38 1993   +1459

Financial futures and options: a guide to markets, applications, and strategies. Todd E. Petzel. New York: Quorum Books, 1989. xviii, 236 p. : ill. *Notes:* Includes index. Bibliography: p. [229]-232. [LC 89003775; ISN 0899301525; $49.95]   HG6024.A3 P48 1989   1460

Financial futures and options in the U.S. economy: a study. by the staff of the Federal Reserve System; edited by Myron L. Kwast... et al. Washington, D.C.: Board of Governors of the Federal Reserve System, 1986. ix, 264 p. : ill. *Notes:* "December 1986." Bibliography: p. [249]-264. [LC 86600598]   HG6024.U5 F56 1986   1461

Financial futures: fundamentals, strategies, and applications. Edward W. Schwarz, Joanne M. Hill, Thomas Schneeweis. Homewood, Ill.: Irwin, 1986. xiii, 460 p. : ill. *Notes:* Includes index. Bibliography: p. 441-450. [LC 85072177; ISN 0256032057]   HG6024.3. S38 1986   1462

Financial futures markets: concepts, evidence, and applications. Robert T. Daigler. New York, NY: HarperCollins College, c1993. xxiii, 500 p. : ill. *Notes:* Includes bibliographical references and index. [LC 92029889; ISN 0065010108] HG6024.9.U6 D35 1993 +1463

Financial futures markets: structure, pricing, and practice. John J. Merrick, Jr. New York: Harper & Row, Ballinger Division, c1990. xi, 228 p. *Notes:* Includes bibliographical references. [LC 89020082; ISN 0887303382; $39.95] HG6024.3. M47 1990 1464

The handbook of currency and interest rate risk management. Robert J. Schwartz and Clifford W. Smith, Jr., editors. New York, N.Y.: New York Institute of Finance, c1990. xlvi, (various pagings): ill. *Notes:* Includes bibliographical references. [LC 90040092; ISN 0133819639; $65.00] HG6024.3. H36 1990 1465

Inside the financial futures markets. Mark J. Powers, Mark G. Castelino. 3rd ed. New York: Wiley, c1991. x, 390 p. : ill. *Notes:* Includes bibliographical references and index. [LC 91009210; ISN 0471536741; $49.95] HG6024.A3 P68 1991 1466

FINANCIAL INSTITUTIONS

Breaking financial boundaries: global capital, national deregulation, and financial services firms. David M. Meerschwam. Boston, Mass.: Harvard Business School Press, c1991. ix, 306 p. : ill. *Notes:* Includes bibliographical references and index. [LC 90015472; ISN 0875842534; $35.00] HG181. M44 1991 1467

Capital city: London as a financial centre. Hamish McRae and Frances Cairncross. New and completely rev. ed. London: Methuen, 1991. xiii, 271 p. *Notes:* Previous ed.: 1985. Includes index. [LC 91026615; ISN 0413654206; £16.99] HG186.G7 M28 1991 1468

City within a state: a portrait of Britain's financial world. Anthony Hilton. London: Tauris, 1987. x, 199 p. *Notes:* Includes bibliographical references and index. [LC 87013850; ISN 1850430446; £12.95 (July)] HG186.G7 H53 1987 1469

Financial institutions and markets. Meir Kohn. New York: McGraw-Hill, c1994. xxvii, 868 p. : ill. (some col.) *Notes:* Includes bibliographical references and indexes. [LC 93038118; ISN 0070359040] HG181. K64 1994 +1470

Financial institutions: understanding and managing financial services. Peter S. Rose, Donald R. Fraser. 3rd ed. Plano, Tex.: Business Publications, 1988. xxii, 762 p. : ill. *Notes:* Includes bibliographies and index. [LC 87072393; ISN 025606153X; $43.95] HG181. R65 1988 1471

Financial markets and institutions: a managerial approach. Kenneth J. Thygerson. New York: HarperCollins College Publishers, c1993. xxxi, 735 p. : ill. (some col.) *Notes:* Includes bibliographical references (p. 715-725) and index. [LC 92022258; ISN 006501278X] HG2491. T49 1993 +1472

The financial services handbook: executive insights and solutions. edited by Eileen M. Friars, Robert N. Gogel. New York: Wiley, c1987. xxiii, 453 p. : ill. (Wiley professional banking and finance series, 0733-8945) *Notes:* "A Wiley-Interscience publication." Includes bibliographies and index. Non-circulating. [LC 86023415; ISN 0471822671] HG175. F55 1987 1473

The gnomes of Tokyo. Jim Powell. 1st ed. New York: Dodd, Mead, c1988. ix, 307 p. *Notes:* Includes index. [LC 88000483; ISN 039608964X] HG187.J3 P68 1988 1474

How the City of London works: an introduction to its financial markets. William M. Clarke. 2nd ed. London: Waterlow, 1988. v, 121 p. : ill. [LC 88047518; ISN 008033105X; £6.95: CIP confirmed] HG186.G7 C552 1988 1475

Marketing financial services: a strategic vision. James H. Donnelly, Jr., Leonard L. Berry, Thomas W. Thompson. Homewood, Ill.: Dow Jones-Irwin, c1985. xiii, 268 p. : ill. *Notes:* Includes bibliographies and index. [LC 84072996; ISN 0870945173] HG174. D66 1985 1476

Money and capital markets in the U.K. and Europe. by Peter J.A. Herbert and John G. Bowdery. [7th ed.]. Henley-on-Thames, England: Administrative Staff College, 1983. 113 p.] HG186.G7 H47 1983 1477

The money machine: how the city works. Philip Coggan. Harmondsworth: Penguin, 1986. 231 p. (The Penguin business library) *Notes:* Includes index. Bibliography: p. 222-223. [LC 87037998; ISN 0140091130; £3.95] HG186.G7 C63 1986 1478

The power structure of American business. Beth Mintz and Michael Schwartz. Chicago: University of Chicago Press, 1985. xix, 327 p. : ill. *Notes:* Includes index. Bibliography: p. 299-318. [LC 84008841; ISN 0226531082] HG181. M556 1985 1479

The second wave: Japan's global assault on financial services. Richard W. Wright and Gunter A. Pauli. New York: St. Martin's Press, 1987. 139 p. : ill. *Notes:* Includes bibliographies and index. [LC 87027138; ISN 0312015585; $30.00 (est.)] HG187.J3 W75 1987 1480

Tokyo: a world financial center. by Brian Robins London: Euromoney, c1987. 285 p. : ill.; ISN 1870031369]　　　　　　　　　　　　　　　　　　　　　　　　　HG188.J3 R6 1987　　1481

The troubled money business: the death of an old order and the rise of a new order. Richard D. Crawford, William W. Sihler. New York, NY: HarperBusiness, c1991. xv, 289 p. *Notes:* Includes index. [LC 91037356; ISN 0887305156; $23.00]　　　　　　　　　HG2491. C73 1991　　1482

Uneasy city: an insider's view of the City of London. Frank Welsh. London: Weidenfeld & Nicolson, 1986. 182 p. : ill. *Notes:* Includes index. Bibliography: p. 174-175. [LC 87024960; ISN 0297789945; £12.95]　　　　　　　　　　　　　　　　　　　　　　　　　　HG186.G7 W34 1986　　1483

FINANCIAL INSTITUTIONS, INTERNATIONAL

The supranationals. edited by S. Melvin Rines and Christine A. Bogdanowicz-Bindert. London: Euromoney Publications, c1986. 200 p. : ill. (some col.) *Notes:* Includes bibliographical references.; ISN 0903121840]　　　　　　　　　　　　　　　　　　　　　　　　HG3881. S86　　1484

FINANCIAL SERVICES INDUSTRY

An analysis of the new financial institutions: changing technologies, financial structures, distribution systems, and deregulation. Alan Gart. New York: Quorum Books, 1989. xx, 376 p. : ill. *Notes:* Includes bibliographical references. [LC 88004933; ISN 0899302718; $59.95]
　　　　　　　　　　　　　　　　　　　　　　　　　　　　　　HG181. G358 1989　　1485

Financial services: perspectives and challenges. edited by Samuel L. Hayes, III. Boston, Mass.: Harvard Business School Press, c1993. xv, 272 p. : ill. *Notes:* Includes bibliographical references and index. [LC 93016967; ISN 0875844022]　　　　　　　　　　　HG174. F526 1993　　1486

The global city: New York, London, Tokyo. Saskia Sassen. Princeton, N.J.: Princeton University Press, c1991. xvi, 397 p. *Notes:* Includes bibliographical references (p. [355]-389) and index. [LC 90023017; ISN 0691078661; $39.50]　　　　　　　　　　　　HG184.N5 S27 1991　　1487

Marketing financial services. edited by David B. Zenoff. Cambridge, Mass.: Ballinger, c1989. xliii, 225 p. : ill. *Notes:* Includes bibliographical references and index. [LC 88034948; ISN 088730298X; $49.50]　　　　　　　　　　　　　　　　　　　　　　　　HG173. M5 1989　　1488

Opportunities in European financial services: 1992 and beyond. edited by Paul Quantock (Spicers Centre for Europe). New York: Wiley, c1990. xiv, 245 p. : ill. *Notes:* Includes bibliographical references. [LC 90031157; ISN 0471522139; $42.50]　　　　　　　HG186.E9 O66 1990　　1489

FINANCIAL STATEMENTS

Analyzing financial statements. John E. McKinley... et al. 3rd ed. Washington, D.C.: American Bankers Association, 1988. vii, 361 p. *Notes:* Includes index. [LC 88009399; ISN 0899823521; $45.00]　　　　　　　　　　　　　　　　　　　　　　　　HF5681.B2 A6464 1988　　1490

Company reports and accounts: their significance and uses. John Blake. London: Pitman, 1987. 322 p. : ill. *Notes:* Includes index. Bibliography: p. [318]. [LC 86027818; ISN 0273026976; £8.95: CIP confirmed]　　　　　　　　　　　　　　　　　　　　　　　HF5681.B2 B52 1987　　1491

Discovery techniques: obtaining and analyzing business financial data. Martin Mellman, Steven B. Lilien, James M. Docherty. Boston: Warren, Gorham & Lamont, c1987. 1 v. (various pagings): ill. *Notes:* Includes index. [LC 86050609; ISN 0887125484]　　HF5681.B2 M375 1987　　1492

Financial statement analysis. George Foster. 2nd ed. Englewood Cliffs, N.J.: Prentice-Hall, 1986. xii, 625 p. : ill. *Notes:* Includes bibliographies and index. [LC 85028112; ISN 0133163172]
　　　　　　　　　　　　　　　　　　　　　　　　　　　　　　HF5681.B2 F64 1986　　1493

Financial statement analysis: a practitioner's guide. Martin S. Fridson. New York: Wiley, c1991. xvi, 285 p. : ill. *Notes:* Includes bibliographical references (p. 279-280) and index. [LC 90044237; ISN 047160173X; $49.95]　　　　　　　　　　　　　　HF5681.B2 F772 1991　　1494

Financial statement analysis: theory, application, and interpretation. Leopold A. Bernstein. 5th ed. Homewood, IL: Irwin, 1992, c1993. xxvii, 1075 p. : ill. *Notes:* Includes bibliographical references and index. [LC 92025686; ISN 0256102236]　　　　　　　HF5681.B2 B46 1992　　1495

Financial statement analysis: using financial accounting information. Charles H. Gibson. 5th ed. Cincinnati, Ohio: College Div., South-Western Pub. Co., 1992. xvi, 783 p. *Notes:* Includes bibliographical references and index. [LC 91027904; ISN 0538821604; $55.95]　　HF5681.B2 G49 1992　　1496

Flow of funds and other financial concepts. Jerry A. Viscione. New York,: National Association of Credit Management, 1981. 138 p. [LC 81002721; ISN 0934914400; $15.50] HF5681.B2 V53 1497

How to analyze businesses, financial statements, and the quality of earnings. Joel G. Siegel. 2nd ed. Englewood Cliffs, N.J.: Prentice Hall, c1991. xxiii, 266 p. *Notes:* Includes bibliographical references and index. [LC 91007532; ISN 0134009959; $49.95] HF5681.B2 S4875 1991 1498

How to interpret financial statements for better business decisions. Barry E. Miller and Donald E. Miller. New York, NY: AMACOM, c1991. xii, 417 p. : ill. *Notes:* Includes index. [LC 90055206; ISN 0814459404; $55.00] HF5681.B2 M46 1991 1499

How to read a financial report: wringing vital signs out of the numbers. John A. Tracy. 4th ed. New York: Wiley, 1993, c1994. 168 p. : ill. *Notes:* "For managers, entrepreneurs, lenders, lawyers, and investors"—Cover. Includes index. [LC 93023783; ISN 0471593915] HF5681.B2 T733 1994 +1500

Keys to reading an annual report. George Thomas Friedlob and Ralph E. Welton. New York: Barron's, c1989. 160 p. *Notes:* Includes index. [LC 88034268; ISN 0812039300; $4.95 ($6.50 Can.)] HF5681.B2 F773 1989 1501

The perceived usefulness of financial statements for investors' decisions. Lucia S. Chang and Kenneth S. Most. Gainesville: Miami: University Presses of Florida; Florida International University Press, c1985. xiii, 127 p. : ill. *Notes:* Bibliography: p. 125-127. [LC 84025788; ISN 0813007526] HF5681.B2 C422 1502

Quality of earnings: the investor's guide to how much money a company is really making. Thornton L. O'glove with Robert Sobel. New York: Free Press, c1987. xviii, 204 p. : ill. *Notes:* Includes index. Bibliography: p. 189-196. [LC 86025631; ISN 0029226309] HG4028.B2 O35 1987 1503

Understanding financial statements. Lyn M. Fraser. 3rd ed. Englewood Cliffs, N.J.: Prentice Hall, c1992. xi, 255 p. *Notes:* Includes bibliographical references and index. [LC 91020209; ISN 0139285814; $29.33] HF5681.B2 F764 1992 1504

Understanding financial statements and corporate annual reports. by Louis O. Foster. Rev., enl. ed. Philadelphia Chilton, 1968. x, 165 p. [LC 68026067] HG4028.B2 F6 1968 +1505

FISCAL POLICY

Debt and taxes. John H. Makin and Norman J. Ornstein. New York: Times Books, c1994. x, 337 p. : ill. *Notes:* "An American Enterprise Institute Book." "How America got into its budget mess and what to do about it"—Dustjacket. Includes bibliographical references (p. 315-322) and index. [LC 93030517; ISN 081292312X; $25.00 ($32.50 Canada)] HJ241. M36 1994 +1506

Taxation and the deficit economy: fiscal policy and capital formation in the United States. edited by Dwight R. Lee; foreword by Michael J. Boskin. San Francisco, Calif.: Pacific Research Institute for Public Policy, c1986. xxvii, 554 p. : ill. (Pacific studies in public policy) *Notes:* Includes bibliographies and index. [LC 85063549; ISN 0936488131; ISN 0936488034; $34.95; $14.95] HJ257.2. T385 1986 1507

FIXED-INCOME SECURITIES

Fixed income masterpieces: insights from America's great investors. edited by Livingston G. Douglas. Homewood, Ill.: Business One Irwin, c1993. xviii, 420 p. : ill. *Notes:* "A collection of classic pieces written on fixed-income investing"—Preface. Includes bibliographical references. [LC 92030857; ISN 1556238622] HG4651. F575 1993 +1508

Fixed-income arbitrage: analytical techniques and strategies. M. Anthony Wong, in collaboration with Robert High. New York: Wiley, c1993. xvii, 254 p. *Notes:* Includes bibliographical references and index. [LC 92045088; ISN 0471555525; $55.00] HG4651. W64 1993 +1509

FLEXIBLE MANUFACTURING SYSTEMS

Human-intelligence-based manufacturing. edited by Y. Ito. London; New York: Springer-Verlag, c1993. x, 228 p. : ill. *Notes:* Includes bibliographical references and index. [LC 93003305; ISN 0387197931; $106.50 (est.)] TS155.6. H835 1993 +1510

FLOOR TRADERS (FINANCE)

Market wizards: interviews with top traders. Jack D. Schwager. New York, N.Y.: New York Institute of Finance, 1989. xviii, 458 p. *Notes:* Includes index. [LC 89032614; ISN 0135560934; $29.50]
HG4621. S28 1989   1511

FOOD INDUSTRY AND TRADE

Altered harvest: agriculture, genetics, and the fate of the world's food supply. by Jack Doyle. New York, N.Y., U.S.A.: Viking, 1985. xix, 502 p. *Notes:* Includes index. Bibliography: p. 388-431. [LC 84040458; ISN 067011524X; $25.00]
HD9006. D65 1985   1512

FOOD

New technologies and the future of food and nutrition: proceedings of the First Ceres Conference, Williamsburg, VA, October 1989. edited by Gerald E. Gaull, Ray A. Goldberg. New York: Wiley, c1991. xiv, 174 p. *Notes:* "A Wiley Interscience publication." Includes bibliographical references and index. [LC 91018915; ISN 0471554081]
TP248.65.F66 C47 1989   1513

FORBES, MALCOLM S

Malcolm Forbes: the man who had everything. by Christopher Winans. 1st ed. New York: St. Martin's Press, 1990. ix, 227 p., [16] p. of plates: ill. *Notes:* "A Thomas Dunne book." [LC 90037255; ISN 0312051344; $19.95]
HC102.5.F67 W56 1990   1514

FORD MOTOR COMPANY

Strategy and the human resource: Ford and the search for competitive advantage. Ken Starkey and Alan McKinlay. Oxford; Cambridge, Mass.: Blackwell Business, 1993. x, 220 p. : ill. *Notes:* Includes bibliographical references (p. [205]-215) and index. [LC 92043004; ISN 0631186743]
HD9710.U54 F694 1993   +1515

Today and tomorrow. Henry Ford in collaboration with Samuel Crowther; foreword by Norman Bodek. Cambridge, Mass.: Productivity Press, c1988. xiv, 286 p., [12] p. of plates: ill. *Notes:* Reprint. Originally published: Garden City, N.Y.: Doubleday, Page, c1926. Includes index. [LC 88042628; ISN 0915299364; $24.95]
HD9710.U54 F583 1988   1516

Turnaround: the new Ford Motor Company. Robert L. Shook. 1st ed. New York: Prentice Hall Press, c1990. xi, 260 p. *Notes:* Includes index. [LC 90036088; ISN 0139320628; $19.45]
HD9710.U54 F687 1990   1517

FORECASTING

Accurate business forecasting. Boston, Mass.: Harvard Business Review, c1991. 101 p. : ill.; 1 chart. *Notes:* Articles reprinted from Harvard Business Review. Includes bibliographical references. *Contents:* Manager's guide to forecasting—Decision analysis comes of age—Forecasting resurrected—Scenarios: uncharted waters ahead—What working for a Japanese company taught me—Pitfalls in evaluating risky projects—Assessing capital risk: you can't be too conservative—Marketing performance-what do you expect?—Four steps to forecast total market demand—Decision making: going forward in reverse—Are economic forecasters worth listening to?; ISN 0875842917; $19.95]
HD30.27. A28 1991   1518

Trend tracking: the system to profit from today's trends. Gerald Celente with Tom Milton. New York: Wiley, c1990. xv, 303 p. *Notes:* Includes bibliographical references (p. [271]-290) and index. [LC 89029817; ISN 0471502650; $24.95]
H61.4. C45 1990   1519

FOREIGN EXCHANGE

Effective control of currency risks: a practical, comprehensive guide. Enzio von Pfeil. New York: St. Martin's Press, 1988. xiv, 285 p. : ill. *Notes:* Includes index. Bibliography: p. 269-278. [LC 87027134; ISN 0312015747; $30.00 (est.)] HG3851. P49 1988   1520

Finance of foreign trade. D. P. Whiting. 4th ed. Plymouth: Macdonald and Evans, 1977. x, 175 p. (M. & E. handbook series) *Notes:* Includes index.; ISN 0712106294] HG3883.G7 W5 1977   1521

Foreign currency translation and hedging. Coopers & Lybrand. New York: Coopers & Lybrand, 1994. 273 p. *Notes:* Includes bibliographical references and index.] HG3853.7. F774 1994   +1522

The foreign exchange and money markets guide. Julian Walmsley. New York: Wiley, 1992. xiv, 513 p. : ill. *Notes:* Includes index. [LC 91030370; ISN 0471531049; $49.95] HG3851. W386 1992   1523

The foreign exchange handbook: a user's guide. Julian Walmsley. New York: Wiley, c1983. xv, 479 p. : ill. *Notes:* "A Wiley-Interscience publication." Includes index. Bibliography: p. 465-467. [LC 82021804; ISN 0471863882; $39.95 (est.)] HG3851. W387 1983   1524

How the foreign exchange market works. Rudi Weisweiller. Original English language ed. New York, N.Y.: New York Institute of Finance, 1990. xvi, 212 p. *Notes:* "Original English language edition published in the United Kingdom under the title Introduction to Foreign Exchange (2nd Edition)." Includes bibliographical references and index. [LC 90039200; ISN 0134008626; $19.95] HG3821. W45 1990   1525

International financial markets. J. Orlin Grabbe. 2nd ed. New York: Elsevier, c1991. xiii, 421 p. : ill. *Notes:* Includes bibliographical references (p. [381]-387) and index. [LC 91003584; ISN 0444015981; $41.00] HG3851. G64 1991   1526

FOREIGN EXCHANGE FUTURES

Financial swaps: new strategies in currency and coupon risk management. Carl R. Beidleman. Homewood, Ill.: Dow Jones-Irwin, 1985. xix, 304 p. : ill. *Notes:* Includes index. Bibliography: p. 285-288.] HG3853. B44   1527

Foreign exchange handbook: managing risk and opportunity in global currency markets. Paul Bishop, Don Dixon. New York: McGraw-Hill, c1992. xiv, 466 p. : ill. *Notes:* Includes bibliographical references (p. 451-455) and index. [LC 91026927; ISN 0070054746; $64.95] HG3853. B57 1992   1528

Inside the swap market. 2nd ed. London, England: IFR Publishing Ltd., c1986. 211 p. : ill. (International financing library) *Notes:* Includes bibliographical references.; ISN 0946559252] HG3853. I58 1986   1529

Interest rate swaps. edited by Carl R. Beidleman. Rev. ed. Homewood, Ill.: Business One Irwin, c1991. xxiii, 518 p. : ill. *Notes:* Rev. ed. of: Financial swaps / Carl R. Beidleman. c1985. Includes bibliographical references and index. [LC 90033697; ISN 1556232071; $62.50] HG3853. I56 1991   1530

Swap finance. edited by Boris Antl. London: Euromoney Publications, 1986. 2 v. in 1: ill.] HG3853. S92   1531

FOREIGN EXECUTIVES

10 tips for the European executive in an American company. Bernard Guétin; translated from the French by Gary Breunig; postface by Aram J. Kevorkian. Paris: Publi-Union, c1990. 101 p. (The 10 tips series.); ISN 2857900554] HD38.2. G83 1990   1532

FOREIGN LICENSING AGREEMENTS

Licensing in international strategy: a guide for planning and negotiations. Farok J. Contractor. Westport, Conn.: Quorum Books, c1985. xix, 254 p. : ill. *Notes:* Includes index. Bibliography: p. [243]-249. [LC 84022756; ISN 0899300243] HF1429. C66 1985   1533

FOREIGN TRADE PROMOTION

The export cult: a global display of economic distortions. by Alex Rubner. Boulder: Westview Press, 1987. xiv, 318 p. *Notes:* Includes index. Bibliography: p. 305-310 [LC 86051219; ISN 0813305144; $37.50] HF1417.5. R82 1987   1534

FOREIGN TRADE REGULATION

International dimensions of the legal environment of business. Michael Litka. 2nd ed. Boston: PWS-KENT Pub. Co., c1991. xvi, 246 p. *Notes:* Includes bibliographical references and index. [LC 90039367; ISN 0534925057; $17.95] KF390.B8 L58 1991   1535

FRANCHISES (RETAIL TRADE)

Franchising: Forms volume realities and remedies. Harold Brown. New York, N.Y. (111 8th Ave., New York 10011): Law Journal Seminars-Press. 1988- 1 v. (loose-leaf): forms *Notes:* Companion publication to Franchising by Harold Brown published in 1981. Upkeep service. Accompanied by Rev. ed., 1988: Franchising: realities and remedies. [LC 88009117]   KF2023. B7 1981 Suppl.   1536

Franchising in Europe. edited by Martin Mendelsohn. London; New York: Cassell, 1993. iv, 428 p. *Notes:* GB92-10709 "First published in hardback 1992"—T.p. verso. Includes bibliographical references and index. *Contents:* Introduction; European overview and EC competition laws; Techniques for international expansion / Martin Mendelsohn—Tax considerations / Manzoor G.K. Ishani—Belgium / André Lombart—Denmark / Peter Arendorff—France / Gérard Sautereau—Germany / Albrecht Schulz—Greece / Yanos Gramatidis—Ireland / Michael Fitzsimons and Francis Fitzpatrick—Italy / Aldo Frignani—Luxembourg / Charles Duro—The Netherlands / Patricia B. Hamelberg-Scheephorst—Portugal / Manuel P. Barrocas—Spain / Gonzalo de Ulloa—United Kingdom / Martin Mendelsohn. [LC 93165771; ISN 030432812X]   HF5429.235.E86 F73 1993   +1537

Franchising: the inside story: how to start your own business and succeed! by John E. Kinch with John P. Hayes. 1st ed. Wilmington, Del.: TriMark Pub. Co., c1986. 211 p. : ill. *Notes:* Includes index. [LC 85041018; ISN 0914663038; $14.95]   HF5429.235.U5 K56 1986   1538

Roadside empires: how the chains franchised America. by Stan Luxenberg. New York, N.Y., U.S.A.: Viking, 1985. viii, 313 p. *Notes:* Includes bibliographical references and index. [LC 83040231; ISN 0670326585; $17.95]   HF5429.235.U5 L88 1985   1539

FREE ENTERPRISE

Business organization and the myth of the market economy. William Lazonick. Cambridge England; New York: Cambridge University Press, 1991. xiv, 372 p. *Notes:* Includes bibliographical references and index. [LC 91008865; ISN 0521394198; $39.95]   HB95. L39 1991   1540

Free market economics: a critical appraisal. Andrew Schotter. 2nd ed. Cambridge, MA.: B. Blackwell, 1990. xiv, 178 p. : ill. *Notes:* Includes bibliographical references (p.169-174). [LC 89018489; ISN 1557860742]   HB95. S36 1990   1541

Toward the year 2000: world business leaders speak out on the future of free enterprise. compiled, edited, and with an introduction by Ruth Karen. New York: Morrow, c1985. 341 p. [LC 85008808; ISN 0688049168]   HB95. T69 1985   1542

FREE TRADE

The myth of free trade: a plan for America's economic revival. Ravi Batra. New York: C. Scribner's Sons, c1993. 274 p. : ill. *Notes:* "A Robert Stewart book." [LC 92040683; ISN 0684195925; $23.00]   HF1455. B328 1993   1543

The political economy of North American free trade. edited by Ricardo Grinspun and Maxwell A. Cameron. New York: St. Martin's Press, 1993. xv, 348 p. : ill. *Notes:* Includes bibliographical references and index. [LC 93014764; ISN 0312075995]   HF1746. P65 1993   1544

Trade talks: America better listen. C. Michael Aho, Jonathan David Aronson. New York, N.Y.: Council on Foreign Relations, c1985. xiv, 178 p. *Notes:* "Council on Foreign Relations books." Includes bibliographical references and index. [LC 85025; ISN 0876090099; ISN 0876090102]   HF1721. A36 1985   1545

A U.S.-Mexico-Canada free-trade agreement: do we just say no? William McGaughey, Jr. Minneapolis, MN: Thistlerose Publications, c1992. v, 226 p. : ill. *Notes:* Includes bibliographical references (p. [199]-213) and index. [LC 91068572; ISN 0960563024]   HF1756. M33 1992   1546

FUND ACCOUNTING

Fund accounting. by Harry D. Kerrigan. New York McGraw-Hill, 1968, c1969. x, 533 p. (McGraw-Hill accounting series) [LC 68030975] HJ9801. K37 +1547

Introduction to fund accounting. Edward S. Lynn, Joan W. Norvelle. 2nd ed. Reston, Va: Reston Pub. Co., c1984. viii, 134 p. : ill. *Notes:* Includes bibliographical references and index. [LC 83023098; ISN 0835931862; $13.95] HF5681.F84 L96 1984 1548

FUTURES

Institutional investor's guide to managed futures programs. Stephen M. Douglass. New York: McGraw-Hill, c1994. xxii, 232 p. : ill. *Notes:* Includes bibliographical references and index. [LC 93041992; ISN 0070219117; $59.95] HG6024.A3 D68 1994 +1549

GALLO FAMILY

Blood and wine: the unauthorized story of the Gallo wine empire. Ellen Hawkes. New York: Simon & Schuster, c1993. 464 p. *Notes:* Includes bibliographical references and index. [LC 92046789; ISN 0671649868] TP547.G35 H39 1993 1550

GAME THEORY

The economics of bargaining. edited by Ken Binmore and Partha Dasgupta. Oxford, UK; New York, NY, USA: B. Blackwell, 1986, c1987. 260 p. : ill. *Notes:* Includes bibliographies and index. [LC 86017169; ISN 0631142541; $49.95] HB144. E29 1551

Game theory: a nontechnical introduction. Morton D. Davis. Rev. ed. New York: Basic Books, c1983. xix, 252 p. *Notes:* Includes index. Bibliography: p. 229-241. [LC 83070771; ISN 0465026273; ISN 0465026281; $14.95; $6.95] QA269. D38 1983 1552

GATES, BILL

Gates: how Microsoft's mogul reinvented an industry—and made himself the richest man in America. Stephen Manes and Paul Andrews. 1st ed. New York: Doubleday, 1993. viii, 534 p. : ill. *Notes:* Includes bibliographical references and index. [LC 92015994; ISN 0385420757; $25.00] HD9696.C62 G336 1993 1553

Hard drive: Bill Gates and the making of the Microsoft empire. James Wallace, Jim Erickson. New York: Wiley, c1992. v, 426 p. : ports. *Notes:* Includes index. [LC 91048138; ISN 0471568864; $22.95] HD9696.C62 G3378 1992 1554

GAY MEN

The corporate closet: the professional lives of gay men in America. James D. Woods with Jay H. Lucas. New York: Toronto: New York: The Free Press; Maxwell Macmillan Canada; Maxwell Macmillan International, c1993. xviii, 331 p. *Notes:* Includes bibliographical references (p. 315-326) and index. [LC 93019898; ISN 0029356032; $22.95] HQ76.2.U5 W66 1993 +1555

GENEEN, HAROLD

Geneen. Robert J. Schoenberg. 1st ed. New York: Norton, c1985. 429 p. : ill. *Notes:* Includes index. [LC 84005957; ISN 039301858X] HE8846.I64 S36 1985 1556

GENERAL ELECTRIC COMPANY

Control your destiny or someone else will: how Jack Welch is making General Electric the world's most competitive corporation. Noel M. Tichy and Stratford Sherman. 1st ed. New York: Doubleday, 1993. xiii, 384 p. : ill. *Notes:* "A Currency book"—Verso t.p. Includes index. [LC 92025822; ISN 0385248830]   HD9697.A3 U575 1993   1557

The new GE: how Jack Welch revived an American institution. Robert Slater. Homewood, Ill.: Business One Irwin, c1993. xxii, 295 p., [8] p. of plates: ill. *Notes:* Includes bibliographical references and index. [LC 92011676; ISN 1556236700; $24.95]   HD9697.A3 U568 1993   1558

GENERAL MOTORS CORPORATION

GM passes Ford, 1918-1938: designing the General Motors performance-control system. Arthur J. Kuhn. University Park: Pennsylvania State University Press, 1986. xii, 380 p. : ill. *Notes:* Includes indexes. Bibliography: p. [349]-361. [LC 85031965; ISN 0271004320; $34.00]   HD9710.U54 G4745 1986   1559

In the rings of Saturn. Joe Sherman. New York: Oxford University Press, 1994. 337 p. : ill., map *Notes:* Includes bibliographical references (p. 325-328) and index. [LC 93012858; ISN 0195072448; $25.00]   HD9710.U54 G47557 1994   +1560

My years with General Motors. Alfred P. Sloan, Jr.; edited by John McDonald with Catharine Stevens; with a new introduction by Peter F. Drucker. New York: Doubleday/Currency, 1990, c1963. xxiii, 472 p. : ill. *Notes:* Reprint. Originally published: Garden City, N.Y.: Doubleday, 1964, c1963. Includes index. [LC 90003177; ISN 0385242353; $17.50 ($18.95 Can.)]   HD9710.U54 G4756 1990   +1561

My years with General Motors. edited by John McDonald, with Catharine Stevens. Garden City, N.Y.: Doubleday, 1972, c1963. 541 p. (Anchor book, A848) *Notes:* Includes index.; ISN 0385042353]   CT275.S5233 A35 1972   1562

On a clear day you can see General Motors: John Z. De Lorean's look inside the automotive giant. by J. Patrick Wright. Grosse Pointe, Mich.: Wright Enterprises, 1979. xi, 237, [2] p. : ports.]   HD9710.U54 G497   1563

Rude awakening: the rise, fall and struggle for recovery of General Motors. Maryann Keller. New York: Morrow, c1989. 275 p. [LC 89032050; ISN 0688075274; $19.95]   HD9710.U54 G4744 1989   1564

GENETIC ENGINEERING

Superpigs and wondercorn: the brave new world of biotechnology and where it all may lead. Michael W. Fox. New York: Lyons & Burford, c1992. ix, 209 p. *Notes:* Includes bibliographical references and index. [LC 92018003; ISN 1558211529]   TP248.6. F69 1992   1565

GENETIC ENGINEERING INDUSTRY

Gene dreams: Wall Street, academia, and the rise of biotechnology. Robert Teitelman. New York: Basic Books, 1989. xii, 237 p. *Notes:* Bibliography: 217-230. [LC 89042528; ISN 0465026591]   HD9999.G452 T44 1989   1566

GEO. A. HORMEL & COMPANY STRIKE, AUSTIN, MINN., 1985-1986

Hard-pressed in the heartland: the Hormel strike and the future of the labor movement. Peter Rachleff. Boston: South End Press, c1993. 135 p. *Notes:* Includes bibliographical references and index. [LC 92026022; ISN 0896084507]   HD5325.P152 1985 A877 1993   1567

GERMANY (WEST)—ECONOMIC POLICY

The fading miracle: four decades of market economy in Germany. Herbert Giersch, Karl-Heinz Paqué, Holger Schmieding. Cambridge England; New York, NY, USA: Cambridge University Press, 1992. xiv, 302 p. : ill. *Notes:* Includes bibliographical references (p. 277-293) and index. [LC 91022347; ISN 0521353513]   HC286. G54 1992   1568

GETTY OIL COMPANY

The taking of Getty Oil: the full story of the most spectacular—& catastrophic—takeover of all time. Steve Coll. New York: Atheneum, 1987. xiii, 528 p. *Notes:* Includes index. Bibliography: p. 487-517. [LC 87011467; ISN 0689118600]   HD9569.G48 C65 1987   1569

GLOBAL WARMING

Global warming: are we entering the greenhouse century? by Stephen H. Schneider. San Francisco, CA: Sierra Club Books, 1989. xiv, 317 p. : ill. *Notes:* Includes index. Includes bibliographical references. [LC 89006048; ISN 0871566931; $18.95]   QC981.8.G56 S3 1989   1570

GOAL (PSYCHOLOGY)

A theory of goal setting & task performance. Edwin A. Locke, Gary P. Latham with contributions by Ken J. Smith, Robert E. Wood. Englewood Cliffs, N.J.: Prentice Hall, c1990. xviii, 413 p. : ill. *Notes:* "Foreword by Albert Bandura"—Jacket. Includes bibliographical references (p. 365-397). [LC 89016372; ISN 0139131388; $32.80]   BF503. L63 1990   1571

GOING PUBLIC (SECURITIES)

Deciding to go public: understanding the process and the alternatives. S.l.: Ernst & Whinney, c1984. 139 p. : ill. *Notes:* Cover title.]   HG4028.S7 D45 1984   1572

The entrepreneur's guide to going public. James B. Arkebauer with Ron Schultz. Dover, N.H.: Upstart, c1994. xxii, 346 p. *Notes:* Includes index. [LC 94000827; ISN 093689458X; $24.95]   HG4028.S7 A75 1994   +1573

Going public: how to make your initial stock offering successful. by Martin Weiss. 1st ed. Blue Ridge Summit, PA: (1990 printing) Liberty Hall Press, 1988. 155 p. : ill. *Notes:* Includes index. [LC 90006316; ISN 0830670122; $13.60]   HG4963. W45 1988   1574

Going public: MIPS computer and the entrepreneurial dream. Michael S. Malone. 1st ed. New York, NY: E. Burlingame Books, c1991. viii, 291 p. *Notes:* Includes index. [LC 90055933; ISN 0060165197; $22.95]   HG4028.S7 M19 1991   1575

Going public: the entrepreneur's guide. Joseph S. O'Flaherty. New York: Wiley, c1984. xv, 304 p. : forms *Notes:* "A Wiley-Interscience Publication." Includes index. Bibliography: p. 291-294. [LC 83023255; ISN 0471869813]   HG4028.S7 O34 1984   1576

Initial public offerings: all you need to know about taking a company public. David P. Sutton & M. William Benedetto. Paperback ed. Chicago, Ill.: Probus Pub. Co., c1990. viii, 354 p. : ill. *Notes:* Includes index.; ISN 1557381429; $22.95]   HG4963. S87 1990   1577

GOLDSMITH, JAMES

Tycoon: the life of James Goldsmith. Geoffrey Wansell. 1st American ed. New York: Atheneum, 1987. 396 p., [16] p. of plates *Notes:* Includes index. [LC 87011473; ISN 0689118171]   HC252.5.G64 W36 1987   1578

GOVERNMENT CONSULTANTS

The idea brokers: think tanks and the rise of the new policy elite. James Allen Smith. New York: The Free Press, c1991. xxi, 313 p. *Notes:* Includes bibliographical references and index. [LC 90039735; ISN 0029295513; $24.95] JK468.C7 S65 1991 1579

GOVERNMENT MARKETING

Public-sector marketing: a guide for practitioners. Larry L. Coffman. New York: Wiley, c1986. xxi, 191 p. : ill. (Wiley series on business strategy) *Notes:* Includes index. Bibliography: p. 182-184. [LC 86009216; ISN 0471011614; $22.95 (est.)] JF1525.M37 C64 1986 1580

GOVERNMENT SECURITIES

The Dow Jones-Irwin guide to buying and selling Treasury securities. Howard M. Berlin. 2nd ed. Homewood, Ill.: Dow Jones-Irwin, c1988. ix, 319 p. : ill. *Notes:* Includes index. [LC 88070136; ISN 1556230486; $25.00] HG4941. B44 1988 1581

The handbook of U.S. Treasury & government agency securities: instruments, strategies, and analysis. editor, Frank J. Fabozzi. Rev. ed. Chicago, Ill.: Probus Pub. Co., c1990. xiii, 486 p. : ill. *Notes:* Rev. ed. of: The Handbook of treasury securities. c1987. Includes bibliographical references. [LC 90034554; ISN 1557380740; $65.00] HG4941. H36 1990 1582

Inside the US Treasury market. Peter Wann. New York: Quorum Books, 1989. vii, 335 p. : ill. *Notes:* Includes index. [LC 89003632; ISN 0899304923; $59.95] HG4936. W36 1989 1583

GRACE, WILLIAM RUSSELL

Merchant adventurer: the story of W.R. Grace. by Marquis James; with an introduction by Lawrence A. Clayton. Wilmington, Del.: SR Books, 1993. xxxiv, 385 p. : ill. *Notes:* Includes bibliographical references and index. [LC 93007475; ISN 0842024441] CT275.G628 J36 1993 +1584

GRAHAM, BENJAMIN

Benjamin Graham on value investing: lessons from the dean of Wall Street. Janet Lowe. Chicago, Ill.: Dearborn Financial Pub., c1994. xv, 246 p. ill. *Notes:* Includes bibliographical references (p. 231-238) and index. [LC 94026907; ISN 0793107024; $22.95] HG172.G68 L69 1994 +1585

GRAHAM, KATHARINE

Power, privilege, and the Post: the Katharine Graham story. Carol Felsenthal. New York: Putnam, c1993. 511 p. : ill. *Notes:* Includes bibliographical references and index. [LC 92031600; ISN 0399137327; $29.95 ($38.95 Can.)] Z473.G7 F45 1993 +1586

GREAT ATLANTIC & PACIFIC TEA COMPANY

The rise and decline of the Great Atlantic & Pacific Tea Company. by William I. Walsh. Secaucus, N.J.: L. Stuart, c1986. 254 p., [24] p. of plates *Notes:* Includes index. [LC 85024987; ISN 0818403829; $17.95] HD9321.9.G7 W35 1986 1587

GREAT BRITAIN—COMMERCE—HISTORY—18TH CENTURY

The power of commerce: economy and governance in the first British Empire. Nancy F. Koehn. Ithaca: Cornell University Press, 1994. xiv, 239 p. : ill., map *Notes:* Includes bibliographical references (p. [221]-230) and index. [LC 94004314; ISN 0801426995] HF1533. K64 1994 +1588

GREAT BRITAIN—ECONOMIC CONDITIONS—1945-

Organization and technology in capitalist development. William Lazonick. Aldershot, Hants, England; Brookfield, Vt.: Edward Elgar, c1992. xvii, 290 p. : ill. *Notes:* Includes bibliographical references and index. [LC 92002430; ISN 1852787422; $74.95 (U.S.: est.)]   HC256.6. L394 1992   1589

GREAT BRITAIN—INDUSTRIES—HISTORY

The rise of modern business in Great Britain, the United States, and Japan. by Mansel G. Blackford. Chapel Hill: University of North Carolina Press, c1988. xi, 176 p. : ill. *Notes:* Includes bibliographies and index. [LC 87010022; ISN 0807842028]   HC255. B59 1988   1590

GREAT NORTHERN RAILWAY COMPANY (U.S.)

The Great Northern Railway: a history. Ralph W. Hidy. . . et al.; editorial assistance from Elizabeth A. Burnham. Boston, Mass.: Harvard Business School Press, c1988. xv, 360 p. : ill., maps, ports *Notes:* Includes index. Bibliography: p. 329-347. [LC 87025040; ISN 0875841856]   HE2791.G775 G73 1988   1591

GREEN MARKETING

Green business opportunities: the profit potential. Dominik Koechlin & Kaspar Müller. London: Financial Times/Pitman Pub., 1992. x, 246 p. : ill. *Notes:* Includes bibliographical references and index. *Contents:* A primer on the economics of the environment / H. Landis Gabel—Why the Earth's genetic biodiversity cannot be a matter of indifference / Werner Arber and Christian Speich—Environmentally conscious management / Kaspar Müller and Dominik Koechlin—Green marketing / Richard Ford—Some aspects of environmental management within a chemical corporation / James Otter—Japanese management and the environment / Takashi Adachi—Environmental management and investment decisions / Dominik Koechlin and Kaspar Müller—Green funds, or just greedy? / Carlos Joly—The green organisation / Richard Ford—One half of the sky / Piroschka Tutsek-Dossi—Environmental management: the relationship between pressure groups and industry: a radical redesign / Douglas Mulhall—Thoughts about the changeability of corporate cultures / Tilman Peter Oehl—Eco-controlling: an integrated economic-ecological management tool / Stefan Schaltegger and Andreas Sturm. [LC 93137022; ISN 0273039555]   HF5413. K64 1992   +1592

GREEN MOVEMENT

Ecological economics: a practical programme for global reform. the Group of Green Economists; translated by Anna Gyorgy. London; Atlantic Highlands, N.J., USA: Zed Books, 1992. xiv, 162 p. : ill. *Notes:* Includes bibliographical references and index. [LC 92011654; ISN 1856490696]   HC240.9.E5 G7813 1992   1593

GRIEVANCE PROCEDURES

Justice on the job: resolving grievances in the nonunion workplace. David W. Ewing. Boston, Mass.: Harvard Business School Press, 1989. ix, 337 p. : ill. *Notes:* Includes bibliographical references. [LC 89036083; ISN 0875842178]   HF5549.5.G7 E95 1989   1594

GROUP PROBLEM SOLVING

Effective group problem solving: how to broaden participation, improve decision making, and increase commitment to action. William M. Fox. 1st ed. San Francisco: Jossey-Bass, 1987. xvii, 204 p. : ill. *Notes:* Includes index. Bibliography: p. 181-192. [LC 86033742; ISN 1555420338]   HD30.29. F69 1987   1595

In search of solutions: sixty ways to guide your problem-solving group. David Quinlivan-Hall & Peter Renner. Amsterdam; San Diego: Pfeiffer, c1994. xiii, 177 p. : ill. *Notes:* Previously published: Vancouver: Training Associates, c1990. Includes bibliographical references (p. 173-176).; ISN 0893842362; $17.95]   HD30.29. Q56 1994   +1596

GUCCI (FIRM)

Gucci: a house divided. George McKnight. New York: D.I. Fine, c1987. xii, 362 p. : facsims *Notes:* Includes index. [LC 86046390; ISN 1556110375; $18.95]   HD9940.I84 G86 1987   1597

GUINNESS (FIRM)

Is Guinness good for you?: the bid for Distillers—the inside story. Peter Pugh. London: Financial Training Publications, 1987. xv, 175 p., [32] p. of plates: ill., ports. *Notes:* Includes index.; ISN 1851850740]   HD9397.G84 P83 1987   1598

HAMMER, ARMAND

Armand Hammer: the untold story. by Steve Weinberg. 1st ed. Boston: Little, Brown, c1989. x, 501 p., [16] p. of plates: ill. *Notes:* Includes index. Bibliography: p. [469]-484. [LC 89012220; ISN 0316928399; $24.95]   HC102.5.H35 W45 1989   1599
Hammer. Armand Hammer, with Neil Lyndon. New York: Putnam, c1987. 544 p., [32] p. of plates *Notes:* Includes index. [LC 86030289; ISN 0399132759]   HC102.5.H35 A3 1987   1600

HAMPER, BEN

Rivethead: tales from the assembly line. Ben Hamper. New York, NY: Warner Books, c1991. xix, 234 p. [LC 89040469; ISN 0446515019; $19.95]   HD8073.H26 A3 1991   1601

HANDICAPPED

The Americans with Disabilities Act: a review of best practices. Timothy L. Jones. New York: AMA Membership Publications Division, American Management Association, c1993. 122 p. : ill. [LC 92038227; ISN 0814423507; $10.00]   HD7256.U5 J66 1993   1602
Complying with the Americans with Disabilities Act: a guidebook for management and people with disabilities. Don Fersh and Peter W. Thomas; foreword by J. Robert Kerrey. Westport, Conn.: Quorum Books, 1993. xv, 261 p. : ill. *Notes:* Includes bibliographical references (p. [249]-250) and index. [LC 92028478; ISN 0899307140]   HD7256.U5 F47 1993   +1603

HARCOURT GENERAL, INC

The making of Harcourt General: a history of growth through diversification, 1922-1992. by Bettye H. Pruitt, with assistance from George David Smith. Boston, Mass.: Harvard Business School Press, c1994. xiv, 310 p. : ill. *Notes:* Includes bibliographical references (p. 293-297) and index. [LC 93050567; ISN 0875845096]   HD2796.H37 P78 1994   +1604

HARVARD UNIVERSITY

The big time: The Harvard Business School's most successful class—and how it shaped America. Laurence Shames. 1st ed. New York: Harper & Row, c1986. 226 p. *Notes:* Includes index. Includes bibliographical references. [LC 84047398; ISN 0060152788; $17.95]   HF1134.H4 S5 1986   1605

A delicate experiment: the Harvard Business School, 1908-1945. Jeffrey L. Cruikshank; foreword by John H. McArthur. Boston, Mass.: Harvard Business School Press, c1987. xi, 303 p. : ill., ports., maps *Notes:* Includes index. Bibliography: p. [287]- 289. [LC 86020953; ISN 087584135X]
HF1134.H4 C78 1987   1606

The empire builders: inside the Harvard Business School. J. Paul Mark. 1st ed. New York: W. Morrow, 1987. 303 p. : ports. *Notes:* Includes bibliographical references and index. [LC 87013064; ISN 0688069622]
HF1134.H4 M37 1987   1607

Great good fortune: how Harvard makes its money. Carl A. Vigeland. Boston: Houghton Mifflin, 1986. 245 p. *Notes:* "A Richard Todd book"—T.p. verso. [LC 86004711; ISN 0395362318; $18.95]
LD2115. V55 1986   1608

The Harvard century: the making of the university to the nation. Richard Norton Smith. New York: Simon and Schuster, c1986. 397 p., [8] p. of plates: ports.; 24 cm. *Notes:* Includes bibliographical references and index. [LC 86006769; ISN 0671460358]
LD2136. S64 1986   1609

Inside the Harvard Business School: strategies and lessons of America's leading school of business. by David W. Ewing. 1st ed. New York, N.Y.: Times Books, 1990. ix, 292 p. *Notes:* Includes bibliographical references. [LC 89040188; ISN 0812918274; $19.45]
HF1134.H4 E95 1990   1610

What they really teach you at the Harvard Business School. Francis J. Kelly and Heather Mayfield Kelly. New York, NY: Warner Books, Inc., c1986. 260 p. [LC 86011121; ISN 0446383171; $9.95]
HF1134.H4 K45 1986   1611

Women like us: what is happening to the women of the Harvard Business School, Class of '75—the women who had the first chance to make it to the top. by Liz Roman Gallese. 1st ed. New York: Morrow, c1985. 252 p. [LC 84019095; ISN 068802176X]
HF1134.H4 G35 1985   1612

Year one: an intimate look inside Harvard Business School, source of the most coveted advanced degree in the world. Robert Reid. 1st ed. New York: W. Morrow, c1994. 331 p. [LC 94005569; ISN 0688128173; $23.00]
HF1134.H4 R45 1994   +1613

HARVARD-EXPANSION GRAND PRIX

Scenarios and strategic management. by Michel Godet; translated from the French by David Green and Alan Rodney. London; Boston: Butterworths, 1987. xviii, 210 p. : ill. *Notes:* Translation of: Prospective et planification stratégique. " . . . this book was awarded the Harvard-Expansion Grand Prix 1985..." Includes index. Bibliography: p. 207-210. [LC 87015774; ISN 0408028904]
HD30.28. G6313 1987   1614

HAYEK, FRIEDRICH A. VON

Hayek on Hayek: an autobiographical dialogue. F.A. Hayek; edited by Stephen Kresge and Leif Wenar. Chicago: University of Chicago Press, c1994. xi, 170 p. : ill. *Notes:* Supplement to: The collected works of F. A. Hayek. Chicago: University of Chicago Press, 1989- Includes bibliographical references (p. 157-159) and index. [LC 93039289; ISN 0226320626]   HB101.H39 H387 1994   +1615

HAZARDOUS WASTE SITES

Reforming superfund. by James Lis and Melinda Warren. St. Louis: Center for the Study of American Business, 1994. 50 p. : ill. *Notes:* Includes bibliographical references (p. 46-50).]
KF3945. L57 1994   +1616

HEALTH CARE REFORM

The American way of health: how medicine is changing and what it means to you. Janice Castro. 1st ed. Boston: Little, Brown, c1994. x, 282 p. *Notes:* Includes bibliographical references and index. [LC 94005949; ISN 0316132721; ISN 0316132756; $18.95; $9.95]   RA395.A3 C39 1994   +1617

Health security: the President's report to the American people. the White House Domestic Policy Council; foreword by Hillary Rodham Clinton. Washington, D.C.?: The Council?, 1993. xi, 136 p. : ill. *Notes:* Cover title. "October 1993"—P. [iii]. Includes President Clinton's address to the joint session of Congress, Sept. 22, 1993—P. 89.; ISN 0160429617; $5.00]   HD7102.U4 U46 1993   +1618

HEALTH FACILITIES

Essentials of cost accounting for health care organizations. Steven A. Finkler. Gaithersburg, Md.: Aspen Publishers, 1994. xiii, 413 p. : ill. *Notes:* Includes bibliographical references and index. [LC 93036707; ISN 0834205289]   HF5686.H7 F563 1994   +1619

Understanding health care financial management: text, cases, and models. Louis C. Gapenski. Arlington, VA: Ann Arbor, Mich.: AUPHA Press; Health Administration Press, 1993. xiv, 761 p. : ill. *Notes:* Includes bibliographical references and index. [LC 92023431; ISN 091070189X]   RA971.3. G37 1993   1620

HEALTH SERVICES ADMINISTRATION

Creating new health care ventures: the role of management. Regina E. Herzlinger. Gaithersburg, Md.: Aspen Publishers, 1992. xvi, 508 p. : ill. *Notes:* Includes bibliographical references and index. [LC 91022413; ISN 0834202328; $69.50]   RA971. H48 1992   1621

HEDGING (FINANCE)

Hedging: principles, practices, and strategies for the financial markets. Joseph D. Koziol. New York: Wiley, c1990. xxiii, 422 p. : ill. *Notes:* Bibliography: p. 395-414. [LC 89008963; ISN 047163560X; $49.95]   HG6024.A3 K683 1990   1622

HIGH TECHNOLOGY

Marketing high technology: an insider's view. William H. Davidow. New York: London: Free Press; Collier Macmillan, c1986. xix, 194 p. *Notes:* Includes bibliographical references and index. [LC 85028061; ISN 002907990X]   HC79.H53 D38 1986   1623

The technology war: a case for competitiveness. David H. Brandin, Michael A. Harrison. New York, N.Y.: Wiley, c1987. ix, 244 p. *Notes:* Includes index. Bibliography: p. 221-231. [LC 87006127; ISN 0471834556]   T49.5. B736 1987   1624

HIGH TECHNOLOGY INDUSTRIES

Comparative high-technology industrial growth: Texas, California, Massachusetts, and North Carolina. John P. Campbell. Austin: Bureau of Business Research, Graduate School of Business, University of Texas at Austin, c1986. ix, 46 p. : ill. *Notes:* Cover title: Technology in Texas. Bibliography: p. 45-46. [LC 86070060; ISN 0877552975]   HC110.H53 C36   1625

Created in Japan: from imitators to world-class innovators. Sheridan M. Tatsuno. New York: Harper & Row, c1990. xvii, 295 p. : ill. *Notes:* Includes bibliographical references. [LC 89038066; ISN 0887303730; $21.95]   HC465.H53 T375 1990   1626

Entrepreneurial science: new links between corporations, universities, and government. Robert F. Johnston and Christopher G. Edwards. New York: Quorum Books, c1987. 157 p. *Notes:* Includes index. Bibliography: p. [141]-146. [LC 87002518; ISN 0899302602]   HC110.H53 E39 1987   1627

Entrepreneurs in high technology: lessons from M.I.T. and beyond. Edward B. Roberts. New York: Oxford University Press, 1991. xii, 385 p. : ill. *Notes:* Includes bibliographical references and indexes. [LC 90026256; ISN 0195067045; $27.95]   HC108.B65 R62 1991   1628

France high-tech. directed by Thierry Grillet and Daniel Le Conte Des Floris; English editor Mark Hunter Paris, France: Editions Autrement, c1985. 257 p. : ill. *Notes:* Includes index.; ISN 2862601497]   HC280.H53 F7313 1985   1629

High tech America: the what, how, where, and why of the sunrise industries. Ann Markusen, Peter Hall, Amy Glasmeier. Boston: Allen & Unwin, 1986. xvi, 227 p. : ill. *Notes:* Includes index. Bibliography: p. [212]-218. [LC 86017460; ISN 0043381391]   HC110.H53 M373 1986   1630

High tech: window to the future. by Gene Bylinsky; photography by Charles O'Rear; designed by Lawrence Bender. Hong Kong: Intercontinental Publishing, c1985. 278 p. : col. ill. *Notes:* At head of title: Silicon Valley. Includes index. [LC 85060954; ISN 0962276001]   HC110.H53 B94   1631

Human resource management in high-technology firms. edited by Archie Kleingartner, Carolyn S. Anderson (Institute of Industrial Relations, UCLA). Lexington, Mass.: Lexington Books, c1987. x, 243 p. : ill. *Notes:* Includes index. Bibliography: p. 219-233. *Contents:* Human resource management in high technology firms and the impact of professionalism / Carolyn S. Anderson and Archie Kleingartner—High technology labor markets / Richard S. Belous—The educational implications of the high technology revolution / Lewis C. Solmon and Midge A. La Porte—The dynamic relationship between research universities and the development of high technology industry / Karl S. Pister—Human resources at Autotel, Inc. / Fred K. Foulkes—Compensation systems in high technology companies / George T. Milkovich—Key human resource issues for management in high tech firms / Robert C. Miljus and Rebecca L. Smith—Conflict resolution in the nonunion firm / David Lewin—Unions' stake in high tech development / Everett M. Kassalow—Human resource management and business life cycles / Thomas A. Kochan—Summary and conclusions. [LC 86045556; ISN 0669136867] HF5549. H875 1987 1632

Japan's high technology industries: lessons and limitations of industrial policy. edited by Hugh Patrick, with the assistance of Larry Meissner. Seattle, WA: University of Washington Press, c1986. xxi, 277 p. : ill. *Notes:* "Sponsored by the Committee on Japanese Economic Studies"—T.p. verso. Includes bibliographies and index. *Contents:* Japanese high technology industrial policy in comparative context / Hugh Patrick—Regime characteristics of Japanese industrial policy / Daniel I. Okimoto—Industrial policy and factor markets: biotechnology in Japan and the United States / Gary Saxonhouse—Japan's industrial policy for high technology industries / Ken-ichi Imai—Joint research and antitrust: Japanese vs. American strategies / Kozo Yamamura—Technology in transition / Yasusuke Murakami—Japanese high technology policy: what lessons for the United States? / George Eads and Richard Nelson. [LC 85040973; ISN 0295963425] HC465.H53 J37 1986 1633

Managing complexity in high technology organizations. edited by Mary Ann Von Glinow and Susan Albers Mohrman. New York: Oxford University Press, 1990. xvi, 327 p. : ill. *Notes:* Includes index. Includes bibliographical references. [LC 89003030; ISN 0195057201; $29.95] HD62.37. M347 1990 1634

Managing for innovation: leading technical people. Watts S. Humphrey. Englewood Cliffs, N.J.: Prentice-Hall, c1987. xvii, 206 p. : ill. *Notes:* Includes bibliographies and index. [LC 86011262; ISN 0135503027] HD62.37. H85 1987 1635

Managing professionals in innovative organizations: a collection of readings. edited by Ralph Katz. Cambridge, Mass.: Ballinger, 1988. xiv, 593 p. : ill. *Notes:* Includes bibliographies. [LC 88024201; ISN 088730351X] HD62.37. M37 1988 1636

Route 128: lessons from Boston's high-tech community. Susan Rosegrant and David R. Lampe. New York: Basic Books, c1992. xvi, 240 p. *Notes:* Includes bibliographical references and index. [LC 91058600; $25.00] HC108.B65 R67 1992 1637

The technopolis strategy: Japan, high technology, and the control of the twenty-first century. Sheridan Tatsuno. New York, N.Y.: Prentice Hall Press, c1986. xviii, 298 p. : ill., maps *Notes:* Maps on lining papers. "A Brady book." Includes index. Bibliography: p. 277-288. [LC 86009300; ISN 0893038857; $19.95] HC465.H53 T38 1986 1638

Walking the high-tech high wire: the technical entrepreneur's guide to running a successful enterprise. David Adamson. New York: McGraw-Hill, c1994. xv, 229 p. *Notes:* Includes bibliographical references and index. [LC 93024208; ISN 0070004684; $24.95] HD62.37. A33 1994 +1639

Who's bashing whom?: trade conflict in high-technology industries. Laura D'Andrea Tyson. Washington, DC: Institute for International Economics, c1993. xviii, 324 p. : ill. *Notes:* "November 1992." Includes bibliographical references (p. 297-309) and index. [LC 92015646; ISN 0881321516] HC110.H53 T94 1993 1640

Winning in high-tech markets: the role of general management: how Motorola, Corning, and General Electric have built global leadership through technology. Joseph Morone. Boston, Mass.: Harvard Business School Press, c1993. viii, 292 p. : charts *Notes:* Includes bibliographical references and index. [LC 92015842; ISN 0875843255; $29.95] HC110.H53 M67 1992 1641

HILLMAN, SIDNEY

Labor will rule: Sidney Hillman and the rise of American labor. Steven Fraser. Ithaca: Cornell University Press, 1993. xvi, 688 p. *Notes:* Includes bibliographical references (p. 577-669) and index. [LC 93026958; ISN 0801481260; $16.95] HD8073.H5 F73 1993 +1642

HOME ECONOMICS

Never done: a history of American housework. Susan Strasser. New York: Pantheon Books, c1982. xvi, 365 p. : ill. *Notes:* Includes index. Bibliography: p. [313]-316. [LC 81048234; ISN 0394510240; ISN 0394708415; $22.50; $11.95] TX23. S77 1982   1643

HOME LABOR

The invisible work force: transforming American business with outside and home-based workers. Beverly Lozano. New York: London: Free Press; Collier Macmillan, c1989. x, 218 p. *Notes:* Includes index. Bibliography: p. [LC 89011696; ISN 0029194423; $19.95] HD2336.U5 L69 1989   1644

HONG KONG—HISTORY—PROPHECIES

The fate of Hong Kong. Gerald Segal. 1st U.S. ed. New York: St. Martin's Press, 1993. xii, 234 p. *Notes:* "Originally published in England by Simon & Schuster Ltd."—T.p. verso. Includes bibliographical references (p. 212-229) and index. [LC 93002583; ISN 0312098057; $21.95]
DS796.H757 S46 1993   +1645

HOTELS, TAVERNS, ETC

The hotel and restaurant business. Donald E. Lundberg. 5th ed. New York: Van Nostrand Reinhold, c1989. ix, 364 p. : ill. *Notes:* Includes index. Bibliography: p. 357. [LC 88015396; ISN 0442205058; $32.96 (est.)] TX911. L785 1989   1646

HOURS OF LABOR, FLEXIBLE

Alternative work schedules: selecting—implementing—and evaluating. Simcha Ronen. Homewood, Ill.: D. Jones-Irwin, c1984. xiii, 255 p. : ill. *Notes:* Includes index. Bibliography: p. 233-243. [LC 84070601; ISN 0870945114] HD5109. R66 1984   1647

Creating a flexible workplace: how to select and manage alternative work options. Barney Olmsted and Suzanne Smith. New York, NY: American Management Association, c1989. xiv, 461 p. : ill. *Notes:* Includes index. Bibliography: p. [425]-445. [LC 88048027; ISN 0814459196; $49.95]
HD5109.2.U5 O46 1989   1648

HOUSING

Real estate finance. Jerome Dasso, Gerald Kuhn. Englewood Cliffs, N.J.: Prentice-Hall, c1983. xiv, 514 p. : ill. *Notes:* Includes index. Bibliography: p. 471-474. [LC 82020482; ISN 0137627572]
HD7293.Z9 D37 1983   1649

HUMAN-COMPUTER INTERACTION

The art of human-computer interface design. edited by Brenda Laurel. Reading, Mass.: Addison-Wesley Pub. Co., c1990. xvi, 523 p., [16] p. of plates: ill., ports. (some col.) *Notes:* "S. Joy Mountford, Advanced Technology Group, Apple Computer Inc., conceived of and supported the development of this book." Includes bibliographical references (p. 485-506) and indexes. [LC 90034470; ISN 0201517973; $26.95] QA76.9.H85 A78 1990   1650

Handbook of human-computer interaction. edited by Martin Helander. Amsterdam; New York: New York, N.Y., U.S.A.: North-Holland; Sole distributors for the U.S.A. and Canada, Elsevier Science Pub. Co., 1988. xxxiii, 1167 p. : ill. *Notes:* Includes bibliographies and indexes. [LC 88025981; ISN 0444705368; $251.50] QA76.9.H85 H36 1988   1651

The virtual reality primer. L. Casey Larijani; with illustrations by Herschel Stroyman & Anthony Marynowski. New York: McGraw-Hill, c1994. xiii, 274 p. : ill. (some col.) *Notes:* Includes bibliographical references (p. 245-257) and index. [LC 93026466; ISN 0070364168; $24.95]
 QA76.9.H85 L37 1994 +1652

HUNT OIL COMPANY

H.L. and Lyda. Margaret Hunt Hill, with Jane and Burt Boyar. Little Rock: August House Publishers, 1994. 276 p. : ill. *Notes:* Includes index. [LC 93049546; ISN 087483337X; $24.95]
 HD9569.H84 H54 1994 +1653

HYLAND, L. A

Call me Pat: the autobiography of the man Howard Hughes chose to lead Hughes Aircraft. by L.A. "Pat" Hyland; edited by W.A. Schoneberger. Virginia Beach, VA: Donning Co./Publishers, c1993. 415 p. : ill. *Notes:* Includes index. [LC 93020990; ISN 0898658713; $19.95]
 HC102.5.H95 A3 1993 +1654

IACOCCA, LEE A

Iacocca: an autobiography. Lee Iacocca; with William Novak. Toronto; New York: Bantam Books, 1984. xv, 352 p., [16] p. of plates: ill., ports. *Notes:* Includes index. [LC 84045174; ISN 0553050672; $17.95] HD9710.U52 I25 1655

Talking straight. Lee Iacocca, with Sonny Kleinfield. Toronto; New York: Bantam, 1988. xii, 324 p., [16] p. of plates: ill. *Notes:* Includes index. [LC 88175522; ISN 0553052705] HD9710.U52 I27 1988 1656

ICAHN, CARL C

King Icahn: the biography of a renegade capitalist. Mark Stevens; research by Carol Bloom Stevens. New York: Dutton, 1993. x, 326 p. *Notes:* Includes bibliographical references (p. [313]-316) and index. [LC 92037592; ISN 0525936130; $23.00 ($29.99 Canada)] HG172.I27 S74 1993 +1657

IMAGING SYSTEMS

Electronic imaging systems: design, applications, and management. Don Avedon, Joseph R. Levy. New York: McGraw Hill, 1994. xiii, 318 p. : ill. *Notes:* Includes index. [LC 93020955; ISN 0070024847; $40.00] TK8315. A94 1994 +1658

INCOME

Uneven tides: rising inequality in America. edited by Sheldon Danziger and Peter Gottschalk. New York: Russell Sage Foundation, c1993. x, 287 p. : ill. *Notes:* Includes bibliographical references and index. [LC 92014233; ISN 0871542226; $29.95] HC110.I5 U47 1993 1659

INCOME TAX

Untangling the income tax. David F. Bradford. Cambridge, Mass.: Harvard University Press, 1986. x, 386 p. : ill. *Notes:* Includes index. "A Committee for Economic Development publication." Bibliography: p. [370]-376. [LC 85027078; ISN 0674930401] HJ4652. B67 1986 1660

INDEPENDENT REGULATORY COMMISSIONS

The regulators; watchdog agencies and the public interest. by Louis M. Kohlmeier, Jr. [1st ed.] New York Harper & Row, 1969. xi, 339 p. *Notes:* Bibliographical references included in "Notes" (p. [313]-330) [LC 69015314] JK901. K65   +1661

INDUSTRIAL ACCIDENTS

Normal accidents: living with high-risk technologies. Charles Perrow. New York: Basic Books, c1984. x, 386 p. : ill. *Notes:* Includes index. Bibliography: p. 367-375. [LC 83045256; ISN 046505143X; $21.95] T54. P47 1984   1662

INDUSTRIAL CAPACITY

Managing excess capacity. edited by C.W.F. Baden-Fuller. Oxford, UK; Cambridge, Mass., USA: Blackwell, 1990. viii, 263 p. : ill. *Notes:* Includes bibliographical references (p. [247]-254). [LC 89028936; ISN 0631172130; $60.00 (U.S.)] HD69.C3 M34 1990   1663

INDUSTRIAL DEVELOPMENT PROJECTS

Managing the development of new products: achieving speed and quality simultaneously through multifunctional teamwork. Milton D. Rosenau, Jr., John J. Moran. New York: Van Nostrand Reinhold, c1993. xv, 255 p. : ill. *Notes:* Includes bibliographical references (p. 249-252) and index. [LC 93014968; ISN 0442013957] HD69.P75 R668 1993   +1664

INDUSTRIAL ENGINEERING

Handbook of industrial engineering. edited by Gavriel Salvendy. 2nd ed. Norcross, Ga.: New York: Institute of Industrial Engineers; Wiley, c1992. xxvii, 2780 p. : ill. *Notes:* "A Wiley Interscience publication." Includes bibliographical references and index. [LC 91022677; ISN 0471502766; $150.00] T56.23. H36 1992   1665

Handbook of industrial engineering. edited by Gavriel Salvendy. New York: Wiley, c1982. 1 v. (various pagings): ill. *Notes:* "A Wiley-Interscience publication." Includes bibliographies and index. [LC 81023059; ISN 0471058416] T56.23. H36 1982   1666

Industrial engineering and management: a new perspective. Philip E. Hicks. 2nd ed. New York: McGraw-Hill, c1994. xviii, 455 p. : ill. *Notes:* Rev. ed. of: Introduction to industrial engineering and management science. c1977. Includes bibliographical references and indexes. [LC 93038101; ISN 0070288070] T56. H47 1994   +1667

Operations management, a systems model-building approach. by Thomas E. Vollmann. Reading, Mass. Addison-Wesley Pub. Co., 1973. xx, 716 p. illus. *Notes:* Includes bibliographies. [LC 72003463] T56. V63   +1668

INDUSTRIAL EQUIPMENT LEASES

Equipment leasing. Peter K. Nevitt, Frank J. Fabozzi. 3rd ed. Homewood, Ill.: Dow Jones-Irwin, c1988. xi, 588 p. : ill. *Notes:* Includes bibliographical references and index. [LC 87071671; ISN 1556230583] HD39.4. N48 1988   1669

The lease versus buy decision. Harold Bierman, Jr. Englewood Cliffs, N.J.: Prentice-Hall, c1982. xii, 111 p. (Prentice-Hall foundations of finance series) *Notes:* Includes index. Bibliography: p. 107-108. [LC 81023512; ISN 0135279941; ISN 0135279860] HD39.4. B53   1670

INDUSTRIAL HYGIENE

Dying for work: workers' safety and health in twentieth-century America. edited by David Rosner and Gerald Markowitz. Bloomington: Indiana University Press, c1987. xx, 234 p. : ill. (Interdisciplinary studies in history) *Notes:* Includes index. Bibliography: p. 224-225. [LC 86010260; ISN 0253318254]   HD7654. D95 1987   1671

The future of work and health: the Institute for Alternative Futures. Clement Bezold, Rick J. Carlson, Jonathan C. Peck. Dover, Mass.: Auburn House Pub. Co., c1986. xxiv, 191 p. : ill. *Notes:* Includes index. Bibliography: p. 171-182. [LC 85018627; ISN 086569088X; $24.95]   HD7654. B49 1986   1672

Loading the dice: a five-country study of vinyl chloride regulation. Joseph L. Badaracco, Jr. Boston, Mass.: Harvard Business School Press, 1985. 176 p. *Notes:* Includes index. Bibliography: p. [163]-165. [LC 85014107; ISN 0875841627]   HD7269.C45 B33 1985   1673

INDUSTRIAL LAWS AND LEGISLATION

Law and ethics in the business environment. Terry Halbert, Elaine Ingulli. St. Paul, MN: West Pub. Co., c1990. xix, 382 p. *Notes:* Includes bibliographical references. [LC 89049615; ISN 0314668047; $21.95]   KF1600. H35 1990   1674

The legal environment of business. John D. Blackburn, Elliot I. Klayman, Martin H. Malin. 3rd ed. Homewood, Ill.: Irwin, 1988. xvi, 666 p. : ill. *Notes:* Includes bibliographical references and indexes. [LC 87082524; ISN 0256060320; $43.50]   KF1600. B43 1988   1675

INDUSTRIAL MANAGEMENT

American business, a two-minute warning: ten changes managers must make to survive into the 21st century. C. Jackson Grayson, Jr., and Carla O'Dell. New York: London: Free Press; Collier Macmillan, c1988. xvii, 368 p. : ill. *Notes:* Includes index. Bibliography: p. 357-360. [LC 87019391; ISN 0029126800]   HD70.U5 G69 1988   1676

American business: an introduction. Ferdinand F. Mauser, David J. Schwartz. 6th ed. San Diego: Harcourt Brace Jovanovich, c1986. xxiii, 729 p. : ill. (some col.) *Notes:* Includes bibliographical references and index. [LC 85060873; ISN 0155023152; $16.95]   HD31. M339 1986   1677

American business and the quick fix. Michael E. McGill. 1st ed. New York: Holt, c1988. x, 242 p. *Notes:* Includes index. Bibliography: p. 225-230. [LC 87028692; ISN 0805007865; $18.95]   HD70.U5 M35 1988   1678

Behind the factory walls: decision making in Soviet and US enterprises. by Paul R. Lawrence... et al. US ed. / editors, Paul R. Lawrence, Charalambos A. Vlachoutsicos. Boston, Mass.: Harvard Business School Press, c1990. xii, 352 p. : ill. *Notes:* Includes bibliographical references (p. 339-342) and index. *Contents:* A comparative study of Soviet and American management systems—US and USSR cultural characteristics—History of US and Soviet economic institutions—US and Soviet contemporary decision-making theory—Managerial patterns—Trends and conclusions. [LC 89071723; ISN 0875842240; $29.95]   HD70.S63 B395 1990   1679

A better idea: redefining the way Americans work. Donald E. Petersen and John Hillkirk. Boston, Mass.: Houghton Mifflin Co., 1991. xviii, 270 p. *Notes:* Includes bibliographical references (p. 267-270). [LC 91026656; ISN 0395581915; $24.95]   HD5660.U5 P48 1991   1680

Beyond compliance: a new industry view of the environment. edited by Bruce Smart. Washington, D.C.?: World Resources Institute, 1992. xiv, 285 p. : ill., *Notes:* "World Resources Institute book." "April 1992." [LC 92081694; ISN 0915825732; $24.95]   HD69.P6 B49 1992   1681

Break-away thinking: how to challenge your business assumptions (and why you should). Ian I. Mitroff. New York: Wiley, c1988. xii, 196 p. : ill. *Notes:* Includes index. Bibliography: p. [187]-194. [LC 87029524; ISN 0471602027]   HD70.U5 M517 1988   1682

Building the strategically-responsive organization. edited by Howard Thomas... et al. Chichester England; New York: J. Wiley, c1994. xv, 486 p. : ill., map *Notes:* "An outgrowth of the 11th Annual International Strategic Management Society Conference, entitled 'The Greening of Strategy—Sustaining Performance,'... held in Toronto, Canada, in October, 1991"—Ser. pref. Includes bibliographical references and index. [LC 93050782; ISN 0471943991]   HD29. B85 1994   +1683

Bullseyes and blunders: stories of business success & failure. Robert F. Hartley. New York: Wiley, c1987. vii, 253 p. *Notes:* Includes bibliographies. [LC 86023350; ISN 0471849049; ISN 0471849030]   HD38. H2986 1987   1684

Business not as usual: rethinking our individual, corporate, and industrial strategies for global competition. Ian I. Mitroff, in collaboration with Susan A. Mohrman and Geoffrey Little. 1st ed. San Francisco: Jossey-Bass Publishers, 1987. xxi, 194 p. : ill. (The Jossey-Bass management series) *Notes:* Includes index. Bibliography: p. 181-187. [LC 86046333; ISN 1555420303]
  HD70.U5 M52 1987   1685

Business research methods. C. William Emory, Donald R. Cooper. 4th ed. Homewood, IL: Irwin, c1991. xxiii, 760 p. : ill. *Notes:* Includes bibliographical references and index. [LC 90044066; ISN 0256092656; $42.95]   HD30.4. E47 1991   1686

Cases in operations management: strategy and structure. W. Earl Sasser... et al. Homewood, Ill.: R.D. Irwin, 1982. xvi, 433 p. : ill. *Notes:* Written by W. Earl Sasser, Kim B. Clark, David A. Garvin, Margaret B. W. Graham, Ramchandran Jaikumar, David H. Maister. [LC 82080418; ISN 0256029024]   HD31. C3559 1982   1687

Company administration handbook. edited by Derek Beattie. 6th ed. Aldershot, Hants, England; Brookfield, Vt., U.S.A.: Gower Pub., 1988. xxiv, 737 p. : ill. *Notes:* Includes bibliographies and index. [LC 86031876; ISN 0566026678; $100.00 (U.S.: est.)]   HD70.G7 C57 1988   1688

The competitive challenge: strategies for industrial innovation and renewal. edited by David J. Teece. Cambridge, Mass.: Ballinger Pub. Co., 1987. xii, 256 p. : ill. *Notes:* "The Transamerica lectures in corporate strategy, School of Business, University of California, Berkeley." Includes bibliographies and indexes. [LC 87001190; ISN 0887301789]   HD70.U5 C58 1987   1689

Corporate combat. William E. Peacock. New York, N.Y.: Facts on File Publications, c1984. viii, 169 p. *Notes:* Includes index. [LC 84013614; ISN 0871962225; $15.95]   HD38. P35 1984   1690

Data warehousing: the route to mass customisation. Sean Kelly. Chichester England; New York: Wiley, 1994. xiii, 184 p. : ill. *Notes:* Includes bibliographical references (p. [179]-180) and index. [LC 94008497; ISN 0471950823; $40.00]   HD30.2. K457 1994   +1691

Doing business internationally: the guide to cross-cultural success. Terrence Brake, Danielle Medina Walker, Thomas (Tim) Walker. Burr Ridge, Ill.: Irwin Professional Pub., c1995. xiv, 282 p. : ill. *Notes:* Includes bibliographical references and index. [LC 94011217; ISN 0786301171]
  HD31. B7235 1995   +1692

The dynamics of taking charge. John J. Gabarro. Boston, Mass.: Harvard Business School Press, c1987. x, 204 p. : ill. *Notes:* Includes index. Bibliography: p. 189-197. [LC 86025624; ISN 0875841376]   HD38. G225 1987   1693

EcoManagement: the Elmwood guide to ecological auditing and sustainable business. Ernest Callenbach... et al. 1st ed. San Francisco: Berrett-Koehler, 1993. xviii, 188 p. : ill. *Notes:* Includes bibliographical references and index. [LC 93017285; ISN 1881052273; $27.95]   HD69.P6 E28 1993   1694

Effective management and evaluation of information technology. Robert J. Thierauf. Westport, Conn.: Quorum Books, 1994. xxi, 456 p. : ill. *Notes:* Includes bibliographical references (p. [439]-442) and index. [LC 93041816; ISN 0899308384]   HD30.2. T48 1994   +1695

The entrepreneur. John J. Kao. Englewood Cliffs, N.J.: Prentice Hall, c1991. xii, 207 p. : ill. *Notes:* Includes bibliographical references. [LC 90032586; ISN 0132823101; $22.00]   HD70.U5 K37 1991   1696

Enviro-management: how smart companies turn environmental costs into profits. D. Keith Denton. Englewood Cliffs, N.J.: Prentice Hall, c1994. x, 246 p. : ill. *Notes:* Includes bibliographical references and index. [LC 94012332; ISN 0130735035]   HD69.P6 D46 1994   +1697

Environmental business management: an introduction. Klaus North. Geneva: International Labour Office, 1992. vii, 194 p. : ill. *Notes:* Includes bibliographical references (p. 157-161) and index. [LC 92249923; ISN 9221072894; 27.50F]   HD38. N655 1992   1698

The essence of operations management. Terry Hill. New York: Prentice Hall, 1993. ix, 143 p. : ill. *Notes:* Includes bibliographical references and index. [LC 92038466; ISN 0132848457]
  HD31. H4897 1993   +1699

The evolution and future of high performance management systems. Glenn Bassett. Westport, Conn.: Quorum, 1993. xvii, 208 p. : ill. *Notes:* Includes discussion of the Hawthorne Studies. Includes bibliographical references (p. [199]-202) and index. [LC 93012992; ISN 0899308139]
  HD31. B369448 1993   +1700

The executive course: what every manager needs to know about the essentials of business. edited by Gayton E. Germane. Reading, Mass.: Addison-Wesley, c1986. xxv, 405 p. : ill. *Notes:* Includes bibliographies and index. *Contents:* Step one: connect / John B. Fery—Marketing management / Richard P. Bagozzi—Financial management / James C. Van Horne—Managerial accounting / Joel S. Demski—Financial reporting / William H. Beaver—Production operations / Steven C. Wheelwright—Logistics / Gayton E. Germane—Management decision and information systems / Charles P. Bonini and Jeffrey H. Moore—Organizational development / Jerry I. Porras—International business management / David B. Zenoff—Technology management / William F. Miller / Strategic management / L.J. Bourgeois. [LC 85013453; ISN 0201115530; $24.95 (est.)]
    HD31. E863 1986   1701

Executive smart charts & other insider revelations on corporate insanity. by Herb Stansbury. 1st ed. San Francisco: Berrett-Koehler, 1993. xi, 229 p. : ill. [LC 93027144; ISN 1881052370]
    HD38. S75 1993   +1702

Fast cycle time: how to align purpose, strategy, and structure for speed. Christopher Meyer; foreword by Peter M. Senge. New York: Toronto: New York: Free Press; Maxwell Macmillan Canada; Maxwell Macmillan International, c1993. xiii, 290 p. : ill. *Notes:* Includes bibliographical references (p. 273-280) and index. [LC 93007306; ISN 0029211816; $29.95]   HD31. M417 1993   1703

Field guide to business terms: a glossary of essential tools and concepts for today's manager. chief contributor, Tim Hindle; edited by Alistair D. Williamson. Boston, Mass.: Harvard Business School Press, c1993. ix, 277 p. [LC 92044938; ISN 087584412X; $16.95]   HD30.17. H56 1993   1704

Fit, failure, and the hall of fame: how companies succeed or fail. Raymond E. Miles, Charles C. Snow. New York: Toronto: New York: Free Press; Maxwell Macmillan Canada; Maxwell Macmillan International, c1994. iv, 214 p. : ill. *Notes:* Spine title: Fit, failure & the hall of fame. Includes bibliographical references (p. 201-208) and index. [LC 94017717; ISN 0029212650; $24.95]
    HD31. M436 1994   +1705

Framebreak: the radical redesign of American business. Ian I. Mitroff, Richard O. Mason, Christine M. Pearson. 1st ed. San Francisco: Jossey-Bass Publishers, c1994. xxii, 156 p. *Notes:* Includes bibliographical references (p. [141]-149) and index. [LC 93042749; ISN 1555426069; $22.00]
    HD70.U5 M54 1994   +1706

The genius of Sitting Bull. Emmett C. Murphy with Michael Snell. Englewood Cliffs, N.J.: Prentice Hall, c1993. xliii, 340 p. : ill., maps *Notes:* "13 heroic strategies for today's business leaders"—D/Dustjacket. Includes bibliographical references and index. [LC 92030240; ISN 0133492265; $18.95]   HD70.U5 M87 1993   1707

Going green: how to communicate your company's environmental commitment. E. Bruce Harrison. Homewood, IL: Business One Irwin, c1993. xvi, 344 p. : ill. [LC 92039264; ISN 1556239459]
    HD69.P6 H37 1993   +1708

The Hay/Inc. 500 report: managing corporate growth and renewal: lessons in excellence from America's best small companies. Philadelphia, Pa.: HayGroup, c1988. 120 leaves: ill.; $295.00]
    HD62.7. H33 1988   1709

The healthy company: eight strategies to develop people, productivity, and profits. Robert H. Rosen with Lisa Berger; foreword by James A. Autry. 1st ed. Los Angeles: J.P. Tarcher, c1991. xix, 315 p. *Notes:* Includes bibliographical references (p. 303-306) and index. [LC 91023472; ISN 0874776554; $22.95]   HD31. R723 1991   1710

How to compete beyond the 1980s: perspectives from high-performance companies: conference proceedings. sponsored by Federal Reserve Bank of Atlanta. Westport, Conn.: Quorum Books, c1985. xxii, 165 p. : ill. *Notes:* Papers presented at a conference held in Atlanta, Ga. in April 1984. Includes index. Bibliography: p. [157]-158. [LC 84022629; ISN 0899300960]   HD29. H68 1985   1711

I know it when I see it: a modern fable about quality. John Guaspari. New York, N.Y.: American Management Association, c1985. 78 p. [LC 84045814; ISN 0814457878]   HD38. G766 1985   1712

In search of excellence: lessons from America's best-run companies. by Thomas J. Peters and Robert H. Waterman, Jr. 1st ed. New York: Harper & Row, c1982. xxvi, 360 p. *Notes:* Includes bibliographical references and index. [LC 82047530; ISN 0060150424; $19.95]   HD70.U5 P424 1982   1713

The information jungle: a quasi-novel approach to managing corporate knowledge. Clyde W. Holsapple, Andrew B. Whinston; illustrations by Jon Kerry. Homewood, Ill.: Dow Jones-Irwin, c1988. xix, 741 p. : ill. *Notes:* Includes bibliographies and index. [LC 87036780; ISN 0870949772; $34.95]   HD30.2. H65 1988   1714

Inside corporate Japan: the art of fumble-free management. David J. Lu; foreword by Norman Bodek. Stamford, CT: Productivity Press, c1987. xxi, 249 p. : ill. *Notes:* Includes index. Bibliography: p. 225-231. [LC 87060546; ISN 091529916X; $24.50]   HD70.J3 L8 1987   1715

Insight into management. P.A. Lawrence and R.A. Lee. 2nd ed. Oxford England; New York: Oxford University Press, 1989. xii, 231 p. : ill. *Notes:* Includes bibliographies and index. [LC 89009402; ISN 0198562268; ISN 0198562276; $18.75; $45.00]   HD31. L3174 1989   1716

Instant management: the best ideas from the people who have made a difference in how we manage. Carol Kennedy. 1st U.S. ed. New York: W. Morrow, 1993?, c1991. xxi, 201 p. *Notes:* Summaries of the work of 34 management theorists. "First published in 1991 in Great Britain by Business Books Limited..."—Verso t.p. Includes bibliographical references. [LC 92019136; ISN 0688119506]   HD31. K454 1993   1717

Integrative management, innovation, and new venturing: a guide to sustained profitability. M. Terkel. Amsterdam; New York: New York, N.Y., U.S.A.: Elsevier; Distributors for the United States and Canada, Elsevier Science Pub. Co., 1991. 2 v. (xxii, 995 p.): ill. *Notes:* Includes bibliographical references (v. 2, p. [945]-983) and indexes. [LC 91151545; ISN 0444874445; $175.00]   HD31. T46 1991   1718

The Japanese business success factors: how top management, product, money and people's creativity contribute to Japanese enterprise growth. Ryūei Shimizu. Tokyo: Chikura Shobo, 1989. 4, 7, 279, 8 p. : ill. *Notes:* Includes bibliographical references and index. [LC 90109390; ISN 4805105887; $75.00]   HD70.J3 S567 1989   1719

The Japanese industrial system. Charles J. McMillan. 2nd rev. ed. Berlin; New York: W. de Gruyter, 1985. xii, 356 p. : ill. *Notes:* Includes indexes. Bibliography: p. [335]-347. [LC 84023270; ISN 089925005X; $29.95]   HD70.J3 M14 1985   1720

Japanese management: a forward-looking analysis. Kunio Odaka. Tokyo: Asian Productivity Organization, c1986. v, 85 p. *Notes:* Translation of: Nihon-teki Keiei. Includes bibliographical references.; ISN 9283310810; ISN 9283310829]   HD70.J3 O3313 1986   1721

The Japanese temptation. H.J. van Dongen, G.G.J.M. Poeth. Delft: Eburon, 1985. 156 p. : ill. *Notes:* Bibliography: p. 146-156. [LC 85197659; ISN 9070379166]   HD70.J3 D66 1985   1722

Juggernaut: the German way of business: why it is transforming Europe—and the world. Philip Glouchevitch. New York: Simon & Schuster, c1992. 239 p. *Notes:* Includes bibliographical references (p. [221]-224) and index. [LC 92019015; ISN 0671744100; $21.00]   HD70.G2 G58 1992   1723

Kaizen, the key to Japanese competitive success. Masaaki Imai. 1st ed. New York: Random House Business Division, 1986. xxxiii, 259 p. : ill. *Notes:* Includes bibliographical references and index. [LC 85030015; ISN 0394551869; $19.95]   HD70.J3 I547 1986   1724

Levers of control: how managers use innovative control systems to drive strategic renewal. Robert Simons. Boston, Mass.: Harvard Business School Press, c1995. xi, 217 p. : ill. *Notes:* Includes bibliographical references and index. [LC 94009073; ISN 0875845592; $29.95]   HD31. S563 1995   +1725

Making it happen: reflections on leadership. John Harvey-Jones. London: Collins, 1988. 256 p. *Notes:* Includes index. [LC 87034086; ISN 0002176637; £12.95: CIP confirmed]   HD70.G7 H37 1988   1726

Making the future work: unleashing our powers of innovation for the decades ahead. John Diebold. New York: Simon and Schuster, c1984. 466 p. *Notes:* Includes index. Bibliography: p. 439-448. [LC 84013889; ISN 0671456571]   HD70.U5 D53 1984   1727

Management and organizational behavior classics. edited by Michael T. Matteson, John M. Ivancevich. 5th ed. Homewood, IL: Irwin, c1993. xviii, 445 p. : ill. *Notes:* Includes bibliographical references and index. [LC 91047499; ISN 0256087504]   HD31. M2917 1993   +1728

The management control function. by Robert N. Anthony. Boston, Mass.: Harvard Business School Press, c1988. ix, 216 p. : ill. *Notes:* Rev. ed. of: Planning and control systems. 1965. Includes indexes. Bibliography: p. 205-207. [LC 88016336; ISN 0875841848]   HD31. A588 1988   1729

Management control systems. Robert N. Anthony, John Dearden, Norton M. Bedford. 5th ed. Homewood, Ill.: R.D. Irwin, 1984. xiii, 853 p. : ill. (The Robert N. Anthony/Willard J. Graham series in accounting) *Notes:* Includes bibliographies and indexes. [LC 83082134; ISN 025602961X]   HD31. A589 1984   1730

Management rediscovered: how companies can escape the numbers trap. Donald A. Curtis. Homewood, Ill.: Dow Jones-Irwin, c1990. xi, 200 p. [LC 89037611; ISN 1556232764; $24.95]   HD70.U5 C87 1990   1731

Managers and national culture: a global perspective. edited by Richard B. Peterson. Westport, Conn.: Quorum Books, 1993. xiv, 460 p. : ill. *Notes:* Includes bibliographical references and index. [LC 92001747; ISN 0899306020]   HD31. M293948 1993   1732

Managing by the numbers: absentee ownership and the decline of American industry. Christopher Meek, Warner Woodworth, and W. Gibb Dyer. Reading, Mass.: Addison-Wesley Pub. Co., c1988. ix, 293 p. : ill. *Notes:* Includes bibiographies and index. [LC 87016088; ISN 020116129X; $19.95]   HD70.U5 M413 1988   1733

Managing for results: economic tasks and risk-taking decisions. Peter F. Drucker. 1st Perennial Library ed. New York: Perennial Library, 1986. xiv, 240 p. *Notes:* Originally published: New York: Harper & Row, c1964. Bibliography: p. 229-230. [LC 85045683; ISN 0060913398; $8.95]
HD38. D7 1986   1734

Managing in turbulent times. by Peter F. Drucker. 1st ed. New York: Harper & Row, c1980. viii, 239 p. *Notes:* Includes index. [LC 79003389; ISN 0060110945; $10.00]   HD31. D7734   1735

Managing take-off in fast growth companies: innovation in entrepreneurial firms. edited by Raymond W. Smilor and Robert L. Kuhn. New York: Praeger, c1986. x, 191 p. : ill. *Notes:* Includes bibliographies and index. [LC 85016745; ISN 0030057094; $29.95]   HD31. T24 1986   1736

Manufacturing knowledge: a history of the Hawthorne experiments. Richard Gillespie. Cambridge England; New York: Cambridge University Press, 1991. x, 282 p. *Notes:* Includes bibliographical references (p. 274-276) and index. [LC 90025639; ISN 0521403588; $39.50]   HD30.42.U5 G55 1991   1737

Maximum performance: the Dow Jones-Irwin complete guide to practical business management. Joseph Shetzen. Homewood, Ill.: Dow Jones-Irwin, c1990. 2 v.: ill. *Notes:* Bibliography: p. 320. Errata sheet inserted. [LC 89025848; ISN 1556231113; $47.50]   HD31. S453 1990   1738

Micromanaging: transforming business leaders with personal computers. George T. Geis, Robert L. Kuhn. Englewood Cliffs, NJ: Prentice-Hall, c1987. xiv, 233 p. *Notes:* Includes bibliographies and index. [LC 86030470; ISN 0135819016; ISN 013581927X]   HD30.2. G44 1987   1739

The naked manager: games executives play. Robert Heller. 1st ed. New York: T. Talley Books, c1985. xvii, 397 p. *Notes:* Includes index. [LC 85010263; ISN 0525243143]   HD70.G7 H44 1985   1740

The new capitalism. William E. Halal. New York: Wiley, c1986. xi, 486 p. : ill. *Notes:* Includes index. Bibliography: p. 435-475. [LC 86001643; ISN 0471874728; $24.95 (est.)]   HD31. H228 1986   1741

New corporate ventures: how to make them work. Ralph Alterowitz with Jon Zonderman. New York: Wiley, c1988. xiv, 206 p. : ill. *Notes:* Includes index. [LC 87034925; ISN 0471624187]
HD70.U5 A414 1988   1742

The new paradigm in business: emerging strategies for leadership and organizational change. edited by Michael Ray and Alan Rinzler for the World Business Academy. New York: J.P. Tarcher/Perigee, c1993. xiv, 300 p. *Notes:* Includes bibliographical references. [LC 92026205; ISN 0874777267]   HD31. N4542 1993   1743

The new portable MBA. Eliza G.C. Collins, Mary Anne Devanna. [Rev. and expanded]. New York: J. Wiley, c1994. xv, 441 p. : ill. *Notes:* Rev. ed. of: The portable MBA / [edited by] Eliza G.C. Collins, Mary Anne Devanna. 1990. Includes bibliographical references (p. 413-422) and index. [LC 94032608; ISN 0471080047; $27.95 (U.K. £19.95)]   HD31. C6134 1994   +1744

The new shop floor management: empowering people for continuous improvement. Kiyoshi Suzaki. New York: Toronto: New York: Free Press; Maxwell Macmillan Canada; Maxwell Macmillan International, c1993. xvi, 462 p. : ill. *Notes:* Includes bibliographical references and index. [LC 92042549; ISN 0029322650]   HD31. S775 1993   1745

Operations management: production of goods and services. John O. McClain, L. Joseph Thomas, Joseph B. Mazzola. 3rd ed. Englewood Cliffs, N.J.: Prentice Hall, c1992. xii, 740 p. : ill. *Notes:* Includes bibliographical references and index. [LC 91039076; ISN 0136361358; $69.00]
HD30.25. M24 1992   1746

A passion for excellence: the leadership difference. Tom Peters, Nancy Austin. New York: Random House, c1985. xxv, 437 p. : ill. *Notes:* Includes index. Bibliography: p. [427]-428. [LC 84045767; ISN 0394544846]   HD70.U5 P425 1985   1747

Pocket MBA: the essentials of management thinking and theory from A to Z. 2nd ed. London: London; New York: The Economist in association with Hamish Hamilton; Penguin, 1994. vi, 233 p. *Notes:* Previous ed.: London: Century Business: Economist, 1992. "Chief contributor Tim Hindle"—Verso. Includes bibliographical references. [LC 94070774; ISN 0241002362; £9.99]
HD30.17. P62 1994   +1748

Policy formulation and administration: a casebook of senior management problems in business. C. Roland Christensen... et al. 9th ed. Homewood, Ill.: R.D. Irwin, 1985. xiii, 867 p. : ill. *Notes:* Coauthors: Norman A. Berg, Malcolm S. Salter, Howard H. Stevenson. Includes bibliographical references and index.; ISN 025603012X]   HD31. P57 1985   1749

Policy formulation and administration: a casebook of senior management problems in business. C. Roland Christensen, Norman A. Berg, Malcolm S. Salter. 8th ed. Homewood, Ill.: R. D. Irwin, 1980. xix, 836 p. : ill. *Notes:* First-6th ed. by G. A. Smith, Jr. (2d-4th, with C. R. Christensen; 5th, with C. R. Christensen and N. A. Berg; 6th, with C. R. Christensen, and others). Includes bibliographical references. [LC 79091633]   HD31. C523 1980   1750

The portable MBA. Eliza G.C. Collins, Mary Anne DeVanna. New York: Wiley, c1990. xii, 386 p. : ill. *Notes:* Includes bibliographical references. [LC 89027382; ISN 0471619973; $24.95]
HD31. C59 1990   1751

The principles of scientific management. Frederick Winslow Taylor. New York: Norton, 1967, c1947. 144 p. (The Norton library) [LC 67005319]   T58.8. T4 1967   1752

Productive workplaces: organizing and managing for dignity, meaning, and community. Marvin R. Weisbord. 1st ed. San Francisco: Jossey-Bass, 1987. xxv, 405 p. : ill. (The Jossey-Bass management series) *Notes:* Includes index. Bibliography: p. 381-395. [LC 87045425; ISN 1555420540]   HD31. W424 1987   1753

Quantitative analysis for business decisions. Harold Bierman, Jr., Charles P. Bonini, Warren H. Hausman. 8th ed. Homewood, IL: Irwin, c1991. xx, 742 p. : ill. (chiefly col.) *Notes:* Includes bibliographical references and index. [LC 90048928; ISN 0256082677; $52.95]   HD30.25. B53 1991   1754

Quantitative methods in management: case studies of failures and successes. edited by C.B. Tilanus, O.B. de Gans, and J.K. Lenstra; translated by B Knoppers and P. Attwood. Chichester; New York: Wiley, c1986. xvi, 279 p. : ill. *Notes:* Translation of: Kwantitatieve methoden in het management. Includes bibliographies and index. [LC 85012351; ISN 047190841X; $29.92 (U.S.)]   HD30.25. K8313 1986   1755

Readings in management. edited by Max D. Richards. 7th ed. Cincinnati: South-Western Pub. Co., c1986. viii, 641 p. : ill. *Notes:* Includes bibliographies. [LC 85071773; ISN 0538079908]   HD31. R417 1986   1756

Relevance regained: from top-down control to bottom-up empowerment. H. Thomas Johnson. New York: Toronto: New York: Free Press; Maxwell Macmillan Canada; Maxwell Macmillan International, c1992. xi, 228 p. : ill. *Notes:* Includes bibliographical references (p. 207-216) and index. [LC 92006762; ISN 0029165555; $24.95]   HD31. J555 1992   1757

Renewing American industry. Paul R. Lawrence, Davis Dyer. New York: London: Free Press; Collier Macmillan Publishers, c1983. xiii, 384 p. : ill. *Notes:* Includes bibliographical references and index. [LC 82072096; ISN 0029181704]   HD70.U5 L38 1983   1758

Rust to riches: the coming of the second industrial revolution. John Rutledge, Deborah Allen. 1st ed. New York: Harper & Row, c1989. xiv, 207 p. : ill *Notes:* Includes index. [LC 88045905; ISN 0060158816; $19.95]   HD70.U5 R87 1989   1759

Short-term America: the causes and cures of our business myopia. Michael T. Jacobs; foreword by David W. Mullins, Jr. Boston, Mass.: Harvard Business School Press, c1991. xiv, 268 p. : ill. *Notes:* Includes bibliographical references (p. 247-254) and index. *Contents:* Business myopia and U.S. competitiveness—The commoditization of corporate ownership—How corporations are really governed—The truth about takeovers—The demise of relationship banking—The cost-of-capital enigma—Management compensation plans - panacea or placebo?—A cure for myopia. [LC 91004207; ISN 087584300X; $24.95]   HD70.U5 J33 1991   1760

Statistical thinking for managers. David K. Hildebrand, Lyman Ott. 3rd ed. Boston: PWS-Kent Pub. Co., c1991. xviii, 1014 p. : ill. *Notes:* Includes bibliographical references (p. 926-928) and index. [LC 90019988; ISN 0534925618; $52.95]   HD30.215. H54 1991   1761

Strategic management. H. Igor Ansoff. New York: Wiley, c1979. ix, 236 p. : ill. *Notes:* "A Halsted Press book." Includes index. Bibliography: p. 226-233. [LC 78023402; ISN 047026585X]   HD31. A582 1979   1762

Strategic management in developing countries: case studies. James E. Austin with Tomás O. Kohn. New York: London: Free Press; Collier Macmillan, c1990. xi, 691 p. *Notes:* Includes bibliographical references. [LC 90037736; ISN 0029011051]   HD70.D44 A97 1990   1763

Strategy and structure of Japanese enterprises. Toyohiro Kono; foreword by Malcolm Falkus. Armonk, N.Y.: M.E. Sharpe, 1984. xiv, 352 p. : ill. *Notes:* Includes bibliographies and index. [LC 84005382; ISN 0873322878; ISN 0873322886]   HD70.J3 K63 1984   1764

Sunrise—sunset: challenging the myth of industrial obsolescence. Alan M. Kantrow, editor. New York: Wiley, c1985. ix, 552 p. : ill. (Harvard Business Review executive book series, 0275-2492) *Notes:* Includes contributions by several faculty members of the Harvard Graduate School of Business Administration. Includes bibliographical references and indexes. [LC 84019580; ISN 0471805734; $22.95 (est.)]   HD31. S764 1985   1765

Surviving corporate transition: rational management in a world of mergers, layoffs, start-ups, takeovers, divestitures, deregulation, and new technologies. William Bridges. 1st ed. New York: Doubleday, 1988. xii, 227 p. *Notes:* Includes index. Bibliography: p. [205]-213. [LC 87019978; ISN 0385237618; $16.95]   HD31. B7395 1988   1766

Taylorism transformed: scientific management theory since 1945. Stephen P. Waring. Chapel Hill: University of North Carolina Press, c1991. xi, 288 p. *Notes:* Includes bibliographical references (p. [237]-275) and index. [LC 91011027; ISN 0807819727; $34.95]   HD30.5. W37 1991   1767

Thriving on chaos: handbook for a management revolution. Tom Peters. 1st ed. New York: Knopf: Distributed by Random House, 1987. xii, 561 p. : ill. *Notes:* Includes index. "A Borzoi book." Bibliography: p. 527-537. [LC 87045575; ISN 0394567846]   HD70.U5 P426 1987   1768

Top management in Japanese firms. Ryūei Shimizu. Tōkyō: Chikura Shobō, 1986. [227] p. *Notes:* Includes bibliographical references and index.; ISN 4805105429]   HD70.J3 S57   1769

Toppling the pyramids: redefining the way companies are run. Gerald Ross and Michael Kay. 1st ed. New York: Times Books, 1994. vi, 228 p. *Notes:* Includes bibliographical references and index. [LC 94000167; ISN 0812923413; $25.00]   HD38. R596 1994   +1770

Total improvement management: next generation in performance management. H. James Harrington with James S. Harrington. New York: McGraw-Hill, c1995. xviii, 488 p. : ill. *Notes:* Includes bibliographical references and index. [LC 94032868; ISN 0070267707]   HD31. H3454 1995   +1771

Tough choices: the decision-making styles of America's top 50 CEOs. Warren J. Pelton, Sonja Sackmann, Robert Boguslaw. Homewood, IL: Dow Jones-Irwin, c1990. xv, 163 p. : ill. *Notes:* Includes index. Bibliography: p. 157-158. [LC 89011766; ISN 1556232330]   HD30.23. P45 1990   1772

The turnaround manager's handbook. Richard S. Sloma. New York: Free Press, c1985. xiv, 226 p. : ill. *Notes:* Includes index. [LC 85016329; ISN 0029292905; $15.95]   HD31. S5774 1985   1773

Understanding business statistics. John E. Hanke, Arthur G. Reitsch. 2nd ed. Burr Ridge, Ill.: Irwin, c1994. xviii, 1005 p. : ill. *Notes:* Includes index. *Contents:* Introduction to statistics—Data collection—Data presentation—Descriptive statistics—Basic probability and discrete probability distributions—Continuous probability distribution—Sampling distributions—Estimation—Hypothesis testing—Two-population hypothesis tests—Chi-square tests—Variability hypothesis tests and analysis of variance—Quality-control applications—Correlation and simple regression—Multiple regression—Index numbers and time series analysis—Business forecasting—Decision making under uncertainty—Nonparametric statistics. [LC 93016827; ISN 0256112193]   HD30.215. H36 1994   +1774

Unheard voices: labor and economic policy in a competitive world. Ray Marshall. New York: Basic Books, c1987. xi, 339 p. : ill. *Notes:* Includes index. Bibliography: p. [319]-327. [LC 83046084; ISN 0465088694; $19.95]   HD5660.U5 M36 1987   1775

Vanguard management: redesigning the corporate future. James O'Toole. 1st ed. Garden City, N.Y.: Doubleday, 1985. x, 418 p. *Notes:* Includes bibliographical references and index. [LC 84024644; ISN 0385198426; $19.95]   HD70.U5 O75 1985   1776

Visions of modernity: American business and the modernization of Germany. Mary Nolan. New York: Oxford University Press, 1994. x, 324 p. *Notes:* Includes bibliographical references and index. [LC 93020943; ISN 0195088751; $19.95]   HD70.G2 N64 1994   +1777

The vital difference: unleashing the powers of sustained corporate success. Frederick G. Harmon and Garry Jacobs. New York: American Management Association, c1985. vii, 294 p. : ill. *Notes:* Includes bibliographical references and index. [LC 85047674; ISN 0814455697]   HD70.U5 H36 1985   1778

What America does right: learning from companies that put people first. Robert H. Waterman, Jr. New York: Norton, 1994. 318 p. *Notes:* Includes bibliographical references (p. 303-306) and index. [LC 93028837; ISN 0393035972; $23.00]   HD70.U5 W38 1994   +1779

World-class manufacturing: the lessons of simplicity applied. Richard J. Schonberger. New York: London: Free Press; Collier Macmillan, c1986. xi, 253 p. : ill. *Notes:* Includes index. Bibliography: p. 237-242. [LC 85024719; ISN 0029292700]   HD31. S3385 1986   1780

INDUSTRIAL MARKETING

Business marketing management: a strategic view of industrial and organizational markets. Michael D. Hutt, Thomas W. Speh. 4th ed. Fort Worth: Dryden Press, c1992. xxvi, 749 p. : ill. *Notes:* Includes bibliographical references and indexes. [LC 91008610; ISN 0030541670; $52.71]   HF5415.13. H87 1992   1781

Business marketing management: an organizational approach: text and cases. Robert W. Haas. 5th ed. Boston: PWS-KENT Pub. Co., c1992. xi, 899 p. : ill. *Notes:* Rev. ed. of: Industrial marketing management. c1989. Includes bibliographical references and index. [LC 91042284; ISN 0534929761; $54.91]   HF5415.13. H2713 1992   1782

Business-to-business direct marketing: proven direct response methods to generate more leads and sales. Robert W. Bly. Lincolnwood, Ill.: NTC Business Books, c1993. xvii, 267 p. *Notes:* Includes index. [LC 91044519; ISN 0844234729]   HF5415.1263. B58 1993   1783

Industrial marketing: cases and concepts. E. Raymond Corey. 3rd ed. Englewood Cliffs, N.J.: Prentice-Hall, c1983. xiv, 610 p. : ill. *Notes:* Includes bibliographical references. [LC 82024106; ISN 0134615093]   HF5415. C654 1983   1784

New directions in marketing: business-to-business strategies for the 1990s. Aubrey Wilson; foreword by Philip Kotler; afterword by Theodore Levitt. Lincolnwood, Ill., USA: NTC Business Books, 1992. 231 p. : ill. *Notes:* Originally published: London: Kogan Page, 1991. Includes bibliographical references (p. [217]-219) and index.; ISN 0844233641; $34.95] HF5415. W547852 1992   1785

Rethinking business to business marketing. Paul Sherlock; foreword by Tom Peters. New York: Free Press, c1991. xviii, 188 p. : ill. [LC 90043634; ISN 0029286158; $19.95] HF5415.13. S518 1991   1786

INDUSTRIAL ORGANIZATION

Managerial hierarchies: comparative perspectives on the rise of modern industrial enterprise. edited by Alfred D. Chandler, Jr. and Herman Daems. Cambridge: Harvard University Press, 1980. ix, 237 p. : ill. *Notes:* "Essays... originally presented at a conference held at the Harvard Business School on September 11-12, 1977." Includes bibliographical references and index. [LC 79020396; ISN 0674547403] HD30.5. M34   1787

Organization theory: from Chester Barnard to the present and beyond. edited by Oliver E. Williamson. New York: Oxford University Press, 1990. vi, 214 p. : ill. *Notes:* Includes bibliographical references. [LC 89038918; ISN 0195061446; $29.95] HD31. O7385 1990   1788

Organizations in action; social science bases of administrative theory. by James D. Thompson. New York McGraw-Hill, 1967. xi, 192 p. *Notes:* Bibliography: p. 165-177. [LC 67011564] HD38. T448   +1789

INDUSTRIAL ORGANIZATION (ECONOMIC THEORY)

The economic theory of organization and the firm. Richard M. Cyert. Washington Square, New York: New York University Press, 1988. xv, 248 p. : ill. *Notes:* Includes bibliographies and index. [LC 88017688; ISN 0814714277; $40.00] HD2326. C94 1988   1790

The economics of industrial organization. William G. Shepherd. 3rd ed. Englewood Cliffs, N.J.: Prentice Hall, c1990. ix, 566 p. : ill. *Notes:* Includes bibliographical references and indexes. [LC 89072160; ISN 013223694X] HD2326. S46 1990   1791

The economics of industries and firms: theories, evidence and policy. Malcolm C. Sawyer. 2nd ed. London: Croom Helm, c1985. ix, 322 p. : ill. *Notes:* Includes index. Bibliography: p. 302-315. [LC 85023918; ISN 0709944136; £19.95] HD2326. S27 1985   1792

The empirical renaissance in industrial economics. edited by Timothy F. Bresnahan and Richard Schmalensee. New York, NY: Basil Blackwell, Inc., 1987. vi, 261 p. *Notes:* "Published in cooperation with The journal of industrial economics." Includes bibliographies and index.; ISN 0631157433] HC79.C7 E46 1987   1793

The firm, the market, and the law. R.H. Coase. Chicago: University of Chicago Press, 1988. vii, 217 p. *Notes:* Includes bibliographies and index. [LC 87024193; ISN 0226111008; $15.95] HD2326. C6 1988   1794

Handbook of industrial organization. edited by Richard Schmalensee and Robert Willig. Amsterdam; New York: New York, N.Y., U.S.A.: North-Holland; Sole distributors for the U.S.A. and Canada, Elsevier Science Pub. Co., 1989. 2 v. *Notes:* Includes bibliographies. Library has: v. 1, 2. [LC 88025138; ISN 0444704345; ISN 0444704353; ISN 0444704361; $80.93; $81.04] HD2326. H28 1989   1795

Industrial market structure and economic performance. F.M. Scherer, David Ross. 3rd ed. Boston: Houghton Mifflin, c1990. xvi, 713 p. : ill. *Notes:* Includes bibliographical references. [LC 89080961; ISN 0395357144; $49.16] HD2326. S286 1990   1796

Inside the firm: the inefficiencies of hierarchy. Harvey Leibenstein. Cambridge, Mass.: Harvard University Press, 1987. xiv, 276 p. : ill. *Notes:* Includes index. Bibliography: p. [263]-268. [LC 87008426; ISN 0674455150] HD2326. L45 1987   1797

The theory of industrial organization. Jean Tirole. Cambridge, Mass.: MIT Press, c1988. xii, 479 p. : ill. *Notes:* Includes bibliographies and index. [LC 88002700; ISN 0262200716] HD2326. T56 1988   1798

INDUSTRIAL POLICY

Government and the enterprise since 1900: the changing problem of efficiency. Jim Tomlinson. Oxford: New York: Clarendon Press; Oxford University Press, 1994. xv, 455 p. *Notes:* Includes bibliographical references (p. 411-449) and index. [LC 93032725; ISN 0198287496; £40.00] HD3616.G72 T66 1994   +1799

State and business in modern Turkey: a comparative study. Ayşe Buğra. Albany: State University of New York Press, c1994. xi, 328 p. : ill. *Notes:* Includes bibliographical references (p. 307-321) and index. [LC 93018517; ISN 0791417883; ISN 0791417875] HD3616.T873 B84 1994 +1800

INDUSTRIAL PROCUREMENT

Prices, quality and trust: inter-firm relations in Britain and Japan. Mari Sako. Cambridge; New York, NY, USA: Cambridge University Press, 1992. xiii, 270 p. : ill. *Notes:* Includes bibliographical references (p. 257-266) and index. [LC 91040505; ISN 0521413869] HD39.5. S25 1992 1801

Purchasing and materials management. Michiel R. Leenders, Harold E. Fearon, Wilbur B. England. 7th ed. Homewood, Ill.: R. D. Irwin, 1980. xi, 582 p. : ill. *Notes:* Sixth ed. by W. B. England and M. R. Leenders. Includes indexes. Bibliography: p. 563-570. [LC 79091639; ISN 0256023743] HD52.5. L43 1980 1802

Purchasing and materials management. Michiel R. Leenders, Harold E. Fearon, Wilbur B. England. 9th ed. Homewood, IL: Irwin, 1989. xiii, 672 p. : ill. *Notes:* Includes bibliographies and indexes. [LC 88028600; ISN 0256069840; $41.95] HD39.5. L43 1989 1803

Purchasing and materials management: text and cases. Donald W. Dobler, David N. Burt, Lamar Lee, Jr. 5th ed. New York: McGraw-Hill Pub. Co., c1990. xix, 843 p. *Notes:* Includes indexes. Bibliography: p. 823-826. [LC 89012575; ISN 0070370478; $45.95] HD39.5. D62 1990 1804

Purchasing and the management of materials. Gary J. Zenz; with the assistance of George H. Thompson. 7th ed. New York: Wiley, c1994. xvi, 730 p. : ill. *Notes:* Includes bibliographical references and indexes. [LC 93005911; ISN 0471549835] HD39.5. Z47 1994 +1805

INDUSTRIAL PRODUCTIVITY

Britain's productivity gap. Stephen Davies and Richard E. Caves. Cambridge Cambridgeshire; New York: Cambridge University Press, 1987. xiv, 131 p. *Notes:* Includes index. Bibliography: p. 122-127. [LC 86023261; ISN 0521334640] HC260.I52 D38 1987 1806

The challenge of hidden profits: reducing corporate bureaucracy and waste. by Mark Green and John F. Berry. 1st ed. New York: W. Morrow, c1985. 453 p. *Notes:* Includes index. Bibliography: p. 393-436. [LC 85011554; ISN 0688039863] HD56. G73 1985 1807

Improving performance: how to manage the white space on the organization chart. Geary A. Rummler, Alan P. Brache. 1st ed. San Francisco: Jossey-Bass Publishers, 1990. xviii, 227 p. : ill. *Notes:* Includes bibliographical references (p. 215-217) and index. [LC 89043299; ISN 1555422144; $24.95] HD56. R86 1990 1808

Industrial efficiency in six nations. edited by Richard E. Caves in association with Sheryl D. Bailey... et al. Cambridge, Mass.: MIT Press, c1992. vi, 492 p. *Notes:* Includes bibliographical references and index. [LC 92003851; ISN 0262031930] HC79.I52 I53 1992 1809

Innovation and the productivity crisis. Martin Neil Baily and Alok K. Chakrabarti. Washington, D.C.: Brookings Institution, c1988. ix, 133 p. : ill. *Notes:* Includes bibliographical references and index. [LC 88001697; ISN 0815707606; ISN 0815707592; $22.95; $8.95] HC79.I52 B35 1988 1810

Made in America: regaining the productive edge. Michael L. Dertouzos, Richard K. Lester, Robert M. Solow and the MIT Commission on Industrial Productivity. Cambridge, Mass.: MIT Press, c1989. x, 334 p. *Notes:* Includes bibliographical references and index. [LC 89002251; ISN 0262041006] HC110.I52 D46 1989 1811

Measure up!: yardsticks for continuous improvement. Richard L. Lynch and Kelvin F. Cross. Cambridge, Mass.: Blackwell Business, 1993. xi, 212 p. : ill. *Notes:* "Paperback edition"—CIP foreword. Includes bibliographical references and index. [LC 93029888; ISN 1557864616] HC110.I52 L96 1993 +1812

Patton on productivity: proven techniques for effective management. John A. Patton. Englewood Cliffs, N.J.: Prentice-Hall, 1987. xiii, 210 p. *Notes:* Includes bibliographical references and index. [LC 86018745; ISN 0136544010] HD56. P35 1987 1813

Productivity and quality through people: practices of well-managed companies. edited by Y.K. Shetty and Vernon M. Buehler; foreword by John A. Young. Westport, Conn.: Quorum Books, c1985. xvi, 351 p. : ill. *Notes:* Includes index. Bibliography: p. [330]-340. [LC 84024930; ISN 0899301150] HD56. P8214 1985 1814

Productivity growth and the competitiveness of the American economy: a Carolina Public Policy Conference volume. edited by Stanley W. Black. Boston: Kluwer Academic Publishers, c1989. viii, 158 p. : ill. *Notes:* "Based on the First Carolina Public Policy Conference held at the University of North Carolina at Chapel Hill in February, 1988"—P. [4] of cover. Includes bibliographical references. [LC 88034259; ISN 0792390016; $44.00] HC110.I52 P754 1989   1815

Productivity growth and U.S. competitiveness. edited by William J. Baumol and Kenneth McLennan. New York: Oxford University Press, 1985. x, 228 p. *Notes:* "A Supplementary paper of the Committee for Economic Development." Includes bibliographies. *Contents:* [ch.] 6. Productivity: the industrial relations connection / Robert B. McKersie and Janice A. Klein. [LC 84029577; ISN 0195035267] HC110.I52 P756 1985   1816

Productivity management: a practical handbook. Joseph Prokopenko. Geneva: Intenational Labour Office, 1987. xvi, 287 p. : ill. *Notes:* Includes index. Bibliography: p. 275-279.; ISN 9221059014] HD56. P8226 1987   1817

Productivity: the art and science of business management. A. Dale Timpe, series editor. New York: Facts On File Publications, 1989. xii, 371 p. *Notes:* Includes index. Bibliography: p. 357-363. [LC 88021849; ISN 0816019053] HD56. P795 1989   1818

Quality & productivity: the new challenge. by Glenn E. Hayes. Wheaton, IL: Hitchcock Pub. Co., c1985. xi, 293 p. : ill. *Notes:* Includes index. Bibliography: p. 281-289. [LC 84062379; ISN 093393100X; $29.95] HD56. H36   1819

The quest for competitiveness: lessons from America's productivity and quality leaders. edited by Y.K. Shetty and Vernon M. Buehler; foreword by George M.C. Fisher. New York: Quorum Books, 1991. xv, 432 p. *Notes:* Selected lectures sponsored by Utah State University's Partners Program, 1979-1989. Includes bibliographical references (p. [415]-420) and index. [LC 89049433; ISN 0899305466; $45.00] HC110.I52 Q47 1991   1820

Reinventing the factory II: managing the world class factory. / Roy L. Harmon; foreword by Leroy D. Peterson. New York: Toronto: New York: Free Press; Maxwell Macmillan Canada; Maxwell Macmillan International, c1992. xxix, 407 p. : ill. *Notes:* Includes bibliographical references (p. 375-387) and index. [LC 89016944; ISN 0029138620; $35.00] HD56. H35 1992   1821

Reinventing the factory: productivity breakthroughs in manufacturing today. Roy L. Harmon, Leroy D. Peterson. New York: London: Free Press; Collier Macmillan, c1990. xv, 303 p. : ill. *Notes:* Includes bibliographical references. [LC 89016944; ISN 0029138612; $35.00] HD56. H34 1990   1822

The uneasy alliance: managing the productivity-technology dilemma. edited by Kim B. Clark, Robert H. Hayes, Christopher Lorenz. Boston, Mass.: Harvard Business School Press, 1985. x, 485 p. : ill. *Notes:* Includes bibliographical references and index. [LC 85008709; ISN 0875841724] HD56. U53 1985   1823

INDUSTRIAL PROJECT MANAGEMENT

Advanced project management: a structured approach. by F.L. Harrison. 3rd ed. New York: Halsted Press, an imprint of J. Wiley, 1992. xvi, 308 p. : ill. *Notes:* Includes bibliographical references and index. [LC 92025620; ISN 047021970X] HD69.P75 H37 1992   +1824

The anatomy of major projects: a study of the reality of project management. Peter W.G. Morris and George H. Hough. Chichester; New York: Wiley, c1987. viii, 326 p. : ill. *Notes:* Includes index. Bibliography: p. 297-312. [LC 87008176; ISN 0471915513; $38.00 (U.S.)] HD69.P75 M674 1987   1825

Augustine's laws. Norman R. Augustine. Rev. and expanded ed. New York: Viking, 1986. xvii, 380 p. : ill. *Notes:* Includes index. [LC 85040569; ISN 067080942X] T56.8. A93 1986   1826

Customer-driven project management: a new paradigm in total quality implementation. Bruce T. Barkley, James H. Saylor. New York: McGraw-Hill, c1994. xxiii, 508 p. : ill. *Notes:* Includes bibliographical references (p. 501-503) and index. [LC 93034343; ISN 0070037396] HD69.P75 B38 1994   +1827

Global project management handbook. David I. Cleland, Roland Gareis, editors. New York: McGraw-Hill, c1994. 1 v. (various pagings): ill. *Notes:* Includes bibliographical references and index. [LC 93030297; ISN 0070113297] HD69.P75 G56 1994   +1828

Human factors in project management. Paul C. Dinsmore. Rev. ed. New York, NY: American Management Association, c1990. xi, 257 p. : ill. *Notes:* Includes bibliographical references. [LC 89046219; ISN 0814450032; $29.95] HD69.P75 D57 1990   1829

The human side of project management. Ruth Sizemore House. Reading, Mass.: Addison-Wesley Pub. Co., c1988. vi, 327 p. *Notes:* Includes index. Bibliography: p. 253-256. [LC 88000972; ISN 020112355X; $15.47] HD69.P75 H68 1988   1830

The little black book of project management. Michael C. Thomsett. New York, NY: American Management Association, c1990. 182 p. : ill. *Notes:* Includes index. [LC 90055215; ISN 0814477321; $13.95]   HD69.P75 T48 1990   1831

Managing projects and programs. with a preface by Norman R. Augustine. Boston, Mass.: Harvard Business School Press, c1989. xiv, 299 p. : ill. *Notes:* Includes bibliographies and index. [LC 89011032; ISN 0875842135]   HD69.P75 M364 1989   1832

Managing projects in organizations: how to make the best use of time, techniques, and people. J. Davidson Frame. 1st ed. San Francisco: Jossey-Bass, 1987. xvii, 240 p. : ill. (The Jossey-Bass management series) *Notes:* Includes index. Bibliography: p. 231-234. [LC 86033707; ISN 1555420311]   HD69.P75 F72 1987   1833

The people side of project management. Ralph L. Kliem and Irwin S. Ludin. Aldershot, Hants, England; Brookfield, Vt.: Gower, c1992. ix, 190 p. : ill. *Notes:* Includes index. [LC 93129024; ISN 0566073633]   HD69.P75 K59 1992   +1834

Project management: a systems approach to planning, scheduling, and controlling. Harold Kerzner. 4th ed. New York: Van Nostrand Reinhold, c1992. xv, 1023 p. : ill. *Notes:* Includes bibliographical references (p. 1001-1016) and indexes. [LC 91045405; ISN 0442010850]   HD69.P75 K47 1992   1835

Project management: an introduction to issues in industrial research and development. S.A. Bergen. Oxford, OK, UK; New York, NY, USA: B. Blackwell, 1986. xii, 194 p. : ill. *Notes:* Includes index. [LC 86001023; ISN 0631147063; ISN 0631147055; $15.95 (U.S.); $45.00 (U.S.)]   T56.8. B465 1986   1836

Project management handbook. edited by David I. Cleland, William R. King. 2nd ed. New York: Van Nostrand Reinhold, c1988. x, 997 p. : ill. *Notes:* Includes bibliographies and index. [LC 87023151; ISN 0442221142; $63.95]   HD69.P75 P75 1988   1837

Project management handbook. edited by Dennis Lock. Aldershot, Hants, England: Gower Technical Press, c1987. xxii, 625 p. : ill. *Notes:* Includes bibliographies and index. [LC 86025799; ISN 0291397417]   T56.8. P776 1987   1838

Project management: planning and control. Rory Burke. 2nd ed. Chichester; New York: J. Wiley, 1993. xiv, 390 p. : ill. *Notes:* "Reprinted with corrections"—T.p. verso. Includes bibliographical references (p. 386) and index. [LC 93030279; ISN 0471942723]   HD69.P75 B87 1993   +1839

Project management: strategic design and implementation. David I. Cleland. 2nd ed. New York: McGraw-Hill, c1994. xx, 478 p. : ill. *Notes:* Includes bibliographical references and index. [LC 93044757; ISN 0070113513]   HD69.P75 C526 1994   +1840

Project management with CPM, PERT, and precedence diagramming. Joseph J. Moder, Cecil R. Phillips, Edward W. Davis. 3rd ed. New York: Van Nostrand Reinhold, c1983. xiv, 389 p. : ill. *Notes:* Rev. ed. of: Project management with CPM and PERT. 2nd ed. 1970. Includes bibliographical references and index. [LC 82016035; ISN 0442254156]   T56.8. M63 1983   1841

The project manager's survival guide: the handbook for real-world project management. Donald Penner. Columbus: Battelle Press, c1994. ix, 91 p. *Notes:* Includes bibliographical references and index. [LC 93004016; ISN 0935470727; $19.95]   HD69.P75 P46 1994   +1842

Systems analysis and project management. David I. Cleland, William R. King. 3rd ed. New York: McGraw-Hill, c1983. xix, 490 p. : ill. (McGraw-Hill series in management) *Notes:* Includes bibliographies and index. [LC 82014817; ISN 0070113114; $22.95 (est.)]   HD69.P75 C53 1983   1843

INDUSTRIAL PROMOTION

Doing business in Vietnam. James W. Robinson. Rocklin, CA: Prima Pub., 1995. xiii, 288 p. : map *Notes:* Includes bibliographical references and index. [LC 94013044; ISN 1559585919]   HC444.Z9 I537 1995   +1844

Losing time: the industrial policy debate. Otis L. Graham, Jr. Cambridge, Mass.: Harvard University Press, 1992. xiii, 370 p. *Notes:* "A Twentieth Century Fund book." Includes bibliographical references (P. 303-357) and index. [LC 91018461; ISN 0674539192; $29.95]   HC110.I53 G73 1992   1845

INDUSTRIAL RELATIONS

Collective bargaining and industrial relations: from theory to policy and practice. Thomas A. Kochan, Harry C. Katz. 2nd ed. Homewood, Ill.: Irwin, 1988. xii, 496 p. *Notes:* Includes bibliographies and indexes. [LC 87082179; ISN 0256030251]   HD8072.5. K62 1988   1846

The elements of industrial relations. Jack Barbash. Madison, Wis.: University of Wisconsin Press, 1984. xi, 153 p. *Notes:* Includes index. Bibliography: p. 139-148. [LC 83040258; ISN 0299096106; ISN 0299096149; $17.50]   HD6971. B34 1984   1847

Employee relations in Europe. Jeff Bridgford and John Stirling. Oxford, UK; Cambridge, Mass., USA: Blackwell Business, 1994. xii, 268 p. : ill. *Notes:* Includes bibliographical references (p. [252]-262) and index. [LC 93016874; ISN 0631186832; $34.95] HD8376.5. B73 1994 +1848

Industrial relations in a new age. Clark Kerr, Paul D. Staudohar, editors. 1st ed. San Francisco: Jossey-Bass, 1986. xx, 419 p. (The Jossey-Bass management series) *Notes:* Includes bibliographies and indexes. [LC 86045630; ISN 1555420133] HD6971. I548 1986 1849

Industrial relations systems. John T. Dunlop. Rev. ed. Boston, Mass.: Harvard Business School Press, c1993. xiii, 331 p. *Notes:* Includes bibliographical references and index. [LC 92042569; ISN 0875843344; $24.95] HD6971. D85 1993 1850

Invitation to industrial relations. Tom Keenoy. Oxford Oxfordshire; New York: B. Blackwell, 1985. xiv, 287 p. (Invitation series) *Notes:* Includes index. Bibliography: p. 270-282. [LC 85011100; ISN 0631141049; ISN 0631141057; $24.95 (U.S.); $9.95 (U.S.)] HD6971. K392 1985 1851

Labor and an integrated Europe. Lloyd Ulman, Barry Eichengreen, William T. Dickens, editors. Washington, D.C.: Brookings Institution, c1993. viii, 295 p. : ill. *Notes:* Includes bibliographical references and index. *Contents:* Labor and integrated Europe / Lloyd Ulman, Barry Eichengreen, and William T. Dickens—Unionism and unification / Melvin Reder and Lloyd Ulman—Prospects for worker participation in management in the single market / Lowell Turner—The rise and decline of neocorporatism / Wolfgang Streeck—West German labor market institutions and East German transformation / David Soskice and Ronald Schettkat—Employee benefits in the single market / Daniel J. B. Mitchell and Jacques Rojot—European wage equalization since the Treaty of Rome / Robert J. Flanagan—European monetary unification and regional unemployment / Barry Eichengreen—Immigration policies in fortress Europe / Bent Hansen—European economic integration and U.S. wages and employment / Wlilliam T. Dickens—European labor markets: the eastern dimension / Jasminka Sohinger and Daniel Rubinfeld. [LC 92040273; ISN 0815786816; $16.95] HD8380.5. L33 1993 1852

Labor relations. Arthur A. Sloane, Fred Witney. 7th ed. Englewood Cliffs, N.J.: Prentice Hall, c1991. xii, 513 p. : ill. *Notes:* Includes bibliographical references and indexes. [LC 90007431; ISN 0135177987; $57.14] HD8072. S6185 1991 1853

Labor relations: development, structure, process. John A. Fossum. 4th ed. Homewood, Ill.: BPI, Irwin, 1989. xvi, 495 p. : ill. (some color) *Notes:* Includes bibliographies and indexes. [LC 88025837; ISN 0256058237; $39.95] HD8072.5. F67 1989 1854

Labor-management relations. Daniel Quinn Mills. 5th ed. New York: McGraw-Hill, 1993, c1994. xviii, 690 p. : ill. *Notes:* Includes bibliographical references and index. [LC 93021687; ISN 0070425124; $52.95] HD8072.5. M54 1994 +1855

Labor-management relations in a changing environment. Michael Ballot; with contributions from Laurie Lichter-Heath, Thomas Kail, Ruth Wang. New York: Wiley, c1992. xxiii, 563 p. : ill. (some col.) *Notes:* Includes bibliographical references and index. [LC 91025544; ISN 0471620181] HD8072.5. B35 1992 1856

Negotiating the future: a labor perspective on American business. Barry Bluestone and Irving Bluestone. New York, NY: Basic Books, c1992. xv, 335 p. *Notes:* Includes bibliographical references (p. [263]-317) and index. [LC 91059007; ISN 0465049176; $25.00] HD6957.U6 B55 1992 1857

The new unionism: employee involvement in the changing corporation. Charles Heckscher. New York: Basic Books, 1988. xi, 302 p. *Notes:* "A Twentieth Century Fund book." Includes index. Bibliography: p. 280-289. [LC 87047769; ISN 0465050980; $22.95] HD8072.5. H42 1988 1858

The origins & evolution of the field of industrial relations in the United States. Bruce E. Kaufman. Ithaca, N.Y.: ILR Press, c1993. xv, 286 p. *Notes* Includes bibliographical references (p. 253-279) and index. [LC 92019055; ISN 0875461921] HD8066. K38 1993 1859

INDUSTRIAL SITES

Managerial real estate: corporate real estate asset management. Hugh O. Nourse. Englewood Cliffs, N.J.: Chicago, Ill.: Prentice-Hall; Commerical-Investment Council, Realtors National Marketing Institute of the National Association of Realtors, c1990. x, 181 p. : ill. *Notes:* Includes bibliographical references and index. [LC 89003629; ISN 0135520010; $39.00] HD1393.5. N68 1990 1860

INDUSTRIAL SOCIOLOGY

Human relations: a job oriented approach. Andrew J. DuBrin. 5th ed. Englewood Cliffs, N.J.: Prentice Hall, c1992. xv, 558 p.: ill. Notes: Includes bibliographical references and indexes. [LC 91024201; ISN 0133955265; $50.93]   HD6955. D82 1992   1861

Survival in the corporate fishbowl: making it into upper and middle management. by John P. Fernandez. Lexington, Mass.: Lexington Books, c1987. xiii, 314 p.: ill. Notes: Includes index. Bibliography: p. [297]-301. [LC 85040021; ISN 0669103365]   HD6957.U6 F47 1987   1862

INDUSTRIES

The age of giant corporations: a microeconomic history of American business, 1914-1992. Robert Sobel. 3rd ed. Westport, Conn.: Praeger, 1993. xiii, 315 p. Notes: Includes bibliographical references (p. 291-297) and index. [LC 92033332; ISN 0275944700]   HC106. S676 1993   1863

American industry: structure, conduct, performance. Richard E. Caves. 7th ed. Englewood Cliffs, NJ: Prentice Hall, c1992. ix, 132 p.: ill. Notes: Includes bibliographical references (p. 123-125) and index. [LC 91021161; ISN 013029893X]   HC106.5. C34 1992   1864

Corporate responses to environmental challenges: initiatives by multinational management. Ann Rappaport and Margaret Fresher Flaherty; foreword by Willim R. Moomaw; prepared under the auspices of the Center for Environmental Management, Tufts University. New York: Quorum Books, 1992. xxi, 186 p.: ill. Notes: Includes bibliographical references (p. [163]-173) and index. [LC 91044706; ISN 0899307159]   HD69.P6 R36 1992   1865

The environmental economic revolution: how business will thrive and the Earth survive in years to come. Michael Silverstein. 1st ed. New York: St. Martin's Press, 1993. 216 p. Notes: Includes bibliographical references (p. [196]-199) and index. [LC 93002562; ISN 0312097972; $19.95 ($26.99 Can.)]   HC110.E5 S5 1993   +1866

Japan surges ahead; the story of an economic miracle. by P. B. Stone. New York Praeger, 1969. xiv, 206 p. Notes: Bibliography: p. 201-202. [LC 71075417]   HC462.9. S68   +1867

Lean and mean: the changing landscape of corporate power in the age of flexibility. Bennett Harrison. New York: Basic Books, c1994. xi, 324 p.: ill. Notes: Includes bibliographical references (p. [247]-309) and index. [LC 93040397; ISN 0465069428; $25.00 ($33.50 Can.)]   HD69.S5 H367 1994   +1868

Rival capitalists: international competitiveness in the United States, Japan, and Western Europe. Jeffrey A. Hart. Ithaca: Cornell University Press, 1992. x, 305 p.: ill. Notes: Includes bibliographical references and index. [LC 92052757; ISN 0801499496]   HC462.9. H2274 1992   1869

INDUSTRIES, SIZE OF

Downsizing: reshaping the corporation for the future. Robert M. Tomasko. New York: AMACOM, c1987. xi, 290 p.: ill. Notes: Includes index. Bibliography: p. 263-280 [LC 87047709; ISN 0814459072]   HD69.S5 T59 1987   1870

Hypergrowth: applying the success formula of today's fastest growing companies. by H. Skip Weitzen. New York: Wiley, c1991. x, 276 p.: ill. Notes: Includes index. [LC 91009619; ISN 0471531731]   HD69.S5 W45 1991   1871

The theory of the growth of the firm. Edith T. Penrose; with a new foreword by Martin Slater. 2d ed. Oxford: Blackwell, 1980. xxxii, 272 p. Notes: Includes bibliographical references and index.]   HD69.S5 P45 1980   1872

INDUSTRY

Business and society: a managerial approach. Frederick D. Sturdivant, Heidi Vernon-Wortzel. 4th ed. Homewood, Ill.: Irwin, c1990. xxii, 361 p.: ill. Notes: Includes bibliographical references. [LC 89024460; ISN 0256070369; $40.95]   HD60.5.U5 S88 1990   1873

Business and society: corporate strategy, public policy, ethics. 6th ed. / William C. Frederick, Keith Davis, James E. Post. New York: McGraw-Hill, c1988. xxvii, 626 p.: ill. Notes: Davis's name appears first on the earlier editions. Includes indexes. Bibliography: p. [608]-611. [LC 87021436; ISN 0070155615; $36.95]   HD60. D3 1988   1874

Business and society: dimensions of conflict and cooperation. edited by S. Prakash Sethi, Cecilia M. Falbe. Lexington, Mass.: Lexington Books, c1987. xv, 654 p. : ill. *Notes:* Includes bibliographies and index. [LC 86045548; ISN 0669132071] HD60.5.U5 B864 1987 1875

Business, government, and society: a managerial perspective: text and cases. George A. Steiner and John F. Steiner. 5th ed. New York: Random House Business Division, 1988. xxvi, 703 [29] p. : ill. *Notes:* Includes index. Bibliography: p. R-O-R-19. [LC 87028526; ISN 0394374746; $22.00] HD60.5.U5 S8 1988 1876

Corporate social responsibility: guidelines for top management. Jerry W. Anderson, Jr. New York: Quorum Books, 1989. x, 284 p. : ill. *Notes:* Includes bibliographies and indexes. [LC 88023952; ISN 0899302726; $45.00] HD60. A43 1989 1877

Global shift: industrial change in a turbulent world. Peter Dicken. London; New York: Harper & Row, 1986. viii, 456 p. : ill., maps *Notes:* Includes index. Bibliography: p. [430]-446. [LC 85045218; ISN 0063183358; £12.95: CIP confirmed] HD2321. D53 1878

The human side of corporate competitiveness. edited by Daniel B. Fishman, Cary Cherniss. Newbury Park, Calif.: Sage Publications, c1990. 224 p. : ill. *Notes:* Includes bibliographical references and indexes. [LC 90032538; ISN 0803937520; $17.95] HD60. H86 1990 1879

Industrial location: principles and policies. Keith Chapman and David F. Walker. 2nd ed. Oxford, Ox., UK; Cambridge, Mass., USA: Blackwell, 1991, c1990. x, 322 p. : ill. *Notes:* Includes bibliographical references (p. [280]-314). [LC 90000415; ISN 0631167897; $23.90 (U.S.)] HD58. C37 1991 1880

International capitalism and industrial restructuring: a critical analysis. edited by Richard Peet. Boston: Allen & Unwin, 1987. xvi, 315 p. : ill. *Notes:* Includes bibliographies and index. [LC 86028870; ISN 0043381324; ISN 0043381332] HD2321. I58 1987 1881

Management response to public issues: concepts and cases in strategy formulation. Rogene A. Buchholz, William D. Evans, Robert A. Wagley. 2nd ed. Englewood Cliffs, N.J.: Prentice Hall, 1989. xi, 388 p.; 24 cm. *Notes:* Includes index. Bibliography. p. 374-380. [LC 88007569; ISN 0135515327; $21.00] HD60. B83 1989 1882

People in corporations: ethical responsibilities and corporate effectiveness. edited by Georges Enderle, Brenda Almond, Antonio Argandoña. Dordrecht Netherlands; Boston: Kluwer Academic, 1990. vii, 264 p. *Notes:* Includes index. Includes bibliographical references. [LC 90037771; ISN 0792308298; $85.00] HD60. P38 1990 1883

Social issues in business: strategic and public policy perspectives. Fred Luthans, Richard M. Hodgetts, Kenneth R. Thompson. 6th ed. New York: London: Macmillan; Collier Macmillan, c1990. xvi, 646 p. : ill. *Notes:* Includes bibliographical references and indexes. [LC 89032652; ISN 0023729716; $45.00] HD60.5.U5 L872 1990 1884

The social responsibilities of business: company and community, 1900-1960. Morrell Heald. New Brunswick, N.J., USA: Transaction Books, c1988. xxvii, 339 p. *Notes:* Includes index. Bibliography: p. 321-330. [LC 88004795; ISN 0887382312] HD60.U5 H4 1988 1885

INDUSTRY AND EDUCATION

Academics and entrepreneurs: developing university-industry relations. Rikard Stankiewicz. New York: St. Martin's Press, 1986. viii, 155 p. : ill. *Notes:* Includes index. Bibliography: p. [122]-155. [LC 85022227; ISN 0312002009; $25.00 (est.)] LC1085. S83 1886

INDUSTRY AND STATE

Business & government. edited by Joseph R. Frese, S.J. and Jacob Judd. Tarrytown, NY: Sleepy Hollow Press and Rockefeller Archive Center, c1985. xii, 233 p. (Essays in 20th century cooperation and confrontation.) *Notes:* Erratum inserted. Includes bibliographical references and index. [LC 82005590; ISN 0912882522] HD3616.U46 B827 1887

Business and public policy. edited by John T. Dunlop. Boston: Harvard University, Graduate School of Business Administration, Division of Research: distributed by Harvard University Press,; , 1980. xvii, 118 p. *Notes:* Includes bibliographical references. *Contents:* Chandler, A. D. Government versus business: an American phenomenon.—Dunlop, J. T. The educational opportunity.—Uyterhoeven, H. Educational challenges in teaching business-government relations.—Dunlop, J. T. Business and public policy. [LC 80081866] HD3616.U46 B832 1888

Business environment and public policy: implications for management and strategy formulation. Rogene A. Buchholz. 3rd ed. Englewood Cliffs, NJ: Prentice Hall, c1989. xiv, 610 p. : ill. *Notes:* Includes bibliographies and index. [LC 88022407; ISN 0130954578; $29.50]
HD3616.U47 B76 1989   1889

Business, government, and public policy: concepts and practices. Dan Bertozzi, Jr. and Lee B. Burgunder. Englewood Cliffs, NJ: Prentice Hall, c1990. xi, 228 p. *Notes:* Includes bibliographical references. [LC 88036766; ISN 013093402X; $17.00]
HD3616.U47 B525 1990   1890

Business, government, and the public. Murray L. Weidenbaum. 3rd ed. Englewood Cliffs, NJ: Prentice-Hall, c1986. x, 499 p. : ill. *Notes:* Includes bibliographical references and index. [LC 85012359; ISN 0130993344]
HD3616.U46 W44 1986   1891

Can America compete? Robert Z. Lawrence. Washington, D.C.: Brookings Institution, c1984. xiii, 156 p. : ill. *Notes:* Includes bibliographical references and index. [LC 84009401; ISN 0815751761; ISN 0815751753]
HD3616.U47 L39 1984   1892

The competitive advantage of nations. Michael E. Porter. New York: Free Press, c1990. xx, 855 p. : ill. *Notes:* Includes bibliographical references. [LC 89025632; ISN 0029253616; $45.00]
HD3611. P654 1990   1893

The economics of regulation: principles and institutions. Alfred E. Kahn. Cambridge, Mass.: MIT Press, c1988. 2 v. in 1: ill. *Notes:* Includes index. Bibliography: v. 2, p. 331-360. *Contents:* v. 1. Economic principles—v. 2. Institutional issues. [LC 87032484; ISN 0262111292; ISN 0262610523]
HD3616.U47 K28 1988   1894

Government-business cooperation, 1945-1964: corporatism in the post-war era. edited with introductions by Robert F. Himmelberg. New York: Garland Pub., 1994. xvii, 417 p. : ill. *Notes:* A collection of articles that were originally published between 1958 to 1990. [LC 93046105; ISN 0815314116]
HD3616.U46 G643 1994   +1895

Industrial policy of Japan. edited by Ryūtarō Komiya. . . et al. Tokyo; Orlando, FL: Academic Press, 1988. xv, 590 p. : ill. *Notes:* Includes index. Bibliography: p. 559-576. [LC 87001409; ISN 0124186505]
HD3616.J33 I816 1988   1896

Laboratories of democracy. by David Osborne. Boston, Mass.: Harvard Business School Press, c1988. x, 380 p. *Notes:* Includes index. Bibliography: p. 339-363. [LC 88005895; ISN 0875841929]
HD3616.U46 O83 1988   1897

Managing business-government relations: cases and notes on business-government problems. J. Ronald Fox. Homewood, Ill.: R.D. Irwin, c1982. x, 555 p. *Notes:* Includes bibliographical references and index. [LC 81086363; ISN 0256029008]
HD3616.U46 F695 1982   1898

Minding America's business. by Ira C. Magaziner & Robert B. Reich. New York: Law & Business: Harcourt Brace Jovanovich, c1982. xii, 387 p. : charts, graphs *Notes:* Includes index. [LC 81013663; ISN 0151599548; $50.00]
HD3616.U47 M286   1899

Perestroika for America: restructuring U.S. business-government relations for competitiveness in the world economy. George C. Lodge. Boston, Mass.: Harvard Business School Press, c1990. xv, 235 p. : ill. *Notes:* Includes bibliographical references. [LC 90033228; ISN 0875842348]
HD3616.U47 L65 1990   1900

Public policies toward business. William G. Shepherd. 7th ed. Homewood, Ill.: R.D. Irwin, 1985. xviii, 541 p. : ill. (Irwin publications in economics) *Notes:* Includes bibliographical references and indexes. [LC 84081130; ISN 025602815X]
HD3616.U47 S38 1985   1901

State, finance, and industry: a comparative analysis of post-war trends in six advanced industrial economies. edited by Andrew Cox. New York: St. Martin's Press, 1986. ix, 292 p. : ill. *Notes:* Spine title: The state, finance & industry. Includes bibliographies and index. [LC 86001741; ISN 0312756186; $25.00 (est.)]
HD3611. S758 1986   1902

Strategic management in the regulatory environment: cases and industry notes. Richard H.K. Vietor. Englewood Cliffs, NJ: Prentice Hall, 1989. x, 445 p. : ill. *Notes:* Includes bibliographies. [LC 88006010; ISN 0138517266; $17.50]
HD3616.U46 V54 1989   1903

The two faces of management: an American approach to leadership in business and politics. Joseph L. Bower. Boston: Houghton Mifflin, 1983. xi, 303 p. *Notes:* Includes bibliographical references and index. [LC 83000141; ISN 0395331196; $19.95]
HD3616.U46 B68 1983   1904

Uneasy partners: big business in American politics, 1945-1990. Kim McQuaid. Baltimore: Johns Hopkins University Press, c1994. xvi, 224 p. *Notes:* Includes bibliographical references (p. [199]-208) and index. [LC 93017520; ISN 0801846528]
HD3616.U46 M383 1994   +1905

INFLATION (FINANCE)

Capital, inflation, and the multinationals. New York Macmillan, 1972, c1971. 306 p. [LC 71181573]
HG229. L399 1972   +1906

INFORMATION RESOURCES MANAGEMENT

Infotrends: profiting from your information resources. Donald A. Marchand and Forest W. Horton, Jr. New York: Wiley, c1986. xv, 324 p. : ill. *Notes:* Includes index. Bibliography: p. 295-317. [LC 85029438; ISN 0471816809]
T58.64. M37 1986   1907

Total information systems management: a European approach. Hubert Österle, Walter Brenner, Konrad Hilbers. Chichester, West Sussex, England; New York: J. Wiley, c1993. xvi, 305 p. : ill. *Notes:* Includes bibliographical references (p. [296]-302) and index. [LC 93012283; ISN 0471939323]
T58.64. O8713 1993   +1908

INFORMATION STORAGE AND RETRIEVAL SYSTEMS

Competitive intelligence in the computer age. Carolyn M. Vella and John J. McGonagle, Jr. New York: Quorum Books, 1987. xv, 189 p. *Notes:* Includes index. Bibliography: p. [182]-184. [LC 86025565; ISN 089930169X]
HF5548.2. V38 1987   1909

INFORMATION TECHNOLOGY

The Arthur D. Little forecast on information technology and productivity: making the integrated enterprise work. Norman Weizer. . . et al. New York: Wiley, c1991. xxvii, 272 p. : ill. *Notes:* Includes index. [LC 90046325; ISN 0471525111; $32.95]
HC79.I55 A77 1991   1910

Building the information-age organization: structure, control, and information technologies. by James I. Cash. . . et al. 3rd ed. Burr Ridge, Ill.: Irwin, c1994. xi, 498 p. : ill. *Notes:* Includes bibliographical references (p. 484-485) and index. [LC 93040865; ISN 0256124582; $64.00]
HD30.2. B85 1994   +1911

Every manager's guide to information technology: a glossary of key terms and concepts for today's business leader. Peter G.W. Keen. 2nd ed. Boston: Harvard Business School Press, c1995. xii, 290 p. *Notes:* Includes index. [LC 94019892; ISN 0875845711; $18.95]
QA76.15. K43 1995   +1912

Handbook of IT auditing. J. Donald Warren, Lynn W. Edelson, Xenia Ley Parker; Coopers & Lybrand L.L.P. 3rd ed. Boston: Warren, Gorham & Lamont, c1994. 1 v. (various pagings): ill. *Notes:* Rev. ed. of: Handbook of EDP auditing / Michael A. Murphy. c1989. Kept up to date by cumulative supplements. Includes bibliographical references and index. How to audit, control, and secure organizational systems. Reflects the rapid evolution of information technology and the changes in the way organizations work. [LC 94061796; ISN 0791321886]
HF5548.35. W37 1994   +1913

InfoCulture: the Smithsonian book of information age inventions. Steven Lubar. Boston: Houghton Mifflin, 1993. vii, 408 p. : ill. *Notes:* Based on an exhibit at the Smithsonian Institution's National Museum of American History. Includes bibliographical references and index. [LC 93004815; ISN 0395570425]
T58.5. L83 1993   +1914

Investing in information technology: managing the decision-making process. Geoff Hogbin and David V. Thomas. London; New York: McGraw-Hill, c1994. xv, 254 p. : ill. *Notes:* Includes bibliographical references and index. [LC 93039047; ISN 0077077571; £24.95]   HD30.2. H636 1994   +1915

Measuring the value of information technology. John Hares and Duncan Royle. Chichester, West Sussex, England; New York: Wiley, c1994. viii, 268 p. : ill. *Notes:* Includes index. " . . . Describes a structured method of investment appraisal that provides a set of mechanisms for precise financial value calculations."—Back cover. [LC 93038006; ISN 047194307X]   HC79.I55 H37 1994   +1916

Process innovation: reengineering work through information technology. Thomas H. Davenport. Boston: Harvard Business School Press, 1992, c1993. x, 337 p. : ill. *Notes:* Includes bibliographical references and index. [LC 92021959; ISN 0875843662; $29.95]
HC79.I55 D37 1992   1917

The race to the intelligent state: towards the global information economy of 2005. Michael Connors. Oxford, UK; Cambridge, Mass.: Blackwell Business, 1993. viii, 221 p. : ill. *Notes:* Includes bibliographical references (p. [211]-216) and index. [LC 92044816; ISN 0631190724]
HC79.I55 C67 1993   +1918

Techno vision: the executive's survival guide to understanding and managing information technology. Charles B. Wang; with an introd. by Peter Drucker. New York: McGraw-Hill, c1994. xxvi, 198 p. *Notes:* Includes bibliographical references and index. [LC 94019951; ISN 0070681554; $19.95] HC79.I55 W36 1994 +1919

2020 vision. Stan Davis, Bill Davidson. New York: Simon & Schuster, c1991. 223 p. : ill. *Notes:* Includes bibliographical references (p. [207]-209) and index. [LC 91000355; ISN 0671732374; $19.95] HC79.I55 D38 1991 1920

Waves of change: business evolution through information technology. James L. McKenney with Duncan C. Copeland, Richard O. Mason. Boston, Mass.: Harvard Business School Press, c1994. xiv, 230 p. : ill. *Notes:* Includes bibliographical references and index. [LC 94003471; ISN 0875845649; $29.95] HD30.2. M4 1995 +1921

INPUT-OUTPUT ANALYSIS

Input-output economics. Wassily Leontief. 2nd ed. New York: Oxford University Press, c1986. xii, 436 p. : ill. *Notes:* Includes bibliographies and indexes. [LC 84029; ISN 0195035275] HB142. L46 1922

INSIDER TRADING IN SECURITIES

The insiders: the truth behind the scandal rocking Wall Street. Mark Stevens; researched by Carol Bloom Stevens. New York: Putnam, c1987. 256 p. [LC 87002537; ISN 039913266X; $18.95] HG4910. S67 1987 1923

INSTITUTIONAL ECONOMICS

Economic behavior and institutions. Thrainn Eggertsson. Cambridge England; New York: Cambridge University Press, 1990. xv, 385 p. : ill. *Notes:* Includes bibliographical references (p. 359-377) and indexes. [LC 89039485; ISN 0521348919; $17.95] HB99.5. T48 1990 1924

The economic institutions of capitalism: firms, markets, relational contracting. Oliver E. Williamson. New York: London: Free Press; Collier Macmillan, c1985. xiv, 450 p. : ill. *Notes:* Includes index. Bibliography: p. 409-436. [LC 85013080; ISN 002934820X] HB99.5. W55 1985 1925

INSTITUTIONAL INVESTMENTS

Institutional investing: challenges and responsibilities of the 21st century. Arnold W. Sametz, editor, in collaboration with James L. Bicksler. Homewood, Ill.: Business One Irwin, c1991. xiv, 559 p. : ill. *Notes:* "New York University Salomon Center, Leonard N. Stern School of Business." Includes bibliographical references and index. [LC 91009104; ISN 1556234732; $55.00] HG4521. I422 1991 1926

INSTRUCTIONAL SYSTEMS

Handbook of task analysis procedures. David H. Jonassen, Wallace H. Hannum, Martin Tessmer. New York: Praeger, 1989. xiv, 408 p. : ill. *Notes:* Includes bibliographical references and index. [LC 88029272; ISN 0275926842; $59.85] LB1028.35. J66 1989 1927

INSURANCE

Fundamentals of risk and insurance. Emmett J. Vaughan. 5th ed. New York: Wiley, c1989. xiv, 781 p. : forms *Notes:* Includes bibliographies and indexes. [LC 88027783; ISN 0471633526; $47.95] HG8051. V35 1989 1928

The insurance industry in Canada. Jeffrey I. Bernstein, Randall R. Geehan. Vancouver: Fraser Institute, c1988. xvi, 93 p. : ill. *Notes:* Bibliography: p. [89]-93. [LC 88091323; ISN 0889751110; $19.95] HG8550. B47 1988 1929

INSURANCE, BUSINESS

The business insurance handbook. compiled and edited by Gray Castle, Robert F. Cushman, Peter R. Kensicki. Homewood, Ill.: Dow Jones-Irwin, c1931. xvii, 753 p. : ill., forms, ports. *Notes:* Includes bibliographical references and index. [LC 80070437; ISN 0870942379]   HG8059. B87   1930

INSURANCE, HEALTH

Employment and health benefits: a connection at risk. Committee on Employer-Based Health Benefits, Division of Health Care Services, Institute of Medicine; Marilyn J. Field and Harold T. Shapiro, editors. Washington, D.C.: National Academy Press, 1993. xvii, 360 p. : ill. *Notes:* Includes bibliographical references (p. 262-284) and index. [LC 92042468; ISN 0309048273; $29.95]
HG9396. I57 1993   1931

National health care: lessons for the United States and Canada. edited by Jonathan Lemco. Ann Arbor: University of Michigan Press, c1994. x, 287 p. : ill. *Notes:* Includes bibliographical references and index. [LC 94009075; ISN 0472104403]   RA395.A3 N335 1994   +1932

No benefit: crisis in America's health insurance industry. Lawrence D. Weiss. Boulder, Colo.: Westview Press, 1992. xii, 156 p. *Notes:* Includes bibliographical references and index. *Contents:* Placing the social fact of private health insurance in perspective—Historical development and current profile of the commercial health insurance industry—Creating the uninsured—Employer cost-cutting strategies—Fraud and deception—Price fixing and conspiracy—Insolvencies: insurance companies that cannot pay claims—The inefficient private sector—A political question: accommodation, compromise, or struggle?—Summary and conclusions. [LC 92018113; ISN 0813312159]   HG9396. W45 1992   1933

INSURANCE, LIFE

Life insurance: theory and practice. Robert I. Mehr, Sandra G. Gustavson. 4th ed. Plano, Tex.: Business Publications, 1987. xvii, 675 p. *Notes:* Includes bibliographical references and index. [LC 86072999; ISN 0256037078; $43.00]   HG8771. M44 1987   1934

INTEGRATED CIRCUITS INDUSTRY

The chip war: the battle for the world of tomorrow. by Fred Warshofsky. New York: Scribner, c1989. ix, 434 p. *Notes:* Includes index. Bibliography: p. 403-417. [LC 88030537; ISN 0684189275; $22.50]
HD9696.I582 W37 1989   1935

INTEREST

Compounding and discounting tables for project analysis: with a guide to their applications. edited by J. Price Gittinger. 2nd ed., rev. and expanded. Baltimore: published for the Economic Development Institute of the World Bank by Johns Hopkins University Press, 1984. x, 200 p. : ill. (EDI series in economic development) *Notes:* Rev. ed. of: Compounding and discounting tables for project evaluation. 1973. Chiefly tables. Bibliography: p. 200. [LC 83049364; ISN 0801824095]
HG1632. C65 1984   1936

Money, interest, and prices: an integration of monetary and value theory. Don Patinkin. 2nd ed., abridged. Cambridge, Mass.: MIT Press, c1989. lxxix, 560 p. : ill. *Notes:* Includes indexes. Bibliography: p. 527-544. [LC 89034501; ISN 0262151141; $47.50]   HG221. P32 1989   1937

The theory of interest. Friedrich A. Lutz; translated from the German by Claus Wittich. Dordrecht: Chicago: D. Reidel; Aldine, 1968. ix, 336 p. *Notes:* Translation of Zinstheorie. Includes bibliographical references and index. [LC 67017604]   HB539. L87   +1938

INTEREST RATE FUTURES

Financial instruments markets: an advanced study of cash-futures relationships. developed by Jerome Lacey. Chicago: Chicago Board of Trade, c1986. viii, 89 p. : ill.]   HG6024.5. L32 1986   1939

A guide to managing interest-rate risk. Donna M. Howe. New York: New York Institute of Finance, c1992. xii, 348 p. : ill. *Notes:* Includes index. [LC 91017819; ISN 0134707338; $29.95]
HG6024.5. H69 1992 1940

The handbook of interest rate risk management. edited by Jack Clark Francis and Avner Simon Wolf. Burr Ridge, Ill.: Irwin, c1994. xxx, 832 p. : ill. *Notes:* Includes bibliographical references and index. [LC 93001267; ISN 1556233825]
HG6024.5. H37 1994 +1941

The practitioner's guide to interest rate risk management. Bernard Manson. London; Boston: Graham & Trotman, 1992. 488 p. : ill. *Notes:* Includes bibliographical references (p. 477-482) and index.; ISN 1853337412]
HG6024.5. M36 1992 1942

Winning the interest rate game: a guide to debt options. edited by Frank J. Fabozzi. Chicago, Ill.: Probus Pub. Co., c1985. xii, 307 p. : ill. *Notes:* Includes index. [LC 84011473; ISN 0917253019; $25.00]
HG6024.5. W56 1985 1943

INTEREST RATES

Controlling interest rate risk: new techniques and applications for money management. edited by Robert B. Platt. New York: Wiley, c1986. xv, 414 p. : ill. *Notes:* Includes bibliographies and index. [LC 85022504; ISN 0471823546; $29.95 (est.)]
HG1621. C6 1986 1944

Financial market rates and flows. James C. Van Horne. 3rd ed. Englewood Cliffs, N.J.: Prentice Hall, c1990. xi, 340 p. : ill. *Notes:* Cover title: Financial market rates & flows. Includes bibliographies and index. [LC 89035627; ISN 0133149560; $22.00]
HB539. V338 1990 1945

INTERNATIONAL BROTHERHOOD OF TEAMSTERS, CHAUFFEURS, STABLEMEN, AND HELPERS OF AMERICA

Collision: how the rank and file took back the teamsters. Kenneth C. Crowe. New York: Toronto: New York: Scribner's; Maxwell Macmillan Canada; Maxwell Macmillan International, c1993. xii, 303 p., [12] p. of plates: ill. *Notes:* Includes bibliographical references (p. 293-294) and index. [LC 92027881; ISN 0684193736; $22.50 ($28.50 Can.)]
HD6515.T3 C76 1993 1946

INTERNATIONAL BUSINESS ENTERPRISES

Accounting: an international perspective. Gerhard G. Mueller, Helen Gernon, Gary Meek. Burr Ridge, Ill.: Business One Irwin, c1994. xv, 200 p. : ill. *Notes:* Includes bibliographical references and index. [LC 93003989; ISN 0786300078]
HF5686.I56 M835 1994b +1947

Blunders in international business. David A. Ricks. Cambridge, Mass.: Blackwell Business, 1993. ix, 172 p. *Notes:* Includes bibliographical references (p. [161]-164) and indexes. *Contents:* Introduction—Production—Names—Marketing—Translation—Management—Strategic management—Other areas of international business—Lessons learned. [LC 92033483; ISN 1557864144]
HD62.4. R53 1993 +1948

Comparative and multinational management. Simcha Ronen. New York: Wiley, c1986. xix, 636 p. : ill. (Wiley series in international business) *Notes:* Includes index. Bibliography: p. 579-621. [LC 85017971; ISN 0471868752; $27.95 (est.)]
HD62.4. R66 1986 1949

Competing with integrity in international business. Richard T. De George. New York: Oxford University Press, 1993. xi, 233 p. *Notes:* Includes bibliographical references and index. [LC 92039089; ISN 0195082265]
HD2755.5. D42 1993 +1950

The cultural environment of international business. Vern Terpstra, Kenneth David. 3rd ed. Cincinnati, OH: South-Western Pub. Co., c1991. xv, 252 p. : ill. *Notes:* "S187CA." Includes bibliographical references and index. [LC 90061084; ISN 0538800038; $25.00]
HD2755.5. T47 1991 1951

Dislodging multinationals: India's strategy in comparative perspective. Dennis J. Encarnation. Ithaca: Cornell University Press, 1989. xiii, 237 p. : ill. *Notes:* Includes bibliographical references. [LC 89000730; ISN 0801423155; $29.95]
HD2900. E53 1989 1952

The Ernst & Young guide to expanding in the global market. Charles F. Valentine. New York: Wiley, c1991. xiv, 225 p. : ill. *Notes:* Revised ed. of: The Arthur Young international business guide. [LC 90012588; ISN 0471530077; $14.95]
HD62.4. V354 1991 1953

The ethics of international business. by Thomas Donaldson. New York: Oxford University Press, 1989. xvi, 196 p. *Notes:* Includes index. Bibliography: p. 165-185. [LC 89009471; ISN 0195058747]
HD2755.5. D65 1989 1954

Explaining international production. John H. Dunning. London; Boston: Unwin Hyman, 1988. xvii, 378 p. *Notes:* Includes index. Bibliography: p. [348]-371. [LC 88010710; ISN 0044451709] HD2755.5. D863 1988   1955

Financial management for the multinational firm. Fuad A. Abdullah. Englewood Cliffs, N.J.: Prentice-Hall, c1987. xiii, 594 p. : ill. *Notes:* Includes bibliographies and indexes. [LC 86025226; ISN 0133163407; $43.20] HG4027.5. A23 1987   1956

The financial structure of multinational capitalism. Pierre Grou; preface by François Morin, postface by Charles-Albert Michalet; translated by Aline Tayar-Adams. New York: St. Martin's Press, 1986, c1985. viii, 243 p. *Notes:* Translation of: La structure financière du capitalisme multinational. Bibliography: p. 241-243. [LC 85010324; ISN 0312289766; $24.95] HG4027.5. G7613 1986   1957

The firm and the market: studies on multinational enterprises and the scope of the firm. Mark Casson. 1st MIT Press ed. Cambridge, Mass.: MIT Press, 1987. xii, 283 p. : ill. *Notes:* Includes index. Bibliography: p. [262]-273. [LC 86027199; ISN 0262031299] HD2755.5. C392 1987   1958

Foundations of multinational financial management. Alan C. Shapiro. Boston: Allyn and Bacon, c1991. xix, 600 p. : ill. *Notes:* Includes bibliographical references and index. [LC 90042041; ISN 0205126766] HG4027.5. S44 1990   1959

Global business management in the 1900s. managing editor, Robert T. Moran; editors, Fariborz Ghadar. . . et al. Washington, D.C.: Beacham Pub., 1990. xi, 485 p. *Notes:* Includes bibliographical references. [LC 89018440; ISN 0933833075; $65.00] HD62.4. G54 1990   1960

Global dreams: imperial corporations and the new world order. Richard J. Barnet, John Cavanagh. New York: Simon & Schuster, c1994. 480 p. *Notes:* Includes bibliographical references (p. [459]-465) and index. [LC 93036362; ISN 0671633775; $25.00 ($32.50 Canada)] HD2755.5. B378 1994   +1961

Global embrace: corporate challenges in a transnational world. Henry Wendt. 1st ed. New York: HarperBusiness, c1993. xi, 292 p. *Notes:* Includes bibliographical references and index. [LC 92053336; ISN 0887305911; $25.00] HD62.4. W45 1993   1962

The global marketplace: 102 of the most influential companies outside America. Milton Moskowitz. New York: Macmillan, c1987. xi, 708 p. : ill. *Notes:* Includes index. Bibliography: p. 691-694. [LC 87015897; ISN 0025875906] HD2755.5. M675 1987   1963

Global strategic management: the essentials. compiled by Heidi Vernon-Wortzel, Lawrence H. Wortzel. 2nd ed. New York: Wiley, c1991. xiii, 545 p. : ill. *Notes:* Rev. ed. of: Strategic management of multinational corporations. c1985. Includes bibliographical references and index. [LC 90044777; ISN 0471617881; $34.95] HD62.4. V483 1991   1964

Global strategies: insights from the world's leading thinkers. with a preface by Percy Barnevik; afterword by Rosabeth Moss Kanter. Boston, MA: Harvard Business School Press, c1994. xix, 243 p. : ill. *Notes:* Articles originally published in the Harvard Business Review since 1982. Includes index. [LC 94016424; ISN 0875845614; $29.95] HD2755.5. G554 1994   +1965

Global vision: building new models for the corporation of the future. John L. Daniels, N. Caroline Daniels. New York: McGraw-Hill, c1993. xxxvi, 197 p. : ill. *Notes:* Includes bibliographical footnotes and index. [LC 93030294; ISN 0070153507; $27.95] HD2755.5. D35 1993   +1966

The globalization of business: the challenge of the 1990s. John H. Dunning. London; New York: Routledge, 1993. xii, 467 p. : ill. *Notes:* Includes bibliographical references (p. [404]-458) and index. [LC 92042817; ISN 0415096111; $25.00] HD2755.5. D865 1993   +1967

Globalization, technology, and competition: the fusion of computers and telecommunications in the 1990s. edited by Stephen P. Bradley, Jerry A. Hausman, Richard L. Nolan. Boston, Mass.: Harvard Business School Press, c1993. vi, 392 p. : ill. *Notes:* Includes discussion of Saturn Corporation and AT&T. Includes bibliographical references and index. [LC 92036104; ISN 0875843387; $34.95] HD62.4. G554 1993   1968

Globalwork: bridging distance, culture, and time. Mary O'Hara-Devereaux, Robert Johansen. 1st ed. San Francisco: Jossey-Bass, c1994. xxix, 439 p. : ill. *Notes:* Includes bibliographical references (p. 421-429) and index. [LC 94004431; ISN 1555426026] HD62.4. O36 1994   +1969

Going international: how to make friends and deal effectively in the global marketplace. Lennie Copeland and Lewis Griggs. 1st ed. New York: Random House, c1985. xxiii, 279 p. *Notes:* Includes bibliographical references and index. [LC 85001985; ISN 0394544501; $17.95] HD62.4. C66 1985   1970

Government control and multinational strategic management: power systems and telecommunication equipment. Yves L. Doz. New York: Praeger, 1979. xvi, 277 p. : ill.; 24 cm. *Notes:* Includes bibliographical references and index. [LC 79011793; ISN 0030494761] HD69.I7 D69   1971

The growth of international business. edited by Mark Casson; contributors, authors, Peter J. Buckley. . . et al.; reviewers and discussants, Charles E. Harvey. . . et al. London; Boston: Allen & Unwin, 1983. xii, 276 p. : ill. *Notes:* Includes index. Bibliography: p. [258]-272. [LC 82020750; ISN 0043303331] HD2755.5. G76 1983   1972

Handbook of international accounting. edited by Frederick D.S. Choi. New York: J. Wiley, c1991. 1 v. (various pagings): ill. *Notes:* Kept up to date with annual supplements. Includes bibliographical references and index. [LC 91016011; ISN 047151487X; $105.00]   HF5686.I56 H36 1991   1973

The handbook of international business. edited by Ingo Walter; associate editor, Tracy Murray. 2nd ed. New York: Wiley, c1988. 677 p. in various pagings: ill. *Notes:* Includes bibliographies and index. [LC 87035545; ISN 0471842346]   HD62.4. H36 1988   1974

Handbook of international business and management. S.J. Gray, M.C. McDermott, and E.J. Walsh. Oxford England; Cambridge, Mass., USA: B. Blackwell, 1990. xviii, 222 p. : ill. *Notes:* Includes bibliographical references (p. [209]-222) and index. [LC 89077224; ISN 0631150242; $29.95]   HD2755.5. G72 1990   1975

Handbook of international financial management. edited by Allen Sweeny and Robert Rachlin. New York: McGraw-Hill, c1984. 1 v. (various pagings): ill. *Notes:* Includes bibliographies and index. [LC 83025581; ISN 0070625786]   HG4027.5. H36 1984   1976

Handbook of international financial management. Michael Z. Brooke. Houndmills, Basingstoke, Hants England: Macmillan, 1990. xviii, 660 p. : ill. *Notes:* Includes index. [LC 90041390; ISN 0333532031; £95.00]   HG4027.5. B76 1990   1977

Handbook of international management. edited by Ingo Walter; associate editor, Tracy Murray. New York: Wiley, c1988. 1 v. (various pagings): ill. *Notes:* Includes bibliographies and index. [LC 87029461; ISN 047160674X]   HD62.4. H365 1988   1978

Human resource management in international firms: change, globalization, innovation. edited by Paul Evans, Yves Doz, André Laurent. New York: St. Martin's Press, 1990. xvi, 258 p. : ill. *Notes:* Includes bibliographical references (p. 243-250) and index. [LC 89024340; ISN 0312041322]   HF5549.5.E45 H86 1990   1979

International accounting and reporting. Thomas G. Evans, Martin E. Taylor, Oscar Holzmann. New York; London: Macmillan, c1985. xix, 412 p. *Notes:* Includes index. Bibliography: p. 394-407. [LC 84011205; ISN 0023345500]   HF5686.I56 E9 1985   1980

International business. Richard N. Farmer, Barry M. Richman. 4th ed. Bloomington, Ind.: Cedarwood Press, c1984. x, 294 p. *Notes:* Includes bibliographies and index. [LC 80110065; ISN 0930417011]   HD69.I7 F3 1984   1981

International business and governments: issues and institutions. Jack N. Behrman and Robert E. Grosse. Columbia: University of South Carolina Press, c1990. xiv, 434 p. : ill. *Notes:* Includes bibliographical references. [LC 90035691; ISN 0872496961; $29.95]   HD2755.5. B414 1990   1982

International business and multinational enterprises. Stefan H. Robock, Kenneth Simmonds. 4th ed. Homewood, IL: Irwin, 1989. xix, 826 p. : ill. *Notes:* Col. map on lining papers. Includes bibliographical references and indexes. [LC 88009304; ISN 0256036349; $46.95]   HD62.4. R63 1989   1983

International business classics. edited by James C. Baker, John K. Ryans, Jr., Donald G. Howard. Lexington, Mass.: Lexington Books, c1988. xii, 576 p. : ill. *Notes:* Includes bibliographies. [LC 86046029; ISN 0669149314; ISN 0669174157]   HD2755.5. I556 1988   1984

International business, environment and management. Christopher M. Korth. 2nd ed. Englewood Cliffs, N.J.: Prentice-Hall, c1985. xxvi, 580 p. : ill. *Notes:* Rev. ed. of: International business, an introduction to the world of the multinational firm / Richard D. Hays, Christopher M. Korth, Manucher Roudiani. 1971, c1972. Includes bibliographies and index. [LC 84008196; ISN 0134724577]   HD62.4. K67 1985   1985

International business: environments and operations. John D. Daniels, Lee H. Radebaugh. 6th ed. Reading, Mass.: Addison-Wesley Pub. Co., c1992. xxvii, 805, [45] p. : ill. *Notes:* Includes bibliographical references and index. [LC 91022710; ISN 0201571005]   HD2755.5. D35 1992   1986

International business: firm and environment. Alan M. Rugman, Donald J. Lecraw, Laurence D. Booth. New York: McGraw-Hill, c1985. xx, 458 p. : ill. (McGraw-Hill series in management) *Notes:* Includes indexes. Bibliography: p. 435-447. [LC 84015482; ISN 0070542740; $27.95 (est.)]   HD2755.5. R835 1985   1987

International business: issues and concepts. Reed Moyer. New York: Wiley, c1984. xiii, 440 p. (Wiley series in international business) *Notes:* Includes bibliographical references. [LC 83010191; ISN 0471874116; $24.95 (est.)]   HD2755.5. M69 1984   1988

International business strategy and administration. John Fayerweather. 2nd ed. Cambridge, Mass.: Ballinger, c1982. xviii, 547 p. : ill. *Notes:* Includes bibliographical references and index. [LC 82001784; ISN 0884108899]   HD62.4. F39 1982   1989

International corporate finance: markets, transactions, and financial management. edited by Harvey A. Poniachek. Boston: Unwin Hyman, 1989. xxiv, 418 p. : ill. *Notes:* Includes index. Includes bibliographical references. [LC 88036651; ISN 0044453949; $75.00]   HG4027.5. I555 1989   1990

International dimensions of accounting. Dhia D. AlHashim, Jeffrey S. Arpan. 3rd ed. Boston, Mass.: PWS-Kent Pub. Co., c1992. xvii, 252 p. : ill. *Notes:* Includes bibliographical references and index. [LC 91041502; ISN 0534928064; $17.95]   HF5686.I56 A43 1992   1991

International dimensions of business policy and strategy. John Garland, Richard N. Farmer, Marilyn Taylor. 2nd ed. Boston, Mass.: PWS-Kent Pub. Co., c1990. xiv, 235 p. : ill. *Notes:* Includes bibliographical references and index. [LC 90034037; ISN 0534919421; $14.00]   HD62.4. G37 1990   1992

International dimensions of financial management. William R. Folks, Jr., Raj Aggarwal. Boston, Mass.: PWS-Kent Pub. Co., c1988. xv, 239 p. : ill. *Notes:* Includes bibliographies and index. [LC 87029132; ISN 0534871941]   HG4027.5. F65 1988   1993

International dimensions of management. Arvind V. Phatak. 3rd ed. Boston: PWS-Kent Pub. Co., c1992. xv, 235 p. : ill. *Notes:* Includes bibliographical references and index. [LC 91033203; ISN 0534928129; $17.95]   HD62.4. P52 1992   1994

International finance: cases and simulation. Robert S. Carlson... et al. Reading, Mass.: Addison-Wesley Pub. Co., c1980. vii, 392 p. : ill. (Addison-Wesley series in international finance) *Notes:* Another copy. *Contents:* Hekman, C.R. The dollar dilemma.—Hekman, C.R. American Can Company.—International Business Group.—Harvard Business School. Harbison-Walker Refractories Company.—Hekman, C.R. Vick International-Latin America/Far East.—Vernon, R. Sola Chemical Company.—Hekman, C.R. Taxation of Americans working overseas. [LC 80081213; ISN 020100903X]   HG4027.5. I57   1995

International trade and competition: cases and notes in strategy and management. David B. Yoffie, Benjamin Gomes-Casseres. 2nd ed. New York: McGraw-Hill, c1994. xviii, 574 p. : ill. *Notes:* Includes bibliographical references and index. [LC 93035774; ISN 0070723001]   HD62.4. Y64 1994   +1996

Internationalization of business: an introduction. Richard D. Robinson. Chicago: Dryden Press, c1984. xvi, 367 p. : ill. (The Dryden Press series in management) *Notes:* Includes bibliographical references and index. [LC 83011710; ISN 0030606013]   HD62.4. R615 1984   1997

Introduction to business: an international perspective. Robert R. Miller, Janice James Miller. Homewood, Ill.: Irwin, 1987. x, 138 p. : ill. (Irwin perspectives in international business) *Notes:* Includes bibliographies and index. [LC 86082593; ISN 0256056285]   HD62.4. M55 1987   1998

An introduction to the multinationals. Michel Ghertman and Margaret Allen. London: Macmillan for Institute for Research and Information on Multinationals, 1984. vi, 143 p. *Notes:* Translation of: Les multinationales. Includes bibliographical references and index.; ISN 0333364503; ISN 0333364511]   HD2755.5. G4931 1984   1999

Japan's emerging multinationals: an international comparison of policies and practices. edited by Susumu Takamiya, Keith Thurley; with a foreword by Herbert A. Simon. Tokyo?: University of Tokyo Press, c1985. xiii, 287 p. : ill. *Notes:* Includes index. Bibliography: p. 269-281.; ISN 4130470264; ISN 0860083489]   HD62.4. J36   2000

Leadership in action: tough-minded strategies from the global giant. Helmut Maucher. New York: McGraw-Hill, c1994. xii, 160 p. [LC 94011898; ISN 0070410410; $19.95]   HD62.4. M387 1994   +2001

Making decisions in multinational corporations: managing relations with sovereign governments. Amir Mahini. New York: Wiley, c1988. xvi, 225 p. *Notes:* Includes bibliographical references and index. [LC 87037591; ISN 0471840920]   HD62.4. M32 1988   2002

A manager's guide to globalization: six keys to success in a changing world. Stephen H. Rhinesmith. Alexandria, Va.: Homewood, Ill.: Americn Society for Training and Development; Business One Irwin, c1993. xxii, 240 p. : ill. *Notes:* Includes bibliographical references (p. 222-233) and index. [LC 92019470; ISN 1556239041]   HD62.4. R48 1993   2003

Managing across borders: the transnational solution. Christopher A. Bartlett and Sumantra Ghoshal. Boston, Mass.: Harvard Business School Press, c1989. xiv, 274 p. : ill. *Notes:* Includes index. Bibliography: p. [255]-265. [LC 89001867; ISN 0875842097]   HD62.4. B36 1989   2004

Managing cultural differences. Philip R. Harris, Robert T. Moran. 3rd ed. Houston: Gulf Pub. Co., c1991. xv, 639 p. : ill. *Notes:* Includes bibliographical references. [LC 90035354; ISN 0872014568; $32.50]   HD62.4. H37 1991   2005

Managing in developing countries: strategic analysis and operating techniques. James E. Austin. New York: London: Free Press; Collier Macmillan, c1990. xiii, 465 p. : ill. *Notes:* Includes bibliographical references. [LC 89023734; ISN 0029011027; $35.00]   HD62.4. A88 1990   2006

Managing risks and costs through financial innovation. prepared and published by Business International Corporation. New York, N.Y.: Business International Corporation, c1987. i, 299 p. : ill. (A Business International research report) *Notes:* "June 1987." [LC 87071616]   HG4027.5. M362 1987   2007

Managing the global firm. edited by Christopher A. Bartlett, Yves Doz, and Gunnar Hedlund. London; New York: Routledge, 1990. xii, 363 p. : ill. *Notes:* Includes index. Includes bibliographical references. [LC 89034004; ISN 0415037115; $52.50]   HD62.4. M366 1990   2008

The might of the multinationals: the rise and fall of the corporate legend. Alex Rubner. New York: Praeger, 1990. xvi, 292 p. *Notes:* Bibliography: p. [277]-284. [LC 89026526; ISN 0275935310]
    HD2755.5. R82 1990   2009

Multinational corporate strategy: planning for world markets. James C. Leontiades. Lexington, Mass.: Lexington Books, c1985. xxi, 228 p. : ill. *Notes:* Includes bibliographical references and index. [LC 83048686; ISN 0669073814]   HD62.4. L46 1985   2010

Multinational corporations. edited by Mark Casson. Aldershot, Hants, England; Brookfield, Vt., USA: Edward Elgar, 1990. xvii, 609 p. : ill. *Notes:* "An Elgar Reference Collection"—T.p. Includes bibliographical references. [LC 90003542; ISN 1852781920; £95.00]   HD2755.5. M824 1990   2011

Multinational enterprise and world competition: a comparative study of the USA, Japan, the UK, Sweden, and West Germany. Jeremy Clegg; foreword by John H. Dunning. New York: St. Martin's Press, 1987. xiv, 206 p. : ill. *Notes:* Based on the author's thesis (Ph. D.)—Reading University, 1985. Includes index. Bibliography: p. 194-202. [LC 87004735; ISN 031200852X; $39.95]
    HD2755.5. C525 1987   2012

Multinational enterprise in historical perspective. edited by Alice Teichova, Maurice Lévy-Leboyer, and Helga Nussbaum. Cambridge Cambridgeshire; New York: Paris: Cambridge University Press; Maison des sciences de l'homme, 1986. x, 396 p. : ill. *Notes:* Includes bibliographical references and indexes. *Contents:* Technological and organizational underpinnings of modern industrial multinational enterprise / Alfred D. Chandler Jr. [LC 86002253; ISN 0521320402]
    HD2755. M83425 1986   2013

The multinational enterprise in transition: selected readings and essays. edited by Phillip D. Grub, Fariborz Ghadar, Dara Khambata. 3rd ed. Princeton, N.J., USA: Darwin Press, c1986. xvi, 534 p. : ill. *Notes:* Includes bibliographies and index. [LC 86013442; ISN 0878500510; ISN 0878500529]
    HD62.4. M84 1986   2014

Multinational enterprises, economic structure, and international competitiveness. edited by John H. Dunning. Chichester; New York: Wiley, c1985. xxiii, 443 p. (Wiley/IRM series on multinationals) *Notes:* Includes bibliographies and index. [LC 84027149; ISN 0471907006; $30.06]
    HD2755.5. M8385 1985   2015

Multinational excursions. Charles P. Kindleberger. Cambridge, Mass.: MIT Press, c1984. vii, 275 p. *Notes:* Includes bibliographies and index. [LC 84000935; ISN 026211092X]   HD2755.5. K56 1984   2016

Multinational financial management. Alan C. Shapiro. 4th ed. Boston: Allyn and Bacon, 1992. xix, 729 p. : ill. *Notes:* Includes bibliographical references and index. [LC 91019533; ISN 0205132308; $73.93]   HG4027.5. S47 1992   2017

Multinational management. David P. Rutenberg. Boston: Little, Brown, c1982. xvii, 385 p. : ill. *Notes:* Includes bibliographies and index. [LC 81023641; ISN 0316763659]   HD62.4. R87 1982   2018

Multinational management: business strategy and government policy. by Yoshi Tsurumi. 2nd ed. Cambridge, MA: Ballinger Pub. Co., c1984. xxvi, 490 p. *Notes:* Includes bibliographies and index. [LC 83010027; ISN 0884109380]   HD62.4. T78   2019

Multinational managers and host government interactions. Lee A. Tavis, editor. Notre Dame, Ind.: University of Notre Dame Press, c1988. xvi, 328 p. : ill. (Multinational managers and developing country concerns.) *Notes:* Includes bibliographical references. [LC 86040590; ISN 0268013640; $22.95]   HD2932. M847 1988   2020

The multinational mission: balancing local demands and global vision. C.K. Prahalad, Yves L. Doz. New York: London: Free Press; Collier Macmillan, c1987. ix, 290 p. : ill. *Notes:* Includes index. Bibliography: p. 273-281. [LC 87011970; ISN 0029250501]   HD62.4. P69 1987   2021

Multinationals and employment: the global economy of the 1990s. edited by Paul Bailey, Aurelio Parisotto and Geoffrey Renshaw. Geneva: International Labour Office, 1993. xvi, 325 p. : ill. *Notes:* Includes bibliographical references.; ISN 9221071057; 45.00SF]   HD2755.5. M84414 1993   +2022

Multinationals and the restructuring of the world economy: the geography of multinationals, volume 2. edited by Michael Taylor and Nigel Thrift. London; Dover, N.H.: Croom Helm, c1986. viii, 389 p. : ill., maps (Croom Helm series in geography and environment) *Notes:* Includes indexes. Bibliography: p. 360-378. [LC 85029081; ISN 0709924577; $39.00 (U.S.)]
    HD2755.5. M8442 1986   2023

Multinationals—theory and history. edited by Peter Hertner and Geoffrey Jones. Aldershot, Hants, England; Brookfield, Vt., USA: Gower, c1986. vii, 200 p. : *Notes:* Papers originally presented at a conference held at the European University Institute, Florence, during 19-21 Sept. 1983 and sponsored by the European Science Foundation. Includes bibliographical references and index. [LC 85024955; ISN 0566050781; $37.00 (U.S.: est.)]   HD2755.5. M86 1986   2024

Navigating new markets abroad: charting a course for the international businessperson. editor/author, David M. Raddock; with contributions by Robert E. Ebel... et al. Lanham, MD: Rowman & Littlefield, c1993. xi, 257 p. *Notes:* Includes bibliographical references and index. [LC 92044668; ISN 0847678431] HD62.4. N38 1993 +2025

New directions in multinational corporate organization. New York: Business International Corporation, c1981. iv, 158 p. : ill. [LC 80070674] HD2755.5. N48 2026

The new expatriates: managing human resources abroad. Rosalie L. Tung. Cambridge, Mass.: Ballinger Pub. Co., 1987. xiii, 200 p. *Notes:* Includes index. Bibliography: p. [187]-189. [LC 87017835; ISN 0887301339] HF5549. T82 1988 2027

The power of financial innovation: successful corporate solutions to managing interest rate, foreign exchange rate, and commodity exposures on a worldwide basis. John Geanuracos, Bill Millar. New York, N.Y.: HarperBusiness, c1991. x, 239 p. : ill. *Notes:* Includes index. [LC 90025236; ISN 0887304702; $59.95] HG4027.5. G43 1991 2028

Readings in international business. Richard N. Farmer, John V. Lombardi, editors. 3rd ed. Bloomington, Ind.: Cedarwood Press, 1983? 218 p. *Notes:* "December, 1983."—p. 2.] HD2755.5. R418 1983 2029

Readings in international business: a decision approach. edited by Robert Z. Aliber and Reid W. Click. Cambridge, Mass.: MIT Press, c1993. vii, 521 p. : ill. *Notes:* Includes bibliographical references and index. [LC 92021502; ISN 0262510669] HD2755.5. R38 1993 2030

The road to Nissan: flexibility, quality, teamwork. by Peter Wickens. London: Macmillan, c1987. xii, 202 p. (Industrial relations in practice) *Notes:* Includes index. Bibliography: p. 191-194. [LC 87036906; ISN 0333419197; ISN 033345765X; £29.50 (Nov.); £14.95] HD62.4. W52 1987 2031

State-owned multinationals. Jean-Pierre Anastassopoulos, Georges Blanc, and Pierre Dussauge; preface by Eneko Landaburu; translated by Valerie Katzaros. Chichester England; New York: Wiley, c1987. xii, 200 p. : ill (Wiley/IRM series on multinationals) *Notes:* Translation of: Les multinationales publiques. Includes index. Bibliography: p. [183]-193. [LC 87002033; ISN 0471915025; $22.00] HD2755.5. A613 1987 2032

Tomorrow's global executive. Henry Ferguson. Homewood, Ill.: Dow Jones-Irwin, c1988. xiii, 265 p. : ill. *Notes:* Includes index. Bibliography: p. 237-248. [LC 87071259; ISN 1556230575] HD62.4. F47 1988 2033

Winning worldwide: strategies for dominating global markets. Douglas Lamont. Homewood, Ill.: Business One Irwin, c1991. xx, 315 p. *Notes:* Includes bibliographical references. [LC 90043329; ISN 1556234198] HD2755.5. L346 1991 2034

INTERNATIONAL BUSINESS MACHINES CORPORATION

Beyond IBM. Lou Mobley and Kate McKeown. New York: McGraw-Hill, c1989. xxiii, 253 p. : ill. *Notes:* Includes index. Bibliography: p. 229. [LC 88013225; ISN 0070426252] HD9696.C64 I4863 1989 2035

Big blues: the unmaking of IBM. by Paul Carroll. 1st ed. New York: Crown, c1993. vii, 375 p. *Notes:* Includes bibliographical references and index. [LC 93005421; ISN 0517591979; $24.00] HD9696.C64 I48317 1993 2036

Blue magic: the people, power, and politics behind the IBM personal computer. James Chposky and Ted Leonsis. New York, NY: Facts on File, 1988. xi, 213 p. *Notes:* Includes index. [LC 88000509; ISN 0816013918] HD9696.C64 I4832 1988 2037

Father, Son & Co.: my life at IBM and beyond. Thomas J. Watson, Jr. and Peter Petre. New York: Bantam Books, c1990. xi, 468 p., 32 p. of plates: ill. *Notes:* Bibliography: p. 450-451. [LC 90032682; ISN 0553070118; $22.95] HD9696.C64 I4887 1990 2038

The global IBM: leadership in multinational management. David Mercer. 1st ed. New York: Dodd, Mead, 1988. vii, 374 p. *Notes:* Includes index. Bibliography: p. [361]-362. [LC 87034041; ISN 0396092594; $22.95] HD9696.C64 I4849 1988 2039

IBM: how the world's most successful corporation is managed. David Mercer. London: Kogan Page, 1987. 306 p. *Notes:* Includes index. Bibliography: p. 299. [LC 86029319; ISN 1850912874; £12.95 (Jan.)] HD9696.C64 I485 1987 2040

The IBM lesson: the profitable art of full employment. D. Quinn Mills. 1st ed. New York: Times Books, c1988. 216 p. [LC 87040593; ISN 0812916905; $17.95] HF5549.5.T7 M55 1988 2041

IBM, the making of the common view. Michael Killen. 1st ed. Boston: Harcourt Brace Jovanovich, c1988. xx, 284 p. : ill. *Notes:* Includes index. [LC 88002189; ISN 0151434808] HD9696.C64 I48475 1988 2042

IBM vs. Japan: the struggle for the future. Robert Sobel. New York: Stein and Day, 1986. 262 p. *Notes:* Includes index. Bibliography: p. 245-252. [LC 85043058; ISN 0812830717; $18.95]
    HD9696.C64 I4885 1986   2043

The IBM way: insights into the world's most successful marketing organization. F.G. "Buck" Rodgers, with Robert L. Shook. 1st ed. New York: Harper & Row, c1986. xiv, 235 p. *Notes:* Includes index. [LC 85045223; ISN 0060155221; $17.95]   HD9696.C64 I4875 1986   2044

The Silverlake Project: transformation at IBM. Roy A. Bauer, Emilio Collar, Victor Tang with Jerry Wind, Patrick Houston. New York: Oxford University Press, 1992. xvi, 219 p. *Notes:* Includes bibliographical references (p. 203-214) and index. [LC 91032337; ISN 0195067541; $24.95]
    HD9696.C64 I483135 1992   2045

Who's afraid of Big Blue?: how companies are challenging IBM—and winning. Regis McKenna. Reading, Mass.: Addison-Wesley, c1989. iv, 218 p. *Notes:* Includes index. Bibliography: p. [213]-214. [LC 88007493; ISN 0201155745; $17.95]   HD9696.C64 I4852 1989   2046

INTERNATIONAL ECONOMIC RELATIONS

Ethics and markets: co-operation and competition within capitalist economies. edited by Colin Crouch and David Marquand. Oxford, UK; Cambridge, MA, USA: Blackwell, 1993. 150 p. *Notes:* "Political quarterly"—Cover. Includes index. *Contents:* The moral boundaries of the market / Russell Keat—The new politics of economics / David Miliband—Reticulated organisations: the birth and death of the mixed economy / Geoff Mulgan—Catholicism, Christian Democrats and 'reformed capitalism' / Jonathan Boswell—What makes the Japanese different? / Ronald Dore—Co-operation and competition in an institutionalized economy: the case of Germany / Colin Crouch—Human resources and human ingenuity / Judith Marquand—Trade unions and new managerial techniques / David Norman—The informal politics of the European Community / Keith Middlemas—Whither global capitalism? / Will Hutton. [LC 93019171; ISN 0631190333]   HF1359. E84 1993   +2047

International economic institutions. M.A.G. van Meerhaeghe. 5th rev. ed. Dordrecht; Boston: Kluwer Academic, 1987. xxviii, 368 p. *Notes:* Translation of: Internationale economische betrekkingen en instellingen. Includes bibliographies and indexes. [LC 87002959; ISN 9024735130]
    HF1411. M433 1987   2048

International economics: theory and context. Wilson B. Brown, Jan S. Hogendorn. Reading, Mass.: Addison-Wesley Pub. Co., c1994. viii, 648 p. : ill. *Notes:* Includes bibliographical references and indexes. [LC 93025797; ISN 0201554453]   HF1359. B76 1994   +2049

International economics: theory, evidence, and practice. Peter Wilson. Lincoln: University of Nebraska Press, c1986. xiv, 282 p. : ill. *Notes:* Includes index. Bibliography: p. 264-276. [LC 85014111; ISN 0803297106; ISN 0803247370]   HF1411. W567 1986   2050

INTERNATIONAL FINANCE

The ABCs of international finance. by John Charles Pool, Stephen C. Stamos, Patrice Franko Jones. 2nd ed. Lexington, Mass.: Lexington Books, 1991. xvi, 220 p. : ill. *Notes:* Includes bibliographical references (p.[207]-210) and index. [LC 90024529; ISN 0669245224; $24.95]   HG3851. P66 1991   2051

Case problems in international finance. edited by W. Carl Kester, Timothy A. Luehrman. New York: McGraw-Hill, c1993. xiii, 617 p. : ill. *Notes:* Includes index. [LC 92027871; ISN 0070342636; $47.00 (list) ($37.00 net)]   HG3881. C324 1993   2052

Changing fortunes: the world's money and the threat to American leadership. Paul Volcker, Toyoo Gyohten. 1st ed. New York: Times Books, 1992. xix, 394 p., [8] p. of plates: ill. *Notes:* Includes bibliographical references and index. [LC 91051035; ISN 081292018X; $25.00] HG3881. V65 1992   2053

Currencies and crises. Paul R. Krugman. Cambridge, Mass.: MIT Press, c1992. xix, 219 p. : ill *Notes:* Includes bibliographical references (p. [209]-213) and index. [LC 91039568; ISN 0262111659]
    HG3881. K77 1992   2054

Finance: an international perspective. Arthur I. Stonehill, David K. Eiteman. Homewood, Ill.: Irwin, 1987. xiv, 142 p. : ill. *Notes:* Includes bibliographies and index. [LC 86081805; ISN 0256056293]
    HG3881. S747 1987   2055

The financial revolution. Adrian Hamilton. 1st American ed. New York: Free Press, 1986. 268 p. *Notes:* Includes index. Bibliography: p.[254]-257. [LC 86009794; ISN 0029138302]
    HG3881. H266 1986   2056

The global economy in the 90s: a user's guide. Bill Orr. New York: New York University Press, c1992. xxiii, 330 p. : ill. *Notes:* Includes bibliographical references (p. 329-330). [LC 91036551; ISN 0814761763; $50.00] HG3881. O772 1992   2057

The handbook of international financial management. editor, Robert Z. Aliber. Homewood, Ill.: Dow Jones-Irwin, c1989. xvii, 859 p. : ill. *Notes:* Includes bibliographies and index. [LC 89031636; ISN 1556230192; $55.00] HG3881. H267 1989   2058

Innovation and technology in the markets: a reordering of the world's capital market systems. Daniel R. Siegel, editor. Chicago, Ill.: Probus Pub. Co., c1990. xiv, 245 p. (Probus guide to world markets) *Notes:* Includes index. Includes bibliographical references.; ISN 1557381208; $37.50] HG3881. I485 1990   2059

International finance and financial policy. edited by Hans R. Stoll; preface by Paul Volcker. New York: Quorum Books, 1990. xxi, 251 p. *Notes:* Includes bibliographical references. [LC 90008027; ISN 0899305555; $45.00] HG3881. I57615 1990   2060

International financial management. John Holland. 2nd ed. Oxford, UK; Cambridge, Mass.: Blackwell, 1993. xii, 470 p. : ill. *Notes:* Includes bibliographical references (p. [454]-463) and indexes. [LC 93014795; ISN 0631174214] HG3881. H615 1993   +2061

International money and finance. C. Paul Hallwood and Ronald MacDonald. 2nd ed. Oxford, UK; Cambridge, Mass., USA: B. Blackwell, 1994. xvi, 445 p. : ill. *Notes:* Previous ed. published under title: International money. 1986. Includes bibliographical references (p. [396]-425) and indexes. [LC 93025078; ISN 0631181512; $26.95] HG3881. H255 1994   +2062

The international money game. Robert Z. Aliber. 5th ed., rev. New York: Basic Books, c1987. xii, 372 p. : ill. *Notes:* Includes bibliographical references and index. [LC 86070450; ISN 0465033822; ISN 0465033830; $19.95; $9.95] HG3881. A44 1987   2063

Money meltdown: restoring order to the global currency system. Judy Shelton. New York: Toronto: New York: Free Press; Maxwell Macmillan Canada; Maxwell Macmillan International, c1994. viii, 399 p. *Notes:* Includes bibliographical references (p. 353-383) and index. [LC 93048786; ISN 0029291127; $24.95] HG3881. S513 1994   +2064

Money, power, and space. edited by Stuart Corbridge, Nigel Thrift and Ron Martin. Oxford, England; Cambridge, Mass.: Blackwell, 1994. x, 452 p. : ill. *Notes:* Includes bibliographical references and index. [LC 93032882; ISN 0631192018] HG3881. M594 1994   +2065

New developments in international finance. edited by Joel M. Stern and Donald H. Chew Jr. Oxford: Basil Blackwell, 1988. ix, 230 p. : ill. *Notes:* Includes bibliographies and index. [LC 86008364; ISN 063115115X; ISN 0631152040; £25.00; No price] HG3881. N48 1988   2066

Readings in international finance. edited by Joseph G. Kvasnicka 3rd ed. Chicago: Federal Reserve Bank of Chicago, 1986? 372 p. : ill. *Notes:* Includes bibliographical references.] HG3881. R356 1986   2067

Secret money: the world of international financial secrecy. Ingo Walter. London; Boston: Allen & Unwin, 1985. 213 p. : ill. *Notes:* Includes index. Bibliography: p. 204-205. [LC 85035895; ISN 0043321070; £11.95] HG3881. W282   2068

INTERNATIONAL ORGANIZATION

Birth of a new world: an open moment for international leadership. Harlan Cleveland; foreword by Robert S. McNamara. 1st ed. San Francisco: Jossey-Bass, c1993. xxx, 260 p. *Notes:* Includes bibliographical references (p. 231-252) and index. [LC 92040189; ISN 1555425119; $25.95] JX1954. C545 1993   +2069

INTERNATIONAL TELEPHONE AND TELEGRAPH CORPORATION

The ITT wars. by Rand V. Araskog. 1st ed. New York: Holt, c1989. xiii, 241 p. *Notes:* Includes index. [LC 88025109; ISN 080500825X] HE8846.I64 A7 1989   2070

INTERNATIONAL TRADE

Beyond free trade: firms, governments, and global competition. edited by David B. Yoffie. Boston, Mass.: Harvard Business School Press, c1993. xix, 466 p. : ill. *Notes:* Includes bibliographical references and index. [LC 92029834; ISN 0875843441; $39.95] HF71. B49 1993   2071

The do's and taboos of international trade: a small business primer. Roger E. Axtell; foreword by Tommy G. Thompson. Rev. ed. New York: J. Wiley, c1994. xvi, 312 p. : ill. *Notes:* Includes bibliographical references and index. [LC 94008586; ISN 0471007609; $16.95]   HF1379. A96 1994   +2072

The Ernst & Young resource guide to global markets, 1991. Charles F. Valentine, Ginger Lew, Roger M. Poor. New York: Wiley, 1991. x, 223 p. : ill. *Notes:* Includes bibliographical references. [LC 90041068; ISN 0471530069; $14.95]   HF1379. V36 1991   2073

International business handbook. V.H. (Manek) Kirpalani, editor. New York: Haworth Press, c1990. xiv, 667 p. : ill., map: *Notes:* Includes bibliographical references and indexes. *Contents:* An overview. Doing international business: a global interview / V.H. (Manek) Kirpalani—Doing international business: countries/regions. Doing business in the Andean countries / Robert Grosse—International influences affecting Great Britain / Ronald Savitt—Central America / James Makens—China / Joseph Eastlack, Susan Kraemer Watkins—Egypt: international business perspectives / Gillian Rice, Essam Mahmoud—West Germany / Peter Zurn—New perspectives in east-west business: the case of Hungary / Jozsef Beracs, Nicolas Papadopoulos—Israel / Samuel Rabino, Jehiel Zif—Japan / William Lazer, Midori Rynn—Marketing opportunities in the Middle East / M.R. Haque—Poland / Leon Zurawicki—Romania: opportunities and challenges / Jacob Naor—Singapore / Soo Jiuan Tan, Chin Tiong Tan—International business climate in Turkey / Osman Ata Atac, Nizamettin Aydin—Business and marketing dynamics in the United States of America / Eugene J. Kelley, Lisa R. Hearne—The future. Epilogue / V.H. (Manek) Kirpalani... [et al.]. [LC 89026682; ISN 086656862X; $91.94]   HF1379. I567 1990   2074

International trade and investment. Franklin R. Root. 6th ed. Cincinnati, OH: South-Western Pub. Co., c1990. viii, 696 p. : ill. *Notes:* Includes bibliographical references. [LC 89022032; ISN 0538086203; $40.50]   HF1411. R6345 1990   2075

World trade and payments: an introduction. Richard E. Caves, Jeffrey A. Frankel, Ronald W. Jones. 5th ed. Glenview, Ill.: Scott, Foresman / Little, Brown Higher Education, c1990. 784 p. : ill. (some col.) *Notes:* Includes index. Includes bibliographical references. [LC 89010438]   HF1379. C38 1990   2076

World trade and payments: an introduction. Richard E. Caves, Jeffrey A. Frankel, Ronald W. Jones. 6th ed. New York, NY: HarperCollins College Publishers, c1993. xvii, 694 p. : ill. *Notes:* Includes bibliographical references and index. [LC 92024764; ISN 0673522741]   HF1379. C38 1993   2077

INTERNET (COMPUTER NETWORK)

Finding it on the Internet: the essential guide to archie, Veronica, Gopher, WAIS, WWW (including Mosaic), and other search and browsing tools. Paul Gilster. New York: Wiley, c1994. xviii, 302 p. : ill. *Notes:* Includes index. [LC 94017024; ISN 0471038571]   TK5105.875.I57 G53 1994   +2078

INTERPERSONAL RELATIONS

Human relations series. Boston c1952-1969. 2 v. illus. (part col.), ports. *Notes:* Cover title. Reprints from the Harvard Business Review, 1952-1969.]   HF5548.8. H3 1952   +2079

INTRAUTERINE CONTRACEPTIVES INDUSTRY

At any cost: corporate greed, women and the Dalkon Shield. Morton Mintz. 1st ed. New York: Pantheon Books, 1985. xvii, 308 p. *Notes:* Includes bibliographical references and index. [LC 85006389]   HD9995.C62 A234   2080

INVENTORY CONTROL

Decision systems for inventory management and production planning. Edward A. Silver, Rein Peterson. 2nd ed. New York: Wiley, c1985. xxiii, 722 p. : ill. (Wiley series in production/operations management) *Notes:* Includes bibliographies and indexes. [LC 84015179; ISN 0471867829; $36.95 (est.)]   HD40. P48 1985   2081

Managing inventory for cost reduction. Norman Kobert. Englewood Cliffs, NJ: Prentice Hall, c1992. xx, 503 p. : ill. *Notes:* Includes bibliographical references (p. 493-494) and index. [LC 92005762; ISN 0135047889]   TS160. K635 1992   2082

Principles of inventory and materials management. Richard J. Tersine. 3rd ed. New York: North-Holland, c1988. xii, 553 p. : ill. *Notes:* Includes index. Bibliography: p. [537]-542. [LC 87013538; ISN 0444011625] TS160. T4 1988   2083

Procurement and inventory systems analysis. Jerry Banks, W.J. Fabrycky. Englewood Cliffs, N.J.: Prentice-Hall, c1987. xii, 292 p. : ill. (Prentice-Hall international series in industrial and systems engineering) *Notes:* Includes bibliographies and index. [LC 86030540; ISN 0137237197; $39.95] TS160. B25 1987   2084

INVESTMENT ADVISERS

Investing with the best: what to look for, what to look out for in your search for a superior investment manager. Claude N. Rosenberg, Jr. 2nd ed. New York: Wiley, c1993. xv, 237 p. : ill. *Notes:* Includes index. [LC 93007865; ISN 0471558273] HG4521. R775 1993   +2085

Standards of practice handbook: the code of ethics and the standards of professional conduct, with commentary and interpretation. Association for Investment Management and Research. 6th ed. New York, NY: AIMR, 1992. xiii, 225 p. *Notes:* Rev. ed. of: Standards of practice handbook / Financial Analysts Federation. 4th ed. 1988. Cover title. Includes bibliographical references (p. [206]-207) and index.; ISN 187908726X; $20.00] HG4921. F38 1992   2086

The Wall Street gurus: how you can profit from investment newsletters. Peter Brimelow. 1st ed. New York: Random House, c1986. x, 238 p. *Notes:* Includes index. [LC 85028153; ISN 0394542029; $17.95] HG4621. B69 1986   2087

INVESTMENT ANALYSIS

Competing in the new capital markets: investor relations strategies for the 1990s. Bruce W. Marcus and Sherwood Lee Wallace. New York, N.Y.: HarperBusiness, c1991. xvii, 363 p. *Notes:* Includes bibliographical references and index. [LC 90022265; ISN 0887304095; $42.50] HG4529. M37 1991   2088

The financial analyst's handbook. edited by Sumner N. Levine. 2nd ed. Homewood, Ill.: Dow Jones-Irwin, 1988. xvi, 1870 p. : ill. *Notes:* Includes bibliographies and index. [LC 87071362; ISN 0870949195; $65.00] HG4521. F55 1988   2089

Graham and Dodd's security analysis. 5th ed. / Sidney Cottle, Roger F. Murray, Frank E. Block; with the collaboration of Martin L. Leibowitz. New York: McGraw-Hill, c1988. xiii, 656 p. : ill. *Notes:* Rev. ed. of: Security analysis. 4th ed. 1962. Includes bibliographical references and index. [LC 87019990; ISN 0070132356; $49.95] HG4521. G67 1988   2090

Investment analysis and portfolio management. Jerome B. Cohen, Edward D. Zinbarg, Arthur Zeikel. 5th ed. Homewood, Ill.: R.D. Irwin, 1987. xiv, 738 p. : ill. *Notes:* Includes bibliographical references and index. [LC 86081802; ISN 0256036241] HG4529. C63 1987   2091

Managing institutional assets. edited by Frank J. Fabozzi. New York: Harper & Row, c1989. xiii, 691 p. : ill. *Notes:* Includes bibliographical references. [LC 89037651; ISN 0887303870; $69.95] HG4529. M36 1989   2092

Modern investment theory. Robert A. Haugen. 2nd ed. Englewood Cliffs, N.J.: Prentice Hall, 1990. xxiii, 696 p. : ill.; +1 computer disk [LC 89022849; ISN 0135947979; $50.40] HG4529. H38 1990   2093

The new stock market. Diana R. Harrington, Frank J. Fabozzi, H. Russell Fogler. Chicago, Ill.: Probus Pub. Co., c1990. x, 364 p. : ill. *Notes:* Includes bibliographical references and index. [LC 89010257; ISN 1557380562; $38.50] HG4529. H37 1990   2094

Security analysis and portfolio management. Donald E. Fischer, Ronald J. Jordan. 5th ed. Englewood Cliffs, N.J.: Prentice Hall, c1991. xiv, 768 p. : ill. *Notes:* Includes bibliographical references and index. [LC 90046179; ISN 0137991495; $60.00] HG4529. F57 1991   2095

Technical analysis explained: the successful investor's guide to spotting investment trends and turning points. by Martin J. Pring. 3rd ed. New York: McGraw-Hill, c1991. xiii, 521 p. : ill. *Notes:* Includes bibliographical references (p. 509-510) and index. [LC 91009075; ISN 0070510423; $49.95] HG4529. P75 1991   2096

INVESTMENT BANKING

Comeback: the restoration of American banking power in the new world economy. Roy C. Smith. Boston, Mass.: Harvard Business School Press, c1993. x, 357 p. *Notes:* Includes bibliographical references and index. [LC 92023757; ISN 0875843263; $27.95] HG4930.5. S57 1993   2097

Doing deals: investment banks at work. Robert G. Eccles and Dwight B. Crane. Boston, Mass.: Harvard University Press, c1988. ix, 273 p. : ill. *Notes:* Includes index. Bibliography: p. [257]-264. [LC 88014884; ISN 0875841996]   HG1616.I5 E33 1988   2098

Investment banking: a tale of three cities. Samuel L. Hayes III and Philip M. Hubbard. Boston, Mass.: Harvard Business School Press, c1990. 424 p. *Notes:* Includes bibliographical references. [LC 89020019; ISN 0875842208]   HG4534. H39 1990   2099

Investment banking and diligence: what price deregulation? Joseph Auerbach and Samuel L. Hayes, III. Boston, Mass.: Harvard Business School Press, c1986. x, 274 p. : ill. *Notes:* Includes bibliographies and index. [LC 86000319; ISN 0875841716]   HG4910. A94 1986   2100

The investment banking handbook. edited by J. Peter Williamson. New York: John Wiley & Sons, c1988. xvii, 574 p. : ill. *Notes:* Includes bibliographies and index. [LC 88122509; ISN 0471815624; $65.00]   HG4534. I56 1988   2101

Investment banking in Europe: restructuring for the 1990's. Ingo Walter and Roy C. Smith. Oxford, England; New York, N.Y.: Basil Blackwell, 1990. xii, 169 p. : ill. *Notes:* Includes bibliographical references. [LC 89017505; ISN 0631171797; £30.00]   HG5430.5. W36 1990   2102

The library of investment banking. Robert Lawrence Kuhn, editor-in-chief. Homewood, Ill.: Dow-Jones Irwin, 1990. 7 v.: ill. *Notes:* Includes bibliographical references. *Contents:* v. 1. Investing and risk management—v. 2. Capital raising and financial structure—v. 3. Corporate and municipal securities—v. 4. Mergers, acquisitions, and leveraged buyouts—v. 5. Mortgage and asset securitization—v. 6. International finance and investing—v. 7. Index to the Library of investment banking.; $312.00]   HG4534. L537 1990   2103

INVESTMENTS

The alchemy of finance: reading the mind of the market. George Soros. New York: J. Wiley, c1994. x, 367 p. *Notes:* Includes bibliographical references. [LC 94006764; ISN 0471042064; $19.95]   HG4515. S67 1994   +2104

The almanac of investments. edited by Alan Crittenden. Novato, Calif.: Crittenden Books, c1984. 514 p. : ill. *Notes:* Includes bibliographies and index. [LC 83051608; ISN 0913153036; $19.95]   HG4521. A45   2105

The big bang: an investor's guide to the changing city. William Kay. London: Weidenfeld and Nicolson, 1986. vii, 196 p. : ill. *Notes:* Includes index.; ISN 0297789848]   HG5432. K39   2106

Blood in the streets: investment profits in a world gone mad. James Dale Davidson, in collaboration with Sir William Rees-Mogg. New York: Summit Books, c1987. 386 p. : ill. *Notes:* Includes bibliographical references and index. [LC 87009935; ISN 067162735X; $17.95]   HG4516. D38 1987   2107

Classics: an investor's anthology. edited by Charles D. Ellis with James R. Vertin. Homewood, Ill.: Dow Jones-Irwin, 1988, c1989. xxxv, 759 p. : ill. *Notes:* Includes bibliographies. [LC 88017609; ISN 1556230982; $47.50]   HG4522. C57 1989   2108

Classics II: another investor's anthology. edited by Charles D. Ellis with James R. Vertin. Homewood, Ill.: Business One Irwin, c1991. xxii, 626 p. : ill. *Notes:* Includes bibliographical references. [LC 91002939; ISN 1556233582]   HG4522. C58 1991   2109

The Dow Jones-Irwin guide to bond and money market investments. Marcia Stigum, Frank J. Fabozzi. Homewood, IL.: Dow Jones-Irwin, c1987. xiii, 298 p. : ill. *Notes:* Includes bibliographical references and index. [LC 86071921; ISN 087094892X; $25.00]   HG4651. S74   2110

The Dow Jones-Irwin guide to investing with investment software. Thomas A. Meyers. Homewood, Ill.: Dow Jones-Irwin, c1987. xi, 209 p. : ill. *Notes:* Includes index. Bibliography: p. 192-193. [LC 86071442; ISN 0870949381]   HG4515.5. M45   2111

Encyclopedia of investments. editor-in-chief, Jack P. Friedman. 2nd ed. Boston: Warren, Gorham & Lamont, c1990. xvi, 964 p. : ill. *Notes:* Kept up to date by updates with cumulative indexes. Includes bibliographical references. [LC 89050553; ISN 0791303659; $112.70]   HG4527. E5 1990   2112

Fractal market analysis: applying chaos theory to investment and economics. Edgar E. Peters. New York: J. Wiley & Sons, c1994. xviii, 315 p. : ill. *Notes:* Includes bibliographical references (p. 296-305) and index. [LC 93028598; ISN 0471585246; $49.95]   HG4515.3. P47 1994   +2113

Fundamentals of investments. Gordon J. Alexander, William F. Sharpe, Jeffery V. Bailey. 2nd ed. Englewood Cliffs, N.J.: Prentice Hall, c1993. xx, 875 p. : ill. *Notes:* Includes bibliographical references and index. [LC 92020869; ISN 0133354490; $45.00]   HG4521. A419 1993   +2114

Genetic algorithms and investment strategies. Richard J. Bauer, Jr. New York: Wiley, c1994. ix, 308 p. : ill. *Notes:* Includes bibliographical references and index. [LC 93011984; ISN 0471576794]   HG4515.2. B38 1994   +2115

Handbook of financial markets: securities, options, and futures. edited by Frank J. Fabozzi and Frank G. Zarb. 2nd ed. Homewood, Ill.: Dow Jones-Irwin, c1986. xix, 785 p. : ill. *Notes:* Includes bibliographical references and indexes. [LC 85071920; ISN 0870946005]   HG4527. H25 1986   2116

Handbook of investment products and services. Victor L. Harper. 2nd ed. New York, N.Y.: New York Institute of Finance, c1986. xxviii, 510 p. : ill. *Notes:* Includes bibliographical references and index. [LC 85015207; ISN 013378746X; $35.00]   HG4521. H24 1986   2117

High-risk, high-return investing. Lawrence W. Tuller. New York: J. Wiley & Sons, c1994. xii, 260 p. : ill. *Notes:* Includes bibliographical references and index. [LC 93028590; ISN 0471580937; $27.95]   HG4521. T86 1994   +2118

How to keep your savings safe: protecting the money you can't afford to lose. by Walter L. Updegrave. New York: Crown, 1992. vii, 232 p. *Notes:* Includes index. [LC 91036900; ISN 0517587343; $19.00]   HG4521. U63 1992   2119

International financial market investment: a Swiss banker's guide. Erwin W. Heri and Vanessa Rossi. Chichester, West Sussex, England; New York: J. Wiley & Sons, 1994. ix, 167 p. : ill. *Notes:* "A Wiley professional title." Translation, modified and updated, of: Was Anleger eigentlich wissen sollten / Erwin W. Heri. 2. Aufl. 1991. Includes bibliographical references. [LC 93024499; ISN 0471941689; $39.95]   HG4527. H4613 1994   +2120

Investing with a social conscience. Elizabeth Judd. New York: Pharos Books, 1990. 272 p. *Notes:* Includes bibliographical references (p. [258]-259). [LC 89078436; ISN 0886874718; $18.95]   HG4910. J84 1990   2121

Investment analysis and portfolio management. Frank K. Reilly. 3rd ed. Chicago: Dryden Press, c1989. xxiv, 1026, [35] p. : ill. *Notes:* Includes bibliographies and indexes. [LC 88036709; ISN 0030254981; $44.38]   HG4521. R396 1989   2122

Investments. William F. Sharpe, Gordon J. Alexander. 4th ed. Englewood Cliffs, N.J.: Prentice Hall, c1990. xxix, 833 p. : ill. *Notes:* Includes bibliographical references. [LC 89023158; ISN 0135043824; $49.20]   HG4521. S48 1990   2123

Investments, an introduction to analysis and management. Frederick Amling. 6th ed. Englewood Cliffs, N.J.: Prentice Hall, c1989. xx, 780 p. *Notes:* Includes bibliographies and index. [LC 88004174; ISN 0135043417]   HG4521. A54 1989   2124

Investments: analysis and management. Jack Clark Francis. 4th ed. New York: McGraw-Hill, c1986. xix, 935, 16 p. : ill. (McGraw-Hill series in finance) *Notes:* Includes bibliographies and indexes. [LC 85023143; ISN 007021803X; $33.95 (est.)]   HG4521. F685 1986   2125

Investor response to management decisions: a research-based analysis of actions and effects. Richard M. Altman. New York: Quorum Books, 1992. xiv, 375 p. *Notes:* Includes bibliographical references (p. [349]-360) and index. [LC 90008874; ISN 0899304486; $59.95]   HG4515. A48 1992   2126

Leverage: the key to multiplying money. Gerald Krefetz. New York: Wiley, c1986. xiii, 207 p. : ill. *Notes:* Includes index. [LC 85016363; ISN 0471822639; $17.95 (est.)]   HG4910. K68 1986   2127

Management of investments. Jack Clark Francis. 2nd ed. New York: McGraw-Hill, c1988. xx, 826, 16 p. : ill. (some col.) *Notes:* Includes bibliographies and indexes. [LC 87003312; ISN 0070218080; $43.95 (est.)]   HG4521. F688 1988   2128

One up on Wall Street: how to use what you already know to make money in the market. by Peter Lynch with John Rothchild. New York: Simon and Schuster, 1989. 318 p. : ill. *Notes:* Includes index. [LC 88032741; ISN 0671661035]   HG4521. L864 1989   2129

Quantitative methods for financial analysis. edited by Stephen J. Brown, Mark P. Kritzman; sponsored by the Institute of Chartered Financial Analysts. 2nd ed. Homewood, Ill.: Dow Jones-Irwin, c1990. xiii, 266 p. : ill. *Notes:* Includes bibliographical references. [LC 89023271; ISN 1556232829]   HG4515.3. Q36 1990   2130

A random walk down Wall Street: including a life-cycle guide to personal investing. Burton G. Malkiel. 5th ed. New York: Norton, 1990. 440 p. : ill. *Notes:* Includes bibliographical references. [LC 89037092; ISN 0393027937; ISN 0393959619; $22.95]   HG4521. M284 1990   2131

The social investment almanac: a comprehensive guide to socially responsible investing. edited by Peter D. Kinder, Steven D. Lydenberg, Amy L. Domini. 1st ed. New York: H. Holt and Co., 1992. xvii, 904 p. : ill. *Notes:* Includes bibliographical references and indexes. [LC 91036732; ISN 0805017690; $50.00]   HG4527. K525 1992   2132

Socially responsible investing: how to invest with your conscience. Alan J. Miller. New York: New York Institute of Finance, c1991. xvi, 367 p. *Notes:* Includes bibliographical references. [LC 91007757; ISN 0131561839; $19.95]   HG4528. M55 1991   2133

Stocks, bonds, options, futures: investments and their markets. staff of the New York Institute of Finance; edited by Stuart R. Veale. New York, N.Y.: Englewood Cliffs, N.J.: The Institute; Prentice-Hall, c1987. 332 p. : ill. *Notes:* Includes index. [LC 87011324; ISN 0138467188; $24.95]   HG4921. S7945 1987   2134

Supply-side portfolio strategies. edited by Victor A. Canto and Arthur B. Laffer. Westport, Conn.: Quorum Books, 1988. xii, 180 p. : ill. *Notes:* Includes bibliographies and index. [LC 87013091; ISN 0899302866; $35.00] HG4910. S775 1988 2135

Surviving the great depression of 1990: protect your assets and investments—and come out on top. Ravi Batra. New York: Dell Publishing, c1989. 367 p. *Notes:* Includes index. Reprint. Originally published: New York: Simon and Schuster, 1988.; ISN 0440204615; $4.95] HG179. B37 1989 2136

The three Rs of investing: return, risk, and relativity. Austin S. Donnelly. Homewood, Ill.: Dow Jones-Irwin, c1985. xvi, 230 p. : ill. *Notes:* Includes bibliographies and index. [LC 84072830; ISN 0870945572] HG4521. D64 1985 2137

Understanding Wall Street. by Jeffrey B. Little and Lucien Rhodes. 3rd ed. Blue Ridge Summit, PA: Liberty Hall Press, c1991. 259 p. : ill. (some col.); *Notes:* Includes bibliographical references (p. [233]-235) and index. [LC 91021412; ISN 0830604820; ISN 0830604790; $21.95; $10.60] HG4910. L54 1991 2138

Venture's financing and investing in private companies: a guide to understanding entrepreneurs and their relationships with investors, lenders, and advisors. Arthur Lipper III. Rev. ed. Chicago, Ill.: Probus Pub. Co., 1988. xviii, 506 p.; ill. *Notes:* Rev. ed. of: Venture's guide to investing in private companies. c1984. Includes bibliographical references and index. [LC 87032887; ISN 091725399X; $32.50] HG4921. L56 1988 2139

What's next?: how to prepare yourself for the crash of '89 and profit in the 1990's. Paul Erdman. 1st ed. New York: Doubleday, 1988. 172 p. [LC 88000290; ISN 0385246986; $14.95 ($19.95 Can.)] HG4521. E75 1988 2140

William E. Donoghue's complete money market guide: the simple, low-risk way you can profit from inflation and fluctuating interest rates. by William E. Donoghue with Thomas Tilling. 1st ed. New York: Harper & Row, c1981. xiv, 224 p. *Notes:* Includes index. [LC 80008200; ISN 0690020082; $12.95] HG4527. D66 1981 2141

INVESTMENTS, AMERICAN

American multinationals and Japan: the political economy of Japanese capital controls, 1899-1980. Mark Mason. Cambridge, Mass.: Council on East Asian Studies, Harvard University, 1992. xix, 373 p. : ill. *Notes:* Includes bibliographical references (p. 341-362) and index. [LC 92009934; ISN 0674026306] HG5772. M32 1992 2142

Rivals beyond trade: America versus Japan in global competition. Dennis J. Encarnation. Ithaca: Cornell University Press, 1992. xvi, 222 p. : ill. *Notes:* Includes bibliographical references and index. [LC 91057900; ISN 0801427339; $24.95] HG5772. E53 1992 2143

INVESTMENTS, BRITISH

British investment in a united Germany. Economists Advisory Group with Rolf Jungnickel and Georg Koopmann. London: Anglo-German Foundation for the Study of Industrial Society, c1993. ii, 64 p. : ill. *Notes:* "An Anglo-German Foundation report"—Cover. Includes bibliographical references (p. 60-62). [LC 93006293; £5.00 (pbk)] HG5432. E26 1993 2144

INVESTMENTS, FOREIGN

Buying into America: how foreign money is changing the face of our nation. by Martin and Susan Tolchin. 1st ed. New York: Times Books, 1988. xiv, 400 p. *Notes:* Includes index. Bibliography: p. 355-387. [LC 87040198; ISN 0812916670; $18.95] HG4910. T65 1988 2145

Direct foreign investment: costs and benefits. edited by Richard D. Robinson. New York: Praeger, 1987. xviii, 227 p. : ill. *Notes:* Includes bibliographical references and index. [LC 87017750; ISN 0275927172; $39.85 (est.)] HG4538. D557 1987 2146

The Dow Jones-Irwin guide to international securities, futures, and options markets. William E. Nix, Susan Wilkinson Nix. Homewood, Ill.: Dow Jones-Irwin, c1988. xiv, 370 p. : ill. *Notes:* Includes index. Bibliography: p. 349-352. [LC 87071358; ISN 0870947710] HG4538. N59 1988 2147

Emerging stock markets: a complete investment guide to new markets around the world. Margaret M. Price. New York: McGraw-Hill, c1994. xvi, 414 p. : ill. *Notes:* Includes index. [LC 93025979; ISN 0070510490; $39.95] HG4538. P685 1994 +2148

The handbook of international investing. editor, Carl Beidleman. Chicago, Ill.: Probus Pub. Co., c1987. xi, 897 p. : ill. *Notes:* "From a declaration of principles jointly adopted by a committee of the American Bar Association and a committee of publishers"—T.p. verso. Includes bibliographies and index. Non-circulating. [LC 86022515; ISN 0917253647; $59.50] HG4538. H38 1987 2149

How to profit from the coming Russian boom: the insider's guide to business opportunities and survival on the frontiers of capitalism. Richard Poe. New York: McGraw-Hill, c1993. xxvi, 305 p. : ill., maps *Notes:* Includes bibliographical references and index. [LC 93010524; ISN 0070504504; $24.95] HG5572. P64 1993 2150

International investments. Bruno Solnik. 2nd ed. Reading, Mass.: Addison-Wesley Pub. Co., 1991. xi, 404 p. : ill. *Notes:* Includes bibliographical references and index. [LC 90036065; ISN 0201535351; $36.89] HG4538. S52 1991 2151

The international political economy of direct foreign investment. edited by Benjamin Gomes-Casseres and David B. Yoffie. Aldershot, Hants, England; Brookfield, Vt., USA: E. Elgar Pub., c1993. 2 v. *Notes:* Includes bibliographical references and indexes. [LC 92027247; ISN 1852786108; $279.95 (approx.)] HG4538. I634 1993 2152

International portfolio management. edited by Mark Tapley. London: Euromoney, 1986. xvii, 171 p. : ill. *Notes:* Includes bibliographies and index.; ISN 0903121948] HG4529.5. I57 2153

Investing in Cuba: problems and prospects. edited by Jaime Suchlicki and Antonio Jorge. New Brunswick, N.J.: Transaction Publishers, c1994. ix, 175 p. *Notes:* "The papers in this volume were presented at the conference 'Investing in Cuba: problems and prospects' held in Toronto, Canada, September 8, 1993, which was sponsored by the Research Institute for Cuba, Coral Gables, Florida, and the Canadian Institute of Strategic Studies, Toronto, Canada." Includes bibliographical references. [LC 94012389; ISN 1560001550; $32.95] HG5252. I58 1994 +2154

Investing in developing countries: a guide for executives. Thomas L. Brewer, Kenneth David, Linda Y.C. Lim, with the assistance of Robert S. Corredera. Lexington, Mass.: Lexington Books, 1986. xviii, 250 p. *Notes:* Includes bibliographies and index. [LC 85046008; ISN 0669127701] HG5993. B74 1986 2155

The new competitors: how foreign investors are changing the U.S. economy. Norman J. Glickman, Douglas P. Woodward. New York: Basic Books, Inc., c1989. x, 374 p. : ill. *Notes:* Includes index. Bibliography: p. 329-362. [LC 88047901; ISN 0465050050; $19.95] HG4910. G547 1989 2156

Stock answers: a guide to the international equities market. edited by Jonathan Clements. New York: Nichols Pub., 1988. xi, 147 p. *Notes:* Includes index. [LC 88009906; ISN 0893973130; $34.95] HG4538. S749 1988 2157

INVESTMENTS, JAPANESE

Japanese direct manufacturing investment in the United States. Mamoru Yoshida. New York: Praeger, 1987. xiv, 220 p. : ill. *Notes:* Originally presented as the author's thesis (doctoral—University of Miami) Includes index. Bibliography: p. 209-216. [LC 86022689; ISN 0275923479; $34.85] HG5772. Y58 2158

Japanophobia: the myth of the invincible Japanese. Bill Emmott. 1st U.S. ed. New York, N.Y.: Times Books, c1993. 261 p. *Notes:* Includes bibliographical references (p. 247-249) and index. [LC 92050501; ISN 0812919076; $25.00 (Canada $32.50)] HG4538. E53 1993 +2159

The sun that never rose: the inside story of Japan's failed attempt at global financial dominance. Eugene R. Dattel. Chicago, Ill.: Probus Publishing, c1994. xvi, 290 p. *Notes:* Includes bibliographical references (p. 271-272) and index. [LC 94171527; ISN 1557385629; $27.50] HG4538. D28 1994 +2160

ISSUES MANAGEMENT

Managing the new bottom line: issues management for senior executives. Raymond P. Ewing. Homewood, IL: Dow Jones-Irwin, c1987. xiii, 191 p. : ill. *Notes:* Includes bibliographical references and index. [LC 87070726; ISN 087094973X] HD59.5. E95 1987 2161

Strategic issues management: how organizations influence and respond to public interests and policies. Robert L. Heath and associates. 1st ed. San Francisco: Jossey-Bass Publishers, 1988. xxi, 415 p. : ill. (The Jossey-Bass management series) *Notes:* Includes index. Bibliography: p. 395-405. [LC 87046335; ISN 1555420834] HD59.5. H4 1988 2162

JAPAN

Japan: a postindustrial power. Ardath W. Burks. 3rd ed., rev. and updated. Boulder: Westview Press, 1991. xvi, 234 p. : ill., maps *Notes:* Includes bibliographical references (p. 219-224) and index. [LC 90047953; ISN 0813309891; ISN 0813309905]   DS806. B85 1991   2163

The Japanese today: change and continuity. Edwin O. Reischauer. Cambridge, Mass.: Belknap Press, 1987, c1977. 426 p. : ill., plates *Notes:* Rev. ed. of: The Japanese. 1977. Includes index. Bibliography: p. 415-418. [LC 87014904; ISN 0674471814]   DS806. R35 1987   2164

JAPAN—CIVILIZATION

Japan, the fragile superpower. Frank Gibney. 2nd rev. ed. New York: New American Library, c1985. xvi, 430 p. *Notes:* "A Meridian book." Includes bibliographical references and index. [LC 85021577; ISN 0452007763; $8.95 ($11.25 Can.)]   DS821. G513 1985   2165

What is Japan?: contradictions and transformations. Taichi Sakaiya; translated by Steven Karpa. New York: Kodansha International, 1993. xxii, 312 p. : 1 map [LC 93016489; ISN 1568360010; $25.00]   DS821. S24213 1993   2166

JAPAN—CIVILIZATION—1945-

Chrysanthemums and thorns: the untold story of modern Japan. Edwin M. Reingold. New York: St. Martin's Press, 1992. xviii, 298 p., [16] p. of plates: ill. *Notes:* Includes bibliographical references (p. 274-282) and index. [LC 92025053; ISN 031208160X; $24.95]   DS822.5. R45 1992   2167

JAPAN—COMMERCE

The Japan business study program: understanding Japanese business. edited by Hirofumi Matsuo. Austin, Tex.: University of Texas at Austin, Graduate School of Business, Bureau of Business Research and Japan External Trade Organization, c1989. xi, 74 p. : ill. *Notes:* Bibliography: p. 35.; $18.00]   HF3826.5. J357 1989   2168

JAPAN—COMMERCE—DEVELOPING COUNTRIES

The borderless world: power and strategy in the interlinked economy. Kenichi Ohmae. New York: Harper Business, c1990. xv, 223 p. [LC 90033770; ISN 0887304737; $21.95]   HF3838.D44 O43 1990   2169

JAPAN—COMMERCIAL POLICY

Japan's unequal trade. Edward J. Lincoln. Washington, D.C.: Brookings Institution, c1990. xiii, 223 p. : ill. *Notes:* Includes bibliographical references. [LC 90030760; ISN 0815752628; $26.95]
HF1601. L56 1990   2170

Strategic capitalism: private business and public purpose in Japanese industrial finance. Kent E. Calder. Princeton, N.J.: Princeton University Press, c1993. xxii, 373 p. : ill. *Notes:* Includes bibliographical references and index. [LC 92039043; ISN 0691043183; $39.00]   HF1601. C35 1993   +2171

JAPAN—ECONOMIC CONDITIONS

Beyond capitalism: the Japanese model of market economics. Eisuke Sakakibara; with an introduction by Clyde V. Prestowitz, Jr. Lanham, MD: University Press of America, c1993. xxi, 162 p. : ill. *Notes:* "Co-published by arrangement with the Economic Strategy Institute"—T.p. verso. Includes bibliographical references. [LC 93006476; ISN 0819190624; $18.50]   HC462.9. S19255 1993   +2172

JAPAN—ECONOMIC CONDITIONS—1945—CARICATURES AND CARTOONS

Japan Inc.: an introduction to Japanese economics: the comic book. Shōtarō Ishinomori; translated by Betsey Scheiner; with an introduction by Peter Duus. Berkeley: University of California Press, c1988. 313 p. : chiefly ill. *Notes:* Translation of: Manga Nihon keizai nyūmon. [LC 87036766; ISN 0520062884; ISN 0520062892] HC462.9. I7413 1988 2173

JAPAN—ECONOMIC CONDITIONS—1945-

Beyond national borders: reflections on Japan and the world. Kenichi Ohmae. Homewood, Ill.: Dow Jones-Irwin, c1987. xi, 128 p. : ill. *Notes:* Includes bibliographical references. [LC 86072864; ISN 1556230176] HC462.9. O56 1987 2174

Doing business with Japan. H. William Tanaka, Nobuyuki Takashima. New Canaan, Conn.: Business Books International, c1986. 209 p. : ill. *Notes:* Includes bibliographical references and index.; ISN 0916673022] HC462.9. T353 2175

The Japan syndrome: symptoms, ailments, and remedies. Jon Woronoff. New Brunswick N.J.: Transaction Books, 1986. 230 p. : ill. *Notes:* Includes index. Bibliography: p. [225]-226. [LC 85020867; ISN 0887380905] HC462.9. W666 1986 2176

The Japanese economy. Takatoshi Itō. Cambridge, Mass.: MIT Press, c1992. xvi, 455 p. : ill. *Notes:* Includes bibliographical references and index. [LC 91013596; ISN 0262090295; $29.95] HC462.9. I79 1992 2177

Japan—facing economic maturity. Edward J. Lincoln. Washington, D.C.: Brookings Institution, c1988. xiii, 298 p. : ill. *Notes:* Includes bibliographical references and index. [LC 87026103; ISN 0815752601; ISN 0815752598; $31.95; $11.95] HC462.9. L56 1988 2178

The political economy of Japan. Stanford, Calif.: Stanford University Press, 1987-1992. 3 v.: ill. *Notes:* "Under the general editorship of Yasusuke Murakami and Hugh T. Patrick." Includes bibliographies and indexes. *Contents:* v. 1. The Domestic transformation / edited by Kōzō Yamamura and Yasukichi Yasuba—v. 2. The changing international context / edited by Takashi Inoguchi and Daniel I. Okimoto—v. 3. Cultural and social dynamics / edited by Shompei Kumon and Henry Rosovsky. [LC 86030037; ISN 0804713804; ISN 0804714487; ISN 0804719918; $37.50; $12.95] HC462.9. P57 1987 2179

JAPAN—ECONOMIC POLICY

Taking Japan seriously: a Confucian perspective on leading economic issues. Ronald Dore. Stanford, Calif.: Stanford University Press, 1987. ix, 264 p. : ill. *Notes:* Includes index. Bibliography: p. [247]-253. [LC 86061030; ISN 0804713502; ISN 0804714010; $35.00; $11.95 (pbk.)] HC462.9. D673 1987b 2180

JAPAN—ECONOMIC POLICY—1945-

Economic policy and development: new perspectives. edited by Toshio Shishido, Ryuzo Sato. Dover, Mass.: London: Auburn House; Croom Helm, c1985. xv, 320 p. : ill. *Notes:* "Contributions. . . in honor of Dr. Saburo Okita"—P. ix. "Saburo Okita: biographical and bibliographical data": p. 317-320. Includes bibliographies. [LC 85006077; ISN 0865691207; $32.00] HC462.9. E236 1985 2181

JAPAN—ECONOMIC POLICY—1945-1989

Postwar reconstruction of the Japanese economy. edited by the Special Survey Committee, Ministry of Foreign Affairs, Japan (September 1946); compiled by Saburo Okita. Tokyo: University of Tokyo Press, c1992. xxix, 194 p. *Notes:* "Reprinted in 1990 by University of Tokyo Press as vol. 1 of Shiryo: sengo nihon no keizai seisaku koso .. edited by Takafusa Nakamura and Tokuko Omori"—T.p. verso. Includes bibliographical references and index.; ISN 4130470566; ISN 0860084787; $44.50] HC462.9. N5813 1992 2182

JAPAN—FOREIGN ECONOMIC RELATIONS

Japan, Europe, and international financial markets: analytical and empirical perspectives. edited by Ryuzo Sato, Richard M. Levich, Rama V. Ramachandran. Cambridge England; New York, NY, USA: Cambridge University Press, 1994. x, 272 p. : ill. *Notes:* Includes bibliographical references and index. [LC 93003810; ISN 0521452287] HF1601. J3534 1994 +2183

Japan's choices: new globalism and cultural orientations in an industrial state. edited by Masataka Kosaka. London; New York: Pinter Publishers, 1989. 162 p. : ill. *Notes:* Includes bibliographical references. [LC 89008705; ISN 0861877918; $37.50] HF1601. J365 1989 2184

Japan's global reach: the influences, strategies and weaknesses of Japan's multinational companies. Bill Emmott. London: Century, 1991, c1992. xi, 244 p. *Notes:* Includes bibliographical references (p. 233-235) and index. [LC 92040130; ISN 071264928X; £18.99] HD2907. E55 1991 2185

The sun also sets: the limits to Japan's economic power. Bill Emmott. 1st ed. NYC i.e. New York City, NY: Times Books, 1989. xii, 292 p. *Notes:* Includes index. Bibliography: p. 277-279. [LC 89004477; ISN 0812918169; $18.95] HF1601. E49 1989 2186

JAPAN—HISTORY—ALLIED OCCUPATION, 1945-1952

Remaking Japan: the American Occupation as New Deal. Theodore Cohen; edited by Herbert Passin. New York: Free Press, c1987. xxiii, 533 p. : ill. *Notes:* Includes index. Bibliography: p. 475-526. [LC 86033726; ISN 0029060508] DS889.16. C63 1987 2187

JAPAN—INDUSTRIES

Asia's new industrial world. Michael Smith. . . et al. London; New York: Methuen, 1985. 136 p. : ill. [LC 84027273; ISN 0416389201] HC462.9. A843 1985 2188

Japanese industrial performance. Kimio Uno. Amsterdam; New York: New York, N.Y., U.S.A.: North-Holland; Sole distributors for the U.S.A. and Canada, Elsevier, 1987. xix, 439 p. : ill.; 1 computer disk (5 1/4 in.) *Notes:* System requirements for computer disk: IBM PC, XT, or AT. Includes index. Bibliography: p. 417-426. [LC 87015452; ISN 0444702741] HC462.9. U56 1987 2189

JAPAN—INDUSTRIES—1945-

Trading places: how we allowed Japan to take the lead. Clyde V. Prestowitz, Jr. New York: Basic Books, c1988. xvi, 365 p. : ill. *Notes:* Includes index. Bibliography: p. [346]-353. [LC 87047775; ISN 0465086802; $19.95] HC462.9. P69 1988 2190

JAPAN—MILITARY POLICY

Inside Japan's defense: technology, economics & strategy. Michael W. Chinworth. Washington: Brassey's (US), c1992. xxi, 245 p. *Notes:* Includes bibliographical references (p. 228-236) and index. [LC 92008390; ISN 0028810384; $30.00 (est.)] UA845. C45 1992 2191

JAPAN—SOCIAL LIFE AND CUSTOMS—1945-

Dealing with the Japanese. Mark Zimmerman. London: Allen & Unwin, 1985. xv, 316 p. : ill. *Notes:* Includes index. Bibliography: p. [299]-301. [LC 85023055; ISN 0046500022; £12.50 (May)] DS822.5. Z56 2192

JEWISH CAPITALISTS AND FINANCIERS

The new crowd: the changing of the Jewish guard on Wall Street. by Judith Ramsey Ehrlich and Barry J. Rehfeld. 1st ed. Boston, MA: Little, Brown, c1989. 444 p., 16 p. of plates *Notes:* Includes index. Bibliography: p. [414]-423. [LC 89012096; ISN 0316222852; $19.95] F128.9.J5 E45 1989 2193

JOB ANALYSIS

Job analysis: a handbook for the human resource director. Jai Ghorpade. Englewood Cliffs, N.J.: Prentice Hall, 1987. xviii, 348 p. : ill. Notes: Includes index. Bibliography: p.333-340. [LC 87014350; ISN 0135102561]   HF5549.5.J6 G48 1988   2194

Job analysis: an effective management tool. Stephen E. Bemis, Ann Holt Belenky, Dee Ann Soder. Washington, D.C.: Bureau of National Affairs, c1983. xiv, 225 p. Notes: Includes index. Bibliography: p. 187-218. [LC 83018923; ISN 0871794128]   HF5549.5.J6 B42 1983   2195

JOB EVALUATION

Fair pay: the managerial challenge of comparable job worth and job evaluation. Thomas H. Patten, Jr. 1st ed. San Francisco: Jossey-Bass Publishers, 1988. xxii, 272 p. : ill. Notes: Includes index. Bibliography: p. 249-262. [LC 88042796; ISN 1555421202; $28.95]   HF5549.5.J62 P38 1988   2196

JOB SATISFACTION

The Financial Post 100 best companies to work for in Canada. Eva Innes, Jim Lyon & Jim Harris. 2nd ed., rev. Toronto: Harper Collins, c1990. 376 p. Notes: Spine title: The 100 best companies to work for in Canada. [LC 90093086; ISN 0002156733; $27.95]   HF5549.2.C2 I55 1990   2197

Job satisfaction—a reader. edited by Michael M. Gruneberg. New York: Wiley, 1976. xiv, 254 p. : ill. Notes: "A Halsted Press book." Bibliography: p. 250-251. [LC 75043852; ISN 0470329114]   HF5549.5.J63 J6   +2198

The motivation crisis; winding down and turning off. by John R. Hinrichs. New York AMACOM, 1974. vii, 264 p. illus. Notes: Includes bibliographical references. [LC 73090418; ISN 0814453570]   HF5549.5.J63 H5   +2199

Requisite organization: the CEO's guide to creative structure and leadership. Elliott Jaques. Kingston, NY: Cason Hall, c1989. 138 [i.e. 276] p. : ill. Notes: Includes bibliography and index. [LC 88029931; ISN 096210700X; $27.50]   HF5549.5.J63 J37 1989   2200

Work and rewards: redefining our work-life reality. William F. Roth, Jr. New York: Praeger, 1989. x, 196 p. Notes: Bibliography: p. [183]-187. [LC 88025572; ISN 0275931668; $37.85]   HF5549.5.J63 R62 1989   2201

JOB SECURITY

Employment security: balancing human and economic considerations. Paul H. Loseby. Westport, Conn.: Quorum Books, 1992. viii, 181 p. : ill. Notes: Includes bibliographical references (p. [169]-176) and index. [LC 92001132; ISN 0899306926]   HD5708.45.U6 L67 1992   2202

Job security in America: lessons from Germany. Katharine G. Abraham and Susan N. Houseman. Washington, D.C.: Brookings Institution, c1993. xi, 175 p. : ill. Notes: Includes bibliographical references (p. 161-168) and index. [LC 92037545; ISN 0815700768; $26.95]   HD5708.45.U6 A27 1993   2203

JOB STRESS

Abuse in the workplace: management remedies and bottom line impact. Emily S. Bassman. Westport, Conn.: Quorum, 1992. xiv, 206 p. Notes: Includes bibliographical references and index. [LC 92007505; ISN 089930673X]   HF5548.85. B365 1992   2204

Creating healthy work organizations. edited by Cary L. Cooper and Stephen Williams; with a foreword by John Bowis. Chichester England; New York: Wiley, c1994. xiii, 250 p. : ill. Notes: Includes bibliographical references and index. [LC 94002441; ISN 0471943452; $40.00]   HF5548.85. C74 1994   +2205

Job stress and blue collar work. edited by Cary L. Cooper and Michael J. Smith. Chichester West Sussex; New York: Wiley, c1985. ix, 243 p. : ill. Notes: Includes bibliographies and index. [LC 85012022; ISN 0471908118; $36.00]   HF5548.85. J64 1985   2206

JOBS, STEVEN

Steve Jobs: the journey is the reward. Jeffrey S. Young. Glenview, Ill.: Scott, Foresman, c1988. 440 p. : ill. Notes: Bibliography: p. 440. [LC 87028359; ISN 0673188647; $18.95] QA76.2.J63 Y68 1988   2207

JOHNSON, J. SEWARD

Johnson v. Johnson. by Barbara Goldsmith. New York: Knopf, 1987. 285 p., [16] p. of plates, ports.; [LC 86046169; ISN 0394560434]   KF759.J64 G65 1987   2208

JOINT VENTURES

Guide to joint ventures in the USSR: laws, regulations, model documents and practical information = Sovmestnye predpriia tiia v SSSR. The USSR Chamber of Commerce and Industry. Paris: ICC Publishing S.A., 1988. 279 p. : forms Notes: Produced jointly by the USSR Chamber of Commerce and Industry and the International Chamber of Commerce.; ISN 9284210704]
HD62.47. G84 1988   2209

The handbook of joint venturing. edited by John D. Carter, Robert F. Cushman, C. Scott Hartz. Homewood, Ill.: Dow Jones-Irwin, c1988. xxiii, 469 p. : ill., ports. Notes: Includes bibliographical references and index. [LC 88013430; ISN 0870947044; $55.00]   HD62.47. H355 1988   2210

Hands across the ocean: managing joint ventures with a spotlight on China and Japan. Susan Goldenberg. Boston, Mass.: Harvard Business School Press, c1988. xii, 242 p. Notes: Includes index. [LC 88017756; ISN 0875841910]   HD62.47. G65 1988   2211

Industrial collaboration with Japan. Louis Turner; with a foreword by Hiroshi Takeuchi, in association with Ayako Asakura... et al.; The Royal Institute of International Affairs. London; New York: Routledge & K. Paul, 1987. 117 p. Notes: Bibliography: p. 112-117. [LC 86026048; ISN 0710211090; £5.95]   HD62.47. T87 1987   2212

The knowledge link: how firms compete through strategic alliances. Joseph L. Badaracco, Jr. Boston, Mass.: Harvard Business School Press, c1991. xiv, 189 p. Notes: Includes bibliographical references (p. [153]-179) and index. [LC 90044763; ISN 0875842267; $24.95]   HD62.47. B33 1991   2213

Partnerships for profit: structuring and managing strategic alliances. Jordan D. Lewis. New York: London: Free Press; Collier Macmillan, c1990. xiv, 336 p. : ill. Notes: Includes bibliographical references (p. 255-324). [LC 89025633; ISN 0029190509; $27.95]   HD62.47. L48 1990   2214

Strategies for joint ventures. Kathryn Rudie Harrigan. Lexington, Mass.: Lexington Books, c1985. xix, 426 p. : ill. Notes: Includes indexes. Bibliography: p. [385]-404. [LC 85040110; ISN 0669104485]   HD62.47. H37 1985   2215

Teaming up for the 90s: a guide to international joint ventures and strategic alliances. Timothy M. Collins, Thomas L. Doorley. Homewood, Ill.: Business One Irwin, c1991. xxi, 348 p. : ill. Notes: Includes bibliographical references and index. [LC 90003654; ISN 1556234309; $42.50]
HD62.47. C63 1991   2216

Triad power: the coming shape of global competition. Kenichi Ohmae. New York: London: Free Press; Collier Macmillan, c1985. xx, 220 p. : ill. Notes: Includes bibliographical references and index. [LC 84026068; ISN 0029234700]   HD62.47. O36 1985   2217

Venturing abroad: international business expansion via joint ventures. by Jack Enen, Jr. 1st ed. Blue Ridge Summit, PA: Liberty Hall Press, 1991. vi, 243 p. Notes: Includes bibliographical references and index. [LC 90036761; ISN 0830686533; $27.95]   HD62.47. E54 1991   2218

JOURNALISM

Making news. Martin Mayer. Rev. and updated. Boston, Mass.: Harvard Business School Press, c1993. 345 p. Notes: Includes bibliographical references and index. [LC 92037134; ISN 0875843719; $16.95]   PN4731. M3945 1993   2219

News over the wires: the telegraph and the flow of public information in America, 1844-1897. Menahem Blondheim. Cambridge, Mass.: Harvard University Press, 1994. viii, 305 p. Notes: Includes bibliographical references and index. [LC 93028731; ISN 067462212X]   PN4864. B76 1994   +2220

JOURNALISM, COMMERCIAL

The power of the financial press: journalism and economic opinion in Britain and America. Wayne Parsons. New Brunswick, N.J.: Rutgers University Press, 1990, c1989. ix, 266 p. *Notes:* Includes indexes. Bibliography: p. 231-253. [LC 89043066; ISN 0813514975; $24.95] PN4888.C59 P37 1990   2221

The press and the world of money: how the news media cover business and finance, panic and prosperity, and the pursuit of the American dream. John Quirt. Byron, Calif.: Anton/California-Courier, c1993. xi, 364 p. *Notes:* Includes bibliographical references and index. [LC 93022766; ISN 0963550403; $24.95 (Canada $29.95)]   PN4888.C59 Q57 1993   +2222

JUNK BONDS

Fall from grace: the untold story of Michael Milken. by Fenton Bailey; with an introduction by Alan Dershowitz. Secaucus, N.J.: Carol Pub. Group, c1992. xxiii, 330 p. *Notes:* "A Birch Lane Press book." "First published in Great Britain in 1991, under the title The junk bond revolution, by Fourth Estate Limited, London."—Verso t.p. Includes bibliographical references (p. [317]-322) and index. [LC 92025285; ISN 1559721359; $19.95 ($24.95 Can.)]   HG4910. B337 1992   2223

The high-yield debt market: investment performance and economic impact. edited by Edward I. Altman. Homewood, Ill.: Dow Jones-Irwin, c1990. x, 306 p. : ill. *Notes:* "Salomon Brothers Center for the Study of Financial Institutions [and] Leonard N. Stern School of Business, New York University." Includes bibliographical references. [LC 89025996; ISN 1556232357; $45.00]   HG4963. H53 1990   2224

Junk bonds: how high yield securities restructured corporate America. Glenn Yago. New York: Oxford University Press, 1991. xi, 249 p. : ill. *Notes:* Includes bibliographical references. [LC 90035876; ISN 019506111X; $21.95]   HG4963. Y34 1991   2225

JURISTIC PERSONS

Ethics of an artificial person: lost responsibility in professions and organizations. Elizabeth Wolgast. Stanford, Calif.: Stanford University Press, 1992. x, 161 p. *Notes:* Includes bibliographical references and index. [LC 91042508; ISN 0804720347; $29.50]   K650. W65 1992   2226

KEYNESIAN ECONOMICS

Peddling prosperity: economic sense and nonsense in the age of diminished expectations. Paul Krugman. 1st ed. New York: W.W. Norton, c1994. xv, 303 p. : ill. *Notes:* Includes bibliographical references and index. [LC 93029965; ISN 0393036022]   HB99.7. K77 1994   +2227

KIAM, VICTOR

Going for it!: how to succeed as an entrepreneur. by Victor Kiam. New York: Morrow, c1986. 260 p. [LC 85061762; ISN 0688060609; $16.95]   HC102.5.K53 A34 1986   2228

KOHLBERG KRAVIS ROBERTS & CO

The money machine: how KKR manufactured power & profits. Sarah Bartlett. New York, NY: Warner Books, c1991. xv, 345 p., [8] p. of plates: ill. *Notes:* Includes bibliographical references (p. 339-345). [LC 91065482; ISN 0446516082; $24.95]   HG4930.5. B37 1991   2229

KOREA (SOUTH)—ECONOMIC CONDITIONS—1960-

Doing business in Korea. edited by Arthur M. Whitehill. North Ryde, N.S.W.: New York: Croom Helm; Nichols Pub. Co., 1987. xvi, 121 p. : ill. *Notes:* Includes bibliographical references and index. [LC 87005665; ISN 0893972762; $35.00]   HC467. D58 1987   2230

Korea in the world economy. Il SaKong. Washington, DC: Institute for International Economics, 1993. xvii, 302 p. *Notes:* "January 1993." "Marketed and distributed outside the USA and Canada by Longman Group UK Limited, London"—T.p. verso. Includes bibliographical references (p. 287-294) and index. [LC 92037855; ISN 0881321834]   HC467. S225 1993   2231

Korean economic dynamism. Dilip K. Das. New York: St. Martin's Press, 1992. xiv, 230 p. : ill. *Notes:* Includes bibliographical references (p. 213-227) and index. [LC 91020609; ISN 0312067658]
HC467. D37 1992   2232

KURTZIG, SANDRA L

CEO: building a $400 million company from the ground up. by Sandra L. Kurtzig with Tom Parker. Boston, Mass.: Harvard Business School Press, c1994. vii, 307 p. *Notes:* Originally published: New York: Norton, c1991. Includes index. [LC 93038123; ISN 0875845428; $14.95]
HD9696.C62 K8754 1994   +2233

LABOR ECONOMICS

Economics of labor in industrial society. Clark Kerr, Paul D. Staudohar, editors. 1st ed. San Francisco, Calif.: Jorsey-Bass, 1986. xx, 420 p. (The Jossey-Bass management series) *Notes:* Includes bibliographies and indexes. [LC 86045631]   HD4901. E28 1986   2234

Handbook of labor economics. edited by Orley Ashenfelter and Richard Layard. Amsterdam; New York: North-Holland; New York, N.Y., U.S.A.: Sole distributors for the U.S.A. and Canada, Elsevier Science Pub. Co., 1986. 2 v. p. : ill.; 25 cm. *Notes:* Includes bibliographies and indexes. [LC 86016730; ISN 0444878580; ISN 0444878564; ISN 0444878572]   HD4802. H36 1986   2235

Labor economics and industrial relations: markets and institutions. edited by Clark Kerr and Paul D. Staudohar. Cambridge, Mass.: Distributed by Harvard University Press, 1994. xxxvii, 704 p. *Notes:* Includes bibliographical references and index. [LC 94002377; ISN 0674506413]
HD4901. L117 1994   +2236

Labor economics and labor relations. Lloyd G. Reynolds, Stanley H. Masters, Colletta H. Moser. 10th ed. Englewood Cliffs, N.J.: Prentice Hall, c1991. xii, 610 p. : ill. *Notes:* Includes bibliographical references and index. *Contents:* Labor economics: institutions and the market—A first look at labor markets—Labor supply decisions—Human capital: education and job training—Demand—Investments by firms in workers—Wage determination—Discrimination—Real wage rates, productivity, and inflation—Unemployment—American workers in a world economy—The evolution of American unions—Unions, politics, and the law—The decline of private-sector unions—Collective bargaining: union and management goals—Bargaining—Collective bargaining: issues and outcomes—Case studies in collective bargaining—Collective bargaining in the public sector—Union wage effects—Nonwage effects and the balance sheet—Glossary of concepts. [LC 90040155; ISN 0135173760; $66.43]   HD4901. R47 1991   2237

Labor economics: theory, institutions, and public policy. Ray Marshall, Vernon M. Briggs, Jr. 6th ed. Homewood, IL: Irwin, 1989. xv, 654 p. : ill. *Notes:* Includes bibliographies and index. [LC 88013564; ISN 0256070903; $42.95]   HD4901. M282 1989   2238

Readings in labor economics and labor relations. edited by Lloyd G. Reynolds, Stanley H. Masters, Colletta H. Moser. 5th ed. Englewood Cliffs, N.J.: Prentice Hall, c1991. vii, 469 p. : ill. *Notes:* Includes bibliographical references. [LC 90039527; ISN 0137537328; $21.50]   HD4901. R389 1991   2239

LABOR LAWS AND LEGISLATION

Managing employee rights and responsibilities. edited by Chimezie A.B. Osigweh, Yg. New York: Quorum Books, 1989. xxiv, 297 p. : ill. *Notes:* Includes index. Bibliography: p. [253]-280. [LC 88038310; ISN 0899303366; $49.95]   KF3455. M36 1989   2240

A primer on American labor law. William B. Gould, IV. 3rd ed. Cambridge, Mass.: MIT Press, c1993. xvii, 326 p. *Notes:* Includes bibliographical references and index. [LC 93019038; ISN 0262570998]
KF3369. G68 1993   2241

LABOR MARKET

Turbulence in the American workplace. Peter B. Doeringer... et al. New York: Oxford University Press, 1991. xiv, 256 p. : ill. *Notes:* Includes bibliographical references (p. 219-243) and indexes. [LC 90043299; ISN 0195064615; $27.95]   HD5724. T87 1991   2242

LABOR PRODUCTIVITY

America and the new economy: how new competitive standards are radically changing American workplaces. Anthony Patrick Carnevale. 1st ed. San Francisco, Calif.: Jossey-Bass, 1991. xxii, 267 p. *Notes:* Includes bibliographical references (p. 239-255) and index. *Contents:* Discovering the new market standards—Six standards of success: how America measures up—Dynamics of technical change and the new economic cycle—New structures that link organizations, industries, and markets—Competitive prospects in critical industries—Changing quantity, distribution, and quality of jobs—Increasing need for complex and wide-range job skills—Sixteen job skills crucial to success—Organizational strategies for meeting the new competitive standards—Continuous learning: the cornerstone of economic progress. [LC 91019307; ISN 155542371X; $29.95]   HC110.L3 C37 1991   2243

Corporate takeovers and productivity. Frank R. Lichtenberg. Cambridge, Mass.: MIT Press, c1992. x, 153 p. *Notes:* Includes bibliographical references (p. 143-149) and index. [LC 91042262; ISN 0262121646; $29.95]   HC110.L3 L53 1992   2244

A little bit at a time: secrets of productive quality. by Russell O. Wright. Berkeley, Calif.: Ten Speed Press, c1990. xv, 187 p. [LC 89077125; ISN 0898153948; $17.95]   HD57. W75 1990   2245

Productivity and American leadership: the long view. William J. Baumol, Sue Anne Batey Blackman, and Edward N. Wolff. Cambridge, MA: MIT Press, c1989. 395 p. : ill. *Notes:* Includes index. Includes bibliographical references. [LC 88037204; ISN 0262022931; $29.95]   HC110.L3 B38 1989   2246

Productivity in organizations: new perspectives from industrial and organizational psychology. contributions by John P. Campbell, Richard J. Campbell, and associates; foreword by Raymond A. Katzell. 1st ed. San Francisco: Jossey-Bass Publishers, 1988. xxvi, 451 p. : ill. *Notes:* Includes bibliographies and indexes. [LC 88042780; ISN 1555421008; $31.95]   HD57. P6987 1988   2247

LABOR SUPPLY

The future impact of automation on workers. Wassily Leontief Faye Duchin. New York: Oxford University Press, c1986. xiii, 170 p. : ill. *Notes:* Includes bibliographical references and index. [LC 85003082; ISN 0195036239; $27.95]   HD5724. L38 1986   2248

How labor markets work: reflections on theory and practice. by John Dunlop... et al.; edited by Bruce E. Kaufman. Lexington, Mass.: Lexington Books, c1988. viii, 256 p. : port. *Notes:* Includes index. "Selected bibliographies": p. [233]-244. [LC 87022718; ISN 0669151262; ISN 0669151270]   HD5701.3. H68 1988   2249

Technology and employment: concepts and clarifications. Eli Ginzberg, Thierry J. Noyelle, and Thomas M. Stanback, Jr. Boulder: Westview Press, 1986. xi, 111 p. (Conservation of human resources studies in the new economy) *Notes:* Includes bibliographicl references and index. [LC 86005556; ISN 0813303990; $23.50]   HD6331.2.U5 G55 1986   2250

The world at work: an international report of jobs, productivity, and human values: a joint project of the Public Agenda Foundation and the Aspen Institute for Humanistic Studies. by Daniel Yankelovich... et al.; with a Sourcebook for policymakers by Harvey Lauer. New York: Octagon Books, 1984. xxii, 407 p. (Critical issues series) [LC 84020608; ISN 0870520237; $75.00]   HD5706. W679 1984   2251

LABOR THEORY OF VALUE

Competitive advantage on the shop floor. William Lazonick. Cambridge, Mass.: Harvard University Press, 1990. vi, 419 p. : ill. *Notes:* Includes bibliographical references. [LC 90032203; ISN 0674154169; $37.50]   HB206. L39 1990   2252

LABOR-MANAGEMENT COMMITTEES

Mutual gains: a guide to union-management cooperation. Edward Cohen-Rosenthal and Cynthia E. Burton. 2nd ed., rev. Ithaca, N.Y.: ILR Press, c1993. xi, 344 p. *Notes:* Includes bibliographical references (p. 317-330) and index. [LC 93011918; ISN 0875463126; $29.95] HD6490.L33 C64 1993 +2253

LAMONT, THOMAS W

The ambassador from Wall Street: the story of Thomas W. Lamont, J.P. Morgan's chief executive: a biography. by Edward M. Lamont. Lanham, Md.: Madison Books: Distributed by National Book Network, c1994. xv, 564 p., [16] p. of plates: ill. *Notes:* Includes bibliographical references and index. [LC 93027773; ISN 1568330189] HG2463.L3 L35 1994 +2254

LAND, EDWIN HERBERT

Land's Polaroid: a company and the man who invented it. Peter C. Wensberg. Boston: Houghton Mifflin, 1987. 258 p., [24] p. of plates: ill. *Notes:* "A Peter Davison book." Includes index. [LC 87002806; ISN 0395421144; $18.95] TR140.L28 W46 1987 2255

LAUDER, ESTEE

Estée: a success story. Estée Lauder. New York: Random House, c1985. 222 p.: ill., ports. [LC 85019371; ISN 0394551915] HD9999.P3932 L38 1985 2256

Estée Lauder: beyond the magic: an unauthorized biography. by Lee Israel. New York: Macmillan, c1985. x, 186 p., [16] p. of plates: ill. *Notes:* Includes index. Bibliography: p. 150-175. [LC 85024131; ISN 0025221000] HD9970.5.C674 E88 2257

LAUREN, RALPH

Ralph Lauren: the man behind the mystique. by Jeffrey A.Trachtenberg. 1st ed. Boston: Little, Brown, c1988. 302 p., [24] p. of plates: ill. *Notes:* Includes index. Bibliography: p. [292]-293. [LC 88012823; ISN 0316852147; $19.95 ($29.95 Can.)] TT505.L38 T73 1988 2258

LEADERSHIP

Authentic leadership: courage in action. Robert W. Terry; foreword by Harlan Cleveland. 1st ed. San Francisco: Jossey-Bass, c1993. xxv, 315 p.: ill. *Notes:* Includes bibliographical references (p. 293-304) and index. [LC 93017060; ISN 155542547X] HD57.7. T46 1993 +2259

Bass & Stogdill's handbook of leadership: theory, research, and managerial applications. Bernard M. Bass. 3rd ed. New York: London: Free Press; Collier Macmillan, c1990. xv, 1182 p.: ill. *Notes:* Rev. ed. of: Stogdill's handbook of leadership. c1981. Includes bibliographical references. [LC 89017240; ISN 0029015006; $75.00] HM141. S73 1990 2260

Certain trumpets: the call of leaders. Garry Wills. New York: Simon & Schuster, c1994. 336 p.: ill. *Notes:* Includes bibliographical references and index. [LC 94006526; ISN 067165702X; $23.00 ($29.50 Can.)] HM141. W525 1994 +2261

The classic touch: lessons in leadership from Homer to Hemingway. John K. Clemens, Douglas F. Mayer. Homewood, Ill.: Dow Jones-Irwin, 1987. xx, 213 p.: ill. *Notes:* Includes bibliographies and index. [LC 86051667; ISN 0870949039] HD57.7. C53 1987 2262

Contemporary issues in leadership. edited by William E. Rosenbach and Robert L. Taylor; foreword by Howard T. Prince II. 3rd ed. Boulder: Westview Press, 1993. xii, 233 p. *Notes:* Includes bibliographical references. [LC 93001255; ISN 081331755X] HM141. C69 1993 +2263

Contemporary issues in leadership. edited by William E. Rosenbach and Robert L. Taylor; foreword by Thomas E. Cronin. 2nd ed. Boulder: Westview Press, 1989. xiv, 248 p.: ill. *Notes:* Includes bibliographies. [LC 89005718; ISN 0813308291; ISN 0813308305; $49.00] HM141. C69 1989 2264

Credibility: how leaders gain and lose it, why people demand it. James M. Kouzes, Barry Z. Posner. 1st ed. San Francisco: Jossey-Bass, 1993. xxxiii, 332 p. *Notes:* Includes bibliographical references (p. 289-315) and indexes. [LC 93015388; ISN 155542550X] HD57.7. K678 1993 2265

Effective leadership for women and men. Jerome Adams, Janice D. Yoder. Norwood, N.J.: Ablex Pub. Corp., c1985. vi, 173 p. : ill. *Notes:* Includes indexes. Bibliography: p. 153-164. [LC 84028440; ISN 0893911682] HM141. A33 1985 2266

Executive achievement: making it at the top. Robert R. Blake and Jane S. Mouton. New York: McGraw-Hill, 1986. xii, 183 p. *Notes:* Includes bibliographies and index. [LC 85016577; ISN 0070056811] HD57.7. B54 1986 2267

The executive's compass: business and the good society. James O'Toole. New York: Oxford University Press, 1993. xiii, 162 p. : ill. *Notes:* Includes bibliographical references (p. [151]-155) and index. [LC 92032157; ISN 0195081196] HD57.7. O86 1993 2268

Flight of the buffalo: soaring to excellence, learning to let employees lead. James A. Belasco & Ralph C. Staver. New York: Warner Books, 1993. xii, 355 p. : ill. [LC 92050527; ISN 0446517097] HD57.7. B447 1993 2269

A force for change: how leadership differs from management. John P. Kotter. New York: London: Free Press; Collier Macmillan, c1990. xi, 180 p. : ill. *Notes:* Includes bibliographical references. [LC 89077323; ISN 0029184657; $22.95] HD57.7. K66 1990 2270

Frontiers of leadership: an essential reader. edited by Michel Syrett and Clare Hogg. Oxford, UK; Cambridge, Mass., USA: Blackwell Business, c1992. xxii, 585 p. *Notes:* Includes bibliographical references and index. [LC 91030908; ISN 0631183876; $24.95] HD57.7. F76 1992 2271

Get better or get beaten: 31 leadership secrets from GE's Jack Welch. Robert Slater. Burr Ridge, Ill.: Irwin Professional Pub., c1994. viii, 155 p. [LC 93044767; ISN 0786302356; $20.00] HD57.7. S57 1994 +2272

Getting things done when you are not in charge. by Geoffrey M. Bellman. 1st ed. San Francisco: Berrett-Koehler Publishers, c1992. xx, 278 p. : ill. *Notes:* "Based on his award-winning book, The quest for staff leadership." Includes bibliographical references (p. 271-272) and index. [LC 92070094; ISN 1881052028; $27.95] HD57.7. B454 1992 +2273

A higher standard of leadership: lessons from the life of Gandhi. Keshavan Nair. 1st ed. San Francisco: Emeryville, CA: Berrett-Koehler; Publishers Group West distributor, c1994. xiii, 157 p. : ill. *Notes:* Includes bibliographical references (p [145]-147) and index. [LC 94026927; ISN 1881052583; $21.95] HM141. N33 1994 +2274

An invented life: reflections on leadership and change. Warren Bennis; foreword by Tom Peters. Reading, Mass.: Addison-Wesley, c1993. xv, 238 p. *Notes:* Includes bibliographical references (p. 223) and index. [LC 92035270; ISN 0201632128; $22.95 ($29.95 Can.)] HD57.7. B458 1993 2275

The knowledge executive: leadership in an information society. by Harlan Cleveland. 1st ed. New York: Dutton, c1985. xix, 261 p. *Notes:* "A Truman Talley Book." Includes bibliographical references and index. [LC 85004442; ISN 0525243070] HM141. C55 1985 2276

Leaders and followers: challenges for the future. edited by Trudy Heller, Jon Van Til, Louis A. Zurcher. Greenwich, Conn. JAI Press, c1986. xiv, 279 p. : ill. *Notes:* Includes bibliographies and index. [LC 86015369; ISN 0892324953] BF723.L4 L32 1986 2277

The leader's edge: the seven keys to leadership in a turbulent world. Burt Nanus. Chicago: Contemporary Books, c1989. xiv, 224 p. *Notes:* Includes bibliographical references. [LC 89032769; ISN 0809244209; $17.95] HD57.7. N36 1989 2278

Leaders, fools, and impostors: essays on the psychology of leadership. Manfred F. R. Kets de Vries. 1st ed. San Francisco: Jossey-Bass, c1993. xxii, 224 p. *Notes:* Includes bibliographical references (p. 203-216) and index. [LC 93017061; ISN 1555425623] HD57.7. K478 1993 +2279

The leader's window: mastering the four styles of leadership to build high-performing teams. John D.W. Beck, Neil M. Yeager. New York: Wiley, c1994. xiv, 242 p. : ill. *Notes:* Includes bibliographical references and index. [LC 93041890; ISN 0471025542; $14.95] HD57.7. B428 1994 +2280

Leadership and organizations. Alan Bryman. London; Boston: Routledge & Kegan Paul, 1986. xi, 235 p. : ill. *Notes:* Includes index. Bibliography: p. 207-226. [LC 85019342; ISN 0710203241; ISN 0710208006; £20.00 ($25.00 U.S.); £8.95 ($17.00 U.S.)] HD57.7. B79 1986 2281

Leadership and the culture of trust. Gilbert W. Fairholm. Westport, Conn.: Praeger, 1994. viii, 236 p. *Notes:* Includes bibliographical references (p. [219]-229) and index. [LC 93042804; ISN 0275948331] HD57.7. F35 1994 +2282

Leadership and the quest for integrity. Joseph L. Badaracco, Jr., Richard R. Ellsworth. Boston, Mass.: Harvard Business School Press, c1989. xi, 222 p. *Notes:* Includes index. Bibliography: p. 211-216. [LC 88024507; ISN 0875842003] HD57.7. B33 1989 2283

The leadership challenge: how to get extraordinary things done in organizations. James M. Kouzes, Barry Z. Posner; foreword by Thomas J. Peters. 1st ed. San Francisco: Jossey-Bass, 1987. xxx, 362 p. : ill. (The Jossey-Bass management series) *Notes:* Includes index. Bibliography: p. 323-344. [LC 87045428; ISN 1555420613] HD57.7. K68 1987   2284

Leadership dilemmas—Grid solutions. Robert R. Blake, Anne Adams McCanse. Houston: Gulf Pub. Co., c1991. xiv, 377 p. : ill. *Notes:* Includes bibliographical references (p. 366-367) and index. [LC 90038432; ISN 0872014886; $26.95] HD57.7. B55 1991   2285

The leadership factor. John P. Kotter. New York: London: Free Press; Collier Macmillan, c1988. ix, 161 p. *Notes:* Includes index. Bibliography: p. 153-155. [LC 87019805; ISN 0029183316] HD57.7. K67 1988   2286

Leadership for change. Chares W. Joiner, Jr.; with a foreword by William G. Ouchi. Cambridge, Mass.: Ballinger Pub., c1987. xvi, 194 p. *Notes:* Includes index. Bibliography: p. 179-183. [LC 86025940; ISN 088730107X] HD57.7. J65 1987   2287

Leadership in administration; a sociological interpretation. Evanston, Ill. Row, Peterson, 1957. 162 p. [LC 57011350] HD31. S37   +2288

Leadership jazz. Max De Pree. 1st ed. New York: Currency Doubleday, 1992. 228 p. [LC 91045733; ISN 0385420188; $20.00 U.S. ($25.00 Canada)] HD57.7. D47 1992   2289

Leadership: managing in real organizations. Leonard R. Sayles. 2nd ed. New York: McGraw-Hill, c1989. xvii, 310 p. *Notes:* Includes bibliographical references and index. [LC 88023145; ISN 0070550182; ISN 0070550174; $31.95] HD57.7. S29 1989   2290

Leadership without easy answers. Ronald A. Heifetz. Cambridge, Mass.: Belknap Press of Harvard University Press, 1994. xi, 348 p. *Notes:* Includes bibliographical references (p. 279-337) and index. [LC 94015184; ISN 0674518586; $24.95] HM141. H385 1994   +2291

Leading: the art of becoming an executive. Philip B. Crosby. New York: McGraw-Hill, c1990. x, 214 p. *Notes:* Spine title: Leading. [LC 89036427; ISN 0070145679; $19.95] HD57.7. C755 1990   2292

Learning leadership: cases and commentaries on abuses of power in organizations. Abraham Zaleznik. Chicago, Ill.: Bonus Books, c1993. viii, 540 p. : ill. *Notes:* Includes bibliographical references and index. [LC 91077019; ISN 0929387716; $19.95] HD57.7. Z35 1993   2293

On becoming a leader. Warren Bennis. Reading, Mass.: Addison-Wesley Pub. Co., c1989. xiii, 226 p. *Notes:* Includes index. Bibliography: p. 217-220. [LC 89030242; ISN 0201080591; $19.95] BF637.L4 B37 1989   2294

Prisoners of leadership. Manfred F.R. Kets de Vries. New York: Wiley, c1989. ix, 246 p. *Notes:* Includes index. Bibliography: p. 223-242. [LC 88028698; ISN 0471500690; $19.95] HD57.7. K48 1989   2295

Risktaker, caretaker, surgeon, undertaker: the four faces of strategic leadership. William E. Rothschild. New York: Wiley, c1993. vi, 314 p. : ill. *Notes:* Includes bibliographical references (p. 303-307) and index. [LC 92031531; ISN 0471536296; $29.95] HD57.7. R687 1993   2296

Running things: the art of making things happen. Philip B. Crosby. New York: McGraw-Hill, c1986. xiii, 253 p. *Notes:* Includes index. [LC 85023743; ISN 007014513X; $18.95] HD57.7. C76 1986   2297

So you want to be the boss?: a CEO's lessons in leadership. J.W. McLean. Englewood Cliffs, N.J.: Prentice Hall, 1990. xii, 167 p. : ill. *Notes:* Includes bibliographical references. [LC 89028370; ISN 0138154325; $13.95] HD57.7. M35 1990   2298

Tough-minded leadership. Joe D. Batten. New York, NY: AMACOM, c1989. xviii, 236 p. : ill. *Notes:* Includes index. Bibliography: p. 227-229. [LC 88048023; ISN 0814459013; $17.95] HD57.7. B38 1989   2299

Vision, values, and courage: leadership for quality management. Neil H. Snyder, James J.Dowd, Jr., Dianne Morse Houghton. New York: Toronto: New York: Free Press; Maxwell Macmillan Canada; Maxwell Macmillan International, c1994. xiv, 270 p. : ill. *Notes:* Spine title: Vision, values & courage. Includes bibliographical references (p. 246-259) and index. [LC 93023935; ISN 0029297559; $29.95] HD57.7. S69 1994   +2300

Why leaders can't lead: the unconscious conspiracy continues. Warren Bennis. 1st ed. San Francisco: Jossey-Bass Publishers, 1989. xix, 169 p. *Notes:* Includes index. [LC 88046091; ISN 1555421520; $19.95] HM141. B434 1989   2301

Why work: leading the new generation. Michael Maccoby. New York: Simon and Schuster, c1988. 270 p. *Notes:* Includes index. Bibliography: p. 255-259. [LC 87031432; ISN 067147281X] HD57.7. M33 1988   2302

Women and power: how far can we go? Nancy Kline. London: BBC Books, 1993. 182 p. *Notes:* Includes bibliographical references (p. 179-180) and index.; ISN 0563364491] HD57.7. K54 1993   2303

The working leader: the triumph of high performance over conventional management principles. Leonard R. Sayles; foreword by Henry Mintzberg. New York: Toronto: New York: Free Press; Maxwell Macmillan Canada; Maxwell Macmillan International, c1993. viii, 277 p. *Notes:* Includes bibliographical references (p. 255-267) and index. [LC 92034089; ISN 0029277558; $24.95]
HD57.7. S3 1993   2304

LEASE OR BUY DECISIONS

Lease or buy?: principles for sound decision making. James S. Schallheim. Boston: Harvard Business School Press, c1994. x, 215 p. : ill. *Notes:* Includes bibliographical references and index. [LC 94010236; ISN 0875845584; $35.00]
HD39.4. S3 1994   +2305

Lease or purchase: theory and practice. Arthur C.C. Herst. Boston: Hingham, MA, U.S.A.: Kluwer-Nijhoff; Distributors for North America, Kluwer Academic Publishers, c1984. vii, 289 p. (Dimensions of international business) *Notes:* Includes indexes. Bibliography: p. 271-282. [LC 84000938; ISN 0898381266]
HD39.5. H47 1984   2306

LEGAL INVESTMENTS

Modern investment mangaement and the prudent man rule. Bevis Longstreth. New York: Oxford University Press, 1986. xv, 275 p. : ill. *Notes:* Includes bibliographical references and index. [LC 86016294; ISN 0195041968; $34.50]
KF1083. L66 1986   2307

LEHMAN BROTHERS

Greed and glory on Wall Street: the fall of the house of Lehman. Ken Auletta. Warner books ed. New York, NY: Warner Books, 1987, c1986. xi, 260 p., [16] p. of plates: ports. *Notes:* Reprint. Originally published: New York: Random House, 1986. Includes bibliographical references and index. [LC 86023416; ISN 0446384062]
HG5129.N5 A8 1987   2308

LEISURE

The overworked American: the unexpected decline of leisure. Juliet B. Schor. New York, N.Y.: BasicBooks, c1991. xvii, 247 p. : ill. *Notes:* Includes bibliographical references (p. 219-234) and index. [LC 91070057; ISN 0465054331; $21.00]
HD4904.6. S36 1991   2309

LEISURE INDUSTRY

For fun and profit: the transformation of leisure into consumption. edited by Richard Butsch. Philadelphia: Temple University Press, 1990. viii, 259 p. *Notes:* Includes bibliographical references. *Contents:* Introduction: leisure and hegemony in America / Richard Butsch—Pessimism versus populism: the problematic politics of popular culture / John Clarke—Pacifying American theatrical audiences, 1820-1900 / Bruce A. McConachie—"Adopted by all the leading clubs": sporting goods and the shaping of leisure, 1800-1900 / Stephen Hardy—Commercial leisure and the 'woman question' / Kathy Peiss—Big time, small time, all around the town: New York vaudeville in the early twentieth century / Robert W. Snyder—The movie palace comes to America's cities / Douglas Gomery—The United States Forest Service and the postwar commodification of outdoor recreation / L. Sue Greer—A historical comparison of children's use of leisure time / Ellen Wartella and Sharon Mazzarella. *Contents:* "How does it feel when you've got no food?": the past as present in popular music / George Lipsitz—Home video and corporate plans: capital's limited power to manipulate leisure / Richard Butsch. [LC 89027699; ISN 0877226768]
GV188.3.U6 F67 1990   +2310

LEVERAGED BUYOUTS

The vulture investors: the winners and losers of the great American bankruptcy feeding frenzy. Hilary Rosenberg. 1st ed. New York, NY: HarperBusiness, c1992. xiii, 402 p. *Notes:* Includes bibliographical references (p. 345-393) and index. [LC 91058511; ISN 0887305555; $22.00]
HG4028.M4 R67 1992   2311

LEVINE, DENNIS

Inside out: an insider's account of Wall Street. Dennis B. Levine, with William Hoffer. New York: G.P. Putnam's Sons, c1991. 431 p., [8] p. of plates: ill. *Notes:* Includes index. [LC 91003149; ISN 039913655X; $22.95 ($29.95 Can.)]
HG2463.L48 A3 1991   2312

Levine & Co.: Wall Street's insider trading scandal. Douglas Frantz. 1st ed. New York: Holt, c1987. x, 370 p. : ill. *Notes:* "Author's notes": p. 353-359. Includes index. [LC 87008521; ISN 0805004572]
HG2463.L48 F72 1987   2313

LEWIS, MICHAEL

Liar's poker: rising through the wreckage on Wall Street. Michael Lewis. New York: Norton, c1989. 249 p. [LC 89030819; ISN 0393027503; $18.95]
HG4928.5. L48 1989   2314

LEWIS, REGINALD F

"Why should white guys have all the fun?": how Reginald Lewis created a billion-dollar business empire. Reginald F. Lewis and Blair S. Walker. New York: Wiley, 1994, c1995. xvii, 318 p., [16] p. of plates: ill. *Notes:* Includes index. [LC 94017864; ISN 0471042277]
HC102.5.L493 A3 1994   +2315

LINOWITZ, SOL M

The making of a public man: a memoir. by Sol M. Linowitz. 1st ed. Boston: Little, Brown, c1985. xii, 258 p. *Notes:* Includes index. [LC 85015899; ISN 0316526894]
KF373.L533 L56 1985   2316

LITTLE, ROYAL

How to lose $100,000,000 and other valuable advice. Royal Little. 1st ed. Boston: Little, Brown, c1979. xvii, 334 p. : ill. *Notes:* Includes index. [LC 79011628; ISN 0316527866]
HG172.L54 A34   2317

LLOYD'S (FIRM)

Nightmare on Lime Street: whatever happened to Lloyd's of London? Cathy Gunn. London: Smith Gryphon, 1992. vii, 214 p. *Notes:* Includes index. [LC 93024160; ISN 185685017X]
HG8039. G86 1992   +2318

LOANS, FOREIGN

Country risk: assessment and monitoring. Thomas E. Krayenbuehl. Lexington, Mass.: Lexington Books, 1985. x, 180 p. : ill. *Notes:* Includes index. Bibliography: p. 169-172. [LC 85006955; ISN 0669109584]
HG3891.5. K73 1985   2319

Passing the buck: banks, governments, and Third World debt. Philip A. Wellons. Boston, Mass.: Harvard Business School Press, c1987. xiv, 342 p. : ill. *Notes:* Includes bibliographical references and index. [LC 86019508; ISN 0875841465]
HG3891.5. W46 1987   2320

Selling money. by S.C. Gwynne. 1st ed. New York: Weidenfeld & Nicolson, c1986. 183 p. *Notes:* Bibliography: p. 181-182. [LC 86009143; ISN 1555840051; $17.95]
HG3891.5. G98 1986   2321

LOBBYISTS

The lobbyists: how influence peddlers get their way in Washington. Jeffrey H. Birnbaum. 1st ed. New York: Times Books, c1992. xv, 334 p. *Notes:* Includes bibliographical references (p. 305-308) and indexes. [LC 92053673; ISN 0812920864; $24.00 ($31.50 Can.)] JK1118. B47 1992   2322

LOCAL AREA NETWORKS (COMPUTER NETWORKS)

Networking the enterprise: how to build client/server systems that work. Richard H. Baker. New York: McGraw-Hill, c1994. xviii, 381 p. : ill. *Notes:* Includes bibliographical references (p. 333-369) and index. [LC 93002617; ISN 0070050899; $40.00] TK5105.7. B355 1994   +2323

LOCKHEED ADVANCED DEVELOPMENT COMPANY

Skunk Works: a personal memoir of my years at Lockheed. Ben R. Rich and Leo Janos. 1st ed. Boston: Little, Brown, c1994. x, 370 p., [8] p. of plates: ill. *Notes:* Includes index. [LC 94008732; ISN 0316743305; $24.95] TL565. R53 1994   +2324

LOGGING

Never under the table: a story of British Columbia's forests and government mismanagement. Joe Garner. Nanaimo, B.C.: Cinnabar Press, 1991. 274 p. : ill. [LC 92013196; ISN 0969134355; $14.95] SD538.3.C2 G37 1991   2325

LOGIC

Fuzzy thinking: the new science of fuzzy logic. Bart Kosko. 1st ed. New York: Hyperion, c1993. xvi, 318 p. : ill. *Notes:* Includes bibliographical references (p. 299-308) and index. [LC 92042019; ISN 1562828398; $24.95] BC108. K59 1993   2326

LONG ISLAND LIGHTING COMPANY

Power crazy. by Karl Grossman. 1st Grove Press ed. New York, N.Y.: Grove Press, 1986. xx, 372 p. : ill. *Notes:* Includes bibliographies and index. [LC 86003159; ISN 0394554612; ISN 0394622227; $17.95 ($25.95 Can.); $10.95] HD9685.U7 L664 1986   2327

LOUIS VUITTON MOET-HENNESSY (FIRM)

Kings on the catwalk: the Louis Vuitton and Moët-Hennessy affair. Hugh Sebag-Montefiore. London: Chapmans, 1992. 275 p. *Notes:* Includes bibliographical references (p. 258-263) and index.; ISN 1855925257; £9.99] HD9940.F84 L67 1992   2328

LUDWIG, DANIEL KEITH

The invisible billionaire, Daniel Ludwig. by Jerry Shields. Boston: Houghton Mifflin, c1986. xii, 401 p. : maps *Notes:* Maps on lining papers. Includes index. Bibliography included in "Sources" and 'Notes": p. [367]-391. [LC 86007519; ISN 0395354021; $19.95] HE569.L84 S55 1986   2329

MACINTOSH (COMPUTER)

Insanely great: the life and times of Macintosh, the computer that changed everything. Steven Levy. New York: Viking, 1994. x, 292 p. *Notes:* Includes bibliographical references (p. [289]-292). [LC 93030495; ISN 0670852449; $20.95 ($25.99 Canada)] QA76.8.M3 L487 1994   +2330

MACROECONOMICS

The global economy: from meso to macroeconomics. Stuart Holland. New York: St. Martin's Press, c1987. xiv, 443 p. : ill. *Notes:* Includes index. Bibliography: p. [424]-434. [LC 87020566; ISN 031201323X; $30.00 (est.)] HB172.5. H655 1987 2331

Introduction to macroeconomics. Stanley Fischer, Rudiger Dornbusch, Richard Schmalensee. 2nd ed. New York: McGraw-Hill, c1988. xxvii, 460 p. : col. ill. *Notes:* Includes bibliographical references and index. [LC 87029667; ISN 0070210101; $22.95] HB172.5. F52 1988 2332

Macroeconomic decision making in the world economy. Michael G. Rukstad. 3rd ed. Fort Worth: Dryden Press, c1992. ix, 708 p. : ill. *Notes:* Includes bibliographical references and index. [LC 91028950; ISN 0030747333] HB172.5. R85 1992 2333

Macroeconomics. Robert J. Barro. 4th ed. New York: John Wiley & Sons, Inc., c1993. xxi, 599, 14 p. : ill.; 1 MacroView diskette. *Notes:* "MacroView by Tim Krochuk to accompany Macroeconomics 4/E"—Diskette. Includes bibliographical references (p. 575-586) and indexes.; ISN 0471575437; $60.00] HB172.5. B36 1993 2334

Macroeconomics. Robert J. Gordon. 4th ed. Boston: Little, Brown, c1987. xxv, 613 p. : ill. (some col.) *Notes:* Includes bibliographical references and index. [LC 86019983; ISN 0316321419] HB172.5. G67 1987 2335

Macroeconomics: analysis and policy. Lloyd G. Reynolds. 6th ed. Homewood, Ill.: Irwin, 1988. xvii, 471 p. : ill. (some col.) (Irwin publications in economics) *Notes:* Includes bibliographical references and index. [LC 87081706; ISN 0256059128] HB172.5. R49 1988 2336

Macroeconomics: concepts, theories, and policies. Thomas F. Dernburg. 7th ed. New York: McGraw-Hill, c1985. xii, 490 p. : ill. *Notes:* Includes bibliographies and index. [LC 84019474; ISN 007016536X; $26.95] HB172.5. D47 1985 2337

Macroeconomics for management. Mary Louise Hatten. 2nd ed. Englewood Cliffs, N.J.: Prentice-Hall, c1986. xiv, 466 p. : ill. *Notes:* Includes index. Bibliography: p. 456-462. [LC 85019104; ISN 0135424321] HB172.5. H37 1986 2338

Macroeconomics in the global economy. Jeffrey D. Sachs, Felipe Larrain B. Englewood Cliffs, N.J.: Prentice Hall, c1993. xx, 778 p. : ill. *Notes:* Errata booklet (8 p.) enclosed. Includes bibliographical references and index. [LC 91044277; ISN 0135442060] HB172.5. S23 1993 2339

Macroeconomics: theory, performance, and policy. Robert E. Hall, John B. Taylor. 2nd ed. New York: Norton, c1988, 1986. xxiii, 566 p. : ill. *Notes:* Includes bibliographical references and index. [LC 88001788; ISN 039395630X] HB172.5. H35 1988 2340

Principles of economics: macro. Willis L. Peterson. 7th ed. Homewood, Ill.: Irwin, 1989. xi, 331 p. : ill. *Notes:* Includes bibliographical references and index. [LC 88000799; ISN 0256067953; $16.95] HB172.5. P455 1989 2341

Principles of macroeconomics. Edwin Mansfield. 6th ed. New York: Norton, c1989. xiii, 506, 46 p. : ill. *Notes:* Includes bibliographical references. [LC 88011903; ISN 0393957098; $25.95] HB172.5. M36 1989 2342

Principles of macroeconomics: readings, issues, and cases. edited by Edwin Mansfield. 3rd ed. New York: Norton, 1980. vii, 325 p. *Notes:* Companion volume to the 3rd edition of Edwin Mansfield's Principles of macroeconomics. *Contents:* Energy future / Robert Stobaugh and Daniel Yergin.; ISN 0393951200] HB171.5. M2714 1980 suppl. 2343

MACY'S (FIRM)

Macy's for sale. Isadore Barmash. 1st ed. New York: Weidenfeld & Nicolson, c1989. ix, 172, [8] p. of plates: ill. *Notes:* Includes index. [LC 88029408; ISN 1555841392; $19.95] HF5465.U6 M243 1989 2344

MAIL-ORDER BUSINESS

Building a mail order business: a complete manual for success. William A. Cohen. 3rd ed. New York: Wiley, c1991. xviii, 584 p. : ill. *Notes:* Includes index. [LC 90048556; ISN 0471520829; $34.95] HF5466. C56 1991 2345

Building a mail order business: a complete manual for success. William A. Cohen. 2nd ed. New York: Wiley, c1985. xx, 565 p. : ill. *Notes:* Includes index. [LC 85217562; ISN 0471810622; $19.95] HF5466. C56 1985 2346

How to start and operate a mail-order business. Julian L. Simon; with contributions by Paul Bringe... et al. 4th ed. New York: McGraw-Hill, c1987. xxii, 547 p. : ill. *Notes:* Includes index. Bibliography: p. 519-523. [LC 86010508; ISN 0070575312; $29.95]   HF5466. S54 1987   2347

Money in your mailbox: how to start and operate a successful mail-order business. L. Perry Wilbur. 2nd ed. New York: Wiley, c1993. xiv, 240 p. : ill. *Notes:* Includes bibliographical references (p. 235) and index. [LC 92013550; ISN 0471573302; $12.95]   HF5466. W48 1993   +2348

MALAYSIA—COMMERCE

Primary commodity exports and economic development: theory, evidence, and a study of Malaysia. John T. Thoburn. London; New York: Wiley, c1977. xvi, 310 p. *Notes:* Includes indexes. Bibliography: p. [287]-302. [LC 76026337; ISN 0471994413]   HF3800.6.Z5 T48   +2349

MALCOLM BALDRIGE NATIONAL QUALITY AWARD

The Baldrige quality system: the do-it-yourself way to transform your business. Stephen George. New York: J. Wiley, c1992. xii, 308 p. : ill. *Notes:* Includes index. [LC 92008636; ISN 0471557986; $29.95]   HD62.15. G46 1992   2350

MAN

One earth, one future: our changing global environment. by Cheryl Simon Silver with Ruth S. DeFries for the National Academy of Sciences. Washington, D.C.: National Academy Press, c1990. xiii, 196 p. *Notes:* Includes bibliographical references (p. 161-162). [LC 90005939; ISN 0309041414; $14.95]   GF75. S55 1990   2351

MANAGEMENT

AMA management handbook. John J. Hampton, editor. 3rd ed. New York: Amacom, c1994. 1 v. (various pagings): ill. *Notes:* Includes bibliographical references and index. *Contents:* General management / Don E. Marsh—Marketing; Sales and distribution / Noel Capon—Human resources / Michael Z. Sincoff—Accounting / Athar Murtuza—Finance / Gordon Cummings—Research and technology / Mark D. Dibner—Manufacturing / Patricia Turnbaugh—Information systems and technology / Norbert J. Kubilus—Purchasing / Don Bohl and Bobby Zachariah—Corporate relations / John D. Bergen—Risk management and insurance / Sandra Gustavson—Entrepreneurship and small business / Donald A. Straits—International business / Jean Kelly—Service industries / Rachael I. Vecchiotti—Public-sector and nonprofit management / Herrington J. Bryce. [LC 94006802; ISN 0814401058]   HD31. A418 1994   +2352

America's management challenge: capitalizing on change. William B. Miller. Radnor, Pa.: Chilton Book Co., c1983. xi, 334 p. : ill. *Notes:* Includes index. Bibliography: p. 324-326. [LC 83070785; ISN 0801973953; $16.50]   HD70.U5 M43 1983   2353

Beyond the hype: rediscovering the essence of management. Robert G. Eccles and Nitin Nohria with James D. Berkley. Boston, Mass.: Harvard Business School, 1992. xiv, 278 p. *Notes:* Includes bibliographical references and index. [LC 92018707; ISN 087584331X; $22.95]   HD31. E27 1992   2354

Beyond the quick fix: managing five tracks to organizational success. Ralph H. Kilmann. 1st ed. San Francisco: Jossey-Bass, 1984. xxii, 300 p. (A Joint publication in the Jossey-Bass management series and the Jossey-Bass social and behavioral science series) *Notes:* Includes index. Bibliography: p. 277-290. [LC 84047988; ISN 0875896200]   HD31. K467 1984   2355

Business classics: fifteen key concepts for managerial success. Cambridge, Mass.: Harvard Business Review, 1986. 181 p. : ill. *Notes:* Cover title. Reprints from the Harvard Business Review. Includes bibliographical references.]   HD30. B87 1986   2356

The business of business: managing with style. by Robert Heller. 1st ed. New York: Harcourt Brace Jovanovich, c1981. xi, 307 p. *Notes:* Includes index. [LC 81047305; ISN 0151149828]   HD31. H442   2357

Business organisation. M. Richards. 3rd ed. Manchester England: NCC Blackwell, 1993. 225 p. : ill. *Notes:* Includes bibliographical references and index. " . . . An introduction to the organisation of business, particularly those aspects which are relevant to computing, data processing and the use of information technology. Detailed consideration is given to the organisational structures of large and small units, in both the public and private sectors. Topics covered include personnel matters, marketing and sales, production, finance and administration."—Back cover. [LC 93059669; ISN 1855542048; £9.99: Formerly CIP] HD31. R52 1993 +2358

Business research methods. William G. Zikmund. 3rd ed. Chicago: Dryden Press, c1991. xxv, 742 p. : ill. *Notes:* Includes bibliographical references. [LC 90034781; ISN 0030330785] HD30.4. Z54 1991 2359

Centralization and decentralization; which, when and how much. Boston Harvard College, 1966-1972. 162 p. illus. *Notes:* Cover title. Reprints from Harvard Business Review.] HD2741. H3 1966 +2360

Computer concepts for managers. G. Gordon Schulmeyer. New York, N.Y.: Van Nostrand Reinhold Co., c1985. xv, 285 p., [2] folded leaves of plates: ill. *Notes:* Includes bibliographies and index. [LC 84003512; ISN 0442280637] HD30.2. S38 1985 2361

Computer essays for management. Jerome Kanter. Englewood Cliffs, N.J.: Prentice-Hall, 1987, c1986. xi, 109 p. [LC 86030651; ISN 0131659944; $21.95] HD30.2. K36 1987 2362

The corporation of the 1990s: information technology and organizational transformation. edited by Michael S. Scott Morton. New York: Oxford University Press, 1991. xii, 331 p. : ill. *Notes:* Includes bibliographical references and index. [LC 90037886; ISN 0195063589; $24.95] HD30.2. C66 1991 2363

Decentralization: managerial ambiguity by design. by Richard F. Vancil; with the assistance of Lee E. Buddrus. Homewood, Ill.: Dow Jones-Irwin, c1979. xiv, 393 p. : ill. *Notes:* "A research study and report prepared for the Financial Executives Research Foundation." Includes bibliographical references and index. [LC 79051782; ISN 0510586322] HD38. V28 2364

Decision support and expert systems: management support systems. Efraim Turban. 3rd ed. New York: Toronto: New York: Macmillan; Maxwell Macmillan Canada; Maxwell Macmillan International, c1993. 1 v. (various pagings): ill., map *Notes:* Includes bibliographical references and index. [LC 92039523; ISN 0024216917] HD30.2. T87 1993 2365

Decision support systems: putting theory into practice. edited by Ralph H. Sprague, Jr., Hugh J. Watson. 2nd ed. Englewood Cliffs, N.J.: Prentice Hall, c1989. xi, 419 p. : ill. *Notes:* Includes index. Bibliography: p. 403-413. [LC 89003970; ISN 0131990357; $51.40] HD30.23. D393 1989 2366

Designing organizations. Daniel Robey, Carol A. Sales. 4th ed. Burr Ridge, Ill.: Irwin, c1994. xviii, 536 p. : ill. *Notes:* Includes bibliographical references and index. [LC 93003727; ISN 0256116997] HD31. R58 1994 +2367

Educating managers: executive effectiveness through liberal learning. Joseph S. Johnston, Jr. . . . et al.; foreword by Thomas H. Wyman. 1st ed. San Francisco: Jossey-Bass, 1986. xxvi, 242 p. : ill. (The Jossey-Bass higher education series) (The Jossey-Bass management series) *Notes:* Includes index. Bibliography: p. 219-231. *Contents:* Conversations with five managers / Alan M. Kantrow, Stanley T. Burns. [LC 86001441; ISN 0875896847] HD30.42.U5 E39 1986 2368

The EIS book: information systems for top managers. by Alan Paller with Richard Laska. Homewood, IL: Dow Jones-Irwin, c1990. viii, 217 p. : ill. (some col.) [LC 89029819; ISN 1556232446; $24.95] HD30.2. P355 1990 2369

Envisionary management: a guide for human resources professionals in management training and development. William P. Anthony, E. Nick Maddox, and Walter Wheatley, Jr. New York: Quorum Books, c1988. xii, 208 p. : ill. *Notes:* Includes index. Bibliography: p. [199]-204. [LC 87007373; ISN 0899302572] HD38. A526 1988 2370

Escape from management hell: 12 tales of horror, humor, and heroism. Robert D. Gilbreath. 1st ed. San Francisco: Berrett-Koehler, 1993. xiv, 161 p. : ill. [LC 93006596; ISN 1881052265; $19.95] HD31. G4953 1993 2371

The evolution of management thought. Daniel A. Wren. 4th ed. New York: Wiley, c1994. xii, 466 p. : ill. *Notes:* Includes bibliographical references (p. 443-447) and indexes. [LC 93014609; ISN 047159752X] HD30.5. W73 1994 +2372

The executive deskbook. Auren Uris. 3rd ed. New York: Van Nostrand Reinhold Co., c1988. xiv, 427 p. : ill. *Notes:* Includes index. [LC 87010597; ISN 0442287909] HD31. U66 1988 2373

Executive support systems: the emergence of top management computer use. by John F. Rockart and David W. De Long. Homewood, Ill.: Dow Jones-Irwin, 1988. viii, 280 p. *Notes:* Includes index. Bibliography: p. 260-271. [LC 87072026; ISN 0870949551; $29.95] HD30.2. R63 1988 2374

The frontiers of management: where tomorrow's decisions are being shaped today. Peter F. Drucker. 1st ed. New York: Truman Talley Books, c1986. xi, 368 p. *Notes:* Includes index. [LC 86008004; ISN 0525244638] HD31. D7713 1986 2375

The future 500: creating tomorrow's organizations today. by Craig R. Hickman and Michael A. Silva. New York, N.Y.: New American Library, c1987. xiv, 274 p. *Notes:* "NAL books." Includes index. Bibliography: p. 264-267. [LC 87015204; ISN 0453005446] HD31. H4814 1987 2376

Future perfect. Stanley M. Davis. Reading, Mass.: Addison-Wesley, 1987. 243 p. : ill. *Notes:* Includes index. Bibliography: p. 229-[232] [LC 87018669; ISN 0201115131; $16.95] HD31. D325 1987 2377

General management: an analytical approach. Norman A. Berg. Homewood, Ill.: R.D. Irwin, Inc., 1984. xvii, 204 p. (The Irwin series in management and the behavioral sciences) *Notes:* "A substantial modification of the text portion of the eighth edition of Policy formulation and administration."—p. ix. Includes bibliographical references and index. [LC 83082964; ISN 0256029105] HD31. B392 2378

The Gower handbook of management. edited by Dennis Lock and Nigel Farrow. 2nd ed. Aldershot, Hants, England; Brookfield, Vt., U.S.A.: Gower Pub. Co., 1988. xl, 1244 p. : ill. *Notes:* Includes bibliographical references and index. [LC 87000144; ISN 0566026627; $90.00 (U.S.: est.)] HD31. G684 1988 2379

Great ideas in management: lessons from the founders and foundations of managerial practice. W. Jack Duncan. San Francisco: Jossey-Bass Publishers, 1989. xvii, 286 p. *Notes:* Includes index. Bibliography: p. 261-276. [LC 88042787; ISN 1555421229] HD30.5. D86 1989 2380

Handbook of business problem solving. Kenneth J. Albert, editor in chief. New York: McGraw-Hill, c1980. ca. 850 p. in various pagings: ill. *Notes:* Includes bibliographical references and index. [LC 79018680; ISN 0070007527; $24.95] HD31. H3125 2381

A handbook of management techniques. Michael Armstrong. New York: Nichols Pub. Co., 1986. 573 p. : ill. *Notes:* Includes bibliographies and index. [LC 86012764; ISN 0893972576; $54.50] HD31. A72 1986 2382

High-involvement management. Edward E. Lawler III. 1st ed. San Francisco, Calif.: Jossey-Bass, c1986. xvii, 252 p. (The Jossey-Bass management series) (The Jossey-Bass social and behavioral science series) *Notes:* Includes index. Bibliography: p. 235-241. [LC 85045909; ISN 0875896863] HD5650. L38 2383

How corporate truths become competitive traps: how to keep the things that "everyone knows are true" from becoming roadblocks to success. Eileen C. Shapiro. New York: Wiley, c1991. xii, 266 p. *Notes:* Includes bibliographical references (p. 235-256) and index. [LC 90023149; ISN 0471516430; $19.95] HD31. S432 1991 2384

How to manage. by more than 100 of the world's leading business experts; edited and compiled by Ray Wild. New York, N.Y.: Facts on File, c1985. 233 p. [LC 83016413; ISN 0816000263] HD31. H683 1985 2385

Information technology and the corporation of the 1990s: research studies. edited by Thomas J. Allen, Michael S. Scott Morton. New York: Oxford University Press, 1994. xii, 532 p. : ill. *Notes:* "Intended to accompany and support its companion, The corporation of the 1990s"—Pref. Includes bibliographical references and index. [LC 91046832; ISN 0195068068] HD30.2. I528 1994 +2386

The inner game of management: how to make the transition to a managerial role. Eric G. Flamholtz and Yvonne Randle. New York, NY: AMACOM, c1987. xiv, 225 p. *Notes:* Includes index. Bibliography: p. 212-220. [LC 87047705; ISN 081445367X] HD31. F538 1987 2387

Inspiring people at work: how to make participative management work for you. Thomas L. Quick. New York: Executive Enterprises, c1986. 214 p. [LC 85080671; ISN 088057402X] HD5650. Q52 1986 2388

Intuition and management: research and application. Daniel Cappon. Westport, Conn.: Quorum Books, 1994. x, 214 p. : ill. *Notes:* Spine title: Intuition & management. Includes bibliographical references (p. [205]-207) and index. [LC 94002993; ISN 0899308503] HD38. C343 1994 +2389

Joint management and employee participation: labor and management at the crossroads. Neal Herrick. 1st ed. San Francisco: Jossey-Bass, 1990. xxxi, 429 p. : ill. *Notes:* Includes bibliographical references (p. 403-414) and index. [LC 89026949; ISN 1555422381; $33.95] HD5660.U5 H46 1990 2390

Just-in-time: surviving by breaking tradition. Walter E. Goddard. Essex Junction, Vt.: Oliver Wight Limited, c1986. x, 199 p. : ill. *Notes:* Includes index. Bibliography: p. 191-193.; ISN 0939246074; $37.00] HD31. G565 2391

Leadership and the one minute manager: increasing effectiveness through situational leadership. Kenneth H. Blanchard, Patricia Zigarmi, Drea Zigarmi. 1st ed. New York: Morrow, c1985. 111 p. [LC 84062389; ISN 0688039693; $15.00] HD31. B526 2392

The learning edge: how smart managers and smart companies stay ahead. Calhoun W. Wick, Lu Stanton León. New York: McGraw-Hill, c1993. xvi, 232 p. : ill. *Notes:* Includes bibliographical references and index. [LC 92035218; ISN 0070700826; $22.95] HD30.4. W53 1993 2393

Management & organization. Andrew J. DuBrin, R. Duane Ireland, J. Clifton Williams. Cincinnati: South-Western Pub. Co., c1989. xvi, 682 p. : ill. (some col.) *Notes:* Rev. ed. of: Management & organization / J. Clifton Williams, Andrew J. DuBrin, Henry L. Sisk. 5th ed. c1985. Includes bibliographical references and index. [LC 87072806; ISN 0538074515; $36.88]   HD31. S57 1989   2394

Management. Harold Koontz, Heinz Weihrich. 9th ed. New York: McGraw-Hill, c1988. xxix, 687 p. : ill. (some col.) (McGraw-Hill series in management) *Notes:* Includes bibliographies and indexes. [LC 87021519; ISN 0070355525; $39.95]   HD31. K6 1988   2395

Management. James A.F. Stoner, R. Edward Freeman. 5th ed. Englewood Cliffs, N.J.: Prentice Hall, c1992. xxvii, 734 p. : ill. (some col.) *Notes:* Includes bibliographical references and indexes. [LC 91030891; ISN 0135443059]   HD31. S6963 1992   2396

The management challenge: Japanese views. edited by Lester C. Thurow. Cambridge, Mass.: MIT Press, c1985. xi, 237 p. *Notes:* Includes index. [LC 84028881; ISN 0262200538]   HD70.J3 M264 1985   2397

Management for productivity. John R. Schermerhorn, Jr. 4th ed. New York: Wiley, 1992, c1993. xxxii, [808] p. in various pagings: col. ill. *Notes:* Includes bibliographical references and indexes. [LC 92004678; ISN 0471524972]   HD31. S3326 1992   2398

Management for productivity. John R. Schermerhorn, Jr. 3rd ed. New York, N.Y.: Wiley, c1989. xxxv, 715, 22 p. : ill. (chiefly col.) *Notes:* Includes bibliographies and indexes. [LC 88027879; ISN 0471631159; $49.95]   HD31. S3326 1989   2399

Management gurus: what makes them and how to become one. Andrzej A. Huczynski. London; New York: Routledge, 1993. 331 p. : ill. *Notes:* Include bibliographical references (p. [297]-316) and index. [LC 93135553; ISN 0415022444; $27.50]   HD31. H755 1993   +2400

Management in France. Jean-Louis Barsoux and Peter Lawrence. London: Cassell, c1990. xiii, 239 p. : ill. *Notes:* Includes bibliographical references (p. 220-228). [LC 89043096; ISN 0304316776; $37.95]   HD70.F8 B37 1990   2401

Management in small doses. Russell L. Ackoff. New York: Wiley, c1986. xiii, 208 p. : ill. [LC 86007835; ISN 0471848220; $17.95]   HD31. A283 1986   2402

Management in the third wave. H. Alan Raymond. Glenview, Ill.: Scott, Foresman, c1986. xii, 255 p. : ill. *Notes:* Includes index. Bibliography: p. 241-244. [LC 85002333; ISN 0673180352]   HD31. R39 1986   2403

Management in Western Europe: society, culture and organization in twelve nations. editor, David J. Hickson. Berlin; New York: Walter de Gruyter, 1993. xiv, 288 p. *Notes:* Includes bibliographical references and index. [LC 92042234; ISN 0899257690]   HD70.E8 M36 1993   +2404

Management mistakes & successes. Robert F. Hartley. 4th ed. New York: Wiley, c1994. viii, 419 p. : ill. *Notes:* Includes bibliographical references. [LC 93042718; ISN 0471000876; $27.95]   HD38. H3488 1994   +2405

The management of organizations: strategy, structure, behavior. Jay B. Barney, Ricky W. Griffin. Boston: Houghton Mifflin Co., c1992. xxi, 820 p. : ill. (some col.) *Notes:* Includes bibliographical references and indexes. [LC 91072002; ISN 0395574277]   HD31. B3684 1992   2406

Management policy and strategy: text, readings, and cases. George A. Steiner, John B. Miner, Edmund R. Gray. 3rd ed. New York: Macmillan, c1986. xii, 963 p. : ill. *Notes:* Text portion... published separately with minor alterations under the complete title: Management policy and strategy. Includes index. Bibliography: p. 941-963. [LC 85010498; ISN 0024167207]   HD31. M2933 1986   2407

The managerial grid III. Robert R. Blake, Jane S. Mouton. Houston: Gulf Pub. Co., Book Division, c1985. xi, 244 p. : ill. *Notes:* Rev. ed. of: The new managerial grid. c1978. "A new look at the classic that has boosted productivity and profits for thousands of corporations worldwide." Includes index. Bibliography: p. 232-234. [LC 84010875; ISN 0872014703]   HD31. B523 1985   2408

Managerial literacy: what today's managers must know to succeed. Gary Shaw, Jack Weber. Homewood, Ill.: Dow Jones-Irwin, c1990. xvi, 198 p. *Notes:* Includes bibliographical references. [LC 89017211; ISN 1556232624; $19.95]   HD30.15. S48 1990   2409

The managerial mystique: restoring leadership in business. Abraham Zaleznik. 1st ed. New York: Harper & Row, c1989. x, 307 p. *Notes:* "An Edward Burlingame book." [LC 88039086; ISN 0060161051; $19.95]   HD38. Z315 1989   2410

Managerialism: the emergence of a new ideology. Willard F. Enteman. Madison, Wis.: University of Wisconsin Press, c1993. xiv, 258 p. *Notes:* Includes bibliographical references (p. 227-251) and index. [LC 93007444; ISN 0299139247]   HD31. E654 1993   +2411

The manager's desk reference. Cynthia Berryman-Fink. New York, NY: AMACOM, American Management Association, c1989. ix, 371 p. *Notes:* Includes bibliographical references and index. [LC 88048035; ISN 0814459048; $24.95]   HD30.33. B47 1989   2412

Managing for the future: the 1990s and beyond. by Peter F. Drucker. New York, N.Y., U.S.A.: Dutton, c1992. xiii, 370 p. *Notes:* "Truman Talley books." Includes index. [LC 91031454; ISN 0525934146; $25.00] HD31. D7733 1992 2413

Managing in the age of change. edited by Roger A. Ritvo, Anne H. Litwin, Lee Butler. Burr Ridge, Ill.: Irwin Professional Pub., c1995. xxiv, 296 p : ill. *Notes:* Includes bibliographical references and index. [LC 94009331; ISN 0786303034] HD31. M29417 1995 +2414

Managing in the postmodern world: America's revolution against exploitation. David M. Boje, Robert F. Dennehy; with a special foreword by Stewart Clegg. Dubuque, Iowa: Kendall/Hunt Pub., c1993. xxxii, 349 p.: ill. *Notes:* Includes bibliographical references. [LC 92076055; ISN 0840381557] HD70.U5 B64 1993 +2415

Managing operations: a competence approach to supervisory management. Roger Cartwright...et al. Oxford, UK; Cambridge, Mass., USA: Blackwell, 1993. vi, 203 p. : ill. *Notes:* "NVQ/ SVQ level 3." Includes bibliographical references (p. [197]) and index. [LC 93031999; ISN 0631190112; $29.95] HD31. M29325 1993 +2416

Managing the corporate dream: restructuring for long-term success. William R. Torbert. Homewood, IL: Dow Jones-Irwin, c1987. xxi, 250 p. *Notes:* Includes bibliographies and index. [LC 86072274; ISN 0870949225] HD31. T63 2417

Managing with a conscience: how to improve performance through integrity, trust, and commitment. Frank K. Sonnenberg. New York: McGraw-Hill, 1993, c1994. xv, 261 p. : ill. *Notes:* Includes bibliographical references (p. 237-245) and index. [LC 93030795; ISN 0070596328; $22.95] HD30.3. S65 1994 +2418

Mary Parker Follett—prophet of management: a celebration of writings from the 1920s. edited by Pauline Graham; preface by Rosabeth Moss Kanter; introduction by Peter F. Drucker. Boston, Mass.: Harvard Business School Press, c1995. xix, 309 p. *Notes:* Includes index. [LC 94019675; ISN 0875845630; $29.95] HD31. M3326 1995 +2419

MBA field studies: a guide for students and faculty. edited by E. Raymond Corey. Boston, Mass.: Harvard Business School Pub. Division, c1990. viii, 79 p. : ill. *Notes:* Includes bibliographical references. [LC 90037157; ISN 0875842518; $5.95] HD30.4. M465 1990 2420

MBA: management by Auerbach: management tips from the leader of one of America's most successful organizations. Red Auerbach with Ken Dooley. New York: Don Mills, Ont.: New York: Macmillan; Maxwell Macmillan Canada; Maxwell Macmillan International, c1991. xviii, 254 p. *Notes:* "A Wellington Press book." Includes index. [LC 91013061; ISN 0025044818; $19.95] HD31. A819 1991 2421

Milestones in management: an essential reader. edited by Henry M. Strage. Oxford; Cambridge, Mass.: Blackwell, 1992. xiv, 497 p. *Notes:* Includes bibliographical references and index. [LC 91027567; ISN 0631183590; $30.00] HD31. M4373 1992 2422

Mind of a manager, soul of a leader. Craig R. Hickman. New York: Wiley, c1990. xv, 287 p. *Notes:* Includes bibliographical references (p. 282-283) and index. [LC 89028494; ISN 0471617156; $37.95] HD31. H4815 1990 2423

Mintzberg on management: inside our strange world of organizations. Henry Mintzberg. New York: Free Press, c1988. x, 418 p. : ill. *Notes:* Includes bibliographical references and index. [LC 89001241; ISN 0029213711; $24.95] HD31. M456 1988 2424

The new manager's handbook. Brad Lee Thompson. Burr Ridge, Ill.: Irwin Professional Pub., c1994. xvi, 272 p. *Notes:* Includes index. [LC 94000143; ISN 0786302062; $13.95] HD38.15. T48 1994 +2425

The one minute manager. Kenneth Blanchard, Spencer Johnson. 1st Morrow ed. New York: Morrow, 1982. 111 p. : ill. *Notes:* Reprint. Originally published: 2nd ed. La Jolla, CA: Blanchard-Johnson, 1981. [LC 82008106; ISN 0688014291] HD31. B527 1982 2426

Orchestrating success: improve control of the business with sales & operations planning. Richard C. Ling and Walter E. Goddard. Essex Junction, VT.: Oliver Wight Limited Publications, Inc., c1988. x, 191 p. *Notes:* Includes index. [LC 88050483; ISN 0939246112] HD31. L45 1988 2427

Organizations and chaos: defining the methods of nonlinear management. H. Richard Priesmeyer. Westport, Conn.: Quorum Books, 1992. xiv, 253 p. : ill. *Notes:* Includes bibliographical references (p. [247]-249) and index. [LC 92007486; ISN 0899306306] HD31. P727 1992 2428

The paranoid corporation and 8 other ways your company can be crazy: advice from an organizational shrink. William A. Cohen, Nurit Cohen. New York: American Management Association, c1993. xi, 196 p. *Notes:* Includes bibliographical references and index. [LC 93024142; ISN 0814451292; $22.95] HD38. C573 1993 +2429

Participation works: business cases from around the world: an anthology of readings on participation in private companies. James P. Troxel, general editor. Alexandria, Va.: Miles River Press, c1993. xxi, 259 p. *Notes:* Includes bibliographical references (p. 249-259). [LC 93031681; ISN 0917917030; $29.95] HD5650. P3325 1993 +2430

Participative systems at work: creating quality and employment security. edited by Sidney P. Rubinstein; introduction by Bill Bradley. New York, N.Y.: Human Sciences Press, 1987. 180 p. : ill. *Notes:* Includes bibliographical references and index. [LC 86020044; ISN 0898853389]
 HD5660.U5 P38 1987 2431

Personality in industry: the human side of a Japanese enterprise. Hiroshi Tanaka. London: Pinter, 1988. xii, 269 p. : ill. *Notes:* Includes bibliographical references and index. [LC 87039608; ISN 0861879279; £20.00: CIP confirmed] HD70.J3 T36 1988 2432

Power in management. John P. Kotter. New York: AMACOM, c1979. 105 p. : ill. *Notes:* Includes bibliographical references and index. [LC 78031558; ISN 0814455077; $9.95] HD38. K68 2433

The power of tomorrow's management: using the vision-culture balance in organizations. Marc van der Erve. Oxford; Boston: Butterworth Heinemann, 1993. x, 219 p. : ill. *Notes:* Includes bibliographical references (p. [210]-216) and index. [LC 93184805; ISN 0750616423; $34.95]
 HD31. E78 1993 +2434

Principals and agents: the structure of business. edited by John W. Pratt and Richard J. Zeckhauser; contributors, Kenneth J. Arrow... et al. Boston, Mass.: Harvard Business School Press, c1985. x, 241 p. (Research colloquium / Harvard Business School) *Notes:* Proceedings from one of a series of conferences held at the Harvard Business School in 1984. Includes index. [LC 84029039; ISN 0875841643] HD29. P735 1985 2435

Quantitative concepts for management: decision making without algorithms. Gary D. Eppen, F.J. Gould, Charles Schmidt. 3rd ed. Englewood Cliffs, NJ: Prentice Hall, c1988. xxiv, 752 p. : ill. *Notes:* Includes index. [LC 88013128; ISN 013746777X; $32.00] HD30.25. E66 1988 2436

The quest for staff leadership. Geoffrey M. Bellman. Glenview, Ill.: Scott, Foresman, c1986. viii, 343 p. *Notes:* Bibliography: p. 339-341. [LC 85019603; ISN 0673181944; $18.95] HD31. B3785 1986 2437

Radical management: power politics and the pursuit of trust. Samuel A. Culbert, John J. McDonough. New York: London: Free Press; Collier Macmillan, c1985. xv, 234 p. *Notes:* Includes index. [LC 85010150; ISN 0029059402] HD31. C8 1985 2438

Readings in management. Phillip B. DuBose, editor. Englewood Cliffs, NJ: Prentice-Hall, c1988. viii, 343 p. : ill. *Notes:* Designed to be used in conjunction with Management, principles, and practices by David H. Holt. Includes bibliographies. [LC 87002301; ISN 0137551665; $12.95]
 HD31. R4175 1988 2439

Real managers. Fred Luthans, Richard M. Hodgetts, Stuart A. Rosenkrantz. Cambridge, Mass.: Ballinger, 1988. xvi, 192 p. : ill. *Notes:* Includes index. Bibliography: p. 179-183. [LC 87019080; ISN 0887301037] HD31. L865 1988 2440

Reframing organizations: artistry, choice, and leadership. Lee G. Bolman, Terrence E. Deal. 1st ed. San Francisco: Jossey-Bass, c1991. xxvi, 492 p. : ill. *Notes:* Includes bibliographical references and index. [LC 90046853; ISN 155542323X] HD31. B6135 1991 2441

Riding the waves of change: developing managerial competencies for a turbulent world. Gareth Morgan. 1st ed. San Francisco: Jossey-Bass Publishers, 1988. xvii, 213 p. *Notes:* Includes index. Bibliography: p. 201-208. [LC 87046337; ISN 1555420931; $19.95] HD31. M6288 1988 2442

The rise of managerial computing: the best of the Center for Information Systems Research, Sloan School of Management, Massachusetts Institute of Technology. edited by John F. Rockart and Christine V. Bullen. Homewood, Ill.: Dow Jones-Irwin, c1986. xxvii, 443 p. : ill. *Notes:* Includes bibliographies and index. [LC 85073006; ISN 0870947575] HD30.335. R57 1986 2443

The rise of the expert company: how visionary companies are using artifical intelligence to achieve higher productivity and profits. by Edward Feigenbaum, Pamela McCorduck, and H. Penny Nil. 1st ed. New York, N.Y.: Times Books, 1988. xiii, 322 p. *Notes:* "Expert systems catalog by Paul Harmon." [LC 87040588; ISN 0812917316; $18.95] HD30.2. F45 1988 2444

Second to none: how our smartest companies put people first. Charles Garfield. Homewood, Ill.: Business One Irwin, c1992. xiii, 454 p. : ill. *Notes:* Includes bibliographical references (p. 419-442) and indexes. [LC 91020224; ISN 1556233604; $22.95] HD5650. G327 1992 2445

Stealth management: "with shared goals they will hardly know you are leading them". Sheldon Miller. 1st ed. Tulsa, Okla.: Stealth Management Institute, c1993. 290 p. : ill. *Notes:* Includes bibliographical references (p. 283) and index. [LC 92090895; ISN 0963531603; $27.95]
 HD31. M452 1993 +2446

The strategic use of information technology. edited by Stuart E. Madnick. New York: Oxford University Press, 1987. xiii, 206 p. : ill. *Notes:* A selection of articles from the Sloan management review. Includes index. Bibliography: p. 189-195 [LC 87001606; ISN 0195050487]
 HD30.2. S79 1987 2447

Telecommunications for management. Charles T. Meadow, Albert S. Tedesco. New York: McGraw-Hill, c1985. xv, 379 p. : ill. (McGraw-Hill series in management information systems) *Notes:* Includes bibliographies and index. [LC 84004339; ISN 0070411980; $29.95] HD30.335. M43 1985 2448

To flourish among giants: creative management for mid-sized firms. Robert Lawrence Kuhn. New York: Wiley, c1985. xii, 494 p. : ill. *Notes:* Includes bibliographical references and index. [LC 84017233; ISN 047180911X; $19.95 (est.)] HD31. K73 1985 2449

Touchstones: ten new ideas revolutionizing business. William A. Band. New York: J. Wiley, c1994. xi, 306 p. : ill. *Notes:* Includes bibliographical references and index. [LC 94012182; ISN 0471310964] HD70.U5 B34 1994 +2450

Transformational management. George Kozmetsky Cambridge, Mass.: Ballinger Pub. Co., 1985. xviii, 185 p. : ill. *Notes:* Includes bibliographies and index. [LC 84024219; ISN 0887300162] HD31. K655 1985 2451

21st century management: keeping ahead of the Japanese and Chinese. Dan Waters. New York: Prentice Hall, 1991. xvi, 127 p. *Notes:* Includes index. [LC 92239147; ISN 0139323449] HD31. W352 1991 2452

The ultimate advantage: creating the high-involvement organization. Edward E. Lawler III. 1st ed. San Francisco, Calif.: Jossey-Bass, c1992. xvii, 371 p. *Notes:* Includes bibliographical references (p. 349-362) and index. [LC 91041095; ISN 1555424147; $29.95] HD5650. L354 1992 2453

Unconventional wisdom: twelve remarkable innovators tell how intuition can revolutionize decision making. Ron Schultz. 1st ed. New York, NY: HarperBusiness, c1994. x, 212 p. *Notes:* Includes bibliographical references (p. 207) and index. [LC 93036431; ISN 0887306519; $22.00 ($29.50 Canada)] HD38. S3674 1994 +2454

Unexpected Japan: why American business should return to its own traditional values and not imitate the Japanese. Donald R. Riccomini & Philip M. Rosenzweig. New York: Walker, 1985. iv, 132 p. *Notes:* Includes index. Bibliography: p. [129]-130. [LC 85007313; ISN 0802708587; $12.95] HD70.J3 R53 1985 2455

Waging business warfare: lessons from the military masters in achieving corporate superiority. David J. Rogers. 1st ed. New York: Scribner, c1987. x, 341 p. *Notes:* Includes index. Bibliography: p. 317-327. [LC 86031584; ISN 0684185962; $19.95] HD38. R5776 1987 2456

The Wall Street Journal on management 2: adding value through synergy. edited by David Asman. New York, N.Y., U.S.A.: Plume, c1990 (1991 printing) xiv, 256 p. *Notes:* Rev. ed. of: The Wall Street journal on managing. 1st ed. c1990. [LC 90027267; ISN 0452266254; $10.95 ($14.95 Can.)] HD31. W245 1991 2457

What's your game plan?: creating business strategies that work. Milton C. Lauenstein. Homewood, Ill.: Dow Jones-Irwin, 1986. viii, 232 p. *Notes:* Includes index. [LC 85071922; ISN 0870945939] HD30.28. L45 2458

The whole manager. Dennis P. Slevin. New York, NY: American Management Association, c1989. x, 422 p. : ill. *Notes:* Rev. ed. of: Executive survival manual. c1985. Includes index. Bibliography: p. 411-416. [LC 88048033; ISN 081445836X; $22.95] HD31. S5765 1989 2459

MANAGEMENT BUYOUTS

The insider buyout. by Donald R. Dubendorf and M. John Storey. 1st ed. Pownal, Vt.: Storey Commications, Inc., c1985. 267 p. *Notes:* Includes index. [LC 84052258; ISN 0882663879; $19.95] HD2746.5. D83 1985 2460

Leveraged management buyouts: causes and consequences. edited by Yakov Amihud. Homewood, Ill.: Dow Jones-Irwin, c1989. xiii, 268 p. : ill. *Notes:* Papers presented at a conference held at the Leonard N. Stern School of Business, New York University, on May 20, 1988, and sponsored by the Salomon Brothers Center for the Study of Financial Institutions. Includes bibliographies. [LC 89030699; ISN 155623208X; $42.50] HD2746.5. L53 1989 2461

MANAGEMENT BY OBJECTIVES

Executive skills, a management by objectives approach. compiled by George Odiorne, Heinz Weihrich, Jack Mendleson. Dubuque, Iowa: W. C. Brown Co., c1980. xiv, 319 p. : ill. *Notes:* Includes bibliographies. [LC 79054373; ISN 0697080374] HD38. E94 2462

The human side of management: management by intergration and self-control. George S. Odiorne. Lexington, Mass.: Lexington Books, in association with University Associates, Inc., San Diego, Calif., c1987. xiv, 236 p. *Notes:* Includes index. Bibliography: p. [221]-223. [LC 86046314; ISN 0669153508] HD30.65. O35 1987 2463

Management excellence: productivity through MBO. Heinz Weihrich. New York: McGraw-Hill, c1985. xx, 252 p. : ill. (McGraw-Hill series in management) *Notes:* Includes bibliographical references and index. [LC 84026130; ISN 0070690014; ISN 0070690022; $16.95 (est.)]
  HD30.65. W45 1985 2464

MBO updated: a handbook of practices and techniques for managing by objectives. Paul Mali. New York: Wiley, c1986. xii, 834 p. : ill. *Notes:* Includes bibliographies and index. "A Wiley - Interscience publication." [LC 85020381; ISN 0471829870; $49.95 (est.)] HD30.65. M35 1986 2465

MANAGEMENT GAMES

The management game. Ardis Burst and Leonard A. Schlesinger. New York, NY: Viking, 1987. 274 p. : ill. [LC 86040617; ISN 0670812250] HD30.26. B87 1987 2466

MANAGEMENT INFORMATION SYSTEMS

Computer-based information systems: a management approach. Donald W. Kroeber, Hugh J. Watson. 2nd ed. New York: London: Macmillan; Collier Macmillan, c1987. xv, 600 p. : ill. *Notes:* Includes bibliographies and index. [LC 85023711; ISN 0023668709] T58.6. K757 1987 2467

Corporate information systems management: text and cases. James I. Cash, Jr.. . . et al. 3rd ed. Homewood, IL: Irwin, 1992. xvi, 702 p. : ill. *Notes:* Includes bibliographical references (p. 676-679) and index. [LC 91044242; ISN 0256087059; $54.95] T58.6. C674 1992 2468

Corporate information systems management: the issues facing senior executives. F. Warren McFarlan, James L. McKenney. Homewood, Ill.: Richard D. Irwin, 1983. ix, 211 p. : ill. *Notes:* Includes index. [LC 82082122; $17.95] T58.6. M26 2469

Corporate information systems management: the issues facing senior executives. James I. Cash, Jr., F. Warren McFarlan, James L. McKenney. 2nd ed. Homewood, Ill.: Dow Jones-Irwin, c1988. x, 285 p. : ill. *Notes:* Includes index. Bibliography: p. 273-278. [LC 87072682; ISN 1556230842]
  T58.6. C3672 1988x 2470

Development effectiveness: strategies for IS organizational transition. by Vaughan Merlyn and John Parkinson; with Bob Phillips and Roy Youngman. New York: Wiley, c1994. xxi, 390 p. : ill. *Notes:* Includes bibliographical references and index. [LC 93006045; ISN 0471589543]
  HD30.213. M47 1994 +2471

Enterprise information technologies: designing the competitive company. Bruce Love. New York: Van Nostrand Reinhold, c1993. xvi, 255 p. : ill. *Notes:* Series statement from jacket. Includes bibliographical references (p. 237-248) and index. [LC 92040887; ISN 0442009550]
  HD30.3. L68 1993 +2472

Executive information systems: a guide for senior management and MIS professionals. Robert J. Thierauf. New York: Quorum Books, 1991. xix, 364 p. : ill. *Notes:* Includes bibliographical references and index. [LC 90045148; ISN 0899305989] T58.6. T48 1991 2473

Executive information systems: emergence, development, impact. edited by Hugh J. Watson, R. Kelly Rainer, George Houdeshel. New York: Wiley, c1992. ix, 357 p. : ill. *Notes:* Includes bibliographical references and index. [LC 91036471; ISN 0471555541] T58.6. E95 1992 +2474

Handbook of IS management. Robert E. Umbaugh, editor. 3rd ed. Boston: Auerbach Publishers, c1991. xvi, 824 p. : ill. *Notes:* Includes index.; ISN 0791309525; $125.00] T58.6. H33 1991 2475

Information management: the strategic dimension. edited by Michael Earl. Oxford Oxfordshire: New York: Clarendon Press; Oxford University Press, 1988. ix, 294 p. *Notes:* Papers from a conference jointly sponsored by the Oxford Institute of Information Management, Templeton College, Oxford and PA Computers and Telecommunications. Includes bibliographies and indexes. [LC 88006605; ISN 0198285922; $45.00 (U.S.)] T58.6. I47 1988 2476

Information systems concepts. Raymond McLeod, Jr. New York: Toronto: Macmillan Pub. Co.; Maxwell Macmillan Canada, c1994. xxi, 462 p. : col. ill. *Notes:* Includes index. [LC 93025603; ISN 0023794739; $34.00] T58.6. M25 1994 +2477

Information systems for accounting and management: concepts, applications, and technology. Joseph W. Wilkinson, Dan C. Kneer. Englewood Cliffs, N.J.: Prentice-Hall, c1987. x, 338 p. : ill. *Notes:* Includes bibliographies. [LC 86030644; ISN 0134644050] T58. W56 1987 2478

Information systems in management. James A. Senn. 4th ed. Belmont, CA: Wadsworth Pub. Co., 1990. xxx, 1 v. (various pagings): ill. *Notes:* Includes bibliographical references. [LC 90030512; ISN 0534102662; $53.00] T58.6. S42 1990 2479

The Information Systems Research Challenge: proceedings. edited by F. Warren McFarlan; contributors, Robert L. Ashenhurst... et al. Boston, Mass.: Harvard Business School Press, c1984. 420 p. : ill. Notes: "Harvard Business School, Research Colloquium."—cover. Includes bibliographical references.; ISN 0875841619]　　　　　　　　　　　　　　　　　　　HF5548.2. I53 1984　　2480

The information systems research challenge. Boston, Mass.: Harvard Business School, c1989- v. ill.; Notes: Vol. 1 cover title: The information systems resea[r]ch challenge. Includes bibliographical references. Contents: v. 1. Qualitative research methods / James I. Cash, Jr., Paul R. Lawrence, editors—v. 2. Experimental research methods / Izak Benbasat, editor—v. 3. Survey research methods / Kenneth L. Kraemer, editor. [LC 89027313; ISN 0875842305]　　T58.6. H367 1989　　2481

Information systems: theory and practice. John Burch, Gary Grudnitski. 4th ed. New York: Wiley, c1986. xiii, 674 p. : ill. Notes: Includes bibliographies and index. [LC 85026492; ISN 047183758X]　　　　　　　　　　　　　　　　　　　　　　　T58.6. B87 1986　　2482

Management information systems: a managerial end user perspective. James A. O'Brien. Homewood, IL: Irwin, c1990. xxxiv, 670 p. : ill. (chiefly col.) Notes: Includes bibliographical references. [LC 89015519; ISN 0256078629; $44.95]　　T58.6. O26 1990　　2483

Management information systems: a study of computer-based information systems. Raymond McLeod, Jr. 5th ed. New York: Toronto: Macmillan Pub. Co.; Maxwell Macmillan Canada, c1993. xxix, 815 p. : ill. (some col.) Notes: Includes bibliographical references (p. 773-774) and index. [LC 92041221; ISN 002379481X; $66.00]　　HD30.213. M38 1993　　+2484

Management information systems and organizational behavior. Pat-Anthony Federico; with the assistance of Kim E. Brun and Douglas B. McCalla. 2nd ed. New York: Praeger, 1985. ix, 221 p. Notes: Includes index. Bibliography: p. 191-221. [LC 85006497; ISN 0275900975; $37.95]　　　　　　　　　　　　　　　　　　　　　　　T58.6. F35 1985　　2485

Management information systems: conceptual foundations, structure, and development. Gordon B. Davis, Margrethe H. Olson. 2nd ed. New York: McGraw-Hill, c1985. ix, 693 p. : ill. (McGraw-Hill series in management information systems) Notes: Includes bibliographies and indexes. [LC 84012606; ISN 0070158282; $34.95]　　T58.6. D38 1985　　2486

Management information systems: the critical strategic resource. James C. Emery. New York: Oxford University Press, 1987. xvii, 341 p. : ill. (Wharton executive library) Notes: Includes bibliographies and indexes. [LC 87007922; ISN 0195043928]　　T58.6. E46 1987　　2487

The management of information systems. Gary W. Dickson, James C. Wetherbe. New York: McGraw-Hill, c1985. xviii, 493 p. : ill. (McGraw-Hill series in management information systems) Notes: Includes bibliographies and index. [LC 84000767; ISN 0070168253; $29.95]　　T58.6. D45 1985　　2488

Managing information technology in turbulent times. Louis Fried. New York: Wiley, c1995. xx, 339 p. : ill. Notes: Includes bibliographical references and index. "This book helps you anticipate and cope with major management issues facing CIOs [Chief Information Officers] in the coming years, including: the changing business and management role of the CIO, introducing new technology to the firm and anticipating its impact on business procedures, business process redesign, managing software projects, the impact of Object Technology on software management, outsourcing, protecting your company's information assets, keeping users satisfied"—Back cover. [LC 94016470; ISN 0471047422]　　T58.6. F75 1995　　+2489

MIS, concepts and design. Robert G. Murdick, with John C. Munson. 2nd ed. Englewood Cliffs, N.J.: Prentice-Hall, c1986. xii, 691 p. : ill. Notes: Includes bibliographies and index. [LC 85030089; ISN 0135863228]　　　　　　　　　　　　　　　T58.6. M88 1986　　2490

Object-oriented information systems: planning and implementation. David A. Taylor. New York: Wiley, c1992. xx, 357 p. : ill. Notes: Includes index. [LC 91038263; ISN 0471543640]　　　　　　　　　　　　　　　　　　　　　　　T58.6. T39 1992　　+2491

Strategic and operational planning for information systems. Wellesley, Mass.: QED Information Sciences, c1985. vi, 124 p. : ill. (The Chantico technical management series) Notes: Reprint. Originally published: Port Jefferson, N.Y.: Chantico Pub. Co. Includes bibliographies. [LC 85060179; ISN 0894351516]　　　　　　　　　　　　　　　　　　　　T58.6. S75 1985　　2492

Strategic information systems: a European perspective. edited by Claudio Ciborra, Tawfik Jelassi. Chichester England; New York: Wiley, c1994. xx, 242 p. : ill., map Notes: Includes bibliographical references and index. [LC 93008851; ISN 0471941077; $32.00]　　T58.6. S755 1994　　+2493

Strategic information systems: competition through information technologies. Seev Neumann. New York: Toronto: New York: Macmillan College Pub. Co.; Maxwell Macmillan Canada; Maxwell Macmillan International, c1994. xiv, 258 p. : ill. *Notes:* Includes bibliographical references and index. *Contents:* Introduction and overview—Strategic information systems are conventional information systems used in innovative ways—Strategic information systems frameworks—The impact of strategic information systems on industries, firms, and strategies—The impact of strategic information systems on the internal structure and processes of organization—The impact of information technology on strategic alliances—Global strategic information systems—Sustainability of information technology-based competitive advantage—Strategic information systems risks—Organizational requirements for introducing strategic information systems—Identifying strategic information systems opportunities—New technologies for strategic information systems. [LC 93017343; ISN 002386690X] HD30.213. N48 1994 +2494

Strategy and computers: information systems as competitive weapons. Charles Wiseman. Homewood, Il: Dow Jones-Irwin c1985. xii, 246 p. *Notes:* Includes bibliographies and index. [LC 85070567; ISN 0870945904; $25.00] HF5548.2. W4687 2495

The technology payoff: how to profit with empowered workers in the information age. Gerald M. Hoffman. Burr Ridge, Ill.: Irwin Professional Pub., c1994. xxiv, 261 p. : ill. *Notes:* Includes bibliographical references (p. 249-255) and indexes. [LC 93038369; ISN 155623838X; $25.00] HD30.213. H63 1994 +2496

Up and running: integrating information technology and the organization. Richard E. Walton. Boston, Mass.: Harvard Business School Press, c1989. xii, 231 p. : ill. *Notes:* Includes index. Bibliography: p. [219]-226. [LC 89035745; ISN 0875842186] T58.6. W345 1989 2497

MANAGEMENT SCIENCE

Computer simulation in management science. Michael Pidd. 3rd ed. Chichester; New York: Wiley, c1992. xix, 351 p. : ill. *Notes:* Includes bibliographical references and indexes. [LC 92004721; ISN 0471934623] T57.62. P53 1992 2498

Management science. Sang M. Lee, Laurence J. Moore, Bernard W. Taylor III. 2nd ed. Dubuque, Iowa: W.C. Brown, c1985. xvii, 910 p. : ill. *Notes:* Includes bibliographies and index. [LC 85070716; ISN 0697082903] HD30.23. L43 1985 2499

Optimization models for planning and allocation: text and cases in mathematical programming. Roy D. Shapiro. New York: Wiley, c1984. xiv, 650 p. : ill. *Notes:* Includes bibliographies and index. [LC 83021878; ISN 0471094684; $36.95 (est.)] T56.24. S53 1984 2500

Quantitative methods for business. David R. Anderson, Dennis J. Sweeney, Thomas A. Williams. 3rd ed. St. Paul: West Pub. Co., c1986. xxi, 751 p. : ill. (some col.) *Notes:* Includes index. Bibliography: p. 741-744. [LC 85020115; ISN 0314931473; $27.95] T56. A63 1986 2501

MANAGERIAL ACCOUNTING

Accounting & management: field study perspectives. edited by William J. Bruns, Jr., Robert S. Kaplan. Boston, Mass.: Harvard Business School Press, c1987. ix, 374 p. : ill. *Notes:* Proceedings of a colloquium held June 16-18, 1986, at the Harvard Business School. Includes bibliographies and index. [LC 87018373; ISN 0875841864] HF5657.4. A25 1987 2502

Accounting, a management approach. Gordon Shillinglaw, Philip E. Meyer. 8th ed. Homewood, Ill.: Irwin, 1986. xxi, 1058 p. : ill. (The Robert N. Anthony/Willard J. Graham series in accounting) *Notes:* Includes index. [LC 85081222; ISN 0256033277] HF5635. S55288 1986 2503

Accounting for management control. Clive Emmanuel, David Otley and Kenneth Merchant. 2nd ed. London; New York: Chapman and Hall, 1990. xvi, 518 p. : ill. [LC 90012812; ISN 0412374803; $35.00] HF5635. E44 1990 2504

Accounting for managers: text and cases. William J. Bruns, Jr. Cincinnati, Ohio: College Division, South-Western Pub. Co., 1993, c1994. 1 v. (various pagings): ill. *Notes:* Includes bibliographical references. [LC 93008521; ISN 0538833106] HF5657.4. B78 1993 2505

Advanced management accounting. Robert S. Kaplan, Anthony A. Atkinson. 2nd ed. Englewood Cliffs, N.J.: Prentice Hall, c1989. xiv, 817 p. : ill. *Notes:* Includes bibliographical references and indexes. [LC 88027431; ISN 0130114030; ISN 0130115606] HF5635. K15 1989 2506

Case problems in management accounting. edited by M. Edgar Barrett and William J. Bruns, Jr. 2nd ed. Homewood, Ill.: R.D. Irwin, 1985. xii, 480 p : ill. (Robert N. Anthony/Willard J. Graham series in accounting) *Notes:* Includes bibliographical references and index. [LC 84071737; ISN 0256031819]   HF5635. C32 1985   2507

The design of cost management systems: text, cases, and readings. Robin Cooper, Robert S. Kaplan. Englewood Cliffs, N.J.: Prentice Hall, c1991. xii, 580 p. : ill. *Notes:* Includes bibliographical references. [LC 91010186; ISN 0132041243; $45.00]   HF5657.4. C65 1991   2508

Finance & accounting for nonfinancial managers. William G. Droms. 3rd ed. Reading, Mass.: Addison-Wesley, 1990. xii, 244 p. : ill. [LC 89015066; ISN 0201523663; $20.95]   HF5635. D795 1990   2509

Handbook of management accounting. 2nd ed. / edited by Roger Cowe. Aldershot, Hants, England; Brookfield, Vt., U.S.A.: Gower, c1988. xxvi, 468 p. : ill. *Notes:* "In association with the Chartered Institute of Management Accountants." Includes bibliographies and index. [LC 86029616; ISN 0566026155; $80.00 (U.S.: est.)]   HF5635. H228 1988   2510

The information mosaic. Sharon M. McKinnon, William J. Bruns, Jr.; foreword by William E. Langdon. Boston: Harvard Business School Press, c1992. x, 265 p. *Notes:* Includes bibliographical references (p. 227-230) and index. [LC 91046758; ISN 0875843174; $24.95]   HF5657.4. M38 1992   2511

Introduction to management accounting. Charles T. Horngren, Gary L. Sundem. 8th ed. Englewood Cliffs, N.J.: Prentice-Hall, c1990. xx, 826 p. : ill. *Notes:* Includes bibliographical references (p. 782-785). [LC 89038825; ISN 0134870751; $48.20]   HF5635. H814 1990   2512

Management accounting: text and cases. John Dearden. Englewood Cliffs, NJ: Prentice Hall, 1988. xiv, 639 p. : ill. *Notes:* Includes bibliographical references and index. [LC 87019300; ISN 0135491231]   HF5657.4. D42 1988   2513

Management planning and control: the behavioral foundations. edited by Kenneth R. Ferris, J. Leslie Livingstone. Rev. ed. Beavercreek, Ohio: Century VII Pub. Co., c1987. xvii, 249 p. : ill. *Notes:* Rev. ed. of: Managerial accounting. [1975]. Includes bibliographies. [LC 86024930; ISN 0939787008; $15.95]   HF5635. M236 1987   2514

Managerial accounting: concepts for planning, control, decision making. Ray H. Garrison. 6th ed. Homewood, IL: Irwin, c1991. xxii, 810 p. : ill. *Notes:* Includes index. [LC 90004534; ISN 0256081204; $54.95]   HF5657.4. G37 1991   2515

Relevance lost: the rise and fall of management accounting. H. Thomas Johnson and Robert S. Kaplan. Boston, Mass.: Harvard Business School Press, c1987. xiii, 269 p. : ill. *Notes:* Includes bibliographical references and index. [LC 86029474; ISN 0875841805]   HF5605. J64 1987   2516

MANAGERIAL ECONOMICS

Corporate decision making in the world economy: company case studies. Michael G. Rukstad. Fort Worth: Dryden Press, 1992. xvii, 390 p. : ill. *Notes:* Includes bibliographical references and index. [LC 91038381; ISN 0030765269; $36.00]   HD30.22. R84 1992   2517

Economics, organization, and management. Paul Milgrom, John Roberts. Englewood Cliffs, N.J.: Prentice-Hall, c1992. xvii, 621 p. : ill. *Notes:* Includes bibliographical references and index. [LC 91041359; ISN 0132246503; $69.00]   HD30.22. M55 1992   2518

Executive economics: ten essential tools for managers. Shlomo Maital. New York: Toronto: New York: Free Press; Maxwell Macmillan Canada; Maxwell Macmillan International, c1994. ix, 286 p. : ill. [LC 94010300; ISN 0029197856]   HD30.22. M34 1994   +2519

Fundamentals of managerial economics. Mark Hirschey, James L. Pappas. 4th ed. Fort Worth: Dryden Press, c1992. xxii, 713 p. : ill. *Notes:* Pappas's name appeared first on the earlier edition. Includes bibliographical references and index. [LC 91033666; ISN 0030747198; $57.14]   HD30.22. P36 1992   2520

Games for business and economics. Roy Gardner. New York: Wiley, c1995. xvi, 480 p. : ill. *Notes:* Includes bibliographical references and index. [LC 94022110; ISN 0471311502]   HD30.22. G37 1995   +2521

Managerial economics. Bruce T. Allen. New York: Harper & Row, c1988. xix, 647 p. *Notes:* Includes indexes. [LC 87021908; ISN 0060444584]   HD30.22. A4 1988   2522

Managerial economics. Dominick Salvatore. New York: McGraw-Hill, c1989. xxxv, 744 p. : ill. *Notes:* Includes bibliographical references and indexes. [LC 88013188; ISN 0070545340; $38.95]   HD30.22. S247 1989   2523

Managerial economics. Edwin Mansfield. 2nd ed. New York: Norton, c1993. xxiii, 648, 83 p. : ill. *Notes:* Subtitle on cover: Theory, applications, and cases. Includes bibliographical references and index. [LC 92005317; ISN 0393962849]   HD30.22. M354 1993   +2524

Managerial economics. James L. Pappas, Mark Hirschey. 6th ed. Chicago: Dryden Press, c1990. xxii, 826 p. : ill. *Notes:* Includes bibliographies and index. [LC 89035716; ISN 0030312027; $47.50]
HD30.22. P37 1990   2525

Managerial economics: analysis and strategy. Evan J. Douglas; with empirical cases by Scott Callan. 4th ed. Englewood Cliffs, N.J.: Prentice Hall, c1992. xxix, 655 p. : ill. *Notes:* Includes bibliographical references and indexes. [LC 91042640; ISN 0135543460]   HD30.22. D68 1992   2526

Managerial economics and business strategy. Michael R. Baye, Richard O. Beil. Burr Ridge, Ill.: Irwin, c1994. xviii, 538 p. : ill. (some col.) *Notes:* Includes bibliographical references and index. [LC 93002146; ISN 0256123268]   HD30.22. B38 1994   +2527

Managerial economics and operations research: techniques, applications, cases. edited by Edwin Mansfield. 5th ed. New York: Norton, c1987. xiv, 590 p. : ill. *Notes:* Includes bibliographical references. [LC 86021746; ISN 0393955907]   HD30.22. M355 1987   2528

Managerial economics: applied microeconomics for decision making. S. Charles Maurice, Christopher R. Thomas, Charles W. Smithson. 4th ed. Homewood, IL: Irwin, c1992. xvi, 768 p. : ill. *Notes:* Includes bibliographical references and index. [LC 91034073; ISN 0256082685; $49.95]
HD30.22. M36 1992   2529

Managing business transactions: controlling the cost of coordinating, communicating, and decision making. Paul H. Rubin; foreword by Oliver E. Williamson. New York: Toronto: Free Press; Macmillan, c1990. xx, 181 p. : ill. [LC 90034270; ISN 0029275954; $27.95]   HD30.22. R82 1990   2530

Organizational economics. Jay B. Barney, William G. Ouchi, editors. 1st ed. San Francisco: Jossey-Bass, 1986. xix, 495 p. (The Jossey-Bass management series) (The Jossey-Bass social and behavioral science series) *Notes:* Includes indexes. Bibliography: p. 446-480. [LC 86045622; ISN 155542015X]   HD30.22. O74 1986   2531

MANCHESTER BUSINESS SCHOOL (UNIVERSITY OF MANCHESTER)

The Manchester experiment: a history of Manchester Business School, 1965-1990. by John F. Wilson. London: P. Chapman Pub. for Manchester Business School, c1992. xi, 153 p. : ill. *Notes:* Includes bibliographical references (p. [146]-150) and index. [LC 92248699; ISN 1853961582]
HF1142.M3 W55 1992   +2532

MANPOWER PLANNING

The art of managing human resources. edited by Edgar H. Schein. New York: Oxford University Press, 1987. xii, 307 p. : ill. (The Executive bookshelf) *Notes:* Includes index. Bibliography: p. 279-295. [LC 86031107; ISN 0195048822]   HF5549.5.M3 A78 1987   2533

Career management in organizations: a practical human resource planning approach. Elmer H. Burack, Nicholas J. Mathys. Lake Forest, IL: Brace-Park Press, 1980, c1979. xxix, 427 p. : ill. *Notes:* Includes index. [LC 79055540]   HF5549.5.M3 B87   2534

Managing a diverse work force: regaining the competitive edge. John P. Fernandez. Lexington, Mass.: Lexington Books, c1991. viii, 322 p. : ill. *Notes:* Includes bibliographical references (p. [304]-315) and index. [LC 90023171; ISN 0669269034; $22.95]   HF5549.5.M3 F467 1991   2535

Managing workforce 2000: gaining the diversity advantage. David Jamieson, Julie O'Mara; foreword by Warren Bennis. 1st ed. San Francisco: Jossey-Bass, 1991. xxviii, 241 p. : ill. *Notes:* "A Bard Productions book"—T.p. verso. Includes bibliographical references (p. 231-233) and index. [LC 90022120; ISN 1555422640; $27.95]   HF5549.5.M3 J36 1991   2536

Workforce America!: managing employee diversity as a vital resource. Marilyn Loden, Judy B. Rosener. Homewood, Ill.: Business One Irwin, c1991. xviii, 250 p. *Notes:* Includes bibliographical references (p. 233-243) and index. [LC 90044016; ISN 1556233868; $22.95]
HF5549.5.M3 L64 1991   2537

MANPOWER POLICY

Peoplepower: elements of human resource policy. Herbert S. Parnes. Beverly Hills, Calif.: Sage Publications, c1984. 303 p. : ill. *Notes:* Includes index. Bibliography: p. 284-290. [LC 84002085; ISN 0803922760; ISN 0803922779]   HD5713. P37 1984   2538

Work in America; report of a special task force to the Secretary of Health, Education, and Welfare. Cambridge, Mass. MIT Press, 1973. xix, 262 p. *Notes:* Bibliography: p. [219]-253. [LC 73000278; ISN 026208063X] HD5723. U5 1973 +2539

MANUFACTURES

Beyond the bottom line: measuring world class performance. Carol J. McNair, William Mosconi, Thomas Norris. Homewood, Ill.: Dow Jones-Irwin, c1989. xix, 212 p. : ill. *Notes:* Includes bibliographical references (p. 195-200) *Contents:* Turbulent environment—Technology: providing a solution—Technology adaption: lessons from the firing line—Management accounting: barrier to change?—Proactive accountant—New measures for new demands—Overhead: Attacking costs that don't add value—Control it where you spend it—JIT and the management accounting system: principal findings—JIT accounting: a look to the future—AMT adoption - matching the solution to the setting. [LC 89001063; ISN 1556231946; $44.95] HF5686.M3 M38 1989 2540

Integrating service strategy in the manufacturing company. Hervé Mathe, Roy D. Shapiro. 1st ed. London; New York: Chapman & Hall, 1993. viii, 237 p. : ill. *Notes:* Includes bibliographical references (p. [227]-230) and index. [LC 92042178; ISN 0412467801] HD9720.5. M384 1993 2541

Knowledge-based manufacturing management: applications of artificial intelligence to the effective management of manufacturing companies. Roger Kerr. Sydney; Reading, Mass.: (1990 printing) Addison-Wesley Pub. Co., c1991. xii, 460 p. : ill. *Notes:* Includes bibliographical references (p. 431-441) and indexes. [LC 89018617; ISN 0201416220; $41.85] HD9720.5. K45 1990 2542

Managing the manufacturing process: a pattern for excellence. Ralph W. Woodgate. New York: Wiley, c1991. xiv, 240 p. *Notes:* "A Wiley-Interscience publication." Includes index. [LC 90042385; ISN 0471506559; $34.95] HD9720.5. W56 1991 2543

The manufacturers' survival guide: new directions for the 1990s. Arnoud de Meyer, with Avivah Wittenberg-Cox. Burr Ridge, Ill.: Irwin Professional Publishing, c1994. viii, 158 p. : ill. *Notes:* Includes bibliographical references and index. [LC 93029616; ISN 0786301643] HD9720.5. M49 1994 +2544

Manufacturing strategy: the research agenda for the next decade. edited by John E. Ettlie, Michael C. Burstein, Avi Fiegenbaum. Boston: Kluwer Academic Publishers, c1990. 256 p. : ill. *Notes:* "Proceedings of the Joint Industry University Conference on Manufacturing Strategy held in Ann Arbor, Michigan on January 8-9, 1990." Includes bibliographical references. [LC 89026853; ISN 0792390652; $50.00] HD9720.5. J65 1990 2545

The marketing edge: the new leadership role of sales & marketing in manufacturing. George E. Palmatier and Joseph S. Shull. Essex Junction, VT: Oliver Wight Limited Publications, c1989. xviii, 256 p. : ill. [LC 88051917; ISN 0939246082; $39 95] HD9720.5. P35 1989 2546

Measuring up: charting pathways to manufacturing excellence. Robert W. Hall, H. Thomas Johnson, Peter B.B. Turney. Homewood, Ill.: Business One Irwin, 1991. v, 180 p. : ill. *Notes:* Includes bibliographical references and index. [LC 90037490; ISN 1556233590; $42.50] HD9720.5. H35 1991 2547

The new manufacturing challenge: techniques for continuous improvement. Kiyoshi Suzaki. New York: London: Free Press; Collier Macmillan Publishers, c1987. xv, 255 p. : ill. *Notes:* Includes index. Bibliography: p. 251-252. [LC 86033715; ISN 0029320402] HD9720.5. S98 1987 2548

MANUFACTURING PROCESSES

Automation, production systems, and computer integrated manufacturing. Mikell P. Groover. Englewood Cliffs, NJ: Prentice-Hall, c1987. xxi, 808 p. : ill.; 24 cm. *Notes:* Rev. ed. of: Automation, production systems, and computer-aided manufacturing. c1980. Includes bibliographies and index. [LC 86025529; ISN 0130546526] TS183. G76 1987 2549

The design and operation of FMS, flexible manufacturing systems. Paul Ránky. Kempston, Bedford, UK: Amsterdam; New York: IFS (Publications); North-Holland Pub. Co., 1983. 348 p. : ill. *Notes:* Includes index. Bibliography: p. [337]-343.; ISN 0903608448] T59.5. R36 2550

From idea to profit: managing advanced manufacturing technology. Jule A. Miller. New York: Van Nostrand Reinhold, c1986. xvi, 256 p. : ill. *Notes:* Includes index. Bibliography: p. 243-247. [LC 85017975; ISN 0442260830] TS183. M55 1986 2551

MARKET SEGMENTATION

Market segmentation: using demographics, psychographics, and other segmentation techniques to uncover and exploit new markets. by Art Weinstein. Chicago, Ill.: Probus Pub. Co., c1987. xii, 296 p. : ill. *Notes:* Includes index. Bibliography: p. 286-289. [LC 86091440; ISN 0917253590; $27.50] HF5415.127. W45 1987   2552

Was there a Pepsi generation before Pepsi discovered it? Stanley C. Hollander and Richard Germain; foreword by Richard S. Tedlow. Chicago, Ill.: NTC Business Books, 1992. xiv, 144 p. : ill. *Notes:* Includes bibliographical references and index. [LC 92013905; ISN 0844234567; $34.95] HF5415.127. H65 1992   2553

MARKETING

The 22 immutable laws of marketing: violate them at your own risk. Al Ries and Jack Trout. 1st ed. New York, NY: HarperBusiness, c1993. xii, 143 p. : ill. *Notes:* Includes index. [LC 92053334; ISN 088730592X; $20.00 ($26.75 Can.)] HF5415. R54369 1993   2554

The 6 imperatives of marketing: lessons from the world's best companies. Allan J. Magrath. New York, NY: American Management Association, c1992. 196 p. : ill. *Notes:* Includes bibliographical references and index. [LC 91033714; ISN 0814450423; $22.95] HF5415.122. M34 1992   2555

Analysis for strategic market decisions. George S. Day. St. Paul: West Pub. Co., c1986. xvi, 259 p. : ill.: *Notes:* Includes index. Bibliography: p. 241-252. [LC 85013917; ISN 0314852271; $16.95] HF5415.135. D39 1986   2556

Basic marketing: a global-managerial approach. E. Jerome McCarthy, William D. Perreault, Jr. 11th ed. Homewood, IL: Irwin, c1993. xxii, 763, 15, 14 p. : col. ill. *Notes:* Includes bibliographical references (p. 723-760) and indexes. [LC 92031792; ISN 025610509X] HF5415.13. M369 1993   +2557

Beacham's marketing reference. edited by Walton Beacham, Richard T. Hise, Hale N. Tongren. Washington, D.C.: Research Pub., c1986. 2 v. (x, 1045 p.) *Notes:* Includes bibliographies and index. Library has: v. 1-2. *Contents:* v. 1. Account executive-market segmentation—v. 2. Marketing audit-wholesaling. [LC 86020271; ISN 0933833032; ISN 0933833040; ISN 0933833059; $139.00] HF5415. B379 1986   2558

The Best of Inc. guide to marketing and selling. by the editors of Inc. magazine. 1st ed. New York: Prentice Hall Press, c1988. vi, 281 p. *Notes:* Includes index. [LC 88009854; ISN 0134540182; $10.95] HF5415.1. B48 1988   2559

Beyond MaxiMarketing: the new power of caring and daring. Stan Rapp, Thomas L. Collins. International ed. New York: McGraw-Hill, 1993, c1994. xxvii, 319 p. *Notes:* Includes index. [LC 93023545; ISN 0070513430; $21.95] HF5415. R3245 1994   +2560

Contemporary marketing. Louis E. Boone, David L. Kurtz. 7th ed. Fort Worth, TX: Dryden Press, c1992. xxvii, 683, [49] p. : col. ill. *Notes:* Includes bibliographical references and index. [LC 91011467; ISN 0030540186] HF5415. B53 1992   2561

Contemporary perspectives on strategic market planning. Roger A. Kerin, Vijay Mahajan, P. Rajan Varadarajan. Boston: Allyn & Bacon, c1990. x, 453 p. : ill. [LC 89036587; ISN 0205123015; $28.00] HF5415.13. K46 1990   2562

Counterturbulence marketing: a proactive strategy for volatile economic times. A. Coskun Samli. Westport, Conn.: Quorum Books, 1993. xvi, 180 p. *Notes:* Includes bibliographical references (p. [171]-173) and index. [LC 93019116; ISN 0899307965] HF5415.13. S238 1993   +2563

Creating strategic leverage: matching company strengths with market opportunities. Milind M. Lele. New York: Wiley, c1992. xviii, 327 p. : ill. *Notes:* Includes bibliographical references (p. 301-318) and index.; ISN 0471631426] HF5415.13. L436 1992   2564

Crisis marketing: when bad things happen to good companies. Joe Marconi. Chicago: Cambridge England: American Marketing Association; Probus, c1992. ix, 216 p. : ill. *Notes:* Includes bibliographic references (p. 199-208) and index.; ISN 1557382468] HF5415.13. M33 1992   2565

The Dartnell marketing manager's handbook. edited by Steuart Henderson Britt and Norman F. Guess. 2nd ed. Chicago: Dartnell Corp., 1983. 1293 p. : ill. (Dartnell handbooks) *Notes:* Title on spine: Marketing manager's handbook. Includes bibliographies and index. [LC 73084563; ISN 0850131359] HF5415.13. D34 1983   2566

Diagnostic marketing: finding and fixing critical problems. C. Davis Fogg. Reading, Mass.: Addison-Wesley, c1985. xiii, 285 p. : ill. *Notes:* Includes index. [LC 84016743; ISN 0201115069; $19.95] HF5415. F563 1985   2567

The essence of marketing. Simon Majaro. New York: Prentice Hall, 1993. xii, 266 p. : ill. *Notes:* Includes bibliographical references and index. [LC 93022068; ISN 013285354X]
    HF5415. M2692 1993   +2568

Ethics in marketing. N. Craig Smith and John A. Quelch. Homewood, IL: Irwin, c1993. xvi, 838 p. : ill. *Notes:* Includes bibliographical references and index. [LC 91041763; ISN 0256108943; $39.95]
    HF5414.122. S62 1993   2569

Field guide to marketing: a glossary of essential tools and concepts for today's manager. chief contributor, Tim Hindle; edited by Alistair D. Williamson. Boston, Mass.: Harvard Business School Press, 1993, c1994. ix, 195 p. [LC 93023865; ISN 0875844308; $16.95]   HF5415. H5257 1994   +2570

Fundamentals of marketing. William J. Stanton, Charles Futrell. 8th ed. New York: McGraw-Hill, c1987. xx, 666 p. : ill. (some col.) (McGraw-Hill series in marketing) *Notes:* Includes bibliographical references and indexes. [LC 86018492; ISN 0070609438; $36.95]   HF5415. S745 1987   2571

Fundamentals of modern marketing. Edward W. Cundiff, Richard R. Still, Norman A.P. Govoni. 4th ed. Englewood Cliffs, N.J.: Prentice-Hall, c1985. xi, 482 p. : ill. *Notes:* Includes bibliographical references and indexes. [LC 84015962; ISN 0133414396]   HF5415. C793 1985   2572

The great marketing turnaround: the age of the individual, and how to profit from it. Stan Rapp, Tom Collins. Englewood Cliffs, N.J.: Prentice Hall, c1990. xii, 336 p. : ill. *Notes:* Includes bibliographical references (p. 314-321) and index. [LC 90040846; ISN 0133655601; $22.95]
    HF5415. R3247 1990   2573

The great writings in marketing: selected readings together with the authors' own retrospective commentaries. compiled by Howard A. Thompson. 2d ed. Tulsa, Okla.: PennWell Pub. Co., c1981. xiii, 632 p. : ill. (The PennWell marketing and management series) *Notes:* Includes bibliographical references and indexes. [LC 80022637; ISN 0878141464; $12.95]   HF5415. G655 1981   2574

Guerrilla marketing: secrets for making big profits from your small business. Jay Conrad Levinson. Boston: Houghton Mifflin, c1993. viii, 327 p. *Notes:* "Completely revised and updated for the '90s"—Cover. Includes bibliographical references (p. [311]-316) and index. [LC 93022334; ISN 0395644968]   HF5415. L4764 1993   +2575

How to market to consumers: 10 ways to win. John A. Quelch. New York: Wiley, c1989. ix, 224 p. : ill. *Notes:* Includes index. Bibliography: p. 207-214. [LC 88017331; ISN 0471618535]
    HF5415.1. Q45 1989   2576

Introduction to marketing management: text and cases. James D. Scott, Martin R. Warshaw, James R. Taylor. 5th ed. Homewood, Ill.: R.D. Irwin, 1985. xviii, 818 p. : ill. (The Irwin series in marketing) *Notes:* Includes bibliographical references and indexes. [LC 84062315; ISN 025603236X]
    HF5415.13. S36 1985   2577

The manager's guide to competitive marketing strategies. Norton Paley. New York: AMACOM, c1989. ix, 390 p. : ill. *Notes:* Includes index. [LC 88047708; ISN 0814459102; $65.00]
    HF5415.13. P32 1989   2578

Managing the marketing functions: the challenge of customer-centered enterprise. Stewart A. Washburn. New York: McGraw-Hill, c1988. xi, 371 p. : ill. *Notes:* Includes index. [LC 88014828; ISN 0070684413; $29.95]   HF5415.13. W267 1988   2579

Market driven management: prescriptions for survival in a turbulent world. B. Charles Ames and James D. Hlavacek. Homewood, Ill.: Dow Jones-Irwin, c1989. xiii, 186 p. : ill. *Notes:* Includes index. [LC 88003735; ISN 1556230389; $29.95]   HF5415.13. A454 1988   2580

Market driven strategy: processes for creating value. George S. Day. New York: London: Free Press; Collier Macmillan, c1990. ix, 405 p. : ill. *Notes:* Includes bibliographical references. [LC 89071473; ISN 0029072115; $29.95]   HF5415.13. D368 1990   2581

Market smarts: proven strategies to outfox and outflank your competition. Allan J. Magrath. New York: Wiley, c1988. xiv, 249 p. : ill. *Notes:* Includes indexes. Bibliography: p. 235-239. [LC 88000249; ISN 0471611603; ISN 047161159X]   HF5415. M2678 1988   2582

Market strategy. by David J. Luck and Arthur E. Prell. New York Appleton-Century-Crofts, 1968. xi, 202 p. illus. (ACC business series) *Notes:* Bibliography: p. 189-193. [LC 68021056]   HF5415. L77   +2583

The marketer's visual tool kit. Terry Richey. New York: AMACOM, c1994. xix, 152 p. : ill. *Notes:* Includes bibliographical references (p. 147-148) and index. [LC 93043007; ISN 0814402135; $24.95]
    HF5415.122. R53 1994   +2584

Marketing. A. Dale Timpe, series editor. New York: Facts on File, c1989. xiv, 366 p. : ill. *Notes:* Includes bibliographical references. [LC 88026838; ISN 0816019061; $27.95]   HF5415. M2946 1989   2585

Marketing. edited by J. Eliashberg, G.L. Lilien. Amsterdam; New York: North-Holland, 1993. xiv, 895 p. : ill. *Notes:* Includes bibliographical references and index. [LC 93010556; ISN 0444889574]
    HF5415.122. M38 1993   +2586

Marketing. Patrick E. Murphy, Ben M. Enis. Glenview, Ill.: Scott, Foresman, c1985. xvi, 654 p. : ill. (some col.) (Scott, Foresman series in marketing) *Notes:* Includes bibliographies and indexes. [LC 84023520; ISN 0673159256]   HF5415. M835 1985   2587

Marketing 2000 and beyond. William Lazer. . . et al. Chicago, Ill.: American Marketing Association, c1990. xi, 246 p. : ill. *Notes:* Includes bibliographical references. [LC 89029851; ISN 0877572046; $29.95]   HF5415.13. M3445 1990   2588

Marketing: an introduction. Philip Kotler, Gary Armstrong. 3rd ed. Englewood Cliffs, N.J.: Prentice Hall, c1993. xxiv, 632 p. : col. ill. *Notes:* Includes bibliographical references and indexes. [LC 92023928; ISN 0135545935; $41.00]   HF5415. K625 1993   2589

The marketing challenge of 1992. John A. Quelch, Robert D. Buzzell, Eric Salama. Reading, Mass.: Addison-Wesley Pub. Co., c1990. ix, 390 p. : ill. *Notes:* Includes bibliographical references. [LC 89017770; ISN 0201515628; $20.55]   HF5415.12.E82 Q45 1990   2590

Marketing classics: a selection of influential articles. compiled by Ben M. Enis, Keith K. Cox. 7th ed. Boston: Allyn and Bacon, c1991. xii, 578 p. : ill. *Notes:* Includes bibliographical references and index. [LC 90045274; ISN 0205129242; $33.21]   HF5415. M29748 1991   2591

Marketing: concepts, strategies, and decisions. David J. Reibstein. Englewood Cliffs, N.J.: Prentice-Hall, c1985. xvii, 684 p. : ill. *Notes:* Includes bibliographical references and index. [LC 84018206; ISN 0135568617; $28.95]   HF5415. R365 1985   2592

The marketing edge: making strategies work. Thomas V. Bonoma. New York: London: Free Press; Collier Macmillan, c1985. xiii, 241 p. : ill. *Notes:* Includes bibliographical references and index. [LC 85001560; ISN 0029042003]   HF5415. B524 1985   2593

Marketing for public and nonprofit managers. Christopher H. Lovelock, Charles B. Weinberg. New York: Wiley, c1984. xiv, 607 p. : ill. *Notes:* Includes bibliographical references and index. [LC 83010555; ISN 0471037222; $29.95 (est.)]   HF5415. L65 1984   2594

Marketing handbook. With the assistance of Gerald Albaum. 2d ed. New York Ronald Press Co., 1965. 1 v. (various pagings) illus. *Notes:* First ed., edited by P. H. Nystrom, published in 1948. Includes bibliography. [LC 65012748]   HF5415. F794 1965   +2595

The marketing imagination. Theodore Levitt. New, expanded ed. New York: London: Free Press; Collier Macmillan, c1986. xxv, 238 p. : ill. *Notes:* Includes bibliographical references and index. [LC 86000576; ISN 0029191807; ISN 0029190908]   HF5415. L482 1986   2596

The marketing information revolution. edited by Robert C. Blattberg, Rashi Glazer, John D.C. Little. Boston, Mass.: Harvard Business School Press, c1994. vi, 373 p. : ill. *Notes:* Includes bibliographical references and index. [LC 93015849; ISN 0875843298; $35.00 (est.)]   HF5415.125. M366 1994   +2597

Marketing management. Benson P. Shapiro, Robert J. Dolan, John A. Quelch. Homewood, Ill.: R.D. Irwin, 1985. 3 v.: ill. (The Irwin series in marketing) *Contents:* v. l. Marketing management: principles, analysis, and applications—v. 2. Marketing management: strategy, planning, and implementation—v. 3. Marketing management readings: from theory to practice. [LC 84062663; ISN 0256031533]   HF5415.13. S516   2598

Marketing management. C. Whan Park, Gerald Zaltman. Chicago: Dryden Press, c1987. xvi, 656 p., [8] p. of plates: ill. (some col.) *Notes:* Includes bibliographical references and indexes. [LC 86013551; ISN 0030055989]   HF5415.13. P335 1987   2599

Marketing management. Kenneth R. Davis. 5th ed. New York: Wiley, c1985. xviii, 841 p. : ill. *Notes:* Includes bibliographical references and indexes. [LC 84020852; ISN 0471895326]   HF5415.13. D36 1985   2600

Marketing management: a strategic approach. Harper W. Boyd Jr., Orville C. Walker Jr. Homewood, IL: Irwin, c1990. 1 v. (various pagings): ill. (some col.) *Notes:* Includes bibliographical references. [LC 89035302; ISN 025605827X; ISN 0256084009; $44.95]   HF5415.13. B672 1990   2601

Marketing management: analysis, planning, implementation, and control. Philip Kotler. 7th ed. Englewood Cliffs, N.J.: Prentice-Hall, c1991. xxvi, 756 p. : ill. *Notes:* Includes bibliographical references and indexes. [LC 90044468; ISN 0135524806; $60.00]   HF5415.13. K64 1991   2602

Marketing management: analysis, planning, implementation, and control. Philip Kotler. 8th ed. Englewood Cliffs, N.J.: Prentice Hall, c1994. xxix, 801 p. : ill. (some col.), col. map *Notes:* Includes bibliographical references and indexes. [LC 93016057; ISN 0137228511]   HF5415.13. K64 1994   +2603

Marketing management and strategy: a reader. edited by Philip Kotler, Keith K. Cox. 4th ed. Englewood Cliffs, NJ: Prentice-Hall, 1987. x, 406 p. : ill. *Notes:* Includes bibliographical references and index. [LC 87018849; ISN 0135584531]   HF5415.13. M3524 1987   2604

Marketing management: text and cases. John A. Quelch, Robert J. Dolan, Thomas J. Kosnik. Homewood, IL: Irwin, c1993. xiii, 848 p. : ill. *Notes:* Includes bibliographical references (p. 832) and index. [LC 92031499; ISN 0256109559]   HF5415.13. Q45 1993   2605

Marketing management: text and cases. Thomas V. Bonoma, Thomas J. Kosnik. Homewood, IL: Irwin, c1990. xiii, 930 p. : ill. *Notes:* Includes bibliographical references. [LC 89015459; ISN 0256079927; $46.95] HF5415. B5242 1990   2606

Marketing masters: lessons in the art of marketing from those who do it best. Paul B. Brown. 1st ed. New York: Harper & Row, c1988. 216 p. : ill. *Notes:* Includes index. [LC 87045601; ISN 0060158689; $19.95] HF5415.1. B79 1988   2607

Marketing masters: secrets of America's best companies. Gene Walden and Edmund O. Lawler. 1st ed. New York: HarperBusiness, c1993. xiv, 224 p., [16] p. of plates: ill. *Notes:* Includes index. [LC 92054750; ISN 0887305903; $22.50] HF5415.1. W35 1993   2608

Marketing masters. Chicago, Ill.: American Marketing Association, c1991. viii, 274 p. : ill. *Notes:* Includes bibliographical references. [LC 91032691; ISN 0877572194; $25.95] HF5415. M314 1991   2609

Marketing mistakes. Robert F. Hartley. 5th ed. New York: Wiley, c1992. x, 352 p. : ill. *Notes:* Includes bibliographical references. [LC 91043275; ISN 0471548367; $24.95] HF5415.1. H37 1992   2610

The marketing mode; pathways to corporate growth. New York McGraw-Hill, c1969. xiii, 354 p. *Notes:* Includes bibliographical references and index. [LC 79083269] HF5415. L4832   2611

Marketing models. Gary L. Lilien, Philip Kotler. K. Sridhar Moorthy. Englewood Cliffs, N.J.: Prentice-Hall, c1992. xv, 803 p. : ill. *Notes:* Includes bibliographical references (p. 715-776) and indexes. [LC 91034512; ISN 0135446449; $69.00] HF5415.13. L49 1992   2612

Marketing myths that are killing business: the cure for death wish marketing. Kevin J. Clancy, Robert S. Shulman. New York: McGraw-Hill, 1993, c1994. xxxv, 308 p. : ill. *Notes:* Includes index. [LC 93005891; ISN 0070111243; $19.95] HF5415. C5278 1993   +2613

Marketing organisation: an analysis of information processing, power, and politics. Nigel Piercy. London; Boston: Allen & Unwin, 1985. xii, 238 p. : ill. *Notes:* Includes index. Bibliography: p. 214-229.; ISN 0046582452; $25.00] HF5415.3. P543 1985   2614

Marketing performance assessment. Thomas V. Bonoma, Bruce H. Clark. Boston, Mass.: Harvard Business School Press, c1988. xiv, 202 p. : ill. *Notes:* Includes index. Bibliography: p. 185-195. [LC 88021428; ISN 0875842038] HF5415. B5243 1988   2615

Marketing places: attracting investment, industry, and tourism to cities, states, and nations. Philip Kotler, Donald H. Haider, Irving Rein. New York: Toronto: New York: Free Press; Maxwell Macmillan Canada; Maxwell Macmillan International, c1993. vii, 388 p. : ill. *Notes:* Includes bibliographical references (p. 347-363) and index. [LC 92046319; ISN 0029175968; $35.00] HF5415. K6315 1993   2616

The marketing plan: how to prepare it, what should be in it. by Robert K. Skacel. Towson, Md.: MPM Associates, c1990. 72 leaves; $39.95] HF5415.13. S52 1990   2617

Marketing planning & strategy. Subhash C. Jain. 3rd ed. Cincinnati, OH: South-Western Pub., c1990. xxi, 916 p. : ill. *Notes:* Includes bibliographical references. [LC 89039053; ISN 0538802510; $40.00] HF5415.13. J25 1990   2618

Marketing principles. Ben M. Enis. 3d ed. Santa Monica, Calif.: Goodyear Pub. Co., c1980. xxiii, 647 p. : ill. *Notes:* Includes bibliographies and indexes. [LC 79027099; ISN 0830254846] HF5415.13. E54 1980   2619

The marketing renaissance. David E. Gumpert, editor. New York: Wiley, c1985. ix, 578 p. : ill. (Harvard Business Review executive book series) *Notes:* Includes contributions by seven faculty members of the Harvard Graduate School of Business Administration. Includes bibliographical references and indexes. [LC 84026991; ISN 0471813524; $22.95 (est.)] HF5415. M322 1985   2620

The marketing revolution: a radical manifesto for dominating the marketplace. Kevin J. Clancy, Robert S. Shulman. New York, NY: HarperBusiness, c1991. viii, 314 p. : ill. *Notes:* Includes index. Erratum sheet inserted. [LC 91035902; ISN 0837304818] HF5415.13. C546 1991   2621

Marketing strategy: a customer-driven approach. Steven P. Schnaars. New York: Toronto: New York: Free Press; Collier Macmillan Canada; Maxwell Macmillan International, c1991. xvi, 319 p. : ill. *Notes:* Includes bibliographical references and indexes. [LC 90043633; ISN 0029279534; $35.00] HF5415.13. S29 1991   2622

Marketing strategy and plans. 3rd ed. / David J Luck, O.C. Ferrell, George S. Lucas. Englewood Cliffs, N.J.: Prentice Hall, c1989. x, 514 p. : ill. *Notes:* Includes bibliographical references and indexes. [LC 88035736; ISN 0135587190; $35.40] HF5415.13. L75 1989   2623

Marketing successes, historical to present day: what we can learn. Robert F. Hartley. 2nd ed. New York: J. Wiley, c1990. vii, 290 p. : ill. *Notes:* Includes bibliographical references. [LC 89014805; ISN 0471512621; $16.95] HF5415. H2432 1990   2624

Marketing theory: classic and contemporary readings. edited by Jagdish N. Sheth, Dennis E. Garrett. Cincinnatti, OH.: South-Western Pub. Co., 1986. viii, 872 p. : ill. *Notes:* Includes bibliographical references. [LC 85073301; ISN 0538192534] HF5415.1. M37   2625

Marketing theory: evolution and evaluation. Jagdish N. Sheth, David M. Gardner, Dennis E. Garrett. New York: Wiley, c1988. xi, 231 p. *Notes:* Bibliography: p. 203-231. [LC 88010162; ISBN 0471635278; $27.95]   HF5415. S4414 1988   2626

Marketing to win: strategies for building competitive advantage in service industries. Frank K. Sonnenberg. New York: Harper Business, c1990. x, 269 p. : ill. *Notes:* Includes bibliographical references (p. 253-260) and index. [LC 90004178; ISBN 0887304206; $29.95]   HF5415. S6932 1990   2627

Marketing today: successes, failures, and turnarounds. John B. Clark. 2nd ed. Englewood Cliffs, N.J.: Prentice Hall, c1990. xvii, 238 p. : ill. *Notes:* Includes bibliographical references. [LC 89026525; ISBN 0135589665; $22.00]   HF5415.1. C54 1990   2628

Marketing warfare. by Al Ries and Jack Trout. New York: McGraw-Hill, c1986. viii, 216 p. : ill. *Notes:* Includes index. [LC 85014957; ISBN 007052730X]   HF5415. R544 1986   2629

Marketing without mystery: a practical guide to writing a marketing plan. Laura M. Dirks, Sally H. Daniel. New York, NY: Amacom, c1991. xii, 212 p. : ill. *Notes:* Includes bibliographical references (p. 197-208) and index. [LC 91019870; ISBN 081447764X; $22.95]   HF5415.13. D49 1991   2630

MaxiMarketing: the new direction in advertising, promotion, and marketing strategy. Stan Rapp and Thomas L. Collins. New York: McGraw-Hill, c1987. x, 278 p. : ill. *Notes:* Includes index. Bibliography: p. 269-274. [LC 86015345; ISBN 0070511918; $19.95]   HF5415. R325 1987   2631

New and improved: the story of mass marketing in America. Richard S. Tedlow. New York: Basic Books, 1990. xi, 481 p. : ill. *Notes:* Includes bibliographical references. [LC 89018331; ISBN 0465050247; $24.95]   HF5415.1. T44 1990   2632

The new competition. Philip Kotler, Liam Fahey, Somkid Jatusripitak. Englewood Cliffs, N.J.: Prentice-Hall, c1985. xii, 292 p. : ill. *Notes:* Includes index. Bibliography: p. 268-281. [LC 84026596; ISBN 0136120784]   HF5415.12.J3 K68 1985   2633

Organizing and implementing the marketing effort: text and cases. Frank V. Cespedes. Reading, MA: Addison-Wesley, c1991. xiii, 818 p. : ill. *Notes:* Includes bibliographical references. [LC 90000397; ISBN 0201510448; $51.00]   HF5415.13. C43 1991   2634

The PIMS principles: linking strategy to performance. Robert D. Buzzell, Bradley T. Gale. New York: London: Free Press; Collier Macmillan, c1987. xiii, 322 p. : ill. *Notes:* Includes indexes. Bibliography: p. 301-312. [LC 87000416; ISBN 0029044308]   HF5415.13. B893 1987   2635

The practice of marketing management: analysis, planning, and implementation. William A. Cohen. 2nd ed. New York: Toronto: New York: Macmillan; Collier Macmillan Canada; Maxwell Macmillan International, c1991. 1 v. (various pagings): col. ill. *Notes:* Includes bibliographical references and indexes. [LC 90034233; ISBN 0023231718; $57.00]   HF5415.13. C635 1991   2636

Principles of marketing. Philip Kotler, Gary Armstrong. 6th ed. Englewood Cliffs, N.J.: Prentice Hall, c1994. xx, 692, [48] p. : col. ill. *Notes:* Includes bibliographical references and index. [LC 93028976; ISBN 013030560X]   HF5415. K632 1994   +2637

Principles of marketing. Thomas C. Kinnear, Kenneth L. Bernhardt. 3rd ed. Glenview, Ill.: Scott, Foresman/Little, Brown Higher Education, c1990. 765, 36, 18 p. : col. ill. *Notes:* Includes bibliographical references. [LC 89027719; ISBN 0673385655; $55.74]   HF5415. K5227 1990   2638

Product-country images: impact and role in international marketing. Nicolas Papadopoulos, Louise A. Heslop, editors. New York: International Business Press, c1993. xxvi, 477 p. : ill. *Notes:* Includes bibliographical references and index. [LC 91035947; ISBN 156024237X]   HF5415.122. P76 1993   2639

Promotional management. Norman Govoni, Robert Eng, Morton Galper. Englewood Cliffs, N.J.: Prentice-Hall, 1985. xiii, 578 p. : ill. *Notes:* Includes bibliographical references and index. [LC 85009423; ISBN 0137310196]   HF5415. G6243 1985   2640

Promotional strategy: managing the marketing communications process. James F. Engel, Martin R. Warshaw, Thomas C. Kinnear. 8th ed. Burr Ridge, Ill.: Irwin, c1994. xv, 624 p. : ill. (some col.) *Notes:* Includes bibliographical references and index. [LC 93048793; ISBN 0256122407]   HF5415. E65 1994   +2641

Public and nonprofit marketing: cases and readings. Christopher H. Lovelock, Charles B. Weinberg. Palo Alto, Calif.: New York: Scientific Press; Wiley, c1984. xiii, 378 p. : ill. *Notes:* Includes bibliographies.; ISBN 0471885789]   HF5415. L653   2642

Quantitative analysis for marketing management. by William R. King. New York McGraw-Hill, 1967. xviii, 574 p. illus. *Notes:* Includes bibliographies. [LC 67021595]   HF5415.1. K5   +2643

The Regis touch: million-dollar advice from America's top marketing consultant. Regis McKenna. Reading, Mass.: Addison-Wesley Pub. Co., c1985. xii, 179 p. : ill. *Notes:* Includes index. [LC 84028374; ISBN 0201139812; $15.95]   HF5415. M2586 1985   2644

Relationship marketing: successful strategies for the age of the customer. Regis McKenna. Reading, Mass.: Addison-Wesley Pub. Co., c1991. xiii, 242 p. : ill. *Notes:* Includes bibliographical references (p. 228-230) and index. [LC 91020127; ISN 0201567695; $19.95 (Canada $25.95)]
  HF5415. M2616 1991 2645

The rise and fall of mass marketing. edited by Richard S. Tedlow and Geoffrey Jones. London; New York: Routledge, 1993. xii, 239 p. : ill. *Notes:* Includes bibliographical references and index. [LC 92024738; ISN 0415075734; $35.00] HF5411. R57 1993 2646

Selling in Japan: the world's second largest market. Tokyo: Japan External Trade Organization (JETRO), c1985. 291 p. : ill.; ISN 4822403173] HF5415.12.J3 S45 1985 2647

Six timeless marketing blunders. by William Shanklin. Lexington, Mass.: Lexington Books, c1989. xix, 154 p. *Notes:* Includes index. Bibliography: p. [145]-149. [LC 88028116; ISN 0669194999]
  HF5415.13. S46 1989 2648

Strategic market management. David A. Aaker. 4th ed. New York: Wiley, c1995. xv, 379 p. : ill. *Notes:* Includes bibliographical references and index. [LC 94029888; ISN 0471309567]
  HF5415.13. A23 1995 +2649

Strategic market planning: problems and analytical approaches. Derek F. Abell, John S. Hammond. Englewood Cliffs, N.J.: Prentice-Hall, c1979. xii, 527 p. : ill. *Notes:* Includes bibliographical references and index. [LC 79012073; ISN 013851089X; $18.95] HF5415.13. A24 2650

Strategic marketing. David W. Cravens. 4th ed. Burr Ridge, Ill.: Irwin, c1994. 1 v. (various pagings): ill. (some col.) *Notes:* Includes bibliographical references and indexes. [LC 93015608; ISN 0256122121] HF5415.135. C72 1994 +2651

Strategic marketing. John F. Cady, Robert D. Buzzell. Boston: Little, Brown, c1986. viii, 664 p. : ill. *Notes:* Includes bibliographical references. [LC 85023080; ISN 0316123285] HF5415. C233 1986 2652

Strategic marketing: a European approach. Jean-Jacques Lambin. London; New York: McGraw-Hill, c1993. xv, 539 p. : ill. *Notes:* Translation of: Le marketing stratégique. Includes bibliographical references (p. [503]-527) and indexes. [LC 93021714; ISN 0077077954; £22.50]
  HF5415.13. L33213 1993 +2653

Strategic marketing and management. edited by Howard Thomas and David Gardner. Chichester West Sussex; New York: Wiley, c1985. x, 509 p. ill. *Notes:* Papers presented at a conference co-sponsored by the Marketing Education Division of the American Marketing Association and the Dept. of Business Administration, College of Commerce and Business Administration at the University of Illinois at Urbana-Champaign, held May 10-11, 1982 at the university. Includes bibliographies and indexes. [LC 83025902; ISN 0471904236; $52.80] HF5411. S87 1985 2654

Strategic marketing cases and applications. David W. Cravens, Charles W. Lamb, Jr. 2nd ed. Homewood, Ill.: R.D. Irwin, 1986. xxi, 803 p. : ill. *Notes:* Includes bibliographical references. [LC 85060246; ISN 0256033714] HF5415. C6944 1986 2655

The strategic marketing planner. Norton Paley. New York, NY: American Management Association, c1991. ix, 205 p. *Notes:* Includes index. [LC 90053216; ISN 0814411495; $75.00]
  HF5415.13. P323 1991 2656

The supermarketers: marketing for success, rules of the mastermarketers, the naked marketplace. Robert Heller. 1st ed. New York: Dutton, c1987. xiii, 384 p. *Notes:* "A Truman Talley book." Includes index. Bibliography: p. 363-365. [LC 86023977; ISN 0525245200] HF5415. H374 1987 2657

12 simple steps to a winning marketing plan. Geraldine A. Larkin. Chicago: Probus Publishing, Co., c1992. v, 217 p. : ill. *Notes:* Includes bibliographical references and index.; $22.00]
  HF5415. L3265 1992 2658

Understanding business markets: interaction relationships and networks. the Industrial Marketing & Purchasing Group; edited by David Ford. London; San Diego: Academic Press, 1990. viii, 556 p. : ill. *Notes:* Includes bibliographical references and index.; ISN 0122621417; $31.50]
  HF5415. U53 1990 2659

The Wall Street Journal on marketing. Ronald Alsop, Bill Abrams. Homewood, Ill.: Dow Jones-Irwin, c1986. x, 294 p. : ill. *Notes:* Includes bibliographical references. [LC 86071213; ISN 0870948962] HF5415.1. A48 2660

Winning the marketing war: a practical guide to competitive advantage. Robert Durö. Chichester England; New York: Wiley, c1989. xi, 161 p. : ill. [LC 89014631; ISN 0471923826; $29.90]
  HF5415.13. D87 1989 2661

MARKETING CHANNELS

Going to market: distribution systems for industrial products. E. Raymond Corey, Frank V. Cespedes, V. Kasturi Rangan; research associates, Bobbi Carrey et al.. Boston, Mass.: Harvard Business School Press, c1989. xxi, 394 p. : ill. *Notes:* Includes bibliographical references andindex. [LC 89001769; ISN 087584202X; $37.50] HF5415.129. C67 1989   2662

Japan's market: the distribution system. by Michael R. Czinkota and Jon Woronoff. New York: Praeger, 1986. xiv, 145 p. : ill. *Notes:* "Praeger special studies. Praeger scientific." Includes index. Bibliography: p. 131-136. [LC 86008157; ISN 0275921425; $29.95 (est.)] HF5415.129. C95 1986   2663

Marketing channels. Louis W. Stern, Adel I. El-Ansary. 4th ed. Englewood Cliffs, N.J.: Prentice Hall, 1992. xvi, 621 p. : ill. *Notes:* Includes bibliographical references and index. [LC 91040011; ISN 0135537363; $56.00] HF5415.129. S75 1992   2664

Marketing channels: a management view. Bert Rosenbloom. 4th ed. Chicago: Dryden Press, c1991. xxii, 707 p. : ill., maps *Notes:* Includes bibliographical references and indexes. [LC 90013851; ISN 0030327628; $57.14] HF5415.129. R67 1991   2665

MARKETING RESEARCH

Cheap but good marketing research. Alan R. Andreasen. Homewood, Ill.: Dow Jones-Irwin, c1988. xv, 281 p. : ill. *Notes:* Includes bibliographies and index. [LC 88002447; ISN 0870947729; $24.95] HF5415.2. A485 1988   2666

Consumer market research handbook. editors, Robert M. Worcester, John Downham. 3rd rev. and enl. ed. Amsterdam; New York: New York, N.Y., U.S.A.: North-Holland; Sole distributors for the U.S.A. and Canada, Elsevier Science Pub. Co., 1986. ix, 840 p. : ill. *Notes:* Includes index. Published by Elsevier Science Publishers. . . on behalf of E.S.O.M.A.R. Bibliography: p. 773-801. [LC 86006345; ISN 0444876936; ISN 0444700234; ISN 0444700218; ISN 0444700226] HF5415.2. C62 1986   2667

Do-it-yourself marketing research. George Edward Breen, Albert B. Blankenship; illustrated by Howard Munce. 3rd ed. New York: McGraw-Hill, c1989. ix, 261 p. : ill.; ISN 007007450X; $39.95] HF5415.2. B67 1989   2668

Exploring marketing research. William G. Zikmund. 4th ed. Chicago: Dryden Press, 1991. xxiv, 834 p. : ill. *Notes:* Includes bibliographical references and index. [LC 90039282; ISN 0030515629] HF5415.2. Z54 1991   2669

The industrial market research handbook. Paul N. Hague. New York: Franklin Watts, 1988. 344 p. : ill. (Advanced management skills.) *Notes:* Previous ed.: 1985. Includes index. [LC 87051314; ISN 0531155307] HF5415.2. H25 1988   2670

Market research and analysis. Donald R. Lehmann. 3rd ed. Homewood, IL.: Irwin, 1989. xvi, 879 p. : ill. *Notes:* Includes bibliographies and index. [LC 88015734; ISN 0256070385; $40.95] HF5415.2. L388 1989   2671

Market research: using forecasting in business. Peter Clifton, Hai Nguyen, Susan Nutt. London; Boston: Butterworth Heinemann, 1992. xiv, 266 p. : ill. *Notes:* Includes bibliographical references (p. 263) and index. [LC 93118001; ISN 0750601531] HF5415.2. C55 1992   +2672

Marketing research. David A. Aaker, George S. Day. 4th ed. New York: Wiley, c1990. xiv, 739, [29] p. : ill. *Notes:* Includes bibliographical references. [LC 89037850; ISN 0471613517; $47.95] HF5415.2. A12 1990   2673

Marketing research. David J. Luck, Ronald S. Rubin. 7th ed. Englewood Cliffs, N.J.: Prentice Hall, c1987. xvi, 683 p. : ill. *Notes:* Rev. ed. of: Marketing research / David J. Luck. . . [et al.]. 6th ed. c1982. Includes bibliographies and indexes. [LC 86025255; ISN 0135578280; $35.95] HF5415.2. M3555 1987   2674

Marketing research. Peter M. Chisnall. 3rd ed. London; New York: McGraw-Hill, c1986. x, 352 p. : ill. (The McGraw-Hill marketing series) *Notes:* Includes bibliographies and index. [LC 86000899; ISN 0070841551; £10.95 (est.)] HF5415.2. C48 1986   2675

Marketing research: an applied approach. Thomas C. Kinnear, James R. Taylor. 3rd ed. New York: McGraw-Hill, c1987. xviii, 718 p. : ill. (some col.) (McGraw-Hill series in marketing) *Notes:* Includes bibliographical references and indexes. [LC 86020844; ISN 0070347484] HF5415.2. K53 1987   2676

Marketing research: methodological foundations. Gilbert A. Churchill, Jr. 5th ed. Chicago: Dryden Press, c1991. xxxii, 1070 p. : ill. *Notes:* Includes flashcard entitled: "Statistics command summary." Includes bibliographical references and index. [LC 89071542; ISN 0030314720; $56.00] HF5415.2. C5 1991   2677

The marketing research process. Margaret Crimp. 2nd ed. Englewood Cliffs, N.J.: Prentice-Hall International, c1985. xv, 294 p. : ill. *Notes:* Includes bibliographies and index.; ISN 0135577039; 99.95 (Sept.)]   HF5415.2. C73   2678

Marketing research: text and cases. Harper W. Boyd, Jr., Ralph Westfall, Stanley F. Stasch. 7th ed. Homewood, Ill.: Irwin, 1989. xv, 816 p. : ill. *Notes:* Includes bibliographical references and index. [LC 88018573; ISN 0256068135; $49.95]   HF5415.2. B65 1989   2679

Marketing research the right way. Boston, MA: Harvard Business Review, c1991. 73 p. : ill. *Notes:* Articles reprinted from the Harvard Business Review. Includes bibliographical references.; ISN 0875842763; $19.95]   HF5415.2. M36 1991   2680

The naked consumer: how our private lives become public commodities. Erik Larson. 1st ed. New York: H. Holt, 1992. vii, 275 p. *Notes:* Includes bibliographical references (p. 241-261) and index. [LC 92014344; ISN 0805017550]   HF5415.2. L36 1992   2681

The Politz papers: science and truth in marketing research. edited by Hugh S. Hardy; foreword by Darrell B. Lucas and with additional notes by W. Edwards Deming. Chicago, Ill.: American Marketing Association, 1990. xvii, 351 p. : ill. *Notes:* Includes bibliographical references and index. [LC 90036688; ISN 0877572100; $57.44]   HF5415.2. P6 1990   2682

Practical marketing research. Jeffrey L. Pope. New York: AMACOM, c1981. vii, 296 p. : ill. *Notes:* Includes index. [LC 81066232; ISN 0814456510]   HF5415.2. P63   2683

Research for marketing decisions. Paul E. Green, Donald S. Tull, Gerald Albaum. 5th ed. Englewood Cliffs, N.J.: Prentice Hall, c1988. xii, 784 p. : ill. (The Prentice Hall series in marketing) *Notes:* Includes bibliographical references and index. [LC 88005800; ISN 0137741758; $29.50]   HF5415.2. G68 1988   2684

Research traditions in marketing. edited by Gilles Laurent, Gary L. Lilien, Bernard Pras. Boston: Kluwer Academic Publishers, c1994. xxii, 442 p. : ill. *Notes:* Papers based on contributions to the conference that marked the 20th Anniversary of the European Institute for Advanced Studies in Management. Includes bibliographical references. [LC 93014432; ISN 0792393880]   HF5415.2. R444 1994   +2685

State of the art marketing research. A.B. Blankenship, George Edward Breen. Chicago, Ill.: Lincolnwood, Ill.: American Marketing Association; NTC Business Books, c1993. xi, 579 p. : ill. *Notes:* Includes bibliographical references and index. [LC 91003834; ISN 0844234575]   HF5415.2. B555 1993   2686

The survey research handbook. Pamela L. Alreck, Robert B. Settle. Homewood, Ill.: R.D. Irwin, 1985. xix, 429 p. : ill. *Notes:* Includes index. [LC 84080312; ISN 0870945297; $37.50]   HF5415.2. A33 1985   2687

MARRIAGE

Commuter marriage: living together, apart. Fairlee E. Winfield; illustrations by Louise Waller. New York: Columbia University Press, 1985. xvi, 186 p. : ill. *Notes:* Includes index. Bibliography: p. [179]-181. [LC 84017528; ISN 0231059485]   HQ734. W7645 1985   2688

MARRIED PEOPLE

Dual-career families. Uma Sekaran. 1st ed. San Francisco, Calif.: Josey-Bass, 1986. xix, 261 p. : ill. (A Joint publication in the Jossey-Bass social and behavioral science series and the Jossey-Bass management series) *Notes:* Half title: Dual-career families: contemporary organizational and counseling issues. Includes indexes. Bibliography: p. 227-247. [LC 86015206; ISN 1555420052]   HQ536. S42 1986   2689

More equal than others: women and men in dual-career marriages. Rosanna Hertz. Berkeley: University of California Press, c1986. xvi, 245 p. *Notes:* Includes index. Bibliography: p. 227-237. [LC 86004325; ISN 0520058046]   HQ536. H47 1986   2690

MASS MEDIA

Misunderstanding media. Brian Winston. Cambridge, Mass.: Harvard University Press, 1986. xi, 419 p. : ill. *Notes:* Includes bibliographical references and index. [LC 86004802; ISN 0674576632]   P96.T42 W5 1986   2691

MASS PRODUCTION

From the American system to mass production, 1800-1932: the development of manufacturing technology in the United States. David A. Hounshell. Baltimore: Johns Hopkins University Press, c1984. xxi, 411 p. : ill. *Notes:* Includes index. Bibliography: p. 385-398. [LC 83016269; ISN 0801829755]
TS149. H68 1984   2692

MASSACHUSETTS INSTITUTE OF TECHNOLOGY

MIT—shaping the future. edited by Kenneth R. Manning. Cambridge, Mass.: MIT Press, c1991. x, 200 p. : ill. *Notes:* Includes bibliographical references. [LC 91066244; ISN 0262631415]
T171.M495 M57 1991   2693

MASSACHUSETTS—ECONOMIC CONDITIONS

The competitive advantage of Massachusetts. Michael E. Porter in collaboration with Monitor Company, Inc. Cambridge, Mass.: Monitor Company, 1991. 128 leaves: ill. *Notes:* Cover title.]
HC107.M4 P67 1991   2694

MATERIALS MANAGEMENT

Total materials management: the frontier for maximizing profit in the 1990s. Eugene L. Magad, John M. Amos. New York: Van Nostrand Reinhold, c1989. xiii, 551 p. : ill. *Notes:* Includes bibliographies and index. [LC 88029161; ISN 0442208405; $46.95]
TS161. M34 1989   2695

MATHEMATICAL INSTRUMENTS

A history of computing technology. Michael R. Williams. Englewood Cliffs, N.J.: Prentice-Hall, c1985. xi, 432 p. (Prentice-Hall series in computational mathematics) *Notes:* Includes bibliographies and index. [LC 85006357; ISN 0133899179]
QA71. W66 1985   2696

MATHEMATICS

Applied mathematics for business, economics, and the social sciences. Frank S. Budnick. 3rd ed. New York: McGraw-Hill Book Co., c1988. xxi, 907, [135] p. : ill. (some col.) *Notes:* Includes index. [LC 87022559; ISN 0070088764; $37.95]
QA37.2. B83 1988   2697

Innumeracy: mathematical illiteracy and its consequences. John Allen Paulos. 1st ed. New York: Hill and Wang, 1989. 135 p. [LC 88017001; ISN 0809074478; $18.95]
QA93. P38 1989   2698

Mathematics for management series. by Clifford H. Springer, Robert E. Herlihy and Robert I. Beggs. Homewood, Ill. R. D. Irwin, 1965-68. 4 v. illus. *Notes:* Vols. 3-4 include R. T. Mall as joint author. *Contents:* v. 1. Basic mathematics.—v. 2. Advanced methods and models.—v. 3. Statistical inference.—v. 4. Probabilistic models. [LC 65008233]
T57. S67   +2699

200f nothing: an eye-opening tour through the twists and turns of math abuse and innumeracy. A.K. Dewdney. New York: Wiley, c1993. ix, 182 p. : ill. *Notes:* Includes bibliographical references (p. 174-180). [LC 92042173; ISN 0471577766; $19.95]
QA93. D49 1993   +2700

MAXWELL, ELISABETH

A mind of my own: my life with Robert Maxwell. by Elisabeth Maxwell. 1st ed. New York: HarperCollins, 1994. xiii, 536 p., [16] p. of plates: ill. [LC 94022765; ISN 0060171049; $23.00]
Z325.M392 A3 1994   +2701

MAXWELL, ROBERT

Maxwell: the rise and fall of Robert Maxwell and his empire. Roy Greenslade. New York: Carol Pub. Group, c1992. vii, 376 p. : ill. *Notes:* "A Birch Lane Press book." Includes bibliographical references (p. 360-366) and index. [LC 92023957; ISN 1559721235; $19.95] Z325.M394 G73 1992   2702

MAZDA MOTORS OF AMERICA (CENTRAL)

Working for the Japanese: inside Mazda's American auto plant. Joseph J. Fucini and Suzy Fucini. New York: London: Free Press; Collier Macmillan, c1990. viii, 258 p. *Notes:* Includes bibliographical references (p. [231]-252) and index. [LC 90034249; ISN 0029109310; $19.95]   HD9710.U54 M394 1990   2703

MCDONALD'S CORPORATION

McDonald's: behind the arches. John F. Love. Toronto; New York: Bantom Books, 1986. 470 p., [8] p. of plates *Notes:* Includes index. [LC 85048111; ISN 055305127X] TX945.5.M33 L68 1986   2704

MCI COMMUNICATIONS CORPORATION

The history of MCI 1968-1988: the early years. Philip L. Cantelon. Dallas, Texas: Washington, D.C.: Heritage Press; MCI Communications Corp., c1993. 720, [40] p. of plates: ill. *Notes:* Includes bibliographical references (p. 667-673) and index. [LC 93079783] HE8846.M375 C36 1993   +2705

MCNAMARA, ROBERT S

Promise and power: the life and times of Robert McNamara. by Deborah Shapley. 1st ed. Boston: Little, Brown, c1993. xvii, 734 p. : ill. *Notes:* Includes bibliographical references (p. [683]-703) and index. [LC 92015614; ISN 0316782807; $22.95 ($36.95 Can.)] E840.8.M46S47 1993   +2706

MEDICAL CARE

Health care cost management: a basic guide. by Madelon Lubin Finkel. 2nd ed. Brookfield, WI: International Foundation of Employee Benefit Plans, 1991. xvi, 105 p. : ill. *Notes:* Includes bibliographical references and index. *Contents:* Health care costs: an overview—Historical perspective on employee benefits—Cost containment options in the employee benefits field—Managed care: does it work?—Plan redesign / Flexible benefit programs—Wellness and health promotion—Managing mental health and substance abuse costs—Dental, vision and prescription drug benefits—The self-funding option—Costs of retiree health benefits—Thoughts for the future. [LC 90085844; ISN 089154416X; $25.00] RA410. F57 1991   +2707

Health care marketing: a foundation for managed quality. edited by Philip D. Cooper. 3rd ed. Gaithersburg, Md.: Aspen Publishers, 1994. xviii, 526 p. : ill. *Notes:* Includes bibliographical references and index. [LC 94000205; ISN 0834205270] RA410.56. H426 1994   +2708

The health care solution: understanding the crisis and the cure. C. Duane Dauner with Michael Bowker. 1st ed. Sacramento, Calif.: Vision Pub., c1994. ix, 174 p. : ill. *Notes:* Includes bibliographical references (p. 163-167) and index. [LC 93060944; ISN 0963628194] RA395.A3 D38 1994   +2709

Health policy reform: competition and controls. Robert B. Helms, editor. Washington, D.C.: AEI Press, 1993. xxvi, 331 p. : ill. *Notes:* Include bibliographical references. [LC 93036870; ISN 0844738441] RA410.53. H448 1993   +2710

Marketing for health care organizations. Philip Kotler, Roberta N. Clarke. Englewood Cliffs, N.J.: Prentice-Hall, c1987. xiii, 545 p. : ill. *Notes:* Includes bibliographies and index. [LC 86018733; ISN 0135575621] RA410.56. K68 1987   2711

Medicine at the crossroads: the crisis in health care. Melvin Konner. 1st ed. New York: Pantheon Books, c1993. xxii, 298 p. *Notes:* Includes bibliographical references (p. 276-281) and index. [LC 92050463; ISN 0679415459; $23.00 ($29.00 Can.)] RA395.A3 K66 1993   2712

Total quality in healthcare: from theory to practice. Ellen J. Gaucher, Richard J. Coffey. 1st ed. San Francisco: Jossey-Bass Inc., c1993. xxxiii, 615 p. : ill. *Notes:* Includes bibiliographical references (p. 583-598) and index. [LC 92037677; ISN 1555425348]   RA399.A1 M37 1993   2713

MEDICAL ECONOMICS

Economics, medicine, and health care. Gavin Mooney. 2nd ed. Hemel Hempstead, Hertfordshire England: Savage, Md.: Harvester Wheatsheaf; Barnes & Noble Books, 1992. xi, 179 p. : ill. *Notes:* Includes bibliographical references and index. [LC 92007234; ISN 0389209910; $58.50]   RA410.9.G7 M66 1992   2714

The future of health policy. Victor R. Fuchs. Cambridge, Mass.: Harvard University Press, 1993. viii, 255 p. : ill. *Notes:* Includes bibliographical references (p. [225]-244) and index. *Contents:* Conceptual issues—What is health?—What is health economics?—Price of health—Poverty and health—Empirical studies—U.S. health expenditures and the gross national product—How Canada does it: physicians' services—How Canada does it: acute hospital care—Expenditures for reproduction-related health care—America's children—Policy analysis—Cost containment: no pain, no gain—Competition revolution of the 1980s—Counterrevolution in health care financing—Technology assessment and health policy—National health insurance revisited. [LC 93014894; ISN 0674338251]   RA410.53. F8 1993   +2715

The political economy of health care. David Reisman. New York: St. Martin's Press, 1993. v, 267 p. *Notes:* Includes bibliographical references and index. [LC 93010466; ISN 031209986X]   RA410.5. R45 1993   2716

MEDICAL POLICY

Improving health policy and management: nine critical research issues for the 1990s. edited by Stephen M. Shortell, Uwe E. Reinhardt. Ann Arbor, Mich.: AHSR/HAP, 1992. xii, 505 p. *Notes:* "Research syntheses from the Foundation for Health Services Research." Includes bibliographical references and index. [LC 92001436; ISN 0910701822]   RA396.A1 I46 1992   2717

Power and illness: the failure and future of American health policy. Daniel M. Fox. Berkeley: University of California Press, c1993. viii, 183 p. : ill. *Notes:* Includes bibliographical references and index. [LC 93002977; ISN 0520084098]   RA395.A3 F685 1993   +2718

MELLON, THOMAS

Thomas Mellon and his times. Thomas Mellon; foreword by David McCullough; preface to the second edition by Paul Mellon; edited by Mary Louise Briscoe. 2nd ed. Pittsburgh: University of Pittsburgh Press, c1994. xxxii, 478 p., [24] p. of plates: ill., maps Notes: Includes bibliographical references (p. 469-470) and index. [LC 94011892; ISN 0822937778]   HC102.5.M377 A3 1994   +2719

MEN

Staying the course: the emotional and social lives of men who do well at work. Robert S. Weiss. New York: London: Free Press; Collier Macmillan, c1990. xvii, 314 p. *Notes:* Includes bibliographical references (p. 295-302) and index. [LC 89071506; ISN 002934090X; $24.95]   HQ1090.3. W45 1990   2720

MENTORS IN BUSINESS

The mentor connection: strategic alliances in corporate life. Michael G. Zey; with a new introduction by the author. New Brunswick, U.S.A.: Transaction Publishers, c1991. xxvii, 228 p. : ill. *Notes:* Reprint. Originally published: Homewood, Ill.: Dow Jones-Irwin, 1984. Includes bibliographical references (p. 216-217) and index. [LC 90040507; ISN 0887388655]   HF5386. Z49 1991   2721

MERCHANT BANKS

Clay and Wheble's Modern merchant banking. 3rd ed., edited by William Kay. New York; London: Woodhead-Faulkner, 1990. ix, 148 p. *Notes:* Previous ed.: 1983. Includes index. [LC 89049703; ISN 085941602X; $45.00]   HG3000.L82 C52 1990   2722

MEXICO—COMMERCE—UNITED STATES

Business Mexico: business & investment opportunities in North America's hottest economy. Jan Fedorowicz... et al. Chicago, Ill.: Probus Pub. Co., c1994. xiii, 402 p. : ill., maps *Notes:* Includes index. [LC 94152076; ISN 1557385106; $35.00]   HF3238.U5 B87 1994   +2723

MICROCOMPUTERS

Computers for everybody: 1984 buyer's guide. Jerry Willis and Merl Miller. Beaverton, Or.: Dilithium Press, c1984. iv, 584 p. : ill. (some col.) *Notes:* Includes index. [LC 83018977; ISN 0880561327; $19.95]   QA76.5. W5342 1984   2724

Computing today: microcomputer concepts and applications. David R. Sullivan, Theodore G. Lewis, Curtis R. Cook. 2nd ed. Boston: Houghton Mifflin Co., c1988. xxi, 524, [49] p. : col. ill. *Notes:* Includes index. [LC 87081410; ISN 0395423295; $37.16]   QA76.5. S887 1988   2725

MICROECONOMICS

Applied microeconomics. Edwin Mansfield. 1st ed. New York: Norton, c1994. xxi, 684, 64 p. : ill. *Notes:* Includes bibliographical references and index. [LC 92047402; ISN 0393964310]   HB172. M348 1994   +2726

A course in microeconomic theory. David M. Kreps. Princeton, N.J.: Princeton University Press, c1990. xviii, 850 p. : ill. *Notes:* Includes bibliographical references and index. [LC 89027619; ISN 0691042640; $35.00]   HB172. K74 1990   2727

Microeconomic theory. John P. Gould, Jr., Edward P. Lazear. 6th ed. Homewood, IL: Irwin, 1989. xvi, 640 p. : ill. (some col.) *Notes:* Includes indexes Bibliography: p. 621-625. [LC 87081574; ISN 0256029962; $35.95]   HB172. G64 1989   2728

Microeconomics. Richard G. Lipsey, Douglas D. Purvis, Peter O. Steiner. 7th Canadian ed. New York: HarperCollins, c1991. xiv, 546, [39] p. : ill. *Notes:* Includes index. [LC 91004406; $28.57]   HB172. L727 1991   2729

Microeconomics: analysis and policy. Lloyd G. Reynolds. 6th ed. Homewood, Ill.: Irwin, 1988. xix, 486 p. : ill., charts (Irwin publications in economics) *Notes:* Includes bibliographies and index. [LC 87081577; ISN 0256059136]   HB172. R47 1988   2730

Microeconomics: theory, applications. Edwin Mansfield. 6th ed. New York: Norton, c1988. xvi, 599, 72 p. : ill. (some col.) *Notes:* Includes bibliographical references and index. [LC 87022131; ISN 0393956350]   HB172. M36 1988   2731

The price system and resource allocation. Ross D. Eckert, Richard H. Leftwich. 10th ed. Chicago: Dryden Press, c1988. xviii, 648 p. : ill. (some col.) *Notes:* Authors' names reversed on previous ed. Includes bibliographies and indexes. [LC 87005068; ISN 0030125332; $43.70]   HB172. L45 1988   2732

Price theory and applications. Jack Hirshleifer; with the assistance of Michael Sproul. 4th ed. Englewood Cliffs, N.J.: Prentice Hall, c1988. xii, 563 p. : ill. *Notes:* Includes indexes. [LC 87025735; ISN 013699752X; $42.00]   HB172. H55 1988   2733

Principles of economics: MICRO. Willis L. Peterson. 6th ed. Homewood, Ill.: Irwin, 1986. xii, 338 p. : ill. (Irwin publications in economics) *Notes:* Includes bibliographical references and index. [LC 85080350; ISN 025603348X]   HB172. P48 1986   2734

Principles of microeconomics. Edwin Mansfield. 7th ed. New York: Norton, c1992. xiii, 397, 48 p. : ill. *Notes:* Includes index. [LC 91042863; ISN 0393961753; $29.95]   HB172. M363 1992   2735

Understanding microeconomics. Robert L. Heilbroner, James K. Galbraith. 9th ed. Englewood Cliffs, NJ: Prentice Hall, c1990. ix, 449 p. : ill. *Notes:* Includes bibliographical references. [LC 89015936; ISN 0139333673; $27.60]   HB172. H44 1990   2736

MICROELECTRONICS

Siliconnections: coming of age in the electronic era. Forrest M. Mims, III. New York: McGraw-Hill, c1986. viii, 208 p. : ill. *Notes:* Includes index. [LC 85013223; ISN 007042411X]   TK7874. M528 1986   2737

MICROELECTRONICS AND COMPUTER TECHNOLOGY CORPORATION

R & D collaboration on trial: the Microelectronics and Computer Technology Corporation. David V. Gibson and Everett M. Rogers. Boston, Mass.: Harvard Business School Press, c1994. xxix, 607 p. : ill., maps *Notes:* Includes bibliographical references (p. 571-588) and index. [LC 93001374; ISN 0875843646; $35.00]   HD9696.C64 M524 1994   +2738

MICROELECTRONICS INDUSTRY

The big score: the billion-dollar story of Silicon Valley. Michael S. Malone. 1st ed. Garden City, N.Y.: Doubleday, 1985. x, 442 p. *Notes:* Includes index. [LC 82046038; ISN 0385183518; $15.95]   HD9696.A3 U5628   2739

Charged bodies: people, power, and paradox in Silicon Valley. Thomas Mahon. New York: New American Library, c1985. 339 p. *Notes:* Bibliography: p. 333-336. [LC 84018957; ISN 0453004873]   HD9696.A3 U546 1985   2740

Competing for control: America's stake in microelectronics. Michael G. Borrus. Cambridge, Mass.: Ballinger, c1988. xviii, 269 p. : ill. *Notes:* Includes bibliographies and index. [LC 88011965; ISN 0887303064]   HD9696.A3 U528 1988   2741

Microcosm: the quantum revolution in economics and technology. George Gilder. New York: Simon and Schuster, c1989. 426 p. *Notes:* Includes index. Bibliography: p. [385]-402. [LC 89011476; ISN 0671509691; $19.95]   HD9696.A2 G55 1989   2742

Portraits of success: impressions of Silicon Valley pioneers. Carolyn Caddes; research by Barbara Newton; with a foreword by John Bardeen. Palo Alto, Calif.: Tioga Pub. Co., 1986. viii, 138 p. : ports. *Notes:* Includes index. Bibliography: p. 134. [LC 86040032; ISN 0935382569; ISN 0935382577; $40.00; $20.00]   HD9696.A3 U533   2743

MICROSOFT CORPORATION

The making of Microsoft: how Bill Gates and his team created the world's most successful software company. by Daniel Ichbiah and Susan L. Knepper. Rocklin, CA: Prima Pub., 1991. xiv, 304 p. *Notes:* Previously published in France under title: New magicians. 1989. Includes index. [LC 91006639; ISN 1559580712; $19.95]   HD9696.C64 M535 1991   2744

Show-stopper!: the breakneck race to create Windows NT and the next generation at Microsoft. G. Pascal Zachary. New York: Toronto: New York: Free Press; Maxwell Macmillan Canada; Maxwell Macmillan International, c1994. 312 p. *Notes:* Includes bibliographical references and index. [LC 94020749; ISN 0029356717; $22.95]   HD9696.C64 M538 1994   +2745

MIDDLE CLASS

Boiling point: Republicans, Democrats, and the decline of middle-class prosperity. Kevin Phillips. 1st ed. New York: Random House, c1993. xxiv, 307 p. : ill. *Notes:* Includes bibliographical references (p. [261]-278) and index. [LC 92056467; ISN 0679404619; $23.00 ($29.00 Can.)]   HT690.U6 P48 1993   2746

Upward dreams, downward mobility: the economic decline of the American middle class. Frederick R. Strobel. Savage, Md.: Rowman & Littlefield Publishers, c1993. xv, 229 p. *Notes:* Includes bibliographical references and index. [LC 92028014; ISN 0847677567]   HT690.U6 S77 1993   2747

MIDDLE MANAGERS

The death of the organization man. Amanda Bennett. 1st ed. New York: Morrow, c1990. 270 p. *Notes:* Includes bibliographical references. [LC 89013369; ISBN 0877959617; $19.95]
 HD38.25.U6 B46 1990 2748

Managerial performance and promotability: the making of an executive. Mark B. Silber, V. Clayton Sherman. Rev. and expanded. Inverness, Ill.: Beta Group, 1984. xi, 175 p.] HF5500.2. S523 1984 2749

Service within: solving the middle management leadership crisis. Karl Albrecht. Homewood, Ill.: Business One Irwin, c1990. xi, 203 p. : ill. *Notes:* Includes bibliographical references and index. [LC 90033698; ISBN 1556233531; $24.95] HD38.2. A56 1990 2750

MILKEN, MICHAEL

Dangerous dreamers: the financial innovators from Charles Merrill to Michael Milken. Robert Sobel. New York: Wiley, c1993. xi, 260 p. *Notes:* Includes bibliographical references (p. 239-247) and index. [LC 92040748; ISBN 0471577340; $27.95] HG4621. S65 1993 2751

Highly confident: the crime and punishment of Michael Milken. Jesse Kornbluth. New York: Morrow, c1992. 384 p., [16] p. of plates: ill. *Notes:* Includes index. [LC 91043450; ISBN 0688109373; $23.00] HG4621.M55 K67 1992 2752

A license to steal: the untold story of Michael Milken and the conspiracy to bilk the nation. Benjamin J. Stein. New York: Simon & Schuster, c1992. 219 p. : ill. *Notes:* Errata slip inserted. Includes index. [LC 92031121; ISBN 0671742728; $23.00] HG4928.5.M55 S74 1992 2753

MILLIONAIRES

The age of the common millionaire. Robert Heller. 1st ed. New York: Dutton, c1988. x, 387 p. *Notes:* "Truman Talley Books." Includes index. [LC 87019973; ISBN 052524588X; $19.95]
 HG173. H43 1988 2754

MINORITIES

Developing diversity in organizations: a digest of selected literature. Ann M. Morrison, Kristen M. Crabtree. Greensboro, N.C.: Center for Creative Leadership, c1993. xv, 138 p. *Notes:* Includes bibliographical references and index. [LC 93144970; ISBN 091287970X] HF5549.5.M5 M668 1993 +2755

Diversity in the workplace: human resources initiatives. edited by Susan E. Jackson and associates; foreword by Eli Ginzberg. New York: Guilford Press, c1992. xxvi, 356 p. : ill. *Notes:* "A publication sponsored by the Society for Industrial and Organizational Psychology, Inc."—T.p. verso. Includes bibliographical references and index. [LC 92001422; ISBN 0898624762; $40.00]
 HF5549.5.M5 W67 1992 2756

Multiculturalism in the United States: a comparative guide to acculturation and ethnicity. edited by John D. Buenker and Lorman A. Ratner. New York: Greenwood Press, c1992. vi, 271 p. *Notes:* Includes bibliographical references and index. *Contents:* African-Americans / Cynthia Greggs Fleming—American Indians / Vine Deloria, Jr.—German-Americans / James M. Bergquist—Irish-Amricans / Dennis Clark—Scandinavian-Americans / John Robert Christianson—Polish-Americans / Edward R. Kantowicz—Jewish-Americans / Edward Shapiro—Italian-Americans / Dominic Candeloro—Chinese-Americans / Bernard Wong—Mexican-Americans / Louise Ano Nuevo Kerr—Bibliographical essay / John D. Buenker and Lorman A. Ratner. [LC 91035116; ISBN 0313253749] E184.A1 M85 1992 2757

MINORITY BUSINESS ENTERPRISES

Banking on Black enterprise: the potential of emerging firms for revitalizing urban economies. Timothy Bates. Washington, DC: Joint Center for Political and Economic Studies, c1993. xxiii, 153 p. *Notes:* Includes bibliographical references (p. 147-153). [LC 92073360; ISBN 0941410943; $17.50]
 HD2346.U5 B268 1993 +2758

MONAGHAN, TOM

Pizza tiger. Tom Monaghan with Robert Anderson. 1st ed. New York: Random House, 1986. 346 p., [9] p. of plates [LC 86010131; ISN 0394553594; $17.95] TX910.5.M59 A37 1986   2759

MONETARY POLICY

Financial innovation and monetary policy, Asia and the West: proceedings of the second international conference held by the Institute for Monetary and Economic Studies of the Bank of Japan. edited by Yoshio Suzuki and Hiroshi Yomo. Tokyo: University of Tokyo Press, c1986. ix, 339 p. : ill. *Notes:* Conference held in Tokyo on May 29-31, 1985. Includes bibliographical references and index.; ISN 0860083896] HG1270.5. F55   2760

Inside the money market. [1st ed.] New York Random House, 1972. x, 308 p. (The Random House series in finance & investment) *Notes:* Bibliography: p. 293-296. [LC 70037059; ISN 0394478851] HG538. L643   +2761

Macroeconomic policy. Robert J. Barro. Cambridge, Mass.: Harvard University Press, 1990. 379 p. : ill. *Notes:* Includes bibliographical references. [LC 89071679; ISN 0674540808; $37.50] HG230.3. B37 1990   2762

Monetary policy and the financial system. Paul M. Horvitz, Richard A. Ward. 6th ed. Englewood Cliffs, N.J.: Prentice-Hall, 1987. xi, 532 p. : ill. *Notes:* Includes bibliographies and index. [LC 86025447; ISN 0135998611] HG540. H67 1987   2763

Monetary policy for a changing financial environment. William S. Haraf and Phillip Cagan, editors. Washington, D.C.: Lanham, MD: American Enterprise Institute for Public Policy Research; Distributed, UPA, c1990. xv, 212 p. : ill. *Notes:* Includes bibliographical references. [LC 89018102; ISN 084473697X; $22.95] HG230.3. M656 1990   2764

Monetary theory. by Stephen Rousseas. [1st ed.] New York Knopf, 1972. xiv, 286 p. illus. (Alfred A. Knopf books in economics) [LC 70163198; ISN 0394310527] HG255. R64 1972   +2765

Money mischief: episodes in monetary history. Milton Friedman. 1st ed. New York: Harcourt Brace Jovanovich, c1992. xiv, 274 p. : ill. *Notes:* Includes bibliographical references (p. 266-274). [LC 91023760; ISN 0151620423; $19.95] HG230.3. F75 1992   2766

MONEY

The death of money: how the electronic economy has destabilized the world's markets and created financial chaos. Joel Kurtzman. New York: Simon & Schuster, c1993. 256 p. *Notes:* Includes index. [LC 92037530; ISN 0671687999] HG220.A2 K87 1993   2767

Handbook of monetary economics. edited by Benjamin M. Friedman and Frank H. Hahn. Amsterdam; New York: North-Holland, 1990. 2 v.: ill. *Notes:* Includes bibliographical references. [LC 90006983; ISN 0444880275; ISN 0444880259; ISN 0444880267; $157.00] HG221. H24 1990   2768

The Midas touch: understanding the dynamic new money societies around us. Anthony Sampson. 1st ed. New York: Dutton, 1990, c1989. xi, 273 p., [16] p. of plates: ill. *Notes:* "Truman Tally books." [LC 89048385; ISN 0525248919; $19.95] HG221. S2567 1990   2769

Money and the economy. John J. Klein. 6th ed. San Diego: Harcourt Brace Jovanovich, c1986. xi, 560 p. : ill. *Notes:* Includes bibliographies and indexes. [LC 85080078; ISN 0155640070] HG540. K57 1986   2770

Money, banking, and economic activity. Lloyd B. Thomas, Jr. 3rd ed. Englewood Cliffs, N.J.: Prentice-Hall, c1986. xiii, 609 p. : ill. *Notes:* Includes bibliographies and index. [LC 85017004; ISN 0136000576] HG221. T3985 1986   2771

Money, banking, and economic analysis. Thomas D. Simpson. 3rd ed. Englewood Cliffs, N.J.: Prentice-Hall, 1987. xiii, 562 p. : ill. *Notes:* Includes bibliographies and index. [LC 86021244; ISN 0136002226] HG221. S616 1987   2772

Money, banking, and financial markets. Robert D. Auerbach. 3rd ed. New York: London: Macmillan; Collier Macmillan, c1988. xx, 832 p. : ill. *Notes:* Includes bibliographies and index. [LC 87011173; ISN 0023050403] HG221. A914 1988   2773

Money, banking, and the economy. Thomas Mayer, James S. Duesenberry, Robert Z. Aliber. 5th ed. New York: Norton, c1993. xv, 374 p. : ill. *Notes:* Includes bibliographical references and index. [LC 92011926; ISN 0393963004] HG540. M393 1993   +2774

Money, interest, and stagnation: dynamic theory and Keynes's economics. Yoshiyasu Ono. Oxford: New York: Clarendon Press; Oxford University Press, 1994. viii, 202 p. : ill. *Notes:* Includes bibliographical references (p. [186]-194) and index. [LC 94013271; ISN 0198288379; £25.00]
HG221. O544 1994 +2775

Money, whence it came, where it went. John Kenneth Galbraith. Boston: Houghton Mifflin, 1975. 324 p. *Notes:* Includes bibliographical references and index. [LC 75014116; ISN 0395198437]
HG231.G35 +2776

Principles of money, banking, and financial markets. Lawrence S. Ritter, William L. Sibler. 7th ed. New York: Basic Books, c1991. xxvii, 644 p. : ill. *Notes:* Includes bibliographical references and index. [LC 90019852; ISN 0465063535; $40.00]
HG221. R536 1991 2777

Risk & other four-letter words. Walter B. Wriston. 1st ed. New York: Harper & Row, c1986. ix, 243 p. [LC 85045245; ISN 0060155442; $19.95]
HG221. W937 1986 2778

The social meaning of money. Viviana A. Zelizer. New York: BasicBooks, c1994. xi, 286 p. *Notes:* Includes bibliographical references (p. [217]-272) and index. [LC 93042808; ISN 0465078915; $24.00 ($32.00 Can.)]
HG221. Z45 1994 +2779

Study guide to accompany money, banking and the economy: fifth edition: Thomas Mayer, James S. Duesenberry, Robert Z. Aliber. by Steven Beckman, Janet L. Wolcutt. New York: Norton, c1993. viii, 262 p. : ill. *Notes:* Includes bibliographical references. [LC 93048129; ISN 0393963012; $13.95]
HG540. B42 1993 +2780

MONEY LAUNDERING

The money launderers: lessons from the drug wars—how billions of illegal dollars are washed through banks & businesses. Robert E. Powis. Chicago, Ill.: Probus Pub. Co., c1992. xvi, 337 p. *Notes:* Includes index. [LC 92161704; ISN 155738262X]
HV6769. P68 1992 2781

MONEY MARKET

Handbook of the money and capital markets. Alan Gart. New York: Quorum Books, 1988. xx, 306 p. : ill. *Notes:* Includes bibliographies and index [LC 87024938; ISN 089930270X; $49.95]
HG181. G367 1988 2782

Money and capital markets. Miles Livingston. 2nd ed. New York: New York Institute of Finance, c1993. 639 p. : ill. *Notes:* Includes bibliographical references and index. [LC 93022907; ISN 0130544051; $39.95]
HG226. L58 1993 +2783

The repo and reverse markets. Marcia Stigum. Homewood, Ill.: Dow Jones-Irwin, c1989. xix, 375 p. : ill. *Notes:* Includes index. Bibliography: p. 361-366. [LC 88007145; ISN 0870949888; $62.50]
HG226. S75 1989 2784

MONEY SUPPLY

Triumph of the bankers: money and banking in the eighteenth and nineteenth centuries. William F. Hixson. Westport, Conn.: Praeger, 1993. x, 193 p. : ill. *Notes:* Includes bibliographical references (p. [183]-187) and index. [LC 93000296; ISN 027594607X]
HG501. H53 1993 +2785

MONOPOLIES

Optimal regulation: the economic theory of natural monopoly. by Kenneth E. Train. Cambridge, Mass.: MIT Press, c1991. xiv, 338 p. : ill. *Notes:* Includes bibliographical references (p. [329]-333) and index. [LC 91004361; ISN 0262200848; $40.00]
HD2757.2. T73 1991 2786

MOODY'S INVESTORS SERVICE

Global credit analysis: Moody's Investors Service. edited by David Stimpson. London: IFR Pub., c1991. xvi, 639 p. : ill. *Notes:* Includes bibliographical references and index. [LC 90016339; ISN 094655983X; $170.00]
HG3726. G56 1991 +2787

MORGAN GUARANTY TRUST COMPANY OF NEW YORK

The house of Morgan: an American banking dynasty and the rise of modern finance. Ron Chernow. 1st ed. New York: Atlantic Monthly Press, c1990. xvii, 812 p., 32 p. of plates: ill. *Notes:* Includes bibliographical references. [LC 89017542; ISN 0871133385; $29.95]   HG2613.N54 M6613 1990   2788

MORGAN, JUNIUS SPENCER

The Morgans: private international bankers, 1854-1913. Vincent P. Carosso with the assistance of Rose C. Carosso. Cambridge, Mass.: Harvard University Press, 1987. xvi, 888 p., [12] p. of plates: ill. *Notes:* Includes index. Bibliography: p. 649-653. [LC 86014829; ISN 0674587294]
HG2463.A2 C37 1987   2789

MORITA, AKIO

Made in Japan: Akio Morita and the Sony Corporation. Akio Morita with Edwin M. Reingold and Mitsuko Shimomura. 1st ed. New York: Dutton, c1986. viii, 309 p., [8] p. of plates [LC 86011479; ISN 0525244654]   HD9696.A3 J376   2790

MORTGAGE BANKS

Mortgage banking: a handbook of strategies, trends, and opportunities. edited by Jess Lederman. Chicago, Ill.: Probus Pub. Co., c1989. xiii, 573 p. : ill. *Notes:* Includes index. [LC 89003489; ISN 1557380317; $65.00]   HG2040. M637 1989   2791

MORTGAGE BONDS

The handbook of mortgage-backed securities. Frank J. Fabozzi, editor. 3rd ed. Chicago, Ill.: Probus Pub. Co., c1992. xvii, 1254 p. : ill. *Notes:* Includes bibliographical references and index.; ISN 1557382573]   HG4655. H36 1992   2792

MORTGAGE LOANS

Housing and the new financial markets. edited by Richard L. Florida. New Brunswick, N.J.: Center for Urban Policy Research, c1986. xviii, 482 p. : ill. *Notes:* Includes index. Bibliography: p. 469-472. [LC 85022346; ISN 0882851136; $17.95]   HG2040.5.U5 H68 1986   2793
Latest innovations in the US mortgage market. by Jeffrey N. Tuchman. New York, NY: Economist Intelligence Unit, c1987. x, 130 p. : ill. *Notes:* "December 1987." "A much expanded update of a 1986 study, Innovation in the US mortgage market to 1990, by the same author"—P. x.; ISN 0850582857]   HG2040.5.U5 T833 1987   2794
Real estate finance. John P. Wiedemer. 6th ed. Englewood Cliffs, N.J.: Prentice-Hall, c1990. xvi, 328 p. : ill. [LC 89036256; ISN 0137628323; $33.00]   HG2040.5.U5 W54 1990   2795
Real estate finance and investments. William B. Brueggeman, Jeffrey D. Fisher. 9th ed. Homewood, IL: Irwin, c1993. xv, 908 p. : ill. *Notes:* Rev. ed. of: Real estate finance. 1989. Includes index. [LC 92022177; ISN 0256082901]   HG2040.5.U5 B78 1993   2796

MORTGAGE-BACKED SECURITIES

Mortgage and mortgage-backed securities markets. Frank J. Fabozzi, Franco Modigliani. Boston, Mass.: Harvard Business School Press, c1992. viii, 341 p. : ill. *Notes:* Includes bibliographical references and index. [LC 91040849; ISN 0875843220; $40.00]   HG5095. F33 1992   2797

MORTGAGES

Real estate finance. Ronald W. Melicher, Maurice A. Unger. 3rd ed. Cincinnati: South-Western Pub. Co., c1989. viii, 423 p. : ill. *Notes:* Unger's name appears first on previous ed. Includes index. Bibliography: p. 381-390. [LC 88060512; ISN 053880095X; $37.50]   HG2040. U53 1989   2798

The revolution in real estate finance. Anthony Downs. Washington, D.C.: Brookings Institution, c1985. xiii, 345 p. *Notes:* Includes bibliographies and index. [LC 85014941; ISN 0815719183; ISN 0815719175; $26.95; $9.95]   HG5095. D68 1985   2799

MOTHERS

Everything a working mother needs to know: about pregnancy rights, maternity leave, and making her career work for her. Anne C. Weisberg and Carol A. Buckler. 1st ed. New York: Doubleday, 1994. xx, 235 p. *Notes:* Includes bibliographical references and index. [LC 93027207; ISN 0385424108; $14.95]   HD6055.2.U6 W45 1994   +2800

MOTION PICTURE INDUSTRY

Reel power: the struggle for influence and success in the new Hollywood. Mark Litwak. 1st ed. New York: Morrow, c1986. 336 p. *Notes:* Includes index. Bibliography: p. [313]-323. [LC 86008564; ISN 0688048897; $18.95]   PN1993.5.U6 L54 1986   2801

MULTIPLE CRITERIA DECISION MAKING

Decisions with multiple objectives: preferences and value tradeoffs. Ralph L. Keeney and Howard Raiffa. Cambridge England; New York, NY: Cambridge University Press, 1993. xix, 569 p. : ill. *Notes:* Originally published: New York: Wiley, 1976. Includes bibliographical references (p. 549-560) and index. [LC 92031874; ISN 0521438837]   T57.95. K43 1993   2802

MUNICIPAL BONDS

A guide to registered municipal securities. John E. Petersen, Michael P. Buckley. Washington, D.C.: Government Finance Research Center of the Municipal Finance Officers Association, 1983. xi, 284 p. : forms *Notes:* Bibliography: p. 283-284. [LC 83062576]   HG4952. P4845 1983   2803

The handbook of municipal bonds and public finance. compiled and edited by Robert Lamb, James Leigland, Stephen Rappaport. New York: New York Institute of Finance, c1993. xxxii, 879 p. : ill. *Notes:* Includes bibliographical references and index. [LC 92026109; ISN 0133739600]   HG4952. H33 1993   2804

Municipal derivative securities: uses and valuation. Gary Gray, Patrick Cusatis. Burr Ridge, Ill.: Irwin, c1995. xvii, 285 p. : ill. *Notes:* Includes bibliographical references and index. [LC 94017987; ISN 0786302518]   HG4726. G73 1995   +2805

MUNICIPAL FINANCE

Municipal bonds. Robert Lamb, Stephen P. Rappaport. 2nd ed. New York: McGraw-Hill, c1987. xx, 327 p. *Notes:* Includes index. [LC 86027539; ISN 0070360847; $24.95]   HJ9145. L35 1987   2806

MURDOCH, RUPERT

Murdoch. William Shawcross. New York: Simon & Schuster, 1993, c1992. 492 p., [16] p. of plates: ill. *Notes:* Includes bibliographical references and index. [LC 92038399; ISN 0671673270; $27.50]   P92.5.M87 S5 1993   2807

A paper prince. George Munster. Ringwood, Vic., Australia; New York, N.Y., U.S.A.: Viking, 1985. 291 p. : ill. *Notes:* Spine title: Rupert Murdoch, a paper prince. Includes index. Bibliography: [269]-280. [LC 85152011; ISN 0670805033; £12.95]   Z533.3.M87 M86 1985   2808

MUTUAL FUNDS

The Dow Jones-Irwin guide to mutual funds. Donald D. Rugg. 3rd ed. Homewood, Ill.: Dow Jones-Irwin, c1986. xii, 245 p. : ill. *Notes:* Includes bibliographical references and index. [LC 86071451; ISN 0870947567]   HG4530. R83   2809

The Fidelity guide to mutual funds: a complete guide to investing in mutual funds. Mary Rowland. New York: Simon and Schuster, 1990. 316 p. : ill. *Notes:* "A Fidelity Publishing book." [LC 89027708; ISN 0671661043; $22.95]   HG4530. R68 1990   2810

How mutual funds work. Albert J. Fredman, Russ Wiles. New York: New York Institute of Finance, c1993. xviii, 334 p. : ill. *Notes:* Includes bibliographical references and index. [LC 93001259; ISN 0130125016; $15.95]   HG4530. F73 1993   +2811

Straight talk about mutual funds. Dian Vujovich; with a foreword by A. Michael Lipper. New York: McGraw-Hill, c1992. xvii, 205 p. : ill. *Notes:* Includes index. [LC 91045461; ISN 0070670064; $12.95]   HG4530. V85 1992   2812

NASDAQ MARKET SYSTEM

The NASDAQ handbook: the stock market for the next 100 years: a complete reference for investors, registered representatives, company executives, researchers, the financial press and students of finance. [Rev. ed.] Chicago: Probus Pub. Co., c1992. xi, 388 p. : ill. *Notes:* Rev. ed. of: The NASDAQ handbook: the stock market of tomorrow—today. c. 1987. Includes bibliographical references and index.]   HG4551. N35 1992   2813

NATIONAL CHARACTERISTICS, JAPANESE

The outnation: a search for the soul of Japan. Jonathan Rauch; foreword by James Fallows; photographs by Joel Sackett. Boston, Mass.: Harvard Business School Press, c1992. xiii, 180 p. : ill. [LC 91037946; ISN 0875843204; $18.95]   DS830. R38 1992   2814

NATIONAL FOOTBALL LEAGUE

The League: the rise and decline of the NFL. David Harris. Toronto: New York: Bantam Books, 1986. 710 p., [24] p. of plates: ill., ports. *Notes:* Includes bibliographical references and index. [LC 86047575; ISN 0553051679]   GV955.5.N35 H37 1986   2815

NATIONAL INCOME

Measuring the wealth of nations: the political economy of national accounts. Anwar M. Shaikh, E. Ahmet Tonak. Cambridge; New York: Cambridge University Press, 1994. xvii, 380 p. : ill. *Notes:* Includes bibliographical references (p. 361-367) and indexes. [LC 93037399; ISN 0521414245; $59.95]   HB141.5. S52 1994   +2816

NATIONAL SECURITY

"Rich nation, strong Army": national security and the technological transformation of Japan. Richard J. Samuels. Ithaca: Cornell University Press, 1994. xiii, 455 p. : ill. *Notes:* Includes bibliographical references (p. 411-441) and index. *Contents:* The strategic relationship of the military and civilian economies—The ideological basis of Japanese technonationalism—Military technonationalism and arms production in Imperial Japan—The Imperial Japanese aircraft industry—Girding the nation's loins for peace—Forces at work: rebuilding Japan's defense industry—The postwar Japanese aircraft industry—Japan's technology highways—Technonationalism and the protocols of the Japanese economy. [LC 93039156; ISN 0801427053]   UA845. S327 1994   +2817

NATURAL RESOURCES

The economics of natural resource use. John M. Hartwick, Nancy D. Olewiler. New York, NY: Harper & Row, c1986. xii, 530 p. : ill. *Notes:* Includes index. Bibliography: 515-524. [LC 85014076; ISN 0060426950] HC59. H3558 1986 2818

Environmental accounting for the sustainable corporation: strategies and techniques. Daniel Blake Rubenstein. Westport, Conn.: Quorum Books, 1994. xiv, 207 p. : ill. *Notes:* Includes bibliographical references (p. [201]) and index. [LC 93050066; ISN 089930866X] HF5686.N3 R8 1994 +2819

NEGOTIABLE INSTRUMENTS

Commercial paper. edited by Richard Felix. London: Euromoney Publications, c1987. ix, 182 p. : ill. *Notes:* Includes bibliographical references.; ISN 1870031601] JX6288. C65 1987 2820

NEGOTIATION

The complete negotiator. by Gerard I. Nierenberg. 1st ed. New York: Nierenberg & Zeif Publishers, c1986. 345 p. : ill. *Notes:* Rev. ed. of: Fundamentals of negotiating. 1973. Includes index. Bibliography: p. 239-331. [LC 86000671; ISN 0936305002; $19.95] BF637.N4 N5 1986 2821

Getting past no: negotiating with difficult people. William Ury. New York: Bantam Books, 1991. 161 p. *Notes:* Includes bibliographical references. [LC 91010101; ISN 0553072749; $20.00 ($25.00 Can.)] BF637.N4 U79 1991 2822

Getting to yes: negotiating agreement without giving in. by Roger Fisher, William Ury and Bruce Patton. 2nd ed. New York, N.Y.: Penguin Books, 1991. xix, 200 p. [LC 91032444; ISN 0140157352; $8.95] BF637.N4 F57 1991 2823

Give & take: the complete guide to negotiating strategies and tactics. by Chester L. Karrass. New York Crowell, 1974. xv, 280 p. [LC 74004360; ISN 0690005660] BF637.N4 K27 1974 +2824

Negotiating rationally. Max H. Bazerman, Margaret A. Neale. New York: Toronto: New York: Free Press; Maxwell Macmillan Canada; Maxwell Macmillan International, c1992. xii, 196 p. : ill. *Notes:* Includes bibliographical references (p. 177-191) and index.. [LC 91034205; ISN 0029019850; $24.95] BF637.N4 B39 1992 2825

Negotiation basics: concepts, skills, and exercises. Ralph A. Johnson. Newbury Park, Calif.: Sage Publications, c1993. xv, 166 p. *Notes:* Includes bibliographical references (p. 148-153) and index. [LC 92035503; ISN 0803940521] BF637.N4 J64 1993 +2826

Negotiation: strategies for mutual gain: the basic seminar of the Harvard Program on Negotiation. Lavinia Hall, editor. Newbury Park, Calif.: Sage, c1993. x, 212 p. *Notes:* Includes bibliographical references and index. [LC 92030441; ISN 0803948506] BF637.N4 N44 1993 2827

Win-win negotiating: turning conflict into agreement. by Fred Edmund Jandt, with the assistance of Paul Gillette. New York, N.Y.: John Wiley & Sons, 1985. x, 300 p. : ill. *Notes:* Includes index. [LC 84025673; ISN 0471882070] BF637.N4 J36 2828

NEGOTIATION IN BUSINESS

Bargaining across borders: how to negotiate business successfully anywhere in the world. Dean Allen Foster. New York: McGraw-Hill, c1992. xii, 326 p. : ill *Notes:* Includes index. *Contents:* Some basic cross-cultural ground rules—Individualism—Time—Americans, love, and money at the negotiating table—Egalitarianism—The effective international negotiator—International negotiating styles—Coming home out there—Appendix. Global homecoming exercises. [LC 91045342; ISN 0070216479; $24.95] HD58.6. F67 1992 2829

The bargaining manager: enhancing organizational results through effective negotiation. Bernard A. Ramundo. Westport, Conn.: Quorum Books, 1994. xii, 162 p. *Notes:* Includes bibliographical references (p. [155]-156) and index. [LC 93032881; ISN 0899308058; $49.95] HD58.6. R35 1994 +2830

Field guide to negotiation: a glossary of essential tools and concepts for today's manager. Gavin Kennedy. Boston, Mass.: Harvard Business School Press, c1994. x, 246 p. *Notes:* "Based on material first published in Great Britain in 1993 by the Economist Books Ltd."—T.p. verso. [LC 93039920; ISN 0875844812; $16.95] HD58.6. K463 1994 +2831

How to do business with the Japanese. Mark Zimmerman. 1st ed. New York: Random House, c1985. xv, 316 p. *Notes:* Includes index. Bibliography: p. [299]-301. [LC 83043212; ISN 0394533313; $19.95] HD58.6. Z56 1985   2832

Japanese-U.S. business negotiations: a cross-cultural study. Don R. McCreary. New York: Praeger, c1986. viii, 121 p. *Notes:* "Praeger special studies. Praeger scientific." Includes index. Bibliography: p. 109-115. [LC 86000554; ISN 0275920062; $27.95 (est.)] HD58.6. M38 1986   2833

Making deals: the business of negotiating. Marvin Gottlieb and William J. Healy. New York, N.Y.: New York Institute of Finance, c1990. xiii, 194 p. : ill. *Notes:* Includes bibliographical references. [LC 90005762; ISN 0135522900; $29.95] HD58.6. G67 1990   2834

The manager as negotiator: bargaining for cooperation and competitive gain. David A. Lax, James K. Sebenius. New York: London: Free Press; Collier Macmillan, c1986. xv, 395 p. : ill. *Notes:* Includes index. Bibliography: p. 363-376. [LC 86018420; ISN 0029187702] HD58.6. L39 1986   2835

Pocket negotiator: the essentials of successful negotiation from A to Z. Gavin Kennedy. London: London; New York: The Economist in association with Hamish Hamilton; Penguin, c1987. viii, 200 p. *Notes:* Includes bibliographical references.; ISN 0241002389; £9.90] HD58.6. K47 1994   +2836

NESTLE

Multinational corporations and the impact of public advocacy on corporate strategy: Nestle and the infant formula controversy. by S. Prakash Sethi. Boston: Kluwer Academic, c1994. xvi, 413 p. : ill. *Notes:* Includes bibliographical references (p. 385-398) and index. [LC 93032157; ISN 0792393783] HD9015.S94 N387 1994   +2837

NEW BUSINESS ENTERPRISES

American independent business: formation, operations, and philosophy for the 1980s. by Phillip B. Chute. Riverside, Calif.: P.B. Chute Corp., c1985. xii, 407 p. : ill. *Notes:* Includes index. [LC 84072826; ISN 0930981006; $14.95] HD62.5. C49 1985   2838

The art and science of entrepreneurship. edited by Donald L. Sexton, Raymond W. Smilor. Cambridge, Mass.: Ballinger Pub. Co., 1986. xxvii, 422 p. : ill. *Notes:* Papers from a conference held in February 1985 sponsored by the RGK Foundation, the IC^2 Institute at the University of Texas at Austin, and the Center for Entrepreneurship at Baylor University. Includes bibliographical references and index. [LC 85022843; ISN 0887300707] HD62. A78 1986   2839

The Arthur Young business plan guide. Eric S. Siegel, Loren A. Schultz, Brian R. Ford; edited by David C. Carney. New York: Wiley, c1987. xii, 184 p. *Notes:* Includes index. [LC 86032622; ISN 0471858854] HD62.5. S556 1987   2840

Business plans that win $$$: lessons from the MIT Enterprise Forum. Stanley R. Rich and David E. Gumpert. 1st ed. New York: Harper & Row, c1985. xviii, 220 p. *Notes:* Includes index. [LC 84048617; ISN 006015439X; $19.95] HG4027.6. R53 1985   2841

Business plans that win venture capital. Terrence P. McGarty. New York: Wiley, c1989. xi, 368 p. : ill. *Notes:* Includes index. Bibliography: p. 359-362. [LC 88027609; ISN 0471501808] HD62.5. M38 1989   2842

Cutting loose: making the transition from employee to entrepreneur. Thomas A. Easton, Ralph W. Conant. Chicago, Ill.: Probus Pub. Co., c1985. xi, 202 p. : ill. *Notes:* Includes index. Bibliography: p. 187-189. [LC 85017040; ISN 0917253140; $17.95] HD62.5. E38 1985   2843

Ecopreneuring: the complete guide to small business opportunities from the environmental revolution. Steven J. Bennett. New York: Wiley, c1991. x, 308 p. *Notes:* Includes bibliographical references (p. 285-286) and index. [LC 90027593; ISN 0471530743; $17.95] HD62.5. B455 1991   2844

The entrepreneurial experience: confronting career dilemmas of the start-up executive. W. Gibb Dyer, Jr. 1st ed. San Francisco: Jossey-Bass Publishers, c1992. xvii, 268 p. *Notes:* Includes bibliographical references (p. 249-261) and index. [LC 91039474; ISN 1555424171; $28.95] HD62.5. D94 1992   2845

Entrepreneurial systems for the 1990s: their creation, structure, and management. John E. Tropman & Gersh Morningstar; foreword by Sam Zell. New York: Quorum Books, 1989. xvi, 260 p. : ill. *Notes:* Includes index. Bibliography: p. [245]-252. [LC 88015424; ISN 0899302882] HD62.5. T76 1989   2846

The entrepreneur's guide to preparing a winning business plan and raising venture capital. W. Keith Schilit; with a foreword by Victor K. Kiam. Englewood Cliffs, N.J.: Prentice Hall, c1990. xiii, 287 p. *Notes:* Includes bibliographical references and index. [LC 88037103; ISN 0132823020] HG4027.6. S35 1990   2847

The entrepreneur's guide to starting a successful business. James W. Halloran. 2nd ed. New York: McGraw-Hill, c1992. xii, 291 p. : ill. *Notes:* Includes index. [LC 91033435; ISN 0070257981] HD62.5. H35 1992 2848

The entrepreneur's manual: business start-ups, spin-offs, and innovative management. Richard M. White, Jr. 1st ed. Radnor, Pa.: Chilton Book Co., c1977. x, 419 p. *Notes:* Includes indexes. [LC 76055520; ISN 0801964547; $15.00] HD69.N3 W54 +2849

Entrepreneurship for the nineties. Gordon B. Baty. Englewood Cliffs, N.J.: Prentice Hall, c1990. xviii, 270 p. *Notes:* Previously published as: Entrepreneurship for the eighties. Includes bibliographical references and index. [LC 90030552; ISN 0132822946; $19.95] HD62.5. B383 1990 2850

The Ernst & Young business plan guide. Eric S. Siegel, Brian R. Ford, Jay M. Bornstein. 2nd ed. New York: Wiley, c1993. ix, 194 p. : ill. *Notes:* Rev. ed. of: The Arthur Young business plan guide. c1987. Includes index. [LC 92034285; ISN 0471578266] HD62.5. S556 1993 2851

Growing a business. Paul Hawken. New York: Simon and Schuster, c1987. 251 p. *Notes:* Includes index. [LC 87016431; ISN 0671644572] HD62.5. H38 1987 2852

Growing pains: how to make the transition from an entrepreneurship to a professionally managed firm. Eric G. Flamholtz, with the assistance of Yvonne Randle. Rev. ed. San Francisco: Jossey-Bass, 1990. xxxvi, 407 p. : ill. *Notes:* Includes bibliographical references (p. 375-389) and index. [LC 90053088; ISN 1555422721; $27.95] HD62.5. F535 1990 2853

Inc. magazine presents how to really create a successful business plan: featuring the business plans of Pizza Hut, People Express, Ben & Jerry's Ice Cream, Celestial Seasonings, Software Publishing. David E. Gumpert. 1st ed. Boston, MA: Inc. Pub., c1990. vii, 174 p. *Notes:* Includes index. [LC 90212491; ISN 0962614602; $14.95] HG4027.6. G86 1990 2854

Market analysis: assessing your business opportunities. Robert E. Stevens, Philip K. Sherwood, Paul Dunn. New York: Haworth Press, c1993. xiii, 240 p. : ill. *Notes:* Includes bibliographical references and index. [LC 92000220; ISN 156024268X] HD62.5. S745 1993 +2855

The McGraw-Hill guide to starting your own business: a step-by-step blueprint for the first-time entrepreneur. Stephen C. Harper. New York: McGraw-Hill, c1991. xiv, 203 p. : ill. *Notes:* Includes index. *Contents:* Creating a new business—Identifying new business opportunities—The general overview and legal structure—Selecting the right target market—Product-service strategy and price strategy—Promotional strategy and physical distribution strategy—Determining your initial capital requirement—Projecting the financial status for the first years—Applying for a loan—Buying an existing business—Acquiring a franchise—Epilogue: Commencement—You've only just begun. [LC 90044711; ISN 0070266859; $19.95] HD62.5. H3734 1991 2856

The new business incubator: linking talent, technology, capital, and know-how. Raymond W. Smilor, Michael D. Gill, Jr. Lexington, Mass.: Lexington Books, c1986. xix, 199 p. : ill. *Notes:* Includes index. Bibliography: p. 183-187. [LC 85045009; ISN 0669110965] HD62.5. S624 1986 2857

New business ventures and the entrepreneur. Howard H. Stevenson, Michael J. Roberts, H. Irving Grousbeck. 4th ed. Burr Ridge, IL: Irwin, c1994. xii, 740 p. : ill. *Notes:* Includes bibliographical references and indexes. [LC 93024704; ISN 0256110301] HD62.5. S75 1994 +2858

New venture creation: entrepreneurship for the 21st century. Jeffry A. Timmons. 4th ed. Burr Ridge, IL: Irwin, c1994. xix, 796 p. : ill. *Notes:* Includes bibliographical references and index. [LC 93039387; ISN 0256115486] HD62.5. T55 1994 +2859

The new venture handbook. Ronald E. Merrill and Henry D. Sedgwick. New and updated ed. New York: AMACOM, c1993. xiii, 304 p. *Notes:* Includes bibliographical references (p. 297-299) and index. [LC 92027378; ISN 0814450873] HD62.5. M46 1993 2860

New venture mechanics. Karl H. Vesper. Englewood Cliffs, N.J.: Prentice Hall, 1992, c1993. xiii, 380 p. : ill. *Notes:* Includes bibliographical references and indexes. [LC 91043340; ISN 0136207901] HD62.5. V46 1992 2861

New venture strategies. Karl H. Vesper. Rev. ed. Englewood Cliffs, N.J.: Prentice-Hall, c1990. xi, 356 p. : ill. *Notes:* Includes index. Includes bibliographical references. [LC 88036900; ISN 0136159079; $24.60] HD62.5. V47 1990 2862

On your own: how to start, develop, and manage a new business. Robert D. Hisrich, Michael P. Peters. Homewood, IL: Business One Irwin, c1992. xviii, 423 p. : ill. *Notes:* Includes bibliographical references and index. [LC 91032699; ISN 1556236506; $29.95] HD62.5. H579 1992 2863

The perfect business plan made simple. William Lasher. 1st ed. New York: Doubleday, c1994. vii, 278 p. *Notes:* "A Made simple book." [LC 93035669; ISN 0385469349] HD62.5. L37 1994 +2864

A piece of the action: how women and minorities can launch their own successful businesses. Suzanne Caplan. New York: AMACOM, c1994. xi, 145 p. *Notes:* Includes bibliographical references (p. 127-134) and index. [LC 93042510; ISN 0814478697; $17.95] HD62.5. C366 1994 +2865

Planning and financing the new venture. Jeffry A. Timmons. Acton, Mass.: Brick House Pub. Co., c1990. xx, 188 p. : ill. *Notes:* Includes bibliographical references. [LC 89022115; ISN 0931790921; ISN 093179093X; $24.95; $18.95]   HD62.5. T56 1990   2866

Planning and forming your company. Gustav Berle. New York: Wiley, c1990. xiv, 272 p. *Notes:* Includes bibliographical references. [LC 89022430; ISN 047151795X; $49.95]   HD62.5. B484 1990   2867

Secrets of a successful entrepreneur: how to start and succeed at running your own business. Gene Daily. Pleasanton, CA: K&A Publications, c1993. xvi, 334 p. *Notes:* Includes bibliographical references (p. 319-323) and index. [LC 93091403; ISN 1883635012; $24.95]   HD62.5. D35 1993   +2868

The Silver prescription: the eight-step action plan for entrepreneurial success. A Divid Silver. New York: Wiley, c1987. xii, 202 p. : ill. *Notes:* Includes index. [LC 86028135; ISN 0471856371]
                                                                   HD62.5. S557 1987   2869

The small business test. Colin Ingram. Berkeley, Calif.: Ten Speed Press, c1990. 96 p. : ill. [LC 90011063; ISN 0898153719; $8.95]   HD62.5. I54 1990   2870

The start-up entrepreneur: how you can succeed in building your own company into a major enterprise starting from scratch. James R. Cook. New York: E.P. Dutton, c1986. xii, 306 p. *Notes:* "A Truman Talley book." Includes index. Bibliography: p. 293-296. [LC 85016160; ISN 0525243720]
                                                                   HD62.5. C664 1986   2871

Starting and managing the small business. Arthur H. Kuriloff, John M. Hemphill, Jr. 2nd ed. New York: McGraw-Hill, c1988. xxi, 663 p. : ill. *Notes:* Includes bibliographies and index. [LC 87003832; ISN 0070356653; $32.95 (est.)]   HD62.5. K87 1988   2872

Starting and operating a business after you retire: what you need to know to succeed. Bess Ritter May. Garden City Park, N.Y.: Avery Pub. Group, c1993. ix, 246 p. *Notes:* Spine title: Starting & operating a business after you retire. Includes bibliographical references and index. [LC 93023063; ISN 0895295679; $12.95]   HD62.5. M38 1993   +2873

The successful business plan: secrets & strategies. by Rhonda M. Abrams. 2nd ed. Grants Pass, Or.: Oasis Press/PSI Research, c1993. xxviii, 320 p. : ill. *Notes:* Includes index. [LC 93021563; ISN 1555711944; $21.95]   HD62.5. A344 1993   +2874

Sweat equity: what it really takes to build America's best small companies—by the guys who did it. Geoffrey N. Smith, Paul B. Brown. New York: Simon and Schuster, c1986. 254 p. *Notes:* Includes index. [LC 86006622; ISN 0671552104]   HD62.5. S625 1986   2875

The woman entrepreneur: starting, financing, and managing a successful new business. Robert D. Hisrich and Candida G. Brush. Lexington, Mass.: Lexington Books, c1986. xvi, 216 p. : ill. *Notes:* Bibliography: p. [193]-195. [LC 84048256; ISN 0669091898]   HD62.5. H58 1986   2876

NEW PRODUCTS

The art of product development: from concept of market. Erwin A. Frand. Homewood, Ill.: Dow Jones-Irwin, c1989. xvi, 186 p. [LC 88036705; $22.95]   HF5415.153. F73 1989   2877

The best of Japan. 1st ed. Tokyo: New York, N.Y., U.S.A.: Kodansha; Distributed in the U.S. by Kodansha International/USA through Harper & Row, 1987. 288, xiv p. : ill. (some col.) *Notes:* Includes index. [LC 86040432; ISN 0870118013; $24.95 (U.S.)]   HF5415.153. B47 1987   2878

Better mousetraps: product improvements that led to success. by Nathan Aaseng. Minneapolis: Lerner Publications, c1990. 80 p. : ill. *Notes:* Includes bibliographical references (p. 76). Presents brief biographies of individuals who improved, refined, and perfected various products and processes, from cameras to razors. [LC 89012803; ISN 0822506807; $10.95]
                                                                  HF5415.153. A23 1990   2879

Breakthroughs!. P. Ranganath Nayak and John M. Ketteringham. [Newly rev. ed.]. Amsterdam; San Diego, CA: Pfeiffer, c1994. xx, 428 p. *Notes:* Includes bibliographical references (p. 415) and index.; ISN 0893842508; $29.95]   HF5415.153. N38 1994   +2880

Bringing innovation to market: how to break corporate and customer barriers. Jagdish N. Sheth, S. Ram. New York: Wiley, c1987. xii, 247 p. : ill. *Notes:* Includes bibliographies and index. [LC 87017611; ISN 0471849774]   HD69.N4 S494 1987   2881

Essentials of new product management. Glen L. Urban, John R. Hauser, Nikhilesh Dholakia. Englewood Cliffs, N.J.: Prentice-Hall, c1987. x, 340 p. : ill. *Notes:* Includes bibliographical references and index. [LC 86008160; ISN 013286584X]   HF5415.153. U73 1987   2882

From concept to market. Gary S. Lynn. New York: Wiley, c1989. viii, 248 p. : ill. *Notes:* Includes index. Bibliography: p. 240-243. [LC 88027851; ISN 0471501263; $39.95]   HF5415.153. L96 1989   2883

Managing new product and process development: text and cases. Kim B. Clark, Steven C. Wheelwright. New York: Toronto: New York: Free Press; Maxwell Macmillan Canada; Maxwell Macmillan International, c1993. xv, 896 p. : ill. *Notes:* Includes bibliographical references (p. 873-879) and index. [LC 92029067; ISN 0029055172]   HF5415.153. C58 1993   2834

Managing new product innovations. William E. Souder. Lexington, Mass.: Lexington Books, c1987. xviii, 251 p. ill. *Notes:* Includes bibliographies and index. [LC 85040104; ISN 066910809X]   HD69.N4 S634 1987   2835

Managing new products: the power of innovation. Thomas D. Kuczmarski. 2nd ed. Englewood Cliffs, N.J.: Prentice Hall, 1992. xiii, 304 p. : ill. *Notes:* Includes index. [LC 91039058; ISN 0135446694; $37.50]   HF5415.153. K83 1992   2886

Managing the new product development process: cases and notes. Robert J. Dolan. Reading, Mass.: Addison-Wesley, c1993. viii, 392: ill. *Notes:* Includes bibliographical references. [LC 92010721; ISN 0201526271]   HF5415.153. D65 1993   +2887

New product development. George Gruenwald; foreword by Peter G. Peterson. 2nd ed. Lincolnwood, Ill., USA: NTC Business Books, 1992. xxvi, 454 p. : ill. *Notes:* Includes bibliographical references and index. [LC 91030698; ISN 0844233528; $45.94]   HF5415.153. G75 1992   2888

New product development and marketing: a practical guide. Italo S. Servi. New York: Praeger, 1990. xv, 180 p. : ill. *Notes:* Includes bibliographical references (p. [173]-175) and index. [LC 89070956; ISN 0275934039; $42.95]   HF5415.153. S47 1990   2889

New product development checklists: proven checklists for developing new products from mission to market. George Gruenwald. Lincolnwood, Ill., USA: NTC Business Books, c1991. xv, 106 p. [LC 90043722; ISN 0844232173; $22.95]   HF5415.153. G77 1991   2890

The new products handbook. edited by Larry Wizenberg. Homewood, IL.: Dow Jones-Irwin, c1986. x, 337 p. : ill. *Notes:* Includes bibliographical references and index. [LC 85071278; ISN 0870945203]   HD69.N4 N48   2891

New products management. C. Merle Crawford. 3rd ed. Homewood, IL: Irwin, c1991. xxi, 564 p. : ill. *Notes:* Includes bibliographical references (p. 552-554) and index. [LC 90004596; $58.75]   HF5415.153. C72 1991   2892

New venture analysis: research, planning, and finance. Dennis R. Costello. Homewood, Ill.: Dow Jones-Irwin, c1985. xii, 190 p. : ill. *Notes:* Includes index. Bibliography: p. 179-184. [LC 84073197; ISN 087094505X]   HF5415.153. C67 1985   2893

Pioneering new products: a market survival guide. Edwin E. Bobrow, Dennis W. Shafer. Homewood, Ill.: Dow Jones-Irwin, c1987. viii, 234 p. : ill. *Notes:* Includes bibliographical references and index. [LC 86050777; ISN 0870946218]   HF5415.153. B63 1987   2894

Revolutionizing product development: quantum leaps in speed, efficiency, and quality. Steven C. Wheelwright, Kim B. Clark. New York: Toronto: New York: Free Press; Maxwell Macmillan Canada; Maxwell Macmillan International, c1992. xv, 364 p. : ill. *Notes:* Includes bibliographical references and index. [LC 91038170; ISN 0029055156; $35.00]   HF5415.153. W44 1992   2895

NEW YORK (N.Y.)—SOCIAL LIFE AND CUSTOMS

Manhattan passions: true tales of power, wealth, and excess. Ron Rosenbaum. 1st ed. New York: Beech Tree Books, c1987. 285 p. [LC 86017351; ISN 0688066127]   F125. R67 1987   2896

NEW YORK STOCK EXCHANGE

Rebuilding Wall Street: "after the Crash of '87, fifty insiders talk about putting Wall Street together again". Mark Fadiman. Englewood Cliffs, N.J.: Prentice Hall, c1992. xxx, 274 p. *Notes:* Includes bibliographical references (p. 251-253) and index. [LC 92023931; ISN 0137530137; $19.95]   HG4572. F33 1992   2897

Revolution on Wall Street: the rise and decline of the New York Stock Exchange. Marshall E. Blume, Jeremy J. Siegel, and Dan Rottenberg. 1st ed. New York: Norton, c1993. 320 p. *Notes:* Includes bibliographical references (p. [287]-295) and index. [LC 93009238; ISN 0393035263]   HG4572. B67 1993   +2898

NEWHOUSE, SAMUEL I

Newhouse: all the glitter, power, and glory of America's richest media empire and the secretive man behind it. Thomas Maier. 1st ed. New York: St. Martin's Press, 1994. x, 446 p., [16] p. of plates: ill. *Notes:* "A Thomas Dunne book." Includes bibliographical references and index. [LC 94019816; ISN 0312114818; $24.95]   Z473.N47 M35 1994   +2899

NEXT (COMPUTER)

Steve Jobs and the NeXT big thing. Randall E. Stross. New York: Toronto: New York: Atheneum; Maxwell Macmillan Canada; Maxwell Macmillan International, 1993. viii, 374 p. : ill. *Notes:* Includes bibliographical references (p. 353-366) and index. [LC 93020761; ISN 0689121350; $24.00 ($29.95 Can.)]   QA76.5. S786 1993   +2900

NIKE (FIRM)

Intelligent enterprise: a knowledge and service based paradigm for industry. James Brian Quinn; foreword by Tom Peters. New York: Toronto: New York: Free Press; Maxwell Macmillan Canada; Maxwell Macmillan International, c1992. xx, 473 p. : ill. *Notes:* Includes bibliographical references (p. 441-455) and index. [LC 92019384; ISN 0029256151; $29.95]   HD58.9. Q357 1992   2901

Just do it: the Nike spirit in the corporate world. Donald Katz. 1st ed. New York: Random House, c1994. xiii, 336 p. *Notes:* "Portions of this work were originally published in Sports illustrated"—D/T.p. verso. Includes index. [LC 93045893; ISN 0679432752; $23.00]   HD9992.U54 N555 1994   +2902

Swoosh: the unauthorized story of Nike, and the men who played there. J.B. Strasser & Laurie Becklund. 1st ed. New York: Harcourt Brace Jovanovich, 1991. xxi, 682 p. *Notes:* Includes index. [LC 91022830; ISN 0151874301; $24.95]   HD9992.U54 N557 1991   2903

NINTENDO KABUSHIKI KAISHA

Game over: how Nintendo zapped an American industry, captured your dollars, and enslaved your children. David Sheff. 1st ed. New York: Random House, c1993. xiii, 445 p. *Notes:* Includes bibliographical references (p. [429]-432) and index. [LC 92050506; ISN 0679404694; $25.00]   HD9993.E454 N577 1993   2904

NISSAN MOTOR MANUFACTURING (UK)

The Nissan enigma: flexibility at work in a local economy. Philip Garrahan and Paul Stewart. London; New York: Mansell, 1992. xii, 148 p. *Notes:* Includes bibliographical references and index. [LC 91015255; ISN 0720120209; $80.00]   HD9710.G74 N574 1992   2905

NOBEL, ALFRED BERNHARD

Alfred Nobel: a biography. Kenne Fant; translated from the Swedish by Marianne Ruuth. 1st English-language ed. New York: Arcade: Distributed by Little, Brown, c1993. viii, 342 p. : ill. *Notes:* Includes index. [LC 93028235; ISN 1559702222; $24.95 ($31.95 in Canada)]   TP268.5.N7 F3613 1993   +2906

NOMURA SHOKEN KABUSHIKI KAISHA

Deceitful practices: Nomura Securities and the Japanese invasion of Wall Street. John E. Fitzgibbon, Jr. New York: Carol Pub. Group, c1991. xiii, 222 p. *Notes:* "A Birch Lane Press book." Includes index. [LC 91027252; ISN 1559720980; $24.95]   HG5774.5. F57 1991   2907

NONPROFIT ORGANIZATIONS

The complete guide to nonprofit management. Smith, Bucklin & Associates; edited by Robert H. Wilbur, Susan Kudla Finn, and Carolyn M. Freeland. New York: Wiley, c1994. xxiii, 326 p. : ill. *Notes:* Includes bibliographical references. [LC 94022989; ISN 0471309532] HD62.6 .C66 1994 +2908

The entrepreneurial nonprofit executive. Thomas A. McLaughlin. Rockville, Md.: Fund Raising Institute, c1991. xi, 264 p. *Notes:* Includes bibliographical references (p. 259-260) and index. [LC 91071517; ISN 0930807227] HD62.6 .M393 1991 +2909

Executive leadership in nonprofit organizations: new strategies for shaping executive-board dynamics. Robert D. Herman, Richard D. Heimovics. 1st ed. San Francisco: Jossey-Bass, 1991. xx, 151 p. *Notes:* Includes bibliographical references (p. 141-145) and index. [LC 90021028; ISN 1555423345; $22.95] HD62.6 .H47 1991 2910

Filthy rich and other nonprofit fantasies: changing the way nonprofits do business in the 90's. by Richard Steckel with Robin Simons and Peter Lengsfelder. Berkeley, Calif.: Ten Speed Press, c1989. xv, 223 p. : ill. *Notes:* Cover title: Filthy rich & other nonprofit fantasies. Includes index. Bibliography: p. 223. [LC 88026045; ISN 0898152674; $8.95] HD62.6 .S74 1989 2911

Financial accounting and managerial control for nonprofit organizations. Regina E. Herzlinger, Denise Nitterhouse. Cincinnati, Ohio: South-Western Pub., 1993, c1994. xvii, 878 p. : ill. *Notes:* Includes bibliographical references and index. [LC 91017144; ISN 0538816023] HF5686.N56 H47 1993 2912

Financial accounting in nonbusiness organizations: an exploratory study of conceptual issues: research report. Robert N. Anthony. Stamford, Conn.: Financial Accounting Standards Board, c1978. xviii, 205 p. *Notes:* Bibliography: p. 197-205. [LC 78058734; $5.00] HJ9733 .A583 2913

Financial and accounting guide for not-for-profit organizations. Malvern J. Gross, Jr., William Warshauer, Jr., Richard F. Larkin. 4th ed. New York: Wiley, c1991. xvi, 686 p. *Notes:* Rev. ed. of: Financial and accounting guide for nonprofit organizations. 3rd ed. c1979. Includes bibliographical references (p. 663-665) and index. [LC 90021695; ISN 0471542059; $85.00] HF5686.N56 G76 1991 2914

Financial and strategic management for nonprofit organizations. Herrington J. Bryce. 2nd ed. Englewood Cliffs, N.J.: Prentice Hall, 1992. xxi, 625 p. *Notes:* Includes bibliographical references and index. [LC 91029025; ISN 0133775739; $56.35] HD62.6 .B78 1992 2915

Financial management in nonprofit organizations. Richard F. Wacht. 2nd ed. Atlanta, Ga.: Georgia State University Business Press, College of Business Administration, c1991, 1990. xviii, 545 p. : ill. *Notes:* Includes bibliographical references and index. [LC 90044446; ISN 0884062147; $49.95] HG4027.65 .W33 1990 2916

The future of the nonprofit sector: challenges, changes, and policy considerations. Virginia A. Hodgkinson, Richard W. Lyman, and associates. 1st ed. San Francisco: Jossey-Bass, 1989. xxxv, 507 p. : ill. *Notes:* "A publication of Independent Sector." Includes bibliographical references. [LC 89045596; ISN 1555421792; $35.00] HD2769.2.U6 H64 1989 2917

Introduction to nonprofit organization accounting. Emerson O. Henke. 4th ed. Cincinnati, Ohio: College Division, South-Western Pub. Co., c1992. xix, 746 p. *Notes:* Includes bibliographical references and index. [LC 91036278; ISN 0538821825; $55.95] HF5686.N56 H45 1992 2918

Making boards effective: the dynamics of nonprofit governing boards. Alvin Zander. 1st ed. San Francisco: Jossey-Bass, c1993. xviii, 169 p. *Notes:* Includes bibliographical references (p. 155-160) and index. [LC 93019577; ISN 1555425801; $25.95] HD62.6 .Z36 1993 +2919

Management control in nonprofit organizations. Robert N. Anthony, Regina E. Herzlinger. Rev. ed. Homewood, Ill.: R. D. Irwin, 1980. xv, 600 p. : ill. (The Willard J. Graham series in accounting) *Notes:* Includes bibliographical references and index. [LC 79089951; ISN 0256023263] HF5686.N56 A67 1980 2920

Managing a nonprofit organization. Thomas Wolf; illustrated by Barbara Carter. 1st ed. New York: Prentice Hall Press, c1990. ix, 310 p. : ill. *Notes:* Includes bibliographical references (p. 299-302) and index. [LC 89022807; ISN 0135515572; $12.95] HD62.6 .W649 1990 2921

Marketing designs for nonprofit organizations. Jack Christian. Rockville, Md.: Fund Raising Institute, c1992. viii, 250 p. : ill. [LC 92070207; ISN 0930807383] HF5415 .C5268 1992 +2922

Nonprofit corporations, organizations, and associations. Howard L. Oleck. 5th ed. Englewood Cliffs, N.J.: Prentice-Hall, c1988. xxii, 1274 p. : ill. *Notes:* Spine title: Nonprofit corporations, organizations & associations. Includes bibliographies and index. [LC 88004171; ISN 0136233805; $79.95] KF1388 .O44 1988 2923

The nonprofit economy. Burton A. Weisbrod. Cambridge, Mass.: Harvard University Press, 1988. ix, 251 p. *Notes:* Includes index. Bibliography: p. [217]-246. [LC 87023718; ISN 0674626257] HD2769.2.U6 W45 1988 2924

The nonprofit organization: essential readings. edited by David L. Gies, J. Steven Ott, Jay M. Shafritz. Pacific Grove, Calif.: Brooks/Cole Pub. Co., c1990. xxvi, 402 p. *Notes:* Includes bibliographical references. [LC 89017373; ISN 0534125883]   HD62.6. N665 1990   2925

The nonprofit sector: a research handbook. edited by Walter W. Powell. New Haven: Yale University Press, c1987. xiii, 464 p. *Notes:* Includes bibliographies and index. [LC 86015984; ISN 0300037023]   HD62.6. N67 1987   2926

Profiles of excellence: achieving success in the nonprofit sector. E.B. Knauft, Renee A. Berger, Sandra T. Gray. 1st ed. San Francisco: Jossey-Bass Publishers, 1991. xxv, 169 p. *Notes:* Includes bibliographical references (p. 159-162) and index. [LC 90023637; ISN 155542337X; $22.95]   HD62.6. K56 1991   2927

Public & nonprofit marketing. Christopher H. Lovelock & Charles B. Weinberg. 2nd edition. Redwood City, Calif.: Scientific Press, c1989. x, 520 p. : ill. *Notes:* Includes bibliographies and index.; ISN 0894261347; $57.00]   HF5415. L653 1989   2928

Strategic management in non-profit organizations: an administrator's handbook. Robert D. Hay. New York: Quorum Books, c1990. viii, 398 p. : ill. *Notes:* Includes bibliographical references. [LC 89024368; ISN 0899305512; $59.95]   HD62.6. H39 1990   2929

Strategic marketing for nonprofit organizations. Philip Kotler, Alan R. Andreasen. 4th ed. Englewood Cliffs, N.J.: Prentice Hall, c1991. xi, 644 p. : ill. *Notes:* Includes bibliographical references and indexes. [LC 90046176; ISN 0138519323; $56.00]   HF5415. K6312 1991   2930

The third America: the emergence of the nonprofit sector in the United States. Michael O'Neill. 1st ed. San Francisco: Jossey-Bass, 1989. xvii, 215 p. *Notes:* Includes index. Bibliography: p. 183-196. [LC 89033760; ISN 1555421652; $22.95]   HD2785. O54 1989   2931

NORRIS, WILLIAM C

William C. Norris: portrait of a maverick. James C. Worthy. Cambridge, Mass.: Ballinger Pub. Co., 1987. xiv, 259 p. : ill., ports. *Notes:* Includes index. Bibliography: p. [245]-250. [LC 87001808; ISN 0887300871]   HD9696.C62 N689 1987   2932

NORTH AMERICA—COMMERCE

North American free trade: assessing the impact. Nora Lustig, Barry P. Bosworth, and Robert Z. Lawrence, editors. Washington, D.C.: Brookings Institution, c1992. xii, 274 p. : ill. *Notes:* Rev. papers from a Brookings Institution conference entitled "NAFTA: an assessment of the research," held in April 1992. Includes bibliographical references and index. *Contents:* The impact of a North American free trade area: applied general equilibrium models / Drusilla K. Brown—Labor issues in a North American free trade area / Raúl Hinojosa-Ojeda, Sherman Robinson—Modeling the industrial effects of NAFTA / Sidney Weintraub—NAFTA and agriculture: a review of the economic impacts / Tim Josling—NAFTA as the center of an integration process: the nontrade issues / Robert A. Pastor—NAFTA and the rest of the world / Carlos Alberto Primo Braga. [LC 92026402; ISN 0815753160; $31.95]   HF3211. N667 1992   2933

NUCLEAR INDUSTRY

Collapse of an industry: nuclear power and the contradictions of U.S. policy. John L. Campbell. Ithaca, N.Y.: Cornell University Press, 1988. xiii, 231 p. (Cornell studies in political economy) *Notes:* Includes index. Bibliography: p. 199-224. [LC 87047856; ISN 080142111X; ISN 0801495008]   HD9698.U52 C35 1988   2934

OCCUPATIONAL HEALTH SERVICES

The healthy workplace: a blueprint for corporate action. William M. Kizer. New York: Wiley, c1987. xxiii, 187 p. : ill. *Notes:* Includes index. Bibliography: p. 167-178. [LC 86019095; ISN 0471845310]   RC968. K58 1987   2935

OFFICE EQUIPMENT AND SUPPLIES INDUSTRY

Before the computer: IBM, NCR, Burroughs, and Remington Rand and the industry they created, 1865-1956. James W. Cortada. Princeton, N.J.: Princeton University Press, c1993. xx, 344 p. : ill. *Notes:* Includes bibliographical references (p. [289]-329) and index. [LC 92025399; ISN 069104807X] HD9801.U542 C67 1993 2936

OFFICE LAYOUT

Behavioral issues in office design. Jean D. Wineman, editor. New York, N.Y.: Van Nostrand Reinhold, c1986. xvii, 364 p. : ill. *Notes:* Includes index. Bibliography: p. 325-349. [LC 85007339; ISN 0442291817; $40.00] HF5547.2. B43 1986 2937

Making and managing high-quality workplaces: an organizational ecology. Fritz Steele. New York: Teachers College Press, c1986. xiv, 209 p. : ill. *Notes:* Includes bibliographical references and index. [LC 85017386; ISN 0807728128; ISN 0807727776] HF5547.2. S78 2938

OFFICE PRACTICE

The changing workplace: a guide to managing the people, organizational, and regulatory aspects of office technology. Alan F. Westin... et al. White Plains, NY: Knowledge Industry Publications, c1985. 1 v. (various pagings): ill. (Information and communications management guides) *Notes:* Bibliography: p. B1-B15. [LC 84023355; ISN 0867291028; $125.00] HF5548.2. C463 1985 2939

Critical issues in office automation. Walter A. Kleinschrod. New York: McGraw-Hill, c1986. xiv, 223 p. *Notes:* Includes index. Bibliography: p. 205-212. [LC 85019837; ISN 0070350345; $28.95] HF5547.5. K53 1986 2940

The electronic sweatshop: how computers are transforming the office of the future into the factory of the past. Barbara Garson. New York: Simon & Schuster, c1988. 288 p. *Notes:* Includes index. Bibliography: p. [271]-273. [LC 88003045; ISN 0671530496] HF5548. G37 1988 2941

Gendered by design?: information technology and office systems. edited by Eileen Green, Jenny Owen, Den Pain. London; Washington, D.C.: Taylor & Francis, 1993. vii, 218 p. : ill. *Notes:* Includes bibliographical references and index. [LC 93015308; ISN 0748400923] HF5548.2. G44 1993 +2942

Information payoff: the transformation of work in the electronic age. Paul A. Strassmann. New York: London: Free Press; Collier Macmillan, c1985. xix, 298 p. : ill. *Notes:* Includes index. Bibliography: p. 282-289. [LC 84024737; ISN 0029317207] HF5547.5. S79 1985 2943

Re-engineering the networked enterprise. Y. Jayachandra with Raul Medina-More, Gita J. Melkote, Fernando Flores. New York: McGraw-Hill, c1994. xi, 290 p. : ill. *Notes:* Includes index. [LC 93005896; ISN 0070320179; $40.00] HF5548. J39 1994 +2944

The white-collar shuffle: who does what in today's computerized workplace. Richard W. Larson and David J. Zimney. New York, NY: AMACOM, American Management Association, c1990. xvi, 288 p. : ill. *Notes:* Includes bibliographical references (p. 271-278) and index. [LC 89081024; ISN 081445996X; $24.95] HF5548. L28 1990 2945

OLD AGE

Lifetrends: the future of baby boomers and other aging Americans. by Jerry Gerber... et al. New York: Macmillan Pub. Co., c1989. xiv, 271 p. *Notes:* "A Stonesong Press book." Includes index. Bibliography: p. [255]-260. [LC 89008233; ISN 0025172913; $18.95] HQ1064.U5 L553 1989 2946

OLD AGE PENSIONS

Fundamentals of private pensions. Dan M. McGill, Donald S. Grubbs, Jr. 6th ed. Homewood, Ill.: Published for the Pension Research Council, Wharton School, University of Pennsylvania by Irwin, 1989. xxviii, 785 p. : ill. *Notes:* Includes bibliographical references and index. [LC 88010341; ISN 025606041X; $31.00] HD7105.35.U6 M34 1989 2947

Labor's capital: the economics and politics of private pensions. Teresa Ghilarducci. Cambridge, Mass.: MIT Press, c1992. xi, 213 p. *Notes:* Includes bibliographical references (p. [183]-197) and index. [LC 91038544; ISN 0262071398]   HD7105.35.U6 G45 1992   2948

Pension planning: pensions, profit-sharing, and other deferred compensation plans. Everett T. Allen, Jr... et al. 7th ed. Homewood, Ill.: Irwin, c1992. xii, 500 p. *Notes:* Rev. ed. of: Pension planning / Everett T. Allen, Jr. 6th ed. 1988. Includes bibliographical references and index. [LC 91044319; ISN 0256082960; $49.95]   HD7105.35.U6 A44 1992   2949

OLSEN, KENNETH H

The ultimate entrepreneur: the story of Ken Olsen and Digital Equipment Corporation. Glenn Rifkin and George Harrar. Updated. Rocklin, CA: Prima Pub., c1990. xii, 336 p. *Notes:* Includes index. [LC 89010807; ISN 1559580224; $10.95]   HD9696.C62 O487 1990   2950

ONLINE DATA PROCESSING

Managing today and tomorrow with on-line information. Linda Gail Christie. Homewood, Ill.: Dow Jones-Irwin, 1986. xvi, 278 p. : ill. *Notes:* Includes index. [LC 85072257; ISN 0870946668]   HF5548.3. C495   2951

OPERATIONS RESEARCH

Operations research: an introduction. Hamdy A. Taha. 4th ed. New York: London: Macmillan; Collier Macmillan, c1987. xv, 876 p. : ill. *Notes:* Includes index. [LC 86005366; ISN 0024189405]   T57.6. T3 1987   2952

Operations research: applications and algorithms. Wayne L. Winston. 2nd ed. Boston: PWS-Kent Pub. Co., c1991. xvi, 1262 p. : ill. *Notes:* Includes bibliographical references and index. [LC 90007817; ISN 0534980791; $55.95]   T57.6. W645 1991   2953

Operations research: principles and practice. A. Ravindran, Don T. Phillips, James J. Solberg. 2nd ed. New York: Wiley, c1987. xviii, 637 p. : ill. *Notes:* Includes bibliographies and index. [LC 86005561; ISN 0471086088]   T57.6. P48 1987   2954

Principles of operations research for management. Frank S. Budnick, Dennis McLeavey, Richard Mojena. 2nd ed. Homewood, Ill.: Irwin, 1988. xx, 988 p. : ill. (some col.) *Notes:* Includes index. [LC 87081435; ISN 0256026432; $24.50]   T57.6. B76 1988   2955

Quantitative approaches to management. Richard I. Levin... et al. 7th ed. New York: McGraw-Hill, c1989. xiv, 848 p. : ill. (some col.) *Notes:* Includes index. Bibliography: p. 841-843. [LC 88013169; ISN 0070374783; $41.95]   T57.6. Q36 1989   2956

OPM LEASING SERVICES

Bad business: the OPM scandal and the seduction of the establishment. Robert P. Gandossy. New York: Basic Books, c1985. x, 262 p. *Notes:* Includes index. Bibliography: p. [242]-257. [LC 85047556; ISN 0465005705; $17.95]   HD9696.C64 O664 1985   2957

Other people's money: the rise and fall of OPM Leasing Services. Stephen Fenichell. 1st ed. Garden City, N.Y.: Anchor Press/Doubleday, 1985. 305 p. [LC 84024256; ISN 0385193688; $15.95]   HF5548.6. F46 1985   2958

OPTICAL COMMUNICATIONS

The rewiring of America: the fiber optics revolution. C. David Chaffee. Boston: Academic Press, c1988. xii, 241 p. : ill. *Notes:* Includes bibliographical references and index. [LC 87018709; ISN 0121663604]   TK5103.59. C465 1988   2959

OPTIONS (FINANCE)

Financial options: from theory to practice. edited by Stephen Figlewski, William L. Silber, Marti G. Subrahmanyam. Homewood, Ill.: Business One Irwin, c1990. xii, 580 p. : ill. *Notes:* "Salomon Brothers Center for the Study of Financial Institutions, Leonard N. Stern School of Business, New York University." Includes bibliographical references and index. [LC 90003770; ISN 1556232349; $49.95]   HG6024.U6 F56 1990   2960

How the options markets work. Joseph A. Walker. New York: New York Institute of Finance, c1991. xiii, 229 p. : ill. *Notes:* Includes index. [LC 90043549; ISN 013400888X; $17.95]   HG6024.A3 W35 1991   2961

The new options market. Max G. Ansbacher. Rev. ed., 1st paperback ed. New York: Walker, c1987. xvii, 280 p. : ill. *Notes:* Includes index. [LC 87018892; ISN 0802773087; $16.95]   HG6042. A57 1987   2962

Options as a strategic investment. Lawrence G. McMillan. 3rd ed. New York: New York Institute of Finance, c1993. xvi, 882 p. : ill. *Notes:* Includes index. [LC 92026130; ISN 0136360025; $49.95]   HG6042. M35 1993   2963

The options manual. Gary L. Gastineau. 3rd ed. New York: McGraw-Hill, c1988. xvi, 440 p. : ill. *Notes:* Rev. ed. of: The stock options manual. 2nd ed. c1979. Includes index. Bibliography: p. 367-399. [LC 87025987; ISN 0070229813; $42.50]   HG6042. G37 1988   2964

Options: theory, strategy, and applications. Peter Ritchken. Glenview, Ill.: Scott, Foresman, c1987. xiii, 414 p. : ill. (Robert S. Hamada series in finance) *Notes:* Includes bibliographies and index. [LC 86029721; ISN 0673183076]   HG6042. R57 1987   2965

Speculative markets. Robert A. Strong. 2nd ed. New York: HarperCollins College Publishers, c1994. x, 438 p. : ill. *Notes:* Includes bibliographical references (p. 414-427) and index. [LC 93034752; ISN 0065012496]   HG6024.3. S76 1994   +2966

OPTOELECTRONICS INDUSTRY

The new optoelectronics ball game: the policy struggle between the U.S. and Japan for the competitive edge. Philip Seidenberg. New York: IEEE Press, Institute of Electrical and Electronics Engineers, c1992. xi, 132 p. *Notes:* "IEEE order number: PC0301-2"—Verso t.p. Includes bibliographical references (p. 113-127) and index. [LC 91044004; ISN 0780304063]   HD9696.O673 U67 1992   2967

ORGANIZATION

Beyond dispute: the invention of team syntegrity. Stafford Beer. Chichester; New York: Wiley, 1994. xi, 367 p. : ill. *Notes:* Includes bibliographical references (p. [357]-359) and index. [LC 94002439; ISN 0471944513]   HD38. B3627 1994   +2968

Classics of organization theory. edited by Jay M. Shafritz, J. Steven Ott. 3rd ed. Pacific Grove, CA: Brooks/Cole Pub. Co., c1992. ix, 534 p. : ill. *Notes:* Includes bibliographical references. [LC 91032705; ISN 0534173047; $23.95]   HD31. C576 1992   2969

Creative organization theory: a resourcebook. Gareth Morgan. Newbury Park, Calif.: Sage Publications, c1989. 369 p. : ill. *Notes:* Includes bibliographies. [LC 88028288; ISN 0803934386; $19.95]   HD31. M6283 1989   2970

Designing effective organizations: the sociotechnical systems perspective. William A. Pasmore. New York: Wiley, c1988. x, 200 p. : ill. (Wiley series on organizational assessment and change) *Notes:* Includes indexes. Bibliography: p. 187-194. [LC 87029521; ISN 0471887854]   HM131. P3426 1988   2971

Excellent organizations: how to develop & manage them using Theory Z. James Lewis, Jr. New York: J.L. Wilkerson Pub. Co., c1985. xvii, 307 p. : ill. *Notes:* Includes index. Bibliography: p. 295-300. [LC 83051208; ISN 0915253003]   HD31. L423   2972

Human systems development. edited by Robert Tannenbaum, Newton Margulies, Fred Massarik, and associates. 1st ed. San Francisco: Jossey-Bass Publishers, 1985. xxxi, 605 p. : ill. (The Jossey-Bass management series) (The Jossey-Bass social and behavioral science series.) *Notes:* Includes bibliographies and indexes. [LC 85009900; ISN 0875896529]   HD58.7. H86 1985   2973

Organization and management: a systems and contingency approach. Fremont E. Kast, James E. Rosenzweig. 4th ed. New York: McGraw-Hill, c1985. xiii, 720 p. : ill. (McGraw-Hill series in management) *Notes:* Includes indexes. Bibliography: p. 691-699. [LC 84019450; ISN 0070334439; $30.50 (est.)]   HD31. K33 1985   2974

Organization: text, cases, and readings on the management of organizational design and change. Phyllis F. Schlesinger... et al. 3rd ed. Homewood, IL: Irwin, c1992. viii, 599 p. : ill., map *Notes:* Rev. ed. of Organization / John P. Kotter, Leonard A. Schlesinger, Vijay Sathe. 2nd ed. 1986. Includes bibliographical references. [LC 91023122; ISN 0256091846; $45.95] HD31. O73 1992   2975

Organization theory: a macro perspective for management. John H. Jackson, Cyril P. Morgan, Joseph G.P. Paolillo. 3rd ed. Englewood Cliffs, N.J.: Prentice Hall, c1986. xi, 387 p. : ill. *Notes:* Includes bibliographies and index. [LC 85019220; ISN 0136415725; $29.95] HD31. J23 1986   2976

Organization theory: a strategic approach. V.K. (Veekay) Narayanan, Raghu Nath. Homewood, IL: Irwin, c1993. xxiv, 614 p. : ill. (some col.) *Notes:* Includes bibliographical references and index. [LC 92031180; ISN 0256087784] HD31. N25 1993   2977

Organization theory: a structural and behavioral analysis. William G. Scott, Terence R. Mitchell, Philip H. Birnbarum i.e. Birnbaum. 4th ed. Homewood, Ill.: R.D. Irwin, 1981. xiv, 356 p. : ill. (The Irwin series in management and the behavioral sciences) *Notes:* Includes bibliographical references and indexes. [LC 80084322; ISN 0256025150] HD31. S364 1981   2978

Organization theory and management: a macro approach. Warren B. Brown, Dennis J. Moberg. New York: Wiley, c1980. xxv, 685 p. : ill. (Wiley series in management) *Notes:* Includes bibliographical references and indexes. [LC 79018709; ISN 0471020230] HD31. B7668   2979

Organization theory: structure, design, and applications. Stephen P. Robbins. 2nd ed. Englewood Cliffs, N.J.: Prentice-Hall, 1986. xxii, 518 p. : ill. *Notes:* Includes bibliographies and indexes. [LC 86016924; ISN 0136419453] HD31. R565 1986   2980

Organizational theory and design: a strategic approach for management. Edwin A. Gerloff. New York: McGraw-Hill, c1985. xviii, 378 p. : ill. *Notes:* Includes bibliographies and indexes. [LC 84015485; ISN 007023177X; $28.95 (est.)] HD31. G435 1985   2981

Organizations: a micro/macro approach. Richard L. Daft, Richard M. Steers. Glenview, Ill.: Scott, Foresman, c1986. 618 p. : ill. (The Scott, Foresman series in management and organizations) *Notes:* Includes bibliographical references and index. [LC 85027864; ISN 0673182207] HD31. D137 1986   2982

Organizations: a quantum view. Danny Miller, Peter H. Friesen; in collaboration with Henry Mintzberg. Englewood Cliffs, N.J.: Prentice-Hall, c1984. xv, 320 p. : ill. *Notes:* Includes index. Bibliography: p. 300-310. [LC 83015993; ISN 0136419852] HD31. M4375 1984   2983

Organizations: behavior, structure, processes. James L. Gibson, John M. Ivancevich, James H. Donnelly, Jr. 7th ed. Homewood, IL: Irwin, c1991. xxiv, 774 p. : ill. (some col.) *Notes:* Includes bibliographical references and indexes. [LC 90036445; ISN 0256080461; $47.95] HD58.7. G54 1991   2984

Organizations: structures, processes, and outcomes. Richard H. Hall. 5th ed. Englewood Cliffs, N.J.: Prentice Hall, c1991. viii, 344 p. : ill. *Notes:* Includes bibliographical references (p. 292-330) and indexes. [LC 90039915; ISN 0136425623; $44.29] HM131. H237 1991   2985

People in organizations: an introduction to organizational behavior. Terence R. Mitchell, James R. Larson, Jr. 3rd ed. New York: McGraw-Hill, c1987. xi, 602 p. : ill. *Notes:* Earlier ed. entitled: People in organizations understanding their behavior. Includes bibliographies and indexes. [LC 86020043; ISN 0070425345; $33.95] HD31. M478 1987   2986

Strategy implementation: structure, systems, and process. Jay R. Galbraith, Robert K. Kazanjian. 2nd ed. St. Paul: West Pub. Co., c1986. xviii, 187 p. : ill. (The West series in strategic management) *Notes:* Includes index. Bibliography: p. 171-180. [LC 86000024; ISN 0314852360; $15.95] HD31. G248 1986   2987

The structuring of organizations: the synthesis of the research. Henry Mintzberg. Englewood Cliffs, N.J.: Prentice-Hall, 1978. xvi, 512 p. : diagrs. (The Theory of management policy.) *Notes:* Includes index. Bibliography: p. 481-496. [LC 78012448; ISN 0138552703] HD31. M4573   2988

Your organization: what is it for?: challenging traditional organizational aims. John Argenti. London; New York: McGraw-Hill, c1993. viii, 299 p. : ill. *Notes:* Includes bibliographical references (p. 292) and index. [LC 92043398; ISN 0077077997; £24.95] HD31. A6463 1993   +2989

ORGANIZATION OF PETROLEUM EXPORTING COUNTRIES

OPEC, its member states and the world energy market. compiled and written by John Evans. Harlow, Essex, U.K.: Detroit, Mich., USA: Longman; Distributed exclusively in the U.S. and Canada by Gale Research Co., c1986. xxiv, 679 p. : ill., maps (A Keesing's reference publication) *Notes:* Includes indexes. [LC 86020075; ISN 0582902673] HD9560.1.O66 E92 1986   2990

ORGANIZATIONAL BEHAVIOR

The Abilene paradox and other meditations on management. Jerry B. Harvey. Lexington, Mass.: San Diego, Calif.: Lexington Books; University Associates, c1988. viii, 150 p. *Notes:* Bibliography: p. [145]-150. [LC 88045176; ISN 0669191795]   HD58.7. H376 1988   2991

Behavior in organizations. H. Joseph Reitz. 3rd ed. Homewood, Ill.: Irwin, 1987. xiii, 626 p. : ill. (The Irwin series in management and the behavioral sciences) *Notes:* Includes bibliographies and indexes. [LC 86082784; ISN 0256032327]   HD58.7. R44 1987   2992

Behavior in organizations: an experiential approach. James B. Lau, A.B. (Rami) Shani. 4th ed. Homewood, Ill.: Irwin, 1988. xi, 584 p. : ill. *Notes:* Includes bibliographies and index. [LC 87082925; ISN 025603656X; 24.50]   HD58.7. L37 1988   2993

Classic readings in organizational behavior. edited by J. Steven Ott. Pacific Grove, Calif.: Brooks/Cole, c1989. xii, 638 p. : ill. *Notes:* Includes bibliographies. [LC 88007779; ISN 0534110738; $18.00]   HD58.7. C52 1989   2994

Classics of organizational behavior. edited by Walter E. Natemeyer and Jay S. Gilberg. 2nd ed. Danville, Ill.: Interstate Printers & Publishers, Inc., c1989. xiv, 370 p. : ill. *Notes:* Includes bibliographical references. [LC 88080497; ISN 0813428149]   HD58.7. C53 1989   2995

Corporate assessment: auditing a company's personality. Adrian Furnham and Barrie Gunter. London; New York: Routledge, 1993. xiii, 293 p. : ill. *Notes:* Simultaneously published in the USA and Canada. Includes bibliographical references (p. [276]-286) and index. [LC 93009829; ISN 0415081181]   HD58.7. F87 1993   +2996

Culture and related corporate realities: text, cases, and readings on organizational entry, establishment, and change. Vijay Sathe. Homewood, Ill.: R.D. Irwin, 1985. xvi, 579 p. : ill. (The Irwin series in management and the behavioral sciences) *Notes:* Includes indexes. Bibliography: p. 558-565. [LC 84062325; ISN 0256031428]   HD58.7. S287   2997

Effective behavior in organizations: learning from the interplay of cases, concepts, and student experiences. Allan R. Cohen. . . et al. 4th ed. Homewood, Ill.: Irwin, 1988. xxvi, 959 p. : ill. (some col.) (The Irwin series in management and the behavioral sciences) *Notes:* Includes bibliographies and index. [LC 87082176; ISN 0256059675]   HD58.7. E35 1988   2998

The empowered manager: positive political skills at work. Peter Block. 1st ed. San Francisco: Jossey-Bass, 1987. xxii, 204 p. : ill. (The Jossey-Bass management series.) *Notes:* Includes index. Bibliography: p. 197-199. [LC 86045619; ISN 1555420192]   HD58.7. B58 1987   2999

Essentials of organizational behavior. Stephen P. Robbins. 3rd ed. Englewood Cliffs, N.J.: Prentice Hall, c1992. ix, 310 p. : ill. *Notes:* Includes bibliographical references and index. [LC 91011416; ISN 0132827085; $28.00]   HD58.7. R6 1992   3000

The eternally successful organization: the art of corporate wellness. Philip B. Crosby. New York: McGraw-Hill, c1988. xii, 255 p. *Notes:* Includes index. [LC 87037853; ISN 0070145334; $19.95]   HD58.7. C75 1988   3001

The executive dilemma: handling people problems at work. Eliza G.C. Collins, editor. New York: Wiley, 1985. ix, 586 p. (Harvard Business Review executive book series) *Notes:* Includes indexes. [LC 85000613; ISN 0471815195; $22.95 (est.)]   HD58.7. E95 1985   3002

Family ties, corporate bonds. Paula Bernstein. Garden City, N.Y.: Doubleday, 1985. x, 176 p. [LC 82048695; ISN 0385190158; $14.95]   HD58.7. B47 1985   3003

Handbook of organizational behavior. Jay W. Lorsch, editor. Englewood Cliffs, NJ: Prentice-Hall, c1987. ix, 430 p. : ill. *Notes:* Includes bibliographies. [LC 86004866; ISN 0133806502]   HD58.7. H355 1987   3004

International dimensions of organizational behavior. Nancy J. Adler. 2nd ed. Boston, Mass.: PWS-KENT Pub. Co., c1991. xxi, 313 p. : ill. *Notes:* Includes bibliographical references and index. [LC 90008589; ISN 0534922740; $17.95]   HD58.7. A33 1991   3005

Macro organizational behavior. Robert H. Miles. Santa Monica, Calif.: Goodyear Pub. Co., c1980. xvi, 542 p. : ill. (The Goodyear series in administration and business management) *Notes:* Includes indexes. Bibliography: p. [LC 79018683; ISN 0876205112]   HD58.7. M54   3006

Making work systems better: a practitioner's reflections. Luc Hoebeke. Chichester; New York: Wiley, c1994. xiv, 190 p. : ill. *Notes:* Includes bibliographical references and index. [LC 93030452; ISN 0471942480]   HD58.7. H627 1994   +3007

Management live: the video book. Robert Marx, Todd D. Jick, Peter J. Frost. Englewood Cliffs, NJ: Prentice Hall, c1991. xii, 377 p. : ill. *Notes:* Includes bibliographical references. [LC 91011851; ISN 0139467815; $23.00]   HD58.7. M375 1991   3008

Management of organizational behavior: utilizing human resources. Paul Hersey, Kenneth H. Blanchard. 6th ed. Englewood Cliffs, NJ: Prentice Hall, c1993. xxii, 536 p. : ill. *Notes:* Includes bibliographical references (p. 493-517) and index. [LC 92035580; ISN 0135550041; $42.00]
HD58.7. H47 1993   3009

The management of organizations: strategies, tactics, analyses. edited by Michael L. Tushman, Charles O'Reilly, David A. Nadler. New York: Grand Rapids, MI: Harper & Row; Ballinger, 1989. xi, 603 p. *Notes:* Includes bibliographical references. [LC 89014954; ISN 0887303803; $54.95]
HD58.7. H354 1989   3010

Managing behavior in organizations: text, cases, readings. edited by Leonard A. Schlesinger, Robert G. Eccles, John J. Gabarro; with the assistance of Thomas B. Lifson, James P. Ware. New York: McGraw-Hill, c1983. xxiv, 684 p. : ill. (McGraw-Hill series in management) *Notes:* Includes bibliographical references. Contents include cases and readings by Harvard Business School Faculty. [LC 82017308; ISN 0070553327; $23.95]   HD31. M29398 1983   3011

Managing corporate culture. Stanley M. Davis. Cambridge, Mass.: Ballinger Pub. Co., c1984. xiv, 123 p. : ill. *Notes:* Includes bibliographical references. [LC 84011142; ISN 0884109976]
HD58.7. D38 1984   3012

Managing individual and group behavior in organizations. Daniel C. Feldman, Hugh J. Arnold. New York: McGraw-Hill, c1983. xxii, 613 p. : ill. (McGraw-Hill series in management) *Notes:* Includes bibliographies and indexes. [LC 82017245; ISN 0070203865; $22.95 (est.)]
HD58.7. F44 1983   3013

Managing organizational behavior. David A. Nadler, J. Richard Hackman, Edward E. Lawler III. Boston: Little, Brown, c1979. xv, 295 p. : ill. *Notes:* Includes indexes. Bibliography: p. 281-286. [LC 78070453]   HD58.7. N32   3014

Men and women of the corporation. Rosabeth Moss Kanter. New York: Basic Books, c1977. xv, 348 p. *Notes:* Includes index. Bibliography: p. [326]-339. [LC 76043464; ISN 0465044522; $12.00]
HD58.7. K36   +3015

Networks and organizations: structure, form, and action. edited by Nitin Nohria and Robert G. Eccles. Boston, Mass.: Harvard Business School Press, c1992. xvi, 544 p. : ill. *Notes:* Papers originally presented at a conference held in 1990, sponsored by Harvard Business School. Includes bibliographical references and index. *Contents:* Structural alignments, individual strategies, and managerial action: elements toward a network theory of getting things done / Herminia Ibarra—Complementary communication media: a comparison of electronic mail and face-to-face communication in a programming team / James L. McKenney, Michael H. Zack, and Victor S. Doherty—Conclusion: Making network research relevant to practice / Rosabeth Moss Kanter and Robert G. Eccles. [LC 92011442; ISN 0875843247; $39.95]   HD58.7. N47 1992   3016

The neurotic behavior of organizations. Uri Merry, George I. Brown. New York, N.Y.: Gestalt Institute of Cleveland Press in association with the Gardner Press, c1987. xiv, 307 p. : ill. *Notes:* Includes indexes. Bibliography: p. 288-300. [LC 85020558; ISN 0898761166]   HD58.7. M47 1987   3017

The neurotic organization. Manfred F.R. Kets de Vries, Danny Miller. 1st ed. San Francisco: Jossey-Bass, 1984. xviii, 241 p. : ill. (The Jossey-Bass management series) (The Jossey-Bass social and behavioral science series) *Notes:* Subtitle half t.p. : Diagnosing and changing counterproductive styles of management. Includes bibliographical references and index. [LC 84005754; ISN 0875896065]   HD58.7. K465 1984   3018

Novations: strategies for career management. Gene W. Dalton, Paul H. Thompson. Glenview, Ill.: Scott, Foresman, c1986. xii, 280 p. : ill. *Notes:* Includes index. Bibliography: p. 266-274. [LC 85014635; ISN 0673181812]   HD58.7. D35 1986   3019

Organization: a guide to problems and practice. John Child. 2nd ed. London; Hagerstown Md.: Harper & Row, 1984. 309 p. : ill. *Notes:* Includes indexes. Bibliography: p. 294-304. [LC 84159348; ISN 0063182750]   HD58.7. C485 1984   3020

Organization and people: readings, cases, and exercises in organizational behavior. compiled by J.B. Ritchie and Paul Thompson; cartoons by Malcolm Hancock. 3rd ed. St. Paul: West Pub. Co., c1984. xxv, 498 p. : ill. (The West series in management) *Notes:* Includes indexes. Bibliography: p. 483-491. [LC 83025969; ISN 0314777857; $14.00]   HD58.7. O67 1984   3021

The organizational and human resources sourcebook. Douglas B. Gutknecht, Janet R. Miller. 2nd ed. Lanham, MD: University Press of America, c1990. xiv, 412 p. : ill. *Notes:* Includes bibliographical references. [LC 89020352; ISN 0819176230; $32.75]   HD58.7. G88 1990   3022

Organizational behavior. Fred Luthans. 5th ed. New York: McGraw-Hill, c1989. xxiii, 637 p. : ill. *Notes:* Includes bibliographies and indexes. [LC 88012843; ISN 0070391610; $43.95]
HD58.7. L88 1989   3023

Organizational behavior and management. edited by Henry L. Tosi, W. Clay Hamner. 4th ed. Columbus, Ohio: Grid Pub., c1985. x, 569 p. : ill. *Notes:* Includes bibliographical references. [LC 84019768; ISN 0882442775; $18.95 (est.)]   HD58.7. O695 1985   3024

Organizational behavior and performance. Andrew D. Szilagyi, Jr., Marc J. Wallace, Jr. 4th ed. Glenview, Ill.: Scott, Foresman, c1987. 742 p. : ill. *Notes:* Includes bibliographies and indexes. [LC 86026087; ISN 0673166643; $29.95]   HD58.7. S97 1987   3025

Organizational behavior and personnel psychology. Kenneth N. Wexley, Gary A. Yukl. Rev. ed. Homewood, Ill.: R.D. Irwin, 1984. xv, 570 p. : ill. (The Irwin series in management and the behavioral sciences) *Notes:* Includes bibliographies and indexes. [LC 83081174; ISN 0256026424]   HD58.7. W38 1984   3026

Organizational behavior and the practice of management. David R. Hampton, Charles E. Summer, Ross A. Webber. 5th ed. Glenview, Ill.: Scott, Foresman, c1987. 876 p. : ill. *Notes:* Includes bibliographies and indexes. [LC 86024798; ISN 0673183033]   HD58.7. H35   3027

Organizational behavior: concepts, controversies, and applications. Stephen P. Robbins. 4th ed. Englewood Cliffs, N.J.: Prentice Hall, c1989. xxii, 599 p. : ill. *Notes:* Includes bibliographies and indexes. [LC 88015696; ISN 0136417620; $33.90]   HD58.7. R62 1989   3028

Organizational behavior: human behavior at work. John W. Newstrom, Keith Davis. 9th ed. New York: McGraw-Hill, c1993. xxiv, 582 p. : col. ill. *Notes:* Rev. ed. of: Human behavior at work / Keith Davis, John W. Newstrom. 8th ed. c1989. Includes bibliographical references and indexes. [LC 92022097; ISN 0070156034]   HD58.7. N49 1993   3029

Organizational behavior: its data, first principles, and applications. Joe Kelly. 3d ed. Homewood, Ill.: R. D. Irwin, 1980. xviii, 665 p. : ill. (The Irwin series in management and the behavioral sciences) *Notes:* Includes indexes. Bibliography: p. 623-651. [LC 79090542; ISN 0256022844]   HD58.7. K44 1980   3030

Organizational behavior: readings and exercises. edited by John W. Newstrom, Keith Davis. 8th ed. New York: McGraw-Hill, c1989. xxi, 597 p. *Notes:* Includes bibliographies and indexes. [LC 88039360; ISN 0070155194; $24.95]   HD58.7. O74 1989   3031

Organizational behaviour: politics at work. Robert Lee and Peter Lawrence. London: Brookfield, Vt., USA: Hutchinson; Brookfield Pub. Co., 1985. 192 p. : ill. (Hutchinson management studies books) *Notes:* Includes bibliographical references and index. [LC 85007835; ISN 0091616514; $20.00]   HD58.7. L44 1985   3032

Organizational culture. edited by Peter J. Frost... et al. Beverly Hills: Sage Publications, c1985. 419 p. : ill. *Notes:* Bibliography: p. 391-412. [LC 85002172; ISN 0803924593; ISN 0803924607]   HD58.7. O764   3033

Organizational influence processes. edited by Robert W. Allen, Lyman W. Porter. Glenview, Ill.: Scott, Foresman, c1983. 492 p. : ill. *Notes:* Includes bibliographies and index. [LC 82023148; ISN 0673153185; $15.95]   HD58.7. O767 1983   3034

Organizations on the couch: clinical perspectives on organizational behavior and change. Manfred F.R. Kets de Vries and associates. 1st ed. San Francisco: Jossey-Bass, 1991. xxviii, 408 p. *Notes:* Includes bibliographical references and indexes. [LC 91015877; ISN 1555423841; $33.95]   HD58.7. O78 1991   3035

Organizations: structure and behavior. edited by Joseph A. Litterer. 3d ed. New York: Wiley, c1980. xi, 625 p. : ill. (Wiley series in management) *Notes:* Includes bibliographies and indexes. *Contents:* Walker, A. H. and J. W. Lorsch. Organizational choice: production vs. function.—Walton, R. E. and J. M. Dutton. The management of interdepartmental conflict: a model and review.—Lawrence, P. R. and Lorsch, J. W. Differentiation and integration in complex organizations. [LC 80015645; ISN 0471077860]   HD58.7. L57 1980   3036

Perspectives on behavior in organizations. edited by J. Richard Hackman, Edward E. Lawler, III, Lyman W. Porter. 2nd ed. New York: McGraw-Hill, c1983. x, 598 p. : ill. *Notes:* Includes bibliographies. [LC 82000175; ISN 0070254141; $15.50]   HD58.7. P47 1983   3037

The politics of management. Andrew Kakabadse. New York, N.Y.: Nichols, 1984, c1983. ix, 174 p. *Notes:* Includes index. Bibliography: p. 165-169. [LC 83020702; ISN 0893971820; $28.50]   HD58.7. K35 1984   3038

Power plays: a guide to maximizing performance and success in business. Thomas L. Quick. New York: F. Watt, 1985. 248 p. *Notes:* Includes index. [LC 84029091; ISN 0531095827; $15.95]   HD58.7. Q49 1985   3039

A primer on organizational behavior. James L. Bowditch, Anthony F. Buono. 2nd ed. New York: Wiley, 1990. xx, 393 p. : ill. *Notes:* Includes bibliographical references. [LC 89038318; ISN 0471617857; $19.95]   HD58.7. B69 1990   3040

A primer on organizational behavior. James L. Bowditch, Anthony F. Buono. 3rd ed. New York: Wiley, 1993, c1994. xvii, 521 p. : ill. *Notes:* Includes bibliographical references and indexes. [LC 93005187; ISN 0471586420]   HD58.7. B69 1994   +3041

Psychological dimensions of organizational behavior. edited by Barry M. Staw. New York: Toronto: New York: Macmillan; Collier Macmillan Canada; Maxwell Macmillan International, c1991. xii, 676 p. : ill. *Notes:* Includes bibliographical references. [LC 90041493; ISN 0024161500]
     HD58.7. P758 1991   3042

Psychological foundations of organizational behavior. edited by Barry M. Staw. 2nd ed. Glenview, Ill.: Scott, Foresman, c1983. 437 p. : ill. *Notes:* Bibliography: p. 434-437. [LC 83003208; ISN 067316005X; $13.95]   HD58.7. P76 1983   3043

Readings in organizational behavior. compiled by Steven Altman and Richard M. Hodgetts. Philadelphia: Saunders, 1979. vii, 367 p. : ill. *Notes:* Includes bibliographical references. [LC 79106003; ISN 0721611400]   HD58.7. R39   3044

Readings in organizational behavior: dimensions of management actions. selected by Richard C. Huseman, Archie B. Carroll. Boston: Allyn and Bacon, c1979. xiv, 432 p. : ill. *Notes:* Includes bibliographical references. [LC 78027060; ISN 0205065155]   HD58.7. R43   3045

Regional cultures, managerial behavior, and entrepreneurship: an international perspective. edited by Joseph W. Weiss. New York: Quorum Books, c1988. x, 207 p. : ill. *Notes:* Includes index. Bibliography: p. [191]-196. [LC 87032278; ISN 0899303277]   HD58.7. R437 1988   3046

Staying human in the organization: our biological heritage and the workplace. J. Gary Bernhard and Kalman Glantz. Westport, Conn.: Praeger, 1992. viii, 163 p. : ill. *Notes:* Includes bibliographical references (p. [153]-158) and index. [LC 92000892; ISN 0275942953]   HD58.7. B465 1992   3047

The thinking organization. Henry P. Sims, Jr., Dennis A. Gioia, and associates. 1st ed. San Francisco: Jossey-Bass, 1986. xxvii, 375 p. : ill. (A Joint publication in the Jossey-Bass management series and the Jossey-Bass social and behavioral science series) *Notes:* Includes bibliographies and indexes. [LC 85045913; ISN 0875896901]   HD58.7. S584 1986   3048

Understanding organizations. Charles Handy. New York: Oxford University Press, c1993. 445 p. : ill. *Notes:* Originally published: 4th ed. Harmondsworth: Penguin Books, 1976. Includes bibliographical references and index. [LC 93005123; ISN 0195087321; $25.00]   HD58.7. H3683 1993   +3049

Unstable at the top: inside the troubled organization. Manfred F.R. Kets de Vries and Danny Miller. New York: New American Library, 1988, c1987. xiv, 221 p. *Notes:* "NAL books." Includes index. Bibliography: p. 201-209. [LC 87023182; ISN 0453005624]   HD58.7. K475 1988   3050

ORGANIZATIONAL CHANGE

Adhocracy: the power to change. by Robert H. Waterman, Jr. 1st Norton ed. New York: W.W. Norton, 1992. 128 p. *Notes:* Originally published as part of the Whittle Communications Larger Agenda series in 1990. Includes index. [LC 92017590; ISN 0393034143]   HD58.8. W386 1992   3051

Aftershock: helping people through corporate change. Harry Woodward, Steve Buchholz; edited by Kären Hess. New York: J. Wiley, c1987. xix, 233 p. : ill. *Notes:* Includes index. Bibliography: p. 225.; ISN 0471624780; $19.95]   HD58.8. W663 1987   3052

The age of paradox. Charles Handy. Boston, Mass.: Harvard Business School Press, 1994. xiii, 303 p. *Notes:* Originally published in Great Britain as: The empty raincoat. Random House UK, 1994. Includes bibliographical references (p. 289-291) and index. [LC 93036586; ISN 0875844251; $22.50]   HD58.8. H3618 1994   +3053

The age of unreason. Charles Handy; foreword by Warren Bennis. Boston, Mass.: Harvard Business School Press, c1989. xii, 278 p. : ill. *Notes:* Includes bibliographical references and index. [LC 90036849; ISN 0875842461]   HD58.8. H362 1989   3054

Beyond bureaucracy: essays on the development and evolution of human organization. Warren Bennis. 1st ed. San Francisco: Jossey-Bass, c1993. xxvii, 254 p. : ill. (Jossey-Bass classics) *Notes:* Rev. ed. of: Changing organizations. 1966. Includes bibliographical references and index. [LC 92041386; ISN 1555425224]   HM131. B432 1993   3055

Breakpoints: how managers exploit radical business change. Paul Strebel. Boston, Mass.: Harvard Business School Press, c1992. x, 261 p. : ill. *Notes:* Includes bibliographical references (p. 241-251) and index. [LC 92010438; ISN 0875843697; $24.95]   HD58.8. S77 1992   3056

Business as a learning community. Ronnie Lessem. London; New York: McGraw-Hill, c1993. xi, 219 p. : ill. *Notes:* Includes and bibliographical references and index. [LC 92044981; ISN 0077077873; £19.95]   HD58.8. L468 1993   +3057

Catching up?: organizational and management change in the ex-Socialist block. Andrzej K. Kozminski. Albany: State University of New York Press, c1993. viii, 236 p. *Notes:* Includes bibliographical references (p. 225-233) and index. [LC 92040391; ISN 0791415988; $16.95]
    HD58.8. K685 1993 +3058

The challenge of organizational change: how companies experience it and leaders guide it. compiled by Rosabeth Moss Kanter, Barry A. Stein, Todd D. Jick. New York: Toronto: New York: Free Press; Maxwell Macmillan Canada; Maxwell Macmillan International, c1992. xix, 535 p. : ill. *Notes:* Includes bibliographical references and index. [LC 92018386; ISN 0029169917; $35.00]
    HD58.8. C43 1992 3059

Change by design. by Robert R. Blake, Jane Srygley Mouton, Anne Adams McCanse. Reading, MA: Addison-Wesley, c1989. xvii, 221 p. : ill. *Notes:* Includes bibliographical references. [LC 89017621; ISN 020150748X; $19.95]
    HD58.8. B55 1989 3060

Change management: a model for effective organizational performance. Patricia K. Felkins, B. J. Chakiris, and Kenneth N. Chakiris. White Plains, N.Y.: Quality Resources, c1993. xiii, 491 p. : ill. *Notes:* Includes bibliographical references (p. [455]-466) and index. [LC 93006989; ISN 0527917230]
    HD58.8. F437 1993 +3061

The change resisters: how they prevent progress and what managers can do about them. George S. Odiorne. Englewood Cliffs, N.J.: Prentice-Hall, c1981. xi, 275 p. (A Spectrum book) *Notes:* Includes bibliographical references and index. [LC 80028341; ISN 0131279025; ISN 0131278940]
    HD58.8. O34 3062

Changing the essence: the art of creating and leading fundamental change in organizations. Richard Beckhard, Wendy Pritchard. 1st ed. San Francisco: Jossey-Bass Publishers, c1992. xviii, 105 p. *Notes:* Includes bibliographical references (p. 97-100) and index [LC 91037204; ISN 1555424120; $20.95]
    HD58.8. B397 1992 3063

Company reorganization for performance and profit improvement: a guide for operating executives and their staffs. Stanley B. Henrici. New York: Quorum Books, 1986. xiv, 211 p. : ill. *Notes:* Includes bibliographical references and index. [LC 86000613; ISN 0899301592] HD58.8. H46 1986 3064

Company strategy and organizational design. Roger Mansfield. New York: St. Martin's Press, 1986. 184 p. : ill. *Notes:* Includes indexes. Bibliography: p. 177-180. [LC 85025062; ISN 0312153287; $25.00 (est.)]
    HD58.8. M263 1986 3065

Competing with flexible lateral organizations. Jay R. Galbraith. 2nd ed. Reading, Mass.: Addison-Wesley, c1994. xxiii, 152 p. : ill. *Notes:* Rev. ed. of: Designing complex organizations. Bibliography: p. 150-152. [LC 93009857; ISN 0201508362; $26.11]
    HD58.8. G34 1994 +3066

Computing strategies for reengineering your organization. Cheryl Currid & Company. Rocklin, CA: Prima Pub., c1994. xxii, 279 p. : ill. *Notes:* Includes bibliographical references (p. 255-259) and index. [LC 93085965]
    HD58.8. C865 1994 +3067

Conflict management and organization development. Willem F.G. Mastenbroek. Expanded ed. Chichester; New York: J. Wiley, c1993. x, 184 p. : ill. *Notes:* Includes bibliographical references (p. [172]-179) and indexes. [LC 93017955; ISN 0471941417; $30.00] HD58.8. M32513 1993 +3068

Corporate lifecycles: how and why corporations grow and die and what to do about it. Ichak Adizes. Englewood Cliffs, N.J.: Prentice Hall, c1988. xvii, 361 p. : ill. *Notes:* "An Adizes Institute book." Includes index. Bibliography: p. 351. [LC 88028665; ISN 0131744003; $22.95]
    HD58.8. A34 1988 3069

Corporate players: designs for working and winning together. Robert W. Keidel. New York: Wiley, c1988. xxi, 250 p. : ill. *Notes:* Includes indexes Bibliography: p. 211-212. [LC 87028563; ISN 0471631760]
    HD58.8. K45 1988 3070

Corporate restructuring: a guide to creating the premium-valued company. Milton L. Rock, Robert H. Rock, editors in chief with James Kristie. New York: McGraw-Hill, c1990. x, 310 p. : ill. *Notes:* Includes bibliographical references (p. 21-22). [LC 89036429; ISN 0070533512; $29.95]
    HD58.8. C658 1990 3071

Corporate transformations: revitalizing organizations for a competitive world. Ralph H. Kilmann, Teresa Joyce Covin, and associates. 1st ed. San Francisco: Jossey-Bass, 1988. xxxi, 553 p. : ill. (The Jossey-Bass management series) *Notes:* Includes bibliographies and indexes. [LC 87045427; ISN 1555420605]
    HD58.8. K496 1988 3072

Creating strategic change: designing the flexible, high-performing organization. William A. Pasmore. New York: Wiley, c1994. xi, 284 p. : ill. *Notes:* Includes bibliographical references (p. 273-278) and index. [LC 93039202; ISN 0471597295; $29.95] HD58.8. P366 1994 +3073

Current perspectives in organization development. J. Jennings Partin, editor. Reading, Mass. Addison-Wesley Pub. Co., 1973. viii, 279 p. illus. *Notes:* Bibliography: p. 277-279. [LC 72011886; ISN 0201057441]
    HD38. P315 +3074

Developing corporate character: how to successfully change an organization without destroying it. Alan L. Wilkins. San Francisco: Jossey-Bass, 1989. xxi, 227 p. *Notes:* Includes index. Bibliography: p. 209-215. [LC 88026698; ISN 1555421334] HD58.8. W54 1989 3075

The entrepreneurial organization. John J. Kao. Englewood Cliffs, N.J.: Prentice Hall, 1991. viii, 360 p. : ill. *Notes:* Includes bibliographical references. [LC 90034672; ISN 0132823284; $26.00] HD58.8. K37 1991 3076

Forging the productivity partnership. William Sandy. New York: McGraw-Hill Pub. Co., c1990. xv, 224 p. : ill. *Notes:* Bibliography: p. 217-218. [LC 89048841; ISN 0070546762; $19.95] HD58.8. S26 1990 3077

From turmoil to triumph: new life after mergers, acquisitions, and downsizing. Mitchell Lee Marks. New York: Toronto: New York: Lexington Books; Maxwell Macmillan Canada; Maxwell Macmillan International, c1994. xi, 340 p. : ill. *Notes:* Includes bibliographical references (p. [323]-327) and index. [LC 94004758; ISN 0029200555; $24.95] HD58.8. M2653 1994 +3078

Healing the wounds: overcoming the trauma of layoffs and revitalizing downsized organizations. David M. Noer. 1st ed. San Francisco: Jossey-Bass, c1993. xxvi, 248 p. : ill. *Notes:* Includes bibliographical references (p. 235-239) and index. [LC 93013407; ISN 1555425607] HM131. N63 1993 +3079

How to manage change effectively. Donald L. Kirkpatrick; foreword by Joe D. Batten. 1st ed. San Francisco: Jossey-Bass, 1985. xxii, 280 p. : ill. (The Jossey-Bass management series) *Notes:* "Approaches, methods, and case examples"—P. [iii]. Includes index. Bibliography: p. 273-275. [LC 85045060; ISN 0875896596] HD58.8. K52 1985 3080

Implementing organizational change. Gordon L. Lippitt, Petter Langseth, Jack Mossop. 1st ed. San Francisco: Jossey-Bass, c1985. xx, 185 p. : ill. (The Jossey-Bass management series) (The Jossey-Bass social and behavioral science series) *Notes:* Includes index. Bibliography: p. 173-177. [LC 84047990; ISN 0875896227] HD58.8. L57 1985 3081

Innovating to compete: lessons for diffusing and managing change in the workplace. Richard E. Walton; with the assistance of Christopher Allen and Michael Gaffney. 1st ed. San Francisco: Jossey-Bass, 1987. xix, 361 p. : ill. (The Jossey-Bass management series) *Notes:* Includes index. Bibliography: p. 341-351. [LC 87045426; ISN 1555420567] HD58.8. W34 1987 3082

Internal markets: bringing the power of free enterprise inside your organization. William Halal, Ali Geranmayeh, John Pourdehnad; foreword by Russell L. Ackoff. New York: Wiley, c1993. xviii, 301 p. : ill. *Notes:* Includes bibliographical references and index. [LC 93019581; ISN 0471593648] HD58.8. H353 1993 +3083

Ironies in organizational development. Robert T. Golembiewski. New Brunswick, N.J., U.S.A.: Transaction Publishers, c1990. xiii, 303 p. : ill. *Notes:* Includes bibliographical references. [LC 88036466; ISN 0887382932; $34.95] HD58.8. G644 1990 3084

Knowledge for action: a guide to overcoming barriers to organizational change. Chris Argyris. 1st ed. San Francisco: Jossey-Bass, c1993. xviii, 309 p. *Notes:* Includes bibliographical references (p. 287-301) and indexes. [LC 92042861; ISN 1555425194] HD58.8. A744 1993 3085

Large-scale organizational change. Allan M. Mohrman, Jr.. . . et al. 1st ed. San Francisco: Jossey-Bass, 1989. xxi, 314 p. : ill. *Notes:* Largely based on a conference held at the University of Southern California in 1986. Includes bibliographies and index. [LC 89045602; ISN 1555421644; $28.95] HD58.8. L375 1989 3086

The leading edge: CEOs who turned their companies around: what they did and how they did it. Mark Potts, Peter Behr. New York: McGraw-Hill, c1987. iv, 200 p. *Notes:* Includes index. [LC 86010567; ISN 0070505993] HD58.8. P68 1987 3087

Liberation management: necessary disorganization for the nanosecond nineties. Tom Peters. 1st ed. New York: A. A. Knopf, 1992. xxxiv, 834 p. : ill. *Notes:* Includes index. [LC 90053071; ISN 0394559991] HD58.8. P424 1992 3088

Managing at the speed of change: how resilient managers succeed and prosper where others fail. by Daryl R. Conner. New York: Villard Books, 1993. xxxi, 282 p. : ill. [LC 92020753; ISN 0679406840; $22.00] HD58.8. C652 1993 +3089

Managing change: cases and concepts. Todd D. Jick. Homewood, IL: Irwin, c1993. xviii, 489 p. : ill. *Notes:* Includes bibliographical references. [LC 92024166; ISN 0256112312] HD58.8. J53 1993 3090

Managing maturing businesses: restructuring declining industries and revitalizing troubled operations. Kathryn Rudie Harrigan. Lexington, Mass.: Lexington Books, c1988. xx, 170 p. : ill. *Notes:* Includes index. Bibliography: p. [149]-158. [LC 87045966; ISN 0669170828] HD58.8. H365 1988 3091

Managing on the edge: how the smartest companies use conflict to stay ahead. Richard Tanner Pascale. New York: Simon and Schuster, c1990. 350 p. : ill. *Notes:* Includes bibliographical references. [LC 89048997; ISN 0671624423; $21.95] HD58.8. P365 1990 3092

Managing organizational change. Patrick E. Connor & Linda K. Lake. New York: Praeger, 1988. xii, 192 p. : ill. *Notes:* Includes index. Bibliography: p [181]-183. [LC 87012475; ISN 0275923355; ISN 0275928268; $35.85; $14.85] HD58.8. C653 1988 3093

Managing organizational change. Roy McLennan. Englewood Cliffs, N.J.: Prentice Hall, c1989. xxvi, 549 p. : ill. *Notes:* Includes bibliographical references. [LC 88025358; ISN 0135515084; $20.75] HD58.8. M35 1989 3094

Managing the new organization: a blueprint for networks and strategic alliances. David Limerick, Bert Cunnington; foreword by George Kozmetsky. 1st ed. San Francisco: Jossey-Bass, c1993. xxii, 281 p. : ill. *Notes:* Includes bibliographical references and index. [LC 93022371; ISN 155542581X] HD58.8. L545 1993 +3095

Mastering change. the key to business success / by Leon Martel. New York: Simon and Schuster, c1986. 345 p. : ill. *Notes:* Includes index. Bibliography: p. 309-332. [LC 85019600; ISN 0671477463] HD58.8. M38 3096

Mastering the dynamics of innovation: how companies can seize opportunities in the face of technological change. James M. Utterback. Boston, Mass.: Harvard Business School Press, c1994. xxix, 253 p. : ill. *Notes:* Includes bibliographical references (p. 233-240) and index. [LC 93038429; ISN 0875843425; $29.95] HD58.8. U87 1994 +3097

Navigating through change. Harry Woodward with Mary Beckman Woodward. Burr Ridge, Ill.: Irwin Professional Pub., c1994. xiii, 201 p. : ill. *Notes:* Includes bibliographical references (p. 196-198) and index. [LC 93048345; ISN 078630233X] HD58.8. W673 1994 +3098

The new rules of the game: the four key experiences managers must have to thrive in the nonhierarchical 90s and beyond. James R. Emshoff with Teri Denlinger. New York, NY: HarperBusiness, c1991. xiv, 219 p. *Notes:* Includes index. [LC 91006706; ISN 0887305075; $19.95] HD58.8. E49 1991 3099

Organization change and development: a systems view. Michael Beer. Santa Monica, Calif.: Goodyear Pub. Co., c1980. xi, 367 p. : ill.; 25 cm. *Notes:* Includes index. Bibliography: p. 349-360. [LC 79025855; ISN 0830264167] HD58.8. B44 3100

Organization development and transformation: managing effective change. edited by Wendell L. French, Cecil H. Bell, Jr., Robert A. Zawacki. 4th ed. Burr Ridge, Ill.: Irwin, c1994. xiii, 604 p. : ill. *Notes:* 3rd ed. published under title: Organization development. Includes bibliographical references. [LC 93038865; ISN 0256103399] HD58.8. O724 1994 +3101

Organizational change through effective leadership. Robert H. Guest, Paul Hersey, Kenneth H. Blanchard. 2nd ed. Englewood Cliffs, N.J.: Prentice-Hall, c1986. xiii, 235 p. *Notes:* Includes index. Bibliography: p. 225-232. [LC 85028136; ISN 0136413900] HD58.8. G83 1986 3102

Organizational transitions for individuals, families, and work groups. Louis B. Barnes, Colleen Kaftan. Englewood Cliffs, N.J.: Prentice Hall, c1991. ix, 357 p. : ill. *Notes:* Includes bibliographical references. [LC 90047934; ISN 0136405908; $32.00] HD58.8. B37 1991 3103

Organizational transitions: managing complex change. Richard Beckhard, Reuben T. Harris. 2nd ed. Reading, Mass.: Addison-Wesley Pub. Co., c1987. xii, 117 p. : ill. (Addison-Wesley OD series) *Notes:* Includes bibliographical references. [LC 86025863; ISN 0201108879; $12.95] HD58.8. B4 1987 3104

Overcoming organizational defenses: facilitating organizational learning. Chris Argyris. Boston, MA: Allyn and Bacon, 1990. xv, 169 p. : ill. *Notes:* Includes bibliographical references. [LC 89018330; ISN 0205123384; $33.50] HD58.8. A753 1990 3105

Paradox and transformation: toward a theory of change in organization and management. edited by Robert E. Quinn, Kim S. Cameron. Cambridge, Mass.: Ballinger Pub. Co., 1988. xvii, 334 p. : ill. (Ballinger series on innovation and organization change) *Notes:* Includes bibliographies and indexes. [LC 88006220; ISN 0887301568] HD58.8. P36 1988 3106

The postmodern organization: mastering the art of irreversible change. William Bergquist. 1st ed. San Francisco: Jossey-Bass, c1993. xx, 277 p. *Notes:* Includes bibliographical references (p. 255-264) and index. [LC 92043606; ISN 155542533X] HD58.8. B473 1993 3107

Re-engineering your business. Daniel Morris, Joel Brandon. New York: McGraw-Hill, c1993. viii, 247 p. : ill. *Notes:* Includes index. [LC 92038709; ISN 0070431787; $24.95] HD58.8. M65 1993 3108

Readings in organizational decline: frameworks, research, and prescriptions. edited by Kim S. Cameron, Robert I. Sutton, David A. Whetten. Boston, Mass.: Ballinger Pub. Co., 1988. ix, 429 p. : 24 cm. (Ballinger series on innovation and organizational change) *Notes:* Bibliography: p. 425-429. [LC 87027136; ISN 0887302238; ISN 088730270X] HD58.8. R37 1988 3109

Real time strategic change: how to involve an entire organization in fast and far-reaching change. Robert W. Jacobs. 1st ed. San Francisco: Berrett-Koehler Publishers, c1994. xviii, 335 p. : ill. *Notes:* Includes index. [LC 94013444; ISN 1881052451; $27.95] HD58.8. J336 1994 +3110

Rebirth of the corporation. D. Quinn Mills. New York: J. Wiley, c1991. x, 320 p. : ill. *Notes:* Includes bibliographical references (p. 305-311) and index. [LC 90039272; ISN 0471522201; $24.95]   HD58.8. M55 1991   3111

The reengineering handbook: a step-by-step guide to business transformation. Raymond L. Manganelli and Mark M. Klein. New York: Amacom, American Management Association, c1994. xvi, 318 p. : ill. *Notes:* Includes bibliographical references and index. [LC 94026609; ISN 0814402364; $29.95]   HD58.8. M257 1994   +3112

Reengineering the corporation: a manifesto for business revolution. Michael Hammer & James Champy. 1st ed. New York: HarperBusiness, c1993. vi, 223 p. *Notes:* Includes case studies of Hallmark, Taco Bell, Capital Holding, and Bell Atlantic. Includes index. [LC 92054748; ISN 0887306403; $25.00]   HD58.8. H356 1993   3113

Reengineering the organization: a step-by-step approach to corporate revitalization. Jeffrey N. Lowenthal. Milwaukee, Wis.: ASQC Quality Press, c1994. xv, 185 p. : ill. *Notes:* Includes bibliographical references and index. [LC 93044774; ISN 0873892585]   HD58.8. L69 1994   +3114

Rekindling commitment: how to revitalize yourself, your work, and your organization. Dennis T. Jaffe, Cynthia D. Scott, Glenn R. Tobe. 1st ed. San Francisco: Jossey-Bass Publishers, c1994. xxvi, 274 p. : ill. *Notes:* Includes bibliographical references (p. 255-266) and index. [LC 94009266; ISN 1555427049; ISN 1555426735]   HD58.8. J34 1994   +3115

Restructuring and turnaround: experiences in corporate renewal. prepared by Business International S.A. Geneva, Switzerland: Business International S.A., c1987. 141 p. : ill. (Business International research report) *Notes:* Includes bibliographical references.]   HD58.8. R477 1987   3116

The Schuster report: the proven connection between people and profits. Frederick E. Schuster. New York: Wiley, c1986. xvi, 200 p. *Notes:* Includes index. Bibliography: p. 186-187. [LC 86009190; ISN 0471832936; $19.95]   HD58.8. S38 1986   3117

Sons of the machine: case studies of social change in the workplace. Charles H. Savage, Jr. and George F.F. Lombard. Cambridge, Mass: MIT Press, c1986. xvi, 313, [16] p. of plates: ill. *Notes:* Includes index. Bibliography: p. [283]-291. [LC 85015133; ISN 0262192438]   HD58.8. S29 1986   3118

Strategic flexibility: a management guide for changing times. Kathryn Rudie Harrigan. Lexington, Mass.: Lexington Books, 1985. xiv, 208 p. *Notes:* Includes index. Bibliography: p. [187]-204. [LC 84040815; ISN 0669102229]   HD58.8. H367 1985   3119

Strategy, change, and defensive routines. Chris Argyris. Boston: Pitman, c1985. xiii, 368 p. : ill. *Notes:* Includes index. Bibliography: p. 357-361. [LC 85000584; ISN 0273023292]   HD58.8. A755 1985   3120

Stream analysis: a powerful way to diagnose and manage organizational change. Jerry I. Porras. Reading, Mass.: Addison-Wesley, c1987. xvi, 163 p. : ill. (The Addison-Wesley series on organization development) *Notes:* Includes bibliographical references. [LC 86022183; ISN 0201056933; $12.95 (est.)]   HD58.8. P67 1987   3121

Successful corporate turnarounds. Eugene F. Finkin. Pbk. ed. New York: Praeger, 1988. xviii, 211 p. : ill. *Notes:* Includes index. [LC 88015177; ISN 0275931080]   HD58.8. F52 1988   3122

Supermanaging: how to harness change for personal and organizational success. Arnold Brown, Edith Weiner. New York: McGraw-Hill, c1984. xv, 283 p. *Notes:* Includes bibliographical references and index. [LC 83020002; ISN 0070082014]   HD58.8. B76 1984   3123

Time, chance, and organizations: natural selection in a perilous environment. Herbert Kaufman. 2nd ed. Chatham, N.J.: Chatham House Publishers, c1991. xii, 212 p. *Notes:* Includes bibliographical references (p. 193-204) and indexes. [LC 91011731; ISN 0934540934; $21.95]   HD58.8. K38 1991   3124

The Tom Peters seminar: crazy times call for crazy organizations. by Tom Peters. Vintage original, 1st ed. New York: Vintage Books, c1994. xv, 320 p. : ill. *Notes:* Includes index. *Contents:* Beyond change: toward the abandonment of everything—Beyond decentralization: disorganizing to unleash imagination—Beyond empowerment: turning every job into a business—Beyond loyalty: learning to think like an independent contractor—Beyond disintegration: the corporation as Rolodex—Beyond reengineering: creating a corporate talk show—Beyond learning: creating the curious corporation—Beyond TQM: toward wow!—Beyond change (redux): toward perpetual revolution. [LC 94004815; ISN 0679754938]   HD58.8. P483 1994   +3125

The transformational leader. Noel M. Tichy, Mary Anne Devanna. New York: Wiley, c1986. xvi, 306 p. *Notes:* Includes index. Bibliography: p. 291-294. [LC 86004043; ISN 0471822590; $19.95]   HD58.8. T52 1986   3126

Transforming work: a collection of organizational transformation readings/ John D. Adams, general editor. Alexandria, Va. (1009 Duke St., Alexandria 22314): Miles River Press, c1984. ix, 278 p. : ill. *Notes:* Includes bibliographies. [LC 84228397; $16.50 (pbk.)]   HD58.8. T72 1984   3127

The twenty-first century organization: analyzing current trends, imagining the future. Guy Benveniste. 1st ed. San Francisco: Jossey-Bass, c1994. xxiv, 310 p. *Notes:* Includes bibliographical references (p. 279-294) and index. [LC 93035549; ISN 1555426263]   HD58.8. B464 1994   +3128

Values and ethics in organization and human systems development: responding to dilemmas in professional life. William Gellermann, Mark S. Frankel, Robert F. Ladenson. 1st ed. San Francisco: Jossey-Bass, 1990. xxvii, 529 p. *Notes:* Includes bibliographical references. [LC 90004946; ISN 1555422969; $39.95] HD58.8. G45 1990   3129

When giants learn to dance: mastering the challenge of strategy, management, and careers in the 1990s. Rosabeth Moss Kanter. New York: Simon and Schuster, c1989. 415 p. *Notes:* Includes bibliographical references and index. [LC 89004131; ISN 0671617338; $21.95] HD58.8. K365 1989   3130

ORGANIZATIONAL EFFECTIVENESS

Appreciative management and leadership: the power of positive thought and action in organizations. Suresh Srivastva, David L. Cooperrider, and associates. 1st ed. San Francisco: Jossey-Bass, 1990. xxvii, 448 p. : ill. *Notes:* "The culmination of a symposium assembled at Case Western Reserve University in October 1988"—Pref. Bibliography: p. 401-437. [LC 89071651; ISN 1555422365; $35.95] HD58.9. S73 1990   3131

Beyond rational management: mastering the paradoxes and competing demands of high performance. Robert E. Quinn. 1st ed. San Francisco: Jossey-Bass, 1988. xxii, 199 p. : ill. (The Jossey-Bass management series) *Notes:* Includes index. Bibliography: p. 185-191. [LC 87046339; ISN 1555420753] HD58.9. Q36 1988   3132

Building a chain of customers: linking business functions to create the world class company. Richard J. Schonberger. New York: Free Press, 1990. ix, 349 p. : ill. *Notes:* Includes bibliographical references. [LC 89077552; ISN 0029279917; $29.95] HD58.9. S36 1990   3133

Corporate operational analysis: a procedure for evaluating key factors in internal operations, acquisitions, and takeovers. Jerry W. Anderson, Jr. and John B. Camealy. New York: Quorum Books, 1991. xiii, 347 p. : ill. *Notes:* Includes bibliographical references (p. [337]-338) and indexes. [LC 90047592; ISN 0899305350; $59.95] HD58.9. A54 1991   3134

Corporate staying power: how America's most consistently successful corporations maintain exceptional performance. James B. Hobbs. Lexington, Mass.: Lexington Books, c1987. xi, 178 p. : ill. *Notes:* Includes index. Bibliography: p. [165]-172. [LC 85045096; ISN 0669111538] HD58.9. H62 1987   3135

Diagnosing the system for organizations. Stafford Beer Chichester West Sussex; New York: Wiley, c1985. xiii, 152 p. : ill. (The Managerial cybernetics of organization) *Notes:* "Companion volume to Brain of the firm and The heart of enterprise." Includes index. Bibliography: p. 152. [LC 84025795; ISN 0471906751; $18.00] HD58.9. B44 1985   3136

The diversity advantage: how American business can out-perform Japanese and European companies in the global marketplace. John P. Fernandez, with Mary Barr. New York: Toronto: Lexington Books: Maxwell Macmillan International; Maxwell Macmillan Canada, c1993. viii, 344 p. *Notes:* Includes bibliographical references (p. [317]-332) and index. *Contents:* Racism, sexism, ethnocentrism, and xenophobia—Putting Japan in perspective—Japanese women—Japanese ethnocentrism and racism—European community structures, business, and labor—European women—Business impact of European culture clashes—Europe and immigration—Women in the U.S. workplace—U.S. immigration policies: how much better than the EC and Japan?—Racial minorities in the United States—Race discrimination in corporate America—Some important realities—What companies must do to be competitive. [LC 93023793; ISN 0669279781; $24.95] HD58.9. F46 1993   +3137

Diversity and differences in organizations: an agenda for answers and questions. edited by Ronald R. Sims and Robert F. Dennehy; foreword by Jim Noel. Westport, Conn.: Quorum, 1993. xvi, 182 p. : ill. *Notes:* Includes bibliographical references (p. [173]) and index. [LC 93018524; ISN 0899307981] HD58.9. D58 1993   3138

Driving fear out of the workplace: how to overcome the invisible barriers to quality, productivity, and innovation. Kathleen D. Ryan, Daniel K. Oestreich. 1st ed. San Francisco: Jossey-Bass Publishers, 1991. xxi, 253 p. : ill. *Notes:* "A Bard Productions book." Includes bibliographical references and index. [LC 90047648; ISN 1555423175] HD58.9. R93 1991   3139

Empowering people at work. Nancy Foy. Aldershot, Hampshire, England: Brookfield, Vt., USA: Gower, c1994. xx, 268 p. : ill. *Notes:* Includes index. [LC 93035661; ISN 0566074362; $24.95 (est.)] HD58.9. F69 1994   +3140

Entrepreneurs in corporations. by Paul M. Connolly. New York: Pergamon Press, 1986. 80 p. *Notes:* Bibliography: p. 73-80. [LC 86011265; ISN 0080295193; $35.00] HD58.9. C65 1986   3141

The fifth discipline fieldbook: strategies and tools for building a learning organization. Peter M. Senge,... et al. New York: Doubleday Currency, c1994. xiii, 593 p. : ill. *Notes:* Includes bibliographical references and index. [LC 93050130; ISN 0385472560; $29.95] HD58.9. F54 1994 +3142

The fifth discipline: the art and practice of the learning organization. Peter M. Senge. 1st ed. New York: Doubleday, c1990. viii, 424 p. : ill. *Notes:* "A Currency book"—T.p. verso. Bibliography: p. [391]-409. [LC 90002991; ISN 0385260946; $19.95] HD58.9. S46 1990 3143

The flexible organization: a unique new system for organizational effectiveness and success. Barbara Forisha-Kovach. Englewood Cliffs, N.J.: Prentice-Hall, c1984. vii, 159 p. : ill. *Notes:* "A Spectrum book." Includes index. [LC 83024591; ISN 0133223213; ISN 0133223132; $16.95; $7.95]
HD58.9. F67 1984 3144

Getting it to the bottom line: management by incremental gains. Richard S. Sloma. New York: London: Free Press; Collier Macmillian, c1987. ix, 196 p. : ill. *Notes:* Includes bibliographical references and index. [LC 87000411; ISN 0029295408] HD58.9. S56 1987 3145

Influence without authority. Allan R. Cohen, David L. Bradford. New York: J. Wiley, c1990. xv, 319 p. : ill. *Notes:* Includes bibliographical references (p. 307-314) [LC 89024901; ISN 0471622680; $19.95] HD58.9. C64 1990 3146

Managing beyond the quick fix: a completely integrated program for creating and maintaining organizational success. Ralph H. Kilmann in collaboration with Ines Kilmann. 1st ed. San Francisco: Jossey-Bass, 1989. xxvi, 228 p. : ill. *Notes:* Includes index. Bibliography: p. 207-220. [LC 88046084; ISN 1555421326] HD58.9. K48 1989 3147

Managing the unknowable: strategic boundaries between order and chaos in organizations. Ralph D. Stacey. 1st ed. San Francisco: Jossey-Bass, c1992. xvii, 219 p. : ill. *Notes:* Includes bibliographical references (p. 205-210) and index. [LC 92017306; ISN 1555424635] HD58.9. S737 1992 3148

Organizational capability: competing from the inside out. by David Ulrich, Dale Lake. New York: Wiley, c1990. xii, 339 p. : ill. *Notes:* Includes bibliographical references. [LC 90031355; ISN 0471618071; $27.95] HD58.9. U47 1990 3149

Organizational design: the organizational audit and analysis technology. by Kenneth D. Mackenzie. Norwood, N.J.: Ablex Pub. Corp., 1986. xiv, 292 p. : ill. (Communication and information science) *Notes:* Includes indexes. Bibliography: p. 279-284. [LC 85013454; ISN 0893913480]
HD58.9. M34 3150

Organizational entrepreneurship. Jeffrey R. Cornwall, Baron Perlman. Homewood, Ill.: Irwin, c1990. xiv, 241 p. : ill. *Notes:* Includes bibliographical references and index. [LC 89035527; ISN 0256069808; $25.95] HD58.9. C667 1990 3151

The purpose-driven organization: unleashing the power of direction and commitment. Perry Pascarella, Mark A. Frohman. 1st ed. San Francisco: Jossey-Bass Publishers, 1989. xvi, 177 p. *Notes:* Includes index. Bibliography: p. [LC 89015236; ISN 1555421768; $20.95] HD58.9. P37 1989 3152

Quality, productivity, and innovation: strategies for gaining competitive advantage. edited by Y.K. Shetty, Vernon M. Buehler; foreword by Roger Smith. New York: Elsevier, c1987. xx, 427 p. : ill. *Notes:* Includes index. Bibliography: p. [399]-416. [LC 87006815; ISN 0444011943]
HD58.9. Q35 1987 3153

The seamless enterprise: making cross functional management work. Dan Dimancescu. 1st ed. New York, NY: HarperBusiness, c1992. xx, 249 p. : ill. *Notes:* "Lessons for executives and managers on concurrent engineering, continuous improvement, and customer driven product development." Includes bibliographical references (p. [237]-238) and index. [LC 91041605; ISN 088730544X; $30.00 (Canada $40.00)] HD58.9. D56 1992 3154

The smarter organization: how to build a business that learns and adapts to marketplace needs. Michael E. McGill, John W. Slocum. New York: J. Wiley, 1994. xiii, 288 p. *Notes:* Includes bibliographical references (p. 267-278) and indexes. [LC 94010732; ISN 0471598461; $27.95]
HD58.9. M43 1994 +3155

ORGANIZATIONAL SOCIOLOGY

Designing effective organizations: traditional & transformational views. David K. Banner, T. Elaine Gagné. Thousand Oaks, Calif.: Sage Publications, 1994, c1995. xxi, 480 p. : ill. *Notes:* Includes bibliographical references and indexes. [LC 94005921; ISN 0803948484] HM131. B23 1994 +3156

Great writers on organizations. Derek S. Pugh and David J. Hickson. Omnibus ed. Aldershot, Hants, England; Brookfield, Vt.: Dartmouth, c1993. viii, 287 p. : ill. *Notes:* This comprehensive edition contains a description of the work of all the writers included in the previous four editions, which were published under the title: Writers on organizations. Contains contributions on the work of Alfred D. Chandler, Paul Lawrence, Jay Lorsch, Mary Parker Follett, Elton Mayo, Chris Argyris, Rosabeth Moss Kantor, many others. Includes bibliographical references and indexes. [LC 93011088; ISN 1855213834; $59.95 (est.)]   HM131. P74 1993   +3157

Organizations: rational, natural, and open systems. W Richard Scott. 3rd ed. Englewood Cliffs, N.J.: Prentice Hall, c1992. xii, 414 p. *Notes:* Includes bibliographical references and index. [LC 91026278; ISN 0136388914; $45.71]   HM131. S385 1992   3158

PACIFIC AREA—COMMERCE—HANDBOOKS, MANUALS, ETC

The Pacific Rim almanac. edited and written by Alexander Besher; associate editor, John Wilcock. New York, N.Y.: HarperPerennial, c1991. xxii, 824 p. : ill., maps *Notes:* Includes index. [LC 90055996; ISN 0062730657; $19.95]   HF4030.7.Z6 B47 1991   3159

PACIFIC AREA—ECONOMIC CONDITIONS

Coming full circle: an economic history of the Pacific Rim. Eric Jones, Lionel Frost, & Colin White. Boulder: Westview Press, 1993. xv, 188 p. : maps *Notes:* Includes bibliographical references (p. 171-180) and index. [LC 93004130; ISN 0813312415]   HC681. J66 1993   +3160

The Pacific century: economic and political consequences of Asian Pacific dynamism. Staffan Burenstam Linder. Stanford, Calif.: Stanford University Press, 1986. xii, 154 p. *Notes:* Includes index. Bibliography: p. [133]-146. [LC 85022053; ISN 0804712948; ISN 0804713057; $18.95; $5.95]   HC681. L56 1986   3161

PACIFIC SETTLEMENT OF INTERNATIONAL DISPUTES

Beyond Machiavelli: tools for coping with conflict. Roger Fisher, Elizabeth Kopelman, Andrea Kupfer Schneider. Cambridge, Mass.: Harvard University Press, 1994. vi, 151 p. : ill. *Notes:* "A publication of the Harvard Negotiation Project"—P. [1]. [LC 93041916; ISN 0674069161; $16.95]   JX4473. F57 1994   +3162

PACKAGE GOODS INDUSTRY

Packaging for the environment: a partnership for progress. E. Joseph Stilwell... et al. New York: Amacom, c1991. x, 262 p. : ill. *Notes:* Includes bibliographical references and index. [LC 91055507; ISN 0814450741; $27.95]   TD195.P26 P33 1991   3163

PALEY, WILLIAM S

In all his glory: the life of William S. Paley, the legendary tycoon and his brilliant circle. by Sally Bedell Smith. New York: Simon and Schuster, c1990. 782 p., [32] p. of plates: ill. *Notes:* Includes bibliographical references (p. [735]-739) and index. [LC 90042704; ISN 0671617354; $29.95]   HE8689.8.P34 S65 1990   3164

PANICS (FINANCE)

Manias, panics, and crashes: a history of financial crises. Charles P. Kindleberger. Rev. ed. New York: Basic Books, c1989. xiv, 302 p. *Notes:* Includes bibliographical references (p. [258]-286). [LC 89042516; ISN 0465044034; $21.95]   HB3722. K56 1989   3165

PARALLEL PROCESSING (ELECTRONIC COMPUTERS)

A new era in computation. edited by N. Metropolis and Gian-Carlo Rota. 1st MIT Press ed. Cambridge, Mass.: MIT Press, 1993. xii, 241 p. : ill. *Notes:* "Articles originally appeared in the winter 1992 issue of Daedalus, volume 121, number 1"—T.p. verso. Includes bibliographical references. [LC 93008200; ISN 0262631547; $13.95]   QA76.58. N48 1993   +3166

PART-TIME EMPLOYMENT

Flexible work arrangements for managers and professionals: findings from a Catalyst study. New York: Catalyst, c1990. 42 leaves *Notes:* "Catalyst: working with business to effect change for women-through research, advisory services and communication"—Cover. Contains bibliographical references (p. 41-42).]   HD5106. M37 1990   3167

PAY EQUITY

Comparable worth: is it a worthy policy? Elaine Sorensen. Princeton, N.J.: Princeton University Press, c1994. xiii, 166 p. : ill. *Notes:* Includes bibliographical references (p. 153-161) and index. [LC 93023874; ISN 0691032637; $29.95]   HD6061.2.U6 S678 1994   +3168

Doing comparable worth: gender, class, and pay equity. Joan Acker. Philadelphia: Temple University Press, 1989. ix, 254 p. *Notes:* Includes index. Bibliography: p. 237-246. [LC 88026845; ISN 0877226210; $34.95]   HD6061.2.U62 O72 1989   3169

The economics of comparable worth. Mark R. Killingsworth. Kalamazoo, Mich.: W.E. Upjohn Institute for Employment Research, 1990. xi, 306 p. *Notes:* Includes bibliographical references (p. 285-298). [LC 89025044; ISN 0880990864; $27.54]   HD6061.2.U6 K56 1990   3170

PENN SQUARE BANK

Belly up: the collapse of the Penn Square Bank. Phillip L. Zweig. 1st ed. New York: Crown Publishers, c1985. x, 500 p., [8] p. of plates: ill., ports. *Notes:* Includes index. [LC 85001530; ISN 0517557088]   HG2613.O354 P419 1985   3171

PENNZOIL COMPANY

Texaco and the $10 billion jury. James Shannon. Englewood Cliffs, N.J.: Prentice Hall, 1988. xxiii, 545 p., [8] p. of plates: ill. *Notes:* Includes index. Bibliography: p. 527-533. [LC 88009885; ISN 0139119590; $19.95]   KF1866.P46 S5 1988   3172

PENSION TRUSTS

Fortune and folly: the wealth and power of institutional investing. William M. O'Barr, John M. Conley; with economic analysis by Carolyn Kay Brancato. Homewood, Ill.: Business One Irwin, c1992. xiii, 244 p. : ill. *Notes:* Includes bibliographical references and index. [LC 92006936; ISN 1556237057]   HD7105.45.U6 O23 1992   3173

PERFORMANCE

Performance. A. Dale Timpe, series editor. New York: Facts on File Publications, c1988. xiv, 378 p. *Notes:* Includes index. Bibliography: p. 366-373. [LC 87027692; ISN 0816019029; $24.95]   HF5549.5.P35 P37 1988   3174

Performance appraisal series. Boston c1955-1972. 106 p. illus. (part col.) *Notes:* Cover title. Reprints from the Harvard Business Review, 1955-1972.]   HF5549.5.J62 H3 1955   +3175

PERFORMANCE STANDARDS

Analysis for improving performance: tools for diagnosing organizations & documenting workplace expertise. Richard A. Swanson. 1st ed. San Francisco: Berrett-Koehler, c1994. xi, 286 p. : ill. *Notes:* Includes bibliographical references (p. 273-277) and index. [LC 94013445; ISN 1881052486; $32.95]   HF5549.5.P35 S88 1994   +3176

Designing performance appraisal systems: aligning appraisals and organizational realities. Allan M. Mohrman, Jr., Susan M. Resnick-West, Edward E. Lawler III, in collaboration with Michael J. Driver, Mary Ann Von Glinow, J. Bruce Prince. 1st ed. San Francisco: Jossey-Bass Publishers, 1989. xix, 227 p. : ill. *Notes:* Includes bibliographical references. [LC 88032894; ISN 1555421490; $25.95]   HF5549.5.P35 M64 1989   3177

Performance at work: a systematic program for analyzing work behavior. Richard A. Swanson, Deane Gradous. New York: Wiley, c1986. ix, 281 p. : ill., forms *Notes:* "A Wiley-Interscience publication." Includes index. Bibliography: p. 275-276. [LC 85026358; ISN 0471830607; $24.95 (est.)]   HF5549.5.P35 S9 1986   3178

PERFORMANCE TECHNOLOGY

Handbook of human performance technology: a comprehensive guide for analyzing and solving performance problems in organizations. Harold D. Stolovitch, Erica J. Keeps, editors; foreword by Thomas F. Gilbert; afterword by Robert F. Mager. 1st ed. San Francisco: Jossey-Bass, c1992. xliii, 817 p. : ill. *Notes:* "A publication of the National Society for Performance and Instruction"—T.p. verso. Includes bibliographical references (p. 765-789) and indexes. [LC 91027298; ISN 155542385X; $75.00]   HF5549.5.P37 H36 1992   3179

PERFORMING ARTS

Entertainment industry economics: a guide for financial analysis. Harold L. Vogel. 2nd ed. Cambridge; New York: Cambridge University Press, 1990. xvi, 432 p. : ill. *Notes:* Includes bibliographical references. [LC 89023886; ISN 0521385008; $34.50]   PN1590.F55 V6 1990   3180

PEROT, H. ROSS

Perot: an unauthorized biography. by Todd Mason. Homewood, IL: Dow Jones-Irwin, c1990. xiv, 316 p., [8] p. of plates: ill. *Notes:* Includes bibliographical references (p. 291-304). [LC 89071424; ISN 1556232365; $19.95]   HC102.5.P42 M37 1990   3181

PERSIAN GULF WAR, 1991

Moving mountains: lessons in leadership and logistics from the Gulf War. William G. Pagonis with Jeffrey L. Cruikshank. Boston, Mass.: Harvard Business School Press, c1992. xix, 248 p. : ill., maps *Notes:* Includes bibliographical references (p. [231]-235) and index. [LC 92015641; ISN 0875843603; $24.95]   DS79.72. P34 1992   +3182

PERSONALITY

Personality theories: a comparative analysis. Salvatore R. Maddi. 5th ed. Chicago, Ill.: Dorsey Press, c1989. xii, 749 p. : ill. *Notes:* Includes index. Bibliography: p. 675-726. [LC 88001607; ISN 0256032459; $35.00]   BF698. M237 1989   3183

PERSONNEL MANAGEMENT

The acceptance of human resource innovation: lessons for manangement. Ellen Ernst Kossek; foreword by Victor H. Vroom. New York: Quorum Books, c1989. xiv, 161 p. : ill. *Notes:* Includes index. Includes bibliographical references. [LC 88032143; ISN 0899303749]   HF5549.5.C6 K67 1989   3184

Applying psychology in business: the handbook for managers and human resource professionals. edited by John W. Jones, Brian D. Steffy, Douglas W. Bray. Lexington, Mass.: Lexington Books, c1991. 878 p. : ill. *Notes:* Includes bibliographical references. [LC 86046357; ISN 0669158380; $150.00]   HF5549. A8953 1991   3185

Competitive advantage through people: unleashing the power of the work force. Jeffrey Pfeffer. Boston, Mass.: Harvard Business School Press, c1994. ix, 281 p. *Notes:* Includes bibliographical references (p. [255]-272) and index. [LC 93026599; ISN 0875844138; $24.95]   HF5549.2.U5 P5 1994   +3186

Corporate resurgence and the new employment relationships: after the reckoning. Elmer H. Burack. Westport, Conn.: Quorum Books, 1993. xiii, 220 p. : ill. *Notes:* Includes bibliographical references and index. [LC 92016207; ISN 0899307892]   HF5549. B874 1993   3187

Critical skills: the guide to top performance for human resources managers. William R. Tracey. New York, NY: American Management Association, c1988. ix, 356 p. : ill. *Notes:* Includes bibliographies and index. [LC 87047762; ISN 0814459390]   HF5549. T712 1988   3188

The Dartnell personnel administration handbook. by Wilbert E. Scheer. 3d ed. Chicago: Dartnell Corporation, c1985. xix, 1124 p. : ill. *Notes:* Includes index. [LC 76077249; ISN 0850131480; $49.16]   HF5549. S3 1985   3189

Design of jobs. edited by Louis E. Davis and James C. Taylor. 2d ed. Santa Monica, Calif.: Goodyear Pub. Co., c1979. xxi, 250 p. : ill. *Notes:* Includes index. Bibliography: p. 245-246. [LC 78023397; ISN 0876202190]   HF5549. D438 1979   3190

Effective human resource development: how to build a strong and responsive HRD function. Neal E. Chalofsky, Carlene Reinhart. 1st ed. San Francisco: Jossey-Bass Publishers, 1988. xviii, 146 p. : ill. *Notes:* Includes index. Bibliography: p. 137-139. [LC 87046334; ISN 1555420818]   HF5549. C435 1988   3191

The employee handbook: a complete, ready-to-use model with sample policies and procedures. Richard T. Egbert. Englewood Cliffs, N.J.: Prentice Hall, c1991. xxvi, 297 p. : ill. *Notes:* Includes index. [LC 90044685; ISN 0132737159]   HF5549. E424 1991   3192

The European human resource management guide. edited by Chris Brewster... et al. London; New York: Academic, c1992. xiii, 648 p. : ill. *Notes:* Includes bibliographical references and index. [LC 93006280; ISN 012133130X]   HF5549.2.E85 E97 1992   3193

Every employee a manager. M. Scott Myers. 3rd ed. San Diego, Calif.: Pfeiffer & Company, c1991. ix, 354 p. : ill. *Notes:* Includes bibliographical references and index. [LC 90021040; ISN 0883902591; $40.19]   HF5549. M93 1991   3194

Gay issues in the workplace. Brian McNaught. 1st ed. New York: St. Martin's Press, 1993. xvii, 151 p. *Notes:* Includes bibliographical references (p. [149]-151). [LC 93026986; ISN 0312098081; $17.95]   HF5549.5.M5 M4 1993   +3195

A great place to work: what makes some employers so good, and most so bad. by Robert Levering. 1st ed. New York, N.Y.: Random House, 1988. xxii,312 p. *Notes:* Includes index. Bibliography: p. [273]-283. [LC 87043226; ISN 0394557255; $18.95; $17.95]   HF5549.2.U5 L37 1988   3196

The greatest management principle in the world. Michael LeBoeuf. New York: Putnam, c1985. 143 p. : ill. *Notes:* Includes index. [LC 84026597; ISN 0399130527]   HF5549. L38 1985   3197

The handbook of human resource development. edited by Leonard and Zeace Nadler. 2nd ed. New York: Wiley, c1990. 1 v. (various pagings): ill. *Notes:* Includes bibliographical references and index. [LC 89028899; ISN 0471506532; $75.00]   HF5549. H296 1990   3198

Handbook of human resources administration. edited by Joseph J. Famularo. 2nd ed. New York: McGraw-Hill, c1986. 1 v. (various pagings): ill., forms *Notes:* Rev. ed. of: Handbook of modern personnel administration. 1972. Includes bibliographies and index. [LC 85011352; ISN 0070199140]   HF5549. H297 1986   3199

HRM, trends and challenges: human resource management. edited by Richard E. Walton and Paul R. Lawrence. Boston, Mass.: Harvard Business School Press, c1985. xi, 392 p. *Notes:* A collection of papers presented at the Human Resource Futures Colloquium, 1984, sponsored by the Harvard Business School. Includes bibliographical references and index. [LC 85008485; ISN 0875841708]   HF5549. H185 1985   3200

Human resource accounting: advances in concepts, methods, and applications. Eric G. Flamholtz. 2nd ed., rev. and expanded. San Francisco: Jossey-Bass Publishers, 1985. xxiv, 389 p. : ill. (The Jossey-Bass management series) *Notes:* Includes index. Bibliography: p. 356-374. [LC 85045053; ISN 087589657X]   HF5681.H8 F55 1985   3201

Human resource management. George T. Milkovich, John W. Boudreau; with the assistance of Carolyn Milkovich. 6th ed. Homewood, IL: Irwin, c1991. xxvii, 740 p. : ill. (some col.) *Notes:* Rev. ed. of: Personnel/human resource management. 5th ed. 1988. Includes bibliographical references and indexes. [LC 90044216; $51.95]   HF5549. M4736 1991   3202

Human resource management systems: strategies, tactics, and techniques. Vincent R. Ceriello and Christine Freeman. Lexington, Mass.: Lexington Books, 1991. xxvii, 796 p. : ill. *Notes:* Includes bibliographical references and index. [LC 90044799; ISN 0669248789; $69.95]
HF5549.5.D37 C47 1991   3203

Human resources and personnel management. William B. Werther, Jr., Keith Davis. 3rd ed. New York: McGraw-Hill, c1989. xxvii, 628 p. : ill. *Notes:* Rev. ed. of: Personnel management and human resources. 2nd ed. c1985. Includes bibliographical references and index. [LC 88020986; ISN 0070694311; $38.95]
HF5549. W439 1989   3204

Human resources management: readings. edited by Fred K. Foulkes. Englewood Cliffs, N.J.: Prentice Hall, 1989. xx, 300 p. *Notes:* Includes bibliographies. [LC 88036387; ISN 0134459172]
HF5549. H8736 1989   3205

The human side of enterprise: 25th anniversary printing. Douglas McGregor; foreword by Warren Bennis. New York: McGraw-Hill, c1985. x, 246 p. : ill. *Notes:* Includes bibliographies. [LC 85061506; ISN 0070450986]
HF5549. M27 1985   3206

Human value management: the value-adding human resource management strategy for the 1990s. Jac Fitz-enz. 1st ed. San Francisco: Jossey-Bass Publishers, 1990. xvii, 346 p. : ill. *Notes:* Includes bibliographical references and index. [LC 89043457; ISN 1555422284; $27.95]   HF5549. F557 1990   3207

The IFM guide to the preparation of a company policy manual. 2nd ed. Greenvale, N.Y.: Institute for Management, c1987. 1 v. (loose-leaf) *Notes:* Includes index. [LC 87022258; ISN 0916592715; $84.95]
HF5549. I5643 1987   3208

Integrating the individual and the organization. Chris Argyris; with a new introduction by the author. New Brunswick, U.S.A.: Transaction Publishers, c1990. xvii, 330 p. *Notes:* Originally published: New York: Wiley, 1964. Includes bibliographical references and indexes. [LC 89029155; ISN 0887388035; $19.95]
HF5549. A8968 1990   3209

Labor pains and the Gaijin boss: hiring, managing and firing the Japanese. Thomas J. Nevins. 1st ed. Tokyo, Japan: Japan Times; , 1984. xxiv, 293 p.; ISN 4789002500]   HF5549.2.J3 N48   3210

The learning imperative: managing people for continuous innovation. edited, with an introduction by Robert Howard; foreword by Robert D. Haas. Boston, Mass.: Harvard Business School Press, c1993. xxvii, 310 p. *Notes:* Includes bibliographical references and index. *Contents:* Teaching smart people how to learn / Chris Argyris—Why change programs don't produce change / Michael Beer, Russell A. Eisenstat, and Bert Spector. [LC 93009876; ISN 0875844324; $29.95]
HF5549.2.U5 L33 1993   3211

Manage people, not personnel: motivation and performance appraisal. with a preface by Victor H. Vroom. Boston, Mass.: Harvard Business School Pub. Division, 1990. xvi, 267 p. : ill. *Notes:* Articles originally published in the Harvard Business Review. Includes bibliographical references. [LC 89077058; ISN 0875842283; $29.95]   HF5549. M2994 1990   3212

Management and the worker; an account of a research program conducted by the Western electric company, Hawthorne works, Chicago. by F. J. Roethlisberger and William J. Dickson, with the assistance and collaboration of Harold A. Wright. Cambridge, Mass. Harvard university press, 1939. xxiv, 615 p., incl. tables, diagrs. 5 pl. on 4 l. *Notes:* "About twelve years ago the Western electric company, at its Hawthorne plant, began the series of inquiries into the human effect of work and working conditions described in this book... [which] offers for the first time a continuous history of the entire series... It also relates together many different inquiries."—Pref. *Contents:* pt. I. Working conditions and employee efficiency.—pt. II. A plan for the improvement of employee relations.—pt. III. A conceptual scheme for the understanding of employee dissatisfaction.—pt. IV. Social organization of employees.—pt. V. Applications to practice of research results. [LC 39025984]
T58. R62   3213

Management of human resources; readings in personnel administration. edited by Paul Pigors, Charles A. Myers and F. T. Malm. 3d ed. New York McGraw-Hill, 1973. xii, 589 p. illus. *Notes:* Includes bibliographical references. [LC 72010046; ISN 0070500045]   HF5549. P4678 1973   +3214

The management of personnel. Robert E. Sibson. 1st ed. New York: Vantage Press, c1985. ix, 242 p. *Notes:* "An R. B. Keck Book." [LC 84091344; ISN 0533064414]   HF5549. S5852   3215

Managing human resource development. Leonard Nadler, Garland D. Wiggs. 1st ed. San Francisco: Jossey-Bass Publishers, 1986. xix, 294 p. (The Jossey-Bass management series) *Notes:* Includes index. Bibliography: p. 275-285. [LC 86007339; ISN 1555420060]   HF5549. N18 1986   3216

Managing human resources issues: confronting challenges and choosing options. William J. Heisler, W. David Jones, Philip O. Benham, Jr. 1st ed. San Francisco: Jossey-Bass, 1988. xx, 250 p. : ill. *Notes:* Includes index. Bibliography: p. 225-235. [LC 88042790; ISN 1555421245; $27.95]
HF5549. H384 1988   3217

Managing the new work force: the challenge of dual-income families. Cary L. Cooper and Suzan Lewis. Amsterdam; San Diego: Pfeiffer & Co., c1994. xvii, 254 p. : ill. *Notes:* Includes bibliographical references (p. [225]-242) and index.; ISN 0893842532; $14.95]   HF5549.5.C35 C6 1994   +3218

The mutual gains enterprise: forging a winning partnership among labor, management, and government. Thomas A. Kochan, Paul Osterman. Boston: Harvard Business School Press, c1994. x, 260 p. : ill. *Notes:* Includes bibliographical references and index. [LC 94005930; ISN 0875843948; $27.95]   HF5549.2.U5 K63 1994   +3219

Personnel: a book of readings. edited by William F. Glueck. Dallas: Business Publications, 1979. xviii, 494 p. : ill. *Notes:* Includes bibliographies. [LC 78070962; ISN 0256020787]   HF5549. P4475   3220

Personnel management: a human resources approach. Leon C. Megginson. 5th ed. Homewood, Ill.: R.D. Irwin, 1985. xvii, 654 p. : ill. (The Irwin series in management and the behavioral sciences) *Notes:* Includes bibliographies and indexes. [LC 84081125; ISN 0256032297]   HF5549. M342 1985   3221

Personnel management series. Boston c1961-1975. 3 v. illus. (part col.) *Notes:* Cover title. Reprints from the Harvard Business Review, 1961-1975. Title of pt. 2: Personnel management.]   HF5549. H364   +3222

Personnel policies in large nonunion companies. Fred K. Foulkes. Englewood Cliffs, N.J.: Prentice-Hall, c1980. xiv, 354 p. : ill. *Notes:* Includes index. Bibliography: p. 345-348. [LC 80010695]   HF5549.2.U5 F68   3223

Personnel, the human problems of management. George Strauss, Leonard R. Sayles. 4th ed. Englewood Cliffs, N.J.: Prentice-Hall, c1980. xiv, 674 p. : ill. *Notes:* Includes bibliographical references and indexes. [LC 79020082; ISN 0136578098]   HF5549. S89 1980   3224

Personnel, the management of human resources. Stephen P. Robbins. 2nd ed. Englewood Cliffs, N.J.: Prentice-Hall, c1982. xxiii, 520 p. : ill. *Notes:* Includes bibliographies and indexes. [LC 81010724; ISN 013657825X]   HF5549. R56 1982   3225

Personnel/human resource management today: readings and commentary. Craig Eric Schneier, Richard W. Beatty, Glenn M. McEvoy. 2nd ed. Reading, Mass.: Addison-Wesley, 1986. xx, 618 p. : ill. *Notes:* Rev. ed. of: Personnel administration today. c1978. Includes bibliographical references. [LC 85015013; ISN 0201057948; $19.95]   HF5549. P45146 1986   3226

Personnel/human resource management. 3rd ed. / David A. DeCenzo, Stephen P. Robbins. Englewood Cliffs, N.J.: Prentice-Hall, c1988. xvii, 637 p. : ill. *Notes:* Second ed. / Stephen P. Robbins. Includes bibliographies and indexes. [LC 87006983; ISN 0136571980; $38.70]   HF5549. D396 1988   3227

Planning and using a total personnel system. Richard A. Kaumeyer, Jr. New York: Van Nostrand Reinhold, c1982. xi, 195 p. : ill. *Notes:* Includes index. [LC 81010317; ISN 0442213700]   HF5549. K2833   3228

Readings in human resource management. edited by Michael Beer, Bert Spector. New York: London: Free Press; Collier Macmillan, c1985. x, 644 p. : ill. *Notes:* Includes contributions by several faculty members of the Harvard Graduate School of Business Administration. Includes bibliographical references and index. [LC 84025977; ISN 002902370X]   HF5549. R38164 1985   3229

Readings in personnel management. Paul S. Greenlaw. Philadelphia: W. B. Saunders, 1979. ix, 402 p. : ill. *Notes:* Includes bibliographical references. [LC 79105503; ISN 0721642616]   HF5549. R3817   3230

Staffing the contemporary organization: a guide to planning, recruiting, and selecting for human resource professionals. Donald L. Caruth, Robert M. Noe, III, and R. Wayne Mondy. New York: Quorum Books, 1988. xii, 309 p. : ill. *Notes:* Includes index. Bibliography: p. 301-304. [LC 87013092; ISN 089930236X; $45.00]   HF5549. C372 1988   3231

Strategic management of human knowledge, skills, and abilities: workforce decision-making in the postindustrial era. Eugene B. McGregor, Jr. 1st ed. San Francisco: Jossey-Bass Publishers, 1991. xxviii, 348 p. : ill. *Notes:* Includes bibliographical references and index. [LC 90020738; ISN 1555423078; $35.95]   HF5549. M33957 1991   3232

Strategic management of human resources. George S. Odiorne. 1st ed. San Francisco: Jossey-Bass, 1984. xx, 356 p. : ill. (The Jossey-Bass management series) (The Jossey-Bass social and behavioral science series) *Notes:* Subtitle on half t.p. and verso of t.p.: A portfolio approach. Includes indexes. Bibliography: p. 317-337. [LC 84047993; ISN 0875896251]   HF5549. O29 1984   3233

The strategic managing of human resources. John Douglas, Stuart Klein, David Hunt. New York: Wiley, c1985. xiv, 619 p. : ill. (Wiley series in management) *Notes:* Includes bibliographical references and index. [LC 84017419; ISN 0471053155; $24.95 (est.)]   HF5549. D598 1985   3234

Union-free management and how to keep it free. © by James L. Dougherty. Executive ed. Chicago: Dartnell Corp., c1972. 1v. (loose-leaf)]   HF5549. D58 1972   3235

Workplace 2000: the revolution reshaping American business. Joseph H. Boyett & Henry P. Conn. New York, N.Y., U.S.A.: Dutton, 1991. xi, 367 p. *Notes:* Includes bibliographical references (p. [345]-357) and index. [LC 90044753; ISN 0525249362; $22.95]   HF5549.2.U5 B69 1991   3236

PETROLEUM

Oil, from prospect to pipeline. Robert R. Wheeler, Maurine Whited. 5th ed. Houston: Gulf Pub. Co., 1985. xi, 147 p. : ill., maps *Notes:* Includes index. [LC 84015755; ISN 0872016366]
    TN870. W57 1985   3237

PETROLEUM CHEMICALS INDUSTRY

Innovation and competition: the global management of petrochemical products. Robert Stobaugh, with the assistance of James Gange. Boston, Mass.: Harvard Business School Press, c1988. xiv, 208 p. : ill. *Notes:* Includes bibliographical references and index. [LC 87025127; ISN 0875841481]
    HD9579.C33 U576 1988   3238

When markets quake: the management challenge of restructuring industry. Joseph L. Bower. Boston, Mass.: Harvard Business School Press, c1986. xi, 240 p. : ill. *Notes:* Includes bibliographies and index. [LC 86018321; ISN 0875841368]
    HD9579.C32 B69 1986   3239

PETROLEUM INDUSTRY AND TRADE

The control of oil. John M. Blair. 1st ed. New York: Pantheon Books, c1976. xxii, 441 p. : ill. *Notes:* Includes bibliographical references and index. [LC 75038116; ISN 0394494709; $15.00]
    HD9560.6. B55   +3240

Energy futures, trading opportunities for the 1980s. John Elting Treat... et al. Tulsa, Okla.: PennWell, c1984. x, 158 p. : ill. *Notes:* Includes bibliographical references and index. [LC 83021985; ISN 0878142509; $40.00]
    HG6047.P47 E53 1984   3241

Fundamentals of the petroleum industry. by Robert O. Anderson. 1st ed. Norman: University of Oklahoma Press, c1984. xii, 390 p. : ill. (some col.), maps *Notes:* Includes bibliographical references and index. [LC 84040271; ISN 0806119098; ISN 0806119160]
    HD9560.5. A55 1984   3242

Middle East oil crisis since 1973. Benjamin Shwadran. Boulder: Westview Press, 1986. xv, 254 p. : maps *Notes:* Includes index. Bibliography: p. 234-240. [LC 85012316; ISN 0813301505; $35.00]
    HD9576.N36 S546 1986   3243

Oil and world power. Peter R. Odell. 8th ed. Harmondsworth, Middlesex: New York: Penguin Books; Viking Penguin, 1986. 314 p. : ill., maps *Notes:* Includes index. A Pelican original. Bibliography: p. 294-[301].; ISN 0140227318]
    HD9560.5. O33 1986   3244

The prize: the epic quest for oil, money, and power. Daniel Yergin. New York: Simon & Schuster, c1991. 877, xxxii p., [32] p. of plates: ill., maps *Notes:* Includes bibliographical references (p. [848]-873) and index. [LC 90047575; ISN 0671502484; $24.95]
    HD9560.6. Y47 1991   3245

The problems of plenty: energy policy and international politics. Peter F. Cowhey. Berkeley: University of California Press, c1985. xiii, 447 p. : ill. (Science, technology, and the changing world order) *Notes:* Includes bibliographical references and index. [LC 83009275; ISN 0520046935]
    HD9560.6. C68 1985   3246

The seven sisters: the great oil companies and the world they shaped. Anthony Sampson. Bantam rev. 3rd ed. Toronto; New York: Bantam Books, c1984, c1983. xvii, 403 p. : map *Notes:* Includes bibliographical references and index.; ISN 0553242377]
    HD9560.5. S24 1984   3247

PHARMACEUTICAL BIOTECHNOLOGY

The billion-dollar molecule: one company's quest for the perfect drug. Barry Werth. New York: Simon & Schuster, c1994. 445 p. *Notes:* Includes bibliographical references (p. [423]-432) and index. [LC 93032566; ISN 0671723278; $24.50 ($32.50 Can.)]
    RS380. W47 1994   +3248

PHARMACEUTICAL INDUSTRY

The world health market: the future of the pharmaceutical industry. David Tucker. London?: Euromonitor Publications, c1984. x, 220 p. : ill. *Notes:* Bibliography: p. 219-220.; ISN 086338028X]
    HD9665.5. T83 1984   3249

PHILANTHROPISTS

The golden donors: a new anatomy of the great foundations. Waldemar A. Nielsen. 1st ed. New York: Truman Talley Books: E.P. Dutton, c1985. xi, 468 p. [LC 85012894; ISN 0525243666]
HV27. N53 1985 3250

PHYSICAL DISTRIBUTION OF GOODS

Contemporary logistics. James C. Johnson, Donald F. Wood. 5th ed. New York: Toronto: New York: Macmillan; Maxwell Macmillan Canada; Maxwell Macmillan International, c1993. xviii, 573 p. : ill., maps *Notes:* Rev. ed of: Contemporary physical distribution and logistics. 1990. Includes indexes. [LC 92021954; ISN 002360851X]
HF5415.6. J6 1993 3251

The distribution handbook. editor-in-chief, James F. Robeson; associate editor, Robert G. House. New York: London: Free Press; Collier Macmillan, c1985. xxii, 970 p. : ill. *Notes:* Includes index. Bibliography: p. 930-949. *Contents:* ch. 4. A look to the future / Wendell M. Stewart, Bernard J. La Londe, James L. Heskett and Donald J. Bowersox—ch. 29. Organizing for effective distribution management / James L. Heskett. [LC 83049340; ISN 0029227003]
HF5415.7. D55 1985 3252

The Gower handbook of logistics and distribution management. edited by John Gattorna; assistant editors, Gretchel Trost, Andrew Kerr. 4th ed. Aldershot, Hants, England; Brookfield, Vt., USA: Gower, c1990. xxv, 518 p. ill. *Notes:* Fourth ed. of: Handbook of physical distribution management. [LC 91105505; ISN 0566090090; $69.95]
HF5415.7. H33 1990 3253

Logistical management: a systems integration of physical distribution, manufacturing support, and materials procurement. Donald J. Bowersox, David J. Closs, Omar K. Helferich. 3rd ed. New York: London: Macmillan; Collier Macmillan, c1986. xxii, 586 p. : ill. *Notes:* Includes bibliographical references and indexes. [LC 85016822; ISN 0023130903]
HF5415.7. B66 1986 3254

Management of physical distribution and transportation. Charles A. Taff. 7th ed. Homewood, Ill.: R.D. Irwin, 1984. xxi, 545 p. : ill. *Notes:* Includes index. Bibliography: p. 525-532. [LC 83081775; ISN 0256020167]
HF5415.7. T32 1984 3255

The strategy of distribution management. Martin Christopher. Westport, Conn.: Quorum Books, 1985. x, 182 p. : ill. *Notes:* Includes bibliographical references and index. [LC 84018214; ISN 0899301142]
HF5415.7. C566 1985 3256

PICKENS, T. BOONE

Boone. T. Boone Pickens, Jr. Boston: Houghton Mifflin, 1987. xii, 304 p., [8] p. of plates: ill. *Notes:* "A Richard Todd book"—T.p. verso. Includes index. [LC 86027648; ISN 0395414334; ISN 0395432901; $18.95; $150.00]
HD9570.P53 P53 3257

PLANT SHUTDOWNS

Closing plants: planning and implementing strategies. by Coopers & Lybrand, Harold Dankner... et al. Morristown, N.J.: Financial Executives Research Foundation, c1986. xiii, 104 p. : ill. [LC 86080051; ISN 0910586578]
HD5708.5. C56 1986 3258

Plant closings: power, politics, and workers. Lawrence E. Rothstein. Dover, Mass.: Auburn House Pub. Co., c1986. xv, 201 p. : *Notes:* Includes bibliographies and index. [LC 85023025; ISN 0865691215; $27.95]
HD5708.55.U6 R68 1986 3259

Saving plants and jobs: union-management negotiations in the context of threatened plant closing. by Paul F. Gerhart. Kalamazoo, MI: W.E. Upjohn Institute for Employment Research, 1987. vii, 109 p. *Notes:* Includes bibliographies. [LC 87010527; ISN 0880990473; ISN 0880990465]
HD5708.5. G47 1987 3260

PLURALISM (SOCIAL SCIENCES)

Cultural diversity in organizations: theory, research, & practice. Taylor Cox, Jr. 1st ed. San Francisco: Berrett-Koehler, 1993. xiii, 314 p. *Notes:* Includes bibliographical references (p. 263-294) and indexes. [LC 93017920; ISN 1881052192; $29.95]
HM131. C749 1993 +3261

POKER

Poker strategy: winning with game theory. Nesmith C. Ankeny. New York: Basic Books, c1981. xv, 189 p. *Notes:* Includes index. [LC 80068177; ISN 0465058396; $11.95]　　　GV1251. A54　　3262

POLAND—ECONOMIC POLICY—1981-1990

Poland's jump to the market economy. Jeffrey Sachs. Cambridge, Mass.: MIT Press, c1993. xv, 126 p. *Notes:* Based on the Lionel Robbins Memorial Lectures delivered at the London School of Economics, January 1991. Includes bibliographical references (p. [119]-122) and index. [LC 93001738; ISN 0262193124; $19.95]　　　HC340.3. S21 1993　　+3263

POLITICAL CORRUPTION

The Japanese power game: what it means for America. William J. Holstein. New York: Toronto: New York: Scribner; Collier Macmillan Canada; Maxwell Macmillan International, c1990. x, 339 p. : ill. *Notes:* Includes bibliographical references (p. 315-326) and index. [LC 90034087; ISN 0684191768; $22.95]　　　JQ1629.C6 H65 1990　　3264

POLITICAL LEADERSHIP

On leadership. John W. Gardner. New York: Free Press, c1990. xv, 220 p. *Notes:* Includes bibliographical references. [LC 89016894; ISN 0029113113; $19.95]　　　JC330.3. G37 1990　　3265

POLLUTION

Corporate realities and environmental truths: strategies for leading your business in the environmental era. Steven J. Bennett, Richard Freierman, Stephen George. New York: Wiley, c1993. viii, 232 p. *Notes:* Includes index. [LC 93003481; ISN 0471530735]　　　HD69.P6 B46 1993　　3266

PORTFOLIO MANAGEMENT

Eurobonds. by F.G. Fisher. London: Euromoney Publications, 1988. 231 p. : ill. *Notes:* Includes index. Bibliography: p. 227.; ISN 1870031512]　　　HG3896. F56 1988　　3267

The institutional investor focus on investment management. edited by Frank J. Fabozzi. Cambridge, Mass.: Ballinger, c1989. xiv, 780 p. : ill. *Notes:* Includes bibliographical references and indexes. [LC 88038947; ISN 0887303307; $69.95]　　　HG4529.5. I59 1989　　3268

Investment policy: how to win the loser's game. Charles D. Ellis. Homewood, Ill.: Dow Jones-Irwin, c1985. xi, 81 p. : ill. *Notes:* Includes bibliographical references and index. [LC 85071879; ISN 0870947133]　　　HG4529.5. E45 1985　　3269

The management of corporate business units: portfolio stategies for turbulent times. Louis E.V. Nevaer and Steven A. Deck. New York: Quorum Books, c1988. xv, 231 p. : ill. *Notes:* Includes index. Bibliography: p. [223]-224. [LC 87032586; ISN 089930284X]　　　HG4529.5. N485 1988　　3270

Managing investment portfolios: a dynamic process. edited by John L. Maginn, Donald L. Tuttle; sponsored by the Institute of Chartered Financial Analysts. 2nd ed. Boston: Warren, Gorham & Lamont, c1990. 1 v. (various pagings): ill. *Notes:* Includes bibliographical references and index. [LC 89050465; ISN 0791303225; $108.10]　　　HG4529.5. M36 1990　　3271

Modern portfolio theory and investment analysis. Edwin J. Elton, Martin J. Gruber. 4th ed. New York: Wiley, c1991. xvi, 736 p. : ill. *Notes:* Includes bibliographical references and index. [LC 90025120; ISN 0471532487; $54.95]　　　HG4529.5. E47 1991　　3272

Portfolio analysis. Gordon J. Alexander, Jack Clark Francis. 3rd ed. Englewood Cliffs, N.J.: Prentice-Hall, c1986. xiv, 297 p. : ill. (Prentice-Hall foundations of finance series) *Notes:* Rev. ed. of: Portfolio analysis / Jack Clark Francis, Stephen H. Archer. 2nd ed. c1979. Includes index. Bibliography: p. 268-289. [LC 85028317; ISN 0136868258; $29.95]　　　HG4521. A42 1986　　3273

Portfolio theory and investment management. Richard Dobbins, Stephen F. Witt, and John Fielding. 2nd ed. Oxford, OX, UK; Cambridge, Mass., USA: Blackwell Business, 1994. vii, 181 p. : ill. *Notes:* Subtitle on cover: An introduction to modern portfolio theory. Includes bibliographical references (p. [167]-174) and indexes. [LC 93023965; ISN 0631191828]   HG4529.5. D62 1994   +3274

Security evaluation and portfolio analysis. Edited by Edwin J. Elton and Martin J. Gruber. Englewood Cliffs, N.J. Prentice-Hall, 1972. xv, 601 p. *Notes:* Includes bibliographical references. [LC 72162349; ISN 0137990154]   HG4521. E5   +3275

State-of-the-art portfolio selection: using knowledge-based systems to enhance investment performance. Robert R. Trippi, Jae K. Lee. Chicago, Ill.: Probus Pub. Co., c1992. xxi, 214 p. : ill. *Notes:* Includes bibliographical references and index.; ISN 1557382956; $69.00]   HG4529.5. T74 1992   3276

POSITIONING (ADVERTISING)

Positioning: the battle for your mind. by Al Ries and Jack Trout. 1st ed., rev. New York: McGraw-Hill, c1986. x, 213 p. *Notes:* Includes index. [LC 85014898; ISN 0070652643]   HF5827.2. R53 1986   3277

POWER (SOCIAL SCIENCES)

The anatomy of power. John Kenneth Galbraith. Boston: Houghton Mifflin, 1983. xv, 206 p. *Notes:* Includes bibliographical references and index. [LC 83012622; ISN 039534400X; $17.95]   HM271. G27 1983   3278

POWER RESOURCES

Coping with abundance: energy and environment in industrial America. Martin V. Melosi. 1st ed. Philadelphia: Temple University Press, c1985. xii, 355 p. : ill. *Notes:* Includes bibliographies and index. [LC 85004745; ISN 0877223726; $29.95]   HD9502.U52 M44 1985b   3279

Creating abundance: America's least-cost energy strategy. Roger W. Sant, Dennis W. Bakke, Roger F. Naill; James Bishop, Jr., editor. New York: McGraw-Hill, c1984. xiii, 176 p. : ill. *Notes:* Includes bibliographical references and index. [LC 83024853; ISN 0070415188; $16.95 (est.)]   TJ163.25.U6 S26 1984   3280

PRICE MAINTENANCE

How to price your products and services. Boston, Mass.: Harvard Business Review, c1991. vi, 123 p. : ill. *Notes:* Articles reprinted from the Harvard Business Review. Includes bibliographical references.; ISN 087584278X; $19.95]   HF5417. H68 1991   3281

PRICE WATERHOUSE (FIRM)

Accounting for success: a history of Price Waterhouse in America, 1890-1990. David Grayson Allen, Kathleen McDermott. Boston: Harvard Business School Press, c1993. xx, 373 p. : ill. *Notes:* Includes bibliographical references (p. 299-357) and index. [LC 92015492; ISN 087584328X; $35.00]   HF5616.U7 P752 1993   3282

PRICING

Pricing: making profitable decisions. Kent B. Monroe. 2nd ed. New York: McGraw-Hill Pub. Co., c1990. xxiv, 502 p. : ill. *Notes:* Includes bibliographical references and indexes. [LC 90005565; ISN 0070427828; $56.42]   HF5416.5. M66 1990   3283

The strategy and tactics of pricing: a guide to profitable decision making. Thomas T. Nagle. Englewood Cliffs, N.J.: Prentice-Hall, 1987. xiii, 351 p. : ill. *Notes:* Includes bibliographies and index. [LC 86015081; ISN 0138515107]   HF5416.5. N34 1987   3284

PRIVACY, RIGHT OF

Managing privacy: information technology and corporate America. H. Jeff Smith. Chapel Hill: University of North Carolina Press, c1994. xiv, 297 p. : ill. *Notes:* Includes bibliographical references (p. [271]-289) and index. [LC 93033334; ISN 0807321470; ISN 0807844543; $45.00]
    JC596.2.U5 S64 1994   +3285

PRIVATIZATION

Going private: the international experience with transport privatization. José A. Gómez-Ibáñez and John R. Meyer. Washington, D.C.: Brookings Institution, c1993. xiv, 310 p. : maps *Notes:* Includes bibliographical references and index. [LC 93029153; ISN 0815731795; $16.95]   HD3850. G65 1993   +3286

Privatisation: fair shares for all or selling the family silver? John Rentoul, Lord Ezra, Peter Clarke London: Papermac, 1987. viii, 107 p. (Days of decision) [LC 87019230; ISN 0333447700; £4.95 (Apr.)]   HD4148. P67 1987   3287

Privatization and deregulation in global perspective. edited by Dennis J. Gayle and Jonathan N. Goodrich. New York: Quorum Books, 1990. xxii, 473 p. : ill. *Notes:* Includes bibliographical references (p. [445]-452) and indexes. [LC 89024317; ISN 0899304192; $59.00]   HD3850. P75 1990   3288

Privatization: investing in state-owned enterprises around the world. Ernst & Young. New York: Wiley, c1994. xiii, 192 p. : ill. *Notes:* Includes bibliographical references (p. 161-165) and index. [LC 93045615; ISN 0471593230]   HD3850. P747 1994   +3289

When government goes private: successful alternatives to public services. Randall Fitzgerald. New York: Universe Books, 1988. 330 p. *Notes:* Includes index. "A Pacific Research Institute for Public Policy book." Bibliography: p. [300]-316. [LC 88301160; ISN 0876636792; $24.95]
  HD3888. F43 1988   3290

PROBABILITIES

Finite markov chains. by John G. Kemeny and J. Laurie Snell. Princeton, N. J. Van Nostrand, c1960. 210 p. (The University series in undergraduate mathematics) [LC 59015644]   QA273. K33   +3291

Introduction to probability models. Sheldon M. Ross. 4th ed. Boston: Academic Press, c1989. xiv, 544 p. *Notes:* Includes bibliographical references and index. [LC 89006539; ISN 0125984642; $44.50]
  QA273. R84 1989   3292

Introduction to probability theory and statistical inference. Harold J. Larson. 3rd ed. New York: Wiley, c1982. xi, 637 p. : ill. (Wiley series in probability and mathematical statistics. Probability and mathematical statistics 0271-6232) *Notes:* Includes index. [LC 81016246; ISN 0471059099]
  QA273. L352 1982   3293

PROBLEM SOLVING

The complete problem solver: a total system for competitive decision making. by John D. Arnold. New York: Wiley, 1992. xiii, 240 p. *Notes:* Includes index. [LC 91043604; ISN 0471541982]
  HD30.29. A76 1992   3294

How to solve business problems: the consultant's approach to business problem solving. Kenneth J. Albert. 1st McGraw-Hill paperback ed. New York: McGraw-Hill, 1983. ix, 207 p. *Notes:* "Previously published under the title 'How to be your own management consultant'."—label on cover. Includes index. [LC 82014956; ISN 0070007535; $9.95]   HD30.29. A4 1983   3295

Problem solving for managers. by William F. Roth, Jr. New York: Praeger, c1985. 230 p. : ill. *Notes:* Includes index. Bibliography: p. 211-219. [LC 84018280; ISN 0030024633; $27.95]
  HD30.29. R68 1985   3296

Unconventional wisdom: irreverent solutions to tough problems at work. Thomas L. Quick. 1st ed. San Francisco: Jossey-Bass, 1989. xv, 174 p. *Notes:* Bibliography: p. 167-168. [LC 89045594; ISN 1555421776; $19.95]   HD30.29. Q54 1989   3297

PROCTER & GAMBLE COMPANY

Soap opera: the inside story of Procter & Gamble. Alecia Swasy. 1st ed. New York: Times Books, c1993. xvi, 378 p. : ill. *Notes:* Includes bibliographical references (p. 311-341) and index. [LC 93012793; ISN 0812920600; $24.00 ($31.50 Canada)]   HD9999.S74 P7674 1993   +3298

PRODUCT MANAGEMENT

Marketing decisions for new and mature products. Robert D. Hisrich, Michael P. Peters. 2nd ed. New York: Toronto: New York: Macmillan; Collier Macmillan Canada; Maxwell Macmillan International Pub. Group, c1991. xiv, 516 p. : ill. *Notes:* Includes bibliographical references and index. [LC 90049108; ISN 0675206472; $52.00]   HF5415. H5436 1991   3299

Product management: strategy and organization. Edgar A. Pessemier. 2nd ed. Malabar, Fla.: R.E. Kreiger Pub. Co., 1986, c1982. xix, 668 p. : ill. *Notes:* Reprint. Originally published: 2nd ed. New York: Wiley, c1982. Includes bibliographies and indexes. [LC 85023976; ISN 0898749220]   HF5415.15. P39 1986   3300

PRODUCT SAFETY

Consuming fears: the politics of product risks. Harvey M. Sapolsky, editor. New York: Basic Books, c1986. x, 241 p. *Notes:* Includes index. Bibliography: p. [203]-229. *Contents:* Introduction / Harvey M. Sapolsky—The changing politics of cigarette smoking / Harvey M. Sapolsky—Hearts and minds / Janet M. Levine—The politics of salt / Mark J. Segal—The political reality of artificial sweeteners / Linda C. Cummings—Tampons and toxic shock syndrome / Sanford L. Weiner—Banning formaldehyde insulation / Sanford L. Weiner—The politics of product controversies / Harvey M. Sapolsky. [LC 86047503; ISN 0465014119; $18.95]   TS175. C66 1986   3301

PRODUCTION (ECONOMIC THEORY)

Recent developments in production economics: proceedings of the Fourth International Working Seminar on Production Economics, Igls, Austria, February 17-21, 1986. edited by R.W. Grubbström and H.H. Hinterhuber, associate editor, Janerik Lundquist. Amsterdam; New York: Elsevier, 1987. vii, 414 p. : ill. *Notes:* Also published as a special issue of Engineering costs and production economics, vol. 12, issues 1-4. Includes bibliographies and indexes. [LC 87015693; ISN 0444428429]   HB241. I58 1986   3302

The structure of production. Mark Skousen. New York: New York University Press, c1990. xvi, 415 p. : ill. *Notes:* Includes bibliographical references (p. 379-400) and index. [LC 89013181; ISN 081477895X; $40.00]   HB241. S58 1990   3303

PRODUCTION CONTROL

Attaining manufacturing excellence: just-in-time, total quality, total people involvement. Robert W. Hall. Homewood, Ill.: Dow Jones-Irwin, c1987. x, 290 p. : ill. (The Dow Jones-Irwin/APICS series in production management) *Notes:* Includes index. [LC 86071920; ISN 087094925X]   TS157. H34 1987   3304

Handbook of production and inventory control. Nyles V. Reinfeld, editor; with contributions by leading personnel in the field. Englewood Cliffs, N.J.: Prentice-Hall, c1987. xiii, 370 p. : ill. *Notes:* Includes index. [LC 86016887; ISN 0133806685]   TS157. H36 1987   3305

Kanban just-in-time at Toyota: management begins at the workplace. edited by the Japan Management Association; translated by David J. Lu; foreword by Norman Bodek. Rev. ed. Cambridge, Mass.: Productivity Press, c1989. xix, 192 p. : ill. *Notes:* Translation of: Toyota no genba kanri: kanban hōshiki no tadashii susumekata. Includes index. [LC 88043585; ISN 0915299488; $34.95]   TS157. T6913 1989   3306

Production and inventory management. Arnoldo C. Hax, Dan Candea. Englewood Cliffs, N.J.: Prentice-Hall, c1984. x, 513 p. *Notes:* Includes bibliographies and indexes. [LC 83009612; ISN 0137248806]   TS155.8. H38 1984   3307

Production-inventory systems: planning and control. Elwood S. Buffa, Jeffrey G. Miller. 3d ed. Homewood, Ill.: R. D. Irwin, 1979. xii, 744 p. : ill. *Notes:* Includes bibliographies and index. [LC 78061186; ISN 0256020418] TS155.8. B84 1979 3308

PRODUCTION ENGINEERING

Design for manufacturability: a systems approach to concurrent engineering and ergonomics. edited by M. Helander and M. Nagamachi. London; Washington, D.C.: Taylor & Francis, 1992. 409 p. : ill. *Notes:* Papers from the conference on Human Factors in Design for Manufacturability and Process Planning, held in Honolulu in Aug. 1990. "Published in collaboration with the International Ergonomics Association." Includes bibliographical references and index. [LC 92019419; ISN 0748400095; £49.00 ($99.00)] TS176. D46 1992 3309

Handbook of expert systems in manufacturing. Rex Maus, Jessica Keyes, editors. New York: McGraw-Hill, c1991. xxii, 561 p. : ill. *Notes:* Includes bibliographical references (p. 551-553) and index. [LC 90013450; ISN 0070409846; $54.95] TS176. H336 1991 3310

Manufacturing high technology handbook. edited by Donatas Tijunelis, Keith E. McKee. New York: M. Dekker, c1987. xvi, 773 p. : ill. *Notes:* Includes bibliographies and index. Non-circulating. [LC 87006866; ISN 0824777204] TS155. M33336 1987 3311

PRODUCTION MANAGEMENT

The automated factory handbook: technology and management. David I. Cleland, Bopaya Bidanda. 1st ed. Blue Ridge Summit, PA: TPR, c1990. xvii, 812 p. : ill. *Notes:* Includes bibliographical references and index. [LC 90030673; ISN 0830692967; $69.95] TS176. C54 1990 3312

Handbook of statistical methods in manufacturing. Richard Barrett Clements. Englewood Cliffs, N.J.: Prentice Hall, 1991. xiv, 392 p. : ill. *Notes:* Includes bibliographical references (p. 369-371) and index. [LC 90007966; ISN 0133729478; $49.95] TS155. C54 1991 3313

International handbook of production and operations management. edited by Ray Wild. London: Cassell, 1989. xviii, 653 p. : ill. [LC 89014301; ISN 0304315257] TS155. I58 1989 3314

The management of productivity and technology in manufacturing. edited by Paul R. Kleindorfer. New York: Plenum Press, c1985. xiv, 331 p. : ill. *Notes:* "Commissioned papers presented at the Wharton Conference on Productivity, Technology and Organizational Innovation, held December 8-9, 1983, in Philadelphia, Pennsylvania, under the sponsorship of the center for the Study of Organizational Innovation, University of Pennsylvania." Includes bibliographical references and index. [LC 85017022; ISN 0306420325] TS155.A1 M356 1985 3315

Manufacturing, the formidable competitive weapon. Wickham Skinner. New York: Wiley, c1985. xviii, 330 p. : ill. *Notes:* Includes bibliographical references and index. [LC 85003290; ISN 0471817392; $29.95 (est.)] TS155. S553 1985 3316

Operations management: decision making in the operations function. Roger G. Schroeder. 3rd ed. New York: McGraw-Hill, c1989. xix, 794 p. : ill. *Notes:* Includes bibliographies and index. [LC 88013477; ISN 0070556180; $41.95] TS155. S37 1989 3317

Operations management: strategy and analysis. by Lee J. Krajewski & Larry P. Ritzman. 2nd ed. Reading, Mass.: Addison-Wesley, c1990. 1 v. (various pagings): ill. *Notes:* Includes bibliographical references and indexes. [LC 89018172; ISN 0201504103] TS155. K788 1990 3318

Operations management: strategy and analysis. Lee J. Krajewski and Larry P. Ritzman. 3rd ed. Reading, Mass.: Addison-Wesley Pub. Co., c1993. xxiii, 904 p. : ill. (some col.) *Notes:* Includes bibliographical references and index. [LC 92012241; ISN 0201566303] TS155. K788 1993 3319

Production & operations management: a life cycle approach. Richard B. Chase, Nicholas J. Aquilano. 6th ed. Homewood, IL: Irwin, c1992. xxvi, 1062 p. : ill. (some col.) *Notes:* Includes bibliographical references and indexes. [LC 91032076; ISN 025610039X; $55.95] TS155. C424 1992 3320

Production and inventory control handbook. James H. Greene, editor in chief. 2nd ed. New York: McGraw-Hill, c1987. 1 v. (various paagings): ill. *Notes:* "Prepared under the supervision of the Handbook Editorial Board of the American Production and Inventory Control Society (APICS)" Includes bibliographies and index. [LC 86007195; ISN 0070243212; $74.95] TS155. P74 1987 3321

Production and operations management. Keith Lockyer, Alan Muhlemann, and John Oakland. 5th ed. New York: Nichols Pub., 1988. xvi, 576 p. : ill. *Notes:* Rev. ed. of: Factory and production management. 3rd ed. 1974. Includes bibliographies and index. [LC 88003194; ISN 0893973084; $34.95] TS155. L68 1988 3322

Production and operations management: concepts, models, and behavior. Everett E. Adam, Jr., Ronald J. Ebert. 5th ed. Englewood Cliffs, NJ: Prentice Hall, c1992. xviii, 729 p. : ill. *Notes:* Includes bibliographical references and index. [LC 91030247; ISN 013717943X; $43.00]
TS155. A29514 1992   3323

Production handbook. 4th ed. / [edited by] John A. White. New York: Wiley, c1987. 1 v. (various pagings): ill. *Notes:* Includes bibliographies and index. [LC 86026796; ISN 0471863475]
TS155. P747 1987   3324

Production/operations management: concepts and situations. Roger W. Schmenner. 4th ed. New York: London: Macmillan; Collier Macmillan, c1990. xv, 797 p. : ill. *Notes:* Includes bibliographies and index. [LC 89034124; ISN 0024069256; $49.00]
TS155. S322 1990   3325

Production/operations management: concepts, structure, and analysis. Richard J. Tersine. 2nd ed. New York: North-Holland, c1985. xiv, 752 p. : ill. *Notes:* Includes bibliographies and index. [LC 84007992; ISN 044400923X]
TS155. T456 1985   3326

PRODUCTION PLANNING

Manufacturing planning and control systems. Thomas E. Vollmann, William L. Berry, D. Clay Whybark. 3rd ed. Homewood, IL: Irwin, c1992. xx, 844 p. : ill. *Notes:* Includes bibliographical references and index. [LC 91026037; $59.00]
TS176. V63 1992   3327

Manufacturing planning: key to improving industrial productivity. Kelvin F. Cross. New York: M. Dekker, c1986. x, 285 p. : ill. *Notes:* Includes bibliographies and index. [LC 85029360; ISN 0824773241]
TS176. C76 1986   3328

Production planning and inventory control. Dennis W. McLeavey, Seetharama L. Narasimhan. Boston: Allyn and Bacon, c1985. xv, 731 p. : ill. *Notes:* Includes bibliographies and index. [LC 84002829; ISN 0205081479; $29.95]
TS176. M374 1985   3329

PRODUCTS LIABILITY

The product liability mess: how business can be rescued from the politics of state courts. Richard Neely. New York: London: Free Press; Collier Macmillan, c1988. ix, 181 p. *Notes:* Includes bibliographical references and index. [LC 87033196; ISN 0029226805]
KF1296. N44 1988   3330

PROFESSIONAL CORPORATIONS

Managing the professional service firm. David H. Maister. New York: Toronto: New York: Free Press; Maxwell Macmillan Canada; Maxwell Macmillan International, c1993. xvi, 376 p. : ill. *Notes:* Includes bibliographical references (p. 365-366) and index. [LC 93014616; ISN 0029197821; $39.95]
HD62.65. M35 1993   +3331

PROFESSIONAL EMPLOYEES

The clash of cultures: managers and professionals. Joseph A. Raelin. Boston, Mass.: Harvard Business School Press, c1986. xv, 299 p. : ill. *Notes:* Includes index. Bibliography: p. [271]-285. [LC 86014227; ISN 0875841457; ISN 0875841414]
HD8038.A1 R33 1986   3332

The gold-collar worker: harnessing the brainpower of the new workforce. Robert E. Kelley. Reading, Mass.: Addison-Wesley, c1985. x, 196 p. *Notes:* Includes bibliographical references and index. [LC 85001408; ISN 0201117398; $16.95]
HD8038.U5 K44 1985   3333

Managing professional people: understanding creative performance. Albert Shapero. New York: London: Free Press; Collier Macmillan, c1985. xviii, 252 p. *Notes:* Includes index. Bibliography: p. 231-240. [LC 84018728; ISN 0029288703]
HD8038.A1 S53 1985   3334

PROFESSIONAL ETHICS

Corporate ethics: a prime business asset. The Business Roundtable. New York, N.Y. (200 Park Ave., Suite 2222, New York 10166): The Business Roundtable, 1988. 138 p. *Notes:* "A report on policy and practice in company conduct." Includes bibliographical references.]
HF5387. C6 1988   3335

PROFESSIONAL SPORTS

Pay dirt: the business of professional team sports. James Quirk and Rodney D. Fort. Princeton, N.J.: Princeton University Press, c1992. xviii, 538 p., [16] p. of plates: ill. *Notes:* Includes bibliographical references (p. 513-529) and indexes. [LC 92015349; ISN 0691042551] GV716. Q57 1992 3336

PROFESSIONS

Emancipating the professions: marketing opportunities from de-regulation. Aubrey Wilson. Chichester, England; New York: J. Wiley & Sons, c1994. xvi, 383 p. : ill. *Notes:* Includes bibliographical references and index. [LC 93045502; ISN 0471944378; $40.00] HD8038.A1 W547 1994 +3337
Getting new clients. Dick Connor, Jeff Davidson. 2nd ed. New York: Wiley, c1993. xviii, 281 p. : ill. *Notes:* Includes index. [LC 92020197; ISN 0471555282; $27.95] HD8038.A1 C665 1993 3338
Getting new clients. Richard A. Connor, Jr., Jeffrey P. Davidson. New York: Wiley, c1987. xxiii, 305 p. : ill. *Notes:* Includes index. [LC 87021657; ISN 047162778X] HD8083.A1 C65 1987 3339
Marketing your consulting and professional services. Richard A. Conner, Jr., Jeffrey P. Davidson. New York: Wiley, c1985. xiv, 219 p. : ill., forms *Notes:* Includes index. Bibliography: p. 187-190. [LC 84023453; ISN 0471818275; $19.95 (est.)] HD8038.A1 C66 1985 3340
Services marketing. Christopher H. Lovelock. 2nd ed. Englewood Cliffs, N.J.: Prentice Hall, c1991. xvi, 526 p. : ill. *Notes:* Includes bibliographical references (p. 517-518) and index. [LC 90036923; ISN 0138070660; $50.00] HF5415.122. L68 1991 3341

PROFIT

Managing to have profits: the art of hitting your target profit. Arnold J. Olenick. New York: McGraw-Hill, c1989. xiii, 210 p. : ill. *Notes:* Includes bibliographical references and index. [LC 88023146; ISN 0070477590; $19.95] HG4028.P7 O42 1989 3342

PROFIT-SHARING

Profit sharing in perspective, in American medium-sized and small business. by B. L. Metzger. 2d ed. Evanston, Ill. 1966. xiii, 229 p. illus., forms, map. *Notes:* Bibliography: p. 228-229. [LC 65028452] HD2984. M47 1966 +3343

PROGRAM BUDGETING

The planning-programming-budgeting approach to Government decision-making. by Harold A. Hovey. Foreword by William Proxmire. New York Praeger, 1968. xxv, 264 p. (Praeger special studies in U.S. economic and social development) *Notes:* Includes bibliographical references. [LC 68055007] HJ2052. H63 +3344

PROGRAM TRADING (SECURITIES)

Program trading: the new age of investing. Jeffrey D. Miller with Mara Miller and Peter J. Brennan. New York: J.K. Lasser Institute, c1989. xi, 212 p. : ill. *Notes:* Includes bibliographical references and index. [LC 89008141; ISN 0137303181; $19.95] HG4515.5. M55 1989 3345

PROPOSAL WRITING IN BUSINESS

Guidelines for preparing proposals: a manual on how to organize winning proposals for grants, venture capital, R & D projects, other proposals. by Roy Meador. Chelsea, Mich.: Lewis Publishers, c1985. vii, 116 p. : ill. *Notes:* Includes index. Bibliography: p. 111-112. [LC 84025002; ISN 0873710045; $19.95] HF5718.5. M43 1985 3346

PROTECTIONISM

Protectionism. Jagdish Bhagwati. Cambridge, Mass.: MIT Press, c1988. xiii, 147 p. : ill. *Notes:* Includes indexes. Bibliography: p. [131]-142. [LC 88000672; ISN 0262022826; $16.95]
 HF1713. B47 1988 3347

Trade wars against America: a history of United States trade and monetary policy. William J. Gill. New York: Praeger, 1990. xvi, 324 p. *Notes:* Includes bibliographical references. [LC 89029765; ISN 0275933164] HF1756. G53 1990 3348

PSYCHOLOGY, INDUSTRIAL

The applied psychology of work behavior: a book of readings. edited by Dennis W. Organ. 4th ed. Homewood, IL: Irwin, c1991. vi, 522 p. *Notes:* Includes bibliographical references. [LC 90022187; ISN 0256082758; $25.95] HF5548.8. A72 1991 3349

Handbook of industrial and organizational psychology. Marvin D. Dunnette and Leaetta M. Hough, editors. 2nd ed. Palo Alto, Calif.: Consulting Psychologists Press, c1990-1994. 4 v.: ill. *Notes:* Spine title: Handbook of industrial & organizational psychology. Vol. 4 also edited by Harry C. Triandis. Includes bibliographical references and indexes. [LC 90002294; ISN 0891060413; $55.00]
 HF5548.8. H265 1990 3350

Handbook of industrial and organizational psychology. Marvin D. Dunnette, editor. New York: Wiley, 1983,c1976. xxvii, 1740 p. : ill. *Notes:* Reprint. Originally published: Chicago: Rand McNally College Pub. Co., c1976. Includes bibliographies and indexes. Non-circulating. [LC 83005815; ISN 0471886424] HF5548.8. H265 1983 3351

Handbook of work and organizational psychology. edited by P.J.D. Drenth... et al. Chichester West Sussex; New York: Wiley, c1984- v. *Notes:* Includes bibliographies and indexes. [LC 83023316; ISN 0471903442; ISN 0471904007; ISN 0471904015; $72.00; $72.00] HF5548.8. H2655 1984 3352

Industrial and organizational psychology. Ernest J. McCormick, Daniel R. Ilgen. 8th ed. Englewood Cliffs, N.J.: Prentice-Hall, c1985. xii, 468 p. : ill *Notes:* Rev. ed. of: Industrial psychology. 7th ed. c1980. Includes bibliographies and index. [LC 84011718; ISN 0134630920; $27.95]
 HF5548.8. M383 1985 3353

Managerial psychology: managing behavior in organizations. Harold J. Leavitt and Homa Bahrami. 5th ed. Chicago: University of Chicago Press, 1988. x, 353 p. : ill. *Notes:* Includes index. Bibliography: p. 339-344. [LC 87016820; ISN 0226469735; $26.75] HF5548.8. L35 1988 3354

Managing by influence. Kenneth Schatz and Linda Schatz. Englewood Cliffs, N.J.: Prentice-Hall, c1986. xiii, 201 p. *Notes:* Includes index. Bibliography: p. 196-197. [LC 86012199; ISN 0135505917]
 HF5548.8. S34 1986 3355

Men, management, and morality: toward a new organizational ethic. Robert T. Golembiewski. New Brunswick, N.J.: Transaction, c1988. xvi, 320 p. : ill. *Notes:* Reprint. Originally published: New York: McGraw Hill, 1965. Includes bibliographical references and indexes. [LC 88004951; ISN 0887387438] HF5548.8. G59 1988 3356

Organizational psychology: readings on human behavior in organizations. edited by David A. Kolb, Irwin M. Rubin, James M. McIntyre. 4th ed. Englewood Cliffs, N.J.: Prentice-Hall, c1984. xiv, 639 p. : ill. *Notes:* "Designed to be used with the text, Organizational psychology, an experimental approach to organizational behavior"—Pref. Includes bibliographies. [LC 83013946; ISN 0136412904] HF5548.8. O74 1984 3357

Psychology and industry today: an introduction to industrial and organizational psychology. Duane P. Schultz, Sydney Ellen Schultz. 5th ed. New York: Macmillan, c1990. xiv, 667, 67 p. : ill. *Notes:* Includes index. Bibliography: p. 625-667. [LC 89002572; ISN 002407621X; $43.00]
 HF5548.8. S356 1990 3358

Psychology of work behavior. Frank J. Landy. 4th ed. Pacific Grove, Calif.: Brooks/Cole Pub. Co., c1989. x, 715, 44, 14 p. *Notes:* Includes indexes. Bibliography: p. 1-44 (3rd group) [LC 88028536; ISN 0534110916; $40.00; $40.00] HF5548.8. L25 1989 3359

Readings in managerial psychology. 4th ed. / edited by Harold J. Leavitt, Louis R. Pondy and David M. Boje. Chicago: University of Chicago Press, 1989. xiii, 769 p. : ill. *Notes:* Includes bibliographies. [LC 88001159; ISN 0226469913; ISN 0226469921] HF5548.8. L36 1989 3360

Ready, fire, aim: avoiding management by impulse. Harry Levinson; compiled from the Levinson letter and edited by Janet E. Robinson. Cambridge, Mass.: Levinson Institute, c1986. xi, 282 p. *Notes:* Includes index. Bibliography: p. [265]-268. [LC 86010593; ISN 0916516067; $25.00 (est.)]
 HF5548.8. L386 1986 3361

The workplace within: the psychodynamics of organizational life. Larry Hirschhorn. Cambridge, Mass.: MIT Press, c1988. x, 265 p. *Notes:* Includes index. Bibliography: p. [251]-258. [LC 87020144; ISN 0262081695]　　　　　　　　　　　　　　　　　　　　HF5548.8. H493 1988　　3362

PUBLIC OPINION

Inside America. Louis Harris. 1st ed. New York: Vintage Books, c1987. xv, 422 p. *Notes:* "A Vintage original"—Verso t.p. [LC 86046188; ISN 0394750705; $8.95]　　　　HN90.P8 H37 1987　　3363

PUBLIC PROSECUTORS

The prosecutors: inside the offices of the government's most powerful lawyers. James Stewart. New York: Simon and Schuster, c1987. 378 p. *Notes:* Includes index. [LC 87013056; ISN 0671497472]　　　　　　　　　　　　　　　　　　　　　　　　　　　　　　KF9640. S74 1987　　3364

PUBLIC RELATIONS

The Dartnell public relations handbook. Robert L. Dilenschneider, Dan J. Forrestal; with a special section on the health care field. 3rd. rev. ed. Chicago: Dartnell Corporation, 1987. xxiv, 875 p. : ill. *Notes:* Includes index. [LC 87071012; ISN 0850131596]　　HD59. D28 1987　　3365

Excellence in public relations and communication management. edited by James E. Grunig with David M. Dozier. . . et al. Hillsdale, N.J.: L. Erlbaum Associates, 1992. xiv, 666 p. *Notes:* Product of a research project of the IABC Research Foundation. Includes bibliographical references and indexes. [LC 92008200; ISN 0805802274]　　　　　　　　　　　　　　HD59. E95 1992　　3366

Experts in action: inside public relations. edited by Bill Cantor; edited by Chester Burger. 2nd ed. New York: Longman, c1989. viii, 520 p. : ill. *Notes:* Includes bibliographical references and indexes. [LC 87002763; ISN 0582998662; $24.95]　　　　　　　　　HM263. E96 1989　　3367

Good-bye to the low profile: the art of creative confrontation. Herb Schmertz with William Novak. 1st ed. Boston: Little, Brown, c1986. 242 p. : ill. [LC 86000027; ISN 0316773662]　HD59. S33 1986　　3368

Guerrilla P.R.: how you can wage an effective publicity campaign—without going broke. Michael Levine. 1st ed. New York: HarperBusiness, c1993. xxv, 229 p. [LC 92053331; ISN 088730608X; $20.00 ($26.75 Can.)]　　　　　　　　　　　　　　　　　　　　　　　　　HD59. L48 1993　　3369

Lesly's handbook of public relations and communications. edited by Philip Lesly. 4th ed. Chicago, Ill.: Probus Pub. Co., c1991. xxii, 874 p. : ill. *Notes:* Rev. ed. of: Lesly's public relations handbook. 3rd ed. 1983. Includes bibliographical references and index. [LC 90020126; ISN 155738133X; $39.95]　　　　　　　　　　　　　　　　　　　　　　　　　　　　　　　HM263. L46 1991　　3370

Lifestyle and event marketing: building the new customer partnership. Alfred L. Schreiber, with Barry Lenson. New York: McGraw-Hill, c1994. xvi, 263 p. *Notes:* Spine title: Lifestyle & event marketing. Includes bibliographical references (p. 249-258) and index. [LC 93040818; ISN 0070561532; $24.95]　　　　　　　　　　　　　　　　　　　　　　　　　HD59.6.U6 S37 1994　　+3371

The marketer's guide to public relations: how today's top companies are using the new PR to gain a competitive edge. Thomas L. Harris; foreword by Philip Kotler. New York: Wiley, c1991. xiv, 306 p. : ill. *Notes:* Includes bibliographical references (p. 298-299) and index. [LC 90041327; ISN 0471618853; $27.95]　　　　　　　　　　　　　　　　　　　　　　　HD59. H276 1991　　3372

The persuasion explosion: your guide to the power & influence of contemporary public relations. by Art Stevens. Washington, D.C.: Acropolis Books, 1985. 224 p. : ill. *Notes:* Includes index. [LC 85006238; ISN 0874917328; $12.95]　　　　　　　　　　　　　　　HM263. S865 1985　　3373

PUBLIC SCHOOLS

Reinventing education: entrepreneurship in America's public schools. Louis V. Gerstner, Jr.. . . et al. New York: Dutton, 1994. xv, 288 p. [LC 93039205; ISN 0525937498]　　LA217.2. R45 1994　　+3374

PUBLIC SPEAKING

The presentations kit: 10 steps for selling your ideas. Claudyne Wilder. Rev. updated ed. New York: Wiley, 1994. xiii, 266 p. : ill.p *Notes:* Includes bibliograpical references and index. [LC 94021163; ISN 0471310891; $14.95] PN4121. W386 1994 +3375

PUBLIC TELEVISION

Public television for sale: media, the market, and the public sphere. William Hoynes. Boulder, Colo.: Westview Press, 1994. xiv, 207 p. : ill. *Notes:* Includes bibliographical references (p. 187-195) and index. [LC 93027344; ISN 0813318297; $18.95] HE8700.79.U6 H69 1994 +3376

PUBLIC UTILITIES

Unnatural monopolies: the case for deregulating public utilities. edited by Robert W. Poole, Jr. Lexington, Mass.: Lexington Books, c1985. xiv, 224 p. *Notes:* Includes bibliographical references and index. [LC 84040828; ISN 0669101265] HD2766. U57 1985 3377

PUBLIC WELFARE

Poor support: poverty in the American family. David T. Ellwood. New York: Basic Books, c1988. xii, 271 p. : ill. *Notes:* Includes index. Bibliography: p. 245-262. [LC 87047779; ISN 0465059961; $19.95] HV91. E453 1988 3378

PURCHASING

Breakthrough partnering: creating a collective enterprise advantage. Patricia E. Moody. Essex Junction, VT: O. Wight, c1993. xv, 268 p. *Notes:* Includes bibliographical references and index.; ISN 0939246392] HD39.5. M66 1993 +3379

Purchasing: principles and applications. Stuart Heinritz. . . et al. 8th ed. Englewood Cliffs, N.J.: Prentice Hall, c1991. xii, 580 p. : ill. *Notes:* Rev. ed. of: Purchasing / Stuart F. Heinritz. 6th ed. c1981. Includes bibliographical references (p. 573) and index. [LC 90043515; ISN 0137420811; $57.14] HF5437. H4 1991 3380

P'UNGSAN KUMSOK KONGOP CHUSIK HOESA (KOREA)

The culture of Korean industry: an ethnography of Poongsan Corporation. Choong Soon Kim. Tucson: University of Arizona Press, c1992. xix, 248 p. : ill. *Notes:* Includes bibliographical references (p. [223]-238) and index. [LC 92004859; ISN 0816513090] HD9506.K64 P865 1992 3381

QUALITY ASSURANCE

Commit to quality. Patrick L. Townsend with Joan E. Gebhardt. Updated ed. New York: Wiley, c1990. *Notes:* Includes bibliographical references (p. 213-216) and index. [LC 89070565; ISN 0471520187; $12.95] HD66. T65 1990 3382

Planning for quality, productivity, and competitive position. Howard S. Gitlow and Process Management International, Inc. Homewood, Ill.: Dow Jones-Irwin, c1990. xiii, 172 p. : ill. *Notes:* Includes bibliographical references (p. 163-164) and index. [LC 90031206; ISN 1556233574; $39.95] TS156.6. G57 1990 3383

QUALITY CIRCLES

Quality circles handbook. David Hutchins. New York, NY: Nichols, 1985. xi, 272 p. : ill. *Notes:* Includes index. Bibliography: p. 260-267. [LC 84027223; ISN 0893972142] HD66. H88 1985 3384

QUALITY CONTROL

Dr. Deming: the American who taught the Japanese about quality. by Rafael Aguayo. Secaucus, N.J.: Carol Pub. Group, 1990. xvi, 289 p. *Notes:* "A Lyle Stuart book." Includes bibliographical references and index. [LC 90047036; ISN 0818405198; $24.95]   TS156. A35 1990   3385

The improvement process: how America's leading companies improve quality. H.J. Harrington. New York: McGraw-Hill, c1987. xv, 239 p. : ill. *Notes:* Includes index. Bibliography: p. 225-226. [LC 86007359; ISN 0070267545; $24.95]   TS156. H34 1987   3386

Introduction to statistical quality control. Douglas C. Montgomery. 2nd ed. New York: Wiley, c1991. 1 v. (various pagings): ill. *Notes:* "ASQC Quality Press"—Spine. Includes bibliographical references and index. [LC 90031744; ISN 047151988X; $53.95]   TS156. M64 1991   3387

ISO 9000. Brian Rothery. 2nd ed. Aldershot, Hampshire, UK; Brookfield, Vt.: Gower, 1993. ix, 248 p. : ill. *Notes:* Includes index. [LC 92043274; ISN 0566074028; $59.95]   TS156. R68 1993   3388

ISO 9000: an implementation guide for small to mid-sized businesses. Frank Voehl, Peter Jackson, David Ashton. Delray Beach, FL: St. Lucie Press, c1994. x, 261 p. : ill. *Notes:* Includes bibliographical references and index. [LC 93046440; ISN 1884015107; $45.00]   TS156. V63 1994   +3389

Juran on leadership for quality: an executive handbook. J.M. Juran. New York: London: Free Press; Collier Macmillan, c1989. vii, 376 p. *Notes:* Includes index. Bibliography: p. 365-369. [LC 88021306; ISN 0029166829]   TS156. J79 1989   3390

Juran on quality by design: the new steps for planning quality into goods and services. J.M. Juran. New York: Toronto: New York: Free Press; Maxwell Macmillan Canada; Maxwell Macmillan International, c1992. vi, 538 p. : ill. *Notes:* Includes bibliographical references (p. 515-525) and index. [LC 91029206; ISN 0029166837; $35.00]   TS156. J854 1992   3391

Juran's quality control handbook. J.M. Juran, editor-in-chief, Frank M. Gryna, associate editor. 4th ed. New York: McGraw-Hill, c1988. 1 v. (various pagings): ill. *Notes:* Rev. ed. of: Quality control handbook. 3rd ed. 1974. Includes bibliographies and indexes. [LC 88004002; ISN 0070331766]
     TS156. J87 1988   3392

The man who discovered quality: how W. Edwards Deming brought the quality revolution to America: the stories of Ford, Xerox, and GM. by Andrea Gabor. 1st ed. New York: Times Books/ Random House, 1990. x, 326 p. : ill. *Notes:* Includes bibliographical references. [LC 89040788; ISN 081291774X; $21.95]   TS156. G3 1990   3393

Quality by design: Taguchi methods and US industry. Lance A. Ealey. 2nd ed. Dearborn, Mich.: Burr Ridge, Ill.: ASI Press; Irwin, c1994. xxii, 298 p. : ill. *Notes:* Includes bibliographical references (p. 288-290) and index. [LC 93037221; ISN 155623970X; $35.00]   TS156. E25 1994   +3394

Quality management handbook. edited by Loren Walsh, Ralph Wurster, Raymond J. Kimber. New York: Milwaukee, Wis.: M. Dekker; ASQC Quality Press, c1986. xiii, 997 p. : ill. *Notes:* Includes bibliographies and index. [LC 85029354; ISN 0824774388]   TS156. Q363 1986   3395

Statistical quality control. Eugene L. Grant, Richard S. Leavenworth. 6th ed. New York: McGraw-Hill, c1988. xvii, 714 p. : ill. (some col.) *Notes:* Includes indexes. Bibliography: p. 656-663. [LC 87021342; ISN 0070241171; $40.95]   TS156. G7 1988   3396

Statistical quality control for manufacturing managers. William S. Messina. New York: Wiley, c1987. xiii, 331 p. : ill. (Wiley series in engineering management) *Notes:* "A Wiley-Interscience publication." Includes index. Bibliography: p. 317-323. [LC 86034022; ISN 0471857742]
     TS156. M45 1987   3397

Total quality control. A.V. Feigenbaum. 3rd ed., rev. New York: McGraw-Hill, c1991. xxvii, 863 p. : ill. *Notes:* "Fortieth anniversary edition." Includes bibliographical references and index. [LC 90048438; ISN 0070203547; $62.00]   TS156. F44 1991   3398

What is total quality control? The Japanese way. by Kaoru Ishikawa; translated by David J. Lu. Englewood Cliffs, N.J.: Prentice-Hall, c1985. xiv, 215 p. : ill. *Notes:* Includes index. [LC 84026265; ISN 0139524339; $22.50]   TS156. I8313 1985   3399

Zero quality control: source inspection and the poka-yoke system. Shigeo Shingo; translated by Andrew P. Dillon; with a preface by Norman Bodek. Stamford, Conn.: Productivity Press, c1986. xxv, 303 p. : ill. *Notes:* Translation of: Furyō zero e no chōsen. Includes index. Bibliography: p. 289-290. [LC 85063497; ISN 0915299070; $65.00]   TS156. S472513 1986   3400

QUALITY OF PRODUCTS

Managing customer value: creating quality and service that customers can see. Bradley T. Gale with Robert Chapman Wood. New York: Toronto: New York: Free Press; Maxwell Macmillan Canada; Maxwell Macmillan International, c1994. xxii, 424 p. : ill. *Notes:* Includes bibliographical references (p. 407-416) and indexes. [LC 93041905; ISN 0029110459; $27.95]   HF5415.157. G34 1994   +3401

Managing quality: the strategic and competitive edge. David A. Garvin. New York: London: Free Press; Collier Macmillan, c1988. xiv, 319 p. *Notes:* Includes index. Bibliography: p. 251-309. [LC 87015145; ISN 0029113806]   HF5415.157. G37 1988   3402

Managing the total quality transformation. Thomas H. Berry. New York: McGraw-Hill, 1991. xxi, 223 p. : ill. *Notes:* Includes index. [LC 90039437; ISN 0070050716; $24.95]   HF5415.157. B47 1991   3403

The quality imperative. the editors of Business week, with Cynthia Green editor. New York: McGraw-Hill, c1994. x, 214 p. *Notes:* At head of title: A Business week guide. Includes index. [LC 93029344; ISN 0070093458; $12.95]   HF5415.157. Q34 1994   +3404

Theory why: in which the boss solves the riddle of quality. John Guaspari. New York, N.Y.: AMACOM, American Management Association, c1986. 121 p. : ill. [LC 86047593; ISN 0814458769]
HD38. G767 1986   3405

QUALITY OF WORK LIFE

Re-inventing the corporation: transforming your job and your company for the new information society. John Naisbitt and Patricia Aburdene. New York, NY: Warner Books, c1985. xi, 308 p. *Notes:* Includes index. Bibliography: p. 257-286. [LC 85040007; ISN 0446512842]
HD6957.U6 N25 1985   3406

When the canary stops singing: women's perspectives on transforming business. edited by Pat Barrentine; authors, Riane Eisler. . . et al. 1st ed. San Francisco: Berrett-Koehler Publishers, c1993. xiii, 277 p. : ill. *Notes:* Includes bibliographical references (p. 257-263) and index. [LC 93027145; ISN 1881052419; $24.95]   HD6957.U6 W48 1993   +3407

RADIO BROADCASTING

Selling radio: the commercialization of American broadcasting, 1920-1934. Susan Smulyan. Washington: Smithsonian Institution Press, c1994. viii, 223 p. : ill. *Notes:* Includes bibliographical references (p. 169-215) and index. [LC 93012833; ISN 1560983124; $24.95]   HE8698. S6 1994   +3408

RADIO CORPORATION OF AMERICA

RCA. Robert Sobel. New York: Stein and Day/Publishers, c1986. 282 p. *Notes:* Includes index. Bibliography: p. 262-269. [LC 85043395; ISN 0812830849; $19.95]   HD9696.A3 U613 1986   3409

RAILROADS

Railroads triumphant: the growth, rejection, and rebirth of a vital American force. Albro Martin. New York: Oxford University Press, 1992. xiv, 428 p. : ill. *Notes:* Includes bibliographical references and index. [LC 90007845; ISN 0195038533; $29.95]   HE2751. M35 1992   3410

RAND HEALTH INSURANCE EXPERIMENT

Free for all?: lessons from the Rand Health Insurance Experiment. Joseph P. Newhouse and the Insurance Experiment Group. Cambridge, Mass.: Harvard University Press, 1993. x, 489 p: ill *Notes:* "A Rand study." Includes bibliographical references and index. [LC 93001356; ISN 0674318463; $49.95]   RA410.53. N52 1993   +3411

RATIO ANALYSIS

A cross-industry analysis of financial ratios: comparabilities and corporate performance. J. Edward Ketz, Rajib K. Doogar, and David E. Jensen. New York: Quorum Books, 1990. x, 218 p. : ill. *Notes:* Bibliography: p. [213]-214. [LC 90008439; ISN 089930463X; $49.95] HF5681.R25 K48 1990 3412

Handbook of business and financial ratios. Michael R. Tyran. Englewood Cliffs, N.J.: Prentice-Hall, c1986. xiv, 274 p. : ill. *Notes:* Includes index. [LC 85025585; ISN 0133758583; $59.95]
HF5681.R25 T97 1986 3413

REAL ESTATE BUSINESS

The McGraw-Hill real estate handbook. Robert Irwin, editor in chief. 2nd ed. New York: McGraw-Hill, c1993. xxv, 641 p. : ill. *Notes:* Includes bibliographical references and index. [LC 92034533; ISN 0070321493; $69.95] HD1375. M17 1993 3414

Real estate: a case study approach. William J. Poorvu. Englewood Cliffs, N.J.: Regents/Prentice Hall, c1993. xxvi, 431 p. : ill., maps [LC 91028587; ISN 0137634838; $39.21] HD1375. P664 1993 +3415

The real estate handbook. editors-in-chief, Maury Seldin, James H. Boykin. 2nd ed. Homewood, Ill.: Dow Jones-Irwin, c1990. xxx, 1055 p. : ill. *Notes* Includes bibliographical references and index. [LC 89030318; ISN 0870949179; $70.00] HD255. R38 1990 3416

Real estate principles. Bruce Harwood, Charles J. Jacobus. 5th ed. Englewood Cliffs, N.J.: Prentice-Hall, c1990. xvii, 684 p. : ill. *Notes:* Includes bibliographical references and index. [LC 89036932; ISN 0137626673; $32.67] HD1375. H38 1990 3417

Real estate principles and practices. Edmund F. Ficek, Thomas P. Henderson, Ross H. Johnson. 4th ed. Columbus: Merrill Pub. Co., c1987. xiii, 604 p. : ill. *Notes:* Cover title: Real estate principles & practices. Includes bibliographies and index. [LC 86062845; ISN 0675207266; $41.95]
KF2042.R4 F46 1987 3418

Real estate: principles and practices. Jerome Dasso, Alfred A. Ring. 11th ed. Englewood Cliffs, N.J.: Prentice Hall, c1989. xv, 524 p. : ill. *Notes:* Ring's name appears first in earlier editions. Includes bibliographical references and index. [LC 88007593; ISN 0137660154; $45.00] HD1375. R35 1989 3419

Real estate, principles and practices. Maurice A. Unger, George R. Karvel. 8th ed. Cincinnati: South-Western Pub. Co., c1987. ix, 650 p. : ill. (some col.) *Notes:* Rev. ed. of: Real estate, principles & practices. 7th ed. c1983. Includes bibliographical references and index. [LC 86061595; ISN 0538197617] HD1375. U6 1987 3420

REAL ESTATE DEVELOPERS

Risk, ruin & riches: inside the world of big time real estate. Jim Powell. New York: Macmillan, c1986. vi, 376 p., [8] p. of plates *Notes:* Includes index. [LC 86007223; ISN 0025985302]
HD1390. P68 1986 3421

Skyscraper dreams: the great real estate dynasties of New York. Tom Shachtman. 1st ed. Boston: Little, Brown, c1991. viii, 354 p., [16] p. of plates: ill. *Notes:* Includes index. [LC 90025070; ISN 0316782130; $22.95] HD268.N5 S52 1991 3422

REAL ESTATE DEVELOPMENT

High rise: how 1,000 men and women worked around the clock for five years and lost $200 million building a skyscraper. Jerry Adler. 1st ed. New York: HarperCollins, c1993. x, 374 p., [8] p. of plates: ill. *Notes:* Includes index. [LC 92053320; ISN 0060167017; $25.00] HD268.N5 A43 1993 3423

Property development. John McMahan. 2nd ed. New York: McGraw-Hill, c1989. xxi, 488 p. : ill. *Notes:* Includes index. Bibliography: p. 459-469. [LC 88039875; ISN 0070454515; $49.95]
HD1390. M38 1989 3424

REAL ESTATE INVESTMENT

Fundamentals of real estate investment. Austin J. Jaffe, C.F. Sirmans. 2nd ed. Englewood Cliffs, N.J.: Prentice-Hall, c1989. xi, 414 p. : ill. *Notes:* Includes bibliographies and index. [LC 88007981; ISN 0133434761; $36.00] HD1382.5. J32 1989 3425

How to invest in real estate. Maurice A. Unger. 2nd ed. New York: McGraw-Hill, c1991. xii, 162 p. : ill., map *Notes:* Includes index. [LC 90038458; ISN 0070659273; $19.95]   HD1382.5. U53 1991   3426

Investment analysis for real estate decisions. Gaylon E. Greer, Michael D. Farrell. 3rd ed. Chicago, Ill.: Dearborn Financial Pub., c1993. xxi, 532 p. : ill. *Notes:* "Reorder no.: 4106-07"—Cover. Includes bibliographical references and index. [LC 92028538; ISN 0793105099]
HD1382.5. G74 1993   3427

Real estate investment. John P. Wiedemer. 5th ed. Englewood Cliffs, N.J.: Regents/Prentice Hall, c1994. xii, 334 p. *Notes:* Includes bibliographical references and index. [LC 93016922; ISN 0137635583]   HD1381.5. W53 1994   +3428

Real estate investment. John P. Wiedemer. 4th ed. Englewood Cliffs, N.J.: Prentice Hall, c1989. x, 321 p. : ill. *Notes:* Includes index. Bibliography: p. 291-292. [LC 88028853; ISN 0137632363; $21.00]
HD1382.5. W53 1989   3429

Real estate investment strategy. Maury Seldin, Richard H. Swesnik. 3rd ed. New York: Wiley, c1985. xxi, 341 p. *Notes:* Includes index. [LC 84027060; ISN 0471816868; $22.95]   HD1382.5. S435 1985   3430

Real estate market analysis: methods and applications. edited by John M. Clapp, Stephen D. Messner. New York: Praeger, 1988. xvii, 350 p. : ill. *Notes:* Includes index. Bibliography: p. 323-338. [LC 87015832; ISN 0275924149; $45.85 (est.)]   HD1382.5. R396 1988   3431

Real estate syndication: securitization after tax reform. Stephen P. Jarchow. 2nd ed. New York: Wiley, c1988. xxv, 995 p. : forms *Notes:* Includes bibliographical references and index. [LC 87037187; ISN 0471635723; $95.00]   KF1079. J33 1988   3432

REAL ESTATE MANAGEMENT

Global corporate real estate management: a handbook for multinational businesses and organizations. M.A. Hines. New York: Quorum Books, 1990. xiv, 262 p. : ill. *Notes:* Includes bibliographical references. [LC 90032722; ISN 089930530X; $49.95]   HD1394. H56 1990   3433

REAL PROPERTY

The appraisal of real estate. 10th ed. Chicago, Ill.: Appraisal Institute, c1992. vii, 768 p. : ill. *Notes:* Includes bibliographical references (p. 741-749) and index. [LC 92008824; ISN 092215404X]
HD1387. A663 1992   3434

Income property valuation. Jeffrey D. Fisher, Robert S. Martin. Chicago, Ill.: Real Estate Education Co., c1994. xxiv, 593 p. : ill. *Notes:* Includes bibliographical references and index. [LC 93042615; ISN 0884629805]   HD1387. F5293 1994   +3435

Real estate law. Robert Kratovil, Raymond J. Werner. 9th ed. Englewood Cliffs, N.J.: Prentice-Hall, 1988. xii, 639 p. *Notes:* Includes bibliographical references and index. [LC 87024081; ISN 0137633432]   KF570. K7 1988   3436

REAL PROPERTY AND TAXATION

Tax factors in real estate operations. Thomas G. Manolakas, Paul E. Anderson. 7th ed. Englewood Cliffs, N.J.: Prentice Hall, c1990. l, 1004 p. *Notes:* Includes bibliographical references and indexes. [LC 90031472; ISN 0138844615; $89.95]   KF6540. M23 1990   3437

REASON

Voltaire's bastards: the dictatorship of reason in the West. John Ralston Saul. New York: Free Press: Maxwell Macmillan International, c1992. x, 640 p. *Notes:* Includes bibliographical references (p. [587]-620) and index. [LC 92000386; ISN 0029277256; $24.95]   BC177. S28 1992   3438

REASONING

Six thinking hats. Edward de Bono. 1st U.S. ed. Boston: Little, Brown, c1985. 207 p. [LC 85081445; ISN 0316177911]   BC177. D43   3439

REGRESSION ANALYSIS

Applied linear statistical models: regression, analysis of variance, and experimental designs. John Neter, William Wasserman, Michael H. Kutner. 3rd ed. Homewood, Ill.: Irwin, c1990. xvi, 1181 p. : ill. [LC 89049309; ISN 025608338X; $51.95]   QA278.2. N47 1990   3440

REICHMANN FAMILY

Too big to fail: Olympia & York: the story behind the headlines. by Walter Stewart. Toronto: McClelland & Stewart, c1993. 335 p., [8] p. of plates: ill. *Notes:* Includes bibliographical references (p. 325-328) and index. [LC 93094840; ISN 0771001770; ISN 0771083041; $29.99]
HD316.R45. S74 1993   +3441

RESEARCH AGENCIES

Forming R & D partnerships: an entrepreneur's guidebook. by Anthony P. Spohr & Leslie Wat. New York, N.Y.: Deloitte, Haskins & Sells, c1983. 112 p. : ill. (Entrepreneur's guidebook series)]
Q180.U5 S66   3442

RESEARCH

Evaluating R&D impacts: methods and practice. edited by Barry Bozeman and Julia Melkers. Boston: Kluwer Academic, c1993. xiii, 304 p. *Notes:* Includes bibliographical references and index. "Annotated bibliography on evaluation of research, 1985-1990": p. [279]-300. [LC 93022110; ISN 0792393252]   Q180.55.E9 E9 1993   3443

Inventivity: the art and science of research management. John J. Gilman. New York: Van Nostrand Reinhold, c1992. xvii, 187 p. : ill. *Notes:* Includes bibliographical references and index. [LC 92003239; ISN 0442011865; $29.95]   Q180.55.M4 G42 1992   +3444

Research and development limited partnerships: an emerging method of funding research and development. Palo Alto, Ca.: Market Intelligence Research Co., c1985. 344 p. : ill. *Notes:* Cover title: Research and development limited partnership manual. Bibliography: 264-270.]   T175. R47   3445

RESEARCH, INDUSTRIAL

Management of research and development organizations: managing the unmanageable. R.K. Jain, H.C. Triandis. New York: Wiley, c1990. xix, 268 p.; ill.: *Notes:* "A Wiley-Interscience publication." Includes bibliographies and index. [LC 89014687; ISN 0471507911; $44.95]   T175.5. J35 1990   3446

Managing professionals in research and development. Donald Britton Miller. 1st ed. San Francisco: Jossey-Bass, 1986. xxiv, 403 p. (The Jossey-Bass management series) *Notes:* Includes index. Bibliography: p. 387-394. [LC 86007283; ISN 1555420001]   T175.5. M55 1986   3447

Managing technological innovation. Brian C. Twiss. 3rd ed. London; New York: Longman, 1986. 238 p. : ill. *Notes:* Includes bibliographies and index. [LC 85004288; ISN 0582296870]
T175.5. T94 1986   3448

Research and development: project selection criteria. Jackson E. Ramsey. Rev. ed. Ann Arbor, Mich.: UMI Research Press, c1986. 215 p. : ill. *Notes:* Revision of thesis (Ph. D.)—State University of New York at Buffalo, 1976. Includes index. Bibliography: p. [195]-209. [LC 86016085; ISN 0835717089]   T175.5. R26 1986   3449

Third generation R&D: managing the link to corporate strategy. Philip A. Roussel, Kamal N. Saad, Tamara J. Erickson; foreword by John F. Magee. Boston, Mass.: Harvard Business School Press, c1991. xx, 192 p. : ill. *Notes:* Includes bibliographical references and index. [LC 90019497; ISN 0875842526; $29.95]   T175.5. R68 1991   3450

RETAIL TRADE

Contemporary retailing. William H. Bolen. 3rd ed. Englewood Cliffs, N.J.: Prentice Hall, c1988. xviii, 622 p. : ill. *Notes:* Includes bibliographies and index. [LC 87017514; ISN 0131703099; $44.00]
HF5429. B595 1988　　3451

Future trends in retailing: merchandise line trends and store trends 1980-1990. by Eleanor G. May, C. William Ress, and Walter J. Salmon. Cambridge, Mass.: Marketing Science Institute; , 1985. iv, 160 p. : charts *Notes:* "February 1985."]
HF5429.3. M39　　3452

Modern retailing: theory and practice. J. Barry Mason, Morris L. Mayer. 5th ed. Homewood, IL: BPI/Irwin, c1990. xx, 826 p. : ill. *Notes:* Includes bibliographical references. [LC 89015257; ISN 0256079595; $43.50]
HF5429. M328 1990　　3453

Retail management: a strategic approach. Barry Berman, Joel R. Evans. 4th ed. New York: London: Macmillan; Collier Macmillan, c1989. xxiv, 679 p., [12] leaves of plates: ill. (some col.) *Notes:* Includes bibliographies and indexes. [LC 88018935; ISN 0023086416; $42.00]　HF5429. B45 1989　　3454

Retailing management. William R. Davidson, Daniel J. Sweeney, Ronald W. Stampfl. 6th ed. New York: Wiley, c1988. xix, 876 p. : ill. *Notes:* Includes index. Bibliography: p. 835-860. [LC 87010555; ISN 0471850942]
HF5429. D334 1988　　3455

REUTERS LTD

The power of news: the history of Reuters, 1849-1989. Donald Read. Oxford; New York: Oxford University Press, 1992. xii, 431 p. : ill. *Notes:* Includes index. [LC 92027585; ISN 0198217765; £20.00]
PN5111.R4 R43 1992　　3456

REUTHER, WALTER

Walter Reuther. Anthony Carew. Manchester; New York: New York: Manchester University Press; Distributed exclusively in the USA and Canada by St. Martin's Press, c1993. vii, 168 p. : ill. *Notes:* Includes bibliographical references (p. 150-164) and index. [LC 93000077; ISN 071902188X]
HD6509.R4 C3 1993　　3457

REWARD (PSYCHOLOGY)

Punished by rewards: the trouble with gold stars, incentive plans, A's, praise, and other bribes. Alfie Kohn. Boston: Houghton Mifflin Co., 1993. xiv, 398 p. *Notes:* Includes bibliographical references (p. 352-384) and index. [LC 93021897; ISN 0395650283; $22.95]　HF5549.5.I5 K64 1993　+3458

RICH AS CONSUMERS

Marketing to the affluent. Thomas J. Stanley. Homewood, Ill.: Dow Jones-Irwin, c1988. xii, 324 p. *Notes:* Includes index. [LC 88002629; ISN 1556231059; $49.95]
HF5415.3. S73 1988　　3459

RISK MANAGEMENT

Corporate risk management: a financial exposition. Neil A. Doherty. New York: McGraw-Hill, c1985. xvi, 483 p. : ill. (McGraw-Hill insurance series) *Notes:* Includes bibliographies and index. [LC 84017095; ISN 0070173605; $28.95]
HD61. D64 1985　　3460

Risk management and insurance. C. Arthur Williams, Jr., Richard M. Heins. 6th ed. New York: McGraw-Hill, c1989. xii, 836 p. : ill. *Notes:* Includes bibliographies and indexes. [LC 88013273; ISN 0070705674; $42.95]
HG8051. W5 1989　　3461

Strategic risk management: how global corporations manage financial risk for competitive advantage. Mark J. Ahn, William D. Falloon. Chicago, Ill.: Probus Pub. Co., c1991. xxiv, 242 p. : ill. *Notes:* Includes bibliographical references (p. 233-237) and index.; ISN 1557381992; $57.50]
HD61. A35 1991　　3462

Taking risks: the management of uncertainty. Kenneth R. MacCrimmon and Donald A. Wehrung with William T. Stanbury. New York: London: Free Press; Collier Macmillan Publishers, c1986. xv, 380 p. : ill. *Notes:* Includes index. Bibliography p. 342-359. [LC 85016275; ISN 0029195608]
  HD61. M23 1986   3463

RJR NABISCO (FIRM)

Barbarians at the gate: the fall of RJR Nabisco. by Bryan Burrough and John Helyar. 1st ed. New York: Harper & Row, c1990. xvi, 528 p., 16 p. of plates: ill. [LC 89045635; ISN 0060161728; $22.50]
  HD2796.R57 B87 1990   3464

True greed: what really happened in the battle for RJR Nabisco. Hope Lampert. New York, N.Y.: New American Library, c1990. xi, 259 p. *Notes:* "NAL books." [LC 89029474; ISN 0453007198; $18.95]
  HD2796.R57 L36 1990   3465

ROBINSON, PETER

Snapshots from hell: the making of an MBA. Peter Robinson. New York: Warner Books, c1994. 286 p. : ill. [LC 93047682; ISN 0446517860; $22.95 ($27.95 Can.)]
  HF1134.S77 R63 1994   +3466

ROBOTICS

Robotics: a manager's guide. Rex Maus, Randall Allsup. New York: Wiley, c1986. x, 238 p. : ill. *Notes:* Includes index. Bibliography: p. 209. [LC 85029555; ISN 0471842648; ISN 0471842656; $37.95 (est.); $19.95]
  TJ211. M38 1986   3467

Robots, machines in man's image. Isaac Asimov and Karen A. Frenkel. 1st ed. New York: Harmony Books, c1985. 246 p. : ill. *Notes:* Includes index. Bibliography: p. 237-240. [LC 84022758; ISN 0517551101]
  TJ211. A83 1985   3468

The tomorrow makers: a brave new world of living-brain machines. Grant Fjermedal. New York: Macmillan, c1986. xi, 272 p. *Notes:* Includes index. [LC 86021781; ISN 0025385607]
  TJ211.15. F54 1986   3469

ROBOTS, INDUSTRIAL

Handbook of industrial robotics. Shimon Y. Nof, editor; with a foreword by Isaac Asimov. New York: J. Wiley, c1985. xvii, 1358 p. : ill. *Notes:* Includes bibliographies and index. [LC 84020969; ISN 0471896845; $69.95]
  TS191.8. H36 1985   3470

Robots: the application of robots to practical work. by David M. Osborne. Detroit, Mich.: Midwest Sci-Tech, c1984. xiii, 232 p. : ill. *Notes:* Includes index. [LC 84060612; ISN 0910853029; ISN 0910853037]
  TS191.8. O782 1984   3471

ROSS, STEVE

Master of the game: Steve Ross and the creation of Time Warner. Connie Bruck. New York: Simon & Schuster, c1994. 395 p. : ill. *Notes:* Includes bibliographical references (p. [367]-369) and index. [LC 93048609; ISN 0671725742; $25.00 ($32.50 Can.)]
  HC102.5.R67 B78 1994   +3472

ROTH, ARTHUR T

People's banker: the story of Arthur T. Roth and the Franklin National Bank. by Walter S. Ross. New Canaan, Conn.: Keats Pub., c1987. viii, 288 p. *Notes:* Includes bibliographical references and index. [LC 87004066; ISN 0879834293]
  HG2463.R68 A3 1987   3473

SAATCHI & SAATCHI

The brothers: the Saatchi & Saatchi story. Ivan Fallon. Chicago: Contemporary Books, c1989. ix, 372 p., [16] p. of plates: ill. *Notes:* Includes bibliographical references (p. 359-360) and index. [LC 89037680; ISN 0809243105; $22.95]   HF6181.S23 F35 1989   3474

SALE OF BUSINESS ENTERPRISES

The complete guide to selling a business. Michael K. Semanik & John H. Wade. New York: American Management Association, c1994. x, 166 p. *Notes:* Includes index. [LC 93044275; ISN 0814402232; $22.95]   HD1393.25. S45 1994   +3475

The right price for your business. Morris A. Nunes. New York: Wiley, c1988. xxii, 175 p. : ill. *Notes:* Includes index. [LC 88015514; ISN 0471625620]   HD1393.25. N86 1988   3476

SALES FORECASTING

Forecasting and market analysis techniques: a practical approach. George J. Kress & John Snyder. Westport, Conn: Quorum Books, 1994. xiv, 286 p. : ill *Notes:* Includes bibliographical references (p. [281]-282) and index. "The major portion of the book is devoted to the three basic categories of forecasting models—time series, causal, and judgmental—emphasizing the most widely used models in each category. Special attention is also given to the sources for obtaining the data needed to make forecasts and analyze markets. The latter part of the book describes procedures for developing market and sales potentials, methods for segmenting markets, and some analytic techniques such as conjoint analysis and cluster analysis, gaining increased usage among market analysts."—Book jacket. [LC 93011890; ISN 089930835X]   HF5415.2. K748 1994   +3477

SALES MANAGEMENT

The Dartnell sales manager's handbook. John P. Steinbrink, editor. 14th ed. Chicago: The Dartnell Corp., c1989. xxxi, 1272 p. *Notes:* Includes index.; ISN 0850131626; $46.72]   HF5415. D32 1989   3478

Major account sales strategy. Neil Rackham. New York: McGraw-Hill, c1989. xv, 218 p. : ill. *Notes:* Includes index. [LC 88008038; ISN 0070511144; $19.95]   HF5438.4. R33 1989   3479

Management of the sales force. William J. Stanton, Richard H. Buskirk. 7th ed. Homewood, Ill.: Irwin, 1987. xv, 704 p. : ill., forms *Notes:* Includes bibliographical references and index. [LC 86082598; ISN 0256036357]   HF5438.4. S78 1987   3480

Sales force automation: using the latest technology to make your sales force more competitive. George W. Colombo. New York: McGraw-Hill, c1994. xxi, 215 p. : ill. *Notes:* Includes index. [LC 93032387; ISN 007011840X; $27.95]   HF5438.4. C64 1994   +3481

Sales management: decisions, strategies, and cases. Richard R. Still, Edward W. Cundiff, Norman A.P. Govoni. 5th ed. Englewood Cliffs, NJ: Prentice-Hall, c1988. xvi, 638 p. : ill. *Notes:* Includes index. [LC 87025725; ISN 0137865422; $25.50]   HF5438.4. S84 1988   3482

Sales management: the complete marketeer's guide. Chris J. Noonan. London; Boston: Allen & Unwin, 1986. xviii, 408 p. *Notes:* Includes index. [LC 85028590; ISN 0046582541; £25.00 ($40.00)]   HF5438.4. N66 1986   3483

SALES PERSONNEL

Developing a professional sales force: a guide for sales trainers and sales managers. David A. Stumm. New York: Quorum Books, 1986. xvi, 218 p. : ill. *Notes:* Includes index. [LC 86008117; ISN 0899301762; $39.95 (est.)]   HF5439.8. S78 1986   3484

The sales compensation handbook. John K. Moynahan, editor. New York, NY: AMACOM, American Management Association, c1991. xiii, 303 p. : ill. *Notes:* Includes index. [LC 90056191; ISN 0814401104; $65.00]   HF5439.7. S22 1991   3485

Sales force performance. Neil M. Ford, Gilbert A. Churchill, Jr., Orville C. Walker, Jr.; with contributions by R. Kenneth Teas... et al. Lexington, Mass.: Lexington Books, c1985. xvi, 306 p. : ill. *Notes:* Includes bibliographies and indexes. [LC 84017166; ISN 0669093769]   HF5439.5. F67 1985   3486

SALES PROMOTION

Sales promotion: concepts, methods, and strategies. Robert C. Blattberg, Scott A. Neslin. Englewood Cliffs, N.J.: Prentice Hall, c1990. xiii, 513 p. : ill. *Notes:* Includes bibliographical references (p. 482-501) and indexes. [LC 89029223; ISN 0137881673] HF5438.5. B57 1990 3487

Sales promotion management. John A. Quelch. Englewood Cliffs, N.J.: Prentice Hall, 1989. xi, 350 p. : ill. *Notes:* Includes bibliographical references. [LC 88025278; ISN 0137881185] HF5438.5. Q45 1989 3488

Your advertising's great—how's business?: the revolution in sales promotion. Bud Frankel, H.W. Phillips. Homewood, Ill.: Dow Jones-Irwin, 1986. xi, 232 p. : ill. *Notes:* Includes bibliographical references and index. [LC 85072254; ISN 0870945432; $17.95] HF5438.5. F73 3489

SALOMON BROTHERS

Nightmare on Wall Street: Salomon Brothers and the corruption of the marketplace. Martin Mayer. New York: Simon & Schuster, c1993. 272 p., [8] p. of plates: ill. *Notes:* Includes bibliographical references (p. [257]-260) and index. [LC 93014703; ISN 0671781871; $23.00] HG4936. M39 1993 3490

Salomon Brothers, 1910-1985: advancing to leadership. by Robert Sobel. New York, N.Y.: Salomon Brothers, c1986. xiii, 240 p. : ill. *Notes:* Includes index. Bibliography: p. 215-221. [LC 86061339] HG4930.5. S62 1986 3491

SARNOFF, DAVID

The general: David Sarnoff and the rise of the communications industry. Kenneth Bilby. 1st ed. New York: Harper & Row, c1986. ix, 326 p. *Notes:* Includes index. Bibliography: p. 317-318. [LC 85045621; ISN 006015568X; $20.95] HE8689.8. B55 3492

SAVINGS AND LOAN ASSOCIATIONS

The big fix: inside the S & L scandal: how an unholy alliance of politics and money destroyed America's banking system. James Ring Adams. Updated and expanded. New York: Wiley, 1991, c1990. xii, 340 p., [8] p. of leaves: ill. *Notes:* Includes bibliographical references (p. [311]-331) and index. [LC 89027; ISN 0471538442; $12.95] HG2151. A35 1991 3493

The greatest-ever bank robbery: the collapse of the savings and loan industry. Martin Mayer. New York: C. Scribner's Sons: Maxwell Macmillan International, c1990. xii, 354 p. *Notes:* Includes bibliographical references (p. 330-340) and index. [LC 90034790; ISN 0684191520; $22.50 ($29.95 Can.)] HG2151. M39 1990 3494

High rollers: inside the savings and loan debacle. Martin Lowy. New York: Praeger, 1991. x, 321 p. *Notes:* Includes bibliographical references (p. [311]-316) and index. [LC 91008344; ISN 027593988X; $24.95] HG2151. L68 1991 3495

Other people's money: the inside story of the S&L mess. Paul Zane Pilzer with Robert Deitz. New York: Simon and Schuster, c1989. 269 p. *Notes:* Includes bibliographical references (p. 257-258). [LC 89021667; ISN 067168101X; $18.95; $18.95] HG2151. P55 1989 3496

The S&L debacle: public policy lessons for bank and thrift regulation. Lawrence J. White. New York: Oxford University Press, 1991. xiv, 287 p. *Notes:* Spine title: The S & L debacle. Includes bibliographical references (p. 265-275) and index. [LC 90014249; ISN 0195067339; $19.95] HG2151. W47 1991 3497

Saving the savings and loan: the U.S. thrift industry and the Texas experience, 1950-1988. M. Manfred Fabritius and William Borges. New York: Praeger, 1989. xii, 161 p. *Notes:* Includes index. Bibliography: p. [147]-153. [LC 88032942; ISN 0275931617; $37.95] HG2153.T4 F33 1989 3498

SAVINGS AND LOAN BAILOUT, 1989-

Full faith and credit: the great S&L debacle and other Washington sagas. William Seidman. 1st ed. New York: Times Books, c1993. xv, 300 p. *Notes:* Includes index. [LC 92056846; ISN 0812921348; $25.00] HG2152. S44 1993 3499

SCHUMPETER, JOSEPH ALOIS

Schumpeter in the history of ideas. edited bu Yuichi Shionoya and Mark Perlman. Ann Arbor, Mich.: University of Michigan Press, c1994. 135 p. *Notes:* Includes bibliographical references and index. [LC 94034016; ISN 0472105485]   HB119.S35 S377 1994   +3500

SCIENCE

Profits of science: the American marriage of business and technology. Robert Teitelman. New York, NY: BasicBooks, c1994. xi, 258 p. *Notes:* Includes bibliographical references (p. [224]-246) and index. [LC 93033277; ISN 0465039839; $23.00 ($31.00 Can.)]   Q127.U6 T384 1994   +3501

Virtual reality. Howard Rheingold. New York: Summit Books, c1991. 415 p. *Notes:* Includes bibliographical references (p. 392-399) and index. [LC 91010955; ISN 0671693638; $22.95]   Q183.9. R44 1991   3502

SCULLEY, JOHN

Odyssey: Pepsi to Apple, a journey of adventure, ideas, and the future. John Sculley with John A. Byrne. 1st ed. New York: Harper & Row, c1987. xiii, 450 p., [16] p. of plates: ill. *Notes:* Includes index. Bibliography: p.431-433. [LC 87045142; ISN 0060157801; $19.95]   HD9696.C62 S38 1987   3503

SECONDARY MORTGAGE MARKET

The secondary mortgage market: strategies for surviving & thriving in today's challenging markets. editor, Jess Lederman. Rev. ed. Chicago, Ill.: Probus, c1992. x, 770 p. : ill. *Notes:* Includes bibliographical references and index.; ISN 1557382883; $69.95]   HG2040.25. S43 1992   3504

SECURITIES

The Blackwell guide to Wall Street. Bluford H. Putnam and Sandra C. Zimmer. Oxford, UK; New York, NY, USA: Blackwell, 1987. viii, 222 p. : ill. *Notes:* Includes index. [LC 87010299; ISN 0631141839; $17.95]   HG4910. P87 1987   3505

Dynamic planning and management in the securities industry: staying competitive in a changing marketplace. Donald F. Howard. New York, N.Y.: New York Institute of Finance, c1987. ix, 284 p. : ill. *Notes:* Includes bibliographical references and index. [LC 86008574; ISN 013221573X; $45.00]   HG4621. H69   3506

Equity markets: structure, trading, and performance. Robert A. Schwartz. New York: Harper & Row, c1988. xvi, 544 p. : ill. *Notes:* Includes bibliographies and index. [LC 87023173; ISN 0060413220]   HG4963. S38 1988   3507

Fundamentals of securities regulation. Louis Loss. [2nd ed.] Boston: Little, Brown, c1988. xxv, 1175 p. *Notes:* Kept up to date by supplements. Includes bibliographical references and index. [LC 87080721; ISN 0316533351]   KF1439. L68 1988   3508

The globalization of money and securities: the new products, players and markets. Dimitris N. Chorafas. Chicago, Ill.: Probus Pub. Co., c1992. xvi, 403 p. : ill. *Notes:* Includes bibliographical references and index.; ISN 1557382328; $69.00]   HG3881. C56 1992   3509

The new financial instruments: an investor's guide. Julian Walmsley. New York: Wiley, c1988. 454 p. : ill. *Notes:* Includes indexes. Bibliography: p. 439-442. Erratum inserted. [LC 87027024; ISN 047185154X]   HG4521. W184 1988   3510

Reshaping the equity markets: a guide for the 1990s. Robert A. Schwartz; with the assistance of Laura M. Cohen. New York: HarperBusiness, c1991. xii, 452 p. : ill. *Notes:* Includes bibliographical references and index. [LC 91002966; ISN 088730432X; $65.00]   HG4521. S357835 1991   3511

Standard & Poor's debt ratings criteria: municipal overview. New York: Standard & Poor's Corp., 1986. viii, 204 p. : ill. *Notes:* Includes index.]   HG4952. S73 1986   3512

Standard & Poor's structured finance criteria. New York: Standard & Poor's, c1988. x, 297 p. *Notes:* Includes index.]   HG4521. S79 1988   3513

SECURITIES FRAUD

Captain Money and the golden girl: the J. David affair. Donald C. Bauder. 1st ed. San Diego: Harcourt Brace Jovanovich, c1985. 244 p., [8] p. of plates: ill. *Notes:* Includes index. [LC 85005512; ISN 0151155011]　　　　　　　　　　　　　　　　　　HV6770.A2 C24 1985　　3514

Master manipulator. Homer Brickey, Jr. New York: American Management Association, c1985. ix, 161 p. : ill. *Notes:* Includes index. [LC 85047675; ISN 0814458181]　　HV6770.T6 B75 1985　　3515

SECURITIES INDUSTRY

The house of Nomura: the inside story of the legendary Japanese financial dynasty. Albert J. Alletzhauser. 1st U.S. ed. New York: Arcade Pub., c1990. xxiii, 343 p., [16] p. of plates: ill. *Notes:* Includes index. Includes bibliographical references (p. 324-331). [LC 89048502; ISN 1559700890; $22.95]　　　　　　　　　　　　　　　　　　　　　　　　HG5774.5. A45 1990　　3516

Management on Wall Street: making securities firms work. by Stephen P. Rappaport. Homewood, Ill.: Dow Jones-Irwin, c1988. xv, 330 p. *Notes:* Includes index. Bibliography: p. 323-326. [LC 87072841; ISN 1556230311]　　　　　　　　　　　　　　　HG4621. R36 1988　　3517

A perspective on the changing business and financial environment. John J. Phelan, Jr. New York: New York University Press, 1989. 109 p. *Notes:* Lecture delivered at the Undergraduate College of the Stern School, New York University, Mar. 1988. [LC 88026829; ISN 0814766080; $15.00]　　　　　　　　　　　　　　　　　　　　　　　　　HG4910. P46 1989　　3518

Securities operations: a guide to operations and information systems in the securities industry. Michael T. Reddy. New York, N.Y.: New York Institute of Finance, c1990. xxiii, 487 p. : ill. *Notes:* Includes index. [LC 89014497; ISN 0137991231; $75.00]　　HG4515.5. R44 1990　　3519

Simulation, optimization and expert systems. Dimitris N. Chorafas. Chicago, Ill.: Probus Pub. Co., c1992. xxiv, 422 p. : ill. *Notes:* Includes bibliographical references and index.; ISN 155738231X; $74.75]　　　　　　　　　　　　　　　　　　　　　　　　HG4515.5. C47 1992　　3520

SECURITIES, PRIVATELY PLACED

Raising capital: private placement forms & techniques. 2nd ed. / Herbert B. Max. Englewood Cliffs, NJ: Prentice Hall Law & Business, c1989- 1 v. (loose-leaf): forms *Notes:* Rev. ed. of: Raising capital / Robert L. Frome, Herbert B. Max. c1981- Kept up-to-date with supplements. [LC 89027429; ISN 0137528175]　　　　　　　　　　　　　　　　　　　　KF1439. F76 1989　　3521

SELF-DIRECTED WORK GROUPS

Classic readings in self-managing teamwork: 20 of the most important articles. editor, Rollin Glaser; assistant to the editor, Christine Bayley. King of Prussia, Pa.: Organization Design and Development, Inc., c1992. xviii, 492 p. : ill. *Notes:* Includes bibliographical references. [LC 92080011; $40.19]　　　　　　　　　　　　　　　　　　　　　　　　　　HD66. C5 1992　　+3522

SELF-EMPLOYED WOMEN

Work of her own: how women create success and fulfillment off the traditional career track. Susan Wittig Albert; foreword by Diane Fassel. New York: G.P. Putman's Sons, c1992. xxii, 249 p. *Notes:* "A Jeremy P. Tarcher/Putnam book." Includes bibliographical references (p. 240-245) and index. [LC 92007618; ISN 0874777097; $19.95 ($24.95 Can.)]　　　　　　HD6072.5. A43 1992　　3523

SELF-EMPLOYED

Running a one person business. Claude Whitmyer, Salli Rasberry, and Michael Phillips. Berkeley, Calif.: Ten Speed Press, 1989. 204 p. : ill. *Notes:* Includes bibliographical references and index. [LC 88002104; ISN 0898152372; $12.00]　　　　　　　　　　　　　HD8036. W45 1989　　3524

SELLING

Manage globally, sell locally: the art of strategic account management. A. Lee Blackstone. Burr Ridge, Ill.: Irwin Professional Pub., c1995. xv, 198 p. : ill. *Notes:* Includes index. " . . . Addresses the factors that make managing the account relationship different from territory management, and offers tools to help the account manager measure success or position within the account.. . . Outlines how a team approach can be used to successfully sell at all levels of the customer's organization."—Book jacket. [LC 94011218; ISN 0786303301]   HF5438.8.K48 B58 1995   +3525

A nation of salesmen: the tyranny of the market and the subversion of culture. Earl Shorris. 1st ed. New York: W.W. Norton & Co., c1994. 352 p. *Notes:* Includes bibliographical references and index. [LC 94016580; ISN 0393036723]   HF5438.25. S563 1994   +3526

Professional selling. David L. Kurtz, H. Robert Dodge. 6th ed. Homewood, IL: Irwin, c1991. xx, 444 p. : ill. *Notes:* Includes bibliographical references (p. 427-429) and index. [LC 90044067; ISN 0256087253; $48.95]   HF5438.25. K87 1991   3527

Seeking customers. edited, with an introduction by Benson P. Shapiro and John J. Sviokla. Boston, MA: Harvard Business School Press, c1993. xviii, 343 p. : ill. *Notes:* "A Harvard Business Review book." Articles originally published in the Harvard Business Review, 1976-1992. Companion volume to: Keeping customers. Includes bibliographical references and index. [LC 92036862; ISN 0875843328; $29.95]   HF5438.25. S434 1993   3528

Selling: principles and methods. Carlton A. Pederson, Milburn D. Wright, Barton A. Weitz. 9th ed. Homewood, Ill.: Irwin, 1988. xvii, 644 p. : ill. (some col.) *Notes:* Includes bibliographies and indexes. [LC 87081434; ISN 0256036446]   HF5438.25. P42 1988   3529

Selling: principles and practices. Frederic A. Russell, Frank H. Beach, Richard H. Buskirk, with Bruce D. Buskirk. 12th ed. New York: McGraw-Hill, c1988. xviii, 602 p. : ill. (some col.) *Notes:* Includes indexes. [LC 87031110; ISN 0070543658; $38.95]   HF5438.25. R87 1988   3530

Strategic selling: the unique sales system proven successful by America's best companies. Robert B. Miller, Stephen E. Heiman, with Tad Tuleja. New York, N.Y.: Warner Books, c1985. 319 p. : ill. *Notes:* Reprint. Originally published: New York: Morrow, 1985. [LC 85026566; ISN 0446370061]   HF5438.25. M567   3531

SELZNICK, DAVID O

Showman: the life of David O. Selznick. David Thomson. 1st ed. New York: Knopf, 1992. xi, 792 p. : ill. *Notes:* Includes bibliographical references (p. 707-710), filmography (p. 749-759), and index. [LC 91047886; ISN 0394568338; $35.00 ($45.00 Can.)]   PN1998.3.S395 T46 1992   3532

SEMICONDUCTOR INDUSTRY

Restructuring for innovation: the remaking of the U.S. semiconductor industry. David P. Angel. New York: Guilford, c1994. vii, 216 p. : ill. *Notes:* Includes bibliographical references (p. 204-212) and index. [LC 93040423; ISN 0898622972]   HD9696.S43 U443 1994   +3533

SERVICE INDUSTRIES

The AMA handbook of marketing for the service industries. Carole A. Congram, editor, Margaret L. Friedman, associate editor. New York, NY: American Management Association, c1991. xix, 588 p. : ill. *Notes:* Includes bibliographical references and index. [LC 90055204; ISN 081440104X; $75.00]   HD9980.5. A53 1991   3534

At America's service: how corporations can revolutionize the way they treat their customers. Karl Albrecht. Homewood, Ill.: Dow Jones-Irwin, c1988. ix, 241 p. : ill. *Notes:* Includes bibliographies and index. [LC 88003564; ISN 1556230958; $19.95]   HD9981.5. A42 1988   3535

Managing in the service economy. James L. Heskett. Boston, Mass.: Harvard Business School Press, 1986. viii, 211 p. : ill. *Notes:* Includes index. Bibliography: p. 195-204. [LC 85030185; ISN 0875841309]   HD9980.5. H47 1986   3536

Managing services: marketing, operations, and human resources. compiled by Christopher H. Lovelock. 2nd ed. Englewood Cliffs, N.J.: Prentice Hall, c1992. xvi, 472 p. : ill. *Notes:* Includes bibliographical references and index. [LC 91026857; ISN 0135447011; $67.85]   HD9980.5. M345 1992   3537

Managing services marketing: text and readings. John E.G. Bateson. Chicago: Dryden Press, c1989. xv, 591 p. : ill. *Notes:* Includes bibliographies and index. [LC 88025684; ISN 0030081475]
    HD9980.5. B38 1989   3538

Managing the service economy: prospects and problems: essays commissioned for the inaugural conference of the Fishman-Davidson Center for the Study of the Service Sector, Wharton School, University of Pennsylvania. edited by Robert P. Inman. Cambridge Cambridgeshire; New York: Cambridge University Press, 1985. xv, 336 p. : ill. *Notes:* Papers from the ARA/Wharton Conference on the Future of the Service Economy held Nov. 19-20, 1982, at the Wharton School, University of Pennsylvania, sponsored by the Fishman-Davidson Center for the Study of the Service Sector. Includes bibliographies and indexes. [LC 84029318; ISN 0521306477]
    HD9980.5. M35 1985   3539

Marketing strategies for services: globalization, client-orientation, deregulation. edited by M.M. Kostecki. Oxford England; New York: Pergamon Press, 1994. xix, 250 p. : ill. *Notes:* Includes bibliographical references (p. 229-243) and indexes. [LC 93039236; ISN 0080423892]
    HD9980.5. M373 1994   +3540

The service encounter. edited by John A. Czepiel, Michael R. Solomon, Carol F. Surprenant. Lexington, Mass.: Lexington Books, c1985. x, 338 p. : ill. (The Advances in retailing series.) *Notes:* Includes bibliographies and index. *Contents:* ch. 8. The psychology of waiting lines / David H. Maister—ch. 18. Developing and managing the customer-service function in the service sector / Christopher H. Lovelock. [LC 83049532; ISN 0669082732]   HD9980.5. S425 1985   3541

The service management course: cases and readings. W. Earl Sasser, Jr., Christopher W.L. Hart, James L. Heskett. New York: Toronto: New York: Free Press; Maxwell Macmillan Canada; Maxwell Macmillan International, c1991. x, 977 p. : ill. *Notes:* Includes bibliographical references. [LC 91006933; ISN 0029140919; $40.00]   HD9980.5. S27 1991   3542

Service management effectiveness: balancing strategy, organization and human resources, operations, and marketing. David E. Bowen, Richard B. Chase, Thomas G. Cummings, and associates. 1st ed. San Francisco: Jossey-Bass, 1990. xxviii, 414 p. : ill. *Notes:* Includes bibliographical references and indexes. [LC 90004047; ISN 1555422225; $31.95]   HD9980.5. B68 1990   3543

Service management for competitive advantage. James A. Fitzsimmons, Mona J. Fitzsimmons. New York: McGraw-Hill, c1994. xviii, 462 p. : ill. *Notes:* Includes bibliographical references and indexes. [LC 93035762; ISN 0070212171]   HD9980.5. F549 1994   +3544

Service success!: lessons from a leader on how to turn around a service business. Daniel I. Kaplan with Carl Rieser. New York: Wiley, c1994. x, 262 p. : ill. *Notes:* Includes index. [LC 93027197; ISN 0471591297; $24.95]   HD9980.5. K37 1994   +3545

Services in transition: the impact of information technology on the service sector. edited by Gerald Faulhaber, Eli Noam, Roberta Tasley. Cambridge. Mass.: Ballinger Pub. Co., c1986. xix, 218 p. *Notes:* Papers presented at the Conference on the Impact of Information Technology on the Service Sector, held at the Wharton School, University of Pennsylvania, Feb. 7-8, 1985. Includes bibliographies and index. [LC 86007918; ISN 0887300928]   HD9981.5. S448   3546

Trading in a new world order: the impact of telecommunications and data services on international trade in services. edited by Bruno Lanvin. Boulder, Colo.: Westview Press, 1993. xvi, 359 p. *Notes:* Includes bibliographical references (p. [343]-356) and index. [LC 92047265; ISN 0813387272]   HD9980.5. T73 1993   +3547

United States service industries handbook. edited by Wray O. Candilis; foreword by William Proxmire. New York: Praeger, 1988. xvi, 238 p. : ill. *Notes:* Includes index. Bibliography: p. 219-225. [LC 87025865; ISN 0275923673; $45.85 (est.)]   HD9981.5. U59 1988   3548

SEX DISCRIMINATION IN EMPLOYMENT

Gender and diversity in the workplace: learning activities and exercises. Gary N. Powell. Thousand Oaks, Calif.: Sage Publications, c1994. viii, 151 p. : ill.; 28 cm. *Notes:* Includes bibliographical references. [LC 94007488; ISN 0803944861]   HD6060. P69 1994   +3549

Gender in the workplace. Clair Brown and Joseph A. Pechman, editors. Washington, D.C.: Brookings Institution, c1987. xiv, 316 p. : ill. *Notes:* Includes bibliographical references and index. [LC 87000668; ISN 0815711700; ISN 0815711697; $32.95 (est.); $12.95 (est.)]   HD6060.5.U5 G46 1987   3550

Justice, gender, and affirmative action. Susan D. Clayton and Faye J. Crosby. Ann Arbor: University of Michigan Press, c1992. ix, 152 p. *Notes:* "Published in cooperation with the Society for the Psychological Study of Social Issues." Includes bibliographical references (p. 129-144) and index. [LC 92022871; ISN 0472064649]   HD6060.5.U5 C58 1992   3551

Sex discrimination handbook. edited by Barbara S. Gamble. Washington, D.C.: BNA Books, Bureau of National Affairs, c1992. viii, 403 p. *Notes:* "The material in this book is reprinted from BNA's Fair employment practices binders." Includes bibliographical references (p. 400-403). [LC 92024161; ISN 0871797631]   KF3467. S47 1992   3552

Women and Japanese management: discrimination and reform. Alice C.L. Lam. London; New York: Routledge, 1992. xvi, 281 p. : ill. *Notes:* Includes bibliographical references (p. [260]-272) and index. [LC 91048163; ISN 0415063353]   HD6060.5.J3 L36 1992   3553

SEX DISCRIMINATION IN NATIONAL INCOME ACCOUNTING

If women counted: a new feminist economics. Marilyn Waring; introduction by Gloria Steinem. New York: Harper & Row, c1988. xx, 386 p. : ill. *Notes:* Includes index. Bibliography: p. [349]-364. [LC 88045160; ISN 0062509330; $19.95]   HC79.I5 W384 1988   3554

SEX ROLE IN THE WORK ENVIRONMENT

Women vs. women: the uncivil business war. Tara Roth Madden. New York, NY: American Management Association, c1987. xxii, 266 p. *Notes:* Includes index. [LC 87047701; ISN 0814459005]   HD6060. M33 1987   3555

SEXUAL DIVISION OF LABOR

Breaking with tradition: women and work, the new facts of life. Felice N. Schwartz with Jean Zimmerman. New York, NY: Warner Books, c1992. xiii, 332 p. : ill. *Notes:* Includes bibliographical references (p. 317-324) and index. [LC 91050418; ISN 0446516007; $21.95 ($26.95 in Canada)]   HD6060.65.U5 S39 1992   3556

SEXUAL HARASSMENT OF WOMEN

Sex and the workplace. Barbara A. Gutek. 1st ed. San Francisco, Calif.: Jossey-Bass, c1985. xix, 216 p. (Jossey-Bass management series) (Jossey-Bass social and behavioral science series) *Notes:* Includes index. Bibliography: p. 203-210. [LC 85045054; ISN 0875896561]   HD6060.3. G88 1985   3557

You don't have to take it!: a woman's guide to confronting emotional abuse at work. Ginny NiCarthy, Naomi Gottlieb, Sandra Coffman. Seattle, Wash.: Seal Press, c1993. xv, 377 p. *Notes:* Includes bibliographical references (p. 357-370) and index. [LC 93012873; ISN 1878067354; $14.95]   HD6060.3. N53 1993   +3558

SHEARSON/AMERICAN EXPRESS INC

The year they sold Wall Street. Tim Carrington. Boston: Houghton Mifflin, 1985. x, 245 p. *Notes:* Includes index. [LC 85014219; ISN 0395343941; $16.95]   HD2746.5. C375 1985   3559

SHOREBANK CORPORATION (CHICAGO, ILL.)

Community capitalism. by Richard P. Taub; with a new preface. [Paperback ed.] Boston, Mass.: Harvard Business School Press, c1994. xxii, 151 p. : ill. *Notes:* Subtitle on cover: The South Shore Bank's strategy for neighborhood revitalization. Includes bibliographical references and index. [LC 94009875; ISN 0875845533; $14.95]   HN90.C6 T38 1994   +3560

SIMON, RON

The game behind the game: negotiating in the big leagues. Ron Simon; foreword by Harvey B. Mackay. Stillwater, MN: Voyageur Press, c1993. 271 p. : ill. [LC 93017730; ISN 0896581977; $19.95 ($25.95 Can.)]   GV734.5. S59 1993   +3561

SINDONA, MICHELE

Power on earth. Nick Tosches. New York: Arbor House, c1986. x, 290 p. *Notes:* Includes index. [LC 86010778; ISN 0877957967; $18.95] HV6766.S56 T67 1986 3562

SMALL BUSINESS

Basic small business management. Clifford M. Baumback. Englewood Cliffs, N.J.: Prentice-Hall, c1983. x, 540 p. : ill. *Notes:* Includes bibliographical references and index. [LC 82018110; ISN 0130664154; $22.95] HD62.7. B37 1983 3563

The complete guide to buying a business. Richard W. Snowden. New York: American Management Association, c1994. xi, 243 p. *Notes:* Includes index. [LC 93027767; ISN 0814451586; $24.95] HD1393.25. S655 1994 +3564

Corporate comeback: managing turnarounds and troubled companies. Arnold S. Goldstein. New York: Wiley, c1988. xi, 237 p. *Notes:* Includes index. [LC 87027413; ISN 0471844888] HD62.7. G635 1988 3565

Effective small business management. Richard M. Hodgetts, Donald F. Kuratko. 3rd ed. San Diego: Harcourt Brace Jovanovich, c1989. xvii, 590 p. : ill. *Notes:* Includes bibliographical references. [LC 88081032; ISN 0155209183] HD62.7. H625 1989 3566

Entrepreneurship and small business management: text, readings and cases. A. Bakr Ibrahim, Willard H. Ellis. Dubuque, Iowa: Kendall/Hunt Pub. Co., c1990. xx, 659 p. : ill. *Notes:* Includes bibliographical references (p. 651-653) and indexes. [LC 90060880; ISN 0840358733] HD62.7. I27 1990 3567

Entrepreneurship and venture management. compiled by Clifford M. Baumback, Joseph R. Mancuso. 2nd ed. Englewood Cliffs, N.J.: Prentice-Hall, c1986. x, 452 p. : ill. *Notes:* Includes bibliographies and indexes. [LC 86012327; ISN 0132830787] HD62.7. E57 3568

Financial management of the small firm. Ernest W. Walker, J. William Petty II. 2nd ed. Englewood Cliffs, N.J.: Prentice-Hall, c1986. xi, 465 p. : ill. *Notes:* Includes bibliographies and index. [LC 86001925; ISN 0133161676; $28.95] HG4027.7. W35 1986 3569

The five-minute financial manager. Bryan E. Milling. Radnor, Pa.: Chilton Book Co., c1989. vi, 158 p. *Notes:* Includes index. [LC 89042863; ISN 0801979973; $14.95] HG4027.7. M56 1989 3570

Free money from the federal government for small businesses and entrepreneurs. Laurie Blum. New York: Wiley, c1993. xii, 382 p. *Notes:* Includes bibliographical references and index. [LC 93011505; ISN 0471599433] HG4027.7. B6 1993 +3571

From the ground up: the resurgence of American entrepreneurship. John Case. New York: Simon & Schuster, c1992. 256 p. *Notes:* Includes bibliographical references (p. 237-245) and index. [LC 91037972; ISN 067168308X; $22.50] HD2346.U5 C33 1992 3572

How to organize and operate a small business. Clifford M. Baumback. 8th ed. Englewood Cliffs, NJ: Prentice Hall, c1988. xiii, 578 p. : ill. *Notes:* Includes index. [LC 87020455; ISN 0134249879] HD62.7. B39 1988 3573

How to run a small business. J.K. Lasser Institute. 7th ed. New York: McGraw-Hill, 1993, c1994. xiii, 328 p. : ill. *Notes:* Includes index. [LC 93026166; ISN 0070365768; $27.95] HD62.7. H68 1993 3574

How to set up your own small business. Max Fallek. Minneapolis, Minn.: American Institute of Small Business, c1993. 2 v.: ill. *Notes:* Includes index. ISN 0939069431] HD62.7. F35 1993 3575

How to start and run your own business. M. Mogano. 7th ed. London; Boston: Graham & Trotman, 1989. vii, 158 p. [LC 89016975; ISN 1853332887; $13.00] HD62.7. M64 1989 3576

Job creation in America: how our smallest companies put the most people to work. David L. Birch. New York: London: Free Press; Collier Macmillan, c1987. xi, 244 p. : ill. *Notes:* Includes bibliographical references and index. [LC 87008523; ISN 0029036100] HD2346.U5 B54 1987 3577

Legal handbook for small business. Marc J. Lane. Rev. ed. New York, NY: AMACOM, c1989. xiii, 253 p. : ill. *Notes:* Includes index. [LC 88048039; ISN 081445951X; $18.95] KF1659. L36 1989 3578

Life after debt: recapitalizing the troubled business. Edmond P. Freiermuth. Homewood, Ill.: Dow Jones-Irwin, c1988. xii, 141 p. *Notes:* Includes index. [LC 87072744; ISN 1556230443; $24.95] HG4027.7. F73 1988 3579

Managing the small business: insights and readings. edited by Cynthia C. Ryans. Englewood Cliffs, N.J.: Prentice Hall, c1989. x, 358 p. : ill. *Notes:* Includes bibliographical references. [LC 88025239; ISN 0135515653] HD62.7. M353 1989 3580

The small business bible: the make-or-break factors for survival and success. Paul Resnik. New York: J. Wiley, c1988. viii, 230 p. *Notes:* Includes index. Bibliography: p. 223-225. [LC 88017207; ISN 0471629723; ISN 0471629855] HD62.7. R47 1988 3581

The small business handbook: a comprehensive guide to starting and running your own business. by Irving Burstiner. Rev. ed. New York: Prentice Hall Press, 1989. xi, 356 p. : ill. *Notes:* Includes bibliographies and index. [LC 88004585; ISN 0138143447; $16.95]   HD62.7. B84 1989   3582

Small business management. Hal B. Pickle, Royce L. Abrahamson. 5th ed. New York: Wiley, c1990. xix, 7028 p. : ill. *Notes:* Includes bibliographical references. [LC 89036239; ISN 0471500712; $40.95]   HD62.7. P52 1990   3583

Small business USA: the role of small companies in sparking America's economic transformation. Steven Solomon. 1st ed. New York: Crown Publishers, c1986. vii, 358 p. *Notes:* Includes index. Bibliography: p. 333-347. [LC 86004547; ISN 0517562405]   HD2346.U5 S57   3584

Small firm management: ownership, finance, and performance. Kevin Keasey and Robert Watson. Oxford, UK; Cambridge, Mass., USA: Blackwell Business, 1993. ix, 262 p. : ill. *Notes:* Includes bibliographical references (p. [240]-256) and index. [LC 92043006; ISN 063117981X]   HG4027.7. K4 1993   +3585

Small firms in global competition. edited by Tamir Agmon, Richard Drobnick. New York: Oxford University Press, 1994. xiv, 142 p. : ill. *Notes:* "A research book from the International Business Education and Research Program, University of Southern California." Includes bibliographical references and index. [LC 92040074; ISN 019507825X; $32.00]   HD62.7. S613 1994   +3586

Starting and succeeding in your own small business. by Louis L. Allen. Foreword by Frank L. Tucker. Introd. by Wilford L. White. New York Grosset & Dunlap, 1968. xxi, 157 p. [LC 67014763]   HD2341. A6   +3587

Successful business expansion: practical strategies for planning profitable growth. Philip S. Orsino. New York: Wiley, c1994. xii, 241 p. : ill. *Notes:* Includes index. [LC 94000327; ISN 0471597376]   HD69.S6 O8 1994   +3588

A successful business of your own. by Barbara C. Griffin. Los Angeles, Calif.: Sherbourne Press, c1974. 222 p. *Notes:* Includes index. Bibliography: p. 211-217. [LC 75306430; ISN 0820201669; $6.95]   HD2341. G67   +3589

Successful small business management. Leon C. Megginson, Charles R. Scott, William L. Megginson. 6th ed. Homewood, IL: Irwin, c1991. xxvi, 851 p. : ill. *Notes:* Includes bibliographical references and index. [LC 90004566; ISN 0256086354; $41.95]   HD62.7. S9 1991   3590

The ultimate guide to raising money for growing companies. Michael C. Thomsett. Homewood, IL: Dow Jones-Irwin, c1990. vii, 288 p. : ill. [LC 89025745; ISN 1556232403; $34.95]   HG4027.7. T48 1990   3591

Up front financing: the entrepreneur's guide. A. David Silver. Rev. ed. New York: Wiley, c1988. xi, 238 p. : ill. *Notes:* Includes bibliographical references and index. [LC 88020844; ISN 0471634751; $24.95]   HG4027.7. S53 1988   3592

Up your own organization!: a handbook for today's entrepreneur. by Donald M. Dible; edited by Jeannie Marschrer; introduction by Robert Townsend. Rev. ed. Reston, Va.: Reston Pub. Co., c1986. xx, 423 p. *Notes:* Includes bibliographies and index. [LC 85008293; ISN 0835980863; $17.95]   HD62.7. D53 1986   3593

SMART CARDS

Smart cards: the new bank cards. Jerome Svigals. Updated and expanded ed., Rev. ed. New York: London: Macmillan; Collier Macmillan Publishers, 1987. xviii, 212 p. : ill. *Notes:* Includes index. [LC 87013745; ISN 0029489016]   TK7895.S62 S85 1987   3594

SMITH, ADAM

The essential Adam Smith. edited and with introductory readings by Robert L. Heilbroner, with the assistance of Laurence J. Malone. New York: W.W. Norton, 1987, c1986. vii, 341 p. : ill. *Notes:* Includes index. Bibliography: p. 10-11. [LC 85021394; ISN 0393955303]   HB103.S6 A48 1986   3595

SMITH, FRED

Overnight success: Federal Express and Frederick Smith, its renegade creator. Vance H. Trimble. 1st ed. New York: Crown, c1993. 342 p., [16] p. of plates: ill. *Notes:* Includes index. [LC 92017333; ISN 0517585103; $22.00]   HE5896.S65 T75 1993   3596

SMITH, ROGER B

Call me Roger. Albert Lee. Chicago: Contemporary Books, c1988. 324 p. *Notes:* Includes index. [LC 87035223; ISN 0809246309; $19.95]   HD9710.U52 S5455 1988   3597

SOCIAL CHANGE

The illusion of choice: how the market economy shapes our destiny. Andrew Bard Schmookler. Albany: State University of New York Press, c1993. xii, 349 p. *Notes:* Includes bibliographical references (p. 321-335) and index. [LC 91043874; ISN 0791412652]   HM101. S325 1993   3598

The planning of change. edited by Warren G. Bennis, Kenneth D. Benne, Robert Chin. 4th ed. New York: Holt, Rinehart, and Winston, c1985. viii, 487 p. : ill. *Notes:* Includes bibliographies and index. [LC 84019227; ISN 0030636825; $24.95 (est.)]   HM101. P558 1985   3599

Strategies for managing change. William G. Dyer. Reading, Mass.: Addison-Wesley Pub. Co., 1984. vi, 202 p. *Notes:* Rev. ed. of: Insight to impact. 1976. Includes index. Bibliography: p. 191-196. [LC 84006219; ISN 020110346X; $18.95 (est.)]   HM101. D96 1984   3600

SOCIAL HISTORY

Powershift: knowledge, wealth, and violence at the edge of the 21st century. Alvin Toffler. New York: Bantam Books, c1990. xxii, 585 p. *Notes:* Includes bibliographical references. [LC 90001068; ISN 0553057766; $27.95]   HN17.5. T6417 1990   3601

SOCIAL MARKETING

Social marketing: strategies for changing public behavior. Philip Kotler, Eduardo L. Roberto. New York: Free Press, c1989. xii, 401 p. : ill. *Notes:* Includes index. Bibliography: p. 371-389. [LC 89045735; ISN 0029184614; $29.95]   HF5415.122. K68 1989   3602

SOCIAL MOBILITY

Declining fortunes: the withering of the American dream. Katherine S. Newman. New York: BasicBooks, c1993. xiii, 257 p. *Notes:* Includes bibliographical references (p. [223]-250) and index. [LC 92053246; ISN 046501593X; $23.00 ($31.00 Can.)]   HN90.S65 N47 1993   3603

SOCIAL PREDICTION

Future vision: the 189 most important trends of the 1990s. from the editors of Research alert. Naperville, Ill.: Sourcebooks Trade, c1991. vi, 248 p. : ill. *Notes:* Includes bibliographical references. [LC 90049474; ISN 0942061179; $21.95]   HN59.2. F88 1991   3604

The knowledge-value revolution, or, a history of the future. Taichi Sakaiya; translated by George Fields and William Marsh. 1st ed. Tokyo; New York: Kodansha International: Distributed in the U.S. by Kodansha America, 1991. xx, 379 p. *Notes:* Translation of: Chika kakumei. Includes bibliographical references (p. 366-370) and index. [LC 91015253; ISN 0870119427; ISN 4770014422; $22.95]   HN60. S2613 1991   3605

SOCIAL RESPONSIBILITY OF BUSINESS

Business and society: corporate strategy, public policy, ethics. William C. Frederick, James E. Post, Keith Davis. 7th ed. New York: McGraw-Hill, c1992. xxviii, 625 p. : ill. *Notes:* Includes bibliographical references (p. 605-608) and indexes. [LC 91026776; ISN 0070156131] HD60. F72 1992   3606

Corporate environmentalism in a global economy: societal values in international technology transfer. Halina Szejnwald Brown. . . et al. Westport, Conn.: Quorum Books, 1993. viii, 256 p. : ill. *Notes:* Includes bibliographical references (p. [229]-245) and index. [LC 92019851; ISN 0899308023]   HD60.5.D44 C67 1993   3607

Doing well while doing good: the marketing link between business & nonprofit causes. L. Lawrence Embley. Englewood Cliffs, N.J.: Prentice Hall, c1993. xix, 252 p. : ill. *Notes:* Includes index. [LC 92030234; ISN 0132198746; $24.95] HD60.5.U5 E43 1993   3608

The E-factor: the bottom-line approach to environmentally responsible business. Joel Makower. 1st ed. New York: Times Books, c1993. 291 p. *Notes:* "A Tilden Press book." Includes bibliographical references (p. [280]-281) and indexes. [LC 92050504; ISN 0812920570; $23.00 ($29.00 Can.)] HD60. M344 1993   3609

In pursuit of principle and profit: business success through social responsibility. Alan Reder. New York: Putnam, c1994. xi, 274 p. *Notes:* Published simultaneously in Canada. "A Jeremy P. Tarcher/Putnam book." Includes bibliographical references (p. [257]-262) and index. [LC 94011916; ISN 087477781X; $22.95] HD60. R444 1994   +3610

Power and accountability. Robert A.G. Monks, Nell Minow. New York, NY: HarperBusiness, c1991. x, 292 p. *Notes:* Includes bibliographical references (p. 267-283) and index. [LC 91008959; ISN 0887305121; $22.95 ($29.95 Can.)] HD60.5.U5 M646 1991   3611

The role of the modern corporation in a free society. by John R. Danley. Notre Dame, Ind.: University of Notre Dame Press, c1994. xiv, 345 p. *Notes:* Includes bibliographical references (p. 325-336) and index. [LC 93002103; ISN 026801647X] HD60. D26 1994   +3612

SOCIAL SCIENCES

Action science. Chris Argyris, Robert Putnam, Diana McLain Smith. 1st ed. San Francisco: Jossey-Bass, 1985. xx, 480 p. (The Jossey-Bass social and behavioral science series) (The Jossey-Bass management series) *Notes:* Includes index. Bibliography: p. 451-465. [LC 85018054; ISN 0875896650] H62. A663 1985   3613

Basic statistics for business and economics. Paul G. Hoel and Raymond J. Jessen. 3rd ed. New York: Wiley, c1982. x, 629 p. : ill. (Wiley series in probability and mathematical statistics. Applied probability and statistics) *Notes:* Includes index. [LC 81019739; ISN 0471098299] HA29. H66 1982   3614

Basics of qualitative research: grounded theory procedures and techniques. Anselm Strauss, Juliet Corbin. Newbury Park, Calif.: Sage Publications, c1990. 270 p. *Notes:* Includes bibliographical references (p. 260-263) and index. [LC 90039609] HA29. S823 1990   3615

Introduction to business and economic statistics. Charles T. Clark, Eleanor W. Jordan. 7th ed. Cincinnati: South-Western Pub. Co., c1985. vii, 639 p. : ill. *Notes:* Rev. ed. of: Introduction to business and economic statistics / John R. Stockton, Charles T. Clark. 6th ed. c1980. Includes index. [LC 83050803; ISN 0538132604] HA29. C589 1985   3616

Introductory statistics for business and economics. Thomas H. Wonnacott, Ronald J. Wonnacott. 4th ed. New York: Wiley, c1990. xvi, 815 p. : ill. *Notes:* Includes index. Bibliography: p. 781-785. [LC 89033083; ISN 047161517X; $53.95] HA29. W622 1990   3617

Longitudinal research. Scott Menard. Newbury Park, CA: Sage Publications, 1991. 81 p. : ill. *Notes:* Includes bibliographical references (p. 73-80). [LC 90020103; ISN 0803937539] H62. M39 1991   3618

Misused statistics: straight talk for twisted numbers. A.J. Jaffe, Herbert F. Spirer. New York: M. Dekker, 1986. xi, 237 p. : ill. *Notes:* Includes index. Bibliography: p. 217-228. [LC 86016237; ISN 0824776313] HA29. J29 1986   3619

The politics and ethics of fieldwork. Maurice Punch. Beverly Hills: Sage Publications, c1986. 93 p. *Notes:* "A Sage university paper"—Cover. Bibliography: p. 85-91. [LC 85062291; ISN 0803925174; ISN 080392562X] H62. P94 1986   3620

Postmodernism and the social sciences. edited by Joe Doherty, Elspeth Graham and Mo Malek. New York: St. Martin's Press, 1992. x, 253 p. *Notes:* Includes bibliographical references (p. 221-241) and index. [LC 91030379; ISN 0312075081] H61. P615 1992   3621

Statistical analysis for decision making. Morris Hamburg. 4th ed. San Diego: Harcourt Brace Jovanovich, c1987. xv, 701, 130 p. : ill. (some col.) *Notes:* Includes index. [LC 86080751; ISN 0155834533] HA29. H242 1987   3622

Statistical techniques in business and economics. Robert D. Mason, Douglas A. Lind. 7th ed. Homewood, IL: Irwin, c1990. xxvii, 910 p. : ill. (some col.) *Notes:* Includes bibliographical references. [LC 89002224; ISN 0256076960; $43.95] HA29. M268 1990   3623

Statistics for business and economics: problems, exercises, and case studies. Edwin Mansfield. 4th ed. New York: Norton, c1991. 272 p. : ill. *Notes:* Includes bibliographical references. [LC 90045336; ISN 039396051X; $14.95] HA29. M2463 1991   3624

Statistics for management. Richard I. Levin, David S. Rubin. 5th ed. Englewood Cliffs, N.J.: Prentice-Hall, 1991. xiv, 862 p. : ill. *Notes:* Includes bibliographical references (p. 856-858) and index. [LC 90007712; ISN 013851965X; $60.00] HA29. L3887 1991   3625

Statistics for modern business decisions. Lawrence L. Lapin. 5th ed. San Diego: Harcourt Brace Jovanovich, c1990. xxix, 1021 p. : ill. (some col.) *Notes:* Includes index. [LC 89085307; ISN 0155837052; $57.50] HA29. L2664 1990 3626

SOCIAL SECURITY

Too many promises: the uncertain future of social security. Michael J. Boskin. Homewood, Ill.: Dow Jones-Irwin, c1986. xiv, 196 p. : ill. *Notes:* "A Twentieth Century Fund report'. Includes index. Bibliography: p. 183-189. [LC 86070430; ISN 0870947796] HD7125. B585 1986 3627

SOCIAL SURVEYS

Handbook of survey research. edited by Peter H. Rossi, James D. Wright, Andy B. Anderson. New York: Academic Press, c1983. xvi, 755 p. : ill. (Quantitative studies in social relations) *Notes:* Includes bibliographies and index. [LC 83003869; ISN 0125982267] HN29. H294 1983 3628

SOCIOLOGY

Handbook of sociology. Neil J. Smelser, editor. Newbury Park, Calif.: Sage Publications, c1988. 824 p. *Notes:* Includes bibliographies and indexes. [LC 87036762; ISN 0803926650] HM51. H249 1988 3629

SOCIOLOGY, CHRISTIAN (CATHOLIC)

The Catholic ethic and the spirit of capitalism. Michael Novak. New York: Toronto: New York: Free Press; Maxwell Macmillan Canada; Maxwell Macmillan International, c1993. xvii, 334 p. *Notes:* Includes bibliographical references (p. 238-318) and index. [LC 92032151; ISN 002923235X; $24.95] BX1753. N66 1993 3630

Doing well & doing good: the challenge to the Christian capitalist. Richard John Neuhaus. New York, N.Y.: Doubleday, 1992. 312 p. *Notes:* Includes bibliographical references and index. [LC 92008752; ISN 0385425023] BX1753. N484 1992 3631

SONI KABUSHIKI KAISHA

From a 500-dollar company to a global corporation: the growth of Sony. Akio Morita. Pittsburgh: Carnegie-Mellon University Press, 1985. 41 p. : port. (1984 Benjamin F. Fairless Memorial Lecture) [LC 85070383; ISN 0887480195] HD9696.A3 J3637 3632

Funny business: an outsider's year in Japan. Gary J. Katzenstein. 1st ed. New York, N.Y.: Soho Press, c1989. 228 p. *Notes:* Bibliography: p. 225-228. [LC 89011548; ISN 0939149184; $26.93] HD9696.A3 J3622 1989 3633

SOUND RECORDING INDUSTRY

Stiffed: a true story of MCA, the music business, and the Mafia. William Knoedelseder. 1st ed. New York: HarperCollins, c1993. xvi, 480 p., [8] p. of plates: ill., ports *Notes:* Includes index. [LC 92053329; ISN 0060167459; $23.00] ML3790. K56 1993 3634

SOUTH AFRICA—ECONOMIC POLICY

South Africa: prospects for successful transition. edited by Bob Tucker and Bruce R. Scott. Kenwyn: Juta, c1992. xxiii, 314 p. : ill. *Notes:* Includes bibliographical references (p. 313-314). [LC 93171108; ISN 0702129208] HC905. S684 1992 +3635

SOUTH AFRICA—POLITICS AND GOVERNMENT—20TH CENTURY

Black and gold. by Anthony Sampson. 1st American ed. New York: Pantheon Books, 1987. 280 p. *Notes:* Title on jacket: Black gold: tycoons, revolutionaries, and apartheid. Includes bibliographical references and index. [LC 86042978; ISN 0394560531; $19.95] DT770. S26 1987 3636

SOVIET UNION—COMMERCE

Cutting the red tape: how Western companies can profit in the new Russia. Mark Tourevski, Eileen Morgan. New York: Toronto: New York: Free Press; Maxwell Macmillan Canada; Maxwell Macmillan International, c1993. xxiii, 310 p. : ill. *Notes:* Includes bibliographical references and index. [LC 92010751; ISN 0029327156; $24.95] HF3624. T68 1993 3637

SOVIET UNION—ECONOMIC POLICY

The failure of Soviet economic planning: system, performance, reform. Robert W. Campbell. Bloomington: Indiana University Press, c1992. xii, 185 p. : ill. *Notes:* Includes bibliographical references and index. [LC 91039964; ISN 0253313112] HC335. C27 1992 3638

SPACE INDUSTRIALIZATION

Space commerce: free enterprise on the high frontier. Nathan C. Goldman. Cambridge, Mass.: Ballinger Pub. Co., c1985. xiii, 186 p. : ill. *Notes:* Includes index. Bibliography: p. 179-182. [LC 84016761; ISN 0887300030] HD9711.75.U62 G65 1985 3639

SPECULATION

Bear market investment strategies. Harry D. Schultz. [Rev. ed.]. Homewood, Ill.: Dow Jones-Irwin, 1981. xii, 232 p. : ill. *Notes:* Revision of: Bear markets: how to survive and make money in them, 1964. Errata slip inserted. [LC 80070618; ISN 0870942247] HG4539. S35 1981 3640

Famous financial fiascos. by John Train; illustrations by Pierre Le-Tan; foreword by C. Northcote Parkinson. 1st ed. New York: C.N. Potter: Distributed by Crown Publishers, c1985. x, 112 p. : ill. [LC 84014754; ISN 0517545837] HG6005. T73 1985 3641

SPORTS

Money games: the business of sports. Ann E. Weiss. Boston: Houghton Mifflin, 1993. vi, 186 p. *Notes:* On t.p. the "s" in 'games' appears as a dollar sign. Includes bibliographical references (p. 165-179) and index. Discusses the influence and growing importance of money in the complex world of professional and amateur sports. [LC 92025002; ISN 0395574447] GV716. W45 1993 3642

The name of the game: the business of sports. Jerry Gorman, Kirk Calhoun; with Skip Rozin. New York: Wiley, c1994. xvi, 278 p. *Notes:* Includes bibliographical references (p. 253-254) and index. [LC 93006046; ISN 0471594237] GV716. G67 1994 +3643

Sports marketing: competitive business strategies for sports. Christine M. Brooks. Englewood Cliffs, N.J.: Prentice Hall, c1994. xiii, 333 p. : ill. *Notes:* Includes bibliographical references and index. [LC 93039462; ISN 0138358931] GV716. B76 1994 +3644

STATISTICAL DECISION

Basic concepts in quantitative management. Harvard Business Review. Boston, Mass.: Harvard Business Review Reprint Dept., 1986? vii, 228 p. : ill., 3 fold. ([Harvard Business Review reprint series]; no. 13015) *Notes:* Articles reprinted from the Harvard Business Review, 1954-1979. Includes bibliographical references.; ISN 0867352647] HD30.23. H369 1986a 3645

STATISTICS

Basic statistics: a modern approach. Morris Hamburg. 3rd ed. San Diego: Harcourt Brace Jovanovich, c1985. x, 548 p. : ill. (some col.) *Notes:* Includes index. Bibliography: p. 495-501. [LC 84081504; ISN 015505113X]   QA276.12. H35 1985   3646

Business and economics statistics with computer applications. William E. Becker, Donald L. Harnett. Reading, Mass.: Addison-Wesley, c1987. xxiv, 739 p. : ill. *Notes:* Includes index. [LC 85009025; ISN 0201109565; $29.95]   HA29. B3837 1987   3647

Elements of statistical inference. David V. Huntsberger, Patrick Billingsley. 6th ed. Boston: Allyn and Bacon, 1987. xv, 511 p. : ill. *Notes:* Includes bibliographical references and index. [LC 86017220; ISN 0205103197; $21.99]   QA276.12. H86 1987   3648

A handbook of introductory statistical methods. C. Philip Cox. New York: Wiley, 1987. xxi, 272 p. : ill. (Wiley series in probability and mathematical statistics. Applied probability and statistics, 0271-6356) *Notes:* Includes index. Bibliography: p. 251-253. Non-circulating. [LC 86013137; ISN 0471819719; $24.95 (est.)]   QA276.12. C69 1987   3649

Statistical methods for business and economics. Roger C. Pfaffenberger, James H. Patterson. 3rd ed. Homewood, Ill.: Irwin, 1987. xiv, 1246 p. : ill. (The Irwin series in quantitative analysis for business) *Notes:* Includes bibliographies and index. [LC 86082595; ISN 0256036640]   QA276.12. P44 1987   3650

Where we stand: can America make it in the global race for wealth, health, and happiness? by Michael Wolff. . . et al. New York: Bantam Books, c1992. xii, 347 p. : ill. (some col.), maps *Notes:* "A Michael Wolff book." Includes index. [LC 91043831; ISN 0553081195; $24.00]   HA155. W46 1992   3651

STEEL INDUSTRY AND TRADE

American steel: hot metal men and the resurrection of the Rust Belt. Richard Preston. 1st ed. New York: Prentice Hall Press, c1991. x, 278 p. [LC 90020230; ISN 013029604X; $19.95]   HD9515. P76 1991   3652

And the wolf finally came: the decline of the American steel industry. John P. Hoerr. Pittsburgh, PA: University of Pittsburgh Press, 1988. xiv, 689 p., [26] p. of plates: ill. (Pittsburgh series in social and labor history) *Notes:* Includes bibliographical references and index. [LC 87024932; ISN 0822935724; ISN 0822953986]   HD9517.M85 H64 1988   3653

The decline of American steel: how management, labor, and government went wrong. Paul A. Tiffany. New York: Oxford University Press, 1988. xiii, 282 p. : ill. *Notes:* Revision of thesis (Ph. D.)—D/University of California at Berkeley. Includes index. Bibliography: p. 257-273. [LC 87005782; ISN 0195043820]   HD9515. T54 1988   3654

Sparrows Point: making steel: the rise and ruin of American industrial might. by Mark Reutter. New York: Summit Books, c1988. 494 p. : map *Notes:* Includes index. Bibliography: p. 443-485. [LC 88024873; ISN 0671553356; $16.63]   HD9518.S6 R48 1988   3655

STOCK INDEX FUTURES

Stock index options: powerful new tools for investing, hedging, and speculating. Donald T. Mesler. Chicago, Ill.: Probus, c1985. xvii, 213 p. : ill. *Notes:* Includes index. Bibliography: p. 197-199. [LC 84011472; ISN 0917253027; $19.95]   HG6043. M47 1985   3656

STOCK MARKET CRASH, 1987

Black Monday and the future of financial markets. Robert J. Barro. . . et al.; edited by Robert W. Kamphuis, Jr., Roger C. Kormendi, and J.W. Henry Watson. Homewood, Ill.: Chicago, Ill.: Dow Jones-Irwin; Mid America Institute for Public Policy Research, Inc., c1989. xiii, 396 p. : ill. *Notes:* Includes bibliographies and index. [LC 88025749; ISN 1556231385; $47.50]   HG4551. B465 1989   3657

Crash: ten days in October—will it strike again? Avner Arbel, Albert E. Kaff. Chicago, Ill.: Longman Financial Services, c1989. xi, 212 p. : ill. [LC 88032078; ISN 0884628434; $27.54]   HG4551. A67 1989   3658

STOCK PRICE INDEXES

The encyclopedia of technical market indicators. Robert W. Colby and Thomas A. Meyers. Homewood, Ill.: Dow Jones-Irwin, c1988. ix, 581 p. : ill. *Notes:* Includes index. [LC 87073023; ISN 1556230494; $50.00]
HG4915. C56 1988   3659

STOCK WARRANTS

Warrants: analysis and investment strategy. Donald T. Mesler. Chicago, Ill.: Probus Pub., 1986. ix, 213 p. : ill. *Notes:* Includes index. Bibliography: p. 205-209. [LC 85025789; ISN 0917253256]
HG4028.S82 M47 1986   3660

STOCK-EXCHANGE

Apocalypse on Wall Street. David McClain. Homewood, Ill.: Dow Jones-Irwin, c1988. xiv, 187 p. : ill. *Notes:* Includes bibliographical references and index. [LC 88009588; ISN 1556231156; $19.95]
HG4551. M44 1988   3661

Asian stockmarkets: the inside story. Anthony Rowley. Homewood, ILL: Dow Jones-Irwin, 1987. 290 p. : ill. *Notes:* Includes index. Bibliography: p. [286]-290.; ISN 9627010294]   HG5705. R68 1987   3662

Dow Theory redux: the classic investment theory revised & updated for the 1990's. Michael D. Sheimo. Chicago, Ill.: Probus Pub. Co., 1989. viii, 176 p. : ill. *Notes:* Includes bibliographical references.; ISN 1557380813; $22.95]
HG4551. S48 1989   3663

The internationalisation of stockmarkets: the trend towards greater foreign borrowing and investment. D.E. Ayling. Aldershot, Hants, England; Brookfield, Vt.: Gower, c1986. xviii, 224 p. *Notes:* Includes bibliographies and index. [LC 85030595; ISN 0566008254; $37.00 (est.)]
HG4551. A95 1986   3664

The Japanese stock market: pricing systems and accounting information. Shigeki Sakakibara. . . et al. New York: Praeger, 1988. xvi, 156 p. : ill. *Notes:* Includes index. Bibliography: p. [141]-150. [LC 88005844; ISN 0275929302]
HG5772. J38 1988   3665

Market making and the changing structure of the securities industry. edited by Yakov Amihud, Thomas S.Y. Ho, Robert A. Schwartz. Lexington, Mass.: Lexington Books, c1985. vii, 318 p. (Lexington Books/Salomon Brothers Center series on financial institutions and markets) *Notes:* Includes bibliographies and index. [LC 83048658; ISN 0669073350]   HG4910. M365 1985   3666

Markets: who plays, who risks, who gains, who loses. Martin Mayer. 1st ed. New York: Norton, c1988. xxxii, 303 p. *Notes:* Includes index. Bibliography: p. 273-279. [LC 88005207; ISN 0393026027; $18.95]
HG4551. M49 1988   3667

Modern stock market handbook. Martin Torosian. Deerfield, Ill.: Financial Associates, c1978. 309 p.]
HG4551. T67   3668

The new encyclopedia of stock market techniques. A. W. Cohen, editor. Larchmont, N.Y.: Investors Intelligence, c1983. 1 v.: ill. *Notes:* Earlier editions published in 1970 under title: The 1971 encyclopedia of stock market techniques and in 1963 under title: Encyclopedia of stock market techniques. Cover title: The encyclopedia of stock techiques. Loose-leaf for updating. [LC 77072870]
HG4521. E55 1983   3669

The New encyclopedia of stock market techniques. A. W. Cohen, editor. Larchmont, N.Y.: Investors Intelligence, c1978. 1 v.: ill. *Notes:* Earlier editions published in 1970 under title: The 1971 encyclopedia of stock market techniques and in 1963 under title: Encyclopedia of stock market techniques. Cover title: The encyclopedia of stock market techiques. Loose-leaf for updating. [LC 77072870]
HG4521. E55 1978   3670

Regulatory reform of stock and futures markets: a special issue of the Journal of financial services research. edited by Franklin R. Edwards. Boston: Kluwer Academic Publ., c1989. 203 p. *Notes:* "Reprinted from the Journal of financial services research, vol. 3, nos. 2/3 (1989)"; ISN 0792390679; $42.50]
HG6049. R45 1989   3671

The SEC and the future of finance. Joel Seligman. New York: Praeger, 1985. xi, 378 p. *Notes:* Includes index. [LC 84018017; ISN 0030697883; $32.95]
KF1070. S43 1985   3672

The stock market. Richard J. Teweles, Edward S. Bradley. 5th ed. New York: Wiley, c1987. xii, 526 p. (Wiley professional banking and finance series, 0733-8945) *Notes:* "A revision of earlier editions by the late George L. Leffler and Loring C. Farwell." Includes bibliographical references and index. [LC 86033950; ISN 047182044X]
HG4551. T48 1987   3673

Stock market anomalies. edited by Elroy Dimson. Cambridge Cambridgeshire; New York: Cambridge University Press, 1988. xii, 295 p. : ill. *Notes:* Includes bibliographical references and index. [LC 87006622; ISN 0521341043]   HG4551. S82 1988   3674

Trading: inside the world's leading stock exchanges. Susan Goldenberg. 1st ed. San Diego: Harcourt Brace Jovanovich, c1986. xi, 263 p. : ill. *Notes:* Includes index. [LC 85017570; ISN 0151910057]   HG4551. G65 1986   3675

Wall Street in transition: the emerging system and its impact on the economy. Henry G. Manne, Ezra Solomon. New York: New York University Press, 1974. 206 p. : ill. *Notes:* Includes bibliographical references. [LC 74015255; ISN 0814753638]   HG4910. M35   +3676

The warning: the coming great crash in the stock market. Joseph Granville. New York, N.Y.: Freundlich Books, 1985. xvi, 397 p. : ill. *Notes:* Includes bibliographical references and index. [LC 85013107; ISN 0881910341; $17.95 (est.)]   HG4910. G76 1985   3677

STOCKBROKERS

Introduction to brokerage operations department procedures. New York Institute of Finance. 2nd ed. New York, N.Y.: New York Institute of Finance, c1988. xiii, 253 p. : ill. *Notes:* Includes index. [LC 88017846; ISN 013478975X; $14.95]   HG4928.5. I57 1988   3678

Stealing the market: how the giant brokerage firms, with help from the SEC, stole the stock market from investors. Martin Mayer. New York, NY: Basic Books, c1992. xi, 208 p. *Notes:* Includes bibliographical references (p. 193-200) and index. [LC 91055600; ISN 0465053629; $23.00]   HG4928.5. M39 1992   3679

The winner's circle: how ten stockbrokers became the best in the business. R.J. Shook & Robert L. Shook. New York: New York Institute of Finance, c1992. x, 230 p. : ill. *Notes:* Includes index. [LC 92004193; ISN 0135875773; $22.95]   HG4928.5. S56 1992   3680

STOCKS

Beating the Street: the best-selling author of One up on Wall Street shows you how to pick winning stocks and develop a strategy for mutual funds. Peter Lynch with John Rothchild. Rev. & updated pbk. ed. New York: Simon & Schuster, c1994. 332 p. : ill. *Notes:* "A Fireside book." Includes index. [LC 94227861; ISN 0671891634; ISN 0671759159; $12.50 ($16.00 Can.)]   HG4921. L96 1994   +3681

The craft of investing. John Train. 1st ed. New York: HarperBusiness, c1994. x, 213 p. : ill. *Notes:* Includes index. [LC 94006856; ISN 0887306268; $22.00 ($31.00 Can.)]   HG4661. T72 1994   +3682

Creating investor demand for company stock: a guide for financial managers. Richard M. Altman. New York: Quorum Books, c1988. xv, 398 p. *Notes:* Includes index. Bibliography: p. 371-385. [LC 86025566; ISN 0899301738]   HG4661. A57 1988   3683

Guide to high-performance investing. by the editors of Investor's Business Daily. Los Angeles, Calif.: O'Neil Data Systems, Inc., 1993. vi, 124 p. : ill., charts *Notes:* Includes index.]   HG4661. G83 1993   +3684

The incredible January effect: the stock market's unsolved mystery. Robert A. Haugen, Josef Lakonishok. Homewood, Ill.: Dow Jones-Irwin, c1988. vii, 135 p. : ill. *Notes:* Includes index. Bibliography: p. 123-132. [LC 87070918; ISN 1556230427]   HG4915. H38 1988   3685

Martin Zweig's Winning on Wall Street. Martin E. Zweig; with the editorial assitance of Morrie Goldfischer. New York, NY: Warner Books, 1986. x, 293 p. : ill. *Notes:* Includes index. [LC 85043167; ISN 0446512346]   HG6049. Z87 1986   3686

The new game on Wall Street. Robert Sobel. New York: Wiley, c1987. xii, 244 p. : ill. *Notes:* Includes index. Bibliography: p. 236-237. [LC 86033986; ISN 0471845272]   HG4921. S6156 1987   3687

The stock market: theories and evidence. James H. Lorie, Peter Dodd, Mary Hamilton Kimpton. 2nd ed. Homewood, Ill.: Dow Jones-Irwin, 1985. xiii, 192 p. : ill. *Notes:* Includes bibliographies and index. [LC 84073043; ISN 0870946188]   HG4661. L67 1985   3688

Trading for a living: psychology, trading tactics, money management. Alexander Elder. New York: J. Wiley, c1993. ix, 289 p. : ill. *Notes:* Includes bibliographical references (p. 275-277) and index. [LC 92035165; ISN 0471592242; $49.95]   HG4661. E43 1993   +3689

What's wrong with Wall Street: short-term gain and the absentee shareholder. by Louis Lowenstein. Reading, Mass.: Addison-Wesley, c1988. xiv, 268 p. : ill. *Notes:* Includes bibliographical references and index. [LC 87033000; ISN 0201171694; $17.95]   HG4521. L853 1988   3690

STRATEGIC ALLIANCES (BUSINESS)

Alliance capitalism: the social organization of Japanese business. Michael L. Gerlach. Berkeley: University of California Press, c1992. xxii, 351 p. : ill. Notes: "Sponsored by the Center for Japanese Studies, University of California, Berkeley"—T.p. verso. Includes bibliographical references (p. 307-327) and indexes. [LC 92016619; ISN 0520076885]   HD69.S8 G47 1992   3691

Winning combinations: the coming wave of entrepreneurial partnerships between large and small companies. by James W. Botkin and Jana B. Matthews. New York: Wiley, c1992. x, 278 p. Notes: Includes bibliographical references and index. [LC 91035792; ISN 047153658X; $24.95]   HD69.S8 B68 1992   3692

STRATEGIC PLANNING

Adding value: a systematic guide to business-driven management and leadership. Gerard Egan; foreword by Bernard F. Brennan. 1st ed. San Francisco: Jossey-Bass, c1993. xxvi, 236 p. : ill. Notes: Includes bibliographical references (p. 225-227) and index. [LC 93002936; ISN 1555425429]   HD30.28. E33 1993   +3693

The art of the long view. Peter Schwartz. 1st ed. New York: Doubleday/Currency, c1991. x, 258 p. Notes: Includes bibliographical references (p. [235]-241) and index. [LC 90020562; ISN 0385267312; $20.00 ($25.00 Can.)]   HD30.28. S37 1991   3694

Business sense: exercising management's five freedoms. Dan Thomas; foreword by Jeffrey M. Wilkins. New York: Toronto: New York: Free Press; Maxwell Macmillan Canada; Maxwell Macmillan International, c1993. xvi, 299 p. : ill. Notes: Includes bibliographical references (p. 277-288) and index. [LC 93018521; ISN 0029324440; $24.95]   HD30.28. T467 1993   3695

Business strategy in practice. Bengt Karlöf; translated by Alan J. Gilderson. Chichester, England; New York: Wiley, c1987. viii, 184 p. : ill. Notes: Translation of: Strategins kärnfragor. Bibliography: p. 183-184. [LC 87010452; ISN 047191620X; $30.00]   HD30.28. K3613 1987   3696

Competing globally through customer value: the management of strategic suprasystems. edited by Michael J. Stahl and Gregory M. Bounds. New York: Quorum Books, 1991. xxiv, 822 p. : ill. Notes: Includes bibliographical references and index. [LC 90026410; ISN 0899306004; $49.95]   HD30.28. C59 1991   3697

Competitive manufacturing: using production as a management tool. Stanley S. Miller. New York: Van Nostrand Reinhold, c1988. ix, 245 p. : ill. Notes: Includes index. Bibliography: p. 236-237 [LC 87010484; ISN 0442263953]   HD30.28. M52 1988   3698

Corporate strategic analysis. Marcus C. Bogue III, Elwood S. Buffa. New York: London: Free Press; Collier Macmillan, c1986. ix, 246 p. : ill. Notes: Includes index. Bibliography: p. 233-239. [LC 86000571; ISN 0029037603]   HD30.28. B64 1986   3699

Corporate strategic planning. Noel Capon, John U. Farley, and James M. Hulbert. New York: Columbia University Press, 1987, c1988. 482 p. : ill. (Columbia studies in business, government, and society) Notes: Includes indexes. Bibliography: p. [441]-465. [LC 87018239; ISN 0231063806]   HD30.28. C375 1988   3700

Designing interactive strategy: from value chain to value constellation. Richard Normann and Rafael Ramírez. Chichester, England; New York: Wiley, c1994. xxiii, 155 p. : ill. Notes: Includes bibliographical references (p. [149]-150) and index. [LC 94007850; ISN 0471950866; $39.95]   HD30.28. N67 1994   +3701

Developing business strategies. David A. Aaker. 3rd ed. New York: Wiley, c1992. xvi, 394 p. : ill. Notes: Includes bibliographical references and index. [LC 91026262; ISN 0471557226; $29.95]   HD30.28. A23 1992   3702

Dynamic planning: the art of managing beyond tomorrow. Beverly Goldberg and John G. Sifonis. New York: Oxford University Press, 1994. xi, 288 p. : ill. Notes: Includes bibliographical references (p. 267-276) and index. [LC 93035402; ISN 0195083083; $25.00]   HD30. G63 1994   +3703

Effective strategic management: analysis and action. Kenneth J. Hatten, Mary Louise Hatten. Englewood Cliffs, N.J.: Prentice Hall, 1988. xiv, 338 p. : ill. Notes: Includes index. Bibliography: p. 315-331. [LC 87020589; ISN 0132452006]   HD30.28. H378 1988   3704

Field guide to strategy: a glossary of essential tools and concepts for today's manager. chief contributor Tim Hindle; edited, with an introduction by Margaret Lawrence. Boston, Mass.: Harvard Business School Press, c1994. xi, 225 p. [LC 93026047; ISN 0875844316; $16.95]   HD30.28. H553 1994   +3705

Fundamental issues in strategy: a research agenda. edited by Richard P. Rumelt, Dan Schendel, David J. Teece. Boston, Mass.: Harvard Business School Press, c1994. xiii, 636 p. : ill. *Notes:* Includes bibliographical references and index. [LC 93038541; ISN 0875843433; $45.00]
HD30.28. F86 1994 +3706

Handbook of strategic management. edited by Jack Rabin, Gerald J. Miller, W. Bartley Hildreth. New York: M. Dekker, c1989. xxiv, 457 p. : ill. *Notes:* Includes bibliographical references. [LC 89034742; ISN 0824780892; $165.00]
HD30.28. H3664 1989 3707

Implanting strategic management. H. Igor Ansoff and Edward J. McDonnell. 2nd ed. New York: Prentice Hall, 1990. xxi, 520 p. : ill. *Notes:* Includes bibliographical references. [LC 89037248; ISN 0134519159; $53.33]
HD30.28. A534 1990 3708

Jumping the curve: innovation and strategic choice in an age of transition. Nicholas Imparato and Oren Harari; foreword by Tom Peters. 1st ed. San Francisco: Jossey-Bass, c1994. xxv, 324 p. : ill. *Notes:* Includes bibliographical references and index. [LC 94025578; ISN 1555427057]
HD30.28. I45 1994 +3709

Knowledge-based systems for strategic planning. Robert J. Mockler. Englewood Cliffs, NJ: Prentice-Hall, 1989. xvi, 396 p. : ill. *Notes:* Includes index. Bibliography: p. 378-381.; ISN 0135169151]
HD30.28. M62 1989 3710

The management of strategic change. edited by Andrew M. Pettigrew. Oxford Oxfordshire; New York, NY: B. Blackwell, 1988, c1987. vi, 370 p. : ill. *Notes:* Based on the proceedings of an international research seminar held under the auspices of the Centre for Corporate Strategy and Change at Warwick University, Coventry, England, in May 1986. Includes bibliographies and index. [LC 87015634; ISN 063115695X; $45.00 (U.S.)]
HD30.28. M359 1988 3711

Managing strategy in the real world: conclusions and frameworks from field studies of business practice. R. Jeffery Ellis; foreword by Robert J. Allio. Lexington, Mass.: Lexington Books, c1988. xviii, 340 p. : ill. *Notes:* Includes bibliographies and indexes. [LC 87004259; ISN 0669158984]
HD30.28. E45 1988 3712

Managing with dual strategies: mastering the present, preempting the future. Derek F. Abell. New York: Toronto: New York: Free Press; Maxwell Macmillan Canada; Maxwell Macmillan International, c1993. xi, 292 p. : ill. *Notes:* Includes bibliographical references (p. 281-286) and index. [LC 93008016; ISN 0029001455; $29.95]
HD30.28. A243 1993 3713

The new corporate strategy. H. Igor Ansoff assisted by Edward J. McDonnell. New York: Wiley, 1988. xviii, 258 p. : ill. *Notes:* Rev. ed. of: Corporate strategy. 1965. Includes indexes. Bibliography: p. 243-245. [LC 87023266; ISN 0471629502]
HD30.28. A535 1988 3714

The outline of strategy. William C. Waddell. Oxford, Ohio: Planning Forum, c1986. x, 150 p. : ill. (Education series) *Notes:* Includes bibliographical references.; ISN 0912841222]   HD30.28. W32 3715

Planning strategies that work. edited by Arnoldo C. Hax. New York: Oxford University Press, 1987. xii, 287 p. : ill. (The executive bookshelf, Sloan management review.) *Notes:* Includes index. Bibliography: p. 252-275. [LC 86031117; ISN 0195048830]
HD30.28. P57 1987 3716

The portable MBA in strategy. edited by Liam Fahey, Robert Randall. New York: Wiley & Sons, 1994. xii, 484 p. : ill. *Notes:* Includes bibliographical references index. [LC 94004475; ISN 0471584983]
HD30.28. P674 1994 +3717

The practical strategist: business and corporate strategy for the 1990s. Robert J. Allio. Cambridge, Mass.: Ballinger Pub. Co., c1988. xiv, 212 p. : ill. *Notes:* Includes bibliographies and index. [LC 88024200; ISN 0887303196]
HD30.28. A384 1988 3718

Readings in strategic management. Arthur A. Thompson, Jr., William E. Fulmer, A.J. Stickland III. 3rd ed. Homewood, IL: BPI/Irwin, c1990. xi, 511 p. : ill. *Notes:* Includes bibliographical references. [LC 89037683; ISN 0256082804; $24.50]
HD30.28. R418 1990 3719

The rise and fall of strategic planning: reconceiving roles for planning, plans, planners. Henry Mintzberg. New York: Toronto: Free Press; Maxwell Macmillan Canada, c1994. xix, 458 p. : ill. *Notes:* Includes bibliographical references (p. [417]-443) and index. [LC 93027323; ISN 0029216052; $29.95]
HD30.28. M56 1994 +3720

Running American business: top CEOs rethink their major decisions. Robert Boyden Lamb. New York: Basic Books, c1987. x, 315 p. *Notes:* Includes indexes. Bibliography: p. 305-307. [LC 86047732; ISN 0465071503; $17.95]
HD30.28. L355 1987 3721

Step-by-step competitive strategy. Dave Francis. London; New York: Routledge, 1994. x, 183 p. : ill. *Notes:* Includes bibliographical references (p. 177-181) and index. "...Cover[s] crucial skills such as: teambuilding, industry analysis, scenario planning, competitor analysis, idea generation, systematic visioning"—Back cover. [LC 93042359; ISN 0415086981]   HD30.28. F716 1994 +3722

Strategic choices: supremacy, survival, or sayonara. Kenneth I. Primozic, Edward A. Primozic, Joe Leben. New York: McGraw-Hill, c1991. xvi, 272 p. : ill. *Notes:* Includes bibliographical references. [LC 90036642; ISN 0070510369; $24.95]
HD30.28. P75 1991 3723

Strategic control systems. Peter Lorange, Michael F. i.e. S.Scott Morton, Sumantra Goshal. St. Paul: West Pub. Co., c1986. xix, 196 p. : ill. (West series in strategic management) *Notes:* Cover title: Strategic control. Includes index. Bibliography: p. 177-189. [LC 86001315; ISN 0314852581; $15.95] HD30.28. L673 1986   3724

Strategic management: analysis and action. Kenneth J. Hatten, Mary Louise Hatten. Englewood Cliffs, N.J.: Prentice-Hall, c1987. xiv, 1041 p. : ill. *Notes:* Includes index. Bibliography: p. 315-331. [LC 86030453; ISN 0138506949] HD30.28. H384 1987   3725

The strategic management blueprint. Paul Dobson and Ken Starkey. Oxford, UK; Cambridge, Mass., USA: Blackwell Business, 1993. xi, 161 p. : ill. *Notes:* Includes bibliographical references (p. [154]-157) and index. [LC 92031273; ISN 0631186247; $24.95] HD30.28. D62 1993   +3726

Strategic management: formulation and implementation: concepts and cases. Lloyd L. Byars. 3rd ed. New York, NY: HarperCollins Publishers, c1991. xxv, 995, A-10 p. : ill. *Notes:* Rev. ed. of: Strategic management: planning and implementation. 2nd ed. c1987. Includes bibliographical references and index. [LC 90044501; ISN 0060410981; $54.29] HD30.28. B9 1991   3727

Strategic management in public and nonprofit organizations: thinking and acting strategically on public concerns. Jack Koteen. New York: Praeger, 1989. xvii, 227 p. *Notes:* Includes index. Bibliography: p. [219]-221. [LC 89033971; ISN 0275933237; $45.00] HD30.28. K67 1989   3728

Strategic management: text and cases. Peter Wright, Charles D. Pringle, Mark J. Kroll, with contributions by John A. Parnell. 2nd ed. Boston: Allyn and Bacon, c1994. xv, 1022 p. : ill. *Notes:* Includes bibliographical references and index. [LC 93005124; ISN 0205148840; $40.00] HD30.28. W75 1994   +3729

Strategic organization planning: downsizing for survival. David C. Dougherty; foreword by John B. Joynt. New York: Quorum Books, 1989. xviii, 253 p. : ill. *Notes:* Includes index. Bibliography: p. [241]-243. [LC 88011355; ISN 0899303390; $45.00] HD30.28. D68 1989   3730

Strategic planning and management control: systems for survival and success. John C. Camillus. Lexington, Mass.: Lexington Books, c1986. xii, 255 p. : ill. *Notes:* Includes bibliographical references and index. [LC 85040001; ISN 0669103152] HD30.28. C353 1986   3731

Strategic planning and management handbook. edited by William R. King and David I. Cleland. New York: Van Nostrand Reinhold Co., c1987. xii, 644 p. : ill. *Notes:* Includes bibliographies and index. [LC 86009058; ISN 0442247311] HD30.28. S727   3732

Strategic planning: models and analytical techniques. articles selected by Robert G. Dyson. Chichester, West Sussex, England; New York: Wiley, c1990. vi, 313 p. : ill. *Notes:* Includes bibliographical references. [LC 89037612; ISN 0471924911; $49.35] HD30.28. S7265 1990   3733

Strategic planning plus: an organizational guide. Roger Kaufman. Newbury Park, Calif.: Sage, c1992. xxii, 317 p. : ill. *Notes:* Includes bibliographical references and index. [LC 92017898; ISN 0803948042] HD30.28. K38 1992   +3734

Strategic planning: selected readings. edited by J. William Pfeiffer. Rev. San Diego: Pfeiffer, c1991. xxxix, 407 p. *Notes:* Includes bibliographical references (p. 385-403). [LC 91061277; ISN 0883902966; $34.95] HD30.28. S728 1991   3735

Strategic planning workbook. Karsten G. Hellebust, Joseph C. Krallinger. New York: J. Wiley, c1989. x, 331 p. : ill. *Notes:* Includes index. [LC 88017206; ISN 0471620424] HD30.28. H398 1989   3736

Strategic thinking: leadership and the management of change. edited by John Hendry and Gerry Johnson with Julia Newton. Chichester; New York: J. Wiley, 1993. xix, 350 p. : ill. *Notes:* Includes bibliographical references and index. [LC 93007087; ISN 0471939900] HD30.28. S73523 1993   +3737

The strategist CEO: how visionary executives build organizations. Michel Robert. New York: Quorum Books, c1988. viii, 140 p. : ill. *Notes:* Includes index. Bibliography: p. [135]-138. [LC 87010945; ISN 0899302688] HD30.28. R63 1988   3738

The strategy concept and process: a pragmatic approach. Arnoldo C. Hax, Nicolas S. Majluf. Englewood Cliffs, N.J.: Prentice-Hall, 1991. xv, 430 p. : ill. *Notes:* Bibliography: p. 396-403. [LC 90044239; ISN 0138521468; $25.50] HD30.28. H3885 1991   3739

Strategy formulation: power and politics. Ian C. MacMillan, Patricia E. Jones. 2nd ed. St. Paul: West Pub. Co., c1986. xv, 160 p. (The West series in strategic management) *Notes:* Includes index. Bibliography: p. 153-155. [LC 85020389; ISN 0314852603; $15.95] HD30.28. M283 1986   3740

The strategy process: concepts and contexts. Henry Mintzberg and James Brian Quinn. Englewood Cliffs, N.J.: Prentice Hall, c1992. xvi, 480 p. : ill. *Notes:* Adapted from: The strategy process: concepts, contexts, cases / Henry Mintzberg and James Brian Quinn. 2nd ed. c1991. Includes bibliographical references (p. 460-468) and indexes. [LC 91040954; ISN 013855370X] HD30.28. Q52 1992   3741

The strategy process: concepts, contexts, cases. Henry Mintzberg and James Brian Quinn. 2nd ed. Englewood Cliffs, N.J.: Prentice Hall, c1991. xix, 1083 p. : ill. (some col.), maps *Notes:* Quinn's name appears first on the earlier ed. Includes bibliographical references (p. 1051-1059) and index. [LC 90020781; ISN 0138519161] HD30.28. Q53 1991   3742

Strategy: seeking and securing competitive advantage. edited, with an introduction by Cynthia A. Montgomery and Michael E. Porter. Boston: Harvard Business School Press, c1991. xxiii, 475 p. : ill. *Notes:* Includes bibliographical references and index. [LC 91012193; ISN 0875842437; $29.95] HD30.28. S7397 1991   3743

Strategy traps and how to avoid them. Robert A. Stringer, Jr. with Joel L. Uchenick. Lexington, Mass.: Lexington Books, 1986. viii, 207 p. : ill. *Notes:* Bibliography: p. [208]. [LC 84048444; ISN 0669093629] HD30.28. S78   3744

The strategy-led business: step-by-step planning for your company's future. Kerry Napuk. London; New York: McGraw-Hill, c1993. xii, 224 p. : ill. *Notes:* Includes bibliographical references (p. [217]) and index. [LC 93000982; ISN 007707775X; £19.95] HD30.28. N383 1993   +3745

Successful business strategy: how to win in the market place. Len Hardy. London: Kogan Page, 1987. ix,253 p. : ill *Notes:* Includes index. [LC 86028550; ISN 1850911746; £14.95 (Nov.)] HD30.28. H3644   3746

Thinking strategically: the competitive edge in business, politics, and everyday life. by Avinash K. Dixit and Barry J. Nalebuff. 1st ed. New York: Norton, 1991. xi, 393 p. : ill. *Notes:* Includes bibliographical references and index. [LC 90033760; ISN 0393029239; $24.95] HD30.28. D59 1991   3747

The twilight of corporate strategy: a comparative ethical critique. Daniel R. Gilbert, Jr. New York: Oxford University Press, 1992. xx, 244 p. *Notes:* Includes bibliographical references (p. 183-237) and index. [LC 91035656; ISN 019506514X] HD30.28. G53 1992   3748

Writers on strategy and strategic management: the theory of strategy and the practice of strategic management at enterprise, corporate, business and functional levels. J.I. Moore. London; New York: Penguin Books, 1992. xv, 311 p. : ill. (Penguin business) *Notes:* Includes selections by Kenneth R. Andrews, Alfred D. Chandler, Jr., Michael E. Porter, Robert D. Buzzell, Joseph L. Bower, Richard G. Hamermesh, Malcolm S. Salter, many others. Includes bibliographical references and indexes. [LC 93160551; ISN 0140139850; £7.99 ($12.00 U.S.A.)] HD30.28. M6453 1992   +3749

STRUCTURAL ADJUSTMENT (ECONOMIC POLICY)

Industry in Poland: structural adjustment issues and policy options. Paris: Washington, D.C.: Organisation for Economic Co-operation and Development: Centre for Co-operation with the European Economies in Transition; OECD Publications and Information Centre, distributor, 1992. 184 p. : ill., maps *Notes:* "Prepared by Jean Guinet... and Alica Amsden"—Foreword. Includes bibliographical references.; ISN 9264137556; $44.00] HC340.3. G84 1992   3750

SUBCHAPTER S CORPORATIONS

Starting your subchapter "S" corporation: how to build a business the right way. Arnold S. Goldstein. New York: Wiley, c1988. x, 182 p. : forms *Notes:* Includes index. [LC 87030260; ISN 0471606022; ISN 0471606049; $39.95] KF6491. G65 1988   3751

SUCCESS

Dave says well done!: the common guy's guide to everyday success. Dave Thomas with Ron Beyma. Grand Rapids, Mich.: Zondervan Pub. House, c1994. 224 p., [16] p. of plates: ill. *Notes:* Includes bibliographical references and index. [LC 94021184; ISN 0310480000; $18.99] BJ1611.2. T47 1994   +3752

How to get to the top... and stay there. Robert J. McKain. New York: AMACOM, c1981. 210 p. : ill. *Notes:* Sequel to: Realize your potential, 1975. Includes bibliographical references and index. [LC 80067964; ISN 0814456537] HF5386. M195   3753

Letters of a businessman to his son. G. Kingsley Ward. Toronto: Totem, 1987, c1985. 225 p. [LC 87094020; ISN 000217748X; $4.95] HF5386. W22 1987   3754

The paradox of success: when winning at work means losing at life: a book of renewal for leaders. by John R. O'Neil. New York: G.P. Putnam's Sons, c1993. 270 p. : ill. *Notes:* "A Jeremy P. Tarcher/Putnam book." Includes index. [LC 92026057; ISN 0874777070] BF637.S8 O545 1993   3755

Principle-centered leadership. Stephen R. Covey. New York: Summit Books, c1991. 334 p. : ill. *Notes:* Includes index. [LC 91028078; ISN 0671749102]   BF637.S8 C67 1991   3756

Tactics: the art and science of success. Edward de Bono. 1st American ed. Boston: Little, Brown, c1984. xi, 228 p. *Notes:* Includes index. [LC 84016384; ISN 0316177903]   BF637.S8 D365 1984   3757

SUCCESS IN BUSINESS

Built to last: successful habits of visionary companies. James C. Collins, Jerry I. Porras. 1st ed. New York: HarperBusiness, c1994. xiv, 322 p. : ill. *Notes:* Includes bibliograpical references and index. [LC 94020571; ISN 0887306713; $25.00]   HF5386. C735 1994   +3758

Company manners: an insider tells how to succeed in the real world of corporate protocol and power politics. Lois Wyse. New York: McGraw-Hill, c1987. viii, 291 p. [LC 86007394; ISN 0070721939]   HF5386. W97 1987   3759

Company manners: how to behave in the workplace in the '90s. Lois Wyse. 1st ed. New York: Crown Trade Paperbacks, c1992. viii, 243 p. *Notes:* Includes index. [LC 92016435; ISN 0517880199; $12.00]   HF5386. W97 1992   3760

Confessions of a street-smart manager. David Mahoney with Richard Conarroe; introduction by William Safire. New York: Simon and Schuster, c1988. 191 p. [LC 87026374; ISN 0671625365]   HF5386. M292 1988   3761

Doing business boldly: the art of taking intelligent risks. by Daniel Kehrer. New York, N.Y.: Times Books, 1989. 341 p. *Notes:* Includes bibliographical references and index. [LC 88040162; ISN 0812913124; $19.95]   HF5386. K267 1989   3762

Entrepreneur: from zero to hero: how to be a blockbuster entrepreneur. Charles Banfe. New York: Van Nostrand Reinhold, c1991. xviii, 206 p. : ill. *Notes:* Includes indexes. [LC 90020479; ISN 0442239610; $14.95]   HF5386. B2294 1991   3763

Every street is paved with gold: the road to real success. Kim Woo-Choong; introduction by Louis Kraar. 1st ed. New York: Morrow, c1992. 254 p. *Notes:* Translation of: Segue nŭn nŏlko hal il ŭn mant'a. [LC 92000266; ISN 0688113273; $20.00]   HF5386. K54 1992   3764

The great American success story: factors that affect achievement. George Gallup, Jr., Alec M. Gallup with William Proctor. Homewood, Ill.: Dow Jones-Irwin, c1986. xii, 244 p. : charts *Notes:* Includes index. [LC 85072469; ISN 0870946013]   HF5386. G34   3765

Mark my words: letters of a businessman to his son. G. Kingsley Ward. Rev. ed. New York: Prentice Hall Press, c1986. xiv, 194 p. *Notes:* "First Prentice Hall Press edition." [LC 85030047; ISN 0135315182; $15.95]   HF5386. W23 1986   3766

Mentoring at work: developmental relationships in organizational life. Kathy E. Kram. Glenview, Ill.: Scott, Foresman, c1985. xiii, 252 p. (Organizational behavior and psychology series) *Notes:* Includes index. Bibliography: p. 232-242. [LC 84013945; ISN 0673156176; $8.95]   HF5386. K78 1985   3767

Peak performers: the new heroes of American business. Charles Garfield. 1st ed. New York: W. Morrow, c1986. 333 p. *Notes:* Includes index. Bibliography: p. 305-318. [LC 85021711; ISN 0688042430]   HF5386. G216 1986   3768

Rising stars and fast fades: successes and failures of fast-growth companies. W. Keith Schilit. New York: Toronto: New York: Lexington Books; Maxwell Macmillan Canada; Maxwell Macmillan International, c1994. xii, 244 p. *Notes:* Includes bibliographical references and index. *Contents:* Pt. 1. The fast-growth companies. Fast growth—The impact of fast growth—High-tech growth—Low-tech growth—Pt. 2. Characteristics of successful fast-growth companies. Nichemanship—Sustainable competitive advantage—Superior product/service quality—Innovativeness—Strong cultural foundation—Valued customers, valued employees—Quality management—Venture capital support. [LC 93040135; ISN 0029278929; $22.95]   HF5386. S384 1994   +3769

Take a chance to be first: the secrets of entrepreneurial success. Warren Avis. New York: Macmillan, c1986. xii, 222 p. *Notes:* Includes index. [LC 86002948; ISN 0025044109]   HF5386. A94 1986   3770

Tribes: how race, religion, and identity determine success in the new global economy. Joel Kotkin. 1st ed. New York: Random House, 1993, c1992. xv, 343 p. *Notes:* Includes bibliographical references (p. 263-329) and index. [LC 92053638; ISN 0679412824; $24.00 ($30.00 Can.)]   HF5386. K776 1993   3771

What they still don't teach you at Harvard Business School: more notes from a street-smart executive. Mark H. McCormack. New York, N.Y.: Bantam Books, 1989. xiv, 298 p. [LC 89015097; ISN 0553057480; $18.95]   HF5386. M474 1989   3772

Working scared: achieving success in trying times. Kenneth N. Wexley, Stanley B. Silverman. 1st ed. San Francisco: Jossey-Bass, c1993. xvi, 190 p. : ill. *Notes:* Includes bibliographical references and index. [LC 92039967; ISN 1555425127]   HF5386. W456 1993   3773

SUGGESTION SYSTEMS

Kaizen teian 1: developing systems for continuous improvement through employee suggestions. edited by the Japan Human Relations Association; foreword by Peter B. Grazier; publisher's message by Norman Bodek. Cambridge, Mass.: Productivity Press, 1992. xvi, 201 p. : ill. *Notes:* Originally published: Tokyo: Nikkan Kogyo Shimbun, 1989. Includes index. [LC 91026612; ISN 0915299895]   HF5549.5.S8 K3513 1992   3774

Kaizen teian 2 =. Guiding continuous improvement through employee suggestions. edited by the Japan Human Relations Association; foreword by Linda Topolsky; publisher's message by Norman Bodek. Cambridge, Mass.: Productivity Press, c1992. xxiv, 197 p. : ill. *Notes:* Includes index. [LC 91046259; ISN 0915299534]   HF5549.5.S8 K3514 1992   +3775

SUPERCOMPUTERS

Supercomputers: a key to U.S. scientific, technological, and industrial preeminence. edited by J.R. Kirkland and J.H. Poore. New York: Praeger, 1987. xxiii, 242 p. : ill. *Notes:* Includes index. Bibliography: p. [217]-227. [LC 87011808; ISN 0275926222; $29.85 (est.)]   QA76.5. S89474 1987   3776

Supercomputers of today and tomorrow: the parallel processing revolution. Richard A. Jenkins. 1st ed. Blue Ridge Summit, PA: Tab Books, c1986. ix, 213 p., [2] p. of plates: ill. (some col.) *Notes:* Includes index. [LC 85027639; ISN 0830604227; ISN 0830603220; $21.95; $14.95]   QA76.5. J445 1986   3777

SUPERVISION OF EMPLOYEES

The AMA handbook of supervisory management. Florence M. Stone, editor. New York, N.Y.: American Management Association, 1989. ix, 550 p. : ill. *Notes:* Includes index. Includes bibliographical references. [LC 89045457; ISN 0814459722; $49.95]   HF5549. A85 1989   3778

First-line management: approaching supervision effectively. Lawrence L. Steinmetz, H. Ralph Todd, Jr. 4th ed. Plano, Tex.: Business Publications, 1986. xv, 429 p. : ill. *Notes:* Includes index. [LC 85073700; ISN 0256033765]   HF5549. S84286 1986   3779

The first-time manager. Loren B. Belker. 3rd ed. New York: American Management Association, c1993. xii, 196 p. *Notes:* Includes index. [LC 92033135; ISN 0814478026]   HF5549. B355 1993   3780

The human resource problem-solver's handbook. Joseph D. Levesque. New York: McGraw-Hill, c1992. 1 v. (various pagings): ill. *Notes:* Includes bibliographical references and indexes. [LC 91031233; ISN 0070375313; $59.95]   HF5549.12. L49 1992   3781

Improving supervisors' effectiveness. Jack J. Phillips. 1st ed. San Francisco: Jossey-Bass Publishers, 1985. xxiv, 421 p. : ill. (The Jossey-Bass management series) *Notes:* Includes index. Bibliography: p. 403-410. [LC 84043032; ISN 0875896472]   HF5549. P459 1985   3782

Managing the new careerists. C. Brooklyn Derr. 1st ed. San Francisco: Jossey-Bass, c1986. xxii, 288 p. (Jossey-Bass management series) (Jossey-Bass social and behavioral science series) *Notes:* Includes index. Bibliography: p. 277-282. [LC 85045901; ISN 0875896774]   HF5549.2.U5 D47 1986   3783

Supervision in action: the art of managing others. Claude S. George, Jr. 4th ed. Reston, Va.: Reston Pub. Co., c1985. viii, 424 p. : ill. *Notes:* Includes bibliographical references and index. [LC 84013397; ISN 0835971600; $23.95]   HF5549. G427 1985   3784

SWORDPLAY

The way and the power: secrets of Japanese strategy. Fredrick J. Lovret. Boulder, Co.: Paladin Press, 1987. x, 314 p. : ill.; ISN 0873644093]   GV1148. L68 1987   3785

SYSTEM ANALYSIS

Dealing with complexity: an introduction to the theory and application of systems science. Robert L. Flood and Ewart R. Carson. New York: Plenum Press, c1988. xv, 289 p. : ill. *Notes:* Includes index. Bibliography: p. 277-283. [LC 87029814; ISN 030642715X]   QA402. F55 1988   3786

TAGUCHI METHODS (QUALITY CONTROL)

Quality up, costs down: a manager's guide to Taguchi methods and QFD. edited by William E. Eureka, Nancy E. Ryan. Dearborn, Mich.: Burr Ridge, Ill.: ASI Press; Irwin Professional Pub., c1995. xii, 224 p. : ill. *Notes:* Rev. ed. of: Taguchi methods and QFD. c1988. Includes bibliographical references (p. 215-218) and index. [LC 94014951; ISN 0786302186]   TS156. T344 1995   +3787

Taguchi on robust technology development: bringing quality engineering upstream. by Genichi Taguchi; translated by Shih-Chung Tsai. New York: ASME Press, 1993. xvi, 136 p. : ill. *Notes:* Includes index. [LC 92030947; ISN 0791800288]   TS156. T342 1993   3788

TARBELL, IDA M

Ida Tarbell: portrait of a muckraker. Kathleen Brady. Pittsburgh, Pa.: University of Pittsburgh Press, 1989. 286 p. : ill. *Notes:* Originally published: New York: Seaview/Putnam, c1984. Includes index. Bibliography: p. [271]-278. [LC 89040207; ISN 0822958074]   PN4874.T23 B7 1989   +3789

TARIFF

Trade-offs: negotiating the Omnibus Trade and Competitiveness Act. Susan C. Schwab. Boston: Harvard Business School Press, c1994. xii, 275 p. *Notes:* Includes bibliographical references (p. 229-239) and index. [LC 94010392; ISN 087584510X]   KF6659. S39 1994   +3790

TAXATION

Comparative tax systems: Europe, Canada, and Japan. Joseph A. Pechman, editor; contributing authors, Krister Andersson... et al. Arlington, Va.: Tax Analysts, 1987. xiv, 447 p. : ill. *Notes:* Includes bibliographies and index. *Contents:* Introduction / by Joseph A. Pechman—Sweden / by Krister Andersson—Netherlands / by Flip de Kam—France / by Jean-Louis Lienard, Kenneth C. Messere, and Jeffrey Owens—Italy / by Laura Castellucci—Federal Republic of Germany / by Annette Dengel; translated by Birgit Schneider—United Kingdom / by Nick Morris—Canada / by Harry M. Kitchen—Japan / by M. Homma, T. Maeda, and K. Hashimoto. [LC 87050143; ISN 0918255058; $14.95]   HJ2599.5. C65 1987   3791

The growth experiment: how the new tax policy is transforming the U.S. economy. Lawrence Lindsey. New York: Basic Books, c1990. 260 p. : ill. *Notes:* Includes bibliographical references (p. [241]-253) and index. [LC 89043100; ISN 0465027504; $21.95 ($29.95 Can.)]   HJ2381. L53 1990   3792

TAYLOR, FREDERICK WINSLOW

Frederick W. Taylor, the father of scientific management: myth and reality. Charles D. Wrege, Ronald G. Greenwood. Homewood, Ill.: Business One Irwin, c1991. xiii, 286 p. [16] p. of plates: ill. *Notes:* Includes bibliographical references (p. 261-278) and index. [LC 91008345; ISN 1556235011; $29.95]   T55.85.T38 W74 1991   3793

TECHNICAL EDUCATION

Training the technical work force. Anthony P. Carnevale, Leila J. Gainer, Eric R. Schulz. 1st ed. San Francisco: Jossey-Bass Publishers, 1990. xxii, 196 p. *Notes:* Includes bibliographical references (p. 189-191) and index. [LC 89048806; ISN 1555422012; $24.95]   T65. C38 1990   3794

TECHNOLOGICAL INNOVATIONS

The breakthrough illusion: corporate America's failure to move from innovation to mass production. Richard Florida and Martin Kenney. New York, NY: BasicBooks, c1990. x, 262 p. : ill., map *Notes:* Includes bibliographical references (p. 205-251) and index. [LC 90080248; ISN 046500749X; $19.95 ($26.95 Can.)]   HC110.T4 F57 1990   3795

The change masters: innovations for productivity in the American corporation. Rosabeth Moss Kanter. New York: Simon and Schuster, c1983. 432 p. *Notes:* Includes bibliographical references and index. [LC 83004781; ISN 0671428020]   HD45. K335 1983   3796

Decline and prosperity: corporate innovation in Japan. Noboru Makino. 1st ed. Tokyo; New York: New York, N.Y.: Kodansha International; Distributed in the United States by Kodansha International/USA Ltd., through Harper & Row, 1987. 206 p. : ill. *Notes:* Translation of: Suibō to han'ei. Original title appears on verso as: Han'ei to suibō. [LC 86040434; ISN 4770013108; ISN 0870118102; ¥2900; $19.95]   HC465.T4 M35313 1987   3797

Design and innovation: policy and management. edited by Richard Langdon and Roy Rothwell. New York: St. Martin's Press, 1985. xxi, 208 p. : ill. *Notes:* Includes bibliographical references. [LC 85026109; ISN 031219448X; $25.00]   T173.8. D47 1985   3798

The effective management of technology: a challenge for corporations. Sushil K. Bhalla. Columbus Ohio: Reading, Mass.: Battelle Press; Distributed by Addison-Wesley Pub. Co., c1987. xiii, 205 p. : ill. *Notes:* Includes bibliographies and index. [LC 86025847; ISN 0201109298; $22.50]   HD45. B47 1987   3799

Favorites of fortune: technology, growth, and economic development since the Industrial Revolution. edited by Patrice Higonnet, David S. Landes, Henry Rosovsky. Cambridge, Mass.: Harvard University Press, 1991. viii, 558 p. *Notes:* Includes bibliographical references and index. [LC 91012249; ISN 067429520X; $45.00]   HC79.T4 F38 1991   3800

Generating technological innovation. edited by Edward B. Roberts. New York: Oxford University Press, 1987. xii, 299 p. : ill. (The Executive bookshelf) *Notes:* A selection of articles from the Sloan management review. Includes index. Bibliography.: p. 264-285. [LC 86033119; ISN 0195050231]   HD45. G39 1987   3801

Global corporate alliances and the competitive edge: strategies and tactics for management. Martin K. Starr. New York: Quorum Books, 1991. xii, 235 p. : ill. *Notes:* Includes bibliographical references (p. [223]-224) and index. [LC 91008725; ISN 0899305865]   HD45. S753 1991   3802

Industrial product innovation: organisation and management. F.A. Johne. London: New York: C. Helm; Nichols Pub., 1985. 177 p. : ill. *Notes:* Includes index. Bibliography: p. 167-174. [LC 85013580; ISN 0893972339; $29.50]   T173.8. J64 1985   3803

Industrial renaissance: producing a competitive future for America. William J. Abernathy, Kim B. Clark, Alan M. Kantrow. New York: Basic Books, c1983. xii, 194 p. : ill. *Notes:* Includes bibliographical references and index. [LC 82072391; ISN 0465032540; $19.00]   HC110.T4 A58 1983   3804

Innovation and growth in the global economy. Gene M. Grossman and Elhanan Helpman. Cambridge, Mass.: MIT Press, c1991. xiv, 359 p. : ill. *Notes:* Includes bibliographical references (p. [343]-350) and index. [LC 91015795; ISN 0262570971; ISN 0262071363]   HC79.T4 G697 1991   3805

Innovation: the attacker's advantage. Richard N. Foster. New York: Summit Books, c1986. 316 p. : ill. *Notes:* Includes index. Bibliography: p. 287-299. [LC 86001945; ISN 0671622501]   HD45. F67 1986   3806

The innovators: the discoveries, inventions, and breakthroughs of our time. John Diebold. 1st ed. New York: Dutton, c1990. xiii, 303 p., [18] p. of plates: ill. *Notes:* "Truman Talley books." Includes index. Bibliography: p. 285-286. [LC 89034510; ISN 0525248307; $19.95]   T173.8. D54 1990   3807

Inside corporate innovation: strategy, structure, and managerial skills. Robert A. Burgelman, Leonard R. Sayles. New York: London: Free Press; Collier-Macmillan, c1986. viii, 216 p. : ill. *Notes:* Includes index. Bibliography: p. 201-212. [LC 85015846; ISN 0029043409]   HD45. B798 1986   3808

Keeping America at work: strategies for employing the new technologies. Robert T. Lund, John A. Hansen. New York: Wiley, c1986. xi, 260 p. *Notes:* Includes index. Bibliography: p. 251-255. [LC 85017900; ISN 0471815632]   HD45. L86 1986   3809

The lever of riches: technological creativity and economic progress. Joel Mokyr. New York: Oxford University Press, 1990. ix, 349 p. : ill. *Notes:* Includes bibliographical references (p. [305]-328) and index. [LC 89028298; ISN 0195061136; $24.95]   HC79.T4 M648 1990   3810

Managing innovation and entrepreneurship in technology-based firms. Michael J.C. Martin. New York: J. Wiley, c1994. xiv, 402 p. : ill. *Notes:* Rev. ed. of: Managing technological innovation and entrepreneurship. c1984. "A Wiley-Interscience publication." [LC 93036588; ISN 0471572195; $25.00]   HD45. M35 1994   +3811

Managing innovation: from the executive suite to the shop floor. John S. Rydz. Cambridge, Mass.: Ballinger Pub. Co., c1986. xv, 182 p. : ill. *Notes:* Includes bibliographical references and index. [LC 86001156; ISN 0887300286]   HD45. R93 1986   3812

Managing the dynamics of new technology: issues in manufacturing management. Hamid Noori. Englewood Cliffs, N.J.: Prentice Hall, 1990. xvi, 383 p. : ill. *Notes:* Includes bibliographies and index. [LC 89003860; ISN 013551763X; $43.20]   HD45. N63 1990   3813

Mass customization: the new frontier in business competition. B. Joseph Pine II; foreword by Stan Davis. Boston, Mass.: Harvard Business School Press, 1992, c1993. xxi, 333 p. : ill. *Notes:* Includes bibliographical references (p. 301-322) and index. [LC 92017506; ISN 0875843727; $29.95]
HD45. P537 1992   3814

Mastering technology: a management framework for getting results. Rod F. Monger. New York: London: Free Press; Collier Macmillan, c1988. x, 310 p. : ill. *Notes:* Includes index. Bibliography: p. 301-305. [LC 88002810; ISN 002921680X]   HD45. M66 1988   3815

New technology as organizational innovation: the development and diffusion of microelectronics. edited by Johannes M. Pennings and Arend Buitendam. Cambridge, Mass.: Ballinger Pub. Co., c1987. xvi, 308 p. : ill. (Ballinger series on the management of innovation and change) *Notes:* Includes bibliographies and index. [LC 86032110; ISN 088730186X]   HD45. N43 1987   3816

Perpetual innovation: the new world of competition. Don E. Kash. New York: Basic Books, c1989. xi, 269 p. : ill. *Notes:* Includes bibliographical references and index. [LC 89042513; ISN 0465055346; $19.95]   HC110.T4 K37 1989   3817

The positive sum strategy: harnessing technology for economic growth. Ralph Landau and Nathan Rosenberg, editors. Washington, D.C.: National Academy Press, 1986. xiv, 640 p. : ill. *Notes:* Sponsored by the National Academy of Engineering and others. Includes bibliographies and index. [LC 85021713; ISN 0309036305; ISN 0309035902]   T173.8. P67 1986   3818

Profiting from innovation: the report of the three-year study from the National Academy of Engineering. William G. Howard, Jr., Bruce R. Guile, editors. New York: Toronto: New York: Free Press; Maxwell Macmillan Canada; Maxwell Macmillan International, c1992. ix, 154 p. : ill. *Notes:* Prepared by the Academy's Study Committee on Profiting from Innovation. Includes bibliographical references (p. 139-144) and index. [LC 91025638; ISN 0029223857; $22.95]
HD45. P76 1992   3819

The pursuit of innovation: managing the people and processes that turn new ideas into profits. George Freedman. New York: American Management Association, c1988. xvi, 346 p. : ill. *Notes:* Includes bibliographies and index. [LC 87047840; ISN 0814459234]   HD45. F723 1988   3820

Readings in the management of innovation. compiled by Michael L. Tushman, William L. Moore. 2nd ed. Cambridge, Mass.: Ballinger, 1988. xiv, 769 p.: ill. *Notes:* Includes bibliographical references and index. [LC 88024199; ISN 0887302440]   HD45. R3 1988   3821

Research on the management of innovation: the Minnesota studies. edited by Andrew H. Van de Ven, Harold L. Angle, Marshall Scott Poole. Cambridge, Mass.: Ballinger Pub., 1989. xxi, 719 p. : ill. *Notes:* Includes index. Includes bibliographical references. [LC 89000402; ISN 088730334X; $84.00]   HD45. R39 1989   3822

Stimulating innovation: a systems approach. Tudor Rickards. New York: St. Martin's Press, 1985. xi, 221 p. : ill. *Notes:* Includes index. Bibliography: p. [201]-214. [LC 85011977; ISN 0312762038; $25.00 (est.)]   T173.8. R53 1985   3823

The technical enterprise: present and future patterns. Herbert I. Fusfeld. Cambridge, Mass.: Ballinger Pub. Co., c1986. xiii, 312 p. *Notes:* Includes bibliographies and index. [LC 86003340; ISN 0887300332]   HC79.T4 F87 1986   3824

Technology, policy, and economic performance: lessons from Japan. Christopher Freeman. London; New York: Pinter Publishers, 1987. 155 p. : ill. *Notes:* Includes index. Bibliography: p. 139-149. [LC 87018553; ISN 0861879287; $25.00 (U.S.)]   HC465.T4 F74 1987   3825

Technology venturing: American innovation and risk-taking. edited by Eugene B. Konecci and Robert Lawrence Kuhn. New York: Praeger, c1985. xii, 251 p. : ill. *Notes:* Derived from a conference held at the University of Texas at Dallas, Feb. 5-7, 1984. Includes bibliographical references and index. [LC 85012192; ISN 0030051835; $34.95 (est.)]   HC110.T4 T45 1985   3826

What machines can't do: politics and technology in the industrial enterprise. Robert J. Thomas. Berkeley: University of California Press, c1994. xviii, 314 p. : ill. *Notes:* Includes bibliographical references (p. 293-306) and index. [LC 93015746; ISN 0520087011]   HD45. T43 1994   +3827

TECHNOLOGICAL UNEMPLOYMENT

Work, unemployment and the new technology. Colin Gill. Cambridge Cambridgeshire: New York: Polity Press; B. Blackwell, 1985. xii, 204 p. *Notes:* Includes index. Bibliography: p. [185]-194. [LC 85003643; ISN 0745600220; ISN 0745600239; $34.95 (U.S.); $14.95 (U.S.)]   HD6331. G55 1985   3828

TECHNOLOGY

Beyond spinoff: military and commercial technologies in a changing world. John A. Alic... et al. Boston, Mass.: Harvard Business School Press, c1992. vi, 428 p. : ill. *Notes:* Includes bibliographical references and index. [LC 91036175; ISN 0875843182; $35.00]   T15. B48 1992   3829

Future facts: a forecast of the world as we will know it before the end of the century. by Stephen Rosen; ill. by the Chartmakers, Inc. New York: Simon and Schuster, c1976. viii, 535 p. : ill. *Notes:* Includes index. [LC 75015545; ISN 0671220780]   T20. R58 1976   3830

Imagining tomorrow: history, technology, and the American future. edited by Jospeh J. Corn. Cambridge, Mass.: MIT Press, c1986. vi, 237 p. : ill. *Notes:* Includes bibliographies and index. [LC 85015158; ISN 0262031159]   T20. I43 1986   3831

Made in U.S.A.: the secret histories of the things that made America. Phil Patton. 1st ed. New York: Grove Weidenfeld, 1992. viii, 403 p. : ill. *Notes:* Includes bibliographical references and index. [LC 91019961; ISN 0802112765; $24.95]   T21. P38 1992   3832

Managing new technology development. edited by Wm. E. Souder, J. Daniel Sherman. New York: McGraw-Hill, c1994. xvi, 348 p. : ill. *Notes:* "...Explores such key concepts as compressing cycle times, parallel development methods,using teams and task forces, managing customer interfaces, the strategic management of technology, managing technology in global markets, co-venturing..."—Back cover. Includes bibliographical references and index. [LC 93020840; ISN 0070597480]   T49.5. M347 1994   +3833

People, science, and technology: a guide to advanced industrial society. Charles Boyle, Peter Wheale, Brian Surgess sic. Totowa, N.J.: Barnes & Noble Books, 1984. x, 265 p. *Notes:* Includes bibliographies and indexes. [LC 83024368; ISN 0389204552]   T14.5. B69 1984   3834

The social construction of technological systems: new directions in the sociology and history of technology. edited by Wiebe E. Bijker, Thomas P. Hughes, and Trevor J. Pinch. Cambridge, Mass.: MIT Press, c1987. x, 405 p. : ill. *Notes:* Papers of a workshop held at the University of Twente, The Netherlands, in July 1984. Includes indexes. Bibliography: p. [349]-372. [LC 86027600; ISN 0262022621]   T14.5. S6325 1987   3835

Strategic technology management: systems for products and processes. David I. Cleland and Karen M. Bursic. New York, NY: AMACOM, c1992. ix, 198 p. : ill. *Notes:* Includes bibliographical references and index. [LC 91053051; ISN 0814450353; $49.95]   T56.8. C6 1992   3836

Technology-mediated communication. editor, Urs E. Gattiker; managing editor, Rosemarie S. Stollenmaier. Berlin; New York: W. de Gruyter, 1992. viii, 325 p. *Notes:* Includes bibliographical references and indexes. [LC 92005545; ISN 3110134195]   T14.5. T446 1992   3837

Technopoly: the surrender of culture to technology. Neil Postman. 1st ed. New York: Knopf, 1992. xii, 222 p. *Notes:* Includes bibliographical references (p. [207]-210) and index. [LC 91053121; ISN 0394582721; $21.00]   T14.5. P667 1992   3838

Tradeoffs: imperatives of choice in a high-tech world. Edward Wenk, Jr. Baltimore: Johns Hopkins University Press, c1986. xii, 238 p. : ill. *Notes:* Includes index. Bibliography: p. [229]-231. [LC 86045441; ISN 0801833787]   T14.5. W46 1986   3839

Unbounding the future: the nanotechnology revolution. by Eric Drexler and Chris Peterson with Gayle Pergamit. New York: Morrow, 1991. 304 p. : ill. *Notes:* Includes bibliographical references and index. [LC 91006341; ISN 0688091245; S22.50]   T45. D74 1991   3840

The whale and the reactor: a search for limits in an age of high technology. Langdon Winner. Chicago: University of Chicago Press, 1986. xiv, 200 p. *Notes:* Includes index. Bibliography: p. 179-192. [LC 85008718; ISN 0226902102]   T14. W54 1986   3841

Window of opportunity: a blueprint for the future. by Newt Gingrich, with David Drake and Marianne Gingrich. New York: Tom Doherty Associates: distributed by St. Martin's Press, 1984. xvi, 272 p. *Notes:* A Tom Doherty Associates Book. "Published in association with Baen Enterprises."; ISN 0312939221; $14.95]   T14.5. G56   3842

TECHNOLOGY AND CIVILIZATION

Challenges and opportunities: from now to 2001. edited by Howard F. Didsbury, Jr. Bethesda, Md.: World Future Society, 1986. xv, 310 p. *Notes:* "This volume prepared in conjunction with the World Future Society's conference, 'Future Focus: the Next Fifteen Years,' held in New York City, July 13-17, 1986." Includes bibliographical references. [LC 86050617; ISN 0930242319]   T14.5. C52 1986   3843

The underside of high-tech: technology and the deformation of human sensibilities. edited by John W. Murphy, Algis Mickunas, and Joseph J. Pilotta. Westport, Conn.: Greenwood Press, c1986. xiii, 217 p. *Notes:* Includes index. Bibliography: p. [207]-212. [LC 85027265; ISN 0313246122]
    HM221. U53 1986   3844

TECHNOLOGY AND STATE

Empowering technology: implementing a U.S. strategy. edited by Lewis M. Branscomb; with contributions by Lewis M. Branscomb... et al. Cambridge, Mass.: MIT Press, c1993. xi, 315 p. *Notes:* Includes bibliographical references (p. [301]-307) and index. [LC 93023975; ISN 0262521857]
    T21. E53 1993   +3845

The tender ship: governmental management of technological change. Arthur M. Squires; foreword by Harold C. Livesay. Boston: Birkhäuser, c1986. xix, 247 p. : ill. *Notes:* "A Pro scientia viva title." Includes bibliographical references and index. [LC 85012972; ISN 081763312X]   T21. S68 1986   3846

TECHNOLOGY TRANSFER

International collaborative ventures in U.S. manufacturing. edited by David C. Mowery. Cambridge, Mass.: Ballinger Pub. Co., c1988. xiv, 386 p. : ill. *Notes:* "An American Enterprise Institute/Ballinger publication." "Competing in a changing world economy project." Includes bibliographies and index. [LC 87035831; ISN 0887302211; $34.95]   HC110.T4 I57 1988   3847

The keys to the kingdom: the FS-X deal and the selling of America's future to Japan. Jeff Shear. New York: Doubleday, 1994. xvii, 318 p. *Notes:* Includes index. [LC 93047228; ISN 0385473532; $25.00]
    HC110.T4 S53 1994   +3848

TELECOMMUNICATION POLICY

Deregulating telecoms: competition and control in the United States, Japan, and Britain. Jill Hills. New York: Quorum Books, 1986. 220 p. *Notes:* Includes index. Bibliography: p. [208]-217. [LC 86016949; ISN 0899302254]   HE7781. H55 1986   3849

TELECOMMUNICATION

Communication technology: the new media in society. Everett M. Rogers. New York: London: Free Press; Collier Macmillan, c1986. xii, 273 p. : ill. (Series in communication technology and society) *Notes:* Includes indexes. Bibliography: p. 247-260. [LC 85027555; ISN 002927110X; ISN 0029271207]   TK5102.5. R55 1986   3850

Communications deregulation: the unleashing of America's communications industry. Jeremy Tunstall. Oxford, UK; New York, NY, USA: B. Blackwell, 1986. xi, 324 p. *Notes:* Includes index. Bibliography: p. [296]-315. [LC 85022983; ISN 0631148191; $24.95 (U.S.)]   KF2765. T86 1986   3851

Competing in time: using telecommunications for competitive advantage. Peter G.W. Keen. Updated and expanded. Cambridge, Mass.: Ballinger, c1988. viii, 302 p. : ill. *Notes:* Includes index. [LC 88003297; ISN 0887303013; ISN 0887303005]   HF5541.T4 K44 1988   3852

Future competition in telecommunications. edited by Stephen P. Bradley and Jerry A. Hausman. Boston, Mass.: Harvard Business School Press, c1989. x, 340 p. : ill. *Notes:* Includes bibliographies and index. [LC 88035787; ISN 0875842119]   HE7775. F88 1989   3853

Telecommunications in the post-divestiture era: essays in honor of Ben T. Wiggins and Jasper Dorsey. edited by Albert L. Danielsen and David R. Kamerschen. Lexington, Mass.: Lexington Books, c1986. xiv, 252 p. : ill. *Notes:* Includes bibliographical references and index. [LC 86045505; ISN 0669134457]   HE7775. T355 1986   3854

TELEMARKETING

The electronic marketing manual. Cecil C. Hoge, Sr. New York: McGraw-Hill, c1993. xxvi, 480 p. *Notes:* Includes bibliographical references and index. [LC 92044804; ISN 0070293651; $34.95]
    HF5415.1265. H64 1993   +3855

Encyclopedia of telemarketing. edited by Richard L. Bencin, Donald J. Jonovic. Englewood Cliffs, N.J.: Prentice Hall, c1989. xlii, 726 p. : ill. *Notes:* Includes index. Bibliography: p. 602-606. [LC 88032110; ISN 0132759187; $45.00]   HF5415.1263. B46 1989   3856

Marketing in an electronic age. edited by Robert D. Buzzell. Boston, Mass.: Harvard Business School Press, 1985. x, 404 p. : ill. *Notes:* "Harvard Business School, Research Colloquium." Includes bibliographical references and index. [LC 84025166; ISN 0875841597]   HF5415.122. M425 1985   3857

TELEMATICS

The network nation: human communication via computer. Starr Roxanne Hiltz, Murray Turoff; with foreword by Suzanne Keller. Rev. ed. Cambridge, Mass.: MIT Press, 1993. xxxi, 557 p. *Notes:* Includes bibliographical references (p. 515-536) and indexes. [LC 92041470; ISN 0262581205]   TK5105.6. H54 1993   +3858

TELEPHONE

After the breakup: assessing the new post-AT&T divestiture era. edited by Barry G. Cole. New York: Columbia University Press, c1991. xxvi, 480 p. : ill. *Notes:* Includes bibliographical references and index. [LC 90040710; ISN 0231073224]   HE8815. A34 1991   3859

Telecommunications in transition. Richard H.K. Vietor, Davis Dyer editors. Boston: Division of Research, Harvard Business School, c1986. 221 p. : ill. (Course module series) [LC 86000259; ISN 0875841325]   HE8817. T45 1986   3860

TELESHOPPING

Future shop: how new technologies will change the way we shop and what we buy. by James Snider and Terra Ziporyn. 1st ed. New York: St. Martin's Press, c1992. xviii, 316 p. *Notes:* Includes bibliographical references and index. [LC 90029167; ISN 0312063598; $22.95]   TX335. S579 1992   3861

TELEVISION

Please stand by: a prehistory of television. Michael Ritchie. Woodstock, N.Y.: Overlook Press, c1994. 247 p., [48] p. of plates: ill. *Notes:* Includes bibliographical references (p. 237-239) and index. [LC 94019089; ISN 0879515465; $24.95]   TK6637. R58 1994   +3862

TELEVISION ADVERTISING AND CHILDREN

Out of the garden: toys, TV, and children's culture in the age of marketing. Stephen Kline. London; New York: Verso, 1993. x, 406 p. *Notes:* Includes bibliographical references (p. 368-395) and index. [LC 93034292; ISN 086091397X; $27.95]   HQ784.T4 K57 1993   +3863

Sold separately: children and parents in consumer culture. Ellen Seiter. New Brunswick, N.J.: Rutgers University Press, c1993. xii, 257 p. : ill. *Notes:* Includes bibliographical references (p. [235]-248) and index. [LC 92044227; ISN 0813519888; $24.95]   HQ784.T68 S45 1993   +3864

TELEVISION BROADCASTING OF NEWS

Bad news at Black Rock: the sell-out of CBS News. Peter McCabe. New York: Arbor House, c1987. xvi, 302 p. [LC 86028896; ISN 0877959072]   PN4888.T4 M28 1987   3865

TELEVISION BROADCASTING

The future of television: a global overview of programming, advertising, technology, and growth. Marc Doyle. Lincolnwood, Ill.: NTC Business Books, c1992. xvi, 187 p. : ill. *Notes:* "NATPE International, the National Association of Television Program Executives." Includes index. [LC 91044640; ISN 0844234613; $39.95] HE8700.4. D69 1992 +3866

Three blind mice: how the TV networks lost their way. Ken Auletta. 1st trade ed. New York: Random House, c1991. xii, 642 p. *Notes:* Includes bibliographical references (p. [623]-626) and index. [LC 90052925; ISN 0394563581; $25.00 ($33.00 Can.)] PN1992.3.U5 A96 1991 3867

The TV establishment; programming for power and profit. Englewood Cliffs, N.J. Prentice Hall, 1974. vi, 186 p. illus. (A Spectrum book) (The American establishments series) *Notes:* Includes bibliographical references. *Contents:* Epstein, E. J. News from nowhere.—Molotch, H. and Lester, M. Accidents, scandals, and routines: resources for insurgent methodology.—Nix, M. The Meet the press game.—Elliott, P. Selection and communication in a television production: a case study.—Brown, L. Television: the business behind the box.—Cantor, M. G. Producing television for children.—Tuchman, G. Assembling a network talk-show.—Wilensky, H. L. Mass society and mass culture: interdependence or independence?—Sallach, D. L. Class domination and ideological hegemony.—Schiller, H. L. Mass communication and American empire. [LC 74003206; ISN 0139024034] PN1992.5. T8 +3868

Video media competition: regulation, economics, and technology. edited by Eli M. Noam. New York: Columbia University Press, 1985. xii, 468 p. (Columbia studies in business, government, and society) *Notes:* Bibliography: p. [441]-457. [LC 85000435; ISN 023106134X] HE8700.8. V53 1985 3869

TELEVISION PROGRAMS

The fanciest dive: what happened when the giant media empire of TIME/LIFE leaped without looking into the age of high-tech. Christopher M. Byron. 1st ed. New York: W.W. Norton, c1986. 280 p. [LC 85021381; ISN 0393022617; $16.95] PN1992.3.U5 T8734 1986 3870

TEMPORARY EMPLOYMENT

Work styles to fit your life-style: everyone's guide to temporary employment. John Fanning, Rosemary Maniscalco. Englewood Cliffs, N.J.: Prentice-Hall, c1993. xv, 239 p. : ill. *Notes:* Includes index. [LC 93015548; ISN 0130157287; $11.95] HD5854. F36 1993 +3871

TENDER OFFERS (SECURITIES)

Taking America: how we got from the first hostile takeover to megamergers, corporate raiding, and scandal. Jeff Madrick. Toronto; New York: Bantam Books, 1987. 310 p. *Notes:* Includes index. Bibliography: p. [298]-302. [LC 87000928; ISN 0553052292] HG4028.T4 M33 1987 3872

Tender offers: developments and commentaries. edited by Marc I. Steinberg. Westport, Conn.: Quorum Books, c1985. 363 p. *Notes:* Includes index. Bibliography: p. [335]-353. [LC 84024947; ISN 089930088X] KF1477. T45 1985 3873

TEXACO, INC

Oil & honor: the Texaco-Pennzoil Wars. Thomas Petzinger, Jr. New York: Putnam, c1987. 495 p., [8] p. of plates *Notes:* Includes index. Bibliography: p. 468-486. [LC 87002255; ISN 0399132767] HD9569.T4 P48 1987 3874

TEXTILE INDUSTRY

Enterprising elite: the Boston Associates and the world they made. Robert F. Dalzell, Jr. Cambridge, Mass.: Harvard University Press, 1987. xviii, 298 p., [11] p. of plates: ill. *Notes:* Includes index. Bibliography: p. 239-289. [LC 86033649; ISN 0674257650] HD9858.L9 D35 1987 3875

THAILAND—ECONOMIC CONDITIONS

The Thai economy in transition. edited by Peter G. Warr. Cambridge England; New York, NY, USA: Cambridge University Press, 1993. xviii, 468 p. : ill., map *Notes:* Includes bibliographical references (p. [438]-456) and index. [LC 93019011; ISN 052138186X] HC445. T397 1993 +3876

TIME, INC

Time Inc.; the intimate history of a publishing enterprise. by Robert T. Elson. Edited by Duncan Norton-Taylor. [1st ed.] New York Atheneum, 1968-1986. 3 v. illus. *Notes:* Vol. 3 by Curtis Prendergast with Geoffrey Colvin; edited by Robert Lubar. Vols. 2-3 have title: The world of Time Inc. Includes bibliographical references and indexes. *Contents:* [v. 1] 1923-1941.—v. 2. 1941-1960.—v. 3. 1960-1980. [LC 68016868; ISN 068910555X; ISN 0689113153] Z473.T85 E48 3877

TIME MANAGEMENT

Competing against time: how time-based competition is reshaping global markets. George Stalk, Jr., Thomas M. Hout. New York: London: Free Press; Collier Macmillan, c1990. x, 285 p. : ill. *Notes:* Includes bibliographical references. [LC 89023735; ISN 0029152917; $24.95] HD69.T54 S73 1990 3878

The management of time. A. Dale Timpe, series editor. New York, N.Y.: Facts on File, 1987. xv, 375 p. : ill. (The Art and science of business management) *Notes:* Includes index. Bibliography: p. 364-367. [LC 86011511; ISN 0816014612] HD69.T54 M36 1987 3879

Managing management time: who's got the monkey? William Oncken, Jr. Englewood Cliffs, NJ: Prentice-Hall, c1984. xviii, 244 p. : ill. *Notes:* Includes index. [LC 84011659; ISN 0135506905; $19.95] HD38. O53 1984 3880

The time trap. Alec Mackenzie. New York, NY: Amacom, c1990. x, 228 p. : ill. [LC 89046217; ISN 0814459692; $17.95] HD69.T54 M33 1990 3881

TOBACCO INDUSTRY

Merchants of death: the American tobacco industry. Larry C. White. 1st ed. New York: Beech Tree Books, c1988. 240 p. *Notes:* Includes index. [LC 87033762; ISN 0688067069] HD9135. W47 1988 3882

The smoke ring: tobacco, money & multinational politics. Peter Taylor; with a foreword by C. Everett Koop. Rev. and expanded ed. New York: New American Library, c1985. xiv, 386 p. *Notes:* "A Mentor book." Includes index. Bibliography: p. 371-373. [LC 85061718; ISN 0451624262; $4.95] HD9130.5. T39 1985 3883

TOTAL QUALITY MANAGEMENT

Beyond total quality management: toward the emerging paradigm. Greg Bounds. . . et al. New York: McGraw-Hill, c1994. xxviii, 817 p. : ill. *Notes:* Includes bibliographical references and index. [LC 93038388; ISN 0070066787] HD62.15. B49 1994 +3884

Business process reengineering: breakpoint strategies for market dominance. Henry J. Johansson. . . et al. Chichester England; New York: Wiley, 1993. xiv, 241 p. : ill. *Notes:* Includes bibliographical references and index. [LC 93007341; ISN 0471938831; $34.95] HD62.15. B87 1993 +3885

Completeness: quality for the 21st century. Philip B. Crosby. New York, N.Y.: Dutton, 1992. xix, 251 p. *Notes:* Includes index. [LC 91046275; ISN 0525934758; $21.00] HD62.15. C76 1992 3886

The corporate guide to the Malcolm Baldrige National Quality Award: proven strategies for building quality into your organization. Marion Mills Steeples. Milwaukee, Wis.: Homewood, Ill.: ASQC Quality Press; Business One Irwin, c1992. xv, 383 p. : ill. *Notes:* Includes bibliographical references (p. 369-374) and index. [LC 91033968; ISN 1556236530] HD62.15. S74 1992 3887

The five pillars of TQM: how to make total quality management work for you. Bill Creech. New York: Truman Talley Books/Dutton, 1994. 549 p. : ill. *Notes:* Includes index. [LC 93028570; ISN 0525937250; $26.95 ($37.99 Can.)] HD62.15. C74 1994 +3888

Fourth generation management: the new business consciousness. Brian L. Joiner in collaboration with Sue Reynard; with contributions from Yukihiro Ando... et al. New York: McGraw-Hill, c1994. xiii, 289 p. : ill. *Notes:* Includes bibliographical references and index. [LC 93040042; ISN 0070327157; $24.95] HD62.15. J65 1994 +3889

Global quality: the new management culture. John Macdonald and John Piggott. Amsterdam; San Diego: Pfeiffer & Co., c1993. xiv, 320 p. *Notes:* Previously published: London: Mercury, c1990. Includes bibliographical references (p. 309-312) and index. [LC 92050993; ISN 0893842060; $21.95] HD62.15. M33 1993 +3890

It's about time: a fable about the next dimension of quality. John Guaspari. New York: Amacom, c1992. 97 p. : ill. [LC 92017963; ISN 0814451306] HD62.15. G83 1992 3891

Japanese quality concepts: an overview. Katsuya Hosotani. White Plains, N.Y.: Quality Resources, c1992. xii, 270 p. : ill. *Notes:* Includes bibliographical references (p. 259-261) and index. [LC 92012106; ISN 052791651X] HD62.15. H6713 1992 3892

Managing finance for quality: bottom-line results from top-level commitment. James A.F. Stoner, Frank M. Werner. Milwaukee, Wis.: Morristown, N.J.: ASQC Quality Press; Financial Executives Research Foundation, c1994. xxiii, 250 p. : ill. *Notes:* Includes bibliographical references (p. [235]-239) and index. *Contents:* Corporate finance in transition—The global quality revolution—Quality management comes to the corporate finance function—Integrating Tqm into corporate finance—Integrating corporate finance into the organization's Tqm efforts—Lessons learned—What's next? The continuing evolution of corporate finance—Corning, Incorporated—Federal Express—Motorola—Solectron—Southern Pacific. [LC 94004310; ISN 0873892674] HD62.15. S78 1994 +3893

Managing quality in America's most admired companies. Jay W. Spechler. San Francisco: Norcross, Ga.: Berrett-Koehler Publishers; Industrial Engineeering and Management Press, Institute of Industrial Engineers, c1993. xii, 422 p. : ill. *Notes:* Includes studies of: Anheuser-Busch, Monsanto, Centex Telemanagement, Octel Communications Corporation, Xerox, IBM Rochester, Intelligent Electronics, Inc., Novell, Inc., Federal Express, American Express Travel Related Services, AT&T Universal Card Services, Westinghouse, Whirlpool Corporation, Springs Industries, Inc., Hyatt Hotel and Resorts, Marriott Corporation, Ritz-Carlton Hotel Company, New York Life, USAA, Reynolds Metals Company, Cadillac Motor Car, 3M, Photo-Sonics, Inc., SpaceLabs Medical, Inc., Steinway & Sons, Knight-Ridder, Inc., K-Mart Corporation, Lazarus, TIAA-CREF, Delta Air Lines, Inc., Michigan Consolidated Gas Company, and Ohio Edison Company. Includes bibliographical references. [LC 92044147; ISN 0898061180] HD62.15. S646 1993 3894

The next phase of total quality management: TQM II and the focus on profitability. Robert E. Stein. New York: Dekker, c1994. xi, 232 p. : ill. *Notes:* Includes bibliographical references (p. 223-224) and index. [LC 93005802; ISN 082479110X; $45.00] HD62.15. S76 1994 +3895

Quality is just the beginning: managing for total responsiveness. Steve Levit. New York: McGraw-Hill, c1994. xii, 206 p. : ill. *Notes:* Includes index. [LC 93040727; ISN 0070375925; $29.95] HD62.15. L48 1994 +3896

Quality or else: the revolution in world business. Lloyd Dobyns and Clare Crawford-Mason. Boston: Houghton Mifflin, 1991. 309 p. : ill. *Notes:* Includes bibliographical references (p. 300-309). [LC 91024378; ISN 0395574390; $21.95] HD62.15. D63 1991 3897

Total quality management: text, cases, and readings. by Joel E. Ross. Delray Beach, FL: St. Lucie Press, c1993. vi, 325 p. : ill. *Notes:* Includes bibliographical references. [LC 92061645; ISN 0963403001; $39.95] HD62.15. R67 1993 +3898

Total quality management: three steps to continuous improvement. Arthur R. Tenner, Irving J. DeToro. Reading, Mass.: Addison-Wesley, c1992. xvii, 266 p. : ill. *Notes:* Includes bibliographical references and index. [LC 91019024; ISN 0201563053; $28.20] HD62.15. T46 1992 3899

TOURIST TRADE

The complete travel marketing handbook: 37 industry experts share their secrets. edited by Andrew Vladimir. Lincolnwood, Ill.: NTC Business Books, c1988. xvi, 291 p. : ill., ports. *Notes:* Includes bibliographical references. [LC 87082612; ISN 0844231568; $34.95] G155.A1 C65 1988 3900

Marketing in travel and tourism. Victor T.C. Middleton. 2nd ed. Oxford: Butterworth-Heinemann, 1994. xii, 393 p. : ill. *Notes:* Includes bibliographical references and index. *Contents:* Part 6. Marketing Canada: to the US market—Marketing South Pacific Islands: to European countries—Marketing visitor attractions: Old Sturbridge Village, USA—Marketing visitor attractions: "Visions of Japan"—Marketing airlines: British Airways 'The world's biggest offer'—Marketing short-break products for UK hotels: Superbreaks mini holidays—Marketing IT products: Thomson Sun Hotels.; ISN 0750609737] G155.A1 M52 1994 +3901

Tourism marketing and management handbook. editors, Stephen F. Witt, Luiz Moutinho. 2nd ed. New York: Prentice Hall, 1994. xv, 617 p. : ill., maps *Notes:* Includes bibliographical references and index. [LC 93011227; ISN 0139233849; $250] G155.A1 T5924 1994 +3902

TOY INDUSTRY

Toyland: the high-stakes game of the toy industry. Sydney Ladensohn Stern and Ted Schoenhaus. Chicago: Contemporary Books, c1990. xi, 339 p., [16] p. of plates: ill. *Notes:* Includes bibliographical references (p. 313-317). [LC 89071198; ISN 0809245205; $19.95] HD9993.T693 U67 1990 3903

TOYOTA JIDOSHA KOGYO KABUSHIKI KAISHA

Against all odds: the story of the Toyota Motor Corporation and the family that created it. Yukiyasu Togo and William Wartman. 1st ed. New York: St. Martin's Press, 1993. xi, 260 p., [8] p. of plates: ill. *Notes:* Includes index. [LC 93025695; ISN 0312097336] HD9710.J34 T6738 1993 +3904

TRADE REGULATION

Contrived competition: regulation and deregulation in America. Richard H.K. Vietor. Cambridge, Mass.: Belknap Press of Harvard University Press, 1994. 439 p. : ill. *Notes:* Includes bibliographical references (p. [361]-420) and index. [LC 93028975; ISN 067416962X; $35.00] HD3616.U46 V53 1994 +3905

Legal aspects of marketing strategy: antitrust and consumer protection issues. Louis W. Stern, Thomas L. Eovaldi. Englewood Cliffs, N.J.: Prentice-Hall, c1984. xxiv, 550 p. (The Prentice-Hall series in marketing) (Prentice-Hall international series in management) *Notes:* Includes bibliographical references and index. [LC 83024612; ISN 0135280842] KF1609. S74 1984 3906

The legal environment of business. Robert N. Corley, O. Lee Reed, with the assistance of Russell L. Welch. 7th ed. New York: McGraw-Hill Book Co., c1987. xxxii, 793 p. : ill. *Notes:* Appendixes include the United States Constitution and excerpts from the antitrust laws and labor laws. Includes index. [LC 86015171; ISN 0070132569; $32.95] KF1600. C6 1987 3907

Prophets of regulation: Charles Francis Adams, Louis D. Brandeis, James M. Landis, Alfred E. Kahn. Cambridge, Mass.: Belknap Press of Harvard University Press, 1984. ix, 387 p. : ill., [16] p. of plates *Notes:* Includes bibliographical references and index. [LC 84000296; ISN 0674716078; $20.00] HD3616.U46 M315 1984 3908

Public regulation: new perspectives on institutions and policies. edited by Elizabeth E. Bailey. Cambridge, Mass.: MIT Press, c1987. xiv, 404 p. *Notes:* "Essays. . . presented at a conference on public regulation sponsored by Carnegie Mellon University"—Pref. Includes bibliographies and index. [LC 86021302; ISN 0262022583] HD3616.U47 P83 1987 3909

Regulating big business: antitrust in Great Britain and America, 1880 to 1990. Tony Freyer. Cambridge England; New York: Cambridge University Press, 1992. xiii, 399 p. *Notes:* Includes bibliographical references and index. [LC 91014033; ISN 052135207X; $59.95] HD3616.G73 F74 1992 3910

Regulation: politics, bureaucracy, and economics. Kenneth J. Meier. New York: St. Martin's Press, 1985. xviii, 334 p. : ill. *Notes:* Includes index. Bibliography: p. 303-318. [LC 84051842; ISN 0312669712; ISN 0312669720; $32.50; $11.95] HD3616.U46 M39 1985 3911

The transformation of corporate control. Neil Fligstein. Cambridge, Mass.: Harvard University Press, 1990. viii, 391 p. : ill. *Notes:* Includes bibliographical references. [LC 89015586; ISN 0674903587; $35.00] HD3616.U46 F57 1990 3912

Who profits: winners, losers, and government regulation. Robert A. Leone. New York: Basic Books, 1986. xiii, 248 p. *Notes:* Includes index. Bibliography: p. 231-237. [LC 85047992; ISN 0465091830; $15.95] HD3616.U47 L44 1986 3913

TRADE-UNIONS

Can unions survive?: the rejuvenation of the American labor movement. Charles B. Craver. New York: New York University Press, c1993. ix, 213 p. *Notes:* Includes bibliographical references (p. 189-201) and index. [LC 92040980; ISN 0814714986; $40.00]   HD6508. C739 1993   +3914

Grand designs: the impact of corporate strategies on workers, unions, and communities. Charles Craypo and Bruce Nissen, editors. Ithaca, N.Y.: ILR Press, c1993. ix, 285 p. *Notes:* Includes bibliographical references (p. 263-271) and index. *Contents:* Decline of tire manufacturing in Akron / Charles Jeszeck—Strife and decertification at Clinton Corn Products / Adrienne M. Birecree—The closing of Wisconsin Steel / David C. Ranney—Relocation of a Torrington plant / Keith Knauss and Michael Matuszak—Cui bono? / David Fasenfest—Shutdown of a steel foundry / Bruce Nissen—Use of federal funds to support relocations / Gene Daniels—Strike and relocation in meatpacking / Charles Craypo—Successful labor-community coalition building / Bruce Nissen—The impact of corporate strategies / Charles Craypo and Bruce Nissen. [LC 93013434; ISN 087546310X; $22.95]   HD6508. G73 1993   +3915

In labor's cause: main themes on the history of the American worker. David Brody. New York: Oxford University Press, 1993. ix, 250 p. *Notes:* Includes bibliographical references. [LC 92042134; ISN 0195067908]   HD6508. B81125 1993   +3916

Turning the tide: strategic planning for labor unions. David Weil. New York: Toronto: New York: Lexington Books; Maxwell Macmillan Canada; Maxwell Macmillan International, c1994. xvi, 319 p. : ill. *Notes:* Includes bibliographical references (p. 269-301) and index. [LC 93036649; ISN 0029340659]   HD6508. W347 1994   +3917

Unions in transition: entering the second century. edited by Seymour Martin Lipset. San Francisco, Calif.: ICS Press, Institute for Contemporary Studies, c1986. xviii, 506 p. : ill. *Notes:* Includes index. Bibliography: p. 455-477. [LC 86010256; ISN 091761674X; ISN 0917616731; $29.95; $11.95]   HD6508. U46 1986   3918

TRADING COMPANIES

Business history of general trading companies: proceedings of the Fuji conference. International Conference on Business History, 13; edited by Shin'ichi Yonekawa, Hideki Yoshihara. Tokyo: University of Tokyo Press, c1987. xviii, 365 p. : ill. *Notes:* Includes bibliographical references and index.; ISN 4130470337; ISN 0860084086]   HF481. I57 1987   3919

The general trading company: concepts and strategy. Dong-Sung Cho. Lexington, Mass.: Lexington Books, c1987. xv, 159 p. : ill. *Notes:* Includes index. Bibliography: p. [149]-155. [LC 86045755; ISN 0669142964]   HF1009.5. C52 1987   3920

TRANSFER PRICING

The transfer pricing problem: a theory for practice. Robert G. Eccles. Lexington, Mass.: Lexington Books, c1985. xviii, 342 p. : ill. *Notes:* Includes index. Bibliography: p. [325]-332. [LC 85004572; ISN 0669090298]   HF5416.5. E27 1985   3921

TRANSPORTATION, AUTOMOTIVE

Commercial motor transportation. Charles A. Taff. 7th ed. Centreville, Md.: Cornell Maritime Press, 1986. xi, 434 p. : ill. *Notes:* Includes index. Bibliography: p. [417]-426. [LC 85047905; ISN 0870333453]   HE5623. T3 1986   3922

Getting there: the epic struggle between road and rail in the American century. by Stephen B. Goddard. New York: Basic Books, c1994. xi, 351 p., [8] p. of plates: ill. *Notes:* Includes bibliographical references (p. [283]-[334]) and index. [LC 93050543; ISN 0465026397; $28.00 ($38.00 Can.)]   HE5623. G63 1994   +3923

TRUMP, DONALD

Trump: the art of the deal. by Donald J. Trump with Tony Schwartz. New York: Random House, 1987. x, 246 p , [16] p. of plates: ill. Notes: Includes index. [LC 87042663; ISN 0394555287]
HD1382.5. T812 1987   3924

Trump: the saga of America's most powerful real estate baron. by Jerome Tuccille. New York: Donald I. Fine, c1985. 243 p. : ill. Notes: Includes index. [LC 85070277; ISN 091765725X; $17.95]
HD1382.5. T82   3925

TRUST COMPANIES

The management of a trust department. by Walter Kennedy and Philip F. Searle. Boston Bankers Pub. Co., 1967. xvi, 264 p. [LC 66028193]
HG4315. K3   +3926

The trust business. John M. Clarke, Jack W. Zalaha, August Zinsser III. Washington, D.C.: American Bankers Asscciation, c1988. vii, 289 p. : ill. Notes: Includes index. [LC 88010345; ISN 0899823505; $37.50 (est.)]
HG4309. C48 1988   3927

TURNER, TED

It ain't as easy as it looks: Ted Turner's amazing story. Porter Bibb. 1st ed. New York: Crown Publishers, c1993. xii, 468 p. : ill. Notes: Includes bibliographical references (p. 421-423) and index. [LC 93001832; ISN 051759322X; $25.00 ($32.50 Canada)]
HC102.5.T86 B52 1993   +3928

TWENTIETH CENTURY

Global outlook 2000: an economic, social and environmental perspective. by the United Nations. New York: United Nations, c1990. xi, 340 p. : ill. Notes: "Sales no. E.90.II.C.3." Includes bibliographical references.; ISN 9211091187; $19.95]
CB161. U55 1990   3929

TWENTY-FIRST CENTURY

American renaissance: our life at the turn of the 21st century. Marvin Cetron and Owen Davies. 1st ed. New York: St. Martin's Press, 1989. viii. 400 p. : ill. [LC 89004048; ISN 0312028601; $19.95]
CB161. C39 1989   3930

Preparing for the twenty-first century. Paul Kennedy. New York: Random House, c1993. xvi, 428 p. : ill. Notes: Includes bibliographical references (p. 389-405) and index. [LC 91052668; ISN 0394584430: $25.00]
CB161. K44 1993   3931

A short history of the future. W. Warren Wagar; afterword by Immanuel Wallerstein. Chicago: University of Chicago Press, c1989. xiv, 323 p. Notes: Includes index. Bibliography: p. 307-311. [LC 89032019; ISN 0226869016; $24.95]
CB161. W24 1989   3932

Visions for the 21st century. edited by Sheila M. Moorcroft. Westport, Conn.: Praeger, 1993. x, 178 p. Notes: Series statement from cover. Includes bibliographical references (p. 165-167) and index. [LC 92035824; ISN 0275945723]
CB161. V59 1993   3933

TOKYO SHOKEN TORIHIKIJO

Unequal equities: power and risk in Japan's stock market. Robert Zielinski, Nigel Holloway. New York: McGraw-Hill, 1992. xii, 205 p. : ill. Notes. Rev. ed. of: Unequal equities. Tokyo: Kodansha, c1991. Includes bibliographical references (p. 197-198) and index. [LC 92018271; ISN 0070707707; $12.95]
HG4597. Z54 1992   3934

UNEMPLOYED

A job to live: the impact of tomorrow's technology on work and society. Shirley Willilams. Harmondsworth, Middlesex: Penguin Books, 1985. 245 p. *Notes:* Includes index. Bibliography: p. 224-[231]; ISN 0140084266] HD5708.5. W54 1985   3935

UNITED STATES

Eagle on the Street: based on the Pulitzer Prize-winning account of the SEC's battle with Wall Street. David A. Vise, Steve Coll. New York: Toronto: New York: Scribner's; Maxwell Macmillan Canada; Maxwell Macmillan International, c1991. xiii, 395 p. : ill. *Notes:* Includes bibliographical references (p. 383-385) and index. [LC 91009529; ISN 0684193140; $24.95 ($32.50 Can.)] KF1444. V57 1991   3936

The FDA follies. Herbert Burkholz. New York, NY: BasicBooks, c1994. xii, 228 p. *Notes:* Includes bibliographical references (p. [217]-219) and index. [LC 93032913; ISN 046502369X] HD9000.9.U5 B87 1994   +3937

The Federal Reserve: lender of last resort. Gillian Garcia and Elizabeth Plautz. Cambridge, Mass.: Ballinger, c1988. xvii, 310 p. : ill. *Notes:* Includes index. Bibliography: p. 281-289. [LC 88019261; ISN 0887303242; $39.95] HG2562.L6 G37 1988   3938

An introduction to the SEC. K. Fred Skousen. 5th ed. Cincinnati, OH: South-Western Pub. Co., c1991. xii, 180 p. : ill. *Notes:* Includes bibliographical references (p. 151-157) and index. [LC 89077835; ISN 0538808845; $16.95] KF1444. S5 1991   3939

An introduction to the Securities and Exchange Commission. Larry Gene Pointer, Richard G. Schroeder. Plano, Tex.: Business Publications, 1986. viii, 116 p. : ill. *Notes:* Includes bibliographies. [LC 85072807; ISN 0256035261] KF1444. P7 1986   3940

Running in place: inside the Senate. James A. Miller. New York: Simon and Schuster, c1986. 204 p. *Notes:* Includes index. [LC 85027734; ISN 0671499289] JK1161. M55 1986   3941

UNITED STATES—APPROPRIATIONS AND EXPENDITURES

Checks unbalanced: the quiet side of public spending. Herman B. Leonard. New York: Basic Books, c1986. xii, 289 p. *Notes:* Includes index. Bibliography: p. 265-279. [LC 85043103; ISN 0465009735; $18.95] HJ2051. L42   3942

UNITED STATES—ARMED FORCES—PROCUREMENT

The defense management challenge: weapons acquisition. J. Ronald Fox with James L. Field. Boston, Mass.: Harvard Business School Press, c1988. xii, 348 p. : ill. *Notes:* Includes bibliographies and index. [LC 88001713; ISN 0875841872] UC263. F69 1988   3943

UNITED STATES—BIOGRAPHY

The vital few: the entrepreneur and American economic progress. Jonathan Hughes. Expanded ed. New York: Oxford University Press, 1986. xiv, 610 p. *Notes:* Includes index. Bibliography: p. [571]-583. [LC 85028504; ISN 0195040384] HC102.5.A2 H8 1986   3944

UNITED STATES—CIVILIZATION—JAPANESE INFLUENCES

Made in Japan: the methods, motivation, and culture of the Japanese, and their influence on U.S. business and all Americans. Boye De Mente. Lincolnwood, Ill., U.S.A.: Passport Books, c1987. x, 176 p. [LC 86060834; ISN 0844285064; $17.95] E183.8.J3 D45 1987   3945

UNITED STATES—COMMERCE

Strategies in global industries: how U.S. businesses compete. Allen J. Morrison; foreword by Hans Schollhammer. New York: Quorum Books, c1990. xvi, 194 p. : ill. *Notes:* Includes bibliographical references. [LC 89024370; ISN 0899305288; $39.95]   HF3021. M67 1990   3946

UNITED STATES—COMMERCE—CASE STUDIES

Revitalizing American industry: lessons from our competitors. edited by Milton S. Hochmuth and William H. Davidson. Cambridge, Mass.: Ballinger Pub. Co., 1985. xix, 413 p. *Notes:* Includes bibliographies and index. [LC 84018471; ISN 0887300197]   HF3031. R48 1985   3947

UNITED STATES—COMMERCIAL POLICY

The paradox of continental production: national investment policies in North America. Barbara Jenkins. Ithaca: Cornell University Press, 1992. xi, 254 p. : ill. *Notes:* Includes bibliographical references and index. [LC 92052761; ISN 0801426766]   HF1456.5.C2 J46 1992   3948

Saving free trade: a pragmatic approach. Robert Z. Lawrence, Robert E. Litan. Washington, D.C.: Brookings Institution, c1986. xii, 132 p. *Notes:* Includes bibliographical references and index. [LC 86014705; ISN 0815751788; ISN 081575177X; $8.95]   HF1455. L39 1986   3949

The United States in the world economy. edited and with an introduction by Martin Feldstein. Chicago: University of Chicago Press, 1988. x, 693 p. : ill. (A National Bureau of Economic Research conference report) *Notes:* These papers are the results of a conference organized by the NBER in March 1987. Includes bibliographies and indexes. [LC 87027718; ISN 0226240770; ISN 0226240789]   HF1455. U544 1988   3950

UNITED STATES—ECONOMIC CONDITIONS

Challenges to American values: society, business, and religion. Thomas C. Cochran. New York; Oxford: Oxford University Press, 1985. 147 p. *Notes:* Includes index. Bibliography: p. 127-137. [LC 84019102; ISN 0195035348]   HC103. C623 1985   3951

The course of American economic growth and development. by Louis M. Hacker. New York Wiley, 1970. xxvi, 382 p. (The Wiley series in American economic history) *Notes:* Bibliography: p. 359-361. [LC 75105384; ISN 0471338400]   HC103. H1455   +3952

The economic transformation of America: 1600 to the present. Robert L. Heilbroner, Aaron Singer. 2nd ed. San Diego: Harcourt Brace Jovanovich, c1984. ix, 371 p. : ill. *Notes:* Includes index. Bibliography: p. 354-360. [LC 83081132; ISN 0155187996]   HC103. H39 1984   3953

Encyclopedia of American economic history: studies of the principal movements and ideas. Glenn Porter, editor. New York: Scribner, c1980. 3 v. (1236 p.): ill. *Notes:* Includes bibliographies and index. Non-circulating. *Contents:* Chandler, A. D. Rise and evolution of big business.—Vernon, R. and Wortzel, H. Multinational enterprise.—Tedlow, R. S. Advertising and public relations.—Baughman, J. P. Management. [LC 79004946; ISN 0684162717; $120.00]   HC103. E52   3954

Enterprise: the dynamic economy of a free people. Stuart Bruchey. Cambridge, Mass.: Harvard University Press, 1990. xiv, 645 p. *Notes:* Includes bibliographical references. [LC 89011102; ISN 0674218701; $24.95]   HC103. B78845 1990   3955

A history of American business. Keith L. Bryant, Jr. Henry C. Dethloff. 2nd ed. Englewood Cliffs, N.J.: Prentice Hall, 1990. xiii, 384 p. : ill. *Notes:* Includes bibliographies and index. [LC 89003725; ISN 0133892557; $27.00]   HC103. B7888 1990   3956

Shooting ourselves in the foot. Bernard J. O'Keefe. Boston: Houghton Mifflin, 1985. v, 294 p. [LC 85007651; ISN 0395385113; $15.95]   HC103. O44 1985   3957

Trends in American economic growth, 1929-1982. Edward F. Denison. Washington, D.C.: Brookings Institution, c1985. xxv, 141 p. *Notes:* Includes bibliographicl references and index. [LC 85017413; ISN 0815718098; $10.95; $28.95]   HC106.3. D3668 1985   3958

The wealth of the nation: an economic history of the United States. Stuart Bruchey. 1st ed. New York: Harper & Row, c1988. ix, 259 p. *Notes:* Includes index. [LC 87045602; ISN 0060914556; ISN 0060158549; $9.95; $18.95]   HC103. B78855 1988   3959

UNITED STATES—ECONOMIC CONDITIONS—1918-1945

The structure of a modern economy: the United States, 1929-89. Kenneth E. Boulding; with the assistance of Meng Chi. New York: New York University Press, 1993. xii, 215 p. : ill. *Notes:* Includes bibliographical references (p. 126-128) and index. [LC 92029613; ISN 0814712037; $50.00]
HC106. B6883 1993   3960

UNITED STATES—ECONOMIC CONDITIONS—1945-

Beyond our means: how America's long years of debt, deficits and reckless borrowing now threaten to overwhelm us. Alfred L. Malabre, Jr. 1st ed. New York: Random House, c1987. xvi, 174 p. *Notes:* Includes index. Bibliography: p. [163]-166. [LC 86022002; ISN 0394543459]
HC106.5. M24 1987   3961

The economics of chaos: on revitalizing the American economy. Eliot Janeway. 1st ed. New York: Dutton, c1989. xiv, 402 p. *Notes:* "Truman Talley books." Includes index. Bibliography: p. 383-388. [LC 88016063; ISN 0525247114]
HC106.5. J36 1989   3962

Post-industrial America: a geographical perspective. David Clark. New York: Methuen, c1985. xiv, 220 p. : ill. *Notes:* Includes index. Bibliography: p. [207]-215. [LC 84014851; ISN 0416382509; ISN 0416382606; $25.00; $12.00]
HC106.5. C5826 1985   3963

Understanding American economic decline. edited by Michael A. Bernstein and David E. Adler. Cambridge England; New York: Cambridge University Press, 1994. xvii, 403 p. : ill. *Notes:* Includes bibliographical references and index. [LC 93048755; ISN 0521450632; ISN 0521456797]
HC106.5. U42 1994   +3964

The U.S. economy demystified: the meaning of U.S. business statistics and what they portend for the future. Albert T. Sommers with Lucie R. Blau. 3rd ed. New York: Toronto: New York: Lexington Books; Maxwell Macmillan Canada; Maxwell Macmillan International, c1993. xiv, 192 p. : ill. [LC 92034701; ISN 0029301165; $19.95]
HC106.5. S64 1993   3965

UNITED STATES—ECONOMIC CONDITIONS—1971-1981

The logarithmic century. by Ralph E. Lapp. Englewood Cliffs, N.J. Prentice-Hall, 1973. 263 p. illus. [LC 72013545]
HC106.6. L36   +3966

UNITED STATES—ECONOMIC CONDITIONS—1981—MATHEMATICAL MODELS

The DRI model of the U.S. economy. by Otto Eckstein. New York: McGraw-Hill, c1983. xiii, 253 p. : ill. *Notes:* Includes bibliographical references and indexes. [LC 83013528; ISN 0070189722]
HC106.8. E26 1983   3967

UNITED STATES—ECONOMIC CONDITIONS—1981-

America's new economy: the basic guide. Robert Hamrin. New York: F. Watts, 1988. 484 p. : ill *Notes:* Includes index. Bibliography: p. 467-470. [LC 87037153; ISN 0531150771]   HC106.8. H35 1988   3968

The Cuomo Commission report: a new American formula for a strong economy. by the Cuomo Commission on Trade and Competitiveness; introduction by Mario M. Cuomo; foreword by James D. Robinson III; Lewis B. Kaden, chairman; Lee Smith, editor. New York: Simon & Schuster, c1988. xxviii, 270 p. : ill. (A Touchstone book) *Notes:* Includes index. Includes bibliographical references. [LC 88015648; ISN 067166963X; $19.95]
HC106.8. C86 1988   3969

The great u-turn: corporate restructuring and the polarizing of America. Bennett Harrison & Barry Bluestone. New York: Basic Books, c1988. x, 242 p. : ill. *Notes:* Includes index. Bibliography: p. 205-230. [LC 88047675; ISN 0465027199; $19.95]
HC106.8. H364 1988   3970

The misunderstood economy: what counts and how to count it. Robert Eisner. Boston, Mass.: Harvard Business School Press, c1994. xv, 222 p. : ill. *Notes:* Includes bibliographical references and index. [LC 93031481; ISN 087584443X; $22.95]
HC106.82. E45 1994   +3971

Rendezvous with reality: the American economy after Reagan. Murray Weidenbaum. New York: Basic Books, c1988. x, 313 p. *Notes:* Includes index. Bibliography: p. 287-306. [LC 88047671; ISN 0465069142; $19.95]
HC106.8. W43 1988   3972

The zero-sum solution: building a world-class American economy. Lester C. Thurow. New York: Simon and Schuster, c1985. 414 p. *Notes:* Includes bibliographical references and index. [LC 85014480; ISN 0671552325]   HC106.8. T5 1985   3973

UNITED STATES—ECONOMIC CONDITIONS—TO 1865

The agrarian origins of American capitalism. Allan Kulikoff. Charlottesville: University Press of Virginia, 1992. xiv, 341 p. : ill. *Notes:* Includes bibliographical references (p. 275-329) and index. [LC 92011395; ISN 0813914205]   HC105. K87 1992   3974

UNITED STATES—ECONOMIC POLICY

Presidential economics: the making of economic policy from Roosevelt to Reagan and beyond. Herbert Stein. 2nd rev. ed. Washington, D.C.: American Enterprise Institute for Public Policy Research, 1988. 450 p. *Notes:* Includes index. Bibliography: p. 424-433. [LC 88003498; ISN 0844736562]   HC106. S79 1988   3975

UNITED STATES—ECONOMIC POLICY—1981-

America tomorrow: the choices we face: a report from the Governance Project. Edmund S. Muskie, chair... et al.; edited by Maureen S. Steinbruner. Washington, D.C.: Lanham, MD: Center for National Policy Press; Distributed by arrangement with University Press of America, c1989. xvi, 125 p. *Notes:* Bibliography: p. 123-125. [LC 89000799; ISN 0944237304; $13.75]
       HC106.8. A429 1989   3976
America's economic resurgence: a bold new strategy. Richard Rosecrance. 1st ed. New York: Harper & Row, c1990. ix, 230 p. : ill. *Notes:* Includes bibliographical references and index. [LC 89045710; ISN 0060162511; $22.95]   HC106.8. R665 1990   3977
Charting the course for business growth through the 1990's: interviews. conducted by Gene E. Bradley. Washington, D.C.: Lanham Md.: Fowler-McCracken Commission, International Management and Development Institute; University Press of America, 1990. x, 299 p. : ill. *Notes:* "One element of the Fowler-McCracken Commission's continuing educational work on 'Improving government-business cooperation in the conduct of international economic policy'"—T.p. verso. [LC 89029798; ISN 0819176850; $35.75]   HC106.8. C473 1990   3978
The culture of contentment. John Kenneth Galbraith. Boston: Houghton Mifflin Co., 1992. ix, 195 p. *Notes:* Includes bibliographical references and index. [LC 91047038; ISN 0395572282; $24.00]
       HC106.8. G3394 1992   3979
The new economic role of American states: strategies in a competitive world economy. edited by R. Scott Fosler (Committee for Economic Development). New York: Oxford University Press, 1988. x, 370 p. *Notes:* Includes bibliographical references and index. [LC 87012499; ISN 0195050037]
       HC106.8. N495 1988   3980
The power economy: building an economy that works. John Oliver Wilson. 1st ed. Boston: Little, Brown, c1985. xvii, 302 p. *Notes:* Includes index. Bibliography: p. [291]-294. [LC 85000169; ISN 0316945021; $19.95]   HC106.8. W55 1985   3981
The resurgent liberal: (and other unfashionable prophecies). Robert B. Reich. 1st ed. New York, NY: Times Books, c1989. xv, 303 p. *Notes:* Includes index. [LC 89004418; ISN 0812918339; $19.95]
       HC106.8. R454 1989   3982
The seven fat years: and how to do it again. Robert L. Bartley. New York: Toronto: New York: Free Press; Maxwell Macmillan Canada; Maxwell Macmillan International, c1992. xiv, 347 p. : ill. *Notes:* Includes bibliographical references (p. 323-330) and index. [LC 92001137; ISN 002901915X; $22.95]   HC106.8. B35 1992   3983
The supply-side revolution: an insider's account of policymaking in Washington. Paul Craig Roberts. Cambridge, Mass.: Harvard University Press, 1984. 327 p. : ill. *Notes:* Includes bibliographical references and index. [LC 83018340; ISN 0674856201; $18.50]   HC106.8. R6 1984   3984
Winning with synergy: how America can regain the competitive edge. Peter and Susan Corning. 1st ed. San Francisco: Harper & Row, c1986. 274 p. : ill. *Notes:* Includes index. [LC 85045350; ISN 0062501550]   HC106.8. C668 1986   3985

UNITED STATES—ECONOMIC POLICY—1981-1993

The age of diminished expectations: U.S. economic policy in the 1990s. Paul Krugman. Rev. and updated ed. Cambridge, Mass.: MIT Press, c1994. xii, 239 p. : ill. *Notes:* Includes index. [LC 93006411; ISN 0262610922; $12.95]   HC106.8. K78 1994   +3986

American economic policy in the 1980s. edited and with an introductory essay by Martin Feldstein. Chicago: University of Chicago Press, 1994. x, 823 p. : ill. *Notes:* Includes bibliographical references and indexes. *Contents:* American economic policy in the 1980s: a personal view / Martin Feldstein—Monetary policy / Michael Mussa, Paul A. Volcker, James Tobin—Tax policy / Don Fullerton, Charls E. Walker, Russell B. Long—Budget policy / James M. Poterba, David Stockman, Charles Schultze—Exchange rate policy / Jeffrey A. Frankel, C. Fred Bergsten, Michael Mussa—Economic regulation / Paul L. Joskow and Roger G. Noll, William Niskanen, Elizabeth Bailey—Health and safety regulation / W. Kip Viscusi, Christopher DeMuth, James Burnley—Financial regulation / Robert E. Litan, William M. Isaac, William Taylor—Antitrust policy / Phillip Areeda, William F. Baxter, Harry M. Reasoner—Trade policy / J. David Richardson, Lionel H. Olmer, Paula Stern—LDC debt policy / Paul Krugman, Thomas O. Enders, William R, Rhodes—Policy toward the aged / David A. Wise and Richard G. Woodbury, Rudolph Penner. [LC 93027972; ISN 0226240932]   HC106.8. A439 1994   +3987

The CSIS Strengthening of America Commission. Sam Nunn, Pete Domenici, cochairmen. Washington, DC: Center for Strategic and International Studies, c1992. 182 p. *Notes:* On cover: "First report." Spine title: The Strengthening of America Commission: first report. Includes bibliographical references (p. 152-161).; ISN 0892062118; $14.00]   HC106.8. C79 1992   3988

The economy in the Reagan years: the economic consequences of the Reagan administrations. Anthony S. Campagna. Westport, Conn.: Greenwood Press, 1994. xiii, 225 p. *Notes:* Includes bibliographical references (p. [217]-219) and index. [LC 93014125; ISN 0313288666]
    HC106.8. C34 1994   +3989

Facing up: how to rescue the economy from crushing debt and restore the American dream. by Peter G. Peterson; foreword by Warren B. Rudman and Paul E. Tsongas. New York: Simon & Schuster, c1993. 411 p. : ill. (some col.) *Notes:* Includes index. [LC 93030838; ISN 0671796429; $22.00]
    HC106.8. P465 1993   +3990

Growth with equity: economic policymaking for the next century. Martin Neil Baily, Gary Burtless, Robert E. Litan. Washington, D.C.: Brookings Institution, c1993. xv, 239 p. : ill. *Notes:* Includes bibliographical references (p. 208-232) and index. [LC 92044225; ISN 0815707665; $31.95]
    HC106.8. B345 1993   3991

UNITED STATES—ECONOMIC POLICY—TO 1933

Regulating a new economy: public policy and economic change in America, 1900-1933. Morton Keller. Cambridge, Mass.: Harvard University Press, 1990. x, 300 p. *Notes:* Includes bibliographical references and index. [LC 89078193; ISN 0674753623; $27.50]   HC106. K45 1990   3992

UNITED STATES—FOREIGN ECONOMIC RELATIONS

Acquiring the future: America's survival and success in the global economy. Joseph E. Pattison. Homewood, Ill.: Dow Jones-Irwin, c1990. vii, 278 p. *Notes:* Includes bibliographical references. [LC 89017071; ISN 1556231849; $22.95]   HF1455. P33 1990   3993

Keeping pace: U.S. policies and global economic change. edited by John Yochelson. Cambridge, Mass.: Ballinger, c1988. xxi, 274 p. *Notes:* "A Center for Strategic and International Studies book." Includes bibliographies and index. [LC 88010585; ISN 0887302521]   HF1455. K424 1988   3994

U.S. competitiveness in world economy. edited by Bruce R. Scott and George C. Lodge; contributors, Joseph L. Bower... et al. Boston, Mass.: Harvard Business School Press, c1985. x, 543 p. : ill. *Notes:* "Harvard Business School, Research Colloquium." Papers originally prepared for the Harvard Business 75th anniversary colloquium entitled "U.S. Competitiveness in the world Economy." Includes bibliographical references and index. [LC 84015714; ISN 0875841600; $32.50]
    HF1455. U4583 1984   3995

UNITED STATES—FOREIGN ECONOMIC RELATIONS—DEVELOPING COUNTRIES

America's new competitors: the challenge of the newly industrializing countries. edited by Thornton F. Bradshaw... et al. Cambridge, Mass.: Ballinger Pub. Co., 1988. xiv, 290 p. : ill. *Notes:* Includes bibliographies and index. [LC 87019295; ISN 0887301355]   HF1456.5.D44 T65 1988   3996

UNITED STATES—FOREIGN ECONOMIC RELATIONS—JAPAN

Agents of influence. Pat Choate. New York: A.A. Knopf, 1990. xxii, 295 p., 8 p. of plates: ill. *Notes:* Includes bibliographical references. [LC 90053118; ISN 0394579011; $22.95]
  HF1456.5.J3 C54 1990   3997
American power, the new world order and the Japanese challenge. William R. Nester. Houndmills, Basingstoke, Hants England: Macmillan, 1993. vi, 492 p.; ISN 0333578953]
  HF1456.5.J3 N47 1993   3998
Turning the tables: a Machiavellian strategy for dealing with Japan. Daniel Burstein. New York: Simon & Schuster, c1993. 272 p. *Notes:* Includes bibliographical references and index. [LC 92041869; ISN 0671789538; $22.00]   HF1456.5.J3 B78 1993   3999

UNITED STATES—INDUSTRIES

Is new technology enough?: making and remaking U.S. basic industries. edited by Donald A. Hicks. Washington, D.C.: Lanham, Md.: American Enterprise Institute for Public Policy Research; UPA distributor, c1988. xiii, 353 p. : ill. *Notes:* "Competing in a changing world economy project." Includes bibliographies and index. [LC 88019742; ISN 0844736597; ISN 0844736600]
  HC106.8. I78 1988   4000
The new industrial state. John Kenneth Galbraith. 4th ed. Boston: Houghton Mifflin, 1985. xxxv, 438 p. *Notes:* Includes bibliographical references and index. [LC 85011956; ISN 0395389917; $19.95]
  HC106.6. G35 1985   4001

UNITED STATES—INDUSTRIES—HISTORY

The entrepreneurs: an American adventure. Robert Sobel and David B. Sicilia; illustrations compiled by Martin W. Sandler. Boston: Houghton Mifflin, 1986. x, 278 p. : ill. (some col.) *Notes:* Includes index. Bibliography: p. 273-274. [LC 86010650; ISN 0395420202; $29.95]   HC103. S683 1986   4002
Made in the U.S.A.: the history of American business. Thomas V. DiBacco. 1st ed. New York: Harper & Row, c1987. xii, 290 p. *Notes:* Includes index. Bibliography: p. 277-278. [LC 86045652; ISN 0060156244; $19.95]   HC103. D46 1987   4003

UNITED STATES—INDUSTRIES—HISTORY—20TH CENTURY

The rise of the corporate commonwealth: U.S. business and public policy in the twentieth century. Louis Galambos and Joseph Pratt. New York: Basic Books, c1988. xiv, 286 p. : ill. *Notes:* Includes index. Bibliography: p. 267-273. [LC 87047784; ISN 0465070299; $19.95]   HC103. G29 1988   4004

UNITED STATES—INDUSTRIES—LOCATION

The new corporate frontier: the big move to Small Town, USA. David A. Heenan. New York: McGraw-Hill, c1991. x, 262 p. *Notes:* Includes bibliographical references (p. 244-247) and index. [LC 91003165; ISN 0070277702; $19.95]   HC110.D5 H44 1991   4005

UNITED STATES—MANUFACTURES

American manufacturing in a global market. edited by Kenneth W. Chilton, Melinda E. Warren, Murray L. Weidenbaum. Boston: Kluwer Academic Publishers, c1990. xvii, 214 p. : ill. *Notes:* Prepared by the Center for the Study of American Business at Washington University, Saint Louis. Includes bibliographical references. [LC 89039844; ISN 0792390512; $47.50]   HD9725. A74 1990   4006

Competing in world-class manufacturing: America's 21st century challenge. National Center for Manufacturing Sciences; Craig Giffi, Aleda V. Roth, Gregory M. Seal. Homewood, Ill.: Business One Irwin, c1990. xvi, 410 p. : ill. *Notes:* Includes bibliographical references. [LC 90045315; ISN 1556234015; $42.50]   HD9725. G53 1990   4007

Manufacturing matters: the myth of the post-industrial economy. Stephen S. Cohen, John Zysman. New York: Basic Books, c1987. xiv, 297 p. : ill. *Notes:* "A Council on Foreign Relations Book." Includes bibliographical references and index. [LC 86047737; ISN 0465043844]   HD9725. C58 1987   4008

UNITED STATES—MANUFACTURES—CONGRESSES

The American edge: leveraging manufacturing's hidden assets. Janice A. Klein, Jeffrey G. Miller, editors. New York: McGraw-Hill, c1993. xii, 259 p. : ill. *Notes:* Based on the Boston University Roundtable held in 1990. "Explores the... strengths of American business practices and the areas in which American companies actually have an important advantange over foreign competitors."—Dustjacket. Includes bibliographical references and index. *Contents:* 5. Production management / Wickham Skinner—7. Women managers / Lyn Tatum Christiansen and Julie H. Hertenstein. [LC 93025092; ISN 007035040X; $24.95]   HD9725. A69 1993   4009

UNITED STATES—MANUFACTURES—LABOR PRODUCTIVITY

Efficiency in U.S. manufacturing industries. Richard E. Caves, David R. Barton. Cambridge, Mass.: MIT Press, c1990. 194 p. : ill *Notes:* Includes bibliographical references. [LC 89028832; ISN 0262031574; $24.95]   HD9725. C34 1990   4010

UNITED STATES—MANUFACTURES—MANAGEMENT

Dynamic manufacturing: creating the learning organization. Robert H. Hayes, Steven C. Wheelwright, Kim B. Clark. New York: London: Free Press; Collier Macmillan, c1988. x, 429 p. : ill. *Notes:* Includes index. Bibliography: p. 401-409. [LC 88000367; ISN 0029142113]
HD9725. H38 1988   4011

Manufacturing for competitive advantage: becoming a world class manufacturer. Thomas G. Gunn. Cambridge, Mass.: Ballinger Pub. Co., c1987. xvi, 221 p. *Notes:* Includes index. Bibliography: p. 215-216. [LC 87001093; ISN 0887301541]   HD9725. G85 1987   4012

Manufacturing renaissance. edited with an introduction by Gary P. Pisano and Robert H. Hayes. Boston, MA: Harvard Business School Press, c1995. xxvi, 346 p. [LC 94043320; ISN 0875846106; $29.95]   HD9725. M363 1995   +4013

Manufacturing's new mandate: the tools for leadership. by Dan Ciampa. New York: Wiley, c1988. xix, 233 p. : ill. *Notes:* Includes index. [LC 88002515; ISN 0471633755]   HD9725. C49 1988   4014

Restoring our competitive edge: competing through manufacturing. Robert H. Hayes, Steven C. Wheelwright. New York: Wiley, c1984. x, 427 p. : ill. *Notes:* Includes bibliographies and index. [LC 84003710; ISN 0471051594; $19.95]   HD9725. H39 1984   4015

Time-based competition: the next battleground in American manufacturing. Joseph D. Blackburn, editor. Homewood, Ill.: Business One Irwin, c1991. ix, 314 p. : ill. *Notes:* Includes bibliographical referenes and index. [LC 90003471; ISN 1556233213; $34.95]   HD9725. T57 1991   4016

UNITED STATES—MANUFACTURES—TECHNOLOGICAL INNOVATIONS

Strategic manufacturing: dynamic new directions for the 1990s. Patricia E. Moody, editor. Homewood, Ill.: Dow Jones-Irwin, c1990. x, 390 p.; ill. *Notes:* Includes index. [LC 89035044; ISN 1556231938; $39.95]   HD9725. S73 1990   4017

UNITED STATES—MANUFACTURES—TECHNOLOGICAL INNOVATIONS—DECISION MAKING—CASE STUDIES

Deciding to innovate: how firms justify advanced technology. James W. Dean, Jr. Cambridge, Mass.: Ballinger, 1987. xviii, 164 p. *Notes:* Includes bibliographies and index. [LC 87017432; ISN 0887301894]   HD9725. D35 1987   4018

UNITED STATES—MANUFACTURES—TECHNOLOGICAL INNOVATIONS—MANAGEMENT

Revitalizing manufacturing: text and cases. Janice A. Klein. Homewood, IL: Irwin, 1990. xiv, 643 p. : ill. *Notes:* Includes bibliographical references and indexes. [LC 89015222; ISN 0256068097; $44.95]   HD9725. K57 1990   4019

Taking charge of manufacturing: how companies are combining technological and organizational innovations to compete successfully. John E. Ettlie. 1st ed. San Francisco: Jossey-Bass, 1988. xix, 194 p. : ill. (The Jossey-Bass management series) *Notes:* Includes index. Bibliography: p. 173-186. [LC 87046333; ISN 1555420869]   HD9725. E87 1988   4020

UNITED STATES—POLITICS AND GOVERNMENT

American government: institutions and policies. James Q. Wilson. 5th ed. Lexington, Mass.: D.C. Heath, c1992. xv, 665, 84 p. : ill. *Notes:* Includes bibliographical references and indexes. [LC 91071584; ISN 0669247707]   JK274. W67 1992   4021

UNITED STATES—POLITICS AND GOVERNMENT—1945-1989—DECISION MAKING—CASE STUDIES

Thinking in time: the uses of history for decision-makers. Richard E. Neustadt, Ernest R. May. New York: London: Free Press; Collier Macmillan, c1986. xxii, 329 p. : ill. *Notes:* Includes index. Bibliography: p. 295-319. [LC 85029169; ISN 0029227909]   E743. N378 1986   4022

UNITED STATES—POLITICS AND GOVERNMENT—1981-1989

Tales of a new America. Robert B. Reich. 1st ed. New York, N.Y.: Times Books, 1987. xiii, 290 p. *Notes:* Includes index. Bibliography: p. 255-275. [LC 86023139; ISN 0812916247; $19.95]   JK271. R39 1987   4023

UNITED STATES—POLITICS AND GOVERNMENT—1989-

The end of the American century. Steven Schlossstein. New York: Chicago, Ill.: Congdon & Weed; Distributed by Contemporary Books, c1989. xv, 537 p. *Notes:* Maps on lining papers. Includes bibliographical references (p. 505-527). [LC 89038064; $22.95]   E881. S35 1989   4024

Mandate for change. edited by Will Marshall and Martin Schram. Berkley trade paperback ed. New York: Berkley Books, c1993. xxviii, 388 p. *Notes:* "Prepared by the Progressive Policy Institute"—D/P. [4] of cover. Includes bibliograhical references (p. 341-388).; ISN 0425139646; $11.95]   JK421. M36 1993   4025

UNITED STATES—POPULATION

The first universal nation: leading indicators and ideas about the surge of America in the 1990s. Ben J. Wattenberg. New York: Toronto: New York: Free Press; Collier Macmillan Canada; Maxwell Macmillan International, 1991. xiv, 418 p. : ill. [LC 90003803; ISN 0029340012; $22.95]   HB3505. W28 1991   4026

UNITED STATES—RELATIONS—JAPAN

A cold peace: America, Japan, Germany, and the struggle for supremacy. Jeffrey E. Garten. New York: Times Books, c1992. viii, 277 p. *Notes:* "A Twentieth Century Fund book." Includes bibliographical references (p. 258-270) and index. [LC 91058013; ISN 0812919793; $22.00 U.S.A. ($27.50 Canada)]   E183.8.J3 G37 1992   4027

For richer, for poorer: the new U.S.-Japan relationship. Ellen L. Frost. New York, NY: Council on Foreign Relations, c1987. xiii, 198 p. *Notes:* Includes index. Bibliography: p. 181-185. [LC 87009150; ISN 0876090242; ISN 0876090250; $9.95; $19.50]   E183.8.J3 F73 1987   4028

UNITED STATES—SOCIAL CONDITIONS

The ecological vision: reflections on the American condition. Peter F. Drucker. New Brunswick, N.J.: Transaction Publishers, c1993. vii, 466 p. *Notes:* Includes bibliographical references and index. [LC 92003967; ISN 1560000619]   HN57. D76 1993   4029

The road to colossus: a celebration of American ingenuity. Thomas Kiernan. New York: W. Morrow, c1985. 332 p. *Notes:* Includes index. [LC 84010861; ISN 0688004563]   HN57. K525 1985   4030

UNITED STATES—SOCIAL CONDITIONS—1865-1918

The flowering of the third America: the making of an organizational society, 1850-1920. Maury Klein. Chicago: Ivan R. Dee, c1993. 217 p. *Notes:* Includes bibliographical references (p. [204]-211) and index. [LC 93013869; ISN 1566630290]   HN57. K55 1993   +4031

UNITED STATES—SOCIAL CONDITIONS—1945-

The new individualists: the generation after The organization man. Paul Leinberger and Bruce Tucker. 1st ed. New York, N.Y.: HarperCollins Publishers, 1991. x, 454 p. *Notes:* Includes index. [LC 90055932; ISN 006016591X; $22.95]   HN65. L365 1991   4032

UNITED STATES—SOCIAL CONDITIONS—1980-

The clustering of America. Michael J. Weiss. 1st ed. New York: Harper & Row, c1988. xvi, 416 p. : col. ill. *Notes:* "A Tilden Press book." Includes index. [LC 88045070; ISN 0060157909; $22.50]   HN59.2. W45 1988   4033

Megatrends 2000: the new directions for the 1990's. John Naisbitt and Patricia Aburdene. 1st ed. New York: Morrow, c1990. 384 p. *Notes:* Includes bibliographical references (p. 315-364). [LC 89013301; ISN 0688072240; $21.95]   HN59.2. N33 1990   4034

Not like our parents: how the baby boom generation is changing America. D. Quinn Mills. 1st ed. New York: Morrow, c1987. 297 p. *Notes:* Bibliography: p. [291]-297. [LC 87013908; ISN 0688068359]   HN59.2. M55 1987   4035

UNITED STATES—SOCIAL LIFE AND CUSTOMS—1945-1970

The fifties. David Halberstam. New York: Villard Books, 1993. xi, 800 p. : ill. *Notes:* Includes bibliographical references (p. [737]-745) and index. [LC 92056815; ISN 0679415599; $27.50 ($35.00 Can.)]   E169.02. H34 1993   +4036

UNIVAC COMPUTER

A few good men from Univac. David E. Lundstrom. Cambridge, Mass.: MIT Press, c1987. xii, 227 p., [18] p. of plates: ill. (MIT Press series in the history of computing) [LC 87004193; ISN 0262121204]   QA76.8.U6 L86 1987   4037

URBAN TRANSPORTATION

Urban transportation policy: new perspectives. David R. Miller, editor. Lexington, Mass. Lexington Books, c1972. xiv, 209 p. illus. *Notes:* "Sponsored by the Urban Transportation Institute, a part of the Metropolitan Studies Program at Syracuse University." Bibliography: p. 199-200. [LC 72007018; ISN 0669846325]   HE308. U73 1970   +4038

USA TODAY (ARLINGTON, VA.)

The making of McPaper: the inside story of USA today. by Peter Prichard; foreword by Charles Kuralt. Kansas City: Andrews, McMeel & Parker, c1987. xiii, 370 p. : ill. *Notes:* Includes index. [LC 87017537; ISN 0836279395; $19.95]   PN4899.A635 U837 1987   4039

USFL (ORGANIZATION)

The $1 league: the rise and fall of the USFL. Jim Byrne. 1st ed. New York: Prentice Hall Press, 1987, c1986. 352 p. [LC 86030272; ISN 0133317609; $17.95]   GV955.5.U8 B97 1986   4040

VENTURE CAPITAL

The Arthur Young guide to raising venture capital. G. Steven Burrill and Craig T. Norback. 1st ed. Blue Ridge Summit, PA: Liberty House, c1988. xi, 252 p. : ill. *Notes:* Includes index. Bibliography: p. [245]-246. [LC 88001897; ISN 0830630147; $24.95]   HG4751. B87 1988   4041

The complete book of raising capital. Lawrence W. Tuller. New York: McGraw-Hill, c1994. xix, 446 p.; 1 computer disk (3 1/2 in.) *Notes:* System requirements for computer disk: IBM-compatible PC; DOS. Forms in ASCII. "PIN 065490-5"—T.p. verso. Includes bibliographical references and index. [LC 93030891; ISN 0070654905]   HG4751. T84 1994   +4042

Financing and managing fast-growth companies: the venture capital process. George Kozmetsky, Michael D. Gill, Jr., Raymond W. Smilor. Lexington, Mass.: Lexington Books, 1985. xxii, 144 p. : ill. *Notes:* Includes index. Bibliography: p. [133]-136. [LC 84048473; ISN 0669094811]   HG4963. K69 1985   4043

Finding private venture capital for your firm: a complete guide. Robert J. Gaston. New York: Wiley, c1989. ix, 260 p. : ill. *Notes:* Includes bibliographical references and index. [LC 88015519; ISN 0471610089]   HG4963. G37 1989   4044

How to raise venture capital. edited by Stanley E. Pratt & the editors of Venture capital journal. New York: Scribner, c1982. xvii, 254 p. *Notes:* Originally published, with a directory, as: Guide to venture capital sources. 5th ed. Wellesley Hills, Mass.: Capital Pub. Corp., c1981. Includes index. [LC 82003393; ISN 0684174448; $17.95]   HG4027.7. G84 1982   4045

Inside venture capital: past, present, and future. Robert C. Perez. New York, N.Y.: Praeger Publishers, 1986. xiii, 189 p. *Notes:* Includes index. Bibliography: p. 167-176. [LC 85030146; ISN 0275921182]   HG4963. P44 1986   4046

The new venturers: inside the high-stakes world of venture capital. John W. Wilson. Reading, Mass.: Addison-Wesley Pub. Co., c1985. ix, 237 p. *Notes:* Includes bibliographical references and index. [LC 85000755; ISN 0201096811; $17.95 (est.)]   HG4963. W55 1985   4047

Nothing ventured: the perils and payoffs of the great American venture capital game. Robert J. Kunze. New York, N.Y.: HarperBusiness, 1990. 252 p. [LC 90023334; ISN 0887304613; $22.95]   HG4963. K86 1990   4048

Obtaining venture financing: principles and practices. James W. Henderson. Lexington, Mass.: Lexington Books, c1988. xii, 366 p. : ill. *Notes:* Includes bibliographical references and index. [LC 85040234; ISN 0669109312]   HG4963. H44 1988   4049

QED report on venture capital financial analysis. by James L. Plummer, with the assistance of James Walker... et al. Palo Alto, CA (125 California Ave., Palo Alto 94306): QED Research, c1987. 1 v. (various pagings): ill. *Notes:* Includes bibliography. [LC 88120574]   HG4751. P58 1987   4050

Raising venture capital and the entrepreneur. Leonard A. Batterson. Englewood Cliffs, N.J.: Prentice-Hall, c1986. xii, 465 p. *Notes:* Includes indexes. Bibliography: p. 178-179. [LC 85030095; ISN 0137526849; $27.50]   HG4963. B38 1986   4051

Risk and reward: venture capital and the making of America's great industries. Thomas M. Doerflinger, Jack L. Rivkin. 1st ed. New York: Random House, 1987. xiv, 320 p.; 24 cm. *Notes:* Includes index. Bibliography: p. [297]-307. [LC 86010107; ISN 0394549295; $19.95]   HG4963. D66 1987   4052

Venture capital at the crossroads. William D. Bygrave, Jeffry A. Timmons. Boston, Mass.: Harvard Business School Press, c1992. xi, 356 p. : ill. *Notes:* Includes bibliographical references (p. 325-339) and index. [LC 92002603; ISN 0875843042; $35.00]   HG4751. B94 1992   4053

Venture capital handbook. David Gladstone. New and rev. Englewood Cliffs, N.J.: Prentice Hall, c1988. xv, 350 p. *Notes:* Includes index. [LC 87061607; ISN 0139415017; $19.95]
HG4965. G57 1988   4054

Venture capital: law, business strategies, and investment planning. Joseph W. Bartlett. New York: J. Wiley, c1988. xx, 514 p. *Notes:* Includes index. Bibliography: p. 437-478. [LC 87030352; ISN 0471850764]   KF1366. B37 1988   4055

Venture capital today: a practical guide to the venture capital market. Tony Lorenz. 2nd ed. New York; London: Woodhead-Faulkner, 1989. xiii, 242 p. *Notes:* Previous ed.: 1985. Includes index. [LC 89040073; ISN 0859415910; £35.00]   HG5441. L67 1989   4056

Venture Japan: how growing companies worldwide can tap into the Japanese venture capital markets. James W. Borton. Chicago, Ill.: Probus Pub. Co., c1992. xxi, 226 p. : ill. *Notes:* Includes bibliographical references and index.; ISN 1557382662]   HG4751. B67 1992   4057

The Venture magazine complete guide to venture capital. Clinton Richardson; with an introduction by Arthur Lipper III. New York: New American Library, c1987. xxiv, 261 p. : ill. *Notes:* "A Plume book." Includes bibliographical references and index. [LC 87005721; ISN 0452259185]
HG4751. R52 1987   4058

VERBAL SELF-DEFENSE

Genderspeak: men, women, and the gentle art of verbal self-defense. Suzette Haden Elgin. New York: Wiley, c1993. xx, 307 p. : ill. *Notes:* "Powerful techniques for improving communication and disarming verbal attacks"—Cover. Includes bibliographical references (p. [293]-302) and index. [LC 92037933; ISN 0471580163; $12.95]   BF637.V47 E42 1993   4059

VERNON SAVINGS & LOAN

The daisy chain: how borrowed billions sank a Texas S&L. James O'Shea. New York: Pocket Books, c1991. xi, 351 p. *Notes:* Includes bibliographical references (p. 297-337) and index. [LC 90025239; ISN 0671733036; $19.95 ($24.95 Can.)]   HG2626.V47 O84 1991   4060

VERTICAL INTEGRATION

Multinationals and world trade: vertical integration and the division of labour in world industries. Mark Casson in association with David Barry... et al. London; Boston: G. Allen & Unwin, 1986. xi, 401 p. : ill. *Notes:* Includes index. Bibliography: p. [372]-388. [LC 85015734; ISN 0043381251]
HD2748. C37 1986   4061

VIDEO TAPE RECORDER INDUSTRY

Fast forward: Hollywood, the Japanese, and the onslaught of the VCR. James Lardner. 1st ed. New York: Norton, c1987. 344 p. *Notes:* Includes index. [LC 86012874; ISN 0393023893]
HD9696.V532 L37 1987   4062

VIDEODISC PLAYERS

RCA and the VideoDisc: the business of research. Margaret B.W. Graham. Cambridge Cambridgeshire; New York: Cambridge University Press, 1986. xiv, 258 p. : ill. (Studies in economic history and policy) *Notes:* Includes index. Bibliography: p. 238-243. [LC 86002241; ISN 0521322820]   TK6685. G73 1986   4063

VOCATIONAL GUIDANCE FOR WOMEN

The career psychology of women. edited by Nancy Betz, Louise F. Fitzgerald. Orlando: Academic Press, 1987. xiii, 305 p. *Notes:* Includes index. Bibliography: p. 259-299. [LC 86022284; ISN 0120944057]   HF5382.65. C37 1987   4064

VOLCKER, PAUL A

Volcker: portrait of the money man. William R. Neikirk. Chicago: Congdon & Weed; Distributed by Contemporary Books, c1987. xvi, 222 p. *Notes:* Bibliography: p. 221-222. [LC 87019953; ISN 0865531781]   HB119.V6 N45 1987   4065

VOLVO, AKTIEBOLAGET

Alternatives to lean production: work organization in the Swedish auto industry. Christian Berggren. Ithaca, N.Y.: ILR Press, c1992. xiii, 286 p. : ill. *Notes:* Includes bibliographical references (p. [267]-276) and index. [LC 92020986; ISN 087546193X]   HD9710.S84 V64134 1992   4066

WAGES AND LABOR PRODUCTIVITY

Paying for productivity: a look at the evidence. Alan S. Blinder, editor. Washington, D.C.: The Brookings Institution, 1990. xii, 308 p. *Notes:* Includes bibliographical references. [LC 89025328; ISN 0815710003; ISN 0815709994; $28.95; $9.95]   HD4945. P29 1990   4067

WAGES

A future of lousy jobs?: the changing structure of U.S. wages. Gary Burtless, editor. Washington, D.C.: Brookings Institution, c1990. xiv, 242 p. : ill. *Notes:* Includes bibliographical references. [LC 89077414; ISN 0815711808; $29.95]   HD4975. F87 1990   4068

Persistent inequalities: wage disparity under capitalist competition. Howard Botwinick. Princeton, N.J.: Princeton University Press, c1993. xiv, 300 p. : ill. *Notes:* Includes bibliographical references (p. [277]-294) and index. [LC 92041291; ISN 0691042977]   HD4909. B63 1993   +4069

WALL STREET

Bear trap: why Wall Street doesn't work. Paul Gibson. New York: Atlantic Monthly Press, c1993. x, 246 p. [LC 92043735; ISN 0871135345]   HG4572. G47 1993   4070

Behavior of prices on Wall Street: market inclinations help prediction produce profits. by Arthur A. Merrill. 2nd ed., rev. Chappaqua, N.Y.: Analysis Press, c1984. 147 p. : ill. *Notes:* Bibliography: p. 140-145. [LC 84072279; ISN 0911894497]   HG4636. M468   4071

Minding Mr. Market: ten years on Wall Street with Grant's interest rate observer. James Grant. 1st ed. New York: Farrar Straus Giroux, c1993. xxii, 424 p. : ill. *Notes:* Collection of essays previously published in Grant's interest rate observer. Includes bibliographical references and index. [LC 93073197; ISN 0374166013; $25.00]   HG4572. G73 1993   +4072

Once in Golconda: a true drama of Wall Street, 1920-1938. John Brooks. New York: W.W. Norton, 1980, 1969. 307 p. *Notes:* Reprint of the ed. published by Harper & Row. "Portions of this book have appeared in American heritage and The New Yorker." Includes index. Bibliography: p. 289-297. [LC 79028716; ISN 0393013758]   HG4572. B7 1980   4073

101 years on Wall street: an investor's almanac. by John Dennis Brown. Englewood Cliffs, N.J.: Prentice Hall, c1991. xii, 308 p. : ill. *Notes:* Includes bibliographical references and index. [LC 90021454; ISN 0139460136; $24.95]   HG4572. B74 1991   4074

The plungers and the peacocks: an update of the classic history of the stock market. Dana L. Thomas. 1st rev. ed. New York: Morrow, c1989. 384 p. : ill. *Notes:* Includes index. Bibliography: p. [361]-373. [LC 88026056; ISN 0688081363]   HG4572. T46 1989   4075

Trading secrets. R. Foster Winans. 1st ed. New York: St. Martin's Press, c1986. xiv, 320 p., 4 p. of plates: ill. *Notes:* Includes index. [LC 86012700; ISN 0312812272; $17.95]   HG4572. W547 1986   4076

WALL STREET JOURNAL

The power and the money: inside the Wall Street journal. Francis X. Dealy, Jr. Secaucus, N.J.: Carol Pub. Group, c1993. 374 p. : ill. *Notes:* "A Birch Lane Press book." Includes bibliographical references (p. [366]-367) and index. [LC 92035893; ISN 1559721189; $22.50 ($27.95 Can.)]
PN4899.W35 D42 1993   4077

Wordly power: the making of the Wall Street journal. Edward E. Scharff. 1st ed. New York: Beaufort Books, 1986. xiii, 305, [22] p. *Notes:* Includes index. Bibliography: p. 293-295. [LC 85026741; ISN 0825303591]
PN4899.W5 S35   4078

WALLACE, DEWITT

Theirs was the kingdom: Lila and DeWitt Wallace and the story of the Reader's Digest. John Heidenry. New York: Norton, c1993. 701 p. : ill. *Notes:* Includes bibliographical references and index. [LC 93012764; ISN 0393034666]
HC102.5.W34 H44 1993   +4079

WALT DISNEY COMPANY

The Disney touch: how a daring management team revived an entertainment empire. Ron Grover. Homewood, IL: Business One Irwin, c1991. xix, 315 p., [16] p. of plates: ill. (some col.) *Notes:* Includes bibliographical references (p. 283-300) and index. [LC 90027124; ISN 155623385X; $22.95]
PN1999.W27 G76 1991   4080

Prince of the magic kingdom: Michael Eisner and the re-making of Disney. Joe Flower. New York, N.Y.: J. Wiley, c1991. viii, 309 p., [8] p. of plates: ill. *Notes:* Includes index. [LC 91016601; ISN 0471524654; $22.95]
PN1999.W27 F5 1991   4081

WALT DISNEY PRODUCTIONS

Storming the magic kingdom: Wall Street, the raiders and the battle for Disney. by John Taylor. 1st ed. New York: Knopf: Distributed by Random House, 1987. x, 261 p., [16] p. of plates *Notes:* Includes index. A Borzoi book. [LC 86046147; ISN 0394546407; $19.95 (est.)]
PN1999.W27 T39 1987   4082

WALT DISNEY WORLD (FLA.)—FINANCE

Vinyl leaves: Walt Disney World and America. Stephen M. Fjellman. Boulder: Westview Press, 1992. xvii, 492 p. *Notes:* Includes bibliographical references and index. [LC 91043693; ISN 0813314720]
GV1853.3.F62 W344 1992   4083

WALTON, SAM

Sam Walton, made in America: my story. by Sam Walton with John Huey. 1st ed. New York: Doubleday, 1992. xiii, 269 p. : ill. (some col.) *Notes:* Includes index. [LC 92018874; ISN 0385426151; $22.50 ($27.50 Can.)]
HC102.5.W35 A3 1992   +4084

The Sam Walton story: the retailing of middle America: (a revealing look at the man and his empire). by Austin Teutsch. Austin, Tex.: Golden Touch Press, c1991. xiii, 224 p., [10] p. of plates: ill. *Notes:* Includes index.; ISN 096303460X; $9.95]
HC102.5.W35 T48 1991   4085

WANG, AN

Lessons: an autobiography. An Wang, with Eugene Linden. Reading, Mass.: Addison-Wesley, c1986. 248 p., [28] p. of plates: ill. *Notes:* Includes index. [LC 86010768; ISN 0201094002]
HD9696.C62 A3 1986   4086

WARBURG FAMILY

The Warburgs: the twentieth-century odyssey of a remarkable Jewish family. Ron Chernow. 1st ed. New York: Random House, c1993. xvii, 820 p. : ill. *Notes:* Includes bibliographical references (p. [729]-739) and index. [LC 93016599; ISN 0679418237; $30.00 ($39.00 Can.)]
HG1552.W37 C47 1993   +4087

WAREHOUSES

Practical handbook of warehousing. Kenneth B. Ackerman. 2nd ed. Washington: Traffic Service Corp., c1986. xxvii, 612 p. : ill. *Notes:* Includes bibliographical references and index.; ISN 0874080363; $40.00]
HF5485. A249 1986   4088

Reinventing the warehouse: world class distribution logistics. Roy L. Harmon; foreword by William C. Copacino New York: Toronto: New York: Free Press; Maxwell Macmillan Canada; Maxwell Macmillan International, c1993. xix, 364 p. : ill., maps *Notes:* Includes bibliographical references (p. 341-348) and index. [LC 92037644; ISN 0029138639; $39.95]
HF5485. H33 1993   4089

Warehouse distribution and operations handbook. David E. Mulcahy. New York: McGraw-Hill, c1994. 1 v. (various pagings): ill. *Notes:* Cover title: Warehouse distribution & operations handbook. Includes index. [LC 93021578; ISN 0070440026]
TS189.6. M85 1994   +4090

WASHINGTON PUBLIC POWER SUPPLY SYSTEM

Illusions of power: a history of the Washington Public Power Supply System (WPPSS). D. Victor Anderson. New York: Praeger, 1985. xiii, 159 p. *Notes:* Includes index. Bibliography: p. 139-141. [LC 84018329; ISN 0030003695; $27.95]
HD9685.U7 W343 1985   4091

WEALTH

The founding fortunes: a new anatomy of the super-rich families in America. Michael Patrick Allen. 1st ed. New York: Truman Talley Books, c1987. ix, 438 p. : ill. *Notes:* Includes bibliographical references and index. [LC 87009912]
HC110.W4 A44 1987   4092

The moneymakers: the great big new rich in America. by Kenneth Lamott. [1st ed.] Boston Little, Brown, 1969. vi, 328 p. ports. *Notes:* Bibliography: p. 307-310. [LC 69016971]   HC110.W4 L18   +4093

WEDTECH (FIRM)

Feeding frenzy. William Sternberg and Matthew C. Harrison, Jr. 1st ed. New York: H. Holt, c1989. x, 326 p. : ill. *Notes:* "A Donald Hutter book." Includes index. Includes bibliographical references. [LC 89015262; ISN 0805010637; $19.95]
HD9743.U8 W437 1989   4094

Feeding the beast: how Wedtech became the most corrupt little company in America. Marilyn W. Thompson. New York: Scribner, c1990. x, 337 p., [8] p. of plates: ill. [LC 89070073; ISN 0684190206; $22.50 ($31.50 Can)]
HD9743.U8 W438 1990   4095

WESTERN ELECTRIC COMPANY

The human problems of an industrial civilization. Elton Mayo. New York: Viking Press, 1960,c1933. 187 p. : ill. (Compass books, 6) *Notes:* Includes bibliographical references and index. [LC 60002948]
x   4096

WHISTLE BLOWING

Whistleblowing: managing dessent in the workplace. by Frederick Elliston... et al. New York: Praeger, 1985. xi, 147 p. *Notes:* Includes bibliographies. [LC 84013294; ISN 0030707749; ISN 0030707765; $26.95 (est.); $13.95 (est.)]
HD60.5.U5 W473 1985   4097

Whistleblowing research: methodological and moral issues. by Frederick Elliston... et al. New York: Praeger, 1985. xiii, 179 p. *Notes:* Includes bibliographical references and index. [LC 84013293; ISN 0030707773; $26.95 (est.)] HD60.5.U5 W4735 1985 4098

WHITE COLLAR CRIMES

Corporate and governmental deviance: problems of organizational behavior in contemporary society. edited by M. David Ermann, Richard J. Lundman. 3rd ed. New York: Oxford University Press, 1987. viii, 263 p. : ill. *Notes:* Includes bibliographies. [LC 86031090; ISN 019504343X] HV6769. C667 1987 4099

Defending white-collar crime: a portrait of attorneys at work. Kenneth Mann. New Haven: Yale University Press, c1985. xiii, 280 p. (Yale studies on white-collar crime) *Notes:* Includes bibliographical references and index. [LC 84017357; ISN 0300032544] KF9350. M32 1985 4100

WHITNEY, WILLIS RODNEY

Willis R. Whitney, General Electric, and the origins of U.S. industrial research. George Wise. New York: Columbia University Press, 1985. 375 p. : ill. *Notes:* Includes index. Bibliography: p. [355]-367. [LC 84027484; ISN 0231060440] T40.W45 W57 1985 4101

WINE INDUSTRY

Through the grapevine: the real story behind America's $8 billion wine industry. Jay Stuller and Glen Martin. 1st HarperCollins pbk. ed. San Francisco: HarperCollinsWest, c1994. 378 p. *Notes:* Includes index. [LC 93026026; ISN 0062585223; $12.00 ($16.00 CAN)] HD9375. S78 1994 +4102

WOMEN

The best companies for women. Baila Zeitz and Lorraine Dusky. New York: Simon and Schuster, c1988. 413 p. *Notes:* Includes index. [LC 88006706; ISN 0671607413] HD6095. Z45 1988 4103

Equal value/comparable worth in the UK and the USA. edited by Peggy Kahn and Elizabeth Meehan. Houndmills, Basingstoke, Hants England: Macmillan, 1992. xvi, 284 p. *Notes:* Includes bibliographical references (p. 259-273) and index. [LC 93025734; ISN 0333475062] HD6061.2.G7 E63 1992b +4104

50/50 by 2000: the woman's guide to political power. Earth Works Group; edited by Cathernie Dee. 1st ed. Berkeley, CA: The Earth Works Group, c1993. 120 p. *Notes:* "National Association for Female Executives." "A 50 simple things book"—P. 4 of cover.] HV1445. A14 1993 +4105

Hard choices: how women decide about work, career, and motherhood. Kathleen Gerson. Berkeley: University of California Press, c1985. xix, 312 p. (California series on social choice and political economy) *Notes:* Includes index. Bibliography: p. 287-301. [LC 84008602; ISN 0520051742] HQ1420. G4 1985 4106

The integration of women in management: a guide for human resources and management development specialists. Ann-Marie Rizzo and Carmen Mendez; foreword by Donald Klingner. New York: Quorum Books, 1990. xii, 206 p. : ill. *Notes:* Includes bibliographical references. [LC 90008422; ISN 0899304753; $39.95] HD6053. R48 1990 4107

Megatrends for women. Patricia Aburdene and John Naisbitt. 1st ed. New York: Villard Books, 1992. xxiv, 388 p. *Notes:* Includes bibliographical references (p. 327-370) and index. [LC 92000431; ISN 067940337X; U.S.A. $22.50 (Canada $28.50)] HQ1421. A28 1992 4108

Not as far as you think: the realities of working women. Lynda L. Moore. Lexington, Mass.: Lexington Books, c1986. xii, 201 p. *Notes:* Includes bibliographical references. [LC 85040109; ISN 0669108367; ISN 0669119458] HD6095. M66 1986 4109

Otherwise engaged: the personal lives of successful career women. Srully Blotnick. New York, N.Y.: Facts on File Publications, c1985. xii, 296 p. *Notes:* Includes bibliographical references and index. [LC 84028708; ISN 0816010935] HD6095. B59 1985 4110

Too smart for her own good?: the impact of success on the intimate lives of women. by Conalee Levine-Shneidman and Karen Levine. 1st ed. Garden City, N.Y.: Doubleday, 1985. xii, 222 p. [LC 84018803; ISN 038518820X; $15.95] HQ1206. L47 1985 4111

Women and careers: issues and challenges. edited by Carol Wolfe Konek, Sally L. Kitch. Thousand Oaks, Calif.: Sage Publications, c1994. xii, 280 p. : ill. *Notes:* Includes bibliographical references and index. *Contents:* Career women in perspective: The Wichita sample / Nancy McCarthy Snyder—"We're all in this alone": Career women's attitudes toward feminism / Sally L. Kitch—Choosing the high tech path: Career women and technology / Nancy A. Brooks—Mentor: Career women and supervision / Brooke B. Collison—Perceptions of equity: Career women and discrimination / Flo Hamrick—Sharing home responsibilities: Women in dual-career marriages / Wayne Carlisle—Career women and motherhood: Child care dilemmas and choices / Nancy McCarthy Snyder—Career women's leisure: Challenges and realities / Marcia L. McCoy—Is alcoholism the cost of equality?: Career women and alcohol / Elsie R. Shore—Leadership or empowerment?: Reframing our questions / Carol Wolfe Konek—The future of women and careers: Issues and challenges / Carol Wolfe Konek, Sally L. Kitch, and Elsie R. Shore. [LC 93029476; ISN 0803952635]   HD6095. W672 1994   +4112

Women's career development. editors, Barbara A. Gutek and Laurie Larwood. Newbury Park, Calif.: Sage Publications, c1987. 191 p. : ill. *Notes:* Includes bibliographies and index. [LC 86006606; ISN 0803927177]   HD6095. W698 1987   4113

Women's quest for economic equality. Victor R. Fuchs. Cambridge, Mass.: Harvard University Press, 1988. ix, 171 p. : ill. *Notes:* Includes index. Bibliography: p. [155]-163. [LC 88007209; ISN 0674955455; $18.95]   HQ1426. F87 1988   4114

WOMEN CONSUMERS

Marketing to women around the world. by Rena Bartos. Boston, Mass.: Harvard Business School Press, c1989. xvii, 320 p. : ill. *Notes:* Includes index. Bibliography: p. 287-309. [LC 88024379; ISN 0875842011]   HC79.C6 B34 1989   4115

WOMEN EXECUTIVES

Breaking into the boardroom: when talent and hard work aren't enough. Jinx Melia. New York: Putnam, 1987 c1986. 167 p. *Notes:* Reprint. Originally published under title: Why Jenny can't lead. 1986. [LC 87007007; ISN 0399133267]   HD6054.3. M45 1987   4116

Breaking the glass ceiling: can women reach the top of America's largest corporations? Ann M. Morrison, Randall P. White, Ellen Van Velsor, and the Center for Creative Leadership. Reading, Mass.: Addison-Wesley Pub. Co., c1987. ix, 229 p. : ill. *Notes:* Includes index. Bibliography: p. 219-224. [LC 87001853; ISN 020115787X; $15.95]   HD6054.4.U6 M67 1987   4117

Competitive frontiers: women managers in a global economy. edited by Nancy J. Adler and Dafna N. Izraeli. Cambridge, Mass.: Blackwell, 1994. xviii, 414 p. : ill. *Notes:* Includes bibliographical references and index. [LC 93019121; ISN 1557865108]   HD6054.3. C67 1994   +4118

Corporate romance: how to avoid it, live through it, or make it work for you. by Leslie Aldridge Westoff. 1st ed. New York, NY: Times Books, c1985. xiii, 246 p. [LC 85040284; ISN 0812912578; $16.95 ($23.00 Can.)]   HD6054.3. W47 1985   4119

Feminine leadership, or, How to succeed in business without being one of the boys. Marilyn Loden. New York: Times Books, c1985. xiii, 306 p. *Notes:* Includes index. Bibliography: p. 281-289. [LC 85040283; ISN 0812912403]   HD6054.3. L63 1985   4120

A few good women: breaking the barriers to top management. Jane White; foreword by Elizabeth Dole. Englewood Cliffs, N.J.: Prentice Hall, c1992. ix, 229 p. *Notes:* Includes bibliographical references (p. 219-224) and index. [LC 92010228; ISN 0133189406; $19.95]   HD6054.4.U6 W46 1992   4121

How women executives succeed: lessons and experiences from the federal government. Danity Little. Westport, Conn.: Quorum Books, 1994. xiv, 193 p. : ill. *Notes:* Includes bibliographical references (p. [181]-186) and index. [LC 93037027; ISN 0899308678]   HD6054.4.U6 L58 1994   +4122

Management and gender: issues and attitudes. Margaret Foegen Karsten. Westport, Conn.: Quorum, 1994. xvi, 265 p. *Notes:* Includes bibliographical references (p. [237]-255) and index. *Contents:* The management process and a feminist approach to management—Managerial women: yesterday and today—Women's contributions to the evolution of management thought—Equal opportunity employment—Sexual and racial harassment and corporate romance—Diversity management—Sterotypes and their effects on leadership perspectives—The socialization process—Career planning and mentoring—Networking—Power and assertiveness—Balancing career and family/personal life—Stress management—Time management—Women in international management—Case studies. [LC 93004225; ISN 0899308120]   HD6054.4.U6 K37 1994b   +4123

Members of the club: the coming of age of executive women. Dawn-Marie Driscoll and Carol R. Goldberg. New York: Toronto: New York: Free Press; Maxwell Macmillan Canada; Maxwell Macmillan International, c1993. xvi, 424 p. *Notes:* Includes bibliographical references (p. 367-411) and index. [LC 93025796; ISN 0029080657; $22.95]   HD6054.4.U6 D75 1993   +4124

On the line: women's career advancement. New York: Catalyst, c1992. 64 leaves: ill. *Notes:* "This research was funded by Baxter International, Citibank, N.A., NYNEX and The Principal Financial Group." Includes bibliographical references (p. 63) and index.]   HD6054.4.U6 O5 1992   4125

The organization woman: building a career—an inside report. Edith L. Highman; surveys by Arthur Highman. New York, N.Y.: Human Sciences Press, c1985. 204 p. *Notes:* Includes index. Bibliography: p. 199-200. [LC 84027775; ISN 0898852374]   HD6054.3. H54   4126

Reach for the top: women and the changing facts of work life. edited with an introduction by Nancy A. Nichols; foreword by Rosabeth Moss Kanter. Boston, MA: Harvard Business School Pub. Corp., c1994. xxii, 185 p. *Notes:* Includes bibliographical references and index. [LC 93034718; ISN 087584507X; $24.95]   HD6054.4.U6 R43 1994   +4127

Shattering the glass ceiling: the woman manager. by Marilyn J. Davidson and Cary L. Cooper. London: P. Chapman, c1992. iv, 185 p. : ill. *Notes:* Includes bibliographical references (p. [174]-183) and index.; ISN 1853961329; $29.95]   HD6054.2.G7 D38 1992   4128

Success and betrayal: the crisis of women in corporate America. Sarah Hardesty, Nehama Jacobs. New York: Watts, 1986. 464 p. *Notes:* Includes index. Bibliography: p. 449-452. [LC 86013243; ISN 0531150275]   HD6054.4.U6 H37 1986   4129

Unnecessary choices: the hidden life of the executive woman. Edith Gilson with Susan Kane. 1st ed. New York: W. Morrow, c1987. 238 p. : forms *Notes:* Includes index. Bibliography: p. 225-232. [LC 86021676; ISN 068804719X]   HD6054.4.U6 G55 1987   4130

Women & men in management. Gary N. Powell. 2nd ed. Newbury Park, Calif.: Sage Publications, c1993. ix, 274 p. : ill. *Notes:* Includes bibliographical references and index. [LC 93009487; ISN 0803952236]   HD6054.3. P69 1993   4131

Women in charge: dilemmas of women in authority. Aileen Jacobson. New York: Van Nostrand Reinhold, c1985. 234 p. *Notes:* Includes index. Bibliography: p. 224-226. [LC 84019584; ISN 0442245874; $12.95]   HD6054.U6 J33 1985   4132

Women in corporate management: results of a Catalyst survey. New York: Catalyst, 1990. 34, [10] leaves *Notes:* Research funded by Kraft General Foods.]   HD6054.3. W64 1990   4133

Women in management. edited by Bette Ann Stead. 2nd ed. Englewood Cliffs, N.J.: Prentice-Hall, c1985. xv, 400 p. : ill. *Notes:* Bibliography: p. 361-389. [LC 84023717; ISN 0139618716; ISN 0139618635; $22.95; $17.95]   HF5500.3.U54 W648 1985   4134

Women in management worldwide. Nancy J. Adler, Dafna N. Izraeli, editors. Armonk, N.Y.: M.E. Sharpe, c1988. xvii, 285 p. *Notes:* Includes bibliographies and index. [LC 88004520; ISN 087332417X; $27.50]   HD6054.3. W66 1988   4135

Women into management: issues influencing the entry of women into managerial jobs. by Wendy Hirsh and Charles Jackson. Brighton England: Institute of Manpower Studies, 1990. viii, 73 p. : ill. *Notes:* Includes bibliographical references (p. 68-72). [LC 91031570; ISN 1851841105; £24.00]   HD6054.4.G7 H57 1990   4136

Women leading: making tough choices on the fast track. Nancy W. Collins, Susan K. Gilbert, Susan H. Nycum. Lexington, Mass.: S. Greene Press, 1988. xv, 181 p. *Notes:* Bibliography: p. 181. [LC 87025130; ISN 0828905673]   HD6054.4.U6 C64 1988   4137

Women managers: travellers in a male world. Judi Marshall. Chichester Sussex; New York: Wiley, c1984. vii, 251 p. : ill. *Notes:* Includes index. Bibliography: p. 243-248. [LC 83023579; ISN 0471904198; $36.00]   HF5500.2. M248 1984   4138

Women MBAs: a foot in the door. Mary Dingee Fillmore. Boston, MA: G.K. Hall, 1987. xii, 233 p. : ill. (Women's studies publications) *Notes:* Bibliography: p. 217-230. [LC 86032002; ISN 0816187282]   HD6054.4.U6 F54 1987   4139

Women, technology & power: ten stars and the history they made. Marguerite Zientara. New York: AMACOM, c1987. ix, 282 p., [10] p. of plates: ports. *Notes:* Includes index. Bibliography: p. 275-278. [LC 85047670; ISN 0814458203]   HD6054.4.U6 Z54 1987   4140

Women who want to be boss: business revelations and success strategies from America's top female executives. Marlene Jensen. 1st ed. Garden City, N.Y.: Doubleday, 1987. xxi, 170 p. *Notes:* Includes index. [LC 86016707; ISN 0385233752; $15.95]   HD6054.4.U6 J46 1987   4141

Women's career development: a study of high flyers. Barbara White, Charles Cox, and Cary Cooper. Oxford, UK; Cambridge, Mass.: Blackwell Business, 1992. 252 p. : ill. *Notes:* Includes bibliographical references (p. [232]-248) and index. [LC 92005696; ISN 0631186557]   HD6054.4.G7 W49 1992   4142

WOMEN IN BUSINESS

Building an effective corporate women's group. New York, N.Y.: Catalyst, c1988. 50 p. *Notes:* "This research was funded by AT&T Foundation."] HD6054.2.U6 B84 1988 4143

Enterprising women: lessons from 100 of the greatest entrepreneurs of our day. A. David Silver. New York: American Management Association, c1994. xiii, 318 p. : ports. *Notes:* Includes profiles of Mary Kay Ash of Mary Kay Cosmetics, Inc., Debbi Fields of Mrs. Fields Cookies, Inc., and Anita Roddick of The Body Shop, Ltd. Includes bibliographical references and index. [LC 94004849; ISBN 0814402267] HD6054.4.U6 S55 1994 +4144

European women in business and management. edited by Marilyn J. Davidson and Cary L. Cooper. London: P. Chapman Pub., c1993. 199 p. : ill. *Notes:* Includes bibliographical references. [LC 93010938; ISBN 1853961388] HD6054.4.E86 E93 1993 +4145

Hardball for women: winning at the game of business. Pat Heim with Susan K. Golant. Los Angeles: Chicago: Lowell House; Contemporary Books, c1992. x, 290 p. *Notes:* Includes bibliographical references and index. [LC 92007522; ISBN 0929923312] HD6053. H39 1992 4146

Our wildest dreams: women entrepreneurs making money, having fun, doing good. Joline Godfrey. 1st ed. New York, NY: HarperBusiness, 1992. xxv, 246 p. *Notes:* Includes bibliographical references and index. [LC 91043548; ISBN 0887305458; $20.00] HD6054.4.U6 G63 1992 4147

Profiles of female genius: thirteen creative women who changed the world. Gene N. Landrum. Amherst, N.Y.: Prometheus Books, 1994. 437 p. : ill.; 24 cm. *Notes:* Includes bibliographical references and index. [LC 94007579; ISBN 0879758929; $24.95] HD6054. L36 1994 +4148

Self-made women: twelve of America's leading entrepreneurs talk about success, self-image, and the superwoman. Diane Jennings. Dallas: Taylor Pub. Co., c1987. 139 p. *Notes:* Bibliography: p. 139. [LC 87016104; ISBN 0878335501; $9.95] HD6054.3. J46 1987 4149

Woman to woman: street smarts for women entrepreneurs. Geraldine A. Larkin. Englewood Cliffs, N.J.: Prentice Hall, c1993. xvii, 265 p. : ill. *Notes:* Includes bibliographical references (p. 261-262) and index. [LC 93004260; ISBN 0137066589; $14.95] HD6054.4.U6 L37 1993 +4150

WOMEN IN FINANCE

Wall Street women. Anne B. Fisher. 1st ed. New York: Knopf, 1990, c1989. 177 p. *Notes:* Includes index. [LC 89045310; ISBN 0394552717; $19.95] HD6073.F472 U64 1990 4151

WOMEN IN THE PROFESSIONS

Professional women at work: interactions, tacit understandings, and the non-trivial nature of trivia in bureaucratic settings. Jerry Jacobs. Westport, Conn.: Bergin & Garvey, 1994. viii, 144 p. *Notes:* Includes bibliographical references (p. [137]-141) and index. [LC 93037848; ISBN 0897893808] HD6054.2.U6 J33 1994 +4152

The third sex: the new professional woman. Patricia A. McBroom. 1st pbk. ed. New York: Paragon House, 1992. 314 p. *Notes:* "Revised and updated for the 90s"—Cover. Originally published: New York: W. Morrow, c1986. Includes bibliographical references (p. 299-304) and index. [LC 91044163; ISBN 1557784051; $14.95] HD6054.2.U6 M36 1992 4153

What you get when you go for it. Beth Milwid. 1st ed. New York: Dodd, Mead, c1987. 248 p. *Notes:* Includes index. [LC 86029084; ISBN 0396089054] HD6054.2.U6 M55 1987 4154

A woman's place is everywhere: inspirational profiles of female leaders who are expanding the roles of American women. Lindsey Johnson, Jackie Joyner-Kersee. New York: Master Media, 1994. xxx, 248 p. : ill. [LC 94005151; ISBN 0942361970; $9.95] HD6054.2.U6 J64 1994 +4155

WOMEN-OWNED BUSINESS ENTERPRISES

The business amazons. by Leah Hertz. London: Deutsch, 1986. xviii, 264 p. *Notes:* Bibliography: p. 262-[265]. [LC 86047209; ISBN 0233978925; £10.95 (May)] HD2346.G7 H43 4156

Her own business: success secrets of entrepreneurial women. by Joanne Wilkens. New York: McGraw-Hill, c1987. xv, 245 p. *Notes:* Includes index. Bibliography: p. 223-240. [LC 86027780; ISBN 0070508542; $16.95] HD2346.U5 W548 1987 4157

WORDPERFECT CORPORATION

Almost perfect: how a bunch of regular guys built WordPerfect Corporation. W.E. Pete Peterson. Rocklin, CA: Prima Pub., c1994. iv, 236 p. *Notes:* Includes index. [LC 93034366; ISN 1559584777; $18.95 ($25.95 Can.)]
    HD9801.U543 U87 1994   +4158

WORK

The new American workplace: transforming work systems in the United States. Eileen Appelbaum and Rosemary Batt. Ithaca, N.Y.: ILR Press, c1994. ix, 287 p. *Notes:* Includes bibliographical references and index. *Contents:* The challenge—Why change? The breakdown of mass production—The alternatives—Alternative models of production—A comparison of the models—Alternative strategies in the United States—The extent of the change (1982-93)—Experiments with workplace innovation (1970-92)—Organizational change in services—The solutions—American models of high performance—Obstacles to change—Policies to promote high-performance systems—Incidence of organizational change among U.S. firms—Summary of case studies (1970-92) [LC 93031201; ISN 0875463193; $18.95]   HD8072.5. A66 1994   +4159

New patterns of work. edited by David Clutterbuck. New York: St. Martin's Press, 1985. xviii, 136 p. : ill. *Notes:* Includes bibliographical references. [LC 85001960; ISN 0312568428; $25.00]
    HD4901. N48 1985   4160

WORK AND FAMILY

Breaking the mold: women, men, and time in the new corporate world. Lotte Bailyn. New York: Toronto: New York: Free Press; Maxwell Macmillan Canada; Maxwell Macmillan International, c1993. xv, 189 p. *Notes:* Includes bibliographical references (p. 175-179) and index. [LC 93025795; ISN 0029012813; $22.95]   HD4904.25. B33 1993   +4161

Solving the work/family puzzle. Bonnie Michaels, Elizabeth McCarty. Homewood, Ill.: Business One Irwin, c1992. xvii, 288 p. : ill. *Notes:* Includes bibliographical references (p. 271-281) and index. [LC 91046296; ISN 1556236271]   HD4904.25. M53 1992   4162

Women and the work/family dilemma: how today's professional women are finding solutions. Deborah J. Swiss, Judith P. Walker. New York: J. Wiley, c1993. xiv, 255 p. *Notes:* Includes bibliographical references (p. 243-250) and index. [LC 92036038; ISN 0471533181; $24.95]
    HD4904.25. S97 1993   4163

Working women don't have wives: professional success in the 1990s. Terri Apter. 1st ed. New York: St. Martin's Press, 1993. ix, 280 p. *Notes:* Includes bibliographical references (p. 269-276) and index. [LC 93031949; ISN 0312096755; $19.95]   HD4904.25. A68 1993   +4164

WORK ENVIRONMENT

Transforming the workplace. John Nora, C. Raymond Rogers and Robert Stramy. Princeton, N.J.: Princeton Research Press, c1986. x, 178 p. *Notes:* Includes bibliographical references. [LC 85063213; ISN 0936231025]   T59.77. N67   4165

WORK ETHIC

Willing workers: the work ethics in Japan, England, and the United States. Tamotsu Sengoku; translated by Koichi Ezaki and Yuko Ezaki. Westport, Conn.: Quorum Books, 1985. xv, 152 p. : ill. *Notes:* Includes index. Bibliography: p. [141]-148. [LC 85009552; ISN 0899301371]
    HD8726.5. S37 1985   4166

WORK GROUPS

Building productive teams: an action guide and resource book. Glenn H. Varney. 1st ed. San Francisco: Jossey-Bass, 1989. xvii, 150 p. *Notes:* Includes bibliographical references. [LC 89045595; ISN 1555421806; $20.95]   HD66. V36 1989   4167

Business without bosses: how self-managing teams are building high-performing companies. Charles C. Manz, Henry P. Sims, Jr. New York: Wiley, c1993. xvi, 238 p. *Notes:* Includes bibliographical references (p. 225-231) and index. [LC 93007864; ISN 0471577006; $24.95]
HD66. M363 1993   +4163

Designing effective work groups. Paul S. Goodman and associates. 1st ed. San Francisco: Jossey-Bass, 1986. xix, 404 p. : ill. (The Jossey-Bass management series) (The Jossey-Bass social and behavioral science series) *Notes:* Includes bibliographies and indexes. [LC 85045903; ISN 0875896804]
HD66. G66 1986   4169

Developing superior work teams: building quality and the competitive edge. Dennis C. Kinlaw. Lexington, Mass.: Lexington Books, c1991. xxvi, 197 p. : ill. *Notes:* "Published in association with University Associates." Includes bibliographical references and index. [LC 90041348; ISN 0669249831; $29.95]
HD66. K56 1991   4170

Empowered teams: creating self-directed work groups that improve quality, productivity, and participation. Richard S. Wellins, William C. Byham, Jeanne M. Wilson. 1st ed. San Francisco: Jossey-Bass, 1991. xxvii, 258 p. : ill. *Notes:* "A Bard Productions book"—T.p. verso. Includes bibliographical references (p. 247-250) and index. [LC 91009880; ISN 1555423531; $27.95]
HD66. W45 1991   4171

A force of ones: reclaiming individual power in a time of teams, work groups, and other crowds. Stanley M. Herman. 1st ed. San Francisco: Jossey-Bass Publishers, c1994. xxi, 261 p. *Notes:* Includes bibliographical references (p. 255) and index. [LC 93023617; ISN 1555425615; $23.00]
HD66. H47 1994   +4172

Groups that work (and those that don't): creating conditions for effective teamwork. J. Richard Hackman, editor. 1st ed. San Francisco: Jossey-Bass, 1990. xxiii, 512 p. [LC 89045597; ISN 1555421873; $34.95]
HD66. G76 1990   4173

Groupware in the 21st century: computer supported cooperative working toward the millennium. edited by Peter Lloyd; foreword by Robert Watson. Westport, Conn.: Praeger, 1994. xxviii, 307 p. : ill. *Notes:* Includes bibliographical references (p. [287]-293) and index. [LC 94028284; ISN 0275950913; ISN 0275950921]
HD66. G774 1994   +4174

How to lead work teams: facilitation skills. Fran Rees. San Diego: Pfeiffer & Co., c1991. vii, 161 p. : ill. *Notes:* Includes bibliographical references (p. 157-158) and index. [LC 91006561; ISN 0883900564; $29.95]
HD66. R394 1991   4175

Inside teams: how 20 world-class organizations are winning through teamwork. Richard S. Wellins, William C. Byham, George R. Dixon. 1st ed. San Francisco: Jossey-Bass, c1994. xxii, 366 p. *Notes:* Includes case histories of, among others, Miller Brewing, Pfizer, Inc., Colgate-Palmolive, Texas Instruments, Wilson Sporting Goods, Kodak Customer Assistance Center. Includes bibliographical references (p. 346) and index. [LC 94026312; ISN 1555425747]
HD66. W46 1994   +4176

Leading self-directed work teams: a guide to developing new team leadership skills. Kimball Fisher. New York: McGraw-Hill, c1993. xxiii, 263 p. : ill. *Notes:* Includes bibliographical references and index. [LC 92028418; ISN 0070210713]
HD66. F56 1993   4177

Leading the team organization: how to create an enduring competitive advantage. Dean Tjosvold, Mary M. Tjosvold. New York: Toronto: New York: Lexington Books; Maxwell Macmillan Canada; Maxwell Macmillan International, c1991. xii, 198 p. *Notes:* Includes bibliographical references (p. [187]-192) and index. [LC 91024664; ISN 0669279722; $22.95]
HD66. T54 1991   4178

The manager and the working group. William B. Eddy. New York: Praeger, 1985. ix, 179 p. *Notes:* Includes bibliographical references and index. [LC 84026283; ISN 0030014387; $23.95 (est.)]
HD66. E325 1985   4179

Mining group gold: how to cash in on the collaborative brain power of a group. Thomas A. Kayser. 1st ed. El Segundo, Calif.: Serif Pub., 1990. xxv, 178 p. : ill. *Notes:* Includes bibliographical references (p. 171-173) and index. [LC 91198910; ISN 1878567020; $12.95]
HD66. K39 1990   +4180

Spectacular teamwork: how to develop the leadership skills for team success. Robert R. Blake, Jane S. Mouton, Robert L. Allen. New York: Wiley, c1987. viii, 219 p. : ill. *Notes:* Includes bibliographical references and index. [LC 86028123; ISN 0471853119]
HD66. B54 1987   4181

Team building: issues and alternatives. William G. Dyer. 2nd ed. Reading, Mass.: Addison-Wesley, c1987. xiii, 171 p. *Notes:* Includes bibliographical references. [LC 86020635; ISN 0201180375; $12.95 (est.)]
HD66. D94 1987   4182

Team players and teamwork: the new competitive business strategy. Glenn M. Parker. 1st ed. San Francisco: Jossey-Bass Publishers, c1990. xxi, 173 p. *Notes:* Includes bibliographical references (p. 165-169) and index. [LC 90053093; ISN 1555422578; $20.95]
HD66. P346 1990   4183

Turf wars: moving from competition to collaboration. by Harvey Robbins. Glenview, IL: Scott, Foresman, 1990. xxii, 229 p. : ill. *Notes:* Includes index.; ISN 0673460797; $24.95]
HD66. R58 1990   4184

The we-force in management: how to build and sustain cooperation. Lawrence G. Hrebiniak. New York: Toronto: New York: Lexington Books; Maxwell Macmillan Canada; Maxwell Macmillan International, c1994. vi, 154 p. : ill. *Notes:* Includes bibliographical references (p. 147-148) and index. [LC 94010294; ISN 002915345X; $19.95]   HD66. H73 1994   +4185

The wisdom of teams: creating the high-performance organization. Jon R. Katzenbach, Douglas K. Smith. Boston, Mass.: Harvard Business School Press, 1992, c1993. xii, 291 p. : ill. *Notes:* Includes bibliographical references and index. [LC 92020395; ISN 0875843670; $24.95]   HD66. K384 1992   4186

WORK MEASUREMENT

Behavioral analysis and measurement methods. David Meister. New York: Wiley, c1985. xiii, 509 p. : ill. *Notes:* "A Wiley-Interscience publication." Includes bibliographies and index. [LC 85003205; ISN 0471896403; $45.00 (est.)]   T60.2. M45 1985   4187

Work measurement: principles and practice. edited by Richard L. Shell. Norcross, Ga.: Industrial Engineering and Management Press, c1986. ix, 320 p. : ill. *Notes:* Bibliography: p. 309-318.; ISN 0898060850]   T60.2. W67   4188

WORKING CLASS

Labor in the twentieth century. edited by John Dunlop, Walter Galenson. New York: Academic Press, c1978. viii, 329 p. *Notes:* Includes bibliographical references and index. [LC 78003335; ISN 0122243501]   HD4854. L26   4189

Workforce 2000: work and workers for the 21st century. William B. Johnston, Arnold E. Packer; with contributions by Matthew P. Jaffe. . . et al. Indianapolis, Ind.: Washington, D.C.?: Hudson Institute; U.S. Dept. of Labor, 1987. xxvii, 117 p. : ill. *Notes:* "June 1987." "HI-3796-RR." [LC 87601910; ISN 1558130047]   HD8072.5. J64 1987   4190

WORLD BANK

Mortgaging the earth: the World Bank, environmental impoverishment, and the crisis of development. Bruce Rich. Boston, Mass.: Beacon Press, c1994. xiv, 376 p. *Notes:* Includes bibliographical references (p. [319]-362) and index. [LC 93003848; ISN 080704704X]   HG3881.5.W57 R53 1994   +4191

WORLD POLITICS

The new realities: in government and politics, in economics and business, in society and world view. by Peter F. Drucker. 1st ed. New York: Harper & Row, c1989. xi, 276 p. *Notes:* Includes index. [LC 89001992; ISN 0060161299; $19.95]   D849. D78 1989   4192

WRITTEN COMMUNICATION

The articulate executive: improving written, interpersonal, and group communication. Boston: Harvard Business Review, c1991. vi, 123 p. : ill. *Notes:* Articles originally published in the Harvard Business Review. Includes bibliographical references. *Contents:* "What do you mean I can't write?" / John S. Fielden—Clear writing means clear thinking means. . . / Marvin H. Swift—"What do you mean you don't like my style?" / John S. Fielden—Barriers and gateways to communication / Carl R. Rogers and F.J. Roethlisberger—Listening to people / Ralph G. Nichols and Leonard A. Stevens—The hidden messages managers send / Michael B. McCaskey—Nobody trusts the boss completely—now what? / Fernando Bartolomé—Management communication and the grapevine / Keith Davis—Skilled incompetence / Chris Argyris—Overcoming group warfare / Robert R. Blake and Jane S. Mouton—How to run a meeting / Antony Jay—Meetings that work, plans bosses can approve / Paul D. Lovett—ABCs of job interviewing / James M. Jenks and Brian L.P. Zevnik.; ISN 0875842682; $19.95]   HF5718. A75 1991   4193

XEROX CORPORATION

Prophets in the dark: how Xerox reinvented itself and beat back the Japanese. David T. Kearns, David A. Nadler. 1st ed. New York: HarperBusiness, c1992. xvi, 334 p. : ill. *Notes:* Includes index. [LC 91058506; ISN 0887305644; $22.50 ($30.00 Can.)]   HD9802.3.U64 X476 1992   4194

Xerox, American samurai. Gary Jacobson, John Hillkirk. New York: Macmillan, c1986. ix, 338 p. *Notes:* Includes index. [LC 85030922; ISN 0025516000]   HD9802.3.U64 X475 1986   4195

YOUNG ADULTS

Late bloomers: coming of age in today's America: the right place at the wrong time. David Lipsky and Alexander Abrams. 1st ed New York: Time Books, c1994. viii, 224 p. *Notes:* Includes bibliographical references (p. 177-222). [LC 94015951; ISN 0812922905; $18.00 ($25.00 Canada)]
      HQ799.7. L57 1994   +4196

YOUTH AS CONSUMERS

Youthtrends: capturing the $200 billion youth market. Lawrence Graham and Lawrence Hamdan. 1st ed. New York: St. Martin's Press, c1987. xx, 282 p. *Notes:* Includes index. [LC 87004426; ISN 0312007043; $15.95]   HC110.C6 G67 1987   4197

MISCELLANEOUS

Beyond management by objectives. J. D. Batten. [Updated ed.] New York: AMACOM, 1980, c1966. 112 p. : ill. [LC 66029660; ISN 0814456146]   HD31. B3695   4198

Effective communication. Boston: The Review, c1952-1974. 148 p. : ill. (A Harvard Business reprint series) *Notes:* Cover title. Reprints from the Harvard Business Review, 1952-1974. Includes bibliographical references.]   HF5718. H3   +4199

Global financial services: strategies for building competitive strengths in international commercial and investment banking. Roy C. Smith and Ingo Walter. New York: Harper & Row, 1990. viii, 805 p. : ill. *Notes:* Includes bibliographical references. [LC 90032811; ISN 0887303358]
      HG3881. S544 1990   4200

Service America!: doing business in the new economy. Karl Albrecht and Ron Zemke. Warner Books ed. New York, NY: Warner Books, 1990, c1985. ix, 203 p. *Notes:* Reprint. Originally published: Homewood, Ill.: Dow Jones-Irwin, c1985. Includes index. Includes bibliographical references (p. 198-199). [LC 90011925; ISN 0446390925]   HD9981.5. A43 1990   4201

Training & developing executives. Boston c1963-1973. 140 p. illus. (part col.) *Notes:* Cover title. Reprints from the Harvard Business Review, 1963-1973.]   HF5549.5.T7 H37   +4202

Understanding and meeting consumerism's challenges. Boston: The Review, c1925-1974. 161, [6] p. : ill. (A Harvard Business Review reprint series) *Notes:* Cover title. Reprints from the Harvard Business Review, 1925-1974. Bibliography: p. [157]. Includes bibliographical references.]
      HC110.C63 H38   +4203

APPENDIX

PUBLISHERS' NAMES AND ADDRESSES

A&C Black Ltd. c/o Talman Co.
Abacus Press, 973 Central St., Stoughton, MA 02072
Ablex Publishing Corp., 355 Chestnut St., Norwood, NJ 07648
Abt Books, 19 Follen St., Cambridge, MA 02138
Academic Press, 525 B St., Ste. 1900, San Diego, CA 92101
Academic Research Associates, 15 Cole Rd., Armonk, NY 10504
Acropolis Books, 2311 Calvert St., NW, No. 300, Washington, DC 20008-2644
Addison Wesley, 1 Jacob Way, Reading, MA 01867
Adler & Adler Publishers, Inc., 5530 Wisconsin Ave., Ste. 1460, Chevy Chase, MA 20815-4301
Adler Publishing Co., Box 25333, Panorama Plaza, Rochester, NY 14625 (ceased publishing)
Association for Investment Management and Research (AIMR), P.O. Box 3668, Charlottesville, VA 22903
Aldine de Gruyter c/o Walter de Gruyter
Allyn & Bacon, 160 Gould St., Needham Heights, MA 02194
Amacom, 135 W. 50th St., 15th Flr., New York, NY 10020
American Council on Education, 1 Dupont Cir., NW, Washington, DC 20036
American Enterprise Institute for Public Policy Research, 1150 17th St., NW, Washington, DC 20036
American Lawyer Media, L.P., 600 3rd Ave., New York, NY 10016
American Management Association, 135 W. 50th St., New York, NY 10020
American Marketing Association, 250 S. Wacker Dr., No. 200, Chicago, IL 60606-5819
Analysis Press, 3300 Darby Rd., No. 3325, Haverford, PA 19041
Andersen, Arthur & Co., 69 W. Washington St., Chicago, IL 60602
Appraisal Institute, 875 N. Michigan Ave., Ste. 2400, Chicago, IL 60611-1980
Apt Books, Inc., 56-16 Seabury St., Apt. 3C, Flushing, NY 11373
Arcade Publishing, Inc. 141 5th Ave. New York, NY 10010
Ashgate Publishing, Old Post Rd., Brookfield, VT 05036
Asia Society, 725 Park Ave., New York, NY 10021
ASME Press, 345 E. 47th St., New York, NY 10017
Aspen Publishers, 200 Orchard Ridge Dr. Gaithersburg, MD 20878
ASQC Quality Press, 611 East Wisconsin Ave., Milwaukee, WI 53201
Assoc. for Systems Mgmt., 1433 W. Bagley Road, Berea, OH 44017
Atlantic Monthly Press c/o Grove Atlantic
Auburn House Pub. Co. c/o Greenwood Publishing Group
Auerbach Publishers, One Penn Plaza, New York, NY 10119
Auerbach Publishers, 31 Saint James Ave., Boston, MA 02116

AUPHA Press, 1911 N. Fort Myer Drive, Suite 503, Arlington, VA 22209
Austin Press, P.O. Box 9774, Austin, TX 78766 (ceased publishing)

Ballinger Publishing Co. c/o HarperCollins Publishers
Bantam Books c/o Bantam Doubleday Dell
Bantam Doubleday Dell, 1540 Broadway, New York, NY 10036-4094
Barnes & Noble Books C/o HarperCollins
Barricade Books, 61 Fourth Ave, New York, NY 10003
Barrington Press, P.O. Box 291, Boston University Station,
Boston, MA 02215
Barron's Educational Series, 250 Wireless Blvd., Hauppauge, NY 11788
Basic Books c/o HarperCollins
Battelle Press, 505 King Ave., Columbus, OH 43201-2693
Beacham Publishing Inc., 2100 'S' Street, NW, Washington, DC 20008
Beaufort Books, 9 E. 40th St., New York, NY 10016 (ceased publishing)
Beech Tree Books, c/o Morrow, Wm. & Co.
Belknap Press of Harvard University Press, 79 Garden St., Cambridge, MA 02138
Bell Publishing, 15 Surrey Ln., East Brunswick, NJ 08816
Berkley Publishing Group/Berkley Books, 200 Madison Ave., New York, NY 10016
Berrett-Koehler, 155 Montgomery St., San Francisco, CA 94104-4109
Birkhauser Boston, 675 Massachusetts Avenue, Cambridge, MA 02139
Blackwell, Basil, 432 Park Avenue S., Ste. 1503, New York, NY 10016
Blackwell Publishers, 238 Main St., Cambridge, MA 02142
Bonus Books, 160 East Illinois St., Chicago, IL 60611
Brace-Park Press, P.O. Box 526, Lake Forest, IL 60045
Brassey's US, 8000 West Park Dr., 1st. Flr., McLean, VA 22102
Braziller, George, Inc., 60 Madison Ave., Ste. 1001, New York, NY 10010
Brookfield Publishing Co., Old Post Rd., Brookfield, VT 05036
Brookings Institution, 1775 Massachusetts Ave., NW, Washington, DC 20036
Brooks/Cole Publishing Co., 511 Forest Lodge Rd., Pacific Grove, CA 93950
Brown, Wm. C., Publishers, 2460 Kerper Blvd., Dubuque, IA 52001
Bureau of National Affairs, 1231 25th St., NW, Washington, DC 20037
Burlingame, E., Books c/o HarperCollins Pubs.
Business Books International, P.O. Box 1587, New Canaan, CT 06840
Business International Corp., 215 Park Avenue S., New York, NY 10003

Business One Irwin, c/o R.D. Irwin
Butterworth-Heinemann, 313 Washington St., Newton, MA 02158

Cambridge University Press, 40 W. 20th St., New York, NY 10011
Carnegie-Mellon University Press, P.O. Box 2l, Schenley Park, Pittsburgh, PA 15213
Carol Publishing Group, 600 Madison Ave., 11th Flr., New York, NY 10022
Cason Hall and Co., P.O. Box 2346, Arlington, VA 22202
Cassell, 215 Park Ave., S., New York, NY 10003
Catalyst, 250 Park Avenue South, New York, NY 10003
Cato Institute, 1000 Massachusetts Ave., NW, 6th Flr., Washington, DC 20001
Center for Strategic and International Studies, 1800 K St. NW, Suite 400, Washington, DC 20006
ChainStorePub. Corp., Lebhar-Friedman Books, 3922 Coconut Palm Dr., Tampa, FL 33619
Chapman and Hall, 1 Penn Plaza, New York, NY 10119
Chatham House Publishers, Box 1, Chatham, NJ 07928
Chelsea Green Publishing Co., P.O. Box 428, 205 Gates-Brigg Bldg, White River Junction, VT 05001
Chicago Board of Trade, 141 W. Jackson Blvd., Ste. 2210, Chicago, IL 60604
Chilton Co., Chilton Way, Radnor, PA 19089-9931
Chrysler Corporation, 12000 Chrysler Dr., Highland Park, MI 48288
Chute, P.B., Corp., 4100 Central Ave., No. 201, Riverside, CA 92506
Clarendon Press c/o Oxford University Press
Collage, 19365 Detroit Rd., Cleveland, OH 44116
Columbia University Press, 562 W. 113th St., New York, NY 10025
Commerce Clearing House, 4025 W. Peterson Ave., Chicago, IL 60646
Committee for Economic Development, 477 Madison Ave., New York, NY 10022
Congdon & Weed, 2 Prudential Plaza, Chicago, IL 60501
Congressional Quarterly, 1414 22nd St., NW, Washington, DC 20037
Consulting Psychologists Press, Inc, 3803 E. Bayshore Rd., Palo Alto, CA 94303
Consultants News c/o Kennedy Publications
Contemporary Books, 2 Prudential Plaza, Ste. 1200, Chicago, IL 60601
Cornell Maritime Press, P.O. Box 456, Centreville, MD 21617
Cornell University Press, P.O. Box 250, Ithaca, NY 14851-0250
Cornerstone Library, c/o Simon & Schuster
Council Oak Books, 1350 E. 15th St., Tulsa, OK 74120-5801
Council of Logistics Management, 2803 Butterfield Road, Ste. 380, Oak Brook, IL 60521
Council on Competitiveness, 1331 Pennsylvania Avenue, NW, Ste. 900, North Lobby, Washington, DC 20004
Council on East Asian Studies c/o Harvard University Press

Council on Foreign Relations Press c/o AIDC, 64 Depot Rd., Colchester, VT 05446
Crain Books c/o NTC Publishing Group
Cresheim Publications c/o Swansea Press, P.O. Box 27785, Philadelphia, PA 19118
Crittenden Publishing, P.O. Box 1150, Novato, CA 94949
Croom Helm c/o Routledge, Chapman and Hall
Crown Publishing Group, 201 E. 50th St., New York, NY 10022
Currency Press c/o State Mutual Book and Periodical Service, Ltd

Darwin Press, Box 2202, Princeton, NJ 08543
D.C. Heath, 125 Spring St., Lexington, MA 02173
De Gruyter, Walter, 200 Saw Mill River Road, Hawthorne, NY 10532
Dearborn Financial Publishing, Inc., 520 N. Dearborn, Chicago, IL 60610
Dekker, M., 270 Madison Ave., New York, NY 10016
Delacorte Press c/o Bantam Doubleday Dell
Dell Publishing Company c/o Bantam Doubleday Dell
Dellen Publishing Co., 400 Pacific Ave, 3rd Fl., San Francisco, CA 94133
Delmar Publishers Inc., Box 15-015, Albany, NY 12212
Deloitte, Haskins & Sells, 144 Avenue of the Americas, New York, NY 10036
Digital Press, 12 Crosby Dr., Bedford, MA 01730 (ceased publishing)
Dorrance & Co., 643 Smithfield St., Pittsburgh, PA 15222
Dorsey Press c/o Wadsworth Publishing Co.
Doubleday and Co. c/o Bantam Doubleday Dell
Dryden Press, 301 Commerce Street, Fort Worth, TX 76102
Duke University Press, Box 90660, College Station, Durham, NC 27708
Dutton c/o NAL/Dutton
Duxbury Press c/o PWS Publishing Co.

Elgar, Edward, Publishing Co., Ltd. c/o Ashgate Publishing Co.
Elsevier Science, P.O. Box 945, Madison Square Station, New York, NY 10160-0757
Empire Publishing Inc., Rte. 3, Box 83, Hwy., 220 S. Madison, NC 27025
Employee Benefit Research Institute, 2121 'K' St., NW, Ste. 600, Washington, DC 20037-1896
Enterprise-Dearborn c/o Dearborn Financial Publishing
Erlbaum, Lawrence, Associates, 365 Broadway, Hillsdale, NY 07642
Euromoney Publishers, Ltd. c/o State Mutual Book and Periodical Service
Euromonitor Publications c/o Gale Research, 835 Penobscot Bldg., Detroit, MI 48226-4094
Evans, M. & Co., 216 E. 49 St., New York, NY 10017

Facts on File, 460 Park Ave., S., New York, NY 10016
Farrar, Straus & Giroux, Inc., 19 Union Sq., W., New York, NY 10003
Fell, Frederick, Pubs. c/o LIFETIME Books, 2131

Hollywood Blvd., Ste. 204, Hollywood, FL 33020
Financial Executives Research Foundation, 10 Madison Ave., P.O. Box 1938, Morristown, NJ 07962-1938
Fine, Donald I., 19 W. 21st St., New York, NY 10010
Free Press, c/o Macmillan Publishing Co.
Freundlich Books, 1 Penn Plaza, Ste. 1714, New York, NY 10019

Garland Publishing Co., 717 5th Ave., Ste. 2500, New York, NY 10022-8102
Georgia State University Business Press, University Plaza, Atlanta, GA 30303-3093
Gestalt Institute of Cleveland Press c/o Gardner Press, 6801 Lake Worth Rd., No. 104, Lake Worth, FL 33467-2965
GoldenTouch Press, 13022 Amarillo Ave., Austin, TX 78729-7539
Golembe Associates, 1025 Thomas Jefferson St., NW, Washington, DC 20007
Gower Publishing Co. c/o Ashgate Publishing Co.
Graceway Publishing Co., P.O. Box 159, Station C, Flushing, NY 11367
Greenwood Publishing Group, Box 5007, 88 Post Rd. W, Westport, CT 06881
Grid Publishing (ceased publishing)
Grove/Atlantic, 841 Broadway, 4th Flr., New York, NY 10003-4793
Guilford Press, 72 Spring St., New York, NY 10012
Gulf Publishing Co., Box 2608, Houston, TX 77252-2608

Halsted Press, 605 Third Ave., New York NY 10158
Hamilton Press c/o Madison Books
Harcourt Brace and Co., 525 B St., Ste. 1900, San Diego, CA 92101
Harcourt Brace Jovanovich (HBJ) c/o Harcourt Brace and Co.
Harmony Books c/o Crown Publishing Group
Harper Business c/o HarperCollins Publishing
HarperCollins Publishing, 10 E. 53rd St., New York, NY 10022-5299
Harvard Business Review, Reprint Department, 230 Western Avenue, Harvard Business School, Boston, MA 02163
Harvard Business School Press, C/O McGraw Hill, 1221 Avenue of the Americas, New York, NY 10020
Harvard University Press, 79 Garden St., Cambridge, MA 02138
Hayden c/o Paramount, 201 W. 103rd St., Indianapolis, IN 46290
Heinemann, 361 Hanover St., Portsmouth, NH 03801-3912
Heinemann Educational Books c/o Smithsonian Institution Press, 470 L'Enfant Plaza, Ste. 7100, Washington, DC 20560
Hill & Wang c/o Farrar, Straus and Giroux
Hitchcock Publishing Co., 191 S. Gary Ave., Carol Stream, IL 60188
Hodder & Stoughton, P.O. Box 257, N. Pomfret, VT 05053
Holden Day Inc., P.O. Box 2499, Merrifield, VA 22116-2499

Holt, Henry, and Co., 115 W. 18th St., New York, NY 10011
Holt, Rinehart & Winston, 1120 S. Capitol of Texas Hwy., No. II-100, Austin, TX 78746-6487
Hoover Institution Press, Stanford University, Stanford, CA 94305-6010
Houghton Mifflin Co., 222 Berkeley St., Boston, MA 02116
Human Resource Planning Society, 41 E. 42nd St., Ste. 1509, New York, NY 10017
Human Sciences Press, 233 Spring St., New York, NY 10013-1578
Humanities Press International, 165 1st Ave., Atlantic Highlands, NJ 07716-1289
Hyperion, 114 5th Ave., New York, NY 10011

ICS Press, 720 Market St., San Francisco, CA 94102
IEEE (Institute of Electrical and Electronic Engineers) Press, 345 E. 47th St., New York, NY 10017-2394
ILR Press, New York State School of Industrial & Labor Relations, Cornell University, Ithaca, NY 14853
Inc. Publishing, 38 Commercial Wharf, Boston, MA 02110
Indiana University Press, 601 N. Morton St., Bloomington, IN 47404
Industrial Engineering and Management Press, 25 Technology Park, Norcross, GA 30092
Information Economics Press, 55 Talmadge Hill, New Canaan, CT 06840
Information Industry Association, 555 New Jersey Ave., NW, Ste. 800, Washington, DC 20001
Institute for Business Planning c/o Prentice Hall
Institute for Management, IFM Building, Old Saybrook, CT 06475
Institute for International Economics, Publications Department, 11 Dupont Cir., NW, Washington, DC. 20036
Institute of Internal Auditors Inc., 249 Maitland Ave., Altamonte Springs, FL 32701-4201
Intercontinental Publishing, 6/f, 69 Wyndham Street, Center, Hong Kong, HONG KONG
International Business Press, P.O. Box 130746, Houston, TX 77219-0746
International Labour Office, 1828 L St., NW, Ste. 801, Washington, DC 20036
International Monetary Fund, 700 19th St., NW, Bldg. IS5-1300, Washington DC 20431
International Publishers Co., P.O. Box 3042, JAF Station, New York, NY 10016
International Universities Press, 59 Boston Post Rd., Madison, CT 06443-1524
International Publishing Corporation, 625 N. Michigan Ave., Ste. 1920, Chicago, IL 60611
Interstate Printers & Publishers, Box 50, Danville, IL 61834-0500
Investor Publications, 219 Parkade, Cedar Falls, IA 50613
Investor Responsibility Research Center, 1755 Massachussetts Ave., NW, Ste. 600, Washington, DC 20036
Investors Intelligence, Inc. c/o Chartcraft, 30 Church St., Box 2046, New Rochelle, NY 10538
Irwin, R.D., 1333 Burr Ridge Rd., Burr Ridge, IL 60521

Irwin/Dow Jones c/o R.D. Irwin
Irwin Professional Pubs. c/o R.D. Irwin
Island Press, P.O. Box 7, Covelo, CA 95428
Issue Action Publications, 207 Loudon St., SE, Leesburg, VA 22075

JAI Press, 55 Old Post Rd., No. 2, P.O. Box 1678, Greenwich, CT 06836
Johns Hopkins University Press, 2715 N. Charles St., Baltimore, MD 21218-4319
Jossey-Bass, 350 Sansome St., San Francisco, CA 94104

Kendall/Hunt Publishing Co., 4050 Westmark Dr., P.O. Box 1840, Dubuque, IA 52004-1840
Kennedy Publications, Templeton Road, Fitzwilliam, NH 03447
Kent Publishing Co. c/o PWS Publishing Co.
Kiplinger Washington Editors, 1729 H St., NW, Washington, DC 20006
Kluwer Academic Publishers, 101 Philip Dr., Assinippi Pk., Norwell, MA 02061
Kluwer Law Book Publishers c/o The Michie Co., P.O. Box 7587, Charlottesville, VA 22906
Knopf, Alfred A. c/o Random House
Knowledge Industry Publishers, 701 Westchester Ave., White Plains, NY 10604
Kodansha International, 114 5th Ave., 18th Flr., New York, NY 10011
Kogan Page, 120 Pentonville Rd., London, NI 9JN, ENGLAND

Lasser, J.K., Institute c/o Prentice Hall General Reference and Law & Business c/o Harcourt Brace and Co.
Law Journal Seminars-Press, 111 8th Ave, New York, NY 10011
Learning Concepts, 7622 Palmerston Dr., Mentor, OH 44060
Lerner Publications Co., 241 1st Avenue N., Minneapolis, MN 55401
Levinson Institute, 404 Wyman St., Waltham, MA 02154
Lexington Books c/o Simon and Schuster
Liberty House, c/o TAB Books
Linden Press, c/o Simon & Schuster Trade Publications, 1230 Ave of the Americas, New York, NY 10020
Little, Brown and Co., 1271 Avenue of the Americas, New York, NY 10020
Lyons & Burford Publications, 31 W. 21st Street, New York, NY 10010

Macmillan Publishing Co., 866 3rd Ave., New York, NY 10022
Madison Books c/o University Press of America, 4720 Boston Way, Lanham, MD 20706
Magee, John Inc., 65 Broad Street, Boston, MA 02109
Mandarin Books Ltd., c/o Heinemann
Mansell (ceased publishing)
Martinus-Nijhof Publishers c/o Kluwer Academic Pubs.
Mathematical Association of America, 1529 18th St., NW, Washington, DC 20036
Maxwell Macmillan c/o Macmillan Publishing Co.

Maxwell Macmillan International c/o Macmillan Publishing Co.
McGraw-Hill Publishing Co., 1221 Avenue of the Americas, New York, NY 10020
Mercer University Press, 1400 Coleman Ave., Macon, GA 31207
Merrill Publishing Co., Box 508, Columbus, OH 43216
Methuen Inc. c/o Routledge, Chapman & Hall
Michigan State University Press, 1405 S. Harrison Road, 25 Manly Miles Bldg., E. Lansing, MI 48823-5205
Microsoft Press, 1 Microsoft Way, Redmond, WA 98073-9717
Morrow, Wm., & Co., 1350 Avenue of the Americas, New York, NY 10019
Municipal Finance Officers Association of the U.S. & Canada, 180 N. Michigan Ave., Suite 800, Chicago, IL 60601
MIT Press, 55 Hayward St., Cambridge, MA 02142

NAL/Dutton, 375 Hudson St., New York, NY 10014-3657
NTC Business Books, 4255 West Touhy Avenue, Lincolnwood, IL 60646
National Association of Credit Management, 8815 Centre Park Dr., Ste. 200, Columbia, MD 21045
National Center for Employee Ownership, 2201 Broadway, Ste. 807, Oakland, CA 94612
National Academy Press, 2101 Constitution Avenue NW, Lockbox 285, Washington, DC 20055
Nelson-Hall, 111 N. Canal Street, Chicago, IL 60606
Nelson, T., P.O. Box 141000, Nelson Place at Elm Hill Pike, Nashville, TN 37214
New American Library c/o Penguin USA
New York Institute of Finance, 2 Broadway, New York, NY 10004
New York University Press, 70 Washington Sq., S., New York, NY 10012
Nichols Publishing Co., P.O. Box 6036, East Brunswick, NJ 08816-6036
Nierenberg & Zeif Publishers, 341 Madison Ave., 20th Flr., New York, NY 10017-3705
Nomos Verlagsgesellschaft c/o International Book Import Service, Inc., 2995 Wall Triana Hwy, Ste. B4, Huntsville, AL 35824-1532
North-Holland c/o Elsevier Science
North River Press, Inc., Box 567, Great Barrington, MA 01230
Northwestern University Press, 625 Colfax St., Evanston, IL 60208-4210
Norton, W.W. and Co., 500 5th Ave, New York NY 10110
Noyes Publications, 120 Mill Rd., Park Ridge, NJ 07656

Oryx Press, 4041 N. Central Ave., Ste. 700, Phoenix, AZ 85012-3397
Osborne/McGraw-Hill, 2600 10th St., Berkeley CA 94710
Out of Your Mind and Into The Marketplace, 13381 White Sand Dr., Tustin, CA 92680
Owen, WM., 885 Heather Rd., Deerfield, MI 60015
Oxford University Press, 200 Madison Ave., New York NY 10016

Pacific Institute for Public Policy Research, 755 Sansome St., No. 450, San Francisco, CA 94111-1703
Paladin Press, Box 1307, Boulder, CO 80306
Pan Books Ltd. c/o Trans-Atlantic Publications, 311 Bainsbridge St., Philadelphia, PA 19147
Panel Publishers, 7201 McKinney Cir., Frederick, MD 21701-9782
Pantheon Books Inc., 201 E. 50th St., New York, NY 10022
Paragon House Publishers, 370 Lexington Ave., New York, NY 10017-6503
Peachtree Publishers, 494 Armour Circle NE, Atlanta, Ga 30324
Penguin Books(UK) c/o Viking/Penguin
Penguin USA, 120 Woodbine Rd., Bergenfield, NJ 07621
Pennsylvania State University Press, Barbara Bldg., Ste. C, University Park, PA 16802
PennWell Books, 1421 S. Sheridan, Tulsa, OK 74112
Pergamon Press c/o Elsevier Science
Petrocelli Books, 174 Brookstone Dr., Research Park, Princeton, NJ 08540-2404
Pfeiffer & Co., 8517 Production Ave., San Diego, CA 92121
Pharos Books c/o The World Almanac, 1 International Blvd., Mahwah, NJ 07495-0017
Pitman, 120 Plain St., Marshfield, MA 02050 (ceased publishing)
Planning Forum, P.O. Box 70, Oxford, OH 45056
Plenum Press, 233 Spring St., New York, NY 10013
Plume c/o NAL/Dutton
Pocket Books c/o Simon and Schuster
Potter, Clarkson, Publishing c/o Crown Publishing Group
Praeger Publications c/o Greenwood Publishing Group
Prentice Hall, 113 Sylvan Ave., Rte. 9W, Englewood Cliffs, NJ 07632
Prima Publishing, 3875 Atherton Rd., Rocklin, CA 95765
Princeton Research Press, Research Road, P.O. Box 704, Princeton NJ 08540
Princeton University Press, 41 William St., Princeton, NJ 08540
Probus Publishing Company c/o Irwin Professional Publishing
Productivity Press, Box 13390, Portland, OR 97213-0390
Professional Communications, P.O. Box 7585, Phoenix, AZ 85011
Publishing Horizons, 8233 Via Paseo Del Norte, Ste. F400, Scottsdale, AZ 85258
Putnam Publishing Group/Putnam Berkley Group, 200 Madison Ave., New York, NY 10016
PWS Publishing Co., 20 Park Plaza, 13th Flr., Boston, MA 02116
PWS/Kent Publishing Co. c/o PWS Publishing Co.

Quality Resources c/o Kraus Organization, Ltd., 1 Water St., White Plains, NY 10601
Quorum Books, c/o Greenwood Publishing Group

Random House, 201 E. 50th St., New York, NY 10022
Rawson Associates c/o Macmillan Publishing Co.
Reston Publishing Co. c/o Prentice Hall

Rodale Press, 33 E. Minor St., Emmaus, PA 18049
Ronald Press c/o John Wiley and Sons
Roosevelt Center for American Policy Studies, 316 Pennsylvania Ave., SE, Ste. 500, Washington, DC 20003 (ceased publishing)
Routledge c/o Routledge, Chapman and Hall
Routledge, Chapman and Hall, 29 W. 35th St., New York, NY 10001-2209
Routledge Kegan Paul c/o Routledge, Chapman and Hall
Rowman & Allanheld c/o Rowman and Littlefield Publishers
Rowman & Littlefield Publishers, 4720 Boston Way, Ste. A, Lanham, MD 20706
Russell Sage Foundation, 112 E. 64th St., New York, NY 10021
Rutgers University Press, 109 Church St., New Brunswick, NJ 08901

Sage Publications, 2455 Teller Rd., Thousand Oaks, CA 91320
Saunders, W.B., Curtis Center, Independence Sq., W, Philadelphia, PA 19106
Schocken Books c/o Random House
Science Research Associates, 250 Old Wilson Bridge Rd., Ste. 310, Worthington, OH 43085
Scientific Press, 507 Seaport Ct., Redwood City, CA 94063 (ceased publishing)
Scott, Foresman & Co., 1900 E. Lake Ave., Glenview, IL 60025
Scribner's, Charles & Sons c/o Macmillan Publishing Co.
Scribner Educational Publishers c/o Macmillan Publishing Co.
Sharpe, M.E., 80 Business Park Dr., Armonk, NY 10504
Shepard's/McGraw-Hill, 555 Middle Creek Pkwy, Box 35300, Colorado Springs, CO 80935-3530
Sierra Club Books, 100 Bush St., 13th Flr., San Francisco, CA 94104
Simon & Schuster, 1230 Ave. of the Americas, New York, NY 10020
Sleepy Hollow Press, 150 White Plains Road, Tarrytown, NY 10591
Social Philosophy & Policy Center c/o Transaction Publishers
Soho Press, 853 Broadway, New York, NY 10003
Sourcebooks Trade, P.O. Box 313, Napierville, IL 60566
South End Press, 116 St. Botolph St., Boston, MA 02115
South-Western Publishing Co., 5101 Madison Rd., Cincinnati, OH 45227
Springer Verlag New York, 175 5th Ave, 19th Fl., New York, NY 10010
Saint Martin's Press, 175 5th Ave., Rm. 1715, New York, NY 1001
Society of Industrial and Office Realtors (SIR), 777 14th Street NW, Suite 400, Washington, DC 20005
Stanford University Press, Stanford CA 94305-2355
State Mutual Book and Periodical Service, Ltd., 521 5th Ave., 17th Flr., New York, NY 10175
State University of New York Press, State University Plaza, Albany, NY 12246-0001
Stein & Day/Scarborough Hse. c/o Madison Books

Stone Bridge Press, P.O. Box 8208, Berkeley, CA 94707
Storey Communications, Schoolhouse Road, Pownal, VT 05261
Stuart, Lyle c/o Carol Publishing Group
Summit Books, c/o Simon & Schuster

TAB Books, P.O. Box 40, Blue Ridge Summit, PA 17294-0850
Talman Co., 131 Spring Rd., Ste. 201E-N, New York, NY 10012
Tarcher, J.P., Inc., 5858 Wilshire Blvd., Ste. 200, Los Angeles, CA 90036
Tauris, I.B. & Co., Ltd. c/o Saint Martin's Press
Taylor & Francis, Ltd., 1900 Frost Rd., Ste. 101, Bristol, PA 19007
Taylor Publishing Co., 1550 W. Mockingbird Ln., Dallas, TX 75235
Teachers College Press, Teachers College, Columbia University, 1234 Amsterdam Ave., New York, NY 10027
Temple University Press, 1601 N. Broad St, University Services Building 306, Philadelphia, PA 19122
Ten Speed Press, P.O. Box 7123, Berkeley, CA 94707
Thames & Hudson, 500 5th Ave., New York, NY 10110
Thistlerose Publications, 1702 Glenwood Ave., Minneapolis, MN 55404-1238
Ticknor & Fields, 215 Park Ave., S., New York, NY 10003
Time Inc., 1271 Avenue of the Americas, New York, NY 10020
Times Books, 201 E. 50th St., 22nd Flr., New York NY 10022
Tioga Publications, 6010 NY Rte. 79E, Chenango Forks, NY 13746
Touche Ross, 1633 Broadway, 9th Floor, New York NY 10019
Traffic Service Corp. c/o International Thomson Transport Press, 424 W. 33rd St., New York, NY 10001
Transaction Publishers, Rutgers University, New Brunswick, NJ 08903
Travel, 15 Columbus Cir., New York, NY 10023
Twayne Publishers c/o Macmillan Publishing Co.
TPR c/o TAB Books

United Nations, 2 U.N. Plaza, Sales Section, Publications Division, Rm. DC2-853, New York, NY 10017
University of Arizona Press, 1230 N. Park Ave., Ste. 102, Tucson, AZ 85719
University of California Press, 2120 Berkeley Way, Berkeley, CA 94720
University of Chicago Press, 5801 S. Ellis Ave., 4th Flr. Chicago, IL 60637
University of Illinois Press, 1325 S. Oak St., Champaign, IL 61820
University of Michigan Press, Box 1104, Ann Arbor, MI 48106
University of Nebraska Press, 312 N. 14th St., Lincoln, NE 68588-0484
University of Notre Dame Press, P.O. Box L, Notre Dame, IN 46556
University of Pennsylvania Press, Blockley Hall, 418 Service Dr., 13th Flr., Philadelphia, PA 19104
University of Pittsburgh Press, 127 N. Bellefield Ave., Pittsburgh, PA 15260
University of Texas Press, Box 7819, Austin, TX 78713-7819
University of Washington Press, Box 50096, Seattle WA 98145-5096
University of Wisconsin Press, 114 N Murray St., Madison, WI 53715-1199
Universitetsforlaget c/o i.b.d. Ltd., 24 Hudson St., Kinderhook, NY 12106
University of North Carolina Press, P.O. Box 2288, Chapel Hill, NC 27515
University of South Carolina Press, 1716 College St., Columbia, SC 29208
University of Texas at Austin, Bureau of Business Research, P.O. Box 7459, Austin, TX 78713-7459
University of Tokyo Press c/o Columbia University Press
University Associates c/o Pfeiffer and Co.
University Press of America, 4720 Boston Way, Lanham, MD 20706
University Press of Kansas, 2501 W. 15th St., Lawrence, KS 66049
University Press of New England, 23 South Main St., Hanover, NH 03755-2048
University Press of Virginia, P.O. Box 3608, University Station, Charlottesville, VA 22903
University Press of Florida, 15 NW 15th St., Gainesville, FL 32611
Upjohn, W.E., Institute for Employment Research, 300 S. Westridge Ave., Kalamazoo, MI 49007-4686
Urban Institute Press, 2100 M St., NW, Washington, DC 20037

Van Nostrand Reinhold, 115 5th Ave., New York, NY 10003
Vantage Press, 516 W. 34th St., NY NY 10001
Viking Penguin, 375 Hudson St., New York, NY 10014-3657
Villard Books c/o Random House
Vintage Books, Mail Drop 28-2, 201 E. 50th St. New York, NY 10022

Wadsworth Publishing Co., 10 Davis Dr., Belmont, CA 94002
Walker & Co., 435 Hudson St., New York, NY 10014
Warner Books, 1271 Avenue of the Americas, New York, NY 10103
Warren, Gorham & Lamont, 31 Saint James St., 4th Flr., Boston, MA 02116-4101
Watts, Franklin, 95 Madison Ave., S, New York, NY 10016
Waveland Press, Box 400, Prospect Heights, IL 60070
West Publishing Co., 620 Opperman Dr., St. Paul, MN 55164
Westview, Press, 5500 Central Ave., Boulder CO 80301
Wight, Oliver, Publishers, Ltd., Inc., 85 Allen Martin Dr., Essex Junction, VT 05452
Wiley, John & Sons, Inc., 605 3rd Ave., New York, NY 10158

Wilkerson, J.L., Publishing Co., P.O. Box 948, Westbury, NY 11590

Woodstead Press, 1755 Woodstead Ct., The Woodlands, TX 77380

World Future Society, 7910 Woodmont Ave., Ste. 450, Bethesda, MD 20814-3032

World Resources Institute, 1709 New York Ave., NW, Washington, DC 20006

Yale University Press, 302 Temple St., New Haven, CT 06511

Yourdon Press, c/o Prentice Hall

INDEXES

AUTHOR INDEX

The numbers after each entry in the list below refer to page numbers in the main section.

Aaker, David A., 6, 191, 192, 268
Aaseng, Nathan, 208
Abdullah, Fuad A., 145
Abegglen, James C., 66, 81
Abell, Derek F., 60, 191, 269
Abernathy, William J., 14, 275
Abo, Tetsuo, 68
Abraham, Katharine G., 161
Abrahamson, Royce L., 260
Abrams, Alexander, 307
Abrams, Bill, 191
Abrams, Rhonda M., 208
Aburdene, Patricia, 246, 294, 300
Aby, Carroll D., 65
Academy Industry Program (National Research Council (U.S.), 19
Acker, Joan, 228
Ackerman, Kenneth B., 299
Ackoff, Russell Lincoln, 176
Adam, Everett E., 240
Adams, James Ring, 16, 253
Adams, Jerome, 167
Adams, John D., 224
Adams, Walter, 53
Adamson, David, 122
Adizes, Ichak, 221
Adler, David E., 288
Adler, Jerry, 247
Adler, Nancy J., 217, 301, 302
Aggarwal, Raj, 147
Agmon, Tamir, 260
Aguayo, Rafael, 245
Aguilar, Francis J., 29, 40
Ahn, Mark J., 250
Aho, C. Michael, 113
AlHashim, Dhia D., 147
Albaum, Gerald S., 102, 193
Albert, Kenneth J., 61, 175, 237
Albert, Michel, 36
Albert, Susan Wittig, 255
Albion, Mark S., 6
Albrecht, Karl, 70, 73, 199, 256, 307
Albrecht, Steven, 70
Aldcroft, Derek Howard, 98
Alexander, David, 4
Alexander, Gordon J., 154, 155, 235
Alexander, Marcus, 52
Alexander, Roy, 100
Alexandrides, Costas G., 70
Aliber, Robert Z., 149, 151, 200
Alic, John A., 277
Alkhafaji, Abbass F., 55
Allen & Overy (Firm), 59
Allen, Bruce T., 183
Allen, Christopher, 222
Allen, David Grayson, 236
Allen, Deborah, 131
Allen, Everett T., 214
Allen, Franklin, 107
Allen, Louis L., 260
Allen, Margaret, 147

Allen, Michael Patrick, 299
Allen, Robert L., 305
Allen, Robert W., 219
Allen, Thomas J., 175
Alletzhauser, Albert J., 255
Allio, Robert J., 269
Allsup, Randall, 251
Almond, Brenda, 139
Alreck, Pamela L., 57, 193
Alsop, Ronald, 191
Alterowitz, Ralph, 130
Altman, Edward I., 65, 66, 105, 163
Altman, Mary Ann, 3
Altman, Richard M., 155, 267
Altman, Steven, 220
Amacom, 168
Ameiss, Albert P., 3
Amemiya, Takeshi, 82
American Association for the Advancement of Science, 56
American Bankers Association, 18
American Compensation Association, 91
American Enterprise Institute for Public Policy Research, 105
American Institute of Small Business, 259
American Management Association, 8, 23, 24, 31, 35, 55, 64, 71, 74, 78, 92, 132, 138, 161, 173, 174, 246, 255, 256, 258, 271, 273, 276
American Marketing Association, 189
American Marketing Association. Marketing Education Division, 191
American Production and Inventory Control Society. Handbook Editorial Board, 239
American Productivity Center, 91
American Society for Quality Control, 78
American Telephone and Telegraph Company, 10, 246
Ames, B. Charles, 187
Amihud, Yakov, 179, 266
Amling, Frederick, 155
Amos, John M., 194
Amrine, Harold T., 103
Amsden, Alice H., 271
Anastassopoulos, J. P., 149
Anderla, Georges, 50
Anders, George, 54
Andersen, Erling B., 87
Anderson, Andy B., 263
Anderson, Carolyn S., 122
Anderson, D. Victor, 299
Anderson, David Ray, 182
Anderson, Jerry W., 139, 225
Anderson, Paul Edward, 248
Anderson, Quentin, 9
Anderson, Robert, 200
Anderson, Robert O., 233
Andersson, Ake E., 45
Andersson, Krister, 274
Ando, Yukihiro, 282
Andreasen, Alan R., 192, 212
Andrews, Kenneth Richmond, 29, 60, 271

Andrews, Paul, 114
Andrulis, Richard S., 30
Angel, David P., 256
Angle, Harold L., 276
Anglo-German Foundation for the Study of Industrial Society, 156
Ankeny, Nesmith C., 235
Ansary, Adel I., 192
Ansbacher, Max G., 215
Ansoff, H. Igor, 101, 131, 269
Anthony, Robert Newton, 3, 4, 5, 65, 129, 211
Anthony, William P., 174
Antl, Boris, 112
Apilado, Vincent P., 17
Apostolou, Nicholas G., 105
Appelbaum, Eileen, 304
Appraisal Institute (U.S.), 248
Apter, T. E., 304
Aquilano, Nicholas J., 239
ARA/Wharton Conference on the Future of the Service Economy (1982 : University of Pennsylvania), 257
Aram, John D., 79
Araskog, Rand V., 151
Arbel, Avner, 265
Archer, Simon, 4
Arens, Alvin A., 13
Arens, William F., 6
Argandoña Rámiz, Antonio, 139
Argenti, John, 216
Argenti, Paul A., 45
Argyris, Chris, 46, 176, 222, 223, 224, 227, 231, 262
Arkebauer, James B., 116
Armstrong, David M., 45
Armstrong, Gary, 138, 190
Armstrong, Michael, 175
Arnold, Hugh J., 218
Arnold, John D., 237
Arnott, Robert D., 12
Aronson, J. Richard, 82
Aronson, Jonathan David, 113
Arpan, Jeffrey S., 147
Arrow, Kenneth Joseph, 86, 178
Arthur D. Little, Inc, 141
Arthur Young & Company, 53
Arthur Young International, 54
Ashenfelter, Orley, 164
Ashenhurst, Robert L., 181
Ashton, David, 245
Asian Productivity Organization, 129
Asimov, Isaac, 251
Asman, David, 179
Aspen Institute for Humanistic Studies, 165
Association for Investment Management and Research, 153
Atkinson, Anthony A., 182
Auerbach, Alan J., 53, 54
Auerbach, Arnold, 177
Auerbach, Joseph, 154
Auerbach, Robert D., 200
Augustine, Norman R., 135
Auld, David D., 57
Auletta, Ken, 169, 279
Austin, James E., 131, 147
Austin, Nancy, 130
Australian National University, 106
Avedon, Don M., 124

Avis, Warren E., 272
Awad, Elias M., 24
Axtell, Roger E., 152
Ayling, D. E., 266
Ayton, Peter, 83

Babcock, Bruce, 44
Bach, George Leland, 86
Backer, Bill, 70
Badaracco, Joseph, 126, 162, 167
Baden Fuller, C., 61, 125
Bagranoff, Nancy A., 3
Bahrami, Homa, 242
Baida, Peter, 30
Bailey, Elizabeth E., 7, 283
Bailey, Fenton, 163
Bailey, Jeffery V., 154
Bailey, Paul J., 148
Bailey, Sheryl D., 134
Baily, Martin Neil, 134, 290
Bailyn, Lotte, 304
Baird, Bruce F., 75
Bairoch, Paul, 84
Baker, C. B., 9
Baker, James Calvin, 146
Baker, Richard H., 171
Baker, Wayne E., 45
Bakke, Dennis, 236
Balassa, Bela A., 84
Balkin, David B., 47
Ball, Ben C., 93
Ballance, Robert H., 84
Ballot, Michael, 137
Ballou, Ronald H., 32
Bamber, Greg, 12
Band, William A., 72, 179
Bandrowski, James F., 60
Banfe, Charles, 272
Banks, Jerry, 153
Banner, David K., 226
Bansal, Vipul K., 107
Banta, William F., 9
Barabba, Vincent P., 75
Baragiola, Patrick, 97
Barbash, Jack, 136
Barcus, Sam W., 25
Barkley, Bruce, 135
Barmash, Isadore, 172
Barnard, Chester Irving, 101
Barnes, Louis B., 33, 223
Barnet, Richard J., 145
Barnett, George A., 46
Barney, Jay B., 176, 184
Barr, Mary, 225
Barrentine, Pat, 246
Barrett, M. Edgar, 183
Barro, Robert J., 172, 200, 265
Barry, David, 296
Barry, Peter J., 9
Barsoux, Jean-Louis, 176
Barth, James R., 17
Bartlett, Christopher A., 147
Bartlett, Joseph W., 296
Bartlett, Sarah, 163
Bartley, Robert L., 289
Barton, David R., 292
Bartos, Rena, 301

Baskin, Otis W., 24
Bass, Bernard M., 166
Bassett, Glenn A., 127
Bassman, Emily S., 161
Bate, Paul, 59
Bates, Timothy Mason, 199
Bateson, John E. G., 257
Batra, Rajeev, 6
Batra, Raveendra N., 84, 113, 156
Batt, Rosemary L., 304
Batten, Joe D., 168, 307
Batterson, Leonard A., 295
Baty, Gordon B., 207
Bauder, Donald C., 255
Bauer, Richard J., 154
Bauer, Roy A., 150
Baughman, James P., 287
Baughn, William Hubert, 17
Baumback, Clifford Mason, 259
Baumol, William J., 135, 165
Baye, Michael R., 184
Bayley, Christine, 255
Baylor University. Center for Entrepreneurship, 206
Bazerman, Max H., 205
Beach, Frank Herman, 256
Beacham, Walton, 186
Beal, Edwin Fletcher, 42
Beams, Floyd A., 4
Beattie, Derek, 127
Beatty, Richard W., 232
Beaty, Jonathan, 16
Beauchamp, Tom L., 29
Beck, John C., 100
Beck, John D. W., 167
Beck, Martha Nibley, 100
Becker, Gary Stanley, 88, 103
Becker, Manning H., 103
Becker, William E., 265
Beckhard, Richard, 221, 223
Becklund, Laurie, 210
Beckman, Steven, 201
Bedeian, Arthur G., 101
Bedford, Norton M., 129
Beer, Michael, 122, 223, 232
Beer, Stafford, 215, 225
Beggs, Robert I., 194
Begin, James P., 42
Behr, Peter, 222
Behrman, Jack N., 28, 146
Beidleman, Carl R., 112, 157
Beierlein, James G., 8
Beil, Richard O., 184
Belasco, James A., 167
Belenky, Ann Holt, 161
Belitsos, Byron, 23
Belker, Loren B., 273
Bell, Arthur H., 25
Bell, Cecil, 223
Bell, Chip R., 72
Bell, Philip W., 4
Bellman, Geoffrey M., 56, 167, 178
Belveal, L. Dee, 44
Bemis, Stephen E., 161
BenDaniel, David J., 53
Benbasat, Izak, 181
Bencin, Richard L., 279
Benedetto, M. William, 116

Beneyto, José, 97
Benham, Philip O., 231
Beniger, James R., 45
Benne, Kenneth Dean, 261
Bennett, Amanda, 199
Bennett, James T., 39
Bennett, Steven J., 81, 206, 235
Bennis, Warren G., 167, 168, 220, 261
Bensman, David, 39
Benson, Ian, 89
Benston, George J., 18
Bentley College. Center for Business Ethics, 95
Benveniste, Guy, 224
Berg, Norman A., 130, 175
Bergen, S. A., 136
Berger, Lance A., 47
Berger, Lisa, 128
Berger, Peter L., 36
Berger, Renee A., 212
Berggren, Christian, 297
Bergquist, William H., 223
Berkley, James D., 173
Berle, Adolf Augustus, 66
Berle, Gustav, 208
Berlet, K. Richard, 47
Berlin, Howard M., 117
Berliner, Callie, 70
Berman, Barry, 250
Berndt, Ernst R., 82
Bernhard, J. Gary, 220
Bernstein, Jacob, 26
Bernstein, Jeffrey Ian, 142
Bernstein, Leopold A., 109
Bernstein, Michael A., 288
Bernstein, Paula, 217
Bernstein, Peter L., 74, 104
Berry, John F., 134
Berry, Leonard L., 108
Berry, Peggy J., 100
Berry, Thomas H., 246
Berry, William L., 240
Berryman-Fink, Cynthia, 176
Berton, Lee, 5
Bertozzi, Dan, 140
Besher, Alexander, 227
Best, Larry, 68
Best, Roger J., 56
Bettinger, Cass, 15
Betz, Nancy E., 297
Beyer, Janice M., 58
Beyma, Ronald, 271
Bezold, Clement, 126
Bhagwati, Jagdish N., 242
Bhalla, Sushil K., 275
Bhatia, Tarun K., 54
Bianco, Anthony, 19
Bibb, Porter, 285
Bibler, Richard S., 53
Bicksler, James L., 142
Bidanda, Bopaya, 239
Bieber, Roland, 98
Bierman, Harold, 35, 65, 125, 131
Bigda, John P., 55
Bijker, Wiebe E., 277
Bilby, Kenneth W., 253
Billingsley, Patrick, 265
Binhammer, H. H., 106

Binmore, Ken, 114
Birch, David L., 259
Bird, Barbara J., 94
Birdzell, L. E., 98
Birley, Sue, 94
Birnbaum, Jeffrey H., 171
Birnbaum-More, Philip H., 216
Bishop, James, 236
Bishop, Paul, 112
Black, Homer A., 69
Black, Stanley W., 135
Black, Tyrone, 106
Blackburn, John D., 126
Blackburn, Joseph D., 292
Blackford, Mansel G., 63, 118
Blackman, Irving L., 41
Blackman, Sue Anne Batey, 165
Blackstone, A. Lee, 256
Blackwell, David W., 105
Blackwell, Roger D., 56
Blair, John Malcolm, 233
Blair, Margaret M., 53
Blake, Gary, 33
Blake, John, 109
Blake, Robert Rogers, 52, 167, 168, 176, 221, 305
Blanc, Georges, 149
Blanchard, Kenneth H., 30, 175, 177, 218, 223
Blanchard, Olivier, 96
Blanding, Warren, 73
Blankenship, Albert Breneman, 192, 193
Blasi, Joseph R., 91
Blattberg, Robert C., 188, 253
Blau, Lucie R., 288
Blaug, Mark, 87
Blecker, Robert A., 15
Blejer, Mario I., 85
Blinder, Alan S., 86, 297
Bloch, H. I. Sonny, 106
Block, Frank E., 153
Block, Peter, 217
Block, Stanley B., 65
Block, Zenas, 94
Blondheim, Menahem, 162
Bloom, Robert, 64
Bloomfield, Caroline L., 25
Blotnick, Srully, 99, 300
Bluestone, Barry, 137
Bluestone, Barry, 288
Bluestone, Irving, 137
Blum, Laurie, 259
Blumberg, Donald F., 72
Blume, Marshall, 209
Bly, Robert W., 33, 132
Board of Governors of the Federal Reserve System (U.S.), 107
Bobrow, Edwin E., 209
Bodily, Samuel E., 76
Boesky, Ivan F., 11
Bogdanowicz-Bindert, Christine A., 109
Bogue, Marcus C., 268
Boguslaw, Robert, 132
Boje, David M., 177, 242
Bok, Derek Curtis, 38, 100
Bolen, William H., 250
Boll, Carl R., 11
Bollenbacher, George M., 15
Bolman, Lee G., 178

Bonini, Charles P., 131
Bonoma, Thomas V., 188, 189
Booher, Dianna Daniels, 25
Boone, Louis E., 40, 186
Booth, Laurence D., 146
Borges, William, 253
Bormann, Ernest G., 46
Bornstein, Jay, 207
Borrus, Michael, 198
Borton, James W., 296
Bos, Theodore, 31
Boskin, Michael J., 263
Boston University. School of Management, 36
Bosworth, Barry, 212
Botkin, James W., 26, 268
Botwinick, Howard, 297
Boudreau, John W., 230
Boulding, Kenneth Ewart, 288
Bounds, Gregory M., 268, 281
Bovée, Courtland L., 6, 25
Bowdery, John G., 108
Bowditch, James L., 54, 219, 220
Bowe, Michael, 96
Bowen, Charles, 80
Bowen, David, 102
Bowen, David Earl, 257
Bowen, Earl K., 32
Bowen, William G., 59
Bower, Joseph L., 140, 233, 271, 290
Bowers, Barbara L., 70
Bowersox, Donald J., 48, 234
Bowes, Lee, 92
Bowie, Norman E., 27, 29
Bowker, Michael, 195
Bowlin, Oswald Doniece, 27
Bowling Green State University. Social Philosophy & Policy Center, 38
Boxwell, Robert J., 19
Boyadjian, Haig J., 27
Boyar, Burt, 124
Boyar, Jane, 124
Boyd, Charles, 23
Boyd, Harper W., 188, 193
Boyett, Joseph H., 232
Boykin, James H., 247
Boyle, Charles, 277
Bozeman, Barry, 249
Brache, Alan P., 134
Bradford, David F., 124
Bradford, David L., 226
Bradford, Lawrence J., 73
Bradley, Edward S., 266
Bradley, Gene E., 289
Bradley, Stephen P., 145, 278
Bradshaw, Thornton F., 291
Brady, Kathleen, 274
Braiotta, Louis, 79
Brake, Terence, 127
Brancato, Carolyn Kay, 228
Brandin, David, 121
Brandon, Joel, 223
Brandt, Steven C., 94
Brannen, Christalyn, 30
Branscomb, Lewis M., 278
Bray, Douglas Weston, 10, 230
Brealey, Richard A., 66
Brebner and Co International Division, 62

Breen, George Edward, 192, 193
Brennan, Peter J., 241
Brenner, Reuven, 48
Brenner, Walter, 141
Bresnahan, Timothy F., 133
Brewer, Thomas L., 157
Brewster, Chris, 230
Brickey, Homer, 255
Bridges, William, 131
Bridgford, Jeff, 137
Briggs, Vernon M., 164
Brigham, Eugene F., 27, 64, 65, 66
Brimelow, Peter, 153
Brimson, James A., 70
Briscoe, Mary Louise, 196
Britt, Steuart Henderson, 186
Brock, James W., 53
Brockway, George P., 86
Brody, David, 284
Broehl, Wayne G., 33
Brooke, Michael Z., 146
Brookings Institution, 14, 50, 69, 134, 159, 203, 257, 287
Brooks, Chris, 264
Brooks, John, 55, 297
Brown, Arnold, 224
Brown, Charles, 92
Brown, Clair, 257
Brown, George Isaac, 218
Brown, Halina Szejnwald, 261
Brown, Harold, 113
Brown, John Dennis, 297
Brown, Marvin T., 30
Brown, Michael Harold, 9
Brown, Paul B., 189, 208
Brown, Richard, 98
Brown, Stephen J., 155
Brown, Warren B., 216
Brown, Wilson B., 150
Bruce, Brian R., 62
Bruchey, Stuart Weems, 287
Bruck, Connie, 55, 251
Brue, Stanley L., 86
Brueggeman, William B., 202
Brumbaugh, R. Dan, 17
Brun, Kim E., 181
Bruns, William J., 182, 183
Brush, Candida G., 208
Bryan, Lowell L., 17
Bryant, Keith L., 287
Bryce, Herrington J., 211
Bryman, Alan, 167
Buğra, Ayşe, 134
Buchanan, James M., 86
Buchholz, Rogene A., 24, 95, 139, 140
Buchholz, Steve, 220
Buckler, Carol A., 203
Buckley, Michael P., 203
Buckley, Peter J., 145
Buddrus, Lee E., 174
Budnick, Frank S., 194, 214
Buehler, Vernon M., 134, 135, 226
Buenker, John D., 199
Buffa, Elwood Spencer, 239, 268
Buitendam, Arend, 276
Buitoni, Bruno, 22
Bulgatz, Joseph, 95

Bullen, Christine V., 178
Bulloch, James, 68
Bumba, Lincoln, 7
Bunc, Mirko, 84
Buono, Anthony F., 54, 220
Bupp, Irvin C., 93
Burack, Elmer H., 184, 230
Burandt, Gary, 22
Burch, John G., 181
Bureau of National Affairs (Washington, D.C.), 161, 258
Burgelman, Robert A., 275
Burger, Chester, 243
Burgunder, Lee B., 140
Burke, Rory, 136
Burkholz, Herbert, 286
Burks, Ardath W., 158
Burrill, G. Steven, 295
Burrough, Bryan, 251
Bursic, Karen M., 277
Burst, Ardis, 180
Burstein, Daniel, 291
Burstein, Michael C., 185
Burstiner, Irving, 260
Burt, David N., 134
Burt, Ronald S., 48
Burtless, Gary T., 290, 297
Burton, Cynthia E., 166
Burton, E. James, 61
Burton, Mary Lindley, 37
Burton, Richard M., 48
Busch, Dennis H., 72
Business Council for Sustainable Development, 82
Business International Corporation, 63, 147, 149
Business International S.A, 54, 69, 224
Business Roundtable, 240
Buskirk, Bruce D., 256
Buskirk, Richard Hobart, 252, 256
Butcher, Lee, 11
Butler, Lee, 177
Butsch, Richard, 169
Buzzell, Robert D., 102, 188, 190, 191, 271, 279
Byars, Lloyd L., 270
Bygrave, William D., 296
Byham, William C., 305
Bylinsky, Gene, 121
Byrne, Jim, 295
Byrne, John A., 34, 101, 254
Byron, Christopher, 280

Caddes, Carolyn, 198
Cady, John F., 191
Cagan, Phillip, 200
Cairncross, Frances, 95, 108
Calder, Kent E., 158
Calhoun, Kirk, 264
Calingaert, Michael, 98
Callahan, Robert E., 51
Callan, Scott, 184
Callenbach, Ernest, 127
Camealy, John B., 225
Cameron, Kim S., 223
Cameron, Maxwell A., 113
Cameron, Rondo E., 84
Camillus, John C., 270
Camp, James L., 23
Campagna, Anthony S., 290

Campbell, Andrew, 52, 59
Campbell, John Creighton, 14
Campbell, John L., 212
Campbell, John P., 121
Campbell, John Paul, 165
Campbell, Richard J., 165
Campbell, Robert Wellington, 264
Campsey, B. J., 66
Canadian Institute of Strategic Studies, 157
Canals, Jordi, 17
Candea, Dan, 238
Candilis, Wray O., 257
Cannie, Joan Koob, 57
Cannon, Edward, 89
Cantelon, Philip L., 195
Canto, Victor A., 156
Cantor, Bill, 243
Cape, Ronald E., 19
Caplan, Suzanne, 207
Caplin, Lee Evan, 11
Capon, Noel, 268
Cappon, Daniel, 175
Carew, Anthony, 250
Carlson, Rick J., 126
Carlson, Robert S., 147
Carmichael, D. R., 3, 13
Carnegie Commission on Higher Education, 42
Carnegie-Mellon University, 283
Carnes, W. Stansbury, 85
Carnevale, Anthony Patrick, 92, 165, 274
Carney, David C., 206
Carnoy, Martin, 84
Carolina Public Policy Conference (1st : 1988 : University of North Carolina at Chapel Hill), 135
Carosso, Rose C., 202
Carosso, Vincent P., 202
Carpenter, Donna Sammons, 88
Carrington, Tim, 258
Carroll, Archie B., 24, 220
Carroll, Paul, 149
Carrubba, Eugene R., 78
Carson, Ewart R., 273
Carter, John D., 162
Carter, John Mack, 34
Carter, William K., 68
Cartwright, Roger, 177
Caruth, Donald L., 232
Carver, John, 79
Case, John, 259
Case Western Reserve University, 225
Cash, James I., 18, 23, 141, 180, 181
Casson, Mark, 94, 145, 148, 296
Castelino, Mark G., 108
Castle, Emery N., 103
Castle, Gray, 143
Castro, Janice, 120
Catalyst, Inc, 228, 302, 303
Catania, Patrick J., 44
Cateora, Philip R., 102, 103
Cater, Erlet, 88
Cato Institute, 16
Cavanagh, Gerald F., 27, 29
Cavanagh, John, 145
Caves, Richard E., 134, 138, 152, 292
Celente, Gerald, 111
Celi, Louis J., 38

Center for Creative Leadership, 301
Center for Economic Progress and Employment, 297
Centre for Co-operation with European Economies in Transition, 271
Centre for Economic Policy Research (Great Britain), 17
Ceres Conference (1st : 1989 : Williamsburg, VA.), 111
Ceriello, Vincent R., 231
Cespedes, Frank V., 190, 192
Cetron, Marvin J., 285
Chaffee, C. David, 214
Chakiris, B. J., 221
Chakiris, Kenneth Nicholas, 221
Chakrabarti, Alok K., 134
Chalofsky, Neal, 230
Chamberlain, Neil W., 42
Champy, James, 224
Chandler, Alfred Dupont, 133, 139, 148, 227, 271, 287
Chandler, Alfred Dupont, 19, 27
Chang, Lucia S., 110
Chapman, Keith, 139
Charkham, Jonathan P., 59
Charmasson, Henri, 32
Chase, Richard B., 239, 257
Chen, Tong, 30
Cherniss, Cary, 139
Chernow, Ron, 202, 299
Chetley, Andrew, 80
Chew, Donald H., 67, 151
Chi, Meng, 288
Chiang, Thomas C., 67
Chicago Board of Trade, 44, 143
Child, John, 218
Childers, Peter G., 70
Chilton, Kenneth, 55
Chilton, Kenneth W., 292
Chimerine, Lawrence, 27
Chin, Robert, 261
Chinworth, Michael W., 160
Chiron, Robert J., 93
Chisnall, Peter M., 192
Cho, Tong-sŏng, 284
Choate, Pat, 291
Choi, Frederick D. S., 146
Chorafas, Dimitris N., 41, 254, 255
Chou, Ya-lun, 37
Chposky, James, 149
Christensen, C. Roland, 33, 42, 63, 130
Christian, Jack, 211
Christie, Linda Gail, 214
Christopher, Martin, 234
Christopher, Robert C., 67
Christy, George A., 105
Chung, Kwang S., 55
Churchill, Gilbert A., 192, 252
Chute, Phillip B., 206
Ciampa, Dan, 292
Ciborra, Claudio, 181
Clampitt, Phillip G., 45
Clancy, John J., 24
Clancy, Kevin J., 189
Clapes, Anthony Lawrence, 58
Clapp, John M., 248
Clark, Bruce H, 189

Clark, Charles Tallifero, 262
Clark, David, 288
Clark, John B., 190
Clark, John J., 35, 53, 67
Clark, Kim B., 14, 127, 135, 209, 275, 292
Clark, Peter J., 53
Clark, Robert Charles, 62
Clarke, John M., 285
Clarke, Peter, 237
Clarke, Roberta N., 195
Clarke, William M., 108
Clawson, Dan, 25
Clawson, James G., 38
Clay, C. J. J., 197
Clayton, Susan D., 257
Clegg, Jeremy, 148
Cleland, David I., 135, 136, 239, 270, 277
Clemence, Richard V., 86
Clemens, John, 166
Clements, Jonathan, 157
Clements, Richard Barrett, 239
Cleveland, Harlan, 151, 167
Click, Reid W., 149
Clifton, Peter, 192
Clinton, Bill, 120
Clippinger, Marni, 7
Clipson, Colin, 77
Closs, David J., 234
Clough, Bryan, 49
Club de Bruxelles, 97
Club of Rome, 84
Club of Rome. Council, 83
Clutterbuck, David, 304
Coase, R. H., 86, 133
Cobb, Clifford W., 82
Cobb, John B., 82
Cochran, Thomas Childs, 287
Cody, Thomas G., 26
Coffey, Richard James, 196
Coffman, Larry L., 117
Coffman, Sandra, 258
Coggan, Philip, 108
Cohen, A. W., 266
Cohen, Allan R., 217, 226
Cohen, Benjamin J., 18
Cohen, Jerome Bernard, 65, 153
Cohen, Michael D., 42
Cohen, Nurit, 177
Cohen, Sanford, 76
Cohen, Stephen S., 292
Cohen, Theodore, 160
Cohen, William A., 26, 61, 172, 177, 190
Cohen-Rosenthal, Edward, 166
Colby, Robert W., 266
Cole, Barry G., 279
Cole, Robert Hartzell, 71
Colford, James P., 58
Coll, Steve, 10, 116
Coll, Steve, 286
Collar, Emilio, 150
Collier, David A., 73
Collins, Eliza G. C., 130, 217
Collins, James C., 272
Collins, Nancy W., 302
Collins, Orvis F., 94
Collins, Thomas L., 186, 190
Collins, Timothy M., 162

Collins, Tom, 187
Colloquium on Human Resource Futures (1984 : Harvard University Graduate School of Business Administration), 230
Colman, Robert Douglas, 27
Colombo, George W., 252
Colvin, Geoffrey, 281
Committee for Economic Development, 9, 124, 135, 289
Committee for Economic Development. Research and Policy Committee, 9
Committee on Japanese Economic Studies (U.S.), 122
Commons, Dorman L., 55
Compton, Eric N., 18
Conant, Ralph Wendell, 206
Conarroe, Richard R., 272
Coney, Kenneth A., 56
Conference on the Impact of Information Technology on the Service Sector (1985 : Wharton School, University of Pennsylvania), 257
Conger, Jay Alden, 99
Congram, Carole A., 256
Conley, John M., 228
Conn, Henry P., 232
Conner, Daryl, 222
Connolly, Michael A., 68
Connolly, Paul M., 225
Connor, Patrick E., 223
Connor, Richard A., 241
Connors, Michael, 141
Contractor, Farok J., 112
Conway, Robert P., 64
Cook, Curtis R., 197
Cook, James R., 208
Cooke, Terence E., 54, 55
Cooley, Philip L., 63
Coombs, Jerrold R., 96
Cooper, Cary L., 161, 232, 302, 303
Cooper, Donald R., 127
Cooper, Douglas, 282
Cooper, Philip D., 195
Cooper, Robin, 69, 183
Cooper, S. Kerry, 17
Cooperrider, David L., 225
Coopers & Lybrand, 112, 141, 234
Copacino, William C., 32
Copeland, Duncan C., 142
Copeland, Lennie, 145
Copeland, Thomas E., 65, 66, 67
Copetas, A. Craig, 94
Corbin, Juliet M., 262
Corbridge, Stuart, 151
Cordier, Jean E., 44
Corey, E. Raymond, 132, 177, 192
Corley, Robert Neil, 43, 283
Corn, Joseph J., 277
Corning, Peter A., 289
Corning, Susan, 289
Cornwall, Jeffrey R., 226
Corrado, Frank M., 45
Cortada, James W., 213
Costello, Dennis, 209
Côté, Marcel, 82
Cottle, Sidney, 153
Council of Logistics Management (U.S.), 32, 48

Council on Competitiveness (U.S.), 35
Council on Foreign Relations, 294
Cousin, Edward J., 44
Covey, Stephen R., 272
Covin, Teresa Joyce, 221
Cowe, Roger, 183
Cowen, Scott S., 79
Cowhey, Peter F., 233
Cowking, Philippa, 21
Cox, Allan J., 99, 100
Cox, Andrew W., 140
Cox, C. Philip, 265
Cox, Charles, 302
Cox, Eli Peace, 75
Cox, Keith Kohn, 188
Cox, Taylor, 234
Crabtree, Kristen M., 199
Crandall, Robert W., 14
Crane, Dwight B., 154
Crano, William D., 46
Cravens, David W., 191
Cravens, Douglas M., 47
Craver, Charles B., 284
Crawford, C. Merle, 209
Crawford, Richard, 109
Crawford-Mason, Clare, 282
Craypo, Charles, 284
Creech, Bill, 281
Crevier, Daniel, 12
Crimp, Margaret, 193
Cringely, Robert X., 50
Crittenden, Alan, 154
Cronin, Mary J., 27
Cropanzano, Russell, 91
Crosby, Faye J., 257
Crosby, Philip B., 168, 217, 281
Cross, Kelvin F., 134, 240
Cross, Richard, 72
Crouch, Colin, 150
Crowe, Kenneth C., 144
Crowther, Samuel, 111
Cruikshank, Jeffrey L., 120, 229
Crumbley, D. Larry, 105
Crystal, Graef S., 101
CSIS Strengthening of America Commission, 290
Culbert, Samuel A., 178
Cummings, Thomas G., 257
Cundiff, Edward W., 102, 187, 252
Cunnington, Bert, 223
Cuomo Commission on Trade and Competitiveness (N.Y.), 288
Curran, Ward S., 66
Currid, Cheryl C., 221
Curtis, Donald A., 129
Cusatis, Patrick, 203
Cushing, Barry E., 3
Cushman, Robert Frank, 27, 55, 62, 143, 162
Cusumano, Michael A., 14, 50
Cyert, Richard Michael, 133
Czepiel, John A., 257
Czinkota, Michael R., 192

Daems, Herman, 133
Daft, Richard L., 216
Dahl, Robert Alan, 91
Daigler, Robert T., 107
Dailey, Gene, 208

Dalton, Gene W., 218
Daly, Herman E., 82, 83
Dalzell, Robert F., 280
D'Amico, Marianne, 63
Daniel, Donnie L., 106
Daniel, Sally H., 190
Daniels, Caroline, 145
Daniels, John D., 146
Daniels, John L., 145
Danielsen, Albert L., 278
Dankner, Harold, 234
Danley, John R., 262
Danziger, Sheldon, 124
Darby, Edwin, 37
Dartnell Corporation, 7, 230, 252
Das, Dilip K., 164
Dasgupta, Partha, 114
Dasso, Jerome J., 123, 247
Datar, Srikant M., 68
Date, C. J., 73, 74
Dattel, Eugene R., 157
Dauner, C. Duane, 195
Dauwalder, David P., 25
Davenport, Thomas H., 141
David, Donald K., 29
David, Kenneth H., 144, 157
Davidow, William H., 121
Davidson, Greg, 86
Davidson, James Dale, 154
Davidson, Jeffrey P., 241
Davidson, Kenneth M., 54
Davidson, Marilyn, 302, 303
Davidson, Paul, 86
Davidson, Wallace N., 27
Davidson, William Harley, 142, 287
Davidson, William R., 250
Davies, Owen, 285
Davies, S. W., 134
Davis, Edward Willmore, 136
Davis, Gordon Bitter, 181
Davis, Keith, 138, 219, 231, 261
Davis, Kenneth Rexton, 188
Davis, Louise, 230
Davis, Morton D., 114
Davis, Stanley M., 26, 142, 175, 218
Davis, William, 34
Day, George S., 61, 186, 187, 192
De Bono, Edward, 248, 272
De George, Richard T., 27, 144
D'Egidio, Franco, 73
De Long, David W., 174
De Mente, Boye, 30, 286
De Mozota, Brigitte Borja, 77
De Pree, Max, 168
DeBonis, J. Nicholas, 40
DeBruicker, Stewart, 57
DeCenzo, David A., 232
DeFries, Ruth S., 173
DeLuca, Matthew J., 47
DeToro, Irving J., 282
Deal, Terrence E., 178
Dealy, Francis X., 298
Dean, James W., 293
Dearden, John, 129, 183
Deboeck, Guido, 106
Deck, Steven A., 235
Dee, Catherine, 300

Deeks, John, 58
Deitz, Robert, 253
Della Bitta, Albert J., 56
Deloitte, Haskins & Sells, 249
Deming, W. Edwards, 193
Denison, Daniel R., 58
Denison, Edward Fulton, 287
Denlinger, Teri E., 223
Dennehy, Robert F., 177, 225
Denton, D. Keith, 23, 127
Dernburg, Thomas Frederick, 172
Derr, C. Brooklyn, 273
Derrick, Lucile, 32
Dertouzos, Michael L., 134
DesJardins, Joseph R., 28
Desatnick, Robert L., 72
Dethloff, Henry C., 287
Detzel, Denis H., 72
Deutschman, Alan, 24
Devanna, Mary Anne, 130, 224
Devinney, Timothy Michael, 97
Dewdney, A. K., 194
Dholakia, Nikhilesh, 208
DiBacco, Thomas V., 291
DiGaetani, John Louis, 45
DiLorenzo, Thomas J., 39
DiNapoli, Dominic, 62
Diamond, David, 30
Diamond, Michael R., 41
Diamond, Stephen C., 54
Dible, Donald M., 260
Dicken, Peter, 139
Dickens, Floyd, 8
Dickens, Jacqueline B., 8
Dickens, William T., 137
Dickie, Robert B., 36
Dickinson, David G., 26
Dickson, Gary W., 181
Dickson, William John, 231
Didsbury, Howard F., 277
Diebold, John, 23, 24, 129, 275
Dilenschneider, Robert L., 243
Dimancescu, Dan, 226
Dimson, Elroy, 267
Dinsmore, Paul C., 135
Dirks, Laura M., 190
Dixit, Avinash K., 271
Dixon, Don, 112
Dixon, George R., 305
Dizard, Wilson P., 45
Dobbins, Richard, 236
Dobler, Donald W., 134
Dobson, Paul, 270
Dobyns, Lloyd, 282
Docherty, James M., 109
Dodd, David L., 153
Dodd, Peter, 267
Dodge, H. Robert, 256
Doerflinger, Thomas M., 296
Doeringer, Peter B., 165
Doherty, Joe, 262
Doherty, Neil A., 250
Dolan, Robert J., 188, 209
Domenici, Pete, 290
Domestic Policy Council (U.S.), 120
Domini, Amy L., 155
Donahue, John D., 41

Donaldson, Gordon, 63, 65, 66
Donaldson, John, 29
Donaldson, Thomas, 28, 29, 144
Dongen, H. J. van, 129
Donnahoe, Alan S., 67
Donnelly, Austin S., 156
Donnelly, James H., 108, 216
Donoghue, William E., 156
Doogar, Rajib K., 247
Dooley, Ken, 177
Doorley, Thomas L., 162
Dore, Ronald Philip, 159
Dorfman, Nancy S., 50
Dorio, Marc A., 92
Dornbusch, Rudiger, 85, 172
Dorsey, Jasper N., 278
Dougall, Herbert Edward, 35
Dougherty, David C., 270
Dougherty, James L., 232
Douglas, Evan J., 184
Douglas, John, 232
Douglas, Livingston G., 110
Douglass, Stephen M., 114
Dow Jones-Irwin, 64, 130, 154, 204
Dowd, James J., 168
Dowling, Edward Thomas, 32
Downey, W. David, 8
Downham, John, 192
Downs, Anthony, 203
Doyle, Jack, 111
Doyle, Marc, 279
Doz, Yves L., 145, 146, 147, 148
Drake, David, 277
Drath, Wilfred H., 100
Drenth, Pieter J. D., 242
Drexler, K. Eric, 277
Driscoll, Dawn-Marie, 302
Drobnick, Richard, 260
Droms, William G., 183
Drucker, Peter Ferdinand, 81, 84, 100, 130, 174, 177, 294, 306
DuBose, Philip B., 178
DuBrin, Andrew J., 138, 176
Dubendorf, Donald R., 179
Ducatel, Ken, 92
Duchin, Faye, 165
Dudick, Thomas S., 68
Dudley, James W., 96
Duerig, Alfred W., 10
Duesenberry, James Stemble, 200
Duke, Benjamin C., 88
Dumaine, Deborah, 46
Duncan, W. Jack, 175
Dunfee, Thomas W., 28
Dunlop, Charles, 51
Dunlop, John Thomas, 137, 139, 165, 306
Dunn, Paul, 207
Dunn, S. Watson, 6
Dunnette, Marvin D., 242
Dunning, Anthony, 50
Dunning, John H., 145, 148
Durö, Robert, 191
Duska, Ronald F., 27
Dusky, Lorraine, 300
Dussauge, Pierre, 149
Dutta, Soumitra, 24
Dyckman, Thomas R., 88

Dyer, Davis, 13, 131, 279
Dyer, W. Gibb, 129, 206
Dyer, William G., 261, 305
Dyson, Robert G., 270

Ealey, Lance A., 245
Earl, Michael J., 180
Earth Works Group (U.S.), 300
Easton, Thomas A., 206
Ebel, Robert E., 149
Ebert, Ronald J., 240
Eccles, Robert G., 154, 173, 218, 284
Eckert, Ross D., 197
Eckstein, Otto, 289
Economic Development Institute (Washington, D.C.), 143
Economist Books, 32
Economist Intelligence Unit (New York, N.Y.), 60, 99
Economist Publications (Firm), 130
Economists Advisory Group, 106, 156
Eddy, William B., 305
Edelson, Lynn W., 141
Edwards, Christopher G., 121
Edwards, Franklin R., 266
Edwards, J. S. S., 17, 67
Edwards, James Don, 5
Edwards, James Don, 69
Edwards, Ward, 75
Eells, Richard Sedric Fox, 31
Egan, Gerard, 268
Egbert, Richard T., 230
Ehrhardt, Michael C., 67
Ehrlich, Judith Ramsey, 160
Eichengreen, Barry J., 137
Eilon, Samuel, 26
Ein-Dor, Phillip, 89
Eisenberg, Richard, 106
Eisler, Riane Tennenhaus, 246
Eisner, Robert, 288
Eiteman, David K., 150
Ekelund, Robert B., 86
Elder, Alexander, 267
Elgin, Suzette Haden, 296
Eli, Max, 52
Eliashberg, Jehoshua, 187
Elkington, John, 57
Ellis, Charles D., 154, 235
Ellis, Dennis F., 26
Ellis, R. Jeffery, 269
Ellis Willard H., 259
Elliston, Frederick, 299, 300
Ellsworth, Richard R., 167
Ellwood, David T., 244
Elmwood Institute, 127
Elson, Robert T., 281
Elton, Edwin J., 235, 236
Emanuel, Myron, 46
Embley, L. Lawrence, 262
Emery, James C., 181
Emmanuel, Clive R., 182
Emmott, Bill, 157, 160
Emory, William, 127
Employee Benefit Research Institute (Washington, D.C.), 90
Emshoff, James R., 223

Encarnation, Dennis J., 67, 144, 156
Enderle, Georges, 139
Enen, Jack, 162
Eng, Robert J., 190
Engel, James F., 56, 190
England, Catherine, 16
England, Wilbur B., 134
English, J. Morley, 35
Enis, Ben M., 188, 189
Enteman, Willard F., 176
Entrepreneur (1983 : Harvard University Graduate School of Business Administration), 94
Eovaldi, Thomas L., 283
Eppen, Gary D., 178
Epstein, Charles B., 62
Erdman, Paul Emil, 156
Erickson, Jim, 114
Erickson, Steven P., 8
Erickson, Tamara J., 249
Ermann, M. David, 300
Ernst & Whinney, 32, 116
Ernst & Young, 55, 64, 144, 152, 237
Erve, Marc van der, 178
Esomar, 192
Etter-Lewis, Gwendolyn, 8
Ettlie, John E., 185, 293
Etzioni, Amitai, 87
Eureka, William E., 274
Euro-Japanese Management Studies Association, 68
Euro-Japanese Management Studies Association. (2nd), 68
Euro-Japanese Management Studies Association. International Conference (4th : 1987 : Tokyo, Japan), 68
Euromoney Publications Ltd, 96, 112
European Bond Commission, 21, 44
European Institute for Advanced Studies in Management, 48, 193
European Science Foundation, 148
European University Institute. European Policy Unit, 98
Evans, John, 216
Evans, Paul, 146
Evans, Thomas G., 146
Evans, William D., 139
Ewen, Elizabeth, 6
Ewen, Stuart, 6
Ewing, David W., 43, 118, 120
Ewing, Raymond P., 157
Ezra, Derek, 237

Fabozzi, Frank J., 12, 21, 35, 117, 125, 144, 153, 154, 155, 202, 235
Fabozzi, T. Dessa, 21
Fabra, Paul, 85
Fabritius, M. Manfred, 253
Fabrycky, W. J., 153
Fadiman, Mark, 209
Fahey, Liam, 97, 190, 269
Fairholm, Gilbert W., 167
Fairley, Irene R., 25
Falbe, Cecilia M., 139
Fallek, Max, 259
Fallon, Ivan, 252
Falloon, William D., 250
Falsey, Thomas A., 58
Famularo, Joseph J., 230

Fanning, John, 280
Fant, Kenne, 210
Farley, John U., 268
Farmer, Richard N., 146, 147, 149
Farrell, Michael D., 248
Farrell, Peter, 76
Farren, Caela, 37
Farris, Paul, 6
Farrow, Nigel, 175
Faulhaber, Gerald R., 10, 257
Fay, Charles H., 47, 76
Fay, Stephen, 16
Fayerweather, John, 146
Fear, Richard A., 93
Fearon, Harold E., 134
Federal Reserve Bank of Atlanta, 128
Federal Reserve Bank of Chicago, 151
Federico, Pat-Anthony, 181
Fedorowicz, J. K., 197
Feduniak, Robert B., 44
Feeney, Joan, 34
Feigenbaum, A. V., 245
Feigenbaum, Edward A., 178
Feinstein, Irwin K., 32
Feldman, Daniel C., 218
Feldstein, Martin S., 287, 290
Felix, Richard, 205
Felkins, Patricia K., 221
Feloni, John, 88
Felsenthal, Carol, 117
Fenichell, Stephen, 214
Ferguson, Henry, 149
Fernandez, John P., 92, 138, 184, 225
Ferrell, O. C., 189
Ferris, Kenneth R., 183
Ferris, Paul, 16
Fersh, Don, 119
Fertakis, John P., 64
Fess, Philip E., 3
Ficek, Edmund F., 247
Fiegenbaum, Avi, 185
Field, Barry C., 95
Field, James L., 286
Field, Marilyn J., 143
Fielding, John, 236
Fields, Debbi, 104
Figgie, Harry E., 69, 83
Figlewski, Stephen, 215
Fillmore, Mary Dingee, 302
Financial Accounting Standards Board, 211
Financial Analysts Federation, 153
Financial Executives Research Foundation, 63, 234
Financial Times Business Information Ltd, 17
Fine, Ben, 36
Fink, Robert E., 44
Fink, Steven, 71
Finkel, Madelon Lubin, 195
Finkin, Eugene F., 224
Finkler, Steven A., 121
Finn, Susan Kudla, 211
Finnerty, John D., 64
Finney, H. A., 4
Fischer, Donald E., 153
Fischer, K., 17
Fischer, Stanley, 85, 172
Fisher, Anne B., 303
Fisher, Frederick G., 235

Fisher, Jeffrey D., 202, 248
Fisher, Kimball, 305
Fisher, Roger, 205, 227
Fishman, Daniel B., 139
Fishman-Davidson Center for the Study of the Service Sector, 257
Fitz-enz, Jac, 231
Fitzgerald, Louise F., 297
Fitzgerald, Randall, 237
Fitzgibbon, John E., 210
Fitzsimmons, James A., 257
Fitzsimmons, Mona J., 257
Fjellman, Stephen M., 298
Fjermedal, Grant, 251
Flaherty, Margaret Fresher, 138
Flamholtz, Eric, 175, 207, 230
Flamm, Kenneth, 50
Fleenor, C. Patrick, 40, 51
Fleischer, Arthur, 53
Fletcher, Jerry L., 91
Fliehman, Deborah G., 57
Fligstein, Neil, 284
Flood, Robert L., 273
Florida International University. International Banking Center, 96
Florida, Richard L., 202, 274
Flower, Joe, 298
Fogg, C. Davis, 186
Fogler, H. Russell, 153
Folks, William R., 147
Follett, Mary Parker, 227
Forbes, J. Benjamin, 40
Forbes, Malcolm S., 94
Ford, Brian R., 206, 207
Ford, David, 191
Ford, Henry, 111
Ford, Neil M., 252
Ford, Roger H., 79
Forester, Tom, 51
Forisha-Kovach, Barbara, 226
Forrestal, Dan J., 243
Fort, Rodney D., 241
Fosler, R. Scott, 289
Fossum, John A., 137
Foster, Dean Allen, 205
Foster, George, 68, 109
Foster, Louis Omar, 110
Foster, Richard N., 275
Foulkes, Fred K., 100, 231, 232
Foundation for Health Services Research, 196
Fowler-McCracken Commission (International Management and Development Institute), 289
Fox, Daniel M., 196
Fox, J. Ronald, 140, 286
Fox, Michael W., 115
Fox, William M., 118
Foy, Nancy, 225
Fraleigh, Cynthia, 77
Frame, J. Davidson, 136
Francis, Dave, 269
Francis, Diane, 90
Francis, Dick, 70
Francis, Jack Clark, 144, 155, 235
Frand, Erwin A., 208
Frangos, Stephen J., 81
Frank, Robert H., 85, 90
Frankel, Bud, 253

Frankel, Jeffrey A., 152
Frankel, Mark S., 225
Frantz, Douglas, 16, 170
Fraser, Donald R., 17, 108
Fraser, George C., 8
Fraser Institute (Vancouver, B.C.), 142
Fraser, Lyn M., 110
Fraser, Steve, 122
Frederick, Robert, 95
Frederick, William Crittenden, 138, 261
Fredman, Albert J., 204
Freedman, George, 276
Freeland, Carolyn M., 211
Freeman, Christine, 231
Freeman, Christopher, 82, 276
Freeman, R. Edward, 28, 60, 176
Freemantle, Brian, 32
Freier, Jerold L., 55
Freierman, Richard, 235
Freiermuth, Edmond P., 259
French, Wendell L., 223
Frenkel, Karen A., 251
Frese, Joseph R., 139
Freudberg, David, 23
Freund, John E., 43
Frey, Albert Wesley, 188
Freyer, Tony Allan, 283
Friars, Eileen M., 108
Fridson, Martin S., 109
Fried, Louis, 181
Friedlob, G. Thomas, 110
Friedman, Alan, 8
Friedman, Benjamin M., 63, 200
Friedman, David H., 17
Friedman, Jack P., 154
Friedman, Jon, 9
Friedman, Margaret L., 256
Friedman, Milton, 200
Friedman, Raymond A., 42
Friesen, Peter H., 216
Frohman, Mark A., 226
Frome, Robert L., 255
Fromm, Bill, 73
Froot, Kenneth, 96
Frost, Ellen L., 294
Frost, Lionel, 227
Frost, Peter J., 217, 219
Fruhan, William E., 63, 65
Frumkin, Norman, 85
Fryburger, Vernon Ray, 6
Fuchs, Victor R., 196, 301
Fucini, Joseph J., 34, 195
Fucini, Suzy, 34, 195
Fuess, Billings S., 94
Fujimoto, Takahiro, 14
Fuld, Leonard M., 31
Fulmer, William E., 269
Furchtgott-Roth, Harold W., 50
Furlong, Carla B., 57
Furnham, Adrian, 217
Furst, Alan, 104
Fusfeld, Herbert I., 276
Futrell, Charles, 187

Gabarro, John J., 127, 218
Gabor, Andrea, 245
Gaebler, Ted, 5
Gaffney, Michael, 222
Gagné, T. Elaine, 226
Gainer, Leila J., 92, 274
Galambos, Louis, 10
Galambos, Louis, 291
Galbraith, James K., 85, 197
Galbraith, Jay R., 216, 221
Galbraith, John Kenneth, 84, 86, 201, 236, 289, 291
Gale, Bradley T., 190, 246
Gale, Douglas, 107
Galenson, Walter, 306
Galeries nationales du Grand Palais (France), 78
Gallaway, Edward A., 41
Gallese, Liz Roman, 120
Gallinger, George W., 38
Gallo, Giampaolo, 22
Gallup, Alec, 272
Gallup, George, 272
Galper, Morton, 190
Gamache, R. Donald, 71
Gamble, Barbara S., 258
Gandossy, Robert P., 214
Gange, James, 233
Gans, O. B. de, 131
Gapenski, Louis C., 27, 65, 121
Garbett, Thomas F., 60
Garcia, G. G., 286
Gardener, Edward P. M., 17
Gardner, David Morgan, 190, 191
Gardner, John William, 235
Gardner, Roy, 183
Gareis, R., 135
Garfield, Charles A., 178, 272
Garland, John S., 147
Garlicki, T. Dessa, 21
Garner, Daniel R., 64
Garner, Joe, 171
Garrahan, Philip, 210
Garrett, Dennis E., 189, 190
Garrett, Echo Montgomery, 74
Garrett, Thomas M., 28
Garrison, Michael A., 27
Garrison, Ray H., 183
Garrison, Sharon Hatten, 27
Garson, Barbara, 213
Gart, Alan, 109, 201
Garten, Helen A., 16
Garten, Jeffrey E., 294
Garvin, David A., 42, 127, 187, 246
Gassée, Jean-Louis, 51
Gastineau, Gary L., 215
Gaston, Robert J., 295
Gattiker, Urs E., 277
Gattorna, John, 234
Gaull, Gerald E., 111
Gaumnitz, Jack E., 35
Gayle, Dennis John, 237
Geanuracos, John, 149
Gebhardt, Joan E., 244
Geehan, Randall, 142
Geis, George T., 130
Geisst, Charles R., 35
Gelernter, David Hillel, 12
Gellermann, William, 225
Gentile, Mary C., 28
Gentry, James A., 4
George, Claude S., 273

George, Stephen, 173, 235
Georgia State University. College of Business Administration, 68
Geranmayeh, Ali, 222
Gerber, Jerry, 213
Gercik, Patricia, 30
Gerhart, Paul F., 234
Gerlach, Michael L., 268
Gerloff, Edwin A., 216
Germain, Richard, 186
Germane, Gayton E., 128
Gernon, Helen Morsicato, 144
Gerrard & National PLC, 106
Gerson, Kathleen, 300
Gerstein, Marc Saul, 61
Gerstner, Louis V., 243
Gerston, Larry N., 77
Gessford, John Evans, 24
Ghadar, Fariborz, 145, 148
Ghemawat, Pankaj, 48
Ghertman, Michel, 147
Ghilarducci, Teresa, 214
Ghorpade, Jai, 161
Ghosh, Arabinda, 67
Ghoshal, Sumantra, 147
Gibb, Richard, 98
Gibney, Frank, 81, 158
Gibson, Charles H., 109
Gibson, David V., 198
Gibson, James L., 216
Gibson, Paul, 297
Giersch, Herbert, 116
Gies, David L., 212
Gies, Thomas George, 17
Giffi, Craig, 292
Giges, Nancy, 22
Gilberg, Jay Steven, 217
Gilbert, Daniel R., 60, 75, 271
Gilbert, Susan K., 302
Gilbreath, Robert D., 174
Gilder, George F., 78, 94, 198
Gill, Colin, 276
Gill, Edward K., 17
Gill, Michael Doud, 207, 295
Gill, William J., 242
Gillespie, Richard, 130
Gillette, Paul J., 205
Gillis, Malcolm, 78
Gilman, John J., 249
Gilson, Edith, 302
Gilster, Paul, 152
Gingrich, Marianne, 277
Gingrich, Newt, 277
Gini, A. R., 28
Ginsburg, Douglas H., 14
Ginzberg, Eli, 100, 165
Gioia, Dennis A., 220
Gitlow, Howard S., 77, 244
Gitlow, Shelly J., 77
Gitman, Lawrence J., 66
Gittes, David L., 4
Gittinger, J. Price, 143
Gladstone, David, 296
Glaister, Stephen, 69
Glantz, Kalman, 220
Glaser, Rollin O., 255
Glass, Harold E., 61

Glassner, Barry, 37
Glazer, Rashi, 188
Gleick, James, 104
Glezen, G. William, 13
Glickman, Norman J., 157
Global Conference on Entrepreneurship Research (2nd : 1992 : London, England), 94
Glouchevitch, Philip, 129
Glover, John Desmond, 19
Glueck, William F., 60, 232
Goddard, Stephen B., 285
Goddard, Walter E., 175, 177
Godet, Michel, 120
Godfrey, Joline, 303
Gogel, Robert N., 108
Golant, Susan K., 303
Goldberg, Beverly, 268
Goldberg, Carol R., 302
Goldberg, Ray Allan, 111
Goldenberg, Susan, 162, 267
Goldhaber, Gerald M., 45, 46
Goldman, Jordan, 46
Goldman, Nathan C., 264
Goldsmith, Barbara, 162
Goldsmith, Walter, 79
Goldstein, Arnold S., 259, 271
Goldstein, Bernard, 50
Goldstein, Irwin L., 92
Goldstein, Morris, 36
Goldston, Mark R., 62
Goldwasser, Thomas, 103
Golembiewski, Robert T., 222, 242
Gomes-Casseres, Benjamin, 147, 157
Gómez-Ibáñez, José A., 237
Gomez-Mejia, Luis R., 47
Goodman, John B., 18
Goodman, Jordan Elliot, 106
Goodman, Paul S., 305
Goodrich, Jonathan N., 237
Goold, Michael, 52
Gordon, Gilbert, 76
Gordon, Robert J., 26, 172
Gordon, Ronald D., 78
Gorman, Jerry, 264
Goshal, Sumantra, 270
Gottlieb, Marvin, 206
Gottlieb, Naomi, 258
Gottschalk, Peter, 124
Gould, F. J., 178
Gould, John P., 197
Gould, William B., 164
Governance Project (Center for National Policy (U.S.), 289
Government Finance Research Center (U.S.), 203
Govindarajan, Vijay, 69
Govoni, Norman A. P., 187, 190, 252
Grabbe, J. Orlin, 112
Gradous, Deane, 229
Graff, Richard P., 51
Graham, Benjamin, 153
Graham, David R., 7
Graham, Elizabeth Candler, 42
Graham, Elspeth, 262
Graham, Lawrence, 307
Graham, Margaret, 296
Graham, Margaret B. W., 127
Graham, Otis L., 136

Graham, Pauline, 177
Graham, Willard J., 5
Granger, C. W. J., 83
Granof, Michael H., 4
Grant, Eugene Lodewick, 93, 245
Grant, James, 71, 297
Grantham, Charles E., 46
Granville, Joseph E., 267
Graulich, David J., 23
Gray, Edmund R., 176
Gray, Gary, 203
Gray, John, 174
Gray, Pamela A., 89
Gray, Paul, 75
Gray, S. J., 146
Gray, Sandra T., 212
Grayson, C. Jackson, 126
Green, Eileen, 213
Green, Mark J., 134
Green, Paul E., 193
Greenbaum, Thomas L., 56
Greene, James H., 239
Greenlaw, Paul Stephen, 232
Greenshields, Rod, 20
Greenslade, Roy, 195
Greenwood, Ronald G., 274
Greer, Gaylon E., 248
Gregory, Gene, 90
Gregory, William H., 76
Greider, William, 20
Greiff, Barrie S., 101
Greyser, Stephen A., 6
Griff, Catherine, 64
Griffin, Barbara C., 260
Griffin, Ricky W., 176
Griggs, Lewis, 145
Grillet, Thierry, 121
Grinspun, Ricardo, 113
Groover, Mikell P., 185
Gross, Malvern J., 211
Grosse, Robert E., 146
Grossman, Gene M., 275
Grossman, Karl, 171
Grossman, Peter Z., 9
Grou, Pierre, 145
Group of Green Economists, 118
Grousbeck, H. Irving, 207
Grover, Ron, 298
Grub, Phillip Donald, 148
Grubbs, Donald S., 213
Grubbström, Robert W., 238
Gruber, Martin Jay, 235, 236
Grudnitski, Gary, 181
Gruenwald, George, 209
Gruneberg, Michael M., 161
Grunig, James E., 243
Gryna, Frank M., 245
Guétin, Bernard, 112
Guaspari, John, 128, 246, 282
Guerard, John, 65
Guess, Norman F., 186
Guest, Robert H., 223
Guile, Bruce R., 276
Guillén, Mauro F., 47
Guinet, Jean, 271
Gummesson, Evert, 73
Gumpert, David E., 189, 206, 207

Gunderson, Gerald, 95
Gunn, Cathy, 170
Gunn, Thomas G., 292
Gunter, Barrie, 217
Gurwin, Larry, 16
Gustafson, James M., 67
Gustavson, Sandra G., 143
Gutek, Barbara A., 258, 301
Gutknecht, Douglas B., 218
Gutteridge, Thomas G., 37
Guy, Dan M., 13
Guy, Mary E., 28
Gwynne, S. C., 16, 170
Gyohten, Toyoo, 150

Haas, Robert W., 132
Hacker, Louis Morton, 287
Hacking, Andrew J., 20
Hackman, J. Richard, 218, 219, 305
Hadady, R. Earl, 44
Hadden, Susan G., 56
Haefner, James E., 6
Hagen, Everet Einar, 82
Hagstrom, Robert G., 22
Hague, Paul N., 192
Hahn, Frank, 200
Haider, Donald H., 189
Haigh, Tim, 101
Hailes, Julia, 57
Halal, William E., 130, 222
Halberstam, David, 14, 294
Halbert, Terry, 126
Haley, Charles W., 66
Hall, Douglas T., 37
Hall, Edward Twitchell, 46
Hall, Lavinia, 205
Hall, Maximilian, 104
Hall, Mildred Reed, 46
Hall, Peter, 121
Hall, Richard H., 216
Hall, Robert Ernest, 172
Hall, Robert W., 185, 238
Hall, William D., 29
Hallman, G. Victor, 107
Hallmark Cards, Inc, 103
Halloran, James W., 207
Hallstein, Richard W., 74
Hallwood, Paul, 151
Halper, Jan, 101
Hamburg, Morris, 262, 265
Hamdan, Lawrence, 307
Hamel, Gary, 48
Hamermesh, Richard G., 271
Hamilton, Adrian, 150
Hamilton, James, 92
Hammer, Armand, 119
Hammer, Lawrence H., 68
Hammer, Michael, 224
Hammer, William E., 13
Hammond, John S., 191
Hamner, W. Clay, 219
Hampden-Turner, Charles, 75
Hamper, Ben, 119
Hampton, David R., 219
Hampton, John J., 173
Hamrin, Robert D., 288
Hanan, Mack, 61, 101

Hancock, William A., 32
Handy, Charles B., 220
Hanke, John E., 30, 31, 43, 132
Hankinson, Graham, 21
Hannum, Wallace H., 142
Hansen, Abby J., 33
Hansen, John A., 275
Hanson, Kristine R., 29
Haraf, William S., 200
Harari, Oren, 269
Hardesty, Sarah, 302
Hardy, Hugh S., 193
Hardy, Len, 271
Hares, John S., 141
Haried, Andrew A., 4
Harmon, Frederick G., 132
Harmon, Paul, 23, 24, 178
Harmon, Roy L., 135, 299
Harnett, Donald L., 87, 265
Harper, Stephen C., 207
Harper, Victor L., 155
Harrar, George, 214
Harrigan, Kathryn Rudie, 162, 222, 224
Harrington, Diana R., 35, 153
Harrington, H. J., 132, 245
Harrington, James S., 132
Harrington, Jon, 59
Harris, David, 204
Harris, Jim, 161
Harris, Louis, 243
Harris, Philip R., 58, 147
Harris, Reuben T., 223
Harris, Thomas L., 243
Harrison, Bennett, 138, 288
Harrison, E. Bruce, 128
Harrison, E. Frank, 75
Harrison, F. L., 135
Harrison, Matthew C., 299
Harrison, Michael A., 121
Harrison, Walter T., 3, 4
Harroch, Richard D., 62
Harry, Lois, 8
Hart, Christopher W. L., 73, 257
Hart, Jeffrey A., 138
Hartley, Robert F., 126, 176, 189
Hartwick, John M., 205
Hartz, C. Scott, 162
Harvard Business Review, 35
Harvard Business School Club of New York, 37
Harvard Business School Project on the Auto Industry and the American Economy, 13
Harvard Business School Research Colloquium (1989), 181
Harvard Business School Symposium on Government, Technology, and the Automotive Future (1978), 14
Harvard Negotiation Project, 205, 227
Harvard University. Center for International Affairs, 95
Harvard University. Council on East Asian Studies, 14
Harvard University. Graduate School of Business Administration, 35, 93, 99, 101, 131, 133, 181, 189, 218, 230, 232, 279, 290
Harvey, A. C., 82
Harvey, Jerry B., 217
Harvey, John L., 54

Harvey-Jones, John, 129
Harwood, Bruce M., 247
Hastings, Colin, 46
Hatala, Lewis J., 10
Hatch, Richard A., 23
Hatcher, Rosemary, 60
Hatcher, Thomas, 60
Hatten, Kenneth J., 268, 270
Hatten, Mary Louise, 172, 268, 270
Haueisen, William D., 23
Haugen, Robert A., 153, 267
Hauser, John R., 208
Hausman, Jerry A., 145, 278
Hausman, Warren H., 131
Hawdon, David, 93
Hawken, Paul, 207
Hawkes, Ellen, 114
Hawkins, Barbara A., 63
Hawkins, David F., 63, 64
Hawkins, Del I., 56
Hax, Arnoldo C., 61, 238, 269, 270
Hay Group, 128
Hay, Leon Edwards, 107
Hay, Robert D., 212
Hayek, Friedrich A. von, 120
Hayes, Glenn E., 135
Hayes, John Phillip, 113
Hayes, Robert H., 135, 292
Hayes, Roger, 23
Hayes, Samuel L., 16, 109, 154
Hays, Richard D., 146
Hazard, Geoffrey C., 53
Heald, Morrell, 139
Healey, P. Basil, 38
Healy, William J., 206
Heath, Chip, 76
Heath, Robert L., 157
Hébert, Robert F., 86, 94
Heckscher, Charles C., 137
Hector, Gary, 16
Hedlund, Gunnar, 147
Heenan, David A., 291
Heidenry, John, 298
Heifetz, Ronald A., 168
Heilbroner, Robert L., 36, 37, 74, 84, 85, 86, 87, 197, 260, 287
Heim, Pat, 303
Heiman, Stephen E., 256
Heimovics, Richard, 211
Heinritz, Stuart F., 244
Heins, Richard M., 250
Heirs, Ben J., 76
Heisler, William J., 231
Hekman, Christine Ries, 147
Helander, Martin, 123, 239
Helferich, Omar Keith, 234
Helfert, Erich A., 67
Hellebust, Karsten G., 270
Heller, Robert, 33, 130, 173, 191, 199
Heller, Trudy, 167
Helms, Robert B., 195
Helpman, Elhanan, 275
Helyar, John, 18, 251
Hemphill, John Mearl, 208
Henderson, Bruce D., 61
Henderson, David R., 86
Henderson, James W., 295

Henderson, Richard I., 47
Henderson, Thomas P., 247
Hendrickson, Robert A., 71
Hendrie, Anne, 17
Hendriksen, Eldon S., 3
Hendry, John, 270
Henke, Emerson O., 211
Hennessy, John H., 53
Henning, Charles N., 105
Henrici, Stanley B., 221
Herbers, John, 41
Herbert, Peter J.A., 108
Herbst, Anthony F., 35, 44
Heri, Erwin W., 155
Herlihy, Robert E., 194
Herman, Robert D., 211
Herman, Stanley M., 305
Hermanson, Roger H., 5
Herrick, Neal Q., 175
Hersey, Paul, 218, 223
Herst, Arthur C. C., 169
Hertenstein, Julie Huffman, 68
Hertner, Peter, 148
Hertz, Leah, 303
Hertz, Rosanna, 193
Herzlinger, Regina E., 121, 211
Heskett, James L., 32, 58, 73, 234, 256, 257
Heslop, Louise, 190
Hess, Kären M., 220
Hey, John Denis, 85
Heymann, H. G., 64
Hickman, Bert G., 35
Hickman, Craig R., 76, 175, 177
Hicks, Donald A., 291
Hicks, Philip E., 125
Hickson, David John, 76, 176, 227
Hidy, Ralph Willard, 118
Higgins, Robert C., 63
High, Robert, 110
Highman, Arthur, 302
Highman, Edith L., 302
Hightower, William C., 97
Higonnet, Patrice L. R., 275
Hikino, Takashi, 19
Hilbers, Konrad, 141
Hildebrand, David K., 131
Hildebrandt, Herbert William, 43
Hildreth, W. Bartley, 269
Hilger, Marye Tharp, 102
Hill, Joanne M., 107
Hill, Linda A., 37
Hill, Margaret Hunt, 124
Hill, Terry, 127
Hillkirk, John, 126, 307
Hills, Jill, 278
Hilton, Anthony, 108
Hilton, Ronald W., 22
Hiltz, Starr Roxanne, 279
Himmelberg, Robert F., 140
Hindelang, Thomas J., 35
Hindle, Tim, 128, 130, 187, 268
Hines, Mary Alice, 248
Hinrichs, John R., 161
Hinterhuber, Hans H., 238
Hiraki, Takato, 36
Hirschey, Mark, 183, 184
Hirschhorn, Larry, 243

Hirsh, Wendy, 302
Hirshleifer, Jack, 197
Hirt, Geoffrey A., 65
Hise, Richard T., 186
Hisrich, Robert D., 207, 208, 238
Hitt, Michael A., 80
Hitt, William D., 29
Hixson, William F., 201
Hlavacek, James D., 187
Ho, Thomas S. Y., 266
Hoag, Susan, 55
Hobbs, James B., 225
Hochmuth, Milton S., 287
Hodgetts, Richard M., 139, 178, 220, 259
Hodgkinson, Virginia Ann, 211
Hodgson, Richard S., 7
Hoebeke, Luc, 217
Hoel, Paul Gerhard, 262
Hoerr, John P., 265
Hoffer, William, 170
Hoffman, Gerald M., 182
Hoffman, W. Michael, 95
Hogan, James, 97
Hogarth, Robin M., 75
Hogbin, Geoff, 141
Hoge, Cecil C., 278
Hogendorn, Jan S., 150
Hogg, Clare, 167
Holcombe, Marya W., 33
Holland, John, 151
Holland, Max, 23
Holland, P. R. J., 59
Holland, Stuart. 36, 172
Hollander, Stanley C., 186
Holloway, Nigel, 285
Holsapple, C. W., 128
Holstein, William J., 235
Holt, David H., 178
Holtham, Clive 75
Holtz, Herman, 25, 26, 55, 56
Holusha, John, 72
Holzmann, Oscar, 146
Honigsblum, Bonnie Birtwistle, 80
Honkapohja, Seppo, 86
Hopkin, John A., 9
Horngren, Charles T., 3, 4, 68, 183
Horton, Forest W., 141
Horton, Thomas R., 100, 101
Horvitz, Paul M., 200
Hoskisson, Robert E., 80
Hosmer, LaRue T., 29
Hosotani, Katsuya, 282
Houck, John W., 29
Houdeshel, George, 180
Hough, George H., 135
Hough, Leaetta M., 242
Houghton, Dianne Morse, 168
Hounshell, David A., 194
House, Robert G., 234
House, Ruth, 135
Houseman, Susan N., 161
Houston, William, 26
Hout, Thomas M., 281
Hovey, Harold A., 241
Howard, Ann, 10
Howard, Donald F., 254
Howard, Donald G., 146

Howard, John A., 56
Howard, Robert, 231
Howard, William G., 276
Howe, Donna M., 144
Howe, R. Edwin, 32
Hoyer, Wayne D., 57
Hoynes, William, 244
H & R Block, 103
Hrebiniak, Lawrence G., 61, 306
Huang, Quanyu, 30
Hubbard, Philip M., 154
Huczynski, Andrzej, 176
Hudson Institute, 306
Hudson, W. J., 31
Huertas, Thomas F., 16
Huey, John, 298
Hughes, Janice, 106
Hughes, Jonathan R. T., 286
Hughes, Thomas Parke, 277
Huhne, Christopher, 74
Hulbert, James M., 268
Hultman, Charles W., 18
Humphrey, Watts S., 122
Hunt, David, 232
Hunter, Mark, 121
Huntsberger, David V., 265
Huseman, Richard C., 220
Hussey, D. E., 61
Hutchins, David C., 244
Hutchinson, Harry D., 18
Hutchison, Robert A., 41
Hutt, Michael D., 132
Hyland, L. A., 124

IABC Research Foundation, 243
Iacocca, Lee A., 124
Ibarra, Herminia, 218
Ibrahim, A. Bakr, 259
IC² Institute, 57, 71, 206
Ichbiah, Daniel, 198
Ichbiah, Daniel, 198
Ijiri, Yuji, 71
Ilgen, Daniel R., 242
Imai, Masaaki, 129
Imdieke, Leroy F., 4
Imparato, Nicholas, 269
Indiana University, Bloomington. Workshop in Political Theory and Policy Analysis, 95
Industrial Marketing & Purchasing Group, 191
Information Systems Research Challenge, 181
Ingberman, Monroe J., 38
Ingram, Colin, 208
Ingrassia, Paul J., 14
Ingulli, Elaine, 126
Inman, Robert P., 257
Inmon, William H., 50
Innes, Eva, 161
Institute for Alternative Futures (U.S.), 126
Institute for Contemporary Studies, 284
Institute for Management, 231
Institute for Research and Information on Multinationals, 147
Institute of Chartered Financial Analysts, 155, 235
Institute of Industrial Engineers (1981-), 13, 306
Institute of Management, 98
Institute of Manpower Studies (Great Britain), 302
Institute of Medicine (U.S.), 19, 143

International Association of Business Communicators, 46
International Chamber of Commerce, 162
International Conference on Business History (13th : 1987 Fuji Education Center), 284
International Conference on Creative and Innovative Management (2nd : 1984 : Miami, Fla.), 71
International Conference on Creative and Innovative Management (3rd : 1987 : Pittsburgh, Pa.), 71
International Conference on Decision Support Systems, 74
International Ergonomics Association, 239
International Financing Review, 112
International Labour Office, 135, 148
International Monetary Fund, 36
International Paper Company, 94
International Service Quality Association, 73
International Strategic Management Society Conference (11th : 1991 : Toronto, Ont.), 126
International Working Seminar on Production Economics (4th : 1986 : Igls, Austria), 238
Investor Responsibility Research Center, 27
Investor's Business Daily, Inc, 267
Investors Intelligence, 266
Ireland, R. Duane, 176
Ireson, William Grant, 93
Irons, Edward D., 8
Irwin, Robert, 247
Ishikawa, Kaoru, 245
Ishinomori, Shōtarō, 159
Islam, Shafiqul, 97
Israel, Lee, 166
Itō, Takatoshi, 159
Itō, Y., 110
Ivancevich, John M., 129, 216
Izraeli, Dafna N., 301, 302

Jablin, Fredric M., 45
Jablonsky, Stephen F., 63
Jackall, Robert, 30
Jackson, Barbara B., 89
Jackson, Charles, 302
Jackson, John Harold, 216
Jackson, Peter, 102, 245
Jackson, Susan E., 199
Jackson, Tim, 98
Jacobs, Garry, 62, 132
Jacobs, Jane, 30
Jacobs, Jerry, 303
Jacobs, Michael T., 131
Jacobs, Nehama, 302
Jacobs, Robert W., 223
Jacobson, Aileen, 302
Jacobson, Gary, 307
Jacobson, Marjory, 63
Jacobsson, Staffan, 19
Jacobus, Charles J., 247
Jaffe, Abram J., 262
Jaffe, Austin J., 247
Jaffe, Dennis T., 224
Jaffe, Jeffrey F., 64
Jahnsson, Hilma Gabriella, 86
Jain, R. K., 249
Jain, Subhash C., 102, 189
James, Marquis, 117

Jamieson, David, 184
Jamison, Andrew, 19
Jandt, Fred Edmund, 205
Janelli, Dawnhee Yim, 58
Janelli, Roger L., 58
Janeway, Eliot, 288
Janis, Irving Lester, 75
Janos, Leo, 171
Japan. Gaimushō, 159
Jaques, Elliott, 161
Jarchow, Stephen P., 248
Jarrett, Jeffrey, 31
Jarrow, Robert A., 105
Jauch, Lawrence R., 60
Jayachandra, Y., 213
Jeffries, Francis M., 15
Jelassi, Tawfik, 181
Jenkins, Barbara, 287
Jenkins, Richard A., 273
Jennings, Diane, 303
Jensen, David E., 247
Jensen, Marlene, 302
Jensen, Michael C., 63
Jensen, Niels-Erik, 87
Jessen, Raymond James, 262
Jick, Todd, 217, 221, 222
Jinnett, Jerry, 60
J.K. Lasser Institute, 259
J.K. Lasser Tax Institute, 241
Johansen, Elaine, 95
Johansen, Robert, 145
Johansson, Henry J., 281
John, Richard R., 66
Johne, F. A., 275
Johnson, Charles J., 64
Johnson, Clark H., 54
Johnson, Gerry, 270
Johnson, Glenn Laurence, 4
Johnson, H. Thomas, 131, 183, 185
Johnson, James C., 234
Johnson, James M., 77
Johnson, Leland L., 34
Johnson, Lindsey, 303
Johnson, Michael, 5
Johnson, Ralph A., 205
Johnson, Ramon E., 66
Johnson, Ross H., 247
Johnson, Spencer, 177
Johnson Wax, 103
Johnston, David, 38
Johnston, Joseph Shackford, 174
Johnston, Moira, 15
Johnston, Robert F., 121
Johnston, William B., 306
Joiner, Brian L., 282
Joiner, Charles W., 168
Joint Center for Political and Economic Studies
Joint Industry University Conference on Manufacturing
Jonassen, David H., 142
Jones, Carl R., 89
Jones, David M., 20
Jones, E. L., 227
Jones, E. Philip, 63
Jones, Frank Joseph, 44
Jones, Geoffrey, 148, 191
Jones, Jeffrey D., 27

Jones, John Philip, 7
Jones, John W., 230
Jones, Patrice Franko, 150
Jones, Patricia E., 270
Jones, Ronald Winthrop, 152
Jones, Timothy L., 119
Jones, W. David, 231
Jones-Parker, Janet, 100
Jonovic, Donald J., 279
Jordan, Eleanor W., 262
Jordan, John M., 93
Jordan, Ronald J., 153
Jorge, Antonio, 157
Josephson, Matthew, 37
Joyce, William F., 61
Joyner-Kersee, Jacqueline, 303
Judd, Elizabeth, 155
Judd, Jacob, 139
Jungnickel, Rolf, 156
Junkus, Joan C., 44
Juran, J. M., 245
Jutkins, Ray, 79

Kaff, Albert E., 265
Kaftan, Colleen, 223
Kahn, Alfred E., 140
Kahn, E. J., 10, 11
Kahn, Peggy, 300
Kakabadse, Andrew, 219
Kamerschen, David R., 17, 278
Kamphuis, Robert W., 265
Kane, Susan, 302
Kanfer, Stefan, 78
Kanter, Jerome, 174
Kanter, Rosabeth Moss, 14, 122, 177, 218, 221, 225, 275
Kantor, Rosabeth Moss, 227
Kantrow, Alan M., 58, 131, 174, 275
Kanuk, Leslie Lazar, 56
Kanungo, Rabindra Nath, 99
Kao, John J., 71, 94, 127, 222
Kaplan, Daniel I., 257
Kaplan, Daniel P., 7
Kaplan, Robert E., 76, 100
Kaplan, Robert S., 69, 71, 182, 183
Kapur, Basant, 106
Karen, Ruth, 113
Kargas, Nicholas A., 3
Karlöf, Bengt, 268
Karrass, Chester Louis, 205
Karsten, Margaret Foegen, 301
Karvel, George R., 247
Kasarda, John D., 94
Kash, Don E., 276
Kassarjian, Harold H., 56
Kast, Fremont Ellsworth, 215
Katz, Donald R., 210
Katz, Harry Charles, 136
Katz, Ralph, 122
Katzenbach, Jon R., 306
Katzenstein, Gary J., 263
Kaufman, Bruce E., 137, 165
Kaufman, George G., 17, 106
Kaufman, Henry, 105
Kaufman, Herbert, 224
Kaufman, Mike, 35
Kaufman, Perry J., 44

Kaufman, Roger A., 270
Kaumeyer, Richard A., 232
Kawasaki, Guy, 11
Kay, Ira T., 40
Kay, Michael, 132
Kay, Robert S., 4
Kay, William, 34, 154, 197
Kaye, Beverly L., 37
Kaynak, Erdener, 12, 102
Kayser, Thomas A., 305
Kazanjian, Robert K., 216
Kazmier, Leonard J., 43
Kearns, David T., 307
Kearns, Robert L., 68
Keasey, Kevin, 260
Keating, Maryann O., 86
Keating, Patrick J., 63
Keaveney, Susan M., 102
Keegan, Warren J., 102
Keen, Peter G. W., 24, 141, 278
Keene, Margaret Rahn, 15
Keeney, Ralph L., 76, 203
Keenoy, Tom, 137
Keeps, Erica J., 229
Kehrer, Daniel M., 272
Keidel, Robert W., 221
Keil, John M., 70
Keller, Donald E., 68
Keller, Maryann, 14, 115
Keller, Morton, 290
Keller, Robert, 101
Keller, Thomas F., 4
Kelley, Robert Earl, 56, 240
Kelly, Charles M., 28
Kelly, Francis, 120
Kelly, Heather Mayfield, 120
Kelly, Joe, 40, 219
Kelly, Sean, 127
Kemeny, John G., 237
Kennedy, Carol, 129
Kennedy, Gavin, 205, 206
Kennedy, James H., 26
Kennedy, Paul M., 285
Kennedy, Peter, 82
Kennedy, Walter, 285
Kenney, Martin, 19, 274
Kensicki, Peter R., 143
Kent State University. Dept. of Economics, 54
Kent State University. Graduate School of Management, 54
Keohane, Robert O., 95
Keren, Michael, 97
Kerin, Roger A., 186
Kerr, Andrew, 234
Kerr, Clark, 137, 164
Kerr, K. Austin, 63
Kerr, Roger, 185
Kerrigan, Harry D., 114
Kerzner, Harold, 136
Kester, W. Carl, 54, 150
Kestin, Hesh, 49
Kets de Vries, Manfred F. R., 101, 167, 168, 218, 219, 220
Ketteringham, John M., 208
Kettl, Donald F., 20
Ketz, J. Edward, 247
Key, Stephen L., 53

Keyes, Jessica, 239
Khambata, Dara, 148
Khanna, Raman, 89
Kiam, Victor, 163
Kidder, Tracy, 49
Kidwell, David S., 105
Kiernan, Thomas, 294
Kiesler, Sara B., 90
Kieso, Donald E., 4
Kight, Leila K., 85
Killen, Michael, 149
Killingsworth, Mark R., 228
Kilmann, Ines, 48, 226
Kilmann, Ralph H., 48, 58, 173, 221, 226
Kilpatrick, Andrew, 22
Kim, Choong Soon, 244
Kim, U-jung, 272
Kim, W. Chan, 81
Kimber, Raymond J., 245
Kimpton, Mary Hamilton, 267
Kinch, John E., 113
Kinder, Peter D., 155
Kindleberger, Charles Poor, 36, 105, 148, 227
Kindred, Alton R., 89
King, Alexander, 83
King, William Richard, 136, 190, 270
Kingstone, Brett, 33
Kinlaw, Dennis C., 95, 305
Kinnear, Thomas C., 190, 192
Kiplinger, Austin H., 83
Kiplinger, Knight A., 83
Kirdar, Üner, 77
Kirkland, J. R., 273
Kirkpatrick, Donald L., 222
Kirpalani, V. H., 152
Kishimoto, Yoriko, 84
Kitch, Sally, 301
Kizer, William M., 212
Klahr, Philip, 101
Klayman, Elliot I., 126
Klein, Janice Anne, 135, 292, 293
Klein, John J., 200
Klein, Katherine J., 91
Klein, Mark M., 224
Klein, Maury, 294
Klein, Sherwin, 28
Klein, Stuart M., 232
Kleindorfer, Paul R., 75, 239
Kleinfield, Sonny, 15, 124
Kleingartner, Archie, 122
Kleinschrod, Walter A., 213
Kleppner, Otto, 7
Kliem, Ralph L., 136
Kline, Nancy, 168
Kline, Stephen, 279
Kling, Rob, 51
Klipper, Miriam Z., 53
Klonoski, Richard J., 28
Knauft, E. B., 212
Kneer, Dan C., 180
Knepper, Susan L., 198
Knight, Martin, 102
Knoedelseder, William, 263
Knopf, Kenyon A., 87
Koźmiński, Andrzej K., 221
Kobayashi, Kōji, 78
Kobert, Norman, 152

Kochan, Thomas A., 136, 232
Kōdansha Intōanashonaru Kabushiki Kaisha, 208
Koechlin, Dominik, 118
Koehn, Nancy F., 117
Koenig, Fredrick, 60
Koestenbaum, Peter, 24
Kofodimos, Joan R., 99, 100
Koh, Sung-soo, 81
Kohl, Atlee M., 55
Kohl, John C., 55
Kohlmeier, Louis M., 125
Kohn, Alfie, 250
Kohn, Meir G., 108
Kohn, Tomás O., 131
Kolb, David A., 242
Kolbe, Kathy, 71
Koller, Tim, 67
Komiya, Ryūtarō, 140
Konecci, Eugene B., 276
Konek, Carol, 301
Konner, Melvin, 195
Kono, Toyohiro, 61, 131
Koontz, Harold, 176
Koopmann, Georg, 156
Kopelman, Elizabeth, 227
Kopp, Robert J., 6
Kopp, Rochelle, 59
Kormendi, Roger C., 17, 104, 265
Korn, Lester, 99
Kornbluth, Jesse, 199
Korth, Christopher M., 70, 146
Kōsaka, Masataka, 160
Kosko, Bart, 171
Kosnik, Thomas J., 188, 189
Kossek, Ellen Ernst, 229
Kostecki, M. M., 257
Koteen, Jack, 270
Kotkin, Joel, 84, 272
Kotler, Philip, 188, 189, 190, 195, 212, 261
Kotter, John P., 58, 99, 100, 167, 168, 178, 216
Kounalakis, Markos, 11
Kousgaard, Nils, 87
Kouzes, James M., 167, 168
Koziol, Joseph D., 121
Kozmetsky, George, 179, 295
Kraemer, Kenneth L., 181
Kraft General Foods, 302
Krajewski, Lee J., 239
Krallinger, Joseph C., 54, 270
Kram, Kathy E., 272
Kratovil, Robert, 248
Kraus, Constantine Raymond, 10
Kraus, George, 68
Kraus, Willy, 12
Krause, Axel, 96
Krayenbuehl, Thomas E., 170
Krefetz, Gerald, 155
Kreps, David M., 197
Kresge, Stephen, 120
Kress, George, 252
Kristie, James, 221
Kristof, Nicholas D., 40
Kritzman, Mark P., 155
Krochuk, Tim, 172
Kroeber, Donald W., 180
Kroenke, David, 23
Kroll, Mark J., 270

Krugman, Paul R., 150, 163, 290
Krum, James R., 97
Kuczmarski, Thomas, 209
Kuhn, Arthur J., 115
Kuhn, Gerald, 123
Kuhn, James W., 42
Kuhn, Robert Lawrence, 71, 130, 154, 179, 276
Kulikoff, Allan, 289
Kunreuther, Howard, 75
Kunze, Robert J., 295
Kuratko, Donald F., 259
Kuriloff, Arthur H., 208
Kurtz, David L., 40, 186, 256
Kurtzig, Sandra L., 164
Kurtzman, Joel, 200
Kutner, Michael H., 249
Kvasnicka, Joseph G., 151
Kwast, Myron L., 107

Labuszewski, John, 44
Lacey, Jerome, 143
Ladenson, Robert F., 225
Laffer, Arthur B., 156
Lager, Fred, 42
Lake, Dale G., 226
Lake, Linda K., 223
Lakonishok, Josef, 267
Lam, Alice C. L., 258
Lamb, Charles W., 191
Lamb, Robert, 203, 269
Lambert, Douglas M., 32
Lambin, Jean-Jacques, 191
Lambro, Donald, 83
Lamm, Richard D., 83
Lamming, Richard, 14
Lamont, Douglas F., 149
Lamont, Edward M., 166
Lamott, Kenneth Church, 299
Lampe, David, 122
Lampert, Hope, 17, 251
Landau, Ralph, 276
Landes, David S., 275
Landrum, Gene N., 34, 303
Landsburg, Steven E., 85
Landy, Frank J., 242
Lane, Marc J., 259
Lane, W. Ronald, 7
Lane and Edson, 53
Langdon, Richard, 275
Langenderfer, Harold Q., 5
Langseth, Petter, 222
Lanham, Richard A., 51
Lanvin, Bruno, 257
Lapin, Lawrence L., 76, 263
Lapp, Ralph Eugene, 288
Lardner, James, 296
Larijani, L. Casey, 124
Larkin, Geraldine A., 191, 303
Larkin, Richard F., 211
LaRoe, Ross M., 87
Larraín B., Felipe, 172
Larsen, E. John, 5
Larson, Erik, 193
Larson, Harold J., 237
Larson, James R., 216
Larson, Kermit D., 4
Larson, Richard W., 213

Larwood, Laurie, 301
Lasher, William, 207
Laska, Richard, 174
Latham, Gary P., 116
Lau, James Brownlee, 217
Lauder, Estée, 166
Lauenstein, Milton C., 179
Lauer, Harvey, 165
Laurel, Brenda, 123
Laurent, André, 146
Laurent, Gilles, 193
Lauterborn, Robert F., 46
Law, Warren A., 105
Lawler, Ed, 189
Lawler, Edward E., 47, 175, 179, 218, 219, 229
Lawrence, Margaret, 268
Lawrence, Paul R., 126, 131, 181, 219, 230
Lawrence, Peter A., 129, 176, 219
Lawrence, Robert Z., 69, 140, 212, 287
Lawson, G. H., 21
Lawton, Robin L., 72
Lax, David A., 206
Layard, P. R. G., 69, 164
Lazear, Edward P., 197
Lazer, William, 188
Lazonick, William, 113, 118, 165
Le Conte des Floris, Daniel, 121
León, Lu Stanton, 175
LeBoeuf, Michael, 230
Leach, William, 77
Leavenworth, Richard S., 93, 245
Leavitt, Harold J., 242
Leben, Joe, 269
Lebergott, Stanley, 57
Lecraw, Donald J., 146
Lederman, Jess, 202, 254
Lee, Albert, 261
Lee, Dwight R., 110
Lee, Jae Kyu, 236
Lee, Kam-Hon, 12
Lee, Lamar, 134
Lee, R. A., 129, 219
Lee, Sang M., 182
Lee, Susan, 106
Lee, Thomas H., 93
Leebaert, Derek, 51
Leenders, Michiel R., 134
Leffler, George Leland, 266
Leftwich, Richard H., 197
Lehigh University. Center for Social Research, 82
Lehigh University. Dept. of Economics, 82
Lehmann, Donald R., 192
Leibenstein, Harvey, 133
Leibowitz, Martin L., 21
Leibowitz, Zandy B., 37
Leigland, James, 203
Leinberger, Paul, 294
Lele, Milind M., 186
Lemco, Jonathan, 143
Lengsfelder, Peter, 211
Lenson, Barry, 243
Lenstra, J. K., 131
Lenz, Allen J., 15
Lenz, Elinor, 104
Leonard, Herman B., 286
Leonard N. Stern School of Business, 163
Leone, Robert A., 284

Leonsis, Ted, 149
Leontiades, James C., 148
Leontiades, Milton, 52
Leontief, Wassily W., 142, 165
Lepper, Ian, 10
Lesikar, Raymond Vincent, 33, 43
Lesly, Philip, 243
Lessem, Ronnie, 47, 220
Lester, Richard K., 134
Leuthold, Raymond M., 44
Lever, Harold, 74
Levering, Robert, 230
Levesque, Joseph D., 273
Levey, Irv, 91
Levi, Maurice D., 87
Levich, Richard M., 96, 160
Levin, Doron P., 54
Levin, Richard I., 214, 262
Levine, Dennis, 170
Levine, Karen, 300
Levine, Michael, 243
Levine, Sumner N., 53, 153
Levine-Shneidman, Conalee, 300
Levinson, Charles, 141
Levinson, Harry, 100
Levinson, Harry, 242
Levinson, Jay Conrad, 187
Levinson, Robert E., 74
Levit, Steve, 282
Levitt, Theodore, 188, 189
Levy, Joseph, 124
Levy, Steven, 171
Lévy-Leboyer, Maurice, 148
Lew, Ginger, 152
Lewellen, Wilbur G., 100
Lewis, Flora, 99
Lewis, James, 215
Lewis, Jordan D., 162
Lewis, Michael, 22, 170
Lewis, Phillip V., 45
Lewis, Reginald F., 170
Lewis, Ronald J., 5
Lewis, Sherman L., 65
Lewis, T. G., 197
Lichtenberg, Frank R., 165
Liebig, James E., 34
Lifson, Thomas B., 52
Light, J. O., 105
Lilien, Gary L., 187, 189, 193
Lilien, Steven B., 3, 109
Lim, Linda, 157
Limerick, David, 223
Lincoln, Edward J., 158, 159
Lind, Douglas A., 262
Linden, Eugene, 298
Linder, Staffan Burenstam, 227
Lindow, Wesley, 200
Lindsey, Jennifer, 64
Lindsey, Lawrence, 274
Ling, Richard C., 177
Link, Albert N., 94
Linowitz, Sol M., 170
Lipkin, Lawrence, 32
Lipper, Arthur, 156
Lippitt, Gordon L., 25, 222
Lippitt, Ronald, 25
Lipset, Seymour Martin, 284

Lipsey, Richard G., 85, 87, 197
Lipsky, David, 307
Lipton, James, 23
Lipton, Kedakai, 23
Lis, James, 120
Lissakers, Karin, 74
Litan, Robert E., 17, 69, 287, 290
Litka, Michael P., 113
Litterer, Joseph August, 219
Little, Danity, 301
Little, Geoffrey, 127
Little, Jeffrey B., 156
Little, John D. C., 188
Little, Royal, 170
Litwak, Mark, 203
Litwin, Anne H., 177
Livingston, Miles, 201
Livingstone, John Leslie, 183
Ljungren, Roy G., 78
Lloyd, Peter, 305
Lloyd, Tom, 66
Lock, Dennis, 136, 175
Locke, Edwin A., 116, 239
Loden, Marilyn, 184, 301
Lodge, George C., 49, 140, 290
Lodge, Juliet, 97
Lodish, Leonard M., 6
Loebbecke, James K., 13
Logue, Dennis E., 105
Lombard, George F. F., 224
Lombardi, John V., 149
Lombardo, Michael M., 99
London, Manuel, 100
Longstreth, Bevis, 169
Lorange, Peter, 270
Lorentzen, Mel, 91
Lorenz, Christopher, 77, 135
Lorenz, Tony, 296
Loretta, Ralph G., 66
Lorie, James Hirsch, 267
Lorsch, Jay William, 79, 217, 219, 227
Loseby, Paul H., 161
Loss, Louis, 254
Loudon, David L., 56
Love, Bruce, 180
Love, John F., 195
Lovelock, Christopher H., 73, 188, 190, 212, 241, 256, 257
Lovret, Fredrick J., 273
Lowe, Janet, 117
Lowenstein, Louis, 267
Lowenthal, Jeffrey N., 224
Lowman, Gwen, 88
Lowy, Martin E., 253
Lozano, Beverly, 123
Lu, David John, 128, 238
Lubar, Steven D., 141
Lucas, Georges, 189
Lucas, Jay H., 114
Lucas, Robert E., 26
Luck, David Johnston, 187, 189, 192
Ludin, Irwin S., 136
Luehrman, Timothy A., 150
Lund, Robert T., 275
Lundberg, Donald E., 123
Lundman, Richard J., 300
Lundquist, Janerik, 238

Lundstrom, David E., 294
Lustig, Nora, 212
Luthans, Fred, 139, 178, 218
Lütkenhorst, Wilfried, 12
Lutz, Friedrich A., 143
Luxenberg, Stan, 113
Lydenberg, Steven D., 155
Lyman, Richard W., 211
Lynch, Peter, 155, 267
Lynch, Richard L., 134
Lynch, Roberta, 39
Lyndon, Neil, 119
Lynn, Edward S., 114
Lynn, Gary S., 208
Lyon, Jim, 161

MacCrimmon, Kenneth R., 251
MacDonald, John, 282
MacDonald, Ronald, 151
MacIver, Elizabeth, 79
MacMillan, Ian C., 94, 270
MacPhee, William A., 94
Maccoby, Michael, 168
Macfarlane, Robert, 62
Mackenzie, Alec, 281
Mackenzie, Kenneth D., 226
Mackiewicz, Andrea, 60
Macrae, Chris, 21
Madden, Tara Roth, 258
Maddi, Salvatore R., 229
Maddox, E. Nick, 174
Madnick, Stuart E., 178
Madrick, Jeffrey G., 11, 54, 280
Magad, Eugene L., 194
Magaziner, Ira C., 49, 140
Maggin, Donald L., 96
Magidson, Susan, 51
Maginn, John L., 235
Magrath, Allan J., 186, 187
Mahajan, Vijay, 186
Mahini, Amir, 147
Mahon, Thomas, 198
Mahoney, David J., 272
Maier, Steven F., 38
Maier, Thomas, 210
Maister, David H., 127, 240, 257
Maital, Shlomo, 183
Majaro, Simon, 187
Majluf, Nicolás S., 61, 270
Makela, Benjamin R., 63
Makin, John H., 110
Makino, Noboru, 275
Makower, Joel, 57, 262
Makridakis, Spyros G., 31, 83
Malabre, Alfred L., 87, 288
Malek, Mohammed H., 262
Mali, Paul, 180
Malin, Martin H., 126
Malkiel, Burton Gordon, 155
Malm, F. T., 231
Malone, Laurence J., 260
Malone, Michael S., 116, 198
Mamorsky, Jeffrey D., 90
Manchester Business School (University of Manchester), 184
Mancuso, Joseph, 259
Mandelbaum, Michael, 97

Manes, Stephen, 114
Manganelli, Raymond L., 224
Maniscalco, Rosemary, 280
Manley, Walter W., 28, 29
Mann, Charles C., 12
Mann, Jim, 10
Mann, Kenneth, 300
Mann, Robert I., 24
Manne, Henry G., 267
Manning, Kenneth R., 194
Manolakas, Thomas G., 248
Mansfield, Edwin, 172, 184, 197, 262
Mansfield, Harvey Claflin, 99
Mansfield, Roger, 221
Manson, Bernard, 144
Manz, Charles C., 305
March, James G., 42, 75, 76
Marchand, Donald A., 141
Marconi, Joe, 186
Marcus, Bruce W., 153
Margulies, Newton, 215
Marino, Bernard D., 35
Mark, J. Paul, 120
Market Intelligence Research Company, 249
Marketing and the New Information/
    Communication Technologies (1983 : Harvard
    University), 279
Markoff, John, 51
Markowitz, Gerald E., 126
Marks, Mitchell Lee, 222
Markusen, Ann R., 121
Marquand, David, 150
Marren, Joseph H., 54
Marriott Corporation, 103
Marsh, David, 78
Marshall, F. Ray, 132, 164
Marshall, John F., 107
Marshall, Judi, 302
Marshall, Will, 293
Marszalek-Gaucher, Ellen, 196
Martel, Leon, 223
Martin, Albro, 246
Martin, Glen, 300
Martin, John D., 26, 27
Martin, Michael J. C., 275
Martin, Robert S., 248
Martin, Ron, 151
Martin, Thomas John, 67
Marx, Robert, 217
Marx, Thomas G., 23
Mason, Joseph Barry, 250
Mason, Mark, 67, 156
Mason, Richard O., 128, 142
Mason, Robert Deward, 262
Mason, Scott P., 63
Mason, Todd, 229
Masonson, Leslie N., 38
Massarik, Fred, 215
Mastenbroek, W. F. G., 221
Masters, Stanley H., 164
Masulis, Ronald W., 64
Matasar, Ann B., 34
Mathe, Hervé, 185
Matheny, Philip R., 100
Mathys, Nicholas J., 184
Matsuo, Hirofumi, 158
Matteson, Michael T., 129

Matthews, Jana B., 268
Mattis, Mary C., 228
Matz, Adolph, 68
Maucher, Helmut, 147
Maurice, S. Charles, 184
Maus, Rex, 24, 239
Maus, Rex, 251
Mauser, Ferdinand F., 126
Max, Herbert B., 255
Maximon, Hillel M., 38
Maxwell, Elisabeth, 194
May, Bess Ritter, 208
May, Eleanor G., 250
May, Ernest R., 293
Mayer, Douglas F., 166
Mayer, Martin, 7, 162, 253, 266, 267
Mayer, Morris Lehman, 250
Mayer, Richard J., 51
Mayer, Thomas, 200, 201
Mayo, Elton, 227, 299
Mazzola, Joseph B., 130
McAdams, Jerry, 91
McAuley, John J., 31, 87
McBride, W. Blan, 61
McBroom, Patricia, 303
McCabe, Peter, 280
McCahery, Joseph, 59
McCall, J. B., 103
McCall, John J., 28
McCall, Morgan W., 76, 99
McCalla, Douglas B., 181
McCanse, Anne Adams, 168, 221
McCarthy, E. Jerome, 186
McCarthy, George D., 53
McCartney, Laton, 18
McCarty, Elizabeth, 304
McClain, David, 266
McClain, John O., 130
McCloskey, Donald N., 87
McCollom, James P., 57
McConnell, Campbell R., 86
McCorduck, Pamela, 51, 178
McCormack, Mark H., 272
McCormick, Ernest J., 242
McCraw, Thomas K., 19, 283
McCreary, Don R., 206
McDermott, Kathleen, 236
McDermott, Michael C., 146
McDonald, John, 115
McDonnell, Edward J., 269
McDonough, John J., 178
McEvoy, Glenn M., 232
McFarlan, F. Warren, 23, 180, 181
McGarty, Terrence P., 206
McGaughey, William, 113
McGee, Robert W., 27
McGill, Dan Mays, 213
McGill, Michael E., 126, 226
McGinnis, Michael Dean, 95
McGonagle, John J., 31, 141
McGovern, Arthur F., 29
McGraw-Hill Book Company, 44
McGregor, Douglas, 231
McGregor, Eugene B., 232
McGuire, Simon R., 58
McIntyre, James M., 242
McKain, Robert J., 271

McKee, David L., 54
McKee, Keith E., 239
McKenna, Regis, 150, 190, 191
McKenney, James L., 23, 142, 180, 218
McKenzie, Carole, 25
McKenzie, Richard B., 86
McKeown, Kathleen R., 149
McKersie, Robert B., 42
McKinlay, Alan, 111
McKinley, John E., 109
McKinney, Jerome B., 107
McKinney, Mary Jane, 65, 105
McKinniss, Candace Bancroft, 30
McKinnon, Sharon M., 183
McKnight, Gerald, 119
McLaughlin, Harold J., 60
McLaughlin, Thomas A., 211
McLean, J. W., 168
McLean, Stuart K., 21
McLeavey, Dennis W., 214, 240
McLennan, Kenneth, 135
McLennan, Roy, 223
McLeod, Raymond, 180, 181
McMahan, John, 247
McMahon, Robert J., 15
McMillan, Charles J., 129
McMillan, L. G., 215
McNair, Carol Jean, 185
McNaught, Brian, 230
McQuaid, Kim, 140
McQuown, Judith H., 65
McRae, Hamish, 31, 108
Meador, Roy, 241
Meadow, Charles T., 178
Meadows, Dennis L., 82
Meadows, Donella H., 82, 84
Means, Gardiner Coit, 66
Meckling, William H., 63
Medoff, James L., 92
Meehan, Elizabeth M., 300
Meehan, John, 9
Meek, Christopher, 129
Meek, Gary, 144
Meek, Gary E., 43
Meerhaeghe, Marcel Alfons Gilbert van, 150
Meerschwam, David M., 108
Megginson, Leon C., 232, 260
Megginson, William L., 260
Mehr, Robert Irwin, 143
Meier, Gerald M., 82
Meier, Kenneth J., 283
Meigs, Robert F., 3
Meigs, Walter B., 3
Meissner, Larry, 122
Meister, David, 306
Meister, Jeanne C., 92
Melamed, Leo, 106
Melia, Jinx, 301
Melicher, Ronald W., 203
Melkers, Julia, 249
Mellman, Martin, 3, 109
Mellon, Thomas, 196
Melosi, Martin V., 236
Melton, William C., 104
Meltzer, Ann S., 92
Menard, Scott W., 262
Mendell, Jay S., 31

Mendelsohn, M., 113
Mendez, Carmen, 300
Mendleson, Jack, 179
Menuez, Doug, 11
Mercer, David, 149
Merchant, Kenneth A., 57, 101, 182
Merlyn, Vaughan, 180
Merrick, John, 108
Merrill, Arthur A., 297
Merrill, Ronald E., 207
Merry, Uri, 218
Merton, Robert C., 104
Mesler, Donald T., 265, 266
Messina, William S., 245
Messner, Stephen D., 248
Metropolis, N., 228
Metzger, Bert L., 241
Metzger, Michael B., 43
Meyer, Arnoud de, 185
Meyer, Christopher, 128
Meyer, Herbert E., 31
Meyer, John Robert, 7, 67, 237
Meyer, Michael, 33
Meyer, Philip E., 182
Meyers, Gerald C., 72
Meyers, Thomas A., 154, 266
Michaels, Bonnie, 304
Michel, Allen, 55
Michigan State University, 48
Mickunas, Algis, 278
Mid America Institute for Public Policy Research, 104
Middleton, Victor T. C., 283
Miles, Raymond E., 128
Miles, Robert H., 24, 217
Milgrom, Paul R., 183
Milkovich, Carolyn, 230
Milkovich, George T., 47, 230
Millar, Bill, 149
Miller, Alan J., 155
Miller, Alan S., 77
Miller, Arthur Selwyn, 62
Miller, Barry E., 110
Miller, Danny, 30, 216, 218, 220
Miller, David R., 295
Miller, Deborah H., 105
Miller, Donald Britton, 249
Miller, Donald E., 110
Miller, Gerald, 259
Miller, Herbert E., 4
Miller, James A., 286
Miller, Janet R., 218
Miller, Janice James, 147
Miller, Jeffrey D., 241
Miller, Jeffrey G., 239, 292
Miller, Jule A., 185
Miller, Mara, 241
Miller, Merl K., 197
Miller, Morris, 74
Miller, Richard Bradford, 16
Miller, Richard Kendall, 12
Miller, Robert B., 256
Miller, Robert R., 147
Miller, Sheldon, 178
Miller, Stanley S., 268
Miller, William B., 173
Miller, William C., 70

Milliken & Company, 246
Milling, Bryan E., 259
Millman, Nancy, 7
Mills, Daniel Quinn, 101, 137, 149, 224, 294
Mills, Dominic, 102
Mills, Geoffrey, 79
Milton, Tom, 111
Milwid, Beth, 303
Mims, Forrest M., 198
Miner, John B., 176
Miniard, Paul W., 56
Minkes, A. L., 60
Minkin, Barry Howard, 83
Minow, Nell, 262
Minowitz, Peter, 87
Minshull, G. N., 98
Mintz, Beth, 108
Mintz, Morton, 152
Mintzberg, Henry, 177, 216, 269, 270, 271
MIPS Computer Systems, Inc, 116
Mishkin, Frederic S., 104
Misra, Jay, 23
MIT Commission on Industrial Productivity, 134
Mitchell, Terence R., 216
Mitroff, Ian I., 71, 126, 127, 128
Miyashita, Kenichi, 52
Moberg, Dennis J., 216
Mobley, Lou, 149
Mockler, Robert J., 269
Moder, Joseph J., 136
Modigliani, Franco, 35, 202
Moebs, Eva, 18
Moebs, G. Michael, 18
Mogano, M., 259
Mohrman, Allan M., 222, 229
Mohrman, Susan Albers, 122, 127
Mojena, Richard, 214
Mokhiber, Russell, 64
Mokyr, Joel, 275
Molyneux, Philip, 17
Monaghan, Tom, 200
Mondy, R. Wayne, 232
Monger, Rod F., 276
Monitor Company, 194
Monks, Robert A. G., 262
Monroe, Kent B., 236
Montgomery, Cynthia A., 271
Montgomery, Douglas C., 245
Montgomery, Robert Hiester, 13
Moody, Patricia E., 244, 292
Moody's Investors Service, 201
Moog, Carol, 6
Mookerjee, Ajay S., 18
Mooney, Gavin H., 196
Moorcroft, Sheila, 285
Moore, Curtis, 77
Moore, David G., 94
Moore, Geoffrey Hoyt, 85
Moore, Gilbert, 8
Moore, J. I., 271
Moore, Laurence J., 182
Moore, Lynda L., 300
Moore, William L., 276
Moorhouse, John C., 89
Moorthy, K. Sridhar, 189
Moran, John J., 125
Moran, Robert T., 5, 145, 147

Morgan, Cyril P., 216
Morgan, Eileen, 264
Morgan, Gareth, 178, 215
Morgan, Hal, 92
Morici, Peter, 49
Morikawa, Hidemasa, 103
Morita, Akio, 202, 263
Moritz, Michael, 41
Morningstar, Gersh, 206
Morone, Joseph G., 122
Morris, Charles R., 83
Morris, Daniel C., 223
Morris, James R., 64
Morris, Joseph M., 51
Morris, Peter W. G., 135
Morrison, Allen J., 287
Morrison, Ann M., 99, 199, 301
Morrison, Charles Edward, 12
Morrison, J. Ian, 83
Morrissey, William, 24
Morse, Dale, 88
Morse, Wayne J., 68
Mosconi, William, 185
Moscove, Stephen A., 3
Moser, Colletta H., 164
Moses, V., 19
Mosich, A. N., 4, 5
Moskowitz, Milton, 145
Mossop, Jack, 222
Most, Kenneth S., 110
Mountford, S. Joy, 123
Moutinho, Luiz, 283
Mouton, Jane Srygley, 52, 167, 176, 221, 305
Mowen, John C., 75
Mowery, David C., 278
Moyer, Reed, 146
Moynahan, John K., 252
Moynihan, Michael, 99
Mueller, Gerhard G., 144
Mueller, Robert Kirk, 45, 59, 79
Muhlemann, Alan, 239
Muksian, Robert, 32
Mulcahy, David E., 299
Müller, Kaspar, 118
Mullineux, A. W., 18, 26
Mungo, Paul, 49
Munson, John C., 181
Munson, Richard, 89
Munster, George, 203
Munter, Mary, 25
Munter, Paul, 80
Munter, Preston K., 101
Murakami, Yasusuke, 159
Murdick, Robert G., 181
Murfin, Andy, 36
Murphy, Emmett C., 128
Murphy, Herta A., 43
Murphy, James L., 87
Murphy, John J., 44
Murphy, John W., 278
Murphy, Joseph E., 62
Murphy, Michael A., 141
Murphy, Patrick E., 188
Murray, Roger F., 153
Murray, Tracy, 146
Murrin, Jack, 67
Muskie, Edmund S., 289

Myerhoff, Barbara G., 104
Myers, Charles Andrew, 231
Myers, John G., 6
Myers, M. Scott, 230
Myers, Rochelle, 71
Myers, Stewart C., 66, 105

Nader, Ralph, 7, 19
Nadler, David, 218, 307
Nadler, Leonard, 92, 230, 231
Nadler, Paul S., 17
Nadler, Stephen D., 26
Nadler, Zeace, 92, 230
Nagamachi, Mitsuo, 239
Nagayasu, Yukimasa, 28
Nagle, Thomas T., 236
Naill, Roger F., 236
Nair, Keshavan, 167
Naisbitt, John, 246, 294, 300
Nakamura, Takafusa, 159
Nalebuff, Barry, 271
Nanus, Burt, 167
Napuk, Kerry, 271
Narasimhan, Seetharama L., 240
Narayanan, V. K., 216
Nash, Edward L., 79
Nash, Laura L., 29
Nash, Michael, 91
Natella, Arthur A., 30
Natemeyer, Walter E., 217
National Academy of Engineering, 19, 61, 276
National Academy of Engineering. Study Committee on Profiting from Innovation, 276
National Academy of Sciences (U.S.), 173
National Association for Female Executives (U.S.), 300
National Association of Accountants, 32, 68, 79
National Association of Securities Dealers, 204
National Bureau of Economic Research Conference on Business Cycles (1984 : Puerto Rico), 26
National Bureau of Economic Research, 53, 55, 64, 287
National Center for Employee Ownership (U.S.), 91
National Center for Manufacturing Sciences (U.S.), 292
National Conference on Business Ethics (8th : 1990 : Bentley
National Endowment for the Arts, 11
National Institute of Economic and Social Research, 134
National Museum of American History (U.S.), 141
National Planning Association, 98
National Research Council (U.S.). Computer Science and Technology Board, 50
National Society for Performance and Instruction, 229
NATO Economics Colloquium (21st : 1992 : Brussels, Belgium), 97
NATPE International, 280
Nayak, P. Ranganath, 208
Naylor, Thomas H., 60
Nazemetz, John W., 13
Neale, Margaret Ann, 205
Neely, Richard, 70, 240
Nehemkis, Peter Raymond, 31
Neiditz, Minerva Heller, 33
Neikirk, William, 297

Nelson, A. Gene, 103
Nelton, Sharon, 70
Neslin, Scott A., 253
Nester, William R., 291
Neter, John, 249
Neuhaus, Richard John, 263
Neuhauser, Peg, 45
Neumann, Seev, 182
Neustadt, Richard E., 293
Neustadtl, Alan, 25
Nevaer, Louis E. V., 235
Nevins, Thomas J., 231
Nevitt, Peter K , 125
New York Institute of Finance, 44, 107, 155, 254, 267
New York (State). Governor (1983- : Cuomo), 288
New York University. Salomon Center, 36
Newbold, Paul, 31
Newgarden, Albert, 54
Newhouse, Joseph P., 246
Newman, James A., 100
Newman, Jerry M., 47
Newman, Katherine S., 261
Newstrom, John W., 219
Newton, Julia, 270
Nguyen, Hai, 192
NiCarthy, Ginny, 258
Nicholas, Ted, 25
Nichols, Larry D., 46
Nichols, Nancy A., 302
Nicholson, Nigel, 101
Nicholson, Robert H., 32
Nickerson, Clarence B., 3
Nickerson, Raymond S., 51
Nielsen, Waldemar A., 234
Nierenberg, Gerard I., 205
Nihon Bōeki Shinkōkai, 158, 191
Nihon Ginkō. KinyūKenkyūkyoku, 200
Nihon HR Kyōkai, 273
Nihon Nōritsu Kyōkai, 238
Nihon Sōgō Kenkyūjo, 64
Nii, Penny, 178
Nisbet, James D., 33
Nissen, Bruce, 284
Nitterhouse, Denise, 211
Nix, Susan W., 156
Nix, William E., 156
Noam, Eli M., 257, 280
Nobes, Christopher, 47
Noblet, Jocelyn de, 78
Noe, Robert M., 232
Noer, David M., 222
Nof, Shimon Y., 251
Nohria, Nitin, 173, 218
Nolan, Mary, 132
Nolan, Richard L., 145
Nomura International Ltd, 68
Noonan, Chris J., 252
Noori, Hamid, 275
Nora, John, 304
Norback, Craig T., 295
Nordhaus, William D., 85
Normann, Richard, 268
Norris, Thomas, 185
North Atlantic Treaty Organization, 97
North, Klaus, 127
North-Holland Publishing Company, 66

Norvelle, Joan W., 114
Nourse, Hugh O., 137
Novak, Michael, 263
Novak, William, 124, 243
Nowak, Laura S., 20
Noxell Corporation, 103
Noyelle, Thierry J., 165
NPA Committee on Changing International Realities, 49
Nunes, Morris A., 62, 252
Nunn, Sam, 290
Nussbaum, Helga, 148
Nutt, Paul C., 75
Nutt, Susan, 192
Nycum, Susan H., 302
Nystrom, Paul H., 188

Oakland, John S., 239
Oakley, Mark, 77
O'Barr, William M., 228
Obel, Børge, 48
O'Brien, James A., 17, 24, 181
O'Connor, William E., 9
Odaka, Kunio, 129
O'Dell, Carla S., 91, 126
Odell, Peter R., 233
Odiorne, George S., 179, 221, 232
Oestreich, Daniel K., 225
Ofer, Gur, 97
O'Flaherty, Joseph S., 116
O'glove, Thornton L., 110
O'Hara, Patrick D., 61
O'Hara-Devereaux, Mary, 145
Ōkita, Saburō, 159
Oleck, Howard Leoner, 211
Olenick, Arnold J., 241
Olewiler, Nancy D., 205
Olins, Wally, 60
Olive, David, 29
Oliver, Richard L., 73
Oliver, Thomas, 42
Olmsted, Barney, 123
Olson, Gerard T., 67
Olson, Jerry C., 57
Olson, Margrethe H., 181
Olson, Steve, 19
O'Keefe, Bernard J., 287
Ōmae, Ken, 158, 159, 162
O'Mara, Julie, 184
Ōmori, Tokudo, 159
Oncken, William, 281
O'Neil, John R., 271
O'Neill, Michael, 212
Ono, Yoshiyasu, 201
O'Reilly, Charles, 218
O'Reilly, Vincent M., 13
Organ, Dennis W., 242
Organisation for Economic Co-operation and Development, 83, 271
Ornstein, Norman J., 110
Orr, Bill, 151
Orsino, Philip S., 260
Osborne, David, 5, 140
Osborne, David M., 251
Osburn, Donald D., 8
O'Shea, James, 296
Osigweh, Chimezie A. B., 164

Oster, Clinton V., 7
Oster, Sharon M., 48
Österle, Hubert, 141
Osterman, Paul, 232
Ostrom, Elinor, 95
Otley, David T., 182
O'Toole, James, 132, 167
Ott, J. Steven, 212, 215, 217
Ott, Lyman, 131
Ouchi, William G., 184
Overholt, William H., 40
Owen, Jenny, 213
Owen, Robert R., 64
Owen, William M., 53
Oxford Institute of Information Management, 180
Oxford Law Colloquium (2nd : 1992), 59

PA Computers and Telecommunications (Firm), 180
Pacific Institute for Public Policy Research, 237
Pacific Research Institute for Public Policy, 41, 89, 110
Pacific Trade and Development Conference (14th : 1984 : Singapore), 106
Packer, Arnold E., 306
Pagonis, William G., 229
Pain, Den, 213
Painter, William H., 41
Paley, Norton, 187, 191
Paliwoda, Stanley J., 102
Paller, Alan, 174
Pallister, David, 10
Palmatier, George E., 185
Paolillo, Joseph G. P., 216
Papadopoulos, N. G., 190
Pappas, James L., 183, 184
Paqué, Karl-Heinz, 116
Parisotto, Aurelio, 148
Park, C. Whan, 188
Park, Yung Chul, 105
Parker, Glenn M., 305
Parker, R. H., 47
Parker, Thomas Trebitsch, 164
Parker, Xenia Ley, 141
Parkinson, J. E., 62
Parkinson, John, 180
Parks, Sharon Daloz, 28
Parnes, Herbert S., 184
Parsons, D. W., 163
Partin, J. Jennings, 221
Pascale, Richard T., 222
Pascarella, Perry, 226
Pasmore, William A., 215, 221
Passin, Herbert, 160
Pastin, Mark, 29
Patinkin, Don, 143
Patinkin, Mark, 49
Patrick, Hugh T., 105, 122, 159
Patten, Thomas Henry, 161
Patterson, James Herbert, 265
Pattison, Joseph E., 290
Patton, Bruce, 205
Patton, John A., 134
Patton, Phil, 277
Pauchant, Thierry C., 71
Paul, Karen, 27
Pauli, Gunter A., 108
Paulos, John Allen, 194

Pavlik, Ellen L., 40, 63
Peacock, William E., 127
Peale, Norman Vincent, 30
Pearson, Christine M., 128
Pechman, Joseph A., 257, 274
Peck, Jonathan C., 126
Pederson, Carlton A., 256
Peet, John, 95
Peet, Richard, 139
Pelton, Warren J., 132
Pendergrast, Mark, 42
Peng, Wensheng, 26
Penner, Donald, 136
Pennings, Johannes M., 76, 276
Penrose, Edith Tilton, 138
Perdue Farms, 246
Perez, Robert C., 295
Pergamit, Gayle, 277
Perles, Benjamin M., 43
Perlman, Baron, 226
Perlman, Mark, 254
Perreault, William D., 186
Perrow, Charles, 125
Perry, Lee Tom, 48
Perry, Robert H., 100
Perry, William E., 89
Pescow, Jerome K., 3
Pessemier, Edgar A., 238
Pessolano, F. John, 31
Peter, J. Paul, 57
Peters, Edgar E., 154
Peters, Michael P., 207, 238
Peters, Robert A., 35
Peters, Roger, 99
Peters, Thomas J., 128, 130, 131, 222, 224
Petersen, Donald E., 126
Petersen, John E., 203
Peterson, Chris, 277
Peterson, Leroy D., 135
Peterson, Peter G., 290
Peterson, Raymond H., 34
Peterson, Rein, 152
Peterson, Richard B., 129
Peterson, Richard Lewis, 105
Peterson, Robert A., 57
Peterson, W. E., 304
Peterson, Willis L., 172, 197
Petre, Peter, 149
Petry, Edward S., 95
Pettigrew, Andrew M., 269
Pettit, John D., 33
Petty, J. William, 259
Petzel, Todd E., 107
Petzinger, Thomas, 280
Peyton, David, 80
Pfaffenberger, Roger C., 265
Pfeffer, Jeffrey, 75, 230
Pfeiffer, J. William, 270
Pfeil, Enzio, 112
Phatak, Arvind V., 147
Phelan, John J., 255
Phillips, Bob, 180
Phillips, Cecil R., 136
Phillips, Don T., 214
Phillips, H. W., 253
Phillips, Jack J., 273
Phillips, Kevin P., 198

Phillips, Michael, 255
Picciotto, Sol, 59
Pickens, T. Boone, 234
Pickle, Hal B., 260
Pidd, Michael, 182
Pierce, James L., 17
Piercy, James E., 40
Piercy, Nigel, 189
Piggott, John, 282
Pigors, Paul John William, 231
Pigott, William, 105
Pike, Earl C., 9
Pilbeam, Keith, 87
Pilotta, Joseph J., 278
Pilzer, Paul Zane, 253
Pinch, T. J., 277
Pincus, J. David, 40
Pine, B. Joseph, 276
Pinsdorf, Marion K., 60
Pinson, Linda, 60
Piper, Thomas R., 28
Pirkl, James Joseph, 8
Pisano, Gary P., 292
Pitts, Robert E., 15
Planning Forum, 269
Platt, Robert B., 144
Plautz, Elizabeth, 286
Plenert, Gerhard Johannes, 47
Plummer, James L., 295
Plummer, Mark L., 12
Pocock, M. A., 27
Poe, Richard, 157
Poeth, G. G. J M., 129
Pohl, Norval F., 43
Pointer, Larry Gene, 286
Policy formulation and administration, 175
Pondy, Louis R., 242
Poniachek, Harvey A., 146
Pool, John Charles, 87, 150
Poole, Marshall Scott, 276
Poole, Robert W., 244
Poor, Roger M., 152
Poore, J. H., 273
Poorvu, William J., 247
Popcorn, Faith, 31
Pope, Jeffrey L., 193
Popov, Vladimir Mikhaĭlovich, 39
Poppel, Harvey L., 50
Porras, Jerry I., 224, 272
Porter, Glenn, 287
Porter, Grover L., 5
Porter, Lyman W., 219
Porter, Michael E., 35, 48, 140, 194, 218, 271
Porter, Michhael E., 271
Porter, Sylvia Field, 107
Porter, W. Thomas, 89
Posner, Barry Z., 167, 168
Post, James E., 138, 261
Postman, Neil, 277
Potts, Mark, 222
Pourdehnad, John, 222
Powell, Gary N., 257, 302
Powell, Jim, 108, 247
Powell, Walter W., 212
Powers, Mark J., 108
Powis, Robert E., 201
Poza, Ernesto J., 41

Prahalad, C. K., 48, 148
Pras, Bernard, 193
Pratt, John W., 178
Pratt, Joseph A., 291
Pratt, Shannon P., 67
Pratt, Stanley E., 295
Prell, Arthur Ely, 187
Prendergast, Curtis, 281
Prentice, Daniel D., 59
Prentice-Hall, Inc, 3
Pressman, Israel, 76
Preston, Richard, 265
Prestowitz, Clyde V., 160
Price, Margaret M., 156
Prichard, Peter, 295
Prichett, Gorden D., 32
Priesmeyer, Henry Richard, 177
Primozic, Edward A., 269
Primozic, Kenneth I., 269
Pring, Martin J., 44, 153
Pringle, Charles D., 270
Pritchard, Robert E., 35
Pritchard, Wendy, 221
Pritchett, Price, 53
Process Management International, Inc., 244
Proctor, William, 272
Profit-Sharing Research Foundation, 241
Progressive Policy Institute (U.S.), 293
Prokopenko, Joseph, 135
Pruitt, Bettye Hobbs, 119
Public Agenda Foundation, 165
Pugh, Derek Salman, 227
Pugh, Peter, 119
Punch, Maurice, 262
Purvis, Douglas D., 85, 87, 197
Putnam, Bluford H., 254
Putnam, Robert, 262
Pyle, William W., 4

QED Research, Inc, 295
Quantock, Paul, 109
Quelch, John A., 6, 57, 102, 187, 188, 253
Quick, Thomas L., 175, 219, 237
Quinlivan-Hall, David, 119
Quinn, Brian Scott, 96
Quinn, James Brian, 210, 270, 271
Quinn, Jane Bryant, 106
Quinn, Robert E., 223, 225
Quirk, James P., 241
Quirt, John, 163

Rabin, Jack, 269
Rabushka, Alvin, 41
Rachleff, Peter J., 115
Rachlin, Robert, 146
Rackham, Neil, 252
Raddock, David M., 149
Radebaugh, Lee H., 146
Raelin, Joseph A., 240
Raghu, Nath, 216
Rahim, M. Afzalur, 52
Raiffa, Howard, 203
Rainer, R. Kelly, 180
Ram, S., 208
Ramírez, Rafael, 268
Ramachandran, Rama V., 160
Ramsey, Douglas K., 48

Ramsey, Jackson Eugene, 249
Ramundo, Bernard A., 205
Rand Corporation. Insurance Experiment Group, 246
Randall, Robert M., 269
Randers, Jørgen, 82
Randle, Yvonne, 175, 207
Rangan, V. Kasturi, 192
Ranky, Paul G., 185
Rapp, Stan, 186, 187, 190
Rappaport, Ann, 138
Rappaport, Stephen P., 203, 255
Rasberry, Salli, 255
Rasmussen, Douglas B., 38
Ratcliffe, Thomas A., 80
Ratner, Lorman, 199
Rau, Pradeep A., 97
Rauch, Jonathan, 204
Ravindran, A., 214
Ray, Michael L., 71, 130
Rayack, Elton, 40
Rayburn, Letricia Gayle, 69
Raymond, H. Alan, 176
Read, Donald, 250
Reddy, Michael T., 255
Reder, Alan, 262
Redman, Tom, 12
Reece, James S., 3
Reed, Edward Wilson, 17
Reed, O. Lee, 283
Reed, Stanley Foster, 53
Rees, Fran, 305
Rees-Mogg, William, 154
Rehfeld, Barry J., 160
Reibstein, David J., 188
Reich, Robert B., 41, 140, 289, 293
Reid, Peter C., 100
Reid, Robert, 120
Reidenbach, R. Eric, 15
Reilly, Frank K., 29, 155
Rein, Irving J., 189
Reinfeld, Nyles V., 238
Reingold, Edwin M., 158, 202
Reinhardt, Uwe E., 196
Reinhart, Carlene, 230
Reischauer, Edwin O., 158
Reisman, David A., 196
Reitsch, Arthur G., 30, 31, 43, 132
Reitz, H. Joseph, 217
Renner, Peter Franz, 119
Renshaw, Edward F., 31
Renshaw, Geoffrey, 148
Rentoul, John, 237
Res, Zannis, 81
Research Institute for Cuba (Coral Gables, Fla.), 157
Resnick-West, Susan M., 229
Resnik, Michael D., 75
Resnik, Paul, 259
Ress, C. William, 250
Reuss, Carol, 46
Reutter, Mark, 265
Reynard, Sue, 282
Reynolds, Lloyd George, 78, 85, 164, 172, 197
RGK Foundation, 71, 206
Rheingold, Howard, 50, 254
Rhinesmith, Stephen H., 147

Rhodes, Jerry, 70
Rhodes, Lucien, 156
Riahi-Belkaoui, Ahmed, 40, 63, 68
Riccomini, Donald R., 179
Rich, Ben R., 171
Rich, Bruce, 306
Rich, Stanley R., 206
Richards, Margaret, 174
Richards, Max De Voe, 131
Richardson, Clinton, 296
Richardson, Peter R., 69
Richey, Terry, 187
Richman, Barry M., 146
Richter, Paul W., 53
Rickards, Tudor, 276
Ricks, David A., 144
Ries, Al., 186, 190, 236
Rieser, Carl, 257
Rifkin, Glenn, 214
Rima, Ingrid Hahne, 84
Rimmington, Anthony, 20
Rines, S. Melvin, 109
Ring, Alfred A., 247
Rinzler, Alan, 130
Rion, Michael, 30
Ritchie, Berry, 79
Ritchie, J. B., 218
Ritchie, Michael, 279
Ritchken, Peter, 215
Ritter, Lawrence S., 201
Ritvo, Roger A., 177
Ritzman, Larry P., 239
Rivkin, Jack L., 296
Rizzo, Ann-Marie, 300
Robbins, Harvey, 305
Robbins, Sidney M., 65
Robbins, Stephen P., 216, 217, 219, 232
Robert, Michel, 270
Roberto, Eduardo L., 261
Roberts, Edward Baer, 121
Roberts, Edward Baer, 275
Roberts, John, 183
Roberts, John, 54
Roberts, Michael J., 207
Roberts, Paul Craig, 289
Roberts, Ralph, 42
Roberts, William H., 7
Robertson, Jack C., 13
Robertson, Thomas S., 56
Robeson, James F., 32, 234
Robey, Daniel, 174
Robins, Brian, 108
Robinson, Carol A., 68
Robinson, D. F., 94
Robinson, Dana Gaines, 92
Robinson, James C., 92
Robinson, James W., 136
Robinson, Janet E., 242
Robinson, Jeffrey, 34
Robinson, Joan, 85
Robinson, Michael A., 107
Robinson, Peter, 251
Robinson, Richard D., 68, 147, 156
Robinson, Roland I., 105
Robock, Stefan Hyman, 146
Rochell, Carlton C., 13
Rock, Milton L., 47, 54, 221

Rock, Robert H., 54, 221
Rockart, John F., 174, 178
Rockefeller Archive Center, 139
Roddick, Anita, 20
Roden, Peyton Foster, 105
Rodgers, F. G., 91, 150
Roethlisberger, Fritz Jules, 231
Rogers, C. Raymond, 304
Rogers, David, 17
Rogers, David J., 179
Rogers, Everett M., 198, 278
Rogers, R. Mark, 85
Rome, Edwin P., 7
Romney, Marshall B., 3
Ronen, Simcha, 123, 144
Roosevelt Center for American Policy Studies, 22, 74
Root, Franklin R., 152
Root, Steven J., 13
Roper, Michael, 101
Rose, Frank, 11
Rose, Peter S., 106, 108
Rose, Richard C., 74
Rosecrance, Richard N., 42, 289
Rosegrant, Susan, 122
Rosen, Corey M., 91
Rosen, Robert H., 128
Rosen, Stephen, 277
Rosenau, Milton D., 125
Rosenbach, William E., 166
Rosenbaum, Ron, 209
Rosenbaum, Walter A., 93
Rosenberg, Claude N., 153
Rosenberg, Hilary, 170
Rosenberg, Nathan, 98, 276
Rosenberg, Richard S., 51
Rosenbloom, Arthur H., 53
Rosenbloom, Bert, 192
Rosenbloom, Jerry S., 90, 107
Rosener, Judy B., 184
Rosenfeld, Eric, 63
Rosenkrantz, Stuart A., 178
Rosenzweig, James Erwin, 215
Rosenzweig, Philip M., 179
Rosner, David, 126
Rosovsky, Henry, 275
Rosow, Jerome M., 49
Ross, David, 133
Ross, Gerald, 132
Ross, Howard D., 27
Ross, Joel E., 282
Ross, Sheldon M., 237
Ross, Stephen A., 64
Ross, Walter Sanford, 251
Rossi, Peter Henry, 263
Rossi, Vanessa, 155
Roszak, Theodore, 51
Rota, Gian-Carlo, 228
Roth, Aleda V., 292
Roth, Harold P., 68
Roth, William F., 161, 237
Rothchild, John, 155, 267
Rothery, Brian, 245
Rothman, Harry, 19
Rothschild, William E., 168
Rothstein, Lawrence E., 234
Rothwell, Roy, 275

Rottenberg, Dan, 209
Rotzoll, Kim B., 6
Rouner, Leroy S., 36
Rousseas, Stephen William, 200
Roussel, Philip A., 249
Rowan, Roy, 101
Rowe, Alan J., 76
Rowland, Mary, 204
Rowley, Anthony, 266
Royal Geographical Society (Great Britain), 88
Royal Institute of International Affairs, 162
Royle, Duncan, 141
Rozin, Skip, 264
Ruben, Jay, 4
Rubenstein, Daniel Blake, 205
Rubin, David S., 262
Rubin, Irwin M., 242
Rubin, Paul H., 184
Rubin, Ronald S., 192
Rubinstein, Sidney P., 178
Rubner, Alex, 112, 148
Rugg, Donald D., 204
Rugman, Alan M., 146
Rukstad, Michael G., 172, 183
Rumelt, Richard P., 269
Rummler, Geary A., 134
Russell, Cheryl, 83
Russell, David, 52
Russell, Frederic Arthur, 256
Russell, Thomas, 7
Rust, Roland T., 73
Rutenberg, David P., 148
Rutgers University. Center for Urban Policy Research, 202
Rutizer, Barry, 38
Rutledge, John, 131
Ryan, Kathleen, 225
Ryan, Mike H., 24
Ryan, Nancy E., 274
Ryans, Cynthia C., 97, 259
Ryans, John K., 61, 97, 146
Rydz, John S., 275

Saad, Kamal N., 249
Saber, John C., 32
Sachs, Jeffrey, 172, 235
Sachs, Jeffrey, 96
Sackmann, Sonja, 132
Sadowski, Randall P., 13
Sakaiya, Taichi, 158, 261
Sakakibara, Eisuke, 158
Sakakibara, Shigeki, 266
Sako, Mari, 134
SaKong, Il., 164
Salama, Eric, 188
Salerno, Lynn M., 51
Sales, Carol A., 174
Salmon, Walter J., 250
Salmonson, R. F., 5
Salomon Brothers Center for the Study of Financial Institutions, 142, 162, 179, 215
Salter, Malcolm S., 13, 80, 130, 271
Salvatore, Dominick, 183
Salvendy, Gavriel, 125
Sametz, Arnold W., 142
Samli, A. Coskun, 186
Sampson, Anthony, 200, 233, 264

Samuels, Richard J., 204
Samuels, Warren J., 62
Samuelson, Paul Anthony, 85, 86
San Miguel, Joseph G., 5
Sandage, C. H., 6
Sandy, William, 222
Sant, Roger W., 236
Sapolsky, Harvey M., 238
Sarathy, Ravi, 102
Sassen, Saskia, 109
Sasser, W. Earl, 73, 127, 257
Sathe, Vijay, 57, 217
Satō, Ryūzō, 159, 160
Saul, John Ralston, 248
Saunders, Anthony, 36
Saunders, Martha Dunagin, 81
Savage, Charles H., 224
Savage, John E., 51
Savona, Paolo, 96
Sawyer, Brian, 23
Sawyer, Lawrence B., 13
Sawyer, Malcolm C., 133
Saxton, Mary J., 58
Sayles, Leonard R., 168, 169, 232, 275
Saylor, James H., 135
Schaefer, Howard G., 83
Schall, Lawrence D., 66
Schallheim, James S., 169
Schank, Roger C., 70
Scharff, Edward E., 298
Schatz, Kenneth, 242
Schatz, Linda, 242
Scheer, Wilbert E., 230
Schein, Edgar H., 59, 184
Schendel, Dan, 269
Scherer, F. M., 133
Schermerhorn, John R., 176
Schiff, Jonathan B., 5
Schiffman, Leon G., 56
Schilit, W. Keith, 206, 272
Schlesinger, Leonard A., 10, 73, 180, 218
Schlesinger, Phyllis F., 216
Schlossstein, Steven, 293
Schmalensee, Richard, 85, 133, 172
Schmenner, Roger W., 240
Schmertz, Herbert, 243
Schmid, Gregory, 83
Schmidheiny, Stephan, 82
Schmidt, Charles, 178
Schmidt, Richard J., 59
Schmieding, Holger, 116
Schmookler, Andrew Bard, 261
Schnaars, Steven P., 189
Schneeberger, Kenneth C., 8
Schneeweis, Thomas, 107
Schneider, Andrea Kupfer, 227
Schneider, Benjamin, 59
Schneider, Bertrand, 83
Schneider, Stephen Henry, 116
Schneier, Craig Eric, 232
Schoemaker, Paul J. H., 75
Schoenberg, Robert J., 114
Schoenhaus, Ted, 283
Schonberger, Richard, 132, 225
Schor, Juliet, 169
Schotter, A., 113

Schrader, David E., 64
Schrage, Michael, 45
Schram, Martin, 293
Schreiber, Alfred L., 243
Schroeder, Richard G., 286
Schroeder, Roger G., 239
Schulmeyer, G. Gordon, 174
Schultz, Don E., 46
Schultz, Duane P., 242
Schultz, Harry D., 264
Schultz, Loren A., 206
Schultz, Ron, 179
Schultz, Sydney Ellen, 242
Schultze, Charles L., 69
Schulz, Eric R., 274
Schumpeter, Joseph Alois, 86
Schuster, Fred E., 224
Schwab, Robert, 77
Schwab, Susan Carol, 274
Schwager, Jack D., 111
Schwartz, David Joseph, 126
Schwartz, Eli, 82
Schwartz, Felice N., 258
Schwartz, John J., 39
Schwartz, Michael, 25, 108
Schwartz, Peter, 268
Schwartz, Robert A., 254, 266
Schwartz, Robert J., 107, 108
Schwartz, Tony, 285
Schwarz, Edward W., 107
Schweitzer, Marcell, 21
Schweizer, Peter, 31
Scott, Bruce R., 263, 290
Scott, Charles R., 260
Scott, Colin, 59
Scott, Cynthia D., 224
Scott, David F., 27
Scott, Denise, 25
Scott, James Dacon, 187
Scott, John, 64
Scott Morton, Michael S., 174, 175, 270
Scott, Robert Haney, 105
Scott, W. Richard, 227
Scott, William G., 18, 216
Sculley, John, 254
Seal, Gregory M., 292
Seaman, Barrett, 41
Searfoss, D. Gerald, 4
Searle, Philip F., 285
Sebag-Montefiore, Hugh, 171
Sebenius, James K., 206
Sedgwick, Henry D., 207
Segal, Gerald, 123
Segal, Harvey, 64
Seidenberg, Philip N., 215
Seidman, Lewis William, 253
Seiter, Ellen, 279
Sekaran, Uma, 24, 193
Seldin, Maury, 247, 248
Seligman, Joel, 266
Selnow, Gary W., 46
Selznick, Philip, 168
Semanik, Michael K., 252
Semmler, Willi, 26
Senge, Peter M., 226
Sengoku, Tamotsu, 304
Senn, James A., 180

Serpa, Roy, 58
Servi, Italo S., 209
Sethi, S. Prakash, 139, 206
Settle, Robert B., 57, 193
Sexton, Donald L., 94, 206
Shachtman, Tom, 247
Shafer, Dennis W., 209
Shafritz, Jay M., 212, 215
Shaikh, Anwar, 204
Shaked, Israel, 55
Shames, Laurence, 119
Shani, Abraham B., 217
Shank, John K., 69
Shanklin, William L., 61, 191
Shannon, James, 228
Shao, Stephen P., 32
Shao, Stephen Pinyee, 32
Shapero, Albert, 240
Shapiro, Alan C., 66, 145, 148
Shapiro, Benson P., 72, 188, 256
Shapiro, Eileen C., 175
Shapiro, Harold T., 143
Shapiro, Helen, 14
Shapiro, Marilyn, 10
Shapiro, Roy D., 32, 182, 185
Shapley, Deborah, 195
Sharpe, William F., 154, 155
Shaw, Gary, 176
Shawcross, William, 203
Shear, Jeff, 278
Shedd, Peter J., 43
Sheff, David, 210
Sheimo, Michael D., 266
Shell, Richard L., 306
Shelton, Judy, 151
Shenefield, John H., 11
Shenson, Howard L., 25, 56
Shepherd, William G., 133, 140
Sherlock, Paul, 133
Sherman, J. Daniel, 277
Sherman, Joe, 115
Sherman, Stratford, 115
Sherman, V. Clayton, 199
Sherwood, Hugh C., 21
Sherwood, Philip K., 69, 207
Sheth, Jagdish N., 189, 190, 208
Shetty, Y. Krishna, 134, 135, 226
Shetzen, Joseph, 130
Shibagaki, Kazuo, 68
Shields, Jerry, 171
Shillinglaw, Gordon, 182
Shimizu, Ryūei, 64, 129, 132
Shimomura, Mitsuko, 202
Shingō, Shigeo, 245
Shionoya, Yuichi, 254
Shishido, Toshio, 159
Shmelev, N. P., 39
Shook, R. J., 267
Shook, Robert L., 111, 150, 267
Shore, Jane E., 37
Shorris, Earl, 256
Short, Daniel G., 4
Shortell, Stephen M., 196
Shoven, John B., 53
Shrode, William A., 28
Shull, Joseph S., 185
Shulman, Robert S., 189

Shwadran, Benjamin, 233
Sibson, Robert Earl, 47, 231
Sicilia, David B., 291
Siegel, Andrew F., 43
Siegel, Daniel Richard, 151
Siegel, Eric S., 206, 207
Siegel, Jeremy J., 209
Siegel, Joel G., 110
Siegel, Lenny, 51
Sifonis, John G., 268
Sigband, Norman B., 25
Sigler, Jay A., 62
Sigoloff, Sanford C., 62
Sihler, William W., 109
Sikora, Martin J., 54
Silber, Mark B., 199
Silber, William L., 201, 215
Silk, Leonard Solomon, 77, 86
Silva, Michael A., 96, 175
Silver, A. David, 34, 208, 260, 303
Silver, Cheryl Simon, 173
Silver, Edward A., 152
Silverman, Robert A., 43
Silverman, Stanley B., 272
Silverstein, Michael, 138
Silvis, Donn E., 46
Simkin, Mark G., 3
Simmonds, Kenneth, 146
Simon, Herbert Alexander, 76
Simon, Julian Lincoln, 173
Simon, Ron, 258
Simons, Robert, 129
Simons, Robin, 64, 211
Simpson, James R., 19
Simpson, Thomas D., 200
Sims, Henry P., 220, 305
Sims, Ronald R., 225
Sin, Yu-gŭn, 52
Singer, Aaron, 287
Sinquefield, Jeanne Cairns, 44
Sirmans, C. F., 247
Sisk, Henry L., 176
Sissors, Jack Zanville, 7
Sitarz, Dan, 82
Siwek, Stephen E., 50
Sjögren, Bertil, 96
Skacel, Robert K., 189
Skinner, Wickham, 239, 292
Skousen, K. Fred, 5, 286
Skousen, Mark, 238
Skully, Michael T., 105
Slater, Robert, 39, 49, 55, 115, 167
Slevin, Dennis P., 179
Slifer, Stephen D., 85
Sloan, Alfred P., 115
Sloan, Allan, 55
Sloan School of Management. Center for Information Systems Research, 178
Sloane, Arthur A., 137
Slocum, John W., 226
Sloma, Richard S., 132, 226
Smart, Bradford D., 93
Smart, Bruce, 126
Smelser, Neil J., 263
Smidt, Seymour, 35, 65
Smilor, Raymond W., 130, 206, 207, 295
Smith, Adam, 260

Smith, Bucklin & Associates, 211
Smith, Clifford W., 65, 66, 107, 108
Smith, Diana McLain, 262
Smith, Douglas K., 306
Smith, Gary, 105
Smith, Geoffrey N., 208
Smith, George Albert, 130
Smith, George David, 10
Smith, George David, 119
Smith, Gerald W., 93
Smith, Gordon V., 27
Smith, H. Jeff, 237
Smith, James Allen, 117
Smith, Janet, 72
Smith, Jay M., 5
Smith, Jeanette, 6
Smith, Lee, 288
Smith, Michael, 160
Smith, Michael J., 161
Smith, N. Craig, 56, 187
Smith, Ralph Eugene, 4
Smith, Ralph Lee, 81
Smith, Richard Norton, 120
Smith, Roy C., 18, 55, 153, 154, 307
Smith, Sally Bedell, 227
Smith, Suzanne, 123
Smith, Wesley J., 7
Smith, William K., 53
Smithson, C. W., 65, 184
Smulyan, Susan, 246
Snape, Ed, 12
Snell, J. Laurie, 237
Snell, Michael, 128
Snider, Jim, 279
Snow, Charles C., 128
Snowden, Richard W., 259
Snyder, John, 252
Snyder, Neil H., 168
Sobel, Robert, 52, 110, 138, 150, 199, 246, 253, 267, 291
Society for Industrial and Organizational Psychology (U.S.), 199
Society for the Psychological Study of Social Issues, 257
Soder, Dee Ann, 161
Solberg, James J., 214
Solimano, Andrés, 85
Solnik, Bruno H., 157
Solomon, Elinor Harris, 90
Solomon, Ezra, 267
Solomon, Michael R., 257
Solomon, Robert C., 29
Solomon, Steven, 260
Solomons, David, 5
Solow, Robert M., 134
Somkid Jatusripitak, 190
Sommer, A. A., 79
Sommers, Albert T., 288
Sonnenberg, Frank K., 177, 190
Sonnenfeld, Jeffrey A., 40, 101
Sorcher, Melvin, 99
Sorensen, Elaine Joy, 228
Soros, George, 154
Sorter, George H., 38
Souder, Wm. E., 209, 277
Spar, Debora L., 38
Spechler, Jay W., 73, 282

Spector, Bert, 232
Speh, Thomas W., 132
Spellman, Christina, 13
Spencer, Anne, 79
Spencer, Lyle M., 12
Spencer, Signe M., 12
Spicers Centre for Europe, 109
Spiegel, Henry William, 86
Spinelli, Altiero, 97
Spirer, Herbert F., 262
Spiro, Herbert T., 105
Spitzer, Carlton E., 24
Spohr, Anthony P., 249
Spooner, John D., 22
Sprague, Irvine H., 15
Sprague, Ralph H., 174
Springer, Clifford Harry, 194
Sproul, Michael, 197
Sproull, Lee, 90
Squires, Arthur M., 278
Squires, James D., 40
SRI International, 89
Srivastva, Suresh, 29, 100, 225
Stabiner, Karen, 39
Stacey, Ralph D., 226
Stahl, Michael J., 268
Stahl, Pat, 44
Stalk, George, 66, 281
Stamos, Steve, 150
Stampfl, Ronald W., 250
Stanback, Thomas M., 165
Stanbury, W. T., 251
Standard and Poor's Corporation, 21, 254
Stankiewicz, Rikard, 139
Stanley, Thomas J., 250
Stansbury, Herb, 128
Stansfield, Richard H., 6
Stanton, Erwin Schoenfeld, 92
Stanton, William J., 187, 252
Starkey, Ken, 111, 270
Starling, Grover, 24
Starr, Martin Kenneth, 275
Starrett, David A., 107
Stasch, Stanley F., 193
Staudohar, Paul D., 137, 164
Staw, Barry M., 220
Stead, Bette Ann, 302
Stead, Jean Garner, 82
Stead, W. Edward, 82
Steckel, Richard, 64, 211
Steele, Fritz, 213
Steeples, Marion Mills, 281
Steers, Richard M., 52, 216
Steffens, John, 50
Steffy, Brian D., 230
Stein, Alex M., 51
Stein, Barry, 221
Stein, Benjamin, 199
Stein, Herbert, 289
Stein, Jerome L., 44
Stein, Judith K., 33
Stein, Robert E., 282
Steinberg, Marc I., 280
Steinbrink, John P., 252
Steinbruner, Maureen S., 289
Steiner, George Albert, 139, 176
Steiner, John F., 139
Steiner, Peter Otto, 55, 85, 87, 197
Steinmetz, Lawrence L., 273
Steiss, Alan Walter, 61
Stelzer, Irwin M., 11
Sterba, James P., 38
Sterling, Bruce, 49
Stern, Joel M., 67, 151
Stern, Louis W., 192, 283
Stern, Sydney Ladensohn, 283
Sternberg, William, 299
Sterngold, James, 88
Stevens, Art, 243
Stevens, Carol Bloom, 5, 124, 142
Stevens, Catharine, 115
Stevens, Mark, 5, 88, 124, 142
Stevens, Robert E., 69, 207
Stevenson, Howard H., 94, 130, 207
Stewart, Hugh B., 84
Stewart, James B., 243
Stewart, Paul, 210
Stewart, Sarah, 10
Stewart, Walter, 249
Stice, Earl K., 5
Stice, James D., 5
Stickney, Clyde P., 4
Stigum, Marcia L., 154, 201
Still, Richard Ralph, 187, 252
Stillman, Richard Joseph, 80, 106
Stilwell, E. Joseph, 227
Stimpson, David, 201
Stine, G. Harry, 64
Stirling, John, 137
Stobaugh, Robert B., 93, 172, 233
Stock, James R., 32
Stockton, John Robert, 262
Stogdill, Ralph Melvin, 166
Stoll, Hans R., 151
Stolovitch, Harold D., 229
Stone, Alan, 10
Stone, Bob, 79
Stone, Dan G., 80
Stone, Florence M., 273
Stone, Nan Dundes, 66
Stone, Peter Bennet, 138
Stonehill, Arthur I., 150
Stoner, James Arthur Finch, 176, 282
Stopford, John M., 61
Storey, M. John, 66, 179
Storrs, Thomas I., 17
Strage, Henry, 177
Stramy, Robert, 304
Strasser, J. B., 210
Strasser, Susan, 7, 123
Strassmann, Paul A., 23, 213
Strauss, Anselm L., 262
Strauss, George, 232
Strebel, Paul, 220
Streeten, Paul, 9
Strickland, A. J., 269
Stringer, Robert A., 271
Strobel, Frederick R., 198
Strong, Robert A., 215
Stross, Randall E., 210
Stuckey, M. M., 74
Stulberg, Joseph B., 52
Stuller, Jay, 300
Stumm, David Arthur, 252

Sturdivant, Frederick D., 138
Sturgess, Brian T., 277
Stutely, Richard, 32
Subrahmanyam, Marti G., 66, 215
Suchlicki, Jaime, 157
Sullivan, David R., 197
Sullivan, Jeremiah J., 68
Sullivan, Teresa A., 16
Summer, Charles Edgar, 219
Sumners, Glenn E., 13
Sundem, Gary L., 183
Sunkel, Osvaldo, 85
Surprenant, Carol F., 257
Suters, Everett T., 62
Sutija, George, 96
Sutton, Brenda, 29
Sutton, David P., 116
Sutton, Robert I., 223
Suzaki, Kiyoshi, 130, 185
Suzuki, Yoshio, 106, 200
Svigals, Jerome, 260
Sviokla, J. J., 72, 256
Swanson, Carl L., 24
Swanson, Gerald J., 83
Swanson, Richard A., 229
Swasy, Alecia, 238
Sweeney, Daniel J., 250
Sweeney, Dennis J., 182
Sweeny, Allen, 146
Sweet, Ann, 42
Swesnik, Richard H., 248
Swiss, Deborah J., 304
Symposium on the Importance of Biotechnology for Future Economic Development, 20
Syracuse University. Urban Transportation Institute, 295
Syrett, Michel, 167
Szilagyi, Andrew D., 219

Tabors, Richard D., 93
Taff, Charles Albert, 234, 284
Taguchi, Gen, 274
Taha, Hamdy A., 214
Takamiya, Susumu, 147
Takashima, Nobuyuki, 159
Tamarkin, Bob, 39
Tan, Augustine H. H., 106
Tanaka, H. William, 159
Tanaka, Hiroshi, 178
Tang, Victor, 150
Tannenbaum, Robert, 215
Tannenbaum, Stanley I., 46
Tapley, Mark, 157
Tarrant, John J., 33, 101
Tasley, Roberta, 257
Tate, David W., 63
Tatsuno, Sheridan, 121, 122
Taub, Richard P., 258
Tavel, Charles H., 19
Tavis, Lee A., 148
Taviss, Irene, 89
Tawadey, Kiran, 59
Taylor, Anthony Herbert, 27
Taylor, Bernard W., 182
Taylor, David A., 181
Taylor, Donald H., 13
Taylor, Frederick Winslow, 131

Taylor, James C., 230
Taylor, James R., 23, 187, 192
Taylor, John, 298
Taylor, John B., 172
Taylor, Marilyn L., 147
Taylor, Martin E., 146
Taylor, Michael, 148
Taylor, Peter, 281
Taylor, Robert L., 166
Taylor, William, 19
Teagan, Mark, 97
Teas, R. Kenneth, 252
Tedesco, Albert S., 178
Tedlow, Richard S., 27, 66, 190, 191, 287
Teece, David J., 127, 269
Teicholz, Tom, 20
Teichova, Alice, 148
Teitelman, Robert, 115, 254
Temin, Peter, 10
Tenner, Arthur R., 282
Tepper, Ron, 25
Terkel, M., 129
Terpstra, Vern, 102, 144
Terry, Robert W., 166
Tersine, Richard J., 153, 240
Tessmer, Martin, 142
Teutsch, Austin, 298
Teweles, Richard Jack, 44, 266
Thiederman, Sondra B., 25, 46
Thierauf, Robert J., 61, 127, 180
Thill, John V., 25
Thoburn, John T., 173
Thomas, Christopher R., 184
Thomas, Dan R. E., 268
Thomas, Dana Lee, 297
Thomas, David V., 141
Thomas, Howard, 126, 191
Thomas, L. Joseph, 130
Thomas, Lloyd Brewster, 200
Thomas, Peter W., 119
Thomas, R. David, 271
Thomas, Robert Joseph, 276
Thompson, Arthur A., 269
Thompson, Brad Lee, 177
Thompson, George, 134
Thompson, Howard Arthur, 187
Thompson, James D., 133
Thompson, Kenneth R., 139
Thompson, Marilyn W., 299
Thompson, Paul, 218
Thompson, Thomas W., 108
Thomsett, Michael C., 136, 260
Thomson, David, 256
Thord, Roland, 45
Thrainn Eggertsson, 142
Thrift, N. J., 148, 151
Thurley, Keith E., 147
Thurow, Lester C., 84, 86, 176, 288
Thygerson, Kenneth J., 108
Tichy, Noel M., 115, 224
Tiffany, Paul A., 265
Tijunelis, D., 239
Tilanus, C. B., 131
Tilling, Thomas, 156
Time, Inc, 33
Timm, Paul R., 45
Timmons, Jeffry A., 207, 208, 296

Timpe, A. Dale, 71, 135, 187, 228, 281
Tirole, Jean, 133
Tjosvold, Dean, 52, 305
Tjosvold, Mary M., 305
Tobe, Glenn R., 224
Todd, H. Ralph, 273
Toffler, Alvin, 10
Toffler, Alvin, 10, 261
Toffler, Barbara Ley, 30
Tōgō, Yukiyasu, 283
Tolchin, Martin, 156
Tolchin, Susan J., 156
Tomasko, Robert M., 138
Tomaskovic-Devey, Donald, 80
Tomlinson, Jim, 133
Tonak, Ertuğrul Ahmet, 204
Tongren, Hale N., 186
Torbert, William R., 177
Torgovo-promyshlennaia palata SSSR, 162
Torosian, Martin, 266
Tosches, Nick, 259
Tosi, Henry L., 219
Touche Ross & Co, 53
Toulouse-Lautrec, Henri de, 282
Tourevski, Mark, 264
Townsend, Kenneth N., 83
Townsend, Patrick L., 244
Tracey, William R., 92, 230
Trachtenberg, Jeffrey A., 166
Tracy, John A., 110
Traffic Service Corporation, 73
Train, John, 22, 37, 264, 267
Train, Kenneth, 201
Transamerica Corporation, 127
Traub, Marvin, 20
Treat, John Elting, 233
Trevor, Malcolm, 68
Triandis, Harry Charalambos, 242, 249
Trice, Harrison Miller, 58
Trimble, Vance H., 260
Trippi, Robert R., 236
Trompenaars, Fons, 47
Tropman, John E., 206
Trossmann, Ernst, 21
Trost, Gretchel, 234
Trout, Jack, 186, 190, 236
Troxel, James P., 177
Truell, Peter, 16
Trump, Donald, 285
Tsurumi, Yoshi, 148
Tuccille, Jerome, 285
Tuchman, Gaye, 280
Tuchman, Jeffrey N., 202
Tucker, Bob, 263
Tucker, Bruce, 294
Tucker, David, 233
Tucker, Kerry, 92
Tucker, Lewis R., 102
Tucker, Robert B., 71
Tufts University. Center for Environmental Management, 138
Tuleja, Tad, 256
Tull, Donald S., 193
Tuller, Lawrence W., 37, 102, 155, 295
Tung, Rosalie L., 149
Tunstall, Jeremy, 278
Turabian, Kate L., 80

Turban, Efraim, 174
Turnbull, Peter W., 103
Turner, Louis, 162
Turner, Stephen J., 43
Turney, Peter B. B., 185
Turoff, Murray, 279
Tushman, Michael, 218, 276
Tuttle, Donald L., 235
Twiss, Brian C., 249
Tyran, Michael R., 247
Tyson, Kirk W. M., 31
Tyson, Laura D'Andrea, 122
Uchenick, Joel, 271
Ulman, Lloyd, 137
Ulrich, David, 226
Umbaugh, Robert E., 180
Unger, Maurice Albert, 203, 247, 248
Ungson, Gerardo R., 52
United Nations, 285
United Nations Conference on Environment and Development (1992 : Rio de Janeiro, Brazil), 82, 95
United Nations. Economic Commission for Europe, 20
United Nations Institute for Training and Research, 84
United States, 49
United States Competitiveness in the World Economy (1984 : Harvard University Graduate School of Business Administration), 290
United States. Dept. of Education, 70
United States. Dept. of Health, Education, and Welfare, 185
United States. Dept. of Labor, 306
United States. President (1993- : Clinton), 120
University of Bradford. Management Centre, 76
University of California, Berkeley. Center for Japanese Studies, 268
University of California, Berkeley. Center for Research in Management, 127
University of California, Los Angeles. Institute of Industrial Relations, 121
University of Chicago, 90
University of Illinois at Urbana-Champaign. Dept. of Business Administration, 191
University of Michigan. Center for Japanese Studies, 14
University of Oxford. Faculty of Law, 59
University of Pittsburgh. Program in Corporate Culture, 58
University of South Carolina. College of Business Administration, 70
University of Southern California. International Business Education and Research Program, 260
University of Texas at Austin. Bureau of Business Administration, 57
University of Texas at Austin. Bureau of Business Research, 158
University of Texas at Austin. College of Business Research, 121
University of Warwick. Centre for Corporate Strategy and Change, 269
Uno, Kimio, 160
Updegrave, Walter L., 155
Urban, Glen L., 208
Urban Transportation Policy Seminar (1970: Syracuse Institute, 295

Uris, Auren, 174
Ury, William, 205
U.S.-Japan Automotive Industry Conference (5th : 1985 : University of Michigan), 14
Usry, Milton F., 68
Usunier, Jean-Claude, 102
Utterback, James M., 223
Uyterhoeven, Hugo E. R., 139

Vale, Philip A., 65
Valentine, Charles F., 144, 152
Valentine, Lloyd M., 26
Valla, Jean-Paul, 103
Van Breda, Michael F., 3
Van Doren, Glenn H., 26
Van Every, Elizabeth J., 23
Van Horne, James C., 65, 144
Van Til, Jon, 167
Van Velsor, Ellen, 301
Van de Ven, Andrew H., 276
Vancil, Richard F., 40, 63, 174
Vander Weide, James H., 38
Vanderkolk, Barbara Schwarz, 92
Varadarajan, P., 186
Varney, Glenn H., 304
Vaughan, Emmett J., 142
Vaughn, Donald E., 65
Vaught, H. T., 65
Vavra, Terry G., 72
Veale, Stuart R., 155
Velasquez, Manuel G., 28
Vella, Carolyn M., 31, 141
Venedikian, Harry M., 103
Vernon, Raymond, 147, 287
Vernon-Wortzel, Heidi, 138, 145
Vertin, James R., 154
Verzariu, Pompiliu, 70
Vesper, Karl H., 207
Vietor, Richard H. K., 140, 279, 283
Vigeland, Carl A., 120
Vignola, Leonard, 59
Vik, Gretchen N., 43
Viksnins, George J., 105
Viner, Aron, 104, 105
Viscione, Jerry A., 109
Vise, David A., 286
Vlachoutsicos, Charalambos A., 126
Vladimir, Andrew, 283
Vlasho, Louis, 68
Voehl, Frank, 245
Vogel, David, 24
Vogel, Ezra F., 49
Vogel, Harold L., 229
Volcker, Paul A., 150
Vollmann, Thomas E., 125, 240
Von Glinow, Mary Ann Young, 122
Von Hoffman, Nicholas, 37
Von Winterfeldt, Detlof, 75
Vujovich, Dian, 204

Wachowicz, John Martin, 65
Wacht, Richard F., 211
Wachtel, Howard M., 84
Waddell, William C., 269
Wade, John H., 252
Wagar, W. Warren, 285
Wagley, Robert A., 139

Waitley, Denis, 71
Walden, Gene, 189
Waldfogel, Joel, 53
Waldo, Charles N., 79
Walker, Blair S., 170
Walker, Charls E., 17
Walker, Danielle Medina, 127
Walker, David F., 139
Walker, Ernest Winfield, 259
Walker, Joseph A., 215
Walker, Judith P., 304
Walker, Orville C., 188, 252
Walker, Thomas, 127
Wallace, James, 114
Wallace, Marc J., 47, 76, 219
Wallace, Phyllis Ann, 101
Wallace, Sherwood Lee, 153
Wallace, Wanda A., 13
Walley, Brian Halford, 62
Walmsley, Julian, 112, 254
Walsh, E. J., 146
Walsh, Loren, 245
Walsh, William I., 117
Walt Disney Productions, 298
Walter, Ingo, 36, 146, 151, 154, 307
Walton, Clarence Cyril, 29
Walton, Mary, 77
Walton, Richard E., 42, 52, 182, 219, 222, 230
Walton, Sam, 298
Walton, Thomas, 11
Walton, William B., 91
Wang, An, 298
Wang, Charles B., 142
Wann, Peter, 117
Wansell, Geoffrey, 116
Ward, G. Kingsley, 271, 272
Ward, John L., 79, 103
Ward, Michael, 59
Ward, Richard Alexander, 200
Ward, Scott, 57
Wareham, John, 99
Warfield, Gerald, 103
Waring, Marilyn, 258
Waring, Stephen P., 131
Warr, Peter G., 281
Warren, Carl S., 3
Warren, Elizabeth, 16
Warren, J. Donald, 141
Warren, James F., 27
Warren, Melinda, 120, 292
Warrington, M. B., 103
Warsh, David, 87
Warshauer, William, 211
Warshaw, Martin R., 187, 190
Warshofsky, Fred, 143
Wartman, William, 283
Wasendorf, Russell R., 44
Washburn, Stewart A., 187
Washington Researchers, 85
Washington University (Saint Louis, Mo.). Center for the Study of American Business, 55, 120,
Wasserman, William, 249
Wat, Leslie, 249
Waterman, D. A., 101, 102
Waterman, Robert H., 128, 132, 220
Waters, Dan, 179
Watkins, Alfred J., 22, 74

Watson, Hugh J., 24, 174, 180
Watson, J. W. Henry, 265
Watson, Robert, 260
Watson, Thomas J., 149
Wattenberg, Ben J., 293
Watts, Reginald, 23
Wayne, F. Stanford, 25
Weaver, Paul, 67
Webber, Alan M., 13
Webber, Ross A., 99, 219
Weber, Jack, 176
Wedemeyer, Richard A., 37
Wehrung, Donald A., 251
Weichhardt, Reiner, 97
Weidenbaum, Murray L., 55, 140, 288, 292
Weihrich, Heinz, 176, 179, 180
Weil, David N., 284
Weil, Robert I., 3
Weilbacher, William M., 6
Weinberg, Charles B., 188, 190, 212
Weinberg, Steve, 119
Weiner, Edith, 224
Weinhold, Wolf A., 80
Weinstein, Art, 186
Weintraub, Andrew, 82
Weisberg, Anne C., 203
Weisbord, Marvin Ross, 131
Weisbrod, Burton Allen, 211
Weiss, Alan, 56
Weiss, Ann E., 264
Weiss, Joseph W., 28, 220
Weiss, Lawrence David, 143
Weiss, Martin, 116
Weiss, Michael J., 294
Weiss, Robert Stuart, 196
Weisweiller, Rudi, 112
Weitz, Barton A., 256
Weitzen, H. Skip, 138
Weizer, Norman, 141
Welch, Jack, 115
Welch, Russell L., 283
Wellins, Richard S., 305
Wellons, Philip A., 170
Wells, Walter, 43
Welsch, Glenn A., 4, 22
Welsh, Frank, 109
Welton, Ralph E., 110
Wenar, Leif, 120
Wendell, Paul J., 58
Wendt, Henry, 145
Wendy's International, 271
Wenk, E., 277
Wensberg, Peter C., 166
Werhane, Patricia Hogue, 29
Werner, Frank M., 282
Werner, Raymond J., 248
Werth, Barry, 233
Werther, William B., 231
West, Michael, 101
West, Thomas L., 27
Westbrook, Jay Lawrence, 16
Westerfield, Randolph, 64
Western Electric Company, 231
Westfall, Ralph L., 193
Westin, Alan F., 213
Westoff, Leslie Aldridge, 301
Weston, J. Fred, 55, 64, 65, 66

Wetherbe, James C., 181
Wexley, Kenneth N., 219, 272
Weygandt, Jerry J., 4
Wharton School. Pension Research Council, 213
Wheale, Peter, 277
Wheatley, Walter, 174
Wheble, B. S., 197
Wheeler, Robert R., 233
Wheelwright, Steven C., 31, 83, 209, 292
Whetten, David A., 223
Whinston, Andrew B., 128
White, Barbara, 302
White, Barton, 22
White, Colin, 227
White, Jane, 301
White, John A., 240
White, Joseph B., 14
White, Lawrence, 281
White, Lawrence J., 36, 253
White, Merry I., 103
White, Randall P., 301
White, Richard M., 207
White, Thomas I., 28
White, William L., 105
Whited, Maurine, 233
Whitehill, Arthur M., 163
Whiteley, Nigel, 77
Whiteley, Richard C., 72
Whiting, D. P., 112
Whitmyer, Claude, 255
Whittington, Ray, 13
Whybark, D. Clay, 240
Wick, Calhoun W., 175
Wickens, Peter, 149
Wiedemer, John P., 202, 248
Wiggins, Ben T., 278
Wiggs, Garland D., 231
Wilbur, L. Perry, 173
Wilbur, Robert H., 211
Wilcock, John, 227
Wilcox, Kirkland A., 5
Wild, Ray, 175, 239
Wilder, Claudyne, 244
Wilen, Tracey, 30
Wiles, Russ, 204
Wilkens, Joanne, 303
Wilkins, Alan L., 222
Wilkinson, C. W., 43
Wilkinson, Dorothy Colby Menning, 43
Wilkinson, Joseph W., 25, 180
Wilkinson, William R., 100
Willborn, Steven L., 95
Williams, C. Arthur, 250
Williams, Frank Jefferson, 43
Williams, J. Clifton, 176
Williams, Michael R., 194
Williams, Oliver F., 29
Williams, Robert, 97
Williams, Shirley, 286
Williams, Steve, 161
Williams, Thomas Arthur, 182
Williamson, Alistair D., 128, 187
Williamson, J. Peter, 154
Williamson, John N., 101
Williamson, Oliver E., 133, 142
Willig, Robert D., 133
Willingham, John J., 13

Willis, Jerry, 197
Wills, Garry, 166
Willson, James D., 13, 58
Wilson, Aubrey, 133, 241
Wilson, Earl Ray, 107
Wilson, J. F., 184
Wilson, James Q., 96, 293
Wilson, Jeanne M., 305
Wilson, John Donald, 39
Wilson, John Oliver, 289
Wilson, John W., 295
Wilson, Peter, 150
Wilson, R. M. S., 69
Wilson, Richard S., 21
Wilson, William R., 57
Winans, Christopher, 111
Winans, R. Foster, 297
Wineman, Jean D., 213
Winfield, Fairlee E., 193
Winkler, Earl R., 96
Winner, Langdon, 277
Winston, Brian, 193
Winston, Wayne L., 214
Wise, George, 300
Wise, Mark, 98
Wiseman, Charles, 182
Witney, Fred, 137
Witt, Stephen F., 236, 283
Wittenberg-Cox, Avivah, 185
Wizenberg, Larry, 209
Woelfel, Charles J., 64, 104
Wojahn, Ellen, 55
Wokutch, Richard E., 14
Wolcutt, Janet L., 201
Wolf, Avner S., 144
Wolf, Charles, 36
Wolf, Harold Arthur, 107
Wolf, Thomas, 211
Wolff, Edward N., 165
Wolff, Michael, 265
Wolgast, Elizabeth Hankins, 163
Wong, M. Anthony, 110
Wonnacott, Paul, 85
Wonnacott, Ronald J., 82, 85, 262
Wonnacott, Thomas H., 82, 262
Wood, Donald F., 234
Wood, Robert Chapman, 246
Woodgate, Ralph W., 185
Woods, James D., 114
Woods, Michael D., 69
Woodward, Douglas P., 157
Woodward, Harry, 220, 223
Woodward, Mary Beckman, 223
Woodworth, Warner, 129
Worcester, Robert M., 192
World Bank, 81
World Business Academy, 130
World Future Society, 277
World Resources Institute, 126
Woronoff, Jon, 159, 192
Worthy, James C., 212
Wortzel, Lawrence H., 145
Wrege, Charles D., 274
Wren, Daniel A., 174
Wright, David, 50
Wright, George, 83
Wright, Harold A., 231

Wright, J. Patrick, 115
Wright, James D., 263
Wright, Milburn D., 256
Wright, Peter L., 270
Wright, Richard W., 108
Wright, Russell O., 165
Wrightsman, Dwayne, 105
Wriston, Walter B., 201
WuDunn, Sheryl, 40
Wurman, Richard Saul, 45
Wurster, Ralph, 245
Wyse, Lois, 272

Yago, Glenn, 163
Yamamoto, Shichihei, 37
Yamamura, Kōzō, 159
Yankelovich, Daniel, 165
Yate, Martin John, 93
Yates, Douglas, 52
Yeager, Neil M., 167
Yep, Dorothy S. M., 71
Yergin, Daniel, 93, 172, 233
Yochelson, John N., 290
Yoder, Janice D., 167
Yoffie, David B., 50, 147, 151, 157
Yomo, Hiroshi, 200
Yonekawa, Shin, 284
York, Arthur M., 46
Yoshida, Mamoru, 157
Yoshihara, Hideki, 284
Yoshino, M. Y., 52
Young, Allan E., 65
Young, Ardis Armstrong, 92
Young, George, 90
Young, Jeffrey S., 162
Young, Karen M., 91
Young, Philip K. Y., 81, 87
Youngman, Roy, 180
Yukl, Gary A., 219
Yunker, James A., 36

Zachary, G. Pascal, 198
Zalaha, Jack W., 285
Zaleznik, Abraham, 101, 122, 166, 168, 176
Zaltman, Gerald, 75, 188
Zander, Alvin Frederick, 211
Zarb, Frank G., 155
Zawacki, Robert A., 223
Zeckhauser, Richard, 76, 178
Zeff, Stephen A., 4
Zeikel, Arthur, 153
Zeitz, Baila, 300
Zelazny, Gene, 33
Zelizer, Viviana A. Rotman, 201
Zemke, Ron, 307
Zenoff, David B., 109
Zenz, Gary Joseph, 134
Zey, Michael G., 196
Zielinski, Robert, 285
Zientara, Marguerite, 302
Zigarelli, Michael A., 91
Zigarmi, Drea, 175
Zigarmi, Patricia, 175
Zikmund, William G., 174, 192
Zimmer, Sandra C., 254
Zimmerman, Frederick Michael, 62

Zimmerman, Jean, 258
Zimmerman, Mark, 160, 206
Zimney, Dave, 213
Zinbarg, Edward D., 153
Zinsser, August, 285
Ziporyn, Terra Diane, 279
Zlatkovich, Charles T., 4
Zonderman, Jon, 130
Zuboff, Shoshana, 13
Zuckerman, Marilyn R., 10
Zurcher, Louis A., 167
Zweig, Martin, 267
Zweig, Phillip L., 228
Zysman, John, 292

TITLE INDEX

The numbers after each entry in the list below refer to page numbers in the main section.

The ABCs of international finance, 150
The Abilene paradox and other meditations on management, 217
Abuse in the workplace: management remedies and bottom line impact, 161
Academics and entrepreneurs: developing university-industry relations, 139
The acceptance of human resource innovation: lessons for manangement, 229
Accidental empires: how the boys of Silicon Valley make their millions, battle foreign competition, and still can't get a date, 50
Accidental millionaire: the rise and fall of Steven Jobs at Apple Computer, 11
Accountant's desk handbook, 3
Accountant's encyclopedia, revised, 3
Accountant's handbook of formulas and tables, 32
Accountants' cost handbook: a guide for management accounting, 68
Accountants' handbook, 3
Accounting, 3
Accounting & management: field study perspectives, 182
Accounting, a management approach, 182
Accounting: an international perspective, 144
Accounting and its legal implications: a guide for managers, business owners, and entrepreneurs, 63
Accounting, budgeting, and finance: a reference for managers, 104
Accounting for corporate reputation, 63
Accounting for fixed assets, 34
Accounting for governmental and nonprofit entities, 107
Accounting for management control, 182
Accounting for managers: text and cases, 182
Accounting for success: a history of Price Waterhouse in America, 1890-1990, 236
Accounting handbook for nonaccountants, 3
Accounting information systems, 3
Accounting information systems: concepts and practice for effective decision making, 3
Accounting principles, 3
Accounting, text and cases, 3
Accounting, the basis for business decisions, 3
Accounting: the basis for business decisions, 3
Accounting theory, 3
The accounting wars, 5
Accurate business forecasting, 111
Acquiring and merging businesses, 53
Acquiring the future: America's survival and success in the global economy, 290
Acquisitions and mergers, 53
The acquisitions manual, 53
Action science, 262
Active asset allocation: state-of-the-art portfolio policies, strategies & tactics, 12
Activity-based costing for marketing and manufacturing, 5
The adaptive corporation, 10

Adding value: a systematic guide to business-driven management and leadership, 268
Adhocracy: the power to change, 220
Advanced accounting, 4
Advanced management accounting, 182
Advanced project management: a structured approach, 135
Advanced strategies in financial risk management, 107
Advances in bond analysis & portfolio strategies, 21
Advances in business financial management: a collection of readings, 63
Adventures of a bystander, 81
Advertising, 6
The advertising advantage, 6
The advertising and promotion challenge: vaguely right or precisely wrong, 6
Advertising in contemporary society: perspectives toward understanding, 6
Advertising: its role in modern marketing, 6
The advertising kit: a complete guide for small businesses, 6
Advertising management, 6
Advertising media planning, 7
Advertising theory & practice, 6
Advertising's hidden effects: manufacturers' advertising and retail pricing, 6
Advice, a high profit business: a guide for consultants and other entrepreneurs, 55
After the breakup: assessing the new post-AT&T divestiture era, 279
After the merger: managing the shockwaves, 53
Aftermarketing: how to keep customers for life through relationship marketing, 72
Aftershock: helping people through corporate change, 220
Against all odds: the story of the Toyota Motor Corporation and the family that created it, 283
The age of diminished expectations: U.S. economic policy in the 1990s, 290
The age of giant corporations: a microeconomic history of American business, 1914-1992, 138
The age of paradox, 220
The age of the common millionaire, 199
The age of unreason, 220
Agenda 21: the Earth Summit strategy to save our planet, 82
Agents of influence, 291
Agnelli and the network of Italian power, 8
The agrarian origins of American capitalism, 289
Agribusiness management, 8
AI: the tumultuous history of the search for artificial intelligence, 12
AIDS in the workplace: legal questions and practical answers, 9
The alchemy of finance: reading the mind of the market, 154
The Alexander complex: the dreams that drive the great businessmen, 33
Alfred Nobel: a biography, 210

Alliance capitalism: the social organization of Japanese business, 268
The almanac of investments, 154
Almost perfect: how a bunch of regular guys built WordPerfect Corporation, 304
Altered harvest: agriculture, genetics, and the fate of the world's food supply, 111
Alternative work schedules: selecting—implementing—and evaluating, 123
Alternatives to lean production: work organization in the Swedish auto industry, 297
The AMA handbook of marketing for the service industries, 256
The AMA handbook of supervisory management, 273
AMA management handbook, 173
The ambassador from Wall Street: the story of Thomas W. Lamont, J.P. Morgan's chief executive: a biography, 166
Ambitious men: their drives, dreams, and delusions, 99
America and the new economy: how new competitive standards are radically changing American workplaces, 165
America in the global '90s: the shape of the future—how you can profit from it, 83
America tomorrow: the choices we face: a report from the Governance Project, 289
America's economic resurgence: a bold new strategy, 289
America's management challenge: capitalizing on change, 173
America's new competitors: the challenge of the newly industrializing countries, 291
America's new economy: the basic guide, 288
American banking in crisis: views from leading financial services CEOs, 16
American business, a two-minute warning: ten changes managers must make to survive into the 21st century, 126
American business: an introduction, 126
American business and the quick fix, 126
The American business cycle: continuity and change, 26
American business values, 27
American economic policy in the 1980s, 290
The American edge: leveraging manufacturing's hidden assets, 292
American Express: the unofficial history of the people who built the great financial empire, 9
American government: institutions and policies, 293
American independent business: formation, operations, and philosophy for the 1980s, 206
American industry: structure, conduct, performance, 138
American living standards: threats and challenges, 69
American manufacturing in a global market, 292
American multinationals and Japan: the political economy of Japanese capital controls, 1899-1980, 156
American power, the new world order and the Japanese challenge, 291
American renaissance: our life at the turn of the 21st century, 285

American steel: hot metal men and the resurrection of the Rust Belt, 265
The American way of health: how medicine is changing and what it means to you, 120
The Americans with Disabilities Act: a review of best practices, 119
Analysis for financial management, 63
Analysis for improving performance: tools for diagnosing organizations & documenting workplace expertise, 229
Analysis for strategic market decisions, 186
An analysis of the new financial institutions: changing technologies, financial structures, distribution systems, and deregulation, 109
Analyzing financial statements, 109
Anatomy of a business plan, 60
The anatomy of a business strategy: Bell, Western Electric, and the origins of the American telephone industry, 10
The anatomy of a great executive, 99
The anatomy of major projects: a study of the reality of project management, 135
The anatomy of power, 236
And the wolf finally came: the decline of the American steel industry, 265
The antitrust laws: a primer, 11
Apocalypse on Wall Street, 266
Applied ethics: a reader, 96
Applied linear statistical models: regression, analysis of variance, and experimental designs, 249
Applied mathematics for business, economics, and the social sciences, 194
Applied microeconomics, 197
The applied psychology of work behavior: a book of readings, 242
Applying psychology in business: the handbook for managers and human resource professionals, 230
The appraisal of real estate, 248
Appreciative management and leadership: the power of positive thought and action in organizations, 225
Approaching zero: the extraordinary underworld of hackers, phreakers, virus writers, and keyboard criminals, 49
April fools: an insider's account of the rise and collapse of Drexel Burnham, 80
Architecture and the corporation: the creative intersection, 11
"Are they selling her lips?": advertising and identity, 6
Armand Hammer: the untold story, 119
The armchair economist: economics and everyday life, 85
The art and science of entrepreneurship, 206
Art for work: the new renaissance in corporate collecting, 63
The art of human-computer interface design, 123
The art of M&A: a merger acquisition buyout guide, 53
The art of managing human resources, 184
The art of product development: from concept of market, 208
The art of reckoning: analysis of performance criteria, 26
The art of the long view, 268

The **Arthur** D. Little forecast on information technology and productivity: making the integrated enterprise work, 141
The **Arthur** Young business plan guide, 206
The **Arthur** Young guide to raising venture capital, 295
The **Arthur** Young management guide to mergers and acquisitions, 53
The **articulate** executive: improving written, interpersonal, and group communication, 306
Artificial intelligence applications for manufacturing, 12
As we forgive our debtors: bankruptcy and consumer credit in America, 16
Asia's new industrial world, 160
Asian stockmarkets: the inside story, 266
The **aspirin** wars: money, medicine, and 100 years of rampant competition, 12
At America's service: how corporations can revolutionize the way they treat their customers, 256
At any cost: corporate greed, women and the Dalkon Shield, 152
The **atlas** of economic indicators: a visual guide to market forces and the Federal Reserve, 85
Attaining manufacturing excellence: just-in-time, total quality, total people involvement, 238
Audit sampling: an introduction to statistical sampling in auditing, 13
Auditing, 13
Auditing, an integrated approach, 13
Auditing concepts and methods: a guide to current auditing theory and practice, 13
Auditing, integrated concepts and procedures, 13
Augustine's laws, 135
Authentic leadership: courage in action, 166
The **automated** factory handbook: technology and management, 239
Automating global financial management, 63
Automation, production systems, and computer integrated manufacturing, 185
Autopsy of a merger, 53

Bad business: the OPM scandal and the seduction of the establishment, 214
Bad news at Black Rock: the sell-out of CBS News, 279
Bailout: an insider's account of bank failures and rescues, 15
Balancing act: how managers can integrate successful careers and fulfilling personal lives, 99
The **Baldrige** quality system: the do-it-yourself way to transform your business, 173
Bank marketing: a guide to strategic planning, 15
Bank marketing handbook: how to compete in the financial services industry, 15
Bankers, builders, knaves, and thieves: the $300 million scam at ESM, 96
The **bankers'** handbook, 17
Banking deregulation and the new competition in financial services, 17
Banking in the Far East, 1990: structures and sources of finance, 17
Banking markets and financial institutions, 17
Banking on Black enterprise: the potential of emerging firms for revitalizing urban economies, 199
Bankrupt: restoring the health and profitability of our banking system, 17
Bankruptcy 1995: the coming collapse of America and how to stop it, 83
Banks, borrowers, and the establishment: a revisionist account of the international debt crisis, 74
Banks, finance and investments in Germany, 17
Barbarians at the gate: the fall of RJR Nabisco, 251
Bargaining across borders: how to negotiate business successfully anywhere in the world, 205
The **bargaining** manager: enhancing organizational results through effective negotiation, 205
Basic business communication, 43
Basic concepts in quantitative management, 264
Basic financial management, 26
Basic legal forms for business, 62
Basic marketing: a global-managerial approach, 186
Basic small business management, 259
Basic statistics: a modern approach, 265
Basic statistics for business and economics, 43, 262
Basics of qualitative research: grounded theory procedures and techniques, 262
Bass & Stogdill's handbook of leadership: theory, research, and managerial applications, 166
The **battle-weary** executive: a blueprint for new beginnings, 37
Beacham's marketing reference, 186
Bear hunting with the Politburo: a gritty first-hand account of Russia's young entrepreneurs—and why Soviet-style capitalism won't work, 94
Bear market investment strategies, 264
Bear trap: why Wall Street doesn't work, 297
Beating the Street: the best-selling author of One up on Wall Street shows you how to pick winning stocks and develop a strategy for mutual funds, 267
Becoming a courageous manager: overcoming career problems of new managers, 99
Becoming a manager: mastery of a new identity, 37
Before the computer: IBM, NCR, Burroughs, and Remington Rand and the industry they created, 1865-1956, 213
Behavior in organizations, 217
Behavior in organizations: an experiential approach, 217
Behavior of prices on Wall Street: market inclinations help prediction produce profits, 297
Behavioral analysis and measurement methods, 306
Behavioral issues in office design, 213
A **behavioral** theory of labor negotiations: an analysis of a social interaction system, 42
Behind closed doors: wheeling and dealing in the banking world, 17
Behind the boardroom door, 79
Behind the factory walls: decision making in Soviet and US enterprises, 126
Behind the veil of economics: essays in the worldly philosophy, 36
Beijing Jeep: the short, unhappy romance of American business in China, 10

Belly up: the collapse of the Penn Square Bank, 228
Ben & Jerry's, the inside scoop: how two real guys built a business with social conscience and a sense of humor, 42
Benchmarking for competitive advantage, 19
Benjamin Graham on value investing: lessons from the dean of Wall Street, 117
The best companies for women, 300
The Best of Inc. guide to marketing and selling, 186
The best of Japan, 208
A better idea: redefining the way Americans work, 126
Better mousetraps: product improvements that led to success, 208
Beyond ambition: how driven managers can lead better and live better, 100
Beyond blue economic horizons: U.S. trade performance and international competitiveness in the 1990s, 15
Beyond bureaucracy: essays on the development and evolution of human organization, 220
Beyond capitalism: the Japanese model of market economics, 158
Beyond compliance: a new industry view of the environment, 126
Beyond dispute: the invention of team syntegrity, 215
Beyond free trade: firms, governments, and global competition, 151
Beyond IBM, 149
Beyond LANs: client/server computing, 41
Beyond Machiavelli: tools for coping with conflict, 227
Beyond management by objectives, 307
Beyond MaxiMarketing: the new power of caring and daring, 186
Beyond national borders: reflections on Japan and the world, 159
Beyond our means: how America's long years of debt, deficits and reckless borrowing now threaten to overwhelm us, 288
Beyond partnership: strategies for innovation and lean supply, 14
Beyond rational management: mastering the paradoxes and competing demands of high performance, 225
Beyond spinoff: military and commercial technologies in a changing world, 277
Beyond the bottom line: 15 key strategies for today's financial manager, 63
Beyond the bottom line: measuring world class performance, 185
Beyond the deal: optimizing merger and acquisition value, 53
Beyond the hype: rediscovering the essence of management, 173
Beyond the limits: confronting global collapse, envisioning a sustainable future, 82
Beyond the quick fix: managing five tracks to organizational success, 173
Beyond the trust gap: forging a new partnership between managers and their employers, 100
Beyond the twin deficits: a trade strategy for the 1990s, 15

Beyond total quality management: toward the emerging paradigm, 281
The big bang: an investor's guide to the changing city, 154
Big blues: the unmaking of IBM, 149
The big boys: power and position in American business, 19
The big fix: inside the S & L scandal: how an unholy alliance of politics and money destroyed America's banking system, 253
The big score: the billion-dollar story of Silicon Valley, 198
The big six: the selling out of America's top accounting firms, 5
The big time: The Harvard Business School's most successful class—and how it shaped America, 119
The billion-dollar molecule: one company's quest for the perfect drug, 233
The biotechnological challenge, 19
Biotechnology: an industry comes of age, 19
Biotechnology and economic development: [papers from the Economic Commission for Europe Symposium on the Importance of Biotechnology for Future Economic Development, June 1985, Szeged, Hungary, 20
Biotechnology, the science and the business, 19
Biotechnology: the university-industrial complex, 19
Birth of a new world: an open moment for international leadership, 151
Black and gold, 264
The Black manager: making it in the corporate world, 8
The black manager: making it in the corporate world, 8
Black managers: the case of the banking industry, 8
Black Monday and the future of financial markets, 265
The Blackwell guide to Wall Street, 254
Blood and wine: the unauthorized story of the Gallo wine empire, 114
Blood in the streets: investment profits in a world gone mad, 154
Blue magic: the people, power, and politics behind the IBM personal computer, 149
Blunders in international business, 144
Board games: the changing shape of corporate power, 53
Boards of directors and the privately owned firm: a guide for owners, officers, and directors, 79
Boards of directors: their changing roles, structure, and information needs, 79
Boards that make a difference: a new design for leadership in nonprofit and public organizations, 79
Body and soul: profits with principles, the amazing success story of Anita Roddick & the Body Shop, 20
Boiling point: Republicans, Democrats, and the decline of middle-class prosperity, 198
Boone, 234
The borderless world: power and strategy in the interlinked economy, 158
Branding in action: cases and strategies for profitable brand management, 21

Break-away thinking: how to challenge your business assumptions (and why you should), 126
Break-even analyses: basic model, variants, extensions, 21
Breaking financial boundaries: global capital, national deregulation, and financial services firms, 108
Breaking into the boardroom: when talent and hard work aren't enough, 301
Breaking the bank: the decline of BankAmerica, 16
Breaking the glass ceiling: can women reach the top of America's largest corporations, 301
Breaking the mold: women, men, and time in the new corporate world, 304
Breaking up the bank: rethinking an industry under siege, 17
Breaking with tradition: women and work, the new facts of life, 258
Breakpoints: how managers exploit radical business change, 220
The breakthrough illusion: corporate America's failure to move from innovation to mass production, 274
Breakthrough partnering: creating a collective enterprise advantage, 244
Breakthroughs!, 208
Bridging cultural barriers for corporate success: how to manage the multicultural work force, 46
Bringing innovation to market: how to break corporate and customer barriers, 208
Britain's productivity gap, 134
British investment in a united Germany, 156
Broadband: business services, technologies, and strategic impact, 50
The brothers: the Saatchi & Saatchi story, 252
Budgeting: profit planning and control, 22
Building a chain of customers: linking business functions to create the world class company, 225
Building a mail order business: a complete manual for success, 172
Building an effective corporate women's group, 303
Building productive teams: an action guide and resource book, 304
Building the information-age organization: structure, control, and information technologies, 141
Building the strategically-responsive organization, 126
Building your business plan: a step-by-step approach, 60
Built to last: successful habits of visionary companies, 272
Bullseyes and blunders: stories of business success & failure, 126
Burning down the house: how greed, deceit, and bitter revenge destroyed E.F. Hutton, 88
Business & government, 139
The business amazons, 303
Business and economics statistics with computer applications, 265
Business and public policy, 139
Business and society: a managerial approach, 138
Business and society: corporate strategy, public policy, ethics, 138, 261
Business and society: dimensions of conflict and cooperation, 139
Business and society: economic, moral, and political foundations: text and readings, 23
Business and the culture of the enterprise society, 58
Business as a learning community, 220
Business classics: fifteen key concepts for managerial success, 173
Business communication: a process approach, 25
Business cycles and forecasting, 26
Business cycles: theory and evidence, 26
Business enterprise in American history, 63
Business environment and business ethics: the social, moral, and the political dimensions of management, 27
Business environment and public policy: implications for management and strategy formulation, 140
Business ethics, 27, 28
Business ethics & common sense, 27
Business ethics: a managerial, stakeholder approach, 28
Business ethics: a philosophical reader, 28
Business, ethics, and the environment: the public policy debate, 95
Business ethics: concepts and cases, 28
Business ethics: Japan and the global economy, 28
Business ethics: reflections from a Platonic point of view, 28
Business ethics: the state of the art, 28
Business forecasting, 30, 31
Business forecasting methods, 31
Business, government, and public policy: concepts and practices, 140
Business, government, and society: a managerial perspective: text and cases, 139
Business, government, and the public, 140
Business history of general trading companies: proceedings of the Fuji conference, 284
Business in Mexico: managerial behavior, protocol, and etiquette, 30
Business in the age of information, 23
Business information systems: an introduction, 23
The business insurance handbook, 143
Business law and the regulatory environment: concepts and cases, 43
Business logistics management, 32
Business marketing management: a strategic view of industrial and organizational markets, 132
Business marketing management: an organizational approach: text and cases, 132
Business merger and acquisition strategies: a handbook for entrepreneurs and managers, 53
Business Mexico: business & investment opportunities in North America's hottest economy, 197
Business not as usual: rethinking our individual, corporate, and industrial strategies for global competition, 127
The business of art, 11
The business of business: managing with style, 173
The business of ethics and business, 28
Business organisation, 174
Business organization and the myth of the market economy, 113

The business plan guide for independent consultants, 25
Business plans that win $$$: lessons from the MIT Enterprise Forum, 206
Business plans that win venture capital, 206
Business policy and strategic management, 60
Business policy: text and cases, 63
Business policy: texts and cases, 63
Business process reengineering: breakpoint strategies for market dominance, 281
Business research methods, 127, 174
The business researcher's handbook, 85
Business sense: exercising management's five freedoms, 268
Business strategy in practice, 268
Business systems for microcomputers: concept, design, and implementation, 23
Business telematics: corporate networks for the information age, 23
The business value of computers, 23
Business without bosses: how self-managing teams are building high-performing companies, 305
Business without economists: an irreverent guide, 31
Business writing at its best, 33
Business writing with style: strategies for success, 33
The business-to-business direct marketing handbook, 78
Business-to-business direct marketing: proven direct response methods to generate more leads and sales, 132
Buying into America: how foreign money is changing the face of our nation, 156
By way of advice: growth strategies for the market driven world: a view from the garden, 82

Call me Pat: the autobiography of the man Howard Hughes chose to lead Hughes Aircraft, 124
Call me Roger, 261
Can America compete, 140
Can ethics be taught?: perspectives, challenges, and approaches at Harvard Business School, 28
Can they do that?: a guide to your rights on the job, 91
Can unions survive?: the rejuvenation of the American labor movement, 284
The capital budgeting decision: economic analysis of investment projects, 35
The capital budgeting handbook, 35
Capital budgeting: planning and control of capital expenditures, 35
Capital choices: changing the way America invests in industry, 35
Capital city: London as a financial centre, 108
Capital for profit: the triumph of Ricardian political economy over Marx and the neoclassical, 85
Capital ideas: the improbable origins of modern Wall Street, 104
Capital, inflation, and the multinationals, 141
Capital investment series, 35
Capital markets and institutions, 35
Capital markets in Korea and the Far East, 81
Capital markets: institutions and instruments, 35
Capitalism against capitalism, 36

Capitalism versus pragmatic market socialism: a general equilibrium evaluation, 36
Capitalist fools: tales of American business, from Carnegie to Forbes to the Milken gang, 37
The capitalist revolution: fifty propositions about prosperity, equality, and liberty, 36
Captain Money and the golden girl: the J. David affair, 255
The care and feeding of ideas, 70
Career crash: America's new crisis—and who survives, 37
Career development in organizations, 37
Career management in organizations: a practical human resource planning approach, 184
The career psychology of women, 297
Cargill: trading the world's grain, 38
Case problems in finance, 63
Case problems in international finance, 150
Case problems in management accounting, 183
Case studies in business ethics, 28
Cases in advertising and communications management, 6
Cases in advertising and promotion management, 6
Cases in consumer behavior, 57
Cases in operations management: strategy and structure, 127
Cash, cash, cash: the three principles of business survival and success, 38
The cashless society, 71
Catching up?: organizational and management change in the ex-Socialist block, 221
The Catholic bishops and the economy: a debate, 38
The Catholic ethic and the spirit of capitalism, 263
Centralization and decentralization; which, when and how much, 174
CEO: building a $400 million company from the ground up, 154
CEO: who gets to the top in America, 40
Certain trumpets: the call of leaders, 166
The CFO's handbook, 63
The chaebol: Korea's new industrial might, 52
The challenge of hidden profits: reducing corporate bureaucracy and waste, 134
The challenge of organizational change: how companies experience it and leaders guide it, 221
Challenges & opportunities for business in post-apartheid South Africa, 27
Challenges and opportunities: from now to 2001, 277
Challenges to American values: society, business, and religion, 287
Change and challenge in the world economy, 84
Change by design, 221
Change management: a model for effective organizational performance, 221
The change masters: innovations for productivity in the American corporation, 275
The change of a lifetime: employment patterns among Japan's managerial elite, 100
The change resisters: how they prevent progress and what managers can do about them, 221
Changes in western European banking, 17
Changing alliances, 13
Changing course: a global business perspective on

development and the environment: executive summary, 82
Changing fortunes: the world's money and the threat to American leadership, 150
Changing roles of financial management: getting close to the business, 63
Changing the essence: the art of creating and leading fundamental change in organizations, 221
The changing workplace: a guide to managing the people, organizational, and regulatory aspects of office technology, 213
Channels of desire: mass images and the shaping of American consciousness, 6
Charged bodies: people, power, and paradox in Silicon Valley, 198
Charismatic leadership: the elusive factor in organizational effectiveness, 99
Charting commodity market price behavior, 44
Charting the corporate mind: graphic solutions to business conflicts, 75
Charting the course for business growth through the 1990's: interviews, 289
The Chase: the Chase Manhattan Bank, N.A., 1945-1985, 39
Cheap but good marketing research, 192
Checks unbalanced: the quiet side of public spending, 286
Chester I. Barnard and the guardians of the managerial state, 18
Chicago guide to preparing electronic manuscripts: for authors and publishers, 90
China wakes: the struggle for the soul of a rising power, 40
The chip war: the battle for the world of tomorrow, 143
Choices: an introduction to decision theory, 75
Choosing and using a consultant: a manager's guide to consulting services, 56
Choosing the right pond: human behavior and the quest for status, 85
Chronicles of corporate change: management lessons from AT&T and its offspring, 10
Chrysanthemums and thorns: the untold story of modern Japan, 158
The city revolution: causes and consequences, 104
City within a state: a portrait of Britain's financial world, 108
The clash of cultures: managers and professionals, 240
Classic readings in organizational behavior, 217
Classic readings in self-managing teamwork: 20 of the most important articles, 255
The classic touch: lessons in leadership from Homer to Hemingway, 166
Classics: an investor's anthology, 154
Classics II: another investor's anthology, 154
Classics of organization theory, 215
Classics of organizational behavior, 217
Clay and Wheble's Modern merchant banking, 197
Climbing the corporate Matterhorn, 100
Closing plants: planning and implementing strategies, 234
The clustering of America, 294
A cold peace: America, Japan, Germany, and the struggle for supremacy, 294

Collapse of an industry: nuclear power and the contradictions of U.S. policy, 212
Collective bargaining, 42
Collective bargaining and industrial relations: from theory to policy and practice, 136
Collision course: the truth about airline safety, 7
Collision: GM, Toyota, Volkswagen and the race to own the 21st century, 14
Collision: how the rank and file took back the teamsters, 144
Comeback: the fall and rise of the American automobile industry, 14
Comeback: the restoration of American banking power in the new world economy, 153
Coming full circle: an economic history of the Pacific Rim, 227
The coming global boom: how to benefit now from tomorrow's dynamic world economy, 83
The coming information age: an overview of technology, economics, and politics, 45
The coming of managerial capitalism: a casebook on the history of American economic institutions, 27
Commercial banking, 17
Commercial banking in the economy, 17
Commercial motor transportation, 284
Commercial paper, 205
Commit to quality, 244
Commitment: the dynamic of strategy, 48
Commodities trading: the essential primer, 44
Commodity futures: markets, methods of analysis, and management of risk, 44
Commodity trading manual, 44
Communicate with confidence!: how to say it right the first time and every time, 25
Communicating for managerial effectiveness, 45
Communicating in business: an action-oriented approach, 25
Communicating when your company is under siege: surviving public crisis, 60
Communication for management and business, 25
Communication technology: the new media in society, 278
Communications deregulation: the unleashing of America's communications industry, 278
Communications in business, 43
Community capitalism, 258
Commuter marriage: living together, apart, 193
Companies that care: the most family-friendly companies in America, what they offer, and how they got that way, 92
Company administration handbook, 127
Company manners: an insider tells how to succeed in the real world of corporate protocol and power politics, 272
Company manners: how to behave in the workplace in the '90s, 272
Company reorganization for performance and profit improvement: a guide for operating executives and their staffs, 221
Company reports and accounts: their significance and uses, 109
Company strategy and organizational design, 221
Comparable worth: is it a worthy policy, 228
A comparable worth primer, 95
Comparable worth: the myth and the movement, 95

Comparative and multinational management, 144
Comparative high-technology industrial growth: Texas, California, Massachusetts, and North Carolina, 121
Comparative international accounting, 47
Comparative tax systems: Europe, Canada, and Japan, 274
Compensation, 47
The compensation handbook: a state-of-the-art guide to compensation strategy and design, 47
Compensation management: rewarding performance, 47
Compensation theory and practice, 47
Competence at work: models for superior performance, 12
Competing against time: how time-based competition is reshaping global markets, 281
Competing for control: America's stake in microelectronics, 198
Competing for the future, 48
Competing globally through customer value: the management of strategic suprasystems, 268
Competing in the new capital markets: investor relations strategies for the 1990s, 153
Competing in time: using telecommunications for competitive advantage, 278
Competing in world-class manufacturing: America's 21st century challenge, 292
Competing with flexible lateral organizations, 221
Competing with integrity in international business, 144
Competition in global industries, 48
Competitive & green: sustainable performance in the environmental age, 95
Competitive advantage: creating and sustaining superior performance, 48
The competitive advantage of Massachusetts, 194
The competitive advantage of nations, 140
Competitive advantage on the shop floor, 165
Competitive advantage through people: unleashing the power of the work force, 230
The competitive challenge: strategies for industrial innovation and renewal, 127
Competitive frontiers: women managers in a global economy, 301
Competitive intelligence in the computer age, 141
Competitive manufacturing: using production as a management tool, 268
Competitive strategies in European banking, 17
Competitive strategy: techniques for analyzing industries and competitors, 48
Competitor intelligence manual and guide: gathering, analyzing, and using business intelligence, 31
The complete book of raising capital, 295
The complete guide to buying a business, 259
The complete guide to consulting success, 25
The complete guide to nonprofit management, 211
The complete guide to selling a business, 252
The complete negotiator, 205
The complete problem solver: a total system for competitive decision making, 237
The complete travel marketing handbook: 37 industry experts share their secrets, 282
Completeness: quality for the 21st century, 281
Complying with the Americans with Disabilities Act: a guidebook for management and people with disabilities, 119
Compounding and discounting tables for project analysis: with a guide to their applications, 143
Computer briefing: using the trends for better managerial decisions, 51
Computer concepts for managers, 174
Computer essays for management, 174
The computer impact, 89
Computer integrated manufacturing systems: selected readings, 13
Computer models in management, 89
Computer simulation in management science, 182
Computer strategies, 1990-9: technologies, costs, markets, 50
Computer-based information systems: a management approach, 180
Computerization and controversy: value conflicts and social choices, 51
Computers and communications: a vision of C&C, 78
Computers and the information society, 51
Computers for everybody: 1984 buyer's guide, 197
Computers on the job: managing the human side, 51
Computing strategies for reengineering your organization, 221
Computing today: microcomputer concepts and applications, 197
The concept of corporate strategy, 60
Conceptual toolmaking: expert systems of the mind, 70
A concise economic history of the world: from Paleolithic times to the present, 84
Confessions of a corporate headhunter, 100
Confessions of a street-smart manager, 272
Conflict management and organization development, 221
Conflict management: the courage to confront, 51
The conglomerate commotion, 52
Connections: new ways of working in the networked organization, 90
The constraints of corporate tradition: doing the correct thing, not just what the past dictates, 58
The consultant's calling: bringing who you are to what you do, 56
The consultant's manual: a complete guide to building a successful consulting practice, 56
The consultant's proposal, fee, and contract problem-solver, 25
The consulting process in action, 25
Consulting: the complete guide to a profitable career, 56
Consumer and commercial credit management, 71
Consumer behavior, 56
Consumer behavior: concepts and applications, 56
Consumer behavior: implications for marketing strategy, 56
Consumer behavior in marketing strategy, 56
Consumer behavior: marketing strategy perspectives, 57
Consumer market research handbook, 192
Consuming fears: the politics of product risks, 238
Contemporary advertising, 6
Contemporary issues in business ethics, 28
Contemporary issues in corporate governance, 59
Contemporary issues in leadership, 166

Contemporary logistics, 234
Contemporary marketing, 186
Contemporary perspectives on strategic market planning, 186
Contemporary retailing, 250
The Continental affair: the rise and fall of the Continental Illinois Bank, 57
Continuous-time finance, 104
Contrary opinion: how to use it for profit in trading commodity futures, 44
Contrived competition: regulation and deregulation in America, 283
Control in business organizations, 57
The control of oil, 233
The control revolution: technological and economic origins of the information society, 45
Control your destiny or someone else will: how Jack Welch is making General Electric the world's most competitive corporation, 115
Controller involvement in management, 57
Controllership: the work of the managerial accountant, 58
Controlling interest rate risk: new techniques and applications for money management, 144
Controlling interest: who owns Canada, 90
The cooperative edge: the internal politics of international cartels, 38
Coping is not enough!: the international debt crisis and the roles of the World Bank and International Monetary Fund, 74
Coping with abundance: energy and environment in industrial America, 236
Corporate and commercial free speech: first amendment protection of expression in business, 7
Corporate and governmental deviance: problems of organizational behavior in contemporary society, 300
Corporate anti-takeover defenses: the poison pill device, 53
Corporate assessment: auditing a company's personality, 217
Corporate capital structures in the United States, 63
The corporate closet: the professional lives of gay men in America, 114
Corporate combat, 127
Corporate comeback: managing turnarounds and troubled companies, 259
Corporate communication, 45
The corporate conscience: money, power, and responsible business, 23
Corporate control and accountability: changing structures and the dynamics of regulation, 59
Corporate controller's manual, 58
The corporate couple: living the corporate game, 100
Corporate crime and violence: big business power and the abuse of the public trust, 64
Corporate culture and organizational effectiveness, 58
Corporate culture and performance, 58
Corporate decision making in the world economy: company case studies, 183
The corporate director's financial handbook, 64
Corporate environmentalism in a global economy: societal values in international technology transfer, 261
Corporate ethics: a prime business asset, 240
Corporate finance, 64
Corporate finance and the securities laws, 64
Corporate financial analysis: a comprehensive guide to real-world approaches for financial managers, 64
Corporate financial reporting and analysis: text and cases, 64
Corporate growth in Japan, 64
The corporate guide to the Malcolm Baldrige National Quality Award: proven strategies for building quality into your organization, 281
Corporate identity: making business strategy visible through design, 60
Corporate imagination plus: five steps to translating innovative strategies into action, 60
Corporate information systems management: text and cases, 180
Corporate information systems management: the issues facing senior executives, 23, 180
Corporate intelligence and espionage: a blueprint for executive decision making, 31
Corporate law, 62
Corporate legends and lore: the power of storytelling as a management tool, 45
Corporate lifecycles: how and why corporations grow and die and what to do about it, 221
Corporate makeover: reshaping the American economy, 64
Corporate mobility and paths to the top: studies for human resource and management development specialists, 40
Corporate networking: building channels for information and influence, 45
Corporate operational analysis: a procedure for evaluating key factors in internal operations, acquisitions, and takeovers, 225
Corporate PACs and federal campaign financing laws: use or abuse of power, 34
Corporate philosophies and mission statements: a survey and guide for corporate communicators and management, 58
Corporate players: designs for working and winning together, 221
Corporate power and responsibility: issues in the theory of company law, 62
Corporate profitability & logistics: innovative guidelines for executives, 32
Corporate quality universities: lessons in building a world-class work force, 92
Corporate real estate handbook, 43
Corporate realities and environmental truths: strategies for leading your business in the environmental era, 235
Corporate responses to environmental challenges: initiatives by multinational management, 138
Corporate restructuring: a guide to creating the premium-valued company, 221
Corporate restructuring: managing the change process from within, 63
Corporate resurgence and the new employment relationships: after the reckoning, 230
Corporate revolution: new strategies for executive leadership, 23

Corporate risk management: a financial exposition, 250
Corporate romance: how to avoid it, live through it, or make it work for you, 301
Corporate senior securities: analysis and evaluation of bonds, convertibles, and preferreds, 21
Corporate site selection for new facilities: a study conducted among the largest U.S. companies, 1989, 33
Corporate social responsibility: guidelines for top management, 139
Corporate staying power: how America's most consistently successful corporations maintain exceptional performance, 225
Corporate strategic analysis, 268
Corporate strategic planning, 268
Corporate strategy and the search for ethics, 60
The corporate strategy matrix, 60
Corporate strategy, public policy, and the Fortune 500: how America's major corporations influence government, 24
The corporate survivors, 64
Corporate takeovers and productivity, 165
Corporate takeovers: causes and consequences, 53
Corporate transformations: revitalizing organizations for a competitive world, 221
Corporate valuation: a business and professional guide, 27
Corporate venturing: creating new businesses within the firm, 94
The corporate warriors, 48
Corporate-level strategy: creating value in the multibusiness company, 52
The corporation as anomaly, 64
The corporation of the 1990s: information technology and organizational transformation, 174
Corporations and society: power and responsibility, 62
Corporations and the common good, 36
Cost accounting: a managerial emphasis, 68
Cost accounting desk reference book: common weaknesses in cost systems and how to correct them, 68
Cost accounting for the '90s: the challenge of technological change: conference proceedings, 68
Cost accounting: planning and control, 68
Cost accounting: processing, evaluating, and using cost data, 68
Cost containment: the ultimate strategic advantage, 69
Cost control handbook, 69
Cost management for today's advanced manufacturing: the CAM-I conceptual design, 70
The cost of talent: how executives and professionals are paid and how it affects America, 100
The cost reduction and profit improvement handbook, 69
Cost-benefit analysis, 69
Costing the earth: the challenge for governments, the opportunities for business, 95
Countertrade, barter, and offsets: new strategies for profit in international trade, 70
The countertrade handbook, 70

Countertrade: practices, strategies, and tactics, 70
Counterturbulence marketing: a proactive strategy for volatile economic times, 186
Country risk: assessment and monitoring, 170
A course in microeconomic theory, 197
The course of American economic growth and development, 287
The craft of investing, 267
Crash: ten days in October—will it strike again, 265
Created in Japan: from imitators to world-class innovators, 121
Creating a customer-centered culture: leadership in quality, innovation, and speed, 72
Creating a flexible workplace: how to select and manage alternative work options, 123
Creating abundance: America's least-cost energy strategy, 236
Creating effective boards for private enterprises: meeting the challenges of continuity and competition, 79
Creating expert systems for business and industry, 23
Creating healthy work organizations, 161
Creating investor demand for company stock: a guide for financial managers, 267
Creating new health care ventures: the role of management, 121
Creating strategic change: designing the flexible, high-performing organization, 221
Creating strategic leverage: matching company strengths with market opportunities, 186
Creating the computer: government, industry, and high technology, 50
Creating value for customers: designing and implementing a total corporate strategy, 72
The creative attitude: learning to ask and answer the right questions, 70
The creative corporation, 70
The creative edge: fostering innovation where you work, 70
The creative mystique: how to manage it, nurture it, and make it pay, 70
Creative organization theory: a resourcebook, 215
Creativity at work, 71
Creativity in business, 71
The creativity infusion: how managers can start and sustain creativity and innovation, 71
Creativity: the art and science of business management, 71
Credibility: how leaders gain and lose it, why people demand it, 167
Crisis management: planning for the inevitable, 71
Crisis marketing: when bad things happen to good companies, 186
Crisis resolution in the thrift industry: a Mid America Institute report, 104
Critical issues in business conduct: legal, ethical, and social challenges for the 1990s, 28
Critical issues in office automation, 213
Critical path hiring: how to employ top-flight managers, 100
Critical skills: the guide to top performance for human resources managers, 230
A cross-industry analysis of financial ratios: comparabilities and corporate performance, 247

Crucial decisions: leadership in policymaking and crisis management, 75
The CSIS Strengthening of America Commission, 290
The cult of information: the folklore of computers and the true art of thinking, 51
Cultural diversity in organizations: theory, research, & practice, 234
The cultural environment of international business, 144
Culture and related corporate realities: text, cases, and readings on organizational entry, establishment, and change, 217
The culture of contentment, 289
The culture of Korean industry: an ethnography of Poongsan Corporation, 244
The cultures of work organizations, 58
The Cuomo Commission report: a new American formula for a strong economy, 288
Currencies and crises, 150
Current perspectives in organization development, 221
Customer bonding, 72
Customer retention through quality leadership: the Baxter approach, 57
The customer-driven company: moving from talk to action, 72
Customer-driven project management: a new paradigm in total quality implementation, 135
Customers as partners: building relationships that last, 72
Cutting loose: making the transition from employee to entrepreneur, 206
Cutting the red tape: how Western companies can profit in the new Russia, 264

The daisy chain: how borrowed billions sank a Texas S&L, 296
Dangerous dreamers: the financial innovators from Charles Merrill to Michael Milken, 199
Dangerous pursuits: mergers and acquisitions in the age of Wall Street, 53
The Dartnell advertising manager's handbook, 6
The Dartnell direct mail and mail order handbook, 7
The Dartnell marketing manager's handbook, 186
The Dartnell personnel administration handbook, 230
The Dartnell public relations handbook, 243
The Dartnell sales manager's handbook, 252
Data in doubt: an introduction to Bayesian statistical inference for economists, 85
Data systems and management: an introduction to systems analysis and design, 89
Data warehousing: the route to mass customisation, 127
Dave says well done!: the common guy's guide to everyday success, 271
The deal decade: what takeovers and leveraged buyouts mean for corporate governance, 53
The deal of the century: the breakup of AT&T, 10
Dealing with complexity: an introduction to the theory and application of systems science, 273
Dealing with the Japanese, 160
The death of money: how the electronic economy has destabilized the world's markets and created financial chaos, 200

The death of the organization man, 199
Debt and danger: the world financial crisis, 74
Debt and taxes, 110
The debt and the deficit: false alarms/real possibilities, 74
Debt, taxes, and corporate restructuring, 53
The debt/equity choice, 64
Deceitful practices: Nomura Securities and the Japanese invasion of Wall Street, 210
Decentralization: managerial ambiguity by design, 174
Deciding to go public: understanding the process and the alternatives, 116
Deciding to innovate: how firms justify advanced technology, 293
Decision analysis and behavioral research, 75
The decision makers: the men and the million-dollar moves behind today's great corporate success stories, 33
Decision sciences: an integrative perspective, 75
Decision support and executive information systems, 74
Decision support and expert systems: management support systems, 174
Decision support systems in finance and accounting, 64
Decision support systems: putting theory into practice, 174
Decision systems for inventory management and production planning, 152
Decisions and organizations, 75
Decisions with multiple objectives: preferences and value tradeoffs, 203
Decline and prosperity: corporate innovation in Japan, 275
The decline of American steel: how management, labor, and government went wrong, 265
Declining fortunes: the withering of the American dream, 261
Defending white-collar crime: a portrait of attorneys at work, 300
The defense management challenge: weapons acquisition, 286
Defining the business: the starting point of strategic planning, 60
The definitive guide to long range planning, 60
Defying gravity: the making of Newton, 11
A delicate experiment: the Harvard Business School, 1908-1945, 120
Demass: transforming the dinosaur corporation, 74
The Deming guide to quality and competitive position, 76
Deming management at work, 76
The Deming management method, 77
The deregulated society, 77
Deregulating financial services: public policy in flux, 17
Deregulating telecoms: competition and control in the United States, Japan, and Britain, 278
Deregulating the airlines, 7
Deregulation and the new airline entrepreneurs, 7
Design and innovation: policy and management, 275
The design and operation of FMS, flexible manufacturing systems, 185
The design dimension: product strategy and the challenge of global marketing, 77

Design for manufacturability: a systems approach to concurrent engineering and ergonomics, 239
Design for society, 77
Design management: a handbook of issues and methods, 77
The design of cost management systems: text, cases, and readings, 183
Design of jobs, 230
Designing and managing your career, 100
Designing career development systems, 37
Designing effective organizations: the sociotechnical systems perspective, 215
Designing effective organizations: traditional & transformational views, 226
Designing effective work groups, 305
Designing interactive strategy: from value chain to value constellation, 268
Designing organizations, 174
Designing performance appraisal systems: aligning appraisals and organizational realities, 229
Designing training and development systems, 92
The desktop encyclopedia of corporate finance & accounting, 64
The destructive achiever: power and ethics in the American corporation, 28
Determinants of executive compensation: corporate ownership, performance, size, and diversification, 40
Developing a professional sales force: a guide for sales trainers and sales managers, 252
Developing business strategies, 268
Developing corporate character: how to successfully change an organization without destroying it, 222
Developing diversity in organizations: a digest of selected literature, 199
Developing human resources, 92
Developing managers, 100
Developing superior work teams: building quality and the competitive edge, 305
Development effectiveness: strategies for IS organizational transition, 180
Diagnosing the system for organizations, 225
Diagnostic marketing: finding and fixing critical problems, 186
Dial 9 to get out!: commentaries on business life as heard on public radio's Marketplace, 23
Did you know?: fascinating facts & fallacies about business, 23
The digital workplace: designing groupware platforms, 46
Direct foreign investment: costs and benefits, 156
The direct marketing handbook, 79
Direct marketing: strategy, planning, execution, 79
The director's & officer's guide to advisory boards, 59
Directors of industry: the British corporate network, 1904-76, 64
Discovery techniques: obtaining and analyzing business financial data, 109
Dislodging multinationals: India's strategy in comparative perspective, 144
The Disney touch: how a daring management team revived an entertainment empire, 298
Distributed computing: implementation and management strategies, 89
The distribution handbook, 234

Diversification through acquisition: strategies for creating economic value, 80
The diversity advantage: how American business can out-perform Japanese and European companies in the global marketplace, 225
Diversity and differences in organizations: an agenda for answers and questions, 225
Diversity in the workplace: human resources initiatives, 199
The divestiture option: a guide for financial and corporate planning executives, 59
The do's and taboos of international trade: a small business primer, 152
Do-it-yourself marketing research, 192
Does ownership matter?: Japanese multinationals in Europe, 67
Doing best by doing good: how to use public purpose partnerships to boost corporate profits and benefit your community, 64
Doing business boldly: the art of taking intelligent risks, 272
Doing business in Korea, 163
Doing business in Vietnam, 136
Doing business internationally: the guide to cross-cultural success, 127
Doing business on the Internet: how the electronic highway is transforming American companies, 27
Doing business with Japan, 159
Doing business with Japanese men: a woman's handbook, 30
Doing comparable worth: gender, class, and pay equity, 228
Doing deals: investment banks at work, 154
Doing well & doing good: the challenge to the Christian capitalist, 263
Doing well while doing good: the marketing link between business & nonprofit causes, 262
Dow Jones industrial average: history and role in an investment strategy, 80
The Dow Jones-Irwin guide to bond and money market investments, 154
The Dow Jones-Irwin guide to buying and selling Treasury securities, 117
The Dow Jones-Irwin guide to financial modeling, 64
The Dow Jones-Irwin guide to international securities, futures, and options markets, 156
The Dow Jones-Irwin guide to investing with investment software, 154
The Dow Jones-Irwin guide to mutual funds, 204
The Dow Jones-Irwin guide to trading systems, 44
Dow Theory redux: the classic investment theory revised & updated for the 1990's, 266
Downscoping: how to tame the diversified firm, 80
Downsizing: reshaping the corporation for the future, 138
Dr. Deming: the American who taught the Japanese about quality, 245
Dreams betrayed: working in the technological age, 13
The DRI model of the U.S. economy, 288
Driving fear out of the workplace: how to overcome the invisible barriers to quality, productivity, and innovation, 225
Dual-career families, 193

Dying for work: workers' safety and health in twentieth-century America, 126
Dynamic manufacturing: creating the learning organization, 292
Dynamic planning and management in the securities industry: staying competitive in a changing marketplace, 254
Dynamic planning: the art of managing beyond tomorrow, 268
The dynamics of taking charge, 127
The dynamos: who are they anyway, 33

The E-factor: the bottom-line approach to environmentally responsible business, 262
Eagle on the Street: based on the Pulitzer Prize-winning account of the SEC's battle with Wall Street, 286
The East Asian miracle: economic growth and public policy, 81
Eastern's armageddon: labor conflict and the destruction of Eastern Airlines, 81
EC/EFTA, the future European economic area, 97
Ecological economics: a practical programme for global reform, 118
The ecological vision: reflections on the American condition, 294
EcoManagement: the Elmwood guide to ecological auditing and sustainable business, 127
The econometric analysis of time series, 82
Econometrics, 82
Economic aspects of biotechnology, 20
Economic behavior and institutions, 142
The economic development of the Pacific Basin: growth dynamics, trade relations, and emerging cooperation, 12
Economic forecasting for business: concepts and applications, 31
The Economic growth controversy, 82
Economic growth in the Third World, 1850-1980, 78
Economic heresies; some old-fashioned questions in economic theory, 85
The economic institutions of capitalism: firms, markets, relational contracting, 142
Economic policy and development: new perspectives, 159
Economic principals: masters and mavericks of modern economics, 87
The economic problem, 85
The economic theory of organization and the firm, 133
The economic transformation of America: 1600 to the present, 287
Economic trend analysis for executives and investors, 83
Economics, 85
Economics: a general introduction, 85
Economics: analysis, decision making, and policy, 86
Economics and world history: myths and paradoxes, 84
Economics explained: everything you need to know about how the economy works and where it's going, 86
Economics for a civilized society, 86
Economics from the heart: a Samuelson sampler, 86

Economics in perspective: a critical history, 86
Economics in plain English, 86
Economics, medicine, and health care, 196
The economics of bargaining, 114
The economics of chaos: on revitalizing the American economy, 288
The economics of comparable worth, 228
The economics of development, 82
Economics of development, 78
The economics of futures markets, 44
The economics of hope: essays on technical change, economic growth, and the environment, 82
The economics of industrial organization, 133
The economics of industries and firms: theories, evidence and policy, 133
Economics of labor in industrial society, 164
The economics of money, banking, and financial markets, 104
The economics of natural resource use, 205
The economics of regulation: principles and institutions, 140
Economics, organization, and management, 183
Economics: principles, problems, and policies, 86
The Economist guide to business numeracy, 32
The Economist Intelligence Unit global manager, 99
The Economist Intelligence Unit guide to building a global image, 60
The economy in the Reagan years: the economic consequences of the Reagan administrations, 290
Econoquake!: how to survive & prosper in the coming global depression, 83
Ecopreneuring: the complete guide to small business opportunities from the environmental revolution, 206
Ecotourism: a sustainable option, 88
ECU: European currency unit, 96
EDI guide: a step by step approach, 89
EDP, controls and auditing, 89
Educating managers: executive effectiveness through liberal learning, 174
Education for judgment: the artistry of discussion leadership, 42
Effective behavior in organizations: learning from the interplay of cases, concepts, and student experiences, 217
Effective business communications, 43
Effective communication, 307
Effective control of currency risks: a practical, comprehensive guide, 112
The effective executive, 100
Effective financial management in public and non-profit agencies: a practical and integrative approach, 107
Effective group problem solving: how to broaden participation, improve decision making, and increase commitment to action, 118
Effective human resource development: how to build a strong and responsive HRD function, 230
Effective leadership for women and men, 167
Effective management and evaluation of information technology, 127
The effective management of technology: a challenge for corporations, 275

Effective small business management, 259
Effective strategic management: analysis and action, 268
The effectiveness of the annual report as a communication vehicle: a digest of the relevant literature, 63
Efficiency in U.S. manufacturing industries, 292
Efficient capital markets and accounting: a critical analysis, 88
The EIS book: information systems for top managers, 174
Electric power: deregulation and the public interest, 89
Electronic funds transfers and payments: the public policy issues, 90
Electronic imaging systems: design, applications, and management, 124
The electronic marketing manual, 278
The electronic sweatshop: how computers are transforming the office of the future into the factory of the past, 213
The electronic word: democracy, technology, and the arts, 51
Elementary business statistics: the modern approach, 43
The elements of business writing, 33
The elements of industrial relations, 136
Elements of statistical inference, 265
Emancipating the professions: marketing opportunities from de-regulation, 241
Emerging European bond markets, 21
The emerging power of Japanese money, 104
Emerging stock markets: a complete investment guide to new markets around the world, 156
Emperors of adland: inside the advertising revolution, 7
The empire builders: inside the Harvard Business School, 120
The empirical renaissance in industrial economics, 133
Employee benefits handbook, 90
The employee handbook: a complete, ready-to-use model with sample policies and procedures, 230
Employee ownership: a reader, 91
Employee ownership in America: the equity solution, 91
Employee ownership: revolution or ripoff, 91
Employee relations in Europe, 137
Employers large and small, 92
Employment and health benefits: a connection at risk, 143
Employment and technical change in Europe: work organization, skills, and training, 92
Employment security: balancing human and economic considerations, 161
The empowered manager: positive political skills at work, 217
Empowered teams: creating self-directed work groups that improve quality, productivity, and participation, 305
Empowering people at work, 225
Empowering technology: implementing a U.S. strategy, 278
Encyclopedia of American economic history: studies of the principal movements and ideas, 287
Encyclopedia of investments, 154

The encyclopedia of technical market indicators, 266
Encyclopedia of telemarketing, 279
The end of economic man: principles of any future economics, 86
The end of the American century, 293
Energy aftermath, 93
Energy and the ecological economics of sustainability, 95
The energy crisis ten years after, 93
Energy future: report of the Energy Project at the Harvard Business School, 93
Energy future: report of the energy project at the Harvard Business School, 93
Energy futures, trading opportunities for the 1980s, 233
Energy, politics, and public policy, 93
Engineering economy: analysis of capital expenditures, 93
Engines of growth: the state and transnational auto companies in Brazil, 14
Enhancing American competitiveness: a progress report to the President and Congress, 49
Enterprise and competitiveness: a systems view of international business, 94
Enterprise information technologies: designing the competitive company, 180
Enterprise: the dynamic economy of a free people, 287
Enterprising elite: the Boston Associates and the world they made, 280
The enterprising man, 94
Enterprising women: lessons from 100 of the greatest entrepreneurs of our day, 303
Entertainment industry economics: a guide for financial analysis, 229
The entrepreneur, 33, 127
Entrepreneur: from zero to hero: how to be a blockbuster entrepreneur, 272
The entrepreneur: mainstream views & radical critiques, 94
The entrepreneur's guide to building a better business plan: a step-by-step approach, 60
The entrepreneur's guide to capital: the techniques for capitalizing and refinancing new and growing businesses, 64
The entrepreneur's guide to going public, 116
The entrepreneur's guide to preparing a winning business plan and raising venture capital, 206
The entrepreneur's guide to starting a successful business, 207
The entrepreneur's manual: business start-ups, spin-offs, and innovative management, 207
Entrepreneurial behavior, 94
The entrepreneurial experience: confronting career dilemmas of the start-up executive, 206
The entrepreneurial manager: decisions, goals, and business ideas, 60
Entrepreneurial megabucks: The 100 greatest entrepreneurs of the last 25 years and how they did it: A. David Silver, 34
The entrepreneurial nonprofit executive, 211
The entrepreneurial organization, 222
Entrepreneurial science: new links between corporations, universities, and government, 121
Entrepreneurial systems for the 1990s: their creation, structure, and management, 206

Entrepreneuring in established companies: managing toward the year 2000, 94
The entrepreneurs: an American adventure, 291
Entrepreneurs in corporations, 225
Entrepreneurs in high technology: lessons from M.I.T. and beyond, 121
Entrepreneurs, the men and women behind famous brand names and how they made it, 34
Entrepreneurship, 94
Entrepreneurship and small business management: text, readings and cases, 259
Entrepreneurship and venture management, 259
Entrepreneurship, creativity & organization: text, cases & readings, 94
Entrepreneurship for the nineties, 207
Entrepreneurship in a "mature industry", 14
Entrepreneurship research: global perspectives: proceedings of the Second Annual Global Conference on Entrepreneurship Research, London, UK, 9-11 March, 1992, 94
Entrepreneurship: what it is and how to teach it: a collection of working papers based on a colloquium held at Harvard Business School, July 5-8, 1983, 94
Enviro-management: how smart companies turn environmental costs into profits, 127
The environment of international banking, 18
Environmental accounting for the sustainable corporation: strategies and techniques, 205
Environmental business management: an introduction, 127
The environmental economic revolution: how business will thrive and the Earth survive in years to come, 138
Environmental economics: an introduction, 95
Envisionary management: a guide for human resources professionals in management training and development, 174
Equal opportunity in business, 80
Equal value/comparable worth in the UK and the USA, 300
Equipment leasing, 125
Equity markets: structure, trading, and performance, 254
The Ernst & Young business plan guide, 207
The Ernst & Young guide to expanding in the global market, 144
The Ernst & Young guide to financing for growth, 64
The Ernst & Young guide to raising capital, 64
The Ernst & Young management guide to mergers and acquisitions, 53
The Ernst & Young resource guide to global markets, 1991, 152
Escape from management hell: 12 tales of horror, humor, and heroism, 174
Essays on economics and economists, 86
Essays on entrepreneurs, innovations, business cycles, and the evolution of capitalism, 86
Essays on ethics in business and the professions, 28
The essence of international marketing, 102
The essence of marketing, 187
The essence of operations management, 127
The essential Adam Smith, 260
The essential Alfred Chandler: essays toward a historical theory of big business, 19
The essential guide to effective corporate board committees, 79
Essentials of accounting, 4
Essentials of cost accounting for health care organizations, 121
Essentials of managerial finance, 64, 65
Essentials of new product management, 208
Essentials of organizational behavior, 217
Estée: a success story, 166
Estée Lauder: beyond the magic: an unauthorized biography, 166
The eternally successful organization: the art of corporate wellness, 217
Ethical decision making in everyday work situations, 28
Ethical dilemmas in the modern corporation, 29
Ethical issues in business: a philosophical approach, 29
Ethical theory and business., 29
Ethics and economic progress, 86
Ethics and excellence: cooperation and integrity in business, 29
Ethics and leadership: putting theory into practice, 29
Ethics and markets: co-operation and competition within capitalist economies, 150
Ethics and the investment industry, 29
Ethics in marketing, 187
Ethics in practice: managing the moral corporation, 29
Ethics of an artificial person: lost responsibility in professions and organizations, 163
The ethics of international business, 144
The ethics of management, 29
Eurobonds, 96, 235
Eurodollars and international banking, 96
Europe in the year 2000, 98
Europe 1992 and the new world power game, 96
Europe: road to unity, 99
The European adventure: tasks for the enlarged Community, 97
The European bond markets: an overview and analysis for money managers and traders, 21
The European Community and the challenge of the future, 97
The European economy, 1914-1990, 98
The European human resource management guide, 230
The European marketplace, 97
European markets after 1992, 97
The European options and futures markets: the overview and analysis for money managers and traders, 44
European women in business and management, 303
Evaluating complex business reports: a guide for executives, 75
Evaluating corporate investment and financing opportunities: a handbook and guide to selected methods for managers and finance professionals, 65
Evaluating R&D impacts: methods and practice, 249
The evaluation interview, 93
Every employee a manager, 230
Every manager's guide to information technology:

a glossary of key terms and concepts for today's business leader, 141
Every street is paved with gold: the road to real success, 272
Everyone's money book, 106
Everything a working mother needs to know: about pregnancy rights, maternity leave, and making her career work for her, 203
The evolution and future of high performance management systems, 127
The evolution of management thought, 174
An exaltation of business and finance, 23
Excellence in business communication, 25
Excellence in public relations and communication management, 243
Excellent organizations: how to develop & manage them using Theory Z, 215
Executive achievement: making it at the top, 167
Executive compensation: a strategic guide for the 1990s, 100
Executive compensation in large industrial corporations, 100
Executive compensation: who, how much, and when? A Harvard Business Review reprint series, 100
The executive course: what every manager needs to know about the essentials of business, 128
The executive deskbook, 174
Executive development series; reprints from Harvard Business Review, 100
The executive dilemma: handling people problems at work, 217
Executive economics: ten essential tools for managers, 183
Executive information systems: a guide for senior management and MIS professionals, 180
Executive information systems and decision support, 74
Executive information systems: emergence, development, impact, 180
Executive integrity: the search for high human values in organizational life, 29
Executive jobs unlimited, 11
Executive leadership in nonprofit organizations: new strategies for shaping executive-board dynamics, 211
Executive musical chairs, 100
Executive power, 100
The executive search collaboration: a guide for human resources professionals and their search firms, 100
Executive skills, a management by objectives approach, 179
Executive smart charts & other insider revelations on corporate insanity, 128
Executive support systems: the emergence of top management computer use, 174
Executive talent: developing and keeping the best people, 100
The executive's compass: business and the good society, 167
Executive's guide to business law, 32
Executive's handbook of model business conduct codes, 29
Experience, Inc.: men and women who founded famous companies after the age of 40, 34

Expert system technology: development and application, 101
Expert systems: techniques, tools, and applications, 101
Expert systems: tools and applications, 24
Experts in action: inside public relations, 243
Explaining international production, 145
Exploring marketing research, 192
The export cult: a global display of economic distortions, 112
Export finance, 102
Export-import financing, 103
External economic relations of the central and east European countries: colloquium, 8-10 April 1992, Brussels = Relations économiques extérieures des pays d'Europe centrale et orientale: colloque, 8-10 avril 1992, Bruxelles, 97

Facing up: how to rescue the economy from crushing debt and restore the American dream, 290
Facts against fictions of executive behavior: a critical analysis of what managers do, 40
The fading miracle: four decades of market economy in Germany, 116
The failure of Soviet economic planning: system, performance, reform, 264
Fair pay: the managerial challenge of comparable job worth and job evaluation, 161
The fairness of markets: a search for justice in a free society, 86
Fall from grace: the untold story of Michael Milken, 163
The fall of the Bell system: a study in prices and politics, 10
The fall of the House of Hutton, 88
False profits: the inside story of BCCI, the world's most corrupt financial empire, 16
Family pride: profiles of five of America's best-run family businesses, 103
Family ties, corporate bonds, 217
Famous financial fiascos, 264
The fanciest dive: what happened when the giant media empire of TIME/LIFE leaped without looking into the age of high-tech, 280
Farm business management: the decision-making process, 103
Fast cycle time: how to align purpose, strategy, and structure for speed, 128
Fast forward: Hollywood, the Japanese, and the onslaught of the VCR, 296
Fast-growth strategies: how to maximize profits from start-up through maturity, 61
The fate of Hong Kong, 123
Father, Son & Co.: my life at IBM and beyond, 149
Favorites of fortune: technology, growth, and economic development since the Industrial Revolution, 275
The FDA follies, 286
Fed watching and interest rate projections: a practical guide, 20
The Federal Reserve: lender of last resort, 286
Feeding frenzy, 299
Feeding the beast: how Wedtech became the most corrupt little company in America, 299
Feminine leadership, or, How to succeed in business without being one of the boys, 301

The feminization of America: how women's values are changing our public and private lives, 104
A few good men from Univac, 294
A few good women: breaking the barriers to top management, 301
The Fidelity guide to mutual funds: a complete guide to investing in mutual funds, 204
Field guide to business terms: a glossary of essential tools and concepts for today's manager, 128
Field guide to marketing: a glossary of essential tools and concepts for today's manager, 187
Field guide to negotiation: a glossary of essential tools and concepts for today's manager, 205
Field guide to strategy: a glossary of essential tools and concepts for today's manager, 268
The fifth discipline fieldbook: strategies and tools for building a learning organization, 226
The fifth discipline: the art and practice of the learning organization, 226
The fifties, 294
50/50 by 2000: the woman's guide to political power, 300
Filthy rich and other nonprofit fantasies: changing the way nonprofits do business in the 90's, 211
Finance & accounting for nonfinancial managers, 183
Finance: an international perspective, 150
Finance: environment and decisions, 105
Finance for the nonfinancial manager, 105
Finance of foreign trade, 112
Finance theory, 105
Financial accounting, 4
Financial accounting: an events and cash flow approach, 38
Financial accounting and managerial control for nonprofit organizations, 211
Financial accounting and reporting desk handbook, 4
Financial accounting in nonbusiness organizations: an exploratory study of conceptual issues: research report, 211
Financial accounting: principles and issues, 4
Financial accounting theory: issues and controversies, 4
The financial analyst's handbook, 153
Financial and accounting guide for not-for-profit organizations, 211
Financial and strategic management for nonprofit organizations, 211
Financial assets, markets, and institutions, 105
The Financial development of Japan, Korea, and Taiwan: growth, repression, and liberalization, 105
Financial dynamics and business cycles: new perspectives, 26
Financial engineering: a complete guide to financial innovation, 107
Financial forecasting and planning: a guide for accounting, marketing, and planning managers, 27
Financial futures and options: a guide to markets, applications, and strategies, 107
Financial futures and options in the U.S. economy: a study, 107

Financial futures: fundamentals, strategies, and applications, 107
Financial futures markets: concepts, evidence, and applications, 108
Financial futures markets: structure, pricing, and practice, 108
A financial history of western Europe, 105
Financial innovation and monetary policy, Asia and the West: proceedings of the second international conference held by the Institute for Monetary and Economic Studies of the Bank of Japan, 200
Financial innovation and risk sharing, 107
Financial institutions and markets, 108
Financial institutions, markets, and money, 105
Financial institutions: understanding and managing financial services, 108
Financial instruments markets: an advanced study of cash-futures relationships, 143
Financial management and policy, 65
Financial management classics, 65
Financial management for decision making, 65
Financial management for the multinational firm, 145
Financial management handbook, 65
Financial management in agriculture, 9
Financial management in nonprofit organizations, 211
Financial management of the small firm, 259
Financial management: theory and practice, 65
The financial manager, 65
Financial market rates and flows, 144
Financial markets and institutions: a managerial approach, 108
Financial markets and the economy, 105
Financial markets: the accumulation and allocation of wealth, 105
Financial mathematics handbook, 32
Financial options: from theory to practice, 215
Financial planning and control, 27
The Financial Post 100 best companies to work for in Canada, 161
The financial revolution, 150
The financial samurai: the emerging power of Japanese money, 105
The financial services handbook: executive insights and solutions, 108
Financial services: perspectives and challenges, 109
The Financial services resolution: policy directions for the future, 16
Financial statement analysis, 109
Financial statement analysis: a practitioner's guide, 109
Financial statement analysis: a strategic perspective, 4
Financial statement analysis: theory, application, and interpretation, 109
Financial statement analysis: using financial accounting information, 109
Financial strategy: studies in the creation, transfer, and destruction of shareholder value, 65
The financial structure of multinational capitalism, 145
Financial swaps: new strategies in currency and coupon risk management, 112
The financial system, 105
Financial theory and corporate policy, 65

Financing and managing fast-growth companies: the venture capital process, 295

Financing East Asia's success: comparative financial development in eight Asian countries, 105

Finding it on the Internet: the essential guide to archie, Veronica, Gopher, WAIS, WWW (including Mosaic), and other search and browsing tools, 152

Finding private venture capital for your firm: a complete guide, 295

Finite markov chains, 237

Finney and Miller's Principles of accounting, intermediate, 4

Finney and Miller's Principles of accounting-introductory, 4

The firm and the market: studies on multinational enterprises and the scope of the firm, 145

The firm, the market, and the law, 133

The first global revolution: a report by the Council of the Club of Rome, 83

The first universal nation: leading indicators and ideas about the surge of America in the 1990s, 293

First-line management: approaching supervision effectively, 273

The first-time manager, 273

Fit, failure, and the hall of fame: how companies succeed or fail, 128

The five pillars of TQM: how to make total quality management work for you, 281

The five-minute financial manager, 259

Fixed income masterpieces: insights from America's great investors, 110

Fixed-income arbitrage: analytical techniques and strategies, 110

The flexible organization: a unique new system for organizational effectiveness and success, 226

Flexible work arrangements for managers and professionals: findings from a Catalyst study, 228

Flight of the buffalo: soaring to excellence, learning to let employees lead, 167

Flow of funds and other financial concepts, 110

The flowering of the third America: the making of an organizational society, 1850-1920, 294

Fluctuating fortunes: the political power of business in America, 24

FMC corporation's use of current cost accounting, 68

For fun and profit: the transformation of leisure into consumption, 169

For God, country and Coca-Cola: the unauthorized history of the great American soft drink and the company that makes it, 42

For richer, for poorer: the new U.S.-Japan relationship, 294

For the common good: redirecting the economy toward community, the environment, and a sustainable future, 82

A force for change: how leadership differs from management, 167

A force of ones: reclaiming individual power in a time of teams, work groups, and other crowds, 305

Forecasting and market analysis techniques: a practical approach, 252

Forecasting in business amd economics, 83

Forecasting methods for management, 83

Forecasting, planning, and strategy for the 21st century, 31

Foreign currency translation and hedging, 112

The foreign exchange and money markets guide, 112

The foreign exchange handbook: a user's guide, 112

Foreign exchange handbook: managing risk and opportunity in global currency markets, 112

Forging the productivity partnership, 222

Forming R & D partnerships: an entrepreneur's guidebook, 249

Fortune and folly: the wealth and power of institutional investing, 228

The fortune builders, 37

Fortune cookies: management wit and wisdom from Fortune magazine, 24

The Fortune encyclopedia of economics, 86

Foundations of financial management, 65

Foundations of multinational financial management, 145

Foundations of public economics, 107

The founding fortunes: a new anatomy of the super-rich families in America, 299

Fourth generation management: the new business consciousness, 282

Fractal market analysis: applying chaos theory to investment and economics, 154

Framebreak: the radical redesign of American business, 128

France high-tech, 121

Franchising: Forms volume realities and remedies, 113

Franchising in Europe, 113

Franchising: the inside story: how to start your own business and succeed! by John E. Kinch with John P. Hayes. 1st ed. Wilmington, Del.: TriMark Pub. Co., c1986. 211 p. : ill. Notes: Includes index. [LC 85041018; ISN 0914663038; $14.95] HF5429.235.U5 K56 1986, 113

Frederick W. Taylor, the father of scientific management: myth and reality, 274

Free for all?: lessons from the Rand Health Insurance Experiment, 246

Free market economics: a critical appraisal, 113

Free money from the federal government for small businesses and entrepreneurs, 259

Friendly spies: how America's allies are using economic espionage to steal our secrets, 31

Friends in high places: the Bechtel story: the most secret corporation and how it engineered the world, 18

From a 500-dollar company to a global corporation: the growth of Sony, 263

From concept to market, 208

From idea to profit: managing advanced manufacturing technology, 185

From the American system to mass production, 1800-1932: the development of manufacturing technology in the United States, 194

From the ground up: the resurgence of American entrepreneurship, 259

From turmoil to triumph: new life after mergers, acquisitions, and downsizing, 222

Front stage, backstage: the dramatic structure of labor negotiations, 42
Frontiers in creative and innovative management, 71
Frontiers of economics, 86
Frontiers of finance: the Batterymarch Fellowship papers, 105
Frontiers of leadership: an essential reader, 167
The frontiers of management: where tomorrow's decisions are being shaped today, 174
Full faith and credit: the great S&L debacle and other Washington sagas, 253
A full service bank: how BCCI stole billions around the world, 16
The functions of the executive, 101
Fund accounting, 114
Fundamental accounting principles, 4
Fundamental issues in strategy: a research agenda, 269
Fundamentals of business law, 43
Fundamentals of business statistics, 43
Fundamentals of employee benefit programs, 90
Fundamentals of finanacial management, 65
Fundamentals of financial accounting, 4
Fundamentals of financial management, 65
Fundamentals of investments, 154
Fundamentals of managerial economics, 183
Fundamentals of marketing, 187
Fundamentals of modern marketing, 187
Fundamentals of private pensions, 213
Fundamentals of real estate investment, 247
Fundamentals of risk and insurance, 142
Fundamentals of securities regulation, 254
Fundamentals of the petroleum industry, 233
Funny business: an outsider's year in Japan, 263
The future 500: creating tomorrow's organizations today, 175
Future competition in telecommunications, 278
Future facts: a forecast of the world as we will know it before the end of the century, 277
The future impact of automation on workers, 165
The future of American banking, 17
The future of American banking: managing for change, 17
The future of banking, 17
The future of health policy, 196
A future of lousy jobs?: the changing structure of U.S. wages, 297
The future of television: a global overview of programming, advertising, technology, and growth, 280
The future of the nonprofit sector: challenges, changes, and policy considerations, 211
The future of transportation and communication: visions and perspectives from Europe, Japan and the U.S.A, 45
The future of work and health: the Institute for Alternative Futures, 126
Future perfect, 175
Future shop: how new technologies will change the way we shop and what we buy, 279
Future tense: the business realities of the next ten years, 83
Future trends in retailing: merchandise line trends and store trends 1980-1990, 250
Future vision: the 189 most important trends of the 1990s, 261

The futures game: who wins? Who loses? Why, 44
Futures trading: concepts and strategies, 44
Fuzzy thinking: the new science of fuzzy logic, 171

Gaining control of the corporate culture, 58
The game behind the game: negotiating in the big leagues, 258
Game over: how Nintendo zapped an American industry, captured your dollars, and enslaved your children, 210
Game theory: a nontechnical introduction, 114
Games for business and economics, 183
Gates: how Microsoft's mogul reinvented an industry—and made himself the richest man in America, 114
Gay issues in the workplace, 230
Gender & racial inequality at work: the sources and consequences of job segregation, 80
Gender and diversity in the workplace: learning activities and exercises, 257
Gender in the workplace, 257
Gendered by design?: information technology and office systems, 213
Genderspeak: men, women, and the gentle art of verbal self-defense, 296
Gene dreams: Wall Street, academia, and the rise of biotechnology, 115
Geneen, 114
The general: David Sarnoff and the rise of the communications industry, 253
General management: an analytical approach, 175
General managers in action, 40
General managers in action: policies and strategies, 40
The general trading company: concepts and strategy, 284
Generating creativity and innovation in large bureaucracies, 71
Generating technological innovation, 275
Genetic algorithms and investment strategies, 154
The genius of Sitting Bull, 128
Genius: the life and science of Richard Feynman, 104
Gentlemen of fortune: the world's merchant and investment bankers, 16
Get better or get beaten: 31 leadership secrets from GE's Jack Welch, 167
Getting it to the bottom line: management by incremental gains, 226
Getting new clients, 241
Getting past no: negotiating with difficult people, 205
Getting the best out of yourself and others, 91
Getting the word out: how managers can create value with communications, 45
Getting there: the epic struggle between road and rail in the American century, 284
Getting things done when you are not in charge, 167
Getting to yes: negotiating agreement without giving in, 205
Give & take: the complete guide to negotiating strategies and tactics, 205
The global bankers, 18
Global business: Asia-Pacific dimensions, 12
The global business: four key marketing strategies, 102

Global business management in the 1900s, 145
Global cash management, 38
The global city: New York, London, Tokyo, 109
Global corporate alliances and the competitive edge: strategies and tactics for management, 275
Global corporate real estate management: a handbook for multinational businesses and organizations, 248
Global credit analysis: Moody's Investors Service, 201
Global dreams: imperial corporations and the new world order, 145
The global economy: from meso to macroeconomics, 172
The global economy in the 90s: a user's guide, 151
Global economy in the age of science-based knowledge, 84
Global electronic wholesale banking, 18
Global embrace: corporate challenges in a transnational world, 145
Global financial services: strategies for building competitive strengths in international commercial and investment banking, 307
The global IBM: leadership in multinational management, 149
Global management principles, 47
Global marketing management, 102
The global marketplace, 49
The global marketplace: 102 of the most influential companies outside America, 145
Global outlook 2000: an economic, social and environmental perspective, 285
The global partnership for environment and development: a guide to Agenda 21, 95
Global project management handbook, 135
Global quality: the new management culture, 282
Global shift: industrial change in a turbulent world, 139
Global strategic management: the essentials, 145
Global strategies: insights from the world's leading thinkers, 145
Global vision: building new models for the corporation of the future, 145
Global warming: are we entering the greenhouse century, 116
The globalization of business: the challenge of the 1990s, 145
The globalization of money and securities: the new products, players and markets, 254
Globalization, technology, and competition: the fusion of computers and telecommunications in the 1990s, 145
Globalwork: bridging distance, culture, and time, 145
GM passes Ford, 1918-1938: designing the General Motors performance-control system, 115
The gnomes of Tokyo, 108
Going for broke: Lee Iacocca's battle to save Chrysler, 41
Going for it!: how to succeed as an entrepreneur, 163
Going global: new opportunities for growing companies to compete in world markets, 102
Going green: how to communicate your company's environmental commitment, 128

Going international: how to make friends and deal effectively in the global marketplace, 145
Going private: the international experience with transport privatization, 237
Going public: how to make your initial stock offering successful, 116
Going public: MIPS computer and the entrepreneurial dream, 116
Going public: the entrepreneur's guide, 116
Going to market: distribution systems for industrial products, 192
The gold-collar worker: harnessing the brainpower of the new workforce, 240
The golden donors: a new anatomy of the great foundations, 234
Good intentions aside: a manager's guide to resolving ethical problems, 29
Good-bye to the low profile: the art of creative confrontation, 243
Government and the enterprise since 1900: the changing problem of efficiency, 133
Government control and multinational strategic management: power systems and telecommunication equipment, 145
Government, technology, and the future of the automobile, 14
Government-business cooperation, 1945-1964: corporatism in the post-war era, 140
The Gower handbook of logistics and distribution management, 234
The Gower handbook of management, 175
Graham and Dodd's security analysis, 153
Grand designs: the impact of corporate strategies on workers, unions, and communities, 284
The great American success story: factors that affect achievement, 272
Great good fortune: how Harvard makes its money, 120
Great ideas in management: lessons from the founders and foundations of managerial practice, 175
The great marketing turnaround: the age of the individual, and how to profit from it, 187
The Great Northern Railway: a history, 118
A great place to work: what makes some employers so good, and most so bad, 230
The great u-turn corporate restructuring and the polarizing of America, 288
Great writers on organizations, 227
The great writings in marketing: selected readings together with the authors' own retrospective commentaries, 187
The greatest management principle in the world, 230
The greatest-ever bank robbery: the collapse of the savings and loan industry, 253
Greed and glory on Wall Street: the fall of the house of Lehman, 169
Green business opportunities: the profit potential, 118
The green consumer, 57
Green gold: Japan, Germany, the United States, and the race for environmental technology, 77
Groups that work (and those that don't): creating conditions for effective teamwork, 305
Groupware in the 21st century: computer

supported cooperative working toward the millennium, 305
Growing a business, 207
Growing pains: how to make the transition from an entrepreneurship to a professionally managed firm, 207
The growth experiment: how the new tax policy is transforming the U.S. economy, 274
The growth of economic thought, 86
The growth of international business, 145
Growth with equity: economic policymaking for the next century, 290
Gucci: a house divided, 119
Guerrilla marketing: secrets for making big profits from your small business, 187
Guerrilla P.R.: how you can wage an effective publicity campaign—without going broke, 243
A guide to econometrics, 82
Guide to economic indicators, 85
A guide to expert systems, 102
Guide to financial analysis, 27
A guide to financial statement disclosures, 80
Guide to high-performance investing, 267
Guide to joint ventures in the USSR: laws, regulations, model documents and practical information = Sovmestnye predpriia tiia v SSSR, 162
Guide to managerial communication, 25
A guide to managing interest-rate risk, 144
Guide to personal finance: a lifetime program of money management, 106
A guide to registered municipal securities, 203
A guide to successful business relations with the Chinese: opening the Great Wall's gate, 30
A guide to the financial markets, 35
Guidelines for preparing proposals: a manual on how to organize winning proposals for grants, venture capital, R & D projects, other proposals, 241
Guides to corporate responsibility series, 24

H.L. and Lyda, 124
The hacker crackdown: law and disorder on the electronic frontier, 49
Hammer, 119
Handbook for raising capital: financing alternatives for emerging and growing businesses, 27
Handbook of accounting and auditing, 4
Handbook of accounting practice, 4
Handbook of business and financial ratios, 247
Handbook of business problem solving, 175
Handbook of business strategy, 61
Handbook of business valuation, 27
Handbook of capital expenditure management, 35
The handbook of capital investing: analyses and strategies for investment in capital assets, 35
Handbook of compensation management, 47
The handbook of convertibles, 58
The handbook of corporate earnings analysis: company performance and stock market valuation, 62
Handbook of corporate finance, 65
Handbook of cost accounting theory and techniques, 68
The handbook of currency and interest rate risk management, 108

Handbook of depreciation methods, formulas, and tables, 77
The handbook of economic cycles: Jake Bernstein's comprehensive guide to repetitive price patterns in stocks, futures, and financials, 26
The handbook of employee benefits: design, funding, and administration, 90
The handbook of executive communication, 45
Handbook of expert systems in manufacturing, 239
The handbook of financial engineering: new financial product innovations, applications, and analyses, 65
Handbook of financial markets and institutions, 105
Handbook of financial markets: securities, options, and futures, 155
The handbook of financial modeling: the financial executive's reference guide to accounting, finance, and investment models, 65
The handbook of fixed income securities, 21
The handbook of forecasting: a manager's guide, 31
Handbook of human performance technology: a comprehensive guide for analyzing and solving performance problems in organizations, 229
The handbook of human resource development, 230
Handbook of human resources administration, 230
Handbook of human resources communications, 46
Handbook of human-computer interaction, 123
Handbook of industrial and organizational psychology, 242
Handbook of industrial engineering, 125
Handbook of industrial organization, 133
Handbook of industrial robotics, 251
The handbook of interest rate risk management, 144
Handbook of internal accounting controls, 13
Handbook of international accounting, 146
The handbook of international business, 146
Handbook of international business and management, 146
The handbook of international financial management, 151
Handbook of international financial management, 146
The handbook of international investing, 157
Handbook of international management, 146
The handbook of international mergers and acquisitions, 53
A handbook of introductory statistical methods, 265
Handbook of investment products and services, 155
Handbook of IS management, 180
Handbook of IT auditing, 141
The handbook of joint venturing, 162
Handbook of key economic indicators, 85
Handbook of labor economics, 164
Handbook of management accounting, 183
Handbook of management consulting services, 25
A handbook of management techniques, 175
Handbook of modern finance, 105
Handbook of monetary economics, 200
The handbook of mortgage-backed securities, 202

The handbook of municipal bonds and public finance, 203
Handbook of organizational behavior, 217
Handbook of organizational communication, 46
Handbook of organizational communication: an interdisciplinary perspective, 45
Handbook of production and inventory control, 238
Handbook of sociology, 263
Handbook of statistical methods in manufacturing, 239
Handbook of strategic growth through mergers and acquisitions, 53
Handbook of strategic management, 269
Handbook of survey research, 263
Handbook of task analysis procedures, 142
Handbook of the money and capital markets, 201
The handbook of U.S. Treasury & government agency securities: instruments, strategies, and analysis, 117
Handbook of work and organizational psychology, 242
Hands across the ocean: managing joint ventures with a spotlight on China and Japan, 162
Hard choices: how women decide about work, career, and motherhood, 300
Hard drive: Bill Gates and the making of the Microsoft empire, 114
Hard heads, soft hearts: tough-minded economics for a just society, 86
The hard problems of management: gaining the ethics edge, 29
Hard-pressed in the heartland: the Hormel strike and the future of the labor movement, 115
Hardball for women: winning at the game of business, 303
The Harvard century: the making of the university to the nation, 120
The Hay/Inc. 500 report: managing corporate growth and renewal: lessons in excellence from America's best small companies, 128
Hayek on Hayek: an autobiographical dialogue, 120
HBJ Miller comprehensive European accounting guide, 4
Head to head: the coming economic battle among Japan, Europe, and America, 84
The headhunters, 101
Healing the wounds: overcoming the trauma of layoffs and revitalizing downsized organizations, 222
Health care cost management: a basic guide, 195
Health care marketing: a foundation for managed quality, 195
The health care solution: understanding the crisis and the cure, 195
Health policy reform: competition and controls, 195
Health security: the President's report to the American people, 120
The healthy company: eight strategies to develop people, productivity, and profits, 128
The healthy workplace: a blueprint for corporate action, 212
Hearing the voice of the market: competitive advantage through creative use of market information, 75

The heart of business: ethics, power, and philosophy, 24
Hedging: principles, practices, and strategies for the financial markets, 121
Henderson on corporate strategy, 61
Her own business: success secrets of entrepreneurial women, 303
The hero's farewell: what happens when CEOs retire, 40
Hidden differences: doing business with the Japanese, 46
The high cost of high tech: the dark side of the chip, 51
High performance in the 90s: leading the strategic and cultural revolution in banking, 15
High rise: how 1,000 men and women worked around the clock for five years and lost $200 million building a skyscraper, 247
High rollers: inside the savings and loan debacle, 253
High tech America: the what, how, where, and why of the sunrise industries, 121
High tech: window to the future, 121
High-involvement management, 175
High-risk, high-return investing, 155
High-tech society: the story of the information technology revolution, 51
The high-yield debt market: investment performance and economic impact, 163
Higher learning, 88
A higher standard of leadership: lessons from the life of Gandhi, 167
Highly confident: the crime and punishment of Michael Milken, 199
Hiring the best: a manager's guide to effective interviewing, 93
A history of American business, 287
A history of computing technology, 194
A history of economic theory and method, 86
The history of MCI 1968-1988: the early years, 195
Hostile takeovers: issues in public and corporate policy, 54
The hotel and restaurant business, 123
Hothouse management: acquisitions, takeovers, and LBOs, 54
House of cards: inside the troubled empire of American Express, 9
The house of Morgan: an American banking dynasty and the rise of modern finance, 202
The house of Nomura: the inside story of the legendary Japanese financial dynasty, 255
Housing and the new financial markets, 202
How corporate truths become competitive traps: how to keep the things that "everyone knows are true" from becoming roadblocks to success, 175
How labor markets work: reflections on theory and practice, 155
How mutual funds work, 204
How the City of London works: an introduction to its financial markets, 108
How the foreign exchange market works, 112
How the options markets work, 215
How the West grew rich: the economic transformation of the industrial world, 98
How to acquire the perfect business for your company, 54

How to analyze businesses, financial statements, and the quality of earnings, 110
How to avoid a mid-life financial crisis, 106
How to build a corporation's identity and project its image, 60
How to build business-wide databases, 24
How to compete beyond the 1980s: perspectives from high-performance companies: conference proceedings, 128
How to do business with the Japanese, 206
How to get the most out of Dow Jones News/Retrieval, 80
How to get to the top... and stay there, 271
How to interpret financial statements for better business decisions, 110
How to invest in bonds, 21
How to invest in real estate, 248
How to keep your savings safe: protecting the money you can't afford to lose, 155
How to lead work teams: facilitation skills, 305
How to lose $100,000,000 and other valuable advice, 170
How to make a buck and still be a decent human being: a week with Rick Rose at Dataflex, 74
How to make it big as a consultant, 26
How to manage, 175
How to manage change effectively, 222
How to market to consumers: 10 ways to win, 187
How to organize and operate a small business, 259
How to prepare a feasibility study: a step-by-step guide including 3 model studies, 69
How to price your products and services, 236
How to profit from the coming Russian boom: the insider's guide to business opportunities and survival on the frontiers of capitalism, 157
How to raise venture capital, 295
How to read a financial report: wringing vital signs out of the numbers, 110
How to run a small business, 259
How to select and manage consultants: a guide to getting what you pay for, 56
How to set up your own small business, 259
How to solve business problems: the consultant's approach to business problem solving, 237
How to start and operate a mail-order business, 173
How to start and run your own business, 259
How to succeed as an independent consultant, 26
How to turn round a manufacturing company, 62
How to use the power of the printed word: thirteen articles packed with facts and practical information, designed to help you read better, write better, communicate better, 94
How women executives succeed: lessons and experiences from the federal government, 301
HRM, trends and challenges: human resource management, 230
Human capital: a theoretical and empirical analysis, with special reference to education, 88
Human factors in project management, 135
The human problems of an industrial civilization, 299
Human relations: a job oriented approach, 138
Human relations series, 152
Human resource accounting: advances in concepts, methods, and applications, 230
Human resource management, 230

Human resource management in high-technology firms, 122
Human resource management in international firms: change, globalization, innovation, 146
Human resource management systems: strategies, tactics, and techniques, 231
The human resource problem-solver's handbook, 273
Human resources and personnel management, 231
Human resources management: readings, 231
The human side of corporate competitiveness, 139
The human side of enterprise: 25th anniversary printing, 231
The human side of management: management by intergration and self-control, 179
The human side of mergers and acquisitions: managing collisions between people, cultures, and organizations, 54
The human side of project management, 135
Human systems development, 215
Human value management: the value-adding human resource management strategy for the 1990s, 231
Human-intelligence-based manufacturing, 110
Hypergrowth: applying the success formula of today's fastest growing companies, 138

I know it when I see it: a modern fable about quality, 128
Iacocca: an autobiography, 124
IBM: how the world's most successful corporation is managed, 149
The IBM lesson: the profitable art of full employment, 149
IBM, the making of the common view, 149
IBM vs. Japan: the struggle for the future, 150
The IBM way: insights into the world's most successful marketing organization, 150
The Icarus paradox: how exceptional companies bring about their own downfall, 30
Ida Tarbell: portrait of a muckraker, 274
The idea brokers: think tanks and the rise of the new policy elite, 117
Ideology and national competitiveness: an analysis of nine countries, 49
If women counted: a new feminist economics, 258
If you're so smart: the narrative of economic expertise, 87
The IFM guide to the preparation of a company policy manual, 231
The illusion of choice: how the market economy shapes our destiny, 261
Illusions of power: a history of the Washington Public Power Supply System (WPPSS), 299
Imagining tomorrow: history, technology, and the American future, 277
The impact of computers on banking, 17
Implanting strategic management, 269
Implementing activity-based cost management: moving from analysis to action: implementation experiences at eight companies, 69
Implementing organizational change, 222
Implementing strategy, 61
The improvement of corporate financial performance: a manager's guide to evaluating selected opportunities, 65

The improvement process: how America's leading companies improve quality, 245
Improving health policy and management: nine critical research issues for the 1990s, 196
Improving performance: how to manage the white space on the organization chart, 134
Improving supervisors' effectiveness, 273
In all his glory: the life of William S. Paley, the legendary tycoon and his brilliant circle, 227
In labor's cause: main themes on the history of the American worker, 284
In love and in business: how entrepreneurial couples are changing the rules of business and marriage, 70
In pursuit of principle and profit: business success through social responsibility, 262
In search of excellence: lessons from America's best-run companies, 128
In search of excess: the overcompensation of American executives, 101
In search of solutions: sixty ways to guide your problem-solving group, 119
In the age of the smart machine: the future of work and power, 13
In the rings of Saturn, 115
In transition: from the Harvard Business School Club of New York Personal Seminar in Career Management, 37
In whose interest?: international banking and American foreign policy, 18
Inc. magazine presents how to really create a successful business plan: featuring the business plans of Pizza Hut, People Express, Ben & Jerry's Ice Cream, Celestial Seasonings, Software Publishing, 207
Inc. yourself: how to profit by setting up your own corporation, 65
Income property valuation, 248
The incredible January effect: the stock market's unsolved mystery, 267
Incredibly American: releasing the heart of quality, 10
Industrial and organizational psychology, 242
Industrial collaboration with Japan, 162
Industrial design: reflection of a century, 78
Industrial efficiency in six nations, 134
Industrial engineering and management: a new perspective, 125
Industrial location: principles and policies, 139
The industrial market research handbook, 192
Industrial market structure and economic performance, 133
Industrial marketing: cases and concepts, 132
Industrial policy of Japan, 140
Industrial product innovation: organisation and management, 275
Industrial relations in a new age, 137
Industrial relations systems, 137
Industrial renaissance: producing a competitive future for America, 275
Industry in Poland: structural adjustment issues and policy options, 271
Influence without authority, 226
InfoCulture: the Smithsonian book of information age inventions, 141
Information anxiety, 45

Information for corporate directors: the role of the board in the management process, 79
The information jungle: a quasi-novel approach to managing corporate knowledge, 128
Information management: the strategic dimension, 180
The information mosaic, 183
Information payoff: the transformation of work in the electronic age, 213
Information strategies: new pathways to management productivity, 45
Information systems concepts, 180
Information systems for accounting and management: concepts, applications, and technology, 180
Information systems for management: a book of readings, 24
Information systems in management, 180
Information systems management: analytical tools and techniques, 89
The information systems research challenge, 181
The Information Systems Research Challenge: proceedings, 181
Information systems: theory and practice, 181
Information technology and the corporation of the 1990s: research studies, 175
The information technology revolution, 51
Information technology: the trillion-dollar opportunity, 50
Infotrends: profiting from your information resources, 141
Initial public offerings: all you need to know about taking a company public, 116
The inner game of management: how to make the transition to a managerial role, 175
Innovating to compete: lessons for diffusing and managing change in the workplace, 222
Innovation and competition: the global management of petrochemical products, 233
Innovation and entrepreneurship in organizations: strategies for competitiveness, deregulation, and privatization, 48
Innovation and growth in the global economy, 275
Innovation and market structure: lessons from the computer and semiconductor industries, 50
Innovation and technology in the markets: a reordering of the world's capital market systems, 151
Innovation and the productivity crisis, 134
Innovation: the attacker's advantage, 275
The innovators: the discoveries, inventions, and breakthroughs of our time, 275
The innovators: the essential guide to business thinkers, achievers and entrepreneurs, 34
Innumeracy: mathematical illiteracy and its consequences, 194
Input-output economics, 142
Insanely great: the life and times of Macintosh, the computer that changed everything, 171
Inside America, 243
Inside America's fastest growing companies, 66
Inside corporate innovation: strategy, structure, and managerial skills, 275
Inside corporate Japan: the art of fumble-free management, 128
Inside Japan's defense: technology, economics & strategy, 160

Inside Japanese financial markets, 105
Inside organizational communication, 46
Inside out: an insider's account of Wall Street, 170
Inside teams: how 20 world-class organizations are winning through teamwork, 305
Inside the boardroom: governance by directors and trustees, 59
Inside the commodity option markets, 44
Inside the Fed: making monetary policy, 104
Inside the financial futures markets, 108
Inside the firm: the inefficiencies of hierarchy, 133
Inside the Harvard Business School: strategies and lessons of America's leading school of business, 120
Inside the money market, 200
Inside the new Europe, 96
Inside the swap market, 112
Inside the US Treasury market, 117
Inside venture capital: past, present, and future, 295
The insider buyout, 179
The insiders: the truth behind the scandal rocking Wall Street, 142
Insight into management, 129
Inspiring people at work: how to make participative management work for you, 175
The instant economist, 87
Instant management: the best ideas from the people who have made a difference in how we manage, 129
Institutional investing: challenges and responsibilities of the 21st century, 142
The institutional investor focus on investment management, 235
Institutional investor's guide to managed futures programs, 114
The insurance industry in Canada, 142
Integrated marketing communications, 46
Integrating acquired companies: management accounting and reporting issues, 54
Integrating service strategy in the manufacturing company, 185
Integrating the individual and the organization, 231
The integration of women in management: a guide for human resources and management development specialists, 300
Integrative management, innovation, and new venturing: a guide to sustained profitability, 129
Intelligent enterprise: a knowledge and service based paradigm for industry, 210
Intelligent machinery: theory and practice, 89
Interactive corporate compliance: an alternative to regulatory compulsion, 62
Interest rate swaps, 112
Interest rates, the markets, and the new financial world, 105
Intermediate accounting, 4
Intermediate accounting: comprehensive volume, 5
Intermediate financial management, 27
Internal auditing manual, 13
Internal markets: bringing the power of free enterprise inside your organization, 222
International accounting and reporting, 146
International business, 146
International business and governments: issues and institutions, 146

International business and multinational enterprises, 146
International business classics, 146
International business, environment and management, 146
International business: environments and operations, 146
International business: firm and environment, 146
International business handbook, 152
International business: issues and concepts, 146
International business strategy and administration, 146
International capital markets, 36
International capital movements: based on the Marshall lectures given at the University of Cambridge, 1985, 36
International capitalism and industrial restructuring: a critical analysis, 139
International collaborative ventures in U.S. manufacturing, 278
International corporate finance: markets, transactions, and financial management, 146
International countertrade, 70
International dimensions of accounting, 147
International dimensions of business policy and strategy, 147
International dimensions of financial management, 147
International dimensions of management, 147
International dimensions of marketing, 102
International dimensions of organizational behavior, 217
International dimensions of the legal environment of business, 113
International economic institutions, 150
International economics: theory and context, 150
International economics: theory, evidence, and practice, 150
International finance, 87
International finance and financial policy, 151
International finance: cases and simulation, 147
International financial management, 151
International financial market investment: a Swiss banker's guide, 155
International financial markets, 112
International handbook of production and operations management, 239
International industry and business: structural change, industrial policy and industry strategies, 84
International investments, 157
International management and production: survival techniques for corporate America, 47
International marketing, 102
International marketing: a cultural approach, 102
International marketing and export management, 102
International marketing management, 102
International marketing: managerial perspectives, 102
International mergers and acquisitions, 54
International money and banking: the creation of a new order, 18
International money and finance, 151
The international money game, 151
The international political economy of direct foreign investment, 157

International portfolio management, 157
International trade and competition: cases and notes in strategy and management, 147
International trade and investment, 152
International trade in computer software, 50
The internationalisation of stockmarkets: the trend towards greater foreign borrowing and investment, 266
Internationalization of business: an introduction, 147
The internationalization of Japanese business: European and Japanese perspectives, 68
Interpersonal communication in the modern organization, 46
Introducing corporate planning: guide to strategic management, 61
An introduction to airline economics, 9
Introduction to brokerage operations department procedures, 267
Introduction to business: an international perspective, 147
Introduction to business and economic statistics, 262
Introduction to computers, 24
An introduction to database systems, 73
Introduction to expert systems, 102
Introduction to financial accounting, 5
Introduction to financial management, 66
Introduction to fund accounting, 114
Introduction to information systems in business management, 24
Introduction to macroeconomics, 172
Introduction to management accounting, 183
Introduction to marketing management: text and cases, 187
Introduction to nonprofit organization accounting, 211
Introduction to probability models, 237
Introduction to probability theory and statistical inference, 237
Introduction to statistical quality control, 245
Introduction to statistics and econometrics, 82
An introduction to the multinationals, 147
An introduction to the SEC, 286
An introduction to the Securities and Exchange Commission, 286
Introductory business forecasting, 31
Introductory statistics for business and economics, 262
Intuition and management: research and application, 175
The intuitive manager, 101
Invasion of the salarymen: the Japanese business presence in America, 68
An invented life: reflections on leadership and change, 167
Inventing desire: inside Chiat/Day: the hottest shop, the coolest players, the big business of advertising, 39
Inventivity: the art and science of research management, 249
Investing in Cuba: problems and prospects, 157
Investing in developing countries: a guide for executives, 157
Investing in information technology: managing the decision-making process, 141

Investing: the collected works of Martin L. Leibowitz, 21
Investing with a social conscience, 155
Investing with the best: what to look for, what to look out for in your search for a superior investment manager, 153
Investment analysis and portfolio management, 153, 155
Investment analysis for real estate decisions, 248
Investment banking: a tale of three cities, 154
Investment banking and diligence: what price deregulation, 154
The investment banking handbook, 154
Investment banking in Europe: restructuring for the 1990's, 154
Investment demand and U.S. economic growth, 35
Investment policy: how to win the loser's game, 235
Investment strategy and the money connection: tracking the monetary and business cycles—and making them work for you, 44
Investments, 155
Investments, an introduction to analysis and management, 155
Investments: analysis and management, 155
Investor response to management decisions: a research-based analysis of actions and effects, 155
The invisible billionaire, Daniel Ludwig, 171
The invisible link: Japan's sogo shosha and the organization of trade, 52
The invisible powers: the language of business, 24
The invisible work force: transforming American business with outside and home-based workers, 123
Invitation to industrial relations, 137
Ironies in organizational development, 222
Irreconcilable differences: Ross Perot versus General Motors, 54
Is Guinness good for you?: the bid for Distillers—the inside story, 119
Is new technology enough?: making and remaking U.S. basic industries, 291
ISO 9000, 245
ISO 9000: an implementation guide for small to mid-sized businesses, 245
Issues and readings in managerial finance, 66
Issues in business and society: capitalism and public purpose, 24
It ain't as easy as it looks: Ted Turner's amazing story, 285
It's about time: a fable about the next dimension of quality, 282
It's good business, 29
The ITT wars, 151

Japan: a postindustrial power, 158
The Japan business study program: understanding Japanese business, 158
Japan, Europe, and international financial markets: analytical and empirical perspectives, 160
Japan Inc.: an introduction to Japanese economics: the comic book, 159
Japan Inc.: global strategies of Japanese trading corporations, 52
Japan surges ahead; the story of an economic miracle, 138

cThe Japan syndrome: symptoms, ailments, and remedies, 159
The Japan syndrome—is there one?: cases to the point, 68
Japan, the fragile superpower, 158
Japan, the United States, and a changing Southeast Asia, 12
Japan's choices: new globalism and cultural orientations in an industrial state, 160
Japan's emerging multinationals: an international comparison of policies and practices, 147
Japan's global reach: the influences, strategies and weaknesses of Japan's multinational companies, 160
Japan's high technology industries: lessons and limitations of industrial policy, 122
Japan's market: the distribution system, 192
Japan's software factories: a challenge to U.S. management, 50
Japan's unequal trade, 158
Japanese and European management: their international adaptability, 68
The Japanese automobile industry: technology and management at Nissan and Toyota, 14
The Japanese bond markets: an overview and analysis, 21
The Japanese business success factors: how top management, product, money and people's creativity contribute to Japanese enterprise growth, 129
Japanese direct manufacturing investment in the United States, 157
The Japanese economy, 159
Japanese electronics technology: enterprise and innovation, 90
Japanese industrial performance, 160
The Japanese industrial system, 129
Japanese management: a forward-looking analysis, 129
The Japanese overseas: can they go home again, 103
The Japanese power game: what it means for America, 235
Japanese quality concepts: an overview, 282
The Japanese school: lessons for industrial America, 88
The Japanese stock market: pricing systems and accounting information, 266
Japanese takeovers: the global contest for corporate control, 54
The Japanese temptation, 129
The Japanese today: change and continuity, 158
Japanese-U.S. business negotiations: a cross-cultural study, 206
Japanophobia: the myth of the invincible Japanese, 157
Japan—facing economic maturity, 159
Job analysis: a handbook for the human resource director, 161
Job analysis: an effective management tool, 161
Job creation in America: how our smallest companies put the most people to work, 259
Job satisfaction—a reader, 161
Job security in America: lessons from Germany, 161
Job stress and blue collar work, 161

A job to live: the impact of tomorrow's technology on work and society, 286
Johnson v. Johnson, 162
Joint management and employee participation: labor and management at the crossroads, 175
A journey through economic time: a firsthand view, 84
Judgement and choice: the psychology of decision, 75
Judgment calls: high-stakes decisions in a risky world, 75
Judgmental forecasting, 83
Judicial jeopardy: when business collides with the courts, 70
Juggernaut: the German way of business: why it is transforming Europe—and the world, 129
Jumping the curve: innovation and strategic choice in an age of transition, 269
Junk bonds: how high yield securities restructured corporate America, 163
Juran on leadership for quality: an executive handbook, 245
Juran on quality by design: the new steps for planning quality into goods and services, 245
Juran's quality control handbook, 245
Just do it: the Nike spirit in the corporate world, 210
Just rewards: the case for ethical reform in business, 29
Just-in-time: surviving by breaking tradition, 175
Justice, gender, and affirmative action, 257
Justice in the workplace: approaching fairness in human resource management, 91
Justice on the job: resolving grievances in the nonunion workplace, 118

Kaisha, the Japanese corporation, 66
Kaizen teian 1: developing systems for continuous improvement through employee suggestions, 273
Kaizen teian 2 =, 273
Kaizen, the key to Japanese competitive success, 129
Kanban just-in-time at Toyota: management begins at the workplace, 238
Keeping America at work: strategies for employing the new technologies, 275
Keeping customers, 72
Keeping good company: a study of corporate governance in five countries, 59
Keeping pace: U.S. policies and global economic change, 290
Keeping the family business healthy: how to plan for continuing growth, profitability, and family leadership, 103
Keeping the U.S. computer industry competitive: defining the agenda: a colloquium report, 50
Keiretsu: inside the hidden Japanese conglomerates, 52
Key issues in business ethics, 29
Keys to reading an annual report, 110
The keys to the kingdom: the FS-X deal and the selling of America's future to Japan, 278
Keys to understanding the financial news, 106
King Icahn: the biography of a renegade capitalist, 124

Kings on the catwalk: the Louis Vuitton and Moët-Hennessy affair, 171
Kleppner's advertising procedure, 7
The knowledge executive: leadership in an information society, 167
Knowledge for action: a guide to overcoming barriers to organizational change, 222
The knowledge link: how firms compete through strategic alliances, 162
Knowledge processing and applied artificial intelligence, 24
Knowledge-based manufacturing management: applications of artificial intelligence to the effective management of manufacturing companies, 185
Knowledge-based systems for strategic planning, 269
The knowledge-value revolution, or, a history of the future, 261
Korea in the world economy, 164
Korean economic dynamism, 164
Korean etiquette & ethics in business, 30

Labor and an integrated Europe, 137
Labor economics and industrial relations: markets and institutions, 164
Labor economics and labor relations, 164
Labor economics: theory, institutions, and public policy, 164
Labor in the twentieth century, 306
Labor pains and the Gaijin boss: hiring, managing and firing the Japanese, 231
Labor relations, 137
Labor relations: development, structure, process, 137
Labor will rule: Sidney Hillman and the rise of American labor, 122
Labor's capital: the economics and politics of private pensions, 214
Labor-management relations, 137
Labor-management relations in a changing environment, 137
Laboratories of democracy, 140
Land of desire: merchants, power, and the rise of a new American culture, 77
Land of opportunity: the entrepreneurial spirit in America, 83
Land's Polaroid: a company and the man who invented it, 166
Large-scale organizational change, 222
The last empire: De Beers, diamonds, and the world, 78
Late bloomers: coming of age in today's America: the right place at the wrong time, 307
Latest innovations in the US mortgage market, 202
Law and ethics in the business environment, 126
The leader's edge: the seven keys to leadership in a turbulent world, 167
The leader's window: mastering the four styles of leadership to build high-performing teams, 167
The leader-manager, 101
Leaders and followers: challenges for the future, 167
Leaders, fools, and impostors: essays on the psychology of leadership, 167
Leaders on leadership: interviews with top executives, 40

Leadership and ambiguity: the American college president, 42
Leadership and organizations, 167
Leadership and the culture of trust, 167
Leadership and the one minute manager: increasing effectiveness through situational leadership, 175
Leadership and the quest for integrity, 167
Leadership at the Fed, 20
The leadership challenge: how to get extraordinary things done in organizations, 168
Leadership dilemmas—Grid solutions, 168
The leadership factor, 168
Leadership for change, 168
Leadership in action: tough-minded strategies from the global giant, 147
Leadership in administration; a sociological interpretation, 168
Leadership jazz, 168
Leadership: managing in real organizations, 168
Leadership without easy answers, 168
The leading edge: CEOs who turned their companies around: what they did and how they did it, 222
Leading edge logistics: a competitive positioning for the 1990's: comprehensive research on logistics organization strategy and behavior in North America, 48
Leading indicators for the 1990s, 85
Leading issues in economic development, 82
Leading self-directed work teams: a guide to developing new team leadership skills, 305
Leading: the art of becoming an executive, 168
Leading the team organization: how to create an enduring competitive advantage, 305
The League: the rise and decline of the NFL, 204
Lean and mean: the changing landscape of corporate power in the age of flexibility, 138
The learning edge: how smart managers and smart companies stay ahead, 175
The learning imperative: managing people for continuous innovation, 231
Learning leadership: cases and commentaries on abuses of power in organizations, 168
Learning to manage conflict: getting people to work together productively, 52
Lease or buy?: principles for sound decision making, 169
Lease or purchase: theory and practice, 169
The lease versus buy decision, 125
Legal aspects of marketing strategy: antitrust and consumer protection issues, 283
The legal environment of business, 126, 283
Legal handbook for small business, 259
The Legitimate corporation: essential readings in business ethics and corporate governance, 29
Leo Melamed on the markets: twenty years of financial history as seen by the man who revolutionized the markets, 106
Lesly's handbook of public relations and communications, 243
Lessons: an autobiography, 298
The lessons of experience: how successful executives develop on the job, 99
Letters of a businessman to his son, 271
The lever of riches: technological creativity and economic progress, 275

Leverage: the key to multiplying money, 155
Leveraged buyouts, 54
Leveraged management buyouts: causes and consequences, 179
Levers of control: how managers use innovative control systems to drive strategic renewal, 129
Levine & Co.: Wall Street's insider trading scandal, 170
A lexicon of economics, 87
Liar's poker: rising through the wreckage on Wall Street, 170
Liberation management: necessary disorganization for the nanosecond nineties, 222
The library of investment banking, 154
A license to steal: the untold story of Michael Milken and the conspiracy to bilk the nation, 199
Licensing in international strategy: a guide for planning and negotiations, 112
Life after debt: recapitalizing the troubled business, 259
Life after television, 78
Life insurance: theory and practice, 143
Lifestyle and event marketing: building the new customer partnership, 243
Lifetrends: the future of baby boomers and other aging Americans, 213
Like no other store—: the Bloomingdale's legend and the revolution in American marketing, 20
The limits to growth; a report for the Club of Rome's project on the predicament of mankind, 84
Liquidity analysis and management, 38
A little bit at a time: secrets of productive quality, 165
The little black book of project management, 136
Loading the dice: a five-country study of vinyl chloride regulation, 126
The lobbyists: how influence peddlers get their way in Washington, 171
The logarithmic century, 288
A logic for strategy, 75
The logic of business strategy, 61
Logistical management: a systems integration of physical distribution, manufacturing support, and materials procurement, 234
The logistics handbook, 32
Logistics strategy: cases and concepts, 32
Long-range planning of Japanese corporations, 61
Long-term prospects for the world economy, 83
Longitudinal research, 262
Lords of the realm: the real history of baseball, 18
Losing time: the industrial policy debate, 136
Lost prophets: an insider's history of the modern economists, 87

Machine-age ideology: social engineering and American liberalism, 1911-1939, 93
The Macintosh way, 11
Macro organizational behavior, 217
Macroeconomic decision making in the world economy, 172
Macroeconomic policy, 200
Macroeconomics, 172
Macroeconomics: analysis and policy, 172
Macroeconomics and monopoly capitalism, 36
Macroeconomics: concepts, theories, and policies, 172
Macroeconomics for management, 172
Macroeconomics in the global economy, 172
Macroeconomics: theory, performance, and policy, 172
Macy's for sale, 172
Made in America: regaining the productive edge, 134
Made in Japan: Akio Morita and the Sony Corporation, 202
Made in Japan: the methods, motivation, and culture of the Japanese, and their influence on U.S. business and all Americans, 286
Made in the U.S.A.: the history of American business, 291
Made in U.S.A.: the secret histories of the things that made America, 277
Major account sales strategy, 252
Making accounting policy: the quest for credibility in financial reporting, 5
Making acquisitions work: lessons from companies' successes and mistakes, 54
Making Americans: an essay on individualism and money, 9
Making and managing high-quality workplaces: an organizational ecology, 213
Making boards effective: the dynamics of nonprofit governing boards, 211
Making capitalism: the social and cultural construction of a South Korean Conglomerate, 58
Making deals: the business of negotiating, 206
Making decisions in multinational corporations: managing relations with sovereign governments, 147
Making it happen: reflections on leadership, 129
Making markets: economic transformation in Eastern Europe and the post-Soviet states, 97
Making news, 162
The making of a public man: a memoir, 170
The making of economic society, 84
The making of Harcourt General: a history of growth through diversification, 1922-1992, 119
The making of McPaper: the inside story of USA today, 295
The making of Microsoft: how Bill Gates and his team created the world's most successful software company, 198
The making of the achiever: how to win distinction in your company, 99
Making organizations competitive: enhancing networks and relationships across traditional boundaries, 48
Making people productive, 91
Making the future work: unleashing our powers of innovation for the decades ahead, 129
Making the most of entrepreneurial management: decentralizing America's corporations, 74
Making the most of your money: smart ways to create wealth and plan your finances in the '90s, 107
Making the right decision: ethics for managers, 29
Making tough decisions: tactics for improving managerial decision making, 75
Making work systems better: a practitioner's reflections, 217

Malcolm Forbes: the man who had everything, 111
The man who discovered quality: how W. Edwards Deming brought the quality revolution to America: the stories of Ford, Xerox, and GM, 245
Manage globally, sell locally: the art of strategic account management, 256
Manage people, not personnel: motivation and performance appraisal, 231
Management, 176
Management & organization, 176
Management accounting: text and cases, 183
Management advisory services manual, 26
Management and gender: issues and attitudes, 301
Management and organizational behavior classics, 129
Management and the worker; an account of a research program conducted by the Western electric company, Hawthorne works, Chicago, 231
The management challenge: Japanese views, 176
Management consulting, 1990: the state of the profession: a symposium-in-print on the occasion of our 20th anniversary, 26
Management consulting: a game without chips, 26
The management consulting idea book, 26
The management control function, 129
Management control in nonprofit organizations, 211
Management control systems, 129
Management excellence: productivity through MBO, 180
Management for a small planet: strategic decision making and the environment, 82
Management for productivity, 176
The management game, 180
Management guides to mergers & acquisitions, 54
Management gurus: what makes them and how to become one, 176
Management in France, 176
Management in small doses, 176
Management in the third wave, 176
Management in transition, 58
Management in Western Europe: society, culture and organization in twelve nations, 176
Management information systems: a managerial end user perspective, 181
Management information systems: a study of computer-based information systems, 181
Management information systems and organizational behavior, 181
Management information systems: conceptual foundations, structure, and development, 181
Management information systems: the critical strategic resource, 181
Management laureates: a collection of autobiographical essays, 101
Management live: the video book, 217
Management mistakes & successes, 176
The management of a trust department, 285
The management of corporate business units: portfolio stategies for turbulent times, 235
Management of human resources; readings in personnel administration, 231
The management of information systems, 181
Management of investments, 155
Management of organizational behavior: utilizing human resources, 218
The management of organizations: strategies, tactics, analyses, 218
The management of organizations: strategy, structure, behavior, 176
The management of personnel, 231
Management of physical distribution and transportation, 234
The management of productivity and technology in manufacturing, 239
Management of research and development organizations: managing the unmanageable, 249
The management of strategic change, 269
Management of the sales force, 252
The management of time, 281
Management on Wall Street: making securities firms work, 255
Management planning and control: the behavioral foundations, 183
Management policy and strategy: text, readings, and cases, 176
Management rediscovered: how companies can escape the numbers trap, 129
Management response to public issues: concepts and cases in strategy formulation, 139
Management science, 182
The manager and the working group, 305
The manager as negotiator: bargaining for cooperation and competitive gain, 206
The manager's desk reference, 176
The manager's guide to competitive marketing strategies, 187
A manager's guide to globalization: six keys to success in a changing world, 147
Managerial accounting: concepts for planning, control, decision making, 183
The managerial and cost accountant's handbook, 69
Managerial communication: a finger on the pulse, 45
The managerial decision-making process, 75
Managerial decisions under uncertainty: an introduction to the analysis of decision making, 75
Managerial economics, 183, 184
Managerial economics: analysis and strategy, 184
Managerial economics and business strategy, 184
Managerial economics and operations research: techniques, applications, cases, 184
Managerial economics: applied microeconomics for decision making, 184
Managerial finance, 66
The managerial grid III, 176
Managerial hierarchies: comparative perspectives on the rise of modern industrial enterprise, 133
Managerial job change: men and women in transition, 101
Managerial literacy: what today's managers must know to succeed, 176
Managerial lives in transition: advancing age and changing times, 10
The managerial mystique: restoring leadership in business, 176
Managerial performance and promotability: the making of an executive, 199

Managerial psychology: managing behavior in organizations, 242
Managerial real estate: corporate real estate asset management, 137
Managerialism: the emergence of a new ideology, 176
Managers and national culture: a global perspective, 129
Managing a diverse work force: regaining the competitive edge, 184
Managing a nonprofit organization, 211
Managing across borders: the transnational solution, 147
Managing and operating a closely held corporation, 41
Managing at the speed of change: how resilient managers succeed and prosper where others fail, 222
Managing behavior in organizations: text, cases, readings, 218
Managing beyond the quick fix: a completely integrated program for creating and maintaining organizational success, 226
Managing big business: essays from the Business History Review, 66
Managing business transactions: controlling the cost of coordinating, communicating, and decision making, 184
Managing business-government relations: cases and notes on business-government problems, 140
Managing by influence, 242
Managing by storying around, 45
Managing by the numbers: absentee ownership and the decline of American industry, 129
Managing career systems: channeling the flow of executive careers, 101
Managing change: cases and concepts, 222
Managing complexity in high technology organizations, 122
Managing conflict in organizations, 52
Managing conflict: interpersonal dialogue and third-party roles, 52
Managing corporate culture, 218
Managing corporate ethics: learning from America's ethical companies how to supercharge business performance, 29
Managing corporate liquidity: an introduction to working capital management, 38
Managing corporate wealth: the operation of a comprehensive financial goals system, 66
Managing creativity, 71
Managing cultural differences, 147
Managing customer value: creating quality and service that customers can see, 246
Managing employee rights and responsibilities, 164
Managing excess capacity, 125
Managing finance for quality: bottom-line results from top-level commitment, 282
Managing for innovation: leading technical people, 122
Managing for results: economic tasks and risk-taking decisions, 130
Managing for the future: the 1990s and beyond, 177
Managing human resource development, 231

Managing human resources issues: confronting challenges and choosing options, 231
Managing in developing countries: strategic analysis and operating techniques, 147
Managing in the age of change, 177
Managing in the postmodern world: America's revolution against exploitation, 177
Managing in the service economy, 256
Managing in the single market, 98
Managing in turbulent times, 130
Managing individual and group behavior in organizations, 218
Managing information technology in turbulent times, 181
Managing information: the challenge and the opportunity, 24
Managing innovation and entrepreneurship in technology-based firms, 275
Managing innovation: from the executive suite to the shop floor, 275
Managing institutional assets, 153
Managing inventory for cost reduction, 152
Managing investment portfolios: a dynamic process, 235
Managing management time: who's got the monkey, 281
Managing managers: strategies and techniques for human resource management, 12
Managing maturing businesses: restructuring declining industries and revitalizing troubled operations, 222
Managing new product and process development: text and cases, 209
Managing new product innovations, 209
Managing new products: the power of innovation, 209
Managing new technology development, 277
Managing on the edge: how the smartest companies use conflict to stay ahead, 222
Managing operations: a competence approach to supervisory management, 177
Managing organizational behavior, 218
Managing organizational change, 223
Managing privacy: information technology and corporate America, 237
Managing professional people: understanding creative performance, 240
Managing professionals in innovative organizations: a collection of readings, 122
Managing professionals in research and development, 249
Managing projects and programs, 136
Managing projects in organizations: how to make the best use of time, techniques, and people, 136
Managing quality in America's most admired companies, 282
Managing quality: the strategic and competitive edge, 246
Managing risks and costs through financial innovation, 147
Managing service as a strategic profit center, 72
Managing services: marketing, operations, and human resources, 256
Managing services marketing: text and readings, 257
Managing strategy in the real world: conclusions

and frameworks from field studies of business practice, 269
Managing take-off in fast growth companies: innovation in entrepreneurial firms, 130
Managing technological innovation, 249
Managing the corporate dream: restructuring for long-term success, 177
Managing the corporate social environment: a grounded theory, 24
Managing the development of new products: achieving speed and quality simultaneously through multifunctional teamwork, 125
Managing the dynamics of new technology: issues in manufacturing management, 275
Managing the global firm, 147
Managing the manufacturing process: a pattern for excellence, 185
Managing the marketing functions: the challenge of customer-centered enterprise, 187
Managing the new bottom line: issues management for senior executives, 157
Managing the new careerists, 273
Managing the new organization: a blueprint for networks and strategic alliances, 223
Managing the new product development process: cases and notes, 209
Managing the new work force: the challenge of dual-income families, 232
Managing the professional service firm, 240
Managing the service economy: prospects and problems: essays commissioned for the inaugural conference of the Fishman-Davidson Center for the Study of the Service Sector, Wharton School, University of Pennsylvania, 257
Managing the small business: insights and readings, 259
Managing the total quality transformation, 246
Managing the unknowable: strategic boundaries between order and chaos in organizations, 226
Managing the unmanageable: strategies for success within the conglomerate, 52
Managing to have profits: the art of hitting your target profit, 241
Managing to keep the customer: how to achieve and maintain superior customer service throughout the organization, 72
Managing today and tomorrow with on-line information, 214
Managing with a conscience: how to improve performance through integrity, trust, and commitment, 177
Managing with dual strategies: mastering the present, preempting the future, 269
Managing with power: politics and influence in organizations, 75
Managing with style: a guide to understanding, assessing, and improving decision making, 75
Managing workforce 2000: gaining the diversity advantage, 184
Managing your accounting and consulting practice, 3
The **Manchester** experiment: a history of Manchester Business School, 1965-1990, 184
Mandate for change, 293
Manhattan passions: true tales of power, wealth, and excess, 209

Manias, panics, and crashes: a history of financial crises, 227
A **manual** for writers of term papers, theses, and dissertations, 80
The **manufacturers'** survival guide: new directions for the 1990s, 185
Manufacturing for competitive advantage: becoming a world class manufacturer, 292
Manufacturing high technology handbook, 239
Manufacturing knowledge: a history of the Hawthorne experiments, 130
Manufacturing matters: the myth of the post-industrial economy, 292
Manufacturing organization and management, 103
Manufacturing planning and control systems, 240
Manufacturing planning: key to improving industrial productivity, 240
Manufacturing renaissance, 292
Manufacturing strategy: the research agenda for the next decade, 185
Manufacturing, the formidable competitive weapon, 239
Manufacturing's new mandate: the tools for leadership 292
Mark my words: letters of a businessman to his son, 272
Market analysis: assessing your business opportunities, 207
Market driven management: prescriptions for survival in a turbulent world, 187
Market driven strategy: processes for creating value, 187
The **market** economy: from micro to mesoeconomics, 36
Market making and the changing structure of the securities industry, 266
Market research and analysis, 192
Market research: using forecasting in business, 192
Market segmentation: using demographics, psychographics, and other segmentation techniques to uncover and exploit new markets, 186
Market smarts: proven strategies to outfox and outflank your competition, 187
Market strategy, 187
Market wizards: interviews with top traders, 111
The **marketer's** guide to public relations: how today's top companies are using the new PR to gain a competitive edge, 243
The **marketer's** visual tool kit, 187
Marketing, 187, 188
Marketing 2000 and beyond, 188
Marketing: an international perspective, 102
Marketing: an introduction, 188
Marketing by agreement: a cross-cultural approach to business negotiations, 103
The **marketing** challenge of 1992, 188
Marketing channels, 192
Marketing channels: a management view, 192
Marketing classics: a selection of influential articles, 188
Marketing: concepts, strategies, and decisions, 188
Marketing decisions for new and mature products, 238
Marketing designs for nonprofit organizations, 211
The **marketing** edge: making strategies work, 188

The marketing edge: the new leadership role of sales & marketing in manufacturing, 185
Marketing financial services, 109
Marketing financial services: a strategic vision, 108
Marketing for health care organizations, 195
Marketing for keeps: building your business by retaining your customers, 57
Marketing for public and nonprofit managers, 188
Marketing handbook, 188
Marketing high technology: an insider's view, 121
The marketing imagination, 188
Marketing in an electronic age, 279
Marketing in the international environment, 102
Marketing in travel and tourism, 283
The marketing information revolution, 188
Marketing management, 188
Marketing management: a strategic approach, 188
Marketing management: analysis, planning, implementation, and control, 188
Marketing management and strategy: a reader, 188
Marketing management: text and cases, 188, 189
Marketing masters, 189
Marketing masters: lessons in the art of marketing from those who do it best, 189
Marketing masters: secrets of America's best companies, 189
Marketing mistakes, 189
The marketing mode; pathways to corporate growth, 189
Marketing models, 189
Marketing myths that are killing business: the cure for death wish marketing, 189
Marketing organisation: an analysis of information processing, power, and politics, 189
Marketing performance assessment, 189
Marketing places: attracting investment, industry, and tourism to cities, states, and nations, 189
The marketing plan: how to prepare it, what should be in it, 189
Marketing planning & strategy, 189
Marketing principles, 189
The marketing renaissance, 189
Marketing research, 192
Marketing research: an applied approach, 192
Marketing research: methodological foundations, 192
The marketing research process, 193
Marketing research: text and cases, 193
Marketing research the right way, 193
The marketing revolution: a radical manifesto for dominating the marketplace, 189
Marketing strategies for services: globalization, client-orientation, deregulation, 257
Marketing strategies for the new Europe: a North American perspective for 1992, 97
Marketing strategy: a customer-driven approach, 189
Marketing strategy and plans, 189
Marketing successes, historical to present day: what we can learn, 189
Marketing theory: classic and contemporary readings, 189
Marketing theory: evolution and evaluation, 190
Marketing to the affluent, 250
Marketing to win: strategies for building competitive advantage in service industries, 190
Marketing to women around the world, 301
Marketing today: successes, failures, and turnarounds, 190
Marketing warfare, 190
Marketing without mystery: a practical guide to writing a marketing plan, 190
Marketing your consulting and professional services, 241
Markets or governments: choosing between imperfect alternatives, 36
Markets: who plays, who risks, who gains, who loses, 266
Marrying for money: the path from the first hostile takeover to megamergers, insider trading, and the Boesky scandal, 54
Martin Zweig's Winning on Wall Street, 267
Mary Parker Follett—prophet of management: a celebration of writings from the 1920s, 177
Masculinity and the British organization man since 1945, 101
Mass customization: the new frontier in business competition, 276
Master manipulator, 255
Master of the game: Steve Ross and the creation of Time Warner, 251
Mastering change, 223
Mastering technology: a management framework for getting results, 276
Mastering the dynamics of innovation: how companies can seize opportunities in the face of technological change, 223
Masters of deception: a corporate giant confronted by its stockholders, 41
Mathematics for business and economics, 32
Mathematics for management and finance, 32
Mathematics for management series, 194
Mathematics, with applications in management and economics, 32
MaxiMarketing: the new direction in advertising, promotion, and marketing strategy, 190
Maximum performance: the Dow Jones-Irwin complete guide to practical business management, 130
Maxwell: the rise and fall of Robert Maxwell and his empire, 195
MBA field studies: a guide for students and faculty, 177
MBA: management by Auerbach: management tips from the leader of one of America's most successful organizations, 177
MBAs on the fast track: the career mobility of young managers, 101
MBO updated: a handbook of practices and techniques for managing by objectives, 180
McDonald's: behind the arches, 195
The McGraw-Hill construction business handbook: a practical guide to accounting, credit, finance, insurance, and law for the construction industry, 55
The McGraw-Hill guide to starting your own business: a step-by-step blueprint for the first-time entrepreneur, 207
The McGraw-Hill handbook of commodities and futures, 44
The McGraw-Hill handbook of global trade and investment financing, 102
The McGraw-Hill real estate handbook, 247

Measure up!: yardsticks for continuous improvement, 134
Measuring the value of information technology, 141
Measuring the wealth of nations: the political economy of national accounts, 204
Measuring up: charting pathways to manufacturing excellence, 185
Medicine at the crossroads: the crisis in health care, 195
Mega-mergers: corporate America's billion-dollar takeovers, 54
Megalomania, managers & mergers, 54
Megatraumas: America at the Year 2000, 83
Megatrends 2000: the new directions for the 1990's, 294
Megatrends for women, 300
Meltdown: the great '90s depression and how to come through it a winner, 26
Members of the club: the coming of age of executive women, 302
Memoirs of a recovering autocrat: revealing insights for managing the autocrat in all of us, 74
Men and women of the corporation, 218
Men, management, and morality: toward a new organizational ethic, 242
The mentor connection: strategic alliances in corporate life, 196
Mentoring at work: developmental relationships in organizational life, 272
The Merc: the emergence of a global financial powerhouse, 39
Merchant adventurer: the story of W.R. Grace, 117
Merchants of death: the American tobacco industry, 281
Merchants of debt: KKR and the mortgaging of American business, 54
Merchants of vision: people bringing new purpose and values to business, 34
Merger mania: arbitrage, Wall Street's best kept money-making secret, 11
Mergers & acquisitions, 54
The mergers & acquisitions handbook, 54
Mergers & acquisitions: will you overpay, 54
Mergers and acquisitions, 54, 55
Mergers: motives, effects, policies, 55
Mergers, restructuring, and corporate control, 55
The methodology of economics, or, How economists explain, 87
Microcosm: the quantum revolution in economics and technology, 198
Microeconomic theory, 197
Microeconomics, 87, 197
Microeconomics: analysis and policy, 197
Microeconomics: theory, applications, 197
Micromanaging: transforming business leaders with personal computers, 130
The midas touch: the strategies that have made Warren Buffet America's pre-eminent investor, 22
The Midas touch: understanding the dynamic new money societies around us, 200
Middle East oil crisis since 1973, 233
The might of the multinationals: the rise and fall of the corporate legend, 148

Milestones in management: an essential reader, 177
Million dollar consulting: the professional's guide to growing a practice, 56
Mind of a manager, soul of a leader, 177
A mind of my own: my life with Robert Maxwell, 194
Minding America's business, 140
Minding Mr. Market: ten years on Wall Street with Grant's interest rate observer, 297
Mining group gold: how to cash in on the collaborative brain power of a group, 305
Mintzberg on management: inside our strange world of organizations, 177
MIS, concepts and design, 181
Mission and business philosophy, 59
Misunderstanding media, 193
The misunderstood economy: what counts and how to count it, 288
Misused statistics: straight talk for twisted numbers, 262
MIT—shaping the future, 194
Models of business cycles, 26
Models of management: work, authority, and organization in a comparative perspective, 47
Modern advanced accounting, 5
Modern American philanthropy: a personal account, 39
Modern business financing: a guide to innovative strategies and techniques, 27
Modern competitive analysis, 48
Modern corporate finance, 66
The modern corporation and private property, 66
Modern decision making: a guide to modeling with decision support systems, 75
Modern investment mangaement and the prudent man rule, 169
Modern investment theory, 153
Modern portfolio theory and investment analysis, 235
Modern portfolio theory, the capital asset pricing model, and arbitrage pricing theory: a user's guide, 35
Modern retailing: theory and practice, 250
Modern stock market handbook, 266
The modern theory of corporate finance, 66
Monetary policy and investment opportunities, 20
Monetary policy and the financial system, 200
Monetary policy for a changing financial environment, 200
Monetary sovereignty: the politics of central banking in western Europe, 18
Monetary theory, 200
Money & banking, 17
Money and banking, 17
Money and banking: contemporary practices, policies, and issues, 106
Money and capital markets, 201
Money and capital markets in the U.K. and Europe, 108
Money and capital markets: the financial system in an increasingly global economy, 106
Money and the economy, 200
Money, banking, and economic activity, 200
Money, banking, and economic analysis, 200
Money, banking, and financial markets, 200

Money, banking and the Canadian financial system, 106
Money, banking, and the economy, 200
Money, banking, and the United States economy, 18
The **money** culture, 22
Money, finance, and macroeconomic performance in Japan, 106
Money games: the business of sports, 264
Money in your mailbox: how to start and operate a successful mail-order business, 173
Money, interest, and prices: an integration of monetary and value theory, 143
Money, interest, and stagnation: dynamic theory and Keynes's economics, 201
The **money** launderers: lessons from the drug wars—how billions of illegal dollars are washed through banks & businesses, 201
The **money** lords; the great finance capitalists, 1925-1950, 37
The **money** machine: how KKR manufactured power & profits, 163
The **money** machine: how the city works, 108
The **money** mandarins: the making of a new supranational economic order, 84
Money meltdown: restoring order to the global currency system, 151
Money mischief: episodes in monetary history, 200
Money of the mind: borrowing and lending in America from the Civil War to Michael Milken, 71
Money, power, and space, 151
Money talks: corporate PACs and political influence, 25
The **money** wars: the rise and fall of the great buyout boom of the 1980s, 55
Money, whence it came, where it went, 201
The **moneymakers:** the great big new rich in America, 299
Monitoring the competition: find out what's really going on over there, 31
The **monster** under the bed: how business is mastering the opportunity of knowledge for profit, 26
Montgomery's Auditing, 13
The **moral** dimension: toward a new economics, 87
The **moral** manager, 29
Moral mazes: the world of corporate managers, 30
The **moral** sense, 96
Morality and the market: consumer pressure for corporate accountability, 56
More equal than others: women and men in dual-career marriages, 193
The **Morgans:** private international bankers, 1854-1913, 202
Mortgage and mortgage-backed securities markets, 202
Mortgage banking: a handbook of strategies, trends, and opportunities, 202
Mortgaging the earth: the World Bank, environmental impoverishment, and the crisis of development, 306
Moscow meets Madison Avenue: the adventures of the first American adman in the U.S.S.R, 22
The **most** powerful bank: inside Germany's Bundesbank, 78

The **motivation** crisis; winding down and turning off, 161
Moving mountains: lessons in leadership and logistics from the Gulf War, 229
Multiculturalism in the United States: a comparative guide to acculturation and ethnicity, 199
Multinational corporate strategy: planning for world markets, 148
Multinational corporations, 148
Multinational corporations and the impact of public advocacy on corporate strategy: Nestle and the infant formula controversy, 206
Multinational enterprise and world competition: a comparative study of the USA, Japan, the UK, Sweden, and West Germany, 148
Multinational enterprise in historical perspective, 148
The **multinational** enterprise in transition: selected readings and essays, 148
Multinational enterprises, economic structure, and international competitiveness, 148
Multinational excursions, 148
Multinational financial management, 148
Multinational management, 148
Multinational management: business strategy and government policy, 148
Multinational managers and host government interactions, 148
Multinational marketing management: cases and readings, 102
The **multinational** mission: balancing local demands and global vision, 148
Multinationals and employment: the global economy of the 1990s, 148
Multinationals and the restructuring of the world economy: the geography of multinationals, volume 2, 148
Multinationals and world trade: vertical integration and the division of labour in world industries, 296
Multinationals—theory and history, 148
Municipal bonds, 203
Municipal derivative securities: uses and valuation, 203
Murdoch, 203
The **muse** in the machine: computerizing the poetry of human thought, 12
Mutual gains: a guide to union-management cooperation, 166
The **mutual** gains enterprise: forging a winning partnership among labor, management, and government, 232
My soul is my own: oral narratives of African American women in the professions, 8
My years with General Motors, 115
The **mystical** machine: issues and ideas in computing, 51
The **myth** of free trade: a plan for America's economic revival, 113

The **naked** consumer: how our private lives become public commodities, 193
The **naked** entrepreneur, 94
The **naked** manager: games executives play, 130
The **name** is the game: how to name a company or product, 32

The name of the game: the business of sports, 264
The NASDAQ handbook: the stock market for the next 100 years: a complete reference for investors, registered representatives, company executives, researchers, the financial press and students of finance, 204
A nation of salesmen: the tyranny of the market and the subversion of culture, 256
National health care: lessons for the United States and Canada, 143
The nature and logic of capitalism, 36
Navigating new markets abroad: charting a course for the international businessperson, 149
Navigating through change, 223
Negotiating rationally, 205
Negotiating the future: a labor perspective on American business, 137
Negotiation basics: concepts, skills, and exercises, 205
Negotiation: strategies for mutual gain: the basic seminar of the Harvard Program on Negotiation, 205
The network nation: human communication via computer, 279
Networking smart: how to build relationships for personal and organizational success, 45
Networking the enterprise: how to build client/server systems that work, 171
Networks and organizations: structure, form, and action, 218
The neurotic behavior of organizations, 218
The neurotic organization, 218
Never done: a history of American housework, 123
Never under the table: a story of British Columbia's forests and government mismanagement, 171
The new ad media reality: electronic over print, 22
The new American workplace: transforming work systems in the United States, 304
New and improved: the story of mass marketing in America, 190
The new bottom line: people and loyalty in business, 91
The new business incubator: linking talent, technology, capital, and know-how, 207
The new business of banking, 15
New business ventures and the entrepreneur, 207
The new capitalism, 130
The new China: comparative economic development in Mainland China, Taiwan, and Hong Kong, 41
The new commodity trading systems and methods, 44
The new competition, 190
The new competitors: a report on American managers from D. Quinn Mills of the Harvard Business School, 101
The new competitors: how foreign investors are changing the U.S. economy, 157
The new corporate bond market: a complete and insightful analysis of the latest trends, issues, and advances, 21
The new corporate frontier: the big move to Small Town, USA, 291
The new corporate strategy, 269
New corporate ventures: how to make them work, 130
The new critical path method: the state-of-the-art in project modeling and time reserve management, 72
The new crowd: the changing of the Jewish guard on Wall Street, 160
New deals: the Chrysler revival and the American system, 41
New developments in international finance, 151
New directions in creative and innovative management: bridging theory and practice, 71
New directions in marketing: business-to-business strategies for the 1990s, 133
New directions in multinational corporate organization, 149
The new economic role of American states: strategies in a competitive world economy, 289
The new elite: Britain's top chief executives, 79
The New encyclopedia of stock market techniques, 266
The new encyclopedia of stock market techniques, 266
A new era in computation, 228
The new Euromarkets: a theoretical and practical study of international financing in the eurobond, eurocurrency, and related financial markets, 96
The new Europe: into the 1990s, 98
The new expatriates: managing human resources abroad, 149
The new financial instruments: an investor's guide, 254
The new game on Wall Street, 267
The new GE: how Jack Welch revived an American institution, 115
The new global economy in the information age: reflections on our changing world, 84
The new heartland: America's flight beyond the suburbs and how it is changing our future, 41
The new individualists: the generation after The organization man, 294
The new industrial state, 291
The new manager's handbook, 177
The new manufacturing challenge: techniques for continuous improvement, 185
The new money masters, 37
The new options market, 215
The new optoelectronics ball game: the policy struggle between the U.S. and Japan for the competitive edge, 215
The new organization: growing the culture of organizational networking, 46
The new paradigm in business: emerging strategies for leadership and organizational change, 130
New patterns of work, 304
New perspectives on compensation, 47
The new portable MBA, 130
New product development, 209
New product development and marketing: a practical guide, 209
New product development checklists: proven checklists for developing new products from mission to market, 209
The new products handbook, 209
New products management, 209
The new realities: in government and politics, in

economics and business, in society and world view, 306
The new rules of the game: the four key experiences managers must have to thrive in the non-hierarchical 90s and beyond, 223
The new science of management decision, 76
The new shop floor management: empowering people for continuous improvement, 130
The new stock market, 153
New technologies and the future of food and nutrition: proceedings of the First Ceres Conference, Williamsburg, VA, October 1989, 111
New technology as organizational innovation: the development and diffusion of microelectronics, 276
The new unionism: employee involvement in the changing corporation, 137
New venture analysis: research, planning, and finance, 209
New venture creation: entrepreneurship for the 21st century, 207
The new venture handbook, 207
New venture mechanics, 207
New venture strategies, 207
The new venturers: inside the high-stakes world of venture capital, 295
Newgames: strategic competition in the PC revolution, 50
Newhouse: all the glitter, power, and glory of America's richest media empire and the secretive man behind it, 210
News over the wires: the telegraph and the flow of public information in America, 1844-1897, 162
The next battleground: Japan, America, and the new European market, 98
The next phase of total quality management: TQM II and the focus on profitability, 282
The 'nice' company, 66
Nightmare on Lime Street: whatever happened to Lloyd's of London, 170
Nightmare on Wall Street: Salomon Brothers and the corruption of the marketplace, 253
1992, 96
The 1992 challenge from Europe: development of the European Community's internal market, 98
1992, one European market?: a critical analysis of the Commission's internal market strategy, 98
1992: understanding the new European market, 96
The Nissan enigma: flexibility at work in a local economy, 210
No benefit: crisis in America's health insurance industry, 143
No one need apply: getting and keeping the best workers, 92
Nonextrapolative methods in business forecasting: scenarios, vision, and issues management, 31
Nonprofit corporations, organizations, and associations, 211
The nonprofit economy, 211
The nonprofit organization: essential readings, 212
The nonprofit sector: a research handbook, 212
Normal accidents: living with high-risk technologies, 125
North American free trade: assessing the impact, 212

Not as far as you think: the realities of working women, 300
Not like our parents: how the baby boom generation is changing America, 294
Not so free to choose: the political economy of Milton Friedman and Ronald Reagan, 40
Nothing ventured: the perils and payoffs of the great American venture capital game, 295
Novations: strategies for career management, 218

Object-oriented information systems: planning and implementation, 181
Obtaining venture financing: principles and practices, 295
Odyssey: Pepsi to Apple, a journey of adventure, ideas, and the future, 254
Off the books, 41
Offensive strategy: forging a new competitiveness in the fires of head-to-head competition, 48
Oil & honor: the Texaco-Pennzoil Wars, 280
Oil and world power, 233
Oil, from prospect to pipeline, 233
On a clear day you can see General Motors: John Z. De Lorean's look inside the automotive giant, 115
On becoming a leader, 168
On leadership, 235
On organizational learning, 46
On the board, 79
On the edge of the organisation: the role of the outside director, 79
On the line: women's career advancement, 302
On track with the Japanese: a case-by-case approach to building successful relationships, 30
On your own: how to start, develop, and manage a new business, 207
Once in Golconda: a true drama of Wall Street, 1920-1938, 297
The $1 league: the rise and fall of the USFL, 295
One earth, one future: our changing global environment, 173
101 years on Wall street: an investor's almanac, 297
100 predictions for the baby boom: the next 50 years, 83
The one minute manager, 177
One smart cookie: how a housewife's chocolate-chip recipe turned into a multimillion dollar business: the story of Mrs. Field's cookies, 104
One up on Wall Street: how to use what you already know to make money in the market, 155
The only thing that matters: bringing the power of the customer into the center of your business, 73
OPEC, its member states and the world energy market, 216
Open systems: a business strategy for the 1990s, 89
Operations management, a systems model-building approach, 125
Operations management: decision making in the operations function, 239
Operations management: production of goods and services, 130
Operations management: strategy and analysis, 239, 214

Operations research: applications and algorithms, 214
Operations research: principles and practice, 214
Opportunities in European financial services: 1992 and beyond, 109
Optimal regulation: the economic theory of natural monopoly, 201
Optimization models for planning and allocation: text and cases in mathematical programming, 182
Options as a strategic investment, 215
The options manual, 215
Options: theory, strategy, and applications, 215
Orchestrating success: improve control of the business with sales & operations planning, 177
Organization: a guide to problems and practice, 218
Organization and management: a systems and contingency approach, 215
Organization and people: readings, cases, and exercises in organizational behavior, 218
Organization and technology in capitalist development, 118
Organization change and development: a systems view, 223
Organization development and transformation: managing effective change, 223
The organization game: an interactive business game where you make or break the company, 76
Organization: text, cases, and readings on the management of organizational design and change, 216
Organization theory: a macro perspective for management, 216
Organization theory: a strategic approach, 216
Organization theory: a structural and behavioral analysis, 216
Organization theory and management: a macro approach, 216
Organization theory: from Chester Barnard to the present and beyond, 133
Organization theory: structure, design, and applications, 216
The organization woman: building a career—an inside report, 302
The organizational and human resources sourcebook, 218
Organizational behavior, 218
Organizational behavior and management, 219
Organizational behavior and performance, 219
Organizational behavior and personnel psychology, 219
Organizational behavior and the practice of management, 219
Organizational behavior: concepts, controversies, and applications, 219
Organizational behavior: human behavior at work, 219
Organizational behavior: its data, first principles, and applications, 219
Organizational behavior: readings and exercises, 219
Organizational behaviour: politics at work, 219
Organizational capability: competing from the inside out, 226

Organizational career development: benchmarks for building a world-class workforce, 37
Organizational change through effective leadership, 223
Organizational climate and culture, 59
Organizational communication: the essence of effective management, 45
Organizational culture, 219
Organizational culture and leadership, 59
Organizational design: the organizational audit and analysis technology, 226
Organizational economics, 184
Organizational entrepreneurship, 226
Organizational influence processes, 219
Organizational psychology: readings on human behavior in organizations, 242
Organizational strategy and change, 76
Organizational structure and information technology, 59
Organizational theory and design: a strategic approach for management, 216
Organizational transitions for individuals, families, and work groups, 223
Organizational transitions: managing complex change, 223
Organizations: a micro/macro approach, 216
Organizations: a quantum view, 216
Organizations and chaos: defining the methods of nonlinear management, 177
Organizations: behavior, structure, processes, 216
Organizations in action; social science bases of administrative theory, 133
Organizations on the couch: clinical perspectives on organizational behavior and change, 219
Organizations: rational, natural, and open systems, 227
Organizations: structure and behavior, 219
Organizations: structures, processes, and outcomes, 216
Organizing and implementing the marketing effort: text and cases, 190
The origins & evolution of the field of industrial relations in the United States, 137
Other people's money: the inside story of the S&L mess, 253
Other people's money: the rise and fall of OPM Leasing Services, 214
Otherwise engaged: the personal lives of successful career women, 300
Our wildest dreams: women entrepreneurs making money, having fun, doing good, 303
Out of the garden: toys, TV, and children's culture in the age of marketing, 279
The outlaw bank: a wild ride into the secret heart of BCCI, 16
The outline of strategy, 269
The outnation: a search for the soul of Japan, 204
Outperformers: super achievers, breakthrough strategies, high-profit results, 101
Outsmarting the competition: practical approaches to finding and outsmarting the competition, 31
Overcoming organizational defenses: facilitating organizational learning, 223
Overdrawn: the collapse of Financial Corporation of America, 107
Overnight success: Federal Express and Frederick Smith, its renegade creator, 260

The overworked American: the unexpected decline of leisure, 169

The Pacific century: America and Asia in a changing world, 81
The Pacific century: economic and political consequences of Asian Pacific dynamism, 227
The Pacific challenge in international business, 81
Pacific growth and financial interdependence, 106
The Pacific Rim almanac, 227
Packaging for the environment: a partnership for progress, 227
Painter on close corporations: corporate, securities, and tax aspects, 41
A paper prince, 203
Paradox and transformation: toward a theory of change in organization and management, 223
The paradox of continental production: national investment policies in North America, 287
The paradox of success: when winning at work means losing at life: a book of renewal for leaders, 271
The paranoid corporation and 8 other ways your company can be crazy: advice from an organizational shrink, 177
Participation works: business cases from around the world: an anthology of readings on participation in private companies, 177
Participative systems at work: creating quality and employment security, 178
Partnerships for profit: structuring and managing strategic alliances, 162
Passing the baton: managing the process of CEO succession, 40
Passing the buck: banks, governments, and Third World debt, 170
A passion for excellence: the leadership difference, 130
Passions within reason: the strategic role of the emotions, 90
Pasta e cioccolato: una storia imprenditoriale, 22
Patterns of high performance: discovering the ways people work best, 91
Patton on productivity: proven techniques for effective management, 134
Pawns or potentates: the reality of America's corporate boards, 79
Pay dirt: the business of professional team sports, 241
Paying for productivity: a look at the evidence, 297
Peak performers: the new heroes of American business, 272
Peddling prosperity: economic sense and nonsense in the age of diminished expectations, 163
Pension planning: pensions, profit-sharing, and other deferred compensation plans, 214
People in corporations: ethical responsibilities and corporate effectiveness, 139
People in organizations: an introduction to organizational behavior, 216
People, performance, and pay: a full report on the American Productivity Center/ American Compensation Association National survey of non-traditional reward and human resource practices, 91

People, science, and technology: a guide to advanced industrial society, 277
The people side of project management, 136
People's banker: the story of Arthur T. Roth and the Franklin National Bank, 251
Peoplepower: elements of human resource policy, 184
The perceived usefulness of financial statements for investors' decisions, 110
Perestroika for America: restructuring U.S. business-government relations for competitiveness in the world economy, 140
The perfect business plan made simple, 207
Performance, 228
Performance appraisal series, 228
Performance at work: a systematic program for analyzing work behavior, 229
Performance pay as a competitive weapon: a compensation policy model for the 1990s, 47
Perot: an unauthorized biography, 229
Perpetual innovation: the new world of competition, 276
Persistent inequalities: wage disparity under capitalist competition, 297
Personal financial planning, 107
Personality in industry: the human side of a Japanese enterprise, 178
Personality theories: a comparative analysis, 229
Personnel: a book of readings, 232
Personnel management: a human resources approach, 232
Personnel management series, 232
Personnel policies in large nonunion companies, 232
Personnel, the human problems of management, 232
Personnel, the management of human resources, 232
Personnel/human resource management, 232
Personnel/human resource management today: readings and commentary, 232
A perspective on the changing business and financial environment, 255
Perspectives in consumer behavior, 56
Perspectives on behavior in organizations, 219
Perspectives on safe & sound banking: past, present, and future, 18
The persuasion explosion: your guide to the power & influence of contemporary public relations, 243
A piece of the action: how women and minorities can launch their own successful businesses, 207
The PIMS principles: linking strategy to performance, 190
Pioneering new products: a market survival guide, 209
Pizza tiger, 200
Planning and financing the new venture, 208
Planning and forming your company, 208
Planning and using a total personnel system, 232
Planning for quality, productivity, and competitive position, 244
Planning, implementing, and evaluating targeted communication programs: a manual for business communicators, 46
The planning of change, 261
Planning strategies that work, 269

The planning-programming-budgeting approach to Government decision-making, 241
Plant closings: power, politics, and workers, 234
Playing by different rules, 55
Please stand by: a prehistory of television, 279
The plungers and the peacocks: an update of the classic history of the stock market, 297
Pocket MBA: the essentials of management thinking and theory from A to Z, 130
Pocket negotiator: the essentials of successful negotiation from A to Z, 206
Poker strategy: winning with game theory, 235
Poland's jump to the market economy, 235
Policy formulation and administration: a casebook of senior management problems in business, 130
The political economy of global restructuring, 84
The political economy of health care, 196
The political economy of Japan, 159
The political economy of North American free trade, 113
The politics and ethics of fieldwork, 262
The politics and reality of family care in corporate America, 92
The politics of baby foods: successful challenges to an international marketing strategy, 80
The politics of management, 52, 219
The Politz papers: science and truth in marketing research, 193
Ponzi schemes, invaders from Mars & other extraordinary popular delusions, and the madness of crowds, 95
Poor Richard's Legacy: American business values from Benjamin Franklin to Donald Trump, 30
Poor support: poverty in the American family, 244
The Popcorn report: Faith Popcorn on the future of your company, your world, your life, 31
The portable MBA, 130
The portable MBA in economics, 87
The portable MBA in strategy, 269
Portfolio analysis, 235
Portfolio theory and investment management, 236
Portrait of an old lady: turmoil at the Bank of England, 16
Portraits in silicon, 49
Portraits of success: impressions of Silicon Valley pioneers, 198
Positioning: the battle for your mind, 236
The positive sum strategy: harnessing technology for economic growth, 276
Post-capitalist society, 84
Post-industrial America: a geographical perspective, 288
The postmodern organization: mastering the art of irreversible change, 223
Postmodernism and the social sciences, 262
Postwar reconstruction of the Japanese economy, 159
Power and accountability, 262
Power and illness: the failure and future of American health policy, 196
Power and influence, 99
Power and the corporate mind, 101
The power and the money: inside the Wall Street journal, 298
Power crazy, 171

Power direct marketing: how to make it work for you, 79
The power economy: building an economy that works, 289
Power in management, 178
The power makers: the inside story of America's biggest business—and its struggle to control tomorrow's electricity, 89
The power of commerce: economy and governance in the first British Empire, 117
The power of ethical management, 30
The power of financial innovation: successful corporate solutions to managing interest rate, foreign exchange rate, and commodity exposures on a worldwide basis, 149
The power of news: the history of Reuters, 1849-1989, 250
The power of the financial press: journalism and economic opinion in Britain and America, 163
The power of tomorrow's management: using the vision-culture balance in organizations, 178
Power on earth, 259
Power plays: a guide to maximizing performance and success in business, 219
Power, privilege, and the Post: the Katharine Graham story, 117
The power structure of American business, 108
Powershift: knowledge, wealth, and violence at the edge of the 21st century, 261
Practical business statistics, 43
The practical forecasters' almanac: 137 reliable indicators for investors, hedgers, and speculators, 31
Practical handbook of distribution/customer service, 73
Practical handbook of warehousing, 299
Practical intelligence: working smarter in business and everyday life, 99
Practical marketing research, 193
The practical strategist: business and corporate strategy for the 1990s, 269
The practice of collective bargaining, 42
The practice of econometrics: classic and contemporary, 82
The practice of marketing management: analysis, planning, and implementation, 190
The practitioner's guide to interest rate risk management, 144
The Predators' Ball: the junk-bond raiders and the man who staked them, 55
Predicting executive success: what it takes to make it into senior management, 99
A preface to economic democracy, 91
Preparing for the twenty-first century, 285
The presentations kit: 10 steps for selling your ideas, 244
Presenting for women in business, 25
Presidential economics: the making of economic policy from Roosevelt to Reagan and beyond, 289
The press and the world of money: how the news media cover business and finance, panic and prosperity, and the pursuit of the American dream, 163
The price of peace: the future of defense industry and high technology in a post-cold war world, 76

The price system and resource allocation, 197
Price theory and applications, 197
The Price Waterhouse guide to financial management: tools for improving performance, 66
Prices, quality and trust: inter-firm relations in Britain and Japan, 134
Pricing financial services, 18
Pricing: making profitable decisions, 236
Primary commodity exports and economic development: theory, evidence, and a study of Malaysia, 173
A primer on American labor law, 164
A primer on decision making: how decisions happen, 76
A primer on organizational behavior, 219, 220
Prince of the magic kingdom: Michael Eisner and the re-making of Disney, 298
Principals and agents: the structure of business, 178
Principle-centered leadership, 272
Principles of agribusiness management, 8
Principles of auditing, 13
Principles of banking, 18
Principles of business law, 43
Principles of corporate finance, 66
Principles of cost accounting: using a cost management approach, 69
Principles of economics: macro, 172
Principles of economics: MICRO, 197
Principles of engineering economy, 93
Principles of environmental management: the greening of business, 95
Principles of inventory and materials management, 153
Principles of macroeconomics, 172
Principles of macroeconomics: readings, issues, and cases, 172
Principles of managerial finance, 66
Principles of marketing, 190
Principles of microeconomics, 197
Principles of money, banking, and financial markets, 201
Principles of operations research for management, 214
The principles of scientific management, 131
Prisoners of leadership, 168
Privatisation: fair shares for all or selling the family silver, 237
Privatization and deregulation in global perspective, 237
Privatization: investing in state-owned enterprises around the world, 237
The prize: the epic quest for oil, money, and power, 233
The problem solvers: a history of Arthur D. Little, Inc, 11
Problem solving for managers, 237
A problem-finding approach to effective corporate planning, 61
The problems of plenty: energy policy and international politics, 233
Proceedings of a conference on linking local and global commons held at Harvard University, April 23-25, 1992, 95
Process innovation: reengineering work through information technology, 141

Procurement and inventory systems analysis, 153
Product assurance principles: integrating design assurance and quality assurance, 78
Product development performance: strategy, organization, and management in the world auto industry, 14
The product liability mess: how business can be rescued from the politics of state courts, 240
Product management: strategy and organization, 238
Product plus: how product + service = competitive advantage, 73
Product-country images: impact and role in international marketing, 190
Production & operations management: a life cycle approach, 239
Production and inventory control handbook, 239
Production and inventory management, 238
Production and operations management, 239
Production and operations management: concepts, models, and behavior, 240
Production handbook, 240
Production planning and inventory control, 240
Production-inventory systems: planning and control, 239
Production/operations management: concepts and situations, 240
Production/operations management: concepts, structure, and analysis, 240
Productive workplaces: organizing and managing for dignity, meaning, and community, 131
Productivity and American leadership: the long view, 165
Productivity and quality through people: practices of well-managed companies, 134
The productivity dilemma: roadblock to innovation in the automobile industry, 14
Productivity growth and the competitiveness of the American economy: a Carolina Public Policy Conference volume, 135
Productivity growth and U.S. competitiveness, 135
Productivity in organizations: new perspectives from industrial and organizational psychology, 165
Productivity management: a practical handbook, 135
Productivity: the art and science of business management, 135
The professional decision-thinker: America's new management and education priority, 76
Professional selling, 256
Professional women at work: interactions, tacit understandings, and the non-trivial nature of trivia in bureaucratic settings, 303
Profiles of excellence: achieving success in the nonprofit sector, 212
Profiles of female genius: thirteen creative women who changed the world, 303
Profiles of genius: thirteen creative men who changed the world, 34
Profit sharing in perspective, in American medium-sized and small business, 241
Profiting from innovation: the report of the three-year study from the National Academy of Engineering, 276
Profiting in America's multicultural marketplace: how to do business across cultural lines, 25

Profits of science: the American marriage of business and technology, 254
Profits, priests, and princes: Adam Smith"s emancipation of economics from politics and religion, 87
Program trading: the new age of investing, 241
Programmers at work, 89
Project evaluation: a unified approach for the analysis of capital investments, 35
Project management: a systems approach to planning, scheduling, and controlling, 136
Project management: an introduction to issues in industrial research and development, 136
Project management handbook, 136
Project management: planning and control, 136
Project management: strategic design and implementation, 136
Project management with CPM, PERT, and precedence diagramming, 136
The project manager's survival guide: the handbook for real-world project management, 136
Promise and power: the life and times of Robert McNamara, 195
Promotional management, 190
Promotional strategy: managing the marketing communications process, 190
Property development, 247
Prophets in the dark: how Xerox reinvented itself and beat back the Japanese, 307
Prophets of regulation: Charles Francis Adams, Louis D. Brandeis, James M. Landis, Alfred E. Kahn, 283
The prosecutors: inside the offices of the government's most powerful lawyers, 243
Protectionism, 242
Psychological dimensions of organizational behavior, 220
Psychological foundations of organizational behavior, 220
Psychology and industry today: an introduction to industrial and organizational psychology, 242
Psychology of work behavior, 242
Public & nonprofit marketing, 212
Public and nonprofit marketing: cases and readings, 190
Public policies toward business, 140
Public policy toward corporate takeovers, 55
Public regulation: new perspectives on institutions and policies, 283
Public relations in the marketing mix: introducing vulnerability relations, 46
Public television for sale: media, the market, and the public sphere, 244
Public-sector marketing: a guide for practitioners, 117
Punished by rewards: the trouble with gold stars, incentive plans, A's, praise, and other bribes, 250
Purchasing and materials management, 134
Purchasing and materials management: text and cases, 134
Purchasing and the management of materials, 134
Purchasing: principles and applications, 244
Pure instinct: business' untapped resource, 71
The purpose-driven organization: unleashing the power of direction and commitment, 226

Pursuing happiness: American consumers in the twentieth century, 57
The pursuit of innovation: managing the people and processes that turn new ideas into profits, 276

QED report on venture capital financial analysis, 295
Quality & productivity: the new challenge, 135
Quality by design: Taguchi methods and US industry, 245
Quality circles handbook, 244
The quality imperative, 246
Quality is just the beginning: managing for total responsiveness, 282
Quality management handbook, 245
Quality management in service organizations: an interpretation of the service quality phenomenon and a synthesis of international research, 73
Quality of earnings: the investor's guide to how much money a company is really making, 110
Quality or else: the revolution in world business, 282
Quality, productivity, and innovation: strategies for gaining competitive advantage, 226
Quality up, costs down: a manager's guide to Taguchi methods and QFD, 274
Quantitative analysis for business decisions, 131
Quantitative analysis for marketing management, 190
Quantitative approaches to management, 214
Quantitative concepts for management: decision making without algorithms, 178
Quantitative decision making for business, 76
Quantitative methods for business, 182
Quantitative methods for business decisions: with cases, 76
Quantitative methods for financial analysis, 155
Quantitative methods in management: case studies of failures and successes, 131
The quest for competitiveness: lessons from America's productivity and quality leaders, 135
The quest for staff leadership, 178
Quiet desperation: the truth about successful men, 101

R & D collaboration on trial: the Microelectronics and Computer Technology Corporation, 198
The race to the intelligent state: towards the global information economy of 2005, 141
Radical management: power politics and the pursuit of trust, 178
Railroads triumphant: the growth, rejection, and rebirth of a vital American force, 246
Rainmaker: the saga of Jeff Beck, Wall Street's mad dog, 19
Raising capital: private placement forms & techniques, 255
Raising the bottom line: business leadership in a changing society, 24
Raising venture capital and the entrepreneur, 295
Ralph Lauren: the man behind the mystique, 166
A random walk down Wall Street: including a life-cycle guide to personal investing, 155
The rape of Ma Bell: the criminal wrecking of the best telephone system in the world, 10

Rare breed: the entrepreneur, an American culture, 94
Rational accounting concepts: the writings of Willard J. Graham, 5
RCA, 246
RCA and the VideoDisc: the business of research, 296
Re-engineering the networked enterprise, 213
Re-engineering your business, 223
Re-inventing the corporation: transforming your job and your company for the new information society, 246
Reach for the top women and the changing facts of work life, 302
Read all about it!: the corporate takeover of America's newspapers, 40
Read the label: reducing risk by providing information, 56
Readings in human resource management, 232
Readings in international business, 149
Readings in international business: a decision approach, 149
Readings in international finance, 151
Readings in labor economics and labor relations, 164
Readings in management, 131, 178
Readings in managerial psychology, 242
Readings in organizational behavior, 220
Readings in organizational behavior: dimensions of management actions, 220
Readings in organizational decline: frameworks, research, and prescriptions, 223
Readings in personnel management, 232
Readings in strategic management, 269
Readings in the management of innovation, 276
Ready, fire, aim: avoiding management by impulse, 242
The real Coke, the real story, 42
Real estate: a case study approach, 247
Real estate finance, 123, 202, 203
Real estate finance and investments, 202
The real estate handbook, 247
Real estate investment, 248
Real estate investment strategy, 248
Real estate law, 248
Real estate market analysis: methods and applications, 248
Real estate principles, 247
Real estate principles and practices, 247
Real estate, principles and practices, 247
Real estate: principles and practices, 247
Real estate syndication: securitization after tax reform, 248
The real heroes of business—and not a CEO among them, 73
Real managers, 178
The real ones: four generations of the first family of Coca-Cola, 42
Real time strategic change: how to involve an entire organization in fast and far-reaching change, 223
Real-world intelligence: organized information for executives, 31
Reassessing American competitiveness, 49
Rebirth of the corporation, 224
Rebuilding capitalism: alternative roads after socialism and dirigisme, 85

Rebuilding Wall Street: "after the Crash of '87, fifty insiders talk about putting Wall Street together again", 209
Recapturing the spirit of enterprise, 94
Recent advances in corporate finance, 66
Recent developments in corporate finance, 67
Recent developments in production economics: proceedings of the Fourth International Working Seminar on Production Economics, Igls, Austria, February 17-21, 1986, 238
The reckoning, 14
Recollecting the future: a view of business, technology, and innovation in the next 30 years, 84
Red ink II: a guide to understanding the continuing deficit dilemma, 22
Redefining excellence: the financial performance of America's "best-run" companies, 67
Reel power: the struggle for influence and success in the new Hollywood, 203
The reengineering handbook: a step-by-step guide to business transformation, 224
Reengineering the corporation: a manifesto for business revolution, 224
Reengineering the organization: a step-by-step approach to corporate revitalization, 224
Reforming superfund, 120
Reframing organizations: artistry, choice, and leadership, 178
Regional cultures, managerial behavior, and entrepreneurship: an international perspective, 220
The Regis touch: million-dollar advice from America's top marketing consultant, 190
Regular economic cycles, 84
Regulating a new economy: public policy and economic change in America, 1900-1933, 290
Regulating big business: antitrust in Great Britain and America, 1880 to 1990, 283
Regulating the automobile, 14
Regulation: politics, bureaucracy, and economics, 283
The regulators; watchdog agencies and the public interest, 125
Regulatory reform of stock and futures markets: a special issue of the Journal of financial services research, 266
Reinventing education: entrepreneurship in America's public schools, 243
Reinventing government: how the entrepreneurial spirit is transforming the public sector, 5
Reinventing the factory II: managing the world class factory, 135
Reinventing the factory: productivity breakthroughs in manufacturing today, 135
Reinventing the warehouse: world class distribution logistics, 299
Rejuvenating the mature business: the competitive challenge, 61
Rekindling commitment: how to revitalize yourself, your work, and your organization, 224
Relationship marketing: successful strategies for the age of the customer, 191
Relevance lost: the rise and fall of management accounting, 183
Relevance regained: from top-down control to bottom-up empowerment, 131

Remaking Japan: the American Occupation as New Deal, 160
Rendezvous with reality: the American economy after Reagan, 288
Renewing American industry, 131
The repo and reverse markets, 201
Report writing for business, 33
Requisite organization: the CEO's guide to creative structure and leadership, 161
Research and development limited partnerships: an emerging method of funding research and development, 249
Research and development: project selection criteria, 249
Research for marketing decisions, 193
Research methods for business: a skill-building approach, 24
Research on the management of innovation: the Minnesota studies, 276
Research traditions in marketing, 193
Research-based decisions, 76
Reshaping the equity markets: a guide for the 1990s, 254
The responsible manager: practical strategies for ethical decision making, 30
Restoring our competitive edge: competing through manufacturing, 292
Restructuring American corporations: causes, effects, and implications, 55
Restructuring and turnaround: experiences in corporate renewal, 224
Restructuring for innovation: the remaking of the U.S. semiconductor industry, 256
Restructuring Japan's financial markets, 36
The resurgent liberal: (and other unfashionable prophecies), 289
Retail management: a strategic approach, 250
Retailing management, 250
Rethinking business to business marketing, 133
Revitalizing American industry: lessons from our competitors, 287
Revitalizing manufacturing: text and cases, 293
The revolution in corporate finance, 67
The revolution in real estate finance, 203
Revolution on Wall Street: the rise and decline of the New York Stock Exchange, 209
The revolutionary corporations: engines of plenty, engines of growth, engines of change, 19
Revolutionizing product development: quantum leaps in speed, efficiency, and quality, 209
Rewarding results: motivating profit center managers, 101
The rewiring of America: the fiber optics revolution, 214
The rice-paper ceiling: breaking through Japanese corporate culture, 59
"Rich nation, strong Army": national security and the technological transformation of Japan, 204
Riding the waves of change: developing managerial competencies for a turbulent world, 178
Riding the waves of culture: understanding diversity in global business, 47
The right price for your business, 252
The rise and decline of the Great Atlantic & Pacific Tea Company, 117
The rise and fall of mass marketing, 191

The rise and fall of strategic planning: reconceiving roles for planning, plans, planners, 269
The rise and fall of the conglomerate kings, 52
The rise of China: how economic reform is creating a new superpower, 40
The rise of managerial computing: the best of the Center for Information Systems Research, Sloan School of Management, Massachusetts Institute of Technology, 178
The rise of modern business in Great Britain, the United States, and Japan, 118
The rise of the corporate commonwealth: U.S. business and public policy in the twentieth century, 291
The rise of the expert company: how visionary companies are using artifical intelligence to achieve higher productivity and profits, 178
The rise of the trading state: commerce and conquest in the modern world, 42
Rising stars and fast fades: successes and failures of fast-growth companies, 272
Risk & other four-letter words, 201
Risk and reward: venture capital and the making of America's great industries, 296
Risk management and insurance, 250
Risk, ruin & riches: inside the world of big time real estate, 247
The risk takers - five years on, 34
Risks: reading corporate signals, 27
Risktaker, caretaker, surgeon, undertaker: the four faces of strategic leadership, 168
Rival capitalists: international competitiveness in the United States, Japan, and Western Europe, 138
Rivalry: in business, science, among nations, 48
Rivals beyond trade: America versus Japan in global competition, 156
Rivethead: tales from the assembly line, 119
The road to colossus: a celebration of American ingenuity, 294
The road to Nissan: flexibility, quality, teamwork, 149
Roadside empires: how the chains franchised America, 113
Robert T. Moran's cultural guide to doing business in Europe, 5
Robotics: a manager's guide, 251
Robots, machines in man's image, 251
Robots: the application of robots to practical work, 251
ROI: practical theory and innovative applications, 35
The role of affect in consumer behavior: emerging theories and applications, 57
The role of the modern corporation in a free society, 262
Roller coaster: the Bank of America and the future of American banking, 15
Route 128: lessons from Boston's high-tech community, 122
Rude awakening: the rise, fall and struggle for recovery of General Motors, 115
Rumor in the marketplace: the social psychology of commercial hearsay, 60
Running a one person business, 255

Running American business: top CEOs rethink their major decisions, 269
Running in place: inside the Senate, 286
Running things: the art of making things happen, 168
Rust to riches: the coming of the second industrial revolution, 131
Rusted dreams: hard times in a steel community, 39

The **S & L** debacle: public policy lessons for bank and thrift regulation, 253
The **sales** compensation handbook, 252
Sales force automation: using the latest technology to make your sales force more competitive, 252
Sales force performance, 252
Sales management: decisions, strategies, and cases, 252
Sales management: the complete marketeer's guide, 252
Sales promotion: concepts, methods, and strategies, 253
Sales promotion management, 253
Salomon Brothers, 1910-1985: advancing to leadership, 253
Sam Walton, made in America: my story, 298
The **Sam** Walton story: the retailing of middle America: (a revealing look at the man and his empire), 298
Satisfaction guaranteed: the making of the mass market, 7
Saving free trade: a pragmatic approach, 287
Saving plants and jobs: union-management negotiations in the context of threatened plant closing, 234
Saving the savings and loan: the U.S. thrift industry and the Texas experience, 1950-1988, 253
Sawyer's internal auditing, 13
Say it with charts: the executive's guide to successful presentations in the 1990s, 33
Scale and scope: the dynamics of industrial capitalism, 19
Scenarios and strategic management, 120
Schaum's outline of theory and problems of mathematical methods for business and economics, 32
Schumpeter in the history of ideas, 254
The **Schuster** report: the proven connection between people and profits, 224
Sea change: Pacific Asia as the new world industrial center, 81
The **seamless** enterprise: making cross functional management work, 226
The **search** for value: measuring the company's cost of capital, 67
The **SEC** and the future of finance, 266
Second to none: American companies in Japan, 67
Second to none: how our smartest companies put people first, 178
The **second** wave: Japan's global assault on financial services, 108
The **secondary** mortgage market: strategies for surviving & thriving in today's challenging markets, 254
Secret money: the world of international financial secrecy, 151

Secrets of a successful entrepreneur: how to start and succeed at running your own business, 208
Secrets of the temple: how the Federal Reserve runs the country, 20
Securities operations: a guide to operations and information systems in the securities industry, 255
Security analysis and portfolio management, 153
Security evaluation and portfolio analysis, 236
Seeking customers, 256
Self-assessment and career development, 38
Self-made women: twelve of America's leading entrepreneurs talk about success, self-image, and the superwoman, 303
Selling in Japan: the world's second largest market, 191
Selling money, 170
Selling: principles and methods, 256
Selling: principles and practices, 256
Selling radio: the commercialization of American broadcasting, 1920-1934, 246
The **service** advantage: how to identify and fulfill customer needs, 73
Service America!: doing business in the new economy, 307
Service breakthroughs: changing the rules of the game, 73
The **service** encounter, 257
The **service** era: leadership in a global environment, 73
The **service** management course: cases and readings, 257
Service management effectiveness: balancing strategy, organization and human resources, operations, and marketing, 257
Service management for competitive advantage, 257
Service quality: new directions in theory and practice, 73
Service success!: lessons from a leader on how to turn around a service business, 257
Service within: solving the middle management leadership crisis, 199
The **service/quality** solution: using service management to gain competitive advantage, 73
Services in transition: the impact of information technology on the service sector, 257
Services marketing, 241
Setting up a company in the European Community: a country by country guide, 62
The **seven** fat years: and how to do it again, 289
The **seven** sisters: the great oil companies and the world they shaped, 233
Sex and money: behind the scenes with the big-time brokers, 22
Sex and the workplace, 258
Sex discrimination handbook, 258
Shaping the future: business design through information technology, 24
Shared minds: the new technologies of collaboration, 45
Shattering the glass ceiling: the woman manager, 302
Shenson on consulting: success strategies from the consultant's consultant, 56
Shooting ourselves in the foot, 287
A **short** history of the future, 285

Short-term America: the causes and cures of our business myopia, 131
Should business and nonbusiness accounting be different, 5
Show-stopper!: the breakneck race to create Windows NT and the next generation at Microsoft, 198
Showman: the life of David O. Selznick, 256
The silent war: inside the global business battles shaping America's future, 49
Siliconnections: coming of age in the electronic era, 198
The Silver prescription: the eight-step action plan for entrepreneurial success, 208
The Silverlake Project: transformation at IBM, 150
Simulation, optimization and expert systems, 255
Single market to social Europe: the European Community in the 1990s, 98
The 6 imperatives of marketing: lessons from the world's best companies, 186
Six roundtable discussions of corporate finance with Joel Stern, 67
Six thinking hats, 248
Six timeless marketing blunders, 191
Skunk Works: a personal memoir of my years at Lockheed, 171
Skyscraper dreams: the great real estate dynasties of New York, 247
The small business bible: the make-or-break factors for survival and success, 259
The small business handbook: a comprehensive guide to starting and running your own business, 260
Small business management, 260
The small business test, 208
Small business USA: the role of small companies in sparking America's economic transformation, 260
Small firm management: ownership, finance, and performance, 260
Small firms in global competition, 260
Smart cards: the new bank cards, 260
Smart growth: critical choices for business continuity and prosperity, 41
Smart house: the coming revolution in housing, 81
The smart interviewer, 93
The smart way to buy a business: an entrepreneur's guide to questions that must be asked, 55
The smarter organization: how to build a business that learns and adapts to marketplace needs, 226
The smoke ring: tobacco, money & multinational politics, 281
Snapshots from hell: the making of an MBA, 251
So you want to be the boss?: a CEO's lessons in leadership, 168
Soap opera: the inside story of Procter & Gamble, 238
The social construction of technological systems: new directions in the sociology and history of technology, 277
The social investment almanac: a comprehensive guide to socially responsible investing, 155
Social issues in business: strategic and public policy perspectives, 139

Social marketing: strategies for changing public behavior, 261
The social meaning of money, 201
The social responsibilities of business: company and community, 1900-1960, 139
Socially responsible investing: how to invest with your conscience, 155
Software industry accounting, 51
Softwars: the legal battles for control of the global software industry, 58
Sold separately: children and parents in consumer culture, 279
Solving costly organizational conflicts, 52
Solving the work/family puzzle, 304
Sons of the machine: case studies of social change in the workplace, 224
The soul of a new machine, 49
South Africa Inc.: the Oppenheimer empire, 10
South Africa: prospects for successful transition, 263
Space commerce: free enterprise on the high frontier, 264
Sparrows Point: making steel: the rise and ruin of American industrial might, 265
Spectacular teamwork: how to develop the leadership skills for team success, 305
Speculative markets, 215
The spirit of Japanese capitalism and selected essays, 37
Sports marketing: competitive business strategies for sports, 264
Staffing problem solver for human resource professionals and managers, 92
Staffing the contemporary organization: a guide to planning, recruiting, and selecting for human resource professionals, 232
Stalking the headhunter: the smart job-hunter's guide to executive recruiters, 101
Standard & Poor's debt ratings criteria: municipal overview, 254
Standard & Poor's ratings guide: corporate bonds, commercial paper, municipal bonds, international securities, 21
Standard & Poor's structured finance criteria, 254
Standards of practice handbook: the code of ethics and the standards of professional conduct, with commentary and interpretation, 153
Start-up companies: planning, financing, and operating the successful business, 62
The start-up entrepreneur: how you can succeed in building your own company into a major enterprise starting from scratch, 208
Starting and managing the small business, 208
Starting and operating a business after you retire: what you need to know to succeed, 208
Starting and succeeding in your own small business, 260
Starting at the top: America's new achievers: twenty-three success stories told by men and women whose dreams of being boss came true, 34
Starting your subchapter "S" corporation: how to build a business the right way, 271
State and business in modern Turkey: a comparative study, 134
State, finance, and industry: a comparative

analysis of post-war trends in six advanced industrial economies, 140
State of the art marketing research, 193
The state of the art of entrepreneurship, 94
State-of-the-art portfolio selection: using knowledge-based systems to enhance investment performance, 236
State-owned multinationals, 149
Statistical analysis for business and economics, 87
Statistical analysis for business decisions, 43
Statistical analysis for decision making, 262
Statistical methods for business and economics, 265
Statistical quality control, 245
Statistical quality control for manufacturing managers, 245
Statistical techniques in business and economics, 262
Statistical thinking for managers, 131
Statistics for business and economics: problems, exercises, and case studies, 262
Statistics for economics, business administration, and the social sciences, 87
Statistics for management, 262
Statistics for modern business decisions, 263
Staying at the top: the life of a CEO, 15
Staying human in the organization: our biological heritage and the workplace, 220
Staying the course: the emotional and social lives of men who do well at work, 196
The steal: counterfeiting and industrial espionage, 32
Stealing the market: how the giant brokerage firms, with help from the SEC, stole the stock market from investors, 267
Stealth management: "with shared goals they will hardly know you are leading them", 178
Step-by-step competitive strategy, 269
Steve Jobs and the NeXT big thing, 210
Steve Jobs: the journey is the reward, 162
Stiffed: a true story of MCA, the music business, and the Mafia, 263
Stimulating innovation: a systems approach, 276
Stock answers: a guide to the international equities market, 157
Stock index options: powerful new tools for investing, hedging, and speculating, 265
The stock market, 266
Stock market anomalies, 267
The stock market: theories and evidence, 267
Stocks, bonds, options, futures: investments and their markets, 155
Storming the magic kingdom: Wall Street, the raiders and the battle for Disney, 298
Straight talk about mutual funds, 204
Strategic and operational planning for information systems, 181
Strategic capitalism: private business and public purpose in Japanese industrial finance, 158
Strategic choices: supremacy, survival, or sayonara, 269
Strategic control systems, 270
Strategic cost analysis: the evolution from managerial to strategic accounting, 69
Strategic cost reduction: how international companies achieve cost leadership, 69
Strategic divestment, 59
Strategic flexibility: a management guide for changing times, 224
Strategic information systems: a European perspective, 181
Strategic information systems: competition through information technologies, 182
Strategic international marketing, 103
Strategic issues management: how organizations influence and respond to public interests and policies, 157
Strategic logistics management, 32
Strategic management, 131
Strategic management: an integrative perspective, 61
Strategic management: analysis and action, 270
Strategic management and organizational decision making, 61
The strategic management blueprint, 270
Strategic management: formulation and implementation: concepts and cases, 270
The strategic management handbook, 61
Strategic management in developing countries: case studies, 131
Strategic management in information technology, 50
Strategic management in non-profit organizations: an administrator's handbook, 212
Strategic management in public and nonprofit organizations: thinking and acting strategically on public concerns, 270
Strategic management in the regulatory environment: cases and industry notes, 140
Strategic management of human knowledge, skills, and abilities: workforce decision-making in the postindustrial era, 232
Strategic management of human resources, 232
Strategic management: text and cases, 270
The strategic managing of human resources, 232
Strategic manufacturing: dynamic new directions for the 1990s, 292
Strategic market management, 191
Strategic market planning: problems and analytical approaches, 191
Strategic market planning: the pursuit of competitive advantage, 61
Strategic marketing, 191
Strategic marketing: a European approach, 191
Strategic marketing and management, 191
Strategic marketing cases and applications, 191
Strategic marketing for nonprofit organizations, 212
The strategic marketing planner, 191
Strategic organization planning: downsizing for survival, 270
Strategic pay: aligning organizational strategies and pay systems, 47
Strategic planning and management control: systems for survival and success, 270
Strategic planning and management handbook, 270
Strategic planning: models and analytical techniques, 270
Strategic planning plus: an organizational guide, 270
Strategic planning: selected readings, 270
Strategic planning workbook, 270
Strategic risk management: how global

corporations manage financial risk for competitive advantage, 250
Strategic selling: the unique sales system proven successful by America's best companies, 256
Strategic technology management: systems for products and processes, 277
Strategic thinking: leadership and the management of change, 270
The **strategic** use of information technology, 178
Strategies and styles: the role of the centre in managing diversified corporations, 52
Strategies for cultural change, 59
Strategies for international industrial marketing: the management of customer relationships in European industrial markets, 103
Strategies for joint ventures, 162
Strategies for managing change, 261
Strategies in global industries: how U.S. businesses compete, 287
The **strategist** CEO: how visionary executives build organizations, 270
Strategy and choice, 76
Strategy and computers: information systems as competitive weapons, 182
Strategy and structure of Japanese enterprises, 131
The **strategy** and tactics of pricing: a guide to profitable decision making, 236
Strategy and the human resource: Ford and the search for competitive advantage, 111
Strategy, change, and defensive routines, 224
The **strategy** concept and process: a pragmatic approach, 270
Strategy formulation: power and politics, 270
Strategy implementation: structure, systems, and process, 216
The **strategy** of distribution management, 234
The **strategy** process: concepts and contexts, 270
The **strategy** process: concepts, contexts, cases, 271
Strategy: seeking and securing competitive advantage, 271
Strategy traps and how to avoid them, 271
The **strategy-led** business: step-by-step planning for your company's future, 271
Stream analysis: a powerful way to diagnose and manage organizational change, 224
Stressors, beliefs, and coping behaviors of Black women entrepreneurs, 8
Structural holes: the social structure of competition, 48
The **structure** of a modern economy: the United States, 1929-89, 288
The **structure** of power in America: the corporate elite as a ruling class, 25
The **structure** of production, 238
The **structuring** of organizations: the synthesis of the research, 216
Study guide to accompany money, banking and the economy: fifth edition: Thomas Mayer, James S. Duesenberry, Robert Z. Aliber, 201
Success and betrayal: the crisis of women in corporate America, 302
The **success** profile: a leading headhunter tells you how to get to the top, 99
Success runs in our race: the complete guide to effective networking in the African-American community, 8

Successful business expansion: practical strategies for planning profitable growth, 260
A **successful** business of your own, 260
The **successful** business plan: secrets & strategies, 208
Successful business strategy: how to win in the market place, 271
Successful corporate acquisitions: a complete guide for acquiring companies for growth and profit, 55
Successful corporate turnarounds, 224
Successful direct marketing methods, 79
Successful personnel recruiting & selection, 92
Successful small business management, 260
Sudden death: the rise and fall of E.F. Hutton, 88
The **suicidal** corporation, 67
The **sun** also sets: the limits to Japan's economic power, 160
The **sun** that never rose: the inside story of Japan's failed attempt at global financial dominance, 157
Sunrise—sunset: challenging the myth of industrial obsolescence, 131
Supercomputers: a key to U.S. scientific, technological, and industrial preeminence, 273
Supercomputers of today and tomorrow: the parallel processing revolution, 273
Supermanaging: how to harness change for personal and organizational success, 224
Supermarketer to the world: the story of Dwayne Andreas, CEO of Archer Daniels Midland, 10
The **supermarketers**: marketing for success, rules of the mastermarketers, the naked marketplace, 191
Superpigs and wondercorn: the brave new world of biotechnology and where it all may lead, 115
Supervision in action: the art of managing others, 273
Supply-side portfolio strategies, 156
The **supply-side** revolution: an insider's account of policymaking in Washington, 289
The **supranationals**, 109
A **survey** of financial and managerial accounting, 5
The **survey** research handbook, 193
Survival in the corporate fishbowl: making it into upper and middle management, 138
Surviving corporate transition: rational management in a world of mergers, layoffs, start-ups, takeovers, divestitures, deregulation, and new technologies, 131
Surviving the great depression of 1990: protect your assets and investments—and come out on top, 156
Susan Lee's ABZs of money & finance, 106
Sustainable corporate growth: a model and management planning tool, 67
Swap finance, 112
Sweat equity: what it really takes to build America's best small companies—by the guys who did it, 208
Swoosh: the unauthorized story of Nike, and the men who played there, 210
Sylvia Porter's your finances in the 1990s, 107
Systems analysis and project management, 136
Systems of survival: a dialogue on the moral foundations of commerce and politics, 30

Tactics: the art and science of success, 272
Taguchi on robust technology development: bringing quality engineering upstream, 274
Take a chance to be first: the secrets of entrepreneurial success, 272
The takeover game, 55
Takeover madness: corporate America fights back, 55
Taking America: how we got from the first hostile takeover to megamergers, corporate raiding, and scandal, 280
Taking charge of manufacturing: how companies are combining technological and organizational innovations to compete successfully, 293
Taking charge/managing conflict, 52
Taking Japan seriously: a Confucian perspective on leading economic issues, 159
The taking of Getty Oil: the full story of the most spectacular—& catastrophic—takeover of all time, 116
Taking risks: the management of uncertainty, 251
Tales of a new America, 293
Talking straight, 124
Taming the prince: the ambivalence of modern executive power, 99
Targeting the computer: government support and international competition, 50
Tax factors in real estate operations, 248
Taxation and the deficit economy: fiscal policy and capital formation in the United States, 110
Taylorism transformed: scientific management theory since 1945, 131
Teaching and the case method: text, cases, and readings, 33
Team building: issues and alternatives, 305
Team players and teamwork: the new competitive business strategy, 305
Team Zebra: how 1500 partners revitalized Eastman Kodak's black & white film-making flow, 81
Teaming up for the 90s: a guide to international joint ventures and strategic alliances, 162
Technical analysis explained: the successful investor's guide to spotting investment trends and turning points, 153
Technical analysis of the futures markets: a comprehensive guide to trading methods and applications, 44
The technical enterprise: present and future patterns, 276
Techniques of financial analysis, 67
Techno vision: the executive's survival guide to understanding and managing information technology, 142
Technological change in Japan's beef industry, 19
Technology 2001: the future of computing and communications, 51
Technology and employment: concepts and clarifications, 165
Technology and the regulation of financial markets: securities, futures, and banking, 36
Technology and transition: a survey of biotechnology in Russia, Ukraine, and the Baltic States, 20
The technology connection: strategy and change in the Information Age, 61

The technology payoff: how to profit with empowered workers in the information age, 182
Technology, policy, and economic performance: lessons from Japan, 276
Technology venturing: American innovation and risk-taking, 276
The technology war: a case for competitiveness, 121
Technology-mediated communication, 277
Technomics: the economics of technology and the computer industry, 50
The technopolis strategy: Japan, high technology, and the control of the twenty-first century, 122
Technopoly: the surrender of culture to technology, 277
Telecommunications for management, 178
Telecommunications in the post-divestiture era: essays in honor of Ben T. Wiggins and Jasper Dorsey, 278
Telecommunications in transition, 279
Telecommunications in turmoil: technology and public policy, 10
Tell it like it was: a conceptual framework for financial accounting, 5
Temples of chance: how America Inc. bought out Murder Inc. to win control of the casino business, 38
10 tips for the European executive in an American company, 112
Tender offer: the sneak attack in corporate takeovers, 55
Tender offers: developments and commentaries, 280
The tender ship: governmental management of technological change, 278
Texaco and the $10 billion jury, 228
The Thai economy in transition, 281
Theirs was the kingdom: Lila and DeWitt Wallace and the story of the Reader's Digest, 298
The theory and practice of futures markets, 44
A theory of goal setting & task performance, 116
The theory of industrial organization, 133
The theory of interest, 143
The theory of the growth of the firm, 138
Theory why: in which the boss solves the riddle of quality, 246
Thinking economically: how economic principles can contribute to clear thinking, 87
Thinking in time: the uses of history for decision-makers, 293
The thinking organization, 220
Thinking strategically: planning for your company's future, 61
Thinking strategically: the competitive edge in business, politics, and everyday life, 271
The third America: the emergence of the nonprofit sector in the United States, 212
The third apple: personal computers & the cultural revolution, 51
The third century: America's resurgence in the Asian era, 84
Third generation R&D: managing the link to corporate strategy, 249
The third industrial age: strategy for business survival, 19
The third sex: the new professional woman, 303
This—is CBS: a chronicle of 60 years, 39

Thomas Mellon and his times, 196
Three blind mice: how the TV networks lost their way, 280
Three plus one equals billions: the Bendix-Martin Marietta war, 55
The three Rs of investing: return, risk, and relativity, 156
Thriving on chaos: handbook for a management revolution, 131
Through the grapevine: the real story behind America's $8 billion wine industry, 300
Till debt do us part: who wins, who loses, and who pays for the international debt crisis, 74
Time, chance, and organizations: natural selection in a perilous environment, 224
Time horizons and technology investments, 61
Time Inc.; the intimate history of a publishing enterprise, 281
The time trap, 281
Time-based competition: the next battleground in American manufacturing, 292
The titans of takeover, 55
To flourish among giants: creative management for mid-sized firms, 179
Today and tomorrow, 111
Tokyo 2000: the world's third international financial centre, 106
Tokyo: a world financial center, 109
The Tom Peters seminar: crazy times call for crazy organizations, 224
The tomorrow makers: a brave new world of living-brain machines, 251
Tomorrow's global executive, 149
Too big to fail: Olympia & York: the story behind the headlines, 249
Too many promises: the uncertain future of social security, 263
Too smart for her own good?: the impact of success on the intimate lives of women, 300
Top decisions: strategic decision-making in organizations, 76
Top dog, 40
Top management in Japanese firms, 132
Toppling the pyramids: redefining the way companies are run, 132
The total business plan: how to write, rewrite, and revise, 61
Total business planning: a step-by-step guide with forms, 61
Total improvement management: next generation in performance management, 132
Total information systems management: a European approach, 141
Total materials management: the frontier for maximizing profit in the 1990s, 194
Total quality accounting, 69
Total quality control, 245
Total quality in healthcare: from theory to practice, 196
Total quality management: text, cases, and readings, 282
Total quality management: three steps to continuous improvement, 282
Touchstones: ten new ideas revolutionizing business, 179
Tough choices: managers talk ethics, 30

Tough choices: the decision-making styles of America's top 50 CEOs, 132
Tough-minded leadership, 168
Tourism marketing and management handbook, 283
Toward competition in cable television, 34
Toward the year 2000: world business leaders speak out on the future of free enterprise, 113
The toxic cloud, 9
Toyland: the high-stakes game of the toy industry, 283
Trade talks: America better listen, 113
Trade wars against America: a history of United States trade and monetary policy, 242
Trade-offs: negotiating the Omnibus Trade and Competitiveness Act, 274
Tradeoffs: executive, family, and organizational life, 101
Tradeoffs: imperatives of choice in a high-tech world, 277
Trading for a living: psychology, trading tactics, money management, 267
Trading in a new world order: the impact of telecommunications and data services on international trade in services, 257
Trading: inside the world's leading stock exchanges, 267
Trading on the edge: neural, genetic, and fuzzy systems for chaotic financial markets, 106
Trading places: how we allowed Japan to take the lead, 160
Trading secrets, 297
Training & developing executives, 307
Training and development in organizations, 92
Training for impact: how to link training to business needs and measure the results, 92
The training investment: banking on people for superior results, 15
Training the technical work force, 274
The transfer pricing problem: a theory for practice, 284
The transformation of corporate control, 283
The transformational leader, 224
Transformational management, 179
Transforming the crisis-prone organization: preventing individual, organizational, and environmental tragedies, 71
Transforming the workplace, 304
Transforming work: a collection of organizational transformation readings/ John D. Adams, general editor, 224
Transgenerational design: products for an aging population, 8
The transition in Eastern Europe, 96
A treatise on the family, 103
Trend tracking: the system to profit from today's trends, 111
Trends in American economic growth, 1929-1982, 287
Triad power: the coming shape of global competition, 162
Trials of transition: economic reform in the former Communist bloc, 97
Tribes: how race, religion, and identity determine success in the new global economy, 272
Triumph of the bankers: money and banking in the eighteenth and nineteenth centuries, 201

The troubled money business: the death of an old order and the rise of a new order, 109
True greed: what really happened in the battle for RJR Nabisco, 251
Trump: the art of the deal, 285
Trump: the saga of America's most powerful real estate baron, 285
The trust business, 285
Turbulence in the American workplace, 165
Turf wars: moving from competition to collaboration, 305
The turnaround experience: real-world lessons in revitalizing corporations, 62
The turnaround manager's handbook, 132
The turnaround prescription: repositioning troubled companies, 62
Turnaround: the new Ford Motor Company, 111
Turning lost customers into gold: —and the art of achieving zero defections, 57
The turning point: revitalizing the Soviet economy, 39
Turning the tables: a Machiavellian strategy for dealing with Japan, 291
Turning the tide: strategic planning for labor unions, 284
The TV establishment; programming for power and profit, 280
12 simple steps to a winning marketing plan, 191
The twenty-first century organization: analyzing current trends, imagining the future, 224
Twenty-first-century management: the revolutionary strategies that have made Computer Associates a multibillion-dollar software giant, 49
21st century capitalism, 37
21st century management: keeping ahead of the Japanese and Chinese, 179
2020 vision, 142
The 22 immutable laws of marketing: violate them at your own risk, 186
The twilight of corporate strategy: a comparative ethical critique, 271
The two faces of management: an American approach to leadership in business and politics, 140
2000f nothing: an eye-opening tour through the twists and turns of math abuse and innumeracy, 194
Tycoon: the life of James Goldsmith, 116
Tycoons: where they came from and how they made it, 34

A U.S.-Mexico-Canada free-trade agreement: do we just say no, 113
The U.S. business corporation: an institution in transition, 67
U.S. competitiveness in world economy, 290
The U.S. economy demystified: the meaning of U.S. business statistics and what they portend for the future, 288
The U.S. financial system: money, markets, and institutions, 106
The ultimate advantage: creating the high-involvement organization, 179
The ultimate entrepreneur: the story of Ken Olsen and Digital Equipment Corporation, 214

The ultimate guide to raising money for growing companies, 260
Unbounding the future: the nanotechnology revolution, 277
Unconventional wisdom: irreverent solutions to tough problems at work, 237
Unconventional wisdom: twelve remarkable innovators tell how intuition can revolutionize decision making, 179
The underside of high-tech: technology and the deformation of human sensibilities, 278
Understanding American economic decline, 288
Understanding and meeting consumerism's challenges, 307
Understanding business markets: interaction relationships and networks, 191
Understanding business statistics, 132
Understanding financial statements, 110
Understanding financial statements and corporate annual reports, 110
Understanding health care financial management: text, cases, and models, 121
Understanding microeconomics, 197
Understanding organizations, 220
Understanding the Japanese industrial challenge: from automobiles to software, 15
Understanding the new economy, 87
Understanding Wall Street, 156
The uneasy alliance: managing the productivity-technology dilemma, 135
Uneasy city: an insider's view of the City of London, 109
Uneasy partners: big business in American politics, 1945-1990, 140
Unequal equities: power and risk in Japan's stock market, 285
Uneven tides: rising inequality in America, 124
Unexpected Japan: why American business should return to its own traditional values and not imitate the Japanese, 179
Unhealthy charities: hazardous to your health and wealth, 39
Unheard voices: labor and economic policy in a competitive world, 132
Union-free management and how to keep it free / c by James L. Dougherty, 232
Unions in transition: entering the second century, 284
The United States in the world economy, 287
United States service industries handbook, 257
The universal machine: confessions of a technological optimist, 51
The unnatural act of management: when the great leader's work is done, the people say "We did it ourselves", 62
Unnatural monopolies: the case for deregulating public utilities, 244
Unnecessary choices: the hidden life of the executive woman, 302
Unstable at the top: inside the troubled organization, 220
Untangling the income tax, 124
Up and running: integrating information technology and the organization, 182
Up front financing: the entrepreneur's guide, 260
Up your own organization!: a handbook for today's entrepreneur, 260

Upward dreams, downward mobility: the economic decline of the American middle class, 198
Urban transportation policy: new perspectives, 295
Using computers: the human factors of information systems, 51

Valuation: measuring and managing the value of companies, 67
The valuation of privately-held businesses: state-of-the art techniques for buyers, sellers, and their advisors, 41
Valuation reference manual: putting a price tag on a business when you're buying, when you're selling, when you're valuing, 67
Value at the top: solutions to the executive compensation crisis, 40
Value-focused thinking, 76
Values and ethics in organization and human systems development: responding to dilemmas in professional life, 225
Valuing a business: the analysis and appraisal of closely-held companies, 67
Valuing the earth: economics, ecology, ethics, 83
Vanguard management: redesigning the corporate future, 132
Venture capital at the crossroads, 296
Venture capital handbook, 296
Venture capital in high-tech companies: the electronics industry in perspective, 90
Venture capital: law, business strategies, and investment planning, 296
Venture capital today: a practical guide to the venture capital market, 296
Venture Japan: how growing companies worldwide can tap into the Japanese venture capital markets, 296
The Venture magazine complete guide to venture capital, 296
Venture's financing and investing in private companies: a guide to understanding entrepreneurs and their relationships with investors, lenders, and advisors, 156
Venturing abroad: international business expansion via joint ventures, 162
Video media competition: regulation, economics, and technology, 280
Vinyl leaves: Walt Disney World and America, 298
The virtual community: homesteading on the electronic frontier, 50
Virtual reality, 254
The virtual reality primer, 124
Vision, values, and courage: leadership for quality management, 168
Visions for the 21st century, 285
Visions of modernity: American business and the modernization of Germany, 132
The vital corporation: how American businesses—large and small—double profits in two years or less, 62
The vital difference: unleashing the powers of sustained corporate success, 132
The vital few: the entrepreneur and American economic progress, 286
Volcker: portrait of the money man, 297
Voltaire's bastards: the dictatorship of reason in the West, 248

The vulnerable fortress: bureaucratic organization and management in the information age, 23
The vulture investors: the winners and losers of the great American bankruptcy feeding frenzy, 170

Waging business warfare: lessons from the military masters in achieving corporate superiority, 179
Walking the high-tech high wire: the technical entrepreneur's guide to running a successful enterprise, 122
Wall Street and regulation, 16
The Wall Street gurus: how you can profit from investment newsletters, 153
Wall Street in transition: the emerging system and its impact on the economy, 267
The Wall Street Journal book of chief executive style, 30
The Wall Street journal on accounting, 5
The Wall Street Journal on management 2: adding value through synergy, 179
The Wall Street Journal on marketing, 191
Wall Street women, 303
Walter Reuther, 250
The Warburgs: the twentieth-century odyssey of a remarkable Jewish family, 299
Warehouse distribution and operations handbook, 299
The warning: the coming great crash in the stock market, 267
Warrants: analysis and investment strategy, 266
Warren Buffett: the good guy of Wall Street, 22
The Warren Buffett way: investment strategies of the world's greatest investor, 22
Was there a Pepsi generation before Pepsi discovered it, 186
Waves of change: business evolution through information technology, 142
The way and the power: secrets of Japanese strategy, 273
The way it was: an oral history of finance, 1967-1987, 106
We are all living with AIDS: how you can set policies and guidelines for the workplace, 9
We're so big and powerful nothing bad can happen to us: an investigation of America's crisis prone corporations, 71
The we-force in management: how to build and sustain cooperation, 306
The wealth creators: an entrepreneurial history of the United States, 95
The wealth of the nation: an economic history of the United States, 287
West of Eden: the end of innocence at Apple Computer, 11
The whale and the reactor: a search for limits in an age of high technology, 277
What America does right: learning from companies that put people first, 132
What every manager should know about financial analysis, 67
What is Japan?: contradictions and transformations, 158
What is total quality control? The Japanese way, 245
What machines can't do: politics and technology in the industrial enterprise, 276

What price clean air?: a market approach to energy and environmental policy, 9

What price food?: agricultural price policies in developing countries, 9

What they really teach you at the Harvard Business School, 120

What they still don't teach you at Harvard Business School: more notes from a street-smart executive, 272

What works for me: 16 CEOs talk about their careers and commitments, 101

What you get when you go for it, 303

What's in a name?: advertising and the concept of brands, 7

What's next?: how to prepare yourself for the crash of '89 and profit in the 1990's, 156

What's wrong with Wall Street: short-term gain and the absentee shareholder, 267

What's your game plan?: creating business strategies that work, 179

Whatever happened to Madison Avenue?: advertising in the '90s, 7

Whatever it takes: decision makers at work, 76

When America does it right: case studies in service quality, 73

When giants learn to dance: mastering the challenge of strategy, management, and careers in the 1990s, 225

When government goes private: successful alternatives to public services, 237

When it hits the fan: managing the nine crises of business, 72

When markets quake: the management challenge of restructuring industry, 233

When the canary stops singing: women's perspectives on transforming business, 246

When the machine stopped: a cautionary tale from industrial America, 23

Where we stand: can America make it in the global race for wealth, health, and happiness, 265

Whistleblowing: managing dessent in the workplace, 299

Whistleblowing research: methodological and moral issues, 300

The white-collar shuffle: who does what in today's computerized workplace, 213

The whiz kids: the founding fathers of American business—and the legacy they left us, 34

Who profits: winners, losers, and government regulation, 283

Who's afraid of Big Blue?: how companies are challenging IBM—and winning, 150

Who's bashing whom?: trade conflict in high-technology industries, 122

The whole manager, 179

Why bank regulation failed: designing a bank regulatory strategy for the 1990s, 16

Why leaders can't lead: the unconscious conspiracy continues, 168

"Why should white guys have all the fun?": how Reginald Lewis created a billion-dollar business empire, 170

Why they buy: American consumers inside and out, 57

Why work: leading the new generation, 168

Why your corporate culture change isn't working—and what to do about it, 59

William C. Norris: portrait of a maverick, 212

William E. Donoghue's complete money market guide: the simple, low-risk way you can profit from inflation and fluctuating interest rates, 156

Willing workers: the work ethics in Japan, England, and the United States, 304

Willis R. Whitney, General Electric, and the origins of U.S. industrial research, 300

Win-win negotiating: turning conflict into agreement, 205

Window of opportunity: a blueprint for the future, 277

The winner's circle: how ten stockbrokers became the best in the business, 267

Winning combinations: the coming wave of entrepreneurial partnerships between large and small companies, 268

Winning in high-tech markets: the role of general management: how Motorola, Corning, and General Electric have built global leadership through technology, 122

Winning in the new Europe: taking advantage of the single market, 97

Winning on the marketing front: the corporate manager's game plan, 61

Winning the innovation game, 71

Winning the interest rate game: a guide to debt options, 144

Winning the marketing war: a practical guide to competitive advantage, 191

Winning with synergy: how America can regain the competitive edge, 289

Winning worldwide: strategies for dominating global markets, 149

The wisdom of teams: creating the high-performance organization, 306

The woman entrepreneur: starting, financing, and managing a successful new business, 208

Woman to woman: street smarts for women entrepreneurs, 303

A woman's place is everywhere: inspirational profiles of female leaders who are expanding the roles of American women, 303

Women & men in management, 302

Women and careers: issues and challenges, 301

Women and Japanese management: discrimination and reform, 258

Women and power: how far can we go, 168

Women and the work/family dilemma: how today's professional women are finding solutions, 304

Women in charge: dilemmas of women in authority, 302

Women in corporate management: results of a Catalyst survey, 302

Women in management, 302

Women in management worldwide, 302

Women into management: issues influencing the entry of women into managerial jobs, 302

Women leading: making tough choices on the fast track, 302

Women like us: what is happening to the women of the Harvard Business School, Class of '75—the women who had the first chance to make it to the top, 120

Women managers: travellers in a male world, 302
Women MBAs: a foot in the door, 302
Women, technology & power: ten stars and the history they made, 302
Women vs. women: the uncivil business war, 258
Women who want to be boss: business revelations and success strategies from America's top female executives, 302
Women's career development, 301
Women's career development: a study of high flyers, 302
Women's quest for economic equality, 301
Wordly power: the making of the Wall Street journal, 298
The work and family revolution: how companies can keep employees happy and business profitable, 92
Work and rewards: redefining our work-life reality, 161
Work in America; report of a special task force to the Secretary of Health, Education, and Welfare, 185
Work measurement: principles and practice, 306
Work of her own: how women create success and fulfillment off the traditional career track, 255
Work styles to fit your life-style: everyone's guide to temporary employment, 280
Work, unemployment and the new technology, 276
Worker protection, Japanese style: occupational safety and health in the auto industry, 14
Workforce 2000: work and workers for the 21st century, 306
Workforce America!: managing employee diversity as a vital resource, 184
Working ethics: strategies for decision making and organizational responsibility, 30
Working for the Japanese: inside Mazda's American auto plant, 195
The working leader: the triumph of high performance over conventional management principles, 169
Working scared: achieving success in trying times, 272
Working women don't have wives: professional success in the 1990s, 304
Workouts and turnarounds: the handbook of restructuring and investing in distressed companies, 62
Workplace 2000: the revolution reshaping American business, 232
Workplace basics: the essential skills employers want, 92
The workplace within: the psychodynamics of organizational life, 243

The world at work: an international report of jobs, productivity, and human values: a joint project of the Public Agenda Foundation and the Aspen Institute for Humanistic Studies, 165
World class brands, 21
A world fit for people: thinkers from many countries address the political, economic, and social problems of our time, 77
The world health market: the future of the pharmaceutical industry, 233
The world in 2020: power, culture, and prosperity, 31
World trade and payments: an introduction, 152
The world's largest market: a business guide to Europe, 1992, 97
World-class manufacturing: the lessons of simplicity applied, 132
The worldly philosophers: the lives, times, and ideas of the great economic thinkers, 87
Write to the top: writing for corporate success, 46
Writers on strategy and strategic management: the theory of strategy and the practice of strategic management at enterprise, corporate, business and functional levels, 271
Writing and speaking in business, 43
Writing for decision makers: memos and reports with a competitive edge, 33
Writing for results in business, government, the sciences, and the professions, 43
Wrong number: the breakup of AT&T, 10

Xerox, American samurai, 307

Year one: an intimate look inside Harvard Business School, source of the most coveted advanced degree in the world, 120
The year they sold Wall Street, 258
You don't have to take it!: a woman's guide to confronting emotional abuse at work, 258
Your advertising's great—how's business?: the revolution in sales promotion, 253
Your organization: what is it for?: challenging traditional organizational aims, 216
Youthtrends: capturing the $200 billion youth market, 307

Zaibatsu America: how Japanese firms are colonizing vital U.S. industries, 68
Zaibatsu: the rise and fall of family enterprise groups in Japan, 103
Zero quality control: source inspection and the poka-yoke system, 245
The zero-sum solution: building a world-class American economy, 289